D1243256

THE INDEX LIBRARY

General Editor, Probate Volumes: CLIFF WEBB, M.A., F.S.A., F.S.G.

WILLS IN THE

ARCHDEACONRY COURT OF BARNSTAPLE

1506–1858

ISSUED BY
THE BRITISH RECORD SOCIETY
[128]

THE INDEX LIBRARY

THE BRITISH RECORD SOCIETY
Chairman: PROFESSOR DAVID HEY, M.A., PH.D.
General Editor, Probate Volumes: CLIFF WEBB, M.A., F.S.A., F.S.G.

WILLS IN THE

ARCHDEACONRY COURT OF BARNSTAPLE

Edited by
Cliff Webb

THE BRITISH RECORD SOCIETY
INDEX LIBRARY VOLUME 128

Published by The British Record Society

ISBN 978-0-901505–58-3

Printed in Great Britain

CONTENTS

Introduction

England is extremely fortunate in general with the survival of its archives; 1000 years without invasion have left us with a remarkable collection of historical documents at both the local and national levels. The Second World War, however, did cause some serious losses. Perhaps the most serious of these occurred when Exeter was bombed on the night of the 3rd-4th of May, 1942.

During this air raid the Probate Sub-Registry at 6 Bedford Circus, Exeter was burnt out. This building housed all the early wills and other probate records proved in the Dioceses of Exeter and Bath and Wells, including the Peculiar Courts whose jurisdiction lay within those dioceses. In a single night a large proportion of Devon, Cornwall and Somerset's probate material was destroyed.

There are substitutes for some of the lost material. Firstly for all the courts whose records were lost there were lists of testators, parishes and dates apart from those of the Archdeaconry of Totnes. For the latter end of the period, there were central surviving abstracts of some material from 1796 and full copies of many from 1812 in the Estate Duty Office. The Estate Duty Office kept copies of all wills on which Death Duty was payable, its annotated indexes survive and are available online at FindMyPast. In 1796 when introduced, Death Duty only applied where money was left to beneficiaries other than close relatives including the spouse and children. In 1805, the scope of the tax was widened to include close relatives *other than* spouse and children and money raised by sale of real estate. In 1815, it was further extended, and only spouses were exempt. Finally, in 1853 the tax became payable on any property transfer at death.

The original records from Devon and Cornwall were transferred to the appropriate Record Offices. It is a great loss that those for the rest of the country were deliberately destroyed in the 1960s by governmental authority, despite offers to house them, as many small courts have gaps in records these may have filled. Devon Record Office has made every effort to collect copies of wills held in private muniments and also abstracts made of them before the 1942 disaster.

The manuscript list for the Barnstaple Archdeaconry was transcribed as: *Wills and Administrations Relating to the County of Devon Proved in the Court of the Archdeaconry of Barnstaple*, 1563–1858, edited by J.J. Beckerlegge (5 vols.), The Devonshire Association for the Advancement of Science, Literature and Art (1950). Only a handful of copies of this work were made.

Latterly, there has been a big effort to collect and index all Devon wills, surviving or not, under the auspices of the Devon Wills Project. As part of this effort, Beckerlegge's work was transcribed by Pat Gillard, Paul Hockie, Marilyn and Pieter Koops, Pat Norton, Susan Page, John Pitts and Brian Randell. The organisers of the project have been extremely cooperative in the production of this work; indeed it could never even have started without their work.

The Devon Wills Project lists its results freely on GENUKI; it may then be asked why we would publish this index. The work in editing a printed work, and collating various sources inevitably highlights potential errors, and associates entries which are otherwise sundered by archival happenstance. This was especially true here, where the work of many hands was involved in the text to be edited. Furthermore, the printed work enables a series of analyses to be undertaken, analyses which compare different parts of the country and produce new knowledge of will-making in England.

The Beckerlegge entries have been annotated in various ways. Firstly, in some cases where Beckerlegge gives no Christian name, it has been possible to supply it, usually from a parish register. Where this has been done it has, of course, been noted. In addition, the lists of Estate Office Wills have provided extra details – in particular of occupation, sadly missing from Beckerlegge's work.

Christian Names

Table 1 comprises a list of testators' male christian names in alphabetical order

Name	#	%	Name	#	%
Aaron	12	0.04%	Bernard	34	0.10%
Abednego	2	0.01%	Berry	1	0.00%
Abel	11	0.03%	Bethuel	1	0.00%
Abijah	1	0.00%	Bezaleel	1	0.00%
Abraham	100	0.30%	Bowden	2	0.01%
Absalom	1	0.00%	Brian	4	0.01%
Achilles	4	0.01%	Brutus	2	0.01%
Adam	33	0.10%	Cad-Edwards	1	0.00%
Agadius	1	0.00%	Caesar	3	0.01%
Agrippa	1	0.00%	Caleb	11	0.03%
Alan	2	0.01%	Calvin	5	0.01%
Alban	1	0.00%	Canson	1	0.00%
Alden	2	0.01%	Cary	1	0.00%
Aldred	2	0.01%	Chamond	1	0.00%
Alexander	237	0.71%	Charles	180	0.54%
Alfred	22	0.07%	Chichester	1	0.00%
Alphonse	4	0.01%	Christmas	1	0.00%
Alnectius/Haln-	2	0.01%	Christopher	387	1.16%
Ambrose	60	0.18%	Clark	1	0.00%
Amiel	6	0.02%	Clase	10	0.03%
Amory	1	0.00%	Clement	27	0.08%
Amos/Amesius	82	0.25%	Collett	1	0.00%
Ananias	11	0.03%	Conan	2	0.01%
Andrew	173	0.52%	Connaught	1	0.00%
Anthony	425	1.27%	Constantine	2	0.01%
Archelaus	19	0.06%	Copleston	1	0.00%
Armanell	12	0.04%	Coriolanus	1	0.00%
Armiger	1	0.00%	Cornelius	7	0.02%
Arnold	2	0.01%	Cosgaipre	1	0.00%
Arscott	3	0.01%	Courtenay	1	0.00%
Arthur	171	0.51%	Crispin	3	0.01%
Arundell	1	0.00%	Culpepper	1	0.00%
Asa	1	0.00%	Cutcliffe	1	0.00%
Askal	1	0.00%	Cyprian	10	0.03%
Atwell	1	0.00%	Cyrus	1	0.00%
Augustine	34	0.10%	Daniel	118	0.35%
Avery	2	0.01%	Darius	1	0.00%
Azariah	5	0.01%	David/Davy	250	0.75%
Baldwin	42	0.13%	Davis	1	0.00%
Balthazar	6	0.02%	Denham	2	0.01%
Baptist	1	0.00%	Derwent	2	0.01%
Barden	1	0.00%	Devereux	1	0.00%
Barnabas	6	0.02%	Diaphanus	1	0.00%
Bartholomew	135	0.40%	Digory	21	0.06%
Beaton	16	0.05%	Dionysius	5	0.01%
Benedict	6	0.02%	Dominic	1	0.00%
Benjamin	56	0.17%	Dudley	2	0.01%

Name	#	%	Name	#	%
Dunstan	4	0.01%	Heyman	1	0.00%
Edmund	146	0.44%	Hezekiah	3	0.01%
Edulphus	2	0.01%	Honorius	3	0.01%
Edward	565	1.69%	Hugh	435	1.30%
Egline	6	0.02%	Hume	1	0.00%
Eli	10	0.03%	Humphrey	299	0.89%
Elias	36	0.11%	Hursey	2	0.01%
Elijah	1	0.00%	Iolus	1	0.00%
Elisha	4	0.01%	Isaac	29	0.09%
Elizeus	2	0.01%	Israel	8	0.02%
Elkanah	1	0.00%	Jabez	1	0.00%
Elnathan	1	0.00%	Jacob	35	0.10%
Emanuel	57	0.17%	Jacques	1	0.00%
Emott	27	0.08%	James	912	2.73%
English	8	0.02%	Jasper	20	0.06%
Enoch	7	0.02%	Jedidiah	1	0.00%
Ephraim	6	0.02%	Jenkin	12	0.04%
Erasmus	2	0.01%	Jenson	6	0.02%
Ethelred	7	0.02%	Jeremiah/-my/-ome	49	0.15%
Eusebius	5	0.01%	Jesse	2	0.01%
Eustace	1	0.00%	Joachim	4	0.01%
Evan	13	0.04%	Joel	1	0.00%
Ezekiel	12	0.04%	John	8,692	25.98%
Fairfax	1	0.00%	Johnson	3	0.01%
Ferdinand	9	0.03%	Jonah	20	0.06%
Finney	1	0.00%	Jonas	6	0.02%
Francis	233	0.70%	Jonathan	56	0.17%
Frederick	5	0.01%	Jones	1	0.00%
Fulk	5	0.01%	Joseph	267	0.80%
Gabriel	32	0.10%	Joshua	20	0.06%
Gamaliel	1	0.00%	Josiah	30	0.09%
Garnett	1	0.00%	Jude	2	0.01%
Garrett	3	0.01%	Julius	2	0.01%
Gawen	3	0.01%	Justinian	6	0.02%
Geoffrey	48	0.14%	Kelland	1	0.00%
George	1,293	3.86%	Lambert	5	0.01%
German	2	0.01%	Lancelot	2	0.01%
Gideon	3	0.01%	Laumedon	1	0.00%
Giffard	2	0.01%	Lawrence	124	0.37%
Gilbert	29	0.09%	Leonard	37	0.11%
Giles	79	0.24%	Levi	1	0.00%
Gordian	1	0.00%	Lewis	61	0.18%
Gratus	1	0.00%	Lodovic	122	0.36%
Gregory	48	0.14%	Lovell	1	0.00%
Griffith	11	0.03%	Lowglelane	1	0.00%
Hammond	1	0.00%	Luke/Lucas	21	0.06%
Hannibal	12	0.04%	Lye	2	0.01%
Harris	1	0.00%	Macklin	9	0.03%
Harry	17	0.05%	Malachi	2	0.01%
Henry	903	2.70%	Malcolm	1	0.00%
Hercules	4	0.01%	Mallett	1	0.00%

Name	#	%
Mansell	1	0.00%
Marfett	1	0.00%
Marius	1	0.00%
Mark	52	0.16%
Marmaduke	5	0.01%
Marshall	1	0.00%
Martin	25	0.07%
Mathew	151	0.45%
Matthias	4	0.01%
Maurice	12	0.04%
Mayhow	1	0.00%
Melchior/Melior	9	0.03%
Mendon	1	0.00%
Meredith	1	0.00%
Merthoe	1	0.00%
Methusaleh	4	0.01%
Michael	146	0.44%
Miles	13	0.04%
Milner	1	0.00%
Mitchell	1	0.00%
More	1	0.00%
Morgan	8	0.02%
Moses	7	0.02%
Mounsell	1	0.00%
Mulford	1	0.00%
Narcissus	1	0.00%
Nathaniel/Nathan	80	0.24%
Nectan	2	0.01%
Nehemiah	2	0.01%
Neil	1	0.00%
Neville	6	0.02%
Nicholas	589	1.76%
Noah	2	0.01%
Obadiah	8	0.02%
Ogilby	2	0.01%
Olimpe	1	0.00%
Oliver	76	0.23%
Onesimus	2	0.01%
Orris	1	0.00%
Osmond	1	0.00%
Owen	9	0.03%
Parkin	1	0.00%
Paschal	21	0.06%
Pather	3	0.01%
Patrick	6	0.02%
Paul	34	0.10%
Pentecost	10	0.03%
Peter	398	1.19%
Petherick	4	0.01%
Philip	788	2.35%
Philpott	2	0.01%

Name	#	%
Phineas	8	0.02%
Preston	1	0.00%
Ralph	51	0.15%
Rawleigh	1	0.00%
Raymond	8	0.02%
Rees	6	0.02%
Reginald	3	0.01%
Renatus	2	0.01%
Reuben	1	0.00%
Reynold	4	0.01%
Richard	2,471	7.38%
Robert	1,521	4.55%
Roger	407	1.22%
Rowland	30	0.09%
Rudolf	2	0.01%
Salathiel	2	0.01%
Samson	10	0.03%
Samuel	429	1.28%
Saunder	1	0.00%
Savery	1	0.00%
Scipio	13	0.04%
Sebastian	14	0.04%
Septimus	1	0.00%
Setene	2	0.01%
Seth	1	0.00%
Shadrach	3	0.01%
Sidwell	2	0.01%
Silas	1	0.00%
Silvanus	7	0.02%
Silvester	12	0.04%
Simon	206	0.62%
Smarte	1	0.00%
Solomon	2	0.01%
Southcombe	1	0.00%
Squire	2	0.01%
Staff	1	0.00%
Stephen	122	0.36%
Stukeley	3	0.01%
Tammy	2	0.01%
Tebbet	3	0.01%
Theobald	8	0.02%
Theodore	1	0.00%
Theophilus	21	0.06%
Thomas	3,041	9.09%
Timothy	17	0.05%
Tobias	13	0.04%
Tristram	27	0.08%
Ulysses	1	0.00%
Uriah	1	0.00%
Uzziah	1	0.00%
Valentine	14	0.04%

Name	#	%
Vincent	14	0.04%
Wakeman	2	0.01%
Walter	340	1.02%
Warwick	1	0.00%
Wedlake	1	0.00%

Name	#	%
William	4,263	12.74%
Willmore	1	0.00%
Zachariah/-ias/-ry	12	0.04%
TOTAL	33,462	100.00%

Table 2 shows testators' male christian names in their order of frequency.

Name	#	%	Name	#	%
John	8,692	25.98%	Ambrose	60	0.18%
William	4,263	12.74%	Emanuel	57	0.17%
Thomas	3,041	9.09%	Benjamin	56	0.17%
Richard	2,471	7.38%	Jonathan	56	0.17%
Robert	1,521	4.55%	Mark	52	0.16%
George	1,293	3.86%	Ralph	51	0.15%
James	912	2.73%	Jeremiah/-my/-ome	49	0.15%
Henry	903	2.70%	Geoffrey	48	0.14%
Philip	788	2.35%	Gregory	48	0.14%
Nicholas	589	1.76%	Baldwin	42	0.13%
Edward	565	1.69%	Leonard	37	0.11%
Hugh	435	1.30%	Elias	36	0.11%
Samuel	429	1.28%	Jacob	35	0.10%
Anthony	425	1.27%	Augustine	34	0.10%
Roger	407	1.22%	Bernard	34	0.10%
Peter	398	1.19%	Paul	34	0.10%
Christopher	387	1.16%	Adam	33	0.10%
Walter	340	1.02%	Gabriel	32	0.10%
Humphrey	299	0.89%	Josiah	30	0.09%
Joseph	267	0.80%	Rowland	30	0.09%
David/Davy	250	0.75%	Gilbert	29	0.09%
Alexander	237	0.71%	Isaac	29	0.09%
Francis	233	0.70%	Clement	27	0.08%
Simon	206	0.62%	Emott	27	0.08%
Charles	180	0.54%	Tristram	27	0.08%
Andrew	173	0.52%	Martin	25	0.07%
Arthur	171	0.51%	Alfred	22	0.07%
Mathew	151	0.45%	Digory	21	0.06%
Edmund	146	0.44%	Luke/Lucas	21	0.06%
Michael	146	0.44%	Paschal	21	0.06%
Bartholomew	135	0.40%	Theophilus	21	0.06%
Lawrence	124	0.37%	Jasper	20	0.06%
Lodovic	122	0.36%	Jonah	20	0.06%
Stephen	122	0.36%	Joshua	20	0.06%
Daniel	118	0.35%	Archelaus	19	0.06%
Abraham	100	0.30%	Harry	17	0.05%
Amos/Amesius	82	0.25%	Timothy	17	0.05%
Nathaniel/Nathan	80	0.24%	Beaton	16	0.05%
Giles	79	0.24%	Sebastian	14	0.04%
Oliver	76	0.23%	Valentine	14	0.04%
Lewis	61	0.18%	Vincent	14	0.04%

Name	#	%	Name	#	%
Evan	13	0.04%	Eusebius	5	0.01%
Miles	13	0.04%	Frederick	5	0.01%
Scipio	13	0.04%	Fulk	5	0.01%
Tobias	13	0.04%	Lambert	5	0.01%
Aaron	12	0.04%	Marmaduke	5	0.01%
Armanell	12	0.04%	Achilles	4	0.01%
Ezekiel	12	0.04%	Alphonse	4	0.01%
Hannibal	12	0.04%	Brian	4	0.01%
Jenkin	12	0.04%	Dunstan	4	0.01%
Maurice	12	0.04%	Elisha	4	0.01%
Silvester	12	0.04%	Hercules	4	0.01%
Zachariah/-ias/-ry	12	0.04%	Joachim	4	0.01%
Abel	11	0.03%	Matthias	4	0.01%
Ananias	11	0.03%	Methusaleh	4	0.01%
Caleb	11	0.03%	Petherick	4	0.01%
Griffith	11	0.03%	Reynold	4	0.01%
Clase	10	0.03%	Arscott	3	0.01%
Cyprian	10	0.03%	Caesar	3	0.01%
Eli	10	0.03%	Crispin	3	0.01%
Pentecost	10	0.03%	Garrett	3	0.01%
Samson	10	0.03%	Gawen	3	0.01%
Ferdinand	9	0.03%	Gideon	3	0.01%
Macklin	9	0.03%	Hezekiah	3	0.01%
Melchior/Melior	9	0.03%	Honorius	3	0.01%
Owen	9	0.03%	Johnson	3	0.01%
English	8	0.02%	Pather	3	0.01%
Israel	8	0.02%	Reginald	3	0.01%
Morgan	8	0.02%	Shadrach	3	0.01%
Obadiah	8	0.02%	Stukeley	3	0.01%
Phineas	8	0.02%	Tebbet	3	0.01%
Raymond	8	0.02%	Abednego	2	0.01%
Theobald	8	0.02%	Alan	2	0.01%
Cornelius	7	0.02%	Alden	2	0.01%
Enoch	7	0.02%	Aldred	2	0.01%
Ethelred	7	0.02%	Alnectius/Haln-	2	0.01%
Moses	7	0.02%	Arnold	2	0.01%
Silvanus	7	0.02%	Avery	2	0.01%
Amiel	6	0.02%	Bowden	2	0.01%
Balthazar	6	0.02%	Brutus	2	0.01%
Barnabas	6	0.02%	Conan	2	0.01%
Benedict	6	0.02%	Constantine	2	0.01%
Egline	6	0.02%	Denham	2	0.01%
Ephraim	6	0.02%	Derwent	2	0.01%
Jenson	6	0.02%	Dudley	2	0.01%
Jonas	6	0.02%	Edulphus	2	0.01%
Justinian	6	0.02%	Elizeus	2	0.01%
Neville	6	0.02%	Erasmus	2	0.01%
Patrick	6	0.02%	German	2	0.01%
Rees	6	0.02%	Giffard	2	0.01%
Azariah	5	0.01%	Hursey	2	0.01%
Calvin	5	0.01%	Jesse	2	0.01%
Dionysius	5	0.01%	Jude	2	0.01%

Name	#	%	Name	#	%
Julius	2	0.01%	Davis	1	0.00%
Lancelot	2	0.01%	Devereux	1	0.00%
Lye	2	0.01%	Diaphanus	1	0.00%
Malachi	2	0.01%	Dominic	1	0.00%
Nectan	2	0.01%	Elijah	1	0.00%
Nehemiah	2	0.01%	Elkanah	1	0.00%
Noah	2	0.01%	Elnathan	1	0.00%
Ogilby	2	0.01%	Eustace	1	0.00%
Onesimus	2	0.01%	Fairfax	1	0.00%
Philpott	2	0.01%	Finney	1	0.00%
Renatus	2	0.01%	Gamaliel	1	0.00%
Rudolf	2	0.01%	Garnett	1	0.00%
Salathiel	2	0.01%	Gordian	1	0.00%
Setene	2	0.01%	Gratus	1	0.00%
Sidwell	2	0.01%	Hammond	1	0.00%
Solomon	2	0.01%	Harris	1	0.00%
Squire	2	0.01%	Heyman	1	0.00%
Tammy	2	0.01%	Hume	1	0.00%
Wakeman	2	0.01%	Iolus	1	0.00%
Abijah	1	0.00%	Jabez	1	0.00%
Absalom	1	0.00%	Jacques	1	0.00%
Agadius	1	0.00%	Jedidiah	1	0.00%
Agrippa	1	0.00%	Joel	1	0.00%
Alban	1	0.00%	Jones	1	0.00%
Amory	1	0.00%	Kelland	1	0.00%
Armiger	1	0.00%	Laumedon	1	0.00%
Arundell	1	0.00%	Levi	1	0.00%
Asa	1	0.00%	Lovell	1	0.00%
Askal	1	0.00%	Lowglelane	1	0.00%
Atwell	1	0.00%	Malcolm	1	0.00%
Baptist	1	0.00%	Mallett	1	0.00%
Barden	1	0.00%	Mansell	1	0.00%
Berry	1	0.00%	Marfett	1	0.00%
Bethuel	1	0.00%	Marius	1	0.00%
Bezaleel	1	0.00%	Marshall	1	0.00%
Cad-Edwards	1	0.00%	Mayhow	1	0.00%
Canson	1	0.00%	Mendon	1	0.00%
Cary	1	0.00%	Meredith	1	0.00%
Chamond	1	0.00%	Merthoe	1	0.00%
Chichester	1	0.00%	Milner	1	0.00%
Christmas	1	0.00%	Mitchell	1	0.00%
Clark	1	0.00%	More	1	0.00%
Collett	1	0.00%	Mounsell	1	0.00%
Connaught	1	0.00%	Mulford	1	0.00%
Copleston	1	0.00%	Narcissus	1	0.00%
Coriolanus	1	0.00%	Neil	1	0.00%
Cosgaipre	1	0.00%	Olimpe	1	0.00%
Courtenay	1	0.00%	Orris	1	0.00%
Culpepper	1	0.00%	Osmond	1	0.00%
Cutcliffe	1	0.00%	Parkin	1	0.00%
Cyrus	1	0.00%	Preston	1	0.00%
Darius	1	0.00%	Rawleigh	1	0.00%

Name	#	%
Reuben	1	0.00%
Saunder	1	0.00%
Savery	1	0.00%
Septimus	1	0.00%
Seth	1	0.00%
Silas	1	0.00%
Smarte	1	0.00%
Southcombe	1	0.00%
Staff	1	0.00%

Name	#	%
Theodore	1	0.00%
Ulysses	1	0.00%
Uriah	1	0.00%
Uzziah	1	0.00%
Warwick	1	0.00%
Wedlake	1	0.00%
Willmore	1	0.00%
TOTAL	33,462	100.00%

Chart 1 shows the commonest male names.

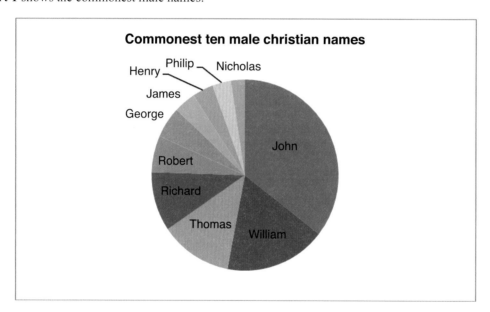

Commonest ten male christian names

Henry · Philip · Nicholas · James · George · Robert · Richard · Thomas · William · John

Just four male christian names (John, William, Thomas and Richard) represent half of all testators.

Table 3 shows testators' female christian names in alphabetical order.

Name	#	%
Abigail	5	0.05%
Admonition	1	0.01%
Agnes	467	4.95%
Alice	331	3.51%
Alison	4	0.04%
Alnette/Alnot	2	0.02%
Amelia	1	0.01%
Amesia	1	0.01%
Amy	16	0.17%
Anastasia	5	0.05%
Angela	3	0.03%
Anica	1	0.01%

Name	#	%
Ann/a	599	6.35%
Anstis	15	0.16%
Apphia	1	0.01%
Appollina	1	0.01%
Audrey	2	0.02%
Avis	25	0.26%
Barbara	14	0.15%
Beata	2	0.02%
Beatrice	7	0.07%
Bernice	1	0.01%
Betsy	3	0.03%
Betty	17	0.18%

Name	#	%	Name	#	%
Blaise	2	0.02%	Honoria	11	0.12%
Blanche	3	0.03%	Ingra	1	0.01%
Bridget	31	0.33%	Isabel	1	0.01%
Candace	1	0.01%	Isott	50	0.53%
Caroline	2	0.02%	Jacquet	9	0.10%
Catherine	253	2.68%	Jacquetta	1	0.01%
Cecilia/Cicely	39	0.41%	Jane	291	3.08%
Charity	57	0.60%	Janora	2	0.02%
Charlotte	4	0.04%	Jean	2	0.02%
Clara	1	0.01%	Jennifer/Jen-	14	0.15%
Clarice	2	0.02%	Joan/na	1,259	13.34%
Clemice	1	0.01%	Jolomia	1	0.01%
Constance	2	0.02%	Joy	1	0.01%
Cresset	1	0.01%	Joyce	5	0.05%
Damaris	5	0.05%	Judith	38	0.40%
Deborah	12	0.13%	Julia	8	0.08%
Dewena	1	0.01%	Juliana	15	0.16%
Diana	2	0.02%	Kitty	1	0.01%
Dinah	2	0.02%	Lectiora	2	0.02%
Dionysia	8	0.08%	Leonora	1	0.01%
Dorcas	7	0.07%	Letitia	3	0.03%
Dorothy	142	1.50%	Lettice	2	0.02%
Dulcibella	1	0.01%	Lois	1	0.01%
Ebbot/a	9	0.10%	Love	1	0.01%
Edith/a	23	0.24%	Loveday	1	0.01%
Eleanor	128	1.36%	Lucilla	1	0.01%
Elicie	1	0.01%	Lucinda	1	0.01%
Eliza	2	0.02%	Lucretia	1	0.01%
Elizabeth	1,329	14.08%	Lucy	17	0.18%
Ellen	34	0.36%	Lydia	2	0.02%
Elma	1	0.01%	Mabel	12	0.13%
Emblem	14	0.15%	Magdalen	6	0.06%
Emma	66	0.70%	Marafiria	1	0.01%
Esther	18	0.19%	Margaret	437	4.63%
Ethel	1	0.01%	Margery	133	1.41%
Ethelreda	1	0.01%	Marian	27	0.29%
Eva	1	0.01%	Martha	59	0.63%
Faith	14	0.15%	Mary	1,376	14.58%
Faithful	4	0.04%	Matilda	9	0.10%
Fanny	3	0.03%	Maud	5	0.05%
Felicia	1	0.01%	Mecholina	1	0.01%
Florence	9	0.10%	Melanie	1	0.01%
Fortune	3	0.03%	Meliora	1	0.01%
Frances	58	0.61%	Mildred	6	0.06%
Frideswide	2	0.02%	Miriam	4	0.04%
Georgina	1	0.01%	Molly	2	0.02%
Gertrude	31	0.33%	Monica	1	0.01%
Grace	306	3.24%	Nancy	2	0.02%
Gwen	2	0.02%	Neriah	4	0.04%
Hannah	65	0.69%	Niobe	1	0.01%
Harriet	2	0.02%	Obedience	2	0.02%
Helen/a	21	0.22%	Parnell	1	0.01%
Honor	64	0.68%	Patience	15	0.16%

Name	#	%
Pauline	10	0.11%
Peggy	4	0.04%
Penelope	8	0.08%
Petronell	40	0.42%
Philadelphia	1	0.01%
Phillippa	42	0.45%
Phoebe	1	0.01%
Phyllis	13	0.14%
Pinilla	1	0.01%
Polinora	2	0.02%
Prestwood	1	0.01%
Priscilla	23	0.24%
Providence	1	0.01%
Prudence	33	0.35%
Rachel	14	0.15%
Radigon	6	0.06%
Rahab	1	0.01%
Rawlina	5	0.05%
Rebecca	77	0.82%
Richarda	1	0.01%
Richelda	1	0.01%
Robina	1	0.01%
Rose	34	0.36%
Ruth	8	0.08%

Name	#	%
Sabboth	1	0.01%
Sally	2	0.02%
Salome	17	0.18%
Sarah	248	2.63%
Sibyl	10	0.11%
Sophia	2	0.02%
Susan/na	204	2.16%
Sybil	28	0.30%
Tabitha	2	0.02%
Tamar	1	0.01%
Temperance	3	0.03%
Thomasine	245	2.60%
Tiffany	1	0.01%
Tryphena	4	0.04%
Unity	2	0.02%
Urithe	13	0.14%
Ursula	12	0.13%
Vital	1	0.01%
Welthian	9	0.10%
Willmot	155	1.64%
Winifred	12	0.13%
Zenobia	3	0.03%
TOTAL	9,438	100.00%

Table 4 shows female names in order of frequency

Name	#	%
Mary	1,376	14.58%
Elizabeth	1,329	14.08%
Joan/na	1,259	13.34%
Ann/a	599	6.35%
Agnes	467	4.95%
Margaret	437	4.63%
Alice	331	3.51%
Grace	306	3.24%
Jane	291	3.08%
Catherine	253	2.68%
Sarah	248	2.63%
Thomasine	245	2.60%
Susan/na	204	2.16%
Willmot	155	1.64%
Dorothy	142	1.50%
Margery	133	1.41%
Eleanor	128	1.36%
Rebecca	77	0.82%
Emma	66	0.70%
Hannah	65	0.69%
Honor	64	0.68%
Martha	59	0.63%

Name	#	%
Frances	58	0.61%
Charity	57	0.60%
Isott	50	0.53%
Phillippa	42	0.45%
Petronell	40	0.42%
Cecilia/Cicely	39	0.41%
Judith	38	0.40%
Ellen	34	0.36%
Rose	34	0.36%
Prudence	33	0.35%
Bridget	31	0.33%
Gertrude	31	0.33%
Sybil	28	0.30%
Marian	27	0.29%
Avis	25	0.26%
Edith/a	23	0.24%
Priscilla	23	0.24%
Helen/a	21	0.22%
Esther	18	0.19%
Betty	17	0.18%
Lucy	17	0.18%
Salome	17	0.18%

Name	#	%	Name	#	%
Amy	16	0.17%	Zenobia	3	0.03%
Anstis	15	0.16%	Alnette/Alnot	2	0.02%
Juliana	15	0.16%	Audrey	2	0.02%
Patience	15	0.16%	Beata	2	0.02%
Barbara	14	0.15%	Blaise	2	0.02%
Emblem	14	0.15%	Caroline	2	0.02%
Faith	14	0.15%	Clarice	2	0.02%
Jennifer/Jen-	14	0.15%	Constance	2	0.02%
Rachel	14	0.15%	Diana	2	0.02%
Phyllis	13	0.14%	Dinah	2	0.02%
Urithe	13	0.14%	Eliza	2	0.02%
Deborah	12	0.13%	Frideswide	2	0.02%
Mabel	12	0.13%	Gwen	2	0.02%
Ursula	12	0.13%	Harriet	2	0.02%
Winifred	12	0.13%	Janora	2	0.02%
Honoria	11	0.12%	Jean	2	0.02%
Pauline	10	0.11%	Lectiora	2	0.02%
Sibyl	10	0.11%	Lettice	2	0.02%
Ebbot/a	9	0.10%	Lydia	2	0.02%
Florence	9	0.10%	Molly	2	0.02%
Jacquet	9	0.10%	Nancy	2	0.02%
Matilda	9	0.10%	Obedience	2	0.02%
Welthian	9	0.10%	Polinora	2	0.02%
Dionysia	8	0.08%	Sally	2	0.02%
Julia	8	0.08%	Sophia	2	0.02%
Penelope	8	0.08%	Tabitha	2	0.02%
Ruth	8	0.08%	Unity	2	0.02%
Beatrice	7	0.07%	Admonition	1	0.01%
Dorcas	7	0.07%	Amelia	1	0.01%
Magdalen	6	0.06%	Amesia	1	0.01%
Mildred	6	0.06%	Anica	1	0.01%
Radigon	6	0.06%	Apphia	1	0.01%
Abigail	5	0.05%	Appollina	1	0.01%
Anastasia	5	0.05%	Bernice	1	0.01%
Damaris	5	0.05%	Candace	1	0.01%
Joyce	5	0.05%	Clara	1	0.01%
Maud	5	0.05%	Clemice	1	0.01%
Rawlina	5	0.05%	Cresset	1	0.01%
Alison	4	0.04%	Dewena	1	0.01%
Charlotte	4	0.04%	Dulcibella	1	0.01%
Faithful	4	0.04%	Elicie	1	0.01%
Miriam	4	0.04%	Elma	1	0.01%
Neriah	4	0.04%	Ethel	1	0.01%
Peggy	4	0.04%	Ethelreda	1	0.01%
Tryphena	4	0.04%	Eva	1	0.01%
Angela	3	0.03%	Felicia	1	0.01%
Betsy	3	0.03%	Georgina	1	0.01%
Blanche	3	0.03%	Ingra	1	0.01%
Fanny	3	0.03%	Isabel	1	0.01%
Fortune	3	0.03%	Jacquetta	1	0.01%
Letitia	3	0.03%	Jolomia	1	0.01%
Temperance	3	0.03%	Joy	1	0.01%

Name	#	%
Kitty	1	0.01%
Leonora	1	0.01%
Lois	1	0.01%
Love	1	0.01%
Loveday	1	0.01%
Lucilla	1	0.01%
Lucinda	1	0.01%
Lucretia	1	0.01%
Marafiria	1	0.01%
Mecholina	1	0.01%
Melanie	1	0.01%
Meliora	1	0.01%
Monica	1	0.01%
Niobe	1	0.01%
Parnell	1	0.01%

Name	#	%
Philadelphia	1	0.01%
Phoebe	1	0.01%
Pinilla	1	0.01%
Prestwood	1	0.01%
Providence	1	0.01%
Rahab	1	0.01%
Richarda	1	0.01%
Richelda	1	0.01%
Robina	1	0.01%
Sabboth	1	0.01%
Tamar	1	0.01%
Tiffany	1	0.01%
Vital	1	0.01%
TOTAL	9,438	100.00%

Chart 2 shows the top ten female christian names

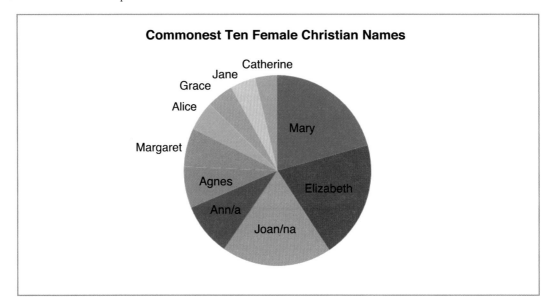

Over half of female testators shared just five names: Mary, Elizabeth, Joan(na), Ann(a) and Agnes.

Places

North Devon was and is overwhelmingly rural, with fishing villages on the coast and a scattering of market towns such as Barnstaple and Bideford. For each parish in the Archdeaconry the number of wills has been calculated and this reduced to a percentage of the total. The number of wills has then been divided by the 1801 census population to give a relativity between places as to their will-making. Places outside the Archdeaconry, including peculiars within its borders, have been excluded from the calculations.

Table 5 Devon parishes by numerical order

Name	#	Name	#	Name	#
Mortehoe	1	Mariansleigh	52	Wembworthy	102
Ilfracombe	2	Rose Ash	53	Chulmleigh	103
Berrynarbor	3	Knowstone	54	Chawleigh	104
Combe Martin	4	Oakford	55	Cheldon	105
Trentishoe	5	West Anstey	56	East Worlington	106
Parracombe	6	East Anstey	57	West Worlington	107
Martinhoe	7	Hartland	58	Eggesford	108
Lynton	8	Welcombe	59	Brushford	109
Countisbury	9	Clovelly	60	Coldridge	110
Brendon	10	Woolfardisworthy		Nymet Rowland	111
Georgeham	11	(by Clovelly)	61	Lapford	112
West Down	12	Parkham	62	Bondleigh	113
Bittadon	13	Alwington	63	Zeal Monachorum	114
Marwood	14	Littleham	64	North Tawton	115
East Down	15	Landcross	65	Bow	116
Kentisbury	16	Monkleigh	66	Clannaborough	117
Shirwell	17	Wear Gifford	67	Witheridge	118
Loxhore	18	Huntshaw	68	Thelbridge	119
Arlington	19	Buckland Brewer	69	Washford Pyne	120
Bratton Fleming	20	Frithelstock	70	Woolfardisworthy	
Challacombe	21	Great Torrington	71	(by Crediton)	121
High Bray	22	St Giles in the Wood	72	Puddington	122
Heanton Punchardon	23	High Bickington	73	Cruwys Morchard	123
Ashford	24	Warkleigh	74	East Putford	124
Pilton	25	Satterleigh	75		
Barnstaple	26	King's Nympton	76		
Goodleigh	27	Romansleigh	77		
Stoke Rivers	28	Meshaw	78		
Charles	29	Creacombe	79		
West Buckland	30	Rackenford	80		
East Buckland	31	Stoodleigh	81		
North Molton	32	Bulkworthy	82		
Twitchen	33	Newton St Petrock	83		
Molland	34	Shebbear	84		
Lundy	35	Langtree	85		
Fremington	36	Peters Marland	86		
Tawstock	37	Buckland Filleigh	87		
Filleigh	38	Sheepwash	88		
South Molton	39	Little Torrington	89		
Northam	40	Merton	90		
Instow	41	Petrockstowe	91		
Westleigh	42	Huish	92		
Horwood	43	Meeth	93		
Newton Tracey	44	Beaford	94		
Abbotsham	45	Roborough	95		
Bideford	46	Dolton	96		
Alverdiscott	47	Dowland	97		
Yarnscombe	48	Iddesleigh	98		
Atherington	49	Burrington	99		
Chittlehampton	50	Ashreigney	100		
George Nympton	51	Winkleigh	101		

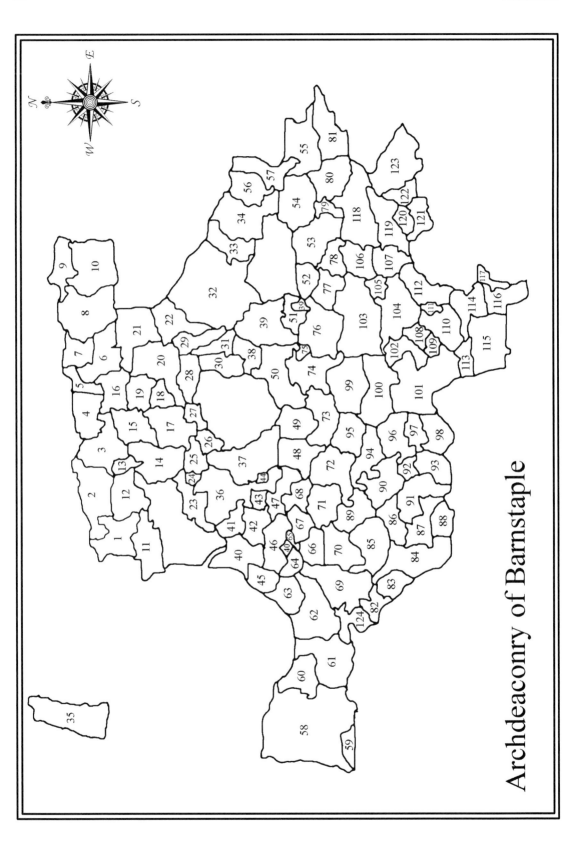

Archdeaconry of Barnstaple

Table 6 Devon parishes by name

Name	#	Name	#	Name	#
Abbotsham	45	High Bickington	73	Stoke Rivers	28
Alverdiscott	47	High Bray	22	Stoodleigh	81
Alwington	63	Horwood	43	Tawstock	37
Arlington	19	Huish	92	Thelbridge	119
Ashford	24	Huntshaw	68	Trentishoe	5
Ashreigney	100	Iddesleigh	98	Twitchen	33
Atherington	49	Ilfracombe	2	Warkleigh	74
Barnstaple	26	Instow	41	Washford Pyne	120
Beaford	94	Kentisbury	16	Wear Gifford	67
Berrynarbor	3	King's Nympton	76	Welcombe	59
Bideford	46	Knowstone	54	Wembworthy	102
Bittadon	13	Landcross	65	West Anstey	56
Bondleigh	113	Langtree	85	West Buckland	30
Bow	116	Lapford	112	West Down	12
Bratton Fleming	20	Little Torrington	89	West Worlington	107
Brendon	10	Littleham	64	Westleigh	42
Brushford	109	Loxhore	18	Winkleigh	101
Buckland Brewer	69	Lundy	35	Witheridge	118
Buckland Filleigh	87	Lynton	8	Woolfardisworthy	
Bulkworthy	82	Mariansleigh	52	(by Clovelly)	61
Burrington	99	Martinhoe	7	Woolfardisworthy	
Challacombe	21	Marwood	14	(by Crediton)	121
Charles	29	Meeth	93	Yarnscombe	48
Chawleigh	104	Merton	90	Zeal Monachorum	114
Cheldon	105	Meshaw	78		
Chittlehampton	50	Molland	34		
Chulmleigh	103	Monkleigh	66		
Clannaborough	117	Mortehoe	1		
Clovelly	60	Newton St Petrock	83		
Coldridge	110	Newton Tracey	44		
Combe Martin	4	Northam	40		
Countisbury	9	North Molton	32		
Creacombe	79	North Tawton	115		
Cruwys Morchard	123	Nymet Rowland	111		
Dolton	96	Oakford	55		
Dowland	97	Parkham	62		
East Anstey	57	Parracombe	6		
East Buckland	31	Peters Marland	86		
East Down	15	Petrockstowe	91		
East Putford	124	Pilton	25		
East Worlington	106	Puddington	122		
Eggesford	108	Rackenford	80		
Filleigh	38	Roborough	95		
Fremington	36	Romansleigh	77		
Frithelstock	70	Rose Ash	53		
Georgeham	11	St Giles in the Wood	72		
George Nympton	51	Satterleigh	75		
Goodleigh	27	Shebbear	84		
Great Torrington	71	Sheepwash	88		
Hartland	58	Shirwell	17		
Heanton Punchardon	23	South Molton	39		

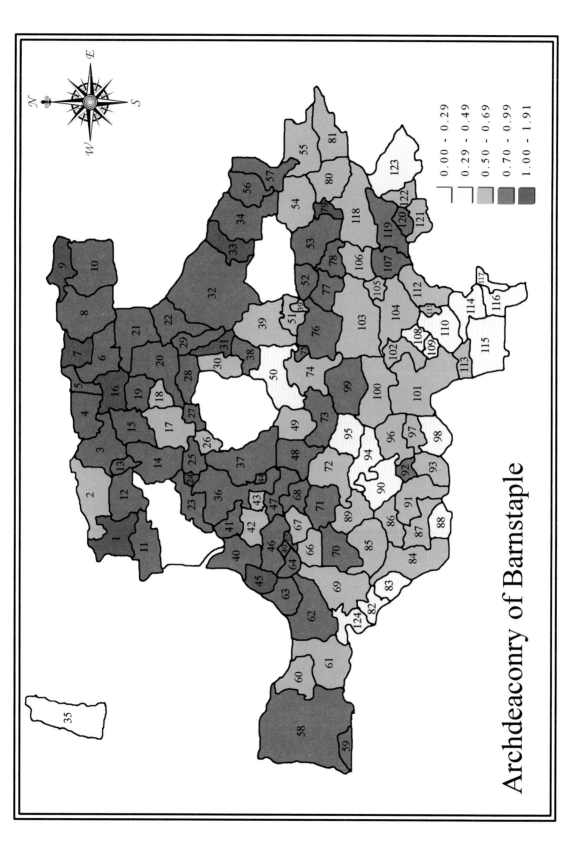

Archdeaconry of Barnstaple

0.00 - 0.29
0.29 - 0.49
0.50 - 0.69
0.70 - 0.99
1.00 - 1.91

Table 7 shows the results of this analysis in alphabetical order of parish.

Parish	# Wills	% of total	1801 Pop	b/d
Abbotsham	409	0.91%	313	1.31
Alverdiscott	202	0.45%	278	0.73
Alwington	223	0.49%	310	0.72
Arlington	190	0.42%	207	0.92
Ashford	112	0.25%	73	1.53
Ashreigney	444	0.98%	726	0.61
Atherington	330	0.73%	484	0.68
Barnstaple	2,952	6.54%	5,748	0.51
Beaford	251	0.56%	516	0.49
Berrynarbor	382	0.85%	532	0.72
Bideford	2,275	5.04%	2,536	0.90
Bittadon	23	0.05%	24	0.96
Bondleigh	177	0.39%	256	0.69
Bow	254	0.56%	677	0.38
Bratton Fleming	388	0.86%	406	0.96
Brendon	189	0.42%	260	0.73
Broad Nymet			included in Bow	
Brushford	60	0.13%	146	0.41
Buckland Brewer	565	1.25%	872	0.65
Buckland Filleigh	148	0.33%	252	0.59
Bulkworthy	52	0.12%	110	0.47
Burrington	544	1.21%	755	0.72
Challacombe	143	0.32%	158	0.91
Charles	194	0.43%	217	0.89
Chawleigh	460	1.02%	755	0.61
Cheldon	55	0.12%	91	0.60
Chittlehampton	1,107	2.45%	3,003	0.37
Chulmleigh	873	1.93%	1,333	0.65
Clannaborough	17	0.04%	59	0.29
Clovelly	396	0.88%	714	0.55
Coldridge	259	0.57%	657	0.39
Combe Martin	658	1.46%	819	0.80
Countisbury	142	0.31%	120	1.18
Creacombe	36	0.08%	29	1.24
Cruwys Morchard	253	0.56%	556	0.46
Dolton	389	0.86%	582	0.67
Dowland	116	0.26%	184	0.63
East Anstey	118	0.26%	165	0.72
East Buckland	139	0.31%	138	1.01
East Down	221	0.49%	311	0.71
East Putford	83	0.18%	179	0.46
East Worlington	114	0.25%	196	0.58
Eggesford	72	0.16%	173	0.42
Filleigh	164	0.36%	220	0.75
Fremington	807	1.79%	875	0.92

Parish	# Wills	% of total	1801 Pop	b/d
Frithelstock	388	0.86%	479	0.81
Georgeham	541	1.20%	617	0.88
George Nympton	157	0.35%	237	0.66
Goodleigh	232	0.51%	248	0.94
Great Torrington	1,616	3.58%	2,044	0.79
Hartland	1,261	2.79%	1,546	0.82
Heanton Punchardon	343	0.76%	418	0.82
High Bickington	517	1.15%	693	0.75
High Bray	230	0.51%	264	0.87
Horwood	52	0.12%	103	0.50
Huish	77	0.17%	97	0.79
Huntshaw	167	0.37%	212	0.79
Iddesleigh	215	0.48%	442	0.49
Ilfracombe	1,231	2.73%	1,838	0.67
Instow	303	0.67%	349	0.87
Kentisbury	246	0.55%	241	1.02
King's Nympton	432	0.96%	510	0.85
Knowstone	282	0.62%	427	0.66
Landcross	40	0.09%	50	0.80
Langtree	338	0.75%	583	0.58
Lapford	304	0.67%	587	0.52
Little Torrington	248	0.55%	449	0.55
Littleham (near Bideford)	216	0.48%	292	0.74
Loxhore	134	0.30%	219	0.61
Lundy	0	0	n.k.	n/a
Lynton	362	0.80%	481	0.75
Mariansleigh	190	0.42%	199	0.95
Martinhoe	315	0.70%	165	1.91
Marwood	553	1.23%	632	0.88
Meeth	147	0.33%	257	0.57
Merton	254	0.56%	689	0.37
Meshaw	116	0.26%	135	0.86
Molland	339	0.75%	473	0.72
Monkleigh	252	0.56%	379	0.66
Mortehoe	254	0.56%	254	1.00
Newton St Petrock	103	0.23%	215	0.48
Newton Tracey	68	0.15%	86	0.79
Northam	1,866	4.14%	2,054	0.91
North Molton	1,186	2.63%	1,521	0.78
North Tawton	482	1.07%	1,436	0.34
Nymet Rowland	45	0.10%	76	0.59
Oakford	221	0.49%	408	0.54
Parkham	469	1.04%	584	0.80
Parracombe	237	0.53%	322	0.74
Peters Marland	182	0.40%	289	0.63
Petrockstowe	258	0.57%	467	0.55

Parish	# Wills	% of total	1801 Pop	b/d
Pilton	788	1.75%	831	0.95
Puddington	81	0.18%	135	0.60
Rackenford	218	0.48%	340	0.64
Roborough	224	0.50%	461	0.49
Romansleigh	149	0.33%	156	0.96
Rose Ash	341	0.76%	397	0.86
St Giles in the Wood	371	0.82%	547	0.68
Satterleigh	54	0.12%	64	0.84
Shebbear	469	1.04%	744	0.63
Sheepwash	161	0.36%	348	0.46
Shirwell	311	0.69%	513	0.61
South Molton	1,663	3.69%	2,753	0.60
Stoke Rivers	160	0.35%	225	0.71
Stoodleigh	186	0.41%	355	0.52
Tawstock	1,118	2.48%	1,131	0.99
Thelbridge	112	0.25%	155	0.72
Trentishoe	99	0.22%	128	0.77
Twitchen	178	0.39%	145	1.23
Warkleigh	185	0.41%	291	0.64
Washford Pyne	79	0.18%	109	0.72
Weare Gifford	213	0.47%	419	0.51
Welcombe	174	0.39%	220	0.79
Wembworthy	163	0.36%	323	0.50
West Anstey	168	0.37%	215	0.78
West Buckland	139	0.31%	257	0.54
West Down	329	0.73%	336	0.98
West Worlington	114	0.25%	158	0.72
Westleigh	255	0.57%	408	0.63
Winkleigh	660	1.46%	1214	0.54
Witheridge	543	1.20%	875	0.62
Woolfardisworthy[1]	432	0.96%	722	0.60
Yarnscombe	314	0.70%	358	0.88
Zeal Monachorum	216	0.48%	622	0.35
TOTAL	45,122	100.00%	67,037	0.67

[1]There are two parishes called Woolfardisworthy, which were not distinguished by testators. Beckerlegge used Woolfardisworthy (East or West), but in this edition Woolfardisworthy only has been used and the two parishes' populations combined for analysis

Table 8 the same results are ordered by proportion of will-making

Parish	# Wills	% of total	1801 Pop	b/d
Martinhoe	315	0.70%	165	1.91
Ashford	112	0.25%	73	1.53
Abbotsham	409	0.91%	313	1.31
Creacombe	36	0.08%	29	1.24
Twitchen	178	0.39%	145	1.23
Countisbury	142	0.31%	120	1.18
Kentisbury	246	0.55%	241	1.02
East Buckland	139	0.31%	138	1.01
Mortehoe	254	0.56%	254	1.00
Tawstock	1,118	2.48%	1,131	0.99
West Down	329	0.73%	336	0.98
Bittadon	23	0.05%	24	0.96
Bratton Fleming	388	0.86%	406	0.96
Romansleigh	149	0.33%	156	0.96
Mariansleigh	190	0.42%	199	0.95
Pilton	788	1.75%	831	0.95
Goodleigh	232	0.51%	248	0.94
Fremington	807	1.79%	875	0.92
Arlington	190	0.42%	207	0.92
Northam	1,866	4.14%	2,054	0.91
Challacombe	143	0.32%	158	0.91
Bideford	2,275	5.04%	2,536	0.90
Charles	194	0.43%	217	0.89
Yarnscombe	314	0.70%	358	0.88
Georgeham	541	1.20%	617	0.88
Marwood	553	1.23%	632	0.88
High Bray	230	0.51%	264	0.87
Instow	303	0.67%	349	0.87
Meshaw	116	0.26%	135	0.86
Rose Ash	341	0.76%	397	0.86
King's Nympton	432	0.96%	510	0.85
Satterleigh	54	0.12%	64	0.84
Heanton Punchardon	343	0.76%	418	0.82
Hartland	1,261	2.79%	1,546	0.82
Frithelstock	388	0.86%	479	0.81
Combe Martin	658	1.46%	819	0.80
Parkham	469	1.04%	584	0.80
Landcross	40	0.09%	50	0.80
Huish	77	0.17%	97	0.79
Welcombe	174	0.39%	220	0.79
Newton Tracey	68	0.15%	86	0.79
Great Torrington	1,616	3.58%	2,044	0.79
Huntshaw	167	0.37%	212	0.79
West Anstey	168	0.37%	215	0.78
North Molton	1,186	2.63%	1,521	0.78
Trentishoe	99	0.22%	128	0.77
Lynton	362	0.80%	481	0.75
High Bickington	517	1.15%	693	0.75
Filleigh	164	0.36%	220	0.75
Littleham (near Bideford)	216	0.48%	292	0.74

Parish	# Wills	% of total	1801 Pop	b/d
Parracombe	237	0.53%	322	0.74
Brendon	189	0.42%	260	0.73
Alverdiscott	202	0.45%	278	0.73
Washford Pyne	79	0.18%	109	0.72
Thelbridge	112	0.25%	155	0.72
West Worlington	114	0.25%	158	0.72
Burrington	544	1.21%	755	0.72
Alwington	223	0.49%	310	0.72
Berrynarbor	382	0.85%	532	0.72
Molland	339	0.75%	473	0.72
East Anstey	118	0.26%	165	0.72
Stoke Rivers	160	0.35%	225	0.71
East Down	221	0.49%	311	0.71
Bondleigh	177	0.39%	256	0.69
Atherington	330	0.73%	484	0.68
St Giles in the Wood	371	0.82%	547	0.68
Ilfracombe	1,231	2.73%	1,838	0.67
Dolton	389	0.86%	582	0.67
Monkleigh	252	0.56%	379	0.66
George Nympton	157	0.35%	237	0.66
Knowstone	282	0.62%	427	0.66
Chulmleigh	873	1.93%	1,333	0.65
Buckland Brewer	565	1.25%	872	0.65
Rackenford	218	0.48%	340	0.64
Warkleigh	185	0.41%	291	0.64
Dowland	116	0.26%	184	0.63
Shebbear	469	1.04%	744	0.63
Westleigh	255	0.57%	408	0.63
Peters Marland	182	0.40%	289	0.63
Witheridge	543	1.20%	875	0.62
Loxhore	134	0.30%	219	0.61
Ashreigney	444	0.98%	726	0.61
Chawleigh	460	1.02%	755	0.61
Shirwell	311	0.69%	513	0.61
Cheldon	55	0.12%	91	0.60
South Molton	1,663	3.69%	2,753	0.60
Puddington	81	0.18%	135	0.60
Woolfardisworthy[1]	432	0.96%	722	0.60
Nymet Rowland	45	0.10%	76	0.59
Buckland Filleigh	148	0.33%	252	0.59
East Worlington	114	0.25%	196	0.58
Langtree	338	0.75%	583	0.58
Meeth	147	0.33%	257	0.57
Clovelly	396	0.88%	714	0.55
Petrockstowe	258	0.57%	467	0.55
Little Torrington	248	0.55%	449	0.55
Winkleigh	660	1.46%	1,214	0.54
Oakford	221	0.49%	408	0.54
West Buckland	139	0.31%	257	0.54
Stoodleigh	186	0.41%	355	0.52
Lapford	304	0.67%	587	0.52
Barnstaple	2,952	6.54%	5,748	0.51

Parish	# Wills	% of total	1801 Pop	b/d
Weare Gifford	213	0.47%	419	0.51
Horwood	52	0.12%	103	0.50
Wembworthy	163	0.36%	323	0.50
Beaford	251	0.56%	516	0.49
Iddesleigh	215	0.48%	442	0.49
Roborough	224	0.50%	461	0.49
Newton St Petrock	103	0.23%	215	0.48
Bulkworthy	52	0.12%	110	0.47
East Putford	83	0.18%	179	0.46
Sheepwash	161	0.36%	348	0.46
Cruwys Morchard	253	0.56%	556	0.46
Eggesford	72	0.16%	173	0.42
Brushford	60	0.13%	146	0.41
Coldridge	259	0.57%	657	0.39
Bow	254	0.56%	677	0.38
Merton	254	0.56%	689	0.37
Chittlehampton	1,107	2.45%	3,003	0.37
Zeal Monachorum	216	0.48%	622	0.35
North Tawton	482	1.07%	1,436	0.34
Clannaborough	17	0.04%	59	0.29
Broad Nymet				
Lundy	0	0	n.k.	n/a
TOTAL	45,122	100.00%	67,037	0.67

[1]There are two parishes called Woolfardisworthy, which were not distinguished by testators. Beckerlegge used Woolfardisworthy (East or West), but in this edition Woolfardisworthy only has been used and the two parishes' populations combined for analysis

It will be readily seen from the map that the nearer Barnstaple, the higher the number of wills proved as a proportion of the population. It may equally be that the nearer to Exeter, the greater the numbers of testators having their wills proved there.

Lundy Island, though clearly in the Archdeaconry, and populated throughout our period, has no wills proved in this Court.

Number of documents

Table 9 shows the number of documents by year.

Year	Count		Year	Count		Year	Count
1506	1		1567	109		1581	148
1512	2		1568	132		1582	150
1522	1		1569	113		1583	170
1527	1		1570	131		1584	128
1528	1		1571	132		1585	147
1531	3		1572	136		1586	219
1551	1		1573	252		1587	218
1552	1		1574	139		1588	243
1560	1		1575	151		1589	196
1563	73		1576	105		1590	215
1564	121		1577	182		1591	290
1565	131		1578	164		1592	264
1566	105		1579	204		1593	235
			1580	229		1594	147

Year	Count			Year	Count			Year	Count
1595	161			1645	141[1]			1702	165
1596	204			1646	5			1703	260
1597	305			1648	1			1704	206
1598	216			1650	1			1705	202
1599	204			1653	1			1706	200
1600	167			1655	1			1707	226
1601	203			1658	1			1708	170
1602	250			1659	1			1709	181
1603	244			1660	110			1710	199
1604	186			1661	205			1711	185
1605	195			1662	140			1712	178
1606	219			1663	283			1713	157
1607	215			1664	256			1714	176
1608	198			1665	201			1715	175
1609	170			1666	205			1716	204
1610	219			1667	199			1717	164
1611	244			1668	193			1718	134
1612	210			1669	241			1719	157
1613	190			1670	241			1720	162
1614	218			1671	190			1721	162
1615	287			1672	238			1722	141
1616	217			1673	200			1723	147
1617	248			1674	187			1724	161
1618	222			1675	204			1725	193
1619	256			1676	206			1726	174
1620	294			1677	170			1727	177
1621	260			1678	165			1728	175
1622	298			1679	241			1729	177
1623	325			1680	214			1730	133
1624	296			1681	219			1731	172
1625	284			1682	214			1732	155
1626	268			1683	119			1733	201
1627	236			1684	217			1734	163
1628	220			1685	226			1735	140
1629	270			1686	169			1736	140
1630	239			1687	171			1737	132
1631	256			1688	218			1738	141
1632	227			1689	180			1739	140
1633	273			1690	259			1740	169
1634	127			1691	197			1741	209
1635	255			1692	175			1742	193
1636	304			1693	233			1743	171
1637	309			1694	189			1744	141
1638	239			1695	162			1745	149
1639	288			1696	186			1746	165
1640	309			1697	190			1747	135
1641	218			1698	180			1748	168
1642	156			1699	140			1749	144
1643	320			1700	185			1750	134
1644	210			1701	139			1751	97

[1] Between late 1645 and 1659 all wills were supposed to be proved in the central court in London, effectively the Prerogative Court of Canterbury, with which Court its records are stored at The National Archives

1752	121	1788	69	1824	96
1753	123	1789	82	1825	116
1754	123	1790	86	1826	127
1755	130	1791	79	1827	126
1756	127	1792	85	1828	92
1757	125	1793	87	1829	128
1758	142	1794	59	1830	115
1759	118	1795	72	1831	117
1760	100	1796	98	1832	113
1761	112	1797	100	1833	105
1762	144	1798	89	1834	123
1763	179	1799	107	1835	103
1764	112	1800	115	1836	132
1765	119	1801	90	1837	147
1766	127	1802	113	1838	95
1767	100	1803	101	1839	114
1768	92	1804	82	1840	103
1769	114	1805	121	1841	113
1770	108	1806	109	1842	95
1771	103	1807	102	1843	112
1772	109	1808	126	1844	92
1773	100	1809	102	1845	117
1774	105	1810	131	1846	108
1775	97	1811	106	1847	116
1776	120	1812	104	1848	124
1777	104	1813	96	1849	104
1778	94	1814	107	1850	90
1779	70	1815	97	1851	130
1780	118	1816	87	1852	131
1781	106	1817	94	1853	112
1782	92	1818	107	1854	113
1783	108	1819	91	1855	132
1784	92	1820	110	1856	125
1785	73	1821	92	1857	119
1786	81	1822	112	1858	10
1787	85	1823	88		

These are charted opposite.

List of abbreviations and explanation of terms

A = administration. Commonly referred to as Admons, this was issued to the person handling the estate of an intestate. Adminstrations could also be granted where there was a problem with probate, e.g. when the named executor was under age, a lunatic or had pre-deceased the testator. In these latter cases, the administration is granted "with will annexed".

dbn = De bonis non administratis, i.e. "of goods not administered". This refers to assets remaining in an estate after the death or removal of the estate administrator. The second administrator was called the administrator de bonis non and distributed the remaining assets. The most common cause of a grant of de bonis non by a court was where the administrator died. However, it could also be granted in cases where the chain of representation was broken. Such happened, for example, when the executor of a will had obtained probate, but then dies intestate. Normally, if the executor died testate, the representation passed to the executor of the first executor's estate upon probate of the latter's own will.

O = other [document]

Chart 3 Will Frequency 1563–1858

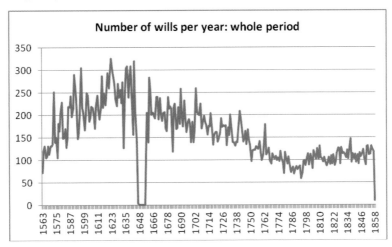

Chart 4 Will Frequency 1801–1858

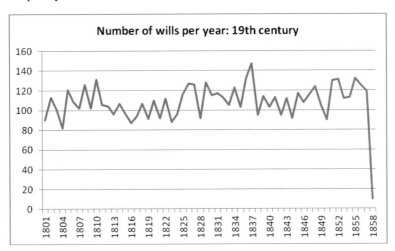

W = registered and original will
[W] = original will only
W* = registered will only

Acknowledgments

This publication would have been impossible without the initial input of material from the Devon Wills Project as mentioned in the introduction proper. Catherine Ferguson, my fellow general editor read the text, saved me from some egregious errors and made some other very helpful suggestions. She also provided invaluable moral support during the long delays which occurred during its preparation. Remaining errors, of course, remain entirely my responsibility.

Cliff Webb, February 2013.

J.J. Beckerlegge

John Joseph Beckerlegge was born at East Lavington, Wiltshire on the 10th August 1887 and died at Penzance towards the end of 1977. He married Lizzie May Harvey at Plymouth in 1922; she survived him by some ten years.

Beckerlegge came from a long line of Cornish nonconformists (see pedigree in Appendix 1). His father with the wonderful Christian name of Barzillai was a Primitive Methodist minister. He moved around the country in his vocation and married Sarah Boorman at Tunbridge in 1882. In later life his father ministered at Mountain Ash in Glamorgan where he and his wife died. It is clear that this religious upbringing caused him to maintain an interest in religion in general, and Methodism in particular throughout his life.

One of six children of whom five lived to adulthood, Beckerlegge appears to have decided on a teaching career fairly early on; his elder sister Marion and younger sister Ellen were also teachers. He attended University College, Reading, and then lived at home with his parents while holding a series of teaching jobs, starting at Abercynon Boys' School in 1905, but in 1916, after a brief sojourn in Somerset, Beckerlegge moved to Plymouth where he spent the rest of his working life. From 1916 to 1942 he was at the Junior Technical School and from 1942 until his retirement in 1945 at Devonport High School. At various times he taught English, but it is clear that History was his love and passion.

He joined the Plymouth Athenaeum in 1920 and the Devonshire Association in 1930 and inaugurated the first local branch of the latter at Plymouth in 1932. He was made an Honorary Member of the Athenaeum in 1951. A founder member of the Old Plymouth Society he served on its committee and published many book reviews in *Devon and Cornwall Notes and Queries*. He twice received the silver medal of the Royal Cornwall Polytechnic Society.

In addition to his historical interests, Beckerlegge was a keen photographer, and was at one time secretary of the Photographic Section of the Plymouth Institution.

Beckerlegge was active to the end of his long life, taking part in a BBC interview within a couple of days of his 90th birthday on the life of the social reformer William Lovett whose biography he had written.

A Provisional Bibliography of J.J. Beckerlegge

'Holbeton church reviewed' *Devonshire Association for the Advancement of Science, Literature and the Arts Report and Transactions* 64, 1932, pp.485–96
'Four hundred years of municipal finance in Plymouth [1532–1932]' *Plymouth Institution and Devon and Cornwall Natural History Society Annual Reports and Transactions* 17 part XI, 1932
'Trevithick, the Cornish engineer: a centenary study' *Plymouth Institution and Devon and Cornwall Natural History Society Annual Reports and Transactions* 17 part XVI, 1937
'Captain Hambly's book [an 18th cent. notebook containing information on the history of Plymouth]' *Plymouth Institution and Devon and Cornwall Natural History Society Annual Reports and Transactions* 17 part XIII, 1934
'The Bell of the Lighthouse on Plymouth Breakwater' *Devonshire Association for the Advancement of Art, Literature and Science Transactions* 68, 1936, pp.325–9
'Presidential Address' *Plymouth Institution and Devon and Cornwall Natural History Society Annual Reports and Transactions* 18–19, 1937
'Fardel Stone' *Devonshire Association Reports and Transactions* 70, 1938, pp.158–9
'Plympton records [overseers' accounts, 1780–1824; work-house accounts, 1775–93]' *Plymouth Institution and Devon and Cornwall Natural History Society Annual Reports and Transactions*, 17 part XIV, 1935
'Plymouth Muniments and Newfoundland' in *Plymouth Institution Annual Reports and Transactions* 18, 1945, pp.2–23
'Thatched Cottages of Newlyn' *Old Cornwall* 4, 1945, p.114

'The Thunderbolt: A Plymouth Newspaper' *Devonshire Association for the Advancement of Art, Literature and Science Transactions* 78, 1946, pp.259–64
William Lovett of Newlyn: The Cornish Social Reformer, 1948
'Plymouth Transport in Recent Years' *Devonshire Association for the Advancement of Art, Literature and Science Transactions* 80, 1948, pp.177–86
'Words heard at Mousehole' *Old Cornwall* 4, 1950, p.417
James Yonge in his 'Plymouth Memoirs', Plymouth Institution, 1951
Two hundred years of Methodism in Mousehole, 1954
'A 'holed stone' near Sancreed' *Devon and Cornwall Notes and Queries* 27, 1956–57
'Overseers' Account, Parish of Crowan, 1730–31' *Devon and Cornwall Notes and Queries* 27, 1956–57
'The inscribed stone at Mawgan-in-Meneage' *Devon and Cornwall Notes and Queries* 28, 1961
'Charles II's visits to Plymouth' *Devonshire Association for the Advancement of Art, Literature and Science Transactions* 100, 1968, pp.219–26
Mousehole: History and Recollections, Nettie Pender (foreword by John J Beckerlegge, 1970)
'Egg Buckland in 1850' *Devonshire Association for the Advancement of Art, Literature and Science Transactions* 103, 1971, pp.123–32
'History and Preaching' (with Hugo Meynell) *Theology* 74, June 1971, pp.266–68

The Beckerlegge lineage of J.J. Beckerlegge

John Beckerlegge. Born c1595. He married Elizabeth … (born c1600) at Paul 1 July 1634. They had children including:

Thomas born 26 Jul, baptised at Paul 5 November 1640. He married Elizabeth Morish at Paul 23 Oct 1669. He died 1708 at Madron. They had children including**:**

Barzillai baptised 5 November 1682 Paul. He married **Catherine Bodinnar** (born 1683) at Paul 14 January 1720. They had children including:

Barzillai. He was baptised 21 Sep 1726 Paul. He married **Margaret Head** (born 1729) at Paul 19 Oct 1749. They had a child:

John baptised 25 March 1754 Paul. He married **Prudence.** He was buried at Paul 1810. They had children including:

Barzillai was baptised 13 November 1788. He married **Elizabeth Nicholls** (born 1791, buried Paul 28 September 1872) 2 February 1812 at Paul. He buried 1 November 1862 at Paul. They had children:

A. **John Nicholls** see below
B. Barzillai baptised 25 Sep 1814 Paul. Master mariner. He married Grace Tonkin (8th daughter of Thomas Tonkin born 1817 died 1884) at Paul 1842. He died 4 Apr 1882. Left £400. They had children:
    1. William baptised 10 Nov 1844. He married Mary Drew at Liverpool 1873. She died 1917 Penzance aged 66. He died at Penzance aged 81, 1926. They had no children.
    2. Grace born 1847. She married James Henry Bennetts (born 1843, died 1922) at Madron 1872. She died 1942. They had children.
    3. Barzillai born 1848. He married Theodora Strick (born 1854, died 1933) at Plymouth 1875. Mariner. He died 2 Oct 1895 at sea. Left £812. They had children:
        a. Theodora born 1876. Music teacher. She married Charles Lawrence Taylor (born 1875) 1897. She died 1961 Hastings. They had children.
        b. William Barzillai born 1879; died 1899.
        c. Thomas born 1881. Bank clerk later manager. Went to Quebec 1935. He died Penzance, 1958.
        d. Charles born 6 May 1881. Royal Navy. Pensioned 1926. He died Dec 1966 aged 88.

    e.   Gertrude May born 1884. She died 1958 Penzance.

    f.   Adolphus born 1887. Mining engineer who visited America and lived in the Philippines. He buried 1944 Madron Cemetery aged 56.

    g.   Mary Grace born 1889. She married Frank Bryant 1912.

    h.   John born 1892. He died in Egypt, 1916.

    i.   James born 1894.

    j.   Barzillai Theodore born 1896. He married Brenda Marshall (born 1893, died 1991) in St John, Milson's Point, New South Wales 1934. He died 1954 Chatswood, New South Wales. She went from England back to Sydney, 1955. They had a child:

        (i)   Peter

  4.   Elizabeth born 1850. She died 1852.

  5.   Thomas born 1851. Mariner. He married Jessie Robbins (9 children 7 living 1911) 1876. Harbourmaster (1911). He died 1940 Penzance aged 80. She born 1856, died Penzance 1945 aged 90. They had children:

    a.   Jessie born 1879. Severely mentally handicapped. Died 1907 aged 29.

    b.   Ida Bessie born 1880. Honours, Trinity College, London, 1895.

    c.   Muriel Grace born 1882. Schoolteacher. She died unmarried 1971.

    d.   Emily Robbins born 1884. She married 1902 William Nicholls. They had children.

    e.   William Robbins born 1886. New Zealand Expeditionary Force. He married Edith Beatrice Flynn (born 1882, died 1979) 1923 at Auckland. He died New Zealand 1942 aged 56. They had children.

    f.   Barzillai alias Barlow born 1889. Blacksmith He married Selina Amelia C. Stone 1910 (she died 1965 aged 78). Went to USA 1923. Came back from Canada 1925. He died 1932 aged 44. They had children:

        (i)   Wilfred Barzillai born 1910. He married 1935 to Marjorie Stevens. He died 1979 Aylesbury.

    g.   Thomas born 1890. He married Minnie Ralph (born 1886 died 1921) 1914. He married secondly Kate Elizabeth Brand nee Church (born 1897, died 1988) 1947.

    h.   Kitty or Kate born 1894. London School of Music and studied violin in Vienna. She married Marcel T. de Rey 1924.

    i.   Doreen born 1898. She died 1902 aged 3.

  6.   John born 1853. Shipwright. He died Medway 1899.

  7.   Adolphus Frederick born and died 1854.

  8.   Elizabeth Tonkin born 1855. She married 1886 to Edward Christopher Corin. She died 1890 aged 35. He died 1941 aged 85. They had children.

  9.   Adolphus Frederick born 1857. He died 1872.

  10. James born 1860. He died 1864.

C.   Margaret born 1819. She married Jacob Corin (born 1819 died 1866) 1852. She died 1879. They had children.

John Nicholls Beckerlegge above born 8 July 1812 Newlyn, baptised 22 August 1813 Paul. He married **Mary Ann Trevelyan** (born 9 Jul 1811, died 18 March 1887) 16 February 1836 at Paul, Cornwall. He died 12 May 1902 aged 89. He left £185. They had children:

A.   William Trevillian born 1837. He married Helen Couch (born 1843 died 1905) at St Austell 1863. He died 1905 at Newton Abbot aged 68. They had children:

  1.   Helen Couch born 1865. She died at Launceston 1892 aged 27.

  2.   Mary Hannah born 1867. Dressmaker. She married Edward C. Enon. He died 1911 at sea aged 39. She died 1934 aged 66.

  3.   William Trevelyan born 1869. He married Mary Elizabeth B. Sargent 1904. Policeman. He died 1942 at Launceston aged 72. They had children:

    a.   William Trevelyan ("Trevie") born 1905. He married Maude Hayne 1936. He died Plymouth 1987. They had children:

        (i)   Geraldine M. born 1938. She married David E. Smith 1960.

        (ii) Lavinia Mary born 1910, died 1991 Taunton unmarried.

4. Kate Couch born 1876. She died unmarried at Newton Abbot 1962 aged 85.
5. Ernest Herbert born 1878. Railway clerk. He married 1911 at Newton Abbot to Mary Elizabeth Dennis (born 1878, died 1958 aged 79). Coal agent. He died at Newton Abbot 1950 aged 71. They had children:
   a. Ernest Trevelyan Dennis born at Newton Abbot 1914. He married at Weymouth to Nancy Sarah M. Evans 1946 (born 1917, died 2005). He died 2004.
   b. Denis H. born at Newton Abbot 1920. He married at Newton Abbot 1947 to Marjorie E. Milliner (born 1918). He died 2011 Sutton Coldfield. They had a daughter.
6. Emma Louise born 1880. She married 1903 at Newton Abbot, William James C. Enon. She died at Newton Abbot 1912 aged 31. They had children.
7. Frances Alice born 1886. She died at Roseberg, 56 Upton Hill, Torquay 1939 aged 53, unmarried.

B. Elizabeth Ann born 1839. She married Richard Cock at Paul 1862. She died 1877. They had children.
C. John Nicholls born 1841 Penzance; aged 19 in 1861. Fisherman. He married Jane Tonkin Baker (born 1846, died 1928) at Newlyn 1868. He died 1910. In 1911 she had had 9 children of whom 8 were living. They had children:
1. John James born 1868. He died 1908 aged 39.
2. William born 1871. Fisherman. He married Elizabeth Mary Trannack Trevaskis 1897 (born 1873, died 1952 aged 79). He died 1952 aged 80.
3. Mary born 1874. She married Jabez Curnow (born 1880, died 1967) 1902. She died 1966. They had children.
4. Jane Tonkin born 1876. She died unmarried 1951.
5. Richard Henry born 1878. Mariner. He married Bertha Jane Harvey (born 1877, died 1972) 1912. He died 1943. They had children:
   a. Cyril born 1915. Exeter University (Chemistry). Pilot officer 1941. He married 1940 Joan P. Mathews. He died Truro 2009. They had child:
      (i) Susan born 1949. She married Sonny Jones 1969. They had children.
   b. Andrew Harvey born 1915. He married Ivy Williams (born 1923, died 2006) 1949. He died 1976 aged 61. They had children.
   c. Ernest E. born 1920. In USA by 1930.
   d. William S. born 1921. He died 1930.
6. Susan Carter born 1881. Tailoress. She married James Brownfield (born 1877 died 1955) 1909. She died 1961. They had children.
7. Elizabeth Ann (Annie) born 1883. Tailoress. She died unmarried 1945.
8. Sarah Nicholls born 1886. Tailoress. She married John Gill 1912. She died 1958 aged 72. They had children.
9. Gertrude born 1890. She died unmarried 1970.

D. Jane born 1847 Penzance. She married (1) William Mark Maddern 1872 and (2) John Thomas Tresize 1879. She died 1917. She had children by husband 2.
E. Sarah Trevelyan born 1849, died 1851.
F. **Barzillai** was born at Newlyn near Penzance in 1854. In 1871 he was a fisherman at Newlyn. He had moved to Tunbridge by 1881, by which time he was a Primitive Methodist minister. He married **Sarah Boorman** at Tunbridge 1882. He died at Amesbury House, Aberdare Road, Mountain Ash, Glamorganshire 18 March 1934 aged 79. He left £271. She died there aged 90, 13 December 1940. She left £1256 10s 8d. They had the following children:
1. Kate born and died at Chichester 1883.
2. Wilfrid born at Chichester 1884. In 1911 he was a 'supplemental clerk'. He married Sarah Jane Barnes (born 1893, died 1982) at Edmonton in 1914. He died at Brighton in 1958 aged 73. They had the following children:
   a. Gwendolyn M. born at Edmonton in 1916.
   b. Alan Philip born at Edmonton 17 October 1920. He married Doris A. Atkins at Edmonton in 1942. He died at Boston, Lincolnshire in 1997. They had the following children:
      (i) Ruth M. born at Colchester 1943. She married Paul E. Newbury at Biggleswade in 1967.

       (ii)   Michael S. born at Wood Green in 1949. He died at Romford in 1955 aged 6.

    c.   Joyce Eileen born at Edmonton 21 August 1923. She died at Brighton unmarried in 1989.

3.   Marion born at Marlborough 1886 and baptised at East Lavington on 25 April that year. She attended Oxford Hall Training College, Warrington and had a series of teaching posts in Abercynon and Mountain Ash. She died unmarried at Cardiff in 1960 aged 74.

4.   **John Joseph** born at Marlborough 10 August 1887 and baptised at East Lavington 13 November of that year. He married Lizzie May Harvey at the Wesleyan Church, Ebrington Street, Plymouth 31 July 1922. He died in Penzance 13 October 1977 aged 90 and was buried in the Sheffield Road Cemetery, Paul. She died at Plymouth 29 February 1988 aged 91 and was buried beside her husband. They had no children.

5.   Ellen born at Colnbrook 31 January 1889. By 1911 she had followed Marion at Oxford Hall Training College, Warrington as a student teacher. She had several qualifications and by 1924 was headmistress of Whitmore Church of England Mixed and Infants' School, Staffordshire and later of Knight Council School near Market Drayton. She died unmarried at Hendon in 1977.

6.   Thomas Trevelyan born at Colnbrook 30 Oct 1890. He married Ethel Bennett at Redruth in 1915 (she died at Cardiff in 1932 aged 54), marriage dissolved. He married secondly Elizabeth Hearle Batten (born 1895) at Cardiff in 1919. He married thirdly Caroline Madeline Bennetts (born 1880, died at Redruth 1958) at Redruth in 1939. He died at Cardiff in 1973 aged 82. He had the following child:

    a.   John Edward (by wife 2) born at Cardiff 16 September 1920. He married Irene Smith at Worth Valley, Yorkshire in 1951. He was a clergyman and vicar of Crowan. He died at Kerrier, Cornwall in 1977. She died at Camborne 1990 aged 89. They had the following children:

       (i)   Catherine M. born at Redruth 1954. She married Daniel J. Duffey at Ealing in 1984.

       (ii)   Anne P. born at Redruth 1956. She married Roger P. Weatherly at North Dorset in 1982.

WILLS

IN THE

ARCHDEACONRY COURT OF BARNSTAPLE

1506–1858

Abbevam see Abevan
Abbinshaw see Abbotsham
Abbot, Abbott, Abbotte, Ebbot, Ebote, Ebott
  ..., Horwood 1606 [W]
  Ebott ..., Bideford 1610 [W]
  Agnes, Frithelstock 1666 W
  Agnes, High Bray 1750 A
  Ann widow of William, Hartland, esquire 1610 [W]; forename
    blank in Ms; supplied from parish register
  Cicely, Frithelstock 1637 W
  Elizabeth, Meeth 1739 W
  Henry, Frithelstock 1615 [W]
  Ebote Isott, Welcombe 1575 W
  James, Great Torrington 1845 W
  Ebbot John, Welcombe 1571 W
  John, Buckland Brewer 1617 [W]
  John, Frithelstock, snr. 1635 A
  John, Frithelstock 1663 A
  John, Frithelstock 1688 W
  John, Langtree 1700 W
  John, North Molton 1718 W
  John (or Thomas), Frithelstock 1727 [W]
  John, Frithelstock 1751 W
  John, North Molton 1793 W
  Jonathan, North Molton 1662 W
  Mary, North Molton, widow 1611 [W]; forename blank in Ms;
    supplied from parish register
  Mary, Langtree 1716 A
  Mary, Frithelstock, widow 1798 W
  Petronell, Frithelstock 1774 W
  Petronell, Frithelstock 1842 W
  Richard, Frithelstock 1663 A
  Richard, North Molton 1686 W
  Richard, Frithelstock 1692 [W]
  Richard, High Bray 1742 W
  Robert, North Molton 1637 W
  Robert, South Molton 1681 A
  Roger, North Molton 1829 W
  Sybil, North Molton 1636 W
  Thomas, North Molton 1610 [W]; forename blank in Ms;
    supplied from parish register
  Thomas, Langtree 1641 W
  Thomas, East or West Anstey 1705 W
  Thomas (or John), Frithelstock 1727 [W]
  Thomas, Langtree, yeoman 1805 W
  William, Hartland, esquire 1570 W
  William, Hartland 1585 A
  William, Frithelstock 1602 W
  William, West Anstey 1663 W
  William, Beaford 1780 W
  William, Rose Ash 1788 A
Abbotsham, Abbinshaw
  ..., Winkleigh 1611 [W]
  Abbinshaw Thomas, Northam 1747 A
Abbott, Abbotte see Abbot
Abell Joseph, Meeth 1840 A to Catherine, widow
Abevan, Abbevam, Abevans, Abuffen, Avivyan
  Abuffen ..., Barnstaple 1602 [W]
  Abevans ..., Northam 1600 [W]
  Edmund, Northam 1687 W
  Abbevam or Avivyan Jenkin, Northam 1579 A
Ableton Dorothy, Witheridge 1714 [W]
  John, Rackenford [no year given] W
  Abolton William, Witheridge 1733 W
Abott see Abbot
Abowen, Abouin, Aboyne
  Aboyne Evan, Northam 1700 W
  Owen, Bideford 1708 W
  Abouin Richard, Combe Martin 1709 W
Abraham, Abram
  Ann, Great Torrington 1761 W
  Elizabeth, South Molton 1812 W
  G ... ., Stoodleigh 1724 [W]
  Joanna, Stoodleigh 1688 W
  Abram John, St Giles in the Wood 1597 [W]
  Abram John, Great Torrington 1695 A

John, Great Torrington 1734 A
John, Tawstock 1790 W
Mary, Oakford, sp. 1807 W
Abram Richard, Great Torrington 1682 A
Richard, Stoodleigh 1724 [W]
Richard, Great Torrington 1752 W
Thomas, Stoodleigh 1761 A
William, Stoodleigh 1762 W
William, Georgeham 1839 A
Abuffen see Abevan
Ace, Ase
  Ase John, Instow 1703 A
  Thomas, Pilton 1682 A
Ache see Arche
Ackford Henry, Dolton 1731 A
Ackie see Atkie
Ackland, Acklond, Acland, Agland
  ..., Challacombe 1608 [W]
  ..., Chittlehampton 1614 [W]
  ... 1726 [W]
  Ann, Monkleigh 1767 W
  Anthony, Chittlehampton 1568 W
  Acklond Anthony, Chittlehampton 1568 W
  Archelaus, Tawstock 1697 W
  Archelaus, Tawstock 1712 A
  Archelaus, Tawstock 1772 W
  Arthur, Barnstaple 1690 W
  Arthur, Winkleigh 1695 A
  Bartholomew, Bideford 1679 W
  Cecilia, Kentisbury 1671 A, 1674 O
  Acland Charles, Bideford 1693 W
  Dorcas, Bratton Fleming 1805 A
  Edward, Clovelly 1695 W
  Agland Edward, Barnstaple 1727 [W]
  Elizabeth, Arlington 1593 [W]
  Elizabeth, East Down 1695 A
  Elizabeth, Clovelly 1724 [W]
  Frances, Fremington 1747 W
  George, Bideford 1743 W
  Hugh, Arlington 1602 W
  Hugh, Chittlehampton 1622 [W]
  Hugh, West Down 1758 W
  Hugh, Meeth 1773 A
  Acland Hugh, Meeth 1801 W
  Humphrey, Bideford 1673 A
  Humphrey, Tawstock 1707 A
  Humphrey, Bideford 1718 W and 1721 [W]
  Acklond James, Woolfardisworthy 1577 A
  James, Arlington 1788 W
  Jane, Bideford 1743 W
  Joan, Roborough 1635 A
  John, Barnstaple 1579 W
  John, West Buckland 1582 A
  Acland John, Alwington 1588 W
  John, Tawstock 1610 [W]; forename blank in Ms; supplied
    from parish register
  John, Bideford 1624 [W]
  John, Peters Marland 1685 W
  John, Clovelly 1719 A
  John, Weare Giffard 1743 W
  John, Chittlehampton 1766 W
  Acland John, Meeth 1826 W
  Acland John, Meeth 1853 W
  Julian, Tawstock 1730 [W]; forename blank in Ms; supplied
    from parish register
  Lodovic, High Bickington 1731 W
  Margaret, Marwood 1672 A
  Mary, East Down 1850 W
  Nicholas, Great Torrington 1641 W
  Peter, Arlington 1664 A
  Peter, Clovelly 1722 [W]
  Philip, Arlington 1716 A
  Rebecca, Bideford 1743 W
  Rebecca, Bideford 1778 W

Richard, Burrington 1719 W
Richard, Burrington 1728 [W]
Robert, Tiverton, 1831 to Frances S. Poole, daughter
Samuel, Shirwell 1773 W
Scipio, Winkleigh 1633 A
Thomas, Arlington 1586 W
Thomas, Goodleigh 1635 A and 1637 O
Thomas, Bideford 1639 W
Thomas, Atherington 1708 W
Thomas, Winkleigh 1742 W
Thomas, Arlington 1744 W
Acland Thomas, St Giles in the Wood 1827 A to Mary, widow
Thomas, East Down 1846 W
Acklond William, Barnstaple 1563 W
William, Arlington 1581 W
William, St Giles in the Wood 1592 [W]
William, Arlington 1619 [W]
William, Tawstock 1714 A and 1717 A
William 1730 [W]
William, Tawstock 1771 W
William, Barnstaple, butcher 1810 W
William, Barnstaple 1840 W
Ackyn see Atkins
Acland see Ackland
Adams, Adam, Adame, Adames, Addam, Addams
...., Hartland 1603 [W]
...., Northam 1604 [W]
Adam ..., Dowland 1607 [W]
Adam ..., Bondleigh 1612 [W]
...., Northam 1613 [W]
...., Mariansleigh 1616 O
... 1723 [W]
Alexander, Mariansleigh 1593 [W]
Alice, Langtree 1673 [W]
Ambrose, Meeth 1811 W*
Amos, Romansleigh 1764 A
Amos, Cheldon, yeoman 1796 W
Amos, Romansleigh 1804 W
Amos, Meshaw, yeoman 1806 A
Amos, Meshaw 1831 A to John, guardian of children
Adam Ann, St Giles in the Wood 1628 [W]
Ann, Beaford 1695 W
Ann, Romansleigh 1814 W
Ann, Tawstock 1821 W
Adam Anstis, Welcombe 1590 [W]
Anthony, Monkleigh 1718 W
Arthur, Northam 1625 [W] and O
Arthur, Buckland Brewer 1671 A
Adam Balthazar, Parkham 1591 [W]
Bartholomew, Bondleigh 1617-37 W
Brutus, Tawstock 1733 W
Charity, Mariansleigh 1818 W
Christopher, Zeal Monachorum 1586 A
Christopher, Abbotsham 1677 A
David, St Giles in the Wood 1696 W
Edmund, Abbotsham 1688 W
Adam Edward, Petrockstowe 1565 W
Edward, Chulmleigh 1789 W
Edward, Mariansleigh 1838 W
Adam Elizabeth, Parkham 1600 W
Elizabeth, St Giles in the Wood 1675 W
Elizabeth, Meshaw 1814 W
Elizabeth, West Worlington 1818 W
Elizabeth, Barnstaple 1826 W
Elizabeth, Pilton 1849 W
Adam Emma, St Giles in the Wood 1595 [W]
Adam George, St Giles in the Wood 1589 A
George, Chulmleigh 1786 W
George, East Worlington 1844 W
Grace, Mariansleigh 1847 W
Adam Henry, Parkham 1596 [W]
Henry, Hartland 1681 W
Henry, Mariansleigh, yeoman 1811 W
Henry, East Down 1818 A to Mary, widow
Adam Hugh, Parkham 1565 W

Jacob, Romansleigh 1779 A
Jacob, South Molton 1815 W
James, Northam 1797 W
James, Chawleigh 1815 W
Adam Jane, Hatherleigh 1567 W
Jane, Fremington 1797 W
Joan 1639 O
Joan, Georgeham 1710 W
Joan, Great Torrington 1786 W
Joan, Meshaw 1794 W
Adam John, Fremington 1580 W
John, Bideford 1586 W
Adam John, Georgeham 1592 [W]
John, Parkham 1610 [W]; forename blank in Ms; supplied
    from parish register
John, Martinhoe 1631 [W]
John, Newton Tracey 1635 A
Adam John, Langtree 1636 W
John, Great Torrington 1640 W
John, Witheridge 1640 W
John, High Bickington 1668 W
John, Beaford 1672 A
John, Mariansleigh 1681 W
John, Instow 1690 W
Addams John, Georgeham 1692 W
John, Bideford 1712 A
John, Meshaw 1756 W
John, Tawstock 1787 W
John, Mariansleigh 1794 W
John, Mariansleigh, jnr., yeoman 1802 W
John, Chulmleigh 1831 W
John, Romansleigh 1837 A
John, Romansleigh 1841 W and 1848 W
John, Newton Tracey 1845 W
John, Rose Ash 1856 A
Joseph, Northam 1707 A
Adam Lawrence, Woolfardisworthy 1589 W
Adam Leonard, Langtree 1670 W
Leonard, Westleigh 1711 W
Adam Mary, Buckland Brewer 1624 [W]
Mary, Bulkworthy 1678 W and 1679 W
Mary, Romansleigh, widow 1801 W
Mary, Instow 1806 W
Mary, Romansleigh 1819 W
Adam Mathew, Bondleigh 1610 [W]; forename blank in Ms;
    supplied from parish register
Monica, Georgeham 1722 A
Nicholas, Buckland Brewer 1663 W
Philip, Ilfracombe 1711 W
Adam Richard, Dowland 1596 [W]
Richard, Tawstock 1688 A
Richard, Tawstock 1749 W and 1759 W
Richard, Tawstock 1827 W
Richard, Witheridge 1844 W
Robert, Combe Martin 1635 A
Sarah, Bideford 1722 [W]
Sarah, Huntsham 1851 W
Thomas, St Giles in the Wood 1621 [W]
Thomas, Langtree 1680 W
Thomas, Winkleigh 1696 W
Thomas, Bideford 1710 W
Thomas, Ilfracombe 1712 W
Thomas, Tawstock 1801 A
Addam Thomasine, Petrockstowe 1580 W
Walter, Georgeham 1622 [W]
Adame William, Fremington 1566 W
Adam William, Dowland 1570 W
Adam William, Clovelly 1571 W
Adam William, St Giles in the Wood 1586 W
Adame William, Parkham 1590 [W]
William, Mariansleigh 1616 [W]
William, St Giles in the Wood 1667 W
William, Parkham 1673 A
William, St Giles in the Wood 1742 W
William, Great Torrington 1760 W

William, St Giles in the Wood 1763 W
William, Mariansleigh 1767 A
William, Cheldon 1789 W
William, Tawstock 1796 A
William, Chulmleigh, thatcher 1816 A to Elizabeth, widow
William, Romansleigh 1825 W
William, Mariansleigh 1831 W
William, Fremington 1841 W
William, Romansleigh 1841 W
William, King's Nympton 1857 W

Addicott, Adecott
Mary, Witheridge 1800 W
Adecott Thomas, Witheridge 1785 A
Thomas, Witheridge 1819 W
Thomas, Witheridge, snr. 1830 A to Mary, widow
Addington William, Bideford 1593 [W]
William, Bideford 1620 [W]
Addren, Addrew see Andrews
Adecott see Addicott
Adeford Robert, Chulmleigh 1566 W
Adgeman see Edgman
Adger, Agger, Agree
Agger alias Nicholls Edward, Woolfardisworthy 1579 W
Jane, Northam 1626 [W]
Agger alias Nicoll John, Woolfardisworthy (West) 1569 W
John, Woolfardisworthy 1643 W
Adger alias Nicholl John, Woolfardisworthy 1643 W
Agree Mary, Rose Ash 1725 [W]
Philip, Woolfardisworthy 1637 W
Adger alias Edger Sabine, Goodleigh 1662 W more than one
   copy
Ager alias Nycolls Thomas, Woolfardisworthy (East or West),
   jnr. 1566 W
Aydger Thomas, Abbotsham 1583 W
William, Abbotsham 1630 [W]
   see also Edger
Adgman, Adgimand see Edgman
Ager, Agger, Agree see Adger
Aeres see Aire
Aiche see Arche
Aighton George, Monkleigh, jnr. 1729 [W]
Aire, Aeres, Airs, Are, Ayer, Ayers, Ayor, Ayre, Ayres, Eare,
   Eyer, Eyre
Alice, Great Torrington 1624 [W]
Eare Alice, Little Torrington 1624 [W]
Ayre Amesius, Romansleigh 1717 W
Eyre Ann, Barnstaple 1597 [W]
Eyer Ann, Knowstone 1734 W
Ayre Arthur, Rackenford 1725 [W]
Aeres Arthur, Northam 1740 W
Ayer Augustine, Weare Giffard 1673 W
Eyre alias Eare Augustine, Weare Giffard 1673 W
Ayre Barbara, Rose Ash 1700 W
Ayre Diaphanus, Barnstaple 1728 [W]
Ayre Dorothy, Marwood 1727 [W]
Ayre Edith, Rose Ash 1718 W
Eare Edmund and Grace, Frithelstock 1635 W
Edward, Witheridge 1599 W
Eare Edward, Peters Marland 1665 W
Ayre Eleanor, Witheridge 1713 W
Ayer Elizabeth, Rose Ash 1619 [W]
Ayer or Eare Elizabeth, Brendon 1675 A
Elizabeth, West Anstey 1676 W
Eare Elnathan, Peters Marland 1725 W
Eare alias Ayre Emanuel, Bideford, snr. 1680 W
Ayre Emanuel, Bideford 1716 W
Eare Frances, Peters Marland 1669 A
Frances, West Down 1680 W
Aire alias Eyre Francis, West Down 1680 W
Ayor Francis, Peters Marland 1742 W
Ayre Francis, Peters Marland 1818 W
Are Fransifeus, Barnstaple 1728 [W]
Ayre George, Witheridge 1733 W
Ayer, Eare alias Grace and Edmund, Frithelstock 1635 W
Eare Henry, Alverdiscott 1696 W

Ayre Henry, Rose Ash 1706 W
Ayre Henry, Bishop's Nympton 1766 W
Ayre Henry, Bishop's Nympton or Molland, yeoman 1810 W
Ayre Henry, Bishop's Nympton or Molland, yeoman 1843 W
   to Barbara, widow
Ayre Honoria, Great Torrington 1686 W
Hugh, Twitchen 1679 W
Are alias Eare Hugh, Twitchen 1679 W
Ayer Joan, Witheridge 1633 W
Ayre Joan, Mariansleigh 1830 W
Ayre Joanna, Rackenford 1700 W
Ayre John, Barnstaple 1579 W
Eare John, Yarnscombe 1586 W
John, West Down 1588 W
Ayer John, Barnstaple 1622 [W]
Ayer or Eare John, West Down 1624 [W]
Ayer John, West Anstey 1626 [W]
Ayer or Eare John, Creacombe 1634 W
Ayres John, Barnstaple 1667 W
Ayre John, Stoodleigh 1694 W
Ayre John, Frithelstock 1702 A
Airs John, Northam 1753 W
Ayre John, Rose Ash 1780 W
Ayre John, Peters Marland 1788 W
Ayre John, Rackenford 1826 W
Ayre John, Peters Marland 1849 W
Ayre John, Fremington 1852 W
Ayer or Eare Joseph, Roborough 1624 [W]
Ayre Joseph, Frithelstock 1706 W
Ayre Justinian, Knowstone 1714 [W]
Ayre alias Walker Mary, Buckland Brewer, snr. 1677 [W]
Ayer or Eare Nicholas, Bideford 1635 W
Ayre Nicholas, West Down 1668 W
Ayer Nicholas, West Anstey 1670 [W]
Ayre Nicholas, Bideford 1700 A
Philip, Witheridge 1698 W
Ayer Richard, West Down 1633 A
Eare Richard, Rose Ash, snr. 1644 W
Ayre Richard, Rose Ash 1663 W and 1668 W
Ayre Richard, Rose Ash 1740 W
Ayre Richard, Witheridge 1768 W
Ayre Richard, Rose Ash, yeoman 1814 A to William, son
Ayre Robert, Rose Ash 1567 W
Ayer Robert, Rose Ash 1668 W
Eare Robert, Bideford 1682 A
Ayer Robert, Rackenford 1703 W
Ayre Robert, Rose Ash 1714 W
Ayre Robert, Rose Ash, gentleman 1810 A
Ayre Robert, South Molton 1848 W
Eare Roger, Lynton 1678 W
Ayer Samuel, Langtree 1670 A
Thomas, Great Torrington 1596 [W]
Ayre Thomas, Witheridge 1693 A
Ayre Thomas, Knowstone 1743 W and 1750 W
Ayre Thomas, Rose Ash 1765 W
Ayre Thomas, Witheridge 1776 W and 1781 W
Ayre Thomas, Rackenford 1794 W
Ayre Thomas, Rackenford 1851 W
Ayre Thomasine, Witheridge 1798 W transmitted to Doctor's
   Commons
Ayer William, Langtree 1621 [W]
Ayer or Eare William, St Giles in the Wood 1635 A and 1636
   O
Ayer William, Weare Giffard 1671 A
Ayre or Eare William, Bideford 1673 W
Eare William, Peters Marland 1725 W
Ayre William, Witheridge 1779 W
Ayre William, Peters Marland 1802 W
Ayre William, Oakford 1803 A
Ayre William, Petrockstowe, yeoman 1807 A
Ayre William, Witheridge 1821 W
Ayre William, Langtree, cordwainer 1847 A to Mary, widow
Aishe see Ash
Aishedon see Ashton
Aishleford see Ashelford
Aishton see Ashton

Aishwick see Ashwick
Aldred William, Barnstaple 1826 W
Alen see Allen
Alexander Ann, South Molton 1854 W
James, South Molton 1845 W
Alford, Alforde, Allford, Alverd
..., Roborough 1726 [W]
Andrew, Winkleigh 1721 [W]
Ann, Bideford 1630 [W]
Ann, Ashreigney 1822 A
Edmund, Winkleigh 1765 A
Edward, King's Nympton 1797 A
Elizabeth, Winkleigh 1704 A
Elizabeth, Merton 1798 W
Elizabeth Ann, Ashreigney, sp. 1841 A to Robert of Tavistock,
    father
George, Ashreigney 1633 A and 1642 A
George, Bondleigh 1699 W
George, Roborough 1713 W
George, Roborough 1736 W
George, Roborough 1769 W
George, High Bickington 1826 W
George, High Bickington 1848 W
Henry, Roborough 1690 W
Henry, Chulmleigh 1694 W
Henry, Roborough, yeoman 1810 W
Isott, Roborough 1614 [W]; forename blank in Ms; supplied
    from parish register
Jacob, Ashreigney 1795 A
Jeremiah, Instow 1804 W
Joan, Ashreigney 1638 A
Joan, Ashreigney 1671 W
Joan, Ashreigney 1800 W
Allford Joanna, Burrington 1720 W
John, Winkleigh 1615 [W]
John, Brushford 1635 W
John, Zeal Monachorum 1642 W
John, Ashreigney 1698 [W]
John, Burrington 1720 W
John, Winkleigh 1755 A
John, Beaford 1763 A
John, Burrington 1771 W
John, Winkleigh 1775 W
John, Roborough 1785 W
John, High Bickington, yeoman 1799 A
John, King's Nympton, yeoman 1810 W
John, King's Nympton 1816 A to Joan, sp., sister
Joseph, Roborough 1686 A
Lawrence, Weare Giffard, limeburner 1803 A
Lewis, High Bickington 1771 W
Lewis, High Bickington 1846 A
Lodovic, Roborough 1711 A
Alverd Mary, Bideford 1701 W
Mary, Mariansleigh 1728 [W]
Mary, High Bickington, widow 1808 W
Mary, Ashreigney 1825 W
Mary Ann, Bideford, widow 1809 W second probate 1832
Nancy, Ashreigney 1840 W
Nathaniel, Beaford 1615 [W]; forename blank in Ms; supplied
    from parish register - surname spelled Alvard there
Nathaniel, Dolton 1615 [W]
Nathaniel, Winkleigh 1788 W
Peter, St Giles in the Wood 1767 W
Peter, High Bickington 1814 A to Susanna, widow
Alforde Ralph, Beaford 1579 W
Ralph, Beaford 1645 W
Richard, Roborough 1592 [W]
Richard, Roborough 1633 A
Richard, Wembworthy 1754 W
Richard, King's Nympton 1756 W
Alforde Robert, Bow 1589 A
Samuel, Ashreigney 1796 A
Simon, Ashreigney 1717 W
Thomas, Bondleigh 1675 A
Thomas, Eggesford 1725 [W]

Thomas, Alverdiscott 1746 A
Thomasine, Zeal Monachorum 1605 W
William, Ashreigney 1689 W and A
William, Winkleigh 1770 A
William, High Bickington 1814 W
Allanson Edward, Barnstaple, gentleman 1679 W
Allen, Alen, Alleyne, Allin, Alling, Allon, Allyn
..., Great Torrington 1600 [W]
..., East Buckland 1608 [W]
..., Chittlehampton 1609 [W]
..., Bideford 1610 [W]
..., Fremington 1612 [W]
... 1730 [W]
Alley [in register] Abigail, Great Torrington, widow 1661 W;
    forename blank in Ms; supplied from parish register
Agnes, Great Torrington 1671 W
Alexander, Great Torrington 1671 W
Ann, Molland 1661 A
Ann, Newton St Petrock 1817 W
Anthony, South Molton 1619 [W]
Anthony, Chittlehampton 1683 A
Bartholomew, Weare Giffard 1608 [W]; forename blank in
    Ms; supplied from parish register
Alleyne Caroline, Ilfracombe 1857 W
Catherine, St Giles in the Wood 1695 W
Catherine, Tawstock 1667 W
Christopher, Fremington 1630 [W]
Christopher, East Buckland 1719 A
Cicely, Pilton, widow 1591 [W]
Deborah, Shebbear 1724 [W]
Edward, Great Torrington 1660 W
Edward, Mariansleigh 1727 [W]
Elizabeth, Marwood 1581 W
Elizabeth, Bideford 1688 A
Elizabeth, Northam 1825 W
Elizabeth, South Molton 1825 W
Ellen, Great Torrington 1636 A
Allyn Gabriel, Northam 1684 A
George, Monkleigh 1615 [W]; forename blank in Ms; supplied
    from parish register
Allyn George, Fremington 1625 [W]
Allyn George, Bideford 1676 W
Allyn George 1685 W
Allyn George, Buckland Filleigh 1690 W
Allyn Gertrude, Chittlehampton 1625 [W]
Grace, Bideford 1623 [W]
Henry, High Bray 1665 A
Henry, Marwood 1676 [W]
Henry, Great Torrington 1683 A
Henry, North Molton, butcher 1806 A
Henry, Buckland Filleigh 1807 W
Henry, North Molton 1808 W
Hercules, Shebbear 1676 W
Hugh, South Molton 1625 [W]
Jacob, Bideford 1671 W
Allyn James, Fremington 1560 W
Allyn Jeremiah, Great Torrington 1686 W
Jerome, Great Torrington 1603 W
Joan, Great Torrington 1569 W
Joan, Shebbear 1589 W
Joan, Weare Giffard 1599 [W]
Joan, Shebbear 1664 W
Alleyne Joanna, Fremington 1688 A
John, Bideford 1571 W
John, Twitchen 1581 A
John, Barnstaple 1592 [W]
John, Fremington 1592 [W]
John, Parkham 1597 [W] and 1598 [W]
John, Chittlehampton 1627 [W]
John, East Buckland 1635 W
John, South Molton 1637 W
Allyn John, Tawstock 1642 W
John, Frithelstock 1660 W
John, Pilton 1661 W and 1670 W
John, Huntshaw 1667 A

Allyn John, St Giles in the Wood 1675 W
John, Tawstock 1676 W
Allyn John, Bideford 1709 W
Allin John, Shebbear 1710 A
Allyn John, Northam 1710 A
John, Parracombe 1711 W
John, Northam 1740 A
Alling John, Mariansleigh 1740 W
Allin John, Atherington 1762 W
Allin John, Parkham, yeoman 1806 W
John, Northam, mariner 1807 A
John, North Molton, yeoman 1808 W
Allyn John, Goodleigh 1825 W
John, South Molton 1843 A
Allin alias Harding John, Woolfardisworthy 1847 W
Julian, Abbotsham 1588 W
Margaret, South Molton 1692 W
Margaret, South Molton, widow 1817 A to Margaret, daughter
Martha, Great Torrington 1661 W
Alling Martha, Yarnscombe 1759 W
Allyn Mary, Great Torrington 1677 A
Mary, South Molton 1692 W
Allin Mary, Berrynarbor 1830 A
Mary, North Molton 1845 W
Mathew, Chittlehampton 1617 [W]
Mathew, Fremington 1618 [W] and 1619 O
Mathew 1629 [W]
Mathew, Barnstaple 1669 W
Allyn alias Larminy Michael (died 1681), Barnstaple 1683 A; forename blank in Ms; supplied from parish register
Nicholas, Peters Marland 1567 W
Nicholas, Shebbear 1629 [W]
Peter, East Buckland 1624 [W]
Peter, Abbotsham 1659 W
Peter, South Molton 1765 W
Philip, Shebbear 1586 W
Philip, Monkleigh 1693 W
Phillippa, Chittlehampton 1690 W
Providence, Molland 1666 W
Ralph, Great Torrington 1630 [W]
Rebecca, Langtree 1744 A
Allin Rebecca, Fremington 1846 W
Richard, Chittlehampton 1596 [W]
Alling Richard, Yarnscombe 1727 [W]
Alen Robert, Shebbear 1565 W
Allyn Robert, Weare Giffard 1585 W
Robert, South Molton 1604 W
Robert, Shebbear 1681 W
Samuel, Bondleigh 1706 W
Alen Simon, Fremington 1576 W
Susanna, Landcross 1844 W
Theophilus, South Molton 1742 W and 1744 A
Theophilus, South Molton, glazier 1807 W
Theophilus, South Molton 1822 A
Theophilus, Barnstaple 1836 A
Thomas, Abbotsham 1619 [W]
Thomas, Twitchen 1631 [W]
Thomas, Molland 1661 A
Allon Thomas, Bideford 1672 W
Allyn Thomas, Stoke Rivers 1674 A
Thomas, Atherington 1682 A
Thomas, North Molton 1729 [W]
Thomas, Northam 1735 A
Thomas, Northam 1745 W
Thomas, North Tawton 1747 W
Allin Thomas, Northam 1820 W
Allin Thomas, Landcross 1828 W
Allyn Thomasine, Fremington 1693 W
Allyn Thomasine, South Molton 1710 W
Thomasine, South Molton, widow 1810 A
Ursula, Fremington 1625 [W]
William, South Molton 1564 W
Alen William, Marwood 1576 W
William, Buckland Brewer 1622 [W]
William, Abbotsham 1633 W

William, Great Torrington 1635 W
Allyn William, South Molton 1644 W
William, Bideford 1664 W and 1667 W
Allyn William, Chittlehampton 1684 W
William, ship *Windsor* 1748 W
William, Parracombe 1750 A
William, Chittlehampton 1764 A
William, Northam 1794 W
William, South Molton 1817 A
Allin William, Fremington 1831 W
Allin William, Little Torrington 1846 W
Aller Alice, Alwington 1580 A
Henry, North Tawton 1625 [W]
Alley, Alleyn see Allen
Allford see Alford
Allin, Alling, Allon, Allyn see Allen
Almsworthy Ann, Filleigh 1755 W
Ann, East Buckland 1778 W
Henry, South Molton 1747 A
Henry, South Molton 1779 A; A dbn
Richard, Witheridge 1699 A
Richard, Charles 1843 A
Valentine, Twitchen 1690 W
Valentine, Filleigh 1749 W
William, East Anstey 1687 A
Alport Thomas Rose, Barnstaple 1855 A to Louisa of Barnstaple, widow
Alverd see Alford
Amery, Amary, Amerye, Amorey, Amory
Amory ..., South Molton 1834 W
Amory Arthur, Chittlehampton 1707 W
Avis, Cruwys Morchard 1597 [W]
Baldwin, Tawstock 1598 [W]
Amory Elizabeth, South Molton 1638 W
Amory Grace, Bideford 1703 W
Amorey Henry, Bideford 1663 W
Henry, Ilfracombe 1672 O
Amory Hugh, South Molton 1618 [W]
Amory James, Zeal Monachorum 1773 A
Amory Joanna, South Molton 1688 W
John, Fremington 1596 [W]
John, Chulmleigh 1606 W
Amory John, South Molton 1633 W
Amory John, Chittlehampton 1702 W
Amory Judith, South Molton 1775 A
Amerye Lewis, Chittlehampton 1579 W
Amory Margaret, South Molton 1637 W
Mary, Abbotsham 1635 W
Paschal, Winkleigh 1598 W
Richard, Chulmleigh 1813 W
Robert, South Molton 1624 [W]
. Amory Robert, South Molton 1670 W and A, and 1672 O
Amory Salathiel, Bideford 1722 W
Amory Thomas, South Molton 1770 W
Amory Thomas, South Molton, gentleman 1804 W
Amerye William, Cruwys Morchard 1569 W
Amory William, South Molton 1633 W
Amary William, Coldridge 1732 W
Amory Willmot, Bideford 1700 W
Ames Ann, Combe Martin 1846 W
William, North Molton 1577 A
Amorey, Amory see Amery
Anderson Agnes, Northam 1742 A
Margaret, Pilton 1683 A
Anderton, Anderdon
Anderdon ..., Shebbear 1601 A
Anderdon ..., Dowland 1607 [W] and O
Anderdon ..., Shebbear 1607 [W]
Jacob, Pilton 1684 A
Joan, Alwington 1703 W
Anderdon John, Shebbear 1602 W
John, Alwington 1703 W
Anderdon Mary, Pilton 1667 W
Anderdon Philip, Shebbear 1696 W
Philip, Northam 1717 A

Anderdon Richard, Shebbear 1616 [W]
Simon, Pilton 1643 W
Anderdon Thomas, Bideford 1636 A
Anderdon William, Shebbear 1567 W
Andrews, Addren, Addrew, Andreews, Andrew, Andrewe, Androw
Andrew ..., Shebbear 1603 [W]
Andrew ..., Great Torrington 1605 [W]
Androw ..., Bideford 1608 [W]
Abraham, Ilfracombe 1809 A
Andrewe Agnes, Winkleigh 1563 W
Alexander, Ilfracombe 1696 A
Andrew Alexander, Monkleigh 1713 [W]
Andrew Alexander, Newton St Petrock 1741 W
Andrewe Ann, Shebbear 1603 W
Ann, Ilfracombe 1696 W
Andrewe Catherine, Bideford 1628 [W]
Andrewe Edward, Combe Martin 1590 [W]
Andreews Edward, Alwington 1719 W
Addren (Addrew) alias Hobbye Eleanor, Bideford 1587 W
Andrewe Elizabeth, Bideford 1584 A
Andrew Elizabeth, Barnstaple 1840 W
Andrew George, Great Torrington 1592 [W]
Andrew George, Bideford 1644 W
George, Great Torrington 1711 W
Andrew George, Molland, yeoman 1807 W
Andrew Grace, Monkleigh 1715 W
Andrewe James, Fremington 1585 W
Andrew James, Shebbear 1722 [W]
Andrew James, East Putford 1770 W
James, Woolfardisworthy 1840 A to Christian, widow
Andrewe Joan, Instow 1595 [W]
Joanna, Ilfracombe 1684 W
John, Ilfracombe 1512 W
Andrew John, Great Torrington 1575 W
John, Great Torrington 1661 W
John, Ilfracombe, jnr. 1676 A
John, Ilfracombe 1677 A
John, Ilfracombe 1688 W
Andrew John, Northam 1692 W
John, Barnstaple 1707 W
John, Great Torrington 1761 A
John, Barnstaple 1763 [W]
Andrew John, Woolfardisworthy, yeoman 1810 W
John, Ilfracombe 1833 A to Ann, widow
John, Little Torrington 1833 W
John, Tawstock 1833 W
John, Pilton 1851 W
Andrew Joseph, Woolfardisworthy 1842 W
Andrew Lawrence, Little Torrington 1766 W
Andrew Mary, Georgeham 1685 W
Mary, Barnstaple 1708 W
Andrew Nicholas, Barnstaple 1848 W
Andrew Philip, Berrynarbor 1596 [W]
Andrew Philip, Northam 1740 A
Philip, Little Torrington 1806 W*
Andrew Philip, Buckland Filleigh 1822 W
Andrew Ralph 1730 [W]
Andrew Richard, Ilfracombe, jnr. 1753 W
Richard, Barnstaple 1779 A
Andrewe Robert, Pilton 1597 [W] (2)
Andrew Robert, Bideford 1599 [W]
Androw Robert, Barnstaple 1623 [W]
Andrew Roger, Instow 1588 W
Andrewe Roger, Instow 1592 [W]
Andrew Roger 1729 [W]
Andrew Samuel, Great Torrington 1793 A
Andrew Thomas, Bideford 1598 [W]
Thomas, ship *Plymouth* 1748 A
Andrew Thomas, East Putford 1838 W
Androw Thomasine, Fremington 1631 [W]
Andrewe William, Great Torrington 1576 [W]
Andrew William, Bideford 1587 A
Andrew William, Martinhoe 1622 [W]
Andrew William, Atherington 1817 W

Androw William, Bideford 1606 [W]; forename blank in Ms; supplied from parish register
Anger ..., Northam 1602 [W]
John, Northam 1567 W
John, Northam 1696 A
William, Northam 1578 A
William, Northam 1621 [W]
Angle Jacob, Chulmleigh 1671 W
Annesly Ann wife of the Earl of Anglesey 1741 A [christian name supplied from peerage]
Ansley see Anstey
Ansteris see Anstice
Anstey, Ansley, Anstie, Ansty
Ansty Barbara, West Anstey 1716 W
Anstie David, East Anstey 1567 W
Ansty Elizabeth, Oakford 1711 W
George, Stoodleigh 1758 A
Hugh, East Anstey 1739 W
James, Tawstock 1622 [W]
Ansley Jenny, Barnstaple 1852 A
Anstie John, East Anstey 1577 W
John, Iddesleigh 1764 A
John, Merton 1841 W
Thomas, West Anstey 1700 W
Ansty William, West Anstey 1695 A and 1704 A
Ansty William, West Anstey 1705 W and 1706 W
William, Witheridge 1856 W
Anstice, Ansteris
David, East Anstey 1611 [W]
Edward, Bideford 1693 A
Ansteris John, South Molton 1587 W
Richard, Lapford 1695 A
Anstie, Ansty see Anstey
Anthony Ann, Bideford 1847 W
George, South Molton, tallow chandler 1822 W to Ann, widow
Gregory, Barnstaple 1756 W
John, South Molton 1739 [W]
Mary, South Molton 1729 W
Mary, South Molton 1758 W
Raymond, Bideford 1617 [W]
Thomas, Tawstock 1622 [W]
Thomas, South Molton 1744 A
Thomas, Bideford 1851 W
Apleton Robert, Witheridge 1715 [W]
William, Witheridge 1696 W
Apley, Aplye
..., Barnstaple 1613 [W] and 1614 [W]
..., Barnstaple 1715 [W]
Aplye alias Pett Agnes, South Molton 1588 W
Dorothy, Barnstaple, widow 1612 [W]; forename blank in Ms; supplied from parish register
Aplin, Aplyn
Aplyn Robert, Meeth 1625 [W]
Robert, Langtree 1726 [W]
Aprise, Apriss
Apriss Henry, Great Torrington 1591 [W]
Richard, Barnstaple 1564 W
Aram Edmund, South Molton 1711 [W]
Mary, South Molton 1755 A
Sarah, South Molton 1715 A
Sarah, South Molton 1743 W
Arche, Ach, Aiche, Arche
Ach ..., Chulmleigh 1602 A
Arche alias Slye Alice, Chulmleigh, widow 1572 W
Aiche William, Chulmleigh 1569 W
Are see Aire
Armstrong John, Monkleigh 1588 W
Arnold, Arnall, Arnell, Arnolde, Arnoll
..., Barnstaple 1836 W
..., Beaford 1851 W
Agnes, Iddesleigh 1759 W
Andrew, Little Torrington 1795 W
Dorothy, Beaford 1849 W
Arnoll Eleanor, Monkleigh 1703 W
Elizabeth, Bideford 1640 W

Arnoll George, Pilton 1730 [W]
George, Petrockstowe 1761 W
George, Winkleigh 1814 A
Arnoll George, Parkham, husbandman 1830 A to Ann, widow
Arnoll Henry, Monkleigh 1682 W
Arnoll Henry, Bideford 1691 W
Arnoll Henry, Monkleigh 1717 W
Hugh, Roborough 1639 A
Arnoll Israel, Iddesleigh 1708 A
Arnolde John, North Tawton 1564 W
Arnoll John, Iddesleigh 1568 W
Arnoll John, Buckland Brewer 1586 W
John, Shebbear 1597 [W]
John, Great Torrington 1602 W
Arnold alias Jennet (Gennet) John, Bideford 1605 W
John, Bideford 1703 W
Arnoll John, Shebbear 1734 W
John, Burrington 1745 A
John, North Tawton 1800 W
John, Iddesleigh, yeoman 1805 W
Arnoll John, Chulmleigh 1831 A to Elizabeth Deldridge, sister
John, Dolton 1843 W
John, Beaford 1856 W
Mary, Great Torrington 1602 W
Michael, Barnstaple 1591 [W]
Arnold alias Gennet Nicholas, Bideford 1642 W
Nicholas, Great Torrington 1739 A
Nicholas, Petrockstowe 1764 A
Nicholas, Little Torrington 1784 A
Nicholas or Philip, Buckland Brewer 1615 [W]
Arnolde alias Marten Richard, Barnstaple 1564 W
Richard, Tawstock 1628 [W]
Arnall Richard, Great Torrington 1629 [W]
Arnoll Robert, Barnstaple 1827 W
Samuel, Little Torrington 1827 W
Thomas, Bideford 1622 [W]
Thomas, Iddesleigh, yeoman 1807 W
William, Great Torrington 1604 W
William, Bideford 1637 W
William, Iddesleigh 1666 A and 1669 O
Arnoll alias Gennet William, Bideford 1686 W
Arnell William, Bideford 1717 W
William, Iddesleigh 1736 W
Arragon William, Northam 1745 W
Arscott, Arscotte, Ascott, Ascotte, Asscott
..., High Bickington 1609 [W] listed twice
..., Langtree 1612 [W]
Arthur, South Molton 1710 W
Ascotte Egline, Winkleigh 1571 W
Eleanor, High Bickington 1616 [W]
Ascott Elizabeth, Westleigh 1640 W
George, Shebbear 1669 A
Ascott Alnectius, Shebbear 1619 [W]
Hugh, Burrington 1590 [W]
Arscotte Humphrey, Westleigh 1601 [W]
Asscott John, Woolfardisworthy 1584 W
Ascott John, Westleigh 1664 W
Ascott Mary, Shebbear 1636 A
Philip, Merton 1615 [W]
Ralph, Northam 1742 W
Richard, Horwood 1594 [W]
Richard, North Tawton 1689 A
Roger, North Tawton 1614 [W]; forename blank in Ms;
   supplied from parish register
Samuel, Bideford 1694 W
Samuel, Wembworthy 1828 W
Thomas, Bideford 1616 [W]
Thomas, Dolton 1663 A
Walter, Zeal Monachorum 1681 A
   see also Huscott
Arthur, Arter, Arthure
..., Northam 1610 [W]
Dorothy, Barnstaple 1818 W
George, Atherington 1854 W
Arthure James, Witheridge 1615 [W]

Mary see Thomas Richards
Arthure alias Greffeth Richard, Barnstaple 1585 O bond
William, Great Torrington 1592 [W]
Arter William, Barnstaple 1852 W
Artute Simon, Bideford 1572 W
Arundell Honor, South Molton 1738 W
Robert, Bideford 1618 [W]
Thomasine, Monkleigh 1679 W
Ascott, Ascotte see Arscott
Ash, Aishe, Ashe, Ayshe
Agnes, Fremington 1701 W
Aishe Ann, Chulmleigh 1619 [W]
Ayshe Daniel, Fremington 1636 W
Daniel, Fremington 1716 W
Ayshe David, Ilfracombe 1639 W
David, Parracombe 1752 A
Ayshe David, Combe Martin 1831 [W]
Dorothy, Fremington 1709 W
Eleanor, Bideford 1721 [W]
Ashe Emett, Ilfracombe 1582 W
Francis, Bideford 1770 A; 1814 A dbn
Humphrey, Combe Martin 1681 W
Aysh alias Rook Jane, Combe Martin 1668 A
Joanna, Northam 1670 W
Aishe John, Ilfracombe 1576 W
Ayshe John, Combe Martin 1583 W
Aishe John, Great Torrington 1621 [W]
Aishe John, Marwood 1629 [W]
Ayshe John, Bideford 1635 A and 1637 O
John, Sheepwash 1644 A
John, Cruwys Morchard 1687 A
John, Fremington 1692 A
John, Bideford 1705 W
Ashe Mary, Northam 1674 W
Philip, Berrynarbor 1762 W
Ayshe Richard, Bondleigh 1581 W
Richard, Fremington 1703 W
Sarah, Fremington 1717 W
Thomas, East Putford 1700 W
Ayshe William, Berrynarbor 1624 [W]
Asham John, Barnstaple 1734 W
Ashby John, Barnstaple 1826 W; A dbn 1836
Ashe see Ash
Asheford see Ashford
Ashelford, Aishleford, Asselford
Joanna, Chulmleigh 1711 W
John, Cruwys Morchard 1611 [W]; forename blank in Ms;
   supplied from parish register
Aishleford John, Cruwys Morchard 1626-28 [W] also dated
   1628
John, Cruwys Morchard 1677 W
Asselford William, Cruwys Morchard 1570 W
Asheton see Ashton
Ashford, Asheford
James, Great Torrington 1832 W
Asheford Leonard, Chawleigh 1694 W
Mary, Great Torrington 1855 W
Thomas, Bondleigh 1670 W
Ashley, Ayshlegh Walter, Winkleigh 1576 A
Ashplant John, High Bickington 1719 W
John, Chulmleigh 1755 W
John, Meeth 1838 W
Thomas, High Bickington 1744 W
Thomas, Bideford 1837 W
William, Merton 1830 A to Mary Gordon and Joan Quance,
   daughters
Ashpole, Ayshpole Stephen, Great Torrington 1587 W
Ashton, Aishedon, Aishton, Asheton, Ayshton
Aishton ..., Welcombe 1606 [W]
Ann, Bideford 1857 W
Elias, Merton 1850 A to Joseph, brother
Francis, Welcombe 1695 A
Gratus, Parkham 1723 [W]
Israel, Welcombe 1691 A
Israel, Welcombe 1771 A

James, Monkleigh 1737 W
James, Alwington 1844 W
Joanna, Little Torrington 1661 W
Aishedon John, Welcombe 1563 W
Asheton John 1582 W
Aishton John, Welcombe 1622 [W] and 1630 [W]
Ayshton John, Bideford 1632 [W]
John, Welcombe 1703 W
Aishton John, Welcombe 1743 W
John, Welcombe 1751 W and 1754 W
Aishton John, Welcombe 1771 W
Aishton John, Welcombe 1782 A
Aishton John, Hartland 1790 A
John, Clovelly, yeoman 1809 A
John, Clovelly 1824 A
Aishton John, Bideford 1850 [W]
Joseph, Merton 1854 A to Elizabeth, widow
Philip, Welcombe 1663 W
Philip, Fremington 1720 A
Aishton Philip, Fremington 1732 A
Phyllis, Bideford 1832 W
Aishton Richard, Hartland 1606 W
Richard, Welcombe 1680 A
Richard, Welcombe 1704 W and 1711 W
Thomas, Welcombe 1698 W
Thomas, Welcombe 1777 A
Thomas, Merton 1819 A to Elizabeth, widow
Aishton Thomas, Welcombe 1831 W
Aishton William, Welcombe 1740 W
William, Great Torrington 1752 A
William, Welcombe 1753 A
William, Buckland Brewer 1754 A
William, Clovelly 1818 W
William, Welcombe 1828 A
Ashwick, Aishwick Thomas, Great Torrington 1681 A
Askhall Thomas, Cruwys Morchard 1725 [W]
Ason Joan, Cruwys Morchard 1746 A
Asscott see Arscott
Asselford see Ashelford
Aston Robert, Ashreigney 1583 W
Atkaines, Atkayne, Atkens see Atkins
Atkey, Ackie, Atkay, Atkae, Atkaie, Atkye
Agnes, Georgeham 1608 [W]; forename blank in Ms; supplied
from parish register
Atkie Alexander, Ilfracombe 1615 [W]
Alexander, Ilfracombe 1675 W
Benjamin, Ilfracombe 1680 W
Dorothy, South Molton 1701 A
Henry, Tawstock 1590 [W]
John, Brendon 1573 A
Atkye John, Ilfracombe 1588 W and 1590 [W]
Margaret, Ilfracombe 1684 W
Mary, Ilfracombe 1668 W
Atkye Oliver, Marwood 1571 W
Atkay Philip, Mortehoe 1625 [W]
Philip, South Molton 1674 W
Philip, South Molton 1701 W
Philip, Ilfracombe 1716 W
Richard, Barnstaple, snr. 1644 W
Richard, Barnstaple 1660 W
Ackie Simon, Marwood 1606 W
Atkie Sybil, Marwood 1615 [W]
Thomas, Ilfracombe 1707 W
Atkins, Ackyn, Atkaines, Atkayne, Atkens, Atkin, Atkyne,
Atkyns
Abel, Bideford 1661 A
Agnes, Hartland 1574 W
Atkayne Cecilia, Dolton 1622 O
Atkin Elizabeth, Bideford 1733 W
Jacob, Witheridge 1676 A
Atkyns Joanna, Hartland 1574 W
Ackyns, John, Hartland 1571 W
Atkens John, Dolton 1574 W
John, Dolton 1614 [W]; forename blank in Ms; supplied from
parish register

Atkin John, Dolton 1645 A
Atkin John, Hartland, gentleman 1710 W; forename blank in
Ms; supplied from parish register
John, King's Nympton 1741 A
Atkin Lawrence, Hartland 1681 W
Atkaines Peter, Hartland 1596 [W]
Atkin Richard, Dolton 1612 [W]; forename blank in Ms;
supplied from parish register
Atkyne Simon, Hartland 1570 W
Thomas, Dolton 1689 W
Atkens William, Hartland 1608 [W]; forename blank in Ms;
supplied from parish register
Atkaines William, Hartland 1615 [W]
Atkin William, Hartland 1678 [W]
Atwell Catherine, Littleham (near Bideford) 1591 [W]
Catherine, South Molton 1752 W
Christiana, Barnstaple 1623 [W]
Francis, South Molton 1734 W
Henry, Littleham (near Bideford) 1622 [W]
Henry, Bideford 1668 W
John, Littleham (near Bideford) 1591 [W]
Juliana, Combe Martin 1629 [W]
Lawrence, South Molton 1623 [W]
Mary, Littleham (near Bideford) 1626 [W]
Mary, South Molton 1695 A
Nicholas, Northam 1663 A
Robert, Combe Martin 1578 W
Robert, Lynton 1621 [W]
Thomasine, South Molton 1631 [W]
Atyoe see Autrie
Auckland Aukland alias Muxworthy Archelaus 1798 A
Austen see Austin
Austin, Austen, Austyn
Austen ..., Combe Martin 1613 [W]
Austen ..., High Bickington 1613 [W]
Austen Alice, Combe Martin 1615 [W]
Anthony, Littleham (near Bideford) 1686 W
Austen Edward, Zeal Monachorum 1624 [W]
Austyn Elizabeth, Shirwell 1639 A
Austin alias Webber Esther 1701 A
Joan, Littleham (near Bideford) 1765 W
Austyn John, Tawstock 1635 W
John, Shirwell 1681 W
John, Parkham 1689 W
Juliana, Shirwell 1682 A
Nathaniel, Littleham (near Bideford) 1661 W
Austyn Simon, Ashreigney 1629 [W]
Austen Thomas, Shirwell 1629 [W]
Autrie, Atyoe
John, North Tawton 1592 [W]
Mathew, North Tawton 1577 W
Avery, Averie, Avereye
..., Clovelly 1608 [W] and 1610 [W]
..., Barnstaple 1730 [W]
Aaron, Abbotsham 1707 W
Alexander, Westleigh 1630 [W]
Alexander, Barnstaple 1689 W
Alexander, Barnstaple 1729 [W]
Avis, Petrockstowe 1640 [W]
Berry, Tawstock 1843 W
Betty, South Molton 1847 W
Catherine, South Molton 1696 W
Charity, South Molton, sp. 1801 W
Christopher, Zeal Monachorum 1631 W
Daniel, Littleham (near Bideford) 1709 A
Edith, Beaford 1625 [W] and 1630 [W]
Averie Elizabeth, North Tawton 1573 W
Averie Elizabeth, Hartland 1574 W
Elizabeth, Dolton 1631 W
Elizabeth, Chittlehampton 1763 W
George, Weare Giffard 1693 W
George, Tawstock, farmer 1806 A
George, Tawstock 1816 W
Georgina, North Molton 1721 A
Honor, Barnstaple 1845 W
Hugh, Dowland 1632 W

Humphrey, South Molton 1691 W
James, Buckland Brewer 1761 W
James, Tawstock 1818 W
Jane, Great Torrington 1602 W
Jane, Little Torrington 1643 A
Jane, Yarnscombe 1691 A
Jane, Abbotsham 1711 W
Joan, Westleigh 1597 [W]
Joanna, South Molton 1722 A
Joanna, South Molton 1745 W
Averie John, Hartland 1577 W
John, South Molton, also of Nymet Tracey Bow 1601 W
John, Dolton 1614 [W]; forename blank in Ms; supplied from
    parish register
John, Dolton 1643 W
John, Barnstaple 1668 A
John, South Molton 1689 W
John, Thelbridge 1698 A
John, Pilton 1716 W and 1717 W
John, South Molton 1741 W
John, Bideford 1753 W
John, Woolfardisworthy 1786 W
John, North Molton, snr. 1839 W
John, Barnstaple 1852 W
John, North Molton 1855 W
John, Ilfracombe 1857 W
Joseph, Woolfardisworthy 1791 W
Joseph, Bulkworthy 1819 W
Joseph, Bulkworthy 1845 W
Mabel, Little Torrington 1620 [W]
Mary, Hartland 1580 W
Mary, Barnstaple, widow 1679 W
Mary, North Molton, widow 1802 W
Averie Matilda, Dolton 1574 W
Richard, North Tawton 1631 A and 1632 O
Richard, North Molton 1763 A
Richard, North Molton, yeoman 1800 A
Richard, Barnstaple 1834 W
Richard, Tawstock 1842 W
Robert, Great Torrington 1594 [W]
Robert, Dowland 1626 [W]
Robert, South Molton 1645 [W]
Robert, West Buckland 1671 [W]
Robert, Marwood 1719 A
Robert, Buckland Brewer 1765 W
Robert, Chittlehampton, blacksmith 1814 A to Mary, daughter
Silvester, North Tawton 1626 [W]
Thomas, Hartland 1613 [W]; forename blank in Ms; supplied
    from parish register
Averye Thomas Bromsam, Hartland 1572 W
Walter, North Tawton 1587 W
Walter, Little Torrington 1622 [W]
Averie William, Dolton, snr. 1565 W
William, Marwood 1719 A
William, South Molton 1720 W
William, West Buckland 1773 W
William, Ilfracombe 1795 A
William, West Buckland 1806 W and 1816 W
William, Pilton 1824 W
Avivyan see Abevan
Axenham Julian, Meshaw 1579 A
Axon John, Cruwys Morchard 1744 W
Aydger see Adger
Ayer see Aire
Ayles John, Bideford 1818 W
Ayor, Ayre, Ayres see Aire
Aysh, Ayshe see Ash
Ayshlegh see Ashley
Ayshpole see Ashpole
Ayshton see Ashton
Aze, Awse, Awze
    Awse (Awze) Daniel, Great Torrington 1758 A; A dbn 1769
    David, Northam, mariner 1705 A
    David, Barnstaple 1749 W

John, High Bray 1674 W
John, Northam 1766 A
    see also Ace

Baarne see Barnes
Babacomb, Babacombe see Babbacombe
Babb David, Ilfracombe 1779 A
    George, Barnstaple 1738 [W]
    George, Lynton 1784 W
    Babbe Joanna, Great Torrington 1623 [W]
    John, North Tawton 1696 W
    Thomas, Lynton 1739 W
    Willmot, North Tawton 1721 W
Babbacombe, Babacomb, Babacombe, Babbacambe,
    Babbacomb, Babercomb, Babercombe, Brabacombe
    Babbacomb ..., Bideford 1607 [W]
    Babercombe ..., Witheridge 1613 [W]
    Babbacomb Agnes, Instow 1702 W
    Charity, Tawstock 1624 [W]
    Charity, Fremington 1639 W
    Babercomb Elizabeth, Witheridge 1616 [W]
    George, Bideford 1620 [W]
    Brabacombe Hugh, Fremington 1684 W
    James, Fremington 1602 W
    Joan, Ashreigney 1597 [W]
    Babbacomb Joan, Bideford 1605 W
    Babercombe Joan, Fremington 1616 [W]
    Babercomb John, Fremington 1616 [W]
    Babbacomb John, Fremington 1644 A
    Babbacomb John, Abbotsham 1678 W
    Babbacomb John, Coldridge 1678 W
    Babbacomb John, Instow 1700 W
    Lawrence, Tawstock 1622 [W] and 1624 O
    Babbacomb Lawrence, Tawstock 1705 W
    Babbacomb Mary, Tawstock 1708 W
    Nathaniel, Instow 1696 A
    Babercomb Richard, Fremington 1593 [W]
    Babercomb Richard, Witheridge 1613 [W]; forename blank in
        Ms; supplied from parish register
    Richard, Northam 1629 [W]
    Babbacomb Richard, Bideford 1664 W
    Babercombe Richard, Bow 1669 A
    Babercombe Richard, High Bickington 1830 W
    Babacomb Roger, Barnstaple 1601 A; forename blank in Ms;
        supplied from parish register
    Babercombe Roger, Winkleigh 1688 W
    Babacomb Simon, Tawstock 1590 [W]
    Babbacomb Simon, Fremington 1615 [W] and 1620 [W]
    Babercombe Thomas, North Tawton 1744 A
    Babacombe Walter, Bideford 1588 W
    Babbacomb William, Bideford 1607 [W]; forename blank in
        Ms; supplied from parish register
    Babercombe William, Burrington 1817 W
Babbage, Babbedge, Babbidge, Babbyde, Babridge, Bobadge,
    Bobage, Bobbage
    Bobbage ..., Wembworthy 1607 [W]
    Ann, Burrington 1815 A
    Ann, Burrington 1834 W
    Edward, Winkleigh 1722 W
    Elizabeth, Winkleigh 1733 W
    Gilbert Pridham, Burrington 1843 W
    James, Ashreigney 1725 A
    James, Burrington 1774 W
    James, Burrington 1816 W
    Babridge Joan, Westleigh, widow 1612 [W]; forename blank
        in Ms; supplied from parish register
    Bobage alias Combe John, Ashreigney 1568 W
    Bobadge John, North Tawton 1632 [W]
    John, Ashreigney 1730 [W]
    John, Ashreigney 1763 A
    John, Ashreigney 1788 W
    John, Burrington 1791 W
    John, Burrington 1799 W
    Mary, Ashreigney 1744 W
    Babbedge Mary, Fremington 1790 W

Mary, Burrington 1834 W
Babbedge Philip, High Bickington or Fremington 1807 W*
Babbidge Richard, Bow 1699 A
Richard, High Bickington 1830 A
Babbyde Roger, Winkleigh 1662 W
Roger, Winkleigh 1688 W
Thomas, North Tawton 1744 A
Bobadge William, Wembworthy 1587 W
William, Burrington 1817 W
Babbe see Babb
Babbedge, Babbidge see Babbage
Babercomb, Babercombe see Babbacombe
Bachelor Elizabeth, Langtree 1587 A
Nicholas, Langtree 1598 [W]
Back Back alias Michall Mary, South Molton 1831 W
Backway John, Hartland 1727 W
John, Bideford 1748 A
Nicholas, Bideford 1725 A
Backwell, Backewell alias Balkwill John, Nymet Rowland 1573
    W
Badcock, Badcocke, Badcoke
..., South Molton 1601 W
..., South Molton 1612 [W]
Badcocke Agnes, South Molton 1624 [W]
Agnes, South Molton 1670 W
Badcocke Alice, Meeth 1626 [W]
Anthony, South Molton 1685 A
Badcocke Augustine, South Molton 1570 W
Badcocke Bridget, South Molton 1625 [W]
Catherine, South Molton 1682 A
David, Huntshaw 1740 W
Badcocke Ferdinand, Shebbear 1628 [W]
Badcocke George, South Molton 1592 [W]
George, South Molton 1693 A
George, South Molton 1783 W
Grace, South Molton 1787 W
Hugh, South Molton 1682 W
Hugh, South Molton 1696 W
Hugh, South Molton 1726 W
Joan, South Molton, widow 1614 [W]; forename blank in Ms;
    supplied from parish register
Badcocke Joanna, South Molton 1628 [W]
Badcocke John, South Molton, snr. 1619 [W]
Badcocke John, South Molton, jnr. 1639 A
Badcocke John, South Molton, snr. 1639 W
John, South Molton, jnr. 1642 A
John, South Molton 1680 W and 1681 A
John, Twitchen 1692 W
John, South Molton 1694 A
John, South Molton 1793 W
John, Georgeham 1851 W
John, South Molton 1709-10 [W]
Badcocke Margaret, Georgeham 1579 A
Badcocke Margaret, South Molton 1640 W
Mary, South Molton 1760 W
Mary, South Molton 1790 W
Mary, South Molton 1825 W
Oliver, South Molton 1617 [W]
Petronell, Barnstaple, widow 1797 W
Reynold, Fremington 1676 W
Badcoke Robert, Meeth 1566 W
Badcocke Robert, South Molton 1592 [W]
Samuel, South Molton 1749 W
Samuel, Northam, mariner 1813 A to Mary wife of Thomas
    Lock
Badcocke Thomas, Chulmleigh 1626 [W]
Badcocke Thomas, South Molton 1635 W
Thomas, Shebbear 1664 W
Thomas, South Molton 1782 W
Badcocke William, Meeth 1599 [W]
Badcocke William, Shebbear 1627 [W]
William, South Molton 1671 W
William, South Molton 1748 W
William, Ashford 1844 W
William Dunn, South Molton 1826 A to John, brother
Badcoke Willmot, South Molton 1585 W

Badge John, North Molton 1628 [W]
Baell see Bale
Bagbear Christopher, Parracombe 1619 [W]
Emma, Littleham (near Bideford) 1622 [W]
Bagglehole, Bagehole, Bagehot, Bagehott, Bagelhole, Baggihole,
    Bagihole, Bagilholl, Bagilholle, Baglehole
Baglehole ..., Hartland 1614 [W]
Abraham, Welcombe 1664 W
Bagihole Abraham, Welcombe 1731 W
Baglehole Alice, Hartland, widow 1612 [W]; forename blank
    in Ms; supplied from parish register
Baglehole Alice, Hartland 1664 A
Bagelhole Ann, Hartland 1851 W
Bernard, Hartland 1586 W
Bagihole Charles, Hartland 1678 A
Bagihole Charles, Bideford 1742 W
Baglehole Christian, Woolfardisworthy 1568 W
Baggihole Christiana, Merton [no year given] W
Baglehole Edward, Hartland 1610 [W]; forename blank in Ms;
    supplied from parish register
Edward, Hartland 1632 [W]
Edward, Bideford 1643 A
Baggihole Edward, Hartland 1663 A
Elizabeth, Hartland 1631 W
Bagehott Elizabeth, Great Torrington 1798 W
Bagihole Geoffrey, Barnstaple 1711 W
Bagilholl Geoffrey, Barnstaple 1722 W
Bagihole Geoffrey, Barnstaple 1750 W
Baglehole alias Stodden Henry, Hartland 1601 W
Henry, Combe Martin 1639 W
Baggelhole Isott, Hartland 1563 W
Isott, Hartland 1640 W
Bagihole Isott, Hartland 1692 A
Jane, Hartland 1631 W
Joan, Little Torrington 1593 [W]
Bagelhole John, Westleigh 1570 W
Baglehole John, Hartland 1586 W
Baglehole John, Hartland 1605 [W]; forename blank in Ms;
    supplied from parish register
John, Hartland 1631 [W]
John, Hartland 1668 W
Baglehole John, Hartland 1715 W
Bagihole John, Welcombe 1738 [W]
Bagehole John, Hartland 1807 W
Baglehole Margaret, Hartland 1602 W
Baglehole Mary, Hartland, widow 1609 [W]; forename blank
    in Ms; supplied from parish register
Nathan, Barnstaple 1643 W
Bagilholle Peter, South Hole, Hartland 1675 A
Baggihole Peter, Bideford 1684 A
Baglehole Philip, Pilton 1703 A
Baggihole Reginald, Hartland 1710 W
Bagihole Richard, Hartland 1582 W
Bagihole Richard, Welcombe 1680 W
Bagihole Richard, Hartland 1692 W
Bagelhole Rose, Hartland 1564 W
Bogalhol Samuel, Hartland 1840 A to Grace, widow
Sarah, Barnstaple 1713 A
Thomas, Northam 1597 [W]
Baglehole Thomas, Hartland 1611 [W]; forename blank in Ms;
    supplied from parish register
Bagihole Thomas, Abbotsham 1676 W
Bagilholl Thomas, Hartland 1707 A
Bagihole Thomas, Barnstaple 1743 W
Bagehott Thomas, Great Torrington 1777 A; A dbn 1778
Bagehot Thomas, Great Torrington, gentleman 1797 W
Thomasine, Hartland 1627 [W]
Bagelholl William, Hartland 1573 W
Baglehole William, Hartland 1607 [W] "of Farford" in
    register; forename blank in Ms; supplied from parish register
William, Hartland 1620 [W] and 1622 [W]
William, Hartland 1663 [W]
Bagihole William, Hartland 1789 W
Baggott John, Georgeham 1856 W
Bagihole, Bagilholl, Bagilholle, Baglehole see Bagglehole

Bagshaw Clarithia, Chulmleigh 1689 W
Bagster, Bagston, Bagter, Bagtor
  Bagter Bartholomew, Georgeham 1623 [W]
  Elizabeth, Georgeham 1834 W
  Elizabeth, Georgeham 1850 W
  Bagtor Emma, North Molton 1570 W
  James, Georgeham 1748 W
  Bagtor John, North Molton 1598 [W]
  Bagtor John, Georgeham 1606 W
  Bagter John, Huish 1623 [W]
  John, Georgeham 1685 W
  John, Georgeham, mariner 1807 W
  Paul, Georgeham 1685 W
  Paul, Georgeham 1780 W
  Paul, Georgeham 1824 W
  Bagston Sarah, Barnstaple 1772 W
  Bagtor Thomas, North Molton 1567 W
  Willmot, Georgeham 1760 W
Bailey, Bailie, Baylegh, Bayley, Baylie, Bayly
  Bailie ..., Barnstaple 1610 O
  Bayly Agnes, Barnstaple 1630 [W], 1637 W and A
  Baylie Alexander, Winkleigh 1617 [W]
  Bayly Alice, Barnstaple 1664 A
  Bailye Anthony, Barnstaple 1605 W
  Baylegh Catherine, Lynton 1587 W
  Bayly Catherine, Barnstaple 1637 W
  Baylie David, Barnstaple 1624 [W]
  David, Bideford 1851 W
  Elizabeth, Great Torrington 1759 W
  Esther see Esther Chibbett
  Bayly Jacob, Barnstaple 1664 A
  Bayly Jacob, Langtree 1666 A
  Bayly James, Clovelly 1824 W
  Bayly Joan, Parkham 1783 W
  Baylie Joanna, Great Torrington 1621 [W]
  Bayley Joanna, Winkleigh 1724 W
  Bayly John, Parkham 1633 W
  John, Buckland Brewer 1753 A
  Bayley John, Ilfracombe 1756 A
  Bayly Margaret, Parkham 1638 W
  Bayly Mary, Chulmleigh 1680 W
  Mary, Woolfardisworthy 1779 W
  Peggy Reid, Ilfracombe, sp. 1853 A to John of Plymouth,
    brother
  Bayley Richard, Alverdiscott 1729 W
  Baylie Robert, Arlington 1607 [W] "of Beeves"; forename
    blank in Ms; supplied from parish register
  Bayly Samuel, Barnstaple 1627 [W]
  Bayly Thomas, Shebbear 1664 [W]
  Bayley Thomas, Shebbear 1736 A
  Bayley Thomas, Alverdiscott 1744 W
  Bayly Thomas, Woolfardisworthy 1773 W
  Bayly William, Chulmleigh 1680 A
  Bayley William, Parkham 1788 W
  Bayly William, Woolfardisworthy, yeoman 1809 W
  William, Weare Giffard 1836 W
  William, Alwington 1847 W
  Baylie Willmot, Combe Martin 1603 W
  Bayley Willmot, Clovelly 1761 W
Baill see Bale
Baitson, Batson
  John, King's Nympton 1679 A
  Mary, Chulmleigh 1726 W
  Batson Richard, Little Torrington 1691 W
Baker, Bakar, Bake, Bakers
  Baker alias Mackland ..., East Worlington 1601 W
  ..., Berrynarbor 1608 [W]
  ..., Sheepwash 1613 [W] and 1615 [W]
  Agnes, West Worlington 1848 W
  Alice, Bratton Fleming 1604 W
  Alice, Shirwell 1643 W
  Ambrose, Twitchen 1591 [W]
  Ann, Bideford 1698 A
  Ann, Twitchen 1716 A
  Anthony, Chulmleigh 1732 W
  Avis, Tawstock 1600 W

  Barbara, Marwood 1629 [W]
  Bernard, Northam 1668 W
  Betsy, South Molton 1857 W
  Bridget, Northam 1698 W
  Charles, Buckland Filleigh 1630 [W]
  David, Georgeham 1624 [W]
  David, Abbotsham 1696 W
  David, Northam 1750 W
  Derwent, Lapford 1589 W
  Dorothy, Tawstock 1665 A
  Dorothy, Winkleigh 1849 A
  Edward, Marwood 1712 W
  Edward, Bratton Fleming 1714 W
  Elizabeth, Sheepwash 1629 [W]
  Elizabeth, Fremington 1668 A
  Elizabeth, Georgeham 1684 W
  Elizabeth, Northam 1695 A
  Elizabeth, Chawleigh 1712 W
  Elizabeth, Chulmleigh 1772 W
  Elizabeth, Chulmleigh 1844 W
  Emma, Georgeham 1635 W
  Frances, Instow 1731 W
  Bake Frances, Northam 1781 W
  Frances, Barnstaple 1826 A to John, brother
  George, Northam 1624 [W] and 1626 O
  George, Barnstaple 1625 [W]
  George, Heanton Punchardon 1675 A
  George, North Molton 1689 A
  George, North Molton 1693 W
  George, North Tawton 1756 A
  Grace, Northam 1798 W
  Hannibal, Northam 1700 A
  Henry, Northam 1688 A
  Henry, Great Torrington 1693 W
  Henry, Chulmleigh 1753 W
  Henry, Stoodleigh 1854 W
  Bake Hugh, Northam, gentleman 1803 W
  Humphrey, West Buckland 1683 W
  Humphrey, Chittlehampton 1700 A
  Bakers Humphrey, Buckland Filleigh no year given I
  Isaac, Barnstaple 1707 A
  James, Ilfracombe 1587 W
  James, Twitchen 1641 W
  James, Warkleigh 1694 A
  James, Chittlehampton 1713 W
  James, Chittlehampton 1762 A
  James, Pilton 1770 A
  James, Chittlehampton 1780 W
  James, Bideford 1836 W
  Bakar John, West Anstey 1563 W
  John, Lynton 1579 W
  John, Georgeham 1580 W
  John, Lynton 1581 W
  John, East Down 1585 A
  John, Stoodleigh 1585 W
  John, Witheridge 1586 A
  John, Shirwell 1588 A
  John, East Down 1606 W
  John, East Down 1619 [W]
  John, West Anstey 1633 W
  John, Shirwell 1640 W
  John, Warkleigh 1641 W
  John, High Bray 1642 W
  John, Great Torrington 1661 A
  John, Northam 1664 W
  John, Barnstaple 1669 A
  John, Tawstock 1669 W
  John, Bratton Fleming 1671 W
  John, Marwood 1676 W
  John, Georgeham 1677 W
  John, Rose Ash 1682 A
  John, Georgeham 1686 A
  John, Georgeham 1694 W
  John, Winkleigh 1694 A
  John, Bideford 1698 W

John, West Down 1709 A
John, Dolton 1714 W
John, Northam 1721 W
John, Bratton Fleming 1724 W
John, Oakford 1726 W
John, Bratton Fleming 1733 W
John, Chittlehampton 1746 W
John, Filleigh 1788 W
John, West Worlington 1793 A
John, Chulmleigh, yeoman 1797 W
John, Yarnscombe, yeoman 1798 W
John, Eggesford, yeoman 1802 A (2)
John, Chulmleigh 1814 W
John, George Nympton 1827 W
John, Ilfracombe 1834 W
John, Chittlehampton 1838 W
John, Molland 1848 W
John, Chittlehampton 1854 W
Joseph, Barnstaple 1667 W
Juliana, Berrynarbor 1623 [W]
Margaret, South Molton 1781 W
Marian, Bratton Fleming 1615 [W]
Marian, Chittlehampton 1712 A
Martha, Chittlehampton 1780 W
Mary, Monkleigh 1615 [W]
Bake Mary, Weare Giffard 1628 [W]
Mary, Northam 1688 A
Mary, Twitchen 1690 W
Mary, Great Torrington 1699 W
Mary, Barnstaple 1738 W
Mary, George Nympton 1764 W
Mary, Chulmleigh 1786 W
Mary, Chulmleigh 1838 A to Elizabeth, mother
Nicholas, Northam 1640 W and 1645 A
Nicholas, Northam 1772 A
Nicholas, Northam 1813 W
Philip, West Anstey 1566 W
Philip, East Anstey 1638 A
Philip, Georgeham 1638 W
Philip, Fremington 1663 W
Philip, Fremington 1700 W
Philip, Barnstaple 1726 W
Philip, Northam 1730 W
Philip, Dolton 1763 W
Richard, Georgeham 1584 W
Richard, Bratton Fleming 1593 [W]
Richard, Burrington 1593 [W]
Richard, East Anstey 1612 [W]; forename blank in Ms;
    supplied from parish register
Richard, Northam 1618 [W]
Richard, Pilton 1621 [W]
Richard, St Giles in the Wood 1623 [W]
Richard, Twitchen 1642 W
Richard, Bratton Fleming 1681 W
Richard, Chulmleigh 1756 W
Richard, Barnstaple, blacksmith 1806 A
Richard, Coldridge, husbandman 1810 W
Richard, Warkleigh 1818 W
Robert, Great Torrington 1588 A
Robert, Stoke Rivers 1621 [W]
Robert, Petrockstowe 1684 A
Roger, Burrington 1622 [W]
Salome, Kentisbury 1581 W and 1585 W
Samuel, Barnstaple 1664 W
Sarah, Abbotsham 1720 W
Simon, George Nympton 1677 W
Sybil, Pilton 1621 [W]
Thomas, Kentisbury 1569 W
Thomas, Georgeham 1592 [W]
Thomas, Tawstock 1626 [W]
Thomas, Barnstaple 1664 A
Thomas, Fremington 1709-10 A
Thomas, Instow 1713 W
Thomas, Ringsash, Ashreigney 1718 W
Thomas, St Giles in the Wood 1734 W
Thomas, Barnstaple 1830 W

Thomas, Lynton 1840 W
Thomas, South Molton 1846 W
Thomasine, Barnstaple 1665 A
Walter, Chulmleigh 1579 W
Walter, Pilton 1618 [W]
William, East Down 1590 [W]
William, Huish 1591 [W]
William, Stoodleigh 1607 [W]; forename blank in Ms;
    supplied from parish register
William, Cheldon 1620 [W]
William, Ilfracombe 1629 [W]
William, Great Torrington 1668 A
William, Barnstaple 1738 [W]
William, Chittlehampton 1750 W
William, Chulmleigh 1758 A
William, East Down 1759 W
William, Chulmleigh 1764 W
William, South Molton 1767 A
William, Instow 1770 A
William, Chittlehampton 1770 W and 1772 W
William, Woolfardisworthy, yeoman 1817 A to Susanna,
    widow
William, Great Torrington 1836 W
William, Ilfracombe 1843 W
Balam Alice, Chittlehampton 1579 W
Balamie, Balamy see Bellamy
Balch ..., Rose Ash 1610 [W] (2) and 1611 [W]
George, Newton Tracey 1673 W
George, Newton Tracey 1723 [W]
George, Tawstock 1742 W
Henry, Barnstaple 1667 A
John, Tawstock 1671 A
John, Georgeham 1704 A
John, Frithelstock 1740 W
Mary, Barnstaple 1679 W
Mary, Tawstock 1745 W
Mary, Fremington 1756 W
Richard, Newton Tracey 1733 W
Richard, Tawstock 1745 W
Richard, Bideford 1842 W
Stephen, Bideford, grocer 1855 A to James Shortridge of
    Bideford, relieving officer and James Lee of Bideford,
    scrivener; cessate A granted at Exeter 31 Mar 1870
Walter, Tawstock 1643 W
William, Tawstock 1742 W
Baldwin, Baldon, Baldwyn
Henry, Bideford 1678 W
Baldon John, Shebbear 1566 W
Baldwyn William, Tawstock 1637 W
Bale, Baell, Baill
Baell ..., Frithelstock 1600 [W]
Baell ..., Martinhoe 1607 [W] and 1609 [W]
..., Countisbury 1609 [W]
Baell ..., North Molton 1614 [W]
Bale alias Pickering Ann, Martinhoe 1645 A
Bale alias Smith Ann, Combe Martin 1776 W
Ann, Lynton, widow 1810 W
Ann, Alwington 1833 A to Julia Hooker of Hartland, daughter
Archelaus, Clovelly 1754 A
Charity, Barnstaple 1730 W
Baell Cicely, Lynton, widow 1610 [W] "of Fursley" in
    register; forename blank in Ms; supplied from parish register
David, Parracombe 1631 W
David, Lynton, snr. 1674 W
David, Barnstaple 1756 A
David, Lynton 1839 T
Edward, Lynton 1705 A
Elizabeth, Barnstaple 1730 W
Elizabeth, Little Torrington 1737 [W]
Elizabeth, Barnstaple 1789 A
Elizabeth, Barnstaple 1831 W
Francis, Peters Marland 1744 W
Francis, Lynton 1813 A (Frances) to Ann Smith, sister
Gabriel, Brendon 1723 [W]
George, Countisbury 1627 [W]

George, Combe Martin, smith 1776 W
Gertrude, Mortehoe 1623 [W]
Hannah, Barnstaple, widow 1796 W
Henry, Combe Martin 1705 A
Henry, Roborough 1748 W
Henry, Molland 1808 W
Hugh, Lynton 1679 W
Hugh, Lynton 1767 A
Hugh, Combe Martin 1817 W
Ilett, Countisbury 1678 W
James, Little Torrington 1756 W
James, Landkey 1857 W
Joanna, North Molton 1642 W
Joanna, Parracombe 1685 W
Joanna, Barnstaple 1697 A
Baell John, Lynton 1607 [W] "of Fursley" in register;
    forename blank in Ms; supplied from parish register
John, Lynton 1624 [W]
John, Countisbury 1629 O
John, Parracombe 1630 [W]
John, Buckland Brewer, snr. 1636 [W]
John, Fremington 1638 A
John, Countisbury 1640 W
John, Bideford 1643 [W]
John, Martinhoe 1684 A
John, Twitchen 1688 W
John, Lynton 1695 W
John, Northam 1702 A
John, Twitchen 1716 W
John, Tawstock 1728 W
John, Parracombe 1729 A
John, Barnstaple 1746 A
John, Clovelly 1759 W
John, Petrockstowe 1759 W
John, Parracombe 1763 W
John, Mortehoe 1776 W
John, Clovelly 1786 W
John, Countisbury 1787 W
John, Alwington, yeoman 1806 A
John, Little Torrington, gentleman 1810 W
John, Molland 1818 W
John, East Down 1821 W
John, Shirwell 1823 A
John, Pilton 1851 W
John, Combe Martin, yeoman 1853 A to Mary wife of William
    Greenslade, of Swansea, Glamorgan, carpenter, daughter
Joseph, Alwington 1827 A to Emlyn, widow
Margaret, Buckland Brewer 1683 W
Margaret, Loxhore 1764 W
Mary, Alwington, widow 1809 A
Mary, Barnstaple 1833 W
Mary, East Down 1837 W
Baell Paschal husband of Ann, Atherington 1605 [W];
    forename blank in Ms; supplied from parish register
Petronell, Countisbury 1672 W
Philip, Great Torrington 1729 W
Baill Richard, Chittlehampton 1588 A
Richard, Pilton 1619 [W]
Richard, Little Torrington 1622 [W]
Richard, Parracombe 1664 W
Richard, Countisbury 1669 W
Richard, Martinhoe 1672 A
Richard, Lynton 1698 W
Richard, Countisbury 1704 W
Richard, Countisbury 1757 W
Richard, Ilfracombe 1766 A
Richard, Countisbury 1784 A
Richard, Countisbury 1822 W
Richard, Swimbridge 1842 W
Robert, West Down 1676 W
Roger, Parracombe 1625 [W]
Ruth, High Bray 1741 W
Baell Simon, Parracombe 1615 [W]
Thomas, Trentishoe 1620 [W]
Thomas, Great Torrington 1638 W

Thomas, Parracombe 1661 A
Thomas, Countisbury 1740 A
Thomasine, Abbotsham 1732 W
Timothy, Barnstaple 1761 W
Walter 1702 A
William, Parracombe 1574 W
Baell William, Mortehoe 1605 W
William, Lynton 1611 [W]; forename blank in Ms; supplied
    from parish register
William, Lynton 1683 W
William, Barnstaple 1718 W and 1725 W
William, High Bray 1726 W
William, Bideford 1729 A
William, Countisbury, gentleman 1810 W
William, Countisbury 1832 W
    see also Ball

Balfron
Balfron alias Barbar Avis, Great Torrington 1574 W
John, Great Torrington 1580 W
Balhatchet Thomas, Bideford 1846 W
Balkwill, Balkwell
..., Sheepwash 1611 [W]
Balkwell Bartholomew, Sheepwash 1698 W
Bartholomew, Sheepwash 1720 W
Bartholomew, Buckland Filleigh 1782 A
Charles, Buckland Filleigh 1745 W
Charles, Buckland Filleigh 1773 W
Elizabeth, Langtree 1734 A
George, Nymet Rowland 1615 [W]
Honor, Buckland Filleigh 1812 W
Balkwell Isaac, Buckland Filleigh 1782 A
Joanna, Buckland Filleigh 1844 W
John alias Backewell, Nymet Rowland 1573 W
John, Nymet Rowland, snr. 1639 W
Balkwell John, Nymet Rowland 1645 W
John, Langtree 1731 W
John, Peters Marland 1834 A to James of Landkey, son
John, Buckland Filleigh, snr. 1841 W
John, Peters Marland 1846 W
Mary, Petrockstowe 1724 W
William, Petrockstowe 1818 W
William, Shebbear 1847 W
Ball, Balle
Agnes, Meeth 1631 [W]
Agnes, Barnstaple 1666 W; forename blank in Ms; supplied
    from parish register
Alexander, Martinhoe 1631 [W]
Alison, Trentishoe 1629 [W]
Ann 1833 A to Julia Hooker of Hartland, daughter
Anthony, Ashreigney 1700 A
Beaton, Tawstock 1638 W
Bennett, Tawstock 1630 [W]
Balle Christopher, Trentishoe 1621 [W]
David, Parracombe 1703 W
Balle Dorothy, Countisbury 1627 [W]
Balle Edward, Meeth 1616 [W]
Edward, Meeth 1629 [W]
Edward, Cruwys Morchard 1689 A
Frances, Lynton 1813 A to Ann Smith, sister
Balle George, Ashreigney 1624 [W]
Hugh, Molland 1690 A
Jeremiah, Northam 1711 A
Balle Joanna, North Molton 1700 A
John, Parracombe 1579 W
Balle John, Heanton Punchardon 1626 [W]
John, Frithelstock 1742 W
John, Frithelstock 1813 W
John, West Anstey 1813 W
John, South Molton 1816 W
John, South Molton 1855 W
John, West Anstey 1857 W
Lawrence, Newton Tracey 1714 [W]
Mary, Frithelstock 1838 W
Richard, Little Torrington 1856 W
Balle Richarda, Ashreigney 1628 [W]

Robert, Kentisbury, gentleman 1643 W
Roger, Frithelstock 1776 W
Salathiel, Clovelly 1695 A
Balle Setene, East Down 1580 W
Thomas, Alwington 1728 W
Thomasine, Sheepwash 1575 W
Walter, Parracombe 1698 W
William, South Molton 1739 W
Balle William, ship *Robert* 1746 A
     see also Bale
Ballamie, Ballamy see Bellemy
Ballen Alice, Chulmleigh 1620 [W]
Baller Benjamin, Barnstaple 1729 W
Edward, Bideford 1853 W
Henry, St Giles in the Wood 1751 W
Joanna, Barnstaple 1688 W
John, Barnstaple 1663 W
John, Bideford 1852 W
Mary, Barnstaple 1690 W
Balliman see Balmant
Ballomy see Bellamy
Balmant, Balliman, Ballyman, Balman, Balment, Balmond,
     Balmont, Bament
Agnes, High Bray 1727 W
Balliman Amesius, Rose Ash 1715 W
Balman Betty, South Molton 1854 W
Elizabeth, North Molton 1598 [W]
Faith, North Molton, widow 1672 [W]
Faith, North Molton 1702 A
George, North Molton 1682 A
George 1705 [W]
Balment George, Chittlehampton 1747 W
James, Molland 1716 W
James, Molland 1717 W
Balmont James, Twitchen 1718 W
Balmont James, Marwood 1796 A
Balmont John, North Molton 1664 W
John, Pilton 1668 W
John, North Molton 1690 A
Balmond John, Ilfracombe 1805 A
Balmont Mary, Chittlehampton 1763 W
Mathew, North Molton 1577 W
Balmont Robert, Chawleigh 1745 W
Balmont Roger, North Molton 1617 [W]
Balmont Roger, North Molton 1628 [W]
Balman Thomas, North Molton 1620 [W]
Ballyman Thomas, Heanton Punchardon 1695 W
Balmont William, North Molton 1616 [W]
Balmont William, North Molton 1703 A
William, North Tawton 1723 [W]
Balmont William, Marwood 1736 W
Balment William, East Down 1767 W
Bament William, Marwood, yeoman 1799 W; 1807 A
Balsdon, Balsedon, Balson
Agnes, Shebbear 1796 W
Alexander, Alverdiscott 1735 W and 1738 [W]
Amos, Sheepwash 1725 W
Amos, Sheepwash 1789 W and A
Daniel, Shebbear 1737 A
Balson Daniel, Shebbear 1738 [W]
Daniel, Shebbear 1825 W
Balson Edmund, Frithelstock 1791 W
Balson Edmund, Frithelstock 1816 W
George, Shebbear 1784 W
George see also John Laramy
Grace, Langtree 1784 A
Grace, Shebbear 1819 W
Balson Grace, Beaford 1828 A to Eliza wife of James Bowen
     of Appledore, daughter
Balson James, Buckland Brewer 1766 A
Balson James, Shebbear 1803 W*
James, Huish 1841 W
Balsedon alias Godinge Joan, Shebbear, widow 1564 W
Balson John, Frithelstock 1615 [W]
Balson John, Shebbear 1630 A

John, Shebbear 1787 W
John, Shebbear 1840 W
John, Weare Giffard 1854 W
Mary, Shebbear 1737 W
William, Shebbear no year given A
William Frost, Marwood 1851 W
Bament see Balmant
Banbury, Bandbury, Barnbury, Bonbury, Burabury
Bunbury or Banbury Charles, Great Torrington 1716 W
Bandbury John, Bideford 1630 [W]
Burabury John, Merton 1724 W
Bonbury Mary, Great Torrington 1747 W
....Banbery Thomas, Great Torrington 1810 W*
Barnbury William, Bideford 1679 A
William, Bideford 1708 A
Band, Bande, Baud, Baunt
..., Cruwys Morchard 1609 [W]
Bande ..., Atherington 1614 [W]
Bande Agnes, Bow 1615 [W]
Bande Anthony, Bow 1630 [W]
Band alias Baud Christopher, Atherington, snr. 1602 W
Bande Emma, Goodleigh 1624 [W], 1626 [O]
Bande George, Lapford 1608 [W]; forename blank in Ms;
     supplied from parish register
Bande Henry, Meeth 1626 [W]
James, Tawstock 1675 A
Bande John, Great Torrington 1591 [W]
John, Tawstock 1597 [W]
Bande John, Bow 1600 W
Bande John, Hartland, snr. 1627 [W]
Baunt John, Welcombe, clerk 1638 W
Baunt John, Abbotsham 1662 W
John, Chittlehampton 1672 W
Bande Marian, Atherington 1623 [W]
Mary, Chittlehampton 1684 A
Bande Peter, Tawstock 1608 [W]; forename blank in Ms;
     supplied from parish register
Bande Peter, Bow 1621 [W]
Bande Petronell, Ashreigney 1595 [W]
Philip, Bow 1679 A
Rawlina, Tawstock 1686 W
Bande Robert, Lapford 1628 [W]
Thomasine, Lapford 1672 W
Bande William, Ashreigney 1598 [W]
Bande alias Bonde William, Bow 1604 W
Bande William, Ilfracombe 1609 [W]; forename blank in Ms;
     supplied from parish register
Bande William, Bow 1611 [W] "Bonde" in register; forename
     blank in Ms; supplied from parish register
Bandbury see Banbury
Bande see Band
Banden see Bawden
Banfield Nathaniel, Hartland 1674 W
Banks, Bancks Eliza, Zeal Monachorum 1687 [W]
Banner John, Ilfracombe 1621 [W]
John, Ilfracombe 1644 W
John, Ilfracombe, jnr. 1705 A
John, Ilfracombe 1707 W
Bannister Joseph, Wembworthy 1850 W
Banou Richard, Barnstaple 1814 W
Baple see Beaple
Barber, Barbar, Barbor
Barbar alias Balfon Avis, Great Torrington 1574 W
Barbor Elizabeth, Barnstaple 1781 W
Jane, Pilton 1843 W
Barbor Petronell, Barnstaple 1739 W
Barbor William, Chittlehampton 1718 W
Bard John, Hartland 1723 [W]
Barett see Barrett
Barhead James, Coldridge 1580 W
Barker Philip, Abbotsham 1714 W
Barkin Ann, South Molton 1670 W
Barlabyn Ellen, North Tawton 1590 [W]
Mark, North Tawton 1623 [W]

Barnacott, Barnecot, Burnacott, Burracott
   Agnes, Fremington 1708 W
   Catherine, Fremington 1678 W
   Catherine, Fremington 1712 A
   Burnacott Elizabeth, Fremington 1580 W
   John, Georgeham 1585 W
   John, Fremington 1597 [W]
   John, Fremington 1681 W
   John, Fremington 1694 W
   Burracott John, Ilfracombe 1754 A
   Susan, Fremington 1640 W
   Barnecot Thomas, Georgeham 1571 W
   William, Fremington 1704 W
Barnard see Burnard
Barnbury see Banbury
Barne see Barnes
Barnecot see Barnacott
Barnehouse see Barnhouse
Barnepole, Barnepoll, Barnepoole, Barnepoule see Barnpole
Barnes, Baarne, Barne, Barns
   ..., Ashreigney 1601 A
   ..., Northam 1608 [W]
   ..., Bow 1610 [W]
   Barne ..., Challacombe 1614 [W]
   Agnes, Filleigh 1705 W
   Barne Anthony, Trentishoe 1568 W
   Arthur, Warkleigh 1787 W
   Charles, Combe Martin 1738 [W]
   George, Weare Giffard 1697 A
   Gregory, Brendon 1686 A
   Gregory, Brendon 1817 A
   Hannah, Barnstaple 1736 W
   Humphrey, Ilfracombe 1838 W
   Barne Jacob, Barnstaple 1644 W
   James, Barnstaple 1612 [W]; forename blank in Ms; supplied
     from parish register
   James, Dowland 1800 A
   James, Lynton 1849 A to John [deceased], father
   Barne Joan, Combe Martin 1591 [W]
   Barne Joan, St Giles in the Wood 1591 [W]
   Barns alias Long Joan, Brendon 1680 W
   Joan, Barnstaple 1698 W; forename blank in Ms; supplied
     from parish register
   Joanna, Barnstaple 1685 W
   John, High Bickington 1600 W
   Barne John, Combe Martin 1622 [W]
   John, Georgeham 1623 [W]
   Barne John, Combe Martin 1629 [W] and 1636 O
   Barne John, St Giles in the Wood 1638 W
   Barne John, Roborough 1684 W
   John, Bideford 1713 A
   John, ship *Culloden* 1761 A
   Barns John, Brendon 1775 A
   Barns John, Brendon 1786 W
   Barns John, Trentishoe 1805 W
   John, Lynton, jnr. 1840 W
   Barns John, Ilfracombe 1845 W
   John, Lynton 1849 W
   Mark, Great Torrington 1632 [W]
   Barne Mary, Combe Martin 1638 W
   Barne Michael, Brendon 1640 W
   Barne Nicholas, Barnstaple 1642 A
   Barne Nicholas, Combe Martin 1661 W
   Nicholas, Combe Martin 1674 A and O
   Nicholas, Filleigh 1703 A
   Nicholas, Filleigh 1728 W
   Nicholas, Ilfracombe 1856 W
   Phyllis, Barnstaple 1723 [W]
   Baarne Prudence, Combe Martin 1691 W
   Barne Richard, Combe Martin 1577 A
   Richard, Kentisbury 1603 W
   Barne Richard, Combe Martin 1623 [W]
   Richard, Barnstaple 1702 W and 1705 W
   Barns Richard, Georgeham 1832 W
   Barne Robert, Combe Martin 1687 W

   Robert, Brendon 1705 W possibly buried 1702; forename
     blank in Ms; supplied from parish register
   Robert, Witheridge 1710 W
   Roger, Barnstaple 1604 [W]; forename blank in Ms; supplied
     from parish register
   Thomas, Combe Martin 1594 [W]
   Thomas, Alverdiscott 1676 A
   Thomas, Barnstaple 1706 A
   Thomas, Weare Giffard 1761 W
   Thomas, Ilfracombe 1818 W
   Ursula, Tawstock, widow 1610 [W]; forename blank in Ms;
     supplied from parish register
   Barne William, Nymet Rowland 1591 [W]
   William, Bideford 1688 A
   William, East Anstey 1731 W
   William, Brendon 1738 W
   William, Landcross 1743 A
   Barns William, Roborough 1791 W
   William, Brendon 1842 W
Barnett, Bornet
   Daniel, Westleigh 1681 W
   Robert, Northam 1703 W
   Bornet Robert, Rose Ash 1813 W
Barnfield, Barnefeild, Barnefeld, Barnfeild, Barnfild
   Barnefeild ..., High Bickington 1611 [W]
   Barnfeild Abraham, East Putford 1688 W
   Abraham, Langtree 1726 W
   Barnfeild Ann, Burrington 1633 W
   Barnfield alias Bamfield Bennett Joan, Buckland Brewer or
     Buckland Filleigh 1732 A
   Barnefeld George, Great Torrington 1580 W
   Barnefeild (Barnfild) John, St Giles in the Wood 1573 W
   Barnefeild John, Atherington 1604 W
   Barnefeild John, jnr., Atherington 1614 [W]; forename blank
     in Ms; supplied from parish register
   Barnfield alias Bamfield John, East Putford 1737 A
   Barnfeild Lodovic, Sheepwash 1716 A
   Margery, Atherington 1596 [W]
   Barnfeild Peter, St Giles in the Wood 1597 [W]
   Barnefield Ralph, St Giles in the Wood 1565 W
   Barnfeild Ralph, St Giles in the Wood 1625 [W]
   Barnfeild Ralph, Barnstaple 1626 [W]
   Barnfeild Ralph, St Giles in the Wood 1662 A
   Thomas, Bulkworthy 1726 W
   Thomasine, Monkleigh 1581 W
Barnhouse, Barnehouse, Barnehowse
   Dennis, Fremington 1579 W
   Barnehouse Elizabeth, Heanton Punchardon 1596 [W]
   Barnehouse John, Combe Martin 1590 [W]
   Barnehouse John, Heanton Punchardon 1633 A
   John, Northam 1736 A
   John, Pilton 1822 W
   Julian, Pilton 1750 W
   Barnehowse Richard, Heanton Punchardon 1619 [W]
   Richard, Bittadon 1714 [W]
   Barnehouse Thomas, Kentisbury 1565 W
   Barnehouse Thomas, Northam 1618 [W]
   William, Bittadon 1725 A
   William, Pilton 1742 W
Barnpole, Barnepoole, Barnepole, Barnepoll, Barnepoule
   Barnepoole alias Ley ..., Fremington 1601 W
   Barnepoll alias Ley Agnes, Fremington 1574 W
   Barnepoole Humphrey, Dowland 1605 W
   Barnepoole John, Barnstaple 1593 [W]
   Barnepoule alias Ley Nicholas, Fremington 1587 W
   Barnepole alias Ley Philip, Fremington 1600 W
   Barnepoole Thomas, Barnstaple 1595 [W]
   Barnepoole William, Fremington 1598 [W]
   Barnepoole alias Ley William, Fremington 1601 W
Barns see Barnes
Baron, Barons see Barron
Barratt see Barrett
Barrawe see Barrow
Barre Richard, Winkleigh 1583 A

Barrett, Barett, Barratt, Barret, Barrott
..., Bideford 1601 A
Agnes, Barnstaple 1620 [W]
Barrott Andrew, Chulmleigh 1724 W
Barratt Cicely, Westleigh 1672 W
Barret Dewena, Bideford 1677 W
Elizabeth, Barnstaple 1757 W
Henry, Barnstaple 1693 W
Henry Frederick, Bideford, mariner 1850 A to Emma, widow
James, Barnstaple 1614 [W]; forename blank in Ms; supplied
     from parish register
John, Barnstaple 1597 [W]
John, Westleigh 1665 W
John, Bideford 1687 A
John, Westleigh 1719 A
John, Bideford 1726 A
Margaret, Westleigh 1675 A
Ralph, Instow 1636 A
Richard, Hartland 1851 W
Robert, Barnstaple 1593 [W]
Robert, South Molton 1603 W
Barett Robert, Ilfracombe 1705 A
Barratt Robert, Clovelly 1709 W
Thomas, Ilfracombe 1744 A
Barret William, Bideford 1676 A
Barratt William, Bideford 1718 W
William, Bideford 1763 A
William, Northam 1765 W
Barrey see Barry
Barrick, Barricke see Barwick
Barrie see Barry
Barron, Baron, Barons
Barons ..., Iddesleigh 1637 A
Baron Arthur, South Molton 1663 A
Elizabeth, High Bray 1668 W
Barron George, Ilfracombe 1841 W
James, Shirwell 1765 W
James, Ilfracombe 1820 W
Barons John, Iddesleigh 1663 A
John, High Bray 1668 W
Margaret, Barnstaple 1832 W
Baron Richard, South Molton 1669 A
Thomas, Bratton Fleming 1639 [W]
Baron Thomas, Barnstaple, victualler 1810 W
Barrott see Barrett
Barrow, Barrawe, Barrowe, Barrows
Barrowe ..., East Buckland 1611 [W]
..., Challacombe 1612 [W]
Ann, Martinhoe 1754 W
Ann, Great Torrington 1833 W
Arthur, Shirwell 1753 W
Betty, Barnstaple 1846 A
Catherine, Bideford 1707 W
Edmund, Stoke Rivers 1674 A
Edmund, Heanton Punchardon, yeoman 1807 W
Elizabeth, High Bray 1621 and 1622 [W]
Elizabeth, Chittlehampton, widow 1809 A
Frances wife of D. see John Haydon
George, East Down 1838 W
Barrawe Humphrey, Challacombe 1604 W
Jeremiah, Barnstaple 1707 A
Joan, Pilton 1622 [W]
Joan, North Molton 1771 W
Barrowe John, Bratton Fleming, jnr. 1597 [W]
John, Pilton 1622 [W]
John, Tawstock 1641 [W]
John, Pilton 1783 W
John, Northam 1786 W
John, Bratton Fleming, tailor 1808 A
John, Marwood, blacksmith 1815 A to Catherine, widow
John, Barnstaple 1829 W
Margaret, East Buckland 1626 [W]
Margaret, North Molton 1702 A
Margaret, Molland 1708 W
Mary Ann, Littleham (near Bideford) 1855 A

Peggy, Barnstaple 1815 W
Barrowe Richard, Bratton Fleming 1572 W
Barrows Richard, South Molton 1660 W
Richard, Bratton Fleming 1676 W
Richard, Charles 1686 W
Richard, Bratton Fleming 1761 W
Richard, Chittlehampton, yeoman 1807 W
Richard, Chittlehampton 1841 A to Mary wife of John Gill,
     widow
Robert, Bratton Fleming 1620 [W]
Robert, Bratton Fleming 1673 W
Robert, Bideford 1686 W
Robert, Filleigh 1821 W
Simon, High Bray 1601 W
Thomas, High Bray 1699 W
Thomas, Shirwell 1773 W
Barrowe Thomasine, East Down 1588 W
Thomasine, Bratton Fleming 1687 W
William, High Bray 1629 [W]
Barrow William, North Molton 1696 A
William, North Molton 1774 W
William, Filleigh 1789 W
Willmot, North Tawton 1663 W
Barry, Barrey, Barrie, Barrye, Barzey
..., Chawleigh 1604 [W]
..., Ashreigney 1612 [W]
Barrey Alden, Chawleigh 1597 [W]
Alexander, Great Torrington 1600 [W]
Alexander, North Tawton 1603 W
David, Buckland Brewer 1596 [W]
Digory, Monkleigh 1639 W
Emblem, Chawleigh 1621 [W]
Giles, Winkleigh 1771 W
Barrye Henry, St Giles in the Wood 1579 W
Honor, Bideford 1637 A
Humphrey, Winkleigh 1588 A
James, Frithelstock, gentleman 1817 A to Grace, widow with
     two children
Barrey John, Chawleigh 1590 [W]
John, High Bickington 1635 W
John, North Tawton 1641 W
John, Ashreigney 1701 W
John, Ashreigney 1722 W
Barzey John, Northam 1799 W
Levi, High Bickington 1679 W
Margaret, North Tawton 1617 [W]
Nicholas, Northam 1636 W
Peter, Atherington 1713 W
Prudence, Northam 1663 A
Barrey Richard, Zeal Monachorum 1594 [W]
Robert, North Tawton 1621 [W]
Barrey Robert, Northam 1773 A
Barrie Simon, North Tawton 1571 W
Thomas, North Tawton 1603 W
Thomasine, Tawstock 1621 [W]
Barrie William, Frithelstock 1573 W
Barten see Barton
Bartholomew, Bartholamy, Bartholemew, Bartolemew
Bartholemew John, Hartland 1786 W
Bartholemew John, Clovelly 1798 A
John, Woolfardisworthy, yeoman 1810 W
Lawrence, Hartland 1829 W
Bartholamy Richard, Hartland 1727 W
Bartholemew Richard, Hartland, yeoman 1808 A
William, Hartland 1828 A
Bartlett, Bartlet, Bartrett
Ann, Bideford 1826 A
Bernard, Landcross 1604 A
Brian, Great Torrington 1799 A
Christopher, Northam 1619 A
Christopher, Northam 1643 A
Daniel, Barnstaple 1772 A
David, Combe Martin 1575 A
Edmund, South Molton 1694 W
Edward, Barnstaple 1628 [W]

Edward, Winkleigh 1641 W
Elizabeth, Bideford 1687 W
Evan, Barnstaple 1617 [W]
Evan, Barnstaple 1638 A
Grace, West Buckland 1795 W
Bartlet Jane, Great Torrington 1821 W
Joan, Chulmleigh 1637 A
Joan, Chulmleigh 1640 [W]
John, Woolfardisworthy 1598 [W]
John, Pilton 1609 [W]; forename blank in Ms; supplied from
   parish register
John, Bideford 1679 W
John, Tawstock 1735 A
John, Horwood 1773 A
Justinian, Combe Martin 1619 [W]
Margaret, Bideford 1685 W
Mary, Fremington 1666 W
Richard, Alwington 1766 W
Richard, East Buckland 1771 W
Bartrett Robert, Barnstaple, jnr. 1599 [W]
Stephen, Fremington 1824 W
Susanna, Bideford 1813 W
Thomas, West Putford 1827 W
William, Combe Martin 1605 W
William, Bideford 1682 W
William 1828 A to Elizabeth of Hartland, widow
William, Great Torrington, jnr. 1847 W
Bartman see Bartram
Barton, Barten, Bortyn
   Barten Elizabeth, Coldridge 1591 [W]
   Bortyn Joan, Barnstaple 1598 [W]
Bartram, Bartman, Battram
   George, Buckland Filleigh 1604 W
   Bartman George, Fremington 1703 A
   Battram John, Huntshaw 1588 W
Bartrett see Bartlett
Bartwycke see Barwick
Battram see Bartram
Barwick, Barrick, Barricke, Bartwycke, Barwicke, Berwicke
   ..., Abbotsham 1601 A
   Agnes, Fremington 1644 W
   Agnes, Pilton 1718 A
   Alice, Pilton 1777 W
   Arthur, Alverdiscott 1671 A
   Bridget, Ilfracombe 1706 W
   Charity, Iddesleigh 1697 W
   Elizabeth, Tawstock 1603 W
   Elizabeth, Combe Martin 1711 W
   Barwicke Ellen, Instow 1593 [W]
   Frances, Bratton Fleming 1695 W
   George, Tawstock 1666 [W]
   Barrick George, Fremington 1679 W
   Humphrey, Parracombe 1825 A
   James, Iddesleigh 1661 W
   James, Iddesleigh 1720 W
   Barwicke Joan, Bratton Fleming 1617 [W]
   Joan, Pilton 1795 W
   Barwicke John, Fremington 1571 W
   Barwicke John, Stoke Rivers 1572 W
   Barwicke John, Bratton Fleming 1587 A
   John, Shirwell 1601 [W]; forename blank in Ms; supplied from
      parish register
   Barwicke John, Buckland Brewer 1627 [W]
   Barwicke John, Fremington 1632 [W]
   Barwicke John, Shirwell 1635 A; 1636 W; 1637 O
   John, Tawstock 1660 W
   John, Combe Martin 1673 W
   John, Pilton 1677 A
   John, Bratton Fleming 1705 A
   John, Tawstock 1712 A
   John, Pilton 1800 W
   Barwick Joseph, Bratton Fleming 1710 W
   Barwicke Margaret, Fremington 1597 [W]
   Barricke Margaret, Lynton 1618 [W]
   Margaret, Pilton 1722 A

Margaret, Iddesleigh 1746 W
Marian, Alverdiscott, widow 1611 [W]; forename blank in Ms;
   supplied from parish register
Mary, Bratton Fleming 1695 A
Mary, Bratton Fleming 1731 A
Nicholas, Tawstock 1669 O
Nicholas, Tawstock 1681 W
Nicholas, Tawstock 1696 W
Nicholas, Tawstock 1715 W
Philip, Fremington 1706 W
Barwicke Richard, Stoke Rivers 1568 W
Barwicke Richard, Bratton Fleming 1620 [W] and 1625 [W]
Richard, Parracombe 1787 W
Richard, Northam 1835 W
Robert, Bratton Fleming 1664 W; 1671 A
Samuel, Fremington 1668 A and 1671 O account
Berwicke Simon, Fremington 1568 W
Barwicke Simon, Alverdiscott 1637 W
Barwicke Thomas, Tawstock 1593 [W]
Thomas, Bratton Fleming 1711 W
Thomas, Pilton 1759 A
William, Pilton 1699 W
Barzey see Barry
Basely, Baseleigh, Baseley, Baslegh, Basley
   Baseleigh Alice, Tawstock 1600 W
   Baseleigh Ann, Tawstock 1605 W
   Basley Clase, Yarnscombe 1600 W
   Baseleigh Edward, Dolton 1618 [W]
   John, Tawstock 1594, 1595 and 1596 [W]
   Margaret, Dolton 1640 W
   Richard, Tawstock 1591 [W]
   Baslegh Thomas, Tawstock 1575 W
   Thomas, Yarnscombe 1596 [W]
Baskavill Sybil, Barnstaple 1622 [W]
Baslegh, Basley see Basely
Bass, Base
   ..., Abbotsham 1602 A
   Bass ..., High Bickington 1608 and 1609 [W]
   Basse Ann, Burrington 1635 W
   Basse Anthony, Satterleigh 1583 A
   Basse Anthony, Marwood 1587 W and A
   Basse Anthony, North Molton 1643 [W]
   Anthony, Barnstaple 1700 W
   Charity wife of William, Tawstock 1610 [W]; forename blank
      in Ms; supplied from parish register
   Basse Dorothy, North Molton 1626 [W]
   Edward, Barnstaple 1709 A
   Basse Giles, Parkham 1626 [W]
   Giles, Abbotsham 1749 W
   Giles, Alwington 1778 A
   Grace, Northam 1749 W
   Basse Jacquet, Parkham 1596 [W]
   Basse James, Tawstock 1627 [W]
   Basse John, Burrington 1605 W
   Mary, Barnstaple 1688 W
   Richard, Barnstaple 1712 W
   Besse Robert, Petrockstowe 1570 W
   Basse Thomas, Parkham 1578 W
   Basse Thomas, Marwood 1582 W
   Thomas, Barnstaple 1703 W
   Thomas, Barnstaple 1717 A
   William, Tawstock 1610 W; forename blank in Ms; supplied
      from parish register
   William, Clovelly 1726 [W]
   William, Molland 1782 W
Bassett Bridget, Buckland Brewer 1692 W
   Emott, Monkleigh 1573 W
   Grace, Shebbear 1808 W
   John, Heanton Punchardon 1660 W
   John, Northam 1846 W
   Joseph David, Berrynarbor 1847 W
   Simon, Heanton Punchardon 1665 A
   Thomas, Tawstock 1732 W
Bassick Adam, Bideford 1727 A
Bastable John, Huntshaw 1678 W

Bastard John, Great Torrington 1703 W
  Phillippa, Northam 1706 W
  Thomas, Petrockstowe 1703 W
Bate Alexander, Abbotsham 1714 W
  Jacob, Welcombe, clerk 1635 W
  Robert, Beaford 1773 W
  Roger, Langtree 1707 W and 1710 W
  Roger, Langtree 1751 A
  William, High Bickington 1730 A
  Bates William, Barnstaple 1823 W
  Willmot, Abbotsham 1714 [W]
Bateman Henry, High Bickington 1605 W
Bater, Bather
  ..., Burrington 1610 [W]
  ..., Brushford 1612 [W]
  Ann, Beaford, widow 1581 W
  Giles, Beaford 1573 W
  John, Beaford, snr. 1636 W
  John, Ashreigney 1679 A
  John, Burrington 1679 A
  John, Burrington 1842 W
  Bather Margaret, Westleigh 1798 W
  Philip, Atherington 1630 [W]
  Richard, Burrington 1633 W
  Richard, Burrington 1711 A
  Roger, Burrington 1585 W
  Roger, Burrington 1693 A
  Thomas, Yarnscombe 1579 W
  Thomas, Burrington 1601 W
  Thomas, Yarnscombe 1639 W
  Urithe, Ashreigney 1694 W
  Walter, Alverdiscott 1592 [W]
  William, Beaford 1591 [W]
  William, Little Torrington 1691 A
Bates see Bate
Bath John, Washford Pyne 1735 W
  Margery, Washford Pyne 1740 W
  William, Chittlehampton 1622 [W]
  William, Shirwell 1714 W
  William, Fremington 1829 W
Bathoe John, Ilfracombe 1729 W
  Robert, Ilfracombe 1689 W
Batson see Baitson
Batt Honor, Beaford 1774 W
  James, Burrington 1814 W
  James, Burrington 1836 A to Mary, widow
  John, Great Torrington 1575 W
  Robert, Burrington 1718 W
Batten, Battin, Battine, Battyn
  Battyn ..., Chulmleigh 1610 [W]
  Augustine, West Worlington 1627 [W]
  Battin Deborah, West Worlington 1697 W
  John, West Worlington 1589 W
  Margaret, Bow 1621 [W]
  Margery, Chawleigh 1566 W
  Battin Philip, South Molton 1706 W
  Battyn Richard, Witheridge 1633 W
  Richard, Knowstone 1665 W
  Battine Robert, West Worlington 1585 W
  Battyn Stephen, Buckland Brewer 1577 W
  Battin Thomas, Rackenford 1568 W
  Battin William, West Worlington 1663 [W]
  William, West Worlington 1675 W
Batteshill, Battershill, Battishill
  Battershill Hannah, North Tawton 1805 A
  Battershill James, North Tawton 1805 W
  Mary, Barnstaple 1668 A
  Robert, North Tawton 1681 A
  Battishill Thomas, Woolfardisworthy 1721 A
  William, Shebbear 1684 W
Battin, Battine see Batten
Battishill see Batteshill
Battram see Bartram
Battyn see Batten
Baud see Band

Bault see Bolt
Baunt see Band
Bawden, Banden, Bauden, Bawdon
  Banden or Bauden Agnes, Barnstaple 1719 A
  Bawdon Christopher, Barnstaple 1740 A
  Clark, Combe Martin 1793 A
  Elizabeth, South Molton 1723 [W]
  Bawdon James, St Giles in the Wood 1643 A
  James, Bideford 1713 A
  James see also Susanna Hill
  John, Bideford, snr. 1617 [W]
  Bawdon John, Northam 1618 [W]
  John, South Molton 1741 W
  John, Ilfracombe 1783 A
  Joseph, Molland 1790 W
  Joshua, South Molton 1749 W
  Joshua, South Molton 1845 A
  Banden Lambert, North Molton 1707 A
  Lambert, North Molton 1850 W
  Mary, Barnstaple, sp. 1798 W
  Bawdon Peter, Barnstaple 1642 W
  Peter, North Molton, mason 1857 A to Fanny, relict
  Bawdon Philip, Northam 1591 [W]
  Banden or Bauden Philip, Bideford 1674 W
  Richard, South Molton 1722 W
  Richard, Barnstaple 1742 W
  Richard, South Molton 1746 W
  Robert, South Molton 1853 W
  Sarah, South Molton 1764 W
  Bawden alias James Sarah, Ilfracombe 1789 A
  Bawdon William, Iddesleigh 1634 [W]
    see also Bowden
Bawman see Bowman
Baxter, Baxtor
  John 1694 W
  Baxtor Paul, Georgeham 1744 A
Baylegh, Bayley, Baylie see Bailey
Baylis Agnes, Charles 1838 W
Bayly see Bailey
Bayne Philip, Ilfracombe 1567 [W]
Bea Hugh, Chittlehampton 1599 [W]
  John, Winkleigh 1595 W
Beaford Margaret, Bideford 1636 A
  Philip, Bideford 1703 A
Beake John, Great Torrington 1591 [W]
Beale, Beal, Beall
  Beal Agnes, Bideford 1643 W
  Beall Alice, Parracombe 1580 W
  Beall Anthony, Lynton 1599 [W]
  Beall Elizabeth, Barnstaple 1597 [W]
  Gabriel, Bideford 1689 W
  Beal Henry, West Anstey 1827 W
  Beall Jasper, Lapford 1599 [W]
  Joan, Bideford 1680 W
  Beal Joan, Chulmleigh 1822 W
  Beall John, Buckland Brewer 1573 W
  Beall John, Mortehoe 1586 W
  Beall John, Countisbury 1590 [W]
  Mary, Bideford 1692 W
  Beall Oliver, Trentishoe 1598 [W]
  Beall Paul, North Molton 1591 [W]
  Philip, Bideford 1667 W
  Beal Philip, South Molton 1839 A to Mary, widow
  Beall Richard, Barnstaple 1580 W
  Beal Robert, Chulmleigh, yeoman 1803 W
  Rose, Lynton 1588 W
  Thomas, Bideford 1681 W
  Thomas, Bideford 1713 W
  Beall Urithe, Atherington 1577 W
  Beall Walter, Frithelstock 1598 [W]
  Beall Walter, Combe Martin 1599 [W]
  William, Atherington 1631 [W]; 1632 O
  Beall Willmot, Buckland Filleigh 1593 [W]
Bealey Mary, North Tawton 1826 W
Bealick William, Parkham 1823 W

Beane Cecilia, Barnstaple 1673 W
  John, Barnstaple, snr. 1665 W
Beaple, Baple, Beapell
  ..., Clovelly 1600 [W]
  Alice, Fremington 1583 A
  Catherine, Clovelly 1620 [W]
  Christiana, Abbotsham 1687 [W]
  Daniel, Instow 1631 [W]
  David, Fremington 1571 W
  David, Newton St Petrock 1624 [W]
  Baple David, Chulmleigh 1772 A
  Baple Dorothy, Chulmleigh 1741 W
  Edward, Abbotsham 1595 [W]
  Eleanor, Tawstock 1670 W
  Elizabeth, Abbotsham 1671 W
  Ethelred, Northam, snr. 1693 W
  George, Instow 1603 W
  George, Abbotsham 1661 W
  Henry, Tawstock 1626 [W] and 1629 O
  Jenkin, Instow 1665 A
  Joanna, Barnstaple 1576 W
  John, Instow 1564 W
  John, Fremington 1581 W
  John, Abbotsham 1602 W
  John, Fremington 1622 [W]
  John, Northam 1643 A
  John, Abbotsham 1645 [W]
  Baple Mary, Martinhoe 1618 [W]
  Oliver, Pilton 1566 W
  Peter, Northam 1592 [W]
  Peter, Abbotsham 1669 A
  Prudence, Barnstaple 1665 A
  Richard, Shebbear 1570 W
  Richard, Northam, jnr. 1573 W
  Richard, Northam 1621 [W] and 1624 O
  Robert, Barnstaple 1622 [W] and 1624 O
  Beapell Salome, Pilton 1583 W
  Sarah, Northam 1700 W
  Simon, Bideford 1606 W
  Thomas, Northam 1575 A
  Thomas, Martinhoe 1590 [W]
  Thomas, Northam 1599 [W]
  Thomas, Northam 1602 A; forename blank in Ms; supplied
    from parish register
  Thomas, Instow 1643 W
  Beaple alias Westlake Thomas, Fremington 1643 W
  Thomas, Barnstaple 1698 A
Bear see Beare
Beard, Bearde
  Ann, North Molton 1679 W and 1683 W
  Christian, Fremington 1620 W
  Elizabeth, North Molton 1676 W
  Elizabeth, Northam 1705 W
  Francis, Great Torrington 1757 W
  George, North Molton 1676 W
  Henry, Arlington 1621 [W] and 1623 O
  Henry, Fremington 1758 W
  Hugh, Bratton Fleming 1773 W
  Jeremiah, Mortehoe 1643 W
  John, Stoke Rivers 1582 A
  Bearde John, Bratton Fleming 1602 W
  John, Mortehoe 1688 W
  John, Bratton Fleming 1816 W
  Mary, Bratton Fleming 1603 W
  Rawlina, Kentisbury 1644 A
  Richard, Stoke Rivers 1575 W
  Richard, Goodleigh 1644 A
  Richard, Northam 1684 W
  Robert, Bratton Fleming 1596 [W]
  Bearde Robert, Chawleigh 1621 [W]
  Robert, Pilton 1793 A
  Thomas, Chawleigh 1581 W
  Thomas, Bratton Fleming 1669 W
  William, Loxhore 1569 W
  William, Northam 1843 W

Beare, Bear, Beere, Byer
  ..., Rose Ash 1600 [W] and 1601 O
  ..., Burrington 1603 and 1604 [W]
  ..., Bideford 1606 [W]
  ..., Loxhore 1608 [W]
  Beere ..., South Molton 1610 [W]
  ..., Abbotsham 1612 [W]
  ..., Ashford 1612 [W]
  ..., Rose Ash 1614 [W]
  Bear Abraham, Marwood 1669 W
  Agnes, Chittlehampton 1673 O account and A
  Bear Agnes, Coldridge 1676 W
  Agnes, Chulmleigh 1686 A
  Alexander, Ashreigney 1592 [W]
  Beere Alexander, Chittlehampton 1638 A
  Alice, Chittlehampton 1585 A
  Alice, South Molton 1624 [W]
  Bear Andrew, Shebbear 1590 [W] and 1597 [W]
  Andrew, Winkleigh 1627 [W]
  Beer Andrew, Bideford 1667 W
  Bear Andrew, Warkleigh 1752 W and 1771 A
  Beere Ann, Hartland 1685 W
  Anthony, Chulmleigh 1699 A
  Anthony, Chittlehampton 1723 [W]
  Arnold, Barnstaple 1686 W
  Bear Augustine, Warkleigh 1596 [W]
  Beere Avis, Tawstock 1639 W
  Bear Azariah, Bulkworthy 1840 W
  Christopher, High Bray 1601 W
  Bear Christopher, Chittlehampton 1619 [W]
  Bere Christopher, Chawleigh 1716 W
  Beere Christopher, St Giles in the Wood 1769 [W] and 1777 A
  Beer Christopher, St Giles in the Wood, jnr. 1784 W
  Beere Christopher, St Giles in the Wood 1803 A
  Daniel, Bideford 1583 W
  Bear Daniel, Great Torrington 1670 W
  Daniel, Great Torrington 1713 A
  Bear Daniel, Bulkworthy 1855 W
  Edmund, Pilton 1605 [W]; forename blank in Ms; supplied
    from parish register
  Beere Edward, Bow 1637 W
  Edward, Buckland Brewer 1661 A
  Beere Edward, Little Torrington 1666 W
  Beere Elizabeth, Pilton 1666 W
  Beere Elizabeth, Pilton 1714 W
  Elizabeth, Barnstaple 1729 A
  Elizabeth, Northam 1729 W
  Bear Elizabeth, Bideford 1742 A
  Beere Elizabeth, Weare Giffard 1804 W
  Beer Elizabeth, Chittlehampton 1826 W
  Gabriel, Tawstock 1730 W
  Bear George, Ashreigney 1590 [W]
  George, George Nympton 1595 [W]
  Beare alias Wedlake George, Barnstaple 1601 W
  Bear George, Romansleigh 1620 [W]
  Bear George, Chittlehampton 1637 W
  George, Barnstaple 1685 W
  George, High Bickington 1708 W
  George, Chulmleigh 1715 W
  Beer George, Frithelstock 1830 W
  Bere George, Stoodleigh 1845 W
  George, West Anstey 1720s W
  Grace, George Nympton 1671 A
  Beere Grace, George Nympton 1679 A
  Bear Grace, Hartland 1775 W
  Beer Grace wife of William see Thomas Hutchings
  Beer Hannah, Chittlehampton, widow 1802 W
  Beere Hannibal, George Nympton 1635 W
  Beere Henry, Romansleigh 1631 [W]
  Beer Henry, Great Torrington 1747 W
  Henry, Meeth, yeoman 1808 W
  Hugh, Chittlehampton 1683 A
  Beere Hugh, Dowland 1684 W
  Humphrey, Chittlehampton 1699 A
  Beere James, St Giles in the Wood 1716 W

Beere James, Beaford 1771 A
Bear James, Bideford 1826 A to Elizabeth, widow
Beer James Gilbert, Bideford 1855 W
Jeremiah, Instow 1716 A
Joan, Clovelly, widow 1571 W
Bear Joan, High Bray 1590 [W]
Bear Joan, Chittlehampton 1621 [W]
Bear Joan, Hartland 1629 [W]
Beere Joan, King's Nympton 1638 A
Beere Joan, Winkleigh 1640 W
Joan, Abbotsham 1687 W
Joan, Pilton 1732 A
Bear Joan, St Giles in the Wood 1750 [W]
John, Ashford 1564 W
John, Burrington 1573 W
John, Hartland 1575 W
John, Bideford 1577 W
John, Combe Martin 1586 A
Beere John, Instow 1586 W
John, High Bray 1588 W
Bear John, Chittlehampton 1590 [W]
Bear John, West Down 1596 [W]
John, Frithelstock 1596 [W]
John, Combe Martin 1605 W
John, North Molton 1612 [W]; forename blank in Ms; supplied
   from parish register
John, Westleigh 1615 [W]
John, Barnstaple 1616 [W]
Beere John, Great Torrington 1633 W
Beere John, Rose Ash 1637 W
Beere John, Dolton 1639 A
Beere John, Clovelly 1644 W
John, Hartland 1670 W
John, Pilton 1683 W
John, Yarnscombe 1683 W
John, Ilfracombe 1691 A
John, Yarnscombe 1693 A
John, Northam 1697 W
John, Barnstaple 1700 W
John, Romansleigh 1714 W
John, Barnstaple 1715 W
Beer John, Chittlehampton 1781 A
John, Frithelstock 1783 W
Bear John, Hartland 1792 A
Beer John, Weare Giffard 1794 W
Beer John, Weare Giffard 1815 W
Beer John, Barnstaple 1818 W
Beer John, Weare Giffard, wheelwright 1822 A to Susanna,
   widow
Beer John, Chulmleigh 1832 W
Beer John, Barnstaple 1842 W
Beer John, St Giles in the Wood 1845 W
Beer John, Frithelstock 1851 W
Beer John, Atherington 1854 W
Leonard, Chulmleigh 1627 [W] and 1629 O
Bere Margaret, Coldridge 1578 W
Margaret, George Nympton 1629 [W]
Beere Margaret, Ashreigney 1773 W
Beer Margaret, St Giles in the Wood 1784 W
Byer Mary, Barnstaple 1625 [W]
Mary, Barnstaple 1703 W
Beere Mary, Little Torrington 1710 A
Mary, Marwood 1729 A
Beere Mary, Great Torrington 1778 A
Beer Mary, Rose Ash 1784 A
Mathew, Chittlehampton 1675 A
Bear Mathew, Rose Ash 1784 A
Beere Nicholas, Fremington 1640 W
Peter, Hartland 1673 A
Beere Petronell, Parkham 1643 W
Philip, Great Torrington 1600 W
Bear Philip, George Nympton 1626 [W]
Philip, South Molton 1630 [W]
Beere Philip, George Nympton 1666 A and 1669 O
Philip, George Nympton 1697 W

Beer Philip, Great Torrington 1837 W
Priscilla, Barnstaple 1675 W
Ralph, Romansleigh 1598 [W]
Richard, Hartland 1565 W
Richard, George Nympton 1584 W
Beere Richard, Combe Martin 1639 W
Beer Richard, Yarnscombe 1822 W
Robert, King's Nympton 1573 W
Robert, Chittlehampton 1581 W
Bear Robert, Frithelstock 1592 [W]
Robert, Romansleigh 1603 W
Robert, Barnstaple 1673 A
Beere Robert, Pilton 1691 A
Robert, Pilton 1726 W
Robert, Barnstaple 1740 A
Robert, South Molton 1741 W
Beer Robert, Barnstaple 1756 W
Roger, Pilton 1617 [W]
Roger, Puddington 1737 A
Beer Ruth, Barnstaple 1821 W
Sabine, Northam 1589 W
Samuel, Ilfracombe 1708 A
Beer Samuel, Marwood, labourer 1849 A to Mary of
   Barnstaple, daughter, sp.
Beer Sarah, Instow 1836 W
Beere Stephen, Buckland Brewer 1621 [W]
Thomas, Parracombe 1570 W
Thomas, Woolfardisworthy 1576 W
Thomas, King's Nympton 1579 W
Thomas, Heanton Punchardon 1592 [W]
Thomas, Ashford 1593 [W]
Beere Thomas, George Nympton 1640 A
Bear Thomas, Abbotsham, snr. 1667 W
Bear Thomas, Chittlehampton 1679 W
Beere Thomas, Meshaw 1684 A
Beere Thomas, Pilton 1704 A
Thomas, Ilfracombe 1728 A
Bear Thomas, Instow, widower 1836 W
Bear Thomasine, Ashford 1565 W
Thomasine, Chulmleigh 1707 W
Bear Tryphena, Romansleigh 1621 [W]
Beere Ursula, Little Torrington 1710 A
Bear Walter, Frithelstock 1568 W
Walter, High Bray 1615 [W]
William, Crenham, Hartland 1569 W
William, Northam 1588 W
Bear William, Winkleigh 1625 [W]
Beere William, Fremington 1644 W
William, Hartland 1681 W
William, Combe Martin 1700 A
William, Pilton 1707 W
Beere William, Great Torrington 1717 W
William, Bideford 1730 W
Beere William, Warkleigh 1777 W
Bear William, Chittlehampton 1790 W
Bear William, Hartland, yeoman 1797 W
William, Pilton, tucker 1811 A
Beer William, Warkleigh 1817 W
Bear William, formerly of Hartland but late of Bideford 1829
   A to Jane, widow
Bear William, Bideford 1842 A
Bear William, Bideford 1846 A
Bearne, Bearnes
  Joanna, High Bray 1663 A
  Bearnes Nicholas, Combe Martin 1665 W
Bease, Beast see Best
Beatham see Betham
Beaton, Beatton
  Beatton Joan, Shebbear 1597 [W]
  John, Yarnscombe 1705 A
  Nathaniel, East Down 1705 A
Beaven, Beavans, Beavin, Beaving, Beavings, Beavins, Bevans,
  Bevens, Bevins
  Bevans Ann, Bideford, widow 1797 W
  Edmund, Northam 1702 A

Bevans Edward, Bideford 1766 W
Beavins John, Ilfracombe 1685 W
Bevins John, Bideford 1696 W
John, Northam 1706 A
Beavins John, Bideford 1707 A
Bevens John, Bideford 1718 A
Beavin John, Heanton Punchardon 1735 A
Beavin John, Georgeham 1752 A
John, Clovelly 1755 W
Beavin John, ship *Fougeux* 1760 W
Beavans John, Clovelly 1766 A
Beavings John, Tawstock 1780 W
Margaret, Clovelly 1769 W
Beavans Mary, Georgeham 1766 W
Beaving Nathaniel, East Down 1689 W
Beavins Philip, Northam 1691 A
Bevans Philip, Bideford 1726 W
Bevans Thomas, Lynton 1818 A
Beavin Thomas, Heanton Punchardon 1761 A
Beavis see Bevis
Beckerlegge, Becalic, Becklick
  Becklick Simon, Parkham 1857 W
  Becalic William, Parkham 1841 A
Beckett Neil, Northam 1571 W
Beckinor see Bickner
Beddell see Beedle
Bedder George, Weare Giffard 1675 A
  Thomas, Pilton 1617 [W]
Beddon Christopher, South Molton 1577 W
Bedford Richard, Shirwell 1775 W
  Thomas, Alverdiscott 1695 W
Beedle, Beddell, Beedell
  Beddell ..., Lapford 1603 [W]
  Elizabeth, South Molton, widow 1803 W
  Philip, Cruwys Morchard 1640 A
  Robert, South Molton, yeoman 1800 W
  Beedell William, Cruwys Morchard 1846 W
Beerman see Burman
Beer, Beere see Beare
Beete Charles, St Giles in the Wood 1736 W
  Beete Elizabeth, Bideford 1631 [W]
Beffis see Bevis
Begbie Elizabeth Jane, Bideford 1846 W
Bekelston John Fenis, Instow 1564 W
Belcher William, Weare Giffard 1696 W
Bell Sarah wife of John see Robert Lamprey
Bellamy, Balamie, Balamy, Ballamie, Ballamy, Ballomy
  Ballamy ..., Bideford 1609 [W]
  Balamy Ann, Bondleigh 1788 A
  Ballamie Catherine, Buckland Brewer 1582 W
  Ballamy Hannah, Bondleigh 1772 W
  John, Zeal Monachorum 1595 [W]
  Ballamy John, Bideford 1605 [W]
  Ballomy John, Bideford 1643 A
  John, North Tawton 1768 W
  Ballamy Robert, North Molton 1632 [W]
  Ballamy Robert, Rose Ash 1696 W
  Ballamy Sarah, Huish 1702 W
  Balamy Thomas, Great Torrington 1597 [W]
  Thomas, Chulmleigh 1731 W
  Balamie Thomasine, Great Torrington, widow 1568 W
  Ballamy Walter, Alverdiscott 1600 W
  William, Buckland Brewer 1579 I
Bellew, Bellewe
  Bellewe Cicely, Bideford 1670 W
  Fulk, Monkleigh, gentleman 1614 [W]; forename blank in Ms;
    supplied from parish register
  George, Huntshaw 1666 W
  Grace, Barnstaple 1701 W
  Henry, Huntshaw 1630 A
  Bellew Henry, Fremington 1691 A
  Henry, Barnstaple, surgeon 1806 A
  James, Bideford 1665 W and 1669 O
  James, Bideford 1699 O account
  Bellewe Jane, Monkleigh 1632 [W]

Joanna, Newton Tracey 1679 [W]
John, Newton Tracey 1662 W
John, Yarnscombe 1672 A and O account
Joseph, Barnstaple 1680 W
Lawrence, Yarnscombe 1714 W
Richard, Yarnscombe 1687 W
Rowland, Frithelstock 1665 W
Susanna, Newton Tracey 1677 A
William, Barnstaple 1689 W
Bellringer Grace, Shirwell 1844 W
Belsforde Philip, Heanton Punchardon 1606 W
Belsworthy, Bilsworthy
  ..., Heanton Punchardon 1608 [W]
  ..., Northam 1613 [W]
  Arthur, Pilton 1643 W
  Bilsworthy Christian, Heanton Punchardon 1618 [W]
Belton, Bylton
  Bylton John, Great Torrington 1587 W
  Richard, Great Torrington 1620 [W]
  Richard, Great Torrington 1721 A
  William, Great Torrington 1704 A
Bendle, Bendell, Bindall
  Bendell ..., Romansleigh 1601 O
  Alice, Cruwys Morchard 1667 A
  Ann, Filleigh 1820 W
  Bindall Hugh, South Molton 1661 A
  Bendell John, King's Nympton 1573 W
  Bendell John, King's Nympton 1587 W
  John, Burrington 1684 W
  John, Burrington 1733 W
  John, Burrington 1782 W
  John, Burrington, yeoman 1804 W
  John, Burrington 1819 W and 1825 W
  Jonas, George Nympton 1624 [W]
  Lodovic, King's Nympton 1623 [W]
  Luke, Burrington 1755 A
  Richard, Chittlehampton 1787 A
  Thomas, Burrington 1592 [W]
  Thomas, Romansleigh 1594 [W]
Benet, Benett see Bennett
Benfold, Benfeild
  Benfeild Margaret, Parkham 1677 W
  Benford alias Canne Thomasine, Dowland 1603 W
  William, Bideford 1597 [W]
Benham, Bennam, Bennem
  Humphrey, Barnstaple 1703 W
  Benham John, St Giles in the Wood 1737 A
  Bennem John, Mortehoe, yeoman 1809 A
  Bennam Robert, Barnstaple 1728 A
Bennett, Benet, Benett, Bennet
  ..., Woolfardisworthy 1604 [W]
  ..., Ilfracombe 1605 [W]
  ..., Bideford 1606 [W]
  ..., Northam 1612 [W]
  Bennet alias Wheake ..., Ilfracombe 1705 W
  Alice, Northam 1595 [W]
  Ananias, Merton 1674 W
  Ananias, Merton 1759 W
  Ann, Barnstaple 1736 W
  Anthony, George Nympton 1609 [W]; forename blank in Ms;
    supplied from parish register
  Charles, Bittadon 1663 A
  Christopher C. see Elizabeth Yeo
  Dinah, Barnstaple 1832 W
  Eleanor, Great Torrington 1675 W
  Bennett alias Weke Emma, West Down 1577 W
  Bennet Geoffrey, Berrynarbor 1706 A
  George, East Down 1605 W
  George, Northam 1692 A
  George, Northam 1709 A
  George, Northam 1726 A
  Grace, Thelbridge 1826 W
  Bennet Gwen, Barnstaple 1577 W
  Hannah, Ilfracombe 1726 A
  Henry, Great Torrington 1793 W

Hugh, Great Torrington 1668 A
Bennet Jenkin, West Down 1661 W
Joan, Winkleigh 1591 [W]
Joan, Marwood 1616 [W]
Joan, Lynton 1625 [W]
Joan, Northam 1631 [W]
Bennet Joan, South Molton 1735 A
Benett John, Clovelly 1569 W
Bennet John, Combe Martin 1569 W
Benet John, Great Torrington 1583 W
John, North Molton 1598 [W]
John, Martinhoe 1618 [W]
John, Berrynarbor 1621 [W]
John, Tawstock 1631 [W]
Bennet John, Merton 1642 W
John, Chulmleigh 1670 A and 1672 O account
Bennett alias Wheake John, Arlington 1732 W
John, Instow 1754 W
John, Great Torrington 1765 A
John, Roborough 1855 W
Leonard, Little Torrington 1691 A
Mark, Roborough, yeoman 1800 A
Mary, Parkham 1633 W
Mary, Merton 1744 A
Mary, Meeth, widow 1796 W
Bennet Mathew, Northam 1574 W
Bennet Mathew, South Molton 1716 A
Bennet Melchior, Northam 1714 [W]
Miriam, Berrynarbor 1666 W
Miriam, North Molton 1783 A
Nathaniel, Thelbridge 1828 A to Grace, widow
Nicholas, George Nympton 1607 [W]; forename blank in Ms;
    supplied from parish register
Penelope, Martinhoe 1633 T
Peter, Northam 1636 T
Peter, Great Torrington 1815 A
Peter, Great Torrington, labourer 1824 A to Henry, son
Benett Philip, Martinhoe 1573 W
Benet or Bounte Philip, Mortehoe 1580 W
Bennet Philip, George Nympton 1582 A
Philip, Barnstaple 1622 [W] and 1624 [W]
Philip, Northam 1691 W
Philip, Instow 1702 W
Bennet Philip, Northam 1737 W
Benett Richard, Northam 1569 W
Bennett alias Gefferie Richard, Combe Martin 1582 W
Richard, Northam 1629 [W]
Richard, Northam 1673 A
Bennet Richard, Barnstaple 1684 A
Richard, Little Torrington 1763 W
Robert, Mortehoe 1580 W
Bennet Robert, Northam 1742 W
Samuel, Martinhoe 1624 [W]
Samuel see also Elizabeth Yeo
Bennet Sarah, Instow 1712 W
Sarah Thomasine, West Anstey 1851 W
Thomas, Marwood 1622 [W]
Thomas, Cruwys Morchard 1830 W
Thomasine, George Nympton 1619 [W] and 1628 A account
Thomasine, Tawstock 1633 W
Benett Walter, Northam 1588 A
Benet William, Northam 1589 A
William, Northam 1624 [W] and O
William, Martinhoe 1628 [W]
Bennet William, Northam 1680 W
William, Northam 1703 W
Bennet alias Wheake William, Ilfracombe 1705 W
William, Ruby 1745 W
William, Witheridge 1825 A to Elizabeth, widow
William, Shirwell 1829 A to Jane of Bideford, widow
William, Thelbridge 1842 W
William, Thelbridge, yeoman 1845 W to Elizabeth, widow
William, Tawstock 1853 W
Willmot, North Molton 1615 [W]
Zachariah, Dolton 1640 W

Bennon Lodovic, Heanton Punchardon 1712 W
Benson Ann, Northam 1680 W
John, Northam 1719 W
John, Parkham 1738 [W]
John, Northam 1809 [W]*; 1811 [W] transmitted to Doctor's
    Commons by monition
Peter, Northam 1700 A
Peter, Knapp, Northam, esquire 1800 W
Bentley, Bently
Bently Elizabeth, Goodleigh 1668 W
John, Barnstaple 1853 W
Thomas, Chittlehampton 1848 W
Benycke William, Meeth 1574 W
Beriman see Berriman
Bernard see Burnard
Berrell, Berell, Berrill
Berell ..., Fremington 1608 O
Elizabeth, Northam 1719 W
Berrill George, Northam 1734 W
Berrill George, Northam 1752 W
Berrill George, Northam 1768 A
Berrill George, Northam 1779 A
John, Fremington 1572 W
Berrill John, Heanton Punchardon 1694 W
Nicholas, Great Torrington 1639 W
Berrill Phillippa, Northam 1734 W
Berrill Richard, Northam 1749 A
Berrill Richard, Northam 1763 W
Berrill Thomas, Northam 1734 W
Berril Thomas, Northam 1765 W
Berrill William, Northam 1742 W
Berriman, Beriman, Berryman, Beryman, Buriman, Buryman
Buryman ..., Little Torrington 1602 [W]
Buriman ..., Abbotsham 1603 [W]
Buryman ..., Northam 1604 [W]
Buriman ..., Northam 1612 and 1613 [W]
Buryman Catherine, Littleham (near Bideford) 1594 [W]
Buryman Daniel, Abbotsham 1590 [W]
Berryman Elizabeth, Parkham 1621 [W]
Florence, Bideford 1670 W
George, Bideford 1667 A
Berryman George, Bideford 1729 W
Buryman Jenson, Bideford 1587 A
Buryman Joan, Abbotsham, widow 1589 W
Beriman John, Shebbear 1578 W
Beryman John, Weare Giffard 1599 [W]
Berryman John, Parkham 1621 [W]
John, Littleham (near Bideford) 1645 A
John, Langtree 1687 W
Buryman Mary, Northam 1593 [W]
Berryman Mary, Bideford 1701 A
Mary, Bideford 1708 A
Mary see also Thomas Finch
Berryman Michael, Abbotsham 1589 A
Beryman Nicholas, Northam 1592 [W]
Beriman Richard, Shebbear 1576 W
Buriman Richard, Westleigh 1612 [W]; forename blank in Ms;
    supplied from parish register
Robert, Clovelly 1856 W
Buryman Roger, Abbotsham 1570 W
Samuel, Bideford 1698 A
Beryman Thomas, Northam 1596 [W] and 1603 W
Thomas, Parkham 1705 W
Buryman William, Iddesleigh 1586 A
Buryman William, Iddesleigh 1591 [W]
Berryman William, Hartland 1766 A
Berry, Berrie, Berrye, Bery, Berye
Bery ..., Alverdiscott 1601 W
..., Martinhoe 1601 [W] and 1607 [W]
Berrye ..., Tawstock 1607 [W]
..., Northam 1615 [W]
Berrie alias Chichester ..., Berrynarbor 1700 or 1790 A
Achilles, Westleigh 1672 W
Agnes, Winkleigh 1588 A

Bery Agnes, Lynton, widow 1606 [W]; forename blank in Ms;
    supplied from parish register
Agnes, Lynton 1633 W
Agnes, Abbotsham 1689 A
Agnes, Chittlehampton 1703 W
Alexander, Twitchen 1703 W
Bery Andrew, Barnstaple 1610 [W]; forename blank in Ms;
    supplied from parish register
Andrew, Tawstock 1633 W
Ann, Northam 1716 A
Ann, Heanton Punchardon 1753 W
Ann, Atherington 1757 A
Ann, Northam, sp. 1821 A to Grace Mullins, sister
Berye Anthony, Westleigh 1579 W
Anthony, Lynton 1617 [W]
Anthony, Brendon 1630 [W]
Anthony, Instow, gentleman 1687 W
Anthony, Lynton 1710 W
Archelaus, Marwood 1743 A
Bartholomew, Chittlehampton 1715 [W]
Bartholomew, Chittlehampton 1736 W and A
Bartholomew, Barnstaple 1741 W
Bartholomew, Chittlehampton 1743 W
Bartholomew, Barnstaple 1762 W
Bartholomew, Chittlehampton 1774 W
Bartholomew, Merton 1814 W
Bartholomew, Shebbear 1853 W
Benjamin, Abbotsham 1677 A
David, Parracombe 1685 W
David, Parracombe 1760 W
Dorothy, Cruwys Morchard 1690 W
Editha, Barnstaple 1663 W
Edmund, Marwood 1702 W
Edward, Barnstaple 1633 A
Edward, Northam 1701 W
Edward, ship *Monarch* 1760 W
Eleanor, Tawstock, gentlewoman 1673 W
Eleanor, Tawstock 1689 W
Berye Elizabeth, Westleigh 1579 W
Elizabeth, Tawstock 1703 W
Berrie Elizabeth, Mortehoe 1717 W
Elizabeth, Barnstaple 1751 W
Enoch, Instow, gentleman 1661 W
Enoch, Pilton 1743 W
Berrie Felicia, Shirwell 1579 W
George, Northam 1628 [W]
George, Yarnscombe, snr. 1672 A
George, Fremington 1691 A
George, Northam 1792 W
George, Heanton Punchardon 1810 W
George, Northam 1823 A to Grace Melhuish, sister
Gilbert, Instow 1722 W
Gilbert, Bideford 1741 W
Grace, Atherington 1707 W
Hannah, Atherington 1752 W
Henry, Bideford 1641 W
Berrie Henry, Tawstock 1698 W
Isott, Tawstock 1616 [W]
Isott, Parkham 1715 W
James, Pilton 1744 W
James, Northam 1854 W
Bery Joan, Tawstock, widow 1613 [W] "of Lake" in register;
    forename blank in Ms; supplied from parish register
Joan, Great Torrington 1640 A
Joan, Tawstock 1704 W
Joan, Chittlehampton 1707 W
Joan, Bratton Fleming 1758 A
Joan, Tawstock 1780 W
Joan, Chulmleigh 1784 W
Joanna, Catherine and Susan, Bideford 1626 [W]
Berye John, Tawstock 1564 W
Berrie John, Chittlehampton 1579 W
Berrie John, Littleham (near Bideford) 1586 W
John, Chulmleigh 1588 W
John, Colley, Kentisbury 1588 W

John, Ashford 1596 [W]
John, Bideford 1596 [W]
John, Parracombe 1596 [W]
John, Lynton 1599 [W]
John, Chulmleigh 1601 W
Bery John, Parracombe 1603 W
Bery John, Tawstock 1603 W
Bery John, Northam 1607 [W]; forename blank in Ms;
    supplied from parish register
John, Lynton 1611 [W] "at Babrooke" in register; forename
    blank in Ms; supplied from parish register
John, Pilton 1626 [W]
John, Shirwell 1627 [W]
John, Brushford 1632 [W]
John, Chittlehampton 1640 A
John, Molland 1643 A
John, Parracombe 1685 A
John, Mortehoe 1689 A
John, Chittlehampton 1691 W
Berrie John, Berrynarbor, esquire 1694 W
John, East Down 1696 A
John, Berryarbor, esquire 1701 W
John, Chittlehampton 1707 A
John, Martinhoe 1716 A
John, Atherington 1721 W
John, Fremington 1736 A
John, Chulmleigh 1751 A
John, Chittlehampton 1779 W
John, Chulmleigh 1781 W
John, North Molton 1784 W
John, Marwood 1796 W
John see also Elizabeth Seager
Lodovic, Bideford 1703 W
Lucas, Dolton 1625 [W]
Margaret, Tawstock 1729 A
Mary, Berrynarbor 1620 [W]
Mary, Marwood 1665 W
Mary, Tawstock 1671 W
Mary, Fremington 1685 A
Mary, Tawstock 1687 W
Berrie Mary, Berrynarbor 1712 W
Mary, Bideford 1760 W
Mary, Fremington 1800 A
Nathaniel, Molland 1616 [W] and 1619 [W]
Nicholas, Chittlehampton 1688 W
Nicholas, Tawstock 1689 W
Nicholas, Berrynarbor, gentleman 1699 W
Nicholas, Georgeham 1751 W
Peter, Parracombe 1677 W
Philip, Merton 1643 W
Philip, Georgeham 1713 W
Philip, Georgeham 1753 A
Berrye Richard, Mortehoe 1579 W
Richard, Barnstaple 1622 [W]
Richard, Combe Martin 1622 [W]
Richard, Molland 1631 [W]
Richard, Tawstock, snr. 1636 W
Richard, Parracombe 1638 W
Berrie Richard, Berrynarbor 1670 W
Richard, Barnstaple 1670 W
Richard, Alverdiscott 1685 W
Richard, Chittlehampton 1685 W
Richard, Cruwys Morchard 1746 W
Richard, Martinhoe 1802 W*
Samuel, Bideford 1748 [W]
Samuel, Barnstaple 1752 A
Samuel, Chittlehampton 1777 W
Samuel, Tawstock 1779 W
Samuel, Barnstaple 1810 A and 1819 A
Simon, Parracombe 1750 W
Stephen, Pilton 1746 W
Stephen, ship *Thetis* 1748 W
Susan, Catherine and Joanna, Bideford 1626 [W]
Berie Thomas, Tawstock 1614 O forename blank in Ms;
    supplied from parish register

Thomas, Woolfardisworthy 1618 [W]
Thomas, Tawstock 1674 W
Thomas, Berrynarbor, esquire 1708 A
Thomas, Great Torrington 1724 [W]
Thomas, Barnstaple 1734 W
Thomas, Great Torrington 1743 W
Thomas, Barnstaple 1754 A
Thomas, Bratton Fleming 1756 W
Thomas, Westleigh, esquire 1802 A
Thomas, Marwood 1834 W
Thomas, Heanton Punchardon 1853 W
Thomasine, Tawstock 1704 W
Walter, Dowland 1602 W
Berrie William, Tawstock 1578 W
Bery William, Tawstock 1597 [W]
William, Fremington 1688 W
Berrie William, Tawstock 1712 W
William, Marwood 1744 W
William, South Molton 1765 W
William, Berrynarbor 1789 W and 1792 W
William, Combe Martin 1819 W
Winifred, Chittlehampton 1736 W
Berryman see Berriman
Berwicke see Barwick
Bery see Berry
Beryman see Berriman
Berye see Berry
Besley, Besly
   Admonition, Barnstaple 1781 W
   Elizabeth, Rose Ash 1838 W
   Besly Oliver, Barnstaple 1777 W
   Richard Thomas William see Richard Thomas Williams
   Besly Sarah, Barnstaple, widow 1807 W
   Sarah, Barnstaple 1844 W
   Susanna, Barnstaple 1722 A
Best, Beast
   Adam, Barnstaple 1617 [W]
   Agnes, Tawstock 1684 W
   Alice, Tawstock 1599 [W]
   Alice, Tawstock, widow 1600 [W]; forename blank in Ms;
     supplied from parish register
   Andrew, Great Torrington 1639 W
   Dorothy, Tawstock 1703 W
   Edith, Great Torrington 1637 [W]
   Elizabeth, Great Torrington 1618 W
   Elizabeth, Great Torrington 1685 W
   George, Tawstock 1623 [W]
   Bease Henry, Great Torrington 1616 [W]
   Bease John, Buckland Brewer 1608 [W]; forename blank in
     Ms; supplied from parish register
   Bease John, Great Torrington 1617 [W]
   John, Great Torrington 1622 [W] and 1624 O
   Bease John, Great Torrington 1635 W
   Beast John, Buckland Brewer 1638 W
   John, Barnstaple 1759 W
   Jonathan, Tawstock 1643 [W]
   Jonathan, Barnstaple 1722 W
   Jonathan, Barnstaple 1736 W
   Margaret, Barnstaple 1585 W
   Richard, Tawstock 1674 W
   Susanna, Great Torrington 1663 A
   Thomas, Tawstock 1585 W
   Beast Thomas, Lapford 1615 [W]
   Thomas, Tawstock 1632 [W]
   Thomas, Tawstock 1694 W
   William, Monkleigh 1565 W
   Best alias Cooke William, Monkleigh 1565 [W]
   Beste William, Great Torrington 1572 W
   Bease William, Buckland Brewer 1669 W
   Best alias Davy William, Atherington 1680 A
   William, Great Torrington 1777 W
   William, Great Torrington, carpenter 1796 W
Betham, Beatham
   ..., Bow 1601 A

Robert, Bow 1606 [W] "young man"; forename blank in Ms;
   supplied from parish register
Beatham Roger, Bow 1670 W
Bethenbye Lawrence, Zeal Monachorum 1583 W
Betson George, Pilton 1609 [W]; forename blank in Ms; supplied
   from parish register
   Mary, Ilfracombe 1734 W
   Philip, Berrynarbor 1701 W
   Richard, Buckland Brewer 1726 W
   William, Barnstaple 1645 W
   William, Sheepwash 1731 A
Beusse see Buss
Bevan, Bevans, Bevens see Beaven
Beverstock Elizabeth, South Molton 1749 A
Bevins see Beaven
Bevis, Beavis, Beffis, Bevys, Bevyse, Beyffes
   Beyffes Agnes, Petrockstowe 1589 W
   Beavis Elizabeth, Chittlehampton 1773 A
   Bevys George, Shebbear 1579 W
   Beffis John, Petrockstowe 1594 [W]
   Bevyse William, Petrockstowe 1578 W
Bewes, Bews, Bewse see Buss
Beyffes see Bevis
Bichford see Bickford
Bickam see Bickham
Bickell ..., Great Torrington 1608 [W]
   William, North Tawton 1848 W
Bickener see Bickner
Bickerstaff, Charles 1746 W
Bickford, Bichford
   Benjamin, East Putford 1695 W
   Bichford John, Atherington 1773 W
Bickham, Bickam
   Ann, South Molton 1768 A
   Bickam John, South Molton 1762 W; 1764 A dbn
Bickley Elizabeth, Great Torrington 1663 A
   Grace, Bow 1598 [W]
   Thomas, King's Nympton 1670 W
Bicknell, Bicknil
   Bicknil George, Stoke Rivers 1665 W
   John, North Molton 1846 W
   Thomasine, Berrynarbor 1683 A
Bickner, Beckinor, Bickener, Bicknor, Byckener, Byckmore
   Anthony, Knowstone 1618 [W]
   Byckmore Edward, Rackenford 1565 W
   Gabriel, Knowstone 1632 [W]
   Honoria, Instow 1688 W
   Bickner alias Hichecocke John, Witheridge 1579 W
   John, Knowstone 1588 W
   Nathaniel, Westleigh 1680 A
   Richard, Westleigh 1602 W
   Bickener Thomas, Westleigh 1580 W
   Beckinor Thomas, Heanton Punchardon 1679 A
   William, Instow 1679 W
   Bicknor William, South Molton 1726 A
Biddell see Biddle
Bidden Edward, South Molton 1591 [W]
Bidder Bartholomew, Marwood 1714 W
   Honoria, Weare Giffard 1694 A
   Humphrey, Monkleigh 1705 A
   John, Bideford 1700 W
   John, Pilton 1758 W
   John, Northam 1799 W
   Margaret, Marwood 1740 W
   Mary, Marwood 1724 W
   Philip, Northam 1732 A
   Richard, Northam 1705 A
   Sarah, Northam 1803 W
   Sarah see also Thomas Cory
   William, Barnstaple 1765 W
Biddle, Biddell, Bidle, Byddle, Bydwill
   Bydwill Francis, North Tawton 1580 A
   Byddle John, Lapford 1631 [W]
   Byddle Richard, Lapford 1627 [W] and O
   Bidle Richard, Iddesleigh 1691 W

Biddell William, Lapford 1587 W
Bidgood, Bydgood
...., Woolfardisworthy 1665 W
Agnes, Woolfardisworthy 1592 [W]
Benjamin, Witheridge 1728 W
George, East Worlington 1669 [W]
Bydgood Hugh, Witheridge 1639 W
Bydgood John, Woolfardisworthy 1572 W
John, Witheridge 1661 W
John, Burrington 1689 A
John, Witheridge 1719 W
John, Witheridge 1820 W
Bydgood Joseph, Stoodleigh 1623 [W]
Bydgood Margaret, Stoodleigh 1589 W
Margaret, Burrington 1675 W
Margery, Bow 1670 W
Richard, Barnstaple, gentleman 1804 W
Robert, South Molton 1719 W
Robert, Witheridge 1729 A
Robert, Witheridge 1772 W
Bydgood Roger, South Molton 1620 [W]
Bydgood Roger, South Molton 1640 W
Simon, Cruwys Morchard 1603 [W]; forename blank in Ms;
    supplied from parish register
William, Woolfardisworthy 1603 W
William, Woolfardisworthy 1730 W
William, Witheridge 1746 A
William, Witheridge 1805 W
William, Witheridge 1827 W
Bidlake Henry, Bideford 1706 W
Bidle see Biddle
Billenger John, Great Torrington 1731 A
Bilsworthy see Belsworthy
Bindall see Bendle
Bindford Emblem, Chulmleigh 1594 [W]
    William, Dowland 1591 [W]
Biner Henry, Great Torrington 1678 W
    Mary, Great Torrington 1684 A
Binford, Bynford
    Bynford alias Canne Thomasine, Dowland 1603 W
Binney John, Bideford 1846 W
Binnock Thomas, Mortehoe 1579 A
Binon see Bynon
Birch, Birche, Birck, Burch, Byrch, Byrche
    ..., Beaford 1604 [W]
    ..., Loxhore 1607 [W], 1612 [W] and 1615 [W]
    Byrche Agnes, Loxhore 1589 W
    Alice, Loxhore 1604 W
    Burche Ambrose, Loxhore 1584 W
    Byrch Baldwin, Barnstaple 1621 [W]
    Beaton, Huntshaw 1603 W
    Burch Catherine, Huntshaw 1714 A
    Birck Catherine, Northam 1767 W
    Burch David, Barnstaple 1721 A
    Burch Dorothy, Filleigh 1619 [W]
    Burch Edward, Shirwell 1633 W
    Byrch Elizabeth, Shirwell 1594 [W]
    Byrch Elizabeth, Huntshaw 1626 [W] and 1627 O
    Burch Fanny, Northam 1857 W
    Burch Gabriel, Huntshaw 1643 W
    Burch Henry, Shirwell 1685 W
    Burch Henry, Loxhore 1689 W
    Burch Henry, Northam 1706 A
    Birche James, Loxhore 1573 A
    Joan, Barnstaple 1642 W
    Burche John, Huntshaw 1586 W
    Byrch John, Loxhore, jnr. 1589 W
    Burch John, Loxhore 1595 [W]
    Byrche John, Shirwell 1619 [W]
    Byrche John, Huntshaw 1620 [W]
    Burch John, West Buckland 1677 W
    Burch John, Brendon 1685 A
    Burch John, Huntshaw 1722 [W]
    Burch John, Bideford 1742 W
    Burch John, South Molton 1762 W

John, Bideford 1777 A
Burch John, Northam 1848 W
Mary, Bideford 1767 W
Burch Philip, Brendon 1717 W
Philip, Langtree 1764 W
Burch Philip, Barnstaple 1825 W
Byrch Richard, Loxhore 1620 [W]
Burch Richard, Brendon 1686 W
Richard, Northam 1851 W
Byrche Robert, Shirwell 1564 W
Byrch Robert, Loxhore 1645 A
Burch Robert, Martinhoe 1703 W
Burch Samuel, Northam 1769 W
Thomas, Lapford 1576 W
Burch Thomas, Shirwell 1591 [W]
Burch Thomas, Bideford 1764 W
Burch Thomas, Bideford 1778 W
Burch William, Loxhore 1616 [W]
Burch William, Huntshaw 1625 [W]
Burch William, East Down 1722 A
Burch William, Northam 1830 W
Bird, Birde, Burd, Byrd, Byrde
    ..., Chawleigh 1792 W
    Byrde Agnes, Chawleigh 1632 [W]
    Ann, Chittlehampton 1687 A
    Ann, South Molton 1847 W
    Byrde Anthony, Chawleigh 1627 [W]
    Anthony, Chittlehampton 1681 W and 1687 A
    Anthony, Eggesford 1713 W
    Anthony, Chawleigh 1757 W
    Catherine, Chulmleigh 1855 W
    Byrde Elizabeth, St Giles in the Wood, widow 1571 W
    Elizabeth, Chawleigh, sp. 1796 W
    George, Chawleigh 1745 A
    Grace, Barnstaple 1801 A*
    Hannibal, King's Nympton 1734 W
    James, North Molton 1843 W
    Jane, Bideford 1800 W
    Byrd John, Chawleigh 1588 A
    Birde John, Bow 1607 [W]; forename blank in Ms; supplied
        from parish register
    Byrde John, Chawleigh 1619 [W]
    Byrde John, North Molton 1640 W
    John, Chulmleigh 1776 W
    Burd John, Beaford 1828 W
    John, Pilton, wool dealer 1854 A to William of North Molton,
        yeoman, father
    John Kemp, Mariansleigh 1852 W
    Loiseau John, Bideford 1739 W
    Margaret, Bideford 1799 W
    Mark, King's Nympton 1690 A
    Mark, Chawleigh 1762 W
    Mark, Chawleigh 1774 W
    Mark, Ashreigney 1777 A
    Mary, King's Nympton 1818 W
    Peter, Chulmleigh 1845 W
    Richard, Chawleigh 1816 W
    Burd Richard, Beaford 1832 W
    Robert, Chawleigh 1716 W
    Robert, Chawleigh 1817 W
    Rose, Chawleigh 1823 W
    Byrde Thomas, Chawleigh 1623 [W]
    Burd Thomas, ship *Ipswich* 1762 A
    Thomas, Chawleigh 1779 W and 1785 W
    Byrd Thomas, Abbotsham 1832 O
    Byrde Vincent, Ashreigney 1620 [W]
    Burd Vincent, North Tawton 1668 W
    Vincent, Ashreigney 1709 A
    William, Northam 1591 [W]
    Byrde William, South Molton 1620 [W]
    William, Chulmleigh 1737 W
    William, Chulmleigh 1845 W
Biscombe, Biscomb
    Joanna, Oakford 1688 W
    Biscomb William, Oakford 1713 W

Bishop, Bishopp, Buishop, Buishope, Bushop, Bushope,
     Bushoppe, Busshope, Buyshope, Buyshopp, Byshop,
     Byshope, Byshopp, Byshoppe
..., Brushford 1612 [W]
..., Bondleigh 1614 [W]
Buishop ..., Bondleigh 1614 [W]
Agnes, Clovelly 1729 W
Ann, Parkham 1820 W
Byshopp Charles, Alwington 1637 W
Charles, Northam 1716 A
Dorothy, Bideford 1787 W
Elias, Bondleigh 1618 [W]
Elizabeth, Bideford 1816 W
Byshopp Emma, Bondleigh 1635 W
Bishopp Emma, Northam 1685 A
George, Alwington 1827 A to Richard, father
Bishop Giles, South Molton 1668 A
Byshopp Grace, Bondleigh 1633 W
Honor, Alwington 1716 [W]; A dbn
Honorius, Great Torrington 1727 W
Byshopp Hugh, Bondleigh 1633 A and 1635 O
Byshopp Jacob, Thelbridge 1638 W
Bishop James, Thelbridge 1709 W
Jane, Thelbridge 1669 O
Bushop Joan, Winkleigh 1574 W
Byshopp Joan, Northam 1630 [W]
Joanna, Littleham (near Bideford) 1803 W
Bishopp John, Ashreigney 1599 [W]
Byshopp John, Northam 1619 [W] and 1622 [W]
Byshopp John, Hartland 1627 [W]
Bishop John, Winkleigh 1637 W
John, Chittlehampton 1641 A
John, East Worlington 1663 W
John, Berrynarbor 1680 W
John, Buckland Brewer 1685 W
Bishopp John, Northam 1693 A
John, Northam 1703 W
John, Bideford 1816 A
John, Woolfardisworthy 1822 W
John, Dolton 1843 W
John, Bideford 1845 W
Byshopp Lodovic, Arlington 1640 W
Busshope Margaret, Bondleigh 1575 W
Bishopp Margaret, Northam 1686 W
Mary, Heanton Punchardon 1680 W
Bishopp Mary, Ilfracombe 1688 W
Byshopp Nicholas, Great Torrington 1629 [W]
Bishopp Peter, Brushford 1598 [W]
Byshopp Richard, Great Torrington 1571 W
Bushope Richard, Brushford 1574 W
Buyshope Richard, Chawleigh 1587 A
Buyshope Richard, Great Torrington 1587 A and 1588 O
     account
Byshopp Richard, Northam 1626 [W]
Byshopp Richard, Great Torrington 1635 W
Byshop Richard, Bondleigh 1635 W and 1636 O
Byshope Robert, Winkleigh 1580 A and 1586 A
Samuel, Parkham 1818 W
Bishopp Sarah, Thelbridge 1666 A
Bushope Simon, Thelbridge 1574 W
Bishopp Stephen, Thelbridge 1666 W
Byshope Thomas, Woolfardisworthy 1580 W
Byshopp Thomas, Hartland 1624 [W]
Byshopp Thomas, Chittlehampton 1628 [W]
Bishopp Thomas, Bideford 1666 A
Bishopp Thomas, Bideford 1695 W
Thomas, Barnstaple 1738 [W]
Buishope William, Winkleigh 1583 W
William, Bondleigh 1595 [W]
Buyshopp William, Brushford 1619 [W]
Byshopp William, Hartland 1629 [W]
William, Pilton 1661 A
Bisick John, Bideford 1751 W
William, Northam 1750 W
Biss Bartholomew, Barnstaple 1694 W
Elizabeth, Barnstaple 1667 W and A

Rebecca, Barnstaple 1660 W
Bissett, Bisset
John, Dowland, husbandman 1805 W
John, Dowland 1840 W
John, Dolton 1844 W
John, Petrockstowe 1845 W
Martha, Petrockstowe 1845 W
Mary, Dolton 1846 W
Bisset Richard, Dowland 1774 W
Bittabear, Byttabere
Byttabere alias Endacott Robert, Winkleigh 1574 W
Bittell Richard, St Giles in the Wood 1715 W
Blaccden see Blagdon
Blachford see Blackford
Black, Blacke
John, Barnstaple 1746 A
Blacke Robert, Chittlehampton 1585 W
Blackdon see Blagdon
Blacke see Black
Blackeford see Blackford
Blackemor, Blackemore see Blackmore
Blackford, Blachford, Blackeford, Blatchford
Blackford alias Doble ..., Parracombe 1666 A
Alexander, Yarnscombe 1616 [W]
Blatchford Grace, Shebbear 1850 W
Blachford Henry, Great Torrington 1664 [W]
Henry, Molland 1716 A
John, West Buckland 1575 W
Blachford John, North Tawton 1577 W
John, Peters Marland 1577 W
John, Martinhoe 1631 [W]
John, Barnstaple 1640 A
Blackford alias Dobell John, Parracombe 1666 A
Blackford alias Dovell John, Parracombe 1719 W
Blatchford Richard, Shebbear 1844 W
Blackeford alias Stodden Robert, Barnstaple 1601 W
Robert, Barnstaple 1635 W
Blackmore, Blackemor, Blackemore, Blackmer, Blackmor,
     Blacmore, Blakemor, Blakemore, Blakmore
..., Northam 1600 [W]
... ... 1604 [W]
..., Bideford 1606 [W]
..., Thelbridge 1607 [W]
..., Great Torrington 1610 [W]
..., Shirwell 1610 [W]
..., Combe Martin 1614 [W]
..., East Worlington 1614 [W]
Agnes, Trentishoe 1574 A
Agnes, Combe Martin 1680 A
Agnes, Kentisbury 1839 W and 1840 W
Alexander, Ilfracombe 1742 A
Alice, Combe Martin 1594 [W]
Alice, Georgeham 1604 W
Alice, Combe Martin 1615 [W]
Alice, Great Torrington 1633 [W]
Alice, North Molton 1637 W
Amy, Great Torrington 1595 [W]
Ann, Parracombe 1633 A and 1634 O
Ann, Chawleigh 1754 A
Ann, Ilfracombe 1820 W
Ann, Countisbury 1830 A to Margaret Jones of Lynton,
     daughter
Anthony, Knowstone 1681 A
Anthony, Ashreigney 1737 A
Anthony, Witheridge 1824 A to Anthony, thatcher, son
Bartholomew, Chulmleigh 1633 W
Catherine, East Anstey 1568 W
Charity, Washford Pyne 1825 W
Charles, Shirwell 1813 W
Charles, Barnstaple 1848 W
Blackmore Christian, Combe Martin 1577 W
Christian, Mortehoe 1598 [W]
Christopher, South Molton 1715 W
Christopher, Ilfracombe 1800 A
Christopher, Arlington 1851 W

Blackemor Clase, Georgeham 1590 [W]
Dorothy, Ashreigney 1708 W
Edward, Shirwell 1735 W
Blackmor Elizabeth, Ilfracombe 1596 [W]
Elizabeth, Beaford 1732 W
Elizabeth, Shirwell 1815 W
Elma, Trentishoe 1575 W
George, Ashreigney 1686 W
Giles, Shirwell 1695 A
Grace, Northam 1609 [W]; forename blank in Ms; supplied
  from parish register
Grace, Great Torrington 1742 W
Grace, North Molton 1789 A
Henry, Marwood 1680 A
Honor, Berrynarbor 1617 [W]
Hugh, Thelbridge 1594 [W]
Hugh, South Molton 1692 A
Blackmore Humphrey, Rackenford 1619 [W]
Humphrey, Ilfracombe 1661 W
Humphrey, Ilfracombe 1765 W
James, Combe Martin 1570 W
James, Georgeham 1578 A
James, Chulmleigh 1634 A
James, Lynton 1642 W
James, Oakford 1666 W
Blackmore alias Read James, Barnstaple 1674 A
James, Bideford 1704 W
James, Barnstaple 1709 A
James, Combe Martin 1727 [W]
James, Northam 1814 W
James, Kentisbury 1831 W
Jane, Combe Martin 1629 [W]
Jane, Combe Martin 1756 W
Joan, Rackenford, widow 1568 [W]
Joan, Rackenford 1578 W
Joan, Great Torrington 1591 [W]
Joan, Knowstone 1596 [W]
Joan, Combe Martin 1627 [W]
Joan, Great Torrington 1631 [W]
Joan, East Anstey 1638 W
Joan, Georgeham 1737 A
Joan, Great Torrington 1747 W
Joan, Combe Martin 1814 A
Blackemore John, Combe Martin 1567 W
John, Trentishoe 1569 W
John, East Down 1573 W
John, Georgeham 1573 A
Blakemore John, Georgeham 1586 W
John, Buckland Brewer 1590 [W]
John, Trentishoe 1592 [W]
John, Barnstaple 1593 [W]
John, Fremington 1595 [W]
John, Combe Martin 1622 [W]
John, Combe Martin 1631 [W] and 1633 O
John, Combe Martin, snr. 1635 W
John, Chawleigh 1640 W
John, Lynton 1640 A
John, Northam 1644 W
John, South Molton 1667 A and 1671 account
John, Burrington 1674 A
John, Ashreigney 1684 W
John, Martinhoe 1684 W
John, Heanton Punchardon 1687 A
John, South Molton 1688 W
John, Northam 1693 W
John, Shirwell 1703 W
John, Chawleigh 1704 W
John, Beaford 1725 W
John, Parracombe 1761 W
John, Beaford 1770 W
John, Chawleigh 1778 W
Blackmer John, Bideford 1805 W
John, Parracombe, yeoman 1805 W
John, Kentisbury, clerk 1809 W
John, Martinhoe 1813 W

John, Chittlehampton 1818 W
John, Fremington 1818 W
John, Parracombe 1822 A to Susanna, widow
John, Fremington 1825 A to Agnes Molland, sister
John, High Bickington 1849 W
John, St Giles in the Wood 1849 W
John, Kentisbury 1853 W
Joseph, Northam, mariner 1809 W
Julian, South Molton 1706 W
Lodovic, Barnstaple 1621 [W]
Lucas, Great Torrington 1679 W
Lucas, Great Torrington 1725 A
Luke, Great Torrington 1680 W
Luke, Great Torrington 1744 W
Blackmore alias Reade Mark, Barnstaple 1695 A; forename
  blank in Ms; supplied from parish register
Mary, Ilfracombe 1703 W
Mary, Great Torrington 1711 W
Mary, Ilfracombe 1726 W
Mary, Barnstaple 1732 W and 1737 A
Mary, Martinhoe 1752 W
Mary, South Molton 1846 W
Michael, Stoodleigh 1617 [W]
Nicholas, ... 1665 W
Nicholas, Thelbridge 1669 A and 1672 O account
Nicholas, Georgeham 1737 A
Paschal, Trentishoe 1628 [W]
Philip, Bondleigh 1663 W and 1670 [W]
Philip, Northam 1718 W
Philip, Ilfracombe 1781 A
Richard, Rackenford 1574 W
Richard, Great Torrington 1618 [W] and 1623 [W]
Richard, Trentishoe 1631 [W]
Richard, Martinhoe, snr. 1633 W
Richard, Parracombe 1666 [W] and 1669 O
Richard, Martinhoe 1672 W
Richard, Combe Martin 1674 O account
Blacmore Richard, South Molton 1718 W
Richard, South Molton 1740 W
Richard, Martinhoe 1744 W
Richard, Kentisbury 1747 W
Richard, St Giles in the Wood 1765 W
Richard, Barnstaple, hatter 1800 W
Richard, Martinhoe, yeoman 1803 W
Richard, St Giles in the Wood 1815 A
Richard, Kentisbury 1828 W
Richard, Roborough 1832 W
Richard, Lynton 1839 A to Mary, widow
Richard, Parracombe 1842 W
Richard, Barnstaple 1843 W
Richard, Shirwell 1848 W
Robert, Combe Martin 1677 A
Robert, Ilfracombe 1742 W
Robert, Kentisbury 1838 W
Blacmore Robert, Pilton 1844 W
Sarah, Kentisbury 1752 W
Sybil, Northam 1662 W
Thomas, Combe Martin 1578 W
Blakmore Thomas, Rackenford 1580 W
Thomas, West Worlington 1591 [W]
Thomas, West Down 1622 [W]
Thomas, Great Torrington 1623 [W]
Thomas, East Anstey 1632 [W]
Thomas, Great Torrington 1694 W and 1702 W
Thomas, Northam 1724 A
Thomas, Yarnscombe 1741 A
Thomas, South Molton 1771 W
Thomasine, Great Torrington 1628 [W]
Blakemor Walter, Northam 1589 W
Walter, Mortehoe 1592 [W]
Walter, Parracombe 1620 [W]
Blakmore William, Chawleigh 1588 A
Blackmor William, East Anstey 1591 [W]
William, Combe Martin 1591 [W]
William, North Molton 1598 [W]

William, Ilfracombe 1599 [W]
William, Hartland 1606 W
William, Combe Martin 1618 [W]
William, Northam 1622 [W]
William, Barnstaple 1727 A
William, Combe Martin 1666 W
William, East Anstey 1671 W
William, Northam 1672 W
William, Oakford 1684 A
William, Ilfracombe 1687 A
William, South Molton 1695 A
William, Ilfracombe 1725 W
William, Northam 1740 W
William, Great Torrington 1742 W
William, St Giles in the Wood 1791 W
Blacmore William, Ilfracombe, yeoman 1807 W
William, Ilfracombe, mariner 1810 A
Willmot, Trentishoe 1666 W
Willmot, South Molton 1686 W
Blackwell, Blackwill
  Blackwill Elizabeth, Barnstaple 1724 W
  Elizabeth see also Joseph Essery
  Frederick, Barnstaple, woolcomber 1848 A to Elizabeth,
    widow and Thomas Clarke Blackwell of Goodleigh,
    basketmaker, son
  James, Barnstaple 1716 W
  Mary see Catherine Tucker
  Blackwill Richard, Barnstaple 1706 W
  Blackwill Thomas, Pilton 1678 W
  Thomas, Sheepwash 1695 W
  Blackwill Thomas, Pilton 1750 A
  Thomas, Barnstaple 1853 W
Blacmore see Blackmore
Blagdon, Blaccden, Blackdon, Blagrone, Blakedon
  ..., Hartland 1614 [W]
  Abraham, Bideford 1636 W
  Blagdon alias Gifford Henry, Abbotsham 1641 W
  Blagrone Innocent, South Molton 1591 [W]
  Isott, Hartland 1668 W
  Blakedon John, Hartland 1569 W
  Blagdon alias Clifford John, Hartland 1600 W
  John, Puddington 1685 W
  Joseph, Hartland 1687 A
  Mary, Hartland 1702 W
  Blaccden Robert 1601 W
  Thomas, Hartland 1584 W
  Blackdon William, Hartland 1571 W
  William, Great Torrington 1620 [W]
  William, Hartland 1620 [W]
Blake, Bleeck, Bleek, Bleeke
  ..., West Worlington 1606 [W]
  ..., Chittlehampton 1610 [W]
  Alexander, Rose Ash 1590 [W]
  Alexander, West Worlington 1626 [W]
  Amos, North Molton 1766 W
  Ann, North Molton 1816 W
  Anthony, Parkham 1681 A
  Catherine, Buckland Brewer 1836 W
  Charity, Stoodleigh 1737 W
  Charles, North Molton 1694 W
  Christopher, North Molton 1673 A
  Christopher, North Molton 1691 A
  Christopher, Roborough 1755 A
  Edward, Littleham (near Bideford) 1603 W
  Edward, Buckland Brewer 1615 [W]; forename blank in Ms;
    supplied from parish register
  George, Rose Ash 1631 [W] and 1633 O
  George, Fremington 1713 W
  George, Warkleigh 1763 A
  Gonnet, High Bray 1624 and 1625 [W]
  Grace, East Buckland 1720 W
  Grace, Instow 1751 A
  James, Northam 1684 A
  Joan, North Molton 1706 W
  Joan, High Bray 1758 W
  John, High Bray 1581 W

John, Rose Ash 1605 W
John, North Molton 1618 [W]
John, Buckland Brewer 1620 [W]
John, North Molton 1629 [W]
John, Buckland Brewer 1631 [W]
John, High Bray 1635 A
John, Littleham (near Bideford) 1638 A
John, High Bray, snr. 1667 W
John, Bulkworthy 1668 W
John, High Bray 1690 A
John, Barnstaple 1699 A
John, Great Torrington, jnr. 1706 A
John, Great Torrington 1712 W
John, Bideford 1723 [W]
John, Stoodleigh 1725 W
John, Warkleigh 1738 [W]
John, Charles 1740 A
John, Barnstaple 1794 W
John, Weare Giffard, yeoman 1802 W
John, Monkleigh, yeoman 1819 A to Ann, widow
John, Chittlehampton 1830 W
Margaret, North Molton 1565 W
Margaret, Great Torrington 1736 W
Mary, Westleigh 1660 W
Mary, Barnstaple 1699 A
Mathew, South Molton 1679 W
Nicholas, Roborough 1752 A
Philip, Great Torrington 1722 [W]
Richard, North Molton 1590 [W]
Richard, Rose Ash 1598 [W]
Richard, North Molton 1685 W
Richard, Great Torrington 1742 W
Richard, South Molton, yeoman 1800 W
Richard, Monkleigh 1834 A to Esther of Fremington, widow
Robert, Buckland Brewer 1599 [W]
Robert, Langtree 1624 [W]
Robert, Brendon 1633 A
Roger, Yarnscombe 1667 W
Roger, Northam 1676 W
Ruth, High Bray 1763 W
Sarah, Bulkworthy 1679 W
Simon, Westleigh 1667 A
Bleeke Susanna, Northam 1688 W
Susanna, Northam 1716 W
Thomas, Filleigh 1596 [W]
Thomas, Langtree 1631 [W]
Thomas, Northam 1675 W
Bleek Thomas, Northam, jnr. 1700 A
Thomas, Buckland Brewer 1721 W
Thomas, Instow 1745 A
Thomas, Little Torrington 1832 W
Thomasine, Buckland Brewer 1613 [W]; forename blank in
  Ms; supplied from parish register
Thomasine, Roborough 1671 A
Walter, Chawleigh 1580 W
William, North Molton 1662 W
William, Roborough 1671 W
Blecke William, Northam 1680 W
William, North Molton 1692 A
William, Northam 1700 W
William, High Bray 1720 W and 1729 A
William, St Giles in the Wood 1773 W
William, South Molton, yeoman 1806 A
William, Roborough, yeoman 1811 W
William, Monkleigh 1834 W
Willmot, Great Torrington 1735 W
Blakedon see Blagdon
Blakemor, Blakemore, Blakmore see Blackmore
Blanch see Blinch
Blanchard Ann, Little Torrington 1598 [W]
  Ann, Frithelstock 1617 [W]
  Christopher, Frithelstock 1617 [W]
  Henry, Little Torrington 1643 W
  John, Little Torrington 1618 [W]
  Margaret, Frithelstock 1573 W

Richard, Frithelstock 1601 W
Richard, Buckland Brewer 1622 [W]
Blaney, Blany
David, West Down 1683 W
Blany David, Heanton Punchardon 1782 W
George, West Down 1691 W
Blasandeacute Robert, Roborough 1762 A
Blatchford see Blackford
Bleeck, Bleek, Bleeke see Blake
Blensham see Blinsham
Blew Edward 1829 A to John of Whitefields, Powick, father
Blight, Bligh
Ann, Buckland Filleigh 1783 A
Elizabeth see Ann Copner
Bligh Gideon, Bulkworthy 1671 [W]
Bligh John, Shebbear 1671 W and 1679 W
John, Bulkworthy 1689 W
John, Buckland Brewer 1751 W
John, Filleigh 1787 A
John, Frithelstock 1831 W
Philip, Great Torrington, husbandman 1806 A
Rebecca, Buckland Filleigh 1766 A
Richard, Bideford 1784 W and 1791 A
Richard, Sheepwash 1838 W
Robert, Great Torrington, labourer 1819 A to Elizabeth, widow
Robert, Bideford 1831 W
Samuel, Abbotsham 1846 W
William, Buckland Filleigh 1748 W
William, Langtree 1837 W
Blinch, Blanch
..., Alwington 1615 [W]
Ann, Buckland Brewer 1733 W
Elizabeth, Bideford 1640 A
George, Northam 1697 A
John, Alwington 1694 W
John, Ashreigney 1733 W
Blanch John, Northam 1745 W
William, Buckland Brewer 1729 A
Blincham see Blinsham
Blincoe Lawrence, Ilfracombe 1695 A
Blinman Elizabeth, Barnstaple 1716 A
Jeremiah, South Molton 1702 W
Blinsham, Blensham, Blincham, Blynsham
Blensham ..., St Giles in the Wood 1609 [W]
Blensham ..., Frithelstock 1611 [W]
Ann, Great Torrington 1828 W
Blensham Henry, Frithelstock 1609 [W]; forename blank in Ms;
  supplied from parish register
Henry, St Giles in the Wood 1696 W
John, St Giles in the Wood 1748 A
Blincham John, Great Torrington 1749 W
Mary, St Giles in the Wood 1680 W
Mary, St Giles in the Wood 1702 A
Mary, Great Torrington, sp. 1800 W
Blynsham Richard, St Giles in the Wood 1623 [W]
Theophilus, St Giles in the Wood 1680 W
Blincham Theophilus, St Giles in the Wood 1742 W
Theophilus, Great Torrington 1818 W
Bloddon, Blowdon
Blowdon William, Rose Ash 1575 W
William, Mariansleigh 1617 [W]
Blow Hugh, Witheridge 1692 W
Blowdon see Bloddon
Blunt Elizabeth, Ilfracombe 1676 W
Blynsham see Blinsham
Blyth John Willis, Northam 1857 W
Boaden, Boadon see Bodden
Boalfield see Boatfield
Board, Borde
Joan, Lynton, widow 1588 W
John, Bideford 1721 W
Boarden see Bodden
Boatfield, Boalfield, Boatfeild, Botefeild, Botefeilde, Botefield
Botefeild ..., Beaford 1610 [W]
Botefeilde ..., Eggesford 1614 [W]

Botefeild Amos, Chawleigh 1605 W
Andrew, Westleigh 1730 A
Andrew, Abbotsham 1777 W
Botefeild Christian, Chawleigh 1598 [W]
Elizabeth, Bideford 1823 W
Botefeild George, Wembworthy 1620 [W]
Boatfeild George, Wembworthy 1643 W
Botefeild George, Wembworthy 1666 W
George, ship *Sunderland* 1762 A
James, Westleigh, yeoman 1815 A to Mary, widow
Jane, Yarnscombe 1763 W
Botefeild John, Wembworthy 1643 W
Botefeild John, Yarnscombe 1725 W
Boalfield John, Yarnscombe 1753 W
John, Northam 1843 A
Judith, Abbotsham 1800 W transmitted to Doctor's Commons,
  13 Aug 1814
Botefeild Marian, Winkleigh 1620 [W]
Michael, Westleigh 1738 [W]
Botefeilde Robert, Eggesford 1617 [W]
Boatfeild Robert, Chawleigh 1701 A
Robert, Bideford 1820 W
Botefeild Thomas, Wembworthy 1636 W
Botefeild Thomas, Wembworthy 1675 W
Bobadge, Bobage, Bobbage see Babbage
Bocher see Butcher
Bodden, Boaden, Boadon, Boarden, Boddyn, Boden
Boarden Andrew, Chittlehampton, jnr. 1705 A
Boaden Elizabeth and Thomas, Dolton 1643 W
Helen, Ilfracombe 1583 W
Boaden Jacquetta, Bideford 1690 W
Boadon James, North Molton 1786 W
Joan, Barnstaple 1582 W
John, Bideford 1583 A
Boaden John, West Anstey 1765 [W]
Boadon Lambert, North Molton 1757 W
Paschal, Bideford 1616 [W]
Boden Philip, Bideford 1620 [W]
Boaden Philip, Bideford 1709 W
Boaden Thomas and Elizabeth, Dolton 1643 W
Boddyn William, Georgeham 1621 [W]
Boden William, Northam 1675 W
Willmot, Bideford 1644 W
Boddy see Body
Boddyn, Boden see Bodden
Bodley, Bodly
Agnes, Cruwys Morchard 1726 A
Amos, Lapford 1763 A
Bodly Edward, Witheridge 1708 W
Edward, Woolfardisworthy 1735 W
Edward, Witheridge 1782 A and 1789 A
Elizabeth, Witheridge 1730 [W]
George, Cruwys Morchard 1642 W
George, Witheridge 1744 W
George, Witheridge 1781 W
Grace, Witheridge 1774 W
Humphrey, Thelbridge 1629 [W]
John, Cruwys Morchard 1740 W
John, Puddington 1795 W
Simon, Puddington 1635 O
Simon, Burrington 1662 A
Thomas, Puddington 1633 A
Thomas, Cruwys Morchard 1748 A
Thomas, Puddington 1762 W
Thomas, Witheridge 1768 W
Thomas, Witheridge 1788 W
Thomas, Cruwys Morchard, snr. , yeoman 1804 W
Thomas, Witheridge 1807 A
William, Witheridge 1840 W
Bodman, Bodmant
Bodmant Avis, Shebbear 1597 [W]
Charles, Northam 1702 W
Joanna, Northam 1708 A
John, Newton St Petrock 1619 [W]
John, Newton St Petrock 1664 W

Robert, Newton St Petrock 1598 [W]
Roger, Newton St Petrock 1591 [W]
William, Northam 1692 W
Body, Boddy
   Boddy Elizabeth, Bideford late wife of John 1825 A
   John, Instow 1763 W
   Margaret, Instow 1771 W
Boddy see Body
Boiles see Boyle
Boldings ..., Barnstaple 1609 [W]
   ..., Berrynarbor 1610 [W]
Bole see Boole
Bolt, Bault, Bolte
   Dorothy, Ashreigney 1854 W
   Elizabeth, Great Torrington 1854 W
   John, Ashreigney 1623 [W]
   Bolte John, Ashreigney 1635 W
   Bault John, Langtree 1662 W
   John, High Bickington, yeoman 1809 W
   Mary, Bideford 1747 A
   Nicholas, St Giles in the Wood 1689 W
   Bolte Robert, Ashreigney 1564 W
   William, Barnstaple 1715 W
   William, Yarnscombe 1839 A to Jane, widow and John
Bolton Mary wife of George see Mary Vye
Bomston John, Chulmleigh 1665 A
Bonbury see Banbury
Bond, Bonde
   Bonde Abraham, Hartland 1635 W
   Agnes, Bideford 1580 A
   Agnes, Bratton Fleming 1729 W
   Bonde Alexander, Lynton 1573 W
   Bonde Alice, Stoodleigh 1639 W
   Alice, Abbotsham 1743 W
   Bonde Ann, Tawstock 1632 [W]
   Anthony, Barnstaple 1642 W
   Bond Anthony, Barnstaple 1718 W
   Baldwin, Ilfracombe 1706 A
   Christopher, ship *Deptford* 1746 W
   Dorothy, Northam 1698 W
   Elizabeth, Bow 1696 [W]
   Elizabeth, Northam 1696 W
   Elizabeth, Chulmleigh 1827 A to John and William, sons
   Enoch, Tawstock 1745 W
   George, Georgeham 1697 W
   Grace, Shirwell 1831 W
   Henry, Atherington 1589 W
   Humphrey, Shirwell, yeoman 1797 W
   James, Northam 1770 W
   Bonde Joan, South Molton 1632 [W]
   Joanna, Shebbear 1708 W
   Joanna, Bideford 1736 W
   Bonde John, Burrington 1571 W
   Bonde John, Northam 1584 W
   Bonde John, Lynton 1589 [W]
   Bonde John, Ashreigney 1590 [W]
   Bonde John, Barnstaple 1627 [W]
   Bonde John, Winkleigh 1631 [W]
   John, Winkleigh, snr. 1672 W
   John, Mortehoe 1685 W
   John, Hartland 1686 A
   John, Stoodleigh 1698 W
   John, Roborough 1708 W
   John, Northam, jnr. 1713 W
   John, Bratton Fleming 1722 W
   Judith, Bow 1722 A
   Bonde Margaret, Tawstock 1626 [W]
   Marian, Georgeham, widow 1568 W
   Mary, Abbotsham 1787 A
   Nicholas, Tawstock 1726 A
   Peter, Bow 1681 W
   Richard, Bow 1683 W
   Richard, Burrington 1740 W
   Bonde Robert, Witheridge 1628 [W]
   Robert, Washford Pyne 1661 A

Robert, Abbotsham 1726 W
Roger, Stoodleigh 1638 A
Roger, North Tawton 1733 A
Roger, Northam 1755 W
Bonde Thomas, Barnstaple 1587 W
Thomas, Bratton Fleming 1661 W
Thomas, South Molton 1724 W
Thomas, Chulmleigh 1819 W
Bonde alias Bande William, Bow 1604 W
Bonde William, Huish 1625 [W]
William, Marwood 1643 W
William, Bow 1695 A
William, Meshaw 1729 W
William, Bideford 1733 A
William, Abbotsham 1768 W
William, Woolfardisworthy 1815 W
Willmot, Meshaw 1738 [W]
Bonifant, Bonivant, Bonnyfant
   Bonnyfant ..., Weare Giffard 1601 A
   ..., Northam 1609 [W]
   Ann, Weare Giffard, widow 1610 W; forename blank in Ms;
      supplied from parish register
   James, Shebbear 1700 A
   James, Weare Giffard 1713 W
   James, Langtree, yeoman 1810 W
   James, Petrockstowe 1837 W
   James, Langtree 1856 W
   Joanna, Pilton 1701 A
   John, Weare Giffard 1580 W
   John, Pilton 1684 W
   John, Great Torrington 1704 A
   John, Petrockstowe 1857 W
   Bonivant Joseph, Barnstaple 1660 A
   Margery, Weare Giffard 1665 W
   Mary, Great Torrington 1854 W
   Oliver, Northam 1593 [W]
   Peter, Weare Giffard 1636 A
   Philip, Northam 1640 W
   Bonnyfant Ralph, Huntshaw 1588 A
   Richard, Great Torrington 1624 [W]
   Samuel, Great Torrington 1691 A
   Samuel, Weare Giffard 1692 [W]
   Samuel, Pilton 1813 W
   Samuel, Langtree, gentleman 1856 A to Henry Perkin
      Bonifant, son
   Bonnyfant Thomas, Northam 1601 W
   Walter, Weare Giffard 1590 [W]
Bonser Alexander, Woolfardisworthy 1676 A
Bont see Bount
Boobeare see Bowbear
Boocher see Butcher
Boode ..., North Molton 1613 [W]
   John, Lynton 1593 [W]
Boole, Bole, Booles, Boolle
   Bole Christopher, Bideford 1596 [W]
   Boolle George, Bideford 1618 [W]
   George, Alwington 1718 [W]
   Boles Mary, Huish 1802 A
   Booles Robert, Bideford 1687 W
   Willmot, Bideford 1636 W
Boone Abraham, Ilfracombe 1792 W
   Abraham, Ilfracombe 1816 W original will proved 11 Apr
     1790
   Charles, Combe Martin 1769 A
   George, Buckland Filleigh 1616 [W]
   Richard, Ilfracombe 1740 W
   Thomas, Great Torrington 1830 W
Boore Susanna, Great Torrington 1728 W
Booth William, Tawstock 1691 W
Borashton William, Countisbury 1580 W
Borde see Board
Bordfild, Borefeild see Borfield
Boreman, Borman
   Borman Ann, Hartland, widow 1807 W
   Lodovic, Beaford 1720 A

Borfield, Bordfild, Borefeild, Borfilde
  Borefeild John, snr., Great Torrington 1608 [W]; forename
    blank in Ms; supplied from parish register
  Borefeild Richard, Winkleigh 1608 [W]; forename blank in
    Ms; supplied from parish register
  Bordfild Robert, Chawleigh 1583 W
  Robert, St Giles in the Wood 1593 [W]
  Borfilde William, Eggesford 1567 W
Borman see Boreman
Born, Borne, Bourne
  Bourne Alexander, Ashreigney 1592 [W]
  Christopher, Coldridge 1775 A
  Christopher, Coldridge 1787 W and 1793 W
  Christopher, Coldridge 1813 W
  Christopher, Bondleigh 1824 W
  John, Coldridge, tailor 1809 W
  Borne or Burie Richard, Great Torrington 1582 A
  Borne Richard, Witheridge 1645 A
  Richard, Coldridge 1816 W
  Robert, Coldridge, carpenter 1807 W
  Robert, Winkleigh, yeoman 1809 W
  Borne alias Hearell William, Ashreigney 1586 W
Bornet see Barnett
Borough, Borowe, Borrough, Borroughe, Borrow, Borrowe
  Borowe Ann, Bratton Fleming, widow 1563 W
  Borroughe Ann, Northam 1589 W
  Borrough Elizabeth, Georgeham 1579 [W]
  Grace, Northam 1675 W
  Borowe Harry, Shebbear 1564 W
  James, Northam 1586 A
  Borowe John, Shebbear 1567 W
  John, Northam 1570 W
  Borrowe John, ship *Duke* 1756 W
  Borrow Richard, Great Torrington 1581 I
  Borowe William, Georgeham 1589 W
Bort Philip, Coldridge 1750 W
Bortyn see Barton
Botefeild, Botefeilde, Botefield see Boatfield
Boteler, Botler
  Balthazar, Parkham 1623 [W]
  Botler Balthazar, Buckland Brewer 1639 W
  Balthazar, Littleham (near Bideford) 1712 W
  Edward, Littleham (near Bideford) 1624 [W]
  Grace, Knowstone 1663 W
  John, Parkham 1587 W
  John, Littleham (near Bideford) 1660 W
  John, Parkham, gentleman 1676 W
  Mary, Buckland Brewer 1675 W
  Philip, Parkham 1617 [W]
  Robert, Parkham 1640 A
  Robert, Parkham 1679 W
  Roger, Buckland Brewer 1666 A
  Thomas, Buckland Brewer 1663 W
  William, Littleham (near Bideford) 1784 W
Boucher, Bouchier, Bowcher, Bowchier, Burcher
  Agnes, Great Torrington 1587 W
  Alice, Martinhoe 1582 W
  Bouchier Caleb, ship *Prince Frederick* 1746 A
  Bowchier Dulcibella, Pilton, widow 1807 W
  George, North Tawton 1673 A
  Bouchier or Buchard alias Rackely George, North Molton
    1674 W
  Bowchier George, North Tawton 1717 W
  Bowchier George, North Tawton 1734 A
  Bowcher George, Barnstaple 1755 W
  Bouchier Henry, Barnstaple 1586 A
  Humphrey, Pilton 1693 W
  Bowcher Joan, Chulmleigh 1637 A
  Joan, Iddesleigh 1675 W
  John, St Giles in the Wood 1568 W
  Bowcher John, Bow 1593 [W]
  Bowcher John, Pilton 1665 A
  Bowcher John, Pilton 1773 W
  Bowchier Joshua, Goodleigh 1778 W
  Richard, Chulmleigh 1570 W

  Robert, Warkleigh 1774 W
  Bouchier Rose, Barnstaple 1746 A
  Bowcher Thomas, Iddesleigh 1672 W
  Bowcher Thomas, Pilton 1725 W
  Burcher Thomas, Rackenford 1745 W
  Burcher William, Rackenford 1761 W
  William, South Molton 1809 A
Bound, Bounde
  Bounde Elizabeth, Ashreigney 1588 W
  Henry, Woolfardisworthy 1576 W
  Bound alias Cale James, Barnstaple 1580 A
  John, Northam 1565 W
  Bounde John, Bow 1566 W
  Bounde John, Dolton 1579 A
  Bounde John, Great Torrington 1585 A
  John, Tawstock 1588 W
  Bound John, Sheepwash 1765 A
  Richard, Atherington 1578 W
  Simon, Zeal Monachorum 1601 W
Boundy, Bountie, Bounty, Bowndy, Bowntye, Bunday
  Bowntye Agnes, Clovelly 1579 W
  Bunday George, Pilton 1737 W
  Bunday James, Barnstaple 1687 W
  Bountie John, Clovelly 1572 W
  Bunday John, Barnstaple 1707 W
  John, Meshaw, butcher 1854 A to Mary, widow
  Mary, Great Torrington 1655 A
  Mary, Meshaw 1855 W
  Bowndy Richard, Bideford 1681 A
  Robert, Clovelly 1624 [W]
  Samuel, Meshaw 1836 W
  Bounday Thomas, Northam 1710 W
  Boundy Thomas, Great Torrington 1761 W
  William, East or West Worlington 1789 W
  William, Meshaw 1823 W
  William, Meshaw 1836 W
  Bounty William, Clovelly 1667 A
Bounshole, Bounsholl
  Bounsholl Walter, Merton 1675 W
  Walter, Merton 1676 W
Bount, Bont, Bounte
  Bont ...., Ilfracombe 1604 [W]
  Alexander, Berrynarbor 1601 W
  Alice, Mortehoe 1590 W
  Catherine, Berrynarbor 1605 W
  George, Alverdiscott 1632 [W]
  Bount John, West Down 1632 [W]
  Bounte or Benet Philip, Mortehoe 1580 W
  Bont Willmot, Landcross 1638 W
Bountie, Bounty, Bowntye see Boundy
Bourne see Born
Boushman William, Countisbury 1580 W
Boutcher see Butcher
Bow Caleb, Chulmleigh 1821 W
  Edmund, Barnstaple 1695 A
Bowbear, Boobeare, Bowbeare
  ..., Knowstone 1612 [W]
  Bowbeare ..., Knowstone 1612 [W]
  English, Monkleigh 1597 [W]
  Boobeare Philip, Molland 1694 W
  Thomas, Knowstone 1593 [W]
Bowbridge Joan, Little Torrington, widow 1569 W
Bowcher, Bowchier see Boucher
Bowden, Bowdene, Bowdon, Bowdowin
  Bowdon ..., Knowstone 1603 [W]
  Bowdon ..., Burrington 1614 [W]
  Bowdon ..., Hartland 1614 [W]
  Bowden alias Tooker ..., Ashford 1666 W
  Bowden alias Tucker ..., Ashford 1677 W
  Bowdon Agnes, Oakford, widow 1563 W
  Bowdon Agnes, Oakford 1619 [W]
  Agnes, Ilfracombe 1812 W
  Bowdon Alice, Little Torrington 1587 A
  Bowdon Alice, Chulmleigh 1627 [W]
  Andrew, Chittlehampton 1729 A

Bowdon Anthony, Little Torrington 1630 [W]
Anthony, Winkleigh 1720 W
Anthony, Winkleigh 1776 A
Anthony, Winkleigh 1812 A to Anthony, son
Arthur, Northam 1664 A
Benjamin, ship *Russell* 1748 W
Bowdon alias Coleman Catherine, Mortehoe 1662 A
Bowdon Christopher, Witheridge 1614 [W]; forename blank in
    Ms; supplied from parish register
Daniel, Northam 1769 W
Bowdon Edward, Berrynarbor 1751 W
Bowdon Elizabeth, West Buckland 1631 [W]
Bowdon Elizabeth, Winkleigh 1707 W
Bowdon Elizabeth, South Molton, widow 1801 W
Elizabeth, South Molton 1805 A
Elizabeth wife of John see Jane Crang
Bowdon Frank, Stoodleigh 1752 W
George, Brendon 1685 W
George, South Molton 1685 A
Bowdowin George, Chittlehampton 1703 W
George, Berrynarbor 1724 W and 1728 A
Bowdon George, Berrynarbor 1742 W
George, Great Torrington 1836 W
Bowdon Henry, Mariansleigh 1753 W
Honoria, Barnstaple 1680 A
Hugh, Knowstone 1573 A
Hugh, George Nympton 1836 W
Humphrey, Rose Ash 1588 W
Bowdon Humphrey, Chawleigh 1610 [W]; forename blank in
    Ms; supplied from parish register
Bowdon Humphrey, Oakford 1618 [W]
Bowdon Isott, North Tawton 1623 [W]
Bowdon alias Clark James, Berrynarbor 1691 W
James, Ilfracombe, jnr. 1821 A
James, heretofore of Monkleigh but late of Buckland Brewer
    1833 W
Bowdon Jane, Little Torrington 1642 A
Bowdon Joanna, Stoke Rivers 1604 W
Bowdon Joanna, Barnstaple 1621 [W]
Bowdon Joanna, Knowstone 1633 W
Joanna, Molland 1709 W
Joanna, Twitchen 1725 W
Bowdon Joanna, Meeth 1736 W
John, Great Torrington 1579 W
Bowdon John, Oakford 1579 W
Bowdon John, North Tawton 1586 W
Bowdon John, Georgeham 1589 W
Bowdon John, North Tawton 1619 [W]
Bowdon John, Oakford 1629 [W]
Bowdon John and Wilmot, Georgeham 1643 A
Bowden alias Tooker John, Barnstaple 1643 W
Bowden alias Tucker John, Barnstaple 1661 O
John, Heanton Punchardon 1663 W
John, Chittlehampton 1664 W
John, West Buckland 1664 A
John, East Putford 1681 W
John, Little Torrington 1682 W
John, Barnstaple 1690 W
Bowdon John, South Molton 1695 A
Bowdon John, Alverdiscott 1703 W
John, Barnstaple 1715 A
John, Twitchen 1715 W
John, North Tawton 1723 [W]
John, South Molton 1746 W
Bowdon John, Pilton 1756 W
John, North Tawton 1764 A
John, Berrynarbor 1766 W
John, Merton 1770 W
John, North Tawton 1775 W
Bowdon John, Berrynarbor 1786 A
John, King's Nympton 1793 A
John, Northam 1803 W
John, Warkleigh 1813 W
John, Ashreigney 1818 A
John, Great Torrington 1848 A

John, Berrynarbor 1851 W
Joseph, Barnstaple 1725 W
Bowdon Mabel, Great Torrington 1597 [W]
Margaret, Langtree 1674 W
Margaret, Oakford 1731 W
Margery, Atherington 1696 W
Mark, Ilfracombe 1677 A
Mary, Molland 1682 A
Mary, Pilton 1719 W
Mary, Berrynarbor 1820 W
Mary, Great Torrington 1835 W
Nicholas, St Giles in the Wood 1803 A
Bowdon alias Woolcomb Philip, Witheridge 1665 W
Bowden alias Tucker Philip, Barnstaple 1669 A
Philip, Frithelstock 1699 W
Phillippa, Little Torrington 1692 W
Prudence, Berrynarbor 1835 W
Ralph, Pilton 1691 A and 1697 A
Bowdon Ralph, Pilton 1755 W
Bowdene Richard, Little Torrington 1586 W
Bowdon Richard, Chulmleigh 1593 [W]
Bowdon Richard, Oakford 1601 A; forename blank in Ms;
    supplied from parish register
Bowdon Richard, Brendon 1602 W
Bowdon Richard, Brendon 1643 W
Richard, Rose Ash 1644 W
Richard, Winkleigh 1644 W
Bowdon Richard, Oakford 1662 W
Richard, Stoodleigh 1676 A
Richard, North Tawton 1688 W
Richard, Winkleigh 1701 W
Richard, North Tawton 1718 W
Richard, Bideford 1735 W
Bowdon Richard, Winkleigh 1741 A
Richard, Berrynarbor 1771 W
Richard, Winkleigh 1802 A
Richard, Berrynarbor, yeoman 1810 W
Richard, Bideford 1856 W
Bowdon Robert, Stoke Rivers 1603 [W]; forename blank in
    Ms; supplied from parish register
Robert, Instow 1698 W
Bowdon Robert, South Molton 1786 A
Robert, Northam, merchant 1801 W
Bowdon Rose, Oakford 1619 [W]
Bowdon Salome, Georgeham 1620 [W]
Samuel, Meeth 1824 W
Samuel, Meeth 1853 W
Bowdon Sarah, Molland 1749 W
Sittarius, Wembworthy 1697 A
Susanna, Pilton 1738 [W]
Thomas, Parracombe 1667 W
Thomas, Northam 1702 A
Thomas, Clovelly 1730 W
Bowdon Thomas, Witheridge 1736 W
Thomas, Ashford 1779 W
Thomas, Northam 1834 W; A dbn 1858
Bowdon Tiffany, North Tawton 1587 W
Bowdon Urithe, High Bickington 1669 W
Bowdon William, Moortown 1586 W
Bowdon William, Georgeham 1588 A
Bowdon William, Alverdiscott 1606 W
William, Oakford 1676 A
William, Barnstaple 1682 A
William, Georgeham 1689 W
Bowdon William, George Nympton 1789 W
William, Chulmleigh 1835 A
William, Northam 1837 A
William, Stoodleigh, snr. 1842 W
Willmot, Alverdiscott 1681 W
Willmot, Northam 1709 W
Bowdon Willmot and John, Georgeham 1643 A
    see also Bawden
Bowdick Elizabeth, Northam 1767 A
Bowen Christopher, Ilfracombe 1711 W and A
    Eliza wife of James see Grace Balsdon

Elizabeth, Barnstaple 1796 W
Evan, Ilfracombe 1638 A
Frances, Bideford 1779 A
George, Ilfracombe 1746 W
George, Bideford 1753 A
Grace, Stoke Rivers 1848 W
John, Ilfracombe 1670 W
John, Northam 1704 W
John, Ilfracombe 1717 W
John, Northam 1741 W
John Light, Bideford 1812 W
Richard, Northam 1769 W
Thomas, Ilfracombe 1724 W
Thomas, Northam 1735 A
Walter, Barnstaple 1765 W
William, Georgeham 1754 A
William 1837 A to John of Barnstaple, son
Bower ...., Zeal Monachorum 1607 [W]
Giles, Broadnymet 1598 [W]
John, North Tawton 1571 W
Mary, Barnstaple 1856 W
Richard, Petrockstowe 1804 A
William, Abbotskerswell 1572 W
Bowhay, Bowhaie, Bowray, Bowstay
..., Petrockstowe 1603 [W]
Christopher, Petrockstowe 1678 A
Christopher, Bideford 1709 W
David, Petrockstowe, yeoman 1804 W
Edward, Chulmleigh 1705 W
Jane, Petrockstowe 1608 [W]; forename blank in Ms; supplied
from parish register
Bowhaie Joan, Petrockstowe 1611 [W]; forename blank in Ms;
supplied from parish register
John, Petrockstowe 1630 [W]
John, Petrockstowe 1720 W
John, Petrockstowe 1780 W
John, Barnstaple 1817 W
Joseph, Great Torrington 1715 A
Joseph, Petrockstowe 1781 W
Robert, Petrockstowe 1570 W
Robert, Petrockstowe 1595 [W]
Bowray Robert, Petrockstowe 1596 [W]
Robert, Tawstock 1640 W
Bowstay Susan, Petrockstowe 1696 A
Thomas, Georgeham 1628 [W]
Thomas, Petrockstowe 1679 [W]
Thomas, Petrockstowe 1731 A
Bowier see Bowyer
Bowlde John, North Tawton 1569 W
Bowles Bridget, Chulmleigh 1667 W
Bowman, Bawman
Catherine, Instow 1719 W
Dorothy, Newton St Petrock 1742 W
Elizabeth, Parkham 1739 A
Bawman George, ship *Torley* 1756 A
Henry, Shebbear 1626 [W]
Jacob, Shebbear 1592 [W]
Bawman James, Marwood 1759 A
John, Bideford 1740 A
John, Parkham 1743 A
John, Shebbear 1778 W
John, Shebbear 1833 W
Mary, Monkleigh 1608 [W] "Bowman alias Norton" in
register; forename blank in Ms; supplied from parish register
Mary, Shebbear 1796 W*
Nicholas, Barnstaple 1597 [W]
Richard, Shebbear 1759 W
Richard, Newton St Petrock 1780 W
Richard, Shebbear 1815 W
Richard, Chittlehampton 1852 W
Roger, Langtree 1663 W
Theophilus, Parkham 1728 A
Thomas, Newton St Petrock 1719 W
Thomas, Bideford 1735 W
Tristram, Shebbear 1621 [W]

Walter, Barnstaple 1612 [W]; forename blank in Ms; supplied
from parish register
William, Littleham (near Bideford) 1672 A
William, Shebbear 1693 W
William, Shebbear 1730 [W]
William, Great Torrington 1739 A
Bowndy see Boundy
Bowray see Bowhay
Bowre see Bowyer
Bowring, Bowringe
Bowringe John, Rackenford 1624 [W]
John, Chulmleigh, snr. 1697 W
John, Chulmleigh 1759 A
Mary, Chulmleigh 1718 W
Bowstay see Bowhay
Bowyer, Bowier, Bowre, Bowyes, Boyer, Boyre
Boyre Elizabeth, Littleham (near Bideford) 1765 A
Boyer John, Stoodleigh 1629 [W]
Bowyes or Boyes Robert, Barnstaple 1589 W
Bowier Sybil, Tawstock, widow 1612 A; forename blank in
Ms; supplied from parish register
Bowre Willmot, Zeal Monachorum 1582 A
Boyce, Boyse
Boyse Arthur, Stoodleigh 1679 W
Boyse Arthur, Stoodleigh 1713 W
Boyse George, Stoodleigh 1687 W
Jacob, Stoodleigh 1666 W
Boyse Jane, Stoodleigh 1679 W
Boyer see Bowyer
Boyle, Boiles, Boyles
Boiles ..., Trentishoe 1610 [W]
Ann, East Down 1663 W
Ann, Northam 1836 W
Anthony, East Down 1719 W
Elizabeth, East Down 1782 W
Boyles Elizabeth, Georgeham 1848 [W]
Boyles Francis, Charles 1713 A
Grace, Barnstaple 1820 W
Boyles Henry, Charles 1758 W
Boyles Isaac, Filleigh 1760 W
James, East Down 1693 A
James, East Down 1714 W
Boyles James, Goodleigh 1765 A
James, East Down 1770 W
James, Marwood 1782 W
John, East Down 1632 [W]
John, East Down, snr. 1640 W
Boyles John, Filleigh 1668 W
Boyles John, Kentisbury 1727 A
Boyles John, East Down 1754 W
John, East Down 1778 W
John, Ashford 1784 W
John, Marwood, yeoman 1821 A to Elizabeth, widow
John, Berrynarbor 1852 W
Michael, Northam 1804 W
Boyles Nicholas, Littleham (near Bideford) 1763 W
Boyles Peter, Berrynarbor 1737 W
Philip, East Down 1712 A
Boyles Philip, East Down 1724 A
Boyles Philip, Kentisbury 1732 W
Richard, East Down 1643 W
Sarah, East Down, widow 1808 W
Thomas, Ilfracombe 1830 W
William, East Down 1638 W
William, Charles 1640 W
Boyles William, Charles 1709 A
William, East Down 1714 W
William, East Down, yeoman 1807 A
Boyles William, Heanton Punchardon 1851 W
Boyne, Boynes, Boyns
Boynes John, Bideford, jnr. 1847 W
Nicholas, Mortehoe 1597 [W]
Boyns Thomas, Northam 1738 [W]
Boyre see Bowyer
Bowse see Bowce

Brabacombe see Babbacombe
Brace John, Ilfracombe 1748 W
Bradbarn John, Petrockstowe 1738 [W]
Braddon ..., Huntshaw 1742 W
  Anthony, Huntshaw 1721 W
  Arthur, Huntshaw 1696 W
  Cyprian, Alverdiscott 1622 [W]
  Eleanor, Huntshaw 1721 A
  Humphrey, Huntshaw 1729 W
  Joanna, Monkleigh 1696 W
  John, Huntshaw 1696 W
  John, Barnstaple 1706 A
  John, Frithelstock 1713 A
  Margery, Clovelly 1637 W
  Peter, Clovelly 1636 W
  Phillippa, Frithelstock 1692 W
  Robert, Monkleigh 1641 W
  Robert, Bideford 1799 A
  Samuel, Parkham 1684 A
  Samuel, Bideford 1711 W
  Stephen, Huntshaw 1583 W
  Stephen, Alverdiscott, gentleman 1607 [W]; forename blank in
    Ms; supplied from parish register
  Thomas, Monkleigh 1700 W
Bradford Andrew, Chulmleigh 1636 A
  Ann, Sheepwash 1763 W
  Ann, Chawleigh 1767 W
  Arthur, Sheepwash 1812 W
  Dorothy, Witheridge 1789 W
  Ellen, East Anstey 1837 W
  Gertrude, Great Torrington 1754 W
  Grace, Washford Pyne 1723 [W]
  Hugh, Witheridge 1692 W
  Humphrey, Lapford 1628 [W]
  John, Woolfardisworthy 1662 A
  John, Thelbridge 1728 W
  Josiah, Woolfardisworthy 1675 W
  Marcus, Washford Pyne 1730 [W]
  Mary, Winkleigh 1596 [W]
  Mary, East Anstey 1816 W
  Michael, Sheepwash 1744 W
  Nathaniel, North Molton 1733 A
  Oliver, North Molton 1573 W
  Robert, Wembworthy 1596 [W]
  Robert, Witheridge 1780 W
  Simon, Rackenford 1579 W
  Thomas, Wembworthy 1633 W
  Thomas, Frithelstock 1640 W
  Vincent, East Anstey 1577 A
  Walter, Washford Pyne 1746 W
  William, East Anstey 1614 W
  William, Ilfracombe 1677 A
  William, Meshaw 1761 A
  William, Chawleigh 1766 W
Bradley Nicholas, Winkleigh 1641 W
  Robert, Romansleigh 1662 A
Bragg, Brag, Bragge
  Bragge ..., Meeth 1610 [W] and 1612 [W]
  Bragge ..., Tawstock 1611 [W]
  Bragge Ann, High Bickington 1671 A
  Ann, Beaford 1697 W
  Ann, Merton 1712 W
  Bragge Anstis, Tawstock 1573 W
  Bartholomew, Beaford 1754 W
  Bragge Blanche, Tawstock 1580 W
  Bridget, Dolton 1663 A
  Bragge Catherine, Tawstock 1620 [W], 1623 [W] and 1624
    [W]
  Edward, Meeth 1684 W
  Edward, Dolton 1707 W
  Edward, Barnstaple 1736 W
  Bragge Elias, Tawstock 1609 [W]; forename blank in Ms;
    supplied from parish register
  Elizabeth, High Bickington 1838 W
  Bragge George, George Nympton 1626 [W]
  Bragge George, Fremington 1629 [W]

  George, Beaford 1685 W
  Hugh, Dolton 1633 A and O
  James, Meeth 1681 A
  James, Langtree 1750 A
  Bragge Joan, Dolton 1572 W
  Brag Joan, Fremington 1592 [W]
  Joanna, Beaford 1718 W
  Brag John, Chittlehampton 1595 [W]
  Bragge John, Tawstock 1625 [W]
  John, Bideford 1667 W
  John, Meeth 1671 W
  John, Hartland 1686 W
  John, Beaford 1698 W
  John, Langtree 1700 W
  John, Merton 1707 A
  John, West Down 1726 A
  John, Langtree 1732 W
  John, Washford Pyne 1747 A
  John, Hartland 1770 W
  John, Woolfardisworthy 1782 W
  John, Hartland 1791 W
  John, High Bickington 1821 W
  Margaret, Dolton 1635 W
  Margaret, Beaford 1701 W
  Matthias, Hartland 1764 W
  Oliver, Hartland 1639 W
  Petronell, Dolton 1635 A
  Philip, Great Torrington 1839 W
  Bragge Richard, Fremington 1605 W
  Bragge Richard, North Tawton, snr. 1673 W
  Richard, Westleigh 1705 W
  Richard, South Molton 1828 W
  Brage Robert, Martinhoe 1573 [W]
  Bragge Robert, Chulmleigh 1585 W
  Bragge Robert, Dolton 1614 [W]; forename blank in Ms;
    supplied from parish register
  Samuel, Hartland 1681 W
  Samuel, Langtree 1722 W
  Samuel, Merton 1772 W
  Sarah, Bideford 1681 W
  Sebastian, Burrington 1814 W
  Sebastian, Cheldon 1841 W
  Thomas, Shebbear 1698 W and 1700 A
  Thomas, Bideford 1704 W
  Thomas, Washford Pyne 1846 W
  Thomasine, Meeth 1691 A
  Tristram, High Bickington 1667 A
  William, Filleigh 1667 W
  William, North Tawton 1685 W
  William, Hartland 1691 W
  William, Dolton 1704 W
  William, Petrockstowe 1780 W
  William, Woolfardisworthy 1794 A
  William, Washford Pyne, yeoman 1797 W
  William, High Bickington 1844 W
  Zachariah, Hartland 1661 W
  Zachariah, Hartland 1708 W
Braggadon see Brockadon
Bragge see Bragg
Braggington, Braginton
  Braginton alias Colwill Ann, Hartland 1846 W
  Digory, Hartland 1746 W
  Bragington Digory, Hartland 1757 W
  Frances, Clovelly 1719 A
  Lawrence, Chittlehampton 1746 A
Braie see Bray
Brailegh, Brailey, Brailie see Brayley
Bramblecombe, Bremacomb, Bremacombe, Bremblecombe,
  Bremellcombe, Bremmacomb, Brimacombe, Brinblecombe,
  Brumelcomb
  Bremacomb ..., Dowland 1600 [W]
  Bremacombe ..., Iddesleigh 1605 [W] and 1608 [W]
  Bremmacomb ..., North Tawton 1607 [W]
  Alice, Dowland 1573 W
  Brimacombe Benjamin, Northam 1684 A

Bremblecombe Digory, Welcombe 1633 W
Bremacombe Edward, Oakford 1588 A
Brinblecombe Elizabeth, Iddesleigh 1620 [W]
Bremblecombe Elizabeth, Winkleigh 1633 W
Bremblecombe Francis, Hartland 1622 [W]
Bremellcombe Henry, Dolton 1583 W
Bremacombe Hugh, Dowland 1598 [W]
Bremblecombe Hugh, Winkleigh 1625 [W]
Brumelcomb Joan, Iddesleigh 1676 A
Brimacombe Joanna, East Putford 1694 A
Bremelcomb John, Winkleigh 1580 A
Brimblecomb John, Huish 1678 A and 1687 A
Brimacomb Judith, Georgeham 1713 W
Bremacombe Leonard, Westleigh 1592 [W]
Bremelcomb Mary, Dowland 1578 W
Bremelcomb Philip, Witheridge 1580 W
Bremacomb Philip, Iddesleigh 1603 W
Ralph, Dowland 1573 W
Richard, Bow 1573 W
Brimblecomb Richard, Georgeham 1711 [W]
Brimbtecomb Roger, Bideford 1749 W
Bremacombe Rowland, Dowland 1598 [W]
Bremacomb William, Little Torrington 1586 W
Bremacombe William, Welcombe 1597 [W]
Brampton
  ..., Bideford 1611 [W]
  Joan, Welcombe 1583 W
  John, Welcombe 1577 W
  Mary, Welcombe 1587 W
  Richard, Northam 1581 W
  Robert, Northam 1601 A; forename blank in Ms; supplied
    from parish register
Bramridge see Brembridge
Branch Diana, Lynton 1828 W
  William, Alwington 1677 W
Brand, Braund, Brawd, Brawn, Brawnd, Brawne
  Brawne Agnes, Barnstaple 1605 W
  Brand Edward, Tawstock 1680 A
  Emma, Huish 1684 W
  Braund Hugh, East Putford 1737 W and 1742 A
  Braund James, Woolfardisworthy 1855 W
  Brawd John, Great Torrington 1576 W
  John, Barnstaple 1663 W
  Jonathan, Barnstaple 1676 W
  Braund Jonathan, Barnstaple 1715 W
  Braund Margaret, Fremington 1771 W
  Brawn Mary, Barnstaple 1677 W
  Mary, Barnstaple 1691 A
  Braund Mary, East Putford 1738 [W]
  Braund Mary, Fremington 1783 W
  Mary, Tawstock 1795 W
  Braund Mary, Parkham 1826 A to Richard of
    Woolfardisworthy, son
  Brawne Richard, Monkleigh 1586 W
  Brawne Robert, Combe Martin 1584 A
  Brawnd Robert, Huish 1707 A
  Braund Samuel, Sheepwash, husbandman 1814 A to William,
    carpenter, brother
  Brawne Simon, Monkleigh 1627 [W]
  Brawne Thomas, Barnstaple 1591 [W]
  Brawne William, Welcombe 1638 W
  Braund William, Littleham (near Bideford) 1810 W*
  Braund William, Parkham, yeoman 1811 W
Branham see Brannam
Branly Mary, Northam 1714 W
Brannam, Branham, Brannan
  Branham Abraham, Bideford, serge weaver 1800 W
  Brannan Ann, Bideford 1839 W
  Mark, Bideford 1846 W
  Nicholas, Bideford 1816 W
Brasier, Brasiare
  ..., Fremington 1600 [W]
  Brasiare Thomas, Chittlehampton 1575 A
Brauley see Brayley

Braunton, Branton, Braunpton
  Abraham, Welcombe 1783 W
  Digory, Welcombe 1716 A
  Branton Grace, Welcombe 1615 [W]
  Jane, Welcombe 1782 A
  Branton or Braunton Joachim, Welcombe 1681 A
  Branton Joan, Northam 1633 A and 1635 O
  Branton Joan, Alverdiscott 1795 W
  John, Northam 1617 [W]
  John, Welcombe 1716 W
  Branton John, Huntshaw 1805 W
  Branton John, Huntshaw 1838 W; A dbn granted at Exeter
    May 1871
  Lawrence, Welcombe 1697 W
  Margaret, Welcombe 1639 W
  Branton Margaret, Welcombe 1706 A
  Branton or Braunton Margaret, Welcombe 1711 A
  Braunpton Philip, Welcombe 1620 [W]
  Branton Philip, Welcombe 1732 W
  Richard, Welcombe 1638 W
  Richard, Welcombe 1711 W
  Branton Richard, Woolfardisworthy 1721 W
  Branton Richard, Alverdiscott 1793 W
  Branton Richard, Bideford 1802 A
  Thomas, Bideford 1711 A
  Thomas, Alverdiscott 1752 W
  Branton Thomas, Monkleigh 1854 W
  Branton William, Alwington 1745 A
  Branton William, Bideford 1779 W
  Braunton alias Sherman Willmot, Northam 1645 W
Braughton see Broughton
Braund see Brand
Bray, Braie, Braye, Brey
  ..., North Molton 1605 W
  Braie ..., Rose Ash 1611 [W]
  Braye ..., Langtree 1614 [W]
  Ann, North Molton 1625 W
  Anthony, Alverdiscott 1616 W
  Anthony, Rose Ash 1640 A
  Archelaus, North Molton 1668 A
  Catherine, North Molton 1728 A
  Christopher, High Bray 1595 [W]
  Christopher, North Molton 1620 [W]
  Christopher, Rose Ash 1643 W
  Edward, South Molton 1675 W
  Elias, Rose Ash 1725 W
  Brey Elias, Rose Ash 1753 W and 1762 W
  Elias, Rose Ash 1806 W*
  Elizabeth, Warkleigh 1615 [W]
  Elizabeth, Buckland Brewer 1661 W
  Elizabeth, Frithelstock 1685 W
  Elizabeth, Rose Ash 1785 W
  Emma, North Molton 1634 [W]
  Faith, North Molton 1679 W
  Jacob, North Molton 1597 [W]
  Jane, North Molton 1677 [W]
  Joanna, North Molton 1620 [W] and 1626 [W]
  Joanna, Rose Ash 1629 [W]
  Joanna, Buckland Brewer 1635 A
  Braye John, Wembworthy 1574 W
  Braye John, Fremington 1580 W
  Braie John, Alverdiscott 1583 W
  John, Warkleigh 1593 [W]
  John, North Molton 1620 [W]
  John, Buckland Brewer 1635 W
  John, Chittlehampton, snr. 1639 O
  John, North Molton 1675 W
  Brey John, Bideford 1683 W
  John, Fremington 1733 W
  John, Rose Ash 1764 W
  John, Bow 1793 A
  John, Knowstone 1825 W
  Braye Julian, Alverdiscott 1586 A
  Margaret, South Molton 1677 W
  Mary, Rose Ash 1724 W

Mary, Rose Ash 1766 W
Mary, South Molton 1799 W
Braie Michael, North Molton 1563 W
Michael, North Molton 1635 A
Nicholas, North Molton 1587 W
Rebecca, North Molton 1676 A
Richard, Rose Ash 1675 W
Richard, Rose Ash 1714 W
Robert, North Molton 1604 W
Robert, South Molton 1691 W
Salvine, King's Nympton 1604 W
Sarah, Rose Ash 1699 W
Sybil, North Molton 1597 [W]
Braye Thomas, Nymet Rowland 1574 W
Thomas, Rose Ash 1600 W
Thomas, South Molton 1617 [W]
Thomas, Woolfardisworthy 1626 [W]
Thomas, Frithelstock 1632 [W]
Thomas, Bideford 1635 W
Thomas, Great Torrington 1644 A
Braye Thomas, Goodleigh 1674 W
Thomas, Rose Ash, yeoman 1800 W
Thomasine, Weare Giffard 1590 [W]
Thomasine, South Molton 1661 W
William, North Molton 1617 [W]
Brayley, Brailegh, Brailey, Brailie, Brauley, Braylegh, Braylie,
    Brayly, Braylye, Brealey, Breayley, Brele, Brelye
Brailie alias Wydlake ..., Filleigh 1601 W
Brailie ..., Goodleigh 1607 [W]
Brailie ... 1608 and 1610 [W]
Agnes, Chulmleigh 1590 [W]
Brayly alias Widlake Agnes, Fremington 1680 A
Braylye Alice, Fremington 1723 [W]
Amesius, Filleigh 1721 A
Breayley Amos, Chittlehampton 1856 W
Andrew, Chittlehampton 1590 [W]
Brayly Andrew, Chittlehampton 1633 A
Braylegh alias Wedlake Ann, West Buckland 1587 A
Brayly Anthony, Filleigh 1630 [W]
Brayly Anthony, East Buckland 1632 [W]
Braylegh Bartholomew, Chittlehampton 1588 W
Bartholomew, Chittlehampton 1732 W
Brayly Charles, Barnstaple 1707 A
Braylie Christian, East Buckland 1617 [W]
Brayly Christiana, Filleigh 1682 A
Cicely, Filleigh 1594 [W]
Brayly Dorothy, Roborough 1625 [W]
Brayly Edward, Filleigh 1665 A
Brayly Edward, Pilton 1700 W
Edward, Ilfracombe 1745 A
Brayly Elizabeth, West Buckland 1623 [W]
Brayly Elizabeth, Filleigh 1637 W
Brayly Elizabeth, West Buckland 1679 W
Brayly Elizabeth, Martinhoe 1695 A
Brailey Elizabeth, Berrynarbor 1762 W
Brayly Emma, Northam 1643 W
Brayly Florence, North Molton 1622 [W]
Brayly alias Widlake Francis, Fremington 1680 W; forename
    blank in Ms; supplied from parish register
Brayly Geoffrey, Fremington 1709 W
George, Chittlehampton 1671 W
Brayly George, West Buckland 1676 A
Brayly George, Northam 1706 W
Brailey George, Northam 1749 A
Brealey George, Ilfracombe 1787 A
George, Bideford 1797 W
George, Northam, gentleman 1800 W
George, Georgeham 1843 W
George see also John Hamlyn
Brayly Henry, Filleigh 1623 [W]
Brayly Henry, Northam 1643 A
Brayly Henry, Martinhoe 1672 W
Brayly Henry, Bideford 1703 W
Henry, Bideford 1742 W
Braylie alias Wydlake Hugh, Filleigh 1602 W

Brayly Humphrey, Ilfracombe 1667 A
Braylie Humphrey, East Buckland 1692 W
Humphrey, Martinhoe 1721 A
Brailegh alias Widlake James, West Buckland 1570 W
Brayly James, Buckland Brewer or Filleigh 1663 A
Brayly James, Beaford 1688 W
Brealey James, Chittlehampton 1839 W
Breayley James, Chittlehampton 1855 W
James Davis, Abbotsham, gentleman 1803 W
Brailey Joan, Ilfracombe 1759 A
Bralie alias Wydlake John, North Molton 1578 A
Bralie alias Wydlake John, Warkleigh 1584 W
Brelye alias Wydlake John, Filleigh 1584 W
Braylegh alias Wedlake John, Martinhoe 1588 W
Brayly John, Fremington 1620 [W] and 1623 [W]
Brayly John, Dowland 1626 [W]
Brayly John, Huntshaw 1626 [W] and 1627 O
Brayly John, Fremington 1628 [W]
Brayly John, Fremington, snr. 1636 A
Brayly John, Chittlehampton 1639 A
Brayly alias Widlake John, South Molton 1667 A
Brayly John, Fremington 1691 A
Brayly John, Fremington 1702 W and 1707 A
John, Chittlehampton 1732 W
Brailey John, Tawstock 1766 W
Brailey alias Wedlake John, South Molton 1776 W
Brailey John, Marwood, husbandman 1806 W
John, Chittlehampton 1834 A to Thomasine, widow
Brailey John, South Molton, painter, jnr. 1856 A to John of
    North Molton, yeoman, father
Brayly Lodovic, Chittlehampton 1620 [W]
Brayly alias Widlake Mary, Chittlehampton 1641 A
Brauly or Branly Mary, Northam 1714 W
Mary, Bideford 1730 A
Mary, Abbotsham 1836 W
Brayly alias Widlake Nicholas, South Molton 1665 W
Braylie Niobe, Tawstock 1616 [W]
Brayly Petronell, Great Torrington 1628 [W]
Brayly Philip, Filleigh 1643 A
Philip, Northam 1742 W
Brayly Priscilla, Goodleigh 1644 W
Brealey Priscilla, Great Torrington 1818 W
Braylie Richard, South Molton 1593 [W]
Brayly Richard, West Buckland 1626 [W]
Brayly Richard, Chittlehampton 1698 A and 1706 A
Brayly Richard and Thomas, Fremington 1626 [W]
Braylegh Robert, Great Torrington 1579 A
Brailey Robert, Tawstock 1755 A
Brayly Samuel, Bideford 1697 W
Brailey Sarah, Northam 1749 W
Brayly Thomas and Richard, Fremington 1626 [W]
Brayly Thomas, Kentisbury 1629 [W]
Brayly Thomas, Ashreigney 1630 [W]
Brayly Thomas, Fremington 1669 W
Brayly Thomas, Martinhoe 1695 W
Brayly alias Widlake Thomas, George Nympton 1704 W
Thomas, Berrynarbor 1729 W
Brailey Thomas, East Down 1777 W
Thomas, Northam 1816 W
Breayley Thomas, Chittlehampton 1853 W
Brayly Thomasine, Martinhoe 1695 W
Brailey Wedlake, South Molton 1776 W
Brele William, Ashreigney 1579 W
Braylie alias Wedlake William, East Buckland 1601 W
Brayly William, Filleigh 1666 A
Brayly alias Widlake William, Filleigh 1669 O
Brayly William, Goodleigh 1706 A
William, Ilfracombe 1732 A
Brailey William, Filleigh 1754 W
Brailey William, Chittlehampton 1765 W
Brailey William, Zeal Monachorum 1769 W
William, Filleigh, yeoman 1807 W
Braily William, Chittlehampton 1812 W
Brailey William, Bideford 1815 W
Brealie William 1841 A to Ann of Parkham, widow

Brayte see Breat
Breach John, Shirwell 1644 W
   Margaret, Shirwell 1636 W
   Nicholas, Shirwell 1740 A
   William, Shirwell 1632 [W]
Bread see Breat
Brealey, Brealie see Brayley
Breat, Brayte, Bread, Breyte
   Agnes, Clovelly 1568 W
   Brayte Joan, Chittlehampton 1578 W
   Breyte John, Clovelly 1580 W
   John, Shebbear 1773 W
   Bread Lodovic, Hartland 1666 A
   Breyte Richard, Clovelly 1580 W
Breayley, Brele, Brelye see Brayley
Bremacomb, Bremacombe see Bramblecombe
Brembridge, Bramridge, Bremeridge, Bremridge, Bremrudge,
   Bremrydge, Bummeridge
   Bremridge ..., Bow 1612 [W]
   Bramridge Ann, Northam 1602 A; forename blank in Ms;
     supplied from parish register
   Bremridge Ann, Newport, Bishop's Tawton 1845 W
   Bremrudge Edmund, Zeal Monachorum 1575 W
   Bremridge Elizabeth, Newton St Petrock 1591 [W]
   Bremrudge Giles, Northam 1589 A
   Bremridge Henry, Hartland 1613 [W]; forename blank in Ms;
     supplied from parish register
   Bremridge James, Hartland 1611 [W]; forename blank in Ms;
     supplied from parish register
   Bremrydge John, Hartland 1627 [W]
   Bremeridge Mary, Winkleigh 1699 A
   Bummeridge Mary, Winkleigh 1741 W
   Brimeridg Petronell, Langtree 1716 W
   Bremridge Samuel, Barnstaple, gentleman 1810 W
   Bremridge Susan, Hartland 1669 W
   Bremrydge Walter, Northam 1626 [W]
   William, Zeal Monachorum 1581 W
   Bremridge William, Langtree 1691 W
Bremile Richard, Huish 1784 W
Bremblecombe, Bremellcombe, Bremmacomb see
   Bramblecombe
Bremridge, Bremrudge, Bremrydge see Brembridge
Brent Dorothy, Shebbear 1776 W
   Dorothy, Shebbear 1782 W
   Ebbot, Newton St Petrock 1820 W
   Hugh, Newton St Petrock 1742 W
   Hugh, Newton St Petrock 1821 W
   Hugh, Shebbear 1845 W
   John, Shebbear 1729 W
   John, Newton St Petrock 1837 A
Bresley John, Berrynarbor 1685 A
Brethren Robert, Lapford 1569 [W]
Brett Robert, Woolfardisworthy 1584 A
Bretton Agnes, Mariansleigh, widow 1610 [W]; forename blank
   in Ms; supplied from parish register
   Alice, Parkham 1618 [W]
   Andrew, Peters Marland 1627 [W]
   Baldwin, Mariansleigh 1615 [W]
   Balthazar, Ilfracombe 1640 W
   George, Bideford 1666 W
   Henry, Ilfracombe 1666 W
   Hugh, Ilfracombe 1640 O
   Humphrey, Ilfracombe 1626 [W] and 1628 [W]
   John, Tawstock 1581 A
   John, Weare Giffard, snr. 1582 W
   John, Tawstock 1602 A
   John, Tawstock 1634 O; forename blank in Ms; supplied from
     parish register
   John, Tawstock 1635 O
   John, Weare Giffard, snr. 1640 W
   Lewis, Parkham 1618 [W]
   Nicholas, Mariansleigh 1593 [W]
   Philip, Ilfracombe 1603 [W] "Bruton" in register; forename
     blank in Ms; supplied from parish register
   Robert, Mortehoe 1602 W
   Thomas, Mortehoe 1629]W

   Walter, Tawstock, snr. 1639 [W]
   William, Tawstock 1581 W
   William, Tawstock 1597 [W]
Brewer, Brewes, Bruer
   Brewes Edward, South Molton 1825 [W]
   Bruer Emblem, East Worlington 1797 W
   John, Combe Martin 1615 [W]
   John, Knowstone 1696 W
   Richard, Molland 1719 A
   Richard, Lapford 1766 W
   Robert, Puddington 1724 [W]
   Robert, South Molton 1768 W
   Roger, Washford Pyne 1727 W
   William, East Anstey 1787 W
   William, Twitchen 1831 A
Brey see Bray
Breyte see Breat
Brian see Bryan
Briant see Bryant
Briddick David, Abbotsham 1725 A
Bridgeman see Bridgman
Bridger, Brigger
   ..., Northam 1602 [W]
   Brigger Harry, Northam 1569 W
Bridges Elizabeth, Sheepwash 1739 A
Bridgman, Bridgeman, Brydgeman, Brydgman
   ..., Newton St Petrock 1608 [W]
   Anthony, Buckland Brewer 1707 W
   Edmund, Newton St Petrock 1660 [W]
   George, Shebbear 1849 W
   Jane, Shebbear 1694 A
   Bridgeman Joan, Iddesleigh, widow 1570 W
   John, Monkleigh 1607 [W]; forename blank in Ms; supplied
     from parish register
   John, Shebbear 1691 A
   John, Barnstaple 1717 W
   Bridgeman John, Peters Marland 1746 W
   John, Great Torrington 1773 W
   John, Shebbear 1815 W
   Bridgeman John, Shebbear 1837 A to Anthony of Buckland
     Filleigh, son
   Mary, Alverdiscott 1717 A
   Bridgeman Petronell, Shebbear 1741 A
   Brydgman Phillippa, Buckland Brewer 1639 W
   Brydgeman Thomas, Great Torrington 1633 W
   Bridgeman William, Buckland Brewer 1633 W
   William, Buckland Brewer 1678 W and 1681 W
   William, Shebbear 1694 W
   William, Buckland Brewer 1731 A and 1732 A
   Bridgeman William, Shebbear 1741 A
   Bridgeman William, Buckland Brewer 1748 A
   Bridgeman William, Shebbear, yeoman 1803 W
   William, Shebbear 1839 W
Bridle Thomas, South Molton 1719 W
Briensmead see Brinsmead
Brigger see Bridger
Bright, Brighte, Bryett
   ..., Dolton 1602 [W] and 1615 [W]
   Abraham, Beaford 1766 W
   Agnes, St Giles in the Wood 1635 W
   Ambrose, Great Torrington 1713 A
   Andrew, Great Torrington 1746 W
   Bryett Ann, Witheridge 1766 A
   Arundell, Burrington 1713 W
   Charles, Chittlehampton 1674 A
   Cyrus, Barnstaple 1636 A
   Daniel, North Molton 1724 W and A
   Daniel, North Molton 1758 W
   Eleanor, High Bray 1644 W
   Ellen, Chittlehampton 1618 [W]
   Francis, Chittlehampton 1621 [W]
   Henry, Dolton 1598 [W]
   James, North Molton 1794 W
   John, King's Nympton 1578 W
   John, Chittlehampton 1580 W

John, High Bray 1610 [W]; forename blank in Ms; supplied
   from parish register
John, High Bray 1629 [W]
John, High Bray, snr. 1641 W
John, Chittlehampton 1641 A
John, Burrington 1664 W
John, High Bickington 1706 A
John, ship *Northumberland* 1758 W
John Adams, Ilfracombe 1853 W
Margaret, Great Torrington 1760 W
Mary, North Molton 1624 [W]
Mary, North Molton wife of ... 1806 A; A dbn
Michael, High Bray 1636 W
Philip, Yarnscombe 1715 [W]
Ralph, Tawstock 1580 W
Brighte Robert, Pilton 1572 W
Robert, Chittlehampton 1688 W
Robert, Filleigh, yeoman 1800 W
Robert, Sheepwash 1841 W
Samuel, Frithelstock 1841 W
Thomas, Charles 1585 A
Thomas, Dolton 1594 [W]
Thomas, Chittlehampton 1618 [W]
Thomas, Great Torrington 1622 [W]
Thomas, Alverdiscott 1737 W
Thomas, North Molton 1768 W
Thomas, South Molton, innholder 1804 W
Thomas, North Molton 1851 W
William, High Bray 1582 A and 1583 A account
William, Monkleigh 1622 [W]
William, Dolton, snr. 1629 [W]
William, Great Torrington 1743 W
William, North Molton, yeoman 1801 W
William, Weare Giffard, butcher 1801 A
William, South Molton 1856 W
Brightwell John, Barnstaple 1849 W
Brimacombe see Bramblecombe
Brimley ..., Northam 1753 A
   George, Ilfracombe 1837 W
   James, Mortehoe, yeoman 1808 W
   James, West Down, yeoman 1820 A to William, son
   John, Mortehoe, yeoman 1819 A to Elizabeth, widow
   Joseph, Northam 1750 W
   Mary, Braunton 1845 W
   Tammy, Ilfracombe 1849 W
   Thomas, Georgeham 1855 W
   William, Heanton Punchardon 1832 A to Mary, widow
   William, West Down 1851 W
Brimson Avis, Pilton 1852 W
   Elias, Pilton 1822 W
Brimsmead see Brinsmead
Brinblecombe see Bramblecombe
Brinsmead, Briensmead, Brimsmead, Brinsmade, Brinsmeade
   Agnes, St Giles in the Wood 1627 [W]
   Brinsmeade Christiana, St Giles in the Wood 1685 A
   Brimsmead Henry, St Giles in the Wood 1701 W
   Briensmead Henry, St Giles in the Wood 1741 W
   Henry, Alverdiscott 1818 W
   John, Witheridge 1718 W
   John, St Giles in the Wood 1857 W
   Robert, St Giles in the Wood 1774 W
   Brinsmade Robert, St Giles in the Wood 1806 W*
   Thomas, St Giles in the Wood 1626 [W]
   Thomas, St Giles in the Wood 1855 W
   William, Great Torrington 1838 W
Brisford Anthony, Oakford 1624 [W]
Bristow John, Barnstaple 1824 W
Britton, Britan, Brittan
   Adam, Barnstaple 1813 [W]
   Adam, West Down 1821 W
   Agnes, Tawstock 1681 W
   Agnes, Chittlehampton 1699 W
   Alexander, Mariansleigh 1728 W
   Alexander 1750 A
   Amos, Warkleigh 1677 W

Ann, Northam 1664 W
Anthony, Parkham 1740 W
Bartholomew, George Nympton 1740 W
Edward, George Nympton 1660 A
George, Tawstock 1753 W
George, West Down 1762 W
Henry, Ilfracombe 1681 W
Brittan Henry, Tawstock 1698 W
Britan Henry, North Molton 1717 W
Henry, Ilfracombe 1828 W
Humphrey, Ilfracombe 1711 W
John, Bideford 1644 A
John, Bideford 1671 W
John, Tawstock 1728 W
John, Barnstaple 1731 W
John, Alwington 1747 A
John, West Down 1797 W
Judith, Tawstock 1665 W
Lawrence, Tawstock 1665 W
Philip, George Nympton 1684 A
Philip, Weare Giffard 1718 W
Rachel, Weare Giffard 1643 A
Richard, Pilton 1667 A
Richard, Tawstock 1668 A
Sally, Barnstaple 1837 W
Brittan Temperance, George Nympton 1696 A
Thomas, Parkham 1728 W
Welthian, Alwington 1748 W
William, Ilfracombe 1667 W
William, Bideford 1677 A
William, South Molton 1710 W
Broad, Broade, Brode
   Elizabeth, Merton 1798 W
   Broade James, South Molton 1660 W
   James, South Molton 1707 A and 1712 A
   Lodovic, South Molton 1641 A
   Margaret, Merton 1765 W
   Broade Mary, South Molton 1663 W
   Robert, Merton 1741 A
   Thomas, Merton 1734 W
   Brode Thomasine, Bideford 1583 W
   Broade Walter, Peters Marland 1688 A
   William, Merton 1789 W
   William, Little Torrington 1828 W
Broadmead, Brodemead
   ..., Barnstaple 1611 [W]
   Brodemead John, Molland 1605 W
   John, South Molton 1644 A.
   Thomas, Molland 1639 W
Brock, Brocke
   Brocke ..., North Tawton 1604 [W]
   ..., Great Torrington 1609 [W]
   Adam, High Bickington 1740 W
   Brocke Henry, Wembworthy 1577 A
   Joan, North Tawton, sp. 1800 W
   Brocke John, Stoodleigh 1577 W
   Brocke John, South Molton 1588 W
   John, Winkleigh 1610 [W]; forename blank in Ms; supplied
     from parish register
   Brocke John, North Tawton 1619 [W]
   John, Winkleigh 1661 W
   John, Bow 1666 W
   John, North Tawton 1677 W
   John, North Tawton 1736 W
   John, Zeal Monachorum 1747 W
   John, Coldridge 1783 W
   John, Iddesleigh 1783 A
   Brocke Richard, Winkleigh 1627 [W]
   Brocke Richard, Bow 1640 W
   Richard, Little Torrington 1690 W
   Richard, Bow 1719 A
   Richard, Iddesleigh 1755 A
   Brocke Robert, Clovelly 1588 W
   Simon, Iddesleigh 1748 A
   Thomas, Bow 1603 W

Thomas, South Molton 1604 W
Brocke alias Phillipe William, North Tawton 1573 W
William, Barnstaple 1674 W
William, North Tawton 1781 W
Willmot, North Tawton 1732 A
Brockadon, Braggadon
  Braggadon Christopher, Westleigh 1644 W
  William, Northam 1639 A
Brode see Broad
Brodemead see Broadmead
Brodfild Thomas, Beaford 1578 A
Broklond see Brookland
Bromham, Broomham
  Bartholomew, Martinhoe 1743 W
  Broomham Elizabeth, Brendon, wife of William 1769 A
  Broomham Hugh, Lynton 1636 A
  John, Martinhoe 1697 W
  Broomham John, Martinhoe 1762 W
  Broomham John, Heanton Punchardon 1766 A
  John, Martinhoe, yeoman 1811 A
  Broomham Richard, Trentishoe 1630 [W]
  Broomham Robert, Pilton 1627 [W]
  Simon, Pilton 1577 W
  William, Ilfracombe 1795 W
  William, Brendon 1848 W
Bromholme, Bromelholme, Bromeholme, Bromhome,
    Broomholme
  ..., Lynton 1612 [W]
  Bromhome Joan, Lynton 1576 W
  Broomholme Joan, Lynton 1640 W
  Bromeholme John, Martinhoe 1590 [W]
  Bromeholme John, Pilton 1593 [W]
  Broomholme John, Lynton 1640 W and A
  Mary, Pilton 1590 [W]
  Richard, Lynton 1676 W
  Bromelholme Robert, Stoke Rivers 1589 O bond
  Bromeholme Robert, Stoke Rivers 1599 [W]
  Roger, Lynton 1590 [W]
  Roger, Martinhoe 1689 A
Bronne see Brown
Brook, Brooke, Brookes, Brooks
  Brooke ..., Cruwys Morchard 1602 [W] and 1614 [W]
  Brooke ..., Barnstaple 1614 [W]
  Brooke ..., South Molton 1614 [W]
  Charles, Mountjoy, Bideford 1844 W
  Brooke Christopher, Tawstock 1597 [W]
  Clase, Bideford 1837 W
  Brooke David, Combe Martin 1592 [W]
  Brooks Edmund, Northam 1817 A to Elizabeth Coward of
    Plymouth and Prudence Gibbs, great nieces
  Edward, Barnstaple 1695 W
  Brooke Elizabeth, Washford Pyne 1763 W
  Brooks Elizabeth, Cruwys Morchard 1767 W
  Elizabeth, Bideford 1834 A to Class, sister
  Elizabeth, Bampton 1846 W
  Gamaliel, Barnstaple 1709 W
  Brooke George, Stoodleigh 1626 [W]
  Brooke George, Cruwys Morchard 1748 W
  Brooke George, Puddington 1769 W
  George, Bideford, brushmaker 1817 A to William, accountant,
    son
  Brooks George, Northam 1852 W
  Henry, Bideford 1825 W
  Henry B., Bideford, gentleman 1855 A (Harry) to Grace of
    Abbotsham, widow
  Brooks Honor, Hartland 1822 W
  Humphrey, Cruwys Morchard 1756 W
  Brooke Isott and John, North Tawton 1623 [W]
  James, Winkleigh 1836 W
  Brooke Joanna, Petrockstowe 1692 W
  Brooke Joanna, Barnstaple 1731 W
  Brooke John, Lynton, minister 1614 [W]; forename blank in
    Ms; supplied from parish register
  Brooke John, Combe Martin 1637 [W]
  John, Heanton Punchardon 1676 A

John, Barnstaple 1703 W
Brooke John, Barnstaple 1731 W
John, Combe Martin 1741 W
Brookes John, Northam 1753 W
Brooke John, South Molton 1757 W
Brooks John, Northam 1764 W
John, Combe Martin 1792 W
John, Winkleigh, labourer 1807 A
Brooks John, Northam 1817 A to Elizabeth Coward of
  Plymouth and Prudence Gibbs, great nieces
Brooks John, Barnstaple 1827 A to Mary, widow
John, Frithelstock 1833 W
Brooks John, Ilfracombe 1856 W
Brooke John and Isott, North Tawton 1623 [W]
Brooke Jonathan, Cruwys Morchard 1685 W and 1690 W
Brooke Lodovic, Northam 1677 W
Margaret, Weare Giffard 1774 A
Brooke Mary, Cruwys Morchard 1692 W
Brooke Mary, Combe Martin 1792 W
Brooks Mary, Northam 1798 W*
Nehemiah, Cruwys Morchard 1757 W
Philip, Bideford 1818 W
Brooks Prudence, Northam 1817 A A to Elizabeth Coward of
  Plymouth and Prudence Gibbs, great nieces
Brooke Richard, Barnstaple 1618 O
Richard, Barnstaple 1715 W
Brooke Richard, Combe Martin 1756 A
Brooks Richard, Northam 1817
Richard, East Anstey 1841 W
Brooke Robert, South Molton 1671 A
Robert, Meeth 1715 W
Brooke Robert, Pilton 1727 A and 1731 A
Brooke Robert, Barnstaple 1733 W
Brooke Robert, Northam 1736 W
Brooke Robert, Pilton 1757 W
Brooks Robert, Northam, mariner 1817 A to Elizabeth Coward
  of Plymouth and Prudence Gibbs wife of Samuel Newman,
  great nieces
Brooke Roger, Cruwys Morchard 1620 [W]
Brooks Roger, Alwington, yeoman 1797 W
Brooke Sarah, Pilton 1731 A
Brooks Susan, Heanton Punchardon 1680 W
Brooke Susanna, Bideford, widow 1806 W
Thomas, Northam 1717 W
Brooke Thomas, Northam 1750 W
Brooks Thomas, Combe Martin, cooper 1811 W
Thomas, Bideford 1832 W
Thomas, Huish 1849 W
Brooks Thomas, Combe Martin 1850 W
Brooke William, Combe Martin 1616 [W]
Brooke William, North Tawton 1632 [W]
William, Barnstaple 1663 W
Brooke William, South Molton 1671 W
Brooke William, Woolfardisworthy 1691 A
William, Abbotsham 1710 W
William, Northam 1714 A
Brooke William, Northam 1754 W
Brooke William, Ilfracombe 1758 W
Brooks William, Alwington 1778 W
Brooke William, Chulmleigh 1808 W*
Brooke William, Barnstaple, tanner 1810 W
William, Iddesleigh 1839 W
Brookland, Broklond, Brookling
  Elizabeth, Bondleigh 1728 A
  Brookling Elizabeth, South Molton 1801 A
  John, Bondleigh 1717 W and 1725 A
  John, Bondleigh 1771 W
  Broklond Thomas, Brushford 1570 W
  Thomas, Lapford 1672 A
  Thomas, Eggesford 1765 A
  William, West Worlington 1829 W
Broom, Broome, Broone
  Broome Elizabeth, Tawstock 1724 W
  Henry, Alwington 1837 W

Jenny, Great Torrington, sp. 1857 A to Elizabeth Short of
  Buckland Brewer, sister
Broome John, Tawstock 1715 W
John, Knowstone 1718 W
John, Parkham 1816 W
Broone Thomas, Hartland 1691 W
Broomham see Bromham
Broomholme see Bromholme
Broone see Broome
Brothers, Brother
  Brother ..., Yarnscombe 1605 [W]
  Brother Brutus, Tawstock 1673 W
  Eleanor, Barnstaple 1672 W
  Brother Emma, Petrockstowe 1599 [W]
  Brother George, Goodleigh 1615 [W]; forename blank in Ms;
    supplied from parish register
  George, Goodleigh 1664 [W]
  Jane, Frithelstock 1700 W
  Brother Joan, Goodleigh 1640 A
  Brother John, Tawstock 1584 W and 1595 [W]
  Brother John, Northam 1606 W
  John, Barnstaple 1632 [W]
  John, Tawstock 1664 W
  John, Goodleigh 1668 W
  Brother Roger, Goodleigh 1578 W
  Brother Roger, Tawstock 1627 [W]
  Brother Walter, Frithelstock 1580 W
  William, Northam 1691 A
  William, Shebbear 1692 A
Broughton, Braughton
  Arthur, Chittlehampton 1665 W
  Braughton George, Stoodleigh 1612 [W]; forename blank in
    Ms; supplied from parish register and 1621 O
  George, Stoodleigh 1640 A and 1641 O
  Humphrey, Stoodleigh 1579 W
  Humphrey, Stoodleigh 1634 W
  Silvanus, Stoodleigh 1629 [W] and 1631 [W]
Brounscombe see Brownscombe
Brown, Bronne, Browne
  Browne ..., Great Torrington 1602 [W]
  Browne ..., Barnstaple 1606 [W]
  Browne ..., Chittlehampton 1614 [W]
  Browne Agnes, Bideford 1631 [W]
  Browne Andrew, Bideford 1638 A
  Browne Cheson, Littleham (near Bideford) 1677 W
  Browne Edward, Bideford 1620 [W]
  Elizabeth, Hartland 1768 W
  Elizabeth, South Molton 1809 W
  Elizabeth, Washford Pyne 1824 W
  Gabriel, Bideford 1709 W
  Browne Giffard, West Buckland 1672 W
  Browne Hannah, Barnstaple 1735 A
  Bronne Henry, Abbotsham 1588 A
  Browne James, Filleigh 1692 W
  Jane, Tawstock 1829 W
  Janus, Northam 1741 A
  Browne Joan, Alwington 1624 [W]
  Browne Joan, Bideford 1639 W
  Browne John, Martinhoe 1606 W
  Browne John, Alwington 1608 [W]; forename blank in Ms;
    supplied from parish register
  Browne John, Abbotsham 1615 [W]
  Browne John, Bow 1619 [W]
  Browne John, Bideford, snr. 1637 W
  Browne John, Bideford 1661 W
  Browne John, Hartland 1681 W
  Browne John, Merton 1683 A
  John, Bideford 1737 W and 1745 W
  Browne John, ship *Jersey* 1746 A
  John, Ilfracombe 1794 W
  John, South Molton, yeoman 1796 A
  Browne John, Barnstaple 1827 A to Jane Hammersley of Lake
    View, Castle Dawson, Londonderry, sister
  John, Great Torrington 1855 W
  Browne Justinian, Bideford 1629 [W]

Martha, Chawleigh, sp. 1811 A
Martha, Chawleigh 1825 A (Chudleigh) to Edward Reed,
  nephew
Browne Mary, Barnstaple 1661 W
Browne Mary, Ilfracombe 1813 W
Browne Mathew, Merton 1665 W
Browne Nicholas, Goodleigh 1684 W
Peter Henry, Ilfracombe 1837 A
Rebecca, Great Torrington 1772 W
Browne Richard, Rackenford 1587 A
Browne Richard, Abbotsham 1596 [W]
Browne Richard, Great Torrington 1686 A
Browne Richard, Atherington 1689 A
Browne Richard, Bideford 1703 W
Browne Robert, Martinhoe 1616 [W]
Browne Robert, Fremington 1632 [W]
Browne Robert, Hartland 1663 W
Browne Robert, Merton 1686 W
Browne Robert, Ilfracombe 1687 W
Robert, Bideford 1745 W
Robert, Weare Giffard 1792 W
Browne Roger, Abbotsham 1583 W and 1585 W
Browne Roger, Great Torrington 1604 W
Samuel, Merton 1840 W
Browne Thomas, Northam 1621 [W]
Browne Thomas, Barnstaple 1734 W
Thomas, Ilfracombe 1754 W
Browne Thomas, West Buckland 1776 A
Thomas John, Pilton 1854 W
Browne Thomasine, Great Torrington 1585 A
Browne Thomasine, Huntshaw 1620 [W]
Tristram, Parkham 1670 A
Browne Urithe, Bow 1638 A
Walter, Barnstaple 1783 W
Browne William, Abbotsham 1565 W
Browne William, Atherington 1639 W
Browne William, Hartland 1670 W
Browne William, Ilfracombe 1670 W
Browne William, Bideford 1685 W
William, Hartland, jnr. 1717 W
William, Barnstaple 1725 A
William, Woolfardisworthy 1793 A
William, Weare Giffard 1818 W
William, Tawstock 1827 W
William, Great Torrington 1831 W
Browne Willmot, Northam 1622 [W]
Browning, Browninge
  Aaron, Northam 1704 W
  Christopher, Northam 1680 W
  Eleanor, Northam 1696 W
  Gregory, Great Torrington 1663 W
  Jennifer, Lynton 1736 W
  John, Northam 1677 [W] and 1680 A
  Mary, Northam 1737 W
  Browninge Maud, Lynton 1597 [W]
  Browninge Peter, Bow 1621 [W]
  Philip, Fremington 1665 W
  Rachel, Chulmleigh 1666 [W]
  Browninge Richard, Northam 1633 A
  Robert, Northam 1718 W
  Robert, Northam 1736 W
  Thomas, Northam 1825 W
  William, Great Torrington 1586 A and 1588 A account
  William, Northam 1723 [W]
  Willmot, Northam 1682 A
  Willmot, Northam 1725 [W]
Brownscombe, Brounscombe, Brownscomb
  ..., Knowstone 1705 W
  Andrew, Witheridge 1780 W
  Catherine, Pilton 1834 W
  Edward, East Buckland 1829 W
  Brownsombe Hugh, Oakford 1693 W
  Brownscomb Hugh, Knowstone 1718 W
  James, Huntshaw 1842 W
  Brownscomb Mary, Bratton Fleming 1823 W

Susanna, Barnstaple 1832 W
Brounscombe Thomas, Zeal Monachorum 1637 W
Thomas, Bratton Fleming 1840 A to Mary Ann, widow
Thomas, Huntshaw 1851 W
William, Bratton Fleming 1819 W
Bruer see Brewer
Bruishford see Brushford
Brumelcomb see Bramblecombe
Brunsdon Constance, South Molton 1604 W
Brusey see Brusy
Brushford, Bruishford
    Bruishford John, Oakford 1604 [W] "Brushford alias Hodge"
      in register; forename blank in Ms; supplied from parish
      register
Brusy, Brusey
    Brusey Edward, Northam 1674 A
    Elizabeth, Bideford 1669 W
    Thomas, Bideford 1692 W
Bruton, Brutton
    Adam, Ilfracombe 1694 W
    Adam, Ilfracombe 1738 [W]
    Catherine, Bideford 1788 W
    Elizabeth, Alwington 1695 W
    George, North Molton 1564 W
    Jane, Alwington 1705 W
    Brutton Jane, Brushford 1711 W
    Brutton Joan, Ilfracombe 1738 W
    John, Alwington 1668 A
    John, Littleham (near Bideford) 1684 W
    John, Great Torrington, yeoman 1801 W
    Richard, West Down 1694 W
    Richard, Ilfracombe 1708 A
    Robert, Georgeham, parish clerk 1614 [W] "Bretton" in
      register; forename blank in Ms; supplied from parish register
Bryan, Brian
    Brian ..., Great Torrington 1606 [W]
    Brian ..., East Putford 1614 [W]
    Ann, Brendon 1709 W
    Henry, Barnstaple 1662 A
    Humphrey, Aram, South Molton 1825 W
    Richard, Parracombe 1752 W
    Winifred, Brendon 1642 W
Bryant, Briant
    Briant ..., Hartland 1608 [W]
    Ann, Ashreigney 1838 W
    Christiana, Fremington 1709-10 W
    Christiana, Fremington 1722 W
    Daniel, Fremington 1698 W
    Edward, West Anstey 1617 [WW]
    Edward, Clovelly 1690 A
    Elias, Twitchen 1675 A
    Briant Elias, Twitchen, snr. 1679 A
    Elizabeth, North Molton 1728 A
    Elizabeth, Molland 1790 W
    Briant Ferdinand, Chulmleigh 1774 W
    Ferdinand, Chulmleigh 1845 W
    George, Clovelly 1824 W
    Gregory, Brendon 1684 A
    Humphrey, Georgeham 1704 W
    Humphrey, Bideford 1713 W
    Briant John, Brendon 1570 W
    John, Iddesleigh 1595 [W]
    John, North Molton 1637 [W]
    John, North Molton 1739 W
    Mary, Buckland Brewer 1599 [W]
    Mary, East Down, widow 1810 W
    Peter, Kentisbury 1691 W
    Peter, East Down 1767 W
    Peter, East Down, yeoman 1804 W
    Peter, Heanton Punchardon 1827 W
    Richard, Great Torrington 1640 W
    Richard, Great Torrington 1805 W limited A
    Robert, West Worlington 1706 W
    Robert, Thelbridge 1765 W
    Robert, Chulmleigh 1817 W
    Thomas, West Down 1589 W

Thomas, Clovelly 1725 W
Thomas, Clovelly 1786 W
Briant Walter, Brendon 1757 A
Briant Walter, Brendon 1768 W
Welthian, West Down 1596 [W]
Bryar John, Great Torrington 1567 W
Brydgeman, Brydgman see Bridgman
Bryett see Bright
Buce see Buss
Bucher see Butcher
Buck Mary, Bideford 1791 W
Buckingham, Buckhingham, Buckinham, Buckkingam,
    Buckyngham
    ..., Charles 1590 [W]
    ..., Twitchen 1611 [W]
    Achilles, West Buckland 1793 W
    Achsah Elizabeth, Rose Ash, sp. 1849 A to Salome, sp., sister
    Agnes, Twitchen 1663 W
    Agnes, Charles 1756 W
    Anica 1643 [W]
    Ann, Charles wife of Dennis 1770 A
    Catherine, Barnstaple 1719 W
    Catherine, West Buckland 1721 W
    Charity, East Buckland 1728 W
    Christopher, East Buckland 1645 W
    Christopher, East Buckland 1724 W
    Christopher, Bideford 1781 W
    Buckkingam Dorothy 1707 W
    Dorothy, Twitchen 1725 W
    Edward, East Buckland 1673 W
    Edward, East Buckland 1729 W
    Buckinham Elizabeth, Barnstaple 1624 [W]
    Elizabeth, Twitchen 1793 W
    Elizabeth, Rose Ash 1832 A to Salome, sp., daughter
    Elizabeth, formerly of Bristol, late of South Molton 1846 A
    Buckyngham Ellen, Winkleigh 1574 W
    Finney, Chittlehampton 1823 W
    Grace, East Buckland 1827 W
    Henry, South Molton 1635 W
    Henry, South Molton 1676 A
    Henry, King's Nympton 1795 W
    Hugh, Twitchen 1681 A
    Hugh, Twitchen 1721 W
    Hugh, Twitchen 1791 W
    James, West Buckland 1695 W
    James, East Buckland 1745 W
    James, West Buckland 1760 W
    James, West Buckland 1775 W
    James, East Buckland 1776 A
    James, West Buckland, yeoman 1807 W
    James, Molland 1845 W
    James, West Buckland 1851 A
    Joan, Twitchen 1616 A
    Joan, Coldridge 1617 A
    John, Bow 1618 A
    John, Twitchen 1622 A and 1624 O
    John, Twitchen 1633 W
    John, South Molton 1676 W and A
    John, East Buckland 1685 W
    John, East Buckland 1703 W
    John, Twitchen 1750 A
    John, Mortehoe 1758 W
    John, North Tawton 1759 A
    John, Chulmleigh 1787 W
    John, West Buckland 1828 W
    John Partridge, Knowstone 1852 W
    Margaret, East Buckland 1725 A
    Margaret see also Christopher Shapland
    Mary, Twitchen 1742 W
    Mary, Barnstaple 1852 W
    Mary see also George Webber
    Paschal, Chulmleigh 1721 A
    Buckyngham Philip, George Nympton 1578 A
    Richard, Twitchen 1664 W
    Richard, East Buckland 1705 W

Richard, King's Nympton 1727 W
Richard, King's Nympton 1740 A
Richard, Chulmleigh, yeoman 1810 W
Richard, King's Nympton 1847 W
Roger, Clovelly 1604 W
Roger, Twitchen 1661 W
Roger, Twitchen 1753 A
Rose, Twitchen 1623 [W]
Salome, Rose Ash 1852 W
Susanna, formerly of St David Exeter, late of Barnstaple 1845
   W
Susanna, Parkham 1848 W
Susanna, Clovelly 1856 W
Thomas, Warkleigh 1746 W
Thomas, Twitchen 1837 W
Thomasine, East Buckland 1709 A
Thomasine, East Buckland 1727 A
William, Barnstaple 1608 [W]; forename blank in Ms;
   supplied from parish register
William, Chulmleigh 1679 W
William, Shirwell 1703 W
William, Twitchen 1707 W
William, East Buckland 1719 A
William, East Buckland 1720 W
William, West Buckland 1748 W
William, Chulmleigh 1753 W
William, Twitchen 1759 W
William, King's Nympton, farmer 1797 W
William, King's Nympton, yeoman 1800 A
William, Twitchen 1800 W
William, Chulmleigh, yeoman 1810 A
William, East Buckland 1815 W
William, West Buckland 1822 W
William, Rose Ash 1840 W
William, Clovelly 1855 W
William, Filleigh 1856 W
William, King's Nympton 1857 W
Buckland John, Beaford 1684 W
Buckler John, Hartland 1699 W
Lectiora, Bideford 1726 W
Mary, Abbotsham 1783 A
Roger, Fremington 1747 W
Thomas, Hartland 1724 [W]
William, Abbotsham 1754 W
Buckman Edward, Bideford 1741 W
Bucknell James, Knowstone, jnr. , yeoman 1800 W
James, Oakford 1815 W
Robert, West Anstey, jnr. 1831 W
Buckpitt ..., Newton St Petrock 1603 [W] and 1604 [W]
..., Buckland Brewer 1610 [W]
Alexander, Great Torrington 1634 A
Clement, Iddesleigh 1619 [W]
John, Newton St Petrock 1589 A
Stephen, Little Torrington 1627 [W]
Buckyngham see Buckingham
Budd, Bud, Budde
Budde ..., Great Torrington 1609 [W]
Budde Adam, Barnstaple 1622 [W]
Budde Alexander, Lynton 1573 A
Alexander, Lynton 1634 W
Ann, Tawstock, widow 1673 W
Anthony, Bratton Fleming 1631 [W]
Budde Catherine, Tawstock, widow 1610 [W]; forename blank
   in Ms; supplied from parish register
Christopher, King's Nympton 1770 A
Daniel, Petrockstowe 1773 W
Daniel, Dolton, yeoman 1809 W
David, Lynton 1625 [W]
David, Brendon 1634 W
Edward Edgar, Barnstaple 1834 W
Elizabeth, Warkleigh 1730 A
Elizabeth, Georgeham 1805 W
Elizabeth, Barnstaple 1857 W
Francis, Newton St Petrock 1713 A
Gabriel, Instow 1639 W
George, Langtree 1700 W

Bud Giles, Great Torrington 1635 W
Henry, Chittlehampton 1636 W
Budde Hugh, Chittlehampton 1619 [W]
Budde John, Chittlehampton 1573 A
Budde John, Great Torrington 1603 W
John, Lynton 1625 [W]
John, Northam 1633 A
John, Goodleigh 1696 A
John, Bideford 1709 A
John, Langtree 1714 W
John, Warkleigh 1722 A
John, Newton St Petrock 1742 A
John, Ashreigney 1796 A
John, Dolton, yeoman 1809 W
John, Dolton 1834 W
Judith, Tawstock 1728 W
Judith, Petrockstowe 1823 W
Lodovic, Bideford 1664 A
Margery, Dolton 1841 W
Mary, Petrockstowe 1719 W
Philip 1838 A
Richard, Barnstaple 1644 W
Richard, Countisbury 1681 A
Richard, Tawstock 1711 W
Richard, Dolton 1725 A
Richard, Dolton 1786 W
Richard, Beaford 1800 W
Richard, Dolton, yeoman 1807 A
Robert, Ilfracombe 1790 A
Robert, Dolton, yeoman 1811 W
Robert, Dolton 1854 W
Roger, Langtree 1737 W
Samuel, North Tawton 1642 W
Samuel, Petrockstowe 1722 A
Samuel, Dolton 1833 W
Sarah, Barnstaple 1640 W
Bud Simon, Instow 1719 A
William, Tawstock 1595 [W]
Bud William, Peters Marland 1711 W
William, Chittlehampton 1764 W
William, Dolton, yeoman 1803 W
William, Dolton 1851 W
Buese, Buesse see Buss
Buishop, Buishope see Bishop
Buishton see Bushton
Buisse see Buss
Bulford, Bullaforde
Bullaforde Agnes, East Buckland 1589 W
Joseph, Instow 1748 W
Bulliford William, Charles 1587 W
Bulhead, Bullhead, Bulhed, Bullead, Bulled, Bullheid, Bullied,
   Bulload, Bullod
Agnes, Ashreigney 1589 W
Agnes and John, Winkleigh 1597 [W]
Arkenold, St Giles in the Wood 1596 [W]
Bullied Elizabeth, Winkleigh 1756 W
Bulled Faith, Witheridge 1739 A
Bulload George, Winkleigh 1745 W
Bullheid Gertrude, Romansleigh 1757 A; A dbn 1769
Bulled Grace, Winkleigh 1712 W
Bulled Grace, Winkleigh 1822 W
Henry, Wembworthy 1579 A
Bulled Henry, Romansleigh 1689 W
Bulled Honor, South Molton 1700 W
Jacquet, Mariansleigh 1641 [W]
James, Winkleigh 1726 W
John, Ashreigney 1589 A
John, Winkleigh 1645 A
John, Mariansleigh 1662 A
John, Bideford 1743 [W]
Bulleid John, Rose Ash 1840 W
John, Witheridge 1841 A
John and Agnes, Winkleigh 1597 [W]
Bulleid Mary, Winkleigh 1736 W
Nicholas, Witheridge 1578 A

Nicholas, Mariansleigh 1633 W
Bulhed Nicholas, St Giles in the Wood 1672 A
Bulled Nicholas, Washford Pyne 1727 W
Robert, Mariansleigh 1591 [W]
Bulleid Robert, Romansleigh 1739 W
Bullod Robert, Romansleigh 1748 A; A dbn 1760
Bulheade Roger, Chittlehampton 1617 W
Bulleid Samuel, Winkleigh 1726 W
Samuel, Winkleigh 1762 A
Simon, Dolton 1630 [W]
Bullead Thomas, Winkleigh 1670 A
Bulled Thomas, Romansleigh 1674 A
Bulled Thomas, Winkleigh 1702 W
Bulled William, North Molton 1839 W
Bulled William, Witheridge 1845 A
Bulled William, Washford Pyne 1849 W
Bullaforde see Bulford
Bullead, Bulled, Bulleid see Bulhead
Bullen, Bulling, Bullyn
Bullen alias Webber Cecilia, Bideford 1706 A
Bulling Humphrey, Shebbear 1663 A
Bulling Joan, Pilton 1617 [W]
John, Chulmleigh 1597 [W] and 1602 W
Bullyn alias Penford John, Chulmleigh 1602 W
Bullyn John, Pilton 1623 [W]
Bulling Miles, Merton 1688 W
Bullyn see Bullen
Buller John, Winkleigh 1723 [W]
Richard, Winkleigh 1725 W
Bulles William, Witheridge 1721 A
Bulley Henry, Pilton 1636 A
Bullhead see Bulhead
Bulliford see Bulford
Bulload, Bullod see Bulhead
Bunday see Boundy
Bunston, Bunsen, Bunstane, Bunstone, Buntson
Buntson ..., Chulmleigh 1611 [W]
Humphrey, Chulmleigh 1645 W
Joan, Chulmleigh 1579 W
Joan, Burrington 1615 [W]
John, Romansleigh 1660 W
John, King's Nympton 1689 W
Mark, Chulmleigh 1675 W
Bunsen Peter, Winkleigh 1625 [W]
Richard, Chulmleigh 1590 [W]
Bunstone Roger, Chulmleigh 1572 W
Bunstane Stephen, Chulmleigh 1623 [W]
William, Alwington 1580 A
Bunstone William, Burrington 1580 W
Bunt John 1837 A to Hugh of Binworthy, Shebbear, brother
Burabury see Banbury
Burage see Burrage
Burch see Birch
Burcher see Boucher
Burcick see Burdick
Burd see Bird
Burden, Burdon, Burdyn
Burdon Edward, Northam, snr. 1640 W
Edward, Little Torrington 1702 A
Edward, Little Torrington 1784 A
Edward, Little Torrington 1826 W
Elizabeth, Northam 1775 W
George, Bideford 1692 W
George, Clovelly 1731 A
George, Horwood 1812 W
Burdon Grace, Bideford wife 1809 W
Henry, Horwood 1773 W
Humphrey, Little Torrington 1776 W
James, Northam 1680 A
James, Clovelly 1729 W
James, Clovelly 1747 A and 1756 A
Burdon Jane, Huntshaw 1782 A
Jane, Frithelstock 1837 W
John, Pitt, Hartland 1573 W
John, Hartland 1577 W

Burdyn John, Georgeham 1582 W
Burdon John, Hartland 1594 [W]
John, Frithelstock 1818 W
Burdon John, Northam 1835 A
Burdon Judith, Northam 1641 W
Mary, Little Torrington, widow 1849 A to Ann, sp., daughter
Burdon Nicholas, Ashreigney, jnr. 1624 [W]
Philip, Northam 1754 [W]
Samuel, Little Torrington 1745 W
Samuel, Little Torrington, yeoman 1810 W
Burdon Thomas, Little Torrington 1618 [W]
Burdon Thomas, Peters Marland 1636 A and 1638 O
Thomas, Frithelstock 1732 A
William, Hartland 1565 W
Burdon William, Westleigh 1782 W
Burdick, Burcick
Elizabeth, Abbotsham 1761 W
Elizabeth, Abbotsham 1836 W
John, Abbotsham, yeoman 1800 A
Burcick Mary, Abbotsham 1788 W
Mary, Abbotsham 1801 A*
Samuel, Abbotsham 1832 W
Thomas, Abbotsham 1844 W
William, Abbotsham, carpenter 1805 W
Burdon, Burdyn see Burden
Burell see Burrell
Burford
Burtford Mansell, South Molton 1671 A account
Mansell, South Molton 1677 A
Burge, Burg, Burgh
George, Oakford 1731 A
Joanna, Twitchen 1583 W
Burgh John, Barnstaple 1664 W
Julian, Molland 1565 W
Margaret, Tawstock, widow 1807 W
Burg Mary, East Anstey 1686 W
Thomas, Lynton 1564 W
Thomas, Heanton Punchardon 1581 W
William, Molland 1565 W
William, Barnstaple 1738 [W]
Burgen see Burgoyne
Burgess, Burges, Burgesse, Burgis, Burgysse
..., Instow 1600 [W]
..., Meshaw 1601 W
Burgesse ..., Twitchen 1611 and 1614 [W]
Burgesse ..., Parracombe 1613 [W]
Burgesse ..., Clovelly 1614 [W]
Burgesse ..., Heanton Punchardon 1614 [W]
Burgess alias Crecomb ..., Lynton 1703 W
Burges Alexander, Rose Ash 1643 W
Burgis Alice, Tawstock 1631 [W]
Burges Angela, North Molton 1627 [W]
Burges Ann, Marwood 1622 [W]
Ann, Bideford 1697 W
Ann, Chittlehampton 1782 W
Anstis, North Molton 1689 W
Anthony, Warkleigh 1723 W
Burgesse Bartholomew, Tawstock 1615 [W]
Burgis Beaton, North Molton 1580 W
Catherine, North Molton 1852 W
Charity, Bratton Fleming, widow 1803 W
Charles, Barnstaple 1790 W
Burges Edward, Instow 1636 W
Burges Elizabeth, Instow 1582 A
Burges Elizabeth, Tawstock 1619 [W]
Burgess alias Hacche Elizabeth, Chittlehampton 1701 A
Elizabeth, Witheridge 1816 W
Elizabeth, North Molton 1857 W
Elizabeth see also Elizabeth Pile
Burgesse Emma, North Molton 1617 [W]
English, Warkleigh 1679 A
Burges George, Heanton Punchardon 1639 W
George, Bideford 1686 W
Giles, Goodleigh 1699 W
Grace, Filleigh 1708 W

Grace, Chulmleigh 1771 W
Grace see also Elizabeth Pile
Hannah, North Molton 1758 W
Burges Henry, Tawstock 1579 A
Burges Henry, North Molton 1626 [W]
Burges Henry, Rose Ash 1629 and 1630 [W]
Henry, Chulmleigh 1734 W
Henry, Rose Ash 1742 A
Henry, North Molton 1770 W and 1784 A
Hugh, North Molton 1690 A
Hugh, Warkleigh 1754 W
James, Chittlehampton, carpenter 1814 W to Judith Ponsford,
    daughter
Burgesse Joan, Heanton Punchardon 1600 W
Burges Joanna, Rose Ash 1624 [W]
Burges Joanna, North Molton 1631 [W]
Burges Joanna, Atherington 1632 [W]
Burges Joanna, Bideford 1635 W
Burges Joanna, Rose Ash 1636 O
Burges Joanna, King's Nympton 1645 A
Burges Joanna, North Molton 1645 W
Burgis John, Twitchen 1569 W
Burges John, Ashford 1570 W
Burgesse John, Instow 1591 [W]
Burgesse John, South Molton 1591 [W]
Burgesse John, Tawstock 1615 [W]
Burgesse John, Rose Ash 1617 [W]
Burges John, Heanton Punchardon 1620 [W]
Burges John, Atherington 1621 [W]
Burges John, Lynton 1628 [W]
Burges John, North Molton 1630 [W]
Burges John, King's Nympton 1634 W
Burges John, North Molton 1636 W and 1643 O
Burges John, Heanton Punchardon 1639 W
John, Twitchen 1660 A
John, Lynton 1661 W
Burges John, South Molton 1669 W
Burges John, North Molton 1671 W
Burges John, Molland 1677 A
John, Martinhoe, snr. 1701 W
John, Barnstaple 1702 A
John, Charles 1703 T
Burges John, Parracombe 1705 A
John, South Molton 1706 A and 1708 T
John, Bideford 1729 W
John, West Down 1734 W
John, Bideford 1738 [W]
John 1749 A no bond
John, Bratton Fleming 1761 W and A
John, North Molton 1766 A
John, Trentishoe 1786 W
John, Bratton Fleming, yeoman 1803 W
John, North Molton, yeoman 1809 W
John, Chittlehampton 1814 W
John, South Molton 1814 W
John, North Molton 1818 W
John, Witheridge 1825 W
John, South Molton 1834 W
John, Kentisbury 1836 W
John, Witheridge 1840 A to Honor, widow
John, Chulmleigh 1854 W
John, Bideford 1709-10 A
John see also Jane Greenslade
Burgesse Margaret, Waish 1617 [W]
Margaret, Northam 1701 W
Margaret, Goodleigh 1709 A
Burgesse Martin, Stoodleigh 1596 [W]
Burgesse Mary, Fremington 1615 [W]
Burges Mary, North Molton 1620 [W]
Burges Mary, Heanton Punchardon 1622 [W]
Mary, South Molton 1748 W
Mary, South Molton, sp. 1843 W (1845) to John, father
Mary, Barnstaple 1856 W
Mary Elizabeth, Mills, North Molton 1757 W
Burges Michael, North Molton 1721 W

Michael, North Molton 1757 W
Nicholas, South Molton 1778 W
Patience, Bideford 1742 W
Burges Paul, North Molton 1579 W
Burges Paul, Parracombe 1621 [W]
Philip, Winkleigh 1824 W
Rachel, South Molton 1725 W
Burges Richard, Rackenford 1586 W
Burges Richard, Lynton 1637 W
Burges Richard, North Molton 1639 W
Richard, Great Torrington 1699 W
Richard, Chittlehampton 1844 A to Jane, widow
Robert, Meshaw 1663 A
Robert, Alverdiscott 1693 W
Robert, Bideford 1702 W
Burgesse Roger, Tawstock 1590 [W]
Burgesse Roger, Twitchen 1598 [W]
Roger, Northam 1695 W
Susanna, North Molton 1741 W
Burges Thomas, Molland 1564 W
Burges Thomas, Heanton Punchardon 1585 W, 1593 [W],
    1595 [W] and 1597 [W]
Burgesse Thomas, Huntshaw 1595 [W]
Thomas, North Molton 1681 W
Thomasine, Barnstaple, widow 1802 W
Burges Ursula, Charles 1673 A
Burgys Walter, Goodleigh 1581 W
Burges William, North Molton 1596 [W]
Burges William, Instow 1601 W
Burgesse William, North Molton 1611 [W]; forename blank in
    Ms; supplied from parish register
Burgesse William, Clovelly 1617 [W]
Burges William, North Molton 1624 [W]
Burgesse William, Bideford 1625 [W]
Burges William, North Molton, snr. 1675 W
William, Rose Ash 1689 W
William, Filleigh 1693 W
William, North Molton 1700 W, 1707 W and 1711 W
William, North Molton 1727 W
Burges William, Parracombe 1743 W
William, Bratton Fleming 1776 W
Burges William, North Molton 1778 W
William, George Nympton 1787 W
William, Witheridge 1810 W
William, Barnstaple, yeoman 1811 W
William, North Molton 1811 A
William, Combe Martin 1814 W
William, Barnstaple 1841 W
Burgh see Burge
Burgis see Burgess
Burgoyne, Burgen, Burgoine, Burgoyn, Burgyn, Burgyne
    Burgen Francis, Bideford 1602 W
    Burgen Geoffrey, Abbotsham 1610 [W]; forename blank in
        Ms; supplied from parish register
    Burgyn Geoffrey, Abbotsham 1638 W
    Burgyn Henry, Yarnscombe 1629 [W]
    Burgyne John, Dolton 1569 W
    Burgen John, Dolton 1618 [W]
    Burgyn Mary, Alwington 1623 [W]
    Richard, Bideford 1578 W
    Burgoyn Richard, Barnstaple 1629 [W]
    Burgyn Robert, Alwington 1623 [W]
    Burgoine Robert, Ilfracombe 1703 W
    Burgen Welthian, Dolton 1601 W
Burgys see Burgess
Burie see Bury
Buriman see Berriman
Burke, Burk
    Burk James, Ilfracombe 1832 W
    Mary, Barnstaple 1680 W
Burleton Ursula, Chulmleigh 1757 W
Burman, Beerman
    Abraham, Hartland 1680 A
    Beerman Richard, Weare Giffard 1696 A
    Richard, Hartland 1753 W

Richard, Hartland 1784 W
Burn see Burne
Burnaberie see Burnbury
Burnacott see Barnacott
Burnade see Burnard
Burnaford Rebecca, St Giles in the Wood 1783 A
　Rebecca, St Giles in the Wood, widow 1801 A
　William, Bideford, shipwright 1809 A
Burnard, Barnard, Bernard, Burnade, Burnarde, Burnerd
　Burnerd ..., Northam 1602 A
　Burnerd ..., Georgeham 1611 [W]
　Burnerd ..., South Molton 1611 [W] and 1613 [W]
　Agnes, Buckland Brewer 1575 W
　Bernard Agnes, Weare Giffard 1731 W
　Alice, Buckland Brewer 1640 W
　Burnerd Ann, Georgeham, widow 1611 O; forename blank in
　　Ms; supplied from parish register
　Edmund, Georgeham 1590 [W]
　Geoffrey, Barnstaple 1624 [W]
　Geoffrey, Barnstaple 1642 W
　Joanna, South Molton 1628 [W]
　John, Monkleigh 1573 W
　Burnerd John, Buckland Brewer 1607 [W]; forename blank in
　　Ms; supplied from parish register
　Margaret, Bideford, widow 1802 W
　Burnard alias Judd Mary, Bideford, wife 1797 W
　Burnarde Peter, King's Nympton 1587 W
　Burnade Richard, Monkleigh 1567 W
　Richard, Hartland 1833 W
　Thomas, South Molton 1578 W
　Thomas, Georgeham 1611 [W]; forename blank in Ms;
　　supplied from parish register
　Thomas, Monkleigh 1630 [W]
　Thomas, Monkleigh 1676 W
　Barnard Thomas, Weare Giffard 1720 W
　Welthian, East Anstey 1619 [W]
　Burnarde William, Buckland Brewer 1564 W
　William, Hartland 1791 W
　William, Hartland 1851 W
　Bernard Willmot, Northam 1741 A
Burnbury, Burnaberie, Burndbury, Burnebury
　Burnebury Christiana, Buckland Brewer 1623 [W]
　Burnaberie John, Buckland Brewer 1580 W
　Mary, Merton 1684 W
　Burndbury Mary, Little Torrington 1690 W
　Burnbury Michael, Little Torrington 1691 W
Burne, Burn, Byrn
　Humphrey, Tawstock 1626 [W]
　Jerome, Woolfardisworthy 1672 W
　John, North Molton 1639 A
　John, Woolfardisworthy 1668 A
　Byrn John, Ilfracombe 1771 W
　Burn Richard, Littleham (near Bideford) 1748 A
　Simon, Winkleigh 1565 A
　Stephen, Witheridge 1607 [W]; forename blank in Ms;
　　supplied from parish register
　Thomas, Winkleigh 1579 W
　Burne alias Harrell Thomas, Winkleigh 1586 W
　Burn William, North Tawton 1622 [W]
Burnebury see Burnbury
Burnerd see Burnard
Burneby Richard, Great Torrington 1637 W
Burnell Ann, Brendon 1852 A
　Robert, Martinhoe 1845 W
Burnett, Burnet
　Burnet James, Shebbear 1805 W
　John, Romansleigh 1856 W
　Margaret, Northam 1734 A
Burracott see Barnacott
Burrage, Burage, Burradge, Burridge, Burrydge
　Burridge ..., Bideford 1609 and 1610 [W]
　Burridge ..., Huntshaw 1611 [W]
　Burridge Anthony, Roborough 1601 W
　Burridge Christopher, Roborough 1684 W
　George, Lapford 1763 A
　Burridge Joan, Zeal Monachorum 1593 [W]

Burradge John, Westleigh 1587 A
　John, Roborough, jnr. 1592 [W]
　Burridge John, Bideford 1595 [W]
　Burridge John, Lapford 1777 A
　Burridge John, Bondleigh, miller 1817 A to Prudence, widow
　Burage Josiah, Merton 1722 W
　Burrydge Nicholas, Roborough 1629 and 1631 [W]
　Burridge Prudence, Bondleigh 1832 W
　Richard, Bideford 1573 A
Burrell, Burell
　John, Fremington 1586 W
　Burell Nicholas, Fremington 1603 W
Burren
　Burren alias Peter Richard, West Down 1600 W
　Thomasine, West Down 1627 [W]
Burridge see Burrage
Burrington ..., Clannaborough 1611 [W]
　Burrington alias Foss Edmund alias Edward, Burrington 1834
　　A
　Robert, Bow, Clannaborough 1603 W
Burrow, Burrough, Burrowe, Burrows
　Burrough ..., Northam 1603 [W]
　Burrowe Cyprian, Northam 1670 A
　Burrows Edward, Ashreigney 1763 W
　Burrough Elizabeth, Woolfardisworthy 1826 W
　Burrowe Joan, Pilton 1591 [W]
　Joan, Pilton 1638 W and O
　Burrough John, Northam 1710 W
　Roger, Sheepwash 1691 A
　Susanna, Witheridge 1660 W
　William, Northam 1639 A
Burrydge see Burrage
Burt Alexander, Ilfracombe 1699 A
　William, Ilfracombe 1675 W
Burtford see Burford
Burton ..., East Buckland 1607 [W]
　Clement, Barnstaple 1593 [W]
　Margaret, East Buckland 1627 [W]
Burtonshaw John, Yarnscombe 1772 A
Bury, Burie, Burye
　Burie Alice, Tawstock 1585 W
　Arthur, Chulmleigh, gentleman 1705 A
　Burie Christian, Kentisbury 1565 W
　Burie Christopher, Northam 1577 A
　Burye Geoffrey, Chittlehampton 1566 W
　Hugh, Cruwys Morchard 1591 [W]
　Burye Humphrey, Berrynarbor 1583 W
　Burie Jane, Berrynarbor 1589 W
　Burye John, Lynton 1570 W
　John, Croscombe, Martinhoe 1575 W
　John, Lapford, esquire 1665 W
　John, Barnstaple, gentleman 1712 A
　John, Oakford 1713 A
　Lawrence, Rose Ash 1619 [W]
　Burie or Borne Richard, Great Torrington 1582 A
　Burie Richard, Berrynarbor 1583 W
　Richard, Martinhoe 1590 [W]
　Burie William, Martinhoe 1565 W
Buryman see Berriman
Burzacott see Bussacott
Bushell ..., Knowstone 1613 [W]
　Agnes, Chulmleigh, widow 1572 W
　Agnes, Countisbury 1676 W
Bushen John, Countisbury 1672 A
　John, Georgeham 1689 W
　John, Kentisbury 1841 W
　Mary, Kentisbury 1836 W
　Thomas, Filleigh 1690 A
Bushop, Bushope, Bushoppe see Bishop
Bushton, Buishton
　Buishton ..., Countisbury 1607 [W]
　Buishton Joan, East Buckland 1617 [W]
　John, East Buckland 1632 [W]
　John, East Buckland 1727 W
　Peter, East Buckland 1680 W

Thomas, Brendon 1590 [W]
Thomas, Brendon 1619 [W]
Thomas, East Buckland 1622 [W]
Thomas, East Buckland 1638 W
Buss, Beusse, Bews, Bewse, Buce, Buese, Buesse, Buisse, Buse,
    Busse, Bysse, Bywes
Buse ..., Welcombe 1602 W and 1604 [W]
Buse ..., Beaford 1610 [W]
Buse Christopher, Abbotsham 1644 A
Buse Dorothy, Abbotsham 1686 W
Buse Francis, Great Torrington 1755 A
Buse Gabriel, Abbotsham 1637 W
Buse Geoffrey, Bideford 1633 A
Buse Geoffrey, Abbotsham 1635 O
Buse Harry, Abbotsham 1605 W
Buse Henry, Abbotsham 1605 W
Buse Henry, Northam 1608 [W]; forename blank in Ms;
    supplied from parish register
Buce Hugh, Hartland 1752 A
Bews Humphrey, Marwood 1694 A
Buse Joan, Hartland, widow 1607 [W]; forename blank in Ms;
    supplied from parish register
Buse Joan, Welcombe 1622 [W]
Buse Joan, Abbotsham 1673 W
Bysse Joanna, Barnstaple 1628 [W]
Bywes John, Hartland 1579 W
Buesse John, Abbotsham 1593 [W]
Buse John, Bideford 1605 W
Buse John, Hartland 1607 [W]; forename blank in Ms;
    supplied from parish register
Buse John, Tawstock 1621 [W]
Buse John, Abbotsham 1637 W
Buse John, Hartland 1671 A and 1673 O account
Buese John, Bideford 1673 A
Buse John, Hartland 1674 W
Buse John, Abbotsham 1685 W
Buse John, ship *Baltimore* 1746 A
Buse Joseph, Hartland 1752 A
Busse Margaret, Abbotsham 1581 A
Buse Nicholas, Great Torrington 1636 A
Buse Nicholas, Hartland 1726 W
Buse Nicholas, Hartland 1763 W
Bewse Peter, Ilfracombe 1690 W
Buse Philip, Hartland 1676 W
Buse Rebecca, Hartland 1745 W
Richard, Bideford 1621 [W]
Buse Richard, Hartland 1669 O
Richard, Abbotsham 1700 W
Buse Robert, Knowstone, snr. 1638 W
Buse Roger, Hartland 1666 A
Buse Sarah, Hartland 1795 W
Buisse or Buysse Thomas, Hartland 1564 W
Buesse Thomas, Beaford 1590 [W]
Buese Thomas, Welcombe 1615 [W] and 1616 O
Beusse William, Beaford 1567 W
William, Northam 1623 [W] and O
William, Peters Marland 1773 W
Bywes William, Welcombe 1584 W
Buse William, Northam 1616 [W]
Buse William, Hartland 1674 A
Buse William, Hartland 1702 W
Buse William, Abbotsham 1711 W
Bussacott, Burzacott, Buzzacott
Alexander, Bideford 1746 W
Edward, East Down 1696 A
Busacott Eleanor, Bideford 1756 A
Burzacott Elizabeth, Barnstaple, widow 1810 W
Burzacott George, Barnstaple 1812 W
Buzzacott Humphrey, Ilfracombe 1782 W
John, East Down 1597 [W]
Mary, East Down 1605 W
Thomasine, Combe Martin 1622 [W]
Bussacott William, Combe Martin 1634 W
Buzzacott William, Barnstaple 1789 W
Bussell George, Witheridge 1568 W
Philip, Knowstone 1671 W

William, Barnstaple 1584 A
William, Witheridge 1590 [W]
Bussen see Buston
Busshope see Bishop
Buston, Bussen, Busten
Alexander, East Buckland 1590 [W]
Ann, Combe Martin 1598 [W]
Bussen Charles, Great Torrington 1821 W
Busten Ellen, Countisbury 1591 [W]
Ilett, Countisbury 1627 [W]
John, East Buckland 1585 W
John, Chulmleigh 1627 and 1628 [W]
Robert, Countisbury 1630 [W]
Salome, East Buckland 1591 [W]
Busvargus James, Bideford 1703 W
Mary, Bideford 1704 W
Butcher, Bocher, Boocher, Boutcher
Boutcher ..., Meeth 1609 [W]
Bernard, Winkleigh 1623 [W]
Bocher Christian, Petrockstowe 1571 W
Bocher Elizabeth, Chulmleigh 1564 W
Bucher alias Roclife Joan, King's Nympton 1582 W
Butcher alias Ratcliffe Joan, Iddesleigh 1674 A
Boocher alias Ratche or Roclyff John, King's Nympton 1572
    W
Boutcher John, King's Nympton 1615 [W]
John, Winkleigh 1643 W
Boutcher Philip, Meeth 1618 [W]
Bocher Robert, Chulmleigh 1587 W
Theobald, Iddesleigh 1660 A
Butler Catherine, Parkham 1624 [W]
Edward, High Bickington 1688 W
Edward, High Bickington 1708 W
Ferdinand, Chittlehampton 1707 A
Ferdinand, Tawstock 1775 W
Frances, Bow 1685 W
Hannah, Littleham (near Bideford) 1850 W
Hugh, Chittlehampton 1692 A
Humphrey, Mariansleigh 1684 W
Humphrey, East Worlington 1719 W
Humphrey, Cruwys Morchard 1806 W
James, Georgeham 1791 W
John, Littleham (near Bideford) 1640 W
John, Barnstaple 1768 A
Joseph, Hartland 1786 W
Mary, East Worlington 1724 W
Melior, Chittlehampton 1682 W
Owen, Littleham (near Bideford) 1591 [W]
Philip, Heanton Punchardon 1752 A
Richard, Warkleigh 1728 W
Richard, Chittlehampton 1760 A
Robert, Great Torrington 1684 A
William, Hartland 1582 W
William, Chittlehampton 1762 A
William, Mortehoe 1800 W*
Wilmot, Alverdiscott, widow 1611 [W]; forename blank in
    Ms; supplied from parish register
Butt John, Chawleigh 1705 A
John, Northam 1817 A to Sarah, widow
Thomas, Northam 1848 W
Butticomb, Buttacombe
Buttacombe Beaton, Eggesford 1596 [W]
Richard, Fremington 1693 W
Thomas, Heanton Punchardon 1666 A
William, Barnstaple 1662 W
Button Daniel, Barnstaple 1684 W
John, Barnstaple 1834 W
Margaret, Bideford 1686 W
Mary, Pilton 1670 W
Buyshope, Buyshopp see Bishop
Buysse see Buss
Buzzacott see Bussacott
Byce Humphrey, Barnstaple 1623 [W]
Byckener, Byckmore see Bickner
Byddle see Biddle

Bydgood see Bidgood
Bydwill see Biddle
Byer see Beare
Bylton see Belton
Bymner, Bynmer
    Bynmer Charity, Northam 1628 [W]
    John, Northam 1618 [W]
Bynford see Binford
Bynmer see Bymner
Bynon, Binon
    Agnes, Combe Martin 1837 W
    Binon Elizabeth, Ashford 1679 A
    Francis, Ashford 1802 W
    George, Ashford 1836 W
    Honor, Ashford 1744 A
    James, Northam 1743 A
    John, Ashford 1740 W
    John, Ashford, yeoman 1800 A
    Lewis, Ashford 1827 [W]
    Lodovic, Ashford 1726 W
    William, Ashford 1856 [W]
Byrch, Byrche see Birch
Byrd, Byrde see Bird
Byrn see Burne
Byshop, Byshope, Byshopp see Bishop
Bysse see Buss
Byttabere see Bittabear

Cabb see Cade
Cadbury, Cadburie
    Francis, Great Torrington 1636 A
    Henry, Great Torrington 1701 W
    Joanna, Great Torrington 1621 [W]
    Cadburie Robert, Great Torrington, alderman in register 1612
      [W]; forename blank in Ms; supplied from parish register
    Robert, Great Torrington 1623 [W] and 1624 O
Cade, Cabb, Cadd, Cadde, Caddie, Caddy, Cadge
    ..., Witheridge 1611 [W]
    Agnes, Witheridge 1636 W
    Alexander, Barnstaple 1623 [W]
    Caddy Amy, Abbotsham 1661 W
    Caddy Andrew, Buckland Brewer 1673 W
    Christopher, Mortehoe 1585 W
    Caddy Christopher, Parkham 1602 [W]; forename blank in Ms;
      supplied from parish register
    David, Barnstaple 1596 [W]
    David, Winkleigh 1598 [W]
    Elizabeth, Northam 1610 [W]; forename blank in Ms; supplied
      from parish register
    Caddy Elizabeth, Dolton 1618 [W]
    Caddy Elizabeth Barber, Parkham 1842 W
    Cadge Francis, Barnstaple 1745 A
    Cadde Geoffrey, Bideford 1582 W
    Grace, Northam 1682 W
    Cadde Henry, Pilton 1602 [W]; forename blank in Ms;
      supplied from parish register and 1603 W
    Cadd, Henry, Bideford 1743 W
    Cadd, Henry, Bideford, potter 1803 W
    Cadd, Henry, Bideford cordwainer 1810 W
    Cadde Joan, Bideford 1583 W
    John, Witheridge 1564 [W]
    John, Witheridge, snr. 1565 W
    Cadde John, Woolfardisworthy 1579 W
    Cadde John, Bideford 1623 [W]
    Caddy John, Frithelstock 1631 and 1632 [W]
    Caddy John, Buckland Brewer 1729 W
    Cabb John, Great Torrington 1740 A
    Cabb John, Clovelly 1745 A
    Caddy John, Buckland Brewer 1784 W
    Caddy John, Buckland Brewer 1822 W
    Caddy John, Parkham 1839 W
    Cabb Joshua, Bideford 1706 W
    Julian, Bideford 1602 W
    Cadd, Margaret, Pilton 1588 W
    Margaret, Northam 1750 W

Cabb Mary, Barnstaple 1723 A
Cadd, Matilda, Langtree 1634 W
    Merthoe, Barnstaple 1632 [W]
Cabb Paul, Bideford 1640 W
Caddy Peter, Parkham 1622 [W]
Peter, Bideford 1696 W
Peter, Northam 1702 W
Philip, Chulmleigh 1645 W
Philip, Northam 1673 A
Philip, Bideford 1713 W
Philip, Northam 1737 W and 1742 A
Phillippa, Northam 1625 [W]
Richard, Witheridge 1588 A
Cadde Richard, Barnstaple 1614 [W]; forename blank in Ms;
    supplied from parish register
Caddy Richard, Abbotsham 1700 W
Cadd Richard Brown, Bideford A dbn 1834 to William, son
Cadd Richard Moon, Bideford, currier 1815 A to Elizabeth,
    widow
Robert, Northam 1843 A; A dbn
Samuel, Northam 1707 A and 1712 A
Samuel, Northam 1747 A
Sarah, Instow 1797 A
Cadd Susanna, Bideford 1684 W
Caddy Susanna, Bideford 1849 W
Thomas, Witheridge 1627 [W]
Thomas, Northam 1705 W
Thomas, Northam 1729 A
Cadde Thomasine, Pilton 1618 and 1619 [W]
Thomasine, Northam 1719 W
Walter, Woolfardisworthy 1573 W
William, Winkleigh 1579 A
Cadde William, Rackenford 1606 W
Caddy William, Northam 1619 [W]
Caddie William, Parkham 1623 [W]
William, Rackenford 1643 W
William, Northam 1682 W
William, Northam 1702 W
William, Bideford 1835 W
Caddy William, Buckland Brewer 1839 W; A dbn
Willmot, Northam 1635 W
Cadewill see Cadwell
Cadlake, Cadelake
    Dorothy, Great Torrington 1760 W and 1770 [W] proved in
      1760
    Cadelake John, Great Torrington 1733 W
Cadmore Nicholas, Little Torrington 1723 A
    Thomas, Chawleigh 1734 W
Cadwell, Cadewill, Cadwill
    Cadewill Christopher, Chittlehampton 1588 W
    Hugh, Bideford 1664 A
    Cadwill William, Frithelstock 1629 [W]
      see also Kedwell, Kidwell
Caldey Richard, Barnstaple 1628 [W]
    Thomas, Northam 1636 A
Cale see Call
Calesey John, Atherington 1700 W
Call, Cale, Calle
    Alexander, Chawleigh 1712 W
    Calle Digory, South Molton 1682 A
    Edmund, Northam 1708 A
    Elizabeth, Great Torrington 1633 A
    Isott, Cheldon 1669 A
    Cale alias Bound James, Barnstaple 1580 A
    Calle alias White James, Barnstaple 1581 A account
    Cale John, King's Nympton, snr. 1625 [W]
    John, Zeal Monachorum 1727 A
    John, Northam 1735 W
    John, Northam 1785 W
    Calle Margaret, Northam 1754 W
    Calle Nicholas, Hartland 1611 [W]; forename blank in Ms;
      supplied from parish register
Callacott John, Abbotsham 1578 W
    John, Shebbear 1687 W and 1691 A

Callard, Calland, Callarde, Callerde
  ..., Ashreigney 1613 [W]
  Callarde Clement, Georgeham 1567 W
  Elizabeth, St Giles in the Wood 1577 W
  George, Burrington 1683 W
  George, Chittlehampton 1692 W
  George, Burrington 1725 W
  Isott, Burrington 1687 W
  John, Winkleigh 1690 A
  John, Burrington 1781 W
  John, Burrington, shoemaker 1806 W
  Mary, Winkleigh 1624 [W]
  Mary, Winkleigh 1687 W
  Calland Mary, Shebbear 1720 W
  Callerde Thomas, Winkleigh 1583 W
Callaway Richard, Hartland 1824 W
  see also Kellaway
Callerde see Callard
Callon William, Great Torrington 1810 W*
Calverley, Calverlyn
  Lawrence, East Anstey 1673 A
  Calverlyn Patrick, Great Torrington 1573 A
Calwoodly, Calewoodley
  Hugh, South Molton 1629 [W] and 1631 [W]
  Calewoodley Richard, South Molton 1591 [W]
Cam Tristram, Langtree, snr. 1679 W
Cambell John, Northam 1703 W
Camp, Campe
  Campe ..., Woolfardisworthy 1605-06 [W]
  Campte ..., Woolfardisworthy 1613 [W]
  James, Ilfracombe 1843 W
  Campe John, Great Torrington 1587 A and 1588 account
  Campe John, Chulmleigh 1617 [W]
  John, Knowstone 1670 W
  Campe Mathew, Woolfardisworthy 1580 W
  Philip, Knowstone 1670 W
  Campe Robert, Woolfardisworthy 1563 W
  Robert, South Molton 1666 W
  Campe Robert, Mariansleigh 1670 W
  Campe Thomas, Woolfardisworthy 1580 W
  Thomas, Stoke Rivers 1847 W
  William, Chittlehampton 1779 W
Campain see Campin
Campe see Camp
Campin, Campain, Campyn
  Campyn Barbara, Yarnscombe 1693 W
  Campyn George, Yarnscombe 1597 [W]
  Campain Grace, Yarnscombe 1766 A
  Henry, Yarnscombe 1733 W
  John, Yarnscombe 1727 W
  Campyn Mathew, Yarnscombe 1632 [W]
  Peter, Great Torrington 1568 W
Can see Cann
Canacot Nicholas, Newton Tracey 1567 W
Cane see Cann
Canell Arthur, Hartland 1567 W
Canham Ann, Arlington 1674 A
Cann, Can, Cane, Canne
  Canne ..., Bow 1601 [W]
  Canne ..., King's Nympton 1607 [W]
  Abraham, Hartland 1688 A
  Can Ann, Buckland Brewer 1669 W
  Christopher, Huntshaw 1688 W
  Cyprian, Alverdiscott 1685 W
  Canne Elizabeth, Bow 1625 [W]
  Emma, Hartland 1711 W
  Canne Hannibal, Coldridge 1597 [W]
  Canne Hugh, Clovelly 1629 [W]
  Canne Hugh, Bideford 1644 W
  Hugh, Hartland 1674 W
  Hugh, Great Torrington 1780 W
  Hugh, Hartland, yeoman 1797 W
  Canne Isott, Hartland 1629 and 1631 [W]
  Cane Jane, Great Torrington 1641 W
  Canne Joan, Hartland 1590 [W]

Canne John, Bow 1571 W
Cane John, Huntshaw 1573 W
Canne John, Hartland 1596 [W]
Canne John, Hartland 1626 [W]
John, East Worlington 1672 W
John, Bow 1690 W
John, Hartland 1704 A
John, East Worlington 1707 A
John, Beaford 1734 W
John, Huntshaw 1746 W
John, Bow 1755 A
John, Coldridge 1755 W
John, Chawleigh 1778 A
John, Merton 1794 W
John, Chawleigh yeoman 1809 A
John, Meeth 1821 W
Lawrence, Hartland 1643 W
Can Leonard, Hartland 1633 [W]
Leonard, Huntshaw 1724 W
Canne Lodovic, Hartland 1621 [W]
Canne Margaret, Alverdiscott 1697 W
Can Mary, Barnstaple 1741 W
Peter, Chawleigh 1732 W
Richard, Great Torrington 1715 A
Richard, ship *Eagle* 1756 W
Richard, Chawleigh 1773 A
Richard, Hartland 1855 W
Robert, Great Torrington 1776 W
Roger, Alverdiscott 1744 W
Roger, Alverdiscott 1780 W
Roger, Westleigh 1813 W
Stephen, Coldridge 1760 A
Stephen, Nymet Rowland, gentleman 1801 W
Susanna, Merton 1819 W
Thomas, Huntshaw 1694 W
Thomas, Bideford 1710 A
Thomas, Westleigh 1785 A
Thomas, Parkham yeoman 1807 W
Canne alias Benford Thomasine, Dowland 1603 W
Can Tristram, Alverdiscott 1638 A
Can William, Yarnscombe 1685 W
William, Langtree 1696 W
Can William, Yarnscombe 1735 A
Cane William, Bideford 1740 A
William, Barnstaple 1740 W
William, West Worlington 1762 W
William, Wembworthy 1774 A
William, Chulmleigh 1802 A
William, Alverdiscott 1829 A
William, Tawstock 1844 W
William, Fremington 1846 A
William, Bideford 1848 W
Cannaford John, South Molton 1599 [W]
Canne see Cann
Canney Eleanor, Frithelstock 1628 [W]
Cannon, Canning
  Catherine, Tawstock 1690 A
  Joanna, Fremington 1685 W
  John, Barnstaple 1575 A
  John, Fremington 1685 [W]
  Nicholas, Hartland 1664 W
  Canning Robert, Langtree 1595 [W]
Cantell, Cantle
  ..., Great Torrington 1603 [W]
  Bernard, Great Torrington 1591 [W] and 1592 [W]
  Cantle William, Great Torrington 1573 W
Canter ..., Great Torrington 1608 [W]
Cannter see Canter
Cantle see Cantell
Canton John, Ilfracombe 1758 A
Capron John, East Anstey 1727 W
  John, Cruwys Morchard 1773 W
Carder, Carde, Carder
  ..., Langtree 1608 [W]
  ..., Mariansleigh 1609 [W] (2)

..., Kentisbury 1613 [W]
..., Bratton Fleming 1680 [W]
Alexander, Ilfracombe 1678 A
Alice, Bratton Fleming 1634 W
Alice, Mortehoe 1640 W
Amos, Arlington 1676 A
Amos, Arlington 1703 W
Amos, Barnstaple 1713 A
Amos, Parracombe 1727 A
Amos, West Down 1743 W
Amos, Arlington 1785 W
Andrew, Bideford 1765 W
Anthony, Arlington 1637 W
Anthony, Bratton Fleming 1637 W
Anthony, Stoke Rivers 1729 W
Arthur, Bratton Fleming 1667 W
Eleanor, Martinhoe 1740 W
Carder Eleanor see William Rawle
Elizabeth, Shirwell 1672 W
Elizabeth, Arlington 1700 W
Elizabeth, Arlington 1725 W
Elizabeth, Bideford 1786 W
Elizabeth, Bideford 1825 W
Emma, Trentishoe 1597 [W]
Emotta, Arlington 1624 [W]
Esther, West Down 1772 W
George, Bratton Fleming 1635 W
Carde George, Witheridge 1674 W
Giles, Berrynarbor 1694 W
Giles, Berrynarbor 1720 A
Grace, Stoke Rivers 1673 W
Honor, Berrynarbor 1672 W
Hugh, North Molton 1672 W
Humphrey, Barnstaple 1795 W
James, Berrynarbor 1636 W
John, Bratton Fleming 1580 W
John, Arlington 1588 W
John, Trentishoe 1590 [W]
John, Mariansleigh 1600 W
John, Great Torrington 1615 [W]
John, Charles 1626 [W] and 1628 O
John, Mortehoe 1634 A
John, Challacombe 1643 A
John, Chittlehampton 1665 A
John, Bratton Fleming 1698 A
John, Barnstaple 1742 [W]
Jonas, Bratton Fleming 1639 W
Macklin, Ilfracombe 1597 [W]
Margaret, Chittlehampton 1704 W
Mary, Bratton Fleming 1708 W
Mary, Bratton Fleming 1726 W
Mary, Bideford 1827 W
Nicholas, Chittlehampton 1664 A
Nicholas, Chittlehampton 1666 W
Peter, Shirwell 1616 [W]
Philip, Mortehoe 1637 W
Richard or John, Bratton Fleming 1608 [W]; forename blank
   in Ms; supplied from parish register
Richard, Bratton Fleming 1640 W
Robert, Bratton Fleming 1568 W
Robert, Goodleigh 1666 A and 1669 O
Thomas, Arlington 1698 A
Thomas, Arlington 1766 W
Thomas, Arlington 1820 A to Eleanor, widow
Walter, Ilfracombe 1670 W
William, Lynton 1609 [W]; forename blank in Ms; supplied
   from parish register
William, Bratton Fleming 1625 [W]
William, Clovelly 1660 W
William, Stoke Rivers 1673 O account
William, Bideford 1755 W
William, South Molton 1827 W
William, East Down 1830 W
William, Marwood 1850 W
Carewe Walter, Great Torrington 1567 W

Carie see Cary
Carnall John, Chulmleigh, snr. 1696 A
Carpenter ..., South Molton 1613 [W]
Ann, South Molton 1570 W
Anthony, Barnstaple 1707 W
Bartholomew, Combe Martin 1597 [W]
Edward, Puddington 1663 W
Edward, Barnstaple 1704 W
Edward, Barnstaple 1728 W
Eleanor, Chulmleigh 1666 [A]
George, Winkleigh yeoman 1805 W
Henry, South Molton 1582 W
John, South Molton 1639 A
John, Rackenford 1640 W
John, Witheridge 1736 W
John, Oakford 1775 W
John, Iddesleigh 1778 A
John, Oakford 1825 A
Lawrence, West Anstey 1616 [W]
Lodovic, South Molton 1626 [W]
Oliver, South Molton 1591 [W]
Philip, Barnstaple 1645 A
Richard, South Molton 1593 [W]
Richard, Rackenford 1600 W
Richard, Rackenford 1624 [W]
Richard, Chulmleigh 1664 A
William, Oakford 1800 W
William, Pilton, jnr. 1814 W
Carr James, Combe Martin 1787 A
John, Combe Martin 1796 W
Carrow, Carrowe
Edward, Barnstaple 1732 W
Hugh, Barnstaple 1710 W
Carrowe Joan, Chittlehampton 1589 W and 1597 A account
John, Barnstaple 1713 W
Carruthers David, Dolton 1733 W
David, Merton 1795 W
Rebecca, Merton. shopkeeper 1803 W
Carslake see Kerslake
Carswell, Kerswill
... 1600 A
Alice, Parkham 1627 [W]
Ann, Ashreigney 1728 W
Kerswill John, South Molton 1628 [W]
Carter Amos, Romansleigh 1834 W
Benedict, Hartland 1758 W
Charles, Hartland 1737 A
Charles, snr., Hartland 1738 W; forename blank in Ms;
   supplied from parish register
Charles, Hartland, gentleman 1811 W
Dionysia and John, Mariansleigh 1631 [W]
Elizabeth, South Molton 1728 W
Elizabeth, Mariansleigh 1732 A
Francis, Knowstone 1678 W
George, Mariansleigh 1759 A
George, Romansleigh, yeoman 1799 W
Joan, South Molton 1756 W
John, Parkham 1564 [W]
John and Dionysia, Mariansleigh 1631 [W]
John, Great Torrington 1643 W
John, Chulmleigh 1678 A
John, Ashreigney 1705 W
John, Barnstaple 1706 W
John, Woolfardisworthy 1744 W
John, Bideford 1779 A
John, Ashreigney 1787 A
John, Ashreigney 1817 W
John, Winkleigh 1829 W
John, Romansleigh 1830 A to Amos, brother
John, Romansleigh 1834 A dbn to Ann Cheldon, guardian to
   daughter
Judith, Hartland 1790 W
Mary, Fremington, widow 18-,   Ann wife of John Nott,
   labourer, daughter
Nicholas, Rose Ash 1704 A

Nicholas, Chulmleigh 1724 A
Nicholas, Ashreigney 1763 W
Philip, Barnstaple 1856 W
Richard, Hartland 1752 W
Robert, South Molton, yeoman 1801 W
Roger, Rose Ash 1749 W
Samuel, Great Torrington 1671 A
Sebastian, Great Torrington 1644 W
Silvanus, Sheepwash 1715 W
Thomas, Barnstaple 1725 A
Thomas, Hartland 1762 W
Thomas, Ashreigney, jnr. 1837 A to Dorothy
Thomas, Ashreigney, snr. 1837 W
William, Hartland 1720 A
William, Chulmleigh 1791 A
William, Hartland 1839 A
William, South Molton 1851 W
Cartway Henry, North Molton 1679 W
   Cartway alias Stick Lodovic, Rose Ash 1671 A and 1673 O
Cartwright Anthony, Newton Tracey 1639 A
   John, Pilton 1624 [W]
   Richard, Newton Tracey 1632 [W]
Cary, Carie, Carye
   ..., Great Torrington 1600 [A] account
   Carie ..., Buckland Brewer 1610 [W]
   Anthony, Clovelly 1694 W
   Catherine, Clovelly 1631 [W]
   Carye Dennis, Great Torrington 1589 A
   Elizabeth, Great Torrington 1678 W
   Elizabeth, Clovelly 1688 W
   Francis, Alwington 1633 W
   George, Clovelly 1702 W
   George, Clovelly 1732 A
   Gertrude, Great Torrington 1673 W
   Jacob, Alwington 1634 W
   John, Buckland Brewer 1604 W
   John, Littleham (near Bideford) 1641 W
   John, Littleham (near Bideford) 1661 W
   John, Littleham (near Bideford) 1673 A
   Jonathan, Littleham (near Bideford) 1676 A
   Margaret, Clovelly 1689 A
   Carey Simon, Great Torrington 1599 [W]
   Thomas, Buckland Brewer 1619 [W]
   Carie Thomasine, Buckland Brewer 1580 W
   William, Great Torrington 1674 W
Caselegh John, North Tawton 1564 [W]
Castle, Castell
   Ann, Combe Martin 1620 [W]
   Castell John, Alwington 1602 W
Castleman Robert, Wembworthy 1619 [W]
Cater Benedict, Pilton 1585 A
   John, St Giles in the Wood 1602 W
   Rebecca, Fremington 1736 W
Catford, Catforde, Catfurd
   Catforde (Catfurd) John, Molland 1564 [W] and 1567 W
   John, West Anstey 1678 A
Caulie see Cawley
Caunter Edward, Bideford 1601 A "Canthor" in register;
   forename blank in Ms; supplied from parish register
   Elizabeth, Pilton 1630 [W]
   Margaret, Clovelly 1633 W
   Richard, Landcross 1606 W
   Richard, Barnstaple 1617 [W]
Causey, Causye see Cawsey
Cawley, Caulie, Cawle
   Caulie alias Pepell John, Buckland Brewer 1572 W
   Cawle John, Chulmleigh 1591 [W]
   Richard, King's Nympton 1732 A
   Cawle William, High Bickington 1567 W
   William, High Bickington 1666 A
Cawsey, Causey, Causye, Cawsie, Cawssie
   ..., King's Nympton 1614 [W]
   Cawsie Ann, Atherington 1629 [W]
   Cawsie Arthur, King's Nympton 1618 [W]
   Cawsie Arthur, King's Nympton 1635 A

Arthur, Bideford 1687 W
Arthur, Barnstaple 1694 W
Causye Baldwin, Coldridge 1602 W
Catherine, High Bickington 1697 A
David, Bideford 1681 A
Eleanor, Chittlehampton 1644 W
Elizabeth, Great Torrington 1712 W
Elizabeth, Atherington 1749 W
Elizabeth, Little Torrington 1772 W
Elizabeth, Cheldon, widow 1807 W
George, Atherington 1607 [W]; forename blank in Ms;
   supplied from parish register
George, Littleham (near Bideford) 1714 W
George, Bideford 1717 A
George, Heanton Punchardon 1726 A and 1731 A
George, Atherington 1755 A
George, Bideford 1763 A
George, Ashford 1768 W
George, Yarnscombe 1825 A
George, Cheldon 1847 W
Cawsie James, Atherington 1596 [W]
James, Bulkworthy 1688 W
James, Bideford 1709 A
Joan, Mortehoe 1765 A
John, Chittlehampton 1577 W
Cawsie John, Bradbury, Chittlehampton 1634 W and 1636 A
Causey John, Chittlehampton 1673 A
John, Atherington 1688 W
John, High Bickington 1693 W
John, Chawleigh 1720 W
John, Bideford 1723 A
John, ship *Peril* 1749 A
John, High Bickington 1775 A
John, Tawstock 1787 W and 1789 W
John, Chawleigh, maltster 1804 W
John, Tawstock 1839 W
Joseph, High Bickington 1737 W
Lewis, Pilton 1791 W
Lewis, Atherington 1831 W
Lodovic, Atherington 1696 W
Causey Margaret, Roborough 1679 W
Margery, King's Nympton 1734 W
Mathew, Roborough 1672 A
Causey Pauline, High Bickington 1677 A.
Cawsie Richard, Atherington 1627 and 1629 [W]
Richard, High Bickington 1690 W
Robert, Atherington 1661 A
Robert, Atherington 1715 A
Robert, Instow 1744 A
Robert, Atherington 1765 A
Roger, Atherington 1706 W
Thomas, High Bickington 1669 W
Causeye Thomas, Northam 1673 W
Thomas, High Bickington 1681 A
William, Chittlehampton 1641 A
William, High Bickington 1669 O
William, Bulkworthy 1740 W
William, Buckland Brewer 1754 W
William, Northam 1836 W
William, Chawleigh 1847 W
Willmot, Atherington 1668 A
Cewlake see Kerslake
Cay Bartholomew, Buckland Brewer 1664 W
Ceely see Sealy
Chadsie, Chadssye
   Chadssye John, Iddesleigh 1576 W
   Thomas, Winkleigh 1625 [W]
   William, Tawstock 1622 [W]
Chaldon, Challon, Cheldon, Chuldon
   Cheldon ..., Romansleigh 1607 and 1609 W
   Cheldon Agnes, Romansleigh 1606 W
   Chuldon Alice, Fremington 1578 W
   Alice, Pilton 1625 [W]
   Cheldon Ann, Bideford 1620 [W]
   Cheldon Ann see also John Carter

Cheldon Edward, Chawleigh 1819 A to Mary, widow
Cheldon Elizabeth, Romansleigh 1626 [W]
Cheldon Elizabeth, Wembworthy 1683 W
Cheldon Hugh, Romansleigh 1568 W
James, Pilton 1642 A
James, Pilton 1663 A
Cheldon James, Bideford 1666 W
Cheldon Jane, Wembworthy 1594 [W]
Cheldon Jane, Winkleigh 1615 [W]
Cheldon Jane, Romansleigh 1621 [W]
Cheldon Jane, Wembworthy 1629 [W]
Cheldon Jane, Wembworthy 1682 A
Cheldon Jane, Romansleigh 1809 W
Cheldon Jane, Romansleigh 1828 A
Cheldon Jane, Romansleigh 1848 W
Chaldon alias Downeman John, Fremington 1601 W
John, Northam 1606 [W]
John, Bideford 1610 [W]
John, Fremington 1611 [W]
John, Pilton 1614 [W]
John, Martinhoe, yeoman 1798 W
John, Romansleigh, yeoman 1809 W
John, Romansleigh 1828 A to Jane, widow
Cheldon Lewis, Romansleigh 1674 A
Cheldon Lewis, Romansleigh 1768 W
Cheldon Mary, Burrington 1827 W
Cheldon Michael, Brushford 1665 W
Challon Peter, Pilton 1710 A
Cheldon Richard, Wembworthy 1580 W
Cheldon Samuel, Romansleigh 1710 W
Cheldon Samuel, Romansleigh 1753 A
Cheldon Samuel, King's Nympton 1836 W
Cheldon Samuel, Romansleigh 1853 W
Susanna, Yarnscombe 1733 W
Cheldon Thomas, Romansleigh 1615 [W]
Thomas, Northam 1632 [W]
William, Fremington 1573 W
William, Bideford 1616 [W]
William, Pilton 1618 O
William, Yarnscombe 1714 A
Chalk Elizabeth, Bideford 1848 W
John, Alwington 1827 A to John, son
Robert, ship *Gramons Sloop* 1746 A
Thomas, Monkleigh 1810 A
Challacombe, Challocombe, Chalncomb, Chalncombe,
   Chollacomb, Chollacombe, Chollacome
Chollacombe ... 1597 [W]
Chollacombe Adam, Ilfracombe 1618 [W]
Chalncombe Agnes, Westleigh, spinster 1672 W
Chalncomb Ann, Combe Martin 1706 W
Ann, Barnstaple, formerly of Braunton 1848 W
Catherine, Combe Martin 1733 W
Chollacombe Christopher, Warkleigh 1621 [W] and 1623 O
Chollacombe Christopher, Chulmleigh 1632 [W]
Chollacombe Clement, Parracombe 1592 [W]
Chollacombe David, Combe Martin 1598 [W]
Edward, Ilfracombe 1752 A
Elizabeth, Combe Martin 1682 W
Esther, Martinhoe 1819 A to Amos Sloley, son
George, Combe Martin 1755 A
George, Combe Martin 1834 W
Chollacombe Henry, Chittlehampton 1634 W
Chollacomb John, Ilfracombe 1631 [W]
Chollacomb John, Ilfracombe 1669 W
Challocombe John, Westleigh 1674 W
Challacomb John, Ilfracombe 1705 A
Chalncombe John, Westleigh 1720 [A]
John, Ilfracombe 1722 W
John, Combe Martin, carpenter 1796 W
John, Mortehoe 1827 W to Mary of St Peter Bristol, sister
John, West Down 1838 W
Chollacombe Julian, Ilfracombe 1636 W
Chollacomb Lewis, Barnstaple 1605 W
Mary, Combe Martin 1743 W
Mary, Barnstaple 1831 W

Chollacombe Nicholas, Combe Martin 1639 O
Nicholas, Berrynarbor, yeoman 1807 W
Peter, Georgeham 1751 W
Chollacombe Philip, Parracombe, snr. 1639 A
Philip, Mortehoe 1776 W
Chollacombe Richard, Combe Martin 1593 [W]
Chollacombe Richard, Combe Martin 1628 [W]
Richard, Combe Martin 1729 W and 1733 A
Challacomb Robert, Atherington 1677 W
Robert, Combe Martin 1790 A
Challacomb Simon, Parracombe 1667 [W]
Chollacome Thomas, Parracombe 1575 W
Chollacombe Thomas, Combe Martin 1632 [W]
Chalncombe Thomas, Combe Martin 1645 A
Thomas, Westleigh 1681 A
Thomas, Combe Martin 1733 A
Thomas, Combe Martin 1743 W and 1749 A
Thomas, Ilfracombe 1763 W
Thomas, Parracombe 1763 A
Thomas, Combe Martin, yeoman 1803 W
Thomas, Combe Martin, yeoman 1810 W
Chollacombe William, Shirwell 1590 [W]
William, Georgeham 1741 A
William, West Down 1787 W
William, Berrynarbor 1809 W
William, West Down 1824 W
Challander Alexander Smith, Instow 1837 W
Challice, Challies, Challish
Challies alias Challish John, Zeal Monachorum 1592 [W]
John, Lapford 1768 W
Richard, Lapford 1706 W
Robert, Lapford 1640 O
Challish Roger, Lapford 1616 [W]
Roger, Lapford 1636 A
Challon see Chaldon
Chambere see Chambers
Chamberlin, Chamberlein, Chamberlinge, Chamberlyn
Chamberlyn Alice, Tawstock 1635 W
Denham, Barnstaple 1827 W
Denham, Barnstaple 1837 W to Ann Dicker, sister
Chamberlyn George, Tawstock 1596 [W]
Chamberlyn George, Tawstock 1694 W
James, Barnstaple 1822 W
Chamberlyn John, Tawstock 1580 W
Chamberlyn John, Dolton 1598 [W]
Chamberlyn John, Cruwys Morchard 1638 W
Chamberlyn Margery, Alverdiscott, widow 1615 [W];
   forename blank in Ms; supplied from parish register
Chamberlein Onesimus, Barnstaple 1757 A
Chamberlyn Richard, Dolton 1640 W
Chamberlyn Robert, Stoodleigh 1581 W
Chamberlinge William, Tawstock 1613 [W]; forename blank
   in Ms; supplied from parish register
Chambers, Chambere
Elizabeth, Winkleigh 1848 W
Joan, Winkleigh 1825 W
Chambere John, St Giles in the Wood 1586 W
John, Winkleigh 1835 W
Robert, Winkleigh 1817 W
Samuel, Winkleigh, cordwainer 1809 W
Samuel, Winkleigh 1851 W
Simon, Winkleigh 1763 W
William, Great Torrington 1800 W
Chamings see Channon
Chammond, Chamond
..., Welcombe 1612 [W]
Chamond Grace, Welcombe 1622 [W]
Champion, Champin
Alexander, Buckland Brewer 1743 [W]; forename blank in
   Ms; supplied from parish register
Edward, South Molton 1699 W
Champin James, Chittlehampton 1676 A
Champin Mary, Chittlehampton 1728 A
William, Atherington 1847 W

Champneys, Champneis, Champness, Changneana
  Champneis Anthony, Barnstaple 1607 [W]; forename blank in
    Ms; supplied from parish register
  Dorothy, Pilton 1700 W
  Champneis John, Chittlehampton 1632 [W]
  Champness Mary, Loxhore 1760 W
  Changneana Peter, Barnstaple 1742 W
Chanish John, Chulmleigh 1729 W
Channon, Chamings, Chaning, Chanon
  James, Chulmleigh 1681 A
  Channing James, Cruwys Morchard 1826 [W]
  Chaning John, Fremington 1670 [W]
  John, Chulmleigh 1742 W
  Chamings Priscilla, Merton 1843 W
  Chanon Thomas, East Anstey, tailor 1814 A to John, son
Channtrell, Channtwill see Chantrell
Chant, Chaunt, Chaunte
  Chaunt ..., Chulmleigh 1600 A
  Chaunt Ann, Chulmleigh 1601 W
  Chaunt Ann, Loxhore 1640 W
  Christopher, Chulmleigh 1700 W
  Chaunt Francis, Ashreigney 1643 W
  Chaunte John, Chulmleigh 1576 W
  Chaunt Peter, Bideford 1627 [W]
  Chaunt Richard, Chulmleigh 1753 W
  Chaunt Roger, Chulmleigh 1621 [W]
  Samuel, Chulmleigh 1690 W
  Chaunte Thomas, Chulmleigh 1589 W
  Chaunte Walter, Chulmleigh 1600 W
Chanter, Chaunter
  Chaunter George, Molland 1623 [W]
  Chaunter Joan, West Anstey 1641 A
  John, Rose Ash 1676 A
  Chaunter Lodovic, Witheridge 1640 W
  Maria, North Molton, sp. 1847 A to Margaret, sp., sister
  Chaunter Peter, Northam 1702 A
  Chaunter William, West Anstey 1639 A
Chantrell, Chantrill, Chauntrell, Chauntrill, Chauntwill
  Chauntrill ..., Ilfracombe 1685 W
  Chauntwill Henry, Marwood 1709 A
  Chauntrell John, Marwood 1579 W and 1585 W
  Chantrill John, Ilfracombe 1685 W
  John, Marwood 1738 A
Chapell, Chapel, Chaple, Chappel, Chappell, Chapple
  Chapell alias Chapinton ..., South Molton 1604 [W]
  Chaple ..., Zeal Monachorum 1607 [W]
  Chaple ..., Ilfracombe 1610 [W]
  ..., Chittlehampton 1612 [W], 1613 [W] and 1615 [W]
  Chaple ..., Langtree 1614 [W]
  Chappell ..., Woolfardisworthy 1686 A
  Alexander, Barnstaple 1621 [W] and 1623 O
  Alice, South Molton 1603 W
  Andrew, Ilfracombe 1589 A
  Chappell Ann, Northam 1756 W
  Chappell Anthony, Chittlehampton 1643 W
  Chappell Anthony, Chittlehampton 1698 A; forename blank in
    Ms; supplied from parish register
  Bartholomew, Chittlehampton 1615 [W]
  Chapple Bartholomew, Warkleigh 1826 W
  Chappell Bridget, Chittlehampton 1627 [W]
  Catherine, South Molton 1598 [W]
  Chappell Catherine Thomson, Northam 1804 W*
  Chappell Charity, Fremington 1791 W
  Chaple alias Scott Christiana, Chittlehampton 1703 A
  Chaple Christopher, Northam 1588 W
  Chappell Christopher, South Molton 1624 [W] & 1625 O
  Chappell Christopher, Northam 1676 A
  Chaple Christopher, Chittlehampton 1711 W
  Clarice, Chittlehampton 1577 W
  Chapple Clement, High Bray 1693 W
  Chapple Clement, North Molton 1712 A
  Chapple Clement, North Molton 1733 A
  Chapple Edward, George Nympton 1714 W
  Chapple Elizabeth, South Molton 1628 [W]
  Chapple Elizabeth, High Bickington 1695 W

Chapple Elizabeth, Northam 1703 W
Chapple Elizabeth, South Molton 1763 W
Chapple Elizabeth, Fremington 1774 W
Chapple Elizabeth, Chittlehampton, widow 1810 W
Chapple Elizabeth, Chittlehampton 1829 W
Chappell Elizabeth, Fremington 1854 A
Chappell Emanuel, Bideford 1662 A
Emma, Northam 1616 [W]
Chappell George, South Molton 1660 A
Chappell George, Chittlehampton 1755 W
Chappell George, Chittlehampton 1802 A
Chapple George, High Bickington 1816 W
Chapple George, West Buckland 1857 W
Chappell Grace, Bideford 1643 A
Chaple Grace, High Bickington 1696 W
Chapple Grace, Cruwys Morchard 1769 W
Chappell Grace, Fremington 1772 W
Chappelle Gregory, Hartland 1576 W
Chappell Henry, South Molton 1681 W
Chaple Henry, South Molton 1699 W
Chapple Hugh, Chittlehampton 1780 W
Chappell James, High Bickington 1686 A
Chappell James, Northam 1755 W
Chapple James, South Molton 1848 W
Chappell Joan, Chittlehampton 1633 W
Chapple Joan, South Molton 1637 A
Chappell Joan, Fremington 1718 A
Chappell Joan, High Bray 1800 A
Chapple Joan, Chittlehampton 1829 W
Chapple Joan, West Buckland 1838 W
Chapple Joan, East Putford 1851 W
Chappell Joan, Blakewell, Chittlehampton 1573 W
John, Shelston 1566 W
John, Woolfardisworthy 1581 A
John, Chittlehampton 1582 W
Chaple John, Northam 1584 A
John, Woolfardisworthy 1585 W
John, Chittlehampton 1590 [W]
John, South Molton 1590 [W]
Chappell John, Frithelstock 1597 [W]
Chappell John, Bideford 1627 [W]
Chappell John, South Molton 1631 [W]
Chapple John, Bideford 1638 W
Chapple John, Chittlehampton 1640 A
Chappell John, Molland 1664 A
Chappell John, Chittlehampton 1667 W
Chappell John, Northam 1670 A
Chappell John, Molland 1682 W
Chapple John, South Molton 1694 W
Chaple John, Bideford 1697 W
Chaple John, Chittlehampton 1699 A
Chappel John, Fremington 1701 A
Chapple John, South Molton 1707 W
Chappel John, Fremington 1715 W
Chappell John, Atherington 1757 W
Chapple John, Chittlehampton 1763 A
Chappell John, North Molton 1771 W
Chapple John, George Nympton 1772 W
Chapple John, Chittlehampton 1773 W
Chappell John, Fremington 1783 W
Chapple John, King's Nympton 1784 W
Chapel John, Buckland Brewer 1822 W
Chapple John, Barnstaple 1839 W
Chapple John, Washford Pyne 1854 W
Chappell Julian, Filleigh 1689 A
Chaple Lice [? Louis], South Molton 1610 [W]
Chapple Lodoix, Chittlehampton 1707 A
Margery, Barnstaple 1607 [W]
Mary, Northam 1621 [W]
Chapple Mary, Chittlehampton 1678 W
Chapple Mary, Woolfardisworthy 1693 W
Chapple Mary, Chittlehampton 1774 W
Chappell Mary, Northam 1828 W
Chappell Mary, Fremington 1831 A

Chappel Mary Ann, North Molton 1849 W
Nicholas, South Molton 1607 [W]
Chappell Nicholas, South Molton 1679 A
Chapple Nicholas, Beaford 1696 A
Chappell Oliver, Chittlehampton 1678 A
Chapple Petronell, South Molton 1673 W
Chappell Philip, Bulkworthy 1676 W
Chappell Prudence, Fremington, widow 1810 W
Richard, Chittlehampton 1579 W
Richard, High Bray 1598 [W]
Richard, Northam 1612 [W]; forename blank in Ms; supplied
    from parish register
Chapple Richard, Chittlehampton 1738 W
Robert, Chittlehampton 1601 W
Robert, Ilfracombe 1606 W
Chapple Robert, South Molton 1631 [W]
Chappell Robert, Chittlehampton 1686 W
Chapple Robert, South Molton 1693 A
Chapple Robert, South Molton 1695 W
Chapple Robert, George Nympton 1753 [W]
Chappel Robert, Chittlehampton 1765 W
Roger, Chittlehampton 1621 [W]
Chapple Roger, Barnstaple 1695 W
Chaple Roger, Fremington 1700 A
Chappell Roger, Fremington 1775 W
Chappeli Roger, Barnstaple 1783 W
Chapple Samuel, Bideford 1705 A
Chapple Samuel, Bideford 1738 A
Chapple Samuel, Fremington 1743 W
Chappell Samuel, Instow 1768 A
Chappell Samuel, Barnstaple 1792 W
Chappell Samuel, Fremington, yeoman 1802 A
Chappell Samuel, Fremington 1817 W; transmitted to Doctor's
    Commons, 5 Feb 1820
Thomas, Chittlehampton 1573 W
Chappell Thomas, South Molton 1592, 1594 [W]
Thomas, Chittlehampton 1606 W
Chappell Thomas, Washford Pyne 1669 W
Chappel Thomas, Northam 1692 W
Chappell Thomas, High Bray 1705 W
Chaple Thomas, Woolfardisworthy 1711 W
Chapple Thomas, Alverdiscott 1779 W
Chappell Thomas, Northam 1819 W
Chapple Thomas, Chittlehampton 1829 W
Walter, Rackenford 1585 A
Chappell William, Chittlehampton 1580 W
William, Sheepwash 1595 [W]
William, Northam 1596 [W]
Chappell William, South Molton 1627 [W]
Chappell William, Chittlehampton 1634 W
Chappell William, High Bray 1690 A
Chappell William, Chittlehampton 1727 A
Chapple William, Chittlehampton 1761 A
Chappell William, Northam 1763 W
Chappell William, South Molton 1763 W
Chappell William, Fremington 1764 W
Chappel William, Chittlehampton, maltster 1798 A
Chappell William, South Molton 1799 W
Chapple William, North Molton 1830 A to Mary, widow
Chapple William, Witheridge 1842 W
Chapple William, Chittlehampton 1850 W
Chappell William, Fremington 1851 W
Chappell Willmot, George Nympton 1728 W
Chapple Willmot, Chittlehampton 1773 W
Chapple Zachariah, Barnstaple 1731 W
Chapelman, Chapleman, Chappellan, Chappelman, Chappleman
Chapleman ..., High Bickington 1610 [W]
Chappelman Agnes, Beaford 1795 A
Chappelman Arthur, Beaford 1748 W
Chapleman Jane, Clovelly 1716 W
Chappleman John, High Bickington 1637 W
Chapleman John, High Bickington 1679 A
Chappelman John, Roborough 1728 W
Julian, Witheridge 1570 W
Chappleman Michael, Clovelly 1758 W

Chappellan Richard, Rackenford 1666 A
Chapington, Chappington
Chapinton alias Chapell ..., South Molton 1604 [W]
Hugh, South Molton 1587 W
Chappington Samuel, South Molton 1696 A
Chaple see Chapell
Chapleman see Chapelman
Chaplen see Chaplin
Chaplin, Chaplen, Chapley, Chaplyn, Chapplein
..., Fremington 1610 [W]
Chapplein Alice, Arlington 1570 W
Elizabeth, Marwood 1665 W
Chaplyn Henry, Woolfardisworthy 1620 [W]
Joan, Marwood 1670 W
Chaplen John, Marwood 1564 [W]
Chapley John, Marwood 1606 [W] "Chaplyn" in register;
    forename blank in Ms; supplied from parish register
Chaplyn John, Marwood 1620 W
Chaplyn Mary, Stoodleigh 1748 A
Chaplyn Roger, Fremington 1634 A
Chaplyn Simon, Marwood 1666 W
Chaplyn see Chaplin
Chapple see Chapell
Chapplein see Chaplin
Chapman, Chepman
..., Alverdiscott 1615 [W]
Ann, Buckland Brewer 1725 W
Ann, Northam, widow 1800 W
Arthur, East Putford 1641 [W]
Edward, Buckland Brewer 1590 [W]
Edward, Monkleigh 1728 A
Edward, Monkleigh 1796 W
Elizabeth, High Bickington 1674 W
Elizabeth, Petrockstowe 1775 W
Emanuel, Northam 1743 A
Emanuel, Northam 1778 W
George, Alverdiscott 1645 W
James, Alverdiscott 1622 [W]
John, Alverdiscott 1585 W
John, Petrockstowe 1626 [W]
John, Alverdiscott, snr. 1628 [W]
John, Great Torrington 1703 A
John, Molland 1725 W
John, Great Torrington 1782 A
Mary, Northam 1682 W
Michael, Shebbear 1726 A
Michael, Shebbear 1741 A
Nicholas, Buckland Brewer 1593 [W]
Nicholas, Monkleigh, yeoman 1798 W
Nicholas, Monkleigh 1836 W
Richard, Rackenford 1577 W
Richard, Rackenford, snr. 1630 [W]
Richard, Buckland Brewer 1691 W
Richard, Ilfracombe 1761 W
Richard, Northam 1835 W
Chepman Thomas, Hartland 1569 W
Thomas, Rose Ash 1576 A
Chepman Thomas, Winkleigh 1589 W
Chepman Thomas, Rose Ash 1600 W
Thomas, Alverdiscott 1630 [W]
Thomas, Ilfracombe 1748 W
Thomasine, Langtree 1623 [W]
Thomasine, Great Torrington 1707 W
Chepman Walter, Alverdiscott 1579 W
William, Alverdiscott 1569 W
William, Northam 1682 A
William, Rackenford 1733 W
Zachary, Buckland Brewer 1740 W
Chappel see Chapell
Chappelman see Chapelman
Chappell, Chappelle see Chapell
Chappington see Chapington
Chappleman see Chapelman
Chapplestone Francis, Merton 1790 W
Thomas, Merton 1742 A

Charck ..., Georgeham 1601 [W]
  ..., Great Torrington 1613 [W]
  ..., St Giles in the Wood 1614 [W]
  Bernard, St Giles in the Wood 1615 [W]
  John, Shebbear 1609 [W]; forename blank in Ms; supplied
    from parish register
  Philip, Dowland 1615 [W]
Chardon, Charden
  Charden ..., South Molton 1608 [W]
  William, Romansleigh 1690 W
Charley, Charlegh, Charly
  Charlegh Catherine, Knowstone 1577 A
  Elizabeth, Great Torrington 1848 W
  Escott, Kentisbury, yeoman 1806 W
  Grace, Tawstock 1772 A
  Grace, Combe Martin 1843 W
  Hugh, Kentisbury 1716 W
  Hugh, Arlington 1741 W
  James, Chittlehampton 1741 W
  Joan, North Molton 1822 W
  Charly John, Kentisbury 1643 A
  John, Kentisbury 1682 A
  John, Kentisbury 1717 W
  John, Kentisbury 1744 W
  John, Tawstock 1769 A; A dbn 1772
  John, Kentisbury 1781 W
  John, Combe Martin 1835 W and 1838 W
  John, Kentisbury 1843 W
  Margaret, Kentisbury 1756 W
  Martha, Barnstaple 1747 W
  Richard, Combe Martin 1857 W
  Robert, West Buckland 1812 A to Thomas, son
  Thomas, Tawstock 1742 W
  William, Arlington 1720 A
  William, Arlington 1731 A
Charter William, Pilton 1761 W
Chaurnley Rose, Stoodleigh, spinster 1625 [W]
Chave James, Barnstaple 1765 A
Cheavener see Chevener
Chedligh see Chidley
Chedsey, Chedsye
  John, Monkleigh, jnr. 1643 A
Cheek, Cheeke
  Cheeke George, Yarnscombe 1714 W
  Mary, Yarnscombe 1728 W
  Cheeke Thomas, Yarnscombe, snr. 1678 W
  Thomas, Yarnscombe 1745 W
  Thomas, Yarnscombe, yeoman 1813 W to John Milton, first
    cousin
Chelcott see Chilcott
Cheldon see Chaldon
Chepman see Chapman
Cheriton, Cherton
  ..., Clannaborough 1844 W
  Cherton Thomas, Bideford 1713 W
Chester Catherine, Winkleigh 1603 W
  David, Burrington 1669 W
  John, Winkleigh 1587 W
  William, Winkleigh 1606 W
Chestley Robert, Roborough 1716 W
Chetvett Michael, Sheepwash 1632 W
Chevener, Cheavener, Chevenor, Chewner
  Chevener alias Clack ..., Beaford 1606 [W]
  Chevener alias Clarck ..., Heanton Punchardon 1611 [W]
  Chewner alias Clarke Agnes, Hartland 1619 [W]
  Chevener alias Clarke John, Heanton Punchardon 1615 [W]
  Chevenor alias Clark John, Heanton Punchardon 1689 T
  Cheavener Martha, Heanton Punchardon 1582 W
  Chevener alias Clarke Richard, Heanton Punchardon 1605 T
Chibbett, Chibbott
  Chibbett alias Kidner ..., Filleigh 1682 A
  Chibbett alias Kitner Emma 1709 W
  Chibbott Esther, Georgeham 1813 A to Mary Williams and
    Esther Bailey, daughters
Chichester ..., Arlington 1608 [W]

..., Frithelstock 1608 [W]
..., Tawstock, snr. widow of Sir John 1694 W "of Hall" in
  register
..., Shirwell 1707 [W]
Chichester alias Berrie ..., Berrynarbor 1700 or 1790 A
Amesius, Arlington 1577 W
Amesius, Arlington 1622 [W] and 1637 O
Amesius 1708 W
Amy, Barnstaple 1845 W
Ann, Barnstaple 1681 W
Arthur, Barnstaple, knight 1718 W
Barbara, Arlington, widow 1644 W
Christopher, Frithelstock 1594 [W]
Edward, Arlington, jnr. 1590 [W]
George, Georgeham, esquire 1676 W
Gregory, Pilton 1631 [W]
Gregory, East Down 1719 W
Henry, Arlington 1601 W
Henry, Arlington 1635 A
Henry, Bittadon, gentleman 1663 W
Henry, Arlington 1684 W
Joan, Arlington 1596 [W]
Joan, King's Nympton 1692 A
John, Arlington, esquire 1644 W
John, Pilton, baronet 1668 W
John, Arlington 1713 W (2)
Lodovic, Arlington 1703 A
Mary, Arlington 1616 [W]
Mary, Arlington 1631 [W]
Philip, Atherington 1641 A
Richard, High Bickington 1639 A
Robert, Arlington 1622 [W]
Robert, Arlington, gentleman 1677 A
Robert, South Molton 1680 W
Robert, Arlington 1684 A
Robert, Berrynarbor 1730 A
Robert, Shirwell 1741 W
Susanna, Tawstock, lady 1694 W
Chick, Chycke
  Elizabeth, Yarnscombe 1820 W
  George, Yarnscombe 1732 W
  George, Yarnscombe 1823 W
  Chycke Joan, South Molton 1631 [W] and 1632 [W]
  Sarah, Yarnscombe 1827 W
  Thomas, Yarnscombe 1767 A
Chidbolt Thomas, Stoke Rivers 1721 A
Chidley, Chedligh, Chidleigh, Chidlight, Chidsley, Chudleigh,
    Chudley
  Chudley Ann, St Giles in the Wood 1721 A
  Chudley Christopher, Merton 1666 W
  Chudleigh Elizabeth, Zeal Monachorum 1779 W
  Chedligh Ellen, Martinhoe 1573 W
  Chudley Grace, Beaford 1703 W
  Chidleigh John, Beaford 1685 A
  John, Beaford 1703 A
  Chudleigh John, Zeal Monachorum 1769 A
  Joseph, Shebbear 1831 W
  Joseph see also John Wonnacott
  Mary, Great Torrington 1828 W
  Richard, Northam 1627 [W]
  Chidlight Richard, Martinhoe, widower 1671 W
  Chudley Richard, Martinhoe 1671 W
  William, Northam 1725 W
  Chidsley William, Buckland Filleigh or Brewer 1741 W
  Chudley William, Northam 1749 W
Chilcott, Chelcott, Chilcot, Chillcott
  Chilcott alias Comens Agnes, Oakford 1619 [W]
  Amory, South Molton 1711 W
  Chelcott Andrew, North Molton 1613 [W]; forename blank in
    Ms; supplied from parish register
  Elizabeth, South Molton 1794 W
  Chelcott George, Witheridge 1594 [W]
  Chillcott Joan, Witheridge 1596 [W]
  John, West Anstey 1626 [W]
  John, Knowstone, jnr. 1670 W

John, Knowstone, snr. 1672 W
John, Knowstone 1695 A
John, Barnstaple 1719 W
Chilcot Mary, South Molton 1717 W
Richard, Knowstone 1637 W
Richard, Knowstone 1671 A
Robert, Instow 1782 W
Roger, Witheridge 1584 W
Chillcott Sarah, George Nympton 1770 W
Thomas, Witheridge, jnr. 1595 [W]
Thomasine, North Molton 1629 [W]
Chelcott William, Fremington 1588 W
Chelcott alias Comens William, Oakford 1605 W "Chilcott" in
    register; forename blank in Ms; supplied from parish register
Ching, Chin, Chinge, Chyn
    Abraham, Bideford 1709 A
    Chin Agnes, Northam 1716 A
    Chinge Edith, Bideford 1601 W
    Hugh, Clovelly 1823 W
    Humphrey, Bideford 1754 W
    John, Burrington 1801 A
    John, Parkham 1850 W
    Chyn Mary, King's Nympton 1705 W
    Chinge Nicholas, Chittlehampton 1588 W
    Paschal, Bideford 1755 W
    Chin Robert, King's Nympton 1685 [W]
    Samuel, Bideford 1851 W
    Chinge Thomas, Hartland 1606 W
    Thomas, Northam 1669 W
    Chin Thomas, Northam 1731 W and A
    Chin Thomas, Northam 1743 W
    Thomas, South Molton 1747 A
    Thomas, Bideford 1785 A
Chinner, Chyner
    Chyner Robert, Clovelly 1705 A
Chinnock, Chynnock
    Chynnock Hugh, Great Torrington 1617 [W]
Chiswell Joanna, Ilfracombe 1826 W
    John, Ilfracombe 1819 W
Choape see Chope
Cholayshe see Chollishe
Chollacomb, Chollacombe, Chollacome see Challacombe
Chollishe, Cholayshe, Cholles
    James, Lapford 1564 [W]
    John, Coldridge 1588 A
    Cholayshe Margaret, Lapford 1587 W
    Cholles Winifred, Winkleigh 1595 [W]
Cholwill, Cholwell
    Cholwell Grace see Hugh Prust
    Joan wife of John, Weare Giffard 1602 [W]; forename blank in
        Ms; supplied from parish register
    John, Hartland 1602 W
    John, Weare Giffard 1603 [W]; forename blank in Ms;
        supplied from parish register
    John, Buckland Brewer 1607 [W] "Colwell" in register;
        forename blank in Ms; supplied from parish register
    John, Abbotsham 1642 W
    Cholwell John, Buckland Brewer 1665 W
    John, Hartland 1768 W
    Mary, Hartland 1596 [W]
    Mary, Parkham 1735 W
    Nicholas, Hartland 1578 W
    Cholwell Nicholas, Hartland 1692 W
    Richard, Great Torrington 1619 [W]
    Richard, Hartland 1622 [W]
    Cholwell Richard, Bideford 1688 W
    Robert, Chittlehampton 1639 W
    Cholwill Thomas, Hartland 1590 [W]
    Thomas, Hartland, snr. 1637 A and 1640 O
    Thomas, Parkham 1688 A
    Thomas, Abbotsham 1725 A
    Thomas, Hartland 1725 W
    Cholwell William, South Molton 1679 W
    William, Hartland 1732 A

Chope, Choape
    ..., Alwington 1610 [W]
    ..., Buckland Brewer 1611 [W]
    Alice, Bideford 1715 W
    Alice, Bideford 1780 A
    Anthony, Parkham 1578 W
    Anthony, Buckland Brewer 1775 A
    Elizabeth, Bideford 1709 W
    Gertrude, Bideford 1774 W
    Henry, Northam 1671 A
    Henry, Bideford 1719 W
    Jenson, Bideford 1625 [W] and 1626 O
    Jerome, Monkleigh 1626 [W]
    Joan, Bideford 1644 W
    Choape John, Hartland 1617 [W]
    John, Woolfardisworthy 1620 [W]
    Joseph, Bideford 1704 W
    Mary, Bideford 1780 A
    Richard, Bideford 1629 [W]
    Richard, Bideford 1643 W
    Robert, Alwington 1583 W
    Robert, Bideford, snr. 1623 [W]
    Robert, Bideford 1635 A and 1637 O
    Robert, Bideford 1679 W
    Robert, Bideford 1707 W and 1711 W
    Robert, Hartland 1790 W
    Robert, Huntshaw 1826 W
    Robert, Hartland 1837 W
Chorne William, Chulmleigh 1591 [W]
Choug see Chugg
Chrispen, Chrispene, Chrispinge, Chrispyne see Crispin
Christian Cecilia, Little Torrington 1622 [W]
Christmas John, Barnstaple 1737 W
    Margaret, Barnstaple 1726 W and 1736 W
    Margaret, Barnstaple 1747 W
    Susan, Barnstaple 1706 W
Christopher, Christophers
    Christophers Catherine, Barnstaple 1712 W
    John, Barnstaple 1709 A
Chruse see Cruse
Chubb, Chube, Chubbe
    Chubbe Alexander, Roborough 1605 W
    Chube John, Roborough 1587 W
    John, Tawstock 1731 W
    Chubbe Thomas, Atherington 1617 [W]
Chudleigh, Chudley see Chidley
Chugg, Choug
    Anthony, Buckland Filleigh 1824 A to Elizabeth wife of John
        Ley of Great Torrington, gentleman, sister
    Elizabeth, West Down 1849 W
    George, Buckland Filleigh, yeoman 1806 W
    George, Peters Marland, yeoman 1819 A to Elizabeth wife of
        John Ley of Great Torrington, gentleman, sister
    George, Georgeham 1824 W
    George, Ilfracombe 1842 W
    Humphrey, Buckland Filleigh 1740 W
    James, West Down 1832 A to Mary, widow
    John, Kentisbury 1830 W
    John, Mortehoe 1836 W
    Joshua, Kentisbury, schoolmaster 1808 W
    Richard, West Down 1822 W
    Richard, West Down 1837 W
    Robert, East Down 1687 W
    Choug Robert, Northam 1722 A
    Susan, Combe Martin 1846 W
    Thomas, Marwood 1832 W
    Thomas, West Down 1837 W
Chuldon see Chaldon
Churley
    Churley alias Tucker Grace, South Molton 1676 A
    John, Knowstone 1577 W
Churton Mary, Barnstaple 1685 W
    Robert, Barnstaple 1679 A; A dbn 1699
Chycke see Chick
Chyn see Ching

Chyner see Chinner
Chynnock see Chinnock
Clack
    Clack alias Chevener ..., Beaford 1606 [W]
Clampitt see Claypitt
Clapham, Clappam
    Culpepper, Barnstaple 1641 W
    Hume, Barnstaple 1629 [W]
    Rawleigh, Barnstaple 1676 W
    Clappam Richard, Chulmleigh 1569 W
Clapp Robert, North Tawton 1787 A
    William, Rackenford 1701 and 1705 A
Clappam see Clapham
Clarck, Clarcke see Clark
Claril
    Claril alias Morcombe Willmot, High Bickington 1580 W
Clark, Clarck, Clarcke, Clarke, Clearke, Clerke
    ..., Heanton Punchardon 1607 [W]
    ..., Northam 1608 [W]
    Clarcke ..., Chulmleigh 1610 [W]
    Clarck alias Chevener ..., Heanton Punchardon 1611 [W]
    ..., Chittlehampton 1611 [W]
    Clarke alias Holmes ..., Winkleigh 1679 W
    Clarke alias Chewner Agnes, Hartland 1619 [W]
    Clarke Alexander, Berrynarbor 1691 W
    Clarke Alice, Chulmleigh 1580 W
    Clarke Alice, Beaford 1625 [W]
    Clarke Alice, Berrynarbor 1745 W
    Ann, Chulmleigh 1663 W
    Clarke Anthony, King's Nympton, butcher 1809 W
    Clarke Catherine, Shirwell 1720 A
    Clarke Catherine, Martinhoe 1741 W
    Clarke David, High Bickington 1592 [W]
    David, Chulmleigh 1644 W
    Clarke alias Langdon Dorothy, Georgeham 1681 W
    Dorothy, Barnstaple 1702 W
    Edward, Chittlehampton 1735 W
    Clarke Edward, Chittlehampton 1771 A
    Clarke Eleanor, Heanton Punchardon 1580 W
    Clarke Elizabeth, Great Torrington 1621 [W]
    Clarke Elizabeth, Chulmleigh 1633 W
    Clarke alias Langdon Elizabeth, Georgeham 1670 W
    Clarke Elizabeth, Chittlehampton 1803 W
    Elizabeth, Berrynarbor, widow 1808 W
    Clarke Elizabeth, Yarnscombe 1842 W
    Clarke Elizabeth, Tawstock 1857 W
    Clarke alias Holmes Fortune, Winkleigh 1667 W
    George, Heanton Punchardon 1677 W
    Clarke George, Barnstaple 1690 W
    George, St Giles in the Wood 1698 A
    George, Bideford 1801 A
    George, Alwington 1818 W
    Hannah, South Molton 1738 W
    Clarke Henry, St Giles in the Wood 1581 W
    Clarke Henry, Coldridge 1746 W
    Clarke Henry, Yarnscombe 1837 W
    Henry, Bideford 1848 W
    Clarke Hugh, Roborough 1769 W
    Clarke Hugh, Chittlehampton 1799 W
    Hugh, Chittlehampton, yeoman 1806 A
    Clarke James, Great Torrington, clerk 1638 A
    Clark alias Bowden James, Berrynarbor 1691 W
    Clarke James, South Molton 1692 A
    James, Heanton Punchardon 1707 W
    Clarke James, Berrynarbor 1717 W
    James, South Molton 1758 W
    Clarke James, North Molton 1767 W
    James, Rose Ash 1852 W
    Clarke Jane, Coldridge 1746 A
    Clarke Joan, Heanton Punchardon 1623 [W]
    Clarke Joan and John, Woolfardisworthy 1630 [W]
    Clarke John, Dowland 1587 W
    Clearke John, Chawleigh 1597 [W]
    Clarcke alias Chevener John, Heanton Punchardon 1615 [W]
    Clarke John, Great Torrington 1623 [W]

Clarke John, West Worlington 1624 [W]
Clarke John, Great Torrington 1638 A
Clark alias Langdon John, Georgeham 1670 W
Clarke John, Northam 1682 W
Clarke John, Heanton Punchardon 1686 W
Clark alias Chevenor John, Heanton Punchardon 1689 W
Clarke John, ship *Lyn* 1748 W
John, Yarnscombe 1752 W
John, Shirwell 1753 W
Clarke John, St Giles in the Wood 1782 W
John, Bideford 1787 W
John, Chittlehampton 1788 W
John, Ashreigney, jnr. 1803 W
John, Chittlehampton, husbandman 1809 W
Clarke John, Yarnscombe 1813 W
Clarke John, Ashreigney 1821 W
Clarke John, Chittlehampton 1822 A to Elizabeth, widow and
    Elizabeth wife of Robert Middleton of East Worlington, jnr.,
    daughter
John, Alwington 1827 A
Clarke John, St Giles in the Wood 1833 A to Elizabeth, widow
Clarke alias Longden John alias Audrey, Great Torrington
    1791 A (John Clarke alias Awdry Longden)
Clarke John and Joan, Woolfardisworthy 1630 [W]
Joseph, Great Torrington 1702 W
Clarke Joseph, Chulmleigh 1726 W
Clarke Margaret, Chittlehampton 1620 [W]
Clarcke Martha, Heanton Punchardon 1618 [W]
Clarke Mary, Berrynarbor 1739 W
Clarke Mary, St Giles in the Wood 1786 W
Mary, Bideford 1801 A
Clarke Nicholas, Berrynarbor 1638 W
Clarke Nicholas, Ilfracombe 1719 W
Clarke Nicholas, Berrynarbor 1738 A
Clarke Nicholas, Combe Martin 1740 A
Clarke Paul, St Giles in the Wood 1680 A
Clarke Peter, Northam 1620 [W]
Clarke alias Crocker Peter, Barnstaple 1623 [W]
Clarke Rachel, Yarnscombe 1771 W
Clarke Richard, Frithelstock 1597 [W]
Clarke alias Chevener Richard, Heanton Punchardon 1605 W
Clarke Richard, Eggesford 1633 A
Richard, Witheridge 1680 A
Clarke Richard, Georgeham 1688 W
Clarke Richard, Witheridge 1695 A
Clarke Richard, Bideford 1744 [W]
Clarke Robert, Roborough 1776 W
Clarke Robert, Bideford 1846 W
Clarke Robert, Buckland Brewer 1857 W
Clarke Roger, Great Torrington 1637 W
Clerke Roger, Frithelstock 1730 A
Clarke Samuel, Bideford 1734 W
Clarke Samuel, Barnstaple 1848 W
Clarke Sarah, Charles 1758 W
Susan, Dolton 1670 W
Clarke Thomas, Marwood 1577 W
Clarke Thomas, Great Torrington 1591 [W]
Clarcke Thomas, St Giles in the Wood 1602 W
Clarke Thomas, Chittlehampton 1625 [W]
Clarke Thomas, Witheridge 1724 A
Clarke Thomas, Berrynarbor 1729 W
Clarke Thomas, Charles 1747 W
Clarke Thomas, Berrynarbor 1815 W; A dbn
Thomas, Bideford 1818 A to Sarah, widow
Clarke Thomasine, Ashreigney 1819 A
Clarke Walter, Barnstaple 1580 W
Clearke William, Georgeham 1598 [W]
Clarke William, St Giles in the Wood 1619 [W]
Clarke William, Clovelly 1631 [W]
Clarke William, Barnstaple 1632 [W]
Clearke William, West Down 1692 A
Clarke William, Molland 1758 W
William, Horwood 1759 W
William, North Tawton 1766 W
Clarke William, East Buckland 1769 A

Clarke William, Horwood 1803 W
Clarke William, Chittlehampton 1804 A
William, Newton Tracey 1825 W
Clarke William, Bideford 1842 W
Clarkson Betty, Great Torrington 1836 W
John, Great Torrington 1818 W
Clase ..., South Molton 1614 [W]
Roger, Chittlehampton 1617 [W]
Clasey Gertrude, Satterleigh 1625 [W]
Clatworthy see Clotworthy
Claw, Clawe, Clow, Clowe
Clow Bridget, Northam 1665 W
Clawe Eleanor, Great Torrington 1603 W
Clawe George, Hartland 1598 [W]
Michael, Great Torrington 1602 W
Nicholas, Northam 1611 [W] "Clowe" in register; forename
blank in Ms; supplied from parish register
Richard, Northam 1621 [W]
Clawe Richard, Northam 1634 A
Clawe Thomas, Great Torrington 1596 [W]
Clawetham William, Alverdiscott 1640 O
Clay Benjamin, East Worlington, clerk 1852 A to Edward
William, Petrockstowe 1791 A
Zachariah, Petrockstowe 1827 W
Claypitt, Clampitt, Clepit, Clepitt, Clippett, Clyppet
Clampitt Bridget, Bideford 1745 A
Clepitt Edward, West Down 1606 [W]; forename blank in Ms;
supplied from parish register
Clyppet Giles, Alwington 1644 A
Clepit Hugh, Alwington 1710 A
Clepitt John, Alwington 1590 [W]
Clippett John, Alwington 1662 W
Clippett Philip, Alwington 1620 [W]
Clippett Richard, Alwington 1703 W
Clayshe John, Bow 1631 [W]
Clayton William, Bideford 1711 W
Clearke see Clark
Cleave, Cleife, Cleive
Cleive Benjamin, Knowstone 1622 [W]
Cleife Eleanor, Martinhoe 1632 [W]
Cleife Elizabeth, Martinhoe 1637 A
Elizabeth, South Molton 1673 W
Cleife Francis, Martinhoe 1620 [W]
Cleive Henry, Oakford 1627 [W]
Cleife John, Knowstone 1619 [W]
John, Great Torrington 1828 W
Cleive Roger, South Molton 1620 [W]
Cleavland John, Northam 1669 A
Clegge William, Great Torrington 1640 [W]
Cleife, Cleive see Cleave
Cleland
Cluland Jane, Northam 1677 W
Clement, Clemens, Clements, Clemett
..., Chawleigh 1610 [W]
Clement alias Ford ..., Barnstaple 1678 A
Abraham, Alwington 1826 W
Clements Agnes, Great Torrington 1713 W
Ann, Monkleigh 1637 W
Anthony, Little Torrington 1578 W
Clemens Anthony, St Giles in the Wood 1806 A*
Clement alias Ford Christian, Barnstaple 1678 [W]
Christopher, Bulkworthy 1681 A
Christopher, Bulkworthy 1708 A
Christopher, Weare Giffard 1743 W
Clemett Christopher, Newton St Petrock 1795 W
Cyprian, Barnstaple 1621 [W]
David, Georgeham 1714 W
Clements Edward, Iddesleigh 1695 W
Elizabeth, Georgeham 1739 W
Clemett Francis, Newton St Petrock 1812 A to William, son
Clements Francis, Langtree 1820 W
George, Chawleigh 1522 [W]
George, Chawleigh 1597 [W]
George, Georgeham 1774 W
Grace, Ilfracombe 1846 W

Henry, Georgeham 1684 W
Joan, Frithelstock 1589 W
Joan, Challacombe 1821 W
Clemente John, Winkleigh 1572 W
John, Monkleigh 1639 A
John, Ilfracombe 1758 A
John, Georgeham 1782 W
John, High Bray 1807 W
Clemens John, St Giles in the Wood 1845 W
Joseph, Parkham, yeoman 1823 A to Mary, widow
Lawrence, Frithelstock 1704 W
Margaret, Ilfracombe 1605 W
Philip, Monkleigh 1613 [W]; forename blank in Ms; supplied
from parish register
Robert, Cruwys Morchard 1620 [W]
Robert, Barnstaple 1731 W
Roger, Chawleigh 1602 [W]; forename blank in Ms; supplied
from parish register
Roger, Lapford 1682 W
Clements Samuel, Great Torrington 1816 W
Stephen, Frithelstock 1586 W
Susan, Barnstaple 1734 W
Thomas, Hartland 1565 [W]
Thomas, Bideford 1629 [W] and 1632 [W]
Thomas, Chawleigh 1643 W
Thomas, Barnstaple 1713 W
Thomas, Great Torrington 1783 W
Thomas see also John Richards
Walter, Barnstaple 1716 W
William, Barnstaple 1625 [W]
William, Frithelstock 1664 W
Clemett William, Newton St Petrock, blacksmith 1808 W
Winifred, Newton St Petrock 1808 [W]
Clench see Clinch
Clepit, Clepitt see Claypitt
Clerke see Clark
Clevanger, Clevenger
Edward, Filleigh 1664 [W]
Clevenger Joan, Chittlehampton 1601 W
Cleverdon, Cleverton, Cliffardon, Cliverton
..., Northam 1602 [W]
..., Clovelly 1608 and 1609 [W]
Ann, Shebbear 1594 [W]
Anthony, St Giles in the Wood 1591 [W]
Anthony, Huntshaw 1669 W
Anthony, Great Torrington 1684 A
Anthony, Great Torrington 1719 W
Anthony, Clovelly 1731 W
Bridget, Hartland 1727 W
Catherine, Abbotsham 1587 W
Catherine, Langtree 1617 [W]
Edmund, Newton St Petrock 1734 A
Elizabeth, Welcombe 1663 W
Elizabeth, Parkham 1677 W
Elizabeth, Hartland 1720 A
Grace, Hartland 1771 W
Henry, Great Torrington 1663 W
Henry, Parkham 1668 A
Henry, Woolfardisworthy 1753 W
Henry, East Putford 1834 W
Joan, Parkham 1641 A
Cleverton John, Parkham 1577 W
John, Shebbear 1588 W
John, Clovelly 1601 W
John, Parkham 1633 W
John, Parkham 1692 W
John, Newton St Petrock 1706 A
John, Buckland Brewer 1740 W
John, Hartland 1767 A
John, Hartland 1814 W
Lawrence, Hartland 1769 W
Margaret, Hartland 1719 W
Cliverton Martha, Buckland Brewer 1768 W
Mary, East Putford 1680 W
Mary, Woolfardisworthy 1851 A

Richard, Clovelly 1572 A
Robert, Parkham 1599 [W]
Robert, Hartland 1661 W
Robert, Woolfardisworthy 1663 A
Robert, Hartland 1682 A
Robert, Hartland 1691 W
Cliverton Susan, Hartland 1768 A
Thomas, Northam 1700 W
Thomas, Clovelly 1712 W
Thomas, Hartland 1720 W
Thomas, Hartland 1744 W
Thomas, Clovelly 1745 W
Thomas, Hartland 1777 A
Thomas, Woolfardisworthy 1818 A to Thomas of
   Broadwoodwidger, son
Thomas, Woolfardisworthy 1840 W
Thomas, East Putford 1847 W
Cliffardon William, Barnstaple 1617 [W]
William, Welcombe 1663 W
William, Woolfardisworthy 1672 W
Cleverton William, Buckland Brewer 1755 W
William, Hartland 1763 A
Willmot, St Giles in the Wood 1625 [W]
Willmot, Woolfardisworthy 1712 W
Zacharias, Littleham (near Bideford) 1725 [W]
Clibbett, Clibbitt Ann, Georgeham 1798 W
Catherine, Northam 1820 W
Esther, Georgeham 1813 A
John, Northam 1757 W
Clibbitt John, Georgeham 1814 W
Philip, Northam 1820 W
William, Northam 1811 W
Clibbitt William, Northam, ship builder 1857 A to William,
   ship builder, son
Cliffardon see Cleverdon
Clifford ..., Great Torrington 1603 [W]
Clifford alias Evans ..., Wembworthy 1691 W
Clifford alias Blagdon John, Hartland 1600 W
John, Parkham 1612 [W]; forename blank in Ms; supplied
   from parish register
Mathew, Wembworthy 1686 A
Clifton James, Bideford 1835 W
Phillippa, Bideford 1720 A
Clinch, Clench, Clinche
..., Creacombe 1610 [W]
Clinche Henry, Barnstaple 1628 [W]
Clench Mary, Barnstaple 1820 W
Clinger, Clynger
Clynger Beaton, Kentisbury 1599 [W]
Clippett see Claypitt
Clive, Clyfe, Clyve
Clyfe John, Martinhoe 1587 W
Clyfe Stephen, Yarnscombe 1587 W
Thomasine, Great Torrington 1851 W
Clyve Walter, Barnstaple 1579 W
Cliverton see Cleverdon
Cloak John, Parkham 1767 W
Margaret, Parkham 1772 W
Clogg, Cloge, Clogge, Cloug, Clougg, Clugg
Clogge ..., Twitchen 1605 [W]
Clogge Alice, Alverdiscott 1573 W
Andrew, Combe Martin 1739 W
Charity, Alwington 1694 A
Edward, Combe Martin 1718 W
Grace, Combe Martin 1795 A
Henry, Combe Martin 1769 W
Henry, Combe Martin 1820 W
James, Ilfracombe 1836 W
Clogge Joan, Twitchen 1591 [W]
Cloge John, Twitchen 1567 W
Cloge John, Fremington 1581 A
Clougg John, West Down 1759 W
Clugg John, Mortehoe 1782 W
Mary, Combe Martin, widow 1811 A
Clougg Mary, West Down 1828 W

Clogge Nicholas, Shirwell 1610 [W]; forename blank in Ms;
   supplied from parish register
Nicholas, Combe Martin, yeoman 1848 A to Nicholas of
   Barnstaple, son
Philip, Tawstock 1696 A
Clogge Richard, Alwington 1625 [W]
Richard, Combe Martin 1697 A
Richard, Combe Martin 1768 W
Richard, Combe Martin 1816 W
Clogge Roger, West Anstey 1590 [W]
Sarah, North Molton 1664 W
Sarah, Puddington 1670 A
Thomas, Bondleigh 1709 W
Clougg Thomas, Tawstock 1729 W
Timothy, Combe Martin 1779 W
Timothy, Combe Martin, yeoman 1846 A to Nicholas, brother
Clogge Walter, Combe Martin 1628 [W]
Walter, Combe Martin 1695 A
Clogge William, Twitchen, jnr. 1597 [W]
Clogge William, Combe Martin 1630 [W]
Clogge William, Great Torrington 1639 W
William, Twitchen, snr. 1642 W
Clogge William, Combe Martin 1672 W
Clougg William, Marwood 1729 W
Clougg William, Ashford 1737 W
Clougg William, Combe Martin 1743 W
Willmot, Pilton 1670 W
Clorigg William, West Down 1810 A
Clotham Thomas, South Molton 1588 A
Clotton Mary, Chittlehampton 1721 A
Clotworthy, Clatworthy, Clottworthie, Clotworthie
..., Burrington 1601 A
..., South Molton 1605 and 1607 [W]
Clotworthie ..., South Molton 1608 [W]
..., North Molton 1609 [W]
..., Meshaw 1632 [W]
Agnes, Meshaw 1667 A
Clotworthie Alice, Burrington 1587 A
Clotworthie Anthony, South Molton 1583 A
Clotworthie Anthony, South Molton 1584 W
Arthur, South Molton 1637 A
Arthur, Coldridge 1665 A
Bartholomew, Meshaw 1626 [W]
Catherine, South Molton 1727 W
Clotworthie Edward, South Molton 1599 [W]
Clotworthie Elizabeth, West Worlington 1594 [W]
Elizabeth, Chulmleigh 1666 W
Elizabeth, South Molton, spinster 1671 W
Elizabeth, Burrington 1686 W
Elizabeth, Chittlehampton 1704 W
Clatworthy Elizabeth, Oakford 1780 [W]
Grace, North Molton 1697 A
Clottworthie Henry, Stoke Rivers 1595 [W]
Humphrey, South Molton 1670 A and O
Humphrey, Chittlehampton 1702 W
James, Winkleigh 1685 W
Clotworthie Joan, Burrington 1586 A
Clatworthy Joan, Oakford 1770 W
Clotworthie John, Burrington 1577 W
Clotworthie John, North Molton 1591 W
Clotworthie John, Burrington 1591 [W]
John, Barnstaple 1607 [W]; forename blank in Ms; supplied
   from parish register
John, George Nympton 1636 [W]
John, Rashleigh 1636 A
John, West Worlington 1639 W
John, Winkleigh 1664 W
Clatworthy John, Winkleigh 1724 W
Clatworthy John, Oakford 1776 W
John, Zeal Monachorum 1826 W
Clatworthy John, Filleigh 1856 W
Joseph, Burrington 1679 W
Joseph, Burrington 1698 W
Clotworthie Lawrence, Berrynarbor 1579 W
Clatworthy Lawrence, Oakford 1757 W

Mary, South Molton 1680 W
Nicholas, Bratton Fleming 1627 [W]
Paschal, Wembworthy 1639 W
Philip, West Worlington 1680 W
Robert, South Molton 1616 [W]
Robert, South Molton 1673 W and 1678 A
Simon, Wembworthy 1630 [A]
Clatworthy Simon, South Molton 1755 A
Susan, Winkleigh 1729 W
Thomas, Wembworthy 1574 W
Thomas, South Molton 1605 W
Thomas, Zeal Monachorum 1670 W
Thomas, Brushford 1683 W
Thomas, North Tawton 1832 W
Thomasine, South Molton 1624 [W]
William, West Worlington 1592 [W]
William, Wembworthy 1639 W
William, West Buckland 1664 W
William, Woolfardisworthy 1670 A (2)
William, Winkleigh 1679 A
Clatworthy William, Winkleigh 1734 A
Cloug, Clougg see Clogg
Cloutman, Cloteman, Cloudman, Clouteman, Clowman,
   Clowteman, Clowtman, Cloydman
Clouteman ..., Stoke Rivers 1601 A
Clowtman Arthur, Trentishoe 1702 A
Clowteman Joan, Stoke Rivers 1605 W
Clowtman Joan, Combe Martin 1625 [W]
Cloteman alias Clowman John, South Molton 1590 [W]
Clowman alias Cloteman John, Northam 1590 [W]
Cloudman or Cloydman John, Marwood 1703 W
John, Bideford 1741 A
John, Hartland 1766 A
Cloutman Lawrence, Pilton 1705 A
Cloutman Lawrence, Pilton 1755 A
Cloutman Margaret, Kentisbury 1664 W
Clowtman Morgan, Martinhoe 1682 A
Clowtman Richard, Pilton 1629 [W]
Cloutman Richard, Marwood 1717 W
Cloutman Thomas, Kentisbury 1663 A
Clowman alias Clowteman William, Pilton 1593 [W]
Clowtman William, Ashford 1625 [W]
Cloverwhaw William, Alverdiscott 1636 A
Clow, Clowe see Claw
Clowman, Clowteman, Clowtman, Cloydman see Cloutman
Clugg see Clogg
Cluland see Cckleland
Clyfe see Clive
Clynger see Clinger
Clyppet see Claypitt
Clyve see Clive
Coake see Cock
Coale see Cole
Coape see Copp
Coarden ..., Huntshaw 1607 [W]
Coateman John, Bideford 1636 A
Coates, Coats, Coattes, Coatts, Coite, Cote, Cotts
   Coite ..., Chulmleigh 1606 [W]
   Coatts Agnes, Lynton, widow 1607 [W]; forename blank in
     Ms; supplied from parish register
   Coats Alexander, Pilton 1718 W
   Anthony, Ilfracombe 1663 W
   Bartholomew, Ilfracombe 1617 [W]
   Catherine, Ilfracombe 1641 W
   Christopher, West Down 1701 W
   Coats David, Lynton 1596 [W]
   David, Lynton 1621 [W]
   Coatts Edmund, Ilfracombe 1599 [W]
   Coatts Edward, Countisbury 1599 [W]
   Elizabeth, West Down 1629 [W]
   Elizabeth, Ilfracombe 1710 W
   George, West Down 1731 W
   Coats George, Ilfracombe 1746 W
   George, Ilfracombe, schoolmaster 1803 A
   Coats George, Ilfracombe 1847 W

George and Mary, Lynton 1629 [W]
Grace, Barnstaple 1730 A
Cote alias Nethercot Henry, Ilfracombe 1578 W
Henry, West Down 1699 W
Coattes Humphrey, West Down 1617 [W]
Cote Jane, Yarnscombe 1718 A
Coats Jane, Ilfracombe 1798 A*
Joan, West Down 1587 W
Coatts Joan, Lynton 1609 [W]; forename blank in Ms;
   supplied from parish register
Joan, West Down 1644 [W]
Coats Joan, Barnstaple 1770 W
John, Lynton 1584 W
Coatts John, Ilfracombe 1610 [W]; forename blank in Ms;
   supplied from parish register
John, Lynton 1620 [W]
Coattes John, Lynton 1672 W
John, West Down 1719 W
Coats John, Berrynarbor 1747 A
Coats John, Barnstaple 1750 W
Coats John, West Down 1819 W
Coats John, West Down 1829 W
Coats John, West Down 1835 W
Coats Joseph, Georgeham 1844 A to George of Ilfracombe and
   Robert of Combe Martin, brothers
Coats Martha, Ilfracombe 1763 A
Mary, Ilfracombe 1699 W
Mary and George, Lynton 1629 [W]
Peter, West Down 1624 [W]
Peter, West Down 1686 A
Peter, West Down 1694 W
Coats Peter, West Down 1756 W
Coats Peter, West Down 1790 W
Coats Peter, West Down 1858 A
Cotts Philip, West Down 1577 W
Philip, West Down 1642 A
Philip, West Down 1644 W
Coats Philip, Marwood 1765 W
Richard, Northam 1620 [W]
Coats Richard, West Down 1720 W
Coats Richard, Ilfracombe 1749 A
Coats Richard, West Down 1817 W
Coats Richard, West Down 1834 W
Cottes Robert, Lynton 1580 W
Robert, Marwood 1623 [W] and O
Coats Robert, West Down 1782 W
Coats Robert, West Down, yeoman 1814 A to Ann, widow
Roger, Lynton 1623 [W]
Coats Ruth, Pilton 1720 A
Thomas, Ilfracombe 1671 W
Thomas, West Down 1677 W
Coats Thomas, Georgeham 1825 A
Walter, West Down 1680 A
Walter, Ilfracombe 1691 W
Coatts William, Ilfracombe 1605 W
Coats William, Lynton 1780 W
Cote alias Nethercot Willmot, Ilfracombe 1578 W
Coatinge Martha, Littleham (near Bideford) 1675 A
Coats, Coattes, Coatts see Coates
Cobbledick, Cobeldick
   Christopher, Frithelstock 1762 W
   John, Frithelstock 1725 W
   Cobeldick John, Newton St Petrock 1853 W
   William, Frithelstock 1755 W
Cobcraft Miles, Great Torrington 1602 [W]
Cobeldick see Cobbledick
Cobley, Cobly
   ... 1640 [W]
   Alice, East Worlington 1591 [W]
   Andrew, East Worlington 1814 W
   Andrew, Chulmleigh 1831 A to Ann, widow
   Augustine, East Worlington 1572 W
   Edward, Woolfardisworthy 1621 [W]
   Edward, East Worlington 1689 W
   Edward, Witheridge 1757 A

Elizabeth, East Worlington, sp. 1816 A to William, gentleman, brother
Elizabeth, Thelbridge 1830 A to James Jackson and Edward Riccard of South Molton, not relatives
George, East Worlington, snr. 1672 W and 1680 A
George, East Worlington, snr. 1753 W
Cobly George, East Worlington 1767 A
George, East Worlington 1780 W
George, Thelbridge 1824 W
Giles, Pilton 1623 [W]
Jacob, East Worlington 1783 W
Jacob, East Worlington, yeoman 1809 W and 1811 W
Jacob, Chulmleigh 1841 W
Coble John, Barnstaple 1573 A
Coblie John, Thelbridge 1588 W
John, Witheridge 1603 W
John, Atherington 1622 W
John, Woolfardisworthy (East or West), snr. 1625 [W]
John, Knowstone 1639 W and 1640 [W]
John, Burrington 1670 A and 1671 O
John, South Molton 1679 W
John, East Worlington 1753 W
John, Chulmleigh 1820 W
John, Chulmleigh 1835 A to Jacob, father
Margaret, South Molton 1688 W
Margaret, East Worlington 1705 W
Margaret, Bow 1739 W
Mary, East Worlington 1817 W
Mary, Chulmleigh 1841 W
Philip, Heanton Punchardon 1589 W
Robert, South Molton 1563 W
Robert, Burrington 1573 W
Robert, Bow 1669 A and O
Roger, Burrington 1615 [W]
Thomas, South Molton 1626 [W]
Cobly Thomas, Kentisbury 1669 O
William, South Molton 1588 A
William, Cheldon 1661 W
William, East Worlington 1824 A to Joan Greenslade of South Molton, sister
William, East Worlington 1832 A to Thomas Comins of Witheridge, guardian to nephew and nieces
Cobner Edward, Northam 1696 W
Elizabeth, Northam 1736 W
Cobner or Colmer Mary, Northam 1718 W
Cobner alias Quick Susan, Northam 1673 W and A
Cock, Coake, Cocke, Cocks
..., Northam 1610 [W]
Cocke ..., Heanton Punchardon 1615 [W]
Agnes, Shirwell 1611 [W]; forename blank in Ms; supplied from parish register
Cocke or Crocke Alice, South Molton 1574 W
Cocke Ambrose, Georgeham 1639 A
Ann, Ilfracombe 1763 W
Ann, South Molton 1843 W
Anthony, Chulmleigh 1676 W
Anthony, Georgeham 1701 W
Bartholomew, Heanton Punchardon 1643 W
Benjamin, Bideford 1698 A
Dennis, Georgeham 1692 W
Cocke Elizabeth, Heanton Punchardon 1625 [W]
Cocke Elizabeth, Heanton Punchardon, snr. 1626 [W] and 1628 O
Elizabeth, Georgeham 1728 A
Elizabeth, Great Torrington 1753 W
Elizabeth, Great Torrington 1771 W
Elizabeth, Winkleigh 1823 W
Coake Francis, Hartland 1696 A
Francis, Chulmleigh 1733 W
George, Fremington, widower 1610 [W]; forename blank in Ms; supplied from parish register
George, Chulmleigh 1690 A
George, Chulmleigh, yeoman 1800 W
George, George Nympton, butcher 1803 W
Grace, Chulmleigh 1705 W

Cocke Harry, Abbotsham 1587 W
Cocke Henry, Arlington 1623 [W]
Hugh, St Giles in the Wood 1727 W
Cocke James, Northam 1624 [W]
Cocks James, Georgeham 1681 A
James, Northam 1700 W
James, St Giles in the Wood 1763 W
James, St Giles in the Wood 1791 W
Cocke Joan, Northam 1621 [W]
Joan, Marwood 1661 W
Joan, Great Torrington 1728 A
Cocke John, Braunton 1573 W
Cocke John, South Molton 1573 W
Cocke John, Buckland Brewer 1582 A
Cocke John, East Putford 1582 A
Cocke John, Marwood 1586 W
Cocke John, Hartland 1587 A
Cocke John, Northam 1622 [W] and 1624 W
John, Chulmleigh 1687 W
John, High Bickington 1691 A
John, Ilfracombe 1695 W
John, Marwood 1724 W (2)
John, Ilfracombe 1732 A
John, Great Torrington 1749 W
John, Meshaw 1790 W
John, Meshaw, yeoman 1800 W
John, Weare Giffard 1827 W
John, Northam 1845 W
John, Shebbear 1845 W
Margaret, Marwood 1688 W
Mark, Fremington 1716 W
Cocke Mary, Marwood 1620 [W]
Mary, Barnstaple 1701 W and 1711 W
Mary, Trentishoe 1716 A
Mary, Fremington 1754 A
Mary, Chulmleigh 1778 W
Mary, South Molton 1798 W
Mary, St Giles in the Wood 1801 W
Mary, Weare Giffard 1847 A; A dbn
Mary see also Richard Lloyd
Mathew, Roborough 1843 W
Cocke Michael, Fremington 1563 W
Cocke Nicholas, Georgeham 1636 W
Nicholas, Barnstaple 1701 W
Nicholas, Georgeham 1729 W
Philip, Marwood 1614 [W] "Cooke" in register; forename blank in Ms; supplied from parish register
Cocke Philip, Northam 1633 W
Cock alias Grendon Philip, Mariansleigh 1695 [W]
Prudence, Instow 1662 W
Cocke Richard, Fremington 1583 W
Richard, Molland 1663 A
Cocke Robert, Shirwell 1639 W
Roger, Chulmleigh 1691 W
Roger, King's Nympton 1712 W
Roger, Atherington 1726 A
Roger, Chulmleigh 1747 A
Roger, South Molton, yeoman 1804 W
Roger, Great Torrington 1805 A
Roger, Meshaw, yeoman 1811 W
Roger, South Molton 1826 A to George, brother
Theophilus, St Giles in the Wood 1835 W
Thomas 1583 A
Cocke Thomas, Hartland 1597 [W]
Cocke Thomas 1597 [W]
Thomas, Northam 1606 W
Thomas, Barnstaple 1682 A
Thomas, Chulmleigh 1700 W
Thomas, Winkleigh 1817 W
Cocke William, Marwood 1567 W
Cocks William, Chulmleigh 1635 A
William, Marwood 1682 W
William, Ilfracombe 1687 W
William, Chulmleigh, snr. 1702 W
William, Instow 1727 W

William, Great Torrington 1828 W
Cock alias Cook William, Hartland 1835 W
Cockaram see Cockram
Cocke see Cock
Cockeram see Cockram
Cockeshead see Coxhead
Cockhill, Cockhil
Agnes, Kentisbury 1622 [W]
Henry, Tawstock 1699 [W]
John, Kentisbury 1618 [W]
John, Fremington 1636 W
Cockhil John, Berrynarbor 1718 W
Marian, Fremington 1644 W
Nicholas, Berrynarbor 1632 [W]
Nicholas, Berrynarbor 1676 W
Reynold, Bideford 1776 W
Richard, Bideford 1706 W
Cockerell Richard, Northam 1743 W
Richard, Bideford 1805 A
Samuel, Bideford 1715 [W]
Thomas, Bideford 1738 A
William, Fremington 1617 [W]
Cocking, Cockings
Joan, North Molton 1748 W
Cockings John, North Molton 1825 W
William, North Molton 1728 A
Cockings William, West Anstey 1775 W
Cockram, Cockaram, Cockeram, Cockrome
Cockeram ... 1600 O account
Cockeram ..., South Molton 1610 [W]
Alexander, ship *Devonshire Tender* 1762 W
Ann, Witheridge 1723 A
Cockeram Christopher, Zeal Monachorum 1595 [W]
Dorothy, Witheridge 1724 A
Edward, Molland, husbandman 1818 A to Susanna Pearse of
  Molland, sister
Cockaram Elizabeth, Meshaw 1782 W
Cockeram Ellen, Chulmleigh 1598 [W]
Cockeram George, South Molton 1629 [W]
George, Witheridge 1731 W
George, Molland 1750 W
George, East Anstey 1830 W
George, Meshaw 1851 W
Grace, Molland 1759 W
Cockeram Henry, Witheridge 1572 W
Cockeram Henry, King's Nympton 1592 [W]
Henry, Witheridge 1669 A
Hugh, Molland 1742 W
Humphrey, Meshaw 1780 W
Humphrey, Meshaw 1814 W
Cockeram Jane, Witheridge 1592 [W]
Cockeram Joan, South Molton 1606 W
Cockeram Joan, Winkleigh, widow 1615 [W]; forename blank
  in Ms; supplied from parish register
Cockerham Joan, Chulmleigh 1705 W
Cawkrame John, East Anstey 1566 W
Cockeram John, Winkleigh 1614 [W]; forename blank in Ms;
  supplied from parish register
Cockeram John, Chulmleigh 1634 A
John, South Molton 1639 W
John, East Anstey 1640 A
Cockeram John, Witheridge 1661 [W]
Cockeram John, Winkleigh 1674 W
Cockeram John, Molland 1703 W
Cockeram John, Coldridge 1706 W
Cockeram John, Winkleigh 1711 W
Cockeram John, Chulmleigh 1713 W
John, East Worlington 1738 A
John, North Molton 1747 A
John, Molland 1770 W
John, Molland 1833 W
John, Meshaw 1853 W
John see also Ann Vicary
Mary, Molland 1844 W
Obadiah, ship *Roy* 1753 A

Cockeram Richard, Winkleigh 1610 [W]; forename blank in
  Ms; supplied from parish register
Cockeram Richard, Martinhoe 1629 [W]
Cockeram Richard, Witheridge 1685 W
Cockeram Richard, Northam 1707 A
Richard, Witheridge 1723 A and 1724 A
Richard, Molland 1742 W
Cockeram Robert, Dolton 1624 [W]
Cockeram Robert, East Anstey 1625 [W]
Robert, West Anstey 1629 A
Robert, Coldridge 1763 W
Cockeram Roger, North Molton 1628 [W]
Cockeram Roger, North Molton 1706 W
Walter, Mariansleigh 1746 A
Cockeram William, King's Nympton 1571 W
Cockeram William, Chulmleigh 1588 W
Cockeram William, Witheridge 1615 [W]; forename blank in
  Ms; supplied from parish register
Cockeram William, Witheridge 1678 A
Cockeram William, Chulmleigh 1681 W
William, East Worlington 1720 W
William, ship *Plymouth* 1748 A
William, Chawleigh, farmer 1850 A to John, farmer, son
Cockrome Willmot, South Molton 1567 W
Cocks see Cock
Cockwell William, Dowland 1807 W
Codeford Nicholas, Roborough 1586 A
Codmore Joan, Petrockstowe 1578 W
Coell see Cole
Coffin, Coffyn
Ann, Alwington 1705 W
Humphrey, Hartland 1685 A
James, Alwington 1663 W
Coffyn James, Alwington 1664 W
James, Alwington 1667 W
John, Alwington, esquire 1608 [W]; forename blank in Ms;
  supplied from parish register
Coffyn John, Bideford, esquire 1622 [W]
Nicholas, Parkham 1669 [W]
Coffyn Richard, Alwington 1635 W
Thomas, Hartland 1812 W
Willmot, Alwington 1584 W
Cogan Ann, Chawleigh 1707 A
Margery, Cheldon 1637 A
Prudence, East Worlington 1637 W
Thomasine, Chawleigh 1715 W
Coham Arscott, Bideford 1778 A; A dbn 1779
Lewis, Great Torrington 1756 W
Richard, Shebbear 1621 [W]
Stephen, Great Torrington 1756 W
William, Bideford 1754 W
Coite see Coates
Cokeman William, Knowstone 1572 W
Cokeshed see Coxhead
Colamer, Colamore see Collamore
Colby Thomas, Barnstaple 1694 W
Thomas, Great Torrington 1774 A
Cole, Coale, Coell, Coles, Coll, Colle, Coul, Coule
..., South Molton 1600 W
..., Bideford 1601 A
..., Knowstone 1609 [W]
..., North Molton 1609 [W] and 1612 [W]
Coles ..., Northam 1610 [W]
Coule Aaron, Ashreigney 1741 W
Aaron, Ashreigney 1797 W
Aaron, Ashreigney 1840 W
Abraham, Ashreigney 1854 W
Agnes, Burrington 1625 [W]
Agnes, Northam 1688 W
Alexander, Lapford 1631 [W]
Alexander, Bideford 1664 W
Coell Alice, Hartland 1577 W
Alice, Hartland 1636 W
Alice, Bideford 1709 W
Ann, High Bickington 1679 W

Ann, Chittlehampton 1733 W
Ann, Northam 1770 A
Ann, Burrington 1831 W
Archelaus, Ashreigney 1753 A
Archelaus, Ashreigney 1803 W
Arthur, Yarnscombe 1671 W
Arthur, East Anstey 1682 A
Arthur, Dolton 1688 A
Christopher, Atherington 1610 [W]; forename blank in Ms;
    supplied from parish register
Christopher, Atherington 1700 W
Christopher, Yarnscombe 1729 W
Clement, Parkham 1621 [W]
Edmund, Combe Martin 1601 W
Coule Edmund, Hartland 1681 W
Coule Edmund, Hartland 1724 W
Edward, Ashreigney 1669 W
Elizabeth, King's Nympton 1594 [W]
Elizabeth, St Giles in the Wood 1645 W
Elizabeth, Westleigh 1751 W
Emanuel, Buckland Brewer 1692 W
Emanuel, Hartland 1785 A
Francis, Ashreigney, snr. 1699 W and 1700 A
Francis, Witheridge 1741 A
Francis, Warkleigh 1769 W
Francis, Witheridge 1 May 1783 W; A dbn 1813
George, Alwington 1641 W
Grace, North Molton 1620 [W]
Gregory, North Molton 1640 W
Henry, Abbotsham 1588 A
Coule Henry, Clovelly 1642 W
Henry, High Bickington 1678 A
Coal Henry, Bideford 1702 W
Henry, Buckland Brewer 1802 W
Henry, Little Torrington 1822 W
Henry, Bideford 1829 A
Honor, Burrington, widow 1848 A to Abraham, yeoman, son
Colle Humphrey, Buckland Brewer 1727 W
Coule Jane, Clovelly 1643 W
Coale Jane, Bideford 1671 W
Jane, Filleigh 1702 W
Joan, North Molton 1579 W
Coule Joan, North Molton 1615 [W]
Joan, East Anstey 1622 [W]
Joan, Atherington 1683 W
Coell John, Combe Martin 1581 W
Colle or Coole John, Hartland 1584 W
Coll John, South Molton 1585 A
Coule John, Atherington 1586 W
John, Combe Martin 1591 [W]
John, Burrington 1619 [W] and 1629 [W]
John, High Bickington 1640 W
John, Ashreigney 1641 A
John, Atherington 1665 W and A
John, North Molton 1672 A
John, Yarnscombe 1690 W
John, Atherington 1692 W
John, South Molton 1694 W
John, Twitchen 1694 W
Coles John, Tawstock 1714 W
Coale John, Great Torrington 1722 A
John, Ashreigney 1747 A
John, Westleigh 1751 W
Coles John, Barnstaple 1757 W
John, Great Torrington 1759 W
Coal John, Ashreigney 1760 W
Coul John, Hartland 1769 W
John, Ashreigney 1777 W
John, Chulmleigh 1790 W
John, South Molton, innholder 1805 W
Coul alias Courtice John, Hartland 1814 W
John, North Molton 1819 W
Coles John, Barnstaple 1822 W
John, South Molton 1829 W
John, Ashreigney 1855 W

Coale Joseph, Warkleigh 1698 W
Coles Joseph, Great Torrington 1710 A
Joseph, Ashreigney 1854 W
Julian, Hartland 1616 [W]
Lawrence, High Bickington 1704 A
Lawrence, Weare Giffard 1754 W
Coles Lawrence, Chulmleigh 1770 A
Lewis, South Molton 1792 A
Mary, Knowstone 1586 W
Mary, North Molton 1622 [W]
Mary, Barnstaple 1681 W
Mary, Beaford 1735 W
Coles Mary, Chulmleigh 1775 A
Mary, South Molton 1814 W
Mary, Witheridge 1822 W
Mary, North Molton 1830 W
More, Newton St Petrock 1603 W
Moses, Ilfracombe, mariner 1815 A to Susanna, widow
Colls Nicholas, Ilfracombe 1565 W
Coles Nicholas, East Down 1715 W
Coles Patrick, Northam 1633 W
Peter, North Molton 1565 W
Peter, North Molton 1620 [W]
Colle Petherick, Hartland 1684 W
Philip, Northam 1624 [W]
Coles Philip, Barnstaple 1645 A
Coles Philip, Barnstaple 1702 A
Philip, Atherington 1705 A
Coll Philip, Roborough 1740 W
Coles Philip, West Down 1751 W
Philip, Burrington 1854 W
Coles Ralph, Bideford 1670 A
Ralph, Ashreigney 1730 W
Colle Richard, Hartland 1586 W
Richard, King's Nympton 1592 [W]
Richard, Parkham 1622 [W]
Richard, Hartland 1628 [W]
Richard, Barnstaple 1634 W
Coles Richard, Great Torrington 1709 A
Richard, Parkham 1712 W
Richard, Roborough 1752 A
Richard, Buckland Brewer 1774 W
Richard, South Molton 1855 W
Robert, Knowstone 1581 W
Colle Robert, Burrington 1588 W
Robert, Yarnscombe 1668 A
Coale Robert, Tawstock 1684 W
Robert, Chulmleigh 1804 W and 1808 W
Coll Roger, Woolfardisworthy 1570 W
Roger, Buckland Brewer 1590 W
Roger, Northam 1593 [W]
Coale Roger, Shirwell 1628 [W]
Samuel, North Molton 1690 W
Samuel, Bideford 1755 W
Samuel, Ashreigney 1820 W
Samuel, Ashreigney 1836 W
Samuel, Burrington 1836 A to Ann, widow
Samuel, Wembworthy 1845 W
Sarah, Huish 1717 A
Coule Sarah, Hartland 1733 A
Sarah, South Molton 1834 W
Colle Simon, Parkham 1579 W
Simon, Atherington 1628 [W]
Simon, Atherington 1643 W
Colles Thomas, Woolfardisworthy 1580 W
Thomas, Parkham 1588 W
Thomas, Mortehoe 1593 [W]
Thomas, Ashreigney 1603 W
Thomas, Fremington 1680 W
Colle Thomas, Chittlehampton 1713 W
Coules Thomas, Ilfracombe 1758 A
Coles Thomas, Mariansleigh 1770 A
Thomas, Buckland Brewer, yeoman 1803 W
Thomas, Chawleigh 1813 W
Thomas, Northam 1856 W

Thomasine, Warkleigh 1622 [W] and 1623 O
Thomasine, Atherington 1635 W
Couls Thomasine, Northam, widow 1706 W
William, Newton St Petrock 1586 I
William, High Bickington 1590 [W]
William, East Anstey 1600 W
William, Buckland Filleigh 1603 W
William, St Giles in the Wood 1632 A
William, King's Nympton 1638 A
William, Northam 1639 A
William, Alwington 1645 W
Cowles William, Northam 1682 W
Coale William, North Molton 1693 W
William, Great Torrington 1737 A
William, Barnstaple 1741 A
Coal William, Langtree 1774 W
William, Ashreigney, yeoman 1802 W
Coles William, St Giles in the Wood 1805 W
William, Bideford 1832 A
William, North Molton 1837 W
William, Ashreigney 1839 W and 1848 W
William, South Molton 1851 W
Willmot, Atherington 1666 W
Coleborne ..., Bow 1590 [W]
Coleman, Collman, Colman, Cowlman
    ..., Bideford 1610 [W]
    ..., Abbotsham 1614 A
    Colman or Collam Ann, Bideford, widow 1673 W
    Ann, Bideford 1697 A
    Catherine, Northam 1662 A
    Coleman alias Bowdon Catherine, Mortehoe 1662 A
    Christopher, Bideford 1637 W
    Emanuel, Northam 1625 [W]
    Colman Gonnet, East Anstey 1580 W
    Henry, East Anstey 1609 [W]; forename blank in Ms; supplied
        from parish register
    Henry, Welcombe 1618 [W]
    Hugh, Langtree 1573 W
    Joan, Bideford, widow 1607 [W]; forename blank in Ms;
        supplied from parish register
    Cowlman John, Langtree 1579 W
    John, Northam 1591 [W]
    John, Langtree 1605 W
    John, Northam 1615 [W] and 1618 O
    John, George Nympton 1621 A
    John, Rose Ash 1671 A
    Colman John, Bideford 1727 W
    Collman Mark, Northam 1639 W
    Colman Mary, Bideford 1729 W
    Philip, Bideford 1629 [W]
    Prudence, South Molton 1617 [W]
    Colman Richard, George Nympton 1591 [W]
    Richard, Bideford 1699 A
    Colman Thomasine, Little Torrington 1577 W
    Thomasine, Langtree 1594 [W]
    William, Thelbridge 1573 [W]
    William, Tawstock 1616 [W]
    William, Bideford 1625 [W] and 1627 O
Colemer see Collamore
Colep Susanna, Barnstaple 1712 W
Coleridge, Colerudge
    John, Woolfardisworthy 1593 [W]
    Colerudge Patrick, Landcross 1573 W
    Robert, Great Torrington 1612 [W]; forename blank in Ms;
        supplied from parish register
Coles see Cole
Colescott, Collocott, Colscott, Coullscott, Coulscott, Cowlescott,
    Cowlscott
    Colscott ..., Goodleigh 1608 [W]
    Cowlescott Ann, Parkham 1623 [W]
    Coulscott Benjamin, Barnstaple 1679 W
    Coulscott Charity, Barnstaple 1669 [W]
    Coullscott Elizabeth, Bideford 1752 A
    George, Woolfardisworthy 1676 A
    Coulscott George, Barnstaple 1721 W and 1739 A

Colscott Henry, Bondleigh 1587 W and A
Colscott John, Bratton Fleming 1577 W
Colscott John, Barnstaple 1583 A account
Colscott John, Barnstaple 1620 [W]
Cowlscott John, Clovelly 1622 [W] and 1624 O
Cowlescott John, Barnstaple 1623 [W]
Coulscott John, Barnstaple 1690 W
Colscott Margery, East Putford 1616 [W]
Colscott Richard, Barnstaple 1621 [W]
Colscott Robert, Buckland Brewer 1598 [W]
Collocott Robert, Shebbear 1806 W
Colescott Rose, Barnstaple 1675 W
Simon, Barnstaple 1638 W
Coulscott Thomasine, Barnstaple 1730 A
Colscott William, Barnstaple 1582 W
Colscott William, Parkham 1615 [W]
Coulscott William, Bideford 1749 A
Coleton, Colliton
    ..., Zeal Monachorum 1607 and 1608 [W]
    Colliton Peter, Zeal Monachorum 1666 W and 1669 O
Colibere see Collibear
Coll see Cole
Collacomb John, Combe Martin 1584 W
Collacott, Collacot ... 1603 [W]
    ..., Abbotsham 1608 [W]
    ..., Bideford 1611 [W]
    Andrew, Shebbear 1680 W
    Cyprian, Sheepwash 1643 A
    David, Shebbear 1695 W
    David, Shebbear 1709 W
    David, Shebbear 1742 W
    Eleanor, Tawstock 1665 A
    Elijah, Bideford 1640 W
    Elizabeth wife of William see Mary Tinson
    Frances, Chawleigh 1680 W
    George, Shebbear 1664 A
    James, Shebbear 1588 A
    Jane, Sheepwash 1799 A
    John, Shebbear 1591 W
    John, Tawstock 1611 [W]; forename blank in Ms; supplied
        from parish register
    John, Shebbear 1673 W
    John, Alwington 1684 W
    John, Abbotsham 1697 A
    John, Shebbear 1731 W
    John, Northam 1784 A
    John, South Molton 1818 W
    Joshua, South Molton 1855 W
    Lewis, Tawstock 1584 W
    Mary, Shebbear 1757 A
    Mathew, Buckland Brewer 1640 W
    Richard, Abbotsham 1596 W
    Robert, Tawstock 1623 [W]
    Robert, Abbotsham 1636 A and 1640 O
    Robert, Shebbear 1642 W
    Collacot Robert, Monkleigh 1733 [W]
    Robert, Shebbear 1763 A
    Robert, Shebbear, yeoman 1806 W
    Sybil, Shebbear 1687 W
    Thomas, Tawstock 1597 [W]
    Thomas, Chittlehampton 1621 [W]
    Thomasine, Tawstock 1597 [W]
    William, Wembworthy 1564 [W]
    William, Abbotsham 1576 W
    William, Abbotsham 1642 W
    William, Pilton 1669 A
    William, Northam, blacksmith 1810 W
    William, Shebbear 1842 W
Collam, Collome
    Collome John, Northam 1695 W
    Collam or Colman Ann, Bideford, widow 1673 W
Collamore, Colamer, Colamore, Colemer, Collemore, Collimore,
    Collmer, Collmore, Collomower
    Collmer Alexander, Barnstaple 1799 W
    Edward, Mortehoe 1776 W and 1788 A

Elizabeth, Bideford 1800 W
Colemer Emma, Fremington, widow 1609 [W]; forename
    blank in Ms; supplied from parish register
Collmore George, Bideford 1750 A
Henry, Ilfracombe 1583 W
Henry, Northam 1718 W
John, Northam 1636 W
John, Northam 1709 W and 1715 W
John, Tawstock 1716 W
John, Bideford 1740 A
Collemore John, Chittlehampton 1745 W
John, Bideford 1765 A
Colamer Margaret, Northam 1588 W
Mary, Northam 1674 W
Peter, Northam 1596 [W]
Robert, Mortehoe 1749 W
Thomas, Northam 1620 [W]
Thomas, Northam 1682 A
Colamore Thomas, Bideford 1718 W
Thomas, Chittlehampton 1741 W
Collomower William, Ilfracombe 1581 A
Collimore William, Mortehoe 1679 W
William, Mortehoe 1695 W
William, Mortehoe 1762 W
Colland, Collande
Collande ..., South Molton 1615 [W]
Cicely, Tawstock 1601 [W]; forename blank in Ms; supplied
    from parish register
John, snr., Tawstock 1602 O forename blank in Ms; supplied
    from parish register
Rose, Tawstock 1574 A
Collander, Collender, Culender
James, Tawstock 1593 [W]
Collander alias Langdon John, Tawstock 1642 W
Culender John, Ashreigney 1792 A
Peter, Georgeham 1619 [W]
Petronell, Georgeham 1620 [W]
Richard, Marwood 1595 [W]
Robert, Chawleigh 1625 [W]
Collander alias Punchard Sarah, Pilton 1670 [W] and A
Collander als Langdon Thomas, Great Torrington 1669 A
Collender Thomas, Tawstock 1688 W
Collard Benjamin, Barnstaple 1796 W
Benjamin, Barnstaple, confectioner 1805 W
George, Burrington 1737 W
John, Witheridge 1705 A
John, Burrington 1737 W
John, Witheridge 1753 A
John, Rackenford 1827 W
Richard, Marwood 1593 [W]
Thomas, North Molton 1837 W
Colle see Cole
Collemore see Collamore
Collender see Collander
Collens see Collins
Colley Catherine, Little Torrington 1813 W
Elizabeth, Barnstaple 1828 W
Henry, Barnstaple proved 22 Sep 1797 W; 1816 A dbn
James, Barnstaple, surgeon 9 Mar 1810 W; re-proved by P.
    Bremridge, guardian to John Bremridge, 20 Nov 1813
Mary, Bideford 1737 W
Mary, Parracombe 1771 W
Rachel, Bideford 1790 W
Susanna, Barnstaple 1795 W
Theodore, Georgeham 1679 A
Colleyne see Collins
Collibear, Colibere, Collibeare, Collibeere, Colliber, Collibies
..., Barnstaple 1611 [W]
..., Fremington 1613 [W]
Alice, Roborough 1643 W
Catherine, Fremington 1616 [W]
Elizabeth, Barnstaple 1729 W
Collibeare Honor, Barnstaple 1681 A
Collibies John, Landcross 1592 [W]
Colibere John, Barnstaple 1622 [W] and 1626 [W]

Collibeere Mary, Barnstaple, widow 1633 [W] & 1637 O
Robert, Barnstaple 1629 [W] and 1631 [W]
Simon, Fremington 1613 [W]; forename blank in Ms; supplied
    from parish register
Simon, Barnstaple 1676 W
Collibeare Sybil, Instow 1628 [W]
William, snr., Fremington 1610 [W]; forename blank in Ms;
    supplied from parish register
William, Instow 1615 [W]
Colibere William, Barnstaple 1620 [W]
Colliber William, Fremington 1725 A
Colibere Willmot, Fremington 1625 [W]
Collier Philip, Buckland Brewer 1613 [W]; forename blank in
    Ms; supplied from parish register
William, Meeth 1595 [W]
Collihole, Colyhole
John, Merton 1835 W
Mary, Merton 1833 W
Colyhole Richard, Winkleigh 1795 A
Richard, Winkleigh 1836 W
Thomas, Lapford, yeoman 1824 W to Elizabeth, widow
William, Winkleigh 1847 W
Collins, Collens, Colleyne, Collinea, Collings, Collyn, Collyns
Collinea Alice, Bratton Fleming 1573 A
Collyn Alice, Bratton Fleming 1637 W
Ann, North Tawton 1677 A
Anthony, Bratton Fleming 1692 W
Catherine, Alwington 1661 W
Edmund, Great Torrington 1726 A
Collings Edward, Westleigh 1724 A
Francis, Coldridge 1682 W
Henry, Bondleigh 1666 A
Henry, Chittlehampton 1688 W
Collyn John, Mortehoe 1567 W
Colleyne John, Bratton Fleming 1571 W
Collings John, Bratton Fleming 1682 W
John, Filleigh 1715 W
John, Bratton Fleming 1724 W and 1732 W
Collings John, Satterleigh 1735 W
Collings John, Great Torrington 1763 A
Collyns Mary, Pilton 1629 [W]
Mary, Marwood 1727 A
Colling Mary, Great Torrington, widow 1798 W
Collings Richard, Great Torrington 1746 A
Collings Richard, North Tawton 1776 W
Collens Robert, Stoke Rivers 1704 A
Collings Robert, Barnstaple 1801 W
Thomas, Newton Tracey 1666 W
Thomas, Ashford 1706 A
Thomas, Marwood 1706 W
Thomas, Satterleigh 1752 A
Collings William, Barnstaple 1760 A
Collings William, Ilfracombe 1828 W
Collman see Coleman
Collimore, Collmer, Collmore see Collamore
Collocott see Colescott
Collome see Collam
Collomower see Collamore
Collows Walter, North Tawton 1591 [W]
Collscott see Colescott
Collwell, Collwill see Colwell
Collyn, Collyns see Collins
Colman see Coleman
Colmer see Comer
Colscott see Colescott
Colwell, Collwell, Collwill, Colwill
Colwill alias Braginton Ann, Hartland 1846 W
Colwill Charles, High Bickington 1762 W
Colwill Charles, Bideford 1826 W
Colwill Elizabeth, South Molton 1724 W
Collwell Florence, Buckland Filleigh 1665 W
Colwill John, Rackenford 1623 [W]
Collwill John, South Molton 1751 W
John, Witheridge 1831 W
John see also Sarah Pulley

Joseph, Tawstock 1689 W
Colwill Lewis, Tawstock 1738 W
Mary, Tawstock 1714 W
Colwill Robert, Little Torrington 1623 [W]
Collwell Roger, Buckland Brewer 1588 W
Collwill Samuel, Great Torrington 1694 W
Colwill William, Buckland Brewer 1618 [W]
Colwill William, South Molton 1723 W
Colwill William, Bideford 1833 W
Colyhole see Collihole
Comack, Comath
Mary, Bideford 1703 W
Comath Matthias, Bideford 1701 A
Coman see Cummins
Comath see Comack
Combe, Comb, Coomb, Coombe, Coome, Cumbe
Comb alias Yeoland Alexander, Pilton 1685 A
Coombe Ann, Burrington 1624 [W]
Coombe Armanell, North Tawton 1757 W
Coome Elizabeth, Pilton 1690 W
Coome Enoch, Bow 1759 W
Coombe George, Pilton 1671 W
Comb George and Mary, Pilton 1696 A
George, Pilton 1729 A
George, Pilton 1741 A
Combe alias Yolland Joan, Pilton 1675 W
Joan, Chawleigh 1746 A
Comb alias John John, Buckland Brewer 1568 W
Combe alias Bobage John, Ashreigney 1568 W
John, Tawstock, Revd 1571 W
Coomb alias Wood John, High Bickington 1663 W
Combe alias Yelland John, Pilton 1667 W, 1670 W and 1673 W
Comb alias Yeolland John, Pilton, snr., widower 1675 [W]
Comb Mary and George, Pilton 1696 A
Mary, Pilton 1751 W
Mary, Pilton 1812 W
Michael, Pilton 1726 W
Cumbe Parkin, Chawleigh 1743 W
Coomb alias Yeoland Richard, Pilton 1663 [W]
Robert, Barnstaple 1672 W
Stephen, Fremington 1697 A
Coombe Thomas, Clannaborough 1633 A
Coombe Thomas, Great Torrington 1834 A
William, Pilton 1591 A
William, Barnstaple 1592 [W]
Comb alias Yeolland William, Barnstaple 1663 W
William, Pilton 1773 A
Comber see Comer
Comens see Cummins
Comer, Colmer, Comber, Coomer
Alice, Tawstock, widow 1571 W
Anna Maria, Marwood 1769 W
Anthony, Stoke Rivers 1729 W
Colmer Baldwin, Tawstock 1598 [W]
Christiana, Tawstock 1703 W
Cormer Dinah, Molland 1717 W
Comers Elizabeth, Stoodleigh 1663 W
Comer or Conler Elizabeth, Bideford 1703 W
Coomer Elizabeth, Bratton Fleming 1724 W
Francis, Clovelly 1704 A
Colmer Geoffrey, Arlington 1668 W
Geoffrey, Arlington 1719 W
Colmer Geoffrey, Hartland, gentleman 1807 W
Colmer George, Tawstock 1595 [W]
Comber Giles, Bratton Fleming 1691 W
Giles, Marwood 1769 W
Hannah, Northam 1699 A
Colmer Henry, Bratton Fleming 1618 [W]
Colmer Henry, Hartland 1754 W
Colmer Henry, Frithelstock 1775 W
Honor, Arlington 1698 W
Hugh, Bratton Fleming 1680 W and 1691 W
James, Northam 1682 A
James, Tawstock 1693 W
James, Northam 1704 [W]

James, Northam 1729 A
James, Northam 1759 A
Colmer John, Woolfardisworthy 1577 W
Colmer John, Tawstock 1635 [W]
Colmer John, St Giles in the Wood 1636 W
John, Bratton Fleming 1696 W
John, Bratton Fleming 1709 W
John, Marwood 1725 W
Colmer John, Fremington 1732 W
John, Tawstock 1764 A
John, Loxhore 1776 W
John, Combe Martin 1791 W
Colmer Mabel, Bratton Fleming, widow 1608 [W]; forename
blank in Ms; supplied from parish register
Margaret, Bratton Fleming 1680 W
Margaret, Bratton Fleming 1712 W
Mary, Bratton Fleming 1685 W
Colmer or Cobner Mary, Northam 1718 W
Mary, Northam 1730 W
Mathew, Bratton Fleming 1673 W
Mathew, Hartland 1676 A
Philip, Arlington 1702 W
Phillippa, Northam 1696 A
Colmer Richard, Tawstock 1602 W
Colmer Richard, Arlington 1641 W
Colmer Robert, Fremington 1599 [W]
Colmer Roger, Barnstaple 1627 [W
Colmer Samuel, Barnstaple 1826 W
Sarah, Ilfracombe 1844 W
Colmer Simon, Fremington 1637 W
Sybil, Bratton Fleming, widow 1570 W
Thomas, Fremington 1620 [W]
Colmer Thomas, Hartland 1639 W
Colmer Thomas, Langtree 1663 W
Thomas, Bratton Fleming 1689 W
Thomas, Clovelly 1709 W
Thomas, Clovelly 1735 W
Thomas, Bratton Fleming 1757 W
Thomas, Bratton Fleming 1852 W
Colmer William, Stoke Rivers 1636 W
William, Hartland 1697 W
William, Marwood 1703 A
Colmer William, ship *Cornwall* 1749 A
Comins, Commins, Comyns see Cummins
Conaclence Robert, Marwood 1615 [W] "Constence" in register;
forename blank in Ms; supplied from parish register
Conding Elizabeth, Fremington 1669 W
Condy Daniel, Great Torrington 1760 W
Mary, Great Torrington 1778 W
Conell see Connell
Congdon John, Merton 1733 A
John, Bideford 1783 W
Robert Allin, Bideford 1850 W
Congram Charity, Chittlehampton 1857 W
Richard, Chittlehampton 1856 W
Conibeare, Conibear, Conibeere, Conibere, Connibear,
Connybear, Connybeare, Connybere, Conybear, Conybeare,
Conybeere, Conyber, Conybere, Cooniber, Cunebear,
Cunebeare, Cunnebeare, Cunnibear, Cunnybeare, Cunybear
Anthony, Heanton Punchardon 1713 A
Cunebear Conan, Pilton 1733 W
Cunebear Elizabeth, Pilton 1735 W
Cunebear George, Goodleigh 1790 W
Cunebear Joan, Tawstock 1728 W
Conibere John, Tawstock 1581 W
Connybear John, Arlington 1599 [W] and 1600 W
Connybeare alias Downeman John, George Nympton 1601 A;
forename blank in Ms; supplied from parish register
Conibear John, Tawstock 1678 W
John, Barnstaple 1689 W
John, Newton Tracey, jnr. 1704 A
John, High Bray 1715 W
Cunybear John, Tawstock 1721 A
Cunebeare John, Westleigh 1726 A
Conybeare John, Bideford 1740 A

Conibeere Mary, Tawstock 1663 W
Cooniber alias Yeoland Mary, Pilton 1663 W
Conybear Mary, Westleigh 1721 W
Connibear Mary, Barnstaple 1750 W
Connybeare Mary, Bideford 1754 W
Conibear Priscilla, Westleigh 1680 A
Ralph, Tawstock 1714 W
Conibear Richard, Tawstock 1676 A
Richard, Atherington 1686 W
Conyber Richard, High Bray 1768 W
Conibear Richard, Ilfracombe 1835 W
Conybeare Robert, Yarnscombe 1615 [W]
Conibear Robert, Combe Martin 1842 W
Conybeere Roger, Tawstock 1639 W
Conybeere Susan, Fremington 1640 W
Connybear Thomas, Tawstock 1603 W
Cunebear Thomas, South Molton 1736 W
Connybear Walter, Tawstock 1603 W
Conybere William, Tawstock 1563 W
Conibear William, Westleigh 1672 A
William, South Molton 1685 A
William, Westleigh 1709 A
Cunnibear William, ship *Royal Oak* 1749 A
Cunnebeare William, Shirwell 1793 W
Connybere Willmot, Tawstock 1629 [W]
Connell, Conell
Conell Cornelius, Great Torrington 1574 W
Conell Richard, Tawstock 1633 A
Simon, Tawstock 1631 [W]
Conner see Connor
Connibear see Conibeare
Connor, Conner, Conniers
Conniers Eli, ship *Weymouth* 1751 W
Conner Hannah, Bideford 1753 W
William, Eggesford, labourer 1850 A to Elizabeth of
    Wembworthy, widow
Connybear, Connybeare, Connybere see Conibeare
Constence see Conacience
Conte Peter, Barnstaple 1714 W
Contyoke Jacquet, Chittlehampton 1569 W
Conybeare, Conybeere, Conyber, Conybere see Conibeare
Cooke, Cook, Couke, Kooke
Agnes, East Worlington 1675 W
Alice, Ford, Hartland 1600 W
Alice, Welcombe 1636 W
Anthony, Chulmleigh 1757 W
Bartholomew, Clovelly 1731 A
Bartholomew, Clovelly 1765 A
Benjamin, Hartland 1731 A
Catherine, South Molton 1580 A
Christopher, Abbotsham 1668 W
Elizabeth, Hartland 1617 [W]
Elizabeth, Hartland 1686 W
Elizabeth, Bideford 1793 W
George, Hartland 1613 [W]; forename blank in Ms; supplied
    from parish register
George, Bideford 1688 W
George, Hartland 1690 A
George, High Bickington 1821 W
George, Bideford 1840 A
Cook Gilbert, Yarnscombe 1703 W
Cook Grace, Hartland 1709 W
Grace, Barnstaple 1748 A
Henry, Bideford 1669 W
Henry, Great Torrington, cordwainer 1809 A
Cook James, Barnstaple 1662 A
James, Hartland 1772 W
James, Hartland 1814 W
Joan, Barnstaple 1664 W
Joan, Bideford 1678 W
Joan, Bideford 1690 W
John, East Putford 1569 W
Kooke John, East Putford 1569 W
John, Brendon 1576 W
John, Buckland Brewer 1582 A

John, Parkham 1610 [W]; forename blank in Ms; supplied
    from parish register
John, Hartland 1610 [W] "of South Hole" in register; forename
    blank in Ms; supplied from parish register
John, Hartland 1611 [W] "of Foord" in register; forename
    blank in Ms; supplied from parish register
Couke John, Barnstaple 1625 O
John, Sheepwash 1630 [W]
John, Hartland 1665 A
John, Barnstaple 1667 A
John, South Molton 1678 W
John, Clovelly 1685 W
John, Hartland, snr. 1686 W
John, Hartland 1686 W
Cook John, Chulmleigh 1703 W
John, Clovelly 1727 A
John, West Worlington 1730 A and 1739 A
Cook John, Hartland 1741 W
John, Zeal Monachorum 1746 W
John, Mariansleigh 1749 A
Cook John, Clovelly 1789 W
John, West Worlington, gentleman 1799 W
John, Witheridge 1814 W
John, South Molton 1827 A to Mary, widow
Cook John, Chulmleigh 1845 W
Joseph, Lapford 1630 [W]
Cooke alias Grendon Joseph, Witheridge 1681 W
Joseph, Lapford 1716 W
Judith, Littleham (near Bideford) 1728 W
Margaret, Hartland 1625 [W]
Martha, Hartland 1687 W
Martha, Clovelly 1784 W
Martha, Chawleigh 1829 A
Mary, Ashreigney 1630 [W]
Mary, West Worlington 1732 W
Mary, Lapford 1762 W
Mary, Fremington 1791 A
Mary, formerly of Westleigh, late of Barnstaple 1850 W
Michael, St Giles in the Wood 1777 W
Molly, Parracombe 1820 W
Nectan, Hartland 1607 [W]; forename blank in Ms; supplied
    from parish register
Nectan, Hartland 1623 [W]
Nicholas, Clovelly 1687 W
Oliver, Eggesford 1638 W
Peter, Hartland 1604 W
Peter, Barnstaple 1757 W
Cooke alias Gaindon Philip, Mariansleigh 1758 A
Richard, Hartland 1604 W
Richard, Northam 1662 W
Richard, Molland 1664 A
Cook Richard, West Worlington 1700 W
Richard, Burrington 1770 W
Richard, Martinhoe 1774 W
Richard, Witheridge 1789 W
Robert, Lapford 1759 W
Robert, Hartland 1769 A (2)
Cook Samuel, East Putford 1714 W
Samuel, Bideford 1832 W
Stephen, Chawleigh 1780 W
Thomas, Hartland 1586 W
Thomas, Barnstaple 1643 W
Cooke alias Grindon Thomas, Witheridge 1644 W
Thomas, Hartland, snr. 1663 W
Thomas, Hartland 1669 W
Thomas, Tawstock 1738 A
Thomas, Atherington 1751 A
Cook Thomas, Lapford 1773 W
Thomas, Hartland 1780 W
Thomas, Chulmleigh 1826 W
Cook Thomas, Hartland 1847 W
Thomasine, West Worlington 1821 W
Cooke alias Best William, Monkleigh 1565 W
Cook William, Abbotsham 1588 W and 1591 [W]

Cooke alias Grendon William, Witheridge 1660 W
William, Chulmleigh 1667 W
Cook alias Grendon William, Lapford 1669 W
William, Clovelly 1686 W
Cook William, Lapford 1697 A
William, Lapford 1806 W
Cook William, Northam 1828 W
Cook alias Cock William, Hartland 1835 W
William, Ilfracombe 1849 W
Cookesly, Cookery, Cookesley
Abednego, North Molton 1640 A
David, High Bray 1639 W
Cookesley James, Pilton 1853 W
Cookesley Joan, High Bray 1689 W
Cookrey Robert, Coldridge 1672 W and 1676 W
Roger, High Bray 1665 A
Cookery Thomas, Coldridge 1633 W
Cookesley Thomas, Knowstone 1722 W
Cookney Nicholas, Creacombe 1617 [W]
Cooling, Couling, Cowling
Cowling Grace, Barnstaple 1776 W
John, Stoodleigh 1718 W
Couling John, Barnstaple 1746 W
Coomb, Coombe, Coome see Combe
Coomer see Comer
Cooper, Cowper
..., Iddesleigh 1614 [W]
Cooper alias Everton ..., Bideford 1663 A
Cowper Agnes, Combe Martin 1582 W
Alexander, Pilton 1774 A
Ann, Alwington 1599 [W]
Catherine, Fremington 1756 W
Christopher, Barnstaple 1693 W
Daniel, Frithelstock 1666 A
Dorothy, Iddesleigh 1637 W
Elizabeth, Fremington 1819 A to Sarah wife of John Nicholls
of Chittlehampton, daughter
George, Chulmleigh 1675 A
George, Fremington 1702 W and 1712 W
James, Burrington 1665 W
Joan, Iddesleigh 1593 [W]
John, Monkleigh 1599 [W]
John, Tawstock 1599 [W] and 1600 W
John, Tawstock 1608 [W]; forename blank in Ms; supplied
from parish register
John, Iddesleigh 1624 [W]
John, Northam 1639 W
John, Barnstaple 1640 A
John, High Bickington 1693 W
John, Fremington 1736 W and 1739 W
John, High Bickington 1748 W
John, High Bickington 1765 W
Joseph, Barnstaple 1681 W
Cooper alias Everton Mary, Bideford 1663 A
Mary Ann see Margaret Cowper Macqueen
Richard, Pilton 1602 W
Richard, Great Torrington 1741 W
Richard, Northam 1825 W
Cowper Robert, Tawstock 1572 W
Rose, Iddesleigh 1625 [W]
Cowper Rowland, Iddesleigh 1579 [W]
Samuel, Beaford 1689 A
Samuel, High Bickington, cooper 1796 A
Simon, Goodleigh 1673 W
Thomas, Beaford 1660 A
Thomas, High Bickington 1796 W
Thomas see also Eleanor Hooper
William, Iddesleigh 1592 [W]
William, Barnstaple 1686 W
William, Fremington 1771 W
Cooze Gilbert, Bideford 1680 W
Cop see Copp
Copinger Ann, heretofore of Hartland but late of Bideford 1833
W
Copland John, Barnstaple 1610 [W] and 1611 O; forename
blank in Ms; supplied from parish register

Coplestone, Copleston, Copplestone
Copleston ..., Instow 1614 [W]
Anthony, Merton 1735 W
Copleston Caesar, Bideford 1683 W
Copleston Catherine, Great Torrington 1584 A
Christopher, Alverdiscott 1637 W
Christopher, Alverdiscott 1662 W
Copplestone Christopher, Abbotsham 1760 W
Copplestone Coriolanus, Bideford 1722 A
Copleston George, Bideford 1570 A
Copleston Humphrey, Instow 1599 [W]
Copplestone Humphrey, Weare Giffard 1672 W
Humphrey, Beaford 1692 W
Copleston John, Eggesford 1585 A
Copleston John, Eggesford 1587 W
John, Little Torrington 1591 [W]
Copleston John, Eggesford, Worshipful, esquire 1606 [W];
forename blank in Ms; supplied from parish register
Copplestone John, Weare Giffard 1644 O
John, Bideford 1681 W
John, Beaford 1692 A
Copplestone John, Merton 1782 W
Joseph, Little Torrington 1692 A
Julius, East Down 1662 W
Lancelot, Alverdiscott 1687 W
Mary, Great Torrington 1620 [W]
Coplestone alias Mills Mary, Bideford 1695 A
Mary, Little Torrington 1704 A
Mary, Langtree 1711 A
Richard, Woodland, Little Torrington 1586 W
Copleston Richard, Woodland 1617 [W]
Richard, Bideford 1709 A
Copplestone Richard, Abbotsham 1761 W
Copplestone Samuel, Bideford, sailor 1705 A
Copplestone Sarah, Bideford 1754 A
Copleston Thomas, Instow 1568 W
Copplestone Thomas, Bideford 1680 A
Thomas, Bideford 1773 W
Thomasine, Little Torrington 1591 [W]
Copner, Coppener
Ann, Northam 1823 W
Ann, Northam, Appledore 1838 A to Elizabeth Bligh, daughter
Jasper, Northam 1786 A
John, Northam 1718 W
Coppener Margery, South Molton 1579 W
Richard, South Molton 1573 W
Simon, Fremington 1617 [W]
Thomas, Barnstaple 1841 W
Ursula, Northam 1786 A
William, Shebbear 1576 W and 1578 W
Copp, Coape, Cop, Coppe, Copps
Coppe ..., Knowstone 1602 [W]
Alexander, Roborough 1779 W
Andrew, North Molton 1837 W
Edmund, Petrockstowe 1812 W
Elizabeth, Merton, widow 1799 W
Coape Gilbert, Chittlehampton 1691 A
Cop Henry, Stoodleigh 1741 A
Henry, Alverdiscott 1809 W
Coppe John, South Molton 1605 W
John, Great Torrington 1766 W
John, Petrockstowe 1776 W
John, Merton, yeoman 1798 W
John, Great Torrington, carrier 1811 W
John, Langtree 1853 W
John, Barnstaple, machine maker 1856 A to Henry of
Alverdiscott, cousin
Jonah, Little Torrington 1833 W
Martha, Great Torrington 1812 A to William Moffitt Copys,
son
Mary see Thomas Reed
Robert, Great Torrington 1799 A
Copps Samuel, Little Torrington 1696 A
Samuel, Merton 1771 W
Susan, Frithelstock 1843 A to Thomas of Horwood, father
Thomas, Little Torrington 1669 W

Coppe William, Hartland 1586 A
Cop William, Barnstaple 1620 [W]
   William, Peters Marland, yeoman 1798 A
   William, Peters Marland, snr. 1799 W
   William, Merton 1804 W
   William, Petrockstowe 1843 W
Copplestone see Coplestone
Copps see Copp
Corby John, Lynton 1772 W
   Peter, Countisbury 1742 W
   William, Lynton 1830 W
Cording Agnes, High Bray 1699 W
   Elizabeth, High Bray 1663 W
   Margaret, High Bray 1724 A
   Mary, Stoke Rivers 1732 W
   Richard, High Bray 1691 A
   William, High Bray 1676 W
Coren Emanuel, King's Nympton 1732 A
   Thomas, Washford Pyne 1719 A
   Thomas, Washford Pyne 1728 A and 1729 A
Corey see Cory
Coridon Margaret, Barnstaple 1722 A
Cormick Henry, Pilton 1838 W
Cormicune Savery, Barnstaple 1574 A
Cornall, Cornell
   Andrew, Chawleigh 1699 W
   Andrew, Chawleigh 1770 W
   Charles, Marwood 1690 A
   Edward, Chawleigh 1690 W
   Francis, Witheridge, mason 1809 A
   Cornell John, Horwood 1596 [W]
   Richard, Chawleigh, yeoman 1809 W
   Simon, Marwood 1712 W
   Thomas, Chulmleigh 1774 W
   William, Arlington 1577 W
Corne
   Corne alias White Beaton, South Molton 1579 A
Cornelius Richard, Coldridge 1587 W
Cornell see Cornall
Corner ..., Molland 1603 [W]
   Anthony, Bratton Fleming 1746 W
   Bennett, Molland 1595 [W]
   Eleanor, Washford Pyne 1579 W
   George, Molland 1685 W
   Harry, Molland 1578 W
   Hugh, Molland 1639 W
   John, Knowstone 1572 W
   John, Twitchen 1574 W
   John, Bratton Fleming 1582 W
   John, Molland 1594 [W]
   Peter, Twitchen 1566 W
   Philip, Molland 1590 [W]
   Richard, Fremington 1573 A
   Richard, Twitchen 1577 W
   Robert, Molland 1596 [W]
   Thomas, Twitchen 1591 [W]
Corneshe see Cornish
Cornew, Cornewe
   Ann, Lapford 1624 [W]
   Cornewe or Korney Gawen, Hartland 1586 W
   George, Hartland 1668 A and 1671 A account
   George, Hartland 1691 A
   Cornewe John, Lapford 1594 [W]
   Cornewe John, Lapford 1613 [W]; forename blank in Ms;
     supplied from parish register
   Cornewe Nicholas, Lapford 1573 W
   Susanna, Hartland 1691 A
   Cornewe Thomas, Lapford 1585 W
Cornewall see Cornwall
Corney James, Hartland no year given W
   John, East Worlington 1625 [W]
   John, Chawleigh 1627 [W]
   William, Marwood 1832 W
Cornish, Corneshe, Cornishe, Cornyshe
   ..., Ashreigney 1607 [W]

Cornyshe Agnes, Hartland 1586 W
   Alexander, Petrockstowe 1723 W
   Alice, Ilfracombe 1626 [W]
   Cornishe Alice, Ilfracombe 1626 [W]
   Amy, Ilfracombe 1661 W
   Corneshe Anstis, Ilfracombe 1583 W
   Bartholomew, West Down 1672 A
   Charity, Little Torrington 1675 A
   Charles, Ilfracombe 1829 W
   David or Thomas, Ilfracombe 1612 [W]; forename blank in
     Ms; supplied from parish register
   Cornyshe Edmund, Bow 1566 W
   Cornishe Edward, Ilfracombe 1596 [W]
   Cornishe Egline, Winkleigh 1631 [W]
   Cornishe Garrett, Ilfracombe 1628 [W]
   Geoffrey, Ilfracombe 1613 [W]; forename blank in Ms;
     supplied from parish register
   Geoffrey, Ilfracombe 1700 W
   George, Ilfracombe 1600 W
   George, Northam 1684 W
   George, Bideford 1711 W
   Grace, Great Torrington 1802 W
   Hannah, Ilfracombe 1756 A
   Cornishe Henry, Ilfracombe 1625 [W]
   Henry, Ilfracombe 1734 W
   Henry, West Down 1758 A
   Cornishe Hugh, Barnstaple 1631 [W]
   James, Barnstaple 1662 W
   James, Barnstaple 1705 W
   James, Barnstaple 1718 W
   Jane, Barnstaple 1847 W
   Joan, Ilfracombe 1617 [W]
   Joan, Bideford 1710 W
   Joan, Great Torrington 1777 W
   Cornyshe John, Ilfracombe 1577 W
   John, Ilfracombe 1614 [W]; forename blank in Ms; supplied
     from parish register
   John, Ilfracombe 1663 W
   John, Ilfracombe 1703 A
   John, Hartland 1710 A
   John, Langtree 1711 W
   John, Merton 1719 W
   John, Petrockstowe 1736 W
   John, Great Torrington 1745 W and 1756 W
   John, Ilfracombe 1827 W
   John, Welcombe 1845 W
   Margaret, Barnstaple 1731 [W]
   Martha, Barnstaple 1746 W
   Mary, Merton 1763 A
   Cornishe Nicholas, Ilfracombe 1591 [W]
   Nicholas, Barnstaple 1608 [W]; forename blank in Ms;
     supplied from parish register
   Nicholas, Ilfracombe 1664 W
   Philip, Bideford 1698 W
   Philip, Bideford 1714 [W]
   Cornishe Richard, Peters Marland 1564 [W]
   Richard, Ilfracombe 1570 W
   Richard, Barnstaple 1715 A
   Cornyshe Thomas, Bow 1566 W
   Cornyshe Thomas, Ilfracombe 1576 A
   David or Thomas, Ilfracombe 1612 [W]; forename blank in
     Ms; supplied from parish register
   Cornishe Thomas, Barnstaple 1623 [W]
   Thomas, Barnstaple 1735 A
   Thomas, Bideford 1788 [W]
   Thomas, Barnstaple 1843 W
   Thomas William, Abbotsham 1857 A to Jane of Ilfracombe,
     widow
   Cornishe Walter, Great Torrington 1596 [W]
   Walter, Ilfracombe 1704 W
   Cornishe William, Peters Marland 1589 A
   Cornishe William, Barnstaple 1628 [W]
   Cornishe William, Winkleigh 1631 [W]
   William, Little Torrington 1641 W
   William, Merton 1719 W

William, Barnstaple 1733 W
Cornwall, Cornewall, Cornole, Cornwell, Corwill
..., Chittlehampton 1614 [W]
Alice, Chittlehampton 1617 [W]
Cornewall Alice, Chittlehampton 1619 O
Amesius, Arlington 1675 W
Cornwell Charles, Marwood 1745 W
Christiana, Barnstaple 1623 [W]
David, Arlington 1610 [W] "of Becott"; forename blank in Ms; supplied from parish register
David, Instow 1766 W
Edward, Chulmleigh 1758 [W]
Elizabeth, Barnstaple 1620 [W]
Elizabeth, Instow 1782 W
Cornewall Henry, Roborough 1593 [W] (2)
Jane, Marwood 1749 W
Joan, Arlington 1612 [W] "of Touching" in register; forename blank in Ms; supplied from parish register
Cornewall John, Marwood 1593 [W]
John, Washford Pyne 1755 W
Corwill Mary, Berrynarbor 1732 W
Cornole Richard, Newton St Petrock 1570 W
Cornewall Robert, Barnstaple 1615 [W]; forename blank in Ms; supplied from parish register
Cornewall Sidwell, Arlington 1673 A
Simon, Marwood 1581 A
Simon, Heanton Punchardon 1731 W
Cornewall Stephen, Marwood 1571 W
Cornewall William, Great Torrington 1572 W
Cornewall William, Great Torrington 1591 [W]
Cory, Corey, Corry
Daniel, Frithelstock 1790 A
Francis, Woolfardisworthy 1855 W
Hugh, Northam 1704 A
Corey Hugh, Northam 1750 A
Hugh, Woolfardisworthy 1833 W
Corry Hugh, Woolfardisworthy 1836 W
James, Great Torrington 1671 A
James, Great Torrington 1724 W
John, Bideford 1625 [W]
John, ship *Romney* 1751 A
John, Hartland 1789 W
John, Woolfardisworthy 1837 W
Joseph, Bow 1748 W
Joseph, Northam 1756 A
Mary, Great Torrington 1728 W
Corry Simon, Atherington 1706 [W]
Susanna, Woolfardisworthy, widow 1855 A to John Davy of Woolfardisworthy, yeoman, brother
Thomas, Heanton Punchardon 1812 A to Sarah Bidder and Mary Cory, daughters
William, Chichester, Heanton Punchardon 1838 W
Cosh Henry, North Molton 1706 W
Cossen see Cousins
Cossington Richard, Great Torrington 1723 A
Coston Edmund, Ilfracombe 1592 [W]
Cote see Coates
Cottell see Cottle
Cotten see Cotton
Cottey, Cothay, Cottie, Cotty
Cottie ..., West Buckland 1607 [W]
Bartholomew, Warkleigh 1680 A
Catherine, North Molton 1673 W
Dorothy, North Molton 1681 W and 1691 W
Cotty Frances, West Buckland 1696 W
Cotty George, Atherington 1744 W
Cothay Henry, Chittlehampton 1720 W
Cothay Henry, Chittlehampton 1776 W
Cotty Humphrey, George Nympton 1697 W
Cotty John, Chittlehampton 1743 A
Cotty John, Chittlehampton, jnr. 1757 W
Cothay John, Chittlehampton 1759 W
John, South Molton 1778 W
Cothay John, Chittlehampton, carpenter 1810 A
Cothay Margaret, Chittlehampton 1806 W
Philip, Littleham (near Bideford) 1592 [W]

Cotty Philip, West Buckland 1813 A to Eleanor Gully, daughter
Cotty William, Chittlehampton 1664 A
William, North Molton 1668 W
Cotty William, North Molton 1695 W
Cotley William, Twitchen 1696 W
Cotty William, Atherington 1721 A
William, Twitchen 1722 A
Cotty William, West Buckland 1735 A
Cothay William, Chittlehampton 1750 W
Cottay William, Chittlehampton 1790 W
Cotty William, West Buckland 1804 W
Cottle, Cottell, Cotwell
Charles, Welcombe 1801 W
James, Clovelly 1750 A
Cotwell John, Hartland 1623 [W]
Mark, North Tawton 1665 W
Mark, North Tawton, esquire 1672 A
Mary, North Tawton 1639 W
Cottell Philip, Northam 1774 W
Richard, North Tawton 1638 A
Richard, North Tawton 1672 A
Robert, Welcombe 1719 [W]
Cottell Thomas, North Tawton 1578 W
Cotton, Cotten, Cottyne
Charles Newell, St Giles in the Wood 1856 W
Cotten John, Barnstaple 1601 W
John, Bideford 1813 W
Cottyne Robert, Westleigh 1576 W
William, Barnstaple, jnr. 1832 W
William, Barnstaple 1836 W
Cotts see Coates
Cotty see Cottey
Cottyne see Cotton
Cotwell see Cottle
Couch, Cooch, Coutch, Cowche
Bartholomew, Dolton 1716 W
Bartholomew, Ashreigney 1801 W
Coutch Gabriel, Huntshaw 1616 [W]
Cowche George, Witheridge 1583 A and 1588 A
George, Monkleigh 1596 [W]
George, Northam 1628 [W]
Cooch George, Hartland 1637 W
George, Bideford 1697 A
George, Iddesleigh 1742 W
Grace, Ashreigney 1803 W
Coutch Henry, Clovelly 1593 [W]
Isott, Swimbridge 1841 A to William
Cowche John, Hartland 1573 W
Coutch John, Frithelstock 1617 [W]
Joseph, Bideford 1693 A
Cooch Josiah, Bideford 1699 W
Lenine Mary, Winkleigh 1736 W
Lodovic, Hartland 1639 A
Marafiria, Frithelstock 1624 [W]
Mary, Beaford 1777 W
Coutch Richard, Hartland 1597 [W]
Thomas, Witheridge 1619 [W]
Thomas, Hartland 1631 [W]
Thomas, Cruwys Morchard 1633 W
Thomas, Iddesleigh 1731 A
Thomas, Bideford 1707 A
Walter, Bideford 1707 A
Cowche William, Westleigh 1571 W
William, Westleigh 1622 [W]
William, Iddesleigh 1727 A
Couchel Lawrence, Witheridge 1565 W
Sybil, Westleigh 1575 W
William, Westleigh 1587 W
Cougeot John, Great Torrington 1738 A
Couke see Cooke
Coul see Cole
Couling see Cooling
Coull see Cole
Coullor see Cowler

Coullscott, Coulscott see Colescott
Courde Amos, Shirwell 1588 W
Court William, North Molton 1848 W
Courteis see Curtis
Courtenay, Courteney see Courtney
Courtes, Courtice see Curtis
Courtier Christian, Stoke Rivers 1662 [W]
   John, Parkham 1630 [W]
   Mary, Bratton Fleming 1637 W
   Thomas, Oakford 1664 W
Courties, Courtis see Curtis
Courtney, Courtenay, Courteney, Courtnay
   ..., Atherington 1603 [W] and 1613 [W]
   ..., Lapford 1613 [W]
   Agnes, Georgeham 1662 [W]
   Courtnay Agnes, Twitchen 1776 W
   Courtenay Amy, Molland 1731 A
   Anastasia, Kentisbury 1714 W
   Courtenay Ann, Bratton Fleming 1683 W
   Courtenay Ann, Rackenford 1701 A
   Ann, Charles 1822 W
   Bartholomew, Rackenford 1695 W
   Courtenay Charles, Pilton 1722 W
   Courtenay Charles, Marwood 1738 W
   David, Swimbridge 1855 W
   Dorothy, Molland 1661 A
   Elizabeth, Barnstaple 1588 A and account
   Elizabeth, Atherington 1627 [W]
   Elizabeth, Barnstaple 1846 W
   Hugh, South Molton 1618 [W]
   Humphrey, Ashford 1675 A
   James, Georgeham 1591 [W]
   James, Georgeham, jnr. 1624 [W]
   James, Bratton Fleming 1674 W
   Courtenay James, Bratton Fleming 1698 A
   Jane, Georgeham 1679 W
   Courtenay Joan, Georgeham 1702 W
   John, Berrynarbor 1624 [W]
   John, Kentisbury 1664 W
   John, Molland 1677 A
   Courtenay John, Berrynarbor 1682 A
   Courtenay John, Molland 1684 A
   John, Instow 1685 W
   John, Northam 1701 W
   Courtenay John, Bratton Fleming 1718 W
   Courtnay John, High Bray 1739 A
   Courtnay John, Twitchen 1742 W
   Courtenay John, Molland, gentleman 1796 W
   Courteney Lewis, Barnstaple 1584 W
   Lewis, Molland 1749 W
   Courtenay Lodovic, High Bray 1727 A
   Courtenay Margaret, Marwood 1738 W
   Courtenay Mary, East Down 1731 W
   Courtenay Mary, Rackenford 1743 A
   Courtenay Mary, Rackenford 1854 A
   Nicholas, Berrynarbor 1680 A
   Philip, Hartland 1577 W
   Philip, Molland 1668 A and 1671 O
   Courtenay Philip, Molland 1685 W
   Courtenay Philip, Molland, yeoman 1805 W
   Richard, Georgeham 1598 [W]
   Richard, Stoke Rivers 1792 A
   Courtenay Richard, Knowstone 1833 W
   Robert, Huntshaw 1576 A
   Robert, Molland 1630 [W]
   Courtenay Robert, Molland 1691 W
   Thomas, Molland 1674 A
   William, Marwood 1716 W
   Courtenay William, Arlington 1814 W
Courtys see Curtis
Cousins, Cossen, Cusens, Gousans
   Cusens David, Georgeham 1691 W
   Gousans David, Northam 1794 T
   Cossen Humphrey, Ilfracombe 1622 [W]
Coutch see Couch
Cove ..., Bondleigh 1606 [W]

..., Bondleigh 1610 [W]
   Alice, Bondleigh 1575 W
   Bartholomew, Bondleigh 1633 W
   Margaret, Bondleigh 1621 [W]
   Richard, Bondleigh 1574 A
   Richard, Bondleigh 1608 [W]; forename blank in Ms; supplied
     from parish register
Coven Robert, Frithelstock 1644 W
   William, Frithelstock 1644 [W]
Coveney, Covenay, Coveny
   Ann, Frithelstock 1663 A
   Ann, Frithelstock 1729 W
   John, Frithelstock 1713 W
   Robert, Frithelstock 1716 W
   Covenay Robert, Frithelstock 1732 W
Coward Elizabeth see Edmund, John, Prudence and Robert
   Brook
Cowche see Couch
Cowell, Cowle
   Cowle Ann, Winkleigh, widow 1848 A to John, son
   Edward, Shirwell 1665 A
   Elizabeth, Weare Giffard 1726 [W]
   Cowle George, Hartland 1703 A
   Cowle Hilary, Trentishoe 1617 [W]
   Cowle James, Iddesleigh 1801 A
   Cowle Joan, North Molton 1571 W
   Cowle John, Winkleigh 1843 W
   Cowle Martin, Hartland 1701 A
   Mary, Barnstaple 1721 W
   Mary, Bideford 1847 W
   Michael, Weare Giffard 1717 W
   Cowle Salome, Combe Martin 1618 [W]
Cowler, Coullor, Cowller
   Christopher, Chittlehampton 1783 A
   ....Coullor Elizabeth, Chittlehampton 1752 A
   Cowller Elizabeth, Chittlehampton, widow 1811 W
   John, Chittlehampton 1727 A
   Mary wife of Richard see John Steer
   Patience, Chittlehampton 1749 W
   Cowler Philip, Chittlehampton 1713 W
   Philip, Chittlehampton 1743 W
   Cowler William, Chittlehampton 1713 W
Cowles see Cole
Cowlescott see Colescott
Cowling see Cooling
Cowller see Cowler
Cowlscott see Colescott
Cowman, Coman
   Christopher, High Bickington 1714 A
   Elizabeth, Shirwell 1693 W
   Francis, Yarnscombe 1725 W
   Henry, High Bickington 1815 A
   John, Rose Ash 1568 W
   John, High Bickington 1782 W
   John, High Bickington 1840 W
   Coman Lucy, Warkleigh, widow 1565 W
   Nathaniel, Shirwell 1679 A
   Nathaniel, Shirwell 1759 A
   Philip, Northam 1668 W
   Richard, Tawstock 1601 W
   Robert, Tawstock 1564 [W]
   William, Bideford 1744 A
Cowper see Cooper
Cox Ann, Barnstaple 1701 W
   Catherine, Northam 1784 W
   George, St Giles in the Wood 1723 A
   James, Knewcastle, Ireland 1742 A
   Joan, Barnstaple 1677 W
   John, Chulmleigh 1763 A
   John George, South Molton 1852 W
   Nathaniel, Barnstaple 1698 W
   Nathaniel, Martinhoe 1762 A
   Phillippa, Barnstaple 1688 W
   Richard, Barnstaple 1689 A
   Thomas, Barnstaple, snr. 1637 W

Thomas, Barnstaple 1676 W
William, Barnstaple 1676 A
William, Barnstaple 1712 A and 1718 A
Coxhead, Cockeshead, Cokeshed
..., Chulmleigh 1611 [W]
Cokeshed Anthony, Chulmleigh 1578 A
Cockeshead Anthony, Chulmleigh 1623 [W]
Frances, Burrington 1629 [W]
Coxheade George, Chulmleigh 1618 [W]
Hugh, Chulmleigh 1629 [W]
Coyde Thomas, Pilton 1627 [W]
Cracknell John, Bideford 1770 W
Cradock, Cradick
Francis, Bideford 1732 W
Cradick George, Barnstaple 1686 W
Cradick John, Barnstaple 1698 A and 1704 A
John, Great Torrington 1729 W
Crailecke, Craleke see Crelake
Cranbury, Cramberie, Crambery, Crambury
Cramberie Edward, Newton St Petrock 1580 A
Crambury Henry, Chittlehampton 1632 [W]
Henry, St Giles in the Wood 1645 W
Crambury John, Barnstaple 1622 [W]
Sarah, Shirwell 1645 W
Crambery Stephen, Great Torrington 1574 A
Crane Josiah, Pilton, gentleman 1814 A to Sarah, widow
Crang, Crange
Crange ..., Mariansleigh 1614 [W]
Crange Agnes, King's Nympton 1590 [W]
Crange Agnes, North Molton 1636 A and 1637 O
Crange Agnes, Mariansleigh 1637 W
Alice, Parracombe 1763 W
Alice, Marwood 1847 W
Andrew, Stoke Rivers, gentleman 1807 A
Catherine, Combe Martin 1852 W
Crange Christopher, North Molton 1573 W
Elizabeth, Kentisbury 1800 W
Elizabeth, Landcross 1849 W
George, Northam 1688 W
James, Monkleigh 1836 A to Thomasine, widow
Jane, Bratton Fleming, widow 1855 A to Elizabeth wife of
  John Bowden of Barnstaple, grocer, daughter
Crange John, North Molton 1628 [W], 1630 [W] and 1631 [W]
  (2)
Crange John, Warkleigh 1638 A and O
John, Mariansleigh 1675 W
John, Chittlehampton 1682 W
John, North Molton 1690 A
John, North Molton 1741 A
John, North Molton 1771 W
John, Kentisbury 1778 W
John, Parracombe 1794 W
John, Parracombe 1835 W
John, Kentisbury 1836 W
Crange Margaret, North Molton 1603 W
Margaret, Marwood 1680 W
Michael, Landcross, yeoman 1807 W
Peter, Abbotsham 1678 W
Crange Richard, North Molton 1586 W and 1597 [W]
Crange Richard, Hartland 1635 A and 1637 O
Crange Richard, Rackenford 1638 A
Richard, Parracombe, snr. 1754 W
Richard, Parracombe, yeoman 1802 A
Richard, Marwood 1850 W to Walter of Georgeham, brother
Crange Robert, Rackenford 1589 W
Crange Roger, Mariansleigh 1579 W
Crange Roger, Mariansleigh 1635 A
Simon, Landcross 1769 W
Crange Thomas, Knowstone 1572 W
Walter, Parracombe 1744 W
Walter, Martinhoe 1813 W
William, Bratton Fleming 1820 W
William, North Molton 1823 W
William, Bratton Fleming 1828 W
Cranninge Ellen, Great Torrington 1592 [W]

Crapp, Crap, Crappe, Crapps, Cropp
Crap ..., Chulmleigh 1603 [W]
Arthur, Heanton Punchardon 1678 A
Crappe Henry, Tawstock 1619 [W]
Crap John, Chulmleigh 1599 [W]
Cropp John, Heanton Punchardon 1685 W
Richard, Woolfardisworthy 1665 A
Crapps Richard, Parkham 1668 W
Tebbet, Beaford 1625 [W]
Thomas, Heanton Punchardon 1676 A
Crascomb, Crascombe see Crosscombe
Crasse see Crosse
Craze William, Chulmleigh 1690 A
Creach, Creash
Margaret, George Nympton 1684 W
Mary, Barnstaple 1720 W
Creash Mathew, Mariansleigh 1742 [W]
Nathaniel, George Nympton 1674 A
Crealake, Crealick, Crealke, Creallake, Crealock see Crelake
Creamer, Creemer, Creemore, Cremer
Creemer Edmund, North Tawton 1703 W
Creemer George, Coldridge 1754 A
John, Zeal Monachorum 1590 [W]
Creemer Mary, Coldridge 1813 W
Cremer Richard, Zeal Monachorum 1582 W
Cremer Richard, Coldridge 1676 W
Cremer Richard, Winkleigh, yeoman 1809 W
Robert, Zeal Monachorum 1571 W
Creemore Roger, Winkleigh 1777 A
Creapin see Crispin
Creash see Creach
Creck see Crick
Crede, Credow
Elizabeth, Buckland Brewer 1567 W
John, Buckland Brewer 1573 A
Credow William, Buckland Brewer, gentleman 1563 W
Creek, Creeke see Crick
Creemore see Creamer
Crelake, Crailecke, Craleke, Crealake, Crealick, Crealke,
  Creallake, Crealock, Crelick, Crelicke, Crelock
Craleke Agnes, Littleham (near Bideford) 1566 W
Crelicke Agnes, Parkham 1672 W
Bartholomew, Parkham 1711 W
Giles, Merton 1683 W
James, Monkleigh 1681 W
Crealake James, Monkleigh 1727 W
Crelock James, Monkleigh 1755 W
Crealock James, Northam 1842 W
Crailecke John, Monkleigh 1566 W
Crelick John, Bideford 1689 W and 1692 W
John, Littleham (near Bideford) 1699 W
Crelocke Philip, Monkleigh 1584 W
Philip, Littleham (near Bideford) 1692 W
Robert, Monkleigh 1639 W
Roger, Monkleigh 1606 [W]; forename blank in Ms; supplied
  from parish register
Creallake William, Meeth 1595 W
Crealick William, Littleham (near Bideford) 1758 W
Crealock William, Monkleigh 1835 W
Cremer see Creamer
Creusey
Creusey alias Mogford Vincent, Chittlehampton 1565 W
Crews, Crewse see Cruse
Crick, Creck, Creek, Creeke
Andrew, Ilfracombe 1681 W
Creeke Joanna, Ilfracombe 1666 W
Creek John, Barnstaple, labourer 1813 A to Thomas, brother
Mary, Martinhoe 1784 W
Creck Nicholas, Ilfracombe 1687 W
Creeke Robert, Ilfracombe 1679 W
Sarah, Brendon 1786 A
Thomas, Brendon 1774 A
Thomas, Martinhoe 1779 A
Thomas, Beaford 1857 W
William, Brendon 1820 W

Cridge Edward, North Molton 1793 A
  Edward, North Molton 1850 A
  John, Charles 1789 W
  John, Barnstaple 1809 W
  John, Charles 1826 W
  Richard, Charles 1791 W
  Richard, South Molton 1838 W
  William, Oakford 1804 W
    see also Crudge
Cridmore Phoebe, Merton 1760 W
Crispin, Chrispen, Chrispinge, Chrispyne, Creapin, Crispen,
    Cryspen, Cryspyn
  Anthony, Barnstaple 1792 W
  Anthony, Great Torrington 1829 W
  Cryspyn Baldwin, Great Torrington 1588 W
  Chrispen Cyprian, Westleigh 1590 [W]
  Crispen Daniel, Rose Ash 1621 [W]
  Chrispen Elias, Winkleigh 1603 W
  Chrispen Elizabeth, Horwood 1595 [W]
  Elizabeth, Bow 1777 W
  George, Rose Ash 1846 A
  George, South Molton 1853 W
  Chrispinge John, Martinhoe 1567 W and 1573 A
  Chrispen John, Romansleigh 1606 W
  John, High Bickington 1729 W
  John, Bow 1756 W
  John, Chawleigh 1771 W
  John, Tawstock 1836 W
  Cryspen Lodovic, South Molton 1640 [W]
  Creapin Lodovic, South Molton 1658 W
  Philip, King's Nympton 1664 W
  Philip, Tawstock, yeoman 1811 W
  Sarah, Barnstaple 1796 W
  Cryspen Thomas, North Molton 1639 W
  Thomas, Lapford 1771 A
  Chrispen William, Westleigh 1571 W
  Chrispene alias Stone William, Berrynarbor 1582 W
Crocke see Croke
Crocker, Croaker, Crooker
  ..., West Down 1602 [W]
  ..., Abbotsham 1607 [W]
  Crocker alias Landman ..., Rose Ash 1692 W
  Agnes, Fremington 1727 W
  Ann, Rose Ash 1741 W
  Bartholomew, Chulmleigh 1664 A
  Beaton, High Bickington 1644 A
  Edward, Abbotsham 1618 [W]
  Edward, Marwood 1663 W
  Elizabeth, Hartland 1632 [W]
  Elizabeth, Northam 1729 W
  Elizabeth, Fremington 1775 W
  Emma, West Down, widow 1610 [W]; forename blank in Ms;
    supplied from parish register
  Faith, Peters Marland 1671 W
  George, Kentisbury 1584 W
  George, Hartland 1619 [W]
  George, Chittlehampton, yeoman 1797 A
  Henry, St Giles in the Wood 1668 W
  Henry, High Bickington 1671 A
  Henry, Bratton Fleming 1708 W
  Henry, High Bickington 1720 W
  Henry, High Bickington 1760 A
  Henry, High Bickington 1800 W*
  Henry, High Bickington 1844 W
  Honor, Fremington 1830 W
  Hugh, Buckland Filleigh 1857 W
  Isota, Hartland 1630 [W]
  Jane, High Bickington 1779 W
  Joan, Buckland Brewer 1706 W and 1710 W
  John, Shebbear 1552 [W]
  Crocker alias Lane John, South Molton 1580 W
  John, Shebbear 1593 [W]
  John, Abbotsham 1603 W
  John, High Bickington 1623 [W]
  John, Huntshaw 1623 [W]

John, St Giles in the Wood 1668 W
John, Rose Ash 1679 A
John, Frithelstock 1681 W
John, Huntshaw 1683 W
John, Mariansleigh 1688 W
John, St Giles in the Wood 1705 W
John, High Bickington 1713 W
John, Littleham (near Bideford) 1731 A
John, Mariansleigh 1759 A
John, High Bickington 1766 A
John, Fremington 1804 W
John, Hartland 1829 A to Rebecca wife of John Hockridge,
  daughter
John, Kentisbury 1620s W
Lawrence, Clovelly 1769 W
Margaret, Shebbear 1616 [W]
Margaret, Chittlehampton, widow 1797 W
Margaret, Chittlehampton 1817 W
Mary, St Giles in the Wood 1665 W
Mathew, St Giles in the Wood 1642 W
Mathew, Frithelstock 1669 [W]
Mathew, High Bickington 1696 A
Mathew, Barnstaple, jnr. 1706 A
Mathew, Roborough 1711 W
Nicholas, Clovelly 1601 W
Croaker Nicholas, Witheridge 1711 W
Crocker alias Clarke Peter, Barnstaple 1623 [W]
Phineas, Northam 1703 W
Crooker Phineas, Northam 1723 [W]
Priscilla, Hartland 1756 A
Richard, Huish 1594 [W]
Richard, Frithelstock 1662 [W]
Richard, St Giles in the Wood 1702 W
Richard, Buckland Brewer 1706 W
Richard, Northam 1727 A
Richard, Chittlehampton 1780 W
Richard, Bideford 1837 W
Richard, Winkleigh 1838 W
Richard, Chittlehampton 1840 W
Robert, Shebbear 1592 [W]
Robert, Barnstaple 1718 W
Robert, Burrington 1782 W
Robert, Coldridge 1786 A
Robert, Coldridge 1805 A
Robert, Zeal Monachorum 1822 A
Roger, Roborough 1715 W
Roger, Barnstaple 1734 A
Samuel, Chittlehampton, yeoman 1814 A to Betty, widow
Samuel, Fremington 1841 W
Sarah, Barnstaple 1739 W
Stephen, Huntshaw 1681 A
Stephen, Fremington 1719 W
Susan, Huntshaw 1682 A
Susan, Bideford 1845 A
Thomas, Fremington 1742 W
Tristram 1747 W
Walter, Rose Ash 1738 W
William, Shebbear 1569 W
William, Kentisbury 1592 [W]
William, Abbotsham 1627 [W]
Crocker alias Landman William, Rose Ash 1669 W and A
William, Rose Ash 1692 A
William, Bideford 1741 A
Crockford Elizabeth, Ilfracombe, widow 1803 W
Crockhay Thomas, Frithelstock 1592 [W], 1593 [W] and A
  account
Crocombe, Crocomb
  Crocomb ..., Bideford 1607 [W]
  Crocomb ..., Goodleigh 1669 [W]
  Crocomb alias Burgess ..., Lynton 1703 W
  Agnes, Brendon 1826 A to John, son
  George, Arlington 1731 W
  George, Lynton 1834 W
  Ilett, Brendon 1686 W
  Joan, Lynton 1634 W

John, Lynton 1575 W
John, Lynton 1619 [W]
John, Brendon 1681 W
John, Lynton 1689 W
John, Brendon, snr., gentleman 1804 W
Rebecca, Arlington 1747 W
Richard, Lynton 1588 W and 1597 [W]
Richard, Arlington, snr. 1706 W
Crocomb Richard, Arlington 1733 W
Richard, Lynton 1792 W
Roger, Lynton 1598 W
Susan, Lynton 1794 W
Thomas, Brendon 1682 W
Crocomb William, snr., Georgeham 1611 [W]; forename blank
   in Ms; supplied from parish register
   see also Crosscombe
Crooke, Crocke, Croke, Crook, Cruck
Crook ..., Romansleigh 1611 [W]
..., Rose Ash 1615 [W]
Agnes, Meshaw 1622 [W]
Crook Agnes, Winkleigh 1680 W
Agnes, Rackenford 1688 W
Alexander, Thelbridge, husbandman 1802 W
Crocke or Cocke Alice, South Molton 1574 [W]
Crook Ann, Rackenford 1665 W
Augustine, Witheridge 1596 [W]
Catherine, North Tawton 1661 [W]
Cicely, Cruwys Morchard 1613 [W]; forename blank in Ms;
   supplied from parish register
Frances, South Molton 1741 W
George, Oakford 1730 A
Hugh, Cruwys Morchard 1613 [W]; forename blank in Ms;
   supplied from parish register
Hugh, Puddington 1615 [W]
Hugh, Stoodleigh 1691 A
Crook Hugh, Puddington 1693 A
Crook Hugh, Oakford 1708 W
Crook Hugh, South Molton 1812 W
James, Rackenford 1619 [W]
Joan, East Anstey 1620 [W]
Joan, Puddington 1686 A
Joan, Witheridge 1724 W
Joan, Rackenford 1761 W
John, East Anstey 1563 W
Croke John, East Anstey 1566 W
Croke John, East Worlington 1571 W
John, Witheridge 1579 W
Crooke alias Grindon John, Witheridge 1580 W
John, Puddington 1619 [W]
John, Beaford 1629 [W]
John, Thelbridge 1635 W
John, Rackenford 1637 W and 1639 W
John, Oakford 1640 W
John, Rackenford 1671 A
Crook John, Rackenford 1704 W
John, Puddington 1813 A to Mary, widow
Crook John, Rackenford 1815 W
Mary, Rackenford 1590 [W]
Crook Mary, Rackenford 1781 [W]
Croke Nicholas, Witheridge 1580 W
Nicholas, Beaford 1633 W
Cruck Nicholas, Winkleigh 1737 W
Crook Peter, Witheridge 1823 W
Raymond, Rackenford 1668 W
Richard, East Anstey 1688 A
Richard, Chulmleigh 1726 W
Robert, Rackenford 1574 A
Robert, Beaford 1629 [W]
Robert, Witheridge 1636 A
Robert, Chulmleigh 1744 A
Crook Roger, Witheridge 1712 W
Susanna see Samuel Downe
Thomas, East Anstey 1600 W
Thomas, Buckland Filleigh 1619 [W]
Thomas, North Tawton 1638 W

Crook Thomas, Rackenford 1664 W
Crook Thomas, Filleigh, yeoman 1802 W
Crook Thomasine, Rackenford 1704 A
Vincent, Rackenford 1641 W
William, Rackenford 1579 W
William, Burrington 1597 [W]
William, Oakford 1644 A
William, Rackenford 1733 W and A
Crook William, Rackenford 1777 W
Crook William, Chittlehampton, yeoman 1802 W
Crook William, South Molton, yeoman 1808 W
Crook William, Rackenford 1818 W
Willmot, Rackenford 1669 A
Crooker see Crocker
Croote, Croot
..., Bideford 1612 [W]
James, North Tawton 1767 W
Robert, West Worlington 1581 W
Robert, North Tawton 1789 W
Croot Thomas, North Tawton 1741 W
William, North Tawton 1615 [W]
Cropp see Crapp
Croscombe see Crosscombe
Crosman see Crossman
Cross, Crasse, Crosse
Crasse ..., Chittlehampton 1609 [W]
Crasse Henry, Barnstaple 1633 A
Crosse Henry, Barnstaple 1643 W
Henry, Pilton 1730 W
Henry, Ilfracombe 1777 W
James, Barnstaple 1754 W
Robert, Fremington 1673 W
Crasse William, Witheridge 1590 [W]
William, Dowland 1771 W
Crosscombe, Crascomb, Crascombe, Croscombe
Crascomb ..., Georgeham 1609 [W]
Croscomb David, Combe Martin 1579 A
Croscomb Isaac, Ilfracombe 1712 W
Crascomb James, Georgeham 1598 [W]
Croscombe James, Georgeham 1663 W
Croscomb James, Northam 1701 W
Croscombe Joan, Georgeham 1618 [W]
Crascomb John, Barnstaple 1721 A
Croscombe alias Crossman John, Bideford, labourer 1808 W
Croscomb Peter, Bratton Fleming 1713 W
Philip, Bideford 1782 A
Croscomb Richard, Georgeham 1706 A
Crascomb Thomas, Pilton 1734 W
Croscombe Thomas, Bideford 1799 W
Crascomb William, Georgeham 1642 W
Crascomb William, Georgeham 1670 [W]
Croscombe William, Bideford 1812 W
Croscombe William, Bideford, mariner 1820 A to Harriet,
   widow
   see also Crocombe
Crossing Francis, Bideford 1755 W
Richard, ship *Eagle* 1756 A
Crossman
Crossman alias Croscombe John 1808 W
Crosman William, Alverdiscott 1580 W
Crowe Thomas, Shebbear 1616 [W]
Cruck see Crooke
Crudge, Crugge
Dorothy, Witheridge 1684 W
Elizabeth, Oakford 1845 W
James, Heightley St Mary ex parochial, but part of Oakford
   appurtenant to Stoodleigh 1831 W
John, Stoodleigh 1593 [W]
John, Hartland 1594 [W]
John, Barnstaple 1610 [W]; forename blank in Ms; supplied
   from parish register
John, West Anstey 1834 W
Margaret, Stoodleigh 1599 [W]
Nicholas, Rackenford 1625 [W]
Richard, Loxhore 1596 [W]

Crugge Simon, Hartland 1570 W
   Stephen, Witheridge 1619 [W]
   William, Oakford 1837 W
     see also Cridge
Crump, Crumpe
   Dorothy, Bideford 1691 W
   Crumpe Samuel, Bideford 1688 W
Crunn John, Northam 1823 W
Cruse, Chruse, Crews, Crewse, Cruste, Crute
   Ambrose, Westleigh 1687 W
   Andrew, East Anstey 1620 [W]
   Anthony, Bideford 1711 W
   Archelaus, Barnstaple 1673 W
   Crews Eleanor, Barnstaple 1712 W
   George, Winkleigh 1670 W
   George, Winkleigh 1688 A
   Crewse Hannibal, Winkleigh 1644 W
   Henry, Cruwys Morchard 1667 W
   Chruse John, Winkleigh 1601 [W]
   John, Winkleigh 1707 W
   John, Dolton 1730 W
   John, Winkleigh 1746 W
   Lewis, Winkleigh 1675 W
   Lodovic, Cruwys Morchard 1641 A
   Mary, Cruwys Morchard 1679 W
   Cruste Nicholas, Great Torrington 1599 [W]
   Crute Peter, Bideford 1705 A
   Preston, Burrington 1783 W
   Thomas, Washford Pyne 1622 [W]
   Thomas, Winkleigh 1667 A
   Crews Tryphena, Barnstaple 1719 W
   William, Barnstaple 1670 [W]
Crute see Cruse
Cryspen see Crispin
Cryspyn see Crispin
Cuddy Philip, Iddesleigh 1690 [W]
Cudemor see Cudmore
Cudlipp Mary, Northam 1636 W
Cudmore, Cudemor
   ..., Buckland Filleigh 1606 [W]
   ..., Petrockstowe 1612 [W]
   Anthony, Petrockstowe 1575 W
   Edmund, Great Torrington 1632 [W]
   Elizabeth, North Tawton 1696 W
   Jane and John, Frithelstock 1669 A
   John, Huntshaw 1576 W
   Cudemor John, Buckland Filleigh 1586 [W]
   John, Rackenford 1593 [W]
   John, Great Torrington 1613 [W]; forename blank in Ms;
     supplied from parish register
   John, Petrockstowe 1674 W
   John, Peters Marland 1719 W
   John, Chawleigh 1749 W
   John and Jane, Frithelstock 1669 A
   Joseph, Petrockstowe 1696 A
   Mary, Rackenford 1645 W
   Robert, Rackenford 1642 W
   Susan, Iddesleigh 1805 A
   Thomas, Alverdiscott 1611 [W]; forename blank in Ms;
     supplied from parish register
   Thomas, Ashreigney 1693 W
   Thomas, Chawleigh 1765 W
   William, Ashreigney 1822 W
Cudwell John, Abbotsham 1645 W
Culender see Collander
Culliford Grace, Rackenford 1622 [W]
   Richard, Rackenford 1610 [W]; forename blank in Ms;
     supplied from parish register
   Zachariah, Rackenford 1506 [W]
Culme Stephen, Berrynarbor 1610 [W]; forename blank in Ms;
     supplied from parish register
Culverwell, Culverwill
   John, West Buckland 1663 A
   Culverwill John, West Buckland 1672 W
Cumbe see Combe

Cummins, Comens, Comins, Commins, Comyns, Cumming
   Comens alias Chilcott Agnes, Oakford 1619 [W]
   Comins Andrew, Witheridge 1858 W
   Comyns Elizabeth, Woolfardisworthy 1791 W
   Comins James, South Molton, yeoman 1810 W
   Comen alias Stockhame John, Knowstone 1574 W
   Commins John, Witheridge 1784 W
   Comins Mary, Witheridge 1790 W
   Cumming Philip, Witheridge 1702 W and 1706 W
   Commins Thomas, Witheridge 1778 W
   Comins Thomas, Witheridge, schoolmaster 1851 A to
     Christian
   Comins Thomas see also William Cobley
   Comens alias Chelcoll William, Oakford 1605 W "Chilcott" in
     register; forename blank in Ms; supplied from parish register
   Commins William, Witheridge 1745 W
   Commins William, Witheridge 1784 W; A dbn
Cundall Amy, Barnstaple 1607 [W]; forename blank in Ms;
     supplied from parish register
   John, Barnstaple 1598 [W]
Cunebear, Cunebeare, Cunnebeare, Cunnibear see Conibeare
Cunningham Ann, South Molton 1831 W
   Joan, South Molton 1852 W
   John, Petrockstowe 1684 A
   John, South Molton 1786 A
   Richard, South Molton 1773 W
   Richard, South Molton 1827 W
   Thomas, South Molton 1775 A
   Thomas, South Molton 1851 W
Cunnybeare, Cunybear see Conibeare
Cupper Daniel, Iddesleigh 1631 [W]
   Joan, Burrington 1687 A
   John, Iddesleigh 1635 W
   John, Burrington 1640 W
   John, Dowland 1672 W
   Margery, Dowland 1675 W
   Petronell, Iddesleigh 1686 W
   Philip, Iddesleigh 1593 [W]
   Walter, Iddesleigh 1700 W and 1708 W
   William, Burrington 1620 [W]
   William, Dowland 1640 W
   William, Burrington 1686 W
Cupy Hannibal, Burrington 1640 W
Cure Agnes and John, Barnstaple 1696 A
   Agnes, Tawstock 1703 W
   Isaac, Tawstock 1672 A
   Joan, Tawstock 1707 W
   John, Barnstaple 1690 A
   John and Agnes, Barnstaple 1696 A
   John, Bideford 1701 W
Curms John, Northam 1733 W
Currie see Curry
Currington John, Fremington 1805 W
Curry Daniel, Frithelstock 1742 A
   Elizabeth, Horwood 1713 W
   Honoria, Tawstock 1711 W
   John, East Buckland 1661 W
   Robert, South Molton 1687 W
   Currie Thomas, Heanton Punchardon 1563 W
Curtis, Cortice, Courteis, Courtice, Courties, Courtis, Curtice,
   Curtys
   Courteis ..., South Molton 1601 A
   Courteis ..., Martinhoe 1605 [W] and 1614 [W]
   Courteis ..., Great Torrington 1608 [W]
   Courteis ..., Knowstone 1613 [W]
   Abraham, Bideford 1729 W
   Courties Agnes, Fremington 1625 [W], 1629 [W] and O
   Courties Alexander, Northam 1622 [W]
   Courtice Ann, Filleigh 1757 W
   Courtice Ann, Martinhoe 1761 W
   Courtie Ann, Bideford 1767 W
   Courtice Ann, Northam 1772 W
   Courtice Ann, Lynton 1824 W
   Courties Anthony, Barnstaple 1633 W
   Curtis Anthony, Filleigh 1678 A
   Cortice Anthony, Filleigh 1779 W

Arthur, Pilton 1735 A
Courties David, Ilfracombe 1620 [W]
Curtys David, Molland 1739 A
Courtis Edmund, Filleigh 1708 A
Courtis Eleanor, Bideford 1676 W
Courteis George, Bideford 1612 [W]; forename blank in Ms;
    supplied from parish register
Courtice George, Ilfracombe 1761 A
Grace, Barnstaple 1723 W
Courtis Helena, Huntshaw 1680 W
Henry, Burrington 1725 W
Honorius, Marwood 1726 W
Curtice Hugh, Chulmleigh 1721 A
Courties Humphrey, Martinhoe 1628 [W]
Courties Jane, Dolton 1593 [W]
Courtice Joan, Barnstaple 1769 W
Courtice Joan, Loxhore 1788 A
Courtis John, Highampton 1563 W
Courtis John, Fremington 1569 W
Courtice John, Atherington 1581 W
Courteis John, Bratton Fleming 1590 [W]
Courteis John, Ilfracombe 1615 [W]
Courtice John, Bratton Fleming 1667 W
Courtice John, Winkleigh 1667 A
Courtis John, Bratton Fleming 1691 W
Courtis John, Barnstaple, snr. 1698 A
Courtis John, Heanton Punchardon 1707 A
Courtis John, Bideford 1710 A
Courtis John, Loxhore 1710 W
John, Bideford 1728 A
John, Loxhore 1736 W
John, Chulmleigh 1744 W
Curtice John, ship *Pembroke* 1750 W
Courtice alias Coul John, Hartland 1814 W
Courtice John, West Buckland 1826 W
Cortice John, Berrynarbor 1830 W
Courtis John, Shirwell 1834 W
Jonathan, Chittlehampton 1730 A
Curtice Joseph, Pilton 1736 W
Courtis Lodovic, Great Torrington 1677 W
Courtis Magdalen, Pilton 1676 W
Miriam, Enmore, sp. 1853 A to William, innkeeper, brother
Courtes Philip, Hartland 1577 W
Curtice Prudence, Northam 1797 W
Courtice Rebecca, Loxhore 1741 W
Courties Richard, Kentisbury 1589 W
Courtis Richard, Bratton Fleming 1641 W
Courtis Richard, Bratton Fleming 1696 W
Richard, Barnstaple 1728 W
Courtis Richard, Pilton 1754 W
Courties Robert, Bratton Fleming 1624 [W]
Courtis Robert, Stoke Rivers 1694 W
Curtice Robert, Bideford 1750 W
Courtice Robert, Buckland Brewer 1818 W
Courties Roger, Fremington 1629 [W]
Courtice Sarah, Bideford 1691 W
Sarah, Bideford 1762 W
Courtis Thomas, Bideford 1579 A
Courties Thomas, Barnstaple 1585 [W]
Courties Thomas, Knowstone 1592 [W]
Courties Thomas, Martinhoe 1592 [W]
Courties Thomas, Challacombe 1596 [W] and 1599 [W]
Courtis Thomas, Bideford 1663 A
Courtice Thomas, Huntshaw 1668 W
Courtis Thomas, Merton 1672 A
Thomas, Northam 1730 A
Courtis Thomas, Lynton 1755 A
Courtice Thomas, Northam 1786 W
Courtis Ursula, Hartland 1673 W
Courties Walter, Westleigh 1589 A
Courtys William, Bratton Fleming 1579 [W]
Courties William, Fremington 1620 [W]
Courties William, Parkham 1631 [W]
Courtis William, Fremington 1676 A
Courtis William, Oakford 1678 W

Courtis William, Bideford 1699 W
Courtis William, Bratton Fleming 1702 W
William, Bideford 1727 W
William, Littleham (near Bideford) 1728 W
Courtis William, Chulmleigh 1816 W
William, Stoodleigh, yeoman 1821 W to Jane, widow
William, Bideford 1829 W
Curtice William, Great Torrington 1833 W
Courtis William, Bideford 1849 W
Curver ..., Brendon 1607 [W]
Cusens see Cousins
Cusick Michael, Northam 1745 A
Cuss Agnes, North Molton 1744 W
Cutcliffe, Cutclif, Cutclife, Cutcliff, Cutclyfe, Cutleffe, Cutliffe,
    Cutlyff, Cuttcliff
    Cutclif ..., Berrynarbor 1600 A
    ..., Kentisbury 1609 [W]
    ..., Berrynarbor 1614 [W]
    Alice, Berrynarbor 1616 [W]
    Ann, Ilfracombe 1637 W
    Ann, Combe Martin 1818 W
    Cutcliff Arthur, Heanton Punchardon 1695 W
    Cutcliff Cecilia, West Down 1688 W
    Charles and Grace, Ilfracombe 1637 W
    Christian, Kentisbury 1638 W
    Cutliffe Edward, Combe Martin 1672 W
    Edward, Combe Martin 1733 W
    Edward, Combe Martin 1786 A
    Edward, Combe Martin, mariner 1846 A to Elizabeth, widow
    Francis, Ilfracombe 1745 A
    George, East Down, yeoman 1805 W
    Grace and Charles, Ilfracombe 1637 W
    Cutcliff Honoria, Combe Martin 1679 A
    James John, Barnstaple 1843 A
    Cutcliff Jane, East Down 1708 W
    Jane, East Down 1804 A
    Joan, Combe Martin 1792 A
    Cutleffe John, Berrynarbor 1566 W
    Cutlyff John, Georgeham 1574 W
    Cutclyfe John, Indicknowle, Berrynarbor 1588 W
    John, Berrynarbor 1622 [W]
    Cuttcliff John, Ilfracombe 1663 W
    Cutcliff John, Combe Martin 1688 W
    Cutcliffe John, Ilfracombe 1730 W
    John, Pilton 1736 A
    John, Bratton Fleming 1771 W
    John, Combe Martin 1778 A
    John, Combe Martin 1794 W
    John, Combe Martin 1817 W
    John 1839 W
    John, Combe Martin 1855 W
    John E. see Richard Pasmore
    Cutcliff Joseph, Ilfracombe 1681 W
    Mary, Berrynarbor 1733 A
    Mary, South Molton 1845 W
    Mathew, West Down 1639 W
    Cutliffe Nicholas, Combe Martin 1776 W
    Nicholas, Combe Martin 1842 W
    Cutliffe Nicholas, Combe Martin 1850 W
    Cutliff Richard, Arlington 1572 W
    Cutclife Richard, East Down 1626 [W]
    Richard, Barnstaple 1769 A
    Richard, Combe Martin, mariner 1816 A to Elizabeth, widow
    Richard, Barnstaple 1825 W
    Cutliffe Robert, Ilfracombe 1748 W
    Cutliffe Susan, Ilfracombe 1749 W
    Thomas, Ilfracombe 1630 [W] and 1632 [W]
    Thomas, Kentisbury 1636 [W]
    Cutcliff Thomas, Great Torrington 1664 A
    Thomas, Bideford 1744 A
    Cutliffe Thomas, Bideford 1747 W
    Cutclife William, Berrynarbor 1603 W
    Cutcliff William, Hartland 1694 A
Cutford Ambrose, West Anstey 1640 A
Cutland ..., Filleigh 1615 [W]

Abraham, Great Torrington 1621 [W]
John, St Giles in the Wood 1591 [W]
Lewis, Fremington 1609 [W]; forename blank in Ms; supplied
   from parish register
Penelope, Great Torrington 1633 W
Richard, Filleigh 1572 W
Cutleffe see Cutcliffe
Cutleigh see Cutley
Cutler Henry, Northam 1745 W
Cutler alias Shapter John, Barnstaple 1568 W
Cutley, Cutlie, Cutly, Cutlye
Beatrice, Pilton 1664 W
Cutly Henry, Heanton Punchardon 1703 A
Cuttlie John, Kentisbury 1575 A
Cutleigh John, Pilton 1686 A
John, Heanton Punchardon 1697 A
Cutly John, Pilton 1698 A
Cutlie Judith, Berrynarbor 1613 [W]; forename blank in Ms;
   supplied from parish register
Mathew, Hartland 1664 A
Cutlye Richard, Combe Martin 1619 [W]
Richard, Combe Martin 1675 W
Thomas, Kentisbury 1666 A
Cutlie William, Berrynarbor 1612 [W] "of Yolaton" in
   register; forename blank in Ms; supplied from parish register
Cutly William, Berrynarbor 1707 A
Cutliff, Cutliffe see Cutcliffe
Cutly, Cutlye see Cutley
Cutlyff, Cuttcliff see Cutcliffe
Cutting George, St Giles in the Wood 1669 [W]
Henry, Great Torrington 1662 A
John, Great Torrington 1661 W

D ...inch James, Bideford 1639 A
Dabb, Dabbe
Francis, Sheepwash 1673 A
Dabbe Harry, Ashreigney 1576 W
John, High Bickington 1686 W and 1688 W
Rebecca, Sheepwash 1682 W
Richard, Ashreigney 1661 W
Dabyn William, Great Torrington 1582 W
Dadds William, South Molton 1852 W
Daft
Daft or Dight John, Shirwell 1602 W
Dagford Hugh, Chulmleigh 1699 W
John, Burrington 1579 W
John, North Molton 1636 A and 1637 O
John, Burrington 1730 W
John, Burrington 1748 W
Roger, Burrington 1730 W
Susan, Burrington 1721 W
Thomas, Burrington 1595 [W]
Thomas, Chulmleigh 1623 [W]
Thomas, Chittlehampton 1629 [W] and 1630 [W]
William, Burrington 1593 [W]
Daie see Day
Dale Caleb, South Molton 1740 W
Richard, Zeal Monachorum 1736 A
William, South Molton 1829 W
Dallen, Dallin, Dalling, Dallinge, Dallyn, Dallyon, Dulin,
   Dulling, Dulon
..., West Buckland 1604 [W]
Dallyn ..., Chittlehampton 1611 [W] and 1613 [W]
..., Bratton Fleming 1612 [W]
..., Heanton Punchardon 1612 [W]
..., Horwood 1613 [W]
Dallyn ..., Heanton Punchardon 1667 A
Agnes, Peters Marland, widow 1570 W
Dallin Alexander, Heanton Punchardon 1747 W
Dalling Alice, Hartland 1734 A
Dallyn Ambrose, Challacombe 1820 A to Thomas, son
Dallyn Ambrose, Challacombe 1826 A
Dallyn Ambrose, West Buckland 1849 W
Dalling Ann, Berrynarbor 1701 W
Dulling Constantine, Great Torrington 1712 W

Edward, Bideford 1604 [W]; forename blank in Ms; supplied
   from parish register
Dalling Edward, Combe Martin 1644 W
Dallin Elizabeth, Ilfracombe 1824 W
Dalling Elizabeth, Ilfracombe 1841 A
Dallyn Francis, Ilfracombe 1626 [W] and 1628 O
George, Marwood 1579 A
Dalling George, Ilfracombe 1687 W
Dalling George, Berrynarbor 1689 W
Dallyn George, Ilfracombe 1700 W
Dalling George, Pilton 1849 W
Gertrude, Martinhoe 1626 [W]
Dallinge Hugh, Hartland 1601 W
Dalling Humphrey, Berrynarbor 1708 W
Dalling James, Heanton Punchardon, merchant 1822 A to
   Mary, widow
Dallyn Jane, West Buckland 1624 [W]
Dallin Jane, Georgeham 1693 W
Dallyn Jane and Simon, Chittlehampton 1696 A
Dallyn John, St Giles in the Wood 1573 W
John, High Bray 1581 W
John, Brendon 1586 W
John, West Buckland 1589 W and A
John, Bratton Fleming 1590 [W]
Dallyn John, Molland 1600 W
Dallyn John, Heanton Punchardon 1605 W
Dulon John, Pilton 1607 [W] "Dillam" in register; forename
   blank in Ms; supplied from parish register
John, Bratton Fleming 1610 [W]; forename blank in Ms;
   supplied from parish register
Dallyn John, Instow 1615 [W]
John, West Buckland 1624 [W]
Dalling John, Berrynarbor 1704 A
Dallyn John, Chittlehampton 1711 A
Dalling John, Hartland 1728 W
Dalling John, Ilfracombe 1738 A
Dalling John, Bideford 1815 A
Dulin Judith, Great Torrington 1717 W
Margaret, Brendon 1596 [W]
Dalling Martha, Pilton 1693 A
Dallyn Mary, Fremington 1642 A
Dallyn Mary, Pilton 1726 A
Dullen Nicholas, Highampton 1577 W
Richard, Heanton Punchardon 1591 [W]
Dallyn Richard, Challacombe 1643 A
Dalling Richard, High Bray 1680 W
Dalling Richard, Martinhoe 1688 W
Dalling Richard, Berrynarbor 1694 W
Dallyon Richard see Thomas Isaac
Robert, Challacombe 1600 W
Dallin Robert, Bideford 1605 W
Dulling Robert, Great Torrington 1733 A
Dallyn Simon, Chittlehampton 1623 [W]
Dallyn Simon and Jane, Chittlehampton 1696 A
Dallyn Susan, Hartland 1675 A
Dallyn Susan, Bratton Fleming 1727 W
Thomas, Hartland 1594 [W]
Dallyn Thomas, Martinhoe 1594 [W]
Dallyn Thomas, Combe Martin 1617 [W]
Thomas, Challacombe 1637 [W]
Dallyn Thomas, Hartland, snr. 1642 W
Dallyn Thomas, Martinhoe 1671 W
Dalling Thomas, Hartland 1700 A
Dalling Thomas, Woolfardisworthy 1709 W
Dalling Thomas, Challacombe 1736 W
Dalling Thomas, Warkleigh 1780 W
Dallin Thomas, Ilfracombe 1793 W
Dalling Thomas, Heanton Punchardon 1818 W
Dallyn Tobias, Berrynarbor 1670 A
Dallyn Tobias, Berrynarbor 1695 W
Dallin Tobias, Berrynarbor 1744 A
Dallin Tobias, Ilfracombe 1780 W
Dallyn William, West Buckland 1565 W
William, Chittlehampton 1587 W
Dallinge William, Fremington 1674 A

Dalling William, Martinhoe 1682 W
Dallyn William, Bratton Fleming 1726 W and A
Dallyn William, Challacombe 1790 W
Dallyn William, Challacombe 1802 W
Dalling William, Ilfracombe 1843 A to Tobias, sailmaker,
    brother
    see also Dollen
Dalley see Dalley
Dallin see Dallen
Dalliner Alice, Tawstock 1605 [W]; forename blank in Ms;
    supplied from parish register
Dalling, Dallinge see Dallen
Dally, Dalley
    Richard, Bittadon 1815 W
    Dalley Richard, Bittadon 1819 W
Dallyn, Dallyon see Dallen
Damerell, Damarel, Damel, Damerall, Damrel
    Damarel Christopher, Bulkworthy 1842 W
    Davy, South Molton 1589 W
    Damerall James, Shebbear, miller 1856 A to Dinah, widow
    Joan, Tawstock 1665 W
    Damrel John, Petrockstowe 1784 A
    Damrel William, Sheepwash 1842 A
Damond see Diamond
Damrel see Damerell
Daniel, Danhill, Daniell, Dannell, Danyell, Danyoll
    Anthony, Great Torrington 1663 W
    Daniell Anthony, East Down 1724 W
    Daniell Augustine, Parkham 1672 W
    Augustine, High Bickington 1713 W
    Danyell David, Barnstaple 1621 [W]
    Edward, Loxhore 1715 W
    Daniell Edward, Westleigh 1729 O
    Daniell Edward, Marwood 1750 W
    Daniell Elizabeth, Marwood 1745 W
    Ezekiel, Marwood 1702 A
    George, East Down 1840 A to John of Kentisbury, son
    Daniell Jenkin, Alverdiscott 1599 [W]
    Joan, Marwood 1707 A
    Daniell John, Barnstaple 1584 A account
    Daniell John, Barnstaple 1609 [W]; forename blank in Ms;
    supplied from parish register
    Danyoll John, Marwood 1619 [W]
    Danyell John, Pilton, jnr. 1622 [W]
    Danyell John, Pilton 1627 [W]
    John, Marwood 1715 W
    Dannell John, Parkham 1721 W
    Daniell John, Bideford 1744 W
    Daniell John, ship *Namur* 1750 W
    Dannell John, Great Torrington 1775 A
    John, Loxhore 1786 W
    Danhill John, Loxhore, yeoman 1808 A
    Dannell John, Parkham 1824 A to Bartholomew, son
    John, Bideford 1854 W
    Mary, Bideford 1682 A
    Mary, Parkham 1716 A
    Daniell Mary, Parkham 1731 A
    Nathaniel, Parkham 1711 W
    Daniell Philip, Pilton 1622 [W]
    Daniell Robert, Westleigh 1607 [W]; forename blank in Ms;
    supplied from parish register
    Danyell Robert, Georgeham 1629 [W]
    Robert, Parkham 1695 A
    Daniell Robert, Barnstaple 1773 A
    Danyell Rose, Barnstaple 1627 [W]
    Daniell Susan, Northam 1745 W
    William, Combe Martin 1845 W
Darby, Darbie, Darbye
    Darbie ..., Martinhoe 1612 [W]
    Darbie John, Martinhoe 1582 W
    Darbye Margaret, Challacombe 1616 [W]
    Darbye Richard, Combe Martin 1628 A
    Walter, Kentisbury 1706 W
Darch, Darche
    ..., Chulmleigh 1607 and 1610 [W]

    Elizabeth, Witheridge 1616 [W]
Darche John, Rose Ash 1564 W
Darche John, Chulmleigh 1589 W
John, Witheridge 1597 [W]
John, Chulmleigh 1598 and 1599 [W]
John, Winkleigh 1752 W
John, Winkleigh, miller 1810 W
Peter, Ilfracombe 1852 A
Richard, High Bickington, yeoman 1797 A
Richard, Tawstock, yeoman 1851 A to Joan
Robert, Winkleigh 1845 W
Rose, Swimbridge 1854 W
Thomas, Chulmleigh 1742 and 1743 W
Thomas, Winkleigh 1849 W
William, Rose Ash 1598 [W]
William, Ashreigney 1720 A
William, Tawstock 1853 W
Darck see Dark
Dare, Dayar
    Dayar Thomas, Satterleigh 1677 W
    William, Bideford 1665 A
Dark, Darck, Darke, Dorke, Durck, Durcke, Durke
    Darck ..., Coldridge 1608 [W]
    Darke ..., Hartland 1610 [W]
    Durke Catherine, Buckland Brewer 1623 [W]
    Darke Charles, Barnstaple 1852 W
    Dorke Edulphus, Georgeham 1687 W
    Durck Giles, Parkham 1618 [W]
    Darke Isota, Coldridge 1626 [W]
    Darke Joan, Great Torrington 1585 W
    Durke John, Woodhouse, Great Torrington 1575 W
    John, Winkleigh 1587 W
    Durcke John, Chawleigh 1594 [W]
    John, Fremington 1620 [W]
    John, Parkham 1622 [W]
    Durke John, Buckland Brewer 1622 [W]
    Durke John, Parkham 1630 [W]
    John, Parkham 1812 W
    John, Alwington 1839 A
    John Allin, Parkham 1826 W
    Joseph Veale, Parkham 1839 A to Honor Sergeant, aunt
    Mary, Alwington 1780 W
    Mary, Parkham 1830 W
    Mary Ann, Petrockstowe 1857 W
    Durck Petherick, Ashreigney 1613 [W]; forename blank in Ms;
    supplied from parish register - surname spelled Darke there
    Durke Ralph, Great Torrington 1575 W
    Dorke Richard, Chawleigh 1568 W
    Durke Richard, Bow 1594 W
    Richard, Alwington 1749 W
    Richard, Wembworthy 1855 [W]
    Thomas, Parkham 1598 [W]
    Durke Thomas, Instow 1598 [W]
    Thomas, Langtree 1840 W
    Walter, Beaford 1621 [W]
    Durke William, Great Torrington 1571 W
    Durcke William, Parkham 1589 W
    William, Langtree 1822 W
    William Whiteborne, formerly of Holsworthy late of
    Barnstaple 1809 W
Darley, Darly
    Darly John, Bideford 1703 W
    Letitia, Bideford 1721 W
Darracoott, Daracott, Darracott, Darrecote, Dorracot, Dorracott,
    Dothacott
    Agnes, Bideford 1748 W
    Dorracott Ambrose, Shirwell 1639 W
    Ann, Northam 1728 A
    Daniel jnr. 1714 W
    Dorracott Dorothy, Barnstaple 1624 [W]
    Dorothy, Bideford 1679 W
    Ethelred, Northam 1751 W
    George, Bideford 1675 W
    Hugh, Shebbear 1772 W
    Humphrey, Huish 1693 W

Dorracot Jacob, Bideford 1633 [W]
Dorracott Jacob, Chittlehampton 1638 A
James, Bideford 1744 A
Daracott Joan, Northam 1635 W
Dorracott John, Bratton Fleming 1590 [W]
Dothacott John, Northam 1599 [W]
John, Instow 1622 A
Dorracott John, Barnstaple 1624 [W]
John, Bideford 1645 W
John, Bideford 1733 A
Joseph, Bideford 1722 A
Joseph, Northam 1766 W
Mark, Northam 1626 [W]
Mark, Heanton Punchardon 1697 A
Mary, Bideford 1675 A
Mary, Barnstaple 1680 W
Obadiah, Instow 1697 W
Peter, Northam 1622 [W] and 1624 O
Richard, Chulmleigh 1727 W and 1738 W
Darrecote Sabine, Tawstock 1569 W
Sarah, Bideford 1714 W
Sarah, Northam 1736 W
Thomas, Heanton Punchardon 1704 A
Walter, Northam 1722 A
Dorracott William, Barnstaple 1598 [W]
Dorracott William, Barnstaple 1640 W
William, Chittlehampton 1685 A
William, Instow 1694 A
William, Bideford 1739 A
Dart, Dartch, Darte
Ann, Coldridge 1721 W
Christian, Burrington 1580 W
Christopher, Bondleigh 1752 W
Christopher, Winkleigh 1833 W
George, Abbotsham 1697 W
George, Pilton 1704 A
Henry, Coldridge 1719 W
Henry, Coldridge 1745 W; 1781 A dbn
Henry, Winkleigh 1795 W
Honorius, Coldridge 1726 W
Darte Humphrey, Winkleigh 1622 [W]
James, Lapford 1690 W
Dartch Joan, Chulmleigh 1620 [W]
Darte John, Burrington 1580 W
Darte John, Pilton 1602 W
John, Cruwys Morchard 1637 W
John, Coldridge 1829 W
John, Molland 1842 W
John, Coldridge 1843 W
John Webber, Burrington 1823 W
Lewis, Barnstaple 1672 A
Margaret, Parkham 1716 A
Darte Mathew, Northam 1584 W
Michael, West Buckland 1730 A
Philip, Mortehoe 1713 A
Philip, Bondleigh 1736 A
Philip, Chawleigh 1813 W
Philip, King's Nympton 1827 W
Richard, Coldridge 1711 A
Richard, Winkleigh 1777 A
Richard, Bideford 1837 W
Darte Robert, Witheridge 1579 W
Roger, Coldridge 1710 W
Roger, Alwington 1762 W
Silvanus, Bow 1842 W
Dart alias Wreford Silvanus, Bow 1842 W
William, Tawstock 1689 A
William, Brushford 1805 W
William, Molland 1805 W
William, Zeal Monachorum 1837 W
Darvote William, High Bickington 1587 W
Dascombe see Datscombe
Dashe Joan, Combe Martin 1587 A
Date Alice, Ilfracombe 1570 W
Dennis, Ilfracombe 1566 W

Datman Agnes, Hartland 1586 W
Anthony, Welcombe 1788 W
Hugh, Hartland 1693 W
John, Hartland 1703 W
John, Hartland 1857 W
Lawrence, Hartland 1660 W
Margaret, Hartland 1663 W
Margaret, Hartland 1677 W
Martin, Hartland 1666 W
Mary, Frithelstock 1693 A
Paschal, Hartland 1693 W
William, Hartland 1767 W
Willmot, Hartland 1698 W
Datscombe, Dascombe ..., Stoodleigh 1617 [W]
Jacob, Stoodleigh 1637 A
Joan, Oakford 1632 [W]
Datscombe alias Hill John, East Anstey 1801 W
Dascombe Lewis, Twitchen 1781 W
Davells, Davels, Davills
Davills John, Peters Marland 1677 A
Davills John, Peters Marland 1692 A
Davels Margaret, Parkham 1578 W
Philip, Peters Marland 1627 W
Davenant James, Barnstaple 1618 [W]
Davey see Davy
David John, Shebbear 1565 W
John, Bideford 1737 A
Walter, Bideford 1565 W
Davies see Davis
Davills see Davells
Davis, Davies, Davyes
Davies Agnes, Bideford 1764 W
Davies Ann, Fremington 1757 W
Davies Catherine, Ilfracombe 1737 W
Davies Catherine, Bideford 1761 A
Davies Eleanor, Ilfracombe 1603 [W]; forename blank in Ms;
    supplied from parish register
Davies Elizabeth, Instow 1772 W
Davies Ellen, Goodleigh 1727 A
Davies Ethelred, Great Torrington 1742 A
Davies George, Parracombe 1735 W
Davies George, Great Torrington, yeoman 1800 W
George, Ilfracombe 1816 A
George, Bideford 1832 W
George, Ilfracombe 1833 W
George, Bideford 1836 AA
Humphrey, Fremington 1831 W
Davies Isaac, Atherington 1769 A
Davies James, West Buckland 1740 A
Davies James, Northam 1744 A and 1752 A
Davies James, Bideford 1748 W
Davies James, Ilfracombe 1764 A
Davies James, Bideford 1766 A
Jane, Great Torrington 1854 W
Davies John, Bideford, jnr. 1703 W
John, Northam 1740 A
Davies John, Bideford 1758 W
Davies John, Barnstaple 1763 W
John, Northam 1783 W
John, Ilfracombe 1789 A
Davies John, Bideford, fellmonger 1806 W
Davies John, Great Torrington 1816 W
Davies John, Burrington 1838 W
John, Lynton 1840 W
Joseph, Ilfracombe 1786 W
Lucinda, Burrington 1856 W
Margaret, Ilfracombe, widow 1802 W
Davies Mary, Clovelly 1723 W
Mary, Instow 1738 W
Davies Mary, Ilfracombe 1773 W
Mary see also Elizabeth Lake
Davies Philip, Ilfracombe 1707 W
Davies Philip, Great Torrington 1784 W
Davies Philip, Huntshaw 1825 W
Davies Richard, Fremington 1702 W

Robert, Instow 1704 W
Robert, Instow 1741 W
Davies Sarah, Northam 1682 W
Davies Thomas, ship *Royal Oak* 1749 A
Davies Thomas, Barnstaple 1772 W
Davyes William, Tawstock 1623 [W]
Davyes William, Barnstaple 1624 [W]
Davies William, Northam 1697 A
William, West Down, miller 1821 A to Mary, sp., daughter
Davison James, Ilfracombe, mariner 1810 A
Podierne, Northam 1735 A
Davy, Davey, Davie, Davye
..., Martinhoe 1604 [W]
Davie ..., Ilfracombe 1605 [W]
Davie ..., Stoke Rivers 1609 and 1610 [W]
Davie ..., Romansleigh 1612 [W]
Davie ..., South Molton 1612 [W]
..., Marwood 1615 [W]
Abraham, Molland 1635 W
Agnes, Marwood 1670 W
Alexander, Loxhore 1639 W
Alexander, West Buckland 1685 A
Davie Alexander, Loxhore 1712 W
Davye Alice, East Buckland 1629 [W]
Alice, Parkham 1678 W
Davie Alice, East Down 1764 W
Amesius, Chittlehampton 1687 A
Davie Amos, Alwington 1747 W
Davie Andrew, Zeal Monachorum 1669 A
Andrew, Rose Ash 1681 W
Davie Andrew, Goodleigh 1695 W
Davye Ann, Bideford 1579 W
Davie Ann, Roborough 1725 W
Davey Ann, Chittlehampton 1743 W
Ann, Heanton Punchardon 1808 W
Ann, Rose Ash 1825 W
Davey Ann, Lynton 1831 W
Anthony, Martinhoe 1604 W
Anthony, Bulkworthy 1681 W
Arthur, Dowland 1603 W
Arthur, Northam 1666 A
Arthur, Roborough 1685 W
Arthur, North Molton 1687 W
Davey Arthur, North Molton 1763 W
Asa, Roborough 1709 W
Bartholomew, Great Torrington 1630 [W]
Davie Benjamin, Ilfracombe 1720 A
Davey Charles, North Molton 1740 W
Charles, Clovelly 1783 W
Davie Christopher, Barnstaple 1613 [W]; forename blank in
   Ms; supplied from parish register
Davye Christopher, Warkleigh 1621 [W] and 1625 O
Christopher, Burrington 1661 W and 1666 A
Davie Cyprian, Molland 1612 [W]; forename blank in Ms;
   supplied from parish register
Daniel, Littleham (near Bideford) 1691 W
Davie Dorothy, Frithelstock 1716 W
Davye Edmund, Huish 1599 [W]
Davye Edward, South Molton 1591 [W]
Edward, Weare Giffard 1686 A
Eleanor, Chittlehampton 1665 W
Eleanor, Northam 1665 W
Davie Eleanor, North Molton 1725 W
Davye Elizabeth, Barnstaple 1589 W
Davye Elizabeth, North Molton 1626 [W]
Elizabeth, Barnstaple 1632 [W]
Elizabeth, Chittlehampton 1666 [W]
Davey Elizabeth, Beaford 1700 W
Davie Elizabeth, Chulmleigh 1759 A
Davie Elizabeth, Winkleigh 1802 A
Davie Elizabeth, Bideford 1819 W
Davey Elizabeth, Barnstaple 1821 W and 1831 W
Davye Emma, Barnstaple 1620 [W]
Ethelred, Great Torrington 1684 W
Davey Ethelred, Great Torrington 1735 A

Evan, East Anstey 1669 A
Evan, Heanton Punchardon 1700 W
Evan, Instow [no year given] [W]
Frances, Roborough 1633 W
Davey Frank, Roborough 1753 A
Davie Gabriel, Lynton 1721 W
Gawen, Roborough 1688 W
Davie Geoffrey, Romansleigh 1571 W
Davye Geoffrey, Warkleigh 1593 and 1595 [W]
Davye George, Bow 1594 [W]
Davye George, Shirwell 1629 [W]
George, Bideford 1709 A
Davie George, North Molton 1710 W
Davey George, Puddington 1750 W
Davey George, ship *Sunderland* 1761 A
George, South Molton 1764 W
George, South Molton 1818 W
Davey George, Pilton 1836 A
Gregory, Bideford 1604 A
Gregory, Stoke Rivers 1633 W
Griffith, South Molton 1688 W
Griffith, Weare Giffard 1707 A
Davie Griffith, Barnstaple 1734 A
Davye Henry, Shirwell 1597 [W]
Davie alias Evans Henry, Romansleigh 1606 W
Davie Henry, North Molton 1614 [W]; forename blank in Ms;
   supplied from parish register
Henry, Hartland 1662 A
Henry, North Molton 1685 W
Henry, Roborough 1690 A
Davey Henry, Bittadon 1709 A
Henry, Bittadon 1711 A
Henry, South Molton 1720 W
Davie Henry, North Molton 1721 W
Davey Henry, Frithelstock 1728 A
Davey Henry, St Giles in the Wood 1741 [W]
Davie Hugh, Abbotsham 1581 A
Davye Hugh, Chittlehampton 1598 [W]
Hugh, Roborough 1675 W
Hugh, Frithelstock 1714 W
Davey Hugh, Chulmleigh 1739 W
Hugh, Roborough 1764 W
Davie Hugh, Pilton 1830 W
Davie Humphrey, Atherington 1681 W
Davie Humphrey, Tawstock 1758 A
Humphrey, Ilfracombe 1853 A
James, High Bray 1615 [W]
James, West Worlington 1662 W
James, Weare Giffard 1685 W
James, Westleigh 1765 W
Davey James, Witheridge 1820 W
James, Rose Ash 1828 A to John Tanner Davy, brother
Davie Jane, Roborough, widow 1611 [W]; forename blank in
   Ms; supplied from parish register
Davie Joan, Ilfracombe, widow 1564 W
Davie Joan, Chawleigh 1578 W
Davye Joan, Tawstock 1598 [W]
Davye Joan, Cheldon 1626 [W]
Joan, Bideford 1630 [W]
Joan, Parracombe 1664 A
Davey Joan, Chittlehampton, widow 1672 W
Davy alias Evans alias Yeovans Joan, Heanton Punchardon,
   widow 1672 W
Joan, Burrington 1672 A
Davy alias Evans Joan, Witheridge 1673 [W]
Joan, North Molton 1688 W
Davie Joan, Great Torrington 1733 A
Davey Joan, Great Torrington 1747 W
Davey Joan, North Molton 1799 W*
Davie John, Stoke Rivers 1563 A
Davye John, Barnstaple 1572 W
Davye John, Martinhoe 1580 W
Davie John, Pilton 1581 W
John, Barnstaple 1581 W
Davie John, Ilfracombe 1582 A

Davie John, Molland 1582 W
John, Ilfracombe 1587 W
Davye John, Roborough 1592 [W]
Davye John, Romansleigh 1592 [W]
John, High Bickington 1594 [W]
Davye John, North Molton 1596 [W]
Davye John, Tawstock 1598 [W]
John, Stoke Rivers 1602 W
Davie John, Beaford 1605 W
John, Barnstaple 1610 [W]; forename blank in Ms; supplied
    from parish register
Davie John, Bideford, mariner 1612 [W]; forename blank in
    Ms; supplied from parish register
Davye John, Chittlehampton 1617 [W]
John, Bideford 1618 [W]
John, Roborough 1630 [W]
John, Parkham, jnr. 1635 W
John, Arlington 1637 W
John, Barnstaple 1637 W
John, Twitchen 1637 W
John, Martinhoe 1661 W
Davy alias Thomas John, Thelbridge 1663 [W]
John, Chittlehampton 1666 A
John, Goodleigh 1667 W
John, Combe Martin 1668 W
John, Burrington 1669 W, 1678 W and 1679 W
John, Ashreigney 1672 A
John, Iddesleigh 1678 W
John, Yarnscombe 1678 W
John, North Molton 1682 W
John, Roborough 1686 W
John, Burrington 1688 W
Davy alias Thomas John, South Molton 1688 W
John, Witheridge 1690 W
Davy alias Thomas John, Hartland 1690 W
John, Roborough 1691 A
John, Bideford 1693 W
Davie John, Goodleigh 1701 W
John, North Molton 1705 A
Davy alias Thomas John, Alverdiscott 1707 A
John, Bideford 1710 A
John, East Down 1710 W
John, Beaford 1711 A
John, North Molton 1712 W, 1714 W and 1717 W
John, Burrington 1715 W
Davy alias Thomas John, Mariansleigh 1717 W
Davie John, Roborough 1720 A
Davie John, King's Nympton 1721 A
Davie John, Great Torrington 1730 A
Davey John, Roborough 1739 A
Davey John, Great Torrington 1740 W
Davie John, Barnstaple 1744 A
Davey John, Great Torrington 1750 W
Davie John, Northam 1755 A
Davie John, Goodleigh 1777 W
Davie John, Winkleigh 1780 W
Davey John, Witheridge 1795 W
John, Rose Ash 1795 W
Davey John, High Bickington 1838 A to John and Eliza,
    children
Davie John, Barnstaple 1839 W
Davey John, Ashford 1842 W
Davey John, Littleham (near Bideford) 1842 W
Davie John, Barnstaple 1852 A
John see also Susanna Cory
John Tanner, Rose Ash 1852 W
Davy alias Evans John Thomas, Thelbridge 1663 A
Joseph, Stoke Rivers 1643 W
Joseph, Pilton 1698 A
Joseph, Rose Ash, yeoman 1806 W
Lawrence, Atherington 1690 A
Margaret, Arlington 1665 A
Margery, Great Torrington 1684 A
Margery, Barnstaple 1690 W
Mark, Barnstaple 1707 A
Davye Martin, South Molton 1592 [W]

Davey Mary, Barnstaple 1732 A
Davie Mary, East Buckland 1752 A
Davey Mary, Barnstaple 1849 A
Mary, North Molton 1850 W
Mary and Thomas, Chawleigh 1775 W
Mathew, North Molton 1635 A
Michael, East Down 1630 [W]
Michael, South Molton 1696 A
Michael, South Molton 1707 W
Michael, North Molton 1765 W
Nathaniel, Romansleigh 1670 W
Nicholas, Bideford 1686 W
Owen, Weare Giffard 1672 W
Davye Peter, Cheldon 1597 [W]
Peter, Bideford 1635 A
Peter, Warkleigh 1701 W
Peter, Chittlehampton 1707 W
Davey Peter, High Bickington 1742 A
Davey Peter, King's Nympton 1742 A
Davie Philip, Barnstaple 1581 A
Philip, Barnstaple 1631 [W]
Davie Philip, Barnstaple 1704 A
Philip, Roborough 1712 W
Davie Philip, North Molton 1759 W
Davie Philip, Winkleigh 1783 W
Philip, North Molton, maltster 1803 W
Davie Phillippa, Iddesleigh 1603 W
Davye Ralph, Barnstaple 1629 [W]
Davie Richard, Great Torrington 1563 W
Richard, Huish 1587 W
Davye Richard, King's Nympton 1591 [W]
Davye Richard, Parkham 1591 [W]
Davye Richard, Tawstock 1598 [W]
Richard, Martinhoe 1624 [W]
Davye Richard, Martinhoe, jnr. 1625 [W]
Davye Richard, Barnstaple 1627 [W]
Richard, Martinhoe 1639 W
Davie Richard, Burrington 1688 A
Richard, Goodleigh 1707 W
Davie Richard, Burrington 1734 A
Davie Richard, Winkleigh 1812 W
Davie Richard, Barnstaple 1834 A to Grace, widow
Richard Cooke, Rose Ash, gentleman 1856 A to John James,
    gentleman, brother
Davye Robert, East Buckland 1626 [W]
Robert, North Molton 1667 W
Davie Robert, North Molton 1700 A
Davie Robert, Barnstaple 1717 W
Davey Robert, Ashreigney 1783 A
Salome, Weare Giffard 1693 W
Salome, Weare Giffard 1714 W
Samuel, Atherington 1682 W
Davey Samuel, Weare Giffard 1741 W
Davie Sarah, Burrington 1822 W
Davey Stephen, Cruwys Morchard 1745 A
Susan, North Molton 1689 W
Theobald, Huish 1603 W
Davie Thomas, Bow 1564 W
Davye Thomas, Chulmleigh 1564 W
Davye Thomas, Barnstaple 1579 W
Davye Thomas, Beaford 1586 W
Davye Thomas, West Worlington 1593 [W]
Davye Thomas, Barnstaple 1627 [W]
Davye Thomas, George Nympton 1628 [W]
Thomas, Barnstaple 1632 [W]
Thomas, Tawstock 1636 [W]
Thomas, Westleigh 1636 A
Thomas, Yarnscombe 1636 A
Thomas, High Bickington 1639 W
Thomas, Marwood 1665 A
Thomas, Charles 1667 W
Thomas, Filleigh 1669 W
Thomas, Ashreigney 1675 A
Thomas, Weare Giffard 1678 A
Thomas, Parkham 1684 W

Thomas, East Down 1687 W
Thomas, Parkham 1697 W
Davey Thomas, Burrington 1714 A
Davie Thomas, North Molton 1715 [W]
Davie Thomas, Barnstaple 1722 W
Davie Thomas, South Molton 1730 A
Davie Thomas, Ashreigney 1737 W and 1740 A
Davey Thomas, Northam 1741 W
Davie Thomas, Winkleigh, yeoman 1802 W
Thomas, Clovelly, yeoman 1803 W
Davie Thomas, Barnstaple 1825 W
Davey Thomas, Pilton 1842 W
Thomas and Mary, Chawleigh 1775 W
Davie Thomas son of John, Bow 1609 [W]; forename blank in
    Ms; supplied from parish register
Thomasine, Barnstaple 1644 W
Davie Thomasine, South Molton 1731 A
Walter, Warkleigh 1602 W
Walter, Great Torrington 1688 W
Walter, Great Torrington 1712 A
Davie William, Chawleigh 1575 W
William, Charles 1576 W
Davie William, Ilfracombe 1585 W
Davye William, Parkham 1591 [W]
Davye William, Barnstaple 1592 [W]
William, Chulmleigh 1602 W
William, King's Nympton 1603 W
Davie William, Meshaw 1607 [W]; forename blank in Ms;
    supplied from parish register
Davye William, Barnstaple 1616 [W]
Davye William, Bideford 1617 [W]
Davye william, Tawstock 1620 [W]
William, Barnstaple 1635 [W]
William, Stoke Rivers 1639 W
Davie William, Bideford 1669 A
William, Chittlehampton 1672 A
Davy alias Best William, Atherington 1680 A
Davey William, East Anstey 1700 W
Davie William, Chittlehampton 1732 W
Davie William, North Molton 1733 A
Davey William, Bideford 1745 W
Davie William, Iddesleigh 1752 W
Davie William, Burrington 1789 W
Davey William, Witheridge, yeoman 1811 W
Davie William, Witheridge 1832 W
Davie William, Burrington 1836 W
Davey William, South Molton 1849 W
Davyes, Davys see Davis
Daw Christopher, Northam 1629 [W]
    Ezekiel, Barnstaple 1636 W
    William, King's Nympton 1742 W
Dawkins, Dawkens, Dawkin
    Alice, Fremington 1669 A
    Arthur, Fremington 1663 W
    Charity, Bideford 1709 W
    Dawkens George, Barnstaple 1581 A, account
    Dawkens George, Pilton 1581 A
    John, Heanton Punchardon 1644 W
    John, Bideford 1721 W
    Dawkin John, Ilfracombe 1772 W
    Dawkin Mary, Ilfracombe 1686 W
    Mary, Fremington 1672 W
    Dawkin Richard, George Nympton 1733 A
    Robert, Fremington 1681 W
    Thomas, Ilfracombe 1699 W
    Walter, Fremington 1631 [W]
    Dawkyns William, Barnstaple 1575 W and A
    Dawkens William, Knowstone 1617 [W]
    William, Fremington 1685 W
Dawne Thomas, Parkham 1733 W
Day, Daie, Daye
    ..., Yarnscombe 1603, 1606 and 1608 [W]
    Daie ..., Molland 1608 [W]
    Daie ..., South Molton 1608 [W]
    Daye Alice, Yarnscombe 1577 W

Arthur, Northam 1626 A
Arthur, Atherington, snr. 1663 W
Catherine, Bideford 1621 [W]
Catherine, South Molton 1697 W
Christopher, South Molton 1690 W
Davy, Beaford 1597 [W]
Edward, Molland 1606 W
Elizabeth, Northam 1804 W
Frances, Barnstaple 1698 W
Francis, Roborough 1766 A
Geoffrey, South Molton 1741 W
George, Roborough 1731 W
George, Roborough, yeoman 1799 W
Grace, South Molton 1663 W
Henry, Great Torrington 1796 A
Honor, Great Torrington 1796 W
Day alias Pollard Honoria, High Bickington 1664 A
Hugh, Molland 1566 W
Jacob, Yarnscombe 1631 and 1633 [W]
John, Northam 1690 W
John, South Molton 1712 A
John, Ilfracombe 1733 A
John, Northam 1748 A
John, Barnstaple 1758 A
Joseph, High Bickington 1748 W
Mary, South Molton 1690 W
Mary, South Molton 1734 A
Nicholas, Ashreigney 1615 [W]
Philip, South Molton 1665 A
Philip, South Molton, snr. 1669 W
Philip, South Molton 1717 A
Robert, Northam, mariner 1811 W
Rowland, Chittlehampton 1662 A
Thomas, Molland 1590 [W]
Thomas, South Molton 1684 W
Thomas, Roborough 1747 W
Thomas, North Tawton 1756 A
Thomas, North Tawton 1779 W
Thomas, Stoke Rivers 1845 W
Thomas, Pilton 1857 W
Walter, South Molton 1679 W
William, Bideford 1617 [W]
William, South Molton 1673 W
William, South Molton 1741 A
William, North Tawton 1767 A
William, Winkleigh 1793 W
William, Hartland, yeoman 1796 W
William Jones, Northam 1854 W
Day Willmot, Roborough 1638 W
Dayar see Dare
Daye see Day
Deacon, Decon
    ..., Combe Martin 1605 [W] and 1606 [W]
    Joan, Heanton Punchardon 1588 W
    Decon John, West Down 1578 W
    John, West Down 1666 W and A
    Mary, Buckland Brewer 1662 A
    Mary, St Giles in the Wood 1663 A
    Nicholas, Combe Martin 1665 A
    Nicholas, Combe Martin 1679 A
    Richard, East Down 1597 [W]
    Richard, Combe Martin 1668 W
    Robert, Westleigh 1710 A
    Thomas, Ilfracombe 1663 W
    Thomas, Mortehoe 1735 A
    Walter, Combe Martin 1595 [W]
    William, Combe Martin 1663 A
    Willmot, Georgeham 1797 A
Deagon, Digon
    Digon Mary, Yarnscombe 1630 [W]
    Maurice, Yarnscombe 1590 [W]
Deamon, Deamond, Deamont see Diamond
Deane, Dean, Dene
    Dean Abraham, Welcombe 1680 A
    Catherine, Monkleigh 1630 [W] and O

Elizabeth, Horwood 1715 A
Ellen 1591 [W]
Dean Emanuel, Monkleigh 1641 W
Emanuel, Bideford 1726 A
George, Merton 1694 W
Gertrude, South Molton, widow 1806 W
Henry, South Molton 1712 W
Humphrey, Horwood 1693 A
Humphrey, Horwood 1762 W
Jane, South Molton 1681 W
Joan, Great Torrington 1599 [W]
Joan, Great Torrington 1682 W
Joan, Great Torrington 1704 A
John, Buckland Brewer 1573 W and A
John, Woolfardisworthy 1594 [W]
John, Shebbear 1599 [W]
John, Great Torrington 1662 W
John, Horwood 1685 W
John, Georgeham 1724 A
John, Northam 1735 A
Dene John, Horwood, gentleman 1808 W
Dene John, Horwood 1857 W
Lucas, Great Torrington 1665 W
Luke, Great Torrington 1684 W
Luke, Great Torrington 1740 A
Magdalen, Mariansleigh 1693 A
Magdalen, South Molton 1697 W
Margaret, Monkleigh 1685 W
Mary, Buckland Brewer 1575 A
Mary, Mariansleigh 1693 W
Michael, Monkleigh 1681 A
Nathaniel, Monkleigh 1669 A
Paul, Bideford 1705 A
Rebecca, Horwood 1715 A
Richard, Langtree 1637 W
Richard, Georgeham, yeoman 1805 W
Robert, Buckland Brewer 1573 W
Robert, South Molton 1664 W
Roger, Great Torrington 1621 [W]
Roger, Frithelstock 1685 W
Dene Stephen, Yarnscombe 1579 A
Dean Thomas, Monkleigh 1642 A
Thomas, Georgeham 1745 A
Tobias, Georgeham 1750 W
William, Shebbear 1729 A
Dean William, Clovelly 1744 A
Deanner see Dinner
Debbe see Dibbe
Debridge, Debbridge, Debridg
  Debridg alias Searle Mary, Knowstone 1716 [W]
  Debbridge Thomas, Tawstock 1642 W
Decon see Deacon
Dee Alice, High Bray 1632 [W]
  Alice, North Molton 1639 A
  Charles, South Molton 1775 W
  Elizabeth, North Molton 1826 A to Michael Lock, brother
  Grace, South Molton, widow 1800 W
  Joan, North Molton 1673 W
  Joan, North Molton 1686 W
  John, North Molton 1598 [W]
  John, North Molton 1629 [W] and 1633 A
  John, Goodleigh 1667 W
  John, Northam 1679 W
  John, South Molton 1697 W
  John, North Molton 1723 W and 1727 A
  John, North Molton 1785 W
  John, North Molton, yeoman 1808 W
  John, North Molton 1845 W
  Jonathan, North Molton 1768 W
  Jonathan, North Molton, yeoman 1808 W
  Margaret, North Molton 1611 [W]; forename blank in Ms;
    supplied from parish register
  Mary, West Buckland, widow 1818 A to John, yeoman, son
  Paul, North Molton 1611 [W]; forename blank in Ms; supplied
    from parish register

Richard, North Molton 1682 A
Roger, High Bray 1593 [W]
Susan, North Molton 1748 W
Thomas, North Molton 1699 W and 1703 A
Thomas, Charles 1738 W
William, High Bray 1631 [W]
William, North Molton 1667 W
William, North Molton 1727 A
William, South Molton, mercer 1800 W
William, West Buckland 1804 A
Winifred, North Molton 1708 W
Deeble see Dibble John, Filleigh 1705 W
Deight ..., Warkleigh 1613 [W]
  Thomas, Warkleigh 1616 [W]
Delaroche, Delaroth
  Elias, Barnstaple 1786 A
  Delaroth William 1749 A granted to the father; no bond
Delatour John, Barnstaple 1767 A
  Peter, Bideford 1746 W
Delbridge, Delbidge, Delbridg, Delbrydge, Deldridge
  Alice, Barnstaple 1617 [W]
  Delbrid Ann, Barnstaple 1660 W
  Bartholomew, Lynton 1689 W
  Edward, Filleigh 1684 W
  Elizabeth, Barnstaple 1590 [W]
  Deldridge Elizabeth see John Arnold
  Delbrydge Emanuel, North Molton 1632 [W]
  George, Atherington 1846 W
  Joan, Filleigh 1706 A
  Delbrid John, Filleigh 1704 W
  Delbrid John, Knowstone 1704 W
  John, Lynton 1769 W
  John, Chittlehampton 1843 W
  Jonathan, Barnstaple 1602 [W]; forename blank in Ms;
    supplied from parish register
  Joseph, Barnstaple 1671 A
  Joseph, Stoodleigh 1799 W
  Delbrid Lois, Monkleigh 1702 W
  Delbrid Mary, Barnstaple 1684 W
  Delbrydge Nicholas, Barnstaple 1636 A
  Delbrid Richard, Barnstaple 1664 A
  Richard, Atherington 1816 W
  Richard, Lynton 1828 W
  Richard, Lynton 1854 W
  Sarah, Atherington 1854 W
  Delbrydge Susan, Barnstaple 1638 [W]
  Delbrid Thomas, Tawstock 1682 W
  Thomas, Atherington, yeoman 1847 A to Sarah, widow
  William, Knowstone 1758 W
  William, Lynton 1768 A
Dell James, King's Nympton 1778 W
  William, Ilfracombe 1844 W
Dellem see Dilham
Delve Daniel, West Buckland 1763 W
  Daniel, Romansleigh, blacksmith 1811 A
  Elizabeth, East Buckland 1596 [W]
  Elizabeth, Romansleigh 1747 A
  Joan, Pilton 1853 W
  John, West Down 1838 W
  John, Loxhore 1843 A to John of Shirwell, yeoman, son
  Peter, Pilton, blacksmith 1802 A
  Roger, East Buckland 1589 W
  William, East Buckland 1597 [W]
  William, Woolfardisworthy 1617 [W]
  William, Romansleigh 1722 W
  William, Romansleigh 1780 A
  William, East Down 1802 W
  William, Pilton 1840 W
Demon, Demonde see Diamond
Dempsy John, Bideford 1714 A
Denbow Elizabeth, North Tawton 1737 W
Dendle George, Combe Martin 1744 A
  George, High Bray 1763 W
  George, Bratton Fleming 1793 A
  George, High Bray, yeoman 1807 W

James, High Bray 1815 W
John, heretofore of North Molton, but late of East Buckland
  1833 W
John, Kentisbury 1843 W
Richard, Marwood 1674 A
Richard, North Molton 1688 W
William, Marwood 1691 A
William, High Bray 1785 W
Dene see Deane
Denford, Denforde, Denvord
  Arthur, Petrockstowe 1727 W
  Bridget, Buckland Filleigh 1640 W
  David, Petrockstowe 1725 W and 1726 A
  Denvord John, Petrockstowe 1580 W
  Denforde John, St Giles in the Wood 1582 W
  Lodovic, St Giles in the Wood 1639 W
  Denforde Margaret, Petrockstowe 1603 W
  Philip, Huish 1796 A
  Phillippa, Petrockstowe 1685 A
  Denforde Richard, Great Torrington 1573 W
  Robert, Petrockstowe 1592 [W]
  Robert, Westleigh 1634 [W]
  Stephen, Petrockstowe 1666 W
Denham, Dinham, Dynham
  Dynham Avis, Yarnscombe 1623 [W]
  Dynham John, Yarnscombe 1645 A
  John, Yarnscombe 1720 W
  Dinham John, Witheridge 1783 W
  Denham alias Dinner John, North Molton 1813 W
  Dynham Mary, Yarnscombe 1623 [W]
Denis see Dennis
Denman Christopher, Fremington 1684 A
  Dorothy, Fremington 1684 A
  Joan, Fremington 1685 W
Dennaford ..., North Tawton 1724 A
Dennard Ann, Bideford 1725 W
  Edward, Bideford 1674 A
  Edward, Bideford 1693 W
  Elizabeth, Bideford, widow 1608 [W]; forename blank in Ms;
    supplied from parish register
  Joseph, Abbotsham 1733 W
  Joseph, Bideford 1734 W
  Oliver, Fremington 1591 [W]
  Petronell, Northam 1685 A
  Philip, Bideford 1708 A
  Sarah, Bideford 1704 A
  William, Instow 1590 [W]
Denner see Dinner
Dennes see Dennis
Denning, Dennynge, Dining, Dyninge
  Dyninge Joan, Northam 1626 [W]
  Dennynge John, Northam 1618 [W]
  Dyninge John, South Molton 1621 [W]
  Dining Nicholas, Westleigh 1671 W
  Dennynge Robert, Bow 1591 [W]
Dennis, Denis, Dennes, Dennys, Denys, Dinis, Dinnis
  Dennys ..., Georgeham 1603 [W]
  ..., Dolton 1610 [W]
  ..., Woolfardisworthy 1611 [W]
  ..., Ilfracombe 1612 [W]
  Abijah, Northam 1746 A
  Abraham, Ilfracombe 1811 W*
  Agnes, Berrynarbor 1701 W
  Agnes, Monkleigh 1702 W
  Alexander, Huntshaw 1735 A
  Alexander, High Bickington 1809 W
  Denys Alice, West Down 1567 W
  Dennys Alice, Martinhoe 1644 A
  Ann, Littleham (near Bideford) 1677 W
  Anthony, Bideford 1671 W
  Anthony, Great Torrington 1680 A
  Dennys Anthony, Monkleigh 1705 A
  Arthur, Frithelstock 1697 W
  Arthur, Bideford 1744 W
  Benjamin, Littleham (near Bideford) 1715 W

Catherine, Buckland Brewer 1605 W
Dennys Charles, Martinhoe 1640 W and 1644 A
Dennys Christian, Littleham (near Bideford) 1624 [W]
Dennys Christian, Mortehoe 1680 W
Christopher, North Molton 1693 W
Christopher, North Molton 1731 W and 1741 W
David, Yarnscombe 1666 W
Dennys Edmund, North Molton 1644 W
Edmund, Charles 1681 A and 1682 A
Edmund, North Molton 1692 W
Dinnis Edmund, Bideford 1723 A
Edmund, Monkleigh 1740 W
Edmund, Fremington, yeoman 1803 W
Edward, Berrynarbor 1692 W
Dennys Elizabeth, Littleham (near Bideford) 1600 W
Elizabeth, Woolfardisworthy 1681 W
Elizabeth, Hartland 1706 W
Elizabeth, Barnstaple 1710 A
Elizabeth 1711 A
Elizabeth, Littleham (near Bideford) 1734 A
Elizabeth, Monkleigh 1748 W
Dennys Gabriel, Monkleigh 1622 [W]
Geoffrey, Heanton Punchardon 1605 W
Dennys George, Beaford 1597 [W]
Dennys George, Littleham (near Bideford) 1597 [W]
Dennys George, Martinhoe 1600 W
Dennys George, Yarnscombe 1620 [W]
George, Merton 1670 W
George, Northam 1690 W
George, Buckland Brewer 1706 A and 1708 A
Dennes George, Littleham (near Bideford) 1720 A
George, Bideford 1750 W
George, Littleham (near Bideford) 1847 W
Gertrude, Mortehoe 1700 W
Gertrude, Merton 1706 W
Grace, High Bickington 1812 A (Chawleigh) to Mary Webber,
  daughter
Dennys Henry, Buckland Brewer 1581 A
Henry, West Down 1612 [W]; forename blank in Ms; supplied
  from parish register
Henry, Woolfardisworthy 1664 W
Henry, Ilfracombe 1720 W
Dennys Hugh, Woolfardisworthy 1632 [W]
Dennys Jacob, King's Nympton 1638 A
James, Frithelstock 1613 [W]; forename blank in Ms; supplied
  from parish register
James, Merton 1687 W
James, Monkleigh 1746 W
James, Littleham (near Bideford) 1748 A (2)
Jane see Ann Pope
Jeremiah, Merton 1733 W
Dennys Jerome, Martinhoe 1615 [W]
Dennys Joan, Bideford 1586 W
Dennys Joan, Monkleigh 1599 [W]
Joan, Buckland Brewer 1606 W
Joan, Little Torrington 1606 W
Dennys Joan, West Down 1618 [W]
Dennys Joan, Frithelstock 1625 [W]
Dennys Joan, Monkleigh 1625 [W]
Dennys Joan, Yarnscombe 1638 A
Joan, Monkleigh 1748 W
Dennys John, Littleham (near Bideford) 1580 W
Dynnes John, Frithelstock 1580 [W]
Dennys John, Winkleigh 1583 A
Denys John, Buckland Brewer 1584 W
Dennys John, Tawstock 1590 [W]
Dennys John, Great Torrington 1592 [W]
Dennys John, Combe Martin 1596 [W]
Dennys John, South Molton 1596 [W]
John, Ilfracombe 1611 [W]; forename blank in Ms; supplied
  from parish register
Dennys John, Littleham (near Bideford) 1619 [W]
Dennys John, Yarnscombe 1627 [W]
Dennys John, Mortehoe 1628 [W]
Dennys John, Sheepwash 1633 W

Dennys John, Northam 1668 A
John, Barnstaple 1675 A
John, Merton 1688 W
John, Hartland 1702 W
John, Bideford 1707 W and 1718 A
Denis John, Monkleigh 1720 W
Dinnis John, Northam 1722 W
John, Great Torrington 1728 W
John, Berrynarbor 1757 W
Dinnis John, Northam 1760 W
John, Hartland 1762 A; A dbn 1769
John, Berrynarbor 1776 A
John, Huntshaw 1781 A
John, Barnstaple 1784 A dbn
John, Hartland 1788 W
John, Great Torrington, yeoman 1803 W
John, Huntshaw 1812 A to Elizabeth and Edward, children
John, Barnstaple 1824 W and 1826 W
John, Tawstock 1829 W
John, Barnstaple 1849 W
John, Hartland 1849 W
John, Great Torrington 1857 W
Dennys Lancelot, Petrockstowe 1618 [W]
Dennys Margery, Woolfardisworthy 1582 W
Dennys Mary, Buckland Brewer 1593 [W]
Dennys Mary, West Down 1636 W
Mary, Monkleigh 1662 W
Mary, Bideford 1665 A
Mary, Merton 1699 W
Dinnis Mary, Arlington 1722 A
Mary, Barnstaple 1784 W
Denys Maud, West Down 1577 W
Methusaleh, Bideford 1707 W
Moses, Northam 1692 W
Nehemiah, Ilfracombe 1675 A
Nicholas, Barnstaple 1678 A
Nicholas, Hartland 1681 A
Peter, Monkleigh 1663 W
Denys Philip, Petrockstowe, esquire 1564 W
Dennys Philip, Woolfardisworthy 1582 W
Dennys Philip, Monkleigh 1591 [W]
Dennys Philip, Buckland Brewer 1593 [W]
Dennys Philip, West Down 1594 [W]
Dennys Philip, Ilfracombe 1671 W
Philip, Merton 1679 A
Philip, West Down 1700 W
Philip, High Bickington 1769 W
Dennys Rebecca, Hartland 1666 W
Dennys Richard, Bideford 1586 A
Denys Richard, Woolfardisworthy 1586 W
Dennys Richard, Monkleigh 1598 [W]
Dennys Richard, Littleham (near Bideford) 1622 [W]
Dennys Richard, Hartland 1640 A
Richard, Woolfardisworthy 1640 A
Richard, Woolfardisworthy 1676 W
Richard, Monkleigh 1715 W
Richard, Langtree 1768 W
Richard, Hartland 1788 A
Richard, Monkleigh 1801 W
Dinis Richard, Clovelly 1802 W*
Richard, Ilfracombe 1826 W to Charles, brother
Richard, Monkleigh 1826 W
Richard, Barnstaple 1850 W
Robert, Bideford 1671 W
Robert, Great Torrington 1691 W
Dinnis Robert, Berrynarbor 1722 W
Roger, Monkleigh 1581 W
Rowland, Monkleigh 1685 A
Samuel, Buckland Brewer 1643 A
Samuel, Bideford 1672 A
Dennys Sarah, Bideford 1668 W and 1669 O account
Sarah, High Bickington 1806 W
Theophilus, Great Torrington 1692 W
Theophilus, Great Torrington 1729 W
Dennys Thomas, Monkleigh 1566 W

Dennys Thomas, West Down 1594 [W]
Dennys Thomas, Buckland Brewer 1595 [W]
Dennys Thomas, Woolfardisworthy 1599 [W]
Dennes Thomas, Martinhoe 1602 W
Dennys Thomas, West Down 1618 [W]
Dennys Thomas, Kentisbury 1619 [W]
Dennys Thomas, Marwood 1620 [W]
Dennys Thomas, Martinhoe 1630 [W]
Dennys Thomas, Littleham (near Bideford) 1641 W
Dennys Thomas, Barnstaple 1665 W
Thomas, Mortehoe 1678 A
Thomas, Bideford 1715 W
Thomas, Mortehoe 1717 W
Thomas, Monkleigh 1719 W
Thomas, Ilfracombe 1740 A
Thomas, Bratton Fleming 1831 A to Mary Ann Ridd, daughter
Dennys Tristram, Sheepwash 1631 [W]
Tristram, Bideford 1700 W
Denys William, Woolfardisworthy 1576 W
Denys William, Little Torrington 1585 W
Dennys William, Horwood 1591 [W]
Dennys William, Woolfardisworthy 1597 [W]
Dennys William, Hartland 1599 [W]
William, Monkleigh 1605 W
Dennys William, Great Torrington 1633 W
Dennys William, Barnstaple 1644 W
William, Woolfardisworthy 1683 W
William, Merton 1684 A
William, Barnstaple 1690 A
William, Bideford 1694 A
William, Merton 1694 W
William, Monkleigh 1706 W
William, Great Torrington 1731 A
William, Buckland Brewer 1819 W
William, Huntshaw 1835 A to Ann, widow
Denis William, Ilfracombe 1849 W and 1852 W
Dennoe George, Bideford 1828 W
Dennynge see Denning
Dennys see Dennis
Densham, Densam, Denshear, Denssam, Densyam, Dunham,
   Dunsham
..., Lapford 1610 and 1614 [W]
Agnes, Shebbear 1627 [W]
Alice, Lapford 1586 W
Denshear Ann, Yarnscombe 1616 [W]
Ann, Chawleigh 1769 A
Ann, Lapford 1772 A
Christopher, Shebbear 1616 [W] and 1618 O
Christopher, Lapford 1643 A
Edmund, Zeal Monachorum 1593 [W]
Elizabeth, Great Torrington 1847 W
Dunham Humphrey, Oakford 1719 A
Joan, Lapford 1618 [W]
Joan, Lapford 1751
Densam John, Lapford 1582 W
John, Coldridge 1616 [W]
Densyam John, Zeal Monachorum 1681 W
Mary, Lapford 1739 A
Nicholas, Lapford 1584 W
Philip, Chulmleigh 1630 [W]
Richard, Lapford 1618 [W]
Denssam Richard, Lapford, jnr. 1630 [W]
Richard, Lapford, snr. 1636 W
Richard, Lapford 1639 W
Richard, Lapford 1681 A
Richard, Lapford 1682 W
Richard, Wembworthy 1687 W
Richard, Lapford 1701 A
Richard, Chulmleigh 1830 A to William, son
Richard, Chulmleigh 1839 W
Robert, Lapford 1645 W
Dunsham Robert, Lapford 1752 A
Robert, Lapford 1788 W
Sybil, Chawleigh 1643 A
Thomas, Burrington 1624 [W]

Thomas, Cheldon 1638 W
Thomasine, Lapford 1762 W
William, Ashreigney 1592 [W]
William, Zeal Monachorum 1634 [W]
William, Dowland 1639 A
William, Lapford 1754 W
Deret, Derte
Derte George, Chawleigh 1564 W
John, Yarnscombe 1564 W
Derver Edward, Northam 1684 A
Derworthy Paschal, Buckland Brewer 1739 W
Deverell James, Bideford 1740 A
Devonshire alias Fuller Thomas, Bideford 1710 A
Dew, Due
..., Chulmleigh 1608 [W]
Due George, Tawstock 1716 W
Richard, North Molton 1632 [W]
Due Susan, Chittlehampton 1674 A
Dewlinge William, Chittlehampton 1600 W
Deyman, Deymand, Deymon, Deymont see Diamond
Deyr see Dyer
Diamond, Damond, Dayman, Daymand, Daymon, Daymond,
    Deamon, Deamond, Deamont, Demon, Demonde, Deyman,
    Deymand, Deymon, Deymont, Dimond, Dyamond, Dyman,
    Dymant, Dyment, Dymon, Dymond, Dymont
Deymont ..., Bideford 1607 [W]
Deymont ..., Bideford, widow 1612 [W]; forename blank in
    Ms; supplied from parish register
Deamont ..., Great Torrington 1660 A
Daymond Alexander, Buckland Brewer 1631 [W]
Deymont Andrew, Hartland 1630 [W] and 1632 W
Daymond Anthony (or Richard), Great Torrington 1626 W
Demonde Avis, Hartland 1570 W
Dyamond Barbara, Little Torrington 1693 A
Deyman Catherine, Woolfardisworthy 1590 [W]
Deyman Catherine, Barnstaple 1620 [W]
Deyman Edmund, Hartland 1607 [W]; forename blank in Ms;
    supplied from parish register
Deamond Elizabeth, Hartland 1585 W
Deyman Elizabeth, Newton Tracey 1601 W
Deyman Ephraim, Barnstaple 1703 A
Deyman Gregory, Hartland 1604 W
Demon Harry, Hartland 1566 W
Deyman Hugh, Hartland 1611 [W]; forename blank in Ms;
    supplied from parish register
Dymond James, Little Torrington 1682 A
Dymond James, Little Torrington 1769 W
Jane, Barnstaple 1766 W
Deyman Joan, Hartland 1623 [W]
Deymont John, Hartland 1579 [W]
Deyman John, Barnstaple 1603 W
Deyman John, Hartland 1606 W
Deyman John, Barnstaple 1617 [W]
Deyman John, Hartland 1620 [W] and 1625 [W]
Daymond John, Hartland 1636 [W] and 1637 W
Dyment John, Buckland Brewer 1675 A
Dymant John, Merton 1679 [W]
Dyment John, Great Torrington 1722 W
Dyman John 1724 W
Dymond John, Barnstaple 1746 W
Daymand John, Hartland 1765 W
Daymond Lawrence, Hartland 1631 [W]
Deyman Lewis, Clovelly 1671 W
Dymond Margaret, Little Torrington 1689 W
Deymand Margaret, Hartland 1706 W
Dyman Margaret 1733 W
Deamond Mary, Hartland 1586 W
Deamond Nicholas, Shirwell 1625 [W]
Dymond Petronell, Hartland 1712 W
Deyman Philip, Hartland 1609 [W]; forename blank in Ms;
    supplied from parish register
Deamon Richard, Hartland 1569 W
Deyman Richard, Hartland 1614 [W]; forename blank in Ms;
    supplied from parish register
Deymon Richard, Buckland Brewer 1622 [W]

Daymond Richard (or Anthony), Great Torrington 1686 W
Deymont Robert, Hartland 1596 W
Dymont Robert, Puddington 1694 W
Dymond Salome, Little Torrington 1661 A
Dymond Solomon, Little Torrington 1661 A
Dimond Stephen, Combe Martin 1773 W
Deyman Thomas, Great Torrington 1625 [W]
Dymond Thomas, Monkleigh 1639 W
Daymand Thomas, Hartland 1692 W
Deamond William, Newton Tracey 1586 W
Deyman William, Roborough 1606 W
Deamond William, Roborough 1621 [W]
Deyman William, Hartland 1638 [W]
Deyman William, Holloford, Hartland 1638 W
Deyman William, Hartland 1642 W and A
Deyman William, Cheristow, Hartland 1672 W
Daymon William, Hartland 1692 W
Daymond William, Hartland 1705 W
Dibbe, Debbe, Dibb, Dybb, Dybbe
John, Buckland Brewer 1567 W
Debbe John, Buckland Brewer 1599 [W]
Dybb Mary, Alwington 1639 A
Dybb Mary, Buckland Brewer 1639 A
Dibb Mary, Northam 1665 W
Debbe Samuel, Buckland Brewer 1623 [W]
Dybbe William, Buckland Brewer 1568 W
Dibble, Deeble, Dibbel, Dible
Dibbel Elizabeth, Knowstone 1755 W
Dible John, Parkham 1608 [W]; forename blank in Ms;
    supplied from parish register
Deeble John, Filleigh 1705 W
John, South Molton 1738 W
Dichett see Ditchett
Dick see Dycke
Dicker Ann see Denham Chamberlin
John, Bondleigh, snr. 1674 W
Dickson Josiah, Bideford 1699 A
Dier see Dyer
Digg, Dig, Digge
Dig Oliver, Frithelstock 1594 [W]
Digge Samuel, Martinhoe 1603 W
Thomas, Frithelstock 1583 W
Dig Thomas, Frithelstock 1593 [W]
Dight John, Warkleigh 1580 W
John, Warkleigh 1592 [W] and 1597 [W]
William, Chawleigh 1592 [W]
Diglegg Mary, Ashreigney 1725 W
Digon see Deagon
Dilham, Dellem
Dellem Francis, Tawstock 1724 A
Dellem Jane, Dolton 1723 W
Nicholas, Tawstock 1719 A
Dillon, Dilling, Dyllen, Dyllon
Abel, Barnstaple 1626 [W]
Dyllon Ann, Puddington 1633 A
Dorothy, Burrington 1812 W
Dyllon Elizabeth and Edward, Chittlehampton 1577 W
Dyllen Edward and Elizabeth, Chittlehampton 1636 A
Dyllon Elizabeth and Edward, Chittlehampton 1577 W
Dyllen Elizabeth and Edward, Chittlehampton 1636 A
Dilling James, Chawleigh 28 Jul 1827 A to Elizabeth, widow;
    further A dbn 1847
John, Burrington, snr., maltster 1802 W
John, Burrington 1844 W and 1853 W
Mary, Chittlehampton 1662 W
Mary, Pilton 1700 A
Dilling Robert, Pilton 1710 W
William, Beaford 1618 [W]
Dimmock Ann, South Molton 1857 W
Thomas, South Molton 1855 W
Dimond see Diamond
Dingle John, Great Torrington 1824 W
Dinham see Denham
Dining see Denning
Dinis see Dennis

Dinner, Deanner, Denner
  Denner ..., East Worlington 1608 [W]
  Denner Alexander, Chulmleigh 1681 A
  Deanner John, Fremington, widower 1588 W
  Dinner alias Denham John, North Molton 1813 W
  William, Witheridge 1813 A
  Denner William, Witheridge 1836 W
Dinnicombe Alice, Combe Martin, sp. 1809 W
  John, Arlington, yeoman 1809 W
  Peter, East Down 1775 W
  William, East Down 1758 W
  William, Martinhoe 1787 W
Dirare John, Countisbury 1586 W
Discombe, Discomb, Discum
  Elizabeth, High Bray 1622 [W]
  Discum Lawrence, Chulmleigh 1679 A
  Discomb Lodovic, Charles 1643 W
  Margaret, Goodleigh 1628 [W]
  Walter, Pilton 1592 [W]
  Dishcombe William, East Down 1618 [W]
Dish ..., Combe Martin 1600 A
Dishcombe see Discombe
Ditchett, Dichett
  ..., Instow 1614 [W]
  Arthur, Witheridge 1782 A
  Dichett Edward, Witheridge 1599 [W]
  James, Chittlehampton 1750 W
  Dichett John, Rose Ash 1572 W
  John, George Nympton 1719 W
  John, Witheridge 1730 A
  Rose, George Nympton 1750 W
  William, Witheridge 1741 A
Dobb, Dobbe
  Dobbe Alice, George Nympton 1608 [W]; forename blank in
    Ms; supplied from parish register
  Dobbe Christian, Chulmleigh 1601 W
  Eleanor, High Bickington 1672 W
  Helena, South Molton 1679 A
  Hugh, George Nympton 1644 W
  John, Witheridge 1572 W
  Dobbe John, George Nympton 1578 A
  Dobbe John, Great Torrington 1588 W
  Dobbe John, Ashreigney 1591 [W]
  Dobbe John, Ashreigney 1616 [W]
  Dobbe John, Burrington 1619 [W]
  Dobbe John, High Bickington 1621 [W] and 1624 O
  John, Burrington 1664 W
  John, Tawstock 1709 W
  John, High Bickington 1722 A
  John, Georgeham 1743 A
  Dobbe Juliana, King's Nympton 1625 [W]
  Dobbe Margaret, Filleigh 1621 [W]
  Dobbe Nicholas, Stoodleigh 1616 [W]
  Dobbe Philip, George Nympton, snr. 1583 W
  Dobbe Philip, George Nympton 1587 W
  Dobbe Philip, Chittlehampton 1593 [W]
  Ralph, Ashreigney 1639 W
  Richard, Ashreigney 1569 W
  Dobbe Roger, Chulmleigh 1621 [W]
  Dobbe Theobald, King's Nympton 1621 [W]
  Thomas, King's Nympton 1571 W
  Dobbe Thomas, Ashreigney 1592 [W]
  Dobbe Walter, Burrington 1615 [W]
  Dobbe William, George Nympton 1583 W
  William, Molland 1645 A
  William, High Bickington 1667 W
  Dobb alias Dubb William, Tawstock 1817 A
Dobbyn, Doben
  Edmund, Great Torrington 1626 [W]
  Doben John, Great Torrington 1583 W
  John, Great Torrington 1628 [W]
Dobe see Dobb
Dobell see Doble
Doben see Dobbyn

Doble, Dobell
  Doble alias Blackford ..., Parracombe 1666 A
  Elizabeth, Great Torrington 1723 W
  Gonnet, Stoodleigh 1627 [W]
  Hannah, Great Torrington 1725 A
  John, Chulmleigh 1581 A
  John, Stoodleigh 1582 W
  John, Stoodleigh 1611 [W]; forename blank in Ms; supplied
    from parish register
  Dobell alias Blackford John, Parracombe 1666 A
  John, Great Torrington 1722 A
  Martha, Goodleigh 1641 W
  Richard, Newton St Petrock 1690 W
  William, Great Torrington 1723 A
Dockham Alice, Chawleigh 1578 W
Dockings Philip, South Molton 1743 W
Docton Alice, Hartland 1620 O
  Elizabeth, Hartland 1627 [W]
  Elizabeth, Northam 1702 W
  Hugh, Hartland 1577 A
  John, Hartland, snr. 1568 W
  John, Clovelly 1636 W
  Nicholas, Northam 1690 A
  Peter, Northam 1676 A
  Philip, Hartland 1742 A and 1750 A
  Richard, Hartland 1569 W
  Richard, Hartland 1665 W
  Susan, Hartland 1719 W
  Thomas, Hartland 1618 O
  Thomas, Hartland, snr. 1682 A
  Thomas, Hartland 1706 W
Dodd William, ship *Lark* 1750 A
Doddridge, Doddridg, Doderidge, Doderudge, Doderydge,
    Dodridg
  Edward, Marwood 1673 W
  Doderudge John, South Molton 1573 W
  Doderidge Richard, North Tawton 1617 [W]
  Doderydge Robert, South Molton 1634 [W]
  Doddridg William, Bideford 1709 A
  William, Marwood 1729 W
Dodge, Doidge
  Elizabeth, Rose Ash 1616 [W]
  Doidge George, Buckland Brewer 1736 W
  Doidge Israel, Barnstaple 1842 W
  James, Creacombe 1601 W
  James, Rose Ash 1679 W
  John, Cheldon 1572 W
  John, Rackenford 1575 W
  John, Creacombe 1601 W
  John, High Bickington 1620 [W]
  John, Rose Ash 1678 W
  Doidge John, Bideford, yeoman 1810 A
  Pentecost, Rackenford 1619 [W]
  Richard, Rose Ash 1633 W
  Richard, Rose Ash 1740 W
  Robert, Rose Ash 1620 [W] and 1623 [W]
  Doidge Samson, Petrockstowe 1721 W
  Thomas, Rackenford 1586 W
  Doidge William, Bideford 1697 A
Dodridg see Doddridge
Dodscombe alias Hill Robert, Oakford 1573 A
Doidge see Dodge
Dolbear, Dolberie
  Dolberie ..., South Molton 1612 [W]
  Lawrence, Great Torrington 1637 W
  Lawrence, Great Torrington 1671 W
Dolbridge John, Lynton 1769 A
Dollen, Dollinge, Dollyn, Dollyne
  Dollyn John, Brendon 1616 [W]
  Dollyne Richard, Stoke Rivers 1566 W
  Dollinge Richard, Martinhoe 1624 [W]
  Simon, Hartland 1566 W
  Stephen, Witheridge 1574 W
  Dollyne Stephen, Witheridge 1574 A
    see also Dallen

Donne, Done, Donn
Donn George, Bideford 1677 A (2)
Giles, Parkham 1612 [W]; forename blank in Ms; supplied
  from parish register
Henry, North Molton 1582 W
John, North Molton 1578 A
Margaret, Tawstock 1637 A
Done or Dove alias Pedler Mary, Monkleigh 1666 A
Robert, Tawstock 1584 W
Done or Dove Thomas, South Molton 1592 [W]
Donynge see Dunning
Doraton Catherine, Barnstaple 1766 A
Dorke see Dark
Dornen Dennis, Barnstaple 1595 [W]
Doron Michael, High Bickington 1809 W
Dorracott see Darracoott
Dorrington John, North Molton, yeoman 1806 W
Dothacott see Darracoott
Doubt Philip, Bideford 1715 W
Williams, Bideford 1721 A
Dove Faith, Hartland 1629 [W]
Dove alias Pedler Mary, Monkleigh 1666 A
Thomas, South Molton 1592 [W]
Thomas, Hartland 1627 [W]
Dovell, Dovel, Dovil, Dovill, Dowle
Dovell alias Blackford ..., Parracombe 1719 W
Dovil Conan, Martinhoe 1692 W
Darius, Parracombe 1763 W
Dowle Dorothy, North Molton 1630 [W]
John, Parracombe 1742 W
John, Martinhoe 1833 W
Joseph, Martinhoe 1857 W
Margaret, Parracombe 1744 W
Margaret, Parracombe 1763 W
Dovel Mary, West Buckland 1716 A
Mary, Martinhoe 1849 A
Mary Ann see Thomas Martin
Philip, Parracombe 1753 W
Philip, Parracombe, yeoman 1810 W
Dovill Richard, Parracombe 1699 W
Richard, Parracombe 1793 W
Susan, Molland 1710 W
William, Parracombe 1715 W
William, West Anstey 1738 W
William, Parracombe, husbandman 1803 W
William, Parracombe 1835 W
Dowdle, Dowdall, Dowdel, Dowdell
Dowdall Alexander, Shirwell 1679 A
Alexander, Heanton Punchardon 1748 W
Elizabeth, Heanton Punchardon 1763 W
Elizabeth, Filleigh, widow 1845 A to John S. Dowdle of
  Filleigh, yeoman and William of Chulmleigh, children
George, Bratton Fleming 1789 W
Jane, Combe Martin 1795 W
Dowdall Joan, Pilton 1619 [W]
John, ship *Orford* 1747 W
Dowdel John, Instow 1772 W
John, Bratton Fleming 1781 A
John, Combe Martin 1795 W
Dowdell John, Alverdiscott, yeoman 1799 A
Samuel, Huntshaw 1816 W
Sarah, Alverdiscott 1803 A
Dowdall Walter, Shirwell 1628 [W]
William, Stoke Rivers 1715 A
Dowdell William, Tawstock 1781 W
William, Huntshaw 1830 W
Dowdon Dennis, Great Torrington 1563 W
Dowe Richard, Dolton 1580 A
Dowell see Dovell
Dowglas Roger, Eggesford 1695 W
Roger, Westleigh 1740 W
Dowling John, Barnstaple 1846 W
Down, Downe
..., Instow 1602 [W]
..., Woolfardisworthy 1607 [W]

..., King's Nympton 1610 [W]
..., Tawstock 1610 [W]
..., Goodleigh 1611 and 1613 [W]
Agnes, Woolfardisworthy 1698 W
Alexander, Pilton 1595 W
Alexander, Great Torrington 1633 W
Alice, Tawstock, widow 1588 W
Ann, Rose Ash 1629 [W]
Anthony, Rose Ash 1587 A
Anthony, Great Torrington 1620 [W]
Anthony, South Molton 1637 [W]
Anthony, Woolfardisworthy 1637 W
Down Anthony, Martinhoe 1644 A
Arthur, South Molton 1666 A
Down Catherine, Pilton 1644 W
Catherine, Pilton 1602 [W]
Christopher, Oakford 1637 [W]
Christopher, Merton 1664 A
Down Cyprian, Newton Tracey 1645 W
Down Daniel, St Giles in the Wood 1818 W
Edmund, Molland 1670 W
Edulphus, Georgeham 1728 W
Edward, East Worlington 1619 [W]
Edward, Bratton Fleming 1666 W
Edward, King's Nympton 1749 A
Down Eleanor, St Giles in the Wood 1824 W
Elizabeth, Barnstaple 1593 [W]
Elizabeth, Woolfardisworthy 1619 [W]
Elizabeth, Goodleigh 1628 [W] and 1631 [W]
Elizabeth, Witheridge 1687 W
Elizabeth, Winkleigh 1749 A
Elizabeth, Pilton 1750 W
Down Elizabeth, King's Nympton 1756 W
Elizabeth, Winkleigh, widow 1806 W
Down Elizabeth, High Bickington 1839 W and 1846 W
Elizabeth daughter of Nicholas, Barnstaple 1615 [W];
  forename blank in Ms; supplied from parish register
Fulk, Barnstaple 1621 [W]
George, Tawstock 1629 [W]
Down George, Bideford 1757 W
George, Great Torrington 1795 W
Grace, George Nympton 1613 [W]; forename blank in Ms;
  supplied from parish register
Henry, Newton Tracey 1583 W
Henry, Barnstaple, M.D. 1671 A
Honor, Northam 1688 W
Isaac, Barnstaple 1636 W
James, Barnstaple 1614 [W]; forename blank in Ms; supplied
  from parish register
James, Barnstaple 1728 W
Down Jane, Bideford 1757 W
Joan, Goodleigh 1588 A
Joan, Newton Tracey 1588 W
Down Joan, Dolton 1642 W
Joan, Molland 1682 W
Joan, Woolfardisworthy 1687 A
Joan, Frithelstock 1728 W
Joan, Winkleigh 1795 A
Joan and William, Great Torrington 1594 [W]
John, Witheridge 1565 W and 1567 W
John, Tawstock 1572 W
John, Thelbridge 1573 A
Downe and Gylle John 1573 A
John, Witheridge 1580 A
John, Goodleigh 1581 W
John, Roborough 1582 W
John, Fremington 1584 W
John, Woolfardisworthy 1588 A
John, Bondleigh 1589 [W]
John, Beaford 1592 [W]
John, Ashreigney 1602 W
John, High Bickington 1616 [W]
John, Newton Tracey 1617 [W]
John, Fremington 1620 [W]
John, Oakford 1623 [W]

John, Witheridge 1626 [W]
Down John, Goodleigh 1643 A
Down John, Tawstock 1644 A
John, Parkham 1661 A
John, Newton Tracey 1665 A
John, Barnstaple 1673 A
John, Woolfardisworthy 1675 W
John, Northam 1688 W
John, Goodleigh 1690 W
Down John, Chulmleigh 1692 W
John, Hartland 1712 W
John, Burrington 1721 W
John, Coldridge 1721 W
Down John, Hartland 1754 W
Down John, Burrington 1780 W
John, High Bickington 1785 W
Down John, Burrington 1804 W
John, Hartland, yeoman 1808 A
Down John, Winkleigh 1831 W
Down John, Merton 1832 W
Down John, Atherington 1839 W
Down John, High Bickington 1849 W
John, snr., Pilton, gentleman 1592 [W]; forename blank in Ms;
    supplied from parish register
Josiah, Winkleigh 1790 W
Lectiora, Barnstaple 1622 [W]
Lewis, Tawstock 1580 W
Margaret, Witheridge 1588 A
Down Margaret, High Bickington 1779 W
Margery, Pilton 1662 A
Mary, Ilfracombe 1665 A
Mary, Barnstaple 1674 W
Mary, Chulmleigh 1689 W
Mary, Merton 1746 A
Mary, Pilton 1750 W
Down Mary, High Bickington 1764 A
Down Mary, King's Nympton 1773 A
Down Mary, Burrington 1806 W*
Down Michael, High Bickington, yeoman 1809 W
Nicholas, Bondleigh 1567 W
Nicholas, Newton Tracey 1627 [W]
Nicholas, Hartland 1695 A
Philip, Woolfardisworthy 1592 [W]
Phillippa, Newton Tracey 1644 W
Phyllis, Barnstaple 1605 W
Polinora, Chulmleigh 1668 W
Down Richard, Roborough 1580 W
Richard, Barnstaple 1583 W and 1588 A
Richard, Barnstaple 1590 [W]
Richard, Bideford 1626 [W]
Richard, Merton 1687 W
Richard, Bideford 1703 W
Richard, Winkleigh 1786 W and 1790 W
Down Richard, Rackenford 1823 W
Down Richard, Barnstaple 1831 W
Down Robert, Lapford 1774 W
Down Robert, Merton 1848 W
Down Robert, Bideford 1856 W
Down Roger, Great Torrington 1644 A
Roger, Chittlehampton 1711 A
Down Roger, Winkleigh 1751 W
Down Roger, Winkleigh 1772 W
Down Samuel, Yarnscombe, thatcher 1811 A
Down Samuel, Rackenford, yeoman 1815 A to Susanna Crook,
    daughter
Down Samuel, Bideford, tallow chandler 1857 A to Edis
    Hammond Down, tallow chandler, son
Sebastian, Chulmleigh 1692 W
Simon, Dolton 1637 W
Simon, Winkleigh 1825 W
Sybil, Bideford 1626 [W]
Thomas, Tawstock 1579 W
Downe alias Winter Thomas, East Worlington 1582 W
Downe alias Elworthy Thomas, Witheridge 1587 A
Thomas, Witheridge 1592 [W]

Thomas, East Worlington 1596 [W]
Thomas, Rose Ash 1680 A
Thomas, Hartland 1757 A
Down Thomas, High Bickington 1825 W
Down Thomas, Great Torrington 1830 W
Down Thomas, Combe Martin 1848 W
Down Thomas, North Molton, farmer 1849 A to Ann, widow
Down Thomas, Atherington 1854 W
Thomasine, Fremington 1595 [W]
Thomasine, Tawstock, widow 1611 [W]; forename blank in
    Ms; supplied from parish register
Thomasine, Barnstaple 1629 [W]
Timothy, Burrington 1762 W
Walter, Clovelly 1572 W
William, Langtree 1579 W
William, Martinhoe 1589 W and 1594 [W]
Downe William and Joan, Great Torrington 1594 [W]
William, Chulmleigh 1598 [W]
William, Instow 1666 W
William, South Molton 1674 A
Down William, Woolfardisworthy 1676 W
William, North Molton 1682 W
Down William, Frithelstock 1722 W
William, Pilton 1727 W
William, Woolfardisworthy 1762 A
Down William, High Bickington 1773 W
Down William, High Bickington, yeoman 1806 W
Down William, High Bickington 1838 W and 1843 W
Down William, Roborough 1844 W
Downeman see Downman
Downey, Downhay
    Downhay John, Zeal Monachorum 1580 W
    Justinian, Witheridge 1710 A
    Downhay Walter, Witheridge 1588 W
    William, Rackenford 1832 W
Downing, Downinge, Downyng, Downynge, Dowyng
    Downinge ..., Hartland 1603 [W]
    Downinge ..., Buckland Brewer 1605 [W]
    Downinge Amy, Hartland 1620 [W]
    Downyng Andrew, Abbotsham 1588 W
    Christopher, Great Torrington 1742 A
    Dominic, Clovelly, yeoman 1807 A
    Downinge Edward, Barnstaple 1638 A
    Downinge Elizabeth, Buckland Brewer 1606 W
    Elizabeth, Hartland 1631 [W]
    George, Georgeham 1839 W
    Henry, Parkham 1847 W
    Downinge James, Buckland Brewer 1604 [W]; forename blank
        in Ms; supplied from parish register
    Jane, Hartland 1677 W
    Downynge Joan, Hartland 1576 A
    Downinge Joan, Buckland Brewer 1624 [W]
    Downynge John, Buckland Brewer 1573 W
    Downinge John, Buckland Brewer 1609 [W] "of Geaton's
        Down"; forename blank in Ms; supplied from parish register
    Downinge John, Hartland 1620 [W]
    John, Buckland Brewer 1637 A
    John, Westleigh 1825 W
    John, Clovelly 1856 W
    Joseph, South Molton 1777 W
    Julian, Frithelstock 1692 W
    Downinge Lawrence, Buckland Brewer 1597 [W]
    Margaret, Frithelstock 1740 A
    Mary, Great Torrington 1856 W
    Mathew, Welcombe 1687 A
    Philip, Frithelstock 1687 A
    Downinge Raymond, Hartland 1624 [W]
    Richard, Weare Giffard 1836 A to Betty, widow
    Downinge Richard, Barnstaple 1840 A to Alice, widow
    Downynge Robert, Hartland 1566 W
    Samuel, Westleigh 1834 W
    Stephen, Northam 1633 W
    Thomas, Frithelstock 1705 A
    Thomas, Weare Giffard, yeoman 1810 W
    Thomas, Alwington 1837 W

Downinge William, Shebbear 1592 [W]
Downinge William, Buckland Brewer 1621 [W]
Downinge William, Frithelstock 1670 A
Downman, Downeman
  Downeman ..., Instow 1607 [W]
  Downeman ..., Warkleigh 1612 [W]
  Andrew, East Buckland 1674 W
  Andrew, Barnstaple 1766 W
  Downman alias Holman Anthony, Knowstone 1566 W
  Charles, Charles 1734 A
  Downeman Christopher, Yarnscombe 1579 W
  Christopher, Atherington 1706 A
  Downeman Edward, Charles 1710 A
  Elizabeth, Instow 1743 W
  Hugh, Westleigh 1761 A
  Downeman Jane, Instow 1692 A
  Downeman Joan, Barnstaple 1637 W
  Joan, Barnstaple 1644 A
  Downeman John, Fremington 1565 W
  Downeman John, Stoke Rivers 1575 W
  Downeman alias Chaldon John, Fremington 1601 W
  Downeman alias Connybeare John, George Nympton 1601 W;
    forename blank in Ms; supplied from parish register
  Downeman John, Twitchen 1638 W
  Downeman John, Instow 1690 W and 1694 A
  Downeman John, Westleigh 1693 A
  John, Westleigh 1706 W
  John, South Molton 1792 W
  Lewis, Peters Marland 1573 A
  Downeman Lodovic, Peters Marland 1635 W
  Downeman Margaret, Twitchen 1638 W
  Mary, Barnstaple 1769 W
  Downeman Mathew, Barnstaple 1630 [W]
  Mathew, Barnstaple 1726 A
  Downeman Paul, Chittlehampton 1621 [W]
  Downeman Philip, Peters Marland 1625 [W]
  Richard, Barnstaple 1676 W
  Richard, Barnstaple 1706 W and 1711 A
  Richard, Barnstaple 1731 A
  Downeman Robert, Barnstaple 1624 [W] and O
  Downeman Samuel, Northam 1717 W
  Downeman Thomas, Heanton Punchardon 1665 W
  Downeman Thomasine, Fremington, widow 1611 [W]
    "Deyman" in register; forename blank in Ms; supplied from
    parish register
  Downeman alias Sandicke William, West Down 1584 W
  Downeman William, Barnstaple 1639 A
  William, Barnstaple 1832 W
Downyng, Downynge, Dowyng see Downing
Drake, Dracke
  Dracke Alexander, Cruwys Morchard 1631 [W] and 1632 [W]
  Alfred, Barnstaple 1852 A
  Alice, Coldridge 1583 W
  Alice, Cruwys Morchard 1624 [W]
  Amesius, Romansleigh 1627 [W]
  Ann, Barnstaple 1719 W
  Avis, Washford Pyne 1632 [W]
  Charles, Shirwell 1855 W
  David, Witheridge 1829 W
  David, formerly of East Worlington but late of West
    Worlington 1831 W
  Elizabeth, Romansleigh 1632 [W]
  Elizabeth, Chawleigh 1725 W
  Elizabeth, King's Nympton 1793 W
  Francis, Clovelly 1748 A
  George, Cruwys Morchard 1616 W
  George, Stoodleigh 1732 A
  George, Romansleigh, yeoman 1849 A to Mary, widow
  Gregory, West Worlington 1702 W
  Henry, Barnstaple 1689 A
  Hugh, Winkleigh 1569 W
  Hugh, Winkleigh 1583 A
  Humphrey, Meshaw 1665 A
  Humphrey, Meshaw 1723 W
  Humphrey, Winkleigh 1816 W

  Isaac, Shebbear 1696 W
  James, Cruwys Morchard 1664 A
  James, Barnstaple 1680 A
  James, Northam 1742 W
  Jane, Barnstaple, widow 1804 W
  Joan, Dolton 1683 W
  Joan, Martinhoe 1716 A
  John, Cruwys Morchard 1614 [W]; forename blank in Ms;
    supplied from parish register
  John, Cruwys Morchard 1622 [W]
  John, Coldridge 1623 [W]
  John, Coldridge, snr. 1666 W
  John, Coldridge 1666 W
  John, Cruwys Morchard 1684 W
  John, Mariansleigh 1693 W
  John, Bondleigh 1710 A
  John, Barnstaple 1712 A
  John, Meshaw 1723 A
  John, Coldridge 1724 W
  John, West Worlington 1727 A
  John, Chulmleigh 1760 W
  John, Barnstaple 1770 W
  Jonah, Coldridge 1666 A
  Margaret, Coldridge 1690 W
  Margery, West Worlington 1594 [W]
  Mary, Barnstaple 1800 A
  Mary, West Worlington 1836 W
  Richard, Lapford 1584 W
  Richard, Cruwys Morchard 1620 [W]
  Richard, Coldridge 1670 W
  Richard, Chittlehampton 1770 W
  Richard, North Tawton 1851 W
  Robert, Cruwys Morchard 1643 W
  Robert, Heanton Punchardon 1847 A
  Roger, Washford Pyne 1618 [W]
  Samuel, Cruwys Morchard 1640 [W]
  Samuel, Shebbear 1726 W
  Samuel, Barnstaple 1795 W
  Stephen, Dolton 1684 W
  Dracke Thomas, Bondleigh 1588 A and 1589 O account
  Thomas, Washford Pyne 1589 W
  Thomas, Dolton 1641 W
  Thomas, Chulmleigh 1706 A
  Thomas, George Nympton 1782 W
  Thomas, Chawleigh 1796 W
  William, West Worlington 1576 W
  William, South Molton 1661 W
  William, Dolton 1663 A
  William, Dolton 1691 A
  William, St Giles in the Wood 1737 W
  William, Romansleigh 1814 W
Draper ..., Combe Martin 1600 A
  Benjamin, Warkleigh 1611 [W]
  Benjamin, Berrynarbor 1837 W
  Benjamin, Lynton 1841 A to Sarah of Berrynarbor, mother
  Benjamin, Combe Martin 1857 W
  Joan, Combe Martin 1812 W
  John, Combe Martin 1588 W
  John, Great Torrington 1591 [W]
  John, Clovelly 1621 [W]
  John, Northam 1699 W
  John, Marwood 1700 W
  John, East Down 1773 W
  John, Combe Martin 1782 W
  Lawrence, Northam 1688 W
  Mary, Shirwell 1830 W
  Philip, Clovelly 1591 [W]
  Philip, Combe Martin 1826 W
  Thomas, Combe Martin 1747 W
  Thomas, Marwood 1749 A
  Thomas, Combe Martin, yeoman 1806 W
  William, East Down 1773 W
Drasher Thomas, Witheridge 1672 A
Drew, Drewe
  Drewe ... 1607 [W]

..., North Molton 1610 [W]
Drewe ..., Buckland Brewer 1610 [W]
Drewe Agnes, Fremington, widow 1607 [W]; forename blank
   in Ms; supplied from parish register
Drewe Agnes, Barnstaple 1628 [W]
Dorothy, Northam 1665 W
Dorothy, Shebbear 1829 W
Drewe Eleanor, Great Torrington 1606 W
Elizabeth, Buckland Brewer 1598 [W]
Elizabeth, Merton 1696 A
George, South Molton 1641 W
Gideon, Merton 1673 W
Drewe Grace, Pilton 1597 [W]
Henry, Ashford 1694 W
Honor, Atherington 1674 A
Jacquet, Great Torrington 1624 [W]
Drewe James, Buckland Brewer 1606 W
Joan, Monkleigh 1640 W
John, Buckland Brewer 1568 W
Drewe John, Tawstock 1587 W
Drewe John, Fremington 1588 W
Drewe John, Barnstaple 1622 A
Drewe John, Barnstaple 1623 [W] and jnr. 1624 O
John, Barnstaple 1669 A and 1672 A
John, Chittlehampton 1676 W
John, Landcross 1728 W
John, Bideford 1730 W
John, Landcross 1765 W
Margaret, Barnstaple 1751 W
Mary, Buckland Brewer 1583 W
Mary, Northam 1762 W
Peter, Bow 1619 [W]
Drewe Peter, Tawstock 1621 [W]
Drewe Richard, Barnstaple 1593 [W]
Drewe Robert, Bow 1593 [W]
Drewe Robert, Buckland Brewer 1596 [W]
Robert, Ashford 1684 A
Robert, Martinhoe 1702 A
Robert, Barnstaple 1737 W
Roger, Buckland Filleigh 1814 W
Samuel, Northam 1690 A
Sarah, St Giles in the Wood 1668 A
Drewe Thomas, Barnstaple 1588 W
Drewe Thomas, Great Torrington 1601 W
Thomas, Northam 1762 W
Walter, Atherington 1636 W
Drewe alias Threwe William, Buckland Brewer 1577 W
Drewett Hannah, Barnstaple 1826 W
Dromant, Dromett, Drommett
   Archelaus, Great Torrington 1668 W
   Elizabeth and John, Great Torrington 1621 [W]
   Dromett Giles, Great Torrington 1636 W
   John, Great Torrington 1621 W
   Drommett John, Great Torrington 1633 W
   Drommett Mary, Great Torrington 1675 A
   Peter, Great Torrington 1628 [W]
   Dromett Richard, Great Torrington 1638 A
   Dromett Roger, Great Torrington 1623 [W]
   William, Great Torrington 1595 [W]
   William, Great Torrington 1629 [W]
Dubb alias Dobb William, Tawstock, labourer 1817 A to Mary,
   widow
Duckett
   Dockett Robert, Tawstock 1785 W
Duckham Joan, Stoodleigh 1616 [W]
   John, Stoodleigh 1593 [W]
   John, Stoodleigh 1682 W
   William 1639 A
Dudall ..., Shirwell 1607 [W]
   Richard, Shirwell 1621 [W]
   Thomas, Shirwell 1592 [W]
   William, Shirwell 1607 [W]; forename blank in Ms; supplied
      from parish register
Duder William, Chulmleigh 1573 W
Due see Dew

Dugan John, Littleham (near Bideford) 1707 A
Duggery James, North Tawton 1668 W
Duke Beaton, Bow 1591 [W]
   John, Great Torrington 1590 [W]
   John, Hartland 1606 W
   Lawrence, Hartland 1590 [W]
   Philip, Winkleigh 1626 [W]
   Robert, Bow 1586 A
   Scipio, Winkleigh 1602 W
   Thomas, Hartland 1623 [W]
   William, Winkleigh 1611 [W]; forename blank in Ms; supplied
      from parish register
Dulham see Dullam
Dulin see Dallen
Dullam, Dulham
   George, Fremington 1851 W
   John, Dolton 1743 A
   Mary, Bideford 1736 W
   Robert, Instow 1781 W
   Robert, Fremington 1782 A
   Dulham Robert, Fremington, yeoman 1826 A to Ann, widow
   Robert, Frithelstock 1854 W
   Thomas, Instow, yeoman 1807 W
   William, Fremington 17 Sep 1847 W second probate 1852
Dullen, Dulling, Dulon see Dallen
Dun see Dunn
Dunacombe see Dunscomb
Dune see Dunn
Dungell, Dungil
   Edmund, Northam 1670 W
   Elizabeth, Northam 1711 W
   Joan, Fremington, widow 1612 [W]; forename blank in Ms;
      supplied from parish register
   Richard, Fremington 1586 W
   Richard, Northam 1619 [W]
   Dungil Robert, Northam 1682 A
Dunham see Densham
Dunier Joan, Tawstock 1746 A
Duning see Dunning
Dunn, Dun, Dune, Dunne
   Dun ..., Great Torrington 1609 [W]
   Dunne Alexander, Shebbear 1641 W
   Dunne Alice, Tawstock 1629 [W]
   Dunne Andrew, Buckland Filleigh 1688 W
   Dun Andrew, Buckland Filleigh 1702 W
   Ann, South Molton 1837 A (1834) to Richard, brother
   Ann, South Molton 1838 W
   Dun Arthur, Atherington 1688 W
   Caroline Elizabeth, South Molton 1855 A to Reuben James
      Dunn, printer, brother (formerly of Minehead, Somerset)
   Dune Catherine, Parkham 1586 W
   Catherine, Filleigh 1798 W*
   Dunne David, Parkham 1578 W
   Edith, South Molton 1855 W
   Dunne Egline, Chulmleigh 1642 A
   Elizabeth, Chulmleigh 1776 A
   Elizabeth, Filleigh 1792 A
   Elizabeth, South Molton, widow 1804 W
   Elizabeth, Little Torrington 1827 W
   Elizabeth, South Molton 1829 W
   Emma, West Down 1639 W
   Dun alias Not George, South Molton 1720 A
   Grace, Shebbear 1673 W
   Griffith, Georgeham 1676 W
   Humphrey, Westleigh 1708 W
   Isaac, Filleigh 1769 A
   Dun James, North Molton 1660 W
   James, South Molton 1842 W
   Dun Joan, South Molton 1699 W
   Joan, Chulmleigh 1725 W
   Dunne John, South Molton 1592 [W]
   Dunne John, North Molton 1596 [W]
   Dunne John, Woolfardisworthy 1597 [W]
   Dun John, South Molton 1606 W
   Dun John, Alverdiscott 1615 [W]

Dun John, West Down 1660 W
John, South Molton 1681 A
John, Ashreigney 1684 A
John, Parkham 1703 A
John, South Molton 1707 W
John, Chulmleigh 1710 W and 1721 W
Dun John, South Molton 1755 W
John, Filleigh 1785 W
John, South Molton 1813 W
John, South Molton 1824 W, 1830 W and 1831 W
John, heretofore of Filleigh, but late of Chittlehampton 1834
    W
John, Parkham 1834 A
Joseph, Woolfardisworthy 1681 A
Joseph, South Molton 1741 W
Joseph, Filleigh 1791 A
Juliana, Bideford 1681 W
Dunne Margaret, Ilfracombe 1581 W
Margaret, Atherington 1632 [W]
Dunne Margery, Bondleigh 1687 W
Dun alias Not Mary, South Molton 1720 W
Mary, High Bickington 1800 W
Mary, Filleigh 1808 A*
Michael, South Molton 1831 W
Philip, Chulmleigh 1633 [W]
Philip, Ilfracombe 1637 W
Philip, Bondleigh 1682 W
Philip, Coldridge 1770 W
Dune Richard, Rose Ash 1580 W
Dunne Richard, Chulmleigh 1670 A
Richard, Chulmleigh 1775 A
Richard, Woolfardisworthy, yeoman 1809 W
Richard, South Molton 1848 W
Robert, Woolfardisworthy 1673 W
Robert, South Molton 1707 A
Robert, South Molton 1793 W
Robert, South Molton 1835 W
Samuel, South Molton 1765 W
Samuel, South Molton 1828 W
Samuel, High Bickington 1857 W
Sybil, Atherington 1680 A
Theophilus, South Molton 1783 A
Thomas, Atherington 1631 [W]
Dunne Thomasine, Woolfardisworthy 1620 [W]
Dunne Walter, Tawstock 1622 [W]
William, Woolfardisworthy 1670 W
William, South Molton 1825 W
William, North Tawton 1830 A to Ann, widow
William, South Molton 1841 W; A dbn 1850
Dunnaford Ann, Northam 1768 W
Dunne see Dunn
Dunning, Donynge, Duning, Dunninge, Dunnynge
Dunninge ..., Northam 1611 [W]
Dunninge Amy, South Molton 1670 W
Ann, Pilton 1837 W
Elizabeth, Winkleigh, widow 1811 W
John or Robert, South Molton 1718 W
Mary, Barnstaple 1772 W
Dunnynge Richard, Bideford 1631 [W]
Richard, Pilton 1818 A to Ann, widow
Donynge Robert, Clovelly 1579 W
Robert or John, South Molton 1718 W
Duning Samuel, South Molton 1749 W
Samuel, South Molton 1768 W
Dunrich, Dunrish
Dunrish Elizabeth, Ilfracombe 1725 W
William, Ilfracombe 1724 A
Dunscomb, Dunacombe, Dunscombe
Dunscombe ..., East Down 1636 O
Dunscomb Abraham, Molland 1641 A
Dunscomb Gillian, Cruwys Morchard 1612 [W]; forename
    blank in Ms; supplied from parish register
Dunscomb Thomas, Cruwys Morchard 1604 [W]; forename
    blank in Ms; supplied from parish register
Dunacombe William, Arlington 1679 W
Dunsham see Densham

Durant see Durrant
Durck, Durcke see Dark
Durdon, Durden
Joan, Great Torrington 1636 W and 1639 A
Robert, Great Torrington 1597 [W]
Durden William, Langtree 1679 W
Durham ..., Burrington 1614 [W]
John, Burrington 1725 A
William, Burrington 1667 W
William, Burrington 1720 A
Durie Charles, Merton, gentleman 1857 A to Alexander, son
Durke see Dark
Durrant, Durant
Durant Christopher, East Putford 1741 W
John, Barnstaple 1607 [W]; forename blank in Ms; supplied
    from parish register
Durant John, Little Torrington 1666 W
Durant John, Buckland Filleigh 1730 W
Durant John, North Tawton 1730 W
Durant alias Rolston Mary, North Tawton 1710 W
Durant Roger, Zeal Monachorum 1747 W
Durant Roger, North Tawton 1792 W
Simon, Barnstaple 1590 [W]
Durant Thomas, Frithelstock 1716 A
Thomas, Petrockstowe 1737 W
Thomas, Petrockstowe 1796 W
Thomasine, Chittlehampton 1632 [W]
Durant William, Bideford 1756 W
Durant William, North Tawton 1849 W
Durvard William, Northam 1589 A
Duynge Roger, Bideford 1583 A
Dyamond see Diamond
Dyare see Dyer
Dybb, Dybbe see Dibbe
Dycke Margery, Northam 1574 W
Dyer, Deyr, Dier, Dyare
..., Puddington 1604 [W]
Dier ..., Lapford 1611 [W]
Dier Agnes, Buckland Brewer 1591 [W]
Agnes, Shirwell 1716 A
Agnes, Lynton 1835 W
Alexander, Marwood 1604 W
Dier Alice, Ilfracombe 1617 [W]
Alice, Marwood 1641 A
Anthony, Fremington 1728 A
Dier David, Ilfracombe 1605 [W]; forename blank in Ms;
    supplied from parish register
Dier Edward, Marwood 1597 [W]
Edward, Barnstaple 1599 [W]
Edward, Northam 1603 W
Dier Edward, Ilfracombe 1617 [W]
Dyar Egline, Zeal Monachorum 1600 W
Eleanor, Buckland Brewer 1635 W
Elizabeth, Ilfracombe 1682 W
Elizabeth, Winkleigh 1693 W
Elizabeth, Ilfracombe 1720 W
Dyar George, Bondleigh 1577 A
George, Barnstaple 1631 [W]
George, North Tawton 1644 W
George, Marwood 1727 W
Henry, Coldridge 1676 and 1677 A
Dyare Humphrey, Bideford 1587 A
Isaac, Beaford 1716 W
James, Chittlehampton 1675 W
Dier Joan, Atherington 1597 [W]
Joan, Ilfracombe 1603 W
Dier Joan, Great Torrington 1618 [W]
Joan, Marwood 1680 W
Joan, Beaford 1715 W
John, West Ilkerton, Lynton 1569 W
John, Chawleigh 1575 W
Dyar John, Yarnscombe 1577 W
John, Ilfracombe 1582 W
Dyare John, Atherington 1586 W
Dier John, Chawleigh 1591 [W]

Dier John, Ilfracombe 1592 [W]
John, Langtree 1599 [W]
Dier John, Ilfracombe 1617 [W]
John, Great Torrington 1619 [W]
John, North Molton 1622 [W]
John, East Buckland 1634 A and 1635 O
John, Frithelstock 1643 W
John, Chittlehampton 1687 A
Dier John, Georgeham 1693 W
John, Lynton 1697 W
John, Buckland Brewer 1707 W
John, Berrynarbor 1708 A
John, Weare Giffard 1710 A
John, Shirwell 1715 A
John, Satterleigh 1724 A
John, South Molton 1726 A
John, Ilfracombe 1735 A
John, Fremington 1741 A
John, Weare Giffard 1778 W
John, Marwood 1781 W
John, Littleham (near Bideford) 1803 W
John, Chittlehampton 1835 A to Ann of Barnstaple, daughter
Joseph, Marwood 1626 [W]
Lodovic, Littleham (near Bideford) 1665 A
Dier Mary, Atherington 1590 [W]
Dier Mary, Ilfracombe 1612 [W]; forename blank in Ms;
    supplied from parish register; 1615 O
Dier Mary, Ilfracombe 1616 [W]
Mary, North Molton 1644 W
Mary, Chittlehampton 1670 W
Mary, Marwood 1727 A
Mary, Ilfracombe 1797 A
Mary, Great Torrington 1855 W
Mary, Weare Giffard 1856 W
Mathew, Marwood 1625 [W]
Deyr Nicholas, St Giles in the Wood 1584 W
Nicholas, Coldridge 1631 [W]
Nicholas, Tawstock 1779 A
Dyare Oliver, South Molton 1585 A
Dier Pauline, Atherington 1618 [W]
Peter, South Molton 1846 W
Philip, ship *Alborough* 1758 A
Dier Richard, Ilfracombe 1598 [W]
Richard, West Down 1672 W
Richard, Lynton 1824 A to James of Ilfracombe, uncle and
    Richard Ward of Lynton
Dyare Robert, North Molton 1577 W
Dier Robert, South Molton 1596 [W]
Robert, Burrington 1664 W
Robert, Weare Giffard 1790 A
Roger, Marwood 1666 W
Roger, Berrynarbor 1730 W
Roger, Marwood 1737 W
Dier Thomas, Huntshaw 1592 [W]
Dier Thomas, Langtree 1595 [W]
Thomas, Ilfracombe 1636 W
Thomas, Burrington 1640 A
Thomas, Chulmleigh 1642 W
Thomas, Lynton 1664 W
Thomas, Atherington 1690 A
Thomas, Ilfracombe 1691 A
Thomas, Satterleigh 1696 W
Thomas, Satterleigh 1714 W
Thomas, Tawstock 1716 W
Thomas, Lynton 1735 W
Thomas, Filleigh 1835 W
Diare Thomasine, Lynton 1586 W
Tobias, Georgeham 1747 A
Dyare William, Marwood 1578 W
William, Ilfracombe 1580 W
Dier William, Brendon 1590 [W]
Dier William, Langtree 1591 [W]
William, Chittlehampton 1606 W
William, Kentisbury 1624 [W]
William, Chittlehampton 1683 W

William, Buckland Brewer 1706 A
William, Tawstock 1819 A to Ann, widow
William, Trentishoe, yeoman 1856 A to William, son
Willmot, Bideford 1733 A
Dyke Elizabeth, Bideford 1746 W
John, Bideford 1745 W
Dyllen, Dyllon see Dillon
Dyman see Diamond
Dymant see Diamond
Dymond see Diamond
Dymont see Diamond
Dynham see Denham
Dyninge see Denham

Eames, Eame
Eame ..., Rose Ash 1615 [W]
Eames alias Zeale Agnes, Romansleigh 1690 W and T
David, Ilfracombe 1718 A
George, North Molton 1758 T
George, Ilfracombe 1830 W
Grace, Ilfracombe 1838 W
Hannah, Ilfracombe 1823 W
Eame Henry, Rose Ash 1624 [W]
Eame alias Seall John, Rose Ash 1583 W
John, Oakford 1635 A
John, Yarnscombe 1638 A
Mary, North Molton 1756 A
Richard, Romansleigh 1685 A and 1689 A
Richard, Ilfracombe 1819 W
Eame Robert, Meeth 1587 W
Eame Thomas, Lynton 1600 W and A
Thomas, North Molton 1603 W
Thomas, North Molton 1675 A
Thomas, North Molton 1700 W
Eame William, Lynton 1638 A
William, Brendon 1743 W
Eare see Aire
Earell see Earlec
Earland Martin, Bow 1723 W
Simon, Bow 1733 W
Earle, Earell
..., Frithelstock 1601 A
Amos, Rackenford 1669 W
Elizabeth, Clovelly 1764 W
Humphrey, Rackenford 1618 [W]
Earell John, Langtree 1586 W
John, Langtree 1640 A
Margaret, Rackenford 1618 O
Philadelphia, Barnstaple 1774 A
Earell Walter, Hartland 1581 W
William, Weare Giffard 1671 A
William, Shebbear 1719 W
Earnest see Ernest
Eascott, Escote, Escott, Estcote
Escott Hugh, Yarnscombe 1705 W
Escott Jane, Barnstaple 1734 W
Estcote John, Abbotsham 1568 W
Eascott alias Winslade John, Northam 1606 W
John, Hartland 1618 [W]
Thomasine, Cheldon 1582 A
Escote William, Meeth 1570 W
William, Cheldon 1587 W
Easement John, Cheldon 1731 W
Easery Anthony, Great Torrington 1762 W
Anthony, East Putford 1814 W
Archelaus, Great Torrington 1748 W
Bridget, Great Torrington 1755 W
Fanny, Bideford 1812 A
Grace, Barnstaple 1857 W
Humphrey, Sheepwash 1793 A
John, Pilton 1810 A
John, Monkleigh 1839 A
John, Little Torrington 1852 W
Joseph, Great Torrington 1856 A
Mary, Bideford 1840 W

Thomas, Great Torrington 1774 W and 1782 W
Thomas, Bideford 1808 W
Thomas, Little Torrington 1830 W
William, Great Torrington 1796 W
William, Bideford 1835 A
  see also Essery
East Francis, Chulmleigh 1708 W
Nicholas, Chulmleigh 1707 W
Eastabrook, Eastabrook see Eastbrooke
Eastaway, Eastway, Estawaye, Estwaie
Estwaie Agnes, Ilfracombe 1569 W
Betty, Barnstaple, sp. 1846 A to Mary, mother
Daniel, Tawstock 1761 W
Edward, Great Torrington 1729 O
Elizabeth, Ilfracombe 1829 W
George, Ilfracombe 1712 A
George, Barnstaple 1830 W
Gertrude, Ilfracombe 1684 W
Eastway Grace, Georgeham 1779 W
Harry, Ilfracombe 1610 [W]; forename blank in Ms; supplied
  from parish register
Henry, Ilfracombe, mariner 1798 W
John, Ilfracombe 1682 A
John, Ilfracombe 1803 A
Lodovic, Ilfracombe, snr. 1635 [W]
Eastway Mary, Georgeham 1779 W
Nicholas, Ilfracombe 1601 [W]; forename blank in Ms;
  supplied from parish register
Estawaye Ralph, Ilfracombe 1589 [W]
Robert, Ilfracombe 1613 [W]; forename blank in Ms; supplied
  from parish register
Robert, Bideford 1729 W
Estawaye Thomas, Combe Martin 1587 W
Thomas, Combe Martin 1674 W
Thomas, Ilfracombe 1743 A
Eastbrooke, Eastabrook, Eastabrooke, Estbrock, Estbrooke
Eastabrook ..., North Tawton 1601 W
Eastabrooke Alexander, North Tawton 1602 W
Eastabrooke Alexander, North Tawton 1672 W
Eastabrooke Alexander, North Tawton 1747 W
Ann, Tawstock 1623 [W]
Eastabrooke Arthur, Bideford 1711 W
Eastabrooke Bridget, North Tawton 1711 A
Eastabrooke Francis, North Tawton 1611 [W] "of Stone" in
  register; forename blank in Ms; supplied from parish register
Eastabrooke Gregory, Great Torrington 1615 [W]
Estbrooke Joan, North Tawton, widow 1569 W
Joan, Tawstock 1620 [W]
Eastabrook Joan, North Tawton 1674 W
Estbrock John, Nymet Rowland 1587 W
Eastabrooke John, Tawstock 1605 W
John, Fremington 1630 [W]
Eastabrooke John, Alverdiscott 1731 W
Eastabrooke John, Bow 1778 A
Eastabrook Joseph, Bow 1817 W
Eastabrooke Lawrence, North Tawton 1613 [W]; forename
  blank in Ms; supplied from parish register
Eastabrook Margaret, North Tawton 1771 W
Estbroucke Mark, North Tawton 1576 W
Eastabrooke Mark, North Tawton 1731 W
Eastabrooke Oliver, North Tawton 1711 A
Eastabrooke Patience, Bideford 1722 A
Estbrocke Richard, North Tawton 1574 W and 1581 W
Eastabrook Roger, Bow 1812 W
Eastabrooke Sabine, Tawstock, widow 1608 [W]; forename
  blank in Ms; supplied from parish register
Thomas, Alverdiscott 1689 W
Estbrooke William, Tawstock 1582 W
Eastabrook William, North Tawton 1769 W
Eastman, Eastmond, Eastmont, Estmond, Estmont
Eastmont ..., South Molton 1612 [W] and 1613 O
Eastmond Armanell, Barnstaple 1662 W
Baldwin, Atherington 1805 W
Eastmont Catherine, Georgeham 1680 W
Elizabeth, Atherington, widow 1811 W

Eastmond George, Marwood, jnr. 1640 W and 1641 A
George, Northam 1856 W
Estmond George and Mary, Marwood 1642 A
Eastmond Henry, Marwood 1578 W
Eastmont James, Marwood 1607 [W]; forename blank in Ms;
  supplied from parish register
Eastmond James, Barnstaple 1847 W
Eastmond James, Mariansleigh 1851 A
Eastmond Joan, Marwood 1635 T
Eastmond Joan, Rose Ash 1674 A
Estmont John, Bratton Fleming 1574 W and 1575 A
Estmond John, Hartland 1576 W
Eastmond John, Atherington 1618 [W]
Eastmond John, Marwood 1633 W
Eastmond John, Mariansleigh, yeoman 1796 W
Eastmont Mary, North Molton 1612 [W]; forename blank in
  Ms; supplied from parish register
Estmond Mary, Marwood 1641 [W]
Mary, Bideford 1844 W
Estmond Mary and George, Marwood 1642 A
Noah, Bideford 1837 A; A dbn granted at Principal Registry,
  Jun 1897
Eastmont Richard, Oakford 1616 [W]
Eastmond Richard, East Anstey 1619 [W]
Eastmond Richard, Georgeham 1677 A
Eastmond Richard, Rose Ash 1703 W
Richard, Bideford 1834 W
Richard, Bideford 1847 W
Robert, Georgeham 1665 A
Eastmond Robert, Rose Ash 1672 A
Eastmond Robert, Rose Ash 1715 A
Robert, South Molton 1805 A
Thomasine, Barnstaple 1622 [W]
Estmont Walter, Hartland 1576 W
Eastmond William, Meshaw 1587 W
William, Bideford 1797 W*
William, Bideford 1826 W
Eastmond William, Mariansleigh 1833 A to Ann, widow
Eastmond William, Bishop's Nympton, farmer 1848 A to
  James of Woolfardisworthy, yeoman, brother
Eastmont Wilmot, Oakford 1611 [W]; forename blank in Ms;
  supplied from parish register
Easton ..., Loxhore 1610 [W]
James, Instow 1831 W
John, Buckland Brewer 1740 W
John, Monkleigh 1755 A
Margaret, Loxhore 1633 W
Samuel, Barnstaple 1741 W
Eastway see Eastaway
Eastwood James, Mariansleigh, miller 1851 A to John
Eates John, Pilton 1663 W
Eaton ..., Barnstaple 1608 [W]
Edward, Barnstaple 1668 W
Robert, Bideford 1645 A
William, Pilton 1645 A
Ebbot, Ebote, Ebott see Abbot
Ebsary, Ebsery
Francis, Merton 1797 W
Ebsery Richard, Atherington 1721 W
Ebsworthy see Edworthy
Edaford see Edford
Edbery William, Combe Martin 1580 W
Edbrooke Robert, Warkleigh 1672 A
Eddy, Eddie
Eddie John, Sheepwash 1588 A
William, Bideford 1729 A
Edford, Edaford
Edaford Edmund, Chawleigh 1580 A
Edford alias Edworth John, Chawleigh 1568 W
Edgecombe, Edgecomb
Mary, Ashford 1632 [W]
Edgecomb Richard, Bideford 1765 W
Edgeley, Edgely, Edgley
Dorothy, Barnstaple 1736 W and 1739 A
Edgely John, South Molton, jnr. 1643 A

Edgley John, South Molton 1749 A
Nathaniel, Barnstaple 1730 W
Edgley Thomas, South Molton 1670 W
Edgley see Edgeley
Edger ..., Woolfardisworthy 1609 [W]
Abraham, Pilton 1675 A
Alice, Pilton 1716 W
Caesar, Northam 1837 W
Daniel, Pilton 1600 A
Elizabeth, Abbotsham 1601 W
John, Charles 1643 W
Edger alias Nicholls John, Woolfardisworthy 1643 W
John, Pilton 1712 W
John, Pilton 1757 W
John, Pilton 1785 W
John, Barnstaple 1820 W
Macklin, Marwood 1760 W
Mary, Marwood 1789 W
Edger alias Nicoll Richard, Woolfardisworthy 1583 W
Robert, Woolfardisworthy 1598 [W]
Edger alias Adger Sabine, Goodleigh 1662 W
Thomas, Woolfardisworthy 1596 [W]
William, Pilton 1630 [W]
William, Pilton 1759 W
   see also Adger
Edgman, Adgman, Adgeman, Adgimand, Edgeman, Edgmam
Edgeman Angela, South Molton 1635 A
Christopher, Rackenford 1597 [W]
Adgman George, Rackenford 1677 W
Edgmam Jane, Mariansleigh 1685 W
John, Witheridge 1617 [W]
Adgimand Mathew, Rackenford 1702 W
Adgeman Richard, Rackenford 1694 W
Robert, Rackenford 1644 A
Roger, Rackenford 1565 W
Edmonds Edward, Shebbear 1833 W
Gertrude, Great Torrington 1751 W
John, North Molton 1670 W
John, Alwington 1767 W
John, Shebbear 1856 W
Edney John, Barnstaple 1715 A
Edwards, Edvards, Edward, Edwardes
Adam, Northam 1573 W
Ann, Barnstaple, widow 1853 A to Elizabeth Thomas, sister
Brian Baker, Barnstaple 1852 W
Charles, Northam 1704 A
Edwardes Elizabeth, Great Torrington 1591 [W]
Gilbert, Barnstaple 1588 A
Hugh, Barnstaple 1669 A
Edward Joan, Northam 1577 W
John, Little Torrington 1696 W
John, Barnstaple 1711 W
John, Combe Martin 1720 W
John, Little Torrington 1738 W
John, Combe Martin 1748 A
John, Ilfracombe 1846 W
Margaret, Littleham (near Bideford) 1772 W
Martha, Ilfracombe 1846 W
Mary, Barnstaple 1686 A
Mary, Barnstaple 1789 W
Phyllis, Combe Martin 1641 W
Richard, Bideford 1587 W
Richard, Bideford 1753 A
Robert, Barnstaple 1745 A
Rowland, Martinhoe 1690 A
Samuel, Bideford 1744 W
Sarah, Northam 1814 W
Theophilus, Barnstaple 1788 W
Edwardes Thomas 1594 [W]
Thomas, Barnstaple 1624 [W]
Edvards Thomas, Bideford 1713 A
Thomas, Barnstaple 1765 W
William, Bideford 1718 W
William, Fremington 1719 W
William, Berrynarbor 1726 A

William, Bideford 1747 W
William, Barnstaple 1755 W
William, Northam 1784 W
William, Ilfracombe 1820 W
William, Stoodleigh 1833 A to Sarah, widow
William, Ilfracombe 1842 W
Willmot, Barnstaple 1625 [W]
Willmot, Combe Martin 1720 W
Edworthy, Ebsworthy
Andrew, High Bickington 1736 W
Elizabeth, Burrington 1708 A
Elizabeth, Chawleigh 1816 W
George, Chawleigh 1781 A
George, Chulmleigh, yeoman 1810 W
Ebsworthy Harry, Clovelly 1838 W
Henry, Pilton 1835 W
Henry see also Susanna Somerton
Joan, Chawleigh 1601 W
Edworth alias Edford John, Chawleigh 1568 W
John, Chawleigh 1626 [W]
John, Burrington 1665 W
John, Chawleigh 1694 W
John, Chawleigh 1767 A
John, Chawleigh 1777 W
John, South Molton 1855 W
Joseph, Chawleigh, yeoman 1810 W
Ebsworthy Richard, Burrington 1670 W
Roger, Chawleigh 1638 W
Roger, Chawleigh 1694 W
Thomas, Bondleigh 1593 [W]
Thomas, Dolton 1836 A
Elett see Elliott
Ellacott see Ellicott
Ellams John, Roborough 1668 A
Eller Thomas, Roborough 1719 A
Elles, Ellice see Ellis
Ellicott, Ellacott
Elizabeth, Dolton 1598 [W]
Elizabeth, Dolton 1839 W
Mary 1831 A to Fanny Letley of Dunster, sister
Ellacott Thomas 1838 A to Elizabeth of Dolton, widow
Elliott, Ellett, Elliett, Elliot, Ellott
Alexander, Great Torrington 1724 A
Elliot Andrew, Bideford 1718 W
Ellett Bartholomew, Georgeham 1580 W
Bartholomew, Welcombe 1633 A and 1635 O
Elliot Edmund, Georgeham 1677 W
Edmund, Marwood 1736 W
Elizabeth, Welcombe 1640 A
Elizabeth, East Putford 1704 W
Elizabeth, Alwington 1716 A
Henry, Kentisbury 1700 W
Ellett Hugh, South Molton 1705 W
Ellett James, Northam 1598 [W]
James, Great Torrington 1762 W
Joan, Marwood 1640 W
Joan, Bideford 1641 A
Ellott John, Georgeham 1599 [W]
John, Marwood 1618 [W]
John, Georgeham 1633 W
John, Georgeham 1661 W
John, Marwood 1668 W
John, Georgeham 1696 W
John, Bideford 1722 A and 1725 A
John, Georgeham 1727 W
John, South Molton 1805 A
Josiah, Bideford 1718 W
Laumedon, South Molton 1644 W
Margaret, Bideford 1731 W
Marian, Georgeham 1637 W
Elliot Mary, Great Torrington 1720 W
Mary, Bideford 1725 A
Phillippa, Bideford 1680 W
Ellett Priscilla, Bideford 1631 [W]
Richard, Bideford 1630 [W]

Robert, Chulmleigh 1835 W
Roger, Barnstaple 1675 W
Elliett Salome, Georgeham 1580 W
Samuel, Bideford 1689 W
Samuel, Bideford 1837 W
Samuel, formerly of South Molton, late of Pilton 1850 W
Stephen, Welcombe 1694 W
Thomas, Woolfardisworthy 1693 W
Thomas, Pilton 1740 W
Thomas, Parkham 1837 W
Ellett Walter, Georgeham 1573 W
Ellis, Elles, Ellice, Ellys, Ellyse, Elys
..., Alverdiscott 1604 [W]
..., Parkham 1608 [W] and 1612 [W]
..., Bideford 1708 [W]
Andrew, Arlington 1638 W
Anthony, Ashreigney 1621 [W]
Avis, Ashreigney 1620 [W]
Catherine and John, Northam 1637 A
Catherine, Northam 1759 A
Edward, Washford Pyne 1592 [W]
Edward, Littleham (near Bideford) 1802 W
Eleanor, Northam 1633 W
Elizabeth, Northam 1625 [W]
Elizabeth, Northam 1799 A
Ellice Emma, Abbotsham 1674 W
George, Northam 1629 [W] and 1631 [W]
George, Fremington 1700 W
George, Bideford 1719 A
George, Monkleigh 1848 W
Ellyse Henry, Witheridge 1582 I
Henry, Bow 1737 W
Henry, Clovelly 1750 A
Humphrey, Arlington 1676 W
James, Bideford 1753 W
James, Northam, joiner 1811 W
Jane, Littleham (near Bideford) 1783 W
Joan, Parkham 1590 [W]
Joan, Northam 1674 W
Joan, Winkleigh 1699 W
Joan, Instow 1717 W
Elys John, Alverdiscott 1568 W
Elles John, Woolfardisworthy 1573 W
John, Westleigh 1615 [W]
Ellis and Fellis John, Alverdiscott 1617 [W]
John, Winkleigh 1639 A
John, Bideford 1667 A
John, Northam 1674 A
John, Washford Pyne 1678 A
John, Woolfardisworthy 1704 W
John, Monkleigh 1834 A to William, son
John, Barnstaple 1841 A to Susan of Tavistock, widow
John, Bideford 1843 W
John, North Tawton 1852 W
John and Catherine, Northam 1637 W
Judith, Bideford 1740 W
Julian, Northam 1606 W
Margery, Parkham, widow 1564 W
Margery, Northam 1638 W
Mary, Winkleigh 1639 A
Miles, Northam 1684 W
Nicholas, Woolfardisworthy 1695 W
Nicholas, Woolfardisworthy 1766 W
Elles Robert, Northam 1577 A
Elles Robert, Washford Pyne 1588 W
Robert, Northam 1668 A
Robert, Northam 1697 W
Samuel, Bideford 1710 A
Sarah, Northam 1754 W
Elles Thomas, Winkleigh 1580 A
Thomas, Chittlehampton 1634 W
Thomas, Winkleigh 1636 A
Thomas, Northam 1636 A
Thomas, Northam 1664 A
Thomas, Northam 1725 W

Thomas, Northam 1739 W
Thomas, Northam 1780 W
Walter, Clovelly 1639 A
Walter, Washford Pyne 1710 A
William, Coldridge 1571 W
Ellys William, Alverdiscott 1601 W
William, Combe Martin 1605 W
William, Georgeham 1666 W
William, Bideford 1695 A
William, Bideford 1707 W
William, West Down 1728 W
William, Bideford 1731 W
William, Abbotsham 1738 W
William, Northam 1759 W
William, Monkleigh 1770 A
William, Northam 1776 W
William, Berrynarbor 1804 A
William, Northam 1809 A limited A
William, Bideford 1841 W
Ellnor John, Roborough 1712 A
Ellott see Elliott
Ellsworthy, Ellworthy see Elworthy
Ellys, Ellyse see Ellis
Elston, Elson, Elstone
..., St Giles in the Wood 1615 [W]
Elstone Agnes, St Giles in the Wood 1586 W
Elston alias Hooper Charles, Stoodleigh 1642 W
Edward, Barnstaple 1794 [W]
Francis, Peters Marland 1729 W
Francis, Langtree 1731 W
Gilbert, Atherington 1640 W
Henry, St Giles in the Wood 1605 W
Henry, Peters Marland 1690 A
Elstone Henry, Little Torrington 1771 W
Elson James, Bideford, joiner 1798 W
Elstone John, St Giles in the Wood 1624 [W]
John, Burrington 1719 W
Elson Jonathan, Bideford 1849 W
Elston alias Hoper Thomas, Molland 1570 W
Thomas, Chulmleigh 1597 [W]
Elstone Thomasine, St Giles in the Wood 1624 [W]
William, Knowstone 1841 W
Elworthy, Ellsworthy, Ellworthy, Elsworthie, Elsworthy
Elsworthy Abraham, Molland 1724 W
Andrew, Thelbridge 1666 W
Andrew, Witheridge 1723 W
Andrew, Witheridge 1768 W
Ann, Witheridge 1776 W
Ann, South Molton 1832 W
Betty, Knowstone 1774 W
Elsworthie Christopher, Great Torrington 1592, 1593 [W]
Dorothy, Thelbridge 1684 W
Elsworthie Elizabeth, Brendon 1598 [W]
Elizabeth, Knowstone 1752 W
Elizabeth, South Molton, sp. 1805 W
Elsworthie Ellen, Thelbridge 1597 [W]
Ellen, Knowstone, widow 1803 W
Elsworthie George, Brendon 1598 [W]
George, Knowstone 1738 W and 1747 A
George, Knowstone 1793 W
Elsworthy Grace, Great Torrington 1759 W
Gwen, Great Torrington 1660 W
Hugh, Witheridge 1615 [W]
Hugh, Knowstone 1691 A
Hugh, Thelbridge 1764 W
Elsworthy James, North Molton 1625 [W]
Jane, Witheridge 1756 W
Joan, Thelbridge 1623 [W] and 1625 [W]
Elsworthy John, North Molton 1603 W
Ellsworthy John, North Molton 1620 [W]
John, Knowstone 1663 W
John, Thelbridge 1666 W
Elsworthy John, Great Torrington 1704 A
John, Witheridge 1725 A
John, Thelbridge 1730 W

John, Witheridge 1736 W
Ellsworthy John, Knowstone 1790 W
John, Molland 1810 A
John, Countisbury 1852 W
Leonard, Witheridge 1628 [W]
Mary, Witheridge 1611 [W] "Ellworthie alias Hole" in
    register; forename blank in Ms; supplied from parish register
Mildred, Witheridge 1774 A
Richard, Molland 1690 W
Richard, Witheridge 1737 W
Richard, Molland 1757 W
Elsworthy Richard, Parracombe 1770 W
Richard, George Nympton, yeoman 1806 W
Elsworthy alias Down Thomas, Witheridge 1587 A
Elsworthie Thomas, Witheridge 1592 [W]
Thomas, Witheridge 1712 W
Thomas, Great Torrington 1731 W
Elsworthy Thomas, Great Torrington 1792 W
Thomas, Witheridge, gentleman 1810 W
Thomas, Chulmleigh 1827 A to Ann, widow
Ellsworthy William, North Molton 1640 A
William, Combe Martin 1660 W
William, Thelbridge 1697 W
Elsworthy William, Clovelly 1771 A
William, Thelbridge 1791 W
Elsworthy William, Clovelly 1837 W
William, Westcott, Witheridge, yeoman 1857 A to William,
    yeoman, son
Elys see Ellis
Emblin, Emblyn, Emlen, Emlin
    Emlin Arthur, Northam 1722 W
    Francis 1681 A
    Emblyn Jane, Barnstaple 1636 A
    Emlen John, Charles 1805 A
Eme Henry, Lynton 1584 W
Emlen, Emlin see Emblin
Emott, Emotts
    Emotts John, Ilfracombe 1617 [W]
    John, Ilfracombe 1619 O
    Thomas, Bideford 1604 W
    William, Ilfracombe 1597 [W]
Enckledon, Encledon
    ... 1601 A and 1608 O
    ..., Heanton Punchardon 1606 A
    ..., Heanton Punchardon 1609 [W]
    ..., Ilfracombe 1610 [W]
    ..., Georgeham 1615 [W]
    Alice, West Down, widow 1608 [W]; forename blank in Ms;
      supplied from parish register
    Edward, Tawstock 1609 [W]; forename blank in Ms; supplied
      from parish register
    Geoffrey, Ilfracombe 1596 [W]
    George, Ilfracombe 1618 [W]
    John, Heanton Punchardon 1591 [W]
    John, Ilfracombe 1595 [W]
    Encledon Richard, West Down 1587 W
    William, Heanton Punchardon 1598 [W]
      see also Incledon
Endacott, Endicott, Endicute
    Endacott John, Wembworthy 1579 W
    Endacott alias Byttabere Robert, Winkleigh 1574 W
    Endicott Sarah 1841 A to William of Dunchideock, brother
    Endecott Thomas, Wembworthy 1597 A
    Endicute Thomasine, Winkleigh, widow 1565 W
Endy Edward, Shebbear 1723 A
England Richard, Northam 1853 A
Enner Thomas, Barnstaple 1746 W
Enyon, Ennyon
    Ennyon Agnes, Northam 1683 A
    Francis, Monkleigh 1685 W
    Thomas, Northam 1618 [W]
    Ennyon Thomas, Instow 1685 W
    Thomas, Northam 1703 A
Ernest, Earnest
    Earnest Agnes, Pilton 1734 W
    Philip, Northam 1664 A

Earnest Thomas, Pilton 1731 W
    William, Mortehoe 1620 [W]
Escote, Escott see Eascott
Esquire John, Cheldon 1822 W
Essery Fanny 1812 A to William of Bideford, son
    John, Little Torrington. carpenter 1852 A to James
      Nancekivell Mills of Great Torrington, accountant, agent to
      the children
    Joseph, Great Torrington, tailor 1856 A to Elizabeth Blackwell
      of Barnstaple, widow, sister
    Thomas, Bideford 1808 W*
    William 1835 A to Robert of Bideford, brother
      see also Easery
Estawaye see Eastway
Estbrock, Estbrocke, Estbrooke, Estbroucke see Eastbrooke
Estcote see Eascott
Estmond, Estmont see Eastman
Estwaie see Eastway
Eugron George, Countisbury 1598 [W]
Evans, Eevens, Evens, Evins
    Evans alias Clifford ..., Wembworthy 1691 W
    Abraham, Abbotsham 1690 A
    Catherine, Abbotsham 1687 W
    David, East Anstey 1700 W
    Henry, Romansleigh 1606 W
    Evans alias Davie Henry, Romansleigh 1606 W
    Henry, Bideford 1733 A
    Humphrey, Coldridge 1605 W
    Jane, South Molton 1672 W
    Evens Jenkin, Northam 1723 W
    Evans alias Yeovans alias Davy (Davie) Joan, Heanton
      Punchardon, widow 1672 W
    Joan, Northam wife of Simon,, snr. 1733 W
    John, Coldridge 1572 W
    Evens John, South Molton 1575 W
    John, Bow 1598 [W]
    John, Abbotsham 1681 W
    John, Bideford 1725 A
    John, Fremington 1733 W
    John, Great Torrington 1736 A
    John, Bideford 1762 W
    Evens John, Buckland Brewer 1802 W
    Joseph, Barnstaple 1836 W
    Margaret, Meshaw 1700 W
    Mary, Northam 1857 W
    Mary see also John Williams
    Maurice, Heanton Punchardon 1713 A
    Nicholas, Bideford 1642 [W]
    Richard, Coldridge 1638 W
    Richard, Coldridge 1690 A
    Richard, Coldridge 1725 W
    Richard, Great Torrington 1725 W
    Eveens Richard, Fremington 1764 W
    Richard, Coldridge 1777 W
    Richard, Coldridge 1804 W
    Roger, ship *Pembroke* 1750 A
    Sabboth, Coldridge 1643 W
    Simon, South Molton, snr. 1625 [W]
    Simon, South Molton 1673 A account
    Simon, South Molton 1676 W
    Thomas, Mariansleigh 1703 W
    Thomas, Bideford 1707 A
    Thomas, South Molton 1733 A
    Thomas, Coldridge 1737 W
    Thomas, Bideford 1778 W
    Thomasine, Bideford 1757 W
    William, Meshaw 1670 A
    William, Meshaw 1685 A
    Evins William, Buckland Brewer 1845 W
    Willmot, Coldridge 1728 A
Eveleigh, Evuley
    ..., Oakford 1734 A
    Elizabeth, Oakford 1717 A
    Evuley Isott, Bideford 1625 [W]
    Joan, West Anstey 1721 W

John, Barnstaple 1625 [W]
Mary, Barnstaple 1797 A
Sarah, Cruwys Morchard 1686 A
William, Cruwys Morchard 1681 W
Evens see Evans
Evered Robert of Kilton, Bridgewater, labourer 1853 A to
    Anthony, labourer, brother
Everton
Henry, Bideford 1699 A
Everton alias Cooper Mary, Bideford 1663 A
William, Northam 1773 W
Every Ann, Bideford 1721 T
John 1684 A
Mary, Bideford 1757 A
Evett Andrew, Witheridge 1610 [W]; forename blank in Ms;
    supplied from parish register
William, Berrynarbor 1605 W
Evins see Evans
Evuley see Eveleigh
Ewart Samuel, Barnstaple 1764 W
Samuel, Lynton 1809 A
Ewdie Richard, Great Torrington 1573 A
Ewins, Ewens
Ewens John, Washford Pyne 1729 A
John, East Anstey 1738 W
Exeter, Excetter, Exter
..., Fremington 1613 and 1614 [W]
Exter Ann, Northam 1785 W
Exter George, Barnstaple 1739 W and 1743 W
Exter Giles, Northam 1770 W
Excetter John, Fremington 1584 W
Exter John, Fremington 1641 A
Exter John, Fremington 1667 W
Exter John, Northam 1722 W
Exter Margaret, Barnstaple 1783 A
Exter Mary, Hartland, wife 1808 W
Richard, Fremington 1613 [W]; forename blank in Ms;
    supplied from parish register
Robert, Fremington 1674 W
Eyer see Aire
Eynon Elizabeth, Bideford 1734 W
Elizabeth, Pilton 1792 W
Eyre see Aire

Facey, Facy, Facye
Facye Anthony, Barnstaple 1625 [W]
Charles, Bideford 1745 A; A dbn
Elizabeth, High Bickington 1632 [W]
Facy Francis, Bideford 1672 W
Grace, Shebbear 1815 W
Facy Joan, Barnstaple 1690 A
Joan, Berrynarbor 1851 W
John, Berrynarbor 1792 A
John, Shirwell 1818 W
John, Chittlehampton 1833 W
John see also John Saunders
Facy Margaret, Great Torrington 1664 W
Philip, Berrynarbor 1788 W
Philip, Berrynarbor 1820 W and 1831 W
Facy Richard, Bideford 1721 W
Samuel, Bideford 1834 W
Fair, Faire see Fare
Fairchild, Fairechilde, Fayrchild, Fayrechilde,
    Fearechild, Ferchild, Ferchilde, Ferechild, Vercheld,
    Verchell, Verchild, Verchilde, Verchylide, Verechild
Ferchide ..., Goodleigh 1612 [W]
Ferchild ..., East Down 1614 [W] (2)
Ferchild ..., Pilton 1614 [W]
Fairechilde Alice, Tawstock 1623 [W]
Benjamin, Pilton 1750 A
Benjamin, Ilfracombe 1781 A
Fayrechilde Catherine, George Nympton 1575 W
Edward, Pilton 1694 [W]
Edward, West Buckland 1759 A
Elizabeth, Barnstaple 1730 W

Francis, Marwood 1853 W
George, Barnstaple 1690 W
Ferchild Gregory, Georgeham 1598 [W]
Hugh, Lynton 1735 W
Fairechilde Humphrey, Ilfracombe 1627 [W]
Ferechild Joan, George Nympton 1585 W
Fayrechilde Joan, Tawstock 1635 A
Fairechild John, Loxhore 1565 W
Verchell John, Loxhore 1565 W and 1568 W
Fearechild John, Berrynarbor 1568 W
Ferchilde John, Tawstock 1602 W
John, Marwood 1694 A
John, Barnstaple 1720 W
John, Barnstaple 1734 W
John, West Buckland, yeoman 1810 W
John, West Buckland 1834 W
Joseph, West Buckland 1733 W
Joseph, Pilton 1746 A and 1755 A
Margaret, widow of John, Marwood 1699 A; forename blank
    in Ms; supplied from parish register
Mary, Barnstaple wife of George of Atherington 1727 W
Fairechilde Mathew, East Down 1567 W
Verchylide Mathew, Marwood 1587 A
Verchild Miles, Lynton 1661 A
Rebecca, Barnstaple 1713 W
Ferchild Richard, Berrynarbor 1568 W
Ferchilde Richard, Combe Martin 1586 A
Ferchilde Richard, Georgeham 1622 A
Verechild Robert, George Nympton 1568 W
Ferchilde Robert, George Nympton 1582 A and account
Susan, Ashford 1684 A
Ferchild Thomas, High Bickington 1591 [W]
Ferchilde William, Fremington 1531 [W]
Verechild William, George Nympton 1584 W
Vercheld William, Loxhore 1588 W
Ferchilde William, Fremington, widower 1612 [W]; forename
    blank in Ms; supplied from parish register
Verchild William, Pilton 1616 [W]
Fayrchild William, Clovelly 1640 A
William, Bratton Fleming 1745 A
William, Barnstaple 1748 W
Fairchild alias Leworthy William, Ilfracombe 1799 W
Faire see Fair
Fairechild, Fairechilde see Fairchild
Fallentyne see Valentine
Falmer John, Hartland 1584 W
Fanning, Faning
Frederick, Chittlehampton 1710 W
Faning Frederick, Bideford 1805 W
John, High Bickington 1756 A
Fanson John, Bideford 1721 W
Fansty, Fanstie
Davy, Alwington 1616 [W]
Fanstie Richard, Alwington 1606 W
Fare Alexander, West Down 1641 W
Alexander, Ilfracombe 1693 W
Alexander, Ilfracombe 1718 A
Henry, West Down 1602 W
Henry, West Down 1730 [W]
Joan, Pilton 1593 [W]
Joan, West Down, widow 1612 [W]; forename blank in Ms;
    supplied from parish register
Joan, Woolfardisworthy 1624 [W] and 1626 [W]
John, Woolfardisworthy 1622 [W]
Fair alias Phare John, Mortehoe 1677 A
John, Ilfracombe 1696 W
John, Mortehoe 1733 W
Faire Juliana, Georgeham 1693 [W]
Margaret, Pilton 1635 W
Oliver, Pilton 1633 A and 1635 O
Philip, West Down 1582 W
Richard, West Down 1584 A and 1586 A account
Richard, Marwood 1703 A
Faire Roger, Northam 1697 A
Sarah, Ilfracombe 1705 W

Thomas, Pilton 1593 W
Walter, West Down 1603 W
Walter, Northam 1711 A
Farley George, North Tawton 1627 [W]
Henry, North Tawton 1758 W
John, Ashreigney 1828 W
Martha, North Tawton 1755 A
Mary, Ashreigney 1843 W
Thomas, North Tawton 1574 W
Thomas, North Tawton 1643 W
William, Chulmleigh 1823 W
Farmer Elizabeth, Tawstock 1736 W
John, Tawstock 1694 W
Joshua, Tawstock, yeoman 1805 W
Farrier David, Weare Giffard 1702 A
John, Weare Giffard 1733 W
Farthing James, Barnstaple 1703 W
Farwell George, North Tawton 1722 A
George, North Tawton 1734 W
John, North Tawton 1772 W
Father, Fathers
Joan, Abbotsham 1628 [W]
John, Hartland 1575 W
John, Hartland 1617 [W]
John, Abbotsham 1628 [W]
Fathers Mary, Northam 1682 A
William, Hartland 1569 W
William, Northam 1632 [W]
Fatts John, Buckland Brewer 1693 A
Faukes, Fawk
Hannah, Bideford 1721 W
Fawk Thomas, Bideford 1718 W
Thomas, Bideford 1737 W (2)
Faulkner Joseph, South Molton 1834 W
Favell John, Pilton 1564 W
Fawk see Faukes
Fay, Fey
John, Brendon 1837 A
William, Heanton Punchardon 1696 W
Fey Willmot, Heanton Punchardon 1710 W
Fayrchild, Fayrechild, Fayrechilde, Fearechild see Fairchild
Featherstone, Fetherstone, Feverston, Feverstone
Alice, South Molton 1752 A
Fetherstone Arthur, Chittlehampton 1683 W
Elizabeth, St Giles in the Wood 1829 W
Feverstone Ellen, Warkleigh 1580 W
Joan, Chittlehampton 1725 A
Feverstone John, Warkleigh 1591 [W]
Fetherstone John, Chittlehampton 1637 W
John, High Bickington 1766 W
John, Roborough 1800 W
Feverston Roger, Warkleigh 1569 W
William, Chawleigh 1696 A
William, Chittlehampton, yeoman 1799 W
Feedavy Vital, Monkleigh 1587 W
Fendell William, Lynton 1570 W
Fender David, Barnstaple 1634 W
Fenys Simon, Instow 1582 W
Ferchild, Ferchilde, Ferechilde see Fairchild
Feret, Ferett see Ferrett
Ferrer John, Filleigh 1832 W
Richard, Filleigh 1750s W
Richard, Filleigh, yeoman 1796 W
Ferrett, Ferett, Feret
..., Chulmleigh 1600 A
Christian, High Bickington 1618 [W]
Edmund, Hartland 1602 [W]; forename blank in Ms; supplied
from parish register
Ferett Emma, Atherington 1577 W
Joan, Tawstock 1749 W
Feret John, Atherington 1570 W
John, Chittlehampton 1576 W and 1578 W
John, Chittlehampton 1596 [W]
John, Chittlehampton 1620 [W]
John, Chittlehampton 1697 W

John, Tawstock 1749 A
Lawrence, Bratton Fleming 1615 [W] and 1620 [W]
Feret Richard, High Bickington 1579 A
Robert, Chittlehampton 1574 W
Ferett William, High Bickington 1568 W
Ferris, Ferries, Ferryes, Pherries
Margaret, Barnstaple 1630 [W]
Ferryes Mary, Barnstaple 1660 W
Ferries or Pherries Philip, Barnstaple 1618 [W]
Thomas, North Molton 1795 A
Thomas, Mariansleigh 1826 A to Ann, widow
Fetherstone, Feverston, Feverstone see Featherstone
Fewell Rabish, Ilfracombe, widow 1602 [W]; forename blank in
Ms; supplied from parish register
Fewen, Fewing, Fewinge, Fewings, Fewyn
..., Yarnscombe 1608 [W]
..., High Bickington 1613 [W]
..., Chittlehampton 1614 [W]
Andrew, High Bickington 1663 W
Bartholomew, High Bickington 1643 A
Catherine, Chittlehampton 1637 W
Elizabeth, High Bickington 1566 W
Fewings Elizabeth, Lapford 1837 W
Elizeus, High Bickington 1629 [W]
Francis, High Bickington 1680 A
Henry, Chittlehampton 1625 [W]
Joan, Filleigh 1619 [W]
John, Northam 1625 [W]
John, High Bickington 1636 W
John, Rose Ash 1637 A
Fewyn John, High Bickington 1643 W
Fewings John, Westleigh 1689 W
Fewings John, Yarnscombe 1718 W
John, High Bickington 1739 W
Fewing John, Tawstock 1792 W
Jonah, Yarnscombe 1623 [W]
Fewings Peter, Westleigh 1710 W
Fewinge Phillippa, High Bickington 1683 W
Fewing Ralph, Westleigh 1686 W
Fewing Roger, High Bickington 1791 A
Simon, High Bickington 1620 [W]
Fewyn Thomas, Yarnscombe 1618 [W]
Thomas, Chittlehampton 1632 [W]
Thomasine, High Bickington 1603 W
Fewing William, Barnstaple 1841 W
Fewett Michael, High Bickington 1643 W
Fewing, Fewinge, Fewings, Fewyn see Fewen
Fey see Fay
Filbey Charles, Bideford 1833 A to Catherine, widow
Filkins Ann, Barnstaple 1742 T
John, Barnstaple 1726 T
Philkins Simon, Bideford 1839 W
Filleux John, Barnstaple 1703 W
Fillipps see Phillips
Filp, Filpe see Philp
Finamore see Finnamore
Finch Mary, Pilton, widow 1809 W
Thomasine, Clovelly 1835 A to Mary Berryman, daughter
William, Barnstaple 1819 W
Finnamore, Finamore, Fynimore
Christopher, Buckland Filleigh 1632 [W]
Christopher, Buckland Filleigh 1671 W
Christopher, Chittlehampton 1680 A
Finamore John, Georgeham 1693 W
Fynimore John, Petrockstowe 1781 W
Stephen, Georgeham 1681 A
Fish Emanuel, Hartland 1750 A; A dbn 1760
John, Hartland 1719 A
John, Hartland 1786 W
John, Welcombe 1853 W
Mary, Hartland 1774 W
Philip, Welcombe 1791 W and A
Philip, Welcombe 1825 W
Thomas, Hartland 1773 A
Thomas, Hartland 1796 W

William, Hartland 1765 A and 1773 A
Fisher, Fysher, Fyshere
Alexander, Yarnscombe 1801 W*
Ann, King's Nympton 1746 W
Barbara, Yarnscombe 1785 W
Charles, Bideford 1836 W
Cicely, Molland 1599 [W]
David, Bideford 1757 W
Edmund, Twitchen 1727 W
Fishere Edward, Molland 1565 W
Edward, King's Nympton 1771 W and 1773 A
Fyshere Ellen, West Anstey 1574 W
Grace, Yarnscombe, sp. 1811 W
Grace, Oakford 1812 W
Grace, West Anstey 1850 W
James, Barnstaple 1789 A
Jane, Chittlehampton 1790 W
Fysher John, Molland 1581 W
John, Molland 1633 A
John, Molland 1725 W
John, Chittlehampton 1784 A
John, Yarnscombe, yeoman 1799 A
John, Oakford, yeoman 1808 W
John, Oakford 1812 A
John, West Anstey 1831 A to Grace, widow
John, West Anstey 1836 W
John, Yarnscombe 1839 W
Mabel, Pilton 1620 [W]
Mary, Molland 1730 W
Mary, Huntshaw 1817 W
Mary see also Samuel Gaskin
Mathew, Knowstone 1829 W
Nicholas, Molland 1662 W
Paul, Pilton 1617 [W]
Peter, Monkleigh 1685 A
Richard, Molland 1612 [W]; forename blank in Ms; supplied
  from parish register
Richard, Molland 1747 [W]
Richard, Yarnscombe, yeoman 1808 W
Richard, Yarnscombe, yeoman 1814 A to Henry, yeoman,
  brother; this A revoked and another granted 5 Aug 1814;
  further A 1818
Samuel, Yarnscombe 1793 W
Samuel, Knowstone, yeoman 1798 W
Thomas, King's Nympton 1761 A
Thomas, Yarnscombe 1763 A
Thomas, Yarnscombe, yeoman 1807 W
Thomas, Knowstone 1819 W
Thomas, Tawstock 1829 A to John, Thomas and William B.,
  sons
Thomas, Northam 1852 W
Walter, South Molton 1590 [W] and 1594 [W]
William, Bondleigh 1664 W
William, Northam, snr. 1803 W
William, Barnstaple, maltster 1803 W
William, Northam 1812 A to Elizabeth, widow
Fishley, Fishleigh
Achilles, Fremington 1627 [W]
Anthony, Fremington 1640 W
George, Instow 1673 A
George, Instow 1769 W
George Yeo, Ilfracombe, yeoman 1837 A to George Yeo
  Fishley, son
Henry, Fremington 1600 W
John, Fremington 1606 W
John, Barnstaple 1730 W
Fishleigh John, Newton St Petrock 1827 W
Oliver, Instow 1676 A
Robert, Instow 1673 [W]
Robert, Buckland Brewer 1732 A
Samuel, Instow 1857 W
William, Instow 1618 [W]
Fishton Elizabeth, King's Nympton 1761 W
Fishwick Fairfax, Northam 1826 A to Mary, widow
Fissick, Fissicke, Fysicke
..., Filleigh 1612 [W]

Joan, Filleigh 1617 [W]
Fissicke Joan, Great Torrington 1591 [W]
Fysicke Margery, Great Torrington 1578 A
Fitch Aaron, Bideford 1707 W
Dorothy, Bideford 1720 W
Richard, Bideford 1691 A
Fitzdavy, Fitsdavye, Fittsdavye
Fittsdavye Christian, Monkleigh 1590 [W] and 1592 [W]
Fitsdavye John, Littleham (near Bideford) 1595 [W]
John, Great Torrington 1616 [W]
Flashman Theophilus, South Molton, saddler 1848 A to Ann,
  widow
Fleamynge see Fleming
Fleat see Fleete
Flecher see Fletcher
Fledman, Flesman
Flesman Roger, Great Torrington 1727 W
Roger, Great Torrington 1745 W
Fleete, Fleat
Sybil, Bideford 1624 [W]
Fleat William, Bideford 1576 A
Fleming, Fleamynge, Fleminge, Flemming, Flemynge, Fleyman
Fleminge ..., Berrynarbor 1608 [W]
Alexander, West Anstey 1678 W
Ann, Alverdiscott 1664 W
Ann, Alverdiscott 1680 W
Ann, West Anstey 1708 W
Charles, West Down 1745 W
Edward, Berrynarbor 1724 W
Flemynge Eleanor, Berrynarbor 1580 W
Elizabeth, Ilfracombe, widow 1797 W
Florence, Barnstaple 1776 W
Flemming George, Fremington 1715 W
George, West Down 1741 A
George, Instow 1815 A
Grace, Ilfracombe 1721 W
Fleminge Humphrey, Ilfracombe 1604 W
Humphrey, Ilfracombe 1625 [W]
Fleamynge John, Berrynarbor 1587 A
John, Instow 1636 W
John, West Down 1742 W
John, Instow 1758 W
John, Ilfracombe 1762 W
Fleminge Julian, Combe Martin 1621 [W]
Mary, Instow 1692 W
Flemynge Nicholas, Ilfracombe 1603 W
Nicholas, Berrynarbor 1639 W
Robert, Bideford 1686 W
Robert, West Anstey 1704 W
Robert, Ilfracombe 1726 A
Robert, Barnstaple 1824 W
Fleyman Thomas, Littleham (near Bideford) 1569 W
Fleminge William 1617 [W]
William, Martinhoe 1670 W
Flencher William, Coldridge 1580 W
Fletcher, Flecher
..., West Worlington 1608 [W]
..., High Bickington 1613 [W]
Agnes, High Bickington 1625 [W]
Augustine, Witheridge 1713 W
Henry, West Worlington 1596 [W]
Hugh, West Worlington 1573 A
Humphrey, Winkleigh 1622 [W]
Jane, West Worlington 1606 W
Flecher Joan, East Worlington 1588 A
Joan, Witheridge 1753 W
Flecher John, Coldridge 1577 W
John, Witheridge 1747 W
Flecher Richard, Chulmleigh 1580 W
William, Witheridge 1718 W
Flexman Adam, Dolton 1796 W
Ann, South Molton 1851 A
Catherine, Great Torrington 1716 A
Elizabeth, Pilton 1850 W

Elizabeth see also Mary Upcott
James, Great Torrington 1714 A
James, Weare Giffard 1761 W
John, Pilton 1835 W
Rebecca, Great Torrington 1793 W
Stephen, Weare Giffard 1798 W
Fleyman see Fleming
Flinger John, Kentisbury 1593 [W]
Flocke Richard, Georgeham 1592 [W]
Floyd David, Monkleigh 1709 A
George, Lynton 1847 W
Jane, Molland 1743 W
John, Chulmleigh 1663 W
Lodovic, Shirwell 1708 W
Fogaty William, Bideford 1826 W
Fogler Agnes, Lapford 1770 W
Foiden John, Chulmleigh 1676 A
Folland Benjamin, Merton 1821 W
Elizabeth, Beaford, widow 1819 A to William, son
Emanuel, Dolton 1838 W
Henry, St Giles in the Wood 1836 W
Hugh, Dolton 1798 W
James, Dolton 1831 A to Robert, son
John, Pilton 1829 W
Michael, Dolton, mason 1806 A
Simon, Dolton 1751 A
Thomas, Bideford 1727 W
Thomas, Dolton 1774 W
Thomasine, Dolton 1842 W
Follett, Follatt, Follet
Catherine, Knowstone 1717 W
Follatt Elizabeth, Chawleigh 1721 W
Geoffrey, Northam 1734 W see entry of his wife Margaret of Molland 1734
George, Northam 1734 A
George, Northam 1738 W
Follet Joan, Knowstone 1706 W
Joan, Knowstone 1731 W and 1741 A
John, Knowstone 1776 W
John, Knowstone 1830 W
Jonah, Molland 1686 W
Margaret, Molland wife of Geoffrey 1734 [W]
Peter, West Anstey 1682 W
Follet Richard, Molland 1672 W
Richard, Collacott, Chittlehampton 1854 W
Thomas, Knowstone 1821 W
Folley Joseph, Great Torrington 1825 W
Peter, Hartland 1857 W
Follington ..., Great Torrington 1612 [W]
Follis and Ellis John, Alverdiscott 1617 [W]
Fooke, Fookes
Fookes Amos, Chittlehampton 1680 A
Eleanor, Georgeham 1637 W
William, Rose Ash 1846 W
Foot, Foots
John, Georgeham 1752 A
Foots Margaret, Buckland Brewer 1706 W
Forbus John, Barnstaple 1636 A
Forchill Thomasine, Loxhore 1574 W
Ford, Forde
Forde ..., Great Torrington 1605 [W]
Alice, Roborough 1716 A
Amos, Barnstaple 1642 W
Amos, Barnstaple 1707 A
Amy, Burrington 1738 W
Forde Andrew, Tawstock 1579 W
Andrew, Chittlehampton 1689 A
Forde Ann, Burrington 1624 [W]
Ann, Pilton 1709 A
Ann, Burrington, wife of John 1847 A to Ann, sp., daughter and William, yeoman
Forde Anstis, Roborough, widow 1612 [W]; forename blank in Ms; supplied from parish register
Ford alias Clement Christian, Barnstaple 1678 A
Forde Dorothy, West Down 1620 [W]

Dorothy, Bideford 1707 A
Edward, Peters Marland, yeoman 1806 A
Eleanor, Chittlehampton 1712 W
Eli, Winkleigh, butcher 1819 A (Elias) to James, father
Elizabeth, Warkleigh 1599 [W]
Elizabeth, Bideford 1711 W
Elizabeth, Peters Marland 1823 A to Grace wife of John Gould of Barnstaple, stonemason, daughter
Elizabeth, Hartland 1855 W
Elizabeth and John, South Molton 1717 A
Francis, Petrockstowe, scrivener 1808 A
Forde Fulk, Sheepwash 1616 [W]
George, Roborough 1664 W
George, Pilton, snr. 1672 [W]
George, Roborough 1714 A
George, Burrington 1716 W
George, Pilton 1725 W
Forde Gilbert, Barnstaple 1625 [W]
Grace, Burrington, widow 1802 W
Forde Henry, Witheridge 1604 W
Hugh, Burrington 1716 W
Forde Isott, Iddesleigh 1593 [W]
James, Burrington 1667 W
James, High Bickington 1778 W
James, Burrington 1789 W
James, Burrington, late of Lime Huron, America 1835 A to Mary, widow
James, Langtree 1846 W
James, Burrington 1857 W
Jane, Chittlehampton 1783 A
Jean, Bideford 1776 W
John, Roborough 1565 W
Forde John, West Worlington 1581 A
Forde John, Great Torrington 1591 [W]
Forde John, Warkleigh 1597 [W]
Forde John, Roborough 1603 W
John, Chittlehampton 1620 [W]
Forde John, Rackenford 1628 [W]
Forde John, Burrington 1638 A
Forde John, Burrington 1639 W and 1641 O
Forde John, Witheridge 1640 A
John, Chittlehampton 1664 W
John, Bideford 1688 W
John, Iddesleigh 1691 A
John, Burrington 1703 A
John, Beaford 1704 W
John, Iddesleigh 1714 W
John, Burrington 1726 W
John, South Molton 1729 A
John, Burrington 1731 W
John, Beaford 1740 A
John, Burrington 1743 W
John, Bideford 1746 W
John, St Giles in the Wood 1773 A
John, Burrington 1785 A
John, Combe Martin 1788 W
John, Abbotsham 1834 W
John, Hartland 1834 W
John, Merton 1841 W
John and Elizabeth, South Molton 1717 A
Joshua, Chulmleigh 1851 W
Margaret, Pilton 1728 W
Mary, Chittlehampton 1676 A
Mary, Pilton 1685 W
Michael, Burrington 1744 W
Forde Nicholas, Roborough 1590 [W]
Nicholas, Winkleigh 1665 W
Richard, Combe Martin 1798 W
Robert, Chawleigh 1711 W
Robert, Merton 1819 W
Sally Lamonia, Langtree 1835 W
Samuel, Peters Marland, yeoman 1805 W
Samuel, Peters Marland, jnr. 1843 W
Samuel, Landcross 1855 W
Sarah, Barnstaple 1713 A

Sarah, Barnstaple 1838 W
Forde Thomas, Burrington 1601 W
Forde Thomas, Iddesleigh 1622 [W]
Thomas, Burrington 1714 A
Thomas, West Buckland 1744 W
Thomas, Burrington 1812 W
Forde Walter, Burrington 1616 [W]
Forde William, Warkleigh 1621 [W]
William, Chittlehampton 1665 A
William, Burrington 1712 W
William, East Buckland 1717 W
William, Chittlehampton 1728 A
William, Dolton 1729 W
William, Bideford 1731 A
William, Burrington 1746 A
William, Barnstaple 1748 [W] no bond; A granted to James,
  his father
William, Hartland 1748 A
William, Burrington 1777 W
William, Chittlehampton 1793 A
William, Chittlehampton 1821 W
William, Ashreigney 1827 W
William, Chittlehampton 1830 W
William, Great Torrington 1833 W
William, Peters Marland 1835 W
William, Chulmleigh 1857 W
Forestreete Samuel, Chittlehampton 1688 W
Forse, Forsse see Fosse
Forten see Fortune
Fortescue, Fortescewe
  ..., Iddesleigh 1606 [W] and 1607 [W]
  ..., Chittlehampton 1609 [W]
  Ann, Weare Giffard 1676 W
  Ann, Northam 1714 W
  Dionysia, Parkham 1690 A
  Elizabeth, Weare Giffard 1630 [W]
  Faithful, Northam 1632 W
  George, Shebbear 1772 A; A dbn 1791
  Gertrude, Barnstaple 1677 W
  James, Shebbear, gentleman 1797 A
  John, Buckland Filleigh 1604 [W]
  John, Parkham 1667 W
  John, Parkham 1730 A
  John, Shebbear 1730 W
  Judith, Plymouth 1832 W
  Lewis, Filleigh 1599 [W]
  Margaret, Weare Giffard 1695 W
  Mary, Witheridge 1838 A
  Mathew, Twitchen 1672 W
  Richard, Filleigh, esquire 1570 W
  Robert, Roborough 1674 A
  Roger, Buckland Filleigh, esquire 1629 [W]
  Roger, Buckland Filleigh 1672 A
  Samuel, Weare Giffard 1681 W
  Samuel, Bideford 1735 W
  Thomasine, Buckland Filleigh 1671 A
  Fortescewe William, Buckland Filleigh 1583 W
  William, Shebbear 1766 A
Fortts or Futts John, Langtree 1665 W
Fortune, Forten
  Forten John, Northam 1607 [W]; forename blank in Ms;
    supplied from parish register
  John, Northam 1610 [W]; forename blank in Ms; supplied
    from parish register
Fosse, Forse, Forsse, Foss
  Foss ..., West Down 1611 [W]
  ..., Barnstaple 1611 [W]
  Alice, West Down 1603 W
  Ambrose, Ilfracombe 1749 A
  Andrew, Marwood 1611 [W]; forename blank in Ms; supplied
    from parish register
  Foss alias Frost Ann, Ilfracombe 1767 A
  Foss Christian, High Bickington 1732 W
  Christopher, Newton Tracey 1674 [W]
  Foss Edmund, Burrington 1795 W

Foss alias Burrington Edmund alias Edward, Burrington 1834
  A to Jeremiah Harris of Winkleigh, son of sister
Foss Eleanor, Mortehoe 1695 A
Elizabeth, West Down, widow 1611 [W]; forename blank in
  Ms; supplied from parish register
Foss Elizabeth see also Betty Webber
Emma, West Down 1631 [W]
Foss Francis, Chulmleigh 1688 A
Henry, West Down 1636 W
Honor, Berrynarbor 1617 [W]
Joan, West Down 1576 W
Forse Joan, Marwood 1635 W
John, West Down 1563 W
John, Ilfracombe 1568 W
John, West Down 1570 W
Foesse John, Huntshaw 1574 W
John, Combe Martin 1588 A
John, Huntshaw 1592 [W]
Foss John, Ilfracombe 1611 [W]; forename blank in Ms;
  supplied from parish register
John, West Down 1616 [W]
John, Mortehoe 1624 [W]
Foss alias Voss John 1679 A
Foss John, Newton Tracey 1680 A
Foss John, West Down 1697 A
Foss John, Huntshaw 1713 W
Foss John, Burrington 1731 W
Foss John, Chulmleigh 1734 W
Foss John, Ilfracombe 1747 W
Foss John, Ilfracombe 1760 W and A
John, Ilfracombe 1795 W
Foss John, Burrington 1805 A
John, Parracombe and Martinhoe, curate 1821 W
Foss Lodovic, Georgeham 1671 A
Foss Paul, High Bickington 1715 W
Peter, Georgeham 1612 [W]; forename blank in Ms; supplied
  from parish register
Peter, West Down 1638 A
Philip, West Down 1630 [W]
Richard, West Down 1588 W
Richard, Pilton 1634 W
Foss Richard, St Giles in the Wood 1681 A
Forsse Robert, West Down 1588 W
Robert, West Down 1623 [W]
Samuel, Ilfracombe 1705 A
Susan, West Down 1672 W
Foss Sybil, Ilfracombe 1748 W
Thomas, West Down 1565 W
Walter, West Down 1578 A
Walter, West Down 1580 W and 1590 [W]
Walter, West Down 1672 W
Foss William, West Down 1685 W
Forse William, Marwood 1730 W
Foss William, Chulmleigh 1756 A
William, Ilfracombe 1848 W
William, Ilfracombe, formerly of Braunton 1852 W
Willmot, Pilton 1633 A
Foster Agnes, Hartland 1689 W
Benjamin, Hartland 1685 A
Bernard, West Down 1664 A
Elizabeth, West Down 1821 W
William, Chulmleigh 1577 W
Found Walter, Hartland 1732 W
Fountain, Fountaine
Fountaine Bridget, Parkham 1666 A
Fountaine John, Barnstaple 1663 A
Mary, Barnstaple 1680 W
Fowell see Fowles
Fowing Richard, ship *Louisa* 1761 W
Fowke Saunder, Meshaw 1563 W
Fowler Bartholomew, Shebbear 1824 W
Fowles, Fowell
Fowell Grace, North Tawton 1638 W
John, Berrynarbor 1851 W

Fox, Foxe
  Agnes, Barnstaple 1686 W
  Amos, Barnstaple 1691 W
  Amos, Barnstaple 1741 W
  Anthony, Oakford 1632 [W]
  Foxe Edward, Oakford 1589 W
  Elizabeth, Northam 1775 W
  Joan, Barnstaple 1729 A
  John, Burrington 1590 [W]
  Jonathan, Barnstaple 1664 A
  Jonathan, Barnstaple 1708 A
  Foxe Margaret, Roborough 1601 W; forename blank in Ms;
    supplied from parish register
  Margaret, Barnstaple 1715 W
  Robert, Pilton 1742 A
Foxford Hugh, Witheridge 1835 W
  John, Witheridge 1829 W
  Samuel, Oakford 1813 W
  Samuel, Oakford 1832 W
  William, Nymet Rowland 1765 W
Frace see Fraze
Fraine, Frain, Frainne, Frayne
  Fraine or Fry Agnes, Barnstaple 1597 [W]
  Frayne Alexander, Langtree 1573 W
  Frayne Alexander, Little Torrington 1700 W
  Frayne Alice, Tawstock 1616 [W]
  Ananias, Great Torrington 1705 W
  Frayne Ananias, Great Torrington 1782 W
  Frain Andrew, Shebbear 1833 W
  Eleanor, Little Torrington 1701 W
  Elizabeth, North Molton 1745 [W]
  Elizabeth, Merton 1790 W
  Frayne Elizabeth, North Tawton 1829 W
  Frayne George, North Molton 1777 W
  Henry, Barnstaple 1694 A
  Henry, Merton 1770 W
  Isott, Shebbear 1597 [W]
  Frayne James, Parkham 1573 A
  Frayne James, Parkham 1577 W
  Frayne James, Chittlehampton 1624 [W]
  Frayne James, Tawstock 1637 A
  Frayne James, Heanton Punchardon 1850 W
  Joan, North Molton 1713 A
  John, Langtree 1590 [W]
  John, Great Torrington 1594 and 1595 [W]
  John, Tawstock 1607 [W]; forename blank in Ms; supplied
    from parish register
  John, High Bickington 1682 W
  John, Petrockstowe 1685 W
  John, Warkleigh 1689 A
  John, Petrockstowe 1706 A
  Frayne John, High Bickington 1725 A
  John, South Molton 1761 A and 1769 A
  John, Merton 1787 W
  Frayne John, North Molton 1818 A to Margaret, widow
  Frain John, Beaford 1829 A
  Frayne John, North Molton 1838 W
  Joseph, Barnstaple, jnr. 1696 A
  Mary, Merton 1756 W
  Frayne Margaret, North Molton 1827 W
  Frayne Peter, North Molton 1738 W and 1745 A
  Richard, North Molton 1643 W
  Samuel, Petrockstowe 1704 W
  Samuel, Merton 1717 W
  Sarah, Petrockstowe 1687 W
  Frayne Thomas, Ashreigney 1573 W
  Frayne Thomas, Petrockstowe 1619 [W]
  Frayne Thomas, Barnstaple 1623 [W]
  Frayne Thomas, Langtree 1663 W
  Thomas, Buckland Filleigh 1684 W
  Thomas, Merton 1776 W
  William, Chittlehampton 1673 [W]
  Frainne William, Satterleigh 1716 A
Francis, Francys
  Francys ..., West Down 1611 [W]

  Alice, South Molton 1624 and 1627 [W]
  George, South Molton 1629 [W]
  George, South Molton 1719 A
  George, South Molton 1734 W
  Hugh, Northam 1709 A
  John, South Molton 1581 W
  Thomas, West Down 1619 [W]
  William, South Molton 1622 [W]
  William, Barnstaple 1664 A
  William, Winkleigh 1822 W
Francke see Frank
Francklin, Francklyn see Franklin
Francys see Francis
Frank, Francke, Franke, Franks
  Edward, Ilfracombe 1752 W
  Franks Hannah, Huntshaw 1770 W
  Joan, Burrington 1741 W
  Francke Robert, Berrynarbor 1687 W
  Franke William, Huntshaw 1770 A
Franklin, Francklin, Francklyn, Franklyn
  Francklin ..., Stoke Rivers 1612 [W]
  Franklyn Alexander, East Buckland 1746 W
  Franklyn John, Great Torrington 1629 [W]
  John, Great Torrington 1676 A
  John, Great Torrington 1737 W
  John, Bideford 1741 W
  Franklyn John, ship *York* 1750 W
  Franklyn John, East Buckland 1766 W
  Francklyn Oliver, Great Torrington 1569 W
  Franklyn Richard, Petrockstowe 1626 [W]
  Franklyn Robert, Stoke Rivers 1632 [W]
  Francklyn Susan, Great Torrington 1716 W
  Francklin alias Hutchings William, Stoke Rivers 1674 A and
    1675 O
Frase see Fraze
Frasier Grace, Hartland 1719 A
Fray Humphrey, East Putford 1695 W
Frayne see Fraine
Fraze, Frace, Frase
  Agnes, Ilfracombe 1680 W
  Anthony, Bideford 1711 W
  Frase Edward, Ilfracombe 1698 A
  Elizabeth, Barnstaple 1725 W
  Joan, Barnstaple 1678 W
  Frase John, North Molton 1597 [W]
  John, Bideford 1742 A
  Robert, Barnstaple 1704 W
  Frace Walter, Ilfracombe 1677 W
Freeman John, Frithelstock 1801 A
  John, Shebbear 1828 W
  Peter, Bideford 1853 W
  Samuel, Bideford 1824 W
  Susan, Frithelstock 1837 W
Freestone John, Barnstaple 1776 W
Freind see Friend
French ... 1607 O
  ..., Heanton Punchardon 1613 [W]
  ..., Instow 1613 and 1614 [W]
  Anthony, Lynton 1798 A
  Christopher, Roborough 1666 W
  Daniel, Brendon 1826 W
  Edward, Barnstaple 1745 A
  Elizabeth, Fremington 1632 [W]
  Henry, Pilton 1695 W
  Henry, Heanton Punchardon 1729 W
  Joan, North Molton 1633 A
  John, Lynton 1784 A
  John, Brendon 1834 W
  Margery, Roborough 1686 W
  Mary, Barnstaple 1660 W
  Richard, Heanton Punchardon 1600 W
  Richard, Lynton 1798 A
  Richard, Brendon 1815 W
  Stephen, Monkleigh 1607 [W]; forename blank in Ms;
    supplied from parish register

Stephen, West Down 1733 W
Thomas, Barnstaple 1580 W
Thomas, Instow 1604 W
Thomas, Heanton Punchardon 1669 A
Frend, Frende see Friend
Frenson John, Washford Pyne 1577 W
Frewin John Perry (Trewin in Beckerlegge), Shebbear, yeoman
  1852 A Holsworthy to Isaac
Frie see Fry
Friend, Freind, Frend, Frende, Frynd, Frynde
  Frende ..., Great Torrington 1608 [W]
  Frynd Agnes, Barnstaple 1635 A
  Andrew 1719 W
  Arthur, Winkleigh 1752 A
  Arthur, Winkleigh 1818 W
  Arthur, Dolton 1851 W
  Frynd Bartholomew, Northam 1637 A
  Candace, Great Torrington 1696 A
  Dennis, Winkleigh 1613 [W]; forename blank in Ms; supplied
    from parish register
  Dorothy, Burrington 1856 W
  Frynde George, Barnstaple 1626 [W]
  Freind George, Combe Martin 1665 A
  Henry, Winkleigh 1616 [W]
  Jane, Winkleigh 1751 W
  Frynde Jasper, Dowland 1645 W
  Joan, Winkleigh 1752 W
  Frynde John, Barnstaple 1622 [W]
  John, Hartland 1692 A
  John, Winkleigh 1778 W and 1788 W
  John, Winkleigh, schoolmaster 1809 W
  John, Dolton 1847 W and 1853 W
  John see also Richard Shute
  Mathew, Bideford 1700 A
  Freind Richard, Winkleigh 1627 [W]
  Richard, Westleigh 1693 W
  Richard, Brushford 1737 W
  Frend or Freud Robert, Meeth 1720 W
  Samuel, Tawstock 1822 A
  Susan, Coldridge 1769 W
  Thomas, Wembworthy 1747 A
  Thomasine, Barnstaple 1716 A
  Frynd William, Pilton 1640 W
  Frynd William, Winkleigh 1644 W
  William, Fremington 1690 W
  William, Dolton 1783 W
  William, Wembworthy, farmer 1809 W
  William, Dolton 1843 W
  William, High Bickington 1852 W
Friendship James, Petrockstowe 1763 W
  John, Great Torrington 1793 W
  Joseph, Great Torrington 1800 A
  Samuel, Frithelstock 1830 A to James, father
  William, Little Torrington 1838 W
  William Gornill, Great Torrington, ropemaker 1857 A to
    Elizabeth Hoyton, widow, sister
Frier see Fryar
Frigare George, Puddington 1745 W
Friscowe ..., Burrington 1613 [W]
  John, Ashreigney 1599 [W]
Frishall Margaret, Chittlehampton 1580 W
Frogler Abraham, Lapford 1767 A
Frost, Froste ..., Ilfracombe 1611 and 1613 [W]
  ..., Twitchen 1613 [W]
  Agnes, Stoke Rivers 1857 A
  Alice, Barnstaple 1622 [W]
  Ambrose, Ilfracombe 1715 W
  Ann, Great Torrington 1704 W
  Frost alias Foss Ann, Ilfracombe 1767 A
  Christopher, Barnstaple 1628 [W] and 1629 O
  Elizabeth, Puddington 1575 [W]
  Elizabeth, Ilfracombe 1618 [W]
  Elizabeth, Great Torrington 1663 W
  Elizabeth, Barnstaple 1751 W
  Elizabeth, Yarnscombe 1805 W

Esther, Alwington 1669 A
George, Beaford 1575 W
George, Beaford 1616 [W]
George, Washford Pyne 1674 A
Giles, Goodleigh, snr. 1643 A
Giles, Pilton 1643 A
Giles, Pilton 1702 A
Giles, Goodleigh 1711 and 1712 A
Henry, Yarnscombe 1805 W
Henry, Barnstaple 1826 W
James, Barnstaple 1606 [W]; forename blank in Ms; supplied
  from parish register
Jane, Great Torrington 1710 W
Joan, Weare Giffard 1591 [W]
Joan, Ilfracombe 1717 A
Joan, Merton 1723 W
John, Great Torrington, snr. 1568 W
John, Puddington 1573 W
Froste alias Gyste John, Bideford 1581 W
Froste John, Great Torrington 1589 A
Froste John, Witheridge 1589 A
John, Winkleigh 1619 [W]
John, Barnstaple 1705 A
Joseph, Great Torrington 1700 W
Joseph, South Molton 1763 W
Josiah, Little Torrington 1684 W
Josiah, Ilfracombe 1702 W
Josiah, Ilfracombe 1742 W and 1745 W
Mary, Great Torrington 1681 A
Mary, Pilton 1720 W
Mary, Barnstaple 1749 A
Michael, Great Torrington 1698 W
Nathaniel, Barnstaple 1716 W
Nicholas, Bideford 1626 [W]
Nicholas, Goodleigh 1665 A
Nicholas, Goodleigh 1719 W
Philip, Pilton 1748 W
Richard, Kentisbury 1821 W
Richard, Kentisbury 1856 W
Robert, Ilfracombe 1690 A
Robert, Pilton 1722 W
Roger, Great Torrington 1625 [W]
Roger, Great Torrington, snr. 1626 [W]
Roger, Great Torrington 1628 [W] and 1629 O
Roger, Little Torrington 1672 W
Thomas, Puddington 1602 W
Thomas, Ilfracombe 1620 [W]
Walter, Ilfracombe 1748 W
William, Pilton 1715 W
William, Ilfracombe 1778 W
William, Huish 1783 W
William, Parracombe 1815 W
William, Berrynarbor 1823 W
William, Berrynarbor, labourer 1857 A to Grace wife of
  Humphrey Hunt of Bratton Fleming, publican, daughter
Froude, Froad, Freud
  Francis, South Molton, widower 1587 W
  Froad Nicholas, Bideford 1731 W
  Freud or Frend Robert, Meeth 1720 W
Fry, Frie, Frye
  ..., Combe Martin 1603 [W]
  Frye ..., Langtree 1605 [W]
  Frye Agnes, Tawstock 1585 W
  Fry or Fraine Agnes, Barnstaple 1597 [W]
  Amos, Ilfracombe 1849 W
  Ann and John, Countisbury 1627 [W]
  Betty, Alverdiscott, widow 1857 A to William Henry of
    Bideford, druggist and John of Alverdiscott, yeoman
  Frye Cicely, Countisbury 1587 W
  Dennis, Burrington 1579 W
  Frie Edward, Ilfracombe 1611 [W]; forename blank in Ms;
    supplied from parish register
  Edward, Heanton Punchardon 1719 W
  Elizabeth, Instow 1638 [W]
  Elizabeth, Barnstaple 1664 W

Elizabeth or John, Fremington 1636 W
Frie George, Countisbury 1583 W
Henry, Langtree 1685 W
Henry, Challacombe 1690 W
Hugh, Shirwell 1697 W
Humphrey, East Putford, jnr. 1755 W
James, Langtree 1663 A
Jane, Parracombe 1817 W
Frye Joan, Countisbury 1586 A
Frye Joan, Challacombe 1597 [W]
Joan, East Putford 1778 A
Joan, Buckland Brewer, widow 1808 W
Joan or John, Chittlehampton 1661 W
Frye John, Shirwell, snr. 1572 W
Frye John, Lynton 1573 A
Frye John, Marwood 1591 [W]
John, Lynton 1599 [W]
John, Countisbury 1600 W
Frye John, Combe Martin 1601 W
John, Challacombe 1603 [W]
Frie John, Shirwell 1610 [W] "of West Plaistow" in register;
    forename blank in Ms; supplied from parish register
John, Shirwell 1620 [W]
John and Anna, Countisbury 1627 [W]
John, Bratton Fleming 1629 [W]
John or Elizabeth, Fremington 1636 W
John, Burrington 1639 A
John, Chittlehampton 1660 and 1661 A
John or Joan, Chittlehampton 1661 W
John, Atherington 1684 W
John, Countisbury 1713 W
John, Lynton 1753 and 1756 A
John, Countisbury 1762 W
John, Merton 1770 W
John, Parracombe 1801 W
John, Brendon, yeoman 1808 W
John, Westleigh, yeoman 1808 A
John 1829 A to Mary of Barnstaple, widow
John, Countisbury 1830 W; 1834 proved by executor on
    attaining the age of 21 years
John, Ilfracombe 1844 W
John, Stoke Rivers 1845 W
John, Phoenix, Jamaica 1849 A to John of Countisbury,
    yeoman, father
John, Alverdiscott 1852 W
John, Lynton 1855 W
Joseph, Lynton 1768 W
Lucy, Shirwell 1718 W
Marian, Shirwell 1604 W
Frye Mary, Shirwell 1617 [W]
Mary, Countisbury 1750 W
Mary, Countisbury 1763 A
Mary, Ilfracombe, widow 1811 W
Mary, Martinhoe 1837 A
Mary, Great Torrington 1851 W
Nicholas, Georgeham 1629 [W]
Nicholas, Trentishoe 1742 W
Frye Philip, Lynton 1577 W
Frye Philip, Shirwell 1580 W
Philip, Witheridge 1829 W
Frie Richard, High Bickington 1568 W
Richard, Countisbury 1577 W
Frye Richard, Buckland Brewer 1585 W
Richard, Stoke Rivers 1624 [W]
Richard, Countisbury, yeoman 1808 A
Richard, jnr. 1825 A
Richard, North Molton 1847 W
Robert, Countisbury 1580 W
Frye Robert, Countisbury 1589 W
Roger, Buckland Brewer, yeoman 1800 A
Samuel, Sheepwash 1721 W
Samuel, Weare Giffard 1839 W
Silvester, Ilfracombe 1684 W
Frye Simon, Shirwell 1609 [W]; forename blank in Ms;
    supplied from parish register

Frye Thomas, Parracombe 1589 W
Thomas, Lynton 1599 [W]
Thomas, Parracombe 1605 W
Thomas, Newton St Petrock 1634 W
Thomas, Little Torrington 1686 A
Thomas, Countisbury 1730 W
Thomas, Weare Giffard 1748 W
Thomas, Langtree 1756 W
Thomas, Great Torrington 1768 W
Thomas, Trentishoe 1802 W
Thomas, Great Torrington, gentleman 1810 A
Thomas see also Thomas Marshall
Frye Walter, Shirwell 1606 W
Walter, Lynton 1750 W and 1756 A
Walter, Trentishoe, yeoman 1804 W
Walter, East Down, yeoman 1809 W
William, Lynton 1741 W
William, South Molton 1811 W
William, Countisbury 1824 W
William, South Molton 1846 W
William, East Putford 1855 W
Fryar, Frier
    Frier ..., Bideford 1608 [W]
    Philip, Hartland 1709 A
Frye see Fry
Frynd, Frynde see Friend
Fuen, Fuin, Fuyn
    Dionysius, Burrington 1587 A
    Fuin John, Filleigh 1585 W
    John, Burrington 1587 W
    John, High Bickington 1589 A and account
    Fuyn Michael, High Bickington 1568 W
Fuere see Furse
Fugars, Fugurs
    John, Buckland Brewer 1573 [W]
    John, Holwell, Buckland Brewer 1573 A
    Robert, Buckland Brewer 1573 A
    Robert, Langtree 1577 W
    Robert, Puddington 1700 W
    Fugurs alias Vagures William, Cruwys Morchard 1663 W
Fuin see Fuen
Fuke Richard, South Molton 1852 W
Fulford, Fullford
    Bartholomew, Buckland Brewer 1826 W
    David, Newton St Petrock 1587 W
    Elizabeth, Buckland Brewer 1828 W
    Henry, Abbotsham 1635 A
    Joan, Peters Marland, widow 1569 W
    John, Bideford 1589 W
    John, Chawleigh 1590 [W]
    John, Littleham (near Bideford) 1691 A
    John, Buckland Brewer 1841 W
    Mary, Langtree 1837 A
    Nicholas, Lapford 1597 [W]
    Fullford Thomas, Bideford no year given W
    Fullford William, Northam 1752 W
Fuller Mathew, Great Torrington 1660 A
    Fuller alias Devonshire Thomas, Bideford 1710 A
Fullford see Fulford
Furchier see Fursier
Furlange see Furlong
Furler John, Great Torrington 1591 [W]
    John, Great Torrington 1591 [W]
Furlong, Furlange, Furlonge
    Elizabeth, Barnstaple 1631 [W]
    Furlonge Nicholas, Barnstaple 1595 [W] and 1597 [W]
    Furlonge Robert, Winkleigh 1585 W
    Furlonge Robert, Barnstaple 1617 [W]
    Thomas, Northam 1633 W
    Furlonge William, Huish 1584 W
Furlott John, Frithelstock, snr. 1666 A
Fursdon Agnes, Chawleigh 1596 [W]
    George, North Tawton 1750 W
    John, Cruwys Morchard 1671 W
    Philip, Cruwys Morchard 1670 W

Roger, North Tawton 1799 A
William, Chawleigh 1592 [W]
William, Northam 1845 W
Furschere see Fursehewer
Furse, Fuere, Furze
..., Great Torrington 1607 [W]
..., St Giles in the Wood 1612 [W]
Catherine, King's Nympton 1619 [W]
Edward, St Giles in the Wood 1601 W
Edward, Bow 1672 W
Elizabeth, King's Nympton 1623 W
George, Great Torrington 1663 A
George, Burrington 1694 A
Henry, Great Torrington 1600 W
Henry, Bideford 1836 W
Hugh, King's Nympton 1618 [W]
Furze James, Abbotsham 1739 W
Jane, King's Nympton 1852 W
Joan, Meeth 1635 W
John, Great Torrington 1572 W
Fuere John, Great Torrington 1574 W
John, King's Nympton 1579 W
John, King's Nympton 1603 W
John, King's Nympton 1639 A
John, Meeth 1665 A
John, King's Nympton 1672 O
John, King's Nympton 1699 A
John, Great Torrington 1703 A
John, King's Nympton 1743 [W]
John, King's Nympton 1765 W
John, King's Nympton 1818 W
John, King's Nympton 1833 W
John, Pilton 1835 A to Hannah, widow
John, East Putford 1846 W
Margery, King's Nympton 1580 W
P.W., Great Torrington 1832 W
Stephen, Great Torrington 1629 [W]
Sybil, Great Torrington 1751 W
Thomas, Great Torrington 1606 W
Thomas, Dolton 1700 A
Walter, Meeth 1602 W
William, Dolton 1580 W
William, St Giles in the Wood 1698 A
Furze William, Shebbear 1843 W
William, Yarnscombe 1854 W
Fursehewer, Furschere, Furshewer, Furshewere
Furshewere Emma, Hartland 1575 A
Furshewer John, Washford Pyne 1593 [W]
Lawrence, Hartland 1606 [W]; forename blank in Ms;
supplied from parish register
Furshewer Philip, Hartland 1640 W
Thomas, Hartland 1607 [W]; forename blank in Ms; supplied
from parish register
Furschere Thomasine, Hartland 1573 A and I
Fursen see Furson
Furshewer, Furshewere see Fursehewer
Fursier, Furchier
Jasper, Hartland 1710 A
John, Hartland 1742 W
Furchier Samuel, Hartland 1757 W and 1763 W
William, Bideford 1800 W
Fursman Thomas, Buckland Brewer 1834 W
Furson, Fursen
Furson alias Snell Elizabeth, Eggesford 1693 A
Fursen John, South Molton, husbandman 1808 A
Samuel, Burrington 1787 A
Fursen Samuel, Burrington 1790 W
Furze see Furse
Futts Elizabeth, Langtree, widow 1796 A
Emanuel, Frithelstock 1772 W
Henry, Horwood 1642 A
Futts or Fortts John, Langtree 1665 W
Samuel, Abbotsham 1747 W
Susan, Frithelstock 1779 W
Thomas, Hartland 1596 [W]
William, Hartland 1563 W

Fuyn see Fuen
Fynimore see Finnamore
Fysher, Fyshere see Fisher
Fysicke see Fissick

Gabriel Richard, Huntshaw, yeoman 1821 A to Mary, widow
Gaddon Sarah, Parkham 1726 W
Gagg, Gag, Gagge
Gagge Barbara, Marwood 1611 [W]; forename blank in Ms;
supplied from parish register
Daniel, Barnstaple 1681 A
Gagge George, Sheepwash 1573 [W]
Gagge George, Pilton 1591 [W]
Humphrey, Barnstaple 1701 A
Humphrey, Barnstaple 1715 W
Joanna, Barnstaple 1727 W
Gagge Richard, Pilton 1585 W
Gag Thomas, Sheepwash 1615 [W]
Gaie see Gay
Gaindon alias Cooke Philip, Mariansleigh 1758 A
Gale Agnes, Goodleigh 1675 W
Amos, Molland 1736 A
John, St Giles in the Wood 1643 A
Robert, Woolfardisworthy 1767 W
Thomas, West Anstey 1712 A
Thomas, Molland 1735 A
Gallen, Gallon
..., West Worlington 1610 [W]
Gallon Alexander, Chittlehampton 1574 W
Gallon Charity, Rose Ash 1746 A
Elizabeth, Knowstone 1689 W
Gallon Iolus, Rose Ash 1746 A
Joan, Mariansleigh 1731 A
John, West Worlington 1588 A
John, Knowstone 1679 W
Peter, South Molton 1698 W
Thomas, George Nympton 1606 W
William, West Worlington 1604 W
Willmot, West Worlington 1617 [W]
Galliford Christopher, Heanton Punchardon, labourer 1851 A to
Ann
Elizabeth, heretofore of Swimbridge but late of Barnstaple
1832 W
Joan, Chittlehampton 1719 A
Thomas, Chittlehampton 1765 A
Gallon see Gallen
Gallsworthie, Gallsworthy see Galsworthy
Galm Alice, West Worlington 1580 W
Galman see Gammon
Galsery Agnes, East Worlington 1690 W
Richard, West Worlington 1678 A
Galsworthy, Gallsworthie, Galsworthie, Galsworthye,
Golsworthy
..., Woolfardisworthy 1607 [W]
Galsworthie ..., King's Nympton 1611 [W]
Alexander, Great Torrington 1676 W
Alexander, Hartland 1823 A to Thomas, husbandman, son
Galsworthye Alice, Alwington 1573 W
Ambrose, Frithelstock 1831 A to John
Ambrose, Merton 1848 W
Gallsworthie Andrew, Parkham 1589 W
Ann, Atherington 1749 W
Augustine, Parkham 1620 [W]
Augustine, Alwington 1706 A
Gallsworthy Baldwin, Buckland Brewer 1635 A and 1637 O
Cecilia, Bideford 1699 W
Gallsworthie Elias, Parkham 1576 W
Elizabeth, Buckland Brewer 1675 W
Elizabeth, Parkham 1689 W
Elizabeth, Hartland 1850 W
Elizabeth, Ilfracombe 1608 [W]; forename blank in Ms;
supplied from parish register
George, Little Torrington 1692 A
Giles, Bideford 1616 [W]
Gallsworthy Giles, Parkham 1640 W

Grace, Hartland, widow 1811 A
Gallsworthy Henry, Fremington 1630 [W]
Honoria, Buckland Brewer 1695 W
James, Atherington 1733 W
Joan, Hartland 1606 W
Galsworthie John, Buckland Brewer, widower 1565 W
Gallsworthie John, Alwington 1566 and 1569 W
Gallsworthie John, Parkham 1578 W
John, Hartland 1606 W
John, Barnstaple 1619 [W]
Gallsworthy John, Hartland 1627 [W]
Gallsworthy John, Buckland Brewer 1632 [W]
Gallsworthy John, Barnstaple 1636 W
John, Parkham, snr. 1641 W
John, Littleham (near Bideford) 1660 W
John, Parkham 1660 and 1666 W
John, Hartland 1667 W
John, Hartland 1683 A
John, Parkham 1685 W
John, Barnstaple 1694 W
John, Northam 1714 A and 1722 A
John, Hartland 1722 A
John, Frithelstock 1835 W
Galsworthie Marfett, Parkham 1594 [W]
Margaret, Hartland 1792 A
Galsworthie Margery, Buckland Brewer 1591 [W]
Margery, Parkham 1620 [W]
Mary, Little Torrington 1692 W
Mary, Northam 1727 W
Nicholas, Hartland 1855 W
Onesimus, East Putford 1681 A
Galsworthie Richard, Parkham 1564 W
Sarah, Hartland 1821 W
Simon, Parkham 1629 [W]
Simon, Buckland Brewer 1718 A
Simon, Parkham 1731 [W]
Gallsworthy Sybil, Barnstaple 1639 W
Galsworthie Thomas, Chittlehampton 1593 [W]
Galsworthie Thomas, Hartland 1594 [W]
Thomas, Parkham 1617 [W]
Gallsworthy Thomas, Buckland Brewer 1638 W
Thomas, Parkham 1688 W
Thomas, East Putford 1699 W
Thomas, Hartland 1724 W
Thomas, Hartland, yeoman 1796 W
Thomas, Hartland, jnr. 1811 A
Galsworthie Thomasine, Alwington 1592 [W]
Walter, Great Torrington 1626 [W]
Gallsworthie William, Parkham 1573 W
William, Parkham 1605 W
Gallsworthy William, Abbotsham 1637 W
Golsworthy William, Northam 1665 W
William, Hartland 1702 W
William, Clovelly 1712 A
William, Westleigh 1724 A
William, Hartland, yeoman 1811 W
Gam Mathew, Shirwell 1616 [W]
Gammon, Galman, Gameing, Gamin, Gaming, Gammen,
    Gamming, Gammons, Gamon, Gamyn, Ganman
Abel, Stoodleigh 1828 W
Gamon Agnes, Pilton 1695 A
Amos, Lynton 1739 A and 1751 A
Amos, Ilfracombe 1791 W
Amos, Ilfracombe 1833 A
Gamon Amos, Ilfracombe 1852 W
Gamon Ann, Berrynarbor 1637 W
Ann, Ilfracombe 1796 W
Gaming Anthony, Rackenford 1720 W
Galman Christian, Shebbear 1577 W
Christopher, Marwood 1728 W
Edward, Brendon 1763 A
Elizabeth, Pilton 1697 W
Elizabeth, Marwood 1742 A
Elizabeth, Marwood 1793 A
Elizabeth, Marwood 1837 W

Elizabeth Lampry(s), Barnstaple 1835 W
Geoffrey, Lynton 1690 W
Gamon Geoffrey, Combe Martin 1698 A
George, Pilton 1690 A
George, Buckland Filleigh 1773 W
Gamon Henry, Pilton 1696 A
Gameing Henry, Bideford 1710 W
Gamon James, Pilton 1675 A
Gamon James, Bideford 1679 W
Ganman James or John, Hartland, yeoman 1806 W
James, Marwood 1813 A to Elizabeth, widow
James, High Bray 1839 W
James, East Down 1851 W
Jasper, Pilton 1693 W
Gamon John, Martinhoe 1674 W
John, Ilfracombe 1681 A
Gaming John, Parracombe 1740 W
John, Bideford 1744 A
John, Loxhore 1763 W
John, Parracombe 1764 W
John, Horwood 1771 W
Ganman John or James, Hartland, yeoman 1806 W
Gaming John, Parracombe, yeoman 1809 W and A
John, Loxhore 1830 W
John, Pilton 1833 W
John, Marwood, snr. 1841 W
John, Ilfracombe 1855 W
Gammons Margaret, Warkleigh 1691 W
Gammen Margaret, Parracombe 1799 W
Mary, Barnstaple 1718 W
Gamon Mary, Bideford 1750 W
Philip, Loxhore 1815 W
Philip, Marwood 1845 W
Richard, Shirwell 1780 A
Richard, Berrynarbor 1844 W
Gamminge Robert, Langtree 1595 [W]
Gamyn Robert, Pilton 1616 [W]
Robert, Pilton 1682 A
Gamon Robert, Georgeham 1692 W
Gamon alias Hancock Sybil, Pilton 1668 A
Gamon Thomas, Ilfracombe 1716 W
Thomas, Ilfracombe 1752 W
Thomas, Ilfracombe 1789 W
Thomas, Ilfracombe, yeoman 1799 W; A dbn 1842
Thomas, Berrynarbor, yeoman 1846 A to Prudence, widow
Gamon Thomasine, Pilton 1696 A
Gamlyn William, Combe Martin 1615 [W]
Gamon William, Marwood 1705 A
William, Stoodleigh 1729 W
Gandy Ann, Chulmleigh 1763 W
William, Chulmleigh 1753 W
Ganlon John, Clovelly 1683 W
Ganming see Gammon
Gard, Garde
Garde Andrew, Chulmleigh 1619 [W]
Ann, North Tawton, sp. 1806 W
Elizabeth, Bideford 1813 W
John, North Tawton 1762 W and 1763 W
Mary, North Tawton 1762 W
Richard, North Tawton 1763 W
Garde Robert, Chittlehampton 1602 W
Garden Elisha, Peters Marland 1754 A
Gardener see Gardner
Gardler Elizeus, Winkleigh 1622 [W]
Gardner, Gardener, Gardiner
Gardener ..., South Molton 1609 [W]
Agnes, Barnstaple 1625 [W]
Alexander, Cruwys Morchard 1707 W
Andrew, South Molton 1681 W
Elizabeth, West Worlington 1848 W
Gardiner Francis, Barnstaple 1781 W
Gardener James, Ashreigney, yeoman 1799 W
Jane, West Worlington 1823 W
John, Barnstaple 1595 [W]

John, South Molton 1740 W and 1748 W
Mary, South Molton 1743 W
Gardener Mary, South Molton 1765 W
Richard, Witheridge 1845 W
Robert, Puddington 1572 W
Thomas, Witheridge 1834 A to Mary, widow
William, South Molton 1676 W
William, Knowstone 1726 W
Gardiner William, East Worlington 1853 W
Gare Ambrose, Marwood 1741 A
William, Marwood 1739 W
Garett see Garrett
Garius or Garins Alice, Goodleigh 1631 [W]
Garland, Garlande
Arthur, Marwood 1643 W
Christiana, Northam 1685 W
Edmund, Northam 1625 [W]
Elizabeth, Bittadon 1643 A
Eusebius, Shirwell 1618 [W]
Eusebius, Bittadon 1644 W
Francis, Marwood, esquire 1643 A
Grace, Barnstaple 1722 W
John, Marwood 1641 W
John, Marwood, esquire 1710 W
John, Mortehoe 1729 W
Lewis, Marwood 1610 [W]; forename blank in Ms; supplied
from parish register
Obedience, Marwood 1679 W
Garlande Richard, Marwood 1586 W
Richard, Marwood 1593 [W]
Richard, Northam 1621 [W]
Richard, Marwood 1623 [W]
Roger, Mortehoe 1664 A
Susan, Mortehoe 1672 W
Susan, Pilton 1792 W
Thomas, Northam 1620 [W]
Thomas, Mortehoe 1689 W
William, Northam 1701 A
Garliford, Garlaforde, Garlford
..., Molland 1600 W
Joan, West Anstey 1629 [W]
Garlaforde John, Twitchen 1572 W
John, Molland 1596 [W]
John, Bow 1640 W
John,, snr., Molland 1614 [W]; forename blank in Ms;
supplied from parish register
Philip, West Anstey 1627 [W]
Richard, South Molton 1585 W
Garlaforde Richard, Twitchen 1588 W
Richard, West Anstey 1631 [W]
Garlford Thomas, Molland 1626 [W]
Walter, Northam 1623 [W]
Garnein ..., Goodleigh 1613 [W]
Garnet John, Northam 1670 A
Garnish, Garnies, Garnis, Garnishe, Garnys, Garnyshe
..., Instow 1614 [W]
Garnis Anthony, Shirwell, snr. 1676 W
Garnys Anthony, Shirwell 1734 W
Garnishe Giles, Barnstaple 1623 [W]
John, Shirwell 1713 [W]
John, Shirwell 1774 A
John, Shirwell, mason 1799 A
Garnies Mary, Barnstaple 1737 W
Garnyshe Thomas, Goodleigh Prior 1602 W
Garnsey John, Beaford, gardener 1801 W
Richard, Tawstock 1814 W
Robert, Witheridge 1640 W
William, Witheridge 1639 W
William, Witheridge 1693 A
Garnys see Garnish
Garrett, Garett, Jerrett
Jerrett ..., Lapford 1785 A
Edward, Alwington 1627 [W]
Garett George, Winkleigh 1632 [W]
Garett Hugh, Winkleigh 1626 [W]

Garett Hugh, Burrington 1688 A
Garett Joan, Winkleigh, snr. 1636 A
Garett John, Clovelly 1636 W
Garret John, Northam 1674 O
John, Bideford 1703 W and 1706 W
Mary, Bideford 1716 A
Jerrett Philip, Northam 1620 [W]
Richard, Bideford 1715 A
Samuel, Bideford 1640 O
William, Bow 1632 [W]
Gartered Hugh, Ilfracombe 1618 [W]
Garvis see Jarvis
Gaskin Bridget, Barnstaple 1799 W
Samuel, Barnstaple, mariner 1821 A to Mary Fisher, widow
Gass Andrew, Mariansleigh 1725 W
Gater ..., Witheridge 1602 O
Edward, Washford Pyne 1575 W
John, Witheridge 1596 [W]
Robert, Witheridge 1593 [W]
Robert, Witheridge, jnr. 1637 W
Robert, Lapford 1704 W
Thomas, George Nympton 1606 [W]; forename blank in Ms;
supplied from parish register
Thomas, Witheridge 1638 O
William, Lapford 1741 W
Gathen Owen, Bideford 1747 A
Gaunt Thomas, Beaford 1660 A
Gausin Cary, Clovelly 1705 A
Gavins Elizabeth, Instow 1591 [W]
William, Instow 1591 [W]
Gawman Bartholomew, Shebbear 1688 W
Joan, Shebbear 1588 W
Joan 1628 [W]
John, Shebbear 1615 [W]
John, George Nympton 1642 [W]
John, Shebbear 1692 A
John Blakway, Shebbear 1577 W
Lodovic, Shebbear 1637 W
Mary, Shebbear 1665 W
Penelope, Shebbear 1663 W
Richard, Shebbear 1588 W
Richard, Shebbear 1618 [W]
Robert, Shebbear 1606 W
Robert, Mariansleigh 1667 W
Samuel, Petrockstowe 1705 A
William, Shebbear 1586 W
Gawtrey Hannah, Great Torrington 1835 W
John, Great Torrington 1831 W
Gay, Gaie, Gaye
..., Huntshaw 1608 [W]
..., Cruwys Morchard 1610 [W]
..., Great Torrington 1612 [W]
Gaie Agnes, Great Torrington, widow 1564 W
Ann, Barnstaple 1717 A
Anthony, Bideford 1722 W
Archelaus, Ashreigney 1743 W
Augustine, Bow 1602 W
Betty, Atherington 1846 W
David, Dowland 1606 W
Dionysia, Great Torrington 1629 [W]
Edmund, Hartland 1574 W
Gaie Edmund, Bow 1568 W
Elizabeth, Barnstaple 1664 W
Elizabeth, Yarnscombe 1747 W
Elizabeth, Barnstaple 1765 W
George, Chulmleigh 1851 W
Grace, Barnstaple 1625 [W]
Grace, Bideford 1721 W
Isaac, Yarnscombe 1815 W
Jane, Frithelstock 1824 W
Jane, Barnstaple 1840 W
Jerome, Great Torrington 1627 [W]
Joan, Great Torrington 1593 [W]
Joan, Ashreigney 1638 A
Gaye John, Ashreigney 1571 W

John, Great Torrington 1592 [W]
John, Barnstaple 1599 [W]
John, Frithelstock 1625 [W]
John, Barnstaple 1677 A
John, Frithelstock 1678 A
John, South Molton 1700 A
John, Wembworthy 1763 W
John, Atherington 1832 W
John, Welcombe 1832 W
John, Chulmleigh 1843 W
Margaret, Frithelstock 1629 [W]
Mark, Bow 1531 [W]
Mary, Bow 1593 [W]
Mary, South Molton 1743 W
Mary, Chawleigh 1771 W
Mary, South Molton, widow 1810 W
Mathew, Yarnscombe 1836 W
Nicholas, Roborough 1621 [W]
Nicholas, Ashreigney 1632 [W]
Oliver, Great Torrington 1628 [W] and 1634 [W]
Peter, Puddington 1732 W
Philip, Ashreigney 1621 [W]
Philip, Wembworthy 1763 W
Ralph, Great Torrington 1599 [W]
Ralph, Great Torrington 1661 W
Gaye Richard, Chulmleigh 1602 W
Richard, Great Torrington 1633 W
Richard, South Molton 1748 A
Richard, South Molton 1806 A
Richard, Chittlehampton 1852 W
Robert, Bratton Fleming 1678 A
Robert, Chawleigh 1764 W
Roger, Winkleigh 1715 A
Gaye Thomas, Great Torrington 1587 W
Thomas, Huntshaw 1642 W
Thomas, Barnstaple 1706 W
Thomasine, Bratton Fleming 1645 A
Thomasine, South Molton 1663 W
Urithe, Bow 1638 A
Gaye William, Lynton 1576 W
Gaye William, Ashreigney 1580 W
William, Great Torrington 1630 [W]
William, Shebbear 1640 A
William, Ashreigney 1662 W
William, Barnstaple 1696 W
William, Ashreigney 1714 A
William, Clovelly 1750 W
William, Clovelly 1765 W
William, formerly of Moorwinter, late of Woolcombe 1798 W
William, Chulmleigh, yeoman 1805 W
William, Chulmleigh 1826 W
Gaydon, Gayton
    Alexander, Barnstaple 1689 W
    Gayton Constantine, Woolfardisworthy 1643 A
    Dorothy, Filleigh 1799 W
    George, Barnstaple 1641 W
    Gayton John 1644 W
    Gayton John, Chittlehampton 1742 W
    John, Barnstaple 1753 A
    John, Barnstaple 1756 W
    John, High Bickington 1806 A*
    John, Pilton 1820 W
    Richard, West Down 1586 W
    Gayton Richard, Roborough 1846 W
    Gayton Susanna, Chittlehampton 1664 W
Gaye see Gay
Gayer or Guyer Robert, Huntshaw 1643 A
Gayton see Gaydon
Geareing see Gerringe
Gearman see German
Geaten see Geaton
Geatly John, Nymet Rowland 1643 W
Geaton, Geaten, Getton
    Geaten Christopher, St Giles in the Wood 1598 [W]
    Edward, Chittlehampton 1637 W

Esther, St Giles in the Wood 1708 A
Henry, St Giles in the Wood 1703 W
Getton Henry, St Giles in the Wood 1706 W
John, Chittlehampton, gentleman 1643 W
John, Chittlehampton 1671 W
John, Horwood 1823 W
John, Fremington 1852 W
William, St Giles in the Wood 1577 W
Gebbe see Gibbs
Gebbens see Gibbons
Gebbes see Gibbs
Gebbins, Gebbons see Gibbons
Geddey see Giddey
Gedleigh see Gidley
Geen, Geene, Geine, Gene, Geyne
    Geine ..., Martinhoe 1614 [W]
    Gene alias Nicoll Alexander, Kentisbury 1582 W
    Geyne Alice, Combe Martin 1619 [W]
    Alice, Trentishoe 1739 W
    Ann, Trentishoe 1793 W
    Ann and Nicholas, Ilfracombe 1727 W
    Geen or Green Dorothy, Great Torrington 1843 W
    Eleanor, East Down 1844 W
    Elizabeth, North Molton 1840 A
    Geene Frances, Westleigh 1707 W
    Geene George, Parracombe 1685 W
    George, Loxhore 1759 W
    Geyne Jenophia, Parracombe 1619 W
    Geyne alias Nicholl John, Shirwell 1606 W
    Geine John, Berrynarbor 1612 [W] "John Nichols alias Geene"
        in register; forename blank in Ms; supplied from parish
        register
    John, Parracombe 1763 W
    John, Marwood 1796 A
    John, formerly of High Bray but late of Swimbridge 1852 W
    Geen or Green alias Nicholls Nicholas, Ilfracombe 1714 W
    Nicholas and Ann, Ilfracombe 1727 W
    Philip, Barnstaple 1829 W
    Richard, East Down 1834 A
    Thomas, Trentishoe 1789 W
    Thomas, Trentishoe 1816 W
    Thomas, West Down 1837 W
    Thomas, Pilton 1844 W
    Geene Walter 1640 W
    Geene William, Tawstock 1691 A
        see also Jeans
Geese Walter, Bideford 1590 [W]
    William, Hartland 1590 [W]
Gefferie see Jeffery
Gefford see Giffard
Geffrey see Jeffery
Gefferie, Geffrie, Geffry, Geffrye see Jeffery
Geine see Geen
Gelbert see Gilbert
Geley John, Wembworthy 1639 W
Gempton James, Great Torrington 1851 W
Gendle Reynold, Hartland 1568 W
Gene see Geen
Genings see Jennings
Genken, Genkinge, Genkyn see Jenkins
Gennens see Jennings
Gennet, Gennett see Jennet
Gennings see Jennings
Gennowe Joan, North Molton 1578 W
    Richard, North Molton 1572 W
Gennyngs see Jennings
Gent John, Winkleigh 1670 A
George Digory, Bideford 1682 W
    Edward, Parkham 1783 W
    Edward, Parkham 1846 W
    Jane, Parkham 1822 W
    John, Merton 1742 W
    John, Parkham 1826 W
    Rees, Winkleigh 1773 W
    William, Bideford 1672 A

William, Heanton Punchardon 1673 A
German, Gearman, Germon, Jerman
  Jerman Daniel, Combe Martin 1688 W
  Gearman David, Chittlehampton 1706 W
  Jerman or German Edward, Peters Marland 1617 [W]
  Jerman or German Elizabeth, Peters Marland 1618, 1621 and
    1622 [W]
  Jerman Francis, Warkleigh 1672 W
  Hannah, Marwood 1742 W
  Jerman Hannibal, Meeth 1709 W
  Jerman Joan, Meeth 1713 W
  John, Dolton 1564 W
  John, Peters Marland 1565 W
  John, Combe Martin 1640 A
  Jerman John, Meeth 1672 W
  John, Meeth 1713 W
  John, Marwood 1725 A
  John, Marwood 1743 A
  John, Parracombe 1785 W
  Jerman Mary, Meeth 1679 W
  Mary, Ilfracombe 1846 W
  Nathaniel, Bideford 1710 A
  Nicholas, Bideford 1620 [W]
  Nicholas, Combe Martin 1665 A
  Jerman Nicholas, Combe Martin 1691 W
  Jerman or German Philip, Bideford 1615 [W]
  Philip, Meeth 1670 W
  Richard, Peters Marland 1570 W
  Richard, Ilfracombe 1830 A to Mary, widow
  Germon Robert, Shebbear 1570 W
  Robert, Ilfracombe 1777 W
  Jerman Samuel, Meeth 1756 W
  Jerman or German Walter, North Tawton 1612 [W]; forename
    blank in Ms; supplied from parish register
  Jerman William, Bideford 1620 [W]
  William, Welcombe 1622 [W]
  German alias Jerman William, Chittlehampton 1664 W
  William, West Anstey 1773 W
  Jerman William, Lynton 1776 A
Gerrard Thomas, Barnstaple 1639 A
Gerringe, Geareing, Gerren, Gerrens, Geryng
  Geareing Joanna, Bideford 1696 W
  Geryng John, Instow 1573 W
  Nicholas, Bideford 1606 W
  Gerren Richard, Hartland 1598 [W]
  Gerrens Robert, Bideford 1589 A
  Geareing Thomas, Bideford 1691 W
Gerry see Jerry
Gerves, Gervis see Jarvis
Geryng see Gerringe
Gest, Geste see Guest
Getton see Geaton
Geyne see Geen
Ghose Richard, Lapford 1572 W
Gibb, Gibbe, Gibbes see Gibbs
Gibbett Elizabeth, Barnstaple 1771 A
  John, Barnstaple 1761 A
Gibbins, Gebbens, Gebbins, Gebbons, Gybbons
  Alexander, North Tawton 1682 A
  Gybbons Andrew, Witheridge 1574 W
  Gebbins Anthony, Barnstaple 1596 [W]
  Bartholomew, North Tawton 1665 A
  Bridget, Tawstock 1642 W
  Gybbons Dorothy, South Molton 1639 A
  Dorothy, North Tawton 1675 W
  Elizabeth, Northam 1765 W
  Frances, Tawstock 1643 A
  Gybbons John, Witheridge 1622 [W] and O
  Gebbons John, South Molton 1635 A
  John, Marwood 1716 A
  John, Coldridge, yeoman 1803 [W]
  Joseph, Alverdiscott 1673 [W]
  Margaret, Alverdiscott 1675 W
  Margaret, Alverdiscott 1698 A
  Mary, Barnstaple 1767 A

Gibbings Mary, Lapford 1815 W
Gibbings Richard, Coldridge 1770 W
  Richard, Coldridge, yeoman 1804 [W]
  Rose, Stoodleigh 1684 A
  Gibbens Thomas, Tawstock 1573 W
  William, Tawstock 1568 W
  Gybbons alias Smytham William, Langtree 1574 A unclear as
    to whether William of Great Torrington and William of
    Langtree were the same person
  Gebbens alias Smytham William, Langtree 1603 W
  William, Tawstock 1641 W
  William, Oakford 1678 A
  William, Northam 1749 T
  Gybbons alias Smytham William, Little Torrington [1574]
    [W]
Gibble John see John Wilkinson
Gibbs, Gebbe, Gebbes, Gibb, Gibbe, Gibbes, Gybbe, Gybbes
  Christopher, Rose Ash 1819 W
  Grace, Georgeham, widow 1811 W
  Grace, Barnstaple 1818 W
  Gybbe Henry, North Molton 1621 [W]
  Henry, Georgeham, yeoman 1800 W
  Henry, East Anstey 1801 W
  Henry, Georgeham 1819 W
  James, Barnstaple 1857 W
  Gybbes John, Great Torrington 1577 A
  Gybbes John, Roborough 1629 [W]
  John, Loxhore 1631 W
  John, Marwood 1680 A
  Gibbe John, Barnstaple 1744 W
  John, Shirwell 1777 W
  Gibb John, Northam, mariner 1807 A
  John, Barnstaple 1832 W
  Mathew, Knowstone 1728 A
  Gibbe Philip, Penrise, Glamorgan 1600 W
  Gibbes Philip, Northam 1614 [W]; forename blank in Ms;
    supplied from parish register
  Philip, Fremington 1671 W
  Philip, Northam 1702 or 1710 W
  Prudence see Edmund, John, Prudence and Robert Brook
  Gebbes Richard, Ilfracombe 1591 [W]
  Richard, Bideford 1669 O
  Richard, Bideford 1765 W
  Richard, South Molton or Buckland Brewer 1772 A
  Richard, North Molton 1838 A to Richard, son
  Richard, North Molton 1845 W
  Richard, Bideford 1849 W
  Gybbes Robert, East Worlington 1587 W
  Gebbes Robert, St Giles in the Wood 1606 W
  Gibb Robert, Littleham (near Bideford) 1669 W
  Sarah, Fremington 1704 W
  Sarah, Abbotsham 1715 W
  Gebbe Thomas, Georgeham 1585 W
  Thomas, Great Torrington 1836 W
  Gybbe William, Hartland 1566 W
  William, Abbotsham 1696 W
Gibson John, Chulmleigh 1602 W
Giddey, Geddey
  Ann, Tawstock 1805 W* (1806)
  George, Bideford 1852 W
  John, Ashford 1826 A to Sally, widow
  Geddey Warwick, Tawstock, mason 1801 W
Gidley, Gedleigh
  John, Ashreigney, victualler 1805 W
  Gedleigh Richard, Winkleigh 1574 W
Giffard, Gefford, Giffards, Gifford
  Gifford ..., Rose Ash 1609 [W]
  Gifford ..., Great Torrington 1610 [W]
  Gifford ..., Atherington 1611 [W]
  Agnes, Parkham 1727 W
  Anthony, Parkham 1701 A
  Caesar, Chittlehampton 1716 W
  Gefford Elizabeth, Barnstaple 1588 W
  Gifford Elizabeth, Parkham 1624 [W]
  Gifford Emanuel, Buckland Brewer 1793 W

Gifford Henry, South Molton 1614 [W]; forename blank in
    Ms; supplied from parish register
Gifford alias Blagdon Henry, Abbotsham 1641 W
Giffards Henry, Chittlehampton, gentleman 1710 A
Gifford Hugh, St Giles in the Wood 1594 [W]
Gifford John, South Molton 1592 [W]
Gifford alias Blagdon John, Hartland 1600 W
John, Landcross 1681 A
John, Chittlehampton, esquire 1688 W
John, Chittlehampton, esquire, jnr. 1704 W; A dbn 1719
John, Chittlehampton 1726 A
John, Buckland Brewer 1752 A
Gifford John, Welcombe 1848 W
Gifford Margaret, Westleigh, widow 1610 [W]; forename
    blank in Ms; supplied from parish register
Giffard Margery, Chittlehampton, widow 1707 W
Gifford Mary, Buckland Brewer 1805 W
Gifford Richard, Bideford 1748 W
Robert, Chittlehampton 1702 W
Roger, Buckland Brewer 1765 W
Sarah, Chittlehampton 1743 W
Thomas, Northam 1708 A
Thomas, Buckland Brewer 1770 W
Gifforde Walter, Chittlehampton 1617 [W]
William, Northam 1741 A
Giffery see Jeffrey
Gifford see Giffard
Gilbert, Gelbert, Gilberte, Gilbord, Jelbert
Gilberte ..., North Tawton 1604 [W]
Gelbert ..., Ilfracombe 1614 [W]
Jelbert ..., Ilfracombe 1614 [W]
Ann, Bideford 1843 W
Canson, Langtree 1736 W
Edmund, Shebbear 1606 W
Eleanor, Buckland Filleigh 1709 W
Elizabeth, Bideford 1812 W
George, Northam 1697 A
Gilbord Henry, Buckland Filleigh 1712 W
Henry, Petrockstowe 1796 W
John, Shebbear 1626 and 1629 [W]
John, Petrockstowe 1720 A
John, Buckland Filleigh 1723 W
John, Hartland 1764 W
John, Bideford 1834 W
Gilberte Margaret, Arlington 1584 W
Paschal, Abbotsham 1675 A
Richard, Sheepwash 1688 A
Richard, Pilton 1805 W
Richard, Buckland Filleigh, tailor 1810 W
Samuel, Langtree 1669 W
Thomas, Bittadon 1855 W
William, Clovelly 1746 W
William, Bideford, cordwainer 1808 W
William, Great Torrington 1854 W
Giles, Gyles, Gylles
Alice, Bideford 1709 W
Gyles Ann, Great Torrington 1625 [W]
Edmund, Heanton Punchardon 1721 W
James, Marwood 1690 A
Joan, Arlington 1725 W
Gylles John, High Bickington, snr. 1580 W
Gyles John, High Bickington 1644 W
John, High Bickington 1693 W
John, Bideford 1754 W
Margaret, High Bickington 1705 W
Mathew, Winkleigh 1617 [W]
Richard, Bideford 1677 A
Richard, Bideford 1700 W
Gyles Roger, St Giles in the Wood 1627 [W]
Sebastian, Great Torrington 1621 [W]
Gyles Sebastian, Great Torrington 1637 O
Thomas, Great Torrington 1619 [W]
Gilford or Gillard Margery, Chittlehampton, widow 1707 W
Gill, Gyll, Gylle
..., Sheepwash 1606 [W]

Alexander, Bratton Fleming 1670 A
Ambrose, Chittlehampton 1670 A
Ann, East Buckland 1792 W
Anthony, Bratton Fleming 1777 A
Catherine, Atherington, widow 1800 W
Frances, Mortehoe 1705 W
Geoffrey, East Down, yeoman 1810 A
Gyll George, Mariansleigh 1587 W
George, Goodleigh 1703 A
George, Atherington 1776 W
George, High Bickington 1823 W
Gregory, Combe Martin 1681 A
Hugh, Filleigh 1673 W
Humphrey, Bratton Fleming 1698 W
Jacob, High Bray 1780 W
Jacob, Bratton Fleming 1854 W
James, Barnstaple 1625 [W]
Joan, Barnstaple 1717 W
Gylle and Down John 1573 A
John, Barnstaple 1625 [W]
John, Mariansleigh 1632 [W]
Gyll John, Mariansleigh 1635 O
John, Cruwys Morchard 1680 A
John, Mortehoe 1704 A
John, Barnstaple 1718 A
John, East Buckland 1782 W
John, Lynton 1798 A
John, Tawstock 1814 W
John, Fremington 1855 W
Mary, Barnstaple 1622 [W]
Mary, Chittlehampton 1717 W
Mary wife of John see Richard Barrow
Nicholas, Pilton 1641 W
Nicholas, Barnstaple 1644 A
Nicholas, Barnstaple 1718 W
Richard, Barnstaple 1627 [W]
Richard, Great Torrington 1643 W
Robert, Chittlehampton 1621 [W]
Robert, Atherington 1747 W
Robert, High Bickington 1757 W
Robert, Atherington, yeoman 1808 A
Robert, High Bickington 1830 A to Susanna, widow
Gylle Roger, North or South Tawton 1569 W
Roger, South Molton 1642 A
Roger, Chittlehampton 1703 W
Thomas, Huish 1642 W
Walter, Parkham 1596 [W]
William, Newton Tracey 1607 [W]; forename blank in Ms;
    supplied from parish register
William, Woolfardisworthy 1620 [W]
Gillams Thomas, Ilfracombe 1620 [W]
Gillard Ann, South Molton 1834 A
Humphrey, Barnstaple 1846 A
John, South Molton 1733 W
John, South Molton 1836 W
Joseph, Molland 1814 W
Mary, Northam 1857 W
Richard, South Molton 1679 W
William, South Molton 1792 A
William, South Molton 1834 W and 1835 W
Willmot, Bideford 1828 W
Gillfard see Gilford
Gillmore Alice, Bideford 1753 W
Gingar Christiana, Barnstaple 1678 W
Nicholas, Barnstaple, esquire, jnr. 1707 A
Thomas, Barnstaple 1660 W
Gininge see Jennings
Gislett John, Buckland Filleigh 1585 W
Gist, Giste, Gyst, Gyste
..., Bideford 1600 A
..., Bideford 1609 and 1610 [W]
..., Bideford 1660 A
Alice, Northam 1614 [W]; forename blank in Ms; supplied
    from parish register
Elizabeth, Welcombe 1616 [W]

Giste Joan, Abbotsham 1590 [W]

Joan and Thomas, Bideford 1689 A Joan might be a typo for
John

Gyste alias Froste John, Bideford 1581 A

Gyst John, Northam 1602 W

Giste John, Welcombe 1620 [W]

John, Monkleigh 1630 [W]

Giste John, Abbotsham 1630 [W]

Margaret, Bideford 1626 [W]

Mary, Bideford 1670 W

Mary, Bideford 1710 W

Nathaniel, Hartland 1689 A

Philip, Welcombe 1595 [W]

Roger, Merton 1700 W

Roger, Merton 1752 A

Giste Thomas, Bideford 1597 [W]

Thomas, Bideford 1703 A

Thomas, Merton 1714 W

Thomas and John, Bideford 1689 A; John might be a typo for
Joan

William, Abbotsham 1644 W

Gitsham

Gyttsham Joan, West Worlington 1638 W

Gitson Andrew, South Molton 1691 W

Philip, South Molton 1710 W

Gittings Grace, Barnstaple 1835 A

Henry, Barnstaple, snr. 1677 W

Henry, Barnstaple 1835 A to Henry, son

Samuel, Bideford 1692 A

Glade ..., South Molton 1603 [W]

Glade alias Slade John, Twitchen 1571 W

Glanvill, Glandvill

Glandvill John, Northam 1751 W

Glanvill alias Glawen Richard, Shebbear 1640 W

Robert, Barnstaple 1663 A

Glandvill Roger, Alverdiscott 1672 W

Glass, Glasse

Glasse Agnes, Great Torrington 1591 [W]

Agnes, Fremington 1728 W

Bartholomew, Yarnscombe 1682 W

Glasse Dorothy, Chulmleigh 1580 W

Glasse George, King's Nympton 1645 W

Gregory, North Molton 1681 W

Glasse Joan, West Worlington 1617 [W]

Glasse John, Bondleigh 1564 W

Glasse John, George Nympton 1593 [W]

Glasse John, Yarnscombe 1626 and 1629 [W]

Glasse John, North Molton 1637 W

John, Winkleigh 1694 A

Glasse Lawrence, Chawleigh 1575 W

Glasse Mary, Filleigh 1624 [W]

Nicholas, Barnstaple 1746 W

Glasse Pentecost, Combe Martin 1621 [W]

Glasse Philip, North Molton, jnr. 1640 W

Glasse Robert, Yarnscombe 1565 W

Sarah, Tawstock 1831 W

Susan, North Molton 1682 W

Glasse Thomas, Bondleigh 1637 A

Thomas, Bondleigh 1660 A

Thomas, Yarnscombe 1690 A

Thomas, Yarnscombe 1750 W

Thomas, Fremington, yeoman 1819 A to Sarah, widow

William, North Molton 1691 [W]

William, Winkleigh 1711 W

Glawen, Glaway, Glawyn, Glowen, Glowin, Glowyn

..., Warkleigh 1600 A

..., East Putford 1603 [W]

Glowyn Alexander, High Bickington 1580 A

Christian, Great Torrington, widow 1564 W

Ethel, Great Torrington 1640 A

Humphrey, Shebbear 1594 [W]

Glowin John, High Bickington 1572 W

John, High Bickington 1602 W

John, Buckland Brewer 1629 [W]

John, High Bickington 1641 A

John, Buckland Filleigh 1645 W

Glowen John, Alwington 1645 W

Glowen John, Sheepwash 1662 W

Glowen John, Bideford 1680 A

John, Sheepwash 1694 W

Margaret or Margery, High Bickington 1592 [W]

Nicholas, Peters Marland 1590 [W]

Phillippa, Great Torrington 1664 W

Richard, Buckland Brewer 1597 [W]

Richard, North Tawton 1627 [W]

Glawen alias Glanvill Richard, Shebbear 1640 W

Glowen Roger, Clovelly 1662 W

Walter, Shebbear 1573 W

Glawyn William, Woolfardisworthy 1567 W

William, High Bickington 1590 [W]

Glaway William, George Nympton 1639 [W]

Gleddon see Gliddon

Glendell John, Great Torrington, snr. 1660 W

Gliddon, Gleddon, Glidon, Glyddon

Glyddon Charles, Sheepwash 1634 W

Gleddon Daniel, Northam 1727 W

James, North Tawton 1717 [W]

John, Clovelly 1725 A

John, Barnstaple 1849 W

Josiah, Marwood 1687 A

Roger, North Tawton 1725 W

Thomas, East Putford 1674 W

Thomas, Parkham 1716 W

Glidon William, Tawstock 1755 W

William, South Molton, jnr. 1829 A to Ann, widow

Glogge Agnes, Alwington 1639 A

John, Alwington 1624 [W]

Glover Andrew, Woolfardisworthy 1780 W

Daniel, Parkham 1732 W

Elizabeth, Parkham 1776 W

Giles, Parkham 1723 W

Jane, Alwington 1693 W

John, Parkham 1564 W and 1566 W

John, Parkham 1669 W

John, Alwington, snr. 1673 W

John, Parkham 1685 W

John, Parkham 1762 W

John, Parkham 1822 A

Philip, Parkham 1587 W

Rebecca, Woolfardisworthy 1713 W

Richard, Parkham 1675 A

Thomas, Parkham 1629 W (2)

Thomas, Winkleigh 1729 W

William, Parkham 1607 [W] mistranscribed as "Blonor?" in
printed edition; forename blank in Ms; supplied from parish
register

Glover alias Whitefield William, Frithelstock 1693 A

William, Northam 1744 W

Glowen, Glowin, Glowyn see Glawen

Gloyne, Gloyn

Esther, Great Torrington 1769 W

George, Oakford 1696 A

Hugh, South Molton 1713 W

Gloyn Hugh, South Molton 1734 A

James, Great Torrington 1702 W

John, Roborough 1577 W

John, Chulmleigh 1707 W and 1717 W

John, Oakford 1793 W

John, Little Torrington 1856 W

Sarah, Bideford 1714 A

Sarah, Bishop's Nympton 1856 W

Glubb Richard, Barnstaple 1669 A

Richard, Great Torrington 1755 W

Thomas, Bideford 1812 A

Glyddon see Gliddon

Goade John, South Molton 1633 A

Goadman John, Hartland 1844 W

Goard Ambrose, Kentisbury 1734 W

Joan, Stoke Rivers 1762 W

John, South Molton 1777 W

Nicholas, Stoke Rivers 1718 and 1719 W
Nicholas, Stoke Rivers 1757 W
Thomas, High Bickington 1597 [W]
Godafraie see Godfrey
Godbear Mary, Chittlehampton 1762 W
　Peter, Chittlehampton 1755 W and 1756 A
　Peter, Chittlehampton, husbandman 1808 A
Godfrey, Godafraie, Goddafray, Godfray
　Godafraie ..., Chawleigh 1607 [W]
　Godfray Alice, Dolton 1574 W
　Charity, Northam 1828 A
　Goddafray Constance, Dolton, widow 1615 [W]; forename
　　blank in Ms; supplied from parish register
　Godfray Joan, Dolton 1642 W
　Godfray John, Bow 1591 [W]
　Godfray Robert, Dolton 1597 [W]
　Rowland, Dolton 1670 A and 1672 O
　Godfray William, Bow 1631 [W]
Godinge, Godynge
　Godynge Emott, Shebbear 1575 W
　Godinge alias Balsdon Joan, Shebbear, widow 1564 W
Godsland, Godisland
　Ann, Burrington 1665 A
　Faith, Burrington 1635 W
　Hugh, Burrington 1698 W
　Godisland James, Barnstaple 1572 W
　John, Burrington 1572 W
　John, Burrington 1723 W
　Lodovic, Woolfardisworthy 1724 A
　Samuel, Rose Ash 1664 [W]
　Scipio, Chulmleigh 1667 W
　Scipio, Burrington 1720 A
　William, Roborough 1586 W
Godswill Hugh, Witheridge 1617 [W]
Godwin, Godwyn
　Godwyn John, Frithelstock 1615 [W]
　Mary, Bideford 1739 W
Godynge see Godinge
Gold, Golde see Gould
Goldringe Bartholomew, Barnstaple 1589 W
Goldsmith Elizabeth, South Molton 1681 W
Goldson Catherine, South Molton 1692 W
Gole see Goole
Golston Samuel, Northam 1727 W
Golsworthy see Galsworthy
Goman Agnes, Chulmleigh 1744 W
　Henry, Chulmleigh 1740 A
　Lewis, Fremington 1745 A
　Thomas, Dowland 1766 A
Gomer
　Gomer or Gorner John, King's Nympton, jnr. 1825 W
　Sarah, South Molton 1725 W
　Sarah, Chittlehampton 1731 W
　Walter, ship *Bideford* 1746 W
　Gomer or Gorner William, King's Nympton 1831 A to Betty,
　　widow
Gonne, Gone
　..., South Molton 1608 [W]
　..., North Molton 1609 [W]
　Agnes, North Molton 1571 W
　Alice, Marwood 1610 [W] "of Middle Marwood" in register;
　　forename blank in Ms; supplied from parish register
　Ellen, North Molton 1591 [W]
　George, Marwood 1608 [W]; forename blank in Ms; supplied
　　from parish register
　Gone Hugh, Iddesleigh 1663 A
　Gone Joan, Iddesleigh 1693 W
　John, Rackenford 1667 A and 1671 O
　Gone Richard, Iddesleigh 1708 W
Good Clement, Ashford 1638 W
　John, Northam 1632 [W]
　John, Northam 1726 W
　Robert, Northam 1677 A
　Robert, Ashreigney 1727 A

Goodanough, Goodanew, Goodenough
　Goodanew John, Buckland Brewer 1782 W
　Goodanew John, Buckland Brewer 1818 W
　John, Buckland Brewer 1837 A
　Goodenough Thomas, Northam 1727 W
　William, Buckland Brewer 1813 W (1833 A to John, father
Goodchild ..., Northam 1614 [W]
Gooddings, Gooden see Gooding
Goodenough see Goodanough
Gooding, Gooddings, Gooden, Goodings
　Gooddings alias Goodwyn Ann, Shebbear 1599 [W]
　Charity, High Bickington 1783 W
　Gooddings John, Shebbear 1630 [W]
　John, Shebbear 1644 A
　John, High Bickington 1814 W; 1824 A
　John, High Bickington 1839 A to John, widow [sic]
　Leonard, High Bickington 1832 W
　Gooddings Richard, Shebbear 1563 W
　Gooden Richard, Shebbear 1600 W
　Samuel, Bideford 1705 A
　Thomas, High Bickington 1846 W
Goodman Agnes, Yarnscombe 1603 W
　Avis, High Bickington 1621 [W]
　George, High Bickington 1636 W
　John, High Bickington 1619 [W]
　Michael, High Bickington 1643 W
　Thomas, High Bickington 1591 [W]
　William, High Bickington 1602 W
Goodnew William, Buckland Brewer 1833 A
Goodwin, Goodwyn
　Andrew, Bideford 1676 W
　Andrew, Bideford 1703 W
　Goodwyn alias Gooddings Ann, Shebbear 1599 [W]
　Goodwyn Henry, Great Torrington, jnr. 1621 [W]
　Goodwyn Henry, Great Torrington 1637 A
　James, Bideford 1793 W
　John, Bideford 1743 W and 1745 A
　John, High Bickington 1760 A
　Margaret, Tawstock 1739 A
　Mary, Bideford 1763 W and 1766 W
　Goodwyn Robert, Shebbear 1599 [W]
　Samuel, Bideford 1749 A
　Sarah, Bideford 1755 W
Goold, Goolde see Gould
Goole, Gole
　Edmund, Chittlehampton 1621 [W]
　George, Stoke Rivers 1682 W
　Henry, Chittlehampton 1598 [W]
　Hugh, Twitchen 1591 [W]
　John, Charles 1576 W
　John, High Bray 1609 [W]; forename blank in Ms; supplied
　　from parish register
　John, Shirwell 1701 A
　Macklin, Shirwell 1635 W
　Gole Margaret 1661 W
　Mary, Berrynarbor 1699 W
　Nicholas, Roborough 1597 [W]
　Peter, Northam 1699 A
　Richard, Chittlehampton 1598 [W]
　Richard, Great Torrington 1639 W
　Richard, North Molton 1681 A
　Robert, Martinhoe 1635 W
　Robert, Filleigh 1661 W
　Silvester, South Molton 1691 W
　Stephen, Northam 1699 A
Goorden see Gorden
Goore see Gord
Gooscott see Goscott
Goosham see Gosham
Gorde see Gourd
Gorden, Goorden, Gording, Gordon, Gourden, Gourdeyn,
　Gourdinge
　Gourden ..., Mortehoe 1613 and 1614 [W]
　Gourden Agnes, Georgeham 1690 [W]
　Gourden Alice, Georgeham 1670 W

Ambrose, Little Torrington 1757 W
Gourden Anthony, Martinhoe 1635 W
Gording Anthony, Mariansleigh 1641 A
Daniel, Great Torrington 1747 W; A dbn 1773
Gourden Edward, Georgeham 1669 W
Elizabeth, Georgeham 1626 [W]
Francis, Merton 1764 A
George, Northam 1757 W
Henry, Northam 1731 W
James, Merton 1735 A
Joan, Northam 1707 A
Gourdeyn John, Mortehoe 1578 W
Gourden John, Barnstaple 1592 [W]
Gourdinge John, Mortehoe 1593 [W]
Goorden John, Martinhoe 1629 [W]
Gording John, Northam 1638 W
Gourding John, Bideford 1677 A
Gourden John, Merton 1706 W
John, Northam 1723 W
John, Georgeham 1743 W
Gordon John, Merton 1854 W
Gourding Margaret, Westleigh 1726 W
Gourding Margaret, Westleigh 1738 W
Margaret, Little Torrington 1766 W
Mary, Merton 1755 W
Gordon Mary see William Ashplant
Gourden Richard, Northam 1551 [W]
Gourdinge Richard, Northam 1602 [W]; forename blank in
    Ms; supplied from parish register
Gourden Richard, Mortehoe 1629 [W]
Gourden Richard, Northam 1691 A
Gourden Richard John, Mortehoe, snr. 1567 W
Gordon Samuel, Peters Marland 1780 W
Sarah, Merton 1741 W
Gourden Thomas, Georgeham 1596 [W]
Thomas, Petrockstowe 1702 W
Thomasine, Northam 1755 A
Gourden William, Georgeham 1578 A
Gourdinge William, Mortehoe 1597 [W]
Gourdinge William, Mortehoe 1627 [W]
Gourden William, Mortehoe 1663 T
Gourding William, Northam 1712 A
William, Little Torrington 1805 A
Gore, Goore
    Goore Hugh, Rose Ash 1587 W
    John, Barnstaple 1746 W
    Goore Robert, Rose Ash 1564 W
    Samuel, Westleigh 1831 W
    Thomas, Barnstaple 1741 A
Gorford, Gorforde
    Gorforde ..., Sheepwash 1601 A
    Joan, Sheepwash 1618 [W] and 1619 O
    John, Sheepwash 1639 W
    John, Buckland Brewer 1731 W and 1740 A
    Simon, South Molton 1740 A
    Susan, Merton 1660 W
    William, Great Torrington 1733 A
Gorner see Gomer
Gorrell see Gorwill
Gorren William, Bideford 1576 A
Gorrill see Gorwill
Gorry Emanuel, Westleigh 1734 W
Gorton Agnes, Loxhore 1640 W
    Gorton alias Holmes Helena, Stoke Rivers 1701 W
    James, Barnstaple 1609 [W]; forename blank in Ms; supplied
       from parish register
    John, Barnstaple 1612 [W]; forename blank in Ms; supplied
       from parish register
    John, Stoke Rivers 1680 W
    Julian, Barnstaple 1621 W
    Lawrence 1598 W
    Rawlina, Loxhore 1622 [W]
Gorvet Christopher, Roborough, labourer 1810 W
Gorwill, Gorrell, Gorrill, Gorwell, Gowle
    ..., Abbotsham 1612 [W]

Gorrell Andrew, Great Torrington 1676 W
Gorrill Eleanor, Barnstaple 1691 A
Grace, Great Torrington 1727 A
Hugh, Barnstaple 1634 W
Gorwell Joan, Barnstaple 1666 A
Margaret, Abbotsham 1624 [W] and O
Gowle Mary, Great Torrington 1684 W
Nicholas, Barnstaple 1683 W
Robert, South Molton 1741 W
Gorwell Samuel, Barnstaple 1664 A
Gorwell Thomas, Barnstaple 1642 A
Gorrell Thomas, Landcross 1662 W
Thomas, Barnstaple 1665 W
William, Barnstaple 1618 [W] and 1625 [W]
William, Barnstaple 1703 W
William, Bideford 1704 A
William, Abbotsham 1733 W
William, Great Torrington 1744 W
William, Great Torrington 1755 W
Willmot, Bideford 1694 A
Goscott, Gooscott
    Gooscott Ellen, Great Torrington 1636 A
    Isaac, Bideford 1702 W
    John, Tawstock 1712 W
    Mary, Bideford 1706 W
Gosham, Goosham
    Goosham Ellen, Frithelstock 1633 A
    John, Yarnscombe 1593 [W]
Gosland John, Burrington 1669 W
    John, Burrington 1680 A
    John, Bow 1737 A
    Robert, East Worlington 1691 W
Gosse, Goss
    ..., West Anstey 1601 O
    Agnes, Lapford 1568 W
    Goss Andrew, Winkleigh 1692 A
    Goss Andrew, Winkleigh, yeoman 1809 W
    Ann, West Anstey 1632 [W]
    Catherine, Molland 1596 W
    Clement, West Anstey 1588 W
    Elizabeth, Knowstone 1599 [W]
    Goss Elizabeth, Wembworthy 1786 W
    Goss Elizabeth, Beaford 1826 A to John, son
    Goss Ellen, Molland 1661 W
    George, Wembworthy 1671 O
    Goss George, Wembworthy 1688 A
    Goss George, West Anstey 1717 A
    Goss George, Georgeham 1840 W
    Goss Gregory, Wembworthy 1778 W
    Henry, Chawleigh 1590 [W]
    Henry, West Anstey 1627 [W]
    Goss Hugh, King's Nympton 1661 A
    Joan, Chawleigh 1589, 1591 and 1592 W
    Goss Joan, West Anstey 1606 W
    Joan, West Anstey 1624 [W]
    Goss Joan, Barnstaple 1805 A
    John, West Anstey 1599 [W]
    Goste John, Bideford 1620 [W]
    John, Rackenford 1640 W
    Goss John, West Anstey 1663 W
    John, Winkleigh 1672 W
    Goss John, West Anstey 1679 A and 1688 A
    Goss John, Chawleigh 1691 W
    Goss John, Winkleigh 1691 W
    Goss John, Barnstaple 1713 W
    Goss John, Chittlehampton 1743 A
    Goss John, Ashreigney 1819 W
    Goss John, Goodleigh 1844 W
    Goss John, Barnstaple 1848 W
    Goss Joseph, Bondleigh 1749 W
    Goss Joseph, Bondleigh 1820 W
    Goss Joseph, Marwood 1852 W
    Josiah, Bondleigh 1625 W
    Lawrence, West Anstey 1582 W
    Lawrence, Creacombe 1594 W

Martin, North Tawton 1594 W
Mary, Chawleigh 1590 W
Goss Mary, Combe Martin 1852 W
Mary see also Ann Pope
Goss Nathaniel, Alverdiscott 1719 A
Pentecost, Rose Ash 1624 W
Peter, Lapford 1568 W
Goss Philip, ship *Blanford* 1758 A
Goss Philip, Georgeham, yeoman 1811 W
Goss Philip, Ilfracombe 1825 W
Goss Richard, Witheridge 1662 W
Robert, Wembworthy 1625 [W]
Goss Robert, Wembworthy 1668 A and 1671 O
Goss Robert, Chawleigh 1685 W
Goss Robert, Molland 1705 A
Goss Robert, Wembworthy 1779 A
Roger, Chawleigh 1630 [W]
Thomas, King's Nympton 1590 [W]
Goss Thomas, North Molton 1726 A
Goss Thomas, Burrington 1782 W
Goss Thomas, Stoodleigh 1837 W
Goss Thomas, Iddesleigh 1849 A
William, West Anstey 1623 [W]
William, South Molton 1675 A
Goss William, Chulmleigh 1723 W
Goss William, Wembworthy 1763 A
Goss William, Combe Martin 1838 W
Gostickle William, North Tawton 1626 A
Gotham, Jotham
John, Chulmleigh 1626 [W]
Jotham Robert, Cruwys Morchard 1620 [W]
Gott Grace, North Molton 1802 W
Gotton Thomas, Beaford 1740 W
Goue see Gove
Gough John, Barnstaple 1799 A
Marius, Bideford 1712 W
Mary, Romansleigh 1781 W
William, Romansleigh 1764 W
Gould, Gold, Goold, Goolde, Goulde, Goule
Goule ..., Charles 1608 [W]
Goule ..., South Molton 1611 [W]
Goolde Agnes, Charles 1635 W
Agnes, Chittlehampton 1771 W
Goule Alice, Charles, widow 1570 W
Goulde alias Walskotte Alice, Warkleigh 1582 W
Ambrose, Westleigh 1742 A
Ambrose, Filleigh 1754 W
Gold Anstis, Barnstaple 1565 W
Goulde Christopher, Charles 1617 [W]
Christopher, Barnstaple 1688 A
Christopher, Stoke Rivers 1711 A
Goolde Clement, Charles 1622 [W]
Daniel, ship *Gloucester* 1746 W
Daniel, ship *Captain* 1757 A
Goule Edmund, Great Torrington 1587 W
Goolde Edward, Charles 1619 [W]
Edward, Heanton Punchardon 1688 W
Elizabeth, Twitchen 1617 [W]
Elizabeth, Barnstaple 1727 A
Elizabeth, North Molton 1759 A
Elizabeth, South Molton, wife 1809 W
Elizabeth, South Molton 1840 W
English, Molland 1668 W
Goold Frances, Barnstaple 1664 W
Goolde George, Charles 1619 [W]
George, Charles 1641 W
George, North Molton 1692 W
Gold George, Marwood 1719 A
George, Charles 1750 W and 1756 W
George, Charles 1770 A and 1777 A
George, Charles 1785 W
George Pincombe, South Molton 1843 A
Grace, Heanton Punchardon 1710 W
Grace wife of John see also Elizabeth Ford
Gregory, Shirwell 1672 A

Henry, Charles 1693 W
Henry, Chittlehampton 1754 W
Henry, North Molton 1766 W
Henry, West Buckland 1780 W
Hugh, Chittlehampton 1698 A
Hugh, South Molton 1739 A
Hugh, Chittlehampton 1766 W
Hugh, Chittlehampton 1855 W
James, Great Torrington 1677 A
James, Molland 1708 W
James, Weare Giffard 1822 W
Jane, Molland 1724 W
Goulde Joan, North Molton 1594 [W]
Goulde Joan, Chittlehampton 1605 W
Goold Joan, South Molton 1686 W
Joan, Barnstaple 1700 A
Joan, Charles 1731 W
Joan, Charles 1785 W
John, Warkleigh 1576 W
Goulde John, North Molton 1579 W
John, South Molton 1599 [W]
Goulde John, Charles 1605 W
Goule John, Berrynarbor 1606 W
John, Charles, jnr. 1643 W
John, Chittlehampton 1644 A
John, North Molton 1673 A
Goule John, Marwood 1678 W
John, Merton 1679 A
Goule John, West Buckland 1694 W
Goule John, High Bray 1695 [W]
John, Heanton Punchardon 1732 W
Gold John, Marwood 1737 A
John, East Anstey 1738 W
John, Molland 1741 W
John, Huntshaw 1745 W
John, Berrynarbor 1746 A
John, South Molton 1746 A
John, Marwood 1747 A
John, North Molton 1752 W
John, Huntshaw 1757 A
John, Chittlehampton 1763 W
John, Yarnscombe 1763 A
John, Tawstock 1794 W
John, Shebbear 1807 W
John, Roborough 1817 W
John, Roborough 1818 A to Mary, widow
John, Barnstaple 1823 W
John, Stoke Rivers 1826 A to Mary, widow
Joseph, Charles 1817 W
Josiah, Ashford 1752 W
Goold Lodovic, South Molton 1682 W
Macklin, Charles 1643 A
Mary, Barnstaple 1666 W
Mary, Chittlehampton 1729 A
Mary, North Molton 1764 W
Mary, Chittlehampton 1855 W
Goule Nicholas, Berrynarbor 1645 W
Nicholas, Charles 1721 A
Philip, North Tawton 1641 W
Philip, Molland 1681 W
Phillippa, Barnstaple 1810 W
Richard, Fremington 1588 W
Richard, Barnstaple 1662 W
Richard, Westleigh 1751 W
Richard, Chulmleigh 1768 A
Richard, Marwood 1826 W
Richard, formerly of Ilfracombe, late of Tenby, Wales 1846 W
Richard, Filleigh 1849 W
Gold Robert, Martinhoe 1577 W
Robert, South Molton 1722 W
Robert, Marwood 1723 A
Roger, South Molton 1594 [W]
Sarah, Merton 1671 W
Sarah, South Molton, widow 1797 W
Sarah, Tawstock, widow 1800 W

Goolde Silvester, Twitchen 1625 [W]
Golde Thomas, Twitchen 1563 W
Goulde Thomas, Warkleigh 1580 W
Goold Thomas, Berrynarbor 1585 W
Goule Thomas, Berrynarbor 1645 A
Gold Thomas, West Anstey 1695 W
Gold Thomas, West Buckland 1732 A
Thomas, Molland 1733 A
Thomas, Charles 1755 A
Thomas, Huntshaw 1759 W
Thomas, Chittlehampton 1774 W
Thomas, Marwood 1833 W
Thomasine, Filleigh 1674 W
Tristram, Filleigh 1685 A
Walter, High Bray 1598 [W]
Goulde William, North Molton 1591 [W]
William, North Molton 1642 W
William, Heanton Punchardon 1710 W
William, North Molton 1744 W and A
William, Marwood 1746 A
William, Chittlehampton 1758 W
William, South Molton, surgeon 1801 W
William, West Buckland 1809 W
William, Chittlehampton 1818 W
Gourrant see Gurrant
Gourd, Gorde, Gourde
  Gorde Anthony, South Molton 1636 A
  Gorde John, Northam 1631 [W]
  Gourde Lawrence, Bratton Fleming 1631 W
  Nicholas, Loxhore 1664 W
  Robert, Bratton Fleming 1631 A
  Gorde Thomasine, South Molton 1638 W
Gourden, Gourdeyn, Gourding, Gourdinge see Gordon
Gourney Elizabeth, Barnstaple 1663 W
Gousans see Cousins
Gove, Goviar, Govier
  Goue ..., Iddesleigh 1607, 1608 and 1612 [W]
  Michael, North Tawton 1643 A
  Richard, Iddesleigh 1581 O account
  Richard, Zeal Monachorum 1781 A
Gover
  Ann, Witheridge 1644 W
  Dorothy and John, Oakford 1639 W
  Grace, Rose Ash 1662 W
  Govier Hugh, Warkleigh 1768 A
  John, Meshaw 1696 W
  Govier John, Pilton 1706 A
  Govier John, Stoodleigh 1757 A
  John and Dorothy, Oakford 1640 W
  Richard, Witheridge 1582 W
  Richard, Warkleigh 1680 A
  Goviar William, Rackenford 1618 [W]
  William, Warkleigh 1710 A
Govett, Govet
  Govet Christopher, Stoke Rivers 1810 [W]
  John, Langtree 1701 W
  John, South Molton 1739 A
  Martha, Langtree 1701 W
Goviar, Govier see Gover
Gowde John, Shirwell 1620 [W]
Gowman Ann, Bideford 1833 A
  Charles, Dolton 1796 W
  Dorothy, Dolton 1776 W
  John, Shebbear 1573 W
  John, Dolton 1761 A
  John, Dolton 1796 A
  Lodovic, Petrockstowe 1695 A
  Richard, Dolton, yeoman 1797 W
Grabell John, Peters Marland 1722 W
Graddon ..., Chittlehampton 1612 [W]
  Ann, Chittlehampton 1620 [W]
  Ann, Chittlehampton, sp. 1845 A to Ann, widow, mother and
    William of Bristol, milkman, brother
  Arthur, Peters Marland 1757 A
  Barbara, Monkleigh 1638 W

Dionysius, Bow 1638 W and 1639 A
Eleanor, Parracombe 1696 A
George, Chittlehampton 1615 [W]
Hezekiah, Parracombe 1699 W
Hugh, South Molton 1668 W
James, Atherington, yeoman 1802 W
James, Chittlehampton 1836 W
John, Buckland Filleigh 1588 W
John, Barnstaple 1618 [W]
John, Roborough 1640 W
John, Peters Marland 1695 W
John, Fremington 1697 W
John, Roborough 1700 W
John, High Bickington 1719 A
John, High Bickington 1732 W
John, Atherington 1769 A
John, Chittlehampton 1853 A
Richard, High Bickington 1703 W
Robert, Bow 1640 O
Susan, Burrington 1694 A
Thomas, Monkleigh 1629 [W]
Thomas, Roborough 1720 W
Thomas, Chittlehampton, yeoman 1857 A to William,
  gentleman, brother
William, Buckland Filleigh, snr. 1636 W
William, Buckland Filleigh 1669 A
William, Atherington 1679 W and 1685 A
William, High Bickington 1719 W
Graham James, Bideford 1740 W
  James, Combe Martin 1759 W
  James, Bideford 1761 W
  John, Bideford 1729 W
Graie see Gray
Grandam John, Hartland 1691 A
Grant, Graunt
  Agnes, Woolfardisworthy 1743 W
  Agnes and Henry, Little Torrington 1710 A
  Benjamin, Bideford 1782 W
  Graunt Elizabeth, Pilton 1665 W
  Elizabeth, Bideford, sp. 1848 A (Eliza) to Fanny, sp.
  Emott, Pilton 1624 [W]
  George Heanes, Great Torrington 1847 A to William, father
  Henry, Great Torrington 1643 W
  Henry and Agnes, Great Torrington 1710 A
  Henry, Great Torrington 1717 A
  Henry, Barnstaple 1732 W
  Grant or Graunt James, Puddington 1695 W
  John, Puddington 1642 A
  John, Great Torrington 1697 W
  Graunt John, Meshaw 1720 A
  John, Great Torrington 1728 W
  John, Witheridge 1731 A
  John, Bideford 1844 W
  Graunt Lucy, Washford Pyne 1639 [W]
  Grant or Graunt Luke, Great Torrington 1683 A
  Margaret, Puddington 1723 A
  Mary, Hartland 1676 W
  Mary, Barnstaple 1735 W
  Mary, Cruwys Morchard 1748 W
  Rebecca, Puddington 1695 [W]
  Grant or Graunt Rebecca, Puddington 1695 [W]
  Rebecca, Puddington 1715 A
  Richard, Pilton 1575 W
  Graunt Richard, Pilton 1605 [W]; forename blank in Ms;
    supplied from parish register
  Graunt Robert, Great Torrington 1601 W
  Robert, Puddington 1661 W
  Stephen, Great Torrington 1675 W
  Stephen, Great Torrington 1710 A
  Thomas, Hartland, gentleman 1679 W
  Graunt Walter, Bideford 1638 A
  Grant or Graunt Walter, Great Torrington 1681 W
Grantland John, Bow 1701 A
Gratcliffe, Gratclyfe, Gratliffe
  ..., Atherington 1602 A

Christopher, Lapford 1637 W
Joan, Bondleigh 1632 [W]
Gratclyfe John, Zeal Monachorum 1571 W
Gratclyfe John, Bondleigh 1580 W
Gratliffe Richard, Barnstaple 1582 W
Robert, Lapford, jnr. 1640 W
Gratclyfe William, Bondleigh 1580 W
Gratdon see Gratton
Grater Arthur, Atherington 1684 W
Charles, Atherington 1702 W
Eleanor, Atherington 1703 A
Elizabeth, Dowland 1702 W
Ethelreda, Langtree 1681 A
Honoria, Clovelly, widow 1676 A
John, Littleham (near Bideford) 1608 [W]; forename blank in
    Ms; supplied from parish register
John, South Molton 1851 W
Mary, Great Torrington 1758 W
Peter, Great Torrington 1746 A
Samuel, Sheepwash 1713 W
Samuel, Chulmleigh 1827 W
Sarah, Ashreigney 1837 A to Susan Vicary, daughter
Gratley Charles, Chawleigh 1707 T
Gratliffe see Gratcliffe
Gratton, Gratdon
Gratdon James, Roborough 1746 A
William, South Molton 1831 A
Graunt see Grant
Gravis John, Bulkworthy 1593 [W]
Gray, Graie, Graye
Graye Alice, Monkleigh, widow 1569 W
Graye Joan, South Molton 1572 W
Rachel, Alverdiscott 1842 W
Graie Richard, Monkleigh 1584 W
Gread, Greade
Greade ..., Chittlehampton 1604 [W]
..., Great Torrington 1609 [W]
Ambrose, Great Torrington 1680 A
Greade Andrew, Chittlehampton 1620 [W]
Gread alias Leyar Ann, Pilton 1683 A
Greade Ann, Barnstaple 1697 A
Greade Anthony, East Putford 1626 [W]
Arthur, Chittlehampton 1668 W
Benjamin, Barnstaple 1704 A
Gread alias Penry Catherine, Barnstaple 1699 A; forename
    blank in Ms; supplied from parish register
Greade David, Chittlehampton 1597 [W]
Eleanor, Barnstaple 1741 W
Francis, Great Torrington 1614 [W]; forename blank in Ms;
    supplied from parish register
Greade Gilbert, Barnstaple 1686, 1694 and 1697 W
Greade Henry, Chittlehampton 1606 W
John, North Molton 1575 W
John, Chittlehampton 1588 A
Greade John, Tawstock 1613 [W]; forename blank in Ms;
    supplied from parish register
John, Chulmleigh 1625 W
Greade John, Barnstaple 1688 W
John, George Nympton 1730 A
John, South Molton 1761 W
John, Bulkworthy 1812 W
Greade Mary, King's Nympton 1571 A
Mary, Barnstaple 1725 W
Mary, George Nympton 1740 W
Greade Pauline, Woolfardisworthy 1603 W
Greade Peter, Tawstock 1579 W
Greade Peter, Bideford 1667 W and 1671 O
Greade Philip, King's Nympton 1566 W
Philip, George Nympton 1662 W
Philip, George Nympton 1694 W
Philip, George Nympton 1762 W
Priscilla, Barnstaple 1681 W
Richard, George Nympton 1606 W
Richard, Heanton Punchardon 1642 W
Richard, Barnstaple 1718 W

Greade Robert, George Nympton 1610 [W]; forename blank
    in Ms; supplied from parish register
Thomas, Chittlehampton 1589 W
Greade Thomas, Barnstaple 1595 A
Thomas, Barnstaple 1663 W
Greade William, Barnstaple 1682 W
William, Barnstaple 1761 W
Greader William, East Putford 1606 W
Grebbell, Grebble, Greble see Gribble
Greby see Greeby
Gredgworthy Thomas, Winkleigh 1671 O
Greeby, Greby
Daniel, Weare Giffard 1705 W
Greby Thomas, Bideford 1723 A
Greek Bernard, Weare Giffard 1775 W
Joseph, Barnstaple 1842 W
Mary, Weare Giffard, sp. 1847 A to William, yeoman, brother
Susan, Great Torrington 1835 W
William, Northam 1733 A
William, Great Torrington 1824 W
William, Weare Giffard 1833 W
Green, Greene, Grene
Abel, Westleigh 1675 A
Greene Catherine, Ilfracombe 1668 [W]
Greene David, Pilton 1622 W
Greene David, Great Torrington 1685 W
Greene David, Great Torrington 1714 W
Dorothy, Great Torrington 1843 W
Edith, South Molton 1644 A
Greene Edward, Combe Martin 1619 [W]
Elizabeth, Great Torrington 1723 W
Elizabeth, Great Torrington 1825 W
Humphrey, St Giles in the Wood 1746 W
James, Great Torrington 1739 A
Jane, Great Torrington 1745 W
John, Peters Marland 1598 [W]
Greene John, Great Torrington 1630 [W]
John, Great Torrington 1731 W
John, Great Torrington 1762 W
Moses, Bideford 1776 W
Greene alias Nicholls Nicholas, Tawstock 1666 W
Philip, Alverdiscott 1819 A to Elizabeth, widow
Philip, Northam 1835 A to Mary, daughter
Greene Richard, Great Torrington 1626 [W]
Richard 1834 A to Eleanor of East Down, widow
Greene Robert, South Molton 1590 [W]
Greene Robert, South Molton 1625 [W]
Greene Roger, South Molton 1631 [W]
Roger, Great Torrington 1766 W
Grene Thomas, Great Torrington 1575 W
Thomas, Great Torrington 1776 W
William, Alverdiscott 1752 W
William, Frithelstock 1758 W
Greenaway see Greenway
Greene see Green
Greeneway see Greenway
Greenhood Agnes, Frithelstock 1782 W
Greening, Grining
Alexander, Bideford 1716 A
Christopher, Bideford 1706 A
Edward, Bideford 1733 W
Elizabeth, Weare Giffard 1697 A
Grining Jasper, Bideford 1675 W
Joan, Bideford 1736 W
John, Bideford 1691 A
Joseph, Bideford 1704 W
Joseph, Weare Giffard 1727 W
Joseph, Bideford 1761 W
Mary, Bideford 1739 W
Richard, Bideford 1698 W
Samuel, Weare Giffard 1717 A
Sarah, Bideford 1769 W
William, Huntshaw 1674 W
William, Huntshaw 1724 W and A
William, Bideford 1737 A

Greenrelier Giles, Barnstaple 1691 A
Greenslade, Greneslade, Grenslad, Grynslade
  ..., Bondleigh 1614 [W]
  Abraham, East Worlington 1729 A
  Agnes, Lapford 1816 W
  Alexander, Chawleigh 1675 A
  Christopher, Chawleigh 1702 A
  Cutcliffe, Ilfracombe 1846 W
  Dorothy, East Worlington 1831 A
  Edward, Northam 1669 A
  Elizabeth, Witheridge 1788 W
  Florence, Oakford 1637 W
  Florence, Oakford 1734 W
  Grace, Chulmleigh 1712 A
  Grace, Chulmleigh 1786 and 1789 A
  Henry, Knowstone 1748 W
  Hugh, Witheridge 1718 W
  Hugh, Thelbridge 1726 W
  Hugh, Witheridge 1775 W
  Isaac, North Molton 1813 W
  Jane, Witheridge, sp. 1817 A to John Burgess, yeoman, cousin
  Joan, Witheridge 1618 [W]
  Joan, Oakford 1639 A
  John, Witheridge 1563 W
  John, Witheridge 1586 A
  John, Knowstone 1594 [W]
  John, Cheldon 1630 [W]
  John, Witheridge 1641 A
  John, Chulmleigh 1779 W
  John, Oakford, yeoman 1808 W
  John, Barnstaple 1856 W
  John see also William Cobley
  Lewis, Thelbridge 1740 W
  Lewis, Chawleigh 1745 W
  Lodovic, Oakford 1663 W
  Lodovic, Oakford 1687 W
  Mary, Rackenford 1728 W
  Mary, Buckland Brewer 1751 A
  Mary, Cruwys Morchard, widow 1797 W
  Mary wife of William see also John Bale
  Melior, Oakford 1684 W
  Nathaniel, Chulmleigh 1748 W
  Nathaniel, Wembworthy 1772 W
  Philip, Barnstaple 1704 A
  Renatus, Heanton Punchardon 1714 W
  Richard, Woolfardisworthy 1581 A
  Richard, East Worlington 1643 W
  Richard, Woolfardisworthy 1671 A and O
  Richard, Oakford 1706 A
  Richard, Witheridge, jnr. 1707 [W]
  Richard, Rose Ash 1721 W
  Richard, Witheridge 1732 W
  Richard, Clovelly 1744 W
  Richard, Thelbridge 1773 W
  Robert, Cruwys Morchard 1775 A
  Sarah, Barnstaple 1844 W
  Stephen, Cruwys Morchard 1759 W
  Susan, Thelbridge 1730 W
  Greneslade Thomas, Oakford 1568 W
  Thomas, Oakford 1635 A
  Thomas, West Worlington 1686 W
  Thomas, Oakford 1706 W
  Greenslade alias Hooper Thomas, Fremington 1709 A
  Thomas, Chawleigh 1724 W
  Thomas, Cheldon 1729 A
  Thomas, Witheridge 1736 W
  Thomas, Buckland Brewer 1750 W
  Thomas, Ilfracombe 1761 W
  Thomas Cutcliffe, Ilfracombe 1840 W
  Grynslade William, Knowstone 1571 W and 1575 W
  Grenslad William, Hartland 1584 W
  William, Witheridge 1705 W
  William, Barnstaple 1711 W
  William, Barnstaple 1722 A
  William, Oakford 1738 W

  William, Barnstaple, maltster 1809 A
  William, Washford Pyne 1819 W
  William, Warkleigh 1829 W
  William, Barnstaple 1837 W
  William, Exford, Minehead, yeoman 1853 A to William, labourer, son
Greenway, Greenaway, Greeneway, Grenewaie, Grenway
  Greeneway ..., Chawleigh 1611 W
  ..., North Molton 1612 [W]
  Christopher, Thelbridge 1729 W
  Elizabeth, North Molton 1619 [W]
  Grenway Joan, North Molton 1602 [W]
  Greenaway John, Charles 1689 W
  Grenewaie Nicholas, King's Nympton 1567 W
  Oliver, North Molton 1602 W
  Richard, South Molton 1636 A
  William, Mariansleigh 1591 [W]
  William, North Molton 1594 [W]
  William, North Molton 1633 W
  William, Thelbridge 1752 A
  William, Witheridge 1822 W
Greenwood Elizabeth, Great Torrington 1632 [W] and 1636 O
  Richard, Bideford 1745 W
  Robert, Great Torrington 1627 and 1631 [W]
  William, East Putford 1855 W
  Zenobia, Great Torrington 1627 and 1631 [W]
Greffen see Griffin
Greffeth, Greffethe see Griffith
Greffey see Griffey
Greffin, Greffinge see Griffin
Greffy see Griffey
Greffyn, Greffynge see Griffin
Gregory, Gregorie, Gregorye
  Agnes, Fremington 1665 A
  Anthony, Petrockstowe 1755 T
  Christopher, Bideford 1710 T
  Gregorie Elizabeth, Barnstaple, widow 1571 W
  Elizabeth, Westleigh 1629 [W]
  Elizabeth, Chittlehampton 1716 A
  Elizabeth, Northam 1796 W
  Emanuel, Filleigh 1666 A
  Frances, Bideford 1661 A
  George, Westleigh 1618 [W]
  George, Bideford 1681 W
  George, Westleigh 1705 W
  George, Northam 1772 W
  George, Instow 1775 A
  Gregorie Henry, Chittlehampton 1575 A
  Gregorie Jacquet, Chittlehampton 1570 W
  James, Westleigh 1710 W
  Joan, Barnstaple 1663 W
  Gregorie John, Barnstaple 1564 W
  Gregorie John, Chittlehampton 1575 W
  Gregorie John, Bow 1616 [W]
  John, Chittlehampton 1624 [W]
  John, Winkleigh 1635 A and 1637 O
  John, Chittlehampton 1640 A
  John, Chittlehampton 1712 W
  John, Littleham (near Bideford) 1712 A
  John, Merton 1725 W
  John, ship *Barfleur* 1758 A
  John, Cruwys Morchard 1763 A
  John, Bideford 1767 W
  John, Petrockstowe 1783 W
  Lewis, Barnstaple 1733 W
  Mary, Northam 1688 W
  Mathew, Winkleigh 1626 [W]
  Oliver, North Tawton 1593 [W]
  Peter, Bow 1601 W
  Gregorie Richard, Atherington 1569 W
  Richard, Chittlehampton 1677 W
  Richard, Westleigh 1690 A
  Richard, Westleigh 1707 A
  Robert, Bow 1611 [W]; forename blank in Ms; supplied from parish register

Robert, Chittlehampton 1712 W
Roger, North Tawton 1713 W
Samuel, Filleigh 1669 O
Simon, Bideford 1677 A
Sybil, Tawstock 1615 [W]
Gregorye Thomas, Westleigh 1586 W
Thomas, Clovelly 1618 [W]
Gregorie Thomasine, Yarnscombe, widow 1564 W
William, Twitchen 1619 [W]
William, Westleigh 1711 A
Willmot, Bondleigh 1636 T
Grendon Joseph, Lapford 1630 [W]
Joseph 1681 see Cooke alias Grendon, Joseph
Mary, Ashreigney 1630 [W]
Philip 1695 see Cock alias Grendon, Philip
Thomas, Buckland Filleigh 1619 [W]
Grendon alias Cooke William, Witheridge 1660 W
Grendon alias Cook William, Lapford 1669 W
William, Alverdiscott 1706 W
Grene see Green
Grenerry John, Barnstaple, exciseman 1823 A to Jemima,
  widow
Greneslade see Greenslade
Grenewaie see Greenway
Grenna John, Chulmleigh 1725 A
Grenny see Grinney
Grenslad see Greenslade
Grenway see Greenway
Gribble, Grebbell, Grebble, Greble, Grible, Grybble
Greble ..., Lapford 1608 and 1613 [W]
Greble Agnes, Bondleigh 1611 [W]; forename blank in Ms;
  supplied from parish register
Grible Bartholomew, Great Torrington 1682 A
Greble Catherine, Barnstaple 1609 [W]; forename blank in
  Ms; supplied from parish register
Catherine, Barnstaple 1627 [W]
Catherine, Barnstaple 1693 W
Grible Edward, Barnstaple 1660 A
Grible Edward, Barnstaple 1694 A and 1703 A
Grible Edward, West Down 1704 A
Edward, Barnstaple 1767 W
Grible Elizabeth, Lapford 1682 A
Elizabeth, Peters Marland 1727 W
Elizabeth, Barnstaple 1752 A
Grebble George, North Tawton 1626 [W]
Grible George, Lapford 1709 W
George, Little Torrington 1732 W
George, Little Torrington 1809 A
George, Little Torrington 1832 A to John, father
Grible Humphrey, South Molton 1660 W
Humphrey, Barnstaple 1677 W
Grebble Isaac, Tawstock 1619 [W] and O
Grebble Joan, Marwood 1570 W
Grebble Joan, Marwood 1621 [W]
Joan, North Tawton 1672 W
John, Parkham 1573 A
Grebbell John, Marwood 1589 W
Greble John, Mortehoe 1593 [W]
Greble John, Barnstaple 1608 [W]; forename blank in Ms;
  supplied from parish register
Greble John, Pilton 1616 [W]
Grebble John, Pilton 1628 [W]
John, Pilton 1642 W
John, Great Torrington 1661 W
Grible John, Pilton 1663 A
John, Barnstaple 1679 W
Grible John, Pilton 1683 A
John, Ilfracombe 1720 A
John, Fremington 1735 A
John, West Down 1747 A
John, mariner 1748 A
John, Little Torrington 1750 A
Jonathan Ivie, Barnstaple 1852 W
Lawrence, Ashreigney 1621 [W]
Lucy, Ilfracombe 1764 A
Grible Margaret, Barnstaple 1696 W

Margaret, Barnstaple 1754 A
Mary, Great Torrington 1678 W
Grible Mary, Barnstaple 1682 W
Grible Mary, Barnstaple 1719 W
Mary Ann, Barnstaple 1832 W
Grebble Oliver, Marwood 1605 W
Greble Philip, Ilfracombe 1577 W
Grebbell Philip, North Tawton 1586 A
Grible Philip, Northam 1674 W
Philip, Northam 1752 W
Greble Richard, Mortehoe 1585 W
Grybble Richard, Tawstock 1630 [W]
Richard, Mortehoe, snr. 1641 W
Grible Richard, Barnstaple 1689 W
Richard, Barnstaple 1738 W
Grebbell Robert, Mortehoe 1581 W
Grebbell Robert, Monkleigh 1594 [W]
Grebble Robert, Great Torrington 1620 [W]
Grible Robert, Lapford 1685 W
Robert, Marwood 1709 A
Robert, Barnstaple 1756 W
Robert Blake, Barnstaple 1836 W
Grybble Roger, Barnstaple 1630 [W] and 1632 O
Grebble Thomas, Tawstock 1586 A
Greble Thomas, Barnstaple 1600 A; forename blank in Ms;
  supplied from parish register
Grebble Thomas, Barnstaple 1626 [W]
Grebble Thomas, Marwood 1628 [W] and 1633 A
Grible Thomas, Pilton 1620 [W]
Grible Thomas, Northam 1686 W
Grible Thomas, Pilton 1706 W
Grible Thomas, Northam 1714 W
Thomas, ship *Royal George* 1746 A
Grebble Thomasine, Mortehoe 1601 W
Greble Thomasine, Tawstock, widow 1603 [W]; forename
  blank in Ms; supplied from parish register
Walter, Barnstaple 1754 A
Grebble William, North Tawton 1634 W
Grible William, South Molton 1700 W
Grible William, Barnstaple 1713 W
Grible William, Great Torrington 1715 W
William, Pilton 1726 W and 1730 W
Grible William, Ilfracombe 1790 W
William, Pilton 1837 W
Griffey, Greffey, Greffy, Griffee, Griffy, Gryffe
Griffy Ann, Pilton 1682 W
Greffy Anthony, Fremington 1626 W
Humphrey, Weare Giffard 1746 W
Humphrey, Northam 1805 A
Gryffe John, Pilton 1576 W
Greffey John, Northam 1712 A
John, Little Torrington 1720 A
John, Monkleigh 1795 W
John, Bideford 1822 A to Richard, carpenter, father
Griffee Richard, Bideford 1735 W
Griffy Thomas, Northam 1629 [W]
Griffy Thomas, Parracombe 1674 A
Thomas, South Molton 1762 W
William, Tawstock, yeoman 1855 A to Elizabeth, widow
Griffies see Griffith
Griffin, Greffen, Greffin, Greffinge, Greffyn, Greffynge,
  Griffine, Griffing, Griffyn, Gryffin, Gryffyn
Greffin Agnes, Mortehoe 1595 [W]
Greffen Agnes, Marwood 1605 W
Amos, Northam 1745 W
Ann, Chittlehampton, widow 1808 A
Greffen Anthony, Ilfracombe 1617 [W]
David, Barnstaple 1699 W
Griffyn Emott, Marwood 1645 W
Greffen Grace, Marwood 1580 W
Greffen Grace, Marwood 1582 A
Henry, Langtree 1718 W
Gryffin Joan, Mortehoe 1643 W
Joan, Bideford 1733 W
Greffyne John, Mortehoe 1566 W

Greffen John, Mortehoe 1584 W
Greffin John, Georgeham 1609 [W]; forename blank in Ms;
    supplied from parish register
Griffyn John, Mortehoe 1642 A
Griffyn John, Marwood 1643 A
John, Marwood 1674 [W]
John, Mortehoe 1687 A
Griffine John, Mortehoe 1696 W
John, Bideford 1733 W
John, Northam 1737 W
John, Chittlehampton 1795 A
John, Shebbear 1830 W
Mary, Northam 1718 W
Mary, Mortehoe 1722 W
Mary, Monkleigh 1749 A
Peter, Berrynarbor 1684 W
Greffen Richard, Mortehoe 1580 A
Greffinge Robert, Mortehoe 1603 W
Griffyn Robert, Ilfracombe 1617 [W]
Greffyn Robert, Ilfracombe 1636 W
Griffing Sarah, Langtree 1713 A
Gryffyn Susan, Ilfracombe 1639 W
Greffen Thomas, Marwood 1609 [W] "of Huish" in register;;
    forename blank in Ms; supplied from parish register
Greffyn Thomas, Nymet Rowland 1616 [W]
Thomas, Marwood 1666 W
Greffyn Thomasine, Marwood 1574 W
Greffyn Walter, Mortehoe 1636 A
William, Chittlehampton, labourer 1857 A to John, labourer,
    father
Griffith, Greffeth, Greffethe, Griffies, Griffita, Griffiths, Griftith
David, Goodleigh 1664 A
Elizabeth, Mortehoe 1792 W
Henry, Marwood 1712 W
Humphrey, Berrynarbor 1775 W
Ingra, Ilfracombe 1638 W
Griffies Jane, Lynton 1818 W
Griffiths Jane, Bideford 1837 W
Greffethe John, Bideford 1581 W
John, Northam 1709 W
Griffies John, Northam 1739 W
John, Little Torrington 1742 A
Griffiths John, Barnstaple 1843 W
Lodovic, Berrynarbor 1702 A
Mary, Weare Giffard 1756 W
Griffiths Mary, Shirwell 1797 A
Mary, Barnstaple 1832 W
Griftith Morgan, Roborough 1664 W
Nathaniel, Bideford 1725 W
Greffeth Oliver, Barnstaple 1603 W
Greffeth alias Arthure Richard, Barnstaple 1585 O bond
Greffeth Richard, Barnstaple 1587 W
Robert, Bideford 1741 A
Samuel, Barnstaple 1756 W
Griffita Thomas, Barnstaple 1731 A
Thomas, Barnstaple 1743 A
Griffiths Thomas, Bideford, druggist 1807 A
William, Pilton 1643 A
William, Pilton 1740 A
Griffiths William, Northam 1754 A
William, Ilfracombe 1815 W
Griffiths William, Berrynarbor 1834 A to Frances, widow
Grigg, Grig, Grigg, Grygg, Grygge
Cecilia, Parkham 1641 W
Grace, Shirwell, widow 1852 A to John, blacksmith, son
Helena, Hartland 1660 A
Grig John, Hartland 1605 W
Grygge John, Hartland 1636 W
John, Bideford 1676 A
John, Littleham (near Bideford) 1692 W
John, Merton 1738 A
John, Monkleigh 1826 W
John, Littleham (near Bideford) 1854 W
Joseph, Peters Marland 1711 W
Josiah, Shebbear 1665 W

Lawrence, Bideford 1682 W
Margaret, Shebbear 1702 W
Mary, Merton 1813 W
Mary, Westleigh 1833 A
Grig Nicholas, Woolfardisworthy 1593 [W]
Grygg Nicholas, Bideford 1637 [W]
Grigge Philip, Parkham 1617 [W]
Reuben, Parkham 1857 W
Richard, Hartland 1720 A
Richard, Littleham (near Bideford) 1819 W
Richard, Parkham 1843 W
Sarah, Hartland 1765 A
Grigge Thomas, Parkham 1612 [W]; forename blank in Ms;
    supplied from parish register
Grigge Thomas, Northam 1623 [W]
William, Bow 1597 [W]
William, 1693 A
William, 1785 A
William, 1845 W
Grigge Willmot, 1639 W
Grills John, Bideford 1667 A
Richard, Langtree 1681 A
Grimshire Elizabeth, Bratton Fleming 1843 A to Mary Ann
    Lashbrook of Lynton, sister
John, Lynton 1799 W
Mary, Lynton 1831 W
Grindham Mary, Barnstaple 1733 W
Grindon
Grindon alias Crooke John, Witheridge 1580 W
Philip, Mariansleigh 1743 A
Grindon alias Cooke Thomas, Witheridge 1644 W
Grining see Greening
Grinney, Grenny
Grenny Joan, Meshaw 1854 W
Philip, Chittlehampton, innholder 1798 A
William, Meshaw 1839 W
Grinshaw Elizabeth, Bratton Fleming 1843 A
Groaes, Groase, Groass see Grosse
Grodon James, Parracombe 1708 W
Grome Agnes, Satterleigh 1583 W
Richard, Satterleigh 1580 W
Groselier Andrew, Bideford 1712 A
Grosse, Groaes, Groase, Groass, Grose
Groass Hugh, Lynton 1703 W
Grose Joan, Mortehoe, widow 1600 W
Grose Joan, Mortehoe 1638 A
Grose Joan, Brendon 1711 W
John, Lynton 1692 A
Groase John, Lynton, snr. 1696 W
Groaes John, Lynton 1771 W
Grove, Groue, Groves
..., Ilfracombe 1610 and 1612 [W]
Groue Ann, Marwood 1677 W
Groves Elizabeth, Lynton 1749 A
Groves Hugh, Lynton 1738 and 1742 A
Israel, Fremington 1786 W
Groue Joan, Ilfracombe 1605 W
John, Ilfracombe 1579 A
Grones John, Mortehoe 1580 W
John, Pilton 1631 [W]
Groves John, Trentishoe, jnr. 1827 W
Groves John, Lynton 1830 W
Groves John Heale, Ilfracombe 1856 A
Lodovic, Georgeham 1643 W
Groves Mary, Lynton 1845 W
Philip, Ilfracombe 1602 W; forename blank in Ms; supplied
    from parish register
Rebecca, Barnstaple 1629 [W]
Rebecca, Shirwell 1770 W
Groves Thomas, Countisbury 1820 A to Elizabeth, widow
Groves William, Barnstaple 1828 W
Grudgeworthy, Grudeworthy, Grudgeworthie, Grudgworthie,
    Grudgworthy
Grudgworthy Anthony, Parkham 1638 W
Grudgworthie Catherine, Westleigh 1584 W

Grudgworthie George, Westleigh 1587 A account
Grudgworthy Humphrey, Winkleigh 1626 [W]
Grudgworthy Humphrey, Winkleigh 1687 W
Isott, Winkleigh 1630 [W]
Joan, Winkleigh 1631 [W]
Grudgworthy John, Bideford 1690 A
Grudgworthy Lydia, Ashreigney 1690 A
Grudgeworthie Nicholas, Parkham 1569 W
Grudgworthy Nicholas, Winkleigh 1724 W
Grudgeworthie Reynold, Westleigh 1579 W
Samuel, Winkleigh 1771 W
Grudgworthy Thomas, Winkleigh 1667 W
Grudeworthy Thomas, Ashreigney 1726 W
Grudgworthy William, Parkham 1664 W
Grute John, Barnstaple 1685 W
Grybble see Gribble
Gryffe see Griffey
Gryffin, Gryffyn see Griffin
Grygg, Grygge see Grigg
Grynslade see Greenslade
Guard Josiah, North Tawton 1700 W
Philip, Chittlehampton 1805 W
Philip, Chittlehampton 1852 W
Thomas, Landcross 1840 A to Sarah, widow
William, Yarnscombe 1730 W
Gubb, Gubbe, Gubbo
Anthony, King's Nympton 1706 A
Anthony, Bratton Fleming 1714 W
Anthony, Bratton Fleming 1748 W
Edward, Bratton Fleming 1720 W
Edward, Bratton Fleming 1738 W
Emanuel, Goodleigh 1639 W
Gubbe Helen, Bratton Fleming 1626 [W]
Gubbo Henry, Bratton Fleming 1577 W
Henry, Bratton Fleming 1745 W
Henry, Marwood 1765 W
Humphrey, Bratton Fleming 1582 W
Jane, Bratton Fleming 1706 W
Joan, Bratton Fleming 1583 W
Joan, King's Nympton 1706 W
Joan, Bratton Fleming 1763 W
Gubbe John, Bratton Fleming 1574 W
John, Burrington 1679 A
John, Bratton Fleming 1682 W
John, Bratton Fleming 1708 W and 1718 A
John, Bratton Fleming 1775 A
John, Kentisbury 1787 A
John, Combe Martin, woolcomber 1808 W
John, Combe Martin 1812 A to Ann, widow
John, Combe Martin, mariner 1815 A to Elizabeth wife of
    John Harris, widow of deceased
Gubbe Margaret, Barnstaple 1624 [W]
Gubbe Margery, South Molton 1629 [W]
Mary, Bratton Fleming 1710 W
Mary, Bratton Fleming 1744 W
Richard, Bratton Fleming 1684 W
Richard, Bratton Fleming, snr. 1700 W
Richard, Arlington 1717 W
Richard, Barnstaple 1728 W
Richard, Kentisbury 1748 A
Richard, West Buckland 1749 W
Robert, Loxhore 1631 [W]
Robert, Shirwell 1700 A
Robert, Bratton Fleming 1704 W
Thomas, Combe Martin 1780 W
Thomas, Combe Martin 1844 W
Gubbe William, Bratton Fleming 1574 W
Gubbe William, West Buckland 1591 [W]
Gubbe William, South Molton 1626 [W]
William, Bratton Fleming 1720 W
William, Combe Martin 1838 W
Guerston Thomas, Scotland 1735 A
Guest, Gest, Geste, Jest
Gest Alfred, Bideford 1576 A
Gest Anthony, Welcombe 1633 A

Charles, Sheepwash 8 Jul 1837 W; 2nd grant 1845
Gest Joan, Bideford 1624 [W]
Gest Joan, Chawleigh 1643 O
Geste John, Great Torrington 1573 W
Gest John, Welcombe 1621 W
John, Barnstaple 1853 W
Jest Marmaduke, Barnstaple 1724 W
Geste Simon, Abbotsham 1577 W
Gest Thomas, Bideford 1644 W
Guilford Robert, Chittlehampton 1706 A
Gulley, Gully
Catherine, Chittlehampton 1843 W
Gully Eleanor see Philip Cottey
Gully George, Kentisbury 1692 A
John, Swimbridge 1840 W
Lawrence, Chittlehampton 1792 W
Richard, Chittlehampton 1827 A to Catherine, widow
Gullock, Gullocks
George, Warkleigh 1693 W
Gullocks John, King's Nympton 1640 W
Gully see Gulley
Gunn, Gun, Gune, Gunne
Absalom, South Molton 1765 A
Gunne Agnes, South Molton 1586 W
Geoffrey, Rackenford 1787 W
Honoria, South Molton 1694 W
Joan, Rackenford 1731 W
Gunne John, North Molton 1580 W
Gune John, South Molton 1584 W
John, Rackenford, husbandman 1801 W
Gun Margaret, South Molton 1665 W
Mary, Great Torrington 1854 W
Gunne Richard, Witheridge 1625 W
Robert, South Molton 1686 W
Robert, South Molton 1760 W
Gune alias Hawkyne Roger, West Buckland 1569 W
Gun Thomas, South Molton 1663 W
Thomas, Rackenford 1754 W
Thomas, Witheridge 1800 W
Thomas, Great Torrington, mason 1821 A to Mary, widow
Walter, Rackenford 1692 A
William, Rackenford 1827 A
Gunnion, Gunnyeon
Sarah, Bideford 1708 W
Gunnyeon Thomas, Bideford 1734 W
Gunter, Guntor
Guntor ..., Lapford 1606 [W]
Robert, Lapford 1599 [W]
Robert, Lapford 1663 W
Gupwill Christopher, Charles 1635 W
Joan, Charles 1581 W
Gurrant, Gourrant
Alice, Great Torrington 1628 [W]
Elizabeth, Clovelly 1565 W
Gourrant John, South Molton 1584 W
John, Great Torrington 1624 [W]
Walter, Great Torrington 1599 [W]
Walter, Great Torrington 1623 [W]
Gurrell Robert, Abbotsham 1674 W
Gutter Joan, Northam 1620 [W]
John, Northam 1620 [W]
Guy Arthur, Barnstaple 1643 A
Joseph, Winkleigh 1669 W
Guyer or Gayer Robert, Huntshaw 1643 A
Gwyn, Guyn
Guyn Jacques, Bideford 1641 W
Thomas, Bideford 1635 W
Gybbe, Gybbes see Gibbs
Gybbons see Gibbons
Gyles see Giles
Gyll see Gill
Gylles see Giles
Gylle see Gill
Gyst, Gyste see Gist
Gyttsham see Gitsham

Hacche, Hache see Hatche
Hackaland Edward, Northam 1668 A
Hacker John, Barnstaple 1578 A
  John, Frithelstock 1586 W
  John, Martinhoe 1619 [W]
  Mary, Combe Martin 1757 W
  Robert, Northam 1675 W
  William, Northam 1705 A
Hackerydge see Hawkridge
Hackwell, Hackewell, Hackwill, Hakewell
  Hackwill Ebbot 1834 [W]
  Jeremiah, St Giles in the Wood 1787 A
  Hackewell Joan, Great Torrington 1575 W
  John, Great Torrington 1808 W*
  Hackwill John, Martinhoe 1832 W
  Hackwill John, St Giles in the Wood 1834 W
  Hackwill Mary, St Giles in the Wood 1727 A
  Hackwill Mary, Martinhoe 1736 W
  Robert, Great Torrington 1666 A
  Thomas, Dolton 1758 W
  Thomas, Little Torrington, yeoman 1813 A to Ebbott, widow
  Hakewell William, Brendon 1698 W
  Hakewell William, Brendon 1710 W
  William, St Giles in the Wood 1715 W
  Hackwill William, St Giles in the Wood, yeoman 1798 W
  Hackwill William, Langtree 1842 W
Hadland John, Dowland 1838 W
Hagley, Haghlegh
  George, Witheridge 1687 W
  Haghlegh Nicholas, Witheridge 1588 A
Haies see Hayes
Haiman see Hayman
Haine, Haines see Haynes
Haiwood see Heywood
Hakewell see Hackwell
Hale John, Northam, jnr. 1772 W
Hall, Halle
  Abigail, Landcross 1750 W
  Elizabeth, Bideford 1830 W
  Emanuel, Instow 1786 W
  Emanuel, Northam 1802 W
  Halle George, Weare Giffard 1595 [W]
  Jacquet, Weare Giffard, widow 1572 W
  Halle James, Weare Giffard 1721 W
  James, Bideford 1740 W
  Jane, Bideford 1804 W
  Joan, Bideford 1665 W
  Halle John, Weare Giffard 1596 [W]
  John, Bideford 1809 W
  Margaret, Bideford 1816 W
  Mathew, Barnstaple 1676 W
  Mathew, Barnstaple 1733 W
  Richard, Weare Giffard 1571 W
  Halle Richard, Weare Giffard 1599 [W]
  Halle Richard, Weare Giffard 1617 [W]
  Richard, Weare Giffard 1681 W
  Halle Roger, Weare Giffard 1601 W
  Samuel, Yarnscombe 1744 A
  Thomas, Fremington 1744 W
  Thomas, Bideford 1821 W
  Halle William, Tawstock 1616 [W]
Hallaford, Halloford
  Giles, Hartland 1663 W
  Halloford Grace, Merton 1670 W
Halle see Hall
Hallitt, Hallote
  Hallote Bernard, Hartland 1662 W
  Peter, Hartland 1660 W
Halloford see Hallaford
Hallote see Hallitt
Hallsbury, Halsbery
  Halsbery or Salisburie ..., Pilton 1615 [W]
  Mabel, Pilton 1621 [W]
Halse, Halls, Hals
  ..., Great Torrington 1608 [W]

  ..., Chittlehampton 1609 [W] and 1611 [W]
  ..., High Bickington 1610 [W]
  ..., Bideford 1611 [W]
  Agnes, Chittlehampton 1641 W
  Alexander, Warkleigh 1686 W
  Alice, Great Torrington 1619 [W]
  Angela, Great Torrington 1629 [W]
  Ann, St Giles in the Wood 1689 W
  Anthony, Atherington 1568 W
  Arthur, Chittlehampton 1717 A
  Baldwin, Chittlehampton 1730 W
  Halls Catherine, Bideford 1731 W
  Halls Catherine, Northam 1769 A
  Dorothy, Bideford 1696 A
  Edward, Fremington 1628 [W] and 1629 O
  Elizabeth, Zeal Monachorum 1578 W
  Elizabeth, Chittlehampton 1630 [W]
  Halls Emanuel, Northam 1832 W
  Emma, Charles 1715 W
  Frances, Chittlehampton 1641 A
  Halls Francis, Chittlehampton 1736 A
  Halls Grace, Bideford 1819 W
  Henry, High Bickington 1643 W
  Halls Hugh, Great Torrington 1744 A
  Halls James, Bideford 1744 W
  Halls James, Yarnscombe 1803 W
  Halls James, Barnstaple 1816 W
  Joan, Chittlehampton 1591 [W]
  John, Little Torrington 1587 W
  John, Great Torrington 1601 W
  Hales John, Barnstaple 1625 [W] and 1626 O
  John, Georgeham 1631 [W]
  John, Fremington 1637 A
  John, St Giles in the Wood 1663 W
  John, Bideford 1664 A
  John, Fremington 1669 A
  John, Great Torrington 1687 A
  John, Warkleigh 1700 A
  Halls John, Barnstaple 1816 W
  Halls John, Merton 1821 W
  Halls John, Tawstock 1833 W
  John, Molland 1853 W
  Halls John Avery, Great Torrington 1843 W
  Halls Joseph, Great Torrington 1775 W
  Halls Joseph, Northam, woolcomber 1808 A
  Lawrence, Chittlehampton 1598 [W]
  Lewis, Molland, yeoman 1803 W
  Lewis, Molland 1841 W
  Mallett, South Molton 1696 A
  Mary, Chittlehampton 1717 W
  Halls Mary, Barnstaple 1732 A
  Mary, Barnstaple 1787 A
  Halse alias Knill Mary wife of William Halls, Fremington
    1709 A; forename blank in Ms; supplied from parish register
  Mathew, Yarnscombe 1598 [W]
  Michael, Bideford 1636 A
  Philip, Georgeham 1643 W
  Philip, Ilfracombe 1692 A
  Philip, King's Nympton 1711 W
  Halls Philip, Northam 1742 W
  Hals Philip, Cheldon 1829 W
  Philip, Molland 1834 W
  Halls Philip, Northam, mason 1848 A (Merton) to William of
    Dolton, mason, son
  Richard, Great Torrington 1616 [W]
  Halls Robert, Northam 1727 W
  Halls Robert, Tawstock 1813 W
  Stephen, Georgeham 1687 W
  Hales Thomas, Chittlehampton 1573 W
  Thomas, Warkleigh 1670 W
  Halls Thomas, Abbotsham 1746 A
  Halls Thomas, Barnstaple 1759 W
  Thomas, West Worlington 1827 A to Ann, widow
  Thomasine, Warkleigh 1688 W
  William, Chittlehampton 1638 A and 1639 O

William, Great Torrington 1669 W and 1671 O
William, Alwington 1703 W
William, Barnstaple 1709 W
Halls William, Bideford 1725 W
William, Great Torrington 1734 W
Halls William, Merton 1743 W
Halls William, Barnstaple 1746 W
Halls William, Bideford 1784 A
Halls William, Barnstaple 1840 W
Halswill, Halswell
... 1603 [W]
..., Abbotsham 1612 O
Halswell Walter, Abbotsham 1593 [W]
Ham John, Northam 1684 A
Hamacot see Honacott
Hamant see Hammond
Hamblin, Hambling, Hambly see Hamlyn
Hamet, Hamett see Hammett
Hamlyn, Hamblin, Hambling, Hambly, Hamlin
..., Parracombe 1612 [W]
Ann, Hartland 1709 W
Hamlin Anthony, Clovelly 1727 A
Hamlin Anthony, Clovelly 1746 A
Beatrice, Ilfracombe 1779 W
Catherine, Tawstock 1709 W
Dorothy, Bideford 1850 W
Hambly Elizabeth, Welcombe 1787 W
Emma, Tawstock 1597 [W]
Grace, Parkham 1679 A
Hannah, Barnstaple 1709 A
Hugh or Philip, Bideford 1612 [W]; forename blank in Ms;
    supplied from parish register
James, Tawstock 1714 W
James, Tawstock 1726 A
Hambly James, Woolfardisworthy 1753 A
James, Buckland Brewer, yeoman 1807 A
Joan, Hartland, widow 1602 [W]; forename blank in Ms;
    supplied from parish register
Joan, Northam 1633 [W]
John, Tawstock 1585 [W]
John, Tawstock 1619 [W]
John, Northam 1625 [W]
John, Abbotsham 1693 W
John, Barnstaple 1693 W
John, Tawstock 1706 A
Hamlin John, Clovelly 1746 W
Hamlin John, Hartland 1768 A
John, Hartland 1772 W
John, Hartland 1822 W
John, Bideford, insurance agent 1857 A to George Brayley of
    Bideford, gentleman, jnr., creditor
Joseph, Clovelly 1702 A
Hamlin Joseph, Clovelly 1725 W
Mary, Tawstock 1643 W
Mary, Tawstock 1726 A
Mary, Clovelly 1788 W
Rebecca, Barnstaple 1697 A
Richard, Tawstock 1628 [W]
Richard, Tawstock 1692 W
Hamblin Robert, Clovelly 1755 A
Robert, Bideford 1849 A
Sidwell, Tawstock 1630 [W]
Thomas, Clovelly 1781 W
Thomas, Clovelly, yeoman 1808 A
William, Frithelstock 1565 W
William, Hartland 1591 [W]
William, Woolfardisworthy 1615 [W]
William, Woolfardisworthy 1639 W
Hambling William, Barnstaple 1681 W
Hamlin William, Barnstaple 1687 W
Hamblyn William, Hartland 1702 W
Hamlin William, Abbotsham 1732 W
Hamlin William, Parkham 1746 W
Hamlin William, Clovelly 1762 A
Willmot, Hartland 1669 A and 1672 O

Hammersley Jane see John Brown
Hammett, Hamet, Hamett, Hammet, Hammott, Hamott
Hamott ..., East Down 1607, 1611 and 1612 [W]
Hamott ..., Heanton Punchardon 1610 [W]
Hamott ..., Bratton Fleming 1612 [W]
Hamott Alice, Tawstock 1603 W
Amy, Northam, Appledore, widow 1797 W
Hamett Ann, Parracombe 1599 [W]
Ann, Clovelly 1768 W
Hamett Anthony, Welcombe 1635 W
Hamett Bernard, Winkleigh 1598 [W]
Hammet Bernard, Clovelly 1690 W
Hamott Christian, Heanton Punchardon 1617 [W]
Hamett Christopher, King's Nympton 1638 [W]
Edward, East Down 1665 A
Hamott Elizabeth, Peters Marland 1669 W
Francis, West Worlington 1700 W
Francis, Chulmleigh 1819 W
Francis see also Ann Rogers
Grace, Winkleigh 1691 A
Grace, Northam 1732 W
Hamott Henry, Winkleigh 1611 [W]; forename blank in Ms;
    supplied from parish register
Henry, Fremington 1728 A
Hamett James, Atherington 1619 [W]
Hammet James, Northam 1704 A
James, Northam 1741 W
James, Clovelly 1750 A
James, Winkleigh 1750 W
James, Bondleigh 1847 W
Jane, South Molton 1740 W
Jesse, Northam 1769 A
Hamett Joan, Ilfracombe 1615 [W]
Hamett Joan, Iddesleigh 1636 W
Hammet Joan, Shebbear 1679 W
Hamett Joel, Iddesleigh 1636 A
Hammott John, East Down 1597 [W]
Hamott John, Tawstock 1603 W
Hamott John, Ilfracombe 1613 [W]; forename blank in Ms;
    supplied from parish register
Hamett John, Northam 1619 [W]
Hamett John, Welcombe 1624 [W]
Hamett John, Ashreigney 1626 [W]
John, Great Torrington 1664 W
Hamett John, Winkleigh 1687 W
John, Zeal Monachorum 1690 A
Hamett John, Tawstock 1704 A
Hamett John, Great Torrington 1709 W
John, Abbotsham 1731 W
John, Bideford 1741 W
John, Zeal Monachorum 1751 W
John, Fremington 1754 A
John, Winkleigh 1763 W
John, Chulmleigh 1782 W
John, West Worlington 1834 A to Philip of Lapford, brother
Jonathan, Great Torrington 1742 A
Lawrence, Bratton Fleming 1664 W
Marshall, Abbotsham 1664 W
Hamett Martha, Winkleigh 1630 [W]
Mary, Northam 1797 W
Mary, Zeal Monachorum 1852 W
Miles, Northam 1631 W
Miles, Northam 1727 W
Hamett Nicholas, Northam 1685 A
Nicholas, ship *York* 1758 A
Hammott Pentecost, Fremington 1592 [W]
Pentecost, Fremington 1682 W
Hammet Peter, Northam 1711 A
Philip, Shirwell 1663 W
Philip, Lapford 1839 W
Hamett Priscilla, Iddesleigh 1639 W
Hamett Ralph, Marwood 1642 W
Hamett Richard, Atherington 1619 [W]
Hamett Richard, Welcombe 1633 W
Richard, Clovelly 1771 A

Hammot Robert, Instow 1678 A
Hamett Roger, Fremington 1637 W
Hammet Sarah, Bideford 1713 W
Hamett Stephen, Northam 1698 A
Hamott Stephen, Northam 1703 W
Stephen, Chulmleigh 1744 W
Hamett Thomas, Kentisbury 1598 [W]
Thomas, Bideford 1729 W
Hamet Tristram, Bideford 1675 A
Hamett Walter, Martinhoe 1622 [W]
Hamett Walter, Northam 1625 [W]
Hammott William, Winkleigh 1581 A
William, Peters Marland 1666 W
William, Chulmleigh 1724 W
Hammet William, Chawleigh 1732 A
William, Northam 1780 W
Willmot, Northam 1741 W
Winifred, Heanton Punchardon 1686 A
Hammond, Hamant, Hammon, Hammonde, Hammont, Hamon,
    Hamond, Hamonde, Hamont, Hamonte, Hamount
Hamond Andrew, East Down 1694 W
Andrew, East Down 1735 W
Andrew Cobley, Charles 1825 A to Edward of Barnstaple,
    brother
Ann, Charles 1817 W
Ann, Loxhore 1827 W
Hamond Anthony, East Down 1618 [W] and O
Anthony, Combe Martin 1775 W
Hamond Dorothy, High Bray 1682 W
Edward, Barnstaple 1720 W
Edward, High Bray 1753 W
Edward, Charles 1789 W
Edward, Loxhore, yeoman 1808 W
Edward, Charles 1822 W
Elizabeth, East Down 1725 W
Elizabeth, Lapford 1759 W
Elizabeth, Fremington 1831 W
George, Georgeham 1748 A
Harriet, Charles 1825 A to Edward of Barnstaple, brother
Hugh, South Molton 1685 W
Hugh, Arlington 1732 W
Hugh, Heanton Punchardon 1780 W
Hugh, Heanton Punchardon, yeoman 1800 W
Hamond Joan, Iddesleigh 1590 [W]
Hamont Joan, Tawstock 1592 [W]
Hamond Joan, Kentisbury 1621 [W]
Hamant or Hamott John, Tawstock 1603 W
Hamond John, East Down 1625 [W]
Hamond John, East Down 1677 W
Hamond John, Winkleigh 1680 W
John, Winkleigh 1681 A
John, Barnstaple 1685 A
John, Heanton Punchardon 1691 W
John, East Down 1725 W
John, Heanton Punchardon 1730 W
John, Loxhore 1732 W
John, Dowland 1734 A
John, East Down 1742 A
John, Arlington 1763 W
John, Barnstaple, beadle 1809 W
Hamonde Margery, Instow 1616 [W]
Hammont Mark, Instow 1715 W
Hamonde Mary, East Down 1618 [W]
Mary, Heanton Punchardon 1821 W
Mathew, Arlington 1692 W
Nicholas, Loxhore 1687 W
Hamond Nicholas, Bratton Fleming 1716 A
Nicholas, High Bray 1722 W
Hamond Philip, Loxhore 1705 W
Hamonte Radigon, Winkleigh 1579 W
Hamant Richard, Great Torrington 1574 W
Hammonde Richard, East Down 1589 A
Hamond Richard, East Down 1629 [W]
Hamond Robert, Instow 1580 W
Hamond Robert, Northam 1591 [W]

Hamond Robert, Arlington 1644 W
Hamond Robert, Atherington 1669 A
Sarah, Combe Martin 1781 W
Hamon Simon, Roborough 1831 A
Thomas, Iddesleigh 1577 W
Hamount alias Watts Thomas, High Bray 1577 W
Walter, West Down 1604 W
Hamond William, Tawstock 1583 W
Hamont William, Buckland Brewer 1588 W
Hamond William, Barnstaple 1589 W
Hamond William, North Molton 1621 [W]
William, Berrynarbor 1665 W
Hamond William, East Down 1672 W
William, Heanton Punchardon 1699 A
William, East Down 1716 W and 1726 W
William, Heanton Punchardon 1739 A
William, North Molton 1744 W
William, Heanton Punchardon, yeoman 1811 W
William, Dowland 1828 W
Hammot, Hammott, Hamott see Hammett
Hamount see Hammond
Hampton, Heannpton, Hempton, Hemyton
Heannpton ..., Chulmleigh 1610 [W]
Hempton ..., Washford Pyne 1612 [W]
Hempton Agnes, Puddington 1634 W
Hemyton Edward, Washford Pyne 1623 [W]
Hanaforde see Handford
Hanam James, South Molton 1703 W
Hance Welthian, Great Torrington 1633 A and O
Hancock, Hancocke, Hancoke, Handcock
Handcock ..., Combe Martin 1609 [W]
Agnes, Ashreigney 1815 W
Hancoke Alice, Berrynarbor 1586 W
Hancocke Andrew, Alverdiscott 1636 W
Hancocke Digory, Petrockstowe 1636 A
Dorothy and Edward, Combe Martin 1664 W
Edward and Dorothy, Combe Martin 1664 W
Edward, Barnstaple 1810 W transmitted to Doctor's Commons
Hancocke Elizabeth, Barnstaple 1628 [W]
Handcock English, Molland 1719 W
George, Ilfracombe 1840 W
Handcock Henry, Knowstone 1757 W
Henry, Knowstone 1790 W
James, Knowstone 1748 A
James, Westleigh 1805 W
Jane, High Bray 1679 W
Handcocke Joan, Marwood 1595 [W]
Joan, Barnstaple 1727 W
Hancoke John, Atherington 1583 W
Hancoke John, Lynton 1584 W
Handcocke John, Combe Martin 1599 [W]
Handcock John, Berrynarbor 1606 W
Handcock John, North Molton 1615 [W] and 1617 W
Hancocke John, Combe Martin 1631 [W]
John, Pilton 1643 A
John, Tawstock 1668 W
Handcock John, High Bray 1685 W
John, Combe Martin, esquire 1693 W
Handcock John, Barnstaple 1721 A
Handcock John, Knowstone 1758 A
Handcock John, Barnstaple 1761 W
Handcock John, Northam 1764 A
Handcock John, West Down 1766 A
John, Ashreigney, yeoman 1819 A to Jennifer, widow
Handcock John, Coldridge 1828 A
John, Northam 1841 W
John, Georgeham 1849 W
John, Marwood 1850 W
John and Margaret, Combe Martin 1688 [W]
Judith, Berrynarbor 1669 W
Margaret and John, Combe Martin 1668 [W]
Mary, Ilfracombe 1706 A
Handcock Mary, South Molton 1751 W
Handcock Mary, Parkham 1843 W
Nathaniel, Parkham 1841 W

Handcock Nicholas, Berrynarbor 1614 [W]; forename blank in
    Ms; supplied from parish register
Nicholas, High Bray 1660 A
Nicholas, Barnstaple 1835 W
Handcock Peter, Barnstaple 1616 [W]
Handcocke Richard, Combe Martin 1593 [W]
Richard, Weare Giffard 1674 W
Handcock Richard, Tawstock 1706 W
Richard, Bideford 1740 A
Handcock Richard, Ilfracombe 1741 W
Robert, Dolton 1686 W
Handcock Robert, Ashreigney 1766 W
Robert, Ashreigney, yeoman 1808 W
Robert, South Molton 1848 W and 1850 W
Handcock Samuel, Stoodleigh 1668 A
Handcock Samuel, Dolton 1777 W
Simon, Barnstaple 1729 A
Handcock Susan, Northam 1771 W
Susan, Pilton 1819 W
Handcock alias Gamon Sybil, Pilton 1668 A
Handcock Thomas, Pilton 1742 W
Handcock Thomas, Ilfracombe 1792 W
Handcock Thomas, Winkleigh 1805 W*
Thomas, Combe Martin 1816 W
Thomas, Ashreigney 1849 W
Thomas, Ilfracombe 1851 A
Hancocke Thomasine, North Molton 1620 [W]
Handcock William, Ilfracombe 1704 W
Handcock William, Ilfracombe, jnr. 1704 W
William, Knowstone 1712 A
Handcock William, Knowstone 1758 A
Handcock William, Ilfracombe 1779 W
Hancocke Willmot, Lynton 1621 [W]
Hander Thomas, Hartland 1763 W
Handford, Hanaforde, Handforde, Hanford, Hunford
..., High Bickington 1602 A and 1604 W
..., Chulmleigh 1604 [W]
Handforde ..., Beaford 1606 [W]
..., Ilfracombe 1607 and 1608 [W]
..., North Tawton 1610 [W]
Alfred, North Tawton 1626 [W]
Amos, Merton 1731 W
Ann, South Molton 1782 W; 1791 A dbn
Anthony, Ilfracombe 1601 W
Anthony, Rackenford 1621 [W]
Hanford Bartholomew, Ilfracombe 1643 W
Christopher, Rackenford 1607 [W]; forename blank in Ms;
    supplied from parish register
Eleanor, South Molton 1771 A
Ellen, West Anstey 1727 W
George, Winkleigh 1634 A
Hunford George, Rackenford 1642 A
George, Roborough 1662 W
George, Northam 1708 W
George, Marwood 1771 W
George, Rackenford 1793 W
Grace, East Anstey 1762 W
Henry, Merton 1688 W
James, Atherington 1758 A
James, South Molton 1790 W
Handforde Joan, Atherington 1584 W
Hanaforde John, Dolton 1580 W
John, High Bickington 1592 [W]
John, Rackenford 1619 [W]
Hanford John, North Tawton 1637 W
John, Burrington 1640 A
John, Roborough 1664 A
Hanford John, Northam 1675 W
Hanford John, Westleigh 1676 A
John, Langtree 1691 W
John, Yarnscombe 1709 W
John, Dolton 1763 W
John, Beaford 1827 W
Margaret, Buckland Brewer 1592 [W]
Margaret, Trentishoe 1663 W

Hanford Martin, Bideford 1666 A
Mary 1833 W
Hanford Nicholas, Bideford 1677 W
Handforde Oliver, Burrington 1575 W
Philip, Ilfracombe 1607 [W]; forename blank in Ms; supplied
    from parish register
Philip, East Anstey 1785 W
Richard, Yarnscombe 1634 W
Hannford Richard, Northam 1669 W
Richard, Rackenford 1714 A
Robert, High Bray 1575 W
Robert, Barnstaple 1632 [W]
Hunford Robert, Chittlehampton 1642 W
Robert, Chittlehampton 1694 W
Robert, Westleigh 1701 W
Rose, High Bickington 1677 W (2)
Hanford Thomas, Rackenford 1597 [W]
Hanford Thomas, Burrington 1641 W
Hanford Thomas, Westleigh 1673 W
Thomas, East Anstey 1750 W
Thomas, Barnstaple 1800 A
Thomas, Bideford, innkeeper 1803 W
Thomas, Winkleigh 1805 W
Thomas, Chittlehampton 1811 W
Hanford Thomasine, Trentishoe 1638 W
Hanford Thomasine, Rackenford 1638 W
Walter, Burrington 1639 A
Handforde William, Dolton 1568 W
William, Atherington 1575 W
William, Bideford 1608 [W]; forename blank in Ms; supplied
    from parish register
Hanford William, Trentishoe 1641 A
William, Rackenford, yeoman 1804 W
Hanger, Honger
Abigail, Parkham 1715 A
Honger David, Bideford 1707 A
Eleanor, Bideford 1660 A
Eleanor, Bideford 1661 W
Elizabeth, Woolfardisworthy 1688 A
John, Woolfardisworthy 1566 W
John, Alwington or Atherington 1646 W
John, Bideford 1661 W
Richard, Woolfardisworthy 1531 [W]
Richard, Woolfardisworthy 1637 [W]
Richard, Woolfardisworthy 1661 A
Richard, Northam 1712 A
Thomas, Woolfardisworthy 1623 [W]
Thomas, Buckland Brewer 1674 [W]
Thomas, Woolfardisworthy 1684 W
Thomas, Dolton 1820 A to Elizabeth, widow
William, Abbotsham 1636 [W]
Hanmer John, Barnstaple 1674 [W]
Harapath see Harrapath
Harbert, Harbett
David, Northam 1693 A
Harbett Henry, Instow 1721 W
Harbottle, Harbottell
Harbottell Ralph, Great Torrington 1606 W
Thomas, Great Torrington 1642 W
Harde see Hearde
Harder see Hearder
Harding, Hardinge, Hearden, Hearding, Heardinge, Herdinge,
    Herdon, Herdynge, Hurdon
Hearding Amesius, Combe Martin 1672 W
Hearding Ann, Arlington 1696 A
Ann, Parracombe 1801 W
Ann Courtenay, Combe Martin, widow 1855 A to James Nott
    Harding of South Molton, gentleman, son
Hardinge Anthony, Marwood 1586 W
Anthony, Marwood 1771 W
Charles, Pilton 1817 W
Charles, Pilton 1828 W
Christopher, ship *Augusta* 1746 W
Hearding David, Tawstock 1632 [W]
Hearding Edward, Mortehoe 1736 W

Hearding Edward, East Down 1742 W
Elizabeth, Fremington 1761 W
Elizabeth, Combe Martin 1763 W
Elizabeth, Weare Giffard 1770 W
Elizabeth, Chulmleigh 1773 W
Elizabeth, Combe Martin 1776 W
Herdinge Elizabeth, Barnstaple 1571 W
Heardinge Geoffrey, Heanton Punchardon 1598 [W]
Grace, Parracombe 1855 W
Hearding Henry, Parracombe 1710 W
Hearding Henry, Barnstaple 1725 W
Hearding Henry, Combe Martin 1728 W
Henry, mariner 1747 A
Henry, Combe Martin 1768 W
Henry, Parracombe 1781 W
Henry, Combe Martin 1782 A
Henry, Trentishoe 1834 A to Elizabeth, widow
Humphrey, Northam 1770 W
James, Berrynarbor 1838 W
James, South Molton, gentleman 4 Aug 1847 A to Elizabeth of
   27 Dorset Street, London, sp., sister and Robert of
   Barnstaple, surgeon; further A dbn 1848
Heardinge Joan, Marwood 1601 W
Hearding Joan, Combe Martin 1661 A
Joan, Combe Martin 1706 W
Hearding Joan, Parracombe 1733 W
Hearding alias Holson John, Filleigh 1591 [W]
Heardinge John, Goodleigh 1595 [W]
Heardinge John, Combe Martin 1597 [W]
Heardinge John, Heanton Punchardon 1598 [W]
Heardinge John, Filleigh 1602 W
Hearding John, Westleigh 1661 A
Hearding John, Kentisbury 1667 W
Hearding John, Shebbear 1670 A
Hearding John, Chittlehampton 1677 A
Hearding John, Tawstock 1688 W
John, Combe Martin 1691 W
Hearding John, Combe Martin 1698 W
John, Combe Martin 1717 W
John, Combe Martin 1735 W
John, ship *Worcester* 1746 W
John, Combe Martin 1767 W
John, Ilfracombe 1784 W
Hearding John, Woolfardisworthy, yeoman 1808 W
John, Combe Martin 1827 W
John, Ilfracombe 1843 W
Harding alias Allin John, Woolfardisworthy 1847 W
John Nott, South Molton 1855 A; A dbn
Hearding Juliana, East Down 1710 W
Hearding Margaret, Atherington 1697 W
Heardinge Margery, Combe Martin 1606 W
Hearding Margery, Monkleigh 1634 W
Hearding Mary, Marwood 1693 W
Hearding Mary, Marwood 1706 A
Mary, Chittlehampton 1820 A to Elizabeth wife of M. Kniele,
   niece
Mary, Ilfracombe 1842 W
Mary, Kentisbury 1857 W
Hearding Nathaniel, South Molton 1633 W
Hurdon Peter, Northam 1856 A to Maria wife of Peter Hurdon
   Oliver of Holsworthy, sister
Hearding Peter, Combe Martin 1633 A
Hearding Peter, Bideford 1703 A
Peter, Mortehoe 1760 A
Peter, Mortehoe 1770 W
Hearding Phillippa, Barnstaple 1733 W
Herdynge Richard, Combe Martin 1575 W
Heardinge Richard, Ilfracombe 1583 W
Richard, Marwood 1585 W
Harden alias Wrath Richard, Knowstone 1587 W
Heardinge Richard, Marwood 1592 [W]
Heardinge Richard, East Down 1638 A
Hearding Richard, Combe Martin 1641 W
Hearding Richard, Tawstock 1671 W
Hearding Richard, Combe Martin 1718 W

Richard, South Molton 1742 A
Hearding Richard, East Down 1742 W
Richard, Combe Martin 1757 A
Hearding Richard, Chulmleigh, yeoman 1809 A
Herdynge Robert, Northam 1576 A
Robert, Fremington 1760 W and 1761 A
Robert, Ashreigney 1776 W
Robert, Fremington 1822 W
Robert, Barnstaple 1857 W
Samuel, Fremington 1752 A
Samuel, Marwood 1752 W
Hearding Samuel, Loxhore 1756 [W]
Samuel, Fremington 1794 W
Samuel, Fremington 1827 W
Sarah, Combe Martin 1780 W
Hearding Susan, Atherington 1723 W
Susan, Barnstaple, sp. 1810 W
Heardinge Thomas, High Bickington 1623 [W]
Herdon Thomas, King's Nympton 1685 W
Thomas, Fremington 1791 W
Thomas, Ilfracombe 1836 W
Thomas, Berrynarbor 1850 W
Timothy, Combe Martin 1732 W
Timothy, Combe Martin 1756 W
Hearden William, Chittlehampton 1582 A
Heardinge William, High Bickington 1585 [W]
Heardinge William, Berrynarbor 1594 [W]
Hearding William, Combe Martin 1631 [W] and 1633 O
Hearding William, Combe Martin 1637 W
Hearding William, Combe Martin 1661 W and A
Hearding William, East Down 1668 W
Hearding William, High Bickington 1671 W
Hearding William, Atherington 1705 A
Hearding William, East Down 1708 W
William, South Molton 1731 W
William, Northam 1740 W
Hearding William, Filleigh 1743 W
William, Kentisbury 1759 W
William, Ashreigney 1771 W
William, Kentisbury 1772 W
William, East Down 1783 W
William Henry, Bideford 1854 W
Hardwick Ann, Hartland 1641 A
Hardy Joan, Lynton 1679 W
John, Romansleigh 1633 W
John, Stoke Rivers 1679 W
Mark, Lynton 1678 W
Harell see Harle
Harendle see Hartnoll
Harford, Harforde, Harfoott, Hartford
Arthur, Barnstaple 1690 A
Hartford Christopher, Goodleigh 1639 A
Harforde Harry, Pilton 1569 W
Hartford James, Pilton 1707 A
Harford alias Sydenham Jane 1690 A
John, Pilton 1622 [W]
Hartford John, Barnstaple 1690 A
Josiah, Pilton 1713 W
Hartford Margaret, Pilton 1665 W
Harfoott Peter, Pilton 1612 [W]; forename blank in Ms;
   supplied from parish register
Hartford Philip, Pilton 1674 [W]
Richard, Pilton 1703 A
Robert, Pilton 1591 [W]
Hargret Michael, South Molton 1670 A and 1672 O
Haries see Harris
Harle, Harell, Harrell, Harrill, Herell, Horrell
Christopher, Ashreigney 1570 W
Elizabeth, Ashreigney 1573 W
Harrill Francis, Tawstock 1732 A
Harell Joan, Dowland 1582 W
Harell Joan, Tawstock 1588 W
Herell John, Tawstock 1575 W
Horrell John, Bideford 1743 A
Herell Richard, St Giles in the Wood 1584 W

Harell alias Burne Thomas, Winkleigh 1586 W
Herell William, Dowland 1571 W
Horrell William, Great Torrington 1684 A
    see also Hearle
Harnaman see Harnaman
Harpathe see Harrapath
Harpur, Harper
    Alexander, Ilfracombe 1682 A
    Alexander, Barnstaple 1726 W
    Ann, Barnstaple 1675 W
    Ann, Stoke Rivers 1701 W
    Edmund, Northam 1733 W
    Edward, Stoke Rivers 1687 W
    Edward, Brendon 1716 A
    Edward, Georgeham 1731 W
    Edward, Ilfracombe 1732 W
    George, Georgeham 1728 A
    Humphrey, Ilfracombe 1703 W and 1706 A
    Humphrey, Brendon 1716 W
    Jane, Ilfracombe 1710 W
    Harper John, Berrynarbor 1640 A
    Harper John, Kentisbury 1641 O
    John, Horwood 1721 A
    Harper John, Clovelly 1741 A
    Mary, Barnstaple 1732 W
    Nicholas, Georgeham 1704 A
    Nicholas, Marwood 1706 W
    Nicholas, Georgeham 1722 W
    Nicholas, Bideford 1731 A
    Harper Philip, Great Torrington 1799 A
    Harper Richard, Berrynarbor, snr. 1627 [W]
    Harper Richard, Berrynarbor 1641 A
    Harper Richard, Great Torrington 1821 W
    Harper Richard, Great Torrington 1855 W
    Robert, Berrynarbor 1682 W
    Sarah, Great Torrington 1724 A
    William, Arlington 1677 W
    William, Berrynarbor 1706 W
Harrapath, Harapath, Harpathe, Harropath, Herapath
    George, Pilton 1643 W
    Harapath George, Pilton 1701 A
    Harropath Joan, Ashford 1577 W
    Joan, Ashford 1589 A account
    Herapath John, Ashford 1667 W
    Herapath John, Ashford 1678 W
    Harpathe Mathew, Ashford 1570 W
    Richard, Ashford 1640 W
    Herapath Samuel, Ashford 1671 W
    Herapath William, Pilton 1820 W
Harre John, Combe Martin 1571 W
Harrell see Harle
Harrie, Harries see Harris
Harrill see Harle
Harrington Gertrude, Shebbear 1778 W
    Robert, Shebbear 1787 W
Harris, Haries, Harrie, Harries, Harrys
    Harries ..., Langtree 1603 [W]
    Harries ..., Iddesleigh 1604 [W]
    Harries ..., Berrynarbor 1606 and 1607 [W]
    Harrie ..., Georgeham 1609 [W]
    Harries ..., Bideford 1611 [W]
    Harries ..., Marwood 1614 [W]
    ..., Ilfracombe 1851 A
    Abraham, Ilfracombe 1755 A
    Adam, Goodleigh 1723 and 1724 W
    Agnes, Chittlehampton 1586 W
    Harries Agnes, Buckland Brewer, widow 1612 [W] "of
      Bulkworthy"; forename blank in Ms; supplied from parish
      register
    Harries Agnes, George Nympton 1613 [W]; forename blank in
      Ms; supplied from parish register
    Agnes, Northam 1668 A
    Harrys Alice, Ashreigney 1567 W
    Ambrose, Arlington 1598 [W]
    Amiel, Marwood 1640 [W]

    Amy, Chulmleigh 1794 W
    Ann, Marwood 1674 W
    Ann, Ashreigney, widow 1802 W
    Ann, Chulmleigh 1847 W
    Ann, Clovelly 1851 A
    Ann and Mary, Pilton 1665 A
    Harries Anthony, South Molton 1598 [W]
    Anthony, Marwood 1619 [W] and 1623 O
    Anthony, Fremington 1625 [W]
    Anthony, Iddesleigh 1700 A
    Anthony, Tawstock 1740 W
    Arthur, Arlington 1643 W
    Harries Bartholomew, Barnstaple 1615 [W]
    Bartholomew, Ilfracombe 1784 W
    Catherine, Barnstaple 1738 W
    Charles, Ilfracombe 1743 W
    Christiana, Horwood 1623 [W]
    Harries Christopher, Alwington 1617 [W]
    Christopher, Atherington 1621 [W]
    Christopher, Hartland 1661 W
    David, Fremington 1620 [W]
    David, Berrynarbor 1679 W
    David, Pilton 1709 W
    David, East Down 1742 W
    David, South Molton 1833 W
    Edmund, Frithelstock 1715 W
    Harries Edward, Atherington 1588 W
    Edward, Instow 1700 A and 1707 A
    Edward, Bideford 1758 W
    Eleanor, East Down 1739 A
    Eli, Combe Martin 1719 A
    Harrie Elizabeth, Arlington 1574 W
    Harries Elizabeth, Barnstaple 1604 W
    Harries Elizabeth wife of John, Marwood 1613 [W]; forename
      blank in Ms; supplied from parish register
    Elizabeth, South Molton 1664 W
    Elizabeth, Georgeham 1670 W
    Elizabeth, Georgeham 1684 W and 1686 W
    Elizabeth, Barnstaple 1700 W and 1701 W
    Elizabeth, Combe Martin 1708 W
    Elizabeth, Marwood 1729 W
    Elizabeth, Ilfracombe, widow 1811 A
    Elizabeth, Ashreigney 1828 A to John, son
    Elizabeth, East Down 1836 A
    Elizabeth, South Molton 1857 W
    Elizabeth wife of John see also John Gubb
    Ephraim, Northam 1808 W
    Esther, Ilfracombe 1724 W
    Faith, Barnstaple 1628 [W]
    Francis, Newton St Petrock 1642 W
    Francis, King's Nympton 1726 A
    Geoffrey, Chittlehampton 1783 W
    Harries George, Arlington 1571 W
    George, West Buckland 1599 [W]
    Haries George, Ilfracombe 1605 W
    George, Ilfracombe 1678 W
    George, Bideford 1689 W
    George, Ilfracombe 1723 W
    George, North Molton 1750 W
    Grace, Ilfracombe 1719 W
    Grace, East Down 1752 W
    Hannah, Sheepwash 1727 W
    Hannah, South Molton 1743 W
    Hannah, East Down 1776 W
    Helen, Parracombe 1693 W
    Henry, Chulmleigh 1701 W
    Henry, Winkleigh 1724 W
    Henry, North Molton 1788 W
    Henry, Mariansleigh, yeoman 1815 A to Sarah, widow
    Henry, Chulmleigh 1823 W
    Honor, Lynton 1640 W
    Haries Hugh, George Nympton 1580 W
    Hugh, Ashreigney 1633 A
    Isott, Ilfracombe 1785 W
    Jacob, Shebbear 1832 W

James, Newton St Petrock 1729 W
James, Langtree 1750 W
James, Tawstock 1762 W
James, Ilfracombe 1782 W
James, Stoodleigh 1784 W
James, Burrington 1791 W
James, Ashreigney 1796 W
James, Burrington 1798 W
James, East Down, jnr. 1816 A to Betty, widow
James, Combe Martin 1818 W
James, Sheepwash 1836 W
James, East Down 1842 W
Harries Jane, Arlington, widow 1612 [W]; forename blank in
    Ms; supplied from parish register
Jane, Tawstock 1684 W
Jane, Goodleigh 1752 W
Jeremiah, Goodleigh 1822 W
Jeremiah see also Edmund Fosse
Joan, Ilfracombe 1593 [W]
Harries Joan, Barnstaple 1605 W
Harries Joan, Northam 1615 [W]
Harrie Joan, Berrynarbor 1616 [W]
Joan, Marwood 1621 [W]
Joan, Georgeham 1644 W
Joan, Northam 1677 A
Joan, Tawstock 1747 A
Joan, Ilfracombe 1754 W
Harrie John, Hartland 1565 W
Harrys John, Burrington 1573 W
Harries John, Northam 1576 W
Harries John, Parracombe 1577 A
Harrie John, Trentishoe 1597 [W]
Harries John, Barnstaple 1604 [W]; forename blank in Ms;
    supplied from parish register
Harries John, Northam 1606 W
Harries John, Marwood 1608 [W] "Harry of Townredden" in
    register; forename blank in Ms; supplied from parish register
Harries John, Hartland 1617 [W]
Harries John, Georgeham 1617 [W] and 1620 [W]
John, West Buckland 1620 [W]
John, Northam 1621 [W]
John, Barnstaple 1623 [W]
John, Lynton 1623 [W]
John, Tawstock 1627 [W]
John, Chittlehampton 1632 [W]
John, Great Torrington 1635 A
John, George Nympton 1639 A
John, West Buckland, snr. 1672 A
John, Goodleigh 1674 A
John, Wembworthy 1679 W
John, Tawstock 1680 W
John, Rackenford 1681 W
John, Ilfracombe 1682 W
John, Georgeham 1684 W
John, Bideford 1685 W
John, Tawstock 1690 A
John, Burrington 1703 W
John, Fremington 1703 A
John, Northam 1705 W
John, Ilfracombe 1706 A
John, Kentisbury 1712 A
John, Marwood 1712 W
Harries John, Huntshaw 1717 W
John, Ilfracombe 1719 W
John, North Molton 1725 W
John, Parkham 1726 W
John, Barnstaple 1733 W
John, Northam 1735 W
John, Tawstock 1736 W
John, East Down 1737 W
John, Marwood 1742 W
John, Pilton 1744 W
John, Arlington 1749 W
John, Coldridge 1757 W
John, Pilton 1757 W

John, Ilfracombe 1770 W and 1780 W
John, East Down 1785 W
John, Combe Martin, mariner 1797 A
John, Atherington, yeoman 1802 W
John, Ilfracombe, mariner 1803 W
John, Shirwell, yeoman 1806 W
John, Stoodleigh, yeoman 1809 A
John, East Down 1820 W
John, Burrington 1825 W
John, East Down 1836 W
John, Atherington 1844 W
Jonah, Tawstock 1643 W
Jonah, Tawstock 1678 W
Jonah, Tawstock 1703 W
Joseph, Barnstaple 1856 W
Joshua, Combe Martin 1853 W
Josiah, George Nympton 1633 A
Julian, Marwood 1592 [W]
Harries Leonard, Pilton 1614 [W]
Lewis, Marwood 1701 W
Lucy, Barnstaple 1684 A
Harries Margaret, Marwood 1617 [W]
Margaret, Ilfracombe 1685 W
Martin, Chittlehampton 1620 [W]
Mary, Ilfracombe 1623 [W]
Mary and Ann, Pilton 1665 A
Mary, Bideford 1697 W
Mary, Parracombe 1703 A
Mary, Bideford 1731 W
Mary, Ilfracombe 1739 W
Mary, Ilfracombe 1830 W
Mary, Barnstaple 1836 A
Mary, East Down 1838 W
Michael, Ilfracombe 1753 W
Morgan, East Down 1682 W
Nathaniel, Bideford 1695 A
Nathaniel, Ilfracombe 1797 W
Nicholas, East Down 1698 W
Nicholas, Westleigh 1749 W
Nicholas, Combe Martin 1774 W
Nicholas, Combe Martin 1807 W
Harrie Oliver, Marwood 1576 W
Harrie Oliver, Marwood 1604 W
Paul, George Nympton 1632 [W]
Peter, Bideford 1764 W
Philip, Great Torrington 1683 W
Philip, Heanton Punchardon 1729 A
Philip, Northam 1750 W
Haries Phillippa, Martinhoe 1623 [W]
Phillippa, Marwood 1642 W
Rebecca, Georgeham 1645 W
Rees, Marwood 1673 A
Harries Richard, Langtree 1567 W
Harries Richard, Georgeham 1580 W
Richard, Instow 1591 [W]
Harries Richard, West Anstey 1600 W
Harrys Richard, Northam 1603 W
Harries Richard, Ilfracombe 1605 W
Harries Richard, Northam 1618 [W]
Richard, West Buckland 1620 [W]
Richard, Ilfracombe 1621 [W]
Richard, Bideford 1623 [W]
Richard, Newton St Petrock 1624 [W]
Richard, Barnstaple 1626 [W]
Richard, Arlington 1633 W
Richard, Hartland 1639 W
Richard, Barnstaple 1683, 1691, 1696 A
Richard, Ilfracombe 1707 W
Richard, Combe Martin 1708 A
Richard, Bideford 1709 W
Richard, Hartland 1710 W
Richard, Burrington 1729 A
Richard, Ilfracombe 1729 A
Richard, Ilfracombe 1795 W
Richelda, Tawstock 1688 W

Harries Robert, South Molton 1574 A
Harries Robert, West Anstey 1574 W
Harries Robert, Warkleigh 1597 [W]
Harries Robert, Atherington 1617 [W]
Robert, Ilfracombe 1623 [W]
Robert, Parracombe 1670 W
Robert, Little Torrington 1671 A
Robert, Wembworthy 1721 W
Robert, Marwood 1726 W
Robert, Chulmleigh 1736 A
Robert, Chulmleigh 1779 A
Robert, Ashreigney 1836 W and 1843 A
Harries Roger, Iddesleigh 1606 W
Roger, Ashreigney 1639 A
Roger, King's Nympton 1724 W
Salome, Combe Martin 1592 [W]
Samuel, Northam 1690 A
Samuel, High Bickington 1717 A
Samuel, Combe Martin 1733 W
Sarah, Bideford 1640 W
Sarah, Ilfracombe 1754 W
Sarah, Burrington 1837 W
Seth, Hartland 1748 A
Simon, Chulmleigh 1720 W and 1730 W
Stephen, Barnstaple 1592 [W]
Stephen, Marwood 1736 W
Susan, Ilfracombe 1742 W
Susan, Ilfracombe 1785 W
Susan, Trentishoe, sp. 1800 W
Susan, Atherington, widow 1805 W
Harries Thomas, Ilfracombe 1574 A
Harries Thomas, South Molton 1584 W
Harries Thomas, Bulkworthy 1600 W
Harriss Thomas, Berrynarbor 1602 W
Harries Thomas, Barnstaple 1614 [W]; forename blank in Ms;
    supplied from parish register
Thomas, Marwood 1621 [W]
Thomas, Newton St Petrock 1664 W
Thomas, Northam 1682 W
Thomas, Parracombe 1693 W
Thomas, Bideford 1698 W
Thomas, Marwood 1699 A
Thomas, Barnstaple 1710 A
Thomas, Barnstaple 1712 W
Thomas, Northam 1718 W
Thomas, Parracombe 1725 W
Thomas, Bideford 1726 W and 1731 W
Thomas, Barnstaple 1744 W
Thomas, South Molton 1748 A
Thomas, Ilfracombe 1761 W and 1762 W
Thomas, Tawstock 1765 W
Thomas, North Molton 1786 W
Thomas, Tawstock 1788 W
Thomas, Bideford 1789 W
Thomas, Ilfracombe 1807 A
Thomas, Ashreigney 1848 W
Thomas, Shebbear 1854 W
Harries Thomas,, snr., Georgeham 1602 [W]; forename blank
    in Ms; supplied from parish register
Harries Thomasine, George Nympton 1614 [W]; forename
    blank in Ms; supplied from parish register
Thomasine, George Nympton 1627 [W]
Harrie William, South Molton 1568 W
Harrie William, Trentishoe 1577 W
Harries William, Atherington 1582 A
William, Barnstaple 1625 [W]
William, Northam 1640 A
William, Woolfardisworthy 1668 W
William, Barnstaple 1674 W
William, Parkham 1677 W
William, Ilfracombe 1715 A
William, Shebbear 1719 A
William, Arlington 1723 W
William, High Bickington 1723 W
William, Bideford 1728 W

William, Ilfracombe 1735 W
William, Berrynarbor 1748 W
William, Georgeham 1756 W
William, ship *Kingston* 1757 W
William, Berrynarbor 1762 W
William, Combe Martin 1763 W
William, Atherington, yeoman 1805 [W]
William, Ashreigney, snr. 1839 W
William, Burrington, yeoman, snr. 1842 A to John of
    Witheridge, husbandman, brother
William, Ashreigney 1857 W
Harrison Charles, Chittlehampton 1682 A
Jane, Bideford 1715 W
John, Barnstaple 1686 W
John, Barnstaple 1710 A
Leonard, Barnstaple 1690 A
Richard, Ilfracombe 1671 W
Richard, Bideford, snr. 1701 W
Susan, Barnstaple 1716 W
Thomas, Barnstaple 1690 W
William, Goodleigh 1640 W
Harriss see Harris
Harropath see Harrapath
Harry, Harrye
Alexander, Marwood 1592 [W]
John, North Molton 1582 W
John, Ashford 1602 W
Peter, Ashford 1701 W
Prudence, Ashford 1704 W
Robert, Marwood 1643 A
Simon, Marwood 1643 W
Harrye Thomas, Ilfracombe 1568 W
Thomas, Barnstaple 1812 W
William, Kentisbury 1587 W
William, Berrynarbor 1595 W
Harrys see Harris
Hart, Harte, Heart, Hert
Harte ..., Zeal Monachorum 1608 [W]
Harte Adam, Zeal Monachorum 1578 W
Harte Alice, Fremington 1630 [W] and 1632 O
Harte Cicely, Ilfracombe 1618 [W]
Geoffrey, Fremington 1606 [W]; forename blank in Ms;
    supplied from parish register
Heart George, Bow 1624 [W]
Harte John, Newton Tracey 1577 W
Harte John, Fremington 1603 W
John, Fremington 1607 [W]; forename blank in Ms; supplied
    from parish register
Harte John, Heanton Punchardon 1622 [W]
John, Cruwys Morchard 1637 W
John, Fremington 1672 W
Margaret, North Molton 1594 [W]
Richard, South Molton 1638 W
Roger, Burrington 1748 A
Harte Rose, Newton Tracey 1577 W
Harte Thomas, Ilfracombe 1581 W
Thomas, Ilfracombe 1610 [W]; forename blank in Ms;
    supplied from parish register
Hert Walter, High Bickington 1735 W
Harte William, Fremington 1653 W
Willmot, Heanton Punchardon 1633 W
Hartford see Harford
Hartnoll, Hartnell, Hartnol, Hartnolle
..., Stoodleigh 1607 [W]
..., Berrynarbor 1610 [W]
..., Ilfracombe 1614 [W]
Agnes, Marwood 1632 [W]
Alexander, Barnstaple 1682 W
Alfred, Ilfracombe 1674 [W]
Alice, Barnstaple 1663 A
Amos, Mortehoe 1696 W
Blanche, Mortehoe 1621 [W]
Charles, West Down 1702 W
Edward, Pilton 1643 [W]
Elizabeth, Bratton Fleming 1761 W

Francis, Bideford 1695 W
Gabriel, Bittadon 1636 W
George, Georgeham 1624 [W]
George, Georgeham 1706 A
George, Heanton Punchardon 1779 A
Harry, Ilfracombe 1579 W
Hartnell Henry, Ilfracombe 1581 A
Henry, Bittadon 1584 W
Henry, Ilfracombe, snr. 1637 [W]
James, Goodleigh 1703 A
James, Georgeham 1802 W
James, Mortehoe, snr. 1834 W
Joan, Mortehoe 1573 A
Joan, Goodleigh 1577 W
Joan, Goodleigh 1593 [W]
Joan, Ilfracombe 1600 W
Joan, Marwood 1623 [W]
Joan, Georgeham 1633 W
Joan, Stoke Rivers 1640 A
Joan, Goodleigh 1641 A
Joan, Ilfracombe 1752 W
Joan, Heanton Punchardon 1761 W
Hartnolle John, Mortehoe 1597 [W]
John, Abbotsham 1641 W
John, Goodleigh 1642 W
John, Marwood, snr. 1645 [W]
John, Goodleigh 1665 W
John, Marwood 1666 and 1667 A
John, George Nympton 1671 A
John, Bideford 1684 W
John, Bideford 1699 A
Hartnol John, Georgeham 1703 A
John, Mortehoe 1712 A
John, Burrington 1717 W
John, East Buckland 1722 W
John, Burrington 1723 W
John, Goodleigh 1736 A
Lewis, Parkham 1596 [W]
Margaret, East Buckland 1676 W
Margery, Pilton, widow 1810 A
Mary, Mortehoe 1605 W
Mary, West Down 1702 A
Mary, Burrington 1727 W
Harendle Mary, Clannaborough 1780 W
Nicholas, Arlington 1596 [W]
Nicholas, Georgeham 1693 W
Nicholas, Georgeham 1735 A
Peter, Marwood 1613 [W]; forename blank in Ms; supplied
     from parish register
Richard, Georgeham 1583 W
Richard, Goodleigh 1607 [W]; forename blank in Ms;
     supplied from parish register
Richard, Mortehoe 1695 W
Richard, Ilfracombe 1744 W
Robert, Stoke Rivers 1628 [W]
Robert, Instow 1660 A
Robert, Goodleigh 1663 W
Samuel, Loxhore 1757 A
Susan, Northam 1668 W
Thomas, Ilfracombe 1575 W
Thomas, Mortehoe 1616 [W]
Thomas, Marwood 1639 O
Thomas, Mortehoe 1642 W
Thomas, Filleigh 1710 W
Thomas, Northam 1740 W
Thomas, Weare Giffard 1838 W
Thomasine, Goodleigh 1603 W
Walter, Goodleigh 1602 W
Walter, North Molton 1636 A
Hartnolle William, Ilfracombe 1624 [W]
William, Marwood 1683 A
William, Goodleigh 1693 W
William, Ilfracombe 1743 W
William, Pilton, husbandman 1797 W

William, Northam, Appledore, mariner 1849 A to Charles,
     cordwainer, jnr., brother
William, Weare Giffard 1856 W
Harton Agnes, Barnstaple 1668 A
Alice, South Molton, widow 1572 W
Edmund, Parracombe 1706 A
John, Witheridge 1577 A
Philip, Parracombe 1721 A
Richard, Barnstaple 1618 [W]
Richard, Parracombe 1724 W
Richard, Parracombe 1782 W
Robert, Chulmleigh 1583 W
William, Parracombe 1768 W
Hartopp see Hortop
Hartree, Hartred, Hartrewe, Harttree
Catherine, Bideford 1797 A
Hartred David, Littleham (near Bideford) 1608 [W]; forename
     blank in Ms; supplied from parish register
Harttree George, Barnstaple 1851 W
Hannah, Barnstaple 1855 W
Prudence, Barnstaple 1797 A
Thomas, Barnstaple 1777 A; A dbn 1794
Hartrewe William, Littleham (near Bideford) 1591 [W]
William, Barnstaple 1722 W
Hartswell, Hartswill, Hartwell, Hatswell, Hatswill, Hurtswell,
     Hutswell
Hutswell Joan, South Molton, widow 1570 W
Hatswill Joan, South Molton 1592 [W]
Hurtswell John, South Molton 1570 W
Hartswill John, South Molton 1592 [W]
John, Chulmleigh 1606 W
John, Chulmleigh 1630 [W]
Hatswell John, Stoodleigh 1664 A
Petronell, Chulmleigh 1625 [W]
Hartwell William, Goodleigh 1594 [W]
Harttree see Hartree
Hartwell see Hartswell
Harvest Martha, Ilfracombe 1852 W
Michael, Ilfracombe 1823 A to Martha, widow
Harvey, Harvie, Harvy, Harvye, Hervey
Harvie Ann, Westleigh 1749 A
Hervey Christopher, Shebbear 1774 W
Christopher, Buckland Brewer 1783 W
Harvy Edmund, Zeal Monachorum 1591 [W]
Elisha, Beaford 1737 W
Elizabeth, Zeal Monachorum 1721 W
Harvy Emanuel, Frithelstock 1681 W
Emanuel, Zeal Monachorum 1688 W
Emanuel, North Tawton, snr. 1696 W
Harvie Giles, Zeal Monachorum 1584 A
Harvy Giles, Zeal Monachorum 1623 [W]
Giles, Zeal Monachorum 1689 A
Grace, Chittlehampton 1696 W
James, Chittlehampton 1633 W
James, Hartland 1755 W
Harvy Joan, Zeal Monachorum 1627 [W]
Harvie John, Yarnscombe 1580 W
Harvye John, Zeal Monachorum 1602 W
John, Frithelstock 1675 W
Harvy John, Zeal Monachorum 1680 W
John, Bideford 1688 A
John, Bideford 1694 W
John, Shebbear 1721 A
John, Zeal Monachorum 1739 A
John, Bideford 1743 W
John, Heanton Punchardon 1789 W
John, Buckland Brewer 1791 W
John, South Molton 1801 W
Jonah, Zeal Monachorum 1685 W
Mary, Zeal Monachorum 1693 W
Harvie Nicholas, Westleigh 1738 W
Peter, Great Torrington 1707 W
Harvy Richard, Zeal Monachorum 1680 W
Richard, Chulmleigh 1728 W
Robert, Zeal Monachorum 1694 A

Samuel, Dolton 1717 A
Sarah, Merton 1740 W
Thomas, Pilton 1753 W
Thomas, Merton 1787 W
Thomasine 1665 A
William, Zeal Monachorum, snr. 1677 [W]
William, Zeal Monachorum 1692 W
William, Winkleigh 1709 W
William, Dolton 1716 A
William, Dolton 1742 A and 1749 A
William, Zeal Monachorum 1783 W
Willmot, Coldridge 1667 W
Harward, Harwood see Horwood
Hasking, Haskings, Haskins
Haskings John, Rackenford 1839 W
John, Charles, yeoman 1842 A to Mary, widow
Haskins Jonah, Great Torrington 1812 W
Haskings Joseph, Zeal Monachorum 1748 W
William, South Molton 1845 W
Haslam James, Clovelly 1768 W
Hastings Abel, Barnstaple 1714 A
Hatche, Hacche, Hatch
Hatch Ann, Abbotsham 1662 A
Anthony, Satterleigh 1586 W
Hatch Arthur, Northam 1644 A
Hacche Arthur, Northam 1699 W
Hatch Bartholomew, Buckland Brewer 1641 W
Hacche alias Burgess Elizabeth, Chittlehampton 1701 A
Hatch Elizabeth, Satterleigh 1597 [W]
Hatch Henry, Pilton 1668 A
Hatch Hugh, Pilton 1642 W
Hugh, Chittlehampton 1671 A
Hacche John, Chittlehampton 1812 W
Lodovic, Chittlehampton 1629 [W]
Hatch Lodovic, Satterleigh 1637 A
Lodovic, Satterleigh 1673 [W]
Margaret, Chittlehampton 1620 [W]
Hacche Mary, Chittlehampton 1824 A to Mary wife of
    Benjamin Radford of Chulmleigh, daughter
Hatch Oliver, East Buckland 1593 [W]
Hatch Robert, Pilton 1643 A
Hatch Robert, Satterleigh 1644 W
Hacche Robert, Satterleigh 1674 [W]
Hacche Robert, Satterleigh 1702 W
Hacche Robert, Northam 1710 W
Thomas, Martinhoe 1584 W
Hatch Thomas, Chittlehampton 1599 [W]
Hacche Thomas, South Molton, esquire 1680 W
Hacche Thomas, South Molton 1724 W
Hache William, Chittlehampton 1573 A
Hache William, Martinhoe 1589 W
Hatherleigh, Hatherlegh, Hatherleghe, Hatherley, Hatherly,
    Hatherlye
..., Bondleigh 1613 [W] and O
Hatherly Agnes, Huntshaw 1704 W
Alice, Clovelly 1618 [W]
Hatherly Arthur, Clovelly 1740 W
Barnabas, Hartland 1634 W
Hatherly Charles, Hartland 1691 W
Hatherly Charles, Bideford 1811 W
Hatherly Dorothy, Shebbear, wife 1805 W
Elizabeth, Chawleigh 1627 [W]
Hatherly Elizabeth, Parkham 1710 W
Hatherly Elizabeth, Bideford 1835 W
Hatherly Frances Grace, Bideford 1825 A to Elizabeth, mother
George, Hartland 1633 A
Henry, Fremington 1618 [W]
Hugh, Winkleigh 1583 W
Hatherlegh Joan, Winkleigh 1575 W
Hatherlegh Joan, Frithelstock 1577 A
Hatherley John, Nether Velly, Hartland 1563 W
Hatherlegh John, Winkleigh 1579 W
Hatherlye John, Frithelstock 1579 [W]
Hatherlegh John, Eggesford 1583 W
John, Bondleigh 1593 [W]

Hatherley John, Winkleigh 1631 [W]
Hatherley John, Chulmleigh 1636 W
Hatherly John, Bondleigh 1683 A
Hatherly John, Bideford 1826 W
Hatherlegh John, Frithelstock c1570s A
Hatherly Margaret, Iddesleigh 1695 A
Hatherly Mary, Bideford, widow 1807 W
Hatherley Mathew, Bondleigh 1563 W
Hatherly Narcissus, Parkham 1701 W
Robert, Chulmleigh 1596 [W]
Hatherley Simon, Huntshaw 1755 W
Hatherly Theobald, Winkleigh 1626 [W]
Hatherlegh William, Hartland 1567 W
Hatherlegh William, Bideford 1576 W
Hatherleghe William 1589 W
William, Hartland 1606 W
William, Hartland 1614 [W]; forename blank in Ms; supplied
    from parish register
Hatherly William, Shebbear 1829 W
William, Shebbear 1844 W
Hatswell, Hatswill see Hartswell
Hatton, Hatting, Hetton
Richard, Tawstock 1632 [W]
Hetton William, South Molton 1675 A
Hatting William, North Molton 1690 A
Haunce see Hance
Hausland, Hauxland see Hawksland
Havers John, Mariansleigh 1620 [W]
Hawckridge, Haweckridge see Hawkridge
Hawkens see Hawkins
Hawkeridg, Hawkeridge, Hawkerydge see Hawkridge
Hawkes, Hawks
Hawks Agnes, Barnstaple 1701 W
Hawks Edmund, Barnstaple 1583 W
Edward, Barnstaple 1697 A
Hawks Frances, Marwood 1663 W
Frances, Parkham 1706 A
George, Bideford 1690 A
Hawks John, Stoodleigh 1622 W
Hawks John, Barnstaple 1674 W
John, Marwood 1681 and 1685 W
John, Marwood 1705 W
John, Barnstaple 1706 A
Hawks John, Parkham 1715 W
John, Huish 1721 A
John, Heanton Punchardon 1758 W
Juliana, East Putford 1682 W
Nathaniel, Barnstaple 1751 W
Thomas, Barnstaple 1663 W
Hawks William, Barnstaple 1663 W
Hawkesland see Hawksland
Hawkesley see Hawksley
Hawkewell, Hawkewill see Hawkwell
Hawkins, Hawkens, Hawkin, Hawkings, Hawkyne, Hawkyns
Hawkyns Alexander, Romansleigh 1625 [W]
Hawkens Ann, North Tawton 1624 W
Hawkin Anthony, Kentisbury 1684 A
Hawkens Catherine, Mariansleigh 1575 W
Catherine, Yarnscombe 1643 W
Hawkin Dorothy, Shebbear 1810 W
Hawkens George, Instow 1588 W
Hawkings George, Coldridge 1746 W
Isott, Shebbear 1634 W
Hawkyns John, Knowstone 1571 W
Hawkens John, Frithelstock 1575 W
Hawkens alias Webber John, Burrington 1585 W
Hawkins alias Webber John, Yarnscombe 1585 W
Hawkens John, Mariansleigh 1596 [W]
Hawkens John, Shebbear 1620 [W]
John, Barnstaple 1672 A
John, Kentisbury 1672 W
Hawking John, Shebbear 1700 A
Hawkings John, Langtree 1783 W
Hawkens Marian, Mariansleigh 1597 [W]
Mary, Barnstaple 1663 W

Nicholas or Richard, Fremington 1718 A
Patience, North Tawton 1771 A
Phillippa, Northam 1701 W
Hawkens Richard, Chulmleigh 1622 [W]
Richard, Newton St Petrock 1667 [W]
Hawkin Richard, Shebbear 1756 A
Richard or Nicholas, Fremington 1718 A
Robert, Bideford 1680 W
Robert, North Tawton 1799 W
Hawkyne alias Gune Roger, West Buckland 1569 W
Hawkens Roger, Bideford 1596 [W]
Simon, High Bickington 1734 W
Hawkens Stephen, Shebbear 1573 A
Thomas, Mariansleigh 1570 W
Thomas, South Molton 1713 W
Urithe, Chulmleigh 1623 [W]
William, North Tawton 1754 W
Hawkings William, North Tawton 1755 W
William, Huish 1760 W; A dbn 1766
Hawkens Willmot, Parkham 1605 W
Hawking Willmot, North Tawton 1630 [W]
Willmot, Romansleigh 1638 W
Hawkridge, Hackerydge, Hawckridge, Haweckridge,
    Hawkeridg, Hawkeridge, Hawkerydge, Hawkrudge,
    Hawridge
Hawckridge Alice, Zeal Monachorum 1591 [W]
Hackerydge Ann, Barnstaple 1705 A
Hawkeridge Copleston, Sheepwash 1616 [W]
Edmund, Little Torrington 1564 W
Hawkrudge Giles, Zeal Monachorum 1567 W
Hawkerydge Hugh, Sheepwash 1631 [W]
Joan, Bideford 1598 [W]
Joan, Barnstaple 1721 W
Hawkrudge John, Zeal Monachorum 1567 W
Haweckridge John, Westleigh 1586 W
Hawckridge John, Fremington 1596 [W]
Hawkeridge John, Barnstaple 1615 [W]
Hawkerydge John, Yarnscombe 1639 [W]
Hawridge John, Pilton 1813 W
Hawkeridge Jonah, Yarnscombe 1661 A
Hawkeridg Lawrence, Barnstaple 1712 A
Hawkeridge Lawrence, Barnstaple 1743 W
Hawkerydge Margaret, Northam 1620 W
Hawkeridg Margaret, Barnstaple 1697 A
Mary, Pilton, widow 1800 W
Hawkrudge Richard, Zeal Monachorum 1583 W
Richard, Abbotsham 1598 [W]
Hawkeridg Richard, Northam 1682 A
Hawkeridg Richard, Abbotsham 1703 W
Hawkeridge Samuel, Bideford 1722 W
Samuel, Bideford 1759 W
Hawkrydge Simon, Bideford 1623 [W] and 1624 O
Hawkeridge Susan, Bideford 1643 W
Hawkrudge Thomas, Fremington 1577 W
Hawckridge Thomas, Parracombe 1594 [W]
Hackerydge Thomas, Northam 1627 [W]
Hawckridge William, Dowland 1590 [W]
Hawckridge William, Alverdiscott 1594 [W]
William, Yarnscombe 1641 A
William, Great Torrington 1673 [W]
William, Bideford 1674 [W]
Hawkeridg William, Yarnscombe 1682 A
Hawks see Hawkes
Hawksland, Hausland, Hauxland, Hawkesland, Hawxland
Hawxland Alice, Zeal Monachorum 1569 W
Hawkesland Gregory, Chittlehampton 1593 [W]
Humphrey, Puddington 1588 A
Hauxland John, Fremington 1566 W
Hawkesland Thomas, Fremington 1620 [W]
Thomasine, Fremington 1585 W
Hawksley, Hawkesley
George, Weare Giffard, yeoman 1800 W
Hawkesley James, Little Torrington 1827 W
Hawkesley John, Bideford 1852 W
Hawxland see Hawksland

Hawkwell, Hawkewell, Hawkewill, Hawkwill
Hawkewill Alice, Brendon 1616 [W]
Hawkwill George, Brendon 1643 W
Gregory, Brendon 1586 W
John, Brendon, jnr. 1642 W
Hawkewell Jonas, Barnstaple 1692 W
Richard, Brendon 1670 W
Hawkewill Roger, Brendon 1635 W
Hawkwill see Hawkwell
Hawkyne, Hawkyns see Hawkins
Hawridge see Hawkridge
Hawsgood John, Mariansleigh 1575 W
Haychcockle see Hitchcock
Haydon, Heydon
Agnes, Heanton Punchardon 1693 W
Heydon Ann, Parkham 1847 W
Anthony, Bratton Fleming 1628 [W]
Elizabeth, Georgeham 1851 W
Francis, South Molton 1812 W
Heydon John, Great Torrington, rug weaver 1820 A to Frances
    wife of D. Barrow, daughter
Heydon Mary, Barnstaple 1682 AP
Nathaniel, Heanton Punchardon 1706 A
Nicholas, Chawleigh 1664 A
Heydon Philip, Parkham 1834 W
Robert, Berrynarbor 1579 W
Heydon Walter, Filleigh 1667 W
William, Heanton Punchardon 1726 W
Heydon William, Bideford 1726 W
Hayen see Haynes
Hayes, Haies
Haies ..., Puddington 1617 [W]
Christopher, Great Torrington 1723 A
Christopher, Molland 1811 W
Haies Nicholas, Witheridge 1568 W
Haies Robert, Puddington 1615 [W]
Hayley Abraham, Chittlehampton 1742 W
Hayman, Haiman, Haymon, Haymond, Haynam, Heighman,
    Heyman
Haiman ..., Bideford 1607 [W]
..., Chulmleigh 1608 [W]
Haiman ..., Beaford 1611 [W]
Heyman Abraham, Bideford 1621 [W]
Haynam Agnes, Oakford 1772 W
Heyman Anthony, Northam 1669 W
Christopher, Great Torrington 1591 [W]
David, Northam 1575 A
Edmund, Great Torrington 1668 A
Heyman Edmund, Frithelstock 1689 W
Elizabeth, Frithelstock 1597 [W]
Elizabeth, Petrockstowe 1698 W
Frideswide, Beaford 1625 [W]
Heyman James, Great Torrington 1643 A
Jane, St Giles in the Wood 1670 W
Joan, Northam 1579 W
Joan, Northam 1637 W
John, Dolton 1586 W
John, Frithelstock 1591 [W]
John, Shebbear 1601 W
John, St Giles in the Wood 1616 [W]
Heighman John, Great Torrington 1618 [W]
Heyman John, Frithelstock, snr. 1630 [W]
John, Sheepwash 1642 W
Heyman John, Bideford 1690 A
Heyman John 1695 W
Heyman John, Iddesleigh 1703 W
Heyman John, Langtree 1713 W
Lodovic, Alwington 1638 W
Mary, Chulmleigh 1620 [W]
Mary, Chulmleigh 1638 W
Nicholas, Chulmleigh 1642 W
Richard, Great Torrington 1591 [W]
Richard, Frithelstock 1599 [W]
Richard, Great Torrington 1626 [W]

Hayman alias Hooper Simon, North Molton 1624 [W]
Thomas, Northam 1621 [W]
Thomas, Frithelstock 1635 W
Haymon William, Northam 1576 A
Haymon William, Northam 1578 W
William, Chulmleigh 1620 [W]
Heyman William, Westleigh 1640 W
William, Dolton 1672 W
Heyman William, Atherington 1694 W
Haymon William, Atherington 1745 W
William, Petrockstowe 1754 A
William, Atherington 1766 A
Haymond Willmot, Frithelstock 1584 A
Haynes, Haine, Haines, Hayen, Hayn, Hayne, Heanes, Heans,
    Hynes
Haine ..., Northam 1614 [W]
Haine ..., Coldridge 1615 [W]
Haine ..., Eggesford 1615 [W]
Hynes Aldred and Catherine, Barnstaple 1640 O
Haine Andrew, Eggesford 1615 [W]
Ann, Abbotsham 1783 W
Hayne Anthony, Monkleigh 1621 [W]
Hayne Baldwin, Tawstock 1577 W
Bartholomew, Monkleigh 1732 W
Bartholomew, Hartland 1777 A
Bartholomew, Hartland 1808 W*
Hayne Charity, North Tawton 1631 W
Daniel, Petrockstowe 1712 A
Hayne David, Barnstaple 1578 W
Heans Elizabeth, Buckland Filleigh 1672 A
Elizabeth, Petrockstowe 1717 W
Heans George, Great Torrington 1752 W
Heanes Grace, Barnstaple, sp. 1808 W
Hayne Henry, Sheepwash 1574 W
Henry, Coldridge 1766 W
Haine Henry, Roborough 1844 W
Humphrey, Huntshaw 1697 W
Hayne Joan, Frithelstock 1572 W
Hayne Joan, Sheepwash 1577 W
Joan, Bideford 1668 W
Joan, Peters Marland 1731 W
Hayne John, Barnstaple 1577 W
Hayne John, Eggesford 1586 A
Haine John, Tawstock 1610 [W]; forename blank in Ms;
    supplied from parish register
Hayne John, Parkham 1620 [W]
Hayne John, Merton 1626 [W]
Hayne alias Wood John, Chulmleigh 1627 [W]
Hayne John, Buckland Brewer 1640 W
Hayn John, Buckland Filleigh 1669 W
Heanes John, Parkham 1681 W
Haines John, Northam 1686 A
John, Northam 1688 W
John, Buckland Brewer, snr. 1701 W
Haines John, Northam 1708 W
Haines John, Peters Marland 1734 W
John, Great Torrington 1756 A
Hayne John, Fremington 1798 W
Hayne Lawrence, Tawstock 1619 [W] and 1623 O
Hayne Lawrence, Tawstock 1665 W
Hayne Lawrence, Tawstock 1676 W
Haine Lawrence, Yarnscombe 1726 W
Haine Martin, Parkham 1615 [W]; forename blank in Ms;
    supplied from parish register
Hayne Mary, Clovelly 1636 W
Hayne Mary, Tawstock 1690 W
Mary, Great Torrington 1783 W
Hayne Nicholas, Parracombe 1661 W
Philip, Northam 1691 A
Hayns Philip, Littleham (near Bideford) 1726 A
Hayne Richard, Ilfracombe 1574 W and A
Hayne Robert, Merton 1594 [W]
Haine Roger, Yarnscombe 1591 [W]
Heanes Samuel, Great Torrington 1778 W
Sarah, Northam 1693 W

Hayne Thomas, Tawstock 1564 W
Hayne Thomas, Tawstock 1580 W
Haine Thomas, Coldridge 1618 [W]
Hayne Thomas, Monkleigh 1634 W
Hayne Thomas, Monkleigh 1702 W
Thomas, Abbotsham 1766 A
Hayne William, Parkham 1576 A
Hayne William, Tawstock 1604 W
William, Parkham 1666 W
Haines William, Huntshaw 1681 W
Hayne William, Tawstock 1686 W
Hayen William, Combe Martin 1723 A
Haywood, Haiwood, Hayward, Haywarde, Haywod, Haywode,
    Haywoode, Hayword, Heawarde, Heyward, Heywod,
    Heywode, Heywood, Heywoode
..., Iddesleigh 1610 [W]
Haiwood ..., Bondleigh 1614 [W]
Haywarde Alison, Meshaw 1566 W
Heywood Ann, Tawstock 1801 A
Heywood Ann, Barnstaple 1828 W
Heywood Arthur, Winkleigh 1692 W
Heywood Arthur, Winkleigh 1704 A
Beata, Dolton 1578 W
Heywood Christiana, Chulmleigh 1708 W
Haywarde Cicely, North Molton 1585 W
Cornelius, Bondleigh 1672 W
Haywode Dunstan, North Tawton 1566 W
Heywood Edward, Iddesleigh 1684 W
Heywood Edward, North Tawton 1696 W
Heywood Elizabeth, Barnstaple 1640 W
Heywood Elizabeth 1699 A
Heywood Elizabeth, King's Nympton 1731 W
Heywood Elizabeth, Chawleigh 1787 W
Heywood Elizabeth, King's Nympton 1814 W
Elizabeth, Petrockstowe 1603 W
Heywood Enoch, Wembworthy 1644 W
Heywood Frances, South Molton 1698 W
Heywood Francis, Chittlehampton 1782 A
George, Petrockstowe 1587 W
Heywood George, Winkleigh 1639 A
Heywood George, Heanton Punchardon 1668 [W]
Heyward George, Chulmleigh 1703 W
Heywood George, Chawleigh 1717 A
Heywood George, Chulmleigh 1736 W
Heywood George, Chawleigh 1760 W
Haywoode Gordian, Witheridge 1604 W
Heywood Grace, South Molton 1682 W
Haywoode Henry, Petrockstowe 1597 [W]
Heywood Humphrey, Winkleigh 1639 W
Heywood Humphrey, Winkleigh 1671 A
James, Great Torrington 1588 W
Heywood Joan, King's Nympton 1569 W
Heywood Joan, Zeal Monachorum 1639 A
Heywood Joan, Winkleigh 1719 W
Haiwood John, South Molton 1567 W
Haywod John, Huish 1571 W
Heywood John, Dolton 1571 W
John, Winkleigh 1574 W
Haiwood John, Bondleigh 1610 [W]; forename blank in Ms;
    supplied from parish register
John, King's Nympton, snr. 1618 [W]
Heywood John, Winkleigh, snr. 1619 [W]
Heywood John, Bondleigh 1626 [W]
Heyward John, Bratton Fleming 1630 [W]
Heywood John, Dolton 1630 [W]
Heywood John, Winkleigh 1630 [W] (2)
Heywood John, North Tawton, snr. 1631 [W]
Heywood John, Dolton 1631 [W]
Heywood John, Eggesford 1635 A
Heywood John, Bondleigh 1636 C
Heywood John, King's Nympton 1639 W
Heywood John, South Molton 1667 A
Heywood John, King's Nympton 1679 W
Heywood John, Winkleigh 1680 W
Heywood John, South Molton 1692 A

Heywood John, Winkleigh 1714 A
Heywood John, King's Nympton 1722 W
Heywood John, ship *Lamester* 1761 A
Heywood John, Winkleigh 1769 W
Heywood John, King's Nympton, yeoman 1810 W
Heywood John, King's Nympton, yeoman 1822 A to
  Elizabeth, widow
Heywood Joseph, Parkham, yeoman 1803 W
Joseph, Parkham 1851 W
Mary, Dolton 1723 W
Michael, Iddesleigh 1590 [W]
Heywood Miriam, Alwington, sp. 1809 W
Nicholas, South Molton 1678 W
Peter, Dolton 1720 W
Haywoode Richard, Huish 1596 [W]
Robert, North Tawton 1587 W
Heywoode Robert, Winkleigh 1590 [W]
Haywoode Robert, Iddesleigh 1598 [W]
Robert, Tawstock 1603 W
Heyward Robert, Barnstaple 1623 [W]
Robert, Winkleigh 1678 A
Hayward Roger, South Molton 1676 A
Hayword Thomas 1633 W
Heyward Thomas, Northam 1684 W
Haywarde Thomasine, Georgeham 1587 W
Hayward Walter, Georgeham 1573 W
Walter, Parkham 1757 A
Heywood Walter 1835 A to Ann of Parkham, widow
Heawarde William, Heanton Punchardon 1572 W
Haywarde William, South Molton 1588 W
William, Ashreigney 1589 W
William, Winkleigh 1678 W
Hayward William, Winkleigh 1703 W
Heywood William Hamlyn, Bideford, esquire 1808 W
Hazard ..., Barnstaple 1601 [A]
Henry, Barnstaple 1627 [W]
Susan, Barnstaple 1623 [W]
William, Pilton 1597 [W]
Hazel James, Pilton 1825 W
Head, Heyde
Heyde Alice, Eggesford 1576 W
Richard, Great Torrington 1738 A
Headdon, Headon see Heddon
Heale, Heal, Heall, Healle, Hele
..., Bideford 1601 [W]
..., Burrington, widow 1605 [W]; forename blank in Ms;
  supplied from parish register
..., Burrington 1613 [W] and 1614 [W]
Abel, Frithelstock 1827 W
Agnes, Bideford, widow 1604 [W]; forename blank in Ms;
  supplied from parish register
Agnes, Winkleigh 1718 W
Healle Alphonse, Ashreigney 1575 W
Ann, Barnstaple 1853 W
Anthony, Ashreigney 1603 W
Heal Anthony, Bratton Fleming, labourer 1812 A to Mary,
  widow
Hele Arthur, North Molton 1645 A
Avis, Ashreigney 1670 W
Bartholomew, South Molton 1763 W
Caleb, Iddesleigh 1839 W
Catherine, Winkleigh 1735 W
David, Bratton Fleming 1706 W
Heal Dorothy, Bulkworthy 1795 W
Edward, Barnstaple 1619 [W] and 1623 [W]
Heal Edward, Tawstock 1834 W
Eleanor, Ashreigney 1677 W
Elizabeth, Winkleigh 1681 W
Hele Elizabeth, South Molton 1805 W
George, Huntshaw 1576 W
George, Marwood 1576 A
George, South Molton 1620 [W]
Heall Henry, Marwood 1580 A
Henry, Chulmleigh 1734 W
Henry, Bratton Fleming 1744 W

Hele Henry, South Molton 1787 W
Heal Henry, Bulkworthy 1789 W
Heal Henry, Buckland Brewer, yeoman 1797 W
Henry, Chulmleigh 1805 W
Heal Henry, Bideford 1834 W
Hele Hugh, King's Nympton 1637 W
Hugh, Chulmleigh 1642 A
James, Chittlehampton 1668 A
James, Great Torrington 1740 W
James, Winkleigh 1772 W
Joan, Tawstock 1643 A
Joan, South Molton 1674 W
John, Burrington 1576 W and 1579 A
John, Bideford 1590 [W]
John, Ashreigney 1591 [W]
John, King's Nympton 1616 [W]
John, Ashreigney 1621 [W]
John, North Tawton 1628 [W]
Hele John, Ashreigney, snr. 1630 [W]
Hele John, Barnstaple 1635 W
John, Marwood 1636 A and 1636 O
John, Ashreigney 1664 W
John, Burrington 1664 W
John, Zeal Monachorum 1665 W
John, High Bickington 1676 W
John, Rose Ash 1689 A
John, Clovelly, snr. 1705 A
John, Winkleigh 1733 W
Hele John, South Molton 1733 W
John, Marwood 1747 A
John, Bratton Fleming 1763 W
Heal John, Ashreigney 1781 W
Heal John, Charles 1790 W
John, Ilfracombe 1806 W
John, Marwood 1818 A
John, South Molton 1818 W
Jonathan, Heanton Punchardon 1760 W and 1763 W
Heal Judith, Littleham (near Bideford) 1834 W
Lawrence, Bulkworthy 1781 A
Heal Lawrence, Bulkworthy, yeoman 1805 A
Margaret, Chawleigh 1673 W
Margaret, Bratton Fleming 1709 A
Margaret, Marwood 1765 W
Margaret, Great Torrington 1845 W
Margery, Bideford 1605 [W]; forename blank in Ms; supplied
  from parish register
Mary, Lapford 1670 W
Mary, Marwood 1673 W
Mary, Marwood 1765 A
Heal Mary, Bow 1788 W
Mary, Marwood, wife 1808 A
Nicholas, Molland 1642 W
Oliver, Burrington 1597 [W]
Paul, Chittlehampton 1732 W
Petronell, Marwood 1805 A
Philip, Ashreigney 1597 [W]
Philip, Burrington 1619 [W]
Heall Richard, Weare Giffard 1565 W
Heall Richard, Bideford 1575 W
Hele Richard, Chawleigh 1645 A
Richard, Ilfracombe 1851 W
Robert, Burrington 1644 W
Hele Robert, George Nympton 1680 W
Hele Robert, Westleigh 1704 W
Robert, Atherington 1780 W
Heal Robert, Northam, yeoman 1804 W
Robert, Buckland Brewer 1849 W
Robert, Iddesleigh, carpenter 1849 A to Mary, widow
Roger, Wembworthy 1691 A
Samuel, High Bickington 1639 A
Samuel, Lapford 1723 W
Samuel, Winkleigh 1749 W
Heal Sarah, Bratton Fleming 1788 W
Heal Sarah, Bratton Fleming 1812 W
Heall Thomas, Littleham (near Bideford) 1580 W

Thomas, Dolton 1610 [W]; forename blank in Ms; supplied
   from parish register
Thomas, Ashreigney 1616 [W]
Thomas, Dowland 1621 [W]
Thomas, Marwood 1631 [W]
Thomas, Lapford 1643 [W]
Thomas, Ilfracombe 1670 W
Thomas, Dowland 1683 A
Thomas, Marwood 1715 W
Thomas, Witheridge 1724 W
Thomas, Marwood 1795 W
Thomasine, Northam 1795 W
Heall William, Ashreigney 1588 W
William, Alverdiscott 1600 W
William, King's Nympton 1600 W
William, Ashreigney 1633 W and A
William, Zeal Monachorum 1641 W
William, Pilton 1643 A
William, High Bickington 1663 A
William, King's Nympton 1690 W
Hele William, King's Nympton 1704 W
Hele William, Ashreigney 1717 W
William, Marwood 1733 W
William, Pilton 1753 A
Heal William, Bow 1791 W
Heaman, Heamaman
   Christopher, Frithelstock 1688 W
   Christopher, Littleham (near Bideford) 1705 W
   Christopher, Iddesleigh 1724 A
   Christopher, Iddesleigh 1727 W
   Joan, Iddesleigh 1709 W
   John, Dolton 1673 [W]
   John, Frithelstock 1709 W
   John, Dolton 1738 W
   John, Dolton 1845 W
   Heamaman Julia, Westleigh 1733 A
   Robert, Burrington 1845 W
   Thomas, Ashreigney 1834 A to Elizabeth, widow
   William, Westleigh 1692 A
   William, Ashreigney 1831 W
   William, Yarnscombe 1852 W
Heanes see Haynes
Heaning Jane, Chulmleigh 1696 W
Heans see Haynes
Heannpton see Hampton
Heard, Harde, Hearde, Herd, Herde, Hurde
   ..., Chittlehampton 1601, 1609 and 1611 [W]
   Hearde ..., Yarnscombe 1602 and 1609 [W]
   Hearde ..., Ashford 1608 [W]
   Hearde ..., Dowland 1609 [W]
   Abigail, Bideford, widow 1807 W
   Hearde Agnes, Dowland 1580 A
   Agnes, Clovelly 1639 W
   Agnes, Stoodleigh 1681 [W]
   Agnes, Buckland Brewer 1727 W
   Herd Alice, King's Nympton, widow 1570 W
   Hearde Alice, Northam 1593 W
   Alice, Clovelly 1700 A
   Hearde Andrew, Eggesford 1603 [W]
   Andrew, Mariansleigh 1668, 1669 and 1674 W
   Ann, St Giles in the Wood 1757 W
   Anthony, Buckland Brewer 1587 W
   Anthony, Clovelly 1704 A
   Arthur, Chittlehampton 1637 W
   Baldwin, Buckland Brewer 1631 [W] and 1633 O
   Barnabas, Hartland 1633 W
   Bartholomew, Winkleigh 1643 A
   Charles, Martinhoe 1635 W
   Charles, Merton 1685 A
   Hearde Clement, Molland 1616 [W] and 1619 O
   Clement, Bideford 1798 A
   David, Northam 1596 [W]
   Dorcas, High Bickington 1731 W
   Edmund, Northam 1626 [W]
   Edward, Chittlehampton 1640 W

Edward, Abbotsham 1683 W
Hearde Elizabeth, Hartland 1615 [W]
Elizabeth, Bideford 1834 A to Thomas S. Heard, son
Ellen, Monkleigh 1680 W
Emma, Yarnscombe 1638 W
Esther, Dolton 1762 A
George, Beaford 1733 W
George, Bideford 1778 W
Hearde Giles, Martinhoe 1587 W
Giles, Bow 1599 [W]
Giles, Parkham 1685 W
Giles, Clovelly 1705 A
Grace, Petrockstowe, widow 1640 A
Grace, Hartland 1837 A to Thomas and Richard, sons
Hearde Henry, Great Torrington 1590 [W]
Henry, Dowland 1599 [W]
Henry, Bow 1624 [W]
Henry, North Tawton 1661 W
Henry, Stoodleigh 1662 A
Henry, Mariansleigh 1667 A, 1671 O and 1674 O
Henry, Dolton 1686 W
Henry, Buckland Brewer 1743 W
Henry, Bow 1744 A
Henry Ellis, Clovelly 1831 A to Margaret Ross of Hartland,
   daughter
Hearde Hugh, Molland 1585 A
Hugh, Clovelly 1596 [W]
Humphrey, Rackenford 1697 W
Isaac, Bow 1763 W
Hearde Isott, Clovelly 1597 [W]
James, Hartland 1592 [W]
James, Clovelly 1601 W
James, Clovelly 1706 W
James, Clovelly 1724 A
James, Hartland 1724 W
Jane, Iddesleigh 1629 [W]
Jane, Hartland 1740 A
Herd Joan, Dolton 1565 W
Joan, Hartland 1565 W and 1569 W
Joan, Dowland 1586 A
Joan, Iddesleigh 1589 [W]
Hearde Joan, Dowland 1590 [W]
Joan, Buckland Brewer, widow 1607 [W] "of Beare" in
   register; forename blank in Ms; supplied from parish register
Joan, Pilton 1611 [W]; forename blank in Ms; supplied from
   parish register
Hearde Joan, Dowland 1617 [W] and 1627 [W]
Joan, Clovelly 1679 W
Joan, Hartland 1691 W
Joan, South Molton 1767 A
Hearde John, Clovelly 1564 W
Hearde John, Dolton 1564 W
Hearde John, Ashford 1567 W
John, Bursdon, Hartland 1568 W
John, Dowland 1568 W and 1578 A
John, Frithelstock 1577 W
Herd John, Parkham 1579 W
Hearde John, Northam 1583 W and 1585 [W]
John, Zeal Monachorum 1586 A
John, Woolfardisworthy 1587 A
John, Dowland 1588 W
John, Northam 1588 W
Hearde John, Meshaw 1593 [W]
John, Great Torrington 1597 [W]
Hearde John, Littleham (near Bideford) 1605 W
Hearde John, Newton St Petrock 1616 [W]
John, Barnstaple 1622 [W]
John, Hartland 1625 [W]
John, Dolton 1630 [W]
John, Ashford 1637 A
John, Knowstone 1640 W
John, Hartland 1642 W
John, Clovelly 1643 W
John, Welcombe 1663 W
John, Iddesleigh 1665 W

John, Chittlehampton 1677 A
John, Ashford 1680 W
John, Clovelly 1695 W
John, Barnstaple 1704 W
John, Ilfracombe 1707 A
John, Roborough 1710 A
John, Coldridge 1712 W
John, Hartland 1712 W
John, Weare Giffard 1715 A
John, Shebbear 1722 W
John, Hartland 1723 W
John, Bow 1739 A and 1740 A
Herd John, Hartland 1751 W
John, Hartland 1782 W
John, Bow, Nymet Tracey 1795 W
John, Hartland 1828 W
John, Chittlehampton 1851 W
John, Warkleigh 1855 A
Joseph, Woolfardisworthy 1689 W
Joseph, Hartland 1845 A to Thomas, brother
Lawrence, Dolton 1700 W
Lawrence, Woolfardisworthy 1757 W
Lovell, Barnstaple 1629 [W]
Hearde Lucy, Ashford 1570 W
Margaret, Barnstaple 1703 W
Margery, Chittlehampton 1620 [W]
Hearde Marian, Dolton 1571 W
Mark, Hartland 1635 W
Mary, Buckland Brewer 1619 [W]
Mary, Bideford 1635 A
Mary, Hartland 1667 A
Mary, High Bickington 1707 W
Mary, Bow, widow 1811 W
Nicholas, Clovelly 1676 A
Nicholas, Hartland 1698 W
Nicholas, Monkleigh 1781 A
Hearde Oliver, Barnstaple 1608 [W]; forename blank in Ms;
    supplied from parish register
Oliver, Barnstaple 1632 [W], 1633 O and 1634 W
Oliver, Barnstaple, snr. 1637 O
Peter, Ashreigney 1629 [W]
Peter, Tawstock 1681 A
Peter, Buckland Brewer 1701 W
Peter, Clovelly 1719 W
Petherick, Tawstock 1593 [W]
Philip, Hartland 1597 [W]
Philip, North Tawton 1627 [W]
Philip, Dowland 1667 A
Philip, Barnstaple 1703 W
Rebecca, Shebbear 1725 W
Harde Richard, Zeal Monachorum 1569 W
Hearde Richard, Clovelly 1587 A and 1588 O account
Richard, Great Torrington 1591 [W]
Hearde Richard, Hartland 1617 [W]
Richard, Bow 1646 W
Richard, Hartland 1755 A
Richard, Hartland 1792 A
Richard, Bideford 1813 W
Richard, Clovelly, mariner 1816 A to Patricia Helton,
    daughter
Herde Robert, Buckland Brewer 1569 W
Robert, Dowland 1577 W
Robert, Molland 1590 [W]
Robert, Yarnscombe 1601 W
Robert, Instow 1683 W
Robert, Beaford 1809 A
Roger, Abbotsham 1615 [W]
Roger, Clovelly 1716 W
Samuel, Alwington 1692 W
Samuel, Mariansleigh 1705 A
Sarah, Hartland 1775 W
Susan, Welcombe 1682 A
Herde Thomas, North Tawton 1573 W
Thomas, Hartland 1577 W
Hearde Thomas, Hartland 1589 W

Thomas, Buckland Brewer 1592 [W]
Hearde Thomas, Hartland 1599 [W]
Hearde Thomas, Dolton 1603 W
Thomas, Hartland 1644 A
Thomas, Hartland 1705 W
Thomas, Bideford 1709 A
Thomas, Beaford, carpenter 1783 A to Elizabeth, widow; A
    dbn 1815 to Rebecca wife of Arthur Stapledon of Merton,
    yeoman, daughter
Thomas, Hartland, husbandman 1814 A to Thomas of
    Plymouth Dock, shipwright, son
Thomas, Hartland 1822 W
Hearde Thomasine, Zeal Monachorum 1593 [W]
Thomasine, Merton 1606 W
Thomasine, Buckland Brewer 1638 W
Thomasine, Marwood 1724 W
Walter, Dowland 1575 W
Walter, Clovelly 1624 [W] and 1626 O
Hearde William, Dowland 1564 W
William, Dolton 1568 W
Herde William, Hartland 1573 W
Hurde William, Welcombe 1578 W
Herde William, Hartland 1579 W
Hearde William, Molland 1591 [W]
Hearde William, Dowland 1597 [W]
Hearde William, Stoodleigh 1610 [W]; forename blank in Ms;
    supplied from parish register
William, Buckland Brewer 1624 [W]
William, Dowland 1630 [W]
William, Northam 1633 W
William, Clovelly, jnr. 1638 W
William, Meeth 1639 A
William, Dowland 1663 W
William, Barnstaple 1685 A
William, Hartland 1707 W
William, Northam 1718 W
William, Bideford 1746 W
William, Beaford 1755 W
William, Bow 1759 W
William, Bideford 1762 W
Herd William, Puddington 1815 W
Willmot, Molland 1590 [W]
Willmot, Parkham 1685 W
Willmot, Clovelly 1687 A
Hearden see Harding
Hearder, Harder
    Agnes, High Bray 1598 [W]
    Harder Alice, Tawstock 1739 W
    Ann, Goodleigh 1590 [W]
    Arthur, West Buckland 1692 A
    Harder Catherine, Marwood 1778 W
    Elizabeth, South Molton 1729 W
    Harder Elizabeth, Marwood 1778 W
    Herder Henry, High Bray 1568 W
    Henry, North Molton 1590 [W]
    Henry, High Bray 1620 [W]
    Henry, South Molton 1622 [W]
    Henry, South Molton 1681 A
    Henry, South Molton 1694 A
    Henry, South Molton 1714 W
    Henry, Tawstock 1826 [W]
    Harder James, West Buckland 1684 A
    Harder John, Romansleigh 1727 A
    Harder John, South Molton 1727 A
    Harder Josiah, Berrynarbor 1723 W
    Margery, North Molton 1595 [W]
    Herder Stephen, Tawstock 1585 [W]
    Susan, South Molton 1696 W
    Walter, Barnstaple 1626 [W]
    William, Tawstock 1571 W
    William, Filleigh 1597 [W]
Heardinge see Harding
Hearle, Hearell
    Agnes, Tawstock 1626 [W]
    Hearell Agnes, Berrynarbor 1632 [W]

Alexander, Ashreigney 1592 [W]
Hearell Alexander, North Tawton 1623 [W]
Alexander, Rose Ash 1673 W
Hearell Ann, Tawstock, widow 1632 [W]
Catherine, Tawstock 1672 W
Hearell Christopher, Tawstock 1622 [W]
Hearell Christopher, Winkleigh 1622 [W]
George, Tawstock 1614 [W]; forename blank in Ms; supplied
    from parish register
Humphrey, Twitchen 1688 W
James, Tawstock 1619 [W]
James, Tawstock 1660 W
James, Tawstock 1704 A
Joan, Great Torrington 1622 [W]
John, Cruwys Morchard 1616 [W]
Hearell John, Zeal Monachorum 1626 [W]
John, Thelbridge 1630 [W]
John, Tawstock 1663 W
John, Tawstock 1702 A
John, Cruwys Morchard 1710 W
Hearell Roger, Tawstock 1636 W
Simon, Ashreigney 1595 [W]
Hearell Thomas, Great Torrington 1588 A
Hearell alias Borne William, Ashreigney 1586 W
William, Ashreigney 1592 [W]
William, Winkleigh 1661 W
William, Arlington 1662 W
    see also Harle
Hearlind William, Kentisbury 1742 W
Hearn see Hearne
Hearnaman, Harnaman, Hornaman, Hurnaman
    ..., Northam 1608 and 1611 [W]
    ..., Rose Ash 1615 [W]
    Arthur, Northam 1625 [W]
    Hurnaman Clement, Knowstone 1569 W
    George, Bow 1630 [W]
    George, Northam 1637 W
    Hornaman Joan, Witheridge 1584 W
    Joan, Burrington 1635 A
    John, Burrington 1597 [W]
    John, Northam 1614 [W]; forename blank in Ms; supplied
       from parish register
    John, Creacombe 1621 [W]
    John, Northam 1621 [W]
    John, South Molton 1637 W
    John, Woolfardisworthy 1707 W
    Mary, Northam 1614 [W]; forename blank in Ms; supplied
       from parish register
    Mathew, Northam 1625 [W]
    Peter, Rose Ash 1624 [W]
    Richard, Tawstock 1713 W
    Susan, Northam 1676 A
    Thomas, Buckland Filleigh 1591 [W]
    Thomas, Burrington 1622 and 1623 [W]
    Thomas, Northam 1623 [W]
    Harnaman alias Poule William, Rose Ash 1564 W
    William, Northam 1593 [W]
    William, Creacombe 1620 [W]
    William, Creacombe 1641 W
Hearne, Hearn, Hern
    ..., East Putford 1604 [W]
    ..., Pilton 1609 [W]
    Amy, Fremington 1591 [W]
    Anthony, Petrockstowe 1602 [W]; forename blank in Ms;
       supplied from parish register
    Hearn Arthur, Great Torrington 1664 A
    Catherine, East Putford 1582 W
    Elizabeth, High Bickington 1730 A
    Elizabeth, Buckland Filleigh 1750 W
    Hearn Elizabeth, Petrockstowe 1752 A
    Hearn Elizabeth see also Mary Ann Larkworthy
    George, High Bickington 1716 W
    George, High Bickington 1730 A
    Hearn Henry, Langtree 1795 W
    Hearn Henry, Beaford, yeoman 1847 A to Hannah, widow

James, Shebbear 1665 W
James, Yarnscombe 1749 W
John, Meeth 1590 [W]
John, East Putford 1596 [W]
John, Petrockstowe 1608 [W]; forename blank in Ms; supplied
    from parish register
Hearn John, High Bickington 1677 A
John, East Putford 1695 W
John, Molland 1713 W
Hearn John, High Bickington 1766 W and 1774 W
Lewis, Buckland Filleigh 1747 W
Lodovic, Petrockstowe 1688 W
Margaret, Monkleigh 1661 W
Hern Mary, High Bickington 1789 W
Michael, High Bickington 1627 [W]
Michael, High Bickington 1674 W
Nicholas, East Putford 1603 W
Richard, Parkham 1666 W
Hearn Richard, Great Torrington, labourer 1855 A to
    Margaret, widow
Robert, Great Torrington 1668 A
Hern Robert, Ilfracombe 1746 A
Hearn Robert, High Bickington 1752 W
Hern Robert, High Bickington 1775 A
Hern Robert, Zeal Monachorum 1833 A to Elizabeth, widow
Susan, Dolton 1637 A
Thomas, Buckland Filleigh or Buckland Brewer 1666 W
Hearn Thomas, Petrockstowe 1705 W
Hearn Thomas, Buckland Filleigh 1785 A
Hearon see Heron
Hearson, Hearston, Herson, Herston
    Agnes, Tawstock 1601 [W]; forename blank in Ms; supplied
       from parish register
    Agnes, South Molton 1686 A
    Hearston Anthony, Tawstock 1630 [W]
    Caleb, Barnstaple 1697 A
    Joan, Barnstaple 1767 W
    Herson John, Ilfracombe 1676 W
    Herson John, Abbotsham 1684 W
    John, Ilfracombe 1703 A
    Herson John, Barnstaple 1723 W
    Jonathan, Barnstaple 1694 W
    Mary, Barnstaple 1754 A
    Nicholas, Ilfracombe 1823 W
    Richard, Barnstaple, puller 1811 W
    Susan, Ilfracombe 1832 A to George of Pilton, son
    Hearston Thomas, Fremington 1578 W
    Herson Thomas, Northam 1688 W
    Thomas, Woolfardisworthy 1718 W
    Thomas, Barnstaple 1754 W
    Herston Walter, Tawstock 1576 W
    Herson William, Bideford 1754 A
Heart see Hart
Heashead Lodovic, Shebbear 1621 [W]
Heath Alice, Chittlehampton 1660 [W]
    Grace, Barnstaple 1795 W
    John, Barnstaple 1622 [W]
    John, Bideford 1644 W
    John, Bideford 1716 W
    Joseph, Bideford 1708 A
    Joseph, Bideford 1746 A
    Margaret, Bideford 1724 W
    William, Pilton 1661 W
Heather Thomasine, East Buckland 1586 A
Heathwood Richard, Barnstaple 1625 [W]
Heawarde see Haywood
Heckett Joan, Barnstaple 1578 W
    Robert, Barnstaple 1633 A
Heclman Melanie, Bideford 1622 [W]
Heddon, Headdon, Headon
    ..., Filleigh 1604 [W]
    ..., Mortehoe 1610 [W]
    ..., Dowland 1611 [W]
    Agnes, Bratton Fleming 1625 [W]
    Alexander, Bratton Fleming 1619 [W]

Alice, West Down 1631 [W]
Ann, Tawstock 1698 W
Ann, Bideford 1727 W
Ann, Stoke Rivers 1776 W
Anthony, Arlington 1598 [W]
Baldwin, Marwood 1643 W
Headon Charity, West Down 1734 W
Christian, Mortehoe 1601 W
Christian, West Down 1625 W
Christopher, Littleham (near Bideford) 1626 [W]
Christopher, West Down 1638 A
David, Bratton Fleming 1632 [W]
Edmund, Bratton Fleming 1628 [W]
Headon Edmund, Tawstock 1688 W
Edward, Ashford 1727 A
Elizabeth, Great Torrington 1708 A
Elizabeth, Mortehoe 1719 W
Elizabeth, Filleigh 1764 W
George, Georgeham 1711 W
George, Heanton Punchardon 1781 W
George, Ilfracombe 1847 W
Gertrude, Mortehoe 1639 W
Headon Henry, Ilfracombe 1585 W
Henry, West Down 1586 A
Henry, Great Torrington 1638 W
Henry, Mortehoe 1643 W
Henry, Combe Martin 1663 W
Hugh, Bratton Fleming 1620 [W]
Headon James, Tawstock 1763 W
James, Barnstaple 1796 W
Joan, West Down, widow 1567 W
Joan, Barnstaple 1588 A
Joan, Barnstaple 1634 W
Joan, Bulkworthy 1726 A
Joan, Georgeham 1728 A
John, Dowland 1576 W
John, Mortehoe 1588 W
John, Bratton Fleming 1611 [W]; forename blank in Ms;
    supplied from parish register
John, West Down 1625 [W]
John, Instow 1637 A
John, Iddesleigh 1643 W
John, West Down 1643 A
John, Mortehoe 1688 W
John, East Buckland 1698 A
John, Mortehoe 1702 A
John, West Down 1713 W
John, Ilfracombe 1724 W
John, Great Torrington 1741 A
John, Weare Giffard 1821 W and 1827 W
John, Georgeham 1831 W
Judith, Barnstaple 1825 A to Nanny, sister
Headdon Julian, Berrynarbor 1586 W
Julian, Ilfracombe 1589 W
Margaret, Georgeham 1727 W
Margery, Great Torrington 1667 W
Mary, Ilfracombe 1744 A
Headon Nathaniel, Heanton Punchardon 1765 A
Nicholas, Goodleigh 1591 [W]
Nicholas, Hartland 1636 A
Philip, Arlington 1631 [W]
Richard, Dowland 1594 [W]
Richard, Bratton Fleming 1611 [W]; forename blank in Ms;
    supplied from parish register
Richard, Bratton Fleming 1636 A and 1640 O
Richard, West Buckland 1696 W
Richard, Georgeham 1717 W
Richard, Heanton Punchardon 1776 A
Richard, West Down 1780 W
Richard, North Molton 1792 W
Richard, North Molton, yeoman 1797 W
Headdon Richard, North Molton 1823 W
Richard, Georgeham 1840 W
Headon Robert, Barnstaple 1669 A
Robert, Barnstaple 1681 A

Robert, Mortehoe 1695 W
Robert, West Down 1721 W
Robert, Mortehoe 1847 W
Roger, Georgeham 1696 W
Roger, Georgeham 1731 A
Roger, Mortehoe, yeoman 1811 W
Samuel, Mortehoe 1642 W
Stephen, Bideford 1711 A
Thomas, West Down 1601 W
Thomas, Georgeham 1619 [W]
Thomas, Bratton Fleming 1628 [W]
Thomas, Roborough 1631 [W]
Thomas, North Tawton 1633 W
Thomas, North Molton 1661 A
Thomas, Georgeham 1685 A
Thomas, ship *Plymouth* 1748 W
Thomas, Heanton Punchardon 1776 W and A
Thomasine, Georgeham 1626 [W] amd O
Thomasine, Georgeham 1637 W
Walter, Bow 1590 [W]
William, Bratton Fleming, jnr. 1568 W
William, Frithelstock 1571 W
William, West Down 1603 W
William, Dowland 1616 [W]
William, Marwood 1639 A
William, Bratton Fleming 1673 W
Headon William, Great Torrington 1702 A
William, Mortehoe 1734 W
William, West Down 1827 W
Headon William, Clovelly 1856 A
Willmot, Littleham (near Bideford) 1711 A
Hedge Richard, Lynton 1628 [W]
Hedgeman, Hedgman
    John, East Worlington 1813 A
    Hedgman William, East Worlington 1823 W
Heiffers John, East Anstey 1605 W
Heimer Samuel, Bideford 1681 A
Heighman see Hayman
Heissett ..., Shebbear 1611 [W]
Heldrewe John, Tawstock 1567 W
Hele see Heale
Heliar, Helier, Helliar, Helliare, Hellyar, Helyar
    ..., Ilfracombe 1512 [W]
    Helliare Ann, Wembworthy 1584 A
    Ann, Little Torrington 1617 [W]
    Helyar Anthony, George Nympton 1628 [W]
    Helyar Charity, Ilfracombe 1619 [W]
    Christopher, Northam 1675 A
    Hellyar Edward, Chulmleigh 1733 A
    Helyar Emblem, Chawleigh 1595 [W]
    Helyar George, Brushford 1629 [W]
    Helyar John, Yarnscombe 1590 [W]
    John, Ashreigney 1613 [W]; forename blank in Ms; supplied
        from parish register
    Helliar John, Ilfracombe 1696 [W]
    Hellier Mary, South Molton 1781 W
    Helier Peter, Chulmleigh 1580 W
    Helyar Philip, Parkham 1599 [W]
    Helyar Philip, Yarnscombe 1615 [W]
    Helyar Richard, Chawleigh 1597 [W]
    Robert, South Molton 1572 W
    Hellyar Thomas, Bideford 1665 A
    Hellyar William, Chulmleigh 1665 W
    Helliar William, Chulmleigh 1719 W and A
    Helliar William, Ilfracombe 1719 W
Hellens see Hellins
Heller Michael, Mariansleigh 1811 W
    William, Winkleigh, yeoman 1809 A to Mary, widow
Helliar, Helliare, Hellier see Heliar
Hellins, Hellens, Helling, Hellings
    Honor, Heanton Punchardon 1824 W
    Hellings alias Hooper John, King's Nympton 1617 [W]
    John, George Nympton 1728 W
    Hellings John, George Nympton 1747 W
    Nathaniel, Burrington 1721 W

Samuel, Heanton Punchardon 1816 W
Helling Susan, Littleham (near Bideford) 1739 A
Hellings William, South Molton 1703 A
Hellens William, ship *Antelope* 1759 W
Hellyar see Heliar
Helmer Richard, Chulmleigh 1567 W
Helton Patricia see Richard Heard
Helyar see Heliar
Hemborow Thomas, Great Torrington 1843 W
Hempton, Hemyton see Hampton
Hender Anthony, Clovelly 1729 W
John, Hartland 1834 W
Susan, Hartland 1789 W
Henley see Hensley
Hennebeare Maurice, Great Torrington 1597 [W]
Henney Philip, Burrington 1758 W
Henning George, Chulmleigh 1691 W
Hensley, Henley, Hensleigh, Hensly
Hensleigh ..., South Molton 1608 [W]
Hensly Anthony, King's Nympton 1687 W
Hensly Anthony, Chittlehampton 1687 W
Anthony, Fremington 1757 W
Hensly Arthur, Instow 1669 A
Jeremiah, Barnstaple 1693 and 1695 W
Hensly John, Barnstaple 1763 W
Henley John, Welcombe 1838 W
Hensly William, Barnstaple 1772 A
Henwood, Henwode
Ann, Bideford 1663 W
Henwode John, King's Nympton 1569 W
Hephey, Hephay, Hepy
Margery, Northam 1589 A
Hephay Margery, Northam 1593 [W]
Hepy Mathew, Chulmleigh 1626 [W]
Hepper see Hopper
Hepy see Hephey
Herapath see Harrapath
Herbert William, Bideford 1671 A
Herd, Herde see Heard
Herder see Hearder
Herdinge, Herdon, Herdynge see Harding
Herell see Harle
Herman Elizabeth, Bideford 1817 W
Hern see Hearne
Hernman, Hermaman, Hernaman, Hernamann
Hernaman Alexander, Winkleigh 1743 W
Arthur, King's Nympton 1755 A
Christopher, Northam 1682 A
Elizabeth, Winkleigh 1845 W
Francis, Northam 1827 W
Hermaman George, Brushford 1693 A
James, Northam 1682 W
James, Bideford 1690 A
John, Burrington 1580 W
John, North Molton 1662 W
John, Northam 1683 W
John, Winkleigh 1832 W
Hermaman Luke, South Molton 1686 W
Mary, Woolfardisworthy 1720 W
Mary, Bideford 1735 W
Phillippa, Northam 1687 W
Prudence, Northam 1755 W
Ralph, Witheridge 1580 W
Richard, South Molton 1776 A
Richard, Knowstone, yeoman 1809 A
Hernamann Richard, Tresidder, Ilfracombe 1855 [W]
   Tresidder possibly a place name
Robert, Stoodleigh 1662 W
Robert, Northam 1682 W
Sarah, Northam 1685 W
Susan, Woolfardisworthy 1736 W
Thomas, Northam 1698 W
Herneman Thomasine, Winkleigh, widow 1571 W
William, Northam 1690 W

William, Northam 1825 and 1826 W
Heron, Hearon
Alexander, High Bickington 1578 A
Hearon Ann, Fremington 1598 [W]
Humphrey, Instow 1589 W
Joan, Ilfracombe 1581 W
John, High Bickington 1574 W
Richard, St Giles in the Wood 1568 W
Thomas, Buckland Brewer 1642 [W]
Hearon William, East Putford 1564 W
Herring John, Barnstaple 1838 A to Maria Mayne Herring,
   widow
Maria Mayne, Barnstaple 1839 A to David
Hersell see Hursell
Herson, Herston see Hearson
Hert see Hart
Hervey see Harvey
Hessott see Hissett
Hetherd, Hethrede
Hethrede Robert, East Buckland 1584 W
Robert, East Buckland 1588 A
Thomasine, East Buckland 1586 A
Hetton see Hatton
Hewes see Hughes
Hewett, Hewet, Huet, Huets, Huett
..., North Tawton 1611 [W]
Ebbota, Northam 1630 [W]
Hewet Edward, South Molton 1743 W
Huett Elizabeth, Parracombe 1774 W
Elizabeth, Barnstaple 1777 W
Henry, Pilton 1763 A
John, North Tawton 1629 [W]
Huet John, Combe Martin, snr. 1680 W
John, Ilfracombe 1792 W
Huets alias Huty Margaret, Goodleigh 1581 W
Sarah, Ilfracombe 1797 W
Thomas, Ilfracombe 1783 A
Thomasine, Ilfracombe 1793 A
William, South Molton 1732 and 1734 W
William, Bideford 1758 A
William, Barnstaple 1766 W
William, Ilfracombe 1807 W
William, South Molton, bootmaker 1814 A to Philip Tapp
Hexhaye John, Northam 1584 A
Hext ..., Buckland Filleigh 1604 [W]
Christian, North Molton 1575 W
Edith, Bideford 1638 W
Hugh, Mortehoe 1582 A
Joan, Mortehoe 1604 W
Hexter John, Winkleigh 1817 [W]
Heyde see Head
Heydon see Haydon
Heyman see Hayman
Heysed, Heysett, Heysset see Hissett
Heysey Thomas, Mariansleigh 1660 W
Heyward, Heywood, Heywoode see Haywood
Hibbert George, Northam 1698 W
Joan, Northam 1701 W
Hickett Joan and John, Marwood 1597 [W]
Hickman ..., Bideford 1610 [W]
John, Bideford 1587 A
Hicks ..., Berrynarbor 1837 A
Grace, Berrynarbor 1752 A
John, Berrynarbor 1755 A
John, Berrynarbor 1837 A to Mary, widow
Philip, Shebbear 1739 A
Philip, Berrynarbor 1843 A
Richard, Berrynarbor 1835 A
William, Shebbear 1817 W
Hiern Blackwill Thomas, Barnstaple, surgeon 1797 A
James, Barnstaple, gentleman 1797 A
Mary, Barnstaple 1791 W
Thomas Blackwill, Barnstaple, surgeon 1797 A
William, Barnstaple 1780 A
William, Litchardon, Fremington, gentleman 1806 [W]

Higgins, Heggins
  Heggins ..., Alwington 1613 [W]
  John, Combe Martin 1629 and 1631 [W]
Higgott Mary, Barnstaple 1664 W
Higgs Arthur, Great Torrington 1660 W
Higher Rebecca, Ilfracombe 1774 A
  William, Ilfracombe 1749 W
  William, Ilfracombe 1830 W
Higman Joseph, Great Torrington, merchant 1810 A
Hile Agnes, Northam 1602 W
  George, Northam 1715 W
  Joan, Northam 1677 W
  Julian, Northam 1676 W
  Mary, Fremington 1716 W
  William, Landcross 1605 W
Hill, Hille, Hyll
  ..., Mortehoe 1600 [W] account
  ..., Fremington 1602 A
  ..., Great Torrington 1605 [W]
  ..., Berrynarbor 1607 [W]
  ..., Loxhore 1607 [W]
  ..., Oakford 1607 [W]
  ..., Heanton Punchardon 1608 [W]
  ..., Chittlehampton 1609 and 1613 [W]
  ..., Martinhoe 1613 [W]
  ... 1672 [W]
  Abraham, Bideford 1636 W
  Agnes, Pilton 1677 A
  Hill alias Saunders Agnes, Buckland Brewer 1707 A
  Alexander, Instow 1626 [W]
  Alice, Molland, widow 1610 [W]; forename blank in Ms;
    supplied from parish register
  Alice, Dowland 1632 [W]
  Amos, South Molton 1747 W
  Amos, Kentisbury 1814 W
  Ann, Shebbear 1595 [W]
  Ann, Littleham (near Bideford) 1740 [W]
  Ann, Barnstaple 1802 W
  Anthony, Barnstaple 1614 [W]; forename blank in Ms;
    supplied from parish register
  Anthony, Buckland Brewer 1618 [W]
  Anthony, Chittlehampton 1628 [W]
  Anthony, Ashreigney 1684 A
  Anthony, Ashreigney 1711 W
  Anthony, Ashreigney 1761 A
  Anthony, Ashreigney 1792 W
  Appollina, Loxhore 1623 [W]
  Arthur, Ashreigney 1663 W
  Baldwin, Barnstaple 1601 W
  Betty, Barnstaple 1823 A to William, cordwainer, son
  Catherine, Tawstock 1771 W
  Charles, Tawstock 1715 A
  Charles, Parkham 1721 A
  Charles, Langtree, yeoman 1810 A
  Christopher, Dolton 1625 [W]
  Christopher, Great Torrington 1638 A
  Christopher, Kentisbury 1667 A and 1671 O
  Christopher, Great Torrington 1682 A
  Christopher, Kentisbury 1686 W
  Christopher, Kentisbury 1776 A
  Clase, Chittlehampton 1580 W
  Daniel, Rose Ash 1669 W
  Daniel, Berrynarbor 1752 W
  Daniel, Arlington 1778 A
  David, Barnstaple 1663 W
  David, Barnstaple 1681 W
  David, Lynton 1704 W
  David, Lynton 1722 W
  David, Lynton 1802 W
  Edmund, Ashreigney 1784 A
  Edward, Berrynarbor 1598 [W]
  Edward, Warkleigh 1661 W
  Edward, East Anstey 1705 W
  Edward, South Molton 1762 A
  Edward, South Molton 1855 W

  Elizabeth, Barnstaple 1630 and 1631 [W]
  Elizabeth, Dolton, widow 1632 [W]
  Elizabeth, Landcross 1680 A
  Elizabeth, Barnstaple 1684 A
  Elizabeth, Winkleigh 1689 W
  Elizabeth, Barnstaple 1710 W
  Elizabeth, Ashreigney 1711 A
  Elizabeth, Parkham 1733 W
  Elizabeth, Barnstaple 1761 W
  Elizabeth, Ashreigney 1811 A
  Francis 1776 W
  George, East Anstey 1578 W
  George, Great Torrington 1580 W
  George, Chawleigh 1641 W
  George, Buckland Brewer 1661 A
  George, Barnstaple 1677 W
  George, Sheepwash 1703 W
  George, Bideford 1719 W
  Gertrude, Pilton 1685 A
  Grace, Stoodleigh 1778 W
  Henry, Little Torrington 1580 W
  Henry, Knowstone 1589 W
  Henry, Knowstone 1631 [W]
  Henry, Pilton 1632 and 1633 [W]
  Henry, Ilfracombe 1644 W
  Henry, Burrington 1684 A
  Henry, Ilfracombe 1701 W
  Henry, ship *Conquerer* 1760 A
  Henry Shapcott, King's Nympton 1841 W
  Hugh, King's Nympton 1589 A
  Hugh, Fremington 1610 [W]; forename blank in Ms; supplied
    from parish register
  Hugh, Great Torrington 1644 A
  Isaac, Northam 1774 A
  James, Shirwell 1610 [W]; forename blank in Ms; supplied
    from parish register
  James, Kentisbury 1624 [W]
  James, Molland 1634 W
  James, Stoodleigh 1637 A
  James, Barnstaple 1644 A
  James, Chawleigh 1734 W
  James, West Anstey 1742 W
  James, Stoodleigh 1749 W
  James, Trentishoe 1756 W
  James, Great Torrington 1758 A
  James, West Anstey 1790 W
  James, West Anstey 1829 W
  Hille Jane, Tawstock 1618 [W]
  Jane, West Anstey 1704 W
  Jane, Winkleigh 1834 W
  Joan, East Anstey 1577 W
  Joan, Fremington 1613 [W]; forename blank in Ms;
    supplied from parish register
  Joan, Chawleigh 1617 [W]
  Hille Joan, Warkleigh 1618 [W]
  Joan, Molland 1624 [W] and 1627 O
  Joan, Barnstaple 1631 [W]
  Joan, Oakford 1632 [W]
  Joan, Buckland Brewer 1634 W
  Joan, South Molton, widow 1639 W
  Joan, Ilfracombe 1665 W
  Joan, Great Torrington 1679 W
  Joan, West Anstey 1719 W
  Joan, West Anstey 1743 A
  Hyll John, King's Nympton 1567 W
  Hyll John, Northam 1567 W
  John, Langaton, Chittlehampton 1569 W
  John, Knightacott, Fremington 1572 W
  Hille John, Chulmleigh 1573 A
  John, Chittlehampton 1578 W
  John, Great Torrington 1578 A
  John, Loxhore 1579 [W] account
  John, Kentisbury 1584 W
  John, Martinhoe 1585 W
  John, Ilfracombe 1587 W

John, East Anstey 1592 and 1593 [W]
John, Rose Ash 1594 [W]
John, East Down 1597 [W]
John, Mortehoe 1599 [W]
John, Martinhoe 1606 W
John, Buckland Brewer 1607 [W]; forename blank in Ms;
    supplied from parish register
John, Trentishoe 1622 [W]
John, Yarnscombe 1626 [W]
John, Dowland 1630 [W]
John, Loxhore 1631 [W]
John, Great Torrington 1663 A
John, Chittlehampton 1669 and 1670 A and jnr. 1670 O
John, Woolfardisworthy 1679 A
John, Barnstaple 1682 W
John, Goodleigh 1685 W
John, Bideford 1688 W
John, Alverdiscott 1690 A
John, Lynton 1695 A
John, Fremington 1697 W
John, East Anstey 1698 A
John, North Molton, jnr. 1703 W
John, North Molton, snr. 1703 W
John, Abbotsham 1707 A
John, Hartland 1708 [W]
John. West Anstey 1711 W
John, Fremington 1716 W
John, Littleham (near Bideford) 1720 A
John, Bideford 1733 A
John, Bideford 1734 W
John, Chittlehampton 1735 A
John, Witheridge 1736 W
John, Bideford 1738 W
John, Warkleigh 1741 W
John, West Anstey 1742 W
John, Chittlehampton 1744 W
John, East Anstey 1752 W
John, Northam 1758 W
John, Witheridge 1762 W
John, Great Torrington 1763 A
John, Berrynarbor 1764 A
John, Winkleigh 1771 W
John, West Anstey 1772 W
John, Chulmleigh 1774 W
John, West Anstey 1775 A
John, Eggesford 1778 W
John, West Anstey 1779 W
John, King's Nympton 1784 W
John, Witheridge 1784 A
John, Barnstaple 1788 A
John, Warkleigh 1793 W
John, Knowstone, yeoman 1798 A
Hill alias Datscombe John, East Anstey, yeoman 1801 W
John, Marwood 1812 W
John, Barnstaple 1818 W
John, Barnstaple, cooper 1819 A to Joanna, widow
John, Heanton Punchardon 1831 A
John, North Molton 1842 W and 1847 W
John, Great Torrington 1847 W
John, Bishop's Nympton 1854 W
John, Fremington 1857 W
Joseph, Knowstone, yeoman 1809 W
Joseph, Warkleigh, yeoman 1809 A
Joseph, Knowstone, yeoman 1821 A to Elizabeth, widow
Joseph, Knowstone 1844 W
Josiah, Great Torrington 1623 [W]
Judith, Westleigh 1846 W
Lewis, Beaford 1568 W
Lodovic, Challacombe 1641 W
Margaret, Knowstone 1591 [W]
Margaret, Ashreigney 1673 W
Margery, Merton 1680 W
Mark, Meeth 1623 [W]
Martha, Pilton 1619 [W]
Mary, South Molton 1643 A

Mary, West Anstey or East Anstey 1661 W
Mary, Ilfracombe 1675 W
Mary, Barnstaple 1679 W
Mary, Hartland 1680 and 1699 W
Mary, Lynton 1706 W
Mary, West Down 1718 W
Mary, Chawleigh 1786 W
Mary, Warkleigh, widow 1809 W
Mary, East Anstey 1825 W
Mary, Barnstaple 1846 W
Michael, Chawleigh 1617 [W] and O
Michael, Stoodleigh 1617 [W]
Miles, Barnstaple 1637 W
Nathaniel, Barnstaple 1734 W
Nicholas, Molland 1616 [W]
Nicholas, Ashreigney 1662 W
Nicholas, Barnstaple 1671 W
Nicholas, Ilfracombe 1684 W
Nicholas, North Molton 1821 W
Paul, Littleham (near Bideford) 1688 W
Hyll Peter, East Anstey 1564 W
Petronell, Pilton 1684 A
Philip, Buckland Brewer 1622 [W]
Philip, Martinhoe 1622 [W]
Philip, Ashreigney 1643 W
Philip, Molland 1660 A, 1666 A and 1669 O bond
Philip, Tawstock 1683 W
Philip, Tawstock 1761 and 1775 A
Radigon, Lynton 1587 W
Richard, Knowstone 1569 W
Richard, Meeth 1570 W
Richard, Stoodleigh 1592 [W]
Richard, Fremington 1616 [W]
Richard, West Anstey 1617 [W]
Richard, Barnstaple 1623 [W]
Richard, Knowstone 1628 [W]
Richard, Alverdiscott 1640 A
Richard, Pilton 1682 A
Richard, Berrynarbor 1689 W
Richard, Horwood 1848 W
Richard, Upton, yeoman 1853 A to Sarah of Ashbrittle, widow
Hill alias Dodscombe Robert, Oakford 1573 A
Robert, Loxhore 1580 W
Robert, Great Torrington 1592 [W]
Robert, Chittlehampton 1604 W
Robert, Barnstaple 1622 [W]
Robert, South Molton 1628 [W]
Robert, Knowstone 1638 W
Robert, Fremington 1643 W
Robert, Barnstaple 1660 W
Robert, Warkleigh 1682 A
Robert, Fremington 1690 W
Robert, Bideford 1719 W
Robert, Lynton 1727 W
Salome, Kentisbury 1597 [W]
Samuel, Bideford 1697 W
Sarah, Barnstaple 1732 A
Simon, Barnstaple 1596 [W]
Simon, Martinhoe 1621 [W]
Simon, George Nympton 1632 [W]
Simon, Instow 1636 W
Simon, Chittlehampton 1675 W
Stephen, Westleigh 1845 W
Susan, Lynton 1695 W
Susan, Barnstaple, widow 1799 W
Hills Susanna, King's Nympton 1854 A to James Bawden,
    labourer, grandson
Hille Thomas, Oakford 1573 A
Thomas, Martinhoe, snr. 1581 W
Thomas, Heanton Punchardon 1602 W
Thomas, East Anstey 1603 W
Thomas, Fremington 1613 [W]; forename blank in Ms;
    supplied from parish register
Thomas, Challacombe 1617 [W]
Thomas, North or South Molton 1668 W

Thomas, Witheridge 1681 and 1686 W
Thomas, Winkleigh 1685 W
Thomas, West Down 1713 W
Thomas, East Anstey 1739 W
Thomas, Ilfracombe 1765 W
Thomas, Chawleigh 1786 W
Thomas, Chittlehampton 1823 W
Thomas, East Anstey 1823 W
Thomas, South Molton, soldier 1854 A to James Bawden of
  King's Nympton, labourer, nephew
Thomasine, Alverdiscott 1708 W
Walter, Lynton 1586 A
Walter, Mortehoe 1698 A
William, Meeth 1583 W
William, Hartland 1588 W
William, Chawleigh 1600 [W]; forename blank in Ms;
  supplied from parish register
William, Barnstaple 1610 [W]; forename blank in Ms;
  supplied from parish register
William, Barnstaple 1622 [W]
William, Buckland Brewer 1623 [W]
William, Dolton 1630 [W]
William, Chittlehampton 1631 and 1632 [W]
William, Barnstaple 1637 W
William, Chittlehampton 1642 A
William, George Nympton 1666 A
William, Buckland Brewer 1679 A
William, George Nympton 1682 W
William, Witheridge 1695 W
William, Barnstaple 1716 W
William, Langtree 1738 W
William, Molland 1748 W
William, Meeth 1755 W
William, Chittlehampton 1771 W
William, South Molton 1783 W
William, Barnstaple 1818 W
William, Bow 1824 W
William, Chittlehampton 1843 W
William, Barnstaple 1845 W
William, Ilfracombe 1852 W
William, Charles 1857 W
William Charles, Fremington 1855 W
Willmot, George Nympton 1627 [W]
Willmot, Ilfracombe 1633 A
Hillman Agnes, Langtree 1629 [W]
Henry, Northam 1598 [W]
Jane, Northam 1736 A
John, Parkham 1629 [W]
John, Northam 1709 W and 1719 W
Peter, Northam 1728 A
Philip, Northam 1735 W
Stephen, Littleham (near Bideford) 1622 [W]
Thomas, Langtree 1624 [W]
Thomas, Northam 1749 A
Thomas, Northam, mariner 1819 A to Susanna, widow
Hillyard Hytteyard Thomas, Westleigh 1576 W
Hilpe Agnes, St Giles in the Wood 1635 W
Hilsdon Hannah, Bow 1719 A
Hilton Mary, Bideford 1827 W
Peter, Alwington 1779 W
Hincksman Thomas, Bondleigh 1564 W
Hindham, Hindam
Hindam John, West Anstey 1677 A
Robert, Oakford 1735 [W]
William, West Anstey 1678 W
Zachariah, Oakford 1669 W
Hiscott, Hiscutt
Elizabeth, Charles 1604 W
Hiscutt Elizabeth, Bideford 1788 W
Henry, Charles 1589 W
Hiscutt Silas, Bideford 1771 W
William, Bratton Fleming 1586 W
Hissett, Hessott, Heysed, Heysett, Heysset, Hissard, Hisset
Heysed Henry, Shebbear 1792 A
Heysett Henry, Petrockstowe 1844 A to Catherine, widow

Hissard Joan, Shirwell 1689 W
Hessott John, Great Torrington 1662 A
Hisset John, Shebbear 1671 W and 1674 O
Lodovic, Shirwell 1682 A
Lodovic, Sheepwash 1707 W
Richard, Chulmleigh 1683 W
Heysset Thomas, Newton St Petrock 1672 W
Heysed William, Shebbear 1680 W
Hitchcock, Haychcockle, Hichcocke, Hichcoke, Hichecocke,
  Hitchcocke, Hychcocke, Hychcoke
..., Bideford 1612 O
Hitchcocke Alexander, Pilton 1591 [W]
Ann, South Molton, widow 1800 W
Hychcocke Henry, Bideford 1589 A
Hitchcocke Joan, Bideford 1623 [W]
Hichcocke alias Wither John, Stoodleigh 1574 W
Hichecocke alias Bickner John, Witheridge 1579 W
Hitchcocke John, Barnstaple 1630 [W]
John, South Molton, innholder 1797 W
John, South Molton, butcher 1797 A
John, South Molton 1829 W
Hychcoke John, Woolfardisworthy [no year given] [W]
Hitchcocke Margaret, Woolfardisworthy 1590 [W]
Haychcockle Margery, Woolfardisworthy 1580 W
Hichcocke alias Wether Richard, Knowstone 1574 A
Hychcocke alias Wither Richard, Creacombe 1574 A
Hichcocke Richard, Bideford 1603 [W]; forename blank in
  Ms; supplied from parish register
Richard, Bideford 1616 [W]
Roger, Bideford 1687 W
Sarah, South Molton 1829 W
Thomas Amory, South Molton 1825 W
Hitchcocke Walter, Pilton 1619 [W]
Hichcoke William, Woolfardisworthy 1575 W
William, South Molton 1818 W
Hoakes Alice, Bideford 1713 W
Hoale see Hole
Hoar, Hoare, Hoor, Hore
Arthur, Great Torrington 1641 A
Catherine, Lapford 1586 A
Christopher, Buckland Brewer 1621 [W]
Christopher, Buckland Brewer 1641 W
Edward, Northam 1841 W
Hoare Emett, Buckland Brewer 1616 [W]
James, Ashreigney 1709 A
James, Dolton 1742 A
John, Lapford 1567 W
Hoare John, Buckland Brewer 1610 [W] "of Hele"; forename
  blank in Ms; supplied from parish register
Hoor John, Abbotsham 1676 A
John, Bideford 1813 A to Mary Willcock, daughter
Lewis, Roborough 1770 W
Phillippa, Ashreigney 1747 W
Roger, Lapford 1568 W
Hoare Roger, Winkleigh 1608 [W]; forename blank in Ms;
  supplied from parish register
Rose, Lapford 1588 W
Hoar Stephen, Buckland Brewer 1599 [W]
William, Ashreigney 1747 W
Willmot, Buckland Brewer 1628 [W]
Hobbs, Hobbes, Hobs
Hobbes ..., South Molton 1602, 1612 and 1613 [W]
Abraham, Bideford 1728 W
Alfred, North Molton 1631 [W]
Alfred, South Molton 1675 W
Ann, North Molton 1639 W
Ann, Countisbury 1836 W
Ann, Great Torrington 1839 A to Nancy, mother
Anstis, North Molton 1669 W
Anthony, Northam 1703 A and 1705 A
Hobbes Bartholomew, North Molton 1594 [W]
Bartholomew, North Molton 1734 W
Beatrice, Brendon 1754 W
Hobbes Cecilia, South Molton 1621 [W]
Daniel, Charles 1676 W

Geoffrey, South Molton, schoolmaster 1801 W
George, South Molton, jnr. 1677 W
George, South Molton 1689 W
Gregory, Brendon 1742 W
Hobbes Henry, South Molton 1623 [W]
Henry, Barnstaple 1696 W
James, Barnstaple 1678 A
James, Barnstaple 1703 A
James, Bideford 1712 A and 1715 A
Hobs Jane, Lynton 1714 W
Hobbes John, South Molton 1599 [W]
John, South Molton, jnr. 1635 W
John, South Molton 1637 W
John, South Molton 1669 W
John, Barnstaple 1675 A
John, Barnstaple 1695 W
John, Chittlehampton 1707 W
John, Northam 1736 W
John, Hartland 1854 W
Julian, Barnstaple 1672 W
Margaret, Barnstaple 1712 W
Mathew, South Molton 1722 A
Hobbe Nicholas, Shebbear 1565 W
Paul, Westleigh 1683 W
Philip, North Molton 1633 O and 1638 A
Philip, South Molton 1690 [W]
Richard, North Molton 1624 [W]
Hobs Richard, South Molton 1637 A
Richard, South Molton 1678 W
Richard, South Molton 1725 W
Richard, Brendon 1728 W
Richard, South Molton 1737 W
Richard, South Molton 1801 A
Silvester, Brendon 1670 W
Thomas, North Molton 1661 W
Thomas, Georgeham 1726 W
Hobbes William, Cheldon 1627 [W]
William, Huntshaw 1631 [W]
William, South Molton 1832 W
Hobbye alias Addren (Addrew) Eleanor, Bideford 1587 W
Hobs see Hobbs
Hobson Alice, Tawstock 1624 [W] and 1626 O
Thomas, Tawstock 1679 W
Hockaday Edward, Northam 1620 [W]
Elizabeth, Roborough 1835 W
Emanuel, Roborough 1825 W
Eustace, Abbotsham 1623 [W]
John, Sheepwash 1626 [W]
John, Buckland Filleigh 1702 W
Nicholas, Barnstaple 1662 W
Nicholas, Bideford 1704 A
Philip, Bideford 1746 A
Thomas, Northam 1621 [W]
Thomas, Buckland Filleigh 1710 W
William, Northam 1708 W
Hockin, Hocken, Hockins, Hockyn
Benjamin, Great Torrington 1645 A
Benjamin, Weare Giffard 1689 W
Benjamin, Frithelstock 1726 A
Hockyn Dorothy, Great Torrington 1640 A
Eleanor, Bideford 1710 W
Hockins George, South Molton 1602 W
Henry, Northam 1685 W
Hocken Hugh, Frithelstock 1630 [W]
Hocken John, Frithelstock 1626 [W]
Hockyn John, Frithelstock, snr. 1638 W
Hockyn John, Oakford 1638 W
John, Frithelstock 1677 W
Richard, Bideford 1686 A
Thomas, Frithelstock 1592 [W]
Thomas, Alverdiscott 1757 W
Hockings William, Burrington 1628 [W]
William, Frithelstock 1664 W
William, Shebbear 1706 A

Hockridge, Hockeridg
Hockeridg Aaron, Abbotsham 1701 W
John, Northam 1728 W
John, Pilton 1839 W
Lawrence, Pilton 1765 W
Rebecca wife of John see John Crocker
Richard, Bideford 1735 W
Hockeridg Robert, Woolfardisworthy 1668 W
Samuel, Northam 1855 W
Sarah, Bideford 1782 W
Thomas, West Down 1829 W
Hockyn see Hockin
Hodge, Hodg, Hodges, Hoydge
..., Northam 1600 A and 1601 A
..., Hartland 1608 [W]
..., Heanton Punchardon 1609 [W]
Alice, West Worlington 1583 W
Ann, Heanton Punchardon 1832 W
Anthony, Oakford 1624 [W]
Avery, South Molton 1741 A
Christopher, North Molton 1593 [W]
Daniel, North Molton 1793 W
Daniel, North Molton 1830 W
Edward, Hartland 1601 A; forename blank in Ms; supplied
    from parish register
Hodges Edward Boucher, Northam 1847 W
Eleanor, Chawleigh 1581 W
Eleanor, Georgeham 1674 A
Elizabeth, Heanton Punchardon 1662 [W]
Elizabeth, Beaford 1836 W
George, Hartland 1644 A
Hodg George, Barnstaple 1719 W
George, North Molton, cordwainer 1824 A to Daniel, builder,
    brother
George, Dolton 1826 W
Grace, Stoodleigh 1726 W
Grace, Oakford 1797 W
Hugh, George Nympton 1578 A
Hugh, Knowstone 1617 [W]
Hugh, Stoodleigh 1685 W
Hugh, East Worlington 1714 W
James, North Tawton 1686 A
Joan, Berrynarbor 1587 A
Joan, Marwood 1593 W
Joan, King's Nympton 1686 W
John, George Nympton 1563 W
John, Nymet Rowland 1564 W
John, Heanton Punchardon 1570 W
John, Berrynarbor 1572 W
John, Chawleigh 1572 W
John, Bulkworthy or Buckland Brewer 1573 W
John, Abbotsham 1584 W
John, Knowstone 1596 [W]
John, Oakford 1604 [W] "Brushford alias Hodge" in register;
    forename blank in Ms; supplied from parish register
John, Barnstaple 1622 [W]
John, Cruwys Morchard 1623 O
John, Pilton 1629 [W]
John, Barnstaple 1643 A
Hodg John, Fremington 1662 A
Hodges John, Goodleigh 1665 A
John, Bratton Fleming 1684 W
John, Knowstone 1699 W
Hodges John, ship *Northumberland* 1756 W
John, Stoodleigh 1763 W
John, Oakford 1776 A
John, South Molton 1795 W
John, Oakford 1814 W
John, Ilfracombe 1817 W
John, Ashford 1830 A to Jane, mother
John, Oakford 1848 W
Juliana, Cruwys Morchard 1619 [W]
Hodg Leonard, Hartland 1698 [W]
Margaret, Nymet Rowland 1586 W
Hodg Mary, Witheridge 1666 A

Mary, Stoodleigh 1760 W
Mary, South Molton, sp. 1810 W
Mary, North Molton 1824 W
Mary, North Molton 1855 W
Mathew, South Molton 1754 W
Mathew, Ashford 1824 W
Mathew, Ashford 1829 W
Nicholas 1667 A
Philip, Pilton 1600 W
Philip, Stoodleigh 1706 W
Philip, Cruwys Morchard 1731 W
Philip, Oakford, yeoman 1811 W
Hoydge Ralph, Chawleigh 1623 [W]
Richard, Abbotsham 1569 W
Richard, South Molton 1586 W
Richard, Bideford 1587 A
Richard, Heanton Punchardon 1599 [W]
Richard, Buckland Brewer 1609 [W] "of Bilsford"; forename
  blank in Ms; supplied from parish register
Richard, Pilton 1633 A
Richard, Barnstaple 1636 W
Richard, Chawleigh 1639 W
Richard, Heanton Punchardon 1642 W
Richard, Lapford 1670 W
Richard, East Worlington 1698 W
Richard, South Molton 1734 W
Richard, North Tawton 1735 W
Richard, King's Nympton 1767 A
Richard, Knowstone 1851 W
Robert, Bideford 1584 A
Robert, Ilfracombe 1757 A
Robert, Ilfracombe 1826 W
Robert, Dolton 1856 W
Sarah, Barnstaple 1633 A
Sebastian, Barnstaple 1815 W
Simon, Barnstaple 1577 W
Hodg Stephen, Burrington 1727 A
Susan, Burrington 1717 A
Thomas, Hartland 1565 W
Thomas, Heanton Punchardon 1606 W
Thomas, Witheridge 1611 [W]; forename blank in Ms;
  supplied from parish register
Thomas, Burrington 1681 A
Thomas, Abbotsham 1708 W
Thomas, East Worlington 1714 W
Thomas, Ilfracombe 1731 W
Thomas, Barnstaple 1759 W
Thomas, Chawleigh 1769 W
Thomas, Dolton, yeoman 1806 W
Thomasine, Knowstone 1599 [W]
Thomasine, Heanton Punchardon 1618 [W]
Hodg Thomasine, Abbotsham 1703 W
Hodg Walter, Knowstone 1662 A
William, West Worlington 1579 W
William, West Buckland 1593 [W]
William, Witheridge 1602 W
William, Witheridge 1639 A
William, Clovelly 1645 A
William, Barnstaple 1663 W
William, Bratton Fleming 1669 A
William, Bratton Fleming 1672 O
William, Bideford 1726 W
William, Mariansleigh 1773 W
William, Knowstone 1802 W
William, Ashford 1825 W
William, Ashford, yeoman 1855 A to Mary, daughter
Willmot, Great Torrington 1571 W
Hodgeman John, East Worlington 1813 A to William, brother
  Roger, Rackenford 1565 W
Hodges see Hodge
Hodgen Thomas, High Bickington 1579 W
Hodgkin Charles James, South Molton, mariner 1853 A to
  Charlotte, mother
Hoell see Hole
Hogegood Thomas, Meshaw 1738 A

Hogg, Hogge
  Hogge ..., Bulkworthy 1612 [W]
  Hogge ..., Northam 1613 [W]
  Hogge Agnes, Bulkworthy 1576 W
  Hogge Agnes, Newton St Petrock 1586 W
  Elizabeth, Northam 1722 W
  Elizabeth, Bideford 1744 A
  Elizabeth, Barnstaple 1816 A
  Francis, Little Torrington 1741 W
  George, Newton St Petrock 1695 A
  George, Bideford, wine merchant 1808 A
  Grace, Newton St Petrock 1690 W
  Jeremiah, Northam 1768 A
  Hogge John, Newton St Petrock 1598 [W]
  Hogge John 1640 A
  John, Northam 1685 A
  John, Newton St Petrock 1722 W
  Mary, Newton St Petrock 1645 [W]
  Mary, Northam 1690 A
  Mary 1774 A
  Peter, ship *Edinburgh* 1765 W
  Philip, Little Torrington 1702 W
  Philip, St Giles in the Wood 1776 W
  Philip, Goodleigh 1839 W
  Hogge Richard, Bulkworthy 1577 W
  Hogge Richard, Buckland Brewer 1624 [W]
  Hogge Richard, Newton St Petrock 1625 [W]
  Hogge Richard 1636 A and 1640 O
  Hogge Roger, Newton St Petrock 1645 W
  Hogge Stephen, Newton St Petrock 1570 W
  Thomas, Knowstone 1577 W
  Hogge Thomas, Bulkworthy 1640 A
  Thomas, Little Torrington 1732 W
  William, Northam 1700 W
  William 1781 A
Hoiles see Hoyle
Holamore see Hollamore
Holand see Holland
Holcombe John, South Molton 1797 W
  Richard, Northam 1687 A
  Sarah, Northam 1689 A
Hold John, Twitchen 1733 W
  Sarah, Twitchen 1737 W
Holdman see Holman
Hole, Hoale, Hoell, Holle, Houle
  ..., Zeal Monachorum 1607 [W]
  Holle ..., Great Torrington 1695 [W]
  Agnes, South Molton 1776 W
  Andrew, Bow 1774 W
  Ann, South Molton 1765 W
  Holle Arthur, Horwood 1736 W
  Christopher, St Giles in the Wood 1665 A
  Christopher, Bow 1731 W
  Elizabeth, North Tawton 1772 W
  Elizabeth, North Tawton, sp. 1805 W
  English, Charles 1712 A
  George, Littleham (near Bideford) 1823 W
  Grace, North Molton 1810 W*
  Henry, St Giles in the Wood 1695 W
  Henry, Great Torrington 1700 W
  Henry, St Giles in the Wood 1750 W
  Hugh, Chulmleigh 1722 W
  James, South Molton 1677 W
  Holle Jean, Clannaborough, widow 1564 [W]
  Joan, Clannaborough 1593 [W]
  Joan 1618 [W]
  Joan, Thelbridge 1625 [W]
  Joan, Cheldon 1732 A
  Joan, Chulmleigh 1747 W
  Hoell John, Tawstock 1592 [W]
  John, Molland 1594 [W]
  Holle John, Clannaborough 1599 [W]
  John, North Tawton 1617 and 1620 [W]
  John 1627 [W]
  John, Merton 1670 W

John, Zeal Monachorum 1680 W
John, North Tawton 1688 W
John, Cheldon 1724 A
Houle John, Charles 1724 W
John, Bow 1732 W
Houle John, Charles 1733 W
John, Chawleigh 1754 A
Houle John, Ashford 1791 A
John, Bideford 1793 W
John, Bow 1808 A
Houle John, High Bray, yeoman 1809 W
John, Bideford 1810 W
John, North Molton 1820 A to Elizabeth, widow
Holl Joyce, Zeal Monachorum 1637 W
Lucy, Ilfracombe 1735 W
Margery, Bow 1663 W
Mary, South Molton 1668 A
Mary, East Worlington 1715 A
Mary, Sandford, North Tawton, widow 1805 W
Mary, Barnstaple 1819 W
Mary 1842 W
Nicholas, Ilfracombe 1680 W
Penelope, Georgeham 1849 W
Holle Peter, Zeal Monachorum 1599 [W]
Peter, Witheridge 1681 W
Peter, Ilfracombe 1698 A
Peter, Witheridge 1701 W
Peter, Ilfracombe 1720 A
Peter, Horwood 1786 W
Ralph, Bondleigh 1695 W
Richard, North Tawton 1644 W
Richard, Bow 1663 W
Richard, Atherington 1697 A
Richard, Brushford 1737 W
Richard, Berrynarbor 1770 A
Richard, North Molton 1805 W
Robert, Chulmleigh 1568 W
Robert, Witheridge 1729 W
Sarah, South Molton, widow 1811 W
Southcombe, South Molton 1793 A
Theophilus, Great Torrington 1771 W
Thomas, Clannaborough 1592 [W]
Thomas, Bow 1621 [W]
Thomas 1621 [W]
Thomas, Chawleigh 1711 W
Hoale Thomas, South Molton 1749 A
Thomas, North Tawton 1751 A
Thomas, North Molton 1829 W
Ursula, Chulmleigh 1738 W
William, Molland 1622 [W]
William, Zeal Monachorum 1622 [W]
Houle William, High Bray 1789 W
Houle William, Bishop's Tawton 1857 W
Holeborne Christian, Marwood 1627 [W]
Holeman see Holman
Holemead, Holemeade
..., East Worlington 1609 [W]
Agnes, Stoodleigh 1590 [W]
Holemeade George, Pilton 1622 [W]
James, Cruwys Morchard 1625 [W]
John, Cruwys Morchard 1601 W
Holemeade Martha, Cruwys Morchard 1623 [W]
Hollacomb, Hollacombe
John, Molland 1615 [W]; forename blank in Ms; supplied
   from parish register
John, Knowstone 1616 [W]
Hollacombe Mary, Barnstaple 1579 W
Hollacombe Silvester, Molland 1638 W
Hollaford, Hollaforde, Holloford, Hullaford
Hollaforde Agnes, Hartland 1584 W
Holloford Hugh, Hartland 1709 A
Hullaford John, Instow 1573 A
Richard, Clovelly 1575 W
Hollaforde William, Hartland 1584 W
William, Hartland 1640 W

Hollamore, Holamore, Hollamor, Hollomer, Holomore,
   Hullamore
..., Beaford 1611 [W]
Alice, Martinhoe 1640 A
Hollomer Andrew, Great Torrington 1707 A
George, North Tawton 1675 A
Holomore Henry, High Bickington 1677 W
Hollamor Joan, Mortehoe 1583 W
John, Martinhoe 1577 W
John, Northam 1616 [W]
John, Merton 1708 W
Margaret, Merton 1715 W
Mary, Beaford 1636 A
Mary, St Giles in the Wood 1689 W
Maurice, High Bickington 1678 W
Philip, Martinhoe 1623 [W]
Philip, Burrington 1665 A
Hullamore Robert, St Giles in the Wood 1580 W
Robert, Northam 1641 A
Samuel, St Giles in the Wood 1664 A
Samuel, Great Torrington 1718 A
Samuel, Barnstaple 1767 A
Holamore Thomas, Beaford 1574 W
Thomas, Beaford 1606 W
Holland, Holand, Hollande
..., Dolton 1611 [W]
Agnes, Instow 1729 W
Anthony, Lynton 1693 W
Christian, Lapford 1580 W
Hollande John, Barnstaple 1571 W
John, Lapford 1641 A
John, Chittlehampton 1663 W
John, King's Nympton 1748 A
John, Fremington 1853 W
Magdalen, Chittlehampton 1681 W
Holand Mary, Sheepwash 1677 A
Peter, Lapford 1576 W
Philip, Barnstaple 1580 W
Robert, Lapford 1577 A
Robert, Fremington 1790 A
Robert, Barnstaple 1838 A to Ann, widow
Holand William, Upcott 1677 W
Hollaway, Hollaways see Holloway
Holloford see Hollaford
Hollomer see Hollamore
Holloway, Hollaway, Hollaways
Elizabeth, Romansleigh 1748 A
Henry, West Buckland 1783 W
John, East Buckland 1724 W
John, East Buckland 1764 A
Hollaway John, West Buckland 1804 W
Peter, North Molton 1763 W
Philip, East Buckland 1698 W
Hollaways Richard, Burrington 1579 W
Richard, North Molton 1793 W
Samuel, Chulmleigh 1724 W
Sarah, East Buckland 1733 A
Susanna, Charles, widow 1807 A
Thomas, Charles 1777 A
Thomas, Charles 1829 A
Hollway see Holway
Holman, Holdman, Holeman, Holmon, Hulman
Holeman ..., Hartland 1610 [W]
Holeman ... 1613 [W]
Holman alias Parnacott Ann, Peters Marland 1674 [W]
Holman alias Downman Anthony, Knowstone 1566 W
Arthur, Beaford 1719 A
Holmon Arthur, Great Torrington 1757 W
Benjamin, Peters Marland 1704 A
Christian, West Down 1564 W
Dorothy, Yarnscombe 1681 W
Edward, Bideford 1837 W
Elizabeth, Hartland 1598 [W]
Elizabeth, North Tawton 1709 W
Emanuel, Peters Marland 1711 A
Gabriel, South Molton 1665 W

Humphrey, Langtree 1664 W
Humphrey, Langtree 1728 W
Holeman Joan, Peters Marland 1633 W
John, Peters Marland 1577 A
John, Hartland 1583 W
Holeman John, Great Torrington 1616 [W]
Holeman John, Buckland Filleigh 1632 [W]
Holeman John 1633 O
Holdman John, Barnstaple 1703 W
John, Yarnscombe 1741 W
John, Bideford 1838 W
Hulman John Morgan, Northam 1853 W
Julius, Westleigh 1695 W
Lodovic, Peters Marland 1625 [W]
Lodovic, Hartland 1665 A and 1669 O
Lodovic, Peters Marland 1669 W
Lodovic, Peters Marland 1687 A
Lodovic, Peters Marland 1722 W
Margery, Great Torrington, sp. 1810 W
Martin, Barnstaple 1675 A
Mary, Bideford 1674 W
Holdman Mary, Bideford 1744 A
Holeman Mary, Abbotsham 1792 W
Nicholas, Buckland Brewer 1641 W
Ralph, Bideford 1688 A
Holeman Richard, Hartland 1592 [W]
Richard, Barnstaple 1645 A
Richard, Peters Marland 1692 A
Robert, Great Torrington 1728 A
Roger, Chulmleigh 1696 W
Hulman Rowland Morgan, Northam 1849 W middle name
    from FreeBMD; initial only in Ms
Holdman Thomas, Hartland 1690 W
Thomas, Abbotsham 1827 W
Thomas, Bideford 1851 W
Thomasine, Hartland 1579 A
Tristram, Hartland 1679 W
Holmon Walter, Peters Marland 1578 W
Willmot, Hartland 1661 W
Willmot, Westleigh 1834 W
Holmead, Holmeade
Holmeade Gertrude, Cruwys Morchard 1666 A
Holmeade Humphrey, Cruwys Morchard 1684 A
Lettice, Pilton 1641 A
Margery, Cruwys Morchard 1602 W
Holmes, Holme
..., Barnstaple 1609 [W]
..., Rose Ash 1615 [W]
Holmes alias Clarke ..., Winkleigh 1679 W
Agnes, South Molton 1590 [W]
Agnes, Loxhore 1640 W
Alexander, Witheridge, blacksmith 1806 A
Anthony, Atherington 1739 W
Crispinus Deacon, Bideford, custom house officer 1822 A to
    Betty, widow
Edith, Creacombe 1717 W
Eleanor, Barnstaple 1755 W
Elizabeth, Mariansleigh 1853 A
Holmes alias Clarke Fortune, Westleigh or Winkleigh 1667 W
Holmes alias Peirse Giles, Creacombe 1695 W
Holmes alias Gorton Helen, Stoke Rivers 1701 W
Isott, North Tawton 1623 [W]
Joan, Stoodleigh 1604 [W]; forename blank in Ms; supplied
    from parish register
Joan, Barnstaple 1612 and 1613 [W]; forename blank in Ms;
    supplied from parish register
Holme John, Stoodleigh 1572 W
John, North Tawton 1584 W
John, Loxhore 1585 W
Holme John, Witheridge 1588 W
Holmes alias Stephens John, Barnstaple 1601 W
John, Rose Ash 1633 A
John, Loxhore 1637 W
John, Witheridge 1663 W
Holmes alias Peirse John, Rose Ash 1681 W

John, North Tawton 1754 W
John, Atherington 1778 W
John, Heanton Punchardon 1799 W
John Deacon, Bideford 1855 W
Lawrence 1599 [W]
Mary, Rose Ash 1597 [W]
Mary, Romansleigh 1756 W
Pauline, Loxhore 1622 [W]
Holmes alias Peres Peter, Rose Ash 1582 W
Richard, Pilton 1624 [W]
Robert, Rose Ash 1732 W
Thomas, Monkleigh 1597 [W]
Thomas, Winkleigh 1598 [W]
Thomas 1598 [W]
Thomas, North Tawton 1629 [W] and 1638 W
Thomas, North Tawton 1719 W
William, Mariansleigh, blacksmith 1844 A to Elizabeth,
    widow, John of West Worlington, yeoman and William of
    Mariansleigh, yeoman, children
Holmon see Holman
Holmyard Samuel, North Tawton 1851 W
Holomore see Hollamore
Holson
Holson alias Hearding John 1591 [W]
Robert, South Molton 1574 W
Holway, Hollway
..., East Buckland 1607 and 1608 [W]
Bartholomew, High Bray 1629 [W]
Catherine, East Buckland 1620 [W]
Hollway Elizabeth, West Buckland 1844 W
Hollway Henry, West Buckland 1845 A
Holway alias Wilkye John, Chittlehampton 1575 A
John, East Buckland 1601 W
Hollway John, Barnstaple 1774 W
Holwaye alias Wilkaye Richard, High Bickington 1582 W
Hollway Susan, Charles 1807 A
Thomas, East Buckland 1576 W
Hollway Thomas, West Buckland 1598 [W]
Holway alias Wilkey Thomas, Wembworthy 1606 W
Hollway Thomas, Chittlehampton 1841 W
Walter, Winkleigh 1661 W
Hollway William, East Buckland 1598 [W]
Holwell, Holwill
John, Great Torrington 1800 A
Holwill John, Great Torrington, saddler 1857 A to Frederick,
    saddler, son
Holworthy ..., West Buckland 1608 [W]
Honacott, Hamacot, Honicott, Honnacott, Hunacott, Huncott,
    Hunnacott
Hunacott ..., West Buckland 1612 [W]
Eleanor, Parkham 1635 [W]
Hunacott Elias, Dolton 1605 W
Huncott Elizabeth, Stoodleigh 1592 [W]
Honnacott Giles, Parkham 1624 [W]
Honnacott Jane, West Buckland 1628 [W]
Honicott John, Barnstaple 1667 A
Huncott Nicholas, Pilton 1616 [W]
Hamacot Robert, East Worlington 1587 W
Hunnacott Robert, Thelbridge 1636 [W]
Honnacott Robert, Parkham 1664 W
William, Alverdiscott 1580 W
Hone Gregory, Georgeham 1676 W
Honey, Honie, Hony, Honye
Hony ..., Northam 1614 [W]
Hony Charles, North Molton 1773 A
Elizabeth, Abbotsham 1757 W
Grace, Bideford 1633 A
Hony Humphrey, South Molton 1632 [W]
James, Northam 1849 W
Honie Joan, South Molton, widow 1564 W
Honie Joan, South Molton 1582 W
Honye John, Combe Martin 1573 A
Hony John, South Molton 157.
Hony Peter, Barnstaple 1611 [W]; ... blank in Ms;
    supplied from parish register

Hony Peter, Barnstaple, gentleman 1612 [W]; forename blank
   in Ms; supplied from parish register
Philip, Burrington 1783 W
Honye Richard, Filleigh 1573 A
Honye Richard, Barnstaple 1577 A
Richard, Northam 1849 W
Samuel, Abbotsham 1744 W
Sarah, Northam 1819 W
Susan, Barnstaple 1832 W
Thomas, Combe Martin 1590 [W]
Honeychurch, Hongchurch, Honichurche, Honychurch
   Barnabas, St Giles in the Wood 1764 W; 1780 A dbn
Christopher, St Giles in the Wood 1765 W
Elizabeth, St Giles in the Wood 1778 W
Elizabeth, Barnstaple 1801 A
Honychurch Henry, North Tawton 1711 W and A
Honychurch alias Marten Humphrey, North Tawton 1585 W
Joan, Roborough 1780 A
Honichurche alias Marten John, North Tawton 1587 W
Honychurch John, North Tawton 1665 A
John, North Tawton 1759 W
Joseph, North Tawton 1766 A
Judith, North Tawton 1782 W
Honychurch Rebecca, North Tawton 1679 W
Samuel 1834 A to Ann of Bideford, widow
Hongchurch Thomas, St Giles in the Wood 1730 W
Thomas, Roborough 1780 A; A dbn
Honeycombe, Hongcomb, Honycombe
   Hongcomb Elizabeth, East Buckland 1729 W
Elizabeth, East Buckland 1760 A
Honycombe Henry, Filleigh 1736 W
Hugh, Weare Giffard 1761 W
Honycombe John, Huntshaw 1720 W
John, Chittlehampton 1748 A
Judith, Littleham (near Bideford) 1776 W
Honeywell, Honeywill see Honywell
Hongchurch see Honeychurch
Hongcomb see Honeycombe
Honger see Hanger
Honichurche see Honeychurch
Honie see Honey
Honiwell, Honiwill see Honeywell
Honiwood Henry, Bow 1666 W
Honnacott see Honacott
Honnybeare Maurice, Great Torrington 1598 [W]
Hony, Honye see Honey
Honychurch see Honeychurch
Honycombe see Honeycombe
Honyede Anthony, Bideford 1602 W
Honywell, Honeywill, Honiwell, Honywill
   Honywill Agnes, Great Torrington 1637 W
Honiwell Esther, Barnstaple 1690 W
Giles, Barnstaple 1714 W
Honywill Henry, Barnstaple 1637 W
John, Shirwell 1568 W
John, Bideford 1577 A
Honywill John, Rackenford 1588 A
Honywill John, Barnstaple 1594 [W]
Honiwill John, Great Torrington 1644 A
Honiwill Mary, Northam 1608 [W]; forename blank in Ms;
   supplied from parish register
Pauline, Brushford 1576 W
Honywill Philip, Barnstaple 1637 W
Honywill Richard, Northam 1589 A
Honiwell Thomas, Barnstaple 1585 W
Honiwell Thomas, Newton 1716 W
Honeywill Thomas, Sheepwash 1756 A
Honiwell William, Abbotsham 1564 W
Hoo see Hooe
Hood, Hoode
   Mary, Tawstock 1717 W
Hoode Thomas, Fremington 1600 W
Hoode William, Berrynarbor 1635 W
William, Tawstock 1689 W

Hooe, Hoo
   ..., Northam 1600 A
..., Abbotsham 1613 [W]
..., Great Torrington 1614 [W]
Arthur, Marwood 1618 [W]
Christopher, Buckland Brewer 1664 W
John, Barnstaple 1596 [W]
John, Brendon 1615 [W]
Thomas, Marwood 1631 [W]
Thomas, Buckland Brewer 1642 W
Hoo William, Buckland Brewer 1570 W
William, Buckland Brewer 1634 W
Hook see Hooke
Hookaway see Hookway
Hooke, Hook
   Atwell, Northam 1735 A
Hook Henry, William, Bideford 1754 A
William Henry, Great Torrington 1737 W
Hooker Julia see Ann Bale or Ball
Hookway, Hookaway
   Juliana, Great Torrington, widow 1807 W
Richard, Bideford 1818 W
Robert, St Giles in the Wood 1809 A
Hookaway Thomas, Winkleigh, yeoman 1796 W
Hoop Agnes, Barnstaple 1592 [W]
   Hugh, Bideford 1587 A
Isott, Puddington 1592 [W]
Philip, Heanton Punchardon 1621 [W]
Thomas, Chulmleigh 1597 [W]
Hooper, Hoopper, Hoper
   ..., Clovelly 1606 [W]
..., Beaford 1608 and 1609 [W]
..., Chulmleigh 1608 [W] and 1617 [W]
..., Thelbridge 1609 [W]
..., Bideford 1614 [W]
Hooper alias Shepherd ..., West Down 1690 A
Abraham, Barnstaple 1686 W
Agnes, Ilfracombe 1626 [W]
Hoopper Alexander, Barnstaple 1782 W
Alice, Chulmleigh 1623 [W]
Howper Ambrose, Chulmleigh 1577 A
Ann, Yarnscombe 1638 A
Ann, Mariansleigh 1818 W
Anthony, Barnstaple 1610 [W]; forename blank in Ms;
   supplied from parish register
Hoopper Armanell, Bondleigh 1764 W
Arthur, Horwood 1680 A
Arthur, Heanton Punchardon 1701 W
Augustine, West Worlington 1617 [W]
Augustine, Parkham 1701 A
Baldwin, Huntshaw 1590 [W]
Hoper Beaton, Hartland 1579 W
Benedict, Chulmleigh 1685 W
Hooper alias Elston Charles, Stoodleigh 1642 W
Charles, Stoodleigh 1679 W
Charles, High Bray, yeoman 1821 A to Mary, widow
Christopher, Northam 1671 W
David, Beaford 1584 W
Hoopper Dennis, Barnstaple 1748 W
Hoopper Edmund, Ilfracombe 1759 A
Edward, Bideford 1629 [W]
Edward, Great Torrington 1636 [W]
Edward, Barnstaple 1645 A
Eleanor, Chawleigh 1830 A to Thomas Cooper, son
Eli, Great Torrington 1663 W
Elizabeth, Martinhoe 1588 W
Elizabeth, Barnstaple 1618 [W]
Elizabeth, Great Torrington 1695 W
Elizabeth, Bideford 1721 W
Hoopper Elizabeth, Monkleigh 1759 W
Elizabeth, Brendon 1835 W
Frances, West Down 1707 W
Francis, Pilton 1725 A
Francis, Barnstaple 1815 W
Francis, South Molton 1833 W

George, Iddesleigh 1673 W
George, Bideford 1678 A
Grace, Parkham 1818 A
Helen, West Down 1664 A
Hoper Henry, Thelbridge 1565 W
Henry, Martinhoe 1606 W
Henry, Chittlehampton 1631 [W]
Henry, Dolton 1700 W
Henry, Barnstaple 1701 A
Henry, North Tawton 1717 W
Hoopper Henry, Parkham 1726 W
Hoopper Henry, Dolton 1732 W
Hoopper Henry, Tawstock 1764 W
Hoopper Henry, Dolton 1765 W
Hoopper Henry, Dolton 1776 W
Hugh, Bideford 1587 A
Hugh, Warkleigh 1696 A
Humphrey, Hartland 1685 W
Humphrey, Chulmleigh 1689 W and 1693 A
Hoopper Jabez, Barnstaple 1746 W
Hoper James, Nymet Rowland 1568 W
James, Fremington 1619 [W]
James, Heanton Punchardon 1680 W
James, Georgeham 1844 W
Hoopper Jane, Lynton 1751 W
Jane, Combe Martin 1854 W
Hoper Joan, Chulmleigh 1589 W
Joan, Dolton, widow 1644 W
Hooper alias Squier Joan, Bideford 1679 A
Joan, Buckland Brewer 1694 W
Hoper John, Martinhoe 1570 W
Hoper John, Cruwys Morchard 1580 W
Howper John, Barnstaple 1581 A
John, Alwington 1584 W
John, Barnstaple 1584 W and 1588 W account
John, Great Torrington 1591 [W]
John, Hartland 1594 [W]
John, West Down 1598 [W]
Hooper alias Hellings John, King's Nympton 1617 [W]
John, Beaford 1618 [W]
John, Ilfracombe 1621 [W]
John, North Molton 1621 [W]
John, Barnstaple 1625 [W]
John, North Molton 1631 [W]
John, Hartland 1639 W
John, Burrington 1640 W
Hooper alias Shepheard John, Instow 1663 W
John, Woolfardisworthy 1678 A
John, Dolton 1693 A
John, Barnstaple 1703 W
John, Shebbear 1711 W
John, Iddesleigh 1714 [W]
John, Parkham 1720 W
John, West Down 1720 A
Hoopper John, West Down 1728 W
John, Tawstock 1729 A
Hoopper John, Barnstaple 1733 W
Hoopper John, Tawstock 1758 W
Hoopper John, Chulmleigh 1759 A
Hoopper John, Tawstock 1766 W
Hoopper John, Chulmleigh 1768 W
Hoopper John, West Down 1770 A
Hoopper John, West Down 1772 W
Hoopper John, Mariansleigh 1786 A
John, Appledore, Northam, merchant 1799 W
John, Barnstaple 1826 A to John, son
John, Dolton 1829 W
John, Northam 1832 W and 1833 W
John, Countisbury 1834 A to Mary, widow
John, Lynton 1840 W
John, Combe Martin 1854 W
John, Coldridge, dissenting minister 1855 A to Mary, widow
Jonathan, Bideford 1709 W
Joseph, Hartland 1847 W
Hoopper Joshua, Goodleigh 1725 A

Hoopper Macklin, Ilfracombe 1785 A
Margaret, Horwood 1681 A
Margery, Martinhoe 1605 W
Mark, Dolton 1633 A
Mark, Barnstaple 1698 W
Hoopper Mary, Countisbury 1754 W
Hoopper Mary, Barnstaple 1764 W
Mary, Lynton, widow 1811 W
Mary, Lynton 1820 W
Mathew, Martinhoe 1640 A
Nicholas, Heanton Punchardon 1688 W
Hoopper Nicholas, High Bickington 1741 W
Oliver, Bideford 1600 W
Peter, Barnstaple 1671 W
Peter, West Down 1700 A
Peter, Countisbury 1720 W
Hoopper Peter, Countisbury 1756 W
Hoopper Peter, Lynton 1783 W
Philip, Dolton 1587 W
Philip, Heanton Punchardon 1627 [W]
Philip, Huish 1667 W
Philip, Dolton 1670 W
Hoopper Philip, Chittlehampton 1752 W
Hoopper Philip, King's Nympton 1771 W
Hoopper Philip, Northam 1774 W
Phillippa, Frithelstock 1640 [W]
Hoper Richard, Chulmleigh 1568 W
Howper Richard, Witheridge 1583 A
Richard, Beaford 1587 W
Richard, Dolton 1589 W and 1599 [W]
Richard, Heanton Punchardon 1617 [W]
Richard, Chulmleigh 1622 [W]
Richard, West Down 1644 W
Richard, West Down 1701 W
Hoopper Richard, Barnstaple 1730 W
Hoopper Richard, Countisbury 1762 A
Hooper alias Shepherd Richard, West Down 1811 W
Richard, Combe Martin 1822 W
Hoper Robert, North Molton 1566 W
Robert, Bideford 1602 [W]; forename blank in Ms; supplied
    from parish register
Robert, Martinhoe 1605 W
Robert, Coldridge 1618 [W]
Robert, Beaford 1635 W
Robert, Alwington 1641 W
Robert, Barnstaple 1641 A
Robert, Parkham 1672 W
Robert, Parkham 1720 A
Hoopper Robert, Tawstock 1744 W
Hoopper Robert, Little Torrington 1765 W
Hooper alias Shepheard Roger, Instow 1703 A
Rowland, Dolton, snr. 1671 W
Rowland, Dolton 1688 W
Rowland, Dolton 1717 W
Hoopper Rowland, Dowland 1780 A
Hoopper Rowland, Dowland 1782 W and 1792 A
Rowland, North Tawton 1798 W
Rowland, Huntshaw 1855 W
Sabine, Barnstaple 1672 W
Samuel, Dolton 1670 W
Samuel, Roborough 1708 A
Sarah, Great Torrington 1720 W
Sarah, Northam, Appledore, sp. 1806 W
Sarah, Great Torrington, widow 1807 W
Hooper alias Juell Sybil, Bideford 1644 W
Hooper alias Hayman Simon, North Molton 1624 [W]
Hoopper Susan, Ashreigney 1767 A
Hoper alias Elston Thomas, Molland 1570 W
Thomas, Bideford 1587 A
Thomas, Burrington 1590 [W]
Thomas, East Worlington 1632 [W]
Thomas, Iddesleigh 1639 W
Thomas, Iddesleigh 1670 W
Thomas, Dolton 1673 W
Thomas, Buckland Brewer 1693 W

Thomas, Dolton 1700 A
Thomas, Dolton 1705 W
Hooper alias Greenslade Thomas, Fremington 1709 A
Thomas, Littleham (near Bideford) 1714 W
Thomas, Atherington 1717 A
Thomas, Barnstaple 1723 A
Hoopper Thomas, Dowland 1725 W
Hoopper Thomas, Barnstaple 1733 A
Hoopper Thomas, Bow 1743 A
Hoopper Thomas, Northam 1757 W; A dbn 1758
Hoopper Thomas, Cheldon 1790 W
Thomas, North Tawton, snr. 1805 W
Thomas, Northam 1848 W
Thomasine, Westleigh 1702 W
Urithe, Heanton Punchardon 1638 W
Walter, Barnstaple 1596 [W]
William, Tawstock 1615 [W]
William, Dolton 1623 [W]
William, North Molton 1623 [W]
William, Heanton Punchardon 1631 [W]
William, Frithelstock 1637 A
William, Monkleigh 1638 W
William, Tawstock 1643 A
William, Bideford 1670 A
William, Heanton Punchardon 1685 A
Hoopper William, Heanton Punchardon 1727 W
Hoopper William, Dolton 1734 W
Hoopper William, Barnstaple 1742 W
Hoopper William, Ashreigney 1748 W
Hoopper William, Merton 1755 A
Hoopper William, ship *Panther* 1759 A
Hoopper William, North Tawton 1762 A
Hoopper William, Northam 1770 W
William, Countisbury, yeoman 1809 W
William, Huntshaw 1813 W
William, North Tawton 1819 W
William, Yarnscombe 1847 W
William, Buckland Filleigh 1849 W
Willmot, Combe Martin 1831 W
Hoor see Hoare
Hooy John, Martinhoe 1625 [W]
Hooy Prudence, Alwington 1623 [W]
Hoper see Hooper
Hopgood John, Bideford 1845 W
Hopkins, Hopkens, Hopkin
Daniel, Heanton Punchardon 1725 A
David, Great Torrington 1705 A
Hopkin Elizabeth, Great Torrington 1723 A
Elizabeth, Bideford 1748 W
Francis, Pilton 1835 W
George, Ilfracombe 1689 W
George, ship *Centaur* 1750 W
Grace, Barnstaple 1726 A
Hopkin John, Puddington 1592 [W]
John, Stoodleigh 1596 [W]
John, Bideford 1697 A
John, Barnstaple 1707 A
John, Bideford 1722 A and 1725 A
John, High Bickington 1731 A
John, Bideford 1742 A
John, Northam 1744 A
John, Bideford 1769 A
John, Littleham (near Bideford) 1789 W
John, Barnstaple 1842 W
Hopkin Malcolm, Marwood 1729 W
Hopkens Margaret, Barnstaple 1574 W
Margaret, Great Torrington 1721 W
Mary, Ilfracombe 1843 W
Hopkin Peter, Northam 1731 W
Philip, Bideford 1768 W
Philip, Woolfardisworthy 1834 W
Hopkin Thomas, Ilfracombe 1616 [W]
Thomas, Ilfracombe 1712 A
Thomas, Tawstock 1764 W
Thomas, Great Torrington, gardener 1798 W

Treane, Abbotsham 1721 W
William, Bideford 1706 A
William, Arlington 1741 W
William, Bideford 1744 W
Hopley Robert, Arlington 1731 W
Hopper, Hepper, Hupper
Charity, Meeth 1770 W
Christopher, Abbotsham 1697 W
Emma and Mathew, Chulmleigh 1628 [W]
George, Langtree 1685 W
Joan, Shebbear 1691 W
John, Thelbridge 1574 W
Hupper John, Thelbridge 1574 W
John, Shebbear 1645 W
John, Shebbear 1685 W
Hupper John, Merton 1746 A
Jonah, Shebbear 1628 [W]
Judith, East Putford 1725 A
Mary, Shebbear 1712 A
Mathew and Emma, Chulmleigh 1628 [W]
Peter, Countisbury 1716 W
Richard, Burrington 1574 A
Hupper Robert, West Down 1678 W
Samuel, Meeth 1814 W
Hepper Simon, Shebbear, snr. 1630 [W]
Simon, Shebbear 1712 A
William, Shebbear 1689 W
William, Meeth, yeoman 1806 A
Hoppin Joseph, Bow 1679 W
Horden, Hordon
Hordon Adam, Loxhore 1679 W
Ann, Instow 1601 W
Ann, Loxhore 1717 W
John, Barnstaple 1792 W
Peter, Barnstaple 1749 W
Rebecca, Bideford 1853 W
Richard, Georgeham 1731 W
William, Meeth 1703 W
Hore see Hoare
Horford Robert, Bratton Fleming 1583 A
Horn see Horne
Hornabrocke, Horneabrooke
Horneabrooke John, Great Torrington 1592 [W]
Samson, Sheepwash 1581 A
Hornaman see Hearnaman
Horneabrooke see Hornabrocke
Horndon William, Petrockstowe 1705 A
Horne, Horn
Armanell, Great Torrington 1688 W
Arthur, Abbotsham 1644 A
Emanuel, Langtree 1718 W
Horn Emanuel, Buckland Brewer 1827 W
Horn Hugh, Shebbear 1798 W
Horn Humphrey, Shebbear, jnr. 1822 W
Jenson, Parkham 1581 W
Joan, Parkham 1586 W
Joan, Parkham 1620 [W]
Joan, Frithelstock 1720 W
John, Parkham 1608 [W]; forename blank in Ms; supplied
    from parish register
John, Parkham 1637 W
John, Parkham 1666 W
John, Frithelstock 1689 W
John, Langtree 1708 W
Horn Mary, Buckland Brewer 1828 W
Horn Petronell, Shebbear 1799 W
Horn Rebecca, Shebbear 1836 W
Richard, Parkham 1615 [W]
Rudolf, Georgeham 1702 A
Tristram, Frithelstock 1637 A and 1640 O
Walter, Parkham 1663 W
William, Frithelstock 1620 [W]
Hornman see Hornaman
Horrell see Harle
Horren Thomas, Dolton 1754 W

Horrwood see Harwood
Horselade see Horslade
Horseman Radigon, St Giles in the Wood 1628 [W]
Horslade, Horselade
   ...., Fremington 1595 [W]
   Horselade Thomas, Fremington 1595 [W]
Horthop see Hortop
Horton William, Rackenford 1616 [W]
Hortop, Hartopp, Horthop, Hortopp
   ... 1606 [W]
   Hortopp Elizabeth, Atherington 1695 W
   John, Great Torrington 1643 A
   John, Parkham 1728 W
   John, Parkham 1766 W
   John, Parkham, yeoman 1800 A
   Hartopp Margery, Atherington 1704 W
   Hortopp Richard, Northam 1621 [W]
   Hartopp William, Bideford 1694 A
   Horthop William, Parkham 1705 A
   William, Parkham 1736 W
Horwood, Harward, Horrwood, Horwode, Horwoode
   ..., Tawstock 1612 [W]
   Agnes, Barnstaple 1609 [W]; forename blank in Ms; supplied
     from parish register
   Alexander, Barnstaple 1666 A
   Alice, West Down 1663 W
   Amesius, Shirwell 1630 [W]
   Ann, South Molton 1620 [W]
   Anthony, Berrynarbor 1679 W
   Catherine, Charles 1630 [W]
   Daniel, Barnstaple 1605 W
   David, Arlington 1609 [W] "Haiwood" in register; forename
     blank in Ms; supplied from parish register
   Edith, Loxhore 1696 W
   Edward, Loxhore 1674 W
   Edward Richard, Georgeham 1818 W
   Elizabeth, Barnstaple 1678 W
   Elizabeth, Combe Martin 1748 W
   Ellen, East Down 1770 W
   Emott, Marwood 1673 W
   Florence, Instow 1733 W
   George, Marwood 1666 W
   George, Shirwell 1671 W
   George, Marwood 1755 W and A
   George, East Down 1757 W
   George, Shirwell 1821 W
   Grace, Barnstaple 1744 W
   Hannah, Barnstaple 1704 A
   Henry, Barnstaple 1673 [W]
   Henry, Georgeham 1713 W
   Hugh, Barnstaple 1733 W
   Humphrey, Ilfracombe 1685 W
   James, Bideford 1697 A
   James, Bideford, gentleman 1797 W
   James, Bideford 1801 W
   Horwode Joan, Shirwell 1566 W
   Joan, Shirwell 1590 [W]
   Horwoode Joan, Barnstaple 1618 [W]
   Joan, Barnstaple 1726 W
   Horwoode John, Instow 1580 W
   John, Shirwell 1589 W
   John, Pilton 1598 [W]
   John, Heanton Punchardon 1615 [W]
   John, Barnstaple 1630 [W]
   John, Shirwell, snr. 1645 W
   John, Barnstaple 1666 A
   John, Barnstaple 1679 A
   John, Shirwell 1690 W
   John, Marwood 1694 W and 1707 A
   Harward Lawrence, Welcombe 1769 A
   Macklin, Marwood 1600 W
   Margaret, Shirwell 1579 W
   Margaret, Berrynarbor 1666 W
   Mathew, Marwood 1643 W
   Nicholas, Barnstaple 1606 W

   Nicholas, Shirwell 1643 W
   Oliver, Barnstaple 1609 [W]; forename blank in Ms; supplied
     from parish register
   Paul, Barnstaple 1703 W
   Rebecca, Barnstaple 1749 W
   Richard, Barnstaple 1642 W
   Harward or Harwood Richard, Pilton 1661 A
   Richard, Instow 1696 W
   Richard, Northam, jnr. 1705 A
   Richard, Georgeham 1787 W
   Robert, Cruwys Morchard 1684 W
   Roger, Coldridge 1716 W
   Roger, Bideford 1740 W
   Horrwood Thomas, Shirwell 1573 W
   Thomas, Barnstaple 1628 [W]
   Walter, Dowland 1678 A
   William, Instow 1615 [W]
   William, Berrynarbor 1623 [W]
   William, Beaford 1673 W
   William, Berrynarbor 1673 [W]
   William, Bideford 1680 A
   William, Instow 1732 W
Hose ..., Alverdiscott 1603 [W]
Hosegood, Hosgood, Housgood
   ..., Washford Pyne 1607 [W]
   Abraham, Meeth 1628 [W]
   Agnes, South Molton 1592 [W]
   Hosgood Agnes, West Worlington 1749 W
   Edmund, West Anstey 1628 [W]
   George, Chulmleigh 1770 W
   George, Woolfardisworthy 1800 W
   George, West Worlington, yeoman 1802 W
   Henry, Tawstock 1593 [W]
   Hosgood Jane, Molland 1581 A
   Hosgood Jane, Northam 1706 A
   Joan, East Anstey 1604 W
   Joan, East Anstey 1635 W
   Joan, West Worlington 1772 W
   Housgood John, East Anstey 1577 W
   Hosgood John, South Molton 1588 A
   John, East Anstey 1595 [W]
   John, Washford Pyne 1598 [W]
   John, Meshaw 1624 [W]
   Hosgood John, Washford Pyne 1641 A
   Hosgood John, Northam 1689 A
   John, West Worlington 1723 A
   John, Chulmleigh 1774 W
   John, West Worlington 1817 W
   John, West Worlington 1834 W
   John, Lapford 1857 W
   Luke, Chulmleigh 1786 W
   Luke, Chulmleigh 1825 W
   Mary, Tawstock 1631 [W]
   Mary, Molland 1640 W
   Mary, West Worlington 1794 W
   Mary, South Molton, widow 1801 W
   Mary, Poughill, sp. 1851 A to Luke
   Mildred, Pilton (formerly of Worlington) 1849 W
   Hosgood Nicholas, West Anstey 1675 W
   Hosgood Nicholas, West Anstey 1711 W
   Housgood Oliver, Molland 1577 W
   Housgood Robert, Mariansleigh 1574 W
   Robert, Nymet Rowland 1663 W
   Thomas, Tawstock 1631 [W]
   Thomas, Northam 1637 [W]
   Hosgood Thomas, Northam 1689 A
   Thomas, West Down 1767 W
   Thomas, Meshaw 1778 W; A dbn
   Thomas, South Molton, innholder 1799 W
   Housgood William, Molland 1574 W
   William, West Worlington 1834 W
Hosier alias Walter John, Barnstaple 1579 W
Hoskins, Hoskin, Huskin
   Jane, East Anstey 1794 W
   Hoskin Richard, Knowstone 1565 W

Huskin Richard, Great Torrington 1837 W
   William Redwood, East Anstey 1829 W
Houle see Hole
Houndle Edward, Barnstaple 1790 A
Houndwell Peter, Lynton 1626 [W]
Housgood see Hosegood
How, Howe
   Catherine, Georgeham 1664 W
   Edward, Little Torrington 1816 [W]; transmitted to Doctor's
     Commons, 7 Sep 1817
   Elizabeth, Parkham 1684 W
   George, Little Torrington 1794 W
   Howe Giles, Parkham 1599 [W]
   Grace, Parkham 1701 A
   Howe Joan, Warkleigh 1765 W
   Howe John, Winkleigh 1575 W
   Howe John, Newton Tracey 1589 W
   John, Parkham 1664 W
   John, Bideford 1680 W
   John, Chawleigh 1693 W
   John, Parkham, snr. 1708 W
   John, East Down 1729 W
   John, Chulmleigh 1737 W
   John, Merton 1756 W
   Howe John, Warkleigh 1764 A
   John, Westleigh 1818 W
   John, Little Torrington 1837 W
   John, Bradford 1848 W
   John, Bideford 1856 W
   Jonathan, Northam 1680 A
   Joseph, Little Torrington 1824 A (Josiah) to Richard of
     Westleigh, brother
   Howe Lawrence, George Nympton 1753 W
   Howe Mary, Monkleigh 1714 A
   Howe Mary, South Molton, widow 1796 W
   Mary, Bideford 1834 W
   Howe Nicholas, Frithelstock 1580 W
   Richard, South Molton 1733 W
   Richard, Yarnscombe 1746 A
   Richard, Great Torrington, minor 1821 A to Mary, mother
   Richard, Weare Giffard 1827 W
   Robert, Molland 1742 A
   Robert, Warkleigh 1754 W
   Robert, Chittlehampton 1758 A
   Samuel, South Molton 1795 W
   Howe Sarah, Little Torrington 1789 A
   Howe Thomas, Winkleigh 1571 W
   Howe Thomas, Hartland 1598 [W]
   Thomas, Abbotsham 1708 A
   Thomas, Merton 1729 W
   Thomas, Little Torrington 1780 W
   Thomas, Combe Martin 1788 A
   Thomas, Little Torrington, snr. 1801 W
   Thomas, Weare Giffard 1808 W
   Thomas, Bideford 1828 W
   Thomas, Little Torrington 1830 A
   Thomas, Little Torrington 1838 W
   Thomasine, Chawleigh 1693 A
   Howe William, Great Torrington 1564 W
   Howe William, Bideford 1595 [W]
Howard Agnes, Heanton Punchardon 1688 A
   Alice, Berrynarbor 1705 W
   Edward, Instow 1696 A
   Elizabeth, Chulmleigh 1707 W
   George, Georgeham 1737 W
   George, Georgeham 1804 W
   James, Knowstone, husbandman 1810 W
   Joan, Northam, widow 1696 A
   John, Great Torrington 1676 W
   John, Heanton Punchardon 1683 A
   John, Heanton Punchardon 1718 A
   John, Great Torrington 1773 W
   John, Welcombe, miller 1855 A to Ann, mother
   Joseph, Georgeham 1855 W
   Mary, Barnstaple 1711 W

   Nathaniel, Barnstaple, jnr. 1705 A
   Peter, Knowstone 1794 A
   Richard, Knowstone 1756 W
   Richard, Welcombe 1853 W
   Robert, Barnstaple 1709 W
   Rudolf, Heanton Punchardon 1695 W
   Thomas, Bideford 1702 A
   Thomas, Heanton Punchardon 1731 A
Howde Richard, Georgeham 1589 W
Howe see How
Howell, Howle
   ..., South Molton 1609 [W]
   Alice, South Molton 1770 W
   Anthony, Georgeham 1736 W
   Catherine, Ilfracombe 1721 W
   David, Bideford 1670 A
   Grace, South Molton 1684 W
   Henry, Great Torrington 1739 A
   Henry, Bideford 1742 A
   Henry, Bideford 1761 W
   Howle Henry, High Bray 1781 W
   Joan, Bideford 1742 W
   Howle John, St Giles in the Wood 1579 W
   John, Ilfracombe 1690 A
   Philip, Bideford 1722 W
   Philip, Bideford 1762 W
   Rees, Ilfracombe 1717 W
   Roger, Chulmleigh 1825 W
   Roger, Chulmleigh 1839 W
   Rose, Bideford 1774 W
   Samuel, Bideford 1754 A
   Thomas, South Molton 1661 W
   Thomas, South Molton 1678 W
   William, ship *Namur* 1759 W and 1762 W
Howp Richard, Martinhoe 1580 W
Hoxland ..., Chittlehampton 1603 [W]
   Catherine, Bideford 1625 [W]
   Christian, Northam 1673 [W]
   John, Witheridge 1575 W
   John, Bideford 1622 [W]
   William, King's Nympton 1827 W
Hoydge see Hodge
Hoyle, Hoiles, Hoyele, Hoyell, Hoyles
   Dorothy, Zeal Monachorum 1685 W
   Hoiles Edward, Heanton Punchardon 1587 W
   Elizabeth, Eggesford 1698 W
   Elizabeth, Northam 1804 W
   Honor, Northam 1695 W
   Joan, South Molton 1701 A
   John, South Molton 1680 A
   John, Heanton Punchardon 1698 W
   John, Marwood 1705 W
   John, South Molton 1715 A
   John, South Molton, yeoman 1799 W
   Hoyles John, Trentishoe 1843 W
   Robert, Zeal Monachorum 1621 [W]
   Robert, Northam 1661 A
   Robert, Martinhoe 1673 W
   Rowland, Zeal Monachorum 1688 A
   Hoyell Samuel, Northam 1737 A
   Hoyele Samuel, Northam 1755 W
   Susan, Northam 1789 W
   Hoyles Thomas, Parracombe 1707 W
Hoyton Elizabeth see William Gornill Friendship
Huchen, Huchens see Hutchings
Huchenson Elizabeth, North Molton 1742 W
   John, South Molton 1729 A
Huchings see Hutchings
Huckmor Emanuel, Hartland 1593 [W]
   Humphrey, Langtree 1605 W
   Humphrey, Abbotsham 1635 A
Huckstable see Huxtable
Huckwell William, Great Torrington 1573 W
Huddle, Huddell, Hudle
   ..., Great Torrington 1605 [W]

..., High Bickington 1605 [W]
Huddell ..., Great Torrington 1609 [W]
Arthur, Buckland Filleigh 1673 A
Huddell John, Monkleigh 1593 [W]
John, Littleham (near Bideford) 1756 W
Margery, Great Torrington 1623 [W]
Pather, Frithelstock 1644 W
Huddell Richard, Monkleigh 1586 W
Thomas, Barnstaple 1628 [W]
Hudle Thomasine, Frithelstock 1679 W
Huddell William, Monkleigh 1597 [W]
Hudford Joan, Rackenford 1687 A
Hudle see Huddle
Hues see Hughes
Huet, Huets, Huett see Hewett
Hughes, Hewes, Hues, Hugh, Hughs
Hugh ..., Stoodleigh 1611 [W]
Hugh alias Knight Anthony, Shirwell 1670 W "Knight" in
    register
Hugh Anthony, Barnstaple 1675 A
Hugh Baldwin, Pilton 1629 [W]
Hughs Charles, Northam 1767 W
Hugh Emanuel, Loxhore 1638 W
Hugh Henry, Pilton 1631 [W]
Hugh James, Pilton 1632 [W]
Hugh alias Knight Joan, Kentisbury 1669 W
Hues Joan, Great Torrington 1675 W
Hues John, Bideford 1637 A
Hues Nicholas, Fremington 1721 A
Hewes Nicholas, Huntshaw 1725 W
Hugh Richard, Pilton 1628 [W]
Hughs Thomas, Great Torrington 1660 A
William, Bideford 1664 A
Hughl William, Bow 1716 W
Hughlegh William, Stoodleigh 1578 A
Hughs see Hughes
Huicksman Thomasine, Bondleigh 1577 W
Huish, Huysh, Huyshe
Huyshe Christopher, Chulmleigh 1666 A
Huyshe John, Oakford 1589 W
John, Barnstaple 1851 W
Huyshe Mathew, Stoodleigh 1578 W
Huysh Willmot, Oakford 1604 W
Hullaford see Hollaford
Hullamore see Hollamore
Hulland, Hullen
Hullen ..., Marwood 1608 [W]
James, King's Nympton 1841 A to Mary
John, Chulmleigh 1760 W
John, Chulmleigh 1785 W
Peter, King's Nympton 1813 W
Richard, King's Nympton 1835 W
Susan, King's Nympton 1846 W
William, King's Nympton, carpenter 1821 A to William, son
William, King's Nympton 1856 W
Hulman see Holman
Humble John, Welcombe 1715 A
Hume George, Pilton 1694 W
George, Pilton 1710 A
Jane, Barnstaple 1754 A
Mary, Brushford 1688 W
Willmot, Pilton 1717 W
Humphreys, Humfre, Humfrie, Humphry
Humphry James, Marwood 1597 [W]
Juliana, Barnstaple 1714 A
Humfre Peter, Highampton 1566 W
Humfrie Peter, Brushford 1566 W
Humfrie Thomas, Heanton Punchardon 1571 W
Hunacott, Huncott, Hunnacott see Hanacott
Hunford see Handford
Hunkin, Hunkings
Hunkings James, Bideford 1682 [W]
James, Northam, yeoman 1799 W
John, Shebbear 1797 A
Jonas, Shebbear 1797 A

Richard, Bideford 1686 W
Hunnacott see Hunacott
Hunt, Hunte
..., South Molton 1606 [W] and 1612 [W]
Abigail, Westleigh 1675 W
Alice, Shebbear 1600 W
Andrew, North Molton 1682 A
Ann, Barnstaple 1850 W
Anthony, South Molton 1617 [W]
Bennett, South Molton 1591 [W]
Christopher, Barnstaple 1679 A
Christopher, Barnstaple 1696 A
Edward, West Worlington 1832 W
Edward, Filleigh 1841 A (1844) to John, shoemaker, son
Eleanor, South Molton 1776 W
Elizabeth, Rackenford 1645 W
Elizabeth, Barnstaple 1727 W
Hunte Emott, South Molton 1623 [W]
George, High Bickington, yeoman 1805 W
George, Winkleigh 1826 W
George, High Bickington 1839 W
George, South Molton 1847 W
Grace see George Webber
Grace wife of Humphrey see William Frost
Hannah, South Molton 1781 W
Henry, South Molton 1634 A and 1637 O
Henry, Iddesleigh 1668 W
Hugh, South Molton 1615 [W]
Hunte Joan, South Molton 1626 [W]
Hunte John, Shebbear 1586 W
Hunte John, South Molton 1603 W
Hunte John, Rackenford 1618 [W]
Hunte John, Lynton 1626 [W]
Hunt, John, Alwington, yeoman 1807 A
Hunt, John, Bratton Fleming, yeoman 1811 A
Hunte Leonard, Huish 1585 W
Mary, South Molton 1681 W
Mary, Barnstaple 1702 A
Mary, Barnstaple 1748 A
Mary, Stoke Rivers 1753 W
Mary, Bratton Fleming 1764 W
Mathew, South Molton 1597 [W]
Hunte Philip, South Molton, snr. 1623 [W]
Philip, Heanton Punchardon 1697 W
Philip, Romansleigh 1820 W
Richard, South Molton 1592 [W]
Richard, North Molton 1632 [W]
Richard, George Nympton 1698 W
Richard, South Molton 1711 W
Richard, Chulmleigh 1754 W
Richard, South Molton 1762 A
Richard, Chulmleigh 1784 W
Richard, Stoke Rivers 1792 A
Richard, Chulmleigh 1837 W
Hunte Robert, South Molton 1626 [W]
Robert, High Bickington 1706 A
Hunte Roger, Chulmleigh 1625 [W]
Roger, Shirwell 1683 A
Hunt alias Marly Sarah, Molland 1710 A
Smarte, North Molton 1631 [W]
Susan, South Molton 1679 W
Tabitha, Barnstaple 1696 W
Hunte Thomas, South Molton 1571 W
Hunte Thomas, South Molton 1617 [W]
Thomas, South Molton 1660 W
Thomas, Molland 1710 W
Thomas, Bratton Fleming 1764 W
Thomas, High Bickington 1839 W
Hunte Thomasine, Huish 1581 W
William, South Molton 1674 W
William, King's Nympton 1699 W
William, Chulmleigh 1729 W
William, Stoke Rivers 1770 W
William, South Molton 1778 W
William, Barnstaple 1794 W

Hunter John, Barnstaple 1853 W
Hupper see Hopper
Hurde see Hearde
Hurdon see Harding
Hurford Christopher 1641 A
Hurler ..., Coldridge 1608 [W]
   Richard, Dowland 1615 [W], 1619 O, and 1625 A
   Robert, Coldridge 1702 W
Hurlestone Alice, South Molton 1632 [W]
   Peter, North Molton 1623 [W]
Hurley Alice, Hartland 1631 [W]
   Hugh, Ilfracombe 1752 A
Hurnaman see Hearnaman
Hurrell Robert, Shebbear 1644 W
Hursell, Hersell, Hussell
   Hersell ..., Combe Martin 1609 [W]
   Hussell Anthony, Ilfracombe 1841 W
   Cecilia, Barnstaple 1621 [W]
   Hussell George, Kentisbury 1821 W
   Hussell George, Kentisbury 1835 W to Elizabeth, widow
   Jonah, Ilfracombe 1598 [W]
Hurtswell see Hartswell
Husband, Husbands
   Agnes, Hartland, widow 1612 [W]; forename blank in Ms;
     supplied from parish register
   Husbands Arthur, Woolfardisworthy 1694 W
   Bartholomew, Bideford 1629 [W]
   Daniel, Northam 1624 [W]
   Husbands Elizabeth, Barnstaple 1719 W
   Elizabeth, Northam, sp. 1819 A to John Blake Husband,
     brother
   George, Hartland 1607 [W]; forename blank in Ms; supplied
     from parish register
   Grace, Bideford, widow 1799 W
   Grace, Bideford 1835 W
   James, Hartland 1602 W
   Husbands Jasper, Northam 1767 W
   John, Kernstone, Hartland 1563 W
   John, Over Velly, Hartland 1569 W
   John, Hartland 1634 A
   Husbands John, Barnstaple 1710 A
   John, Bideford 1711 A
   John, Northam 1792 W and 1793 W
   Johnson, Northam 1703 W
   Martin, Hartland 1621 [W]
   Sarah, Northam 1790 A
   Sarah Whitefield, Bideford 1831 A to Thomas
   William, Hartland 1597 [W]
   William, Pilton 1617 [W]
   William, Parkham 1693 W
   Husbands William, Northam 1754 A
Huscott Richard, Kentisbury 1742 A
   see also Arscott
Huskin see Hoskins
Hussell see Hursell
Hustable see Huxtable
Huswaye Alphonse, North Tawton 1574 W
Hutch Margaret, Goodleigh 1581 W
Hutchings, Huchen, Huchens, Huchings, Hutchen, Hutchens,
   Hutching, Hutchinge, Hutchins, Huthchens
   Hutchen ..., Petrockstowe 1602 W
   Hutchens ..., Buckland Filleigh 1610 [W]
   Hutchens ..., Sheepwash 1610 [W]
   ..., Bideford 1679 A
   Agnes, Petrockstowe 1780 A
   Hutchens Ann, Petrockstowe 1595 [W]
   Benjamin, Barnstaple 1841 W
   Huchens Edmund, Buckland Filleigh 1588 W
   Eleanor, Bideford 1679 W
   Elizabeth, Bideford 1691 W
   Hutching Elizabeth, Georgeham 1698 W
   Elizabeth, Merton 1770 A
   Hutchins Frances, Northam 1697 [W]
   Francis, Petrockstowe 1725 A
   George, West Down 1643 W

   Henry, Petrockstowe 1637 W
   Henry, Petrockstowe 1723 W
   Huthchens Hugh, Fremington 1620 [W]
   Hugh, Shebbear 1712 A
   Hugh, Northam 1729 W
   James, Petrockstowe 1787 W
   James, Barnstaple 1836 W
   Hutchins Jane, Shebbear 1644 W
   Huchens John, Petrockstowe 1583 A
   Hutchens John, Petrockstowe 1590 [W]
   Hutchens John, Mariansleigh 1596 [W]
   Hutchens John, Fremington 1627 [W]
   Hutchens John, Parkham 1629 [W]
   Hutchens John, Little Torrington 1631 [W]
   Hutchen John, King's Nympton, gentleman 1639 W
   John, Parkham 1671 W
   John, Northam 1696 W
   John, Langtree 1697 W
   John, Petrockstowe 1711 W
   John, Shirwell 1751 W
   John, Witheridge 1759 A
   John, Peters Marland 1775 W
   John, Bideford 1805 W
   John, Peters Marland, yeoman 1806 W
   John, Peters Marland 1807 A
   John, Sheepwash, labourer a bastard 1821 A to Mary
     Westlake, natural sister
   Lodovic, Northam 1692 A
   Hutchins Mary, Little Torrington 1715 A
   Mary, Bondleigh 1833 W
   Hutching Nicholas, Landcross 1662 W
   Nicholas, Landcross 1680 W
   Nicholas, Shebbear 1693 A
   Nicholas, Shebbear 1766 W
   Hutchen Nicholas, Shebbear 1637 W
   Hutchens Petronell, Great Torrington 1639 [W]
   Hutchens Richard, Petrockstowe 1594 [W]
   Hutchen Richard, Welcombe 1621 [W]
   Richard, West Down 1679 W
   Richard, Kentisbury 1763 W
   Richard, Charles 1846 W
   Huchen Robert, Petrockstowe 1566 W
   Hutchens Robert, King's Nympton 1581 A
   Hutchins Robert, Petrockstowe 1633 W and 1643 W
   Robert, West Down 1668 A
   Hutchins Hutchings Robert, Petrockstowe 1790 A
   Huchen Roger, Parkham 1573 W
   Hutchens Samuel, Pilton 1620 [W]
   Hutchins Samuel, Peters Marland 1697 W
   Hutchins Samuel, Petrockstowe 1720 A
   Samuel, Petrockstowe 1735 A
   Samuel, Peters Marland 1800 W*
   Sarah, Petrockstowe 1718 W
   Sarah, Abbotsham 1784 A
   Huchens Thomas, Petrockstowe 1588 W, 1590 [W] and 1599
     [W]
   Thomas, Petrockstowe 1623 [W]
   Huchings Thomas, Monkleigh 1708 W
   Thomas, Little Torrington 1711 A
   Thomas, Northam, yeoman 1819 A to Grace wife of William
     Beer of Bridford, daughter
   Thomas, Northam, Appledore 1828 A to Sarah Penhorwood,
     daughter
   Thomasine, Langtree 1623 [W]
   Hutchinge William, Pilton 1591 [W]
   Hutchens William, Sheepwash 1595 [W]
   Hutchins William, Buckland Filleigh 1645 A
   Hutchens William, Bow 1666 A
   Hutchings alias Francklin William, Stoke Rivers 1674 A and
     1675 O
   William, Kentisbury 1792 W
   William, Shebbear 1802 W*
   William, North Molton 1824 W
   Hutchins Willmot, Landcross 1668 W

Hutson, Hutsen
  Hutsen alias Limbery Elizabeth, Fremington 1679 W;
    forename blank in Ms; supplied from parish register
  Hutson alias Lymbery James, Fremington 1661 W
Hutswell see Hartswell
Hutton Thomas, Barnstaple, butcher 1798 W
  William, Tawstock 1734 W
  William, Fremington 1823 W
  William, Fremington 1836 W
  William Thorne, Fremington 1852 W
Huty alias Heuts Margaret, Goodleigh 1581 W
Huxlonde William, Zeal Monachorum 1566 W
Huxtable, Huckstable, Hustable, Huxstable, Huxstaple
  ..., Charles 1610 [W] and 1614 [W]
  ..., High Bray 1614 [W]
  Huxstable ..., Buckland Filleigh 1719 W
  Agnes, Charles 1641 W
  Huxstable Agnes, Dowland 1688 A
  Agnes, Chittlehampton 1739 W
  Amos, Challacombe 1723 A
  Andrew, Bulkworthy 1591 [W]
  Ann, Chittlehampton 1789 W
  Ann, Ilfracombe 1826 W
  Anthony, Arlington 1643 W
  Anthony, Bratton Fleming 1753 W
  Anthony, Bratton Fleming 1789 W
  Cecilia, Warkleigh 1667 [W] and 1676 A
  Charles, North Molton 1740 W
  Hustable Charles, South Molton 1795 W
  Huxstable Christopher, Charles 1593 [W]
  Christopher, Bondleigh, thatcher 1811 A
  Clement, Marwood 1726 W
  Edmund, Charles 1671 W
  Huxstable Edmund, Warkleigh 1691 W
  Huxstable Edmund, Chittlehampton 1710 A
  Edmund, Chittlehampton 1732 W
  Edmund, Chittlehampton 1781 W
  Edmund, Chittlehampton 1830 W
  Edward, Shirwell 1801 W*
  Edward, Bratton Fleming 1849 W
  Eleanor, East Buckland 1822 W
  Elizabeth, Bratton Fleming 1590 [W]
  Elizabeth, Charles 1626 [W]
  Huxstable Elizabeth, Challacombe 1697 W
  Elizabeth, Berrynarbor 1820 W
  Elizabeth, Bratton Fleming 1826 W
  Elizabeth, South Molton 1851 W
  Emblem, Chittlehampton 1732 W
  George, Bratton Fleming 1573 W
  Huxstable George, Buckland Filleigh 1688 A
  Huxstable George, Challacombe 1690 W
  George, Ilfracombe 1750 A
  George, Charles 1780 W
  George, South Molton, yeoman 1806 W
  George, Ilfracombe 1832 W
  Henry, Charles 1642 W
  Jane, Combe Martin 1828 A to Ann, daughter
  Huxstable Joan, Roborough 1588 W
  Huxstable Joan, North Molton 1692 A
  Joan, South Molton 1824 W
  Huckstable John, Charles 1571 W
  John, Barnstaple 1573 A
  Huxstable John, North Molton 1591 [W]
  John, Arlington 1599 [W]
  John, West Down 1611 [W]; forename blank in Ms; supplied
    from parish register
  John, South Molton 1619 [W]
  John, Tawstock 1635 A
  John, Charles 1638 W
  John, Lynton 1643 A
  John, Charles, snr. 1645 A
  John, Charles 1670 W
  John, Ilfracombe 1671 W
  John, North Molton 1676 W
  Huxstable John, Charles 1687 W

Huxstable John, West Down 1698 W
Huxstable John, Ilfracombe 1700 W
Huxstable John, North Molton 1703 A
John, Combe Martin 1705 W
Huxstable John, North Molton 1710 A
Huxstable John, North Molton 1711 W
Huxstable John, Ilfracombe 1715 W
John, High Bickington 1726 W
John, Buckland Filleigh 1732 W
John, Charles 1737 W
John, North Molton 1742 W
John, South Molton 1767 W
John, Bratton Fleming 1769 W
John, Charles 1770 W
John, South Molton 1784 W
John, North Molton 1785 W
John, Ilfracombe 1814 W
John, Ilfracombe 1826 W
John, Chittlehampton 1835 W
John, Lynton 1839 A
John, South Molton 1839 W
Joseph, South Molton 1828 W
Margaret, Charles 1603 W
Huxstable Margaret, Chittlehampton 1687 W
Margaret, Warkleigh 1844 W
Martha, West Down 1622 [W]
Mary, Charles 1633 W
Huxstable Mary, Warkleigh 1697 W
Huxstable Mary, Burrington 1701 W
Mary, South Molton, widow 1802 W
Mary, Chittlehampton 1805 A
Mary, Barnstaple 1845 W
Huxstable Mathew, West Down 1690 W
Molly, Ilfracombe 1817 W
Huxstable Nicholas, Charles 1694 A
Nicholas, Chittlehampton 1761 W
Petronell, Charles 1753 W
Philip, Ilfracombe, formerly of Braunton 1826 W
Rachel, Chittlehampton 1786 W
Richard, Filleigh 1621 [W]
Richard, Charles 1623 [W] and 1633 W
Richard, Tawstock 1670 W
Richard, Northam 1677 A
Huxstable Richard, Ilfracombe 1698 A
Richard, Challacombe 1723 W
Richard, Warkleigh 1739 A
Richard, Coldridge 1742 A
Richard, Fremington 1744 W
Richard, Chittlehampton, yeoman 1807 W
Richard, Fremington 1825 W
Richard, Chittlehampton 1828 A to Susanna of Barnstaple,
  widow
Richard, Warkleigh 1832 W
Richard, Challacombe 1855 W
Roger, Combe Martin 1570 W
Roger, North Tawton 1787 W
Sarah, West Down 1727 W
Huxstaple Thomas, East Buckland 1574 W
Thomas, High Bray 1639 W
Thomas, East Buckland 1673 W
Thomas, North Molton 1706 W
Thomas, Clovelly 1743 W
Thomas, Chittlehampton 1829 W
Thomas, South Molton 1833 W
Thomas, Ilfracombe 1840 W
Huxstaple William, Charles 1585 W
William, Bratton Fleming 1621 [W]
William, Goodleigh 1638 W
William, Bratton Fleming 1663 [W]
William, Northam 1697 A
Huxstable William, North Molton 1707 A
William, Shirwell 1738 W
William, Warkleigh 1754 A
William, North Molton 1765 W
William, Bratton Fleming 1772 W

William, South Molton 1814 A
William, East Buckland, yeoman 1815 A to Eleanor, widow
William, Roborough 1829 A to Joanna, widow
William, Chittlehampton 1849 A
William, Instow 1856 W
Huysh, Huyshe see Huish
Hychcocke, Hychcoke see Hitchcock
Hyll see Hill
Hyman William, Molland 1755 W
Hynam Jane, Burrington 1857 W
William, Burrington 1847 W
Hynes see Haynes

Iland, Ilande
Ilande Catherine, Hartland 1605 W
Thomas, Hartland 1592 [W]
Illman Elizabeth, Bideford, widow 1855 A to William,
    gentleman, son
Incledon, Inckledon, Inckldon, Incleton
Christopher, Ilfracombe 1756 A
Inckledon Elizabeth, Heanton Punchardon 1622 [W]
Inckldon Geoffrey, Ilfracombe 1596 [W]
Inckledon George, Ilfracombe 1618 [W]
Inckledon George, Mortehoe 1642 W
George, Heanton Punchardon 1786 A
Inckledon Henry, West Down 1623 [W]
Inckledon James, Heanton Punchardon 1672 W
James, Heanton Punchardon 1736 A
James, Heanton Punchardon, yeoman 1798 W
John, Ilfracombe 1595 [W]
John, Heanton Punchardon 1856 W
Incleton Mary, Northam 1712 W
Mathew, Barnstaple 1695 A
Inckledon Philip, Marwood 1636 A
Inckledon Philip, Heanton Punchardon 1640 A
Inckledon Philip, Heanton Punchardon 1711 A and 1720 A
Philip, Heanton Punchardon 1776 A
Inckledon Robert, Georgeham 1626 [W]
Inckledon Thomas, Georgeham 1620 [W]
Inckledon Thomas, Yarnscombe 1623 [W]
Inckledon Thomas, Georgeham 1642 A
Thomas, Northam 1693 A
Incleton Thomas, Ilfracombe 1700 W
Inckledon William, Heanton Punchardon 1598 [W]
Inckledon William, Ashreigney 1626 [W] and O
Inckledon William, Heanton Punchardon 1664 [W]
Inckledon William, Heanton Punchardon 1708 W
William, Heanton Punchardon 1731 W
    see also Enckledon
Inclett Richard, Alwington 1568 W
Infram Agnes, Stoodleigh 1625 [W]
Alice, Countisbury 1621 [W]
George, Countisbury 1598 [W]
Rebecca, Stoodleigh 1625 [W]
Thomas, Stoodleigh 1625 [W] (2)
Walter, Lynton 1621 [W]
Innocent Christopher, Meeth 1771 W
Ireland Joan, Chittlehampton 1747 W
William, formerly of High Bray late of Goodleigh 1831 W
Irwin, Irvin, Irwing
Alice, Marwood 1831 W
Benjamin Pile, Pilton 1835 W
Elizabeth, Heanton Punchardon 1852 W
Irvin Grace, Trentishoe 1776 W
James, Combe Martin 1833 W
John, Northam 1743 W
John, Kentisbury 1763 W
John, Northam 1810 A
John, Barnstaple 1814 W
John, Berrynarbor 1826 A (Ilfracombe) to John, son
Joseph, Mortehoe 1818 W
Leonora, Barnstaple 1832 W
Mary, Combe Martin 1841 A to William and John, children
Irwing William, Northam 1741 W
William, Combe Martin 1748 W

William, Combe Martin 1779 W
William, Loxhore 1832 A
William, Combe Martin 1833 A to Mary, widow; A dbn 1841
Isaac, Isaack, Isack, Isacke, Isake
Isaack ..., Chulmleigh 1611 [W] and O
Abraham, Yarnscombe 1627 [W]
Isaack alias Skibbow Agnes, Burrington 1660 A
Isacke Alexander, High Bickington 1593 [W]
Isake Alice, Ashreigney, widow 1570 W
Isaack Ambrose, Yarnscombe 1704 W
Ambrose, High Bickington 1705 A
Ambrose, Yarnscombe 1790 W
Andrew, Burrington 1813 A
Isacke Ann, Chulmleigh 1638 W
Isacke Ann, Cruwys Morchard 1638 W
Isaack Arthur, St Giles in the Wood 1689 or 1690 A
Isaack Catherine, Atherington 1615 [W]
Charity, Winkleigh 1672 A
Isake Christopher, Cruwys Morchard 1587 W
Isack Edith, Cruwys Morchard 1599 [W]
Isake Edward, Burrington 1583 W
Isaack Eleanor, Iddesleigh 1667 W
Elizabeth, Tawstock 1673 W
Isaack Elizabeth, Winkleigh 1704 W
Francis, Bideford, cabinet maker 1811 W
Isaack George, Atherington 1692 [W]
George, Great Torrington 1792 A
George, Newton Tracey, cooper 1802 W
Hugh, Ashreigney 1676 W
Isaack Hugh, Ashreigney 1693 A
Hugh, Ashreigney 1753 W
Hugh, Yarnscombe 1782 A
Hugh, Georgeham 1792 A
Jenny, Atherington 1853 W
Joan, Atherington 1579 W
Joan, Ashreigney 1632 [W]
Joan, Tawstock 1680 W
Isacke alias Skibbowe John, King's Nympton 1569 W
Isacke John, Ashreigney 1571 W
Isake John, Petrockstowe 1573 W
Isake John, Cruwys Morchard 1579 A
Isake John, Ashreigney 1601 W
Isaack John, Oakford 1616 [W]
John, King's Nympton 1628 [W]
Isaack John, Yarnscombe 1668 W
John, East Buckland 1731 W
John, Burrington 1737 W
John, Bondleigh 1753 W
John, West Worlington 1765 A
John, Burrington 1797 A
John, Zeal Monachorum 1831 W
Julian, Wembworthy 1633 W
Isaack Lawrence, Tawstock 1700 W
Lawrence, Atherington 1844 W
Lucy, Yarnscombe, widow 1816 A to Thomas, son
Isaack Margery, West Down 1668 W
Mary, Atherington 1731 W
Oliver, Ashreigney 1735 W
Isaack Philip, Winkleigh 1685 W
Philip, High Bickington 1772 W
Ralph, Bondleigh 1746 W
Isacke Richard, Oakford 1597 [W] and O account
Richard, Ashreigney 1795 A
Richard, Great Torrington 1838 A
Isaack Robert, Atherington 1615 [W]
Isacke Robert, Atherington 1635 W
Isaack Robert, Iddesleigh 1686 W
Robert, Northam 1733 W
Isack Roger, Great Torrington 1715 W
Isaack Samuel, Winkleigh 1697 W
Isake Simon, Atherington 1577 W
Thomas, Ashreigney 1622 [W]
Thomas, Yarnscombe 1667 W
Thomas, Ashreigney 1754 W

Thomas, Yarnscombe 1837 A to John Snell and Richard
  Dallyon of Bishop's Tawton, guardians
William, Great Torrington 1674 A
Isaack William, Winkleigh 1701 W
William, King's Nympton 1725 A
William, Great Torrington 1730 A
William, Yarnscombe 1762 W
William, Dowland 1764 A
William, Yarnscombe, yeoman 1803 A
William, High Bickington 1841 W
Isake Willmot, Cruwys Morchard 1583 W
Isberry Marian, Atherington 1686 W
Ivie Lucy, Barnstaple, sp. 1798 W

Jackman Benjamin, Barnstaple 1644 W
  Damaris, Barnstaple 1682 W
  Frances, Barnstaple 1645 W
  Henry, Sheepwash 1664 A
  Richard, Bideford 1578 W
  Richard, Loxhore 1631 [W]
Jackson William, Bickford, South Molton 1841 W
Jacob, Jacobbe
  ..., Witheridge 1607 [W]
  Agnes, King's Nympton 1634 A and 1637 O
  Elizabeth, Chittlehampton 1683 W
  Elizabeth, East Worlington 1703 W
  Jacobbe James, Barnstaple 1577 W
  Jacob alias Steevens Joan, Bow 1641 W
James Cecilia, Peters Marland 1580 W
  Edward, Shebbear 1663 W
  George, ship *Lark* 1747 W
  James, Shebbear 1670 W
  James, Shebbear 1713 W
  John, Shebbear 1578 A
  John, Great Torrington 1581 W and 1589 O account
  John, Ilfracombe 1597 [W]
  John, Peters Marland 1673 [W]
  Michael, Peters Marland 1677 A
  Nicholas, Combe Martin 1578 W
  Paschal, Huntshaw 1637 W
  Sarah 1789 see Bawden alias James, Sarah
  Thomas, Northam 1664 A
  Walter, Buckland Brewer 1578 W
  William, Peters Marland 1579 W
  William, Shebbear 1639 W
Janes, Jans
  Christopher, ship *Duke* 1763 A
  Jans John, Ilfracombe 1747 A
  Matilda, Kentisbury 1575 W
  Jans Walter, Ilfracombe 1749 A
  William, Great Torrington 1759 A
Janken, Jancken
  Davy, Hartland 1604 W
  Hugh, Chittlehampton 1583 A
  John, Barnstaple 1593 [W]
  Peter, Ilfracombe 1597 [W]
Jancken see Janken
Jans see Janes
Jarman, Jarmin
  Agnes, Goodleigh 1742 A
  Dorothy, Knowstone 1755 W
  Hercules, Sheepwash 1587 A
  John, Bideford 1743 W
  Lucy, Peters Marland 1588 A
  Jarmin Margaret, North Molton 1817 W
  Philip, George Nympton 1841 W
  Richard Bidgood, formerly of Tiverton, late of Barnstaple
    1804 W
  William, Goodleigh 1734 W
Jarvis, Garvis, Gerves, Gervis, Jarves, Jerves, Jervis
  Jervis ..., Woolfardisworthy 1611 [W]
  Jarves Elizabeth, Langtree 1578 W
  Elizabeth, Barnstaple 1808 W
  Garvis Henry, South Molton 1598 [W] and 1599 [W]
  Gerves Joan, Cruwys Morchard, widow 1568 W

Jarves John, Langtree 1572 W
Gervis or Jerves William, Cruwys Morchard 1579 W
Jasper John, Meeth 1684 W
  John, Meeth 1703 A
  Richard, Shebbear 1621 [W]
Jathson Martin, ship *Lowestoft* 1749 W
Jeans, Jeane, Jeanes, Jeen
  Jeen Charles, Alwington 1787 W
  George, High Bickington, husbandman 1806 W
  Jeanes John, Westleigh 1701 W and 1711 A
  Jeane Samuel, Frithelstock 1734 W
  William, High Bickington 1792 W
  see also Geen
Jeffery, Gefferie, Geffery, Geffrey, Geffrie, Geffry, Geffrye,
    Giffery, Jeffrey, Jeffrye, Jeoffery
  Jeffrye or Geffry ..., Abbotsham 1608 [W]
  Geffrye ..., Barnstaple 1606 [W]
  Geffrie or Jeffrie ..., Stoke Rivers 1609 [W]
  Jeffrie ..., Parracombe 1611 [W]
  Geffrie or Jefferie ..., Bideford 1612 [W]
  Geffrie or Jeffrie ..., Shebbear 1614 [W]
  Jeoffery Anthony, Newton St Petrock 1736 W
  Betty, Northam 1819 A to Mary wife of John Prance, daughter
  Catherine, Winkleigh 1641 [W]
  Jeoffery Cornelius, Hartland 1762 A
  Jeoffery Edward, Barnstaple 1730 A
  Jeoffery Edward, Northam 1774 A
  Jeoffery Elizabeth, Northam 1779 W
  Jeoffery Elizabeth, Great Torrington 1780 W
  Francis, Shebbear 1822 W
  Jeffry George, Northam 1626 [W]
  Giffery Gregory, Roborough 1674 [W]
  Jeffry Helen, Stoke Rivers 1622 [W]
  Jeffry or Geffry Henry, Abbotsham 1593 [W]
  Jeffry Henry, Tawstock 1631 [W]
  Henry, Northam 1826 W
  Hugh, Shebbear 1836 W
  James, Northam, mariner 1819 A to Mary wife of John
    Prance, daughter
  Joan, Northam, widow 1697 W
  Geffrey John, Stoke Rivers 1573 W
  Gefferie John, Northam 1582 W
  Jeffry John, Barnstaple 1637 A
  Jeffry John, Burrington 1640 W
  John, Barnstaple 1669 A
  John, ship *Norfolk* 1746 W
  Jeoffery John, ship *Superb* 1747 A
  Jeoffery John, ship *Newcastle* 1756 A
  Jeoffery John, Bideford 1767 A and 1768 A
  Jeoffery John, Northam 1781 A
  Jeffry John, Ilfracombe 1796 W
  John, Shebbear 1816 W
  John, Northam 1818 W to Catherine, sp., niece
  John, Shebbear 1843 W
  Jeoffery Joseph, Zeal Monachorum 1741 A
  Jefferie Margaret, Buckland Brewer 1583 W
  Mark, Hartland 1664 A
  Jeoffery Mary, Shebbear 1756 A
  Jefferies Mary, Bideford, sp. 1810 W
  Jeffrye or Geffrye Pentecost, Abbotsham 1616 [W]
  Jeffry Peter, Barnstaple 1631 [W]
  Jeoffery Philip, Northam 1772 W
  Geffrey Richard, Abbotsham 1577 A
  Gefferie alias Bennett Richard, Combe Martin 1582 W
  Jeffry Richard, Abbotsham 1621 [W]
  Jeffry Richard, Winkleigh 1625 [W]
  Richard, Barnstaple 1666 W
  Richard, Bideford 1693 W
  Jeoffery Richard, Heanton Punchardon 1747 W
  Jeoffery Richard, Heanton Punchardon 1780 W
  Robert, Abbotsham 1685 A
  Robert, Northam 1808 W
  Jeffry Roger, Barnstaple 1606 W
  Roger, Barnstaple 1695 W
  Thomas, Winkleigh 1669 A; A dbn 1670

Thomas, Northam 1689 W and 1690 W
Thomas, Barnstaple 1715 A
Gefferie William, Collingsdown, Buckland Brewer 1583 W
William, Barnstaple 1669 A
Jeoffery William, Newton St Petrock 1764 W
Jeoffery William, Newton St Petrock 1791 W
William, Fremington 1828 W
William, Shebbear 1836 W
Jelbert see Gilbert
Jellett John, Lapford 1589 A
Jenings see Jennings
Jenkins, Genken, Genkinge, Genkyn, Jenkin, Jenkings, Jenkyn
Alice, Barnstaple 1751 A
Jenkin David, Northam 1684 A
David, Northam 1697 A
Jenkin David, Abbotsham 1704 W
Jenkin David, Hartland 1717 A
Jenkyn Edward, Dolton 1636 A
Edward, Northam 1786 A
Edward, Bideford 1787 A
Jenkin Edward, Northam, shipwright 1797 W
Elizabeth, Northam 1747 W
Elizabeth, Bideford 1770 W
Jenkin George, Mortehoe 1669 W
Jenkin Griffith, Northam 1670 A
Henry, East Buckland 1693 A
Jenkyn Hugh, Chittlehampton 1583 W account
Jenkings Hugh, Buckland Brewer 1783 W
Hugh, Frithelstock 1820 W
James, Barnstaple 1709 A
Genken John, Barnstaple 1593 [W]
Genkyn John, Woolfardisworthy 1603 W
John, Alverdiscott 1684 A
John, Northam 1740 A
John, Buckland Brewer 1768 A
Jenkings John, Northam 1792 W
John, Northam 1833 W
John see also Mary Tout
Jenkin Lodovic, Fremington 1673 W
Jenkings Lodovic, Barnstaple 1730 A
Jenkin Margaret, Alverdiscott 1674 W
Jenkyn Mary, Hartland 1619 [W]
Mary, Bratton Fleming 1741 A
Mary, Northam 1778 W
Mary, Frithelstock 1783 A
Mary, Buckland Brewer, widow 1800 W
Genkinge Peter, Ilfracombe 1597 [W]
Priscilla, Northam 1741 W
Richard, Clovelly 1746 A
Susan, Barnstaple 1736 W
Susan, Northam 1841 W
Thomas, Barnstaple 1664 A
Jenkin Thomas, Westleigh 1681 W
Jenkings Thomas, Northam 1741 A
Thomas, Marwood 1741 W
Jenkin William, Heanton Punchardon 1696 A
William, Hartland 1726 W
William, Hartland 1815 W
Jenkin William, Clovelly, mariner 1820 A to Grace, widow
William, Buckland Brewer 1855 W
Jenn Abel, Dolton, gentleman 1805 W
Abraham, Newton St Petrock or Petrockstowe 1745 A
Grace, Dolton 1832 W
John, Woolfardisworthy 1800 A and 1803 A
John, West Putford 1855 W
Joseph, Newton St Petrock 1717 W
Joseph Thomas, Parkham 1832 W; forename may have been
   just Thomas
Jennet, Gennet, Gennett, Jennett
Elizabeth, Bideford 1640 W
Jennett alias Arnold John, Bideford 1605 W
John, Bideford 1717 A
Gennet alias Arnold Nicholas, Bideford 1642 W
Sarah, Bideford 1717 A
Gennett Thomas, Bideford 1622 [W]

Gennett William, Bideford 1637 W
Gennet alias Arnold William, Bideford 1686 W
Jennings, Genings, Gennens, Gennings, Gennyngs, Gennys,
   Gininge, Jenings, Jennins
Abraham, Barnstaple 1733 A
Edward, South Molton, snr. 1670 O "Bond Tyller decd."
Jenings Edward, South Molton, jnr. 1705 W
Edward, South Molton 1720 W
Gennings Henry, Bideford 1728 W
Jenings James, South Molton 1705 A
Gennys John, Langtree 1567 W
Gennings John, Burrington 1592 [W]
Gennings John, Great Torrington 1618 [W]
Genings alias Jenings John, Great Torrington 1679 W
Gennings Mathew, South Molton 1664 W
Mathew, South Molton 1747 W
Gennyngs or Jennins Nicholas, Great Torrington 1615 [W]
Rebecca, Barnstaple 1736 W
Gininge Richard, High Bickington 1572 W
Richard, Littleham (near Bideford) 1846 W
Gennens Thomas, Great Torrington 1573 A
Thomas, South Molton 1591 [W]
Jenings Thomas, Goodleigh 1670 A
Thomas, Bideford 1722 W
Jennynge Walter, High Bickington 1576 W and 1578 W
Jenson Elizabeth, Barnstaple 1583 A
Jeoffery see Jeffery
Jere Richard see John May
Jerman see German
Jerome Philip, Pilton 1627 [W]
Jerrett see Garrett
Jerry, Jery
Jane, Westleigh 1726 W
Jery Thomas, Great Torrington 1664 A
Gerry Thomas, Westleigh 1698 A
Jerves, Jervis see Jarvis
Jery see Jerry
Jeslyn see Jocelyn
Jesse, Jess
Jess Agnes, South Molton 1708 A
Alice, Hartland 1620 [W]
Catherine, Hartland 1607 [W]; forename blank in Ms;
   supplied from parish register
Jess David, South Molton 1674 W
Jess Joan, Hartland 1643 W
Lodovic, Hartland 1623 [W]
Jess Paul, South Molton 1680 W
Peter, South Molton 1621 [W] and O
Petronell, Hartland 1585 W
Jess Philip, South Molton 1705 W
Richard, Hartland 1595 [W]
Walter, Bideford 1590 [W]
William, Hartland 1590 [W]
Jest see Guest
Jeve Richard, Barnstaple 1842 W
Jewell, Jewil, Jewle, Juel, Juell, Jule
Juell ..., Hartland 1616 [W]
Achilles, Instow 1644 A
Agnes, Barnstaple 1638 W
Juell Alice, Kentisbury 1675 W
Ann, Bideford 1711 A
Juell Bartholomew, High Bickington 1604 W
Juel Christopher, Bideford 1640 W
Juell Digory, Bideford 1604 W
Jewle alias Predham Dorothy, Great Torrington 1606 W
Juell Edward, Bideford 1629 [W]
Juell Elias, Tawstock 1566 W
Juell Elizabeth, Instow 1642 W
Elizabeth, Barnstaple 1695 W
Elizabeth, Bideford 1849 W and 1858 A
Juell George, Instow 1604 W
Juell George, Barnstaple 1623 [W]
Juel Grace, Zeal Monachorum 1676 W
Grace, Hartland 1709 W and 1717 W
Juel Grace, Hartland 1772 W

Gregory, Kentisbury 1726 W
Hannah, Bideford 1691 W
Henry, Barnstaple 1622 [W]
Henry, King's Nympton 1640 W
Juell Hugh, Ashreigney 1620 [W]
Isaac, Little Torrington 1716 A
Juell Isott, Ashreigney 1622 [W]
Juell James, Barnstaple 1590 [W]
Juell James, Fremington 1619 [W]
Jane, Barnstaple 1828 W
Jennifer, Hartland 1669 W
Juell Joan, High Bickington 1591 [W]
Juell Joan, Zeal Monachorum 1624 [W]
Joan, Barnstaple 1631 [W] and 1635 O
Joan, South Molton 1661 W
Joan, East Putford 1668 W
Juel alias Pitton John, Bideford 1580 W
Juell John, Hartland 1581 [W]
Juell John, Instow 1582 W
Juell John, Hartland 1587 W
Juell John, Bideford 1597 [W]
Juell John, Zeal Monachorum 1620 [W]
John, Barnstaple 1632 [W]
John, Barnstaple 1668 W
John, Pilton 1684 A
Juell John, Hartland 1705 A
John, Chulmleigh 1712 A
Jule John, Barnstaple 1716 W
John, Bideford, schoolmaster 1800 W
John, Bideford 1804 W
John, Northam 1828 W
John, Bideford 1837 A to Mary Pyke
Jonathan, Clovelly, yeoman 1810 W
Joseph, Barnstaple 1715 W
Jewil Joseph, Instow 1765 W
Joseph, Clovelly 1802 A
Joseph, Barnstaple 1689 or 1690 W
Juell Margaret, Barnstaple 1624 [W]
Margery, Tawstock 1589 W
Martha, Clovelly 1812 W
Mary, Barnstaple 1746 A
Juell Nicholas, Yarnscombe 1576 A
Juell Nicholas, Hartland 1595 [W]
Nicholas, Kentisbury 1700 W
Juell Peter, Little Torrington 1629 [W]
Richard, Hartland 1699 A
Juell Robert, Abbotsham 1597 [W]
Juel Robert, Bideford 1682 A
Robert, Barnstaple 1705 A
Robert, Bideford 1707 W
Robert, Clovelly 1774 W
Robert, Great Torrington 1856 W
Juell Roger, Parkham 1577 A
Roger, Barnstaple 1599 [W]
Roger, Chulmleigh 1740 W
Samuel, Bideford 1682 A and 1688 A
Samuel, mariner 1748 W
Samuel, Hartland 1767 W
Juell alias Hooper Sybil, Bideford 1644 W
Juell Stephen, Great Torrington 1574 W
Jewel Susan, Hartland 1773 A
Jule Thomas, Burrington 1575 W
Juell Thomas, High Bickington 1591 [W]
Juell alias Petton Thomas, Hartland 1606 W
Juell Thomas, Yarnscombe 1644 W
Thomas, South Molton 1668 W
Thomas, St Giles in the Wood, husbandman 1799 W
Thomas, Barnstaple 1809 W
Thomas, Parkham 1812 W
Juell Thomasine, Abbotsham 1584 A
Juell Walter, Winkleigh 1591 [W]
Juell Walter, Ashreigney 1606 W
Juell Walter, Littleham (near Bideford) 1641 A
Juell William, High Bickington 1574 A
Juell William, Bideford 1597 [W]
Juell William, Barnstaple 1619 [W]

Juell William, Zeal Monachorum 1619 [W]
Juell William, Abbotsham 1621 [W]
Juel William, Abbotsham 1643 W
Juel William, Buckland Brewer 1643 A
William, High Bickington 1660 W
William, Bideford 1697 W
Willmot, Great Torrington 1662 W
Jewin John, Northam, merchant 1810 A
Jhones, Joanes, Joans see Jones
Jobson Charles 1634 W no place given, but B .... shown after
    date
Joce, Jose
    Jose ..., Stoke Rivers 1660 W
    Anthony, Great Torrington 1636 W
    Arthur, King's Nympton 1695 W
    Bartholomew, South Molton 1693 W
    David, East Buckland 1627 [W]
    David, East Buckland 1672 A and O
    Edward, Shirwell 1689 or 1690 W
    Elizabeth, Frithelstock 1567 W
    Elizabeth, Marwood 1625 [W]
    Elizabeth, Tawstock 1696 A
    Elizabeth, Tawstock 1834 W
    Joce Elizabeth Buckingham wife of Thomas see Walter
        Thorne
    Emma, Shirwell 1729 W
    Francis, Shirwell 1754 W; A dbn 1756
    James, Ilfracombe 1642 W
    James, South Molton 1701 W
    James, Chittlehampton, yeoman 1800 A
    Jose Joan, West Buckland 1621 [W]
    John, Frithelstock 1566 W
    John, Stoke Rivers 1599 [W]
    John, Stoke Rivers, jnr. 1626 [W]
    John, Stoke Rivers 1633 A and O
    John, Stoke Rivers 1704 W
    John, South Molton 1710 W
    John, South Molton 1735 A
    John, Chittlehampton 1741 W
    John, Tawstock 1795 W
    John, Chittlehampton, yeoman 1797 W
    John, Tawstock, yeoman 1807 W
    John, Chittlehampton 1829 A
    John, Chittlehampton 1853 W
    Joseph, Goodleigh 1770 W and 1775 A
    Mary, Shirwell 1773 W
    Mary, Stoke Rivers 1689 or 1690 W
    Nicholas, Chittlehampton 1762 W
    Nicholas, Chittlehampton, yeoman 1811 W
    Jose Peter, South Molton 1620 [W]
    Peter, Tawstock 1754 W
    Philip, Loxhore 1740 W
    Jose Richard, Stoke Rivers 1573 W, I and A
    Jose Richard, Buckland Brewer 1575 W
    Richard, Shirwell 1600 W
    Richard, Shirwell 1622 [W]
    Richard, Georgeham 1625 [W]
    Richard, Shirwell 1671 A and 1674 O
    Robert, Parkham 1632 [W]
    Robert, Shirwell 1668 W
    Robert, Combe Martin 1830 A to Mary of Loxhore, widow
    Robert Somer, Tawstock 1852 W
    Roger, East Putford 1588 W
    Sarah, Pilton 1825 W
    Thomas, Parracombe 1577 W
    Thomas, Marwood 1632 [W]
    Thomas, West Buckland 1673 [W]
    Thomas, Bideford 1714 A
    Thomas, Tawstock 1756 W
    Thomas, Chittlehampton, druggist 1809 A
    Thomas, Chittlehampton 1832 W
    William, Marwood 1615 [W]
    William, Shirwell 1685 A
    William, Tawstock 1694 W
    William, Tawstock 1795 W
    William, Chittlehampton 1824 W

William, Tawstock 1837 W
William Nicholls, Chittlehampton 1846 A
Winifred, Shirwell 1674 A
Jocelyn, Jeslyn, Joceling, Jocelinge, Joceylin, Joseland, Joselin,
    Josland, Joslene, Joslin, Josline, Josling, Joslyn
    Jocelinge ..., Ashreigney 1607 [W]
    Jocelinge ..., Petrockstowe 1609 [W]
    Joselin Alice, Peters Marland 1620 [W]
    Josling Francis, Mariansleigh 1834 W
    Joslin George, Chulmleigh 1839 W
    Joslin Henry, Burrington 1843 W
    Joslin Hugh, King's Nympton 1739 W
    Joceling Jane, Burrington 1740 A
    Joslene Joan, Eggesford 1583 A
    Jeslyn John, Cruwys Morchard 1617 [W]
    Joceylin John, Ashreigney 1667 A
    Josline John, Ashreigney 1706 A
    Joseland John, North Tawton 1763 A
    Joslyn John, North Molton 1780 W
    Josland Richard, Coldridge 1818 W
    Joslin Thomas, Ashreigney 1678 W and 1683 W
    Josling Thomas, Ashreigney, carpenter 1810 W
    William, Ashreigney, snr. 1640 W
    Josland William, Chawleigh 1832 W
    Joslin William Janes, Chittlehampton 1812 W
Joesse see Joce
Johanes, Johans, Johes see Jones
Johns, John
    ..., Peters Marland 1600 A
    ..., Clovelly 1609 [W]
    ..., Langtree 1613 [W]
    Johns alias Marten ..., Bideford 1697 A
    Benjamin, Pilton 1716 W
    Charles, Merton 1802 W
    Christian, Langtree 1827 A to Grace, mother
    Christiana, Bideford 1624 [W]
    Daniel, Huish 1776 W
    Daniel, Dolton 1831 W
    David, Great Torrington 1575 W
    David, Hartland 1686 A
    Grace, Pilton 1766 W
    Griffith, Fremington 1702 W
    Henry, Bideford 1827 A to Mary A. of Bristol, daughter
    James, Northam 1770 W
    James, Dolton 1816 W
    Joan, Great Torrington 1591 [W] and 1592 [W]
    Joan, Buckland Brewer 1644 W
    John alias Comb John, Buckland Brewer 1568 W
    John, Fremington 1591 [W]
    John, Peters Marland 1599 [W]
    John, Beaford 1625 [W]
    John, Hartland 1660 W
    John, Shebbear 1763 W
    Josiah, Littleham (near Bideford) 1698 A
    Margaret, Parkham 1834 W
    Margery, Hartland 1660 W
    Mary, Bow 1698 W
    Mary, Peters Marland 1788 W
    Mary, North Molton 1791 W
    Obadiah, Hartland 1672 A
    John Peter, Tawstock 1573 W
    Petronell, Langtree 1796 W*
    Philip, Little Torrington 1773 W
    Richard, Bideford 1573 A
    Richard, Merton 1693 W
    Richard, Langtree 1760 W and A
    Robert, Petrockstowe 1594 [W]
    Robert, Pilton 1617 [W]
    John Robert, Merton 1828 W
    Roger, Great Torrington 1592 [W]
    Samuel, Bideford, jnr. 1702 A
    Samuel, Bideford 1708 W
    Samuel, Beaford 1830 W
    Samuel, Dolton 1845 W
    Samuel, Shebbear 1854 W

Simon, Buckland Brewer 1684 W
Thomas, Langtree 1578 W
Thomas, Great Torrington 1589 W
Thomas, Buckland Brewer 1598 [W]
Thomas, Merton 1692 W
Thomas, Bideford 1712 W
Thomas, Bideford 1744 A
Thomas, Sheepwash, yeoman 1809 W
William, Buckland Brewer 1643 W
William, Bideford 1662 A
William, Bondleigh 1715 W
William, Little Torrington 1783 W
William, North Molton 1785 W
William, Langtree 1786 W
William, Langtree, yeoman 1803 W
Johnson, Johnston
    ..., Instow 1611 [W]
    Ann, Bideford 1839 A
    Benjamin, Sheepwash, innkeeper 1806 W
    James, King's Nympton 1721 W
    James, Barnstaple 1741 W
    John, Buckland Brewer 1620 [W]
    Johnston John, Barnstaple 1679 A
    John, Bideford 1697 W and A
    John, Abbotsham 1733 W
    Margaret, Tawstock 1681 W
    Nicholas, Barnstaple 1626 [W]
    Peter, Ashreigney 1772 A
    Richard, Great Torrington 1755 W
    Robert, Tawstock 1633 W
    Robert, Pilton 1740 W and 1750 W
    Samuel, King's Nympton, gentleman 1802 W
    Thomas, ship *Dispatch* 1756 A
    Walter, Barnstaple 1623 [W], 1636 A and 1644 A
    William, Barnstaple 1661 W
Joice see Joyce
Joisten Hugh, Ashreigney 1570 W
Joll, Jole
    Judith, Bideford 1775 A
    Jole Stephen, Northam 1684 W
Jolliff Grace, Woolfardisworthy 1698 W
    John, Woolfardisworthy 1687 W
Jollow, Jollowe
    John, Woolfardisworthy 1621 [W] and 1623 [W]
    John, Shebbear 1753 A
    Thomas, Buckland Brewer 1586 W
Jones, Jhones, Joanes, Joans, Johanes, Johans, Johes
    Joans ..., High Bickington 1607 [W]
    Johans ..., Cruwys Morchard 1610 [W]
    Johans ..., Ilfracombe 1610 [W]
    Agnes, Trentishoe 1820 W
    Jhones Andrew, Shebbear 1572 W
    Ann, South Molton 1825 W
    Ann, Dolton 1841 W
    Ann, Barnstaple 1856 W
    Anthony, Atherington 1665 W
    Catherine, Fremington 1743 A
    Catherine, South Molton, widow 1805 W
    Christopher, Martinhoe 1813 W
    Christopher, Swimbridge, late of East Buckland 1826 W
    Johanes David, Ilfracombe 1582 W
    David, Barnstaple 1677 A and 1683 A
    David, Barnstaple 1837 W
    David, Lynton 1853 W
    Johes Edward, Bideford 1728 W
    Edward, Northam 1750 W
    Edward, High Bray 1770 A
    Edward, Great Torrington 1786 W
    Elizabeth, Bideford 1719 W
    Elizabeth, Barnstaple 1743 A
    Elizabeth, East Buckland 1839 W
    Elizabeth, South Molton 1856 W
    George, Instow 1708 W
    George, Georgeham 1834 A
    Joanes Grace, Barnstaple 1632 [W]

Grace, Bow 1770 W
Grace, Georgeham 1777 A
Griffith, 1633 O
Henry, Barnstaple 1694 W
Honor, Berrynarbor 1682 A
Hugh, Bideford 1709 A
Hugh, Barnstaple 1801 A
Isaac, Northam 1748 A
James, Northam, Appledore, mariner 1806 W
James, Tawstock 1848 W
Jenkin, Alwington 1710 A
John, Northam 1669 A
Joanes John, Barnstaple 1693 A
John, Bideford 1697 A
John, Northam 1700 W
John, Barnstaple 1734 W
John, West Buckland 1735 A
John, Barnstaple 1752 W
John, South Molton 1783 W
John, Lynton 1792 W
John, South Molton, gentleman 1809 W
John, Tawstock 1812 W and 1821 W
John William, Abbotsham 1850 W
Jonathan, Coldridge 1843 W
Lewis, Northam 1764 W
Margaret see Ann Blackmore
Martha, Northam 1731 W
Joans Mary, Ilfracombe 1593 [W]
Joanes Mary, Instow 1693 W
Mary, Barnstaple 1711 W
Mary, Ilfracombe 1738 W
Mary, Bideford 1796 A
Mary, South Molton 1833 W
Mary, Barnstaple 1852 W
Mary wife of Thomas see also Richard Pearse
Mathew, Barnstaple 1669 A
Mathew, Berrynarbor 1679 A
Nicholas, Tawstock 1804 W
Nicholas, Tawstock 1848 W
Nicholas, Lynton 1851 W; A dbn passed at the Principal
    Registry May 1868
Philip, Atherington 1661 W
Philip, Pilton 1725 W
Philip, Pilton 1741 W
Philip, Chittlehampton 1766 A
Philip, Lynton 1775 W
Johes Philip, Lynton 1832 A to Betsy, widow
Phillippa, Clovelly 1709 W
Rees, Barnstaple 1713 W
Joans Richard, Ilfracombe 1606 W
Richard, Bideford 1715 A
Richard, Bideford 1717 W
Richard, Heanton Punchardon 1717 A
Richard, Barnstaple, jnr. 1815 A
Robert, Abbotsham 1681 W
Robert, Ilfracombe 1736 W
Robert, Barnstaple 1811 W
Roger, Fremington 1705 A
Samuel, Bideford 1684 W
Samuel, Barnstaple 1747 A
Sarah, Barnstaple 1850 W
Squire, South Molton 1740 A
Joanes Susan, Barnstaple 1632 [W]
Joanes Susan, Mortehoe 1693 W
Thomas, Fremington 1688 W
Thomas, Fremington 1724 W
Thomas, Northam 1725 W
Thomas, Bideford 1740 W
Thomas, Northam 1748 W
Thomas, South Molton 1759 W
Thomas, Arlington 1777 A
Thomas, Trentishoe 1838 W
Thomas, South Molton 1848 W
Thomas Jenkin, Clovelly 1847 W
Joanes Thomasine, Bideford 1635 A
William, Bideford 1631 [W]

William, Parracombe 1637 W
Joans William, Instow 1692 W
William, Fremington 1706 A
William, Instow 1715 W
William, Molland 1716 W
William, Bideford 1723 W
William, Molland 1768 A
William, Trentishoe, yeoman 1806 W
William, West Buckland 1854 W
Jonkes Margaret, Bideford 1760 W
Jope ..., Ashreigney 1602 [W]
    Catherine, Chawleigh 1641 W
    Diggory, Alwington 1610 [W]; forename blank in Ms;
        supplied from parish register
    Henry, Chittlehampton 1625 [W]
    John, Winkleigh 1567 W
    John, Weare Giffard 1579 W
    Lawrence, Great Torrington 1596 [W]
    Mary, Barnstaple 1643 W
    Michael, Barnstaple 1645 A
    Moses, Winkleigh 1764 W
    Richard, Weare Giffard 1616 [W] and 1626 [W]
    Richard, Barnstaple 1640 W
    Richard, Chulmleigh 1644 W
    Richard, North Tawton 1720 W
    Robert, Chulmleigh 1642 W
    Robert, Ashreigney 1688 W
    Roger, North Tawton 1615 [W]
    Thomas, Ashreigney 1605 W
    Thomas, Great Torrington 1627 [W]
    Thomas, Winkleigh 1636 A
    Thomas, Ashreigney 1641 W
    Thomas, Barnstaple 1692 A
    Walter, Chawleigh 1627 [W]
    William, Chittlehampton 1596 [W]
Jordan, Jordayne, Jorden
    Jorden ..., Beaford 1608 [W]
    Jordayne Ann, Chawleigh 1601 W
    Ann, Barnstaple 1835 W
    Catherine, Barnstaple 1816 W
    Jorden Isott and Richard, Beaford 1619 [W]
    Jourden John, Pilton 1701 A
    Mary, Huntshaw 1676 W
    Mary, Pilton 1706 A
    Mary, Knowstone 1822 W
    Jorden Nicholas, Roborough 1644 A
    Penelope, Barnstaple, widow 1814 A to Catherine, sp.,
        daughter
    Jorden Richard and Isott, Beaford 1619 [W]
    Jorden Robert, Cruwys Morchard 1626 [W]
    Jorden Susan, Iddesleigh 1634 W
    Jorden Thomas, Chawleigh 1598 [W]
Jory see Jury
Jose see Joce
Joseland, Joselin, Josland, Joslene, Joslin, Josline, Josling, Joslyn
    see Jocelyne
Josse see Joce
Jotham see Gotham
Joule, Jowles
    Henry, Clovelly 1740 W
    Jowles John, Bideford 1710 A
    John, Bideford 1754 W
    Stephen, Bideford 1705 A
Jourden see Jordan
Jowles see Joule
Joy, Juye
    Francis, Great Torrington 1668 W
    Joan, Great Torrington 1668 W
    Juye John, Little Torrington 1587 W
    Richard, Great Torrington 1665 W
    Richard, Great Torrington 1753 W
Joyce, Joice
    Hugh, Burrington 1669 A
    Joan, Ilfracombe 1662 W
    Nicholas, King's Nympton 1664 A

Joice Rose, Parracombe 1586 W
Joyner ..., Barnstaple 1616 [W]
    Walter, Barnstaple 1615 [W]
Judd, Judde, Jude
    Judde ..., Great Torrington 1613 [W]
    Alfred, Langtree 1666 W
    Anthony, Great Torrington 1715 A
    Anthony, Great Torrington 1732 W
    Anthony, Great Torrington 1769 W
    Anthony, Great Torrington 1824 A
    Anthony, St Giles in the Wood, yeoman 1824 A to Harriet,
        widow
    Anthony, Great Torrington 1855 W to Frances, widow
    Judde Elias, Parkham 1598 [W]
    Elizabeth, Langtree 1755 W
    Hugh, Great Torrington 1828 A to Fanny, widow
    Hugh, Little Torrington 1849 W
    Judde John, Barnstaple 1613 [W]; forename blank in Ms;
        supplied from parish register
    John, Langtree 1736 W
    John, Little Torrington 1777 W and A
    John, Langtree 1800 W
    John, Great Torrington, yeoman 1816 A to Mary, widow
    John, Great Torrington 1834 W
    Lewis, Langtree 1765 W
    Lewis, Langtree 1843 W
    Judd alias Burnard Mary, Bideford 1797 W
    Mary, Langtree, widow 1798 W
    Mary, Great Torrington 1855 W
    Peter, Langtree 1767 W
    Petronell, Langtree 1759 W
    Richard, Langtree 1701 W
    Richard, Langtree 1748 W
    Jude Thomas, Little Torrington 1623 [W]
    Judde William, Woolfardisworthy 1624 [W]
    William, Langtree 1723 W
    William, Langtree 1746 W
Juel, Juell see Jewell
Jugg Philip, Georgeham 1714 A
    William, Tawstock 1743 W
    William, Ilfracombe 1747 W
    William, East Down 1812 A to Dorothy, widow
Jule see Jewell
Jury, Jory
    Jory ..., Langtree 1615 [W]
    Elizabeth, Langtree 1774 W
    George, Langtree 1805 W
    Joan, Chawleigh 1755 A
    Jory John, Chawleigh 1730 W
    John, Northam 1772 W
    William, Ashreigney 1765 W
Just Margaret, Fremington 1695 A
Justine John, Cruwys Morchard 1567 W
Jutson, Jutsum
    Jutsum John, North Molton 1837 W
    Robert, Pilton 1660 W
Juye see Joy

Kaile, Kayle, Kayll
    ..., Heanton Punchardon 1612 [W]
    Kayle John, Ilfracombe 1579 W
    Mary, Mortehoe 1591 [W]
    Kayll Philip, Trentishoe 1626 [W]
    Robert, Ilfracombe 1595 [W]
    Thomas, Barnstaple 1598 [W]
Karslake see Kerslake
Kates Elizabeth, Great Torrington 1690 A
    Richard, Great Torrington 1679 A and 1690 A
    Richard, Great Torrington, jnr. 1695 A
    Richard, Great Torrington, snr. 1695 A
    Richard, jnr. 1699 A
    Richard, snr. 1699 A
    Roger, Great Torrington 1699 A
Katon Maurice, Barnstaple 1787 A
Kayle, Kayll see Kaile

Keale, Keile, Keill, Keyle
    Keyle Ann, Barnstaple 1638 W
    Edmund, Lynton 1794 W
    Elizabeth, Barnstaple 1639 W
    Keyle Joan, Barnstaple 1617 [W]
    Keile Richard, Challacombe 1727 W
    Keill Roger, Ilfracombe 1565 [W]
Keat, Keate
    Keate Mark, Ashreigney 1622 [W]
    Salome, Ashreigney 1625 [W]
Kebby, Kibby
    Elizabeth, Countisbury 1668 W
    Kibby Elizabeth, Countisbury 1722 W
    Henry, Countisbury 1667 W
Kedwell, Kedewell, Kedwill, Kedwyll
    ..., Bideford 1609 [W]
    ..., Chittlehampton 1609 [W] and 1610 [W]
    Kedwyll Elizabeth, High Bray 1639 W
    Kedewell George, Bideford 1594 [W]
    Kedwill John, Bideford 1695 A
    Kedwill Susan, Bideford 1667 W
    see also Cadwell, Kidwell
Keene, Keen, Kene, Keyne, Kine, Kyne
    ..., Heanton Punchardon 1606 [W]
    ..., South Molton 1607 [W] and O and 1614 [W]
    ..., King's Nympton 1608 [W]
    ..., Clovelly 1613 [W]
    Keen Agnes, King's Nympton 1641 W
    Agnes, George Nympton, widow 1806 W
    Alfred, Ilfracombe 1620 [W]
    Keen Alice, Ilfracombe 1670 W
    Bridget, South Molton 1689 A
    Keen Deborah, Ilfracombe 1745 A
    Edmund, King's Nympton 1661 W
    Elizabeth, Parkham 1620 [W]
    Eva, Shebbear 1729 W
    Francis, Parkham 1694 W
    Geoffrey, Ilfracombe 1636 W
    Keen Henry, Hartland 1643 W
    Henry, George Nympton 1788 W
    Keen Henry, Berrynarbor 1853 A
    Humphrey, Mariansleigh 1616 [W]
    Jerome, Hartland 1592 [W]
    Keen Joan, South Molton 1676 W
    Kene John, Mariansleigh 1573 W
    Kyne John, Bideford 1600 W
    John, Hartland 1640 W
    John, Parkham 1640 A
    John, Burrington 1704 W
    John, Littleham (near Bideford) 1704 W
    John, Ilfracombe 1708 A
    Keen John, Bideford 1709 W
    Keen John, George Nympton 1826 W
    Kene Lawrence, Clovelly 1571 W
    Margaret, Chawleigh 1595 [W]
    Keyne Margery, Dolton 1580 A
    Mary, Parkham 1664 W
    Keen Mary, Merton 1673 [W]
    Mathew, Northam 1607 [W]; forename blank in Ms; supplied
        from parish register
    Nathan, Northam 1731 W
    Keyne Nicholas, Northam 1584 A
    Nicholas, Ilfracombe 1616 [W]
    Nicholas, Parkham 1619 [W]
    Kine Nicholas, Burrington 1667 W
    Keen Orris, Northam 1743 W
    Kyne Philip, Ilfracombe 1578 W
    Philip, Ilfracombe 1661 A
    Richard, Chawleigh 1592 [W]
    Kyne Robert, Chawleigh 1576 W
    Kyne Tebbet, Chawleigh 1586 W
    Kene Thomas, Dolton 1566 W
    Thomas, South Molton 1685 W
    Keen Timothy, Shebbear 1724 W
    Keyne Walter, Northam 1584 A

Keyne William, Parkham 1589 W
Keen Willmot, Littleham (near Bideford) 1725 A
Keener, Keenor
  Elizabeth, Burrington 1740 [W]
  Keenor Giles, Winkleigh 1730 W
  Keenor John, Winkleigh 1844 W
Keeper John, Brendon 1625 [W]
  Keeper alias Parker Richard, Berrynarbor 1663 W
Keese see Keyes
Keft, Keift see Kift
Keigwin John, Pilton 1762 A
Keile, Keill see Keale
Keir Ann, Ilfracombe 1729 [W]
Kelland, Killand, Killande, Kyllond
  Ann, North Tawton 1690 [W]
  Benjamin, Merton 1664 [W]
  Bow, Merton 1744 A
  Christopher, Lapford 1624 [W]
  Christopher, Lapford 1681 A
  Christopher, Merton 1757 A
  Dionysia, Hartland 1666 W
  Elizabeth, Rackenford 1679 W
  Elizabeth, Great Torrington, widow 1811 W
  George, Zeal Monachorum 1837 W
  Kyllond John, Lapford 1580 W
  Killand John, Witheridge 1608 [W]; forename blank in Ms;
    supplied from parish register
  John, Rackenford 1629 [W]
  John, Rackenford 1676 W
  John, Chittlehampton 1694 A
  John, Merton 1746 W
  John, Coldridge 1770 A
  Juliana, George Nympton 1691 W
  Kelland, Merton 1788 W
  Mary, North Tawton 1633 W
  Nicholas, Chittlehampton 1637 W
  Nicholas, Chittlehampton 1694 A
  Nicholas, Chittlehampton 1728 W
  Philip, Lapford 1693 W
  Philip, Zeal Monachorum 1828 W
  Kyllond Richard, Rackenford 1583 W
  Richard, Lapford 1603 W
  Richard, King's Nympton 1665 A
  Richard, Rackenford 1678 A and 1679 A
  Richard, Rackenford 1701 A
  Richard, Zeal Monachorum 1765 W
  Richard, Lapford 1822 W
  Richard, Burrington, yeoman 1855 A to Mary, widow
  Robert, Rackenford 1641 W
  Robert, Rackenford 1663 A
  Thomas, Langtree 1791 W
  Thomasine, Lapford 1679 A
  Kyllond Vincent, Rackenford 1582 W
  Killande William, Rackenford 1617 [W]
  William, North Tawton 1638 W and 1641 A
  William, Lapford, snr. 1670 W
  William, North Tawton 1672 W
  William, Lapford 1686 A
  William, Great Torrington 1790 W
  William, Zeal Monachorum, gentleman 1803 W
  William, Coldridge 1827 W
Kellaway, Kelloway
  Ann, Shebbear 1824 W
  Elizabeth, Little Torrington 1816 W
  Fulk, South Molton 1687 W
  John, Little Torrington 1767 W
  John, Hartland 1855 W
  Mathew, Atherington 1762 W
  Mathew, Little Torrington, yeoman 1810 W
  Kelloway William, Great Torrington 1740 W
  see also Callaway
Kelletre Joan, Martinhoe 1586 W
Kelle, Kelleigh, Kelley, Kellie see Kelly
Kellow Peter, Great Torrington 1739 W
Kelloway see Kellaway

Kelly, Kelle, Kelleigh, Kellie, Kellye
  Kelleigh ..., Great Torrington 1608 [W]
  Abraham, Coldridge, yeoman 1804 W
  Kelley Alice, Huntshaw 1564 W
  Alice, Countisbury 1661 A
  Ananias, Merton 1697 A
  Ann, Chittlehampton 1708 W
  Ann, Peters Marland 1711 A
  Arthur, Peters Marland 1632 [W]
  Arthur, Peters Marland 1664 A
  Arthur, Fremington 1681 A
  Arthur, Peters Marland 1686 A
  Azariah, Bideford 1668 W
  Catherine wife of G. see Thomas Martin
  Kellie Clement, Ilfracombe 1613 [W]; forename blank in Ms;
    supplied from parish register
  Daniel, Martinhoe 1619 [W]
  Edward, Iddesleigh 1844 W
  Kellie Francis, Martinhoe 1617 [W]
  Gregory, Brendon 1620 [W]
  Jane, Lapford 1826 W
  Kellie Joan, Great Torrington 1616 [W]
  Kellye John, Martinhoe 1575 W
  Kelley John, Roborough 1593 [W]
  John, High Bickington 1631 [W]
  John, Bideford 1674 W
  Kelle John, Ashreigney 1714 W
  John, Peters Marland 1727 W
  John, Arlington 1776 A
  John, Marwood 1776 W
  John, Burrington, yeoman 1811 A
  John, Burrington 1845 W
  Jonathan, Coldridge 1623 [W]
  Kelley Lowglelane, Northam 1744 A
  Margaret, Meeth 1712 W
  Mary, Meeth 1676 W
  Nicholas, Coldridge 1602 W
  Peter, Winkleigh 1732 W
  Robert, Marwood 1703 W
  Kelley Robert, Marwood 1753 W; A dbn 1810
  Kellie Roger, Martinhoe 1606 W
  Thomas, Peters Marland 1639 A
  Thomas 1663 [W]
  Thomas, Meeth 1681 W
  Kelley Thomas, Peters Marland 1693 W
  Thomas, Dolton 1826 A
  Walter, Marwood 1690 W
  Walter, Bideford 1708 W
  Walter, Northam 1724 W
  Walter, Atherington 1725 A
  Walter, Marwood 1734 W
  Walter, Countisbury 1738 W
  Kelley William, Martinhoe 1589 A
Kemeys, Kemye
  Edward, Northam 1815 W
  Kemye John, North Molton 1631 [W]
Keming, Kemins, Kening
  Kening Judith, Bideford 1732 W
  Kemins Walter, Barnstaple 1615 [W] and 1616 [W]
Kemp, Kempe, Kemps, Kimp
  Agnes, Shirwell 1736 A
  Kempe Alexander, Rose Ash 1624 [W]
  Kempe Alice, North Molton 1640 W
  Kemps Bartholomew, Meshaw 1680 W
  Kimp Charles, North Molton 1741 A
  Kimp Christopher, Dowland 1827 W
  Edward, Meshaw 1763 W
  Kempe Gonnell, Oakford 1604 [W]; forename blank in Ms;
    supplied from parish register
  Henry, Tawstock 1784 W
  Kempe John, South Molton 1585 A
  Kempe John, Bondleigh 1592 [W]
  Kempe John, North Molton 1632 [W]
  Kempe John, Meshaw 1641 W
  Kempe John, North Molton 1665 A

Kimp John, Meshaw 1749 A
John, Meshaw 1776 W
John, Barnstaple, tailor 1807 W
John, King's Nympton, farmer 1852 A to William
John, Meshaw 1857 W
Julian, Rose Ash 1782 W
Kempe Leonard, Parracombe 1629 [W]
Kimp Philip, Winkleigh 1856 W
Richard, North Molton 1736 A
Kempe Robert, Meshaw 1617 [W]
Shadrach, Dowland 1804 W*
Kimp Shadrach, Dowland 1827 W
Kempe Thomas, Chulmleigh 1595 [W]
Thomas, George Nympton, yeoman 1797 W
William, Tawstock 1713 A; A dbn 1745
William, King's Nympton 1846 W and 1851 W
Kempland, Kemplande, Kimpland, Kympland
..., Rackenford 1600 O account
Kympland Alice, Barnstaple 1629 [W]
Kimpland Ann, Barnstaple 1720 W
Kimpland Ann, Barnstaple 1751 W
Augustine, Barnstaple 1604 [W]; forename blank in Ms;
supplied from parish register
James, Barnstaple 1692 A
Kimpland James, Barnstaple 1786 W
Kimpland Joan, Barnstaple 1782 W
John, Rackenford 1583 W
Kympland John, Barnstaple 1625 [W] and 1627 [W]
Kimpland John, Barnstaple 1832 W
Peter, Barnstaple 1668 W
Priscilla, Barnstaple 1668 W
Kimpland Thomas, Barnstaple 1765 W
Kemplande William, Barnstaple 1617 [W]
Kimpland William, Barnstaple 1779 W
Kympland Willmot, Barnstaple 1623 [W]
Kemps see Kemp
Kempthorne Elizabeth, Hartland 1699 W
John, Hartland 1696 W
Nathan, Hartland 1727 A
Nathan, Hartland 1743 W
Thomas, Hartland 1629 [W]
Kemye see Kemeys
Kene see Keene
Kening see Keming
Kennacott Nathaniel, Langtree 1675 W
Thomasine, Langtree 1692 W
Kennedy Thomas, Barnstaple 1725 W
Kennersley Richard, Ilfracombe 1711 A
Kennick, Kennock, Kennocke. Kerrick, Kyrricke
Kennock Agnes, Buckland Brewer, widow 1609 [W];
forename blank in Ms; supplied from parish register
Kerrick Ann, Beaford 1616 [W]
Ann, Dolton 1715 W
Ann, Chulmleigh 1731 W
Kennocke Anthony, Buckland Brewer 1640 A
George, Chulmleigh 1725 W
Kyrricke John, Beaford 1568 W
John, Shirwell 1694 A
Kennocke Leonatus, Barnstaple 1621 [W]
Kennock Mary, Martinhoe 1581 W
Kennocke Philip, Barnstaple 1620 [W]
Kennocke Thomas, Buckland Brewer 1619 [W]
Thomas, Beaford 1668 A
Kennock William, Buckland Brewer 1606 W
William, Dolton 1710 W
Kenny Frances, Bideford 1716 W
Mary, Bideford 1778 W
Kensbeare see Kentsbeare
Kent, Kente
Anthony, Chittlehampton 1603 W
Anthony, Chawleigh 1693 W
Christopher, North Tawton 1685 A
Kente Elizabeth, Georgeham, widow 1615 [W]; forename
blank in Ms; supplied from parish register
Elizabeth, Chittlehampton 1639 W

Geoffrey, Heanton Punchardon 1593 [W]
James, Oakford, jnr. 1695 W
James, Oakford, snr. 1695 W
Jane, Brendon 1735 W
John, Parkham 1620 [W]
John, Chittlehampton 1644 A
John, Stoodleigh 1732 A
Philip, Bideford 1752 W
Philip, Bideford 1809 A; limited A
Robert, Barnstaple, shipwright 1822 A to Sarah wife of John
Tolland of Pilton, miller, widow
Kente Robert, Georgeham 1609 [W]; forename blank in Ms;
supplied from parish register
Roger, Barnstaple 1591 [W] and 1593 [W]
Thomas, Knowstone 1682 W
Thomas, High Bickington 1742 W
Kente William, Northam 1602 W
Kentin Elizabeth, Bideford 1739 W
Mathew, Bideford 1740 W
Kentsbeare, Kensbeare, Kentsbeere
Kensbeare Bartholomew and Mary, Bow 1695 A
Kensbeare Damaris, Lapford 1681 A
George, Lapford 1708 W
Kentsbeere John, Lapford 1636 [W]
Kensbeare Mary and Bartholomew, Bow 1695 A
Kentsbeare Thomas, Lapford 1672 A
Kenworthie Roger, Winkleigh 1579 W
Kenyoke John, Burrington 1580 W
Kepner Roger, Great Torrington 1573 W
Kerby Richard William, Bideford, clerk 1857 W to Amelia
Harriette, widow
Kerrick see Kennick
Kerry, Kerrie, Kerye
Kerrie Amias, Arlington 1609 [W]; forename blank in Ms;
supplied from parish register
Kerye Lettice, Pilton, widow 1570 W
Philip, Pilton 1701 W
Thomas, Pilton 1691 A
William, Pilton, snr. 1636 W
William, Pilton 1685 W
William, Pilton 1703 W
Kerscote Thomas, Shirwell 1576 W
Kerslake, Carslake, Cewlake, Karslake
Cewlake Alice, Monkleigh 1567 W
Karslake Anastasia, Knowstone 1629 [W]
Ann, Knowstone 1615 [W]
Karslake Bridget, Pilton 1833 W
Karslake Henry, South Molton 1748 A
Karslake Henry, Chulmleigh 1802 A
Henry, George Nympton 1631 [W] and 1633 O
Karslake Philip, Knowstone 1618 [W] and 1622 [W]
Philip, Knowstone 1633 W
Karslake Richard, Knowstone 1624 [W]
Richard, George Nympton 1674 A
Thomas, Yarnscombe 1836 W
Karslake William, George Nympton 1741 W
Kerswill see Carswill
Kerye see Kerry
Kestle Walter, Bideford 1725 W
Kett, Kette
Kette Andrew, Sheepwash 1574 W
Geoffrey, North Molton 1597 [W]
Kewer John, Tawstock 1629 [W]
Rawlina, Tawstock 1629 [W]
Keyle see Keale
Keyne see Keene
Keys Grace, Northam 1713 A
Grace, Great Torrington 1847 A to Mary Ann wife of Henry
Martin of Appledore, sister
Kibby see Kebby
Kidd Thomas, Ilfracombe 1857 W
Kidner alias Chibbett ..., Filleigh 1682 A
Kidwell, Kidwill
Edward, High Bray 1754 A
John, High Bray 1707 W

Kidwill John, Tawstock 1758 A
Kidwill John, Weare Giffard 1824 W
Kidwill Mary, Loxhore 1768 W
Mary wife of William see Susanna Sussex
William, Weare Giffard, yeoman 1845 A to Ann, widow
    see also Cadwell, Kedwell
Keyes, Keese
Keese Richard, Northam 1708 W
Kift, Keft, Keift, Kifte
Charles, Marwood 1713 W
Kifte John, Huntshaw 1624 [W]
John, St Giles in the Wood 1712 W
Mary, Fremington 1778 W
Keift Thomas, Instow, carpenter 1809 W
Keft William, Fremington 1771 W
William, Abbotsham 1780 W
Kill Ann, Ashford 1672 W
Peter, Ashford 1687 W
Killand, Killande see Kelland
Killington ..., East Buckland 1613 [W]
Elizabeth, Barnstaple 1743 W
Kimp see Kemp
Kimpland see Kempland
Kine see Keene
King, Kinge, Kynge
Kinge ..., Chawleigh 1602 [W]
Kinge ..., Northam 1603 [W] and 1605 [W]
Kinge ..., Yarnscombe 1610 [W]
Kinge ..., King's Nympton 1611 [W]
Kinge ..., Bideford 1614 [W]
Kinge ..., Chittlehampton 1614 [W]
Kinge ..., Martinhoe 1614 [W]
Agnes, Northam 1739 W
Alexander, Charles 1850 A
Kinge Ambrose, Buckland Brewer 1615 [W]
Ann, High Bickington 1769 W
Ann, Woolfardisworthy 1803 W*
Kynge Anthony, Chittlehampton 1580 W account
Kinge Anthony, Martinhoe 1597 [W]
Kinge Anthony, Fremington 1620 [W]
Arthur, Chittlehampton 1677 A
Arthur, Chittlehampton 1714 W
Barbara, High Bickington 1822 W
Benjamin, Northam 1754 W
Catherine, Northam 1771 A
Charles, Barnstaple 1715 A
Kinge Christian, Bideford 1615 [W] and 1616 O
Kinge Edward, Barnstaple 1607 [W]; forename blank in Ms;
    supplied from parish register
Elizabeth, Ilfracombe 1761 W
Elizabeth, High Bickington 1847 W
Kynge Emblem, Chittlehampton 1577 W
Kynge Emma, Georgeham, widow 1566 W
Kinge Gabriel, Clovelly 1615 [W]
Kinge Gabriel, Chittlehampton 1637 A
Kinge George, Bideford 1613 [W]; forename blank in Ms;
    supplied from parish register
Kinge George, Bideford 1617 [W]
George, King's Nympton 1703 W
George, South Molton 1754 W
George, Barnstaple 1773 W
Hugh, Tawstock 1840 W
Humphrey, Hartland 1721 W
Isott, Chittlehampton 1733 W
James, South Molton 1674 A
James, Northam 1736 W
James, High Bickington 1820 W and 1825 W
Kinge Jane, Hartland 1696 W
Jane, Barnstaple 1849 W
Kinge Joan, Buckland Brewer 1578 W
Kinge Joan, Combe Martin 1640 A
Joan, Chittlehampton 1669 W
Joan, King's Nympton 1669 W
Joan, King's Nympton 1729 A
Kinge John, Hartland 1563 W
Kinge John, Atherington 1582 W

Kinge John, Hartland 1593 [W]
Kinge John, Martinhoe 1597 [W]
Kinge John, Chawleigh 1605 W
Kinge John, Northam 1615 [W] and 1618 O
Kinge John, Northam 1628 [W], 1629 O and 1630 [W]
John, Northam 1683 W
John, Hartland 1689 W
John, Barnstaple 1704 W
John, Northam 1717 W
John, George Nympton 1746 W
John, Hartland 1778 A and 1781 A
John, Northam 1781 W
John, High Bickington 1808 W*
John, High Bickington 1812 W
John, Newton St Petrock 1840 W
John, Ilfracombe 1856 W
Jonathan, Barnstaple, tailor 1797 W
Joshua, South Molton 1702 A
Kinge Lodovic, Winkleigh 1638 A
Margaret, Abbotsham 1693 W
Mary, Bideford 1834 W
Mary, High Bickington 1847 W
Kinge Mathew, Ilfracombe 1613 [W]; forename blank in Ms;
    supplied from parish register
Kinge Mathew, Ilfracombe 1621 [W]
Mathew, Ilfracombe 1709 A
Kinge Maud, Welcombe, widow 1564 W
Kinge Miles, Northam 1574 W
Miles, Ilfracombe 1697 A
Miles, Ilfracombe 1719 W
Kinge Peter, Bradford 1638 [W]
Peter, Ilfracombe 1716 W
Peter, Hartland 1758 W
Kinge Philip, Dowland 1631 [W]
Philip, Northam 1716 A
Phillippa, Hartland 1641 W
Prudence, Northam 1683 W
Prudence, Northam 1733 W
Kynge Richard, Welcombe 1573 W
Kynge Richard, Buckland Brewer or Filleigh 1577 W
Kinge Richard, Hartland 1601 W
Kinge Richard, Chulmleigh 1638 A
Richard, Northam 1693 W
Richard, ship *Borton* 1750 A
Kinge Robert, Chawleigh 1595 [W] and 1596 [W]
Kinge Robert, Barnstaple 1628 [W] and 1629 [W]
Robert, Abbotsham 1685 W
Robert, Northam 1712 W
Robert, Northam 1730 A
Robert, Barnstaple 1756 A
Kinge alias Saunder Samson, Parkham 1571 W
Samuel, Fremington 1660 A
Scipio, Winkleigh 1718 W
Kynge Thomas, Buckland Brewer 1586 W
Kinge Thomas, Chittlehampton 1602 [W]
Kinge Thomas, High Bickington 1636 W
Thomas, Hartland 1666 A
Thomas, Northam 1680 W
Thomas, Great Torrington 1693 A
Thomas, High Bickington 1760 W
Thomas, Hartland, yeoman 1800 A
Thomas, High Bickington, innholder 1808 W
Thomas, High Bickington 1820 W
Thomas, Hartland, yeoman 1820 A to Ursula Pillman,
    daughter
Thomas, Barnstaple 1850 W
Thomas Bland, Bideford 1805 A
Kynge Thomasine, Hartland 1585 W
Kinge Thomasine, Great Torrington 1595 [W]
Kinge Thomasine, Northam 1609 [W]; forename blank in Ms;
    supplied from parish register
Ursula, Hartland 1772 W
Kinge Walter, Georgeham 1599 [W]
Kinge William, Georgeham 1574 W
Kinge William, Chittlehampton 1602 W

William, Hartland 1631 [W]
Kinge William, Newton St Petrock 1633 A
Kinge William, Chittlehampton 1643 W
William, Barnstaple 1664 A
William, Northam 1682 A
William, Ilfracombe 1711 W and 1714 A
William, Georgeham 1736 A
William, High Bickington 1831 W
Kingdon, Kingdom
..., King's Nympton 1608 [W]
..., Zeal Monachorum 1609 [W]
Abraham, South Molton 1754 W
Abraham, South Molton 1772 W and 1774 W
Abraham, South Molton 1848 W
Agnes, Charles 1707 W
Alice, North Molton 1669 A
Ann, North Molton 1789 W
Ann, Eggesford 1823 W
Cecilia, King's Nympton 1638 A
Christopher, Coldridge 1780 W
Christopher, North Molton 1787 A
Christopher, Rackenford 1791 A
Dorothy, North Molton 1700 W
Edward, Little Torrington 1590 [W]
Elizabeth, Shirwell 1676 A
Elizabeth, Great Torrington 1825 W
Emblem, Great Torrington 1849 W
Francis, Great Torrington 1835 W
George, North Molton 1706 W
Gertrude, Twitchen 1673 W
Grace, North Molton 1784 W
Grace, South Molton 1824 W
Hannah, South Molton 1778 A
Henry, South Molton 1772 W
Henry, High Bray, yeoman 1802 W
Joan, South Molton 1620 [W]
Joan, North Molton 1636 W
Joan, North Molton 1724 W
Joan, South Molton 1769 W
Joan, South Molton 1781 W
John, Peters Marland 1581 W
John, Molland 1595 [W]
John, Coldridge 1596 [W]
John, North Molton 1605 W
John, Shebbear 1612 [W]; forename blank in Ms; supplied
    from parish register
John, North Molton 1619 [W] and 1623 [W]
Kingdom or Kingdon John, King's Nympton 1637 W
John, King's Nympton, snr. 1641 A
John, Shirwell 1663 W
John, George Nympton 1666 W
Kingdom John, South Molton 1669 W
John, Coldridge 1672 W
John, Knowstone 1676 W
John, Coldridge 1691 W
John, Charles 1696 A
John, North Molton 1738 W
John, Chittlehampton 1746 W
John, North Molton 1763 W
John, Great Torrington 1770 W
John, Rose Ash 1774 A
John, Great Torrington 1796 A
John, Rackenford, yeoman 1796 W
John, Romansleigh, yeoman 1811 W
John, Eggesford 1822 A to Richard, yeoman, son
John, Great Torrington 1853 W
Jonathan, North Molton 1622 [W]
Jonathan, North Molton, snr. 1623 [W]
Margaret, South Molton 1766 A
Mary, North Molton 1753 W
Oliver, South Molton 1766 W
Oliver, South Molton, fellmonger 1810 A
Oliver, South Molton 1848 W
Philip, North Molton 1599 [W]
Philip, Twitchen 1633 A

Philip, North Molton 1638 W and 1643 W
Philip, South Molton 1690 W
Philip, South Molton, jnr. 1690 W
Richard, Coldridge 1674 W
Richard, North Molton 1773 W
Richard, North Molton 1833 W
Thomas, George Nympton 1613 [W]; forename blank in Ms;
    supplied from parish register
Thomas, North Molton 1619 [W] and 1623 O
Thomas, Shirwell 1686 W
Thomas, Shirwell 1836 W
Thomas Huxtable, Molland 1847 W
William, North Molton 1570 W
William, Molland 1627 [W]
William, Nymet Rowland 1670 W and 1672 W
Kingdom William, North Molton 1695 W
William, North Molton 1700 W, 1714 W and 1733 A
William, North Molton 1748 A
William, South Molton 1762 W
William, North Molton 1778 W
William, South Molton 1823 W
Kingdom or Kingdon William, Eggesford 1830 W
William, Meshaw 1853 W to John of Rose Ash, brother and
    Margaret Palfreman of Meshaw
Kinge see King
Kingford ..., East Putford 1614 [W] (2)
John, Hartland 1714 A
John, Chulmleigh 1734 A
Mary, Peters Marland 1787 A
Kingsland, Kensman, Kingslande, Kingsman, Kinsland,
    Kinsman, Kyngsland, Kynsman
..., Ashford 1607 [W] and 1614 [W]
..., Great Torrington 1609 [W]
Charles, North Molton 1636 A
David, Bideford 1641 A
Kensman Evan, Shebbear 1583 W
George, Charles 1635 W
Kinsland George, West Buckland 1689 A
George, Goodleigh 1712 W
Kinsman James, Weare Giffard 1663 W
Kinsman Jerome, Woolfardisworthy 1623 [W]
Kyngsland Joan, Charles 1579 W
Kingslande Joan, Ashford 1618 [W]
Joan, North Molton 1644 W
John, Woolfardisworthy 1581 W account, A
John, Charles 1595 [W]
John, Great Torrington 1666 W
Kinsman John, Woolfardisworthy 1729 W
Kensman Joseph, Hartland 1730 W
Kinsman Mary, Holsworthy 1848 A
Kinsland Richard, South Molton 1682 W
Kynsman Robert, Dolton 1570 W
Kinsman Robert, Chulmleigh 1627 [W] and 1630 O
Kinsman Sarah, Weare Giffard 1684 W
Thomas, Northam 1603 W
Kinsman Thomas, Westleigh 1710 W
Thomasine, Clovelly 1592 [W]
Walter, South Molton 1645 A
Kingston, Kingson, Kingstone
Charles, Barnstaple 1694 W
Kingson George, Barnstaple 1827 A to Oliver Veale, creditor
Kingstone John, Barnstaple 1713 W
Kingson John, Barnstaple 1832 W
Richard, Barnstaple 1706 A
Kingson Robert, Little Torrington 1593 [W]
Sarah, Barnstaple 1845 W
Kingwell, Kyngwell
Kyngwell Edmund, Witheridge 1575 W
Kirkham William, King's Nympton 1742 A
Kitner alias Chibbett Emma 1709 W
Kitt, Kytt, Kytte
Kytt John, Parkham 1640 A
Kytte Roger, North Molton 1579 A
Kitto, Kitta
Kitta Elizabeth, Bideford 1710 A

Robert, Bideford 1709 W
Kivell William, Bideford 1857 W
Knapman John, Woolfardisworthy 1586 W
 Philip, Hartland 1618 [W]
 Richard, Woolfardisworthy 1579 W
 William, North Tawton 1733 A
Knashe see Nash
Kneath ..., Ilfracombe 1612 [W]
 ..., Countisbury 1613 [W]
 Nicholas, Pilton 1621 [W]
Kneebone, Kneeband, Kneeborne
 Catherine, Fremington 1733 A
 Kneeband Geoffrey, Fremington 1593 [W]
 Kneeborne John, Fremington 1681 W
Kniele Elizabeth wife of M. see Mary Harding
 see also Knill
Knight, Knyght, Knyghte
 ..., Barnstaple 1614 [W]
 ..., South Molton 1614 [W]
 Agnes, Countisbury 1678 W
 Alice, Lynton 1611 [W]; forename blank in Ms; supplied from
 parish register
 Andrew, Goodleigh 1568 W
 Andrew, Lynton 1582 W
 Anthony, Countisbury 1645 W
 Knight alias Hugh Anthony, Shirwell 1670 W "Knight" in
 register
 Anthony Peake, Combe Martin 1839 W
 Knyghte Baldwin, Loxhore 1569 W
 Baldwin, Pilton 1629 [W]
 Knyght David, Lynton 1580 W and 1584 W
 David, Molland 1621 [W]
 David, Lynton 1641 A, 1642 A (2)
 David, Countisbury 1665 W
 David, Lynton 1709 A
 David, Countisbury 1716 W and A
 David, Lynton 1725 A
 David, Lynton 1742 A
 David, Lynton 1777 W, 1778 W and 1784 A
 David, Lynton 1819 W
 Dorothy, Combe Martin 1748 W
 Edward, South Molton 1699 W
 Edward, South Molton 1725 W
 Elizabeth, South Molton 1775 W
 Elizabeth, Ilfracombe 1817 W
 Emanuel, Loxhore 1638 W
 Emma, Parracombe 1590 [W]
 Francis, Ilfracombe 1703 W
 George, Iddesleigh 1664 W
 George, Ilfracombe 1694 A
 George, Trentishoe 1758 W and 1767 A
 George, Ilfracombe 1840 W
 Gregory, Ilfracombe 1620 [W]
 Gregory, Countisbury 1688 A
 Henry, Bow 1631 [W]
 Henry, Pilton 1631 [W]
 Humphrey, South Molton 1660 W
 Humphrey, South Molton 1735 W
 James, Pilton 1632 [W]
 Joan, Goodleigh 1568 W
 Joan, Lynton 1580 W
 Joan, Lynton 1603 W
 Joan, Pilton 1630 [W]
 Knight alias Hugh Joan, Kentisbury 1669 W
 Joan, Combe Martin 1767 A
 John, Loxhore 1580 A
 Knyght John, Countisbury 1583 W
 John, Lynton 1595 [W]
 John, Molland 1597 [W] and 1599 [W]
 John, Pilton 1622 [W]
 John, Lynton, snr. 1623 [W]
 John, Lynton, snr. 1676 A
 John, Bittadon 1678 W
 John, Northam 1679 W
 John, Lynton 1680 W

John, Lynton 1700 A
John, South Molton 1713 W
John, Lynton 1726 W and 1735 W
John, South Molton 1750 W
John, Lynton 1757 A
John, Lynton 1758 W and 1769 A
John, Bittadon 1776 W
John, South Molton 1776 W
John, Wembworthy 1779 W
John, Bittadon 1790 W
John, Combe Martin 1816 W second A 1839
John, Lynton 1843 W
Mary, Lynton 1812 A to Richard, clerk, son
Nicholas, Countisbury 1687 W
Nicholas, Countisbury 1717 W
Philip, Lynton 1598 [W]
Philip, Pilton 1665 A
Phillippa, Iddesleigh 1672 W
Rebecca, Barnstaple 1738 W
Richard, Pilton 1628 [W]
Richard, Countisbury 1695 W
Richard, Pilton 1702 A
Richard, Lynton 1741 W
Richard, Barnstaple 1765 A
Richard, Barnstaple, mercer 1809 A
Richard, Combe Martin 1829 W and 1831 A
Richard, Barnstaple 1834 W
Robert, Ashreigney 1812 W
Roger, Lynton 1583 W
Roger, Lynton 1603 W
Roger, Buckland Filleigh 1677 W
Samuel, Ilfracombe 1630 [W]
Simon, Countisbury 1678 W
Susan, Ilfracombe 1750 A
Thomas, Lynton 1590 [W]
Thomas, Great Torrington 1627 [W]
Thomas, Goodleigh 1674 A
Thomas, West Buckland 1675 A
Thomas, Ilfracombe 1693 A
Thomas, Ilfracombe 1694 W
Thomas, Countisbury 1695 W
Thomas, Ilfracombe 1741 W
Thomas, Ilfracombe 1759 A
Thomas, Ilfracombe 1766 W
Knight alias Perry Tristram, Pilton 1697 A
Walter, Lynton 1746 W
Knyght William, Lynton 1581 W
William, Arlington 1602 W
William, Barnstaple 1701 A
William, Ilfracombe 1706 A
William, Kentisbury 1739 W
William, mariner 1742 W
William, Lynton 1745 W and 1757 A
William, Wembworthy 1772 W
William, Ilfracombe 1847 W
Knighton ..., Stoodleigh 1611 [W]
Knill, Knille, Knoll, Knyll, Knylle
 ... 1603 [W]
 ..., Parkham 1611 [W]
 Knill alias Ley ..., Pilton 1676 A
 Agnes, Tawstock 1606 W
 Knylle Alice, Berrynarbor 1586 W
 Arthur, Barnstaple 1725 A
 Beatrice, Alverdiscott 1669 A
 Deborah, Parkham 1643 W
 Gilbert, Little Torrington 1711 W
 Gilbert, Pilton 1711 A
 Gilbert, Pilton 1727 W
 Gilbert, Great Torrington 1728 W and 1740 W
 Grace, Barnstaple 1844 W
 Knoll Henry, Barnstaple 1620 [W]
 Humphrey, Tawstock 1709 W
 Knyll James, Alverdiscott 1638 A and 1639 O
 Knyll James, Hartland 1639 A
 James, Alverdiscott 1644 A

James, Fremington 1691 W
James, Fremington 1734 W
Jane, Fremington 1686 W
Knyll Joan, Barnstaple 1635 W
John, Stoke Rivers 1568 W
John, Barnstaple 1613 [W]; forename blank in Ms; supplied
    from parish register
John, Berrynarbor 1617 [W]
Knyll John, Barnstaple 1631 [W]
John, Berrynarbor 1644 A
John, Barnstaple 1664 W
John, Newton Tracey 1671 A
John, Parkham 1673 [W]
John, Pilton 1689 W
John, Ilfracombe 1698 W
John, Georgeham 1702 W
John, Alwington 1728 A
John, Northam 1741 A
John, ship *Lark* 1749 W
John, Barnstaple, yeoman 1799 A
John, Ilfracombe 1825 W
Knyll Julian, Barnstaple 1602 W
Lewis, Barnstaple 1756 A
Lodovic, Barnstaple 1619 [W]
Knyll Marian, Tawstock, widow 1572 W
Knill alias Pugsley Mary, Barnstaple 1697 A
Mary, Berrynarbor 1758 A
Knill alias Halse Mary wife of William Halls, Fremington
    1709 A; forename blank in Ms; supplied from parish register
Mathew, Ilfracombe 1691 W
Michael, Landcross 1700 W
Nicholas, Tawstock 1622 [W]
Knille Peter, Tawstock 1618 [W]
Peter, Barnstaple 1786 W
Peter, Barnstaple 1830 A
Philip, Mortehoe 1671 W
Philip, Berrynarbor 1772 A
Radigon, Barnstaple 1832 W
Knyll Richard, Huntshaw 1638 W
Richard, Woolfardisworthy (East or West), snr. 1675 W
Richard, Northam 1724 W
Richard, ship *Tawstock* 1751 A
Richard, Ilfracombe 1792 W
Knyll Robert, Pilton 1637 W
Robert, Marwood 1672 W
Robert, Barnstaple, brickmaker 1799 W
Sarah, Ashford 1669 A
Thomas, Berrynarbor 1717 W
Thomas, Pilton 1718 W
Thomas, Berrynarbor 1753 A
Thomas, Ilfracombe 1753 A
Knyll William, Berrynarbor 1579 W
William, Clovelly 1687 W
William, Pilton 1708 A
William son of John, Barnstaple 1610 [W]; forename blank in
    Ms; supplied from parish register
    see also Kniele
Knollin, Knowling
  Henry, Northam 1812 A to Ann, widow
  Knowling Richard, Bow 1792 A
Knolman, Knollman, Knowleman, Knowman
  Knowman John, Ilfracombe 1805 A
  Knollman Mary, Bideford 1694 W
  Robert, Bideford 1672 W
  Knowleman Robert, Bideford 1702 W
  Knowman Robert, Heanton Punchardon 1732 A
  Knowleman Thomas, Pilton 1698 A
Knott Anthony, Barnstaple 1708 W
  George, ship *Monmouth* 1757 A
  John, Merton 1714 W
Knowleman see Knolman
Knowling see Knollin
Knowman see Knolman
Knyght, Knyghte see Knight
Knyll, Knylle see Knill

Kooke see Cooke
Korney alias Cornewe Gawen, Hartland 1586 W
Krympe John, Knowstone 1563 W
Kyllond see Kelland
Kymell Thomas, Cruwys Morchard 1632 [W]
Kympland see Kempland
Kyne see Keene
Kynge see King
Kyngsland, Kynsman see Kingsland
Kyngwell see Kingwell
Kyrricke see Kennick
Kytt, Kytte see Kitt

Labbet, Labbett see Lobbett
Labdon see Lobdon
Lacey
  Lasie Joan, Barnstaple 1593 [W]
  Susan, Coldridge 1818 W
Laddewyn Willmot, East Worlington 1575 A
Laishbrook, Laishbrooke, Laishebrooke see Lashbrook
Lake ..., Parkham 1602 [W]
  ..., Satterleigh 1603 [W]
  ..., South Molton 1603 [W]
  ..., Chittlehampton 1609 [W]
  ..., High Bickington 1611 [W]
  ..., Beaford 1612 [W]
  ..., Northam 1612 [W]
  Adam, Huntshaw 1744 A
  Adam, Monkleigh 1827 W
  Agnes, Bideford 1629 [W]
  Alice, Chulmleigh 1700 W
  Anastasia, South Molton 1594 [W]
  Anna Wilmott, Thelbridge, sp. 1857 A to Thomas Cole Lake
    of South Molton, father
  Armanell, Tawstock 1645 W
  Benedict, George Nympton 1722 W
  Catherine, Tawstock 1661 W
  Catherine, Barnstaple 1709 W
  Catherine, Beaford 1637 W
  Christopher, Northam 1591 [W]
  Christopher, Tawstock 1640 [W]
  Christopher, Winkleigh 1770 W
  Edith, High Bickington 1639 W
  Eleanor, Brendon 1606 W
  Elizabeth, Littleham (near Bideford), widow 1609 [W];
    forename blank in Ms; supplied from parish register
  Elizabeth, Chittlehampton 1693 A
  Elizabeth, Molland 1695 A
  Elizabeth, Winkleigh 1729 W
  Elizabeth, Barnstaple 1822 A to Mary Davis, daughter
  Emma, Puddington 1641 W
  Ezekiel, Marwood 1722 W
  Faith, Tawstock 1602 W
  Francis, Hartland 1672 A
  George, Great Torrington 1591 [W]
  George 1591 [W]
  George, Alwington 1720 W
  Giles, Bideford 1667 W
  Grace, Merton 1774 W
  Grace, Bideford 1855 W
  Henry, Barnstaple 1668 W
  Hugh, North Molton 1727 A
  Humphrey, Tawstock 1665 W
  Humphrey, South Molton 1758 W
  Humphrey, Pilton 1761 W
  James, Great Torrington 1619 [W]
  James, Chittlehampton 1758 W
  James, Pilton 1769 W
  James, Weare Giffard 1825 A to James of Bideford, son
  Jeremiah, Wembworthy 1777 W
  Joan, High Bickington 1663 W
  Joan, South Molton 1669 A
  Joan, Northam 1734 W
  John, Knowstone 1573 W
  John, South Molton 1585 W

John, Bideford 1591 [W]
John, Buckland Brewer 1598 [W]
John, Langtree 1599 [W]
John, Satterleigh 1599 [W]
John, Abbotsham 1601 W
John, Buckland Brewer 1607 [W] "of Tothacot" in register;
   forename blank in Ms; supplied from parish register
John, Tawstock 1616 [W]
John, Littleham (near Bideford) 1617 [W] and 1619 O
John, Puddington 1629 [W]
John, Chittlehampton 1641 W
John, Beaford 1665 A
John, South Molton 1669 O
Lakes John, Tawstock 1682 W
John, Merton 1692 A
John, Bideford 1693 W
John, Chulmleigh 1699 A
John, Northam 1707 W
John, Chittlehampton 1710 W
John, Barnstaple 1711 W
John, Marwood 1712 W
John, George Nympton 1713 A
John, Chittlehampton 1732 W
John, Bideford 1733 W
John, West Down 1740 A
John, Chittlehampton 1742 A and 1747 A
John, Witheridge, yeoman 1810 A
John, Roborough 1842 W
Jonathan, Fremington 1708 A
Margaret, Shirwell 1764 A
Margery, Chittlehampton 1629 [W] and 1631 [W]
Margery, Georgeham 1635 W
Martha, Barnstaple 1778 W
Mary, Tawstock 1678 W
Mary, South Molton 1757 W and 1769 W
Mary, Great Torrington 1799 A
Mary, South Molton 1835 W
Michael, Winkleigh 1614 [W]; forename blank in Ms;
   supplied from parish register
Nicholas, Tawstock 1636 W
Oliver, Tawstock 1601 W
Peter, Alwington 1591 [W]
Peter, Brushford 1627 [W]
Philip, Tawstock 1591 [W]
Philip, Martinhoe 1636 W
Philip, Merton 1679 A
Philip, Bideford 1714 A
Richard, Abbotsham 1578 W and 1581 O
Richard, High Bickington 1623 [W]
Richard, Beaford 1624 [W]
Richard, Georgeham 1633 A
Richard, Tawstock 1663 W
Richard, Bideford 1692 W
Richard, Westleigh 1726 A
Richard, Weare Giffard 1816 W
Robert, High Bickington 1606 W
Robert, Molland 1660 W
Robert, Tawstock 1675 W
Robert, Bideford 1788 W
Robert, Bideford 1844 A
Roger, South Molton 1636 A
Samuel, Weare Giffard 1772 A
Samuel, Great Torrington 1781 W
Samuel, Petrockstowe 1827 W
Sybil, Great Torrington 1626 [W]
Simon, Huntshaw 1699 W
Simon, Weare Giffard 1735 W
Simon, Westleigh 1788 A
Susan, Bideford 1705 W
Susan, Cruwys Morchard 1826 W
Thomas, King's Nympton 1570 W
Thomas, Bideford 1578 A
Thomas, Beaford 1584 W
Thomas, Puddington 1588 W
Thomas, Bideford 1597 [W]
Thomas, Littleham (near Bideford) 1599 [W]

Thomas, Abbotsham 1630 [W]
Thomas, South Molton 1636 W
Thomas, Bideford 1690 A
Thomas, Georgeham 1750 W
Thomas, South Molton 1751 W and 1757 W
Thomas, Bideford 1845 W
Thomas, Buckland Brewer, innkeeper 1851 A to Thomas
   Rowe Lake
Thomas, Warkleigh, labourer 1855 A to John, innkeeper,
   brother
Thomasine, Martinhoe 1597 [W]
Walter, Buckland Brewer 1597 [W]
Walter, Tawstock 1639 W
William, Bideford 1599 [W]
William, Abbotsham 1615 [W]
William, Tawstock 1633 W
William, Chittlehampton 1640 W and O
William, Alverdiscott 1641 W
William, South Molton 1667 A
William, Chittlehampton, snr. 1675 A
William, Chittlehampton 1682 W
William, South Molton 1694 A
William, Northam 1720 W
William, Chittlehampton 1727 W
William, South Molton 1741 A
William, South Molton 1749 W
William, Bideford 1750 W
William, South Molton 1755 A and 1758 A
William, North Molton 1761 W
William, Barnstaple 1822 W
William, King's Nympton 1833 A
William, Great Torrington 1848 W
Zachariah, Westleigh 1703 A
Lakeman Catherine, Pilton 1623 [W]
   George, Barnstaple 1721 W
   John, Pilton 1826 W
Laker John, King's Nympton 1775 W
   Philip, Fremington, yeoman 1800 A
Lamb Christopher, Buckland Brewer 1727 W
   Christopher 1792 A
   Elizabeth, Buckland Brewer 1732 W
   Gregory, Atherington 1638 A
   Jane, Buckland Brewer 1732 W
   Joyce, Frithelstock 1711 W
Lambert Anthony, Bideford 1663 A
   Elizabeth, Monkleigh 1590 [W]
   John, Monkleigh 1600 W
   Thomas, Great Torrington, snr. 1645 W
Lamerris, Lamerrish
   ..., Barnstaple 1608 [W]
   Lamerrish Joan, Barnstaple 1610 [W]; forename blank in Ms;
   supplied from parish register
Lamerton Susan, Weare Giffard 1729 A
Lamfill Mary, Barnstaple 1629 [W]
Lamnan Geoffrey, Warkleigh 1567 W
Lamprey, Lamphere, Lamphey, Lampry
   ..., Bideford 1607 [W]
   Amos, Langtree 1688 A
   Elias, Littleham (near Bideford) 1631 [W]
   Lamphey Florence, Marwood 1627 [W]
   John, Newton St Petrock 1619 [W]
   Lamphere John, Tawstock 1665 A
   Lampry John, Northam 1703 A
   Lampry John, Northam 1707 W
   Lampry John, Barnstaple 1761 A
   John, Marwood 1776 W
   John, Pilton 1831 W
   Robert 1598 [W]
   Robert, Monkleigh 1633 W
   Robert, Marwood, maltster 1815 A to Sarah wife of John Bell
   of St George the Martyr
   Roger, Newton St Petrock 1591 [W]
   William, Goodleigh 1718 W
Lance George, Bideford 1819 W
   Humphrey, High Bickington 1683 A

Lancey, Lancy, Launcey, Launcie
  Launcey ..., Combe Martin 1607 [W]
  Alice, Combe Martin 1843 W
  Lancy Bridget, East Down 1687 W
  Launcey David, Combe Martin 1618 [W]
  David, East Down 1664 W
  Launcey Edward, Combe Martin 1638 A
  Lancy Edward, Barnstaple 1671 W
  Edward, Bratton Fleming 1764 A
  Edward, Challacombe 1837 A
  Edward, Bratton Fleming 1846 W
  Elizabeth, Shirwell 1833 W
  Elizabeth Hawkins, Pilton 1823 W
  Ethelred, Barnstaple 1688 W
  Lancy Francis, Barnstaple 1707 A
  Francis, East Down 1748 W
  Launcey George, East Down 1635 W
  Launcey George, Fremington 1639 W
  Grace, Pilton 1778 W
  Launcey alias Land Honor, Fremington 1640 A
  Jacob, ship *Vigilant* 1750 A
  Launcey James, Tawstock 1605 W and 1622 [W]
  James, Kentisbury 1854 W
  Jane, Combe Martin 1843 W
  Launcey Joan, East Down 1589 W
  Launcey Joan, Tawstock 1606 W
  Launcey John, East Down 1571 W
  Launcie John, East Down 1586 W
  Launcey John, Fremington 1625 [W]
  John, Combe Martin 1723 A
  John, Bratton Fleming, yeoman, jnr. 1815 A to Mary Ann,
    widow
  John, Combe Martin 1815 A
  John, Parracombe 1855 W
  Joseph, Northam 1754 A
  Margaret, Barnstaple 1726 W
  Mary, East Down 1710 W
  Mary, Combe Martin 1843 W
  Neville, Barnstaple 1664 W
  Neville, Barnstaple 1685 A
  Launcey, Nicholas, Tawstock 1638 A
  Launcey alias Lande Nicholas, Tawstock 1638 A
  Nicholas, East Down 1688 W
  Nicholas, Combe Martin 1731 A
  Nicholas, Combe Martin 1734 W
  Lancy Philip, East Down, snr. 1697 W
  Philip, East Down 1748 W
  Lancy Rebecca, Barnstaple 1694 A
  Rebecca, Bratton Fleming 1758 W
  Rebecca, Shirwell 1826 A to Thomas, father
  Launcey Richard, Tawstock 1626 [W]
  Lancy Richard, Combe Martin 1716 A
  Richard, Northam 1741 A
  Richard, Combe Martin 1826 W
  Samuel, Northam 1789 W
  Thomas, Pilton 1761 W
  Thomas, Shirwell 1826 W
  Thomas, Combe Martin 1830 A to John of Pilton, brother
  Launcey Walter, East Down 1637 A
  Launcey alias Lande Walter, East Down 1637 A
  Launcey alias Lande Walter, Barnstaple 1638 A and 1639 A
  Lancy Walter, East Down 1681 W
  Walter, East Down 1683 W
  Lancey Walter, Pilton 1702 W
  Launcey alias Lande William, Fremington 1631 [W]
  William, Fremington 1662 W
Land, Lande
  Lande ..., Bideford 1613 [W]
  Lande Alice, Atherington 1645 A
  Charlotte, Exeter 1837 A
  Elizabeth, Bideford 1688 W
  Francis, Bideford 1661 W
  George, Ilfracombe 1641 A
  Lande alias Launcey Honor, Fremington 1640 A
  Lande John, Buckland Brewer 1587 W

  John, Bideford 1714 W
  Mary, Berrynarbor 1698 A
  Nicholas, Bideford 1694 A
  Lande Thomas, Chittlehampton 1620 [W] and 1623 O
  Thomas, Bideford 1694 W
    see also Laund
Landman
  Landman alias Crocker ..., Rose Ash 1692 W
  Alice, South Molton 1712 W
  Benjamin, Fremington 1746 W
  Joan, Pilton 1666 W
  John, Barnstaple 1661 W
  John, South Molton 1713 W
  Joseph, Pilton 1685 W
  Sarah, Barnstaple 1632 [W]
  Landman alias Crocker William, Rose Ash 1669 A
  William, South Molton 1694 A
  William, South Molton 1705 W
Landry Emotta, Goodleigh 1629 [W]
  Lanndry John, Goodleigh 1627 [W]
  Landy, Landye see Landey
Lane Abraham, Roborough 1780 A
  Edward, Ashreigney 1771 A
  Elizabeth, Roborough 1786 A
  Francis, King's Nympton 1789 W
  Henry, Lapford 1627 [W]
  Lane alias Crocker John, South Molton 1580 W
  John, Huntshaw 1592 [W]
  John, Abbotsham 1748 A
  John, King's Nympton 1769 W
  Joseph, Chulmleigh 1827 A to Elizabeth of Tiverton, widow
  Josiah, Parkham 1827 W
  Josiah, Parkham 1841 W
  Margaret, Great Torrington 1575 W
  Margaret, Rackenford 1622 W
  Philip, Ashreigney 1781 A
  Philip, Wembworthy 1816 W
  Roger, Cruwys Morchard 1632 O
  Thomas, Chawleigh 1641 A
  Thomas, King's Nympton 1738 W
  Thomas, Ashreigney 1763 W
  Thomas, Arlington 1812 A to Dorothy, widow
  Thomas, Ashreigney 1835 A to Elizabeth, widow; A dbn 1843
    to Thomas, son
  William, Barnstaple 1611 [W]; forename blank in Ms;
    supplied from parish register
  William, Rackenford 1644 W
  William, Bideford 1748 W
  William, Clovelly 1836 W
Laneman Alexander, Rose Ash 1625 [W]
  John, Barnstaple 1609 [W]; forename blank in Ms; supplied
    from parish register
  Richard, Rose Ash 1615 [W]
  Thomas, Barnstaple 1623 [W]
  Laneman alias Crocker William, Rose Ash 1669 A
Lanercombe, Lunnacombe
  Lunnacomb ..., Wembworthy 1604 [W]
  Agnes, Bratton Fleming 1566 W
Lang, Lange
  Lange ..., East Putford 1610 [W]
  Lange ..., South Molton 1610 [W]
  Lange Agnes, Barnstaple 1575 W
  Lange Agnes, Fremington 1600 W
  Lange Agnes, Chittlehampton 1640 W
  Alfred, Lynton 1582 A
  Alice, Woolfardisworthy 1643 W
  Lange Arthur, Frithelstock 1634 W
  Lange Davy, South Molton 1615 [W]
  Lange Elias, Fremington 1592 [W] and 1593 [W]
  Ellen, Bideford, sp. 1854 A to Mary of St Leonards, Devon,
    widow, mother
  Evan, Northam 1691 A
  Lange Francis, Barnstaple 1604 [W]; forename blank in Ms;
    supplied from parish register
  Lange George, Ilfracombe 1598 [W]

Lange George, North Molton 1619 [W]
George, Heanton Punchardon 1687 W
Lange Henry, Barnstaple 1599 [W]
Lange Henry, Hartland 1639 W
Lange Humphrey, Frithelstock 1604 W
Jane, Frithelstock 1698 A
Lange alias Pawle John, Barnstaple 1570 W
Lange John, Northam 1586 W
Lange John, Barnstaple 1593 [W]
Lange John, North Molton 1598 [W]
Lange John, North Molton 1632 [W]
Lange John, Northam 1632 [W]
Lange John, Chittlehampton 1638 O
John, Knowstone 1661 A
John, Great Torrington 1669 W
John, Great Torrington 1693 W
John, Frithelstock 1730 W
John, South Molton 1746 W
John, Bideford 1840 W
John, Parkham 1856 W
Lange Jonathan, Little Torrington 1624 [W]
Joseph, Lynton 1687 W
Lawrence, Frithelstock 1664 A
Lange Mary, North Tawton 1639 W
Mary, Bideford 1693 W
Lange Mathew, Northam 1633 W
Lange Michael, Northam 1637 W
Lange Nicholas, Barnstaple 1624 [W]
Nicholas, Westleigh 1679 W
Peter, Fremington 1643 A
Peter, Northam 1856 W
Lange Petronell, Georgeham 1619 [W] and 1620 [W]
Philip, Northam 1851 W
Rebecca, Bideford 1679 W
Lang or Langdon Richard, Langtree 1707 W
Lange Robert, Marwood 1640 W
Robert, Chulmleigh 1741 A
Susan, Frithelstock 1679 W
Lange Thomas, Tawstock 1589 W
Thomas, East Putford 1693 W
Thomas, Coldridge 1848 W; A dbn passed at Exeter, Jun 1868
Timothy, Bideford 1677 W
Timothy, Bideford 1728 W
Lange William, Barnstaple 1621 [W]
Lange William, North Molton 1628 [W]
William, Berrynarbor 1663 W
William, Bideford 1673 A
William, Brendon 1678 A
William, Woolfardisworthy 1705 W
Lange Willmot, South Molton 1620 [W]
Langbere, Langebear, Lannbeer
Elicie, St Giles in the Wood 1575 W
Joan, St Giles in the Wood 1578 W
Langebear John, St Giles in the Wood 1590 [W]
Lannbeer John, Great Torrington 1821 W
Langbridge, Langbridg, Langbrydge, Langebridge
Agnes, Romansleigh 1582 W
Edith, Romansleigh 1592 [W]
Edward, Winkleigh 1719 A
Francis, Chulmleigh 1627 [W]
Henry, Romansleigh 1566 W
Jane, Bow 1743 W
Joan, Winkleigh 1739 W
Langebridge John, Chulmleigh 1592 [W]
Langbridg John, Meshaw 1664 W
John, Chulmleigh 1761 W
Josiah, Chulmleigh 1641 A
Philip, Romansleigh 1588 A
Langbrydge Samuel, Meshaw 1631 [W]
Samuel, Chulmleigh 1687 A
Samuel, West Worlington 1712 W
Langdon, Longdon
..., Georgeham 1601 A
..., Hartland 1610 [W]
Abagaiher, Northam 1729 W

Agnes, Atherington 1643 W
Alice, South Molton 1623 [W]
Alice, South Molton 1699 A
Anthony, Barnstaple, currier 1806 A
Longden alias Clarke Audrey Longden alias John Clarke,
    Great Torrington 1791 A
Christopher, Great Torrington 1720 A
Langdon alias Clarke Dorothy, Georgeham 1681 W
Edward, Berrynarbor 1643 A
Elizabeth, Heanton Punchardon 1625 [W]
Langdon alias Clark Elizabeth, Georgeham 1670 W
George, Heanton Punchardon 1699 W
George, Northam 1700 W
George, Heanton Punchardon 1720 W
George, Northam 1745 W
George, Heanton Punchardon 1757 W
George, Heanton Punchardon 1830 W
Henry, Woolfardisworthy 1599 [W]
Henry, Barnstaple 1623 [W]
Henry, Fremington 1799 W
Honor, Heanton Punchardon 1774 W
Hugh, Northam, snr. 1698 W
Humphrey, Barnstaple 1691 W
Humphrey, Barnstaple 1719 W
Humphrey, Great Torrington 1731 A
Humphrey, Great Torrington 1734 W
James, Barnstaple 1707 W
Jane, Heanton Punchardon 1784 W
Jeremiah, Heanton Punchardon 1780 W
Jeremiah, Heanton Punchardon 1832 A
Joan, Tawstock 1627 [W]
Joan and John, Woolfardisworthy 1630 [W]
John, Fremington 1594 [W]
John, Chittlehampton, snr. 1631 [W]
John, Chittlehampton 1635 W
Langdon alias Collander John, Tawstock 1642 W
John, Heanton Punchardon 1675 A and 1675 O
John, Fremington 1677 W
John, Heanton Punchardon 1710 W
John, Northam 1722 A
John, Heanton Punchardon 1723 W
John, Barnstaple 1733 W
John, Heanton Punchardon, yeoman 1800 W
John, Barnstaple 1803 W and 1813 W
John, Chulmleigh 1829 A to John S., son
John, Mortehoe 1853 W
John and Joan, Woolfardisworthy 1630 [W]
Justinian, Barnstaple 1712 W
Kitty, Heanton Punchardon, sp. 1807 A
Lewis, Barnstaple 1808 W*
Lodovic, Great Torrington 1720 W
Lucas, Great Torrington 1707 W
Margaret, Great Torrington 1692 A
Margaret, Marwood 1836 W
Mary, Georgeham 1644 A
Mary, Fremington 1762 W
Mary, Barnstaple 1790 W
Mary, Barnstaple 1834 W
Mary, Barnstaple 1852 W
Mathew, Barnstaple 1697 W
Oliver, Instow 1693 A
Peter, Ilfracombe 1697 A and 1703 A
Philip, Heanton Punchardon 1758 W
Rebecca, Barnstaple 1748 W
Reginald, South Molton 1716 W
Richard, Shirwell 1573 A
Richard, Barnstaple 1682 W
Langdon alias Lang Richard 1707 W
Richard, Heanton Punchardon 1761 A
Robert, Woolfardisworthy 1618 [W]
Robert, Chawleigh 1625 [W]
Robert, King's Nympton 1822 W
Roger, Great Torrington 1757 A
Samuel, Ilfracombe 1771 W
Samuel, Ilfracombe 1807 A

Sarah, Heanton Punchardon 1698 W
Sarah, Bideford 1735 A
Simon, South Molton 1623 [W]
Susan, Northam 1722 A
Susan, Northam 1821 A to Hannah Maine, widow, daughter
Langdon alias Collander Thomas, Great Torrington 1669 A
Thomas, Northam 1716 W
Thomas, Merton 1727 W
Thomas, Ilfracombe 1743 W
Thomas, Great Torrington 1750 W
Thomas, Great Torrington 1850 W
William, Georgeham 1598 [W]
William, Shirwell 1634 W
William, Barnstaple 1739 W
William, formerly of Heanton Punchardon, late of Barnstaple
    1763 A; 16 Aug 1844
Lange see Lang
Langebear see Langbere
Langebridge see Langbridge
Langer John, Twitchen 1768 W
Thomas, Twitchen 1778 W
Langford Elizabeth, Bideford 1723 A
John, Bideford 1698 W
John, Bideford 1720 W; A dbn 1723
Sarah, Bideford 1700 W
Langham   ..., Lapford 1602 [W] and 1607 [W]
Agnes, Lapford 1577 W
Ann, Puddington 1745 W
Nicholas, Woolfardisworthy 1745 A
Robert, Lapford 1580 W
Langman see Longman
Langmede Thomas, Winkleigh 1575 W
Langridge Samuel, Chulmleigh 1644 W
Langwill John, Chittlehampton 1725 W
Robert, Oakford 1617 [W]
Lannbeer see Langbere
Lanndry see Landry
Lanner Mary, Tawstock 1643 A
Lannery John, Barnstaple 1644 A
Lantrow Caleb, Merton 1709 A
Christopher 1728 W
Lanyon Mary, Barnstaple 1620 [W] and 1636 O
Lapthorne Roger, Bideford 1632 [W]
Laramey see Laramy
Laramore, Laramur, Larimer, Larrimer
Laramur Cicely, Westleigh 1585 W
Larimer Henry, Barnstaple 1728 A
Matilda, Alverdiscott 1637 W
Larrimer Nicholas, Kentisbury 1672 W
Larimer Oliver, Great Torrington 1726 W
Larimer William, Huntshaw 1574 W
    see also Lorimer
Laramy, Laramey, Larimy, Larimye, Larmey, Larminey,
    Larramy, Larromy, Loromie, Loromy
Loromie ..., Beaford 1612 [W]
Larramy Alexander, Challacombe 1721 A
Alexander, Shirwell 1793 A
Larmey Alexander, Challacombe 1831 W
Henry, Barnstaple 1726 W
James Warren, Northam, farm bailiff 1856 A to Elizabeth,
    widow
Joan, Frithelstock 1679 W
John, Marwood 1843 A to George Balsdon of Barnstaple,
    maltster, trustee of child
Laramey Jonah, Alverdiscott 1684 W
Larminy alias Allyn Michael (died 1681), Barnstaple 1683 A;
    forename blank in Ms; supplied from parish register
Loromy Richard, Dolton 1597 [W]
Larimy Richard 1681 A
Larromy Robert, Buckland Brewer 1671 A
Sarah, Marwood 1839 W
Larimye Susan, Shirwell 1692 W
William, Shirwell 1672 W
William, Northam 1673 [W]
Laramey William, Challacombe, snr. 1688 W

Larramy William, Challacombe 1737 W
William, Bratton Fleming 1800 W
Larder ..., Great Torrington 1607 [W]
Elizabeth, Great Torrington 1619 [W]
Larg Agnes, Northam 1679 A
Larimer see Laramore
Larimy, Larimye see Laramy
Lark, Larke
Edward, Bideford 1687 W
Samuel, Buckland Brewer 1677 A
Larke Willmot, Clovelly 1642 W
Larkham Thomas, Northam 1690 W
Larkin Elizabeth, Barnstaple 1718 W
George, Barnstaple 1766 A
Josiah, Barnstaple 1799 A
Mary, Barnstaple, widow 1798 W
Thomas, Barnstaple 1737 W
Larkworthy, Larwerthy
James, Shebbear 1753 W
Jane, Shebbear 1829 W
John, Shebbear 1819 W and 1825 W
Mary, Shebbear 1765 W
Mary Ann, Shebbear 1839 A to Elizabeth Hearn of Langtree,
    daughter
Larwerthy Peggy, Shebbear 1827 A to William, brother
William, Shebbear 1826 W and 1831 W
William, Shebbear 1851 W
Larmey, Larminy, Larramy see Laramy
Larrimer see Laramore
Larromy see Laramy
Larwell Thomas, Northam 1695 A
Larwerthy see Larkworthy
Lashbrook, Laishbrook, Laishbrooke, Laishebrooke, Lasbroke,
    Lashbrocke, Lashbrooke
Laishbrook ..., Witheridge 1615 [W]
Elizabeth, Barnstaple 1832 W
Lashbrooke Grace, Barnstaple 1840 W
Lasbroke Joan, Martinhoe 1572 W
Lashbrooke John, Petrockstowe 1728 A
John, Buckland Brewer 1797 W
Mary Ann see Elizabeth Grimshire
Lashbrocke Richard, Martinhoe 1569 W
Lashbrooke Richard, formerly of Huntshaw, late of
    Fremington, yeoman 1804 W
Richard, Buckland Brewer 1845 W
Laishbrooke Robert, Witheridge 1599 [W]
Laishebrooke Robert, Buckland Filleigh 1626 [W]
Lashbrooke William, Dolton 1721 A
William, Buckland Brewer 1833 A to Jane, widow
Lasie see Lacey
Latch Peter, Bideford 1715 W
Thomas, Northam 1698 W
Thomas, Bideford 1738 W
Latey see Laty
Latham, Lathum
John, Martinhoe 1814 W and 1815 W
John, Brendon 1837 W
Philip, Combe Martin 1845 A
Richard, Trentishoe 1803 W*
Richard, Combe Martin 1845 A
Lathum Samuel, Lynton 1731 A
William, Lynton 1856 W
Laty, Latey
John, South Molton 1676 W
Latey John, Chittlehampton 1734 A
Richard, South Molton 1702 A
Thomas, South Molton 1745 A
Launcey, Launcie, Launcy see Lancey
Laund, Lawnd
Lawnd Elizabeth, Ilfracombe 1776 W
Lawnd Joan, Ilfracombe 1753 A
Lawnde Robert, Ilfracombe 1617 [W]
Lawnd Walter, Pilton 1664 W
William, Ilfracombe 1675 A
    see also Land

Launder Alexander, Winkleigh 1700 W
Laurence, Laureme, Laurens, Lawrence
   Lawrence ..., Bideford 1605 [W]
   Lawrence ..., Chulmleigh 1607 [W]
   Agnes, Chulmleigh 1728 W
   Lawrence Dorothy, Chulmleigh, sp. 1797 W
   Lawrence Edward, Chulmleigh 1700 W
   Laurens Emma, Bideford, widow 1567 W
   Lawrence Francis, Chulmleigh 1641 W
   Lawrence Francis, Chulmleigh 1673 W
   Lawreme Francis, Chulmleigh 1740 A
   Lawrence Francis, Chulmleigh 1766 W
   Francis, Ashreigney 1794 W
   Lawrence Giles, Barnstaple 1618 [W]
   Lawrence Grace, Chulmleigh 1768 W
   Lawrence Joan, Chulmleigh 1676 W
   Joan, Chulmleigh 1707 W and 1717 A
   Joan, Chulmleigh 1722 W
   Lawrence Joan, Chulmleigh 1735 A
   Lawrence Joan, Chulmleigh 1751 W
   Lawrence John, Bideford 1635 W
   Lawrence John, Chulmleigh 1704 W
   John, Ashreigney 1827 W
   Lawrence Mary, Ilfracombe 1838 A to Betty, sister
   Lawrence Richard, Abbotsham 1629 [W]
   Laurence alias Searle Richard, Bideford 1661 A
   Lawrence Richard, Chawleigh 1666 A and 1669 O
   Lawrence Richard, Abbotsham 1703 W
   Lawrence Richard, Chulmleigh 1742 A
   Sarah, Bideford 1710 W
   Walter, Bideford 1706 W
   Lawrence William, Bideford 1619 [W]
   Lawrence William, Ashreigney 1713 A
   Lawrence Willmot, Northam 1620 [W]
Lavercomb, Lavercombe
   Alice, Goodleigh 1643 A
   Lavercombe Ann, Northam 1691 W
   Lavercombe Anthony, Stoke Rivers 1690 W
   Arminall, Tawstock 1663 W; forename blank in Ms; supplied
     from parish register
   Lavercombe Elizabeth, Bratton Fleming 1729 A
   Lavercombe Grace, Bratton Fleming 1749 W
   Helen, Tawstock 1645 W
   Henry, Charles 1702 W
   Henry, Bratton Fleming 1716 W
   Humphrey, Bratton Fleming 1700 W
   Lavercombe Joan, Bratton Fleming 1616 [W]
   Lavercombe John, Bratton Fleming 1625 [W]
   John, Bratton Fleming 1707 W
   John, Combe Martin 1716 [W]
   Lavercombe John, Bratton Fleming 1726 W
   Juliana, Combe Martin 1729 A
   Lawrence, Charles 1664 W
   Lawrence, Charles 1702 A
   Mary, Tawstock 1680 W
   Mary, Braunton, widow 1846 A to Mary Symonds, widow,
     daughter
   Lavercombe Paul, Barnstaple 1692 W
   Lavercombe Richard, Bratton Fleming 1682 W
   Lavercombe Richard, Bratton Fleming 1721 A and 1729 A
   Lavercombe Richard, Bratton Fleming 1751 W
   Lavercombe Richard, Bratton Fleming 1812 A to Richard, son
   Lavercombe Thomas, Bratton Fleming 1592 [W]
   Lavercombe Thomas, Tawstock 1639 W
   Thomas, Tawstock 1679 W
   Thomas, Bratton Fleming 1719 W
   Lavercombe Thomas, Bratton Fleming 1793 A
   William, Charles 1702 W
   Lavercombe William, Bratton Fleming 1724 W
Law John, Barnstaple 1692 A
Lawday, Laudey, Laudie, Laudy, Laudye, Lawdaye, Lawdey,
   Lawdie, Lawdy, Lawdye, Lowdey
   Lawdye ..., Burrington 1603 [W]
   Lawdey Agnes, Great Torrington 1592 [W]
   Lawdey Andrew, South Molton 1625 [W]

   Lawdye Anthony, High Bickington 1579 W
   Lawdy Arthur, Chittlehampton 1641 W
   Lawdey Charles, Warkleigh 1755 W and 1760 W
   Lowdey Elizabeth, South Molton 1774 A
   Lawdaye Joan, Little Torrington, widow 1572 W
   Lawdey John, High Bickington 1571 W
   Lawdye John, Barnstaple 1596 [W]
   Lawdye John, Barnstaple 1624 [W]
   Laudey John, Bideford 1628 [W]
   Laudye John, Atherington 1633 W
   John, North Molton 1675 W
   John, Atherington 1688 A
   John, South Molton 1794 W
   John, King's Nympton 1795 A
   John, King's Nympton 1839 W
   Lowdey Jonathan, Barnstaple 1781 A
   Lawrence, Heanton Punchardon 1704 A
   Lawrence, Atherington 1708 A
   Laudie Margery, Burrington 1584 A
   Mary, South Molton 1794 A
   Lawdye Mathew, Satterleigh 1643 W
   Laudy Peter, Satterleigh 1670 A
   Peter, North Molton 1696 W
   Richard, North Molton 1716 W
   Roger, North Molton 1699 W
   Lawdie Thomas, South Molton 1568 W
   Lawdye Thomas, South Molton 1590 [W]
   Lawdye William, High Bickington 1615 [W]
Lawnd, Lawnde see Laund
Lawne Agnes, Barnstaple 1673 [W]
   Catherine, Ilfracombe 1629 [W]
Lawrence see Laurence
Lawry Elizabeth wife of Edward see Thomas Lerwill
Laxton Peter, Winkleigh, miller 1811 W
Lay see Lee
Lea see Lee
Leach, Leache, Leche
   ..., Bideford 1607 [W]
   Ambrose, Washford Pyne 1825 W
   Andrew, Chawleigh 1634 O
   Charles, Northam 1710 W
   George, Barnstaple 1613 [W]; forename blank in Ms; supplied
     from parish register
   Leache George, Barnstaple 1622 [W]
   James, Northam 1760 W
   John, Bideford 1630 [W]
   John, Chawleigh 1634 A
   Leache Mary, Bideford 1628 [W]
   Mary, Bideford 1741 A
   Richard, Barnstaple 1620 [W]
   Leache Richard, Bideford 1621 [W]
   Samuel, Bideford 1708 A
   Sarah, Bideford 1716 W
   Leache Thomas, Bideford 1580 A
   Leche Thomas, Martinhoe 1586 A
   Thomas, Bideford 1594 [W]
   Thomas, Bideford 1694 W
   William, Barnstaple, innkeeper 1822 A to Mary, widow
Leachland Nicholas, Barnstaple 1735 A
Leaker Richard, Fremington 1847 W
Leaman, Leamon, Leman
   Alexander, Weare Giffard 1681 W
   Alice, Bulkworthy 1725 A
   Anthony, Filleigh 1731 W
   Leman Elizabeth, Frithelstock 1744 A
   Leman James, Northam 1716 W
   James, Atherington 1840 A to Mary, widow
   Mary, Shebbear 1693 W
   Leamon Philip, Northam 1727 W
   Robert, Bideford 1715 W
   Stephen, Weare Giffard 1696 W
   Thomas, Shebbear 1687 W
   William, Bulkworthy 1709 W
Leare, Lear
   Henry, Pilton 1704 A

Henry, Barnstaple 1744 W
Margaret, Tawstock 1640 A
Philip, Pilton 1627 [W]
Philip, Pilton 1713 A
Susan, Pilton 1633 W
Lear Thomasine, Pilton 1675 W and 1676 W
William, Pilton 1703 A
Leatheren, Leathern see Letherne
Leaves alias Lecaes ..., Heanton Punchardon 1678 W
Lebbett Thomas, Huish 1693 W
Lecaes alias Leaves ..., Heanton Punchardon 1678 W
Leche see Leach
Lechedon see Lichedon
Lee, Lea, Ley, Leye
Ley ..., Molland 1601 A
Ley alias Barnepoole ..., Fremington 1601 W
..., Instow 1603 [W]
Ley ..., Meeth 1605 [W]
Ley ..., Burrington 1605 [W], 1611 [W] and 1614 [W]
Ley ..., Combe Martin 1609 [W] and 1614 [W]
..., Twitchen 1610 [W]
Ley ..., King's Nympton 1612 [W]
Ley ..., Pilton 1613 [W]
Ley ..., High Bray 1617 [W]
Ley alias Knill ..., Pilton 1676 A
Ley alias Barnepoll Agnes, Fremington 1574 W
Ley Agnes, Great Torrington 1587 W and 1594 [W]
Ley Agnes, Tawstock 1620 [W]
Ley Agnes, Molland 1642 A
Ley Agnes, Tawstock 1667 W
Ley Agnes, Monkleigh 1683 W
Ley Agnes, Barnstaple 1703 W
Ley Alexander, Great Torrington 1735 W
Ley Alice, Atherington 1585 W
Ley Alice, Barnstaple 1703 W
Ley Alice, Combe Martin 1750 A
Ley Andrew, Great Torrington 1602 W
Ley Ann, Tawstock 1661 A
Ann, Shebbear 1831 W
Ann, Fremington 1838 W
Ley Ann, George Nympton 1848 W
Ann see Elizabeth Nankivell
Anthony, Goodleigh 1604 W
Anthony, Alverdiscott 1619 [W]
Ley Anthony, Combe Martin 1708 A
Ley Anthony, Combe Martin 1732 A
Ley Arthur, Barnstaple 1718 W
Ley Charles, Ilfracombe 1591 [W]
Ley David, High Bickington 1696 A
Ley Deborah with Francis and Mary, Atherington 1635 A
Edmund, Twitchen 1586 W
Ley Edmund, Filleigh 1725 W
Ley Edward, St Giles in the Wood 1671 W
Ley Edward, Combe Martin 1752 W
Edward, Woolfardisworthy 1827 W
Edward, Woolfardisworthy 1850 W
Eleanor, Parkham 1612 [W]; forename blank in Ms; supplied
   from parish register
Ley Eleanor, Burrington 1673 W
Ley Elias, Bondleigh 1594 [W]
Ley Elizabeth, Atherington 1617 [W]
Ley Elizabeth, Tawstock 1689 W
Elizabeth, Chawleigh 1843 A
Ley Elizabeth, Bideford 1847 W
Elizabeth, East or West Worlington 1849 W
Ley Elizabeth, Tawstock, widow 1609 [W]; forename blank in
   Ms; supplied from parish register
Ley Elizabeth wife of John see Anthony and George Chugg
Ley Ellen, Challacombe 1580 W
Ley Emma, Frithelstock 1592 [W]
Emott, Parkham 1628 [W]
Francis, Newton Tracey 1670 A
Ley Francis with Mary and Deborah, Atherington 1635 A
Ley Garrett, Tawstock 1599 [W]
Ley George, Pilton 1683 W
Ley George, Burrington 1688 A

Ley George, Pilton 1707 A
Ley George, Combe Martin 1716 W
George, Pilton 1726 A
Ley George, Ilfracombe 1743 A
Ley George, Barnstaple 1757 A
Ley George, Roborough 1768 W
Ley George, Brendon 1784 W
Ley George, Barnstaple 1791 A
Ley George, Marwood 1844 A to Henry, esquire, brother
Ley Giles, Pilton 1633 A and 1635 O
Ley Grace, East Putford 1689 A
Ley Grace, Barnstaple, widow 1804 W
Grace Hamlyn, Barnstaple 1852 A
Ley Hannah, Barnstaple 1663 W
Henry, Chittlehampton 1682 W
Ley Henry, Barnstaple 1705 W
Ley Henry, Beaford 1707 W
Ley Henry, Barnstaple 1730 W
Ley Henry, Barnstaple 1771 W
Hugh, North Molton 1643 W
Ley Hugh, Tawstock, snr. 1697 W
Hugh, Pilton 1706 W
Hugh, Pilton 1725 W
Ley Hugh, Tawstock 1728 W
Ley Hugh and John, Pilton 1664 W
Ley Humphrey, Burrington 1665 A
Ley James, Atherington 1605 W
Ley James, Combe Martin 1638 A
James, Pilton 1678 A and 1692 A
Ley James, Tawstock 1708 A
Ley James, Chittlehampton 1742 W
James, Barnstaple 1743 A
Ley James, formerly of Monkleigh but late of Northam 1831
   A
James, Pilton 1850 W
James see also Stephen Balch
Ley Jane, Chittlehampton 1687 W
Ley Jane, Great Torrington 1733 A
Jane, Barnstaple 1815 W
Ley Jeremiah, Monkleigh 1760 W
Ley Joan, Coldridge 1575 W
Ley Joan, Parkham 1590 [W]
Ley Joan, King's Nympton 1592 [W]
Ley Joan, High Bickington 1596 [W]
Ley Joan, Yarnscombe 1616 [W]
Joan, Alverdiscott 1621 [W]
Joan, Zeal Monachorum 1626 [W]
Ley Joan, Combe Martin 1632 [W]
Joan, Instow 1661 W
Ley Joan, Little Torrington 1663 A
Joan, Lapford 1664 W
Ley Joan, High Bickington 1696 A
Ley Joan, Barnstaple 1700 A
Leye John, East Anstey 1566 W
Ley John, Atherington, snr. 1570 W
Lay John, King's Nympton 1583 W
John, Instow 1586 A
Ley John, Tawstock 1590 [W]
Ley John, Burrington 1591 [W]
Ley John, Barnstaple 1593 [W]
Ley John, Combe Martin 1598 [W]
Ley John, King's Nympton 1600 W
Ley John, Atherington 1603 W
Ley John, Combe Martin 1615 O
Ley John, Yarnscombe 1616 [W] and 1619 [W]
Ley John, Combe Martin 1620 [W]
Ley John, Georgeham 1623 [W]
John, Coldridge 1625 [W]
Ley John, Twitchen 1633 W
John, Frithelstock 1634 A
Ley John, Burrington 1636 W
Ley John, Atherington 1638 W
Ley John, Chulmleigh 1639 A
Ley John, Little Torrington 1663 A
Ley John, Satterleigh 1664 A and 1670 O

Ley John, Barnstaple 1667 A
John, Twitchen 1672 A
John, Pilton 1674 W
Ley John, Combe Martin 1677 A
John, Parkham 1678 W
Ley John, St Giles in the Wood 1695 W
John, Barnstaple 1705 W
Ley John, St Giles in the Wood 1707 A
Ley John, Huish 1711 W
Ley John, Barnstaple 1712 W
Ley John, Tawstock 1713 W
Ley John, Barnstaple 1714 W
Ley John, Monkleigh 1714 W
Ley John, Hartland 1716 A
Ley John, Huish 1716 A
John, Langtree 1723 W
Ley John, Barnstaple 1733 W
John, Hartland 1735 A; A dbn 1752
Ley John, Tawstock 1735 W
Ley John, Combe Martin 1737 A
John, Barnstaple 1740 W
Ley John, Beaford 1741 W
John, Great Torrington 1745 A
Ley John, High Bickington 1748 A
John, Great Torrington 1752 W
Ley John, Chittlehampton 1757 W and 1764 A
John, Winkleigh 1767 W
Ley John, Trentishoe 1769 W
John, Parkham 1770 W
Ley John, Dolton 1771 A
John, Great Torrington 1773 A
John, Chawleigh 1778 W
Ley John, Brendon 1787 A
Ley John, George Nympton, yeoman 1808 W
Ley John, Combe Martin, mariner 1809 A; A dbn 1818 to
   John, son
John, Shebbear 1824 W
Ley John, Cruwys Morchard 1828 A
Ley John, Northam 1834 W
John, Fremington 1835 W
Ley John, Meshaw 1836 W
Ley John, Combe Martin 1852 W
Ley John and Hugh, Pilton 1664 A
Ley John Freestone, Barnstaple 1776 W
Ley Joseph, Tawstock 1666 W
Ley Joseph, Meeth 1703 A
Ley Julian, East Putford 1627 [W]
Ley Julian, Pilton 1766 W
Ley Letitia, High Bickington 1708 W
Ley Lodovic, Pilton 1687 W
Ley Mabel, East Anstey 1569 W
Ley Margaret, Combe Martin, widow 1640 W
Ley Margaret, Barnstaple 1691 W
Margaret, Great Torrington 1718 W
Ley Margery, Atherington, widow 1571 W
Ley Margery, Great Torrington 1583 A
Ley Margery, Great Torrington 1593 [W]
Ley Margery, Burrington 1665 W
Ley Marian, King's Nympton 1596 [W]
Ley Mary, Atherington, widow 1610 [W]; forename blank in
   Ms; supplied from parish register
Ley Mary, Marwood 1664 W
Mary, Twitchen 1672 A
Mary, Twitchen 1689 W
Ley Mary, Tawstock 1708 A
Ley Mary, Chittlehampton 1710 A
Ley Mary, Tawstock 1773 W
Mary, Woolfardisworthy, wife 1809 W
Ley Mary with Francis and Deborah, Atherington 1635 A
Ley alias Barnepoule Nicholas, Fremington 1587 W
Nicholas, Pilton 1681 W
Ley Nicholas, Barnstaple, jnr. 1685 W
Ley Nicholas, Barnstaple, snr. 1696 W
Ley Nicholas, Brendon 1746 W

Ley Nicholas, Ilfracombe, yeoman 1792 W; 1805 W re-proved
   - former probate under value
Ley Nicholas, Combe Martin 1840 W
Ley alias Vouler Oliver, Tawstock 1565 W
Paul, Westleigh 1618 [W]
Peter, Bondleigh 1639 A
Ley Philip, High Bickington 1585 W
Ley Philip, Chittlehampton 1594 [W]
Philip, Alverdiscott 1600 W
Ley alias Barnepole Philip, Fremington 1600 W
Ley Philip, East Down 1626 [W]
Ley Philip, Instow 1632 [W]
Ley Philip, Tawstock 1674 W
Ley Philip, Chittlehampton 1688 W and 1698 A
Philip, Washford Pyne 1700 W
Ley Philip, Chittlehampton 1733 A
Philip, Winkleigh 1758 W
Ley Richard, Combe Martin 1598 [W]
Richard, Twitchen 1617 [W]
Ley Richard, King's Nympton 1635 W
Ley Richard, High Bickington 1639 A
Ley Richard, Combe Martin 1664 A and 1673 A
Ley Richard, Langtree 1687 A
Ley Richard, Barnstaple 1695 A
Ley Richard, Pilton 1755 A
Ley Richard, Combe Martin 1757 W
Ley Richard, Combe Martin 1839 W
Richard, Horwood 1850 W
Ley Robert, Burrington 1565 W
Leye Robert, Instow 1582 A
Ley Robert, East Anstey 1597 [W]
Robert, Parkham 1608 [W]; forename blank in Ms; supplied
   from parish register
Robert, Lapford 1618 [W]
Robert, Clovelly 1623 [W]
Ley Robert, King's Nympton 1625 [W]
Ley Robert, Atherington 1635 W
Robert, Lapford 1645 A
Ley Robert, Barnstaple 1671 W
Robert, Clovelly 1692 W
Ley Robert, Barnstaple 1694 W
Ley Robert, Merton 1710 W
Lea Robert, Knowstone 1711 A
Ley Robert, Dolton 1716 A
Ley Robert, Barnstaple 1731 A
Ley Robert, Atherington 1742 A
Ley Robert, Chittlehampton 1743 A
Robert, West Worlington 1829 W
Ley Roger, Great Torrington, gentleman 1607 [W]; forename
   blank in Ms; supplied from parish register
Ley Samuel, Barnstaple 1693 W
Samuel, Bideford 1741 W
Ley Sarah, Pilton 1755 A
Scipio, Burrington 1670 W
Ley Simon, Chittlehampton 1596 [W]
Ley Simon, High Bickington 1620 [W]
Ley Simon, Chulmleigh 1671 W
Ley Simon, Chittlehampton 1703 W
Ley Simon, Chittlehampton 1723 A
Ley Stephen, East Putford 1686 W
Ley Stephen, Weare Giffard 1716 W
Stephen, Langtree 1744 A
Ley Stephen, Bideford 1760 A
Ley Susan, Combe Martin 1678 A
Ley Susan, Barnstaple 1767 A
Ley Susan, Atherington 1815 W
Sybil, Instow 1690 W
Ley Thomas, King's Nympton 1584 W
Ley Thomas, Buckland Brewer 1618 [W]
Ley Thomas, High Bray 1619 [W]
Thomas, Parkham 1624 [W]
Ley Thomas, Ashreigney 1637 A
Ley Thomas, Monkleigh 1675 W
Ley Thomas, Atherington 1688 W

Thomas, Twitchen 1693 W
Ley Thomas, Chulmleigh 1721 W
Ley Thomas, Tawstock 1742 W
Ley Thomas, Monkleigh 1743 W
Ley Thomas, Beaford 1745 W
Ley Thomas, Cruwys Morchard 1754 W
Ley Thomas, Tawstock 1764 W
Thomas, Atherington 1765 W
Ley Thomas, Bideford 1781 W
Ley Thomas, Combe Martin, mariner 1815 A to Mary, widow
Thomas, Stoke Rivers, yeoman 1826 A to Mary, widow
Ley Thomas, Combe Martin 1826 A to John, brother
Ley Thomas, Chawleigh, farmer 1854 W to John, son
Ley Thomasine, Hartland 1629 [W]
Ley Unity, Ilfracombe, widow 1796 W
Ley Valentine, Great Torrington 1670 [W]
Ley Vincent, King's Nympton 1631 [W]
Ley Walter, Tawstock 1596 [W]
Ley Walter, Great Torrington 1615 [W]
Walter, Clovelly 1639 A
Ley Walter, Fremington 1643 W
Ley William, Atherington 1578 W
Ley William, Great Torrington 1587 W
Ley William, Witheridge 1596 [W]
Ley William, Fremington 1598 [W]
Ley alias Barnepoole William, Fremington 1601 W
William, Pilton 1622 [W]
William, Lapford 1626 [W]
Ley William, Chulmleigh 1630 [W]
William, Charles, snr. 1642 W
William, Barnstaple 1665 A
William, Tawstock 1666 A
Ley William, Combe Martin 1671 W
Ley William, Tawstock 1687 A
Ley William, Tawstock, snr. 1693 W
William, Rackenford 1693 A
William, Great Torrington 1708 W
William, Barnstaple 1710 A
William, Twitchen 1711 W
Ley William, Great Torrington 1714 W
William, Wembworthy 1729 W
Ley William, Tawstock 1733 W
Ley William, Combe Martin 1750 A
Ley William, Pilton 1760 W
William, Frithelstock 1761 W
Ley William, Tawstock 1771 W
Ley William, Chittlehampton 1787 A
William, Goodleigh 1790 W
Ley William, Combe Martin 1798 W
Ley William, Combe Martin 1816 W
William, Northam 1818 W
Ley William, George Nympton 1838 W
William, Goodleigh 1848 W
Ley William, Combe Martin 1848 W
William, Woolfardisworthy 1849 W
William, Stoke Rivers 1852 W
Ley Willmot, Chulmleigh 1734 W
Winifred, Hartland 1729 W; A dbn 1752
Leeden Joan, Rose Ash 1798 W
Leg see Legge
Legall Peter, Northam 1750 W
Legge, Leg, Legg
   ..., Bideford 1608 [W]
   ..., Loxhore 1609 [W]
   Ebbett wife of Richard, Fremington 1607 [W]; forename blank
      in Ms; supplied from parish register
   Legg Joan, Abbotsham 1710 W
   John, Fremington 1580 W
   Leg John, Northam 1617 [W]
   John, Tawstock 1618 [W]
   John, Abbotsham 1629 [W]
   Legg John, Meeth 1666 W
   Margaret, Tawstock 1620 [W]
   Mary, Tawstock 1629 [W]
   Legg Mary, Northam 1723 W

Legg Mathew, Bideford 1740 A
Peter, Atherington 1633 A
Phyllis, Abbotsham 1615 [W]
Legg Prudence, Northam 1710 A
Richard, Fremington 1607 [W]; forename blank in Ms;
   supplied from parish register
Thomas, Tawstock 1633 W
Legg William, Tawstock 1576 W
William, Abbotsham 1600 W
William, Northam 1616 [W] and O
Leigh, Legh, Leighe, Lighe
   Leigh alias Luppingcott ... 1594 [W]
   Agnes, Northam 1620 [W]
   Edward, Cruwys Morchard 1733 A
   Leighe Elizabeth, Twitchen 1573 W
   Elizabeth Cornish, Barnstaple 1829 A to Elizabeth wife of
      Arthur Packer, mother
   Joan, Cruwys Morchard 1734 A
   John, Barnstaple 1664 A
   John, Martinhoe 1685 W
   Lighe Thomas, Twitchen 1573 W
   Legh Thomas, Buckland Brewer or Buckland Filleigh 1574 W
   Thomas, Northam 1629 [W]
   William, Northam, esquire 1663 W
   William, Barnstaple 1827 A to Elizabeth, widow
Leman see Leaman
Lemon Elizabeth, Northam 1742 W
   James, Frithelstock 1739 A
   James, Northam 1742 W
   James, St Giles in the Wood 1800 A
   Mary, Bideford 1728 W
   Mary, Great Torrington 1827 W
   Robert, Barnstaple 1788 W
Lendon, Lenden
   ..., Abbotsham 1605 [W]
   Agnes, Alwington 1571 W
   Christopher, Frithelstock 1683 W
   George, Hartland 1718 W
   George, Great Torrington 1731 A
   Humphrey, Frithelstock 1638 W
   James, Bideford 1707 W
   John, Parkham 1676 W
   Joseph, Bideford 1846 W
   Robert, Chulmleigh 1717 W
   William, Chulmleigh 1725 W
   Lenden William, ship *Sandwich* 1762 A
Lenine George, Winkleigh 1689 W
Lennard, Lennarde
   Lennarde ..., South Molton 1604 [W]
   Roger, South Molton 1592 [W]
Lenton Alice, Landkey 1576 W
   Robert, Alwington 1637 A
Lepalme Charles, Barnstaple 1739 A
Lerwill, Lerawyll, Lerewell, Lerewill, Leriwill, Lerrawill,
      Lerriwill, Lerwell
   Lerewill ..., Kentisbury 1606 [W]
   Lerrawill Agnes, Kentisbury 1722 W
   Lerrawill Alice, Ilfracombe 1743 W
   Amesius, Kentisbury 1694 W
   Lerrawill Amos, Kentisbury 1735 W
   Lerewill Ann, Combe Martin 1631 [W]
   Charles, Combe Martin 1796 W
   Lerrawill Edward, Combe Martin 1735 W
   Elizabeth, Alwington 1796 W
   Grace, Combe Martin 1781 W
   Humphrey, Combe Martin 1666 W and 1669 O
   Lerrawill Humphrey, Kentisbury 1728 W
   Lerewill Joan, Bratton Fleming 1630 [W]
   Joan, Combe Martin 1841 A
   Lerawyll John, Arlington 1581 W
   John, Kentisbury 1645 A
   Lerriwell John, Ilfracombe 1686 W
   John, Kentisbury 1720 W
   Lerrawill John, Ilfracombe 1725 W
   John, Combe Martin 1750 A

John, Combe Martin 1774 W
John, Alwington 1785 W
Lerewell Mary, Arlington 1590 [W]
Nicholas, Kentisbury 1644 W
Lerwell Nicholas, Kentisbury 1712 A
Philip, Arlington 1746 W
Lerewill Richard, Arlington 1606 W
Lerewill Richard, Kentisbury 1615 [W]
Lerewill Richard, Combe Martin 1619 [W]
Richard, Arlington 1637 A and 1641 O
Richard, Combe Martin 1665 W
Lerwell Richard, Combe Martin 1690 W
Richard, Kentisbury 1857 W
Simon, Arlington 1643 W
Thomas, Northam 1697 A
Thomas, Kentisbury 1818 A to Thomas, brother, Walter,
  brother and Elizabeth wife of Edward Lawry, sister
Thomas, Combe Martin 1841 A to John, labourer, brother
Thomas, Kentisbury 1849 W
Thomasine, Combe Martin 1691 W
Walter, Combe Martin, snr. 1747 W
Walter, Combe Martin 1766 W
Walter, Combe Martin 1839 W
Walter, East Down 1844 W
Lerewill William, Combe Martin 1620 [W]
Lerewill William, Kentisbury 1629 [W] and 1631 [W]
Leriwill William, Ilfracombe 1705 A
William, Combe Martin 1782 A
Lesland John, Northam 1693 W
Lester John, Great Torrington 1667 W
Letchland Nathan, Barnstaple 1713 A
Lethaby see Letherby
Lethbridge, Lethbridg, Lethbrydge, Lethebridg, Lethebridge,
  Lethybridge
  Alan, Coldridge 1672 A
  Alice, Coldridge 1671 A
  Lethbrydge Ann, Great Torrington 1640 W
  Anthony, Martinhoe 1645 A
  Lethbrid Anthony, Merton 1687 W
  Benjamin, Hartland 1849 W
  Christopher, Bow 1670 W
  Christopher, Romansleigh 1767 W
  Edward, Bideford, ironmonger 1853 A to Ann, widow
  Edward see also Mary Ann Morrison
  Lethbrydge John, Bow 1636 W
  Lethbrydge John, Great Torrington, snr. 1637 W
  John, Zeal Monachorum 1756 W
  Margaret, Pilton 1723 W
  Lethybridge Richard, Dolton 1619 [W]
  Robert, Zeal Monachorum 1672 W
  Lethebrid Samuel, Chulmleigh 1707 W
  Thomas, Nymet Rowland 1748 A
  Lethbridg Walter, Merton 1684 A
  Lethebridge William, Bow 1598 [W]
  Lethbrydge William, Bow 1639 A
Letherby, Lethaby, Lethibie, Lithaby
  Lethaby Elizabeth, Meshaw 1686 A
  Lithaby John, Ilfracombe, miller 1807 W
  Lethaby John see also George Webber
  Lethaby John Tucker, Ilfracombe 1839 A to Ann, sister
  Lethibie Robert, Chawleigh 1568 W
  Lithaby Robert, Meshaw 1732 A
  Letheby Walter, Lynton, cordwainer 1805 A
  Letheby Walter, Lynton 1838 A
Letherne, Leatheren, Leathern, Letheren, Lethern, Letherra
  George, Winkleigh 1689 W
  George, Winkleigh 1703 A and 1712 O
  Lethern Hannah, Winkleigh 1711 W
  Letheren Humphrey, Winkleigh 1588 W
  Letheren Joan, Winkleigh 1793 A
  John, Winkleigh 1578 W
  John, Winkleigh 1664 A
  John, Winkleigh, snr. 1703 W
  John, Winkleigh, jnr. 1704 A
  Leathern John, Winkleigh 1741 A

Letheren John, Winkleigh 1790 W
Leathern John, Dolton 1832 W
Leatheren Margery, Winkleigh 1740 W
Lethern Mary, Winkleigh 1643 A
Peter, Winkleigh 1578 W
Letheren Peter, Winkleigh 1587 W
Leathern Richard, Northam 1784 W
Letherra Robert, Winkleigh 1728 W
Lethern Robert, Winkleigh 1776 A
Lethern Thomasine, Winkleigh 1722 W
Letherton George, Winkleigh 1716 W
Lethibie see Letherby
Lethybridge see Lethbridge
Letley Fanny see Mary Ellicott
Leusmore see Loosemore
Leverton, Levaton, Leveaton, Levyton, Liverton, Liveton
  ..., Iddesleigh 1607 [W]
  Levaton Agnes, Dolton 1591 [W]
  Levaton Ann, Dolton 1629 [W]
  Dunstan, Bideford 1725 A
  George, Meeth 1758 W
  Levaton Grace, Burrington 1694 W
  Levyton Henry, Dolton 1616 [W]
  Henry, Great Torrington, gentleman 1799 W
  Leveton Humphrey, Bideford 1588 A
  Levaton Joan, Iddesleigh 1633 W
  Leveton John, Dolton 1577 W and 1582 W
  Levaton John, Dolton 1618 [W] and 1629 [W]
  John, Dolton 1709 A
  Leveton Margaret, Iddesleigh 1569 W
  Mary, Merton 1821 W
  Levaton Robert, Dolton 1673 W
  Robert, Peters Marland 1853 W
  Rowland, Dolton 1723 W
  Rowland, Iddesleigh 1738 A
  Levaton Thomas, Dolton 1663 W
  Thomas, Dowland 1701 W
  Levyton William, Dolton 1606 [W]
  Leviton William, Dolton 1611 [W]; forename blank in Ms;
    supplied from parish register
  Levaton William, Dolton 1625 [W] and 1626 O
  Levaton William, Dowland 1682 W
  Liveton William, Dolton, snr. 1686 W
  Levaton William, Dolton 1707 W
  William, Great Torrington 1724 A
  Liverton William, Dowland 1751 W
  William, Dolton 1804 W*
  William, Dolton 1826 W
  Liverton William, Atherington 1838 W
  Willmot, Merton 1762 W
Lewbet see Lobbett
Lewis, Lewes, Lowis
  Lewes Amesius, Tawstock 1677 W
  Lewes Ann, Buckland Filleigh 1681 W
  Ann, Buckland Filleigh 1691 W
  Catherine see Thomas Wilmot
  Christopher, Monkleigh 1769 A
  Christopher, Frithelstock 1849 W
  Daniel, Mortehoe 1738 W
  David, Georgeham 1668 A
  David, High Bray 1714 W
  Edward, Alwington 1721 W
  Edward, Weare Giffard 1773 A
  Edward, Georgeham 1816 W
  Elizabeth, Monkleigh 1790 A
  Elizabeth, Georgeham 1819 W
  Elizabeth, Chittlehampton 1840 W
  Emblem, Buckland Filleigh 1688 W
  Lewes Francis, Little Torrington 1685 A
  Lowis Francis, Lapford 1853 W
  George, Shebbear 1676 W
  Lewes George, Buckland Filleigh 1681 W
  George, Shebbear 1702 W
  George, Buckland Filleigh 1720 W
  George, Petrockstowe 1762 W

George, Merton 1799 A
George, Merton 1855 W
Henry, Heanton Punchardon 1674 A
Hugh, Heanton Punchardon 1680 A
James, Northam 1714 A
James, Fremington 1741 W
Jane, Atherington 1706 A
Lewes John, Atherington 1691 A
John, Tawstock 1704 A
John, Northam 1711 A
John, Northam 1729 W
John, West Down 1740 W
John, Washford Pyne 1745 W
John, Burrington 1750 A
John, Chulmleigh 1760 W
John, Meeth 1761 W
John, Chulmleigh 1789 W
John, Ilfracombe 1812 W
John, East Putford 1820 W
John, Tawstock 1820 W
John, Buckland Filleigh 1827 W
John, Chittlehampton 1835 W
Joseph, Shebbear 1710 A
Joseph, Clovelly 1733 W
Joseph, Buckland Brewer, yeoman 1798 W
Lewes Margery, Fremington 1681 W
Mary, Langtree 1802 W
Mary, Monkleigh, widow 1808 W
Mary, Great Torrington 1843 W
Mary Ann, Hartland 1856 W
Miles, Northam 1782 A
Owen, Bristol 1832 A to Margaret of Hotwell Road, Bristol,
   widow
Lewes Richard, Barnstaple 1629 [W]
Richard, Little Torrington 1718 W
Richard, Monkleigh 1783 W
Richard, Mortehoe 1838 W
Robert, Chulmleigh 1787 W
Lewes Roger, Great Torrington 1591 [W]
Lewes Thomas, Tawstock 1641 W
Thomas, Bideford 1698 W
Thomas, Huntshaw 1725 W
Thomas, Little Torrington 1737 W
Lewes William, Bideford 1709 A
William, Frithelstock 1725 W
William, Fremington 1745 A
William, Monkleigh 1782 W
William, Ilfracombe 1786 W
William, Mortehoe, yeoman 1799 W
William, St Giles in the Wood 1810 W
William, Georgeham 1815 W
William, Chulmleigh 1840 W
Leworthy, Leworthie, Leyworthie, Leyworthy, Luorthie,
   Luworthie
..., South Molton 1609 [W]
..., Northam 1611 [W]
..., St Giles in the Wood 1612 [W]
Anthony, Oakford, blacksmith 1806 A
Christopher, Charles 1624 [W]
Christopher, East Anstey 1679 W
Clement, Charles 1680 A
Clement, North Molton 1775 W
Daniel, High Bray 1645 A
Edmund, Challacombe 1675 W
English, Charles 1594 [W]
George, Charles 1618 [W]
George, Charles 1679 W
George, Charles 1766 W and 1773 W
George, North Molton 1839 A to Mary, widow
Henry, Bratton Fleming 1592 [W]
Henry, Chittlehampton 1744 A
Henry, Barnstaple 1775 W
Henry, Northam 1775 W
Henry, Barnstaple 1829 W
Humphrey, Challacombe 1755 W

Humphrey, Bratton Fleming 1812 W and 1824 W
Jane, Arlington, widow 1805 W
Jane, Barnstaple 1838 W
Joan, St Giles in the Wood 1616 [W]
Joan, Chittlehampton 1634 W
Joan, Barnstaple, widow 1798 W
Luworthie John, Bratton Fleming 1566 W
Leworthie John, Heanton Punchardon 1578 W and 1586 W
Leworthie John, Northam 1590 [W]
John, High Bray 1617 [W] and 1621 [W]
Leyworthy John, Chittlehampton 1620 [W]
John, Goodleigh 1622 [W]
John, Petrockstowe 1630 [W]
John, Barnstaple 1637 W
John, Charles 1645 W
John, Challacombe, yeoman 1798 W
John, Mortehoe, yeoman 1807 W
John, Challacombe, yeoman 1814 A to William, son
John, Charles 1840 A
Leworthie Margaret, Highampton 1580 W
Margaret, Berrynarbor 1809 A*
Mary, Bideford 1639 A
Mary, Charles 1737 A
Mary, East Down 1784 A
Mary, Buckland Filleigh 1800 A
Luorthie Nicholas, Heanton Punchardon 1588 A
Richard, Tawstock 1615 [W]
Robert, Yarnscombe 1623 [W]
Samuel, Charles 1766 A
Luorthie Thomas, Bratton Fleming 1589 W
Thomas 1663 W
Thomasine, North Molton 1724 W
Walter, High Bray 1621 W
Leyworthie William, High Bray 1591 [W]
William, Challacombe 1788 W
Leworthy alias Fairchild William, Ilfracombe 1799 W*
William, Stoke Rivers 1810 W
William, Charles 1835 W
Ley see Lee
Leyar alias Gread Ann, Pilton 1683 A
Leyman Deborah, Francis and Mary, Atherington 1635 A
   Frances with Deborah and Mary, Atherington 1635 A
   James, Frithelstock 1663 W
   John, Atherington 1716 A
   Mary with Deborah and Frances, Atherington 1635 A
   Thomas, Atherington 1627 [W]
   Thomas, Great Torrington, victualler 1808 W
   Walter, Ilfracombe 1629 [W]
   William, Frithelstock 1661 A
Leyworthie, Leyworthy see Leworthy
Lichedon, Lechedon, Litchden
   Lechedon Anstis, Tawstock 1577 W
   Elizabeth, South Molton 1588 W
   John, South Molton 1587 A
   Richard, Barnstaple 1584 A
   Thomas, Chittlehampton 1587 W
   Lechedon Walter, Barnstaple 1577 W
   Litchden William, North Molton 1624 [W]
Lickey, Lyckey, Lykey
   Lyckey Charles, Chittlehampton 1635 A
   Lykey Willmot, Chittlehampton 1641 W
Liddon see Lyddon
Liell see Lyle
Lighe see Leigh
Light George, Barnstaple 1709 A
   George, ship *Eagle* 1760 W
   John, Barnstaple 1723 W
   John, Barnstaple 1756 W
Lightfoot, Lightfoote
   Lightfoote Baldwin, Chulmleigh 1640 W
   Francis, Chulmleigh 1667 W
   Francis, Chulmleigh 1720 W
Lile, Lill see Lyle
Lilleycrop, Lilleycropp see Lillicrop
Lillick George, Bideford 1742 W

Lillicrop, Lilleycrop, Lilleycropp, Lillicrap, Lillicrappe,
  Lillisrop, Lillycrap, Lillycropp, Lyllecrop, Lylleycrop,
  Lylleycropp, Lyllicrop, Lyllycropp, Lyllycrap, Lyllycropp
  Lillicrap ..., Peters Marland 1613 [W]
  Lyllecrop Agnes, Zeal Monachorum 1571 W
  Lyllycropp Anthony, Zeal Monachorum 1631 [W]
  Lillicrappe John, Zeal Monachorum 1585 W
  Lillycrap John, Zeal Monachorum 1615 [W]
  Lillycropp John, Zeal Monachorum 1687 W
  Lilleycrop John, St Giles in the Wood 1792 W
  Lilleycropp Mary, St Giles in the Wood, sp. 1799 W
  Lillisrop Richard, Zeal Monachorum 1721 W
  Robert, Zeal Monachorum 1726 W
  Thomas, Merton 1730 W
  Lyllicrop William, Zeal Monachorum 1629 [W] and O
  Lillycropp Willmot 1661 W
Lilly Thomas, Barnstaple 1835 W
Lillycrap, Lillycropp see Lillicrop
Lilwyer John, Great Torrington 1690 [W]
Limbeare, Lemberie, Lemberry, Lembrey, Limbear,
  Limber, Limberie, Limberry, Limbery, Limebear,
  Limeberry, Linbre, Lymbeare, Lymbeere, Lymber,
  Lymbere, Lymberie, Lymberry, Lymbery, Lymebeere,
  Lymebere, Lymebury
  ..., Burrington 1612 [W] and O
  Limbery ..., Satterleigh 1698 [W]
  Limebear Catherine, Chittlehampton 1673 W
  Lymebeer Christopher, King's Nympton 1643 [W]
  Christopher, Berrynarbor 1690 W
  Christopher, Warkleigh 1694 W
  Lymberie Elizabeth, Warkleigh 1580 W
  Limbery alias Hutsen Elizabeth, Fremington 1679 W;
    forename blank in Ms; supplied from parish register
  Lymbeere Francis, King's Nympton 1632 [W]
  Limbery George, Northam 1704 W
  Lemberry George, Northam 1763 W
  Lymbery alias Hutson James, Fremington 1661 W
  Lymbery James, Fremington 1684 W
  Limbrey Jane, Northam 1781 W
  Lymbere Joan, Burrington 1621 [W]
  Lymbeere Joan, Tawstock 1642 A
  Limberie John, Burrington 1572 W
  Lymbere John, Burrington 1602 W
  John, Mortehoe 1678 W
  Limbrey John, Northam 1748 A
  Lembery John, Northam 1782 W
  Lemberie Margery, Northam, widow 1568 W
  Mary, Northam 1792 W
  Lymberie Peter, Northam 1573 A
  Phillippa, Northam 1704 A
  Limbear Richard, Berrynarbor 1598 [W]
  Lymbeere Richard, Burrington 1641 W
  Lymebury Richard, Tawstock 1641 W
  Limber Richard, Chittlehampton 1680 W
  Lymbeare Richard, King's Nympton 1696 A
  Linbre Richard, Tawstock 1754 W
  Richard, Northam 1853 W
  Lymber Robert, Nymet Rowland 1583 A
  Lymbery Robert, Northam 1583 A
  Lymberry Robert 1600 W
  Limberry Robert, Fremington 1726 W
  Lymbery Roger, Warkleigh 1573 W
  Lymebere Thomas, Chittlehampton 1626 [W]
  Lymbeare Thomas, Petrockstowe 1667 [W]
  Lembry Thomas, Northam 1678 A
  William, Northam 1592 [W] and 1598 [W]
  Limebear William, Satterleigh 1669 W
  Lymbery William, Abbotsham 1695 W
  Limeberry William, Instow 1722 W
  Limberry William, Northam 1733 W
Linch, Linche
  ..., Great Torrington 1608 [W]
  Ann, Barnstaple 1754 W
  Grace, Alwington 1716 W
  Linche James, Great Torrington 1620 [W]
  James Parker, Marwood 1848 W

Linche Jasper, Abbotsham 1628 [W]
  Joan, Parkham 1618 [W]
  John, Parkham 1598 [W]
  John, Great Torrington 1613 [W]; forename blank in Ms;
    supplied from parish register
  Linche John, Parkham 1627 [W]
  John, Combe Martin 1843 W
  Robert, Great Torrington 1591 [W]
  Linche Robert, Parkham 1621 [W]
  Robert, Barnstaple 1722 A
  Robert, Marwood 1787 W
  Thomas, Marwood 1814 W
  William, Parkham 1710 W
Lincomb see Lyncomb
Line Elizabeth, Dolton 1771 W
  John, Chawleigh 1711 A
Ling Mary, Lynton 1713 W
Linnex William, Bideford 1703 W
Linton see Lynton
Lions ..., Mortehoe 1604 [W]
Lisle see Lyle
Lisset, Lyssett
  Lyssett Eliza, Barnstaple 1698 W
  Roger, Barnstaple 1679 A
Lister Edward, Great Torrington 1716 W
Litchden see Licheden
Liteljohn see Littlejohn
Litell see Little
Lithaby see Letherby
Litle see Little
Litlejohn, Litlejon see Littlejohn
Litletar see Littletar
Litson Agnes, Lynton 1799 A
  Alexander, Lynton, carpenter 1814 A to Sarah, widow
  Amy, Countisbury 1823 W
  Ann, Lynton 1795 W
  Ann, Trentishoe 1821 W
  Elizabeth, Lynton, sp. 1846 A to John, innkeeper, brother
  Francis, Lynton 1767 A
  Gabriel, Lynton 1723 W
  Henry, Countisbury 1758 A
  John, Lynton 1792 W, 1796 W, 1799 W
  John, Countisbury 1852 W
  Mary, Lynton 1799 A
  Richard, Brendon 1787 A
  William, Lynton 1764 W
  William, Lynton 1815 W
  William, Lynton 1841 W
  William, Lynton, spirit merchant 1849 A to John, brother
Little, Litell, Litle, Littell, Lytell
  Litell ..., Ashford 1611 [W]
  David, Hartland 1670 W
  Joan, Georgeham 1625 [W]
  Lytell John, Heanton Punchardon 1587 W
  John, Barnstaple 1594 [W]
  Litle John, Georgeham 1684 W
  Litle John, Woolfardisworthy 1703 W
  Litell Richard, Georgeham 1592 [W]
  Litell Roger, Great Torrington 1592 [W]
  Litle Roger, Georgeham 1666 W
  Litell Thomas, Barnstaple 1587 A
  Littell William, Ashreigney 1573 A
  Litell William, Dolton 1581 W
  Litle William, Alwington 1695 A
Littlejohn, Liteljohn, Litlejohn, Littelljohn, Littlejohns
  Littlejohns Abraham 1746 A
  Agnes, Huntshaw 1621 [W]
  Elizabeth, Hartland 1729 W
  Littlejohns Elizabeth, Bideford 1856 W
  Liteljohn George, Barnstaple 1586 A
  Litlejohn Hugh, Hartland 1597 [W]
  Littelljohn John, Westleigh 1576 W
  Litlejohn John, Hartland 1714 W
  Littlejohns John, Hartland 1748 A
  Littlejohns John, Woolfardisworthy, yeoman 1807 A

Margaret, Hartland 1743 A
Littlejohns Margaret, Hartland, sp. 1799 A
Philip, Clovelly 1735 W
Richard, Hartland 1630 [W]
Richard, Hartland 1644 W
Litlejon Richard, Bideford 1707 A
Samson, Hartland 1755 W
Samson, Hartland 1785 A
Thomas, Hartland 1675 W
Thomasine, Hartland 1762 W
William, Hartland 1735 W
William, Fremington 1767 W
Littlejohns William, Hartland 1769 A
William 1837 W
Littlejohns William, Welcombe 1849 W
Littletar, Litletar
Christopher, Petrockstowe 1724 W
Edward, Peters Marland 1622 [W]
Francis, Petrockstowe 1628 [W]
Litletar John, Petrockstowe 1709 A
John, Petrockstowe 1724 W
John, Petrockstowe 1748 A
Thomas, Petrockstowe 1620 [W]
Thomas, Petrockstowe 1724 W
Thomas, Petrockstowe 1757 A
Thomas, Merton 1776 W
Liverton, Liveton see Leverton
Llewellin, Fluelling
Llewellin alias Welling Henry, Barnstaple 1688 A; forename
    blank in Ms; supplied from parish register
Fluelling Thomas, Countisbury 1693 W
Lloyd David, Great Torrington, innkeeper 1818 A to Janet,
    widow
Jane, Great Torrington 1821 W
John, Bideford 1796 W
Richard, Great Torrington 1825 A to Mary Cock formerly of
    St Giles in the Wood now of Great Torrington, sister
Loady Mathew, Heanton Punchardon 1750 W
Lobbett, Labbet, Labbett, Lobbett
..., Great Torrington 1603 [W]
..., Coldridge 1608 O
Agnes, Great Torrington, widow 1613 [W]; forename blank in
    Ms; supplied from parish register
Labbett Elizabeth, Northam 1818 W
Labbett Emma, Roborough 1586 W
Labbett John, Great Torrington 1591 [W]
John, Coldridge 1598 [W]
John, Great Torrington 1603 W
Labbett John, ship *Northumberland* 1758 A
Labbett John, Northam 1814 W
John, Northam 1835 W
Labbet Mary, Huish 1680 W
Mary, Northam 1840 W
Richard, Great Torrington 1592 [W]
Robert, Bratton Fleming 1629 [W]
Lewbet William, Roborough 1570 W
Labbet William, Huish 1680 W
Lobdon, Labdon
John, Winkleigh 1574 W, 1578 W and 1581 O account
Labdon Michael, Winkleigh 1588 W
Lock, Locke
..., Burrington 1603 [W]
..., North Molton 1607 [W]
..., Molland 1614 [W]
Aaron, South Molton 1742 W
Aaron, ship *Chester* 1746 W
Agnes, East Worlington 1643 W
Agnes, North Molton 1669 A
Agnes, Kentisbury 1741 W
Agnes, Parracombe 1767 A
Agnes, Trentishoe 1773 A
Locke Alexander, Molland 1629 [W]
Locke Alfred, Knowstone 1631 [W]
Alfred, Molland 1643 W
Alfred, Kentisbury 1710 W
Alice, Kentisbury 1724 W

Alice, Parracombe 1764 W
Locke Ann, Barnstaple 1635 W
Ann, Rackenford 1674 A
Ann, North Molton 1733 W
Ann, Chittlehampton 1819 W
Ann, South Molton 1850 W
Locke Bartholomew, East Worlington 1638 W
Bartholomew, South Molton 1802 W
Bartholomew, Chittlehampton 1853 W
Catherine, North Molton 1781 W
Locke Charity, North Molton 1626 [W]
Charles, North Molton 1699 A
Charles, Winkleigh 1775 W
Charles, North Tawton 1836 W
Locke Christopher, King's Nympton 1625 [W]
Christopher, Ilfracombe 1663 A
Christopher, Atherington 1699 A
Christopher, North Molton 1761 W
David, Parracombe 1742 A
David, Parracombe 1787 A
David, Combe Martin 1841 W
Edmund, Bideford 1790 W
Locke Edward, South Molton 1628 [W]
Elizabeth, North Molton 1730 W
Elizabeth, North Molton 1752 A
Elizabeth, North Molton 1761 W
Elizabeth, North Molton 1812 W
Elizabeth, North Molton 1825 W
Elizabeth, Petrockstowe 1842 A to Grace Mitchell, sister
Esther, Great Torrington 1780 W
Francis, Martinhoe 1742 A
Francis, Martinhoe 1840 W
Geoffrey, Combe Martin 1765 W
Locke George, North Molton 1636 W
George, Chulmleigh 1783 W
George, Northam, baker 1807 W
George, Chittlehampton 1843 W
Giles, South Molton 1681 A
Locke Grace, Chittlehampton 1627 [W]
Grace, North Molton 1711 W
Grace, North Molton 1784 W
Harris, Huntshaw 1753 A
Henry, North Molton 1573 W and 1578 W
Henry, Knowstone 1616 [W]
Locke Henry, North Molton 1621 [W]
Locke Henry, Filleigh 1630 [W]
Henry, North Molton 1641 A
Henry, North Molton 1706 W
Henry, West Anstey 1782 W
Honor, North Molton 1777 W
Hugh, North Molton 1667 W
Hugh, King's Nympton 1671 O
Hugh, Stoke Rivers 1763 W
Isota, Atherington 1704 W
Locke James, Witheridge 1570 [W]
James, Barnstaple 1685 W
James, North Molton 1819 W
Locke Joan, North Molton 1596 [W]
Joan, North Molton 1699 W
Joan, Parracombe 1734 W
Joan, Tawstock 1747 W
Joan, North Molton 1760 W
Joan, Barnstaple 1841 W
Locke John, North Molton 1567 W and 1573 [W]
Locke John, North Molton 1582 W
Locke John, Bow 1595 [W]
John, Molland 1614 [W]; forename blank in Ms; supplied
    from parish register
John, Burrington 1616 [W]
Locke John, Chittlehampton 1621 [W]
Locke John, Bideford 1625 [W]
Locke John, North Molton 1627 [W]
John, Kentisbury, snr. 1643 W
John, North Molton 1662 W
John, Knowstone 1670 W

John, Knowstone, snr. 1672 A
John, Stoke Rivers 1681 A
John, North Molton 1684 W
John, West Down 1697 A
John, King's Nympton 1699 W
John, Kentisbury 1700 W
John, North Molton, snr. 1703 W
John, Winkleigh 1710 A
John, Martinhoe 1712 A
John, North Molton 1719 A
John, South Molton 1720 W
John, Parracombe 1729 W
John, Stoke Rivers 1737 W
John, North Molton 1741 W
John, Parracombe 1744 W
John, North Molton 1757 W
John, Great Torrington 1768 W
John, North Molton 1778 W
John, Knowstone 1787 W
Locke John, East Buckland, yeoman 1797 W
John, Great Torrington, yeoman 1800 W
John, Lynton, gentleman 1803 W
John, Parracombe, yeoman 1808 A
John, Tawstock, butcher 1808 W
John, Martinhoe 1813 W
John, Winkleigh 1827 W
John, Meeth 1849 W
John, Parracombe 1849 A
Kestell John, North Molton 1816 W
Lawrence, North Molton 1734 A
Locke Margaret, Knowstone 1631 [W]
Margaret, South Molton 1643 W
Mary, Lynton, widow 1807 W
Mary, Northam, widow 1854 A to Susanna and Jane, sps.,
     daughters
Mary see also Samuel Badcock
Michael, North Molton 1768 W
Michael, North Molton 1828 A to Mary wife of William
     Slader and Susanna wife of Richard Passmore, daughters
Michael, South Molton 1830 A
Michael see also Elizabeth Dee
Nicholas, East Buckland 1588 W
Nicholas, North Molton 1702 W
Nicholas, Kentisbury 1738 W
Locke Philip, North Molton 1622 [W]
Philip, Rose Ash 1854 W
Rebecca, Parracombe 1770 W
Locke Richard, Buckland Brewer 1622 [W]
Locke Richard, North Molton 1633 W
Richard, Georgeham 1760 W
Locke Richard, North Molton 1851 W
Locke Robert, Fremington 1617 [W]
Robert, Knowstone 1712 A
Robert, Dolton 1772 W
Locke Roger, North Molton 1581 W
Locke Samuel, Romansleigh 1639 W
Sarah, Northam 1840 A
Thomas, Loxhore 1679 A
Lock alias Lux Thomas, Coldridge 1690 A
Thomas, North Molton 1752 W
Thomas, North Molton 1774 W
Thomas, Romansleigh 1797 W
Thomas, West Anstey, yeoman 1798 W
Thomas, Chittlehampton, yeoman 1810 W
Thomas, North Molton 1848 A
Vincent, Rackenford 1672 W
Locke Walter, Great Torrington 1592 [W]
Walter, Parracombe 1667 W
Walter, Parracombe, jnr. 1696 W
Walter, Dolton 1762 A
Walter, Parracombe 1762 A
Walter, Martinhoe, yeoman 1810 W
Locke William, North Molton 1572 W
Locke William, North Molton 1598 [W]
Locke William, North Molton 1623 [W] and 1636 W

Locke William, East Buckland 1640 W
William, Warkleigh 1641 A
William, North Molton 1690 A
William, North Molton 1703 W and 1714 W
William, South Molton 1718 W
William, Trentishoe 1724 A
William, North Molton 1726 W and 1728 A
William, North Molton 1753 A, 1763 A; A dbn 1764
William, High Bray 1773 A
William, North Molton 1784 W and 1791 W
William, Ashreigney 1797 A
William, North Molton 1823 W
William, Parracombe 1834 W
William, South Molton 1837 W
William, Barnstaple 1841 W
William, Combe Martin 1847 W
William, Burrington 1855 W
Locke William see also Mary Sage
Lockeford, Louckforde
     Catherine, Fremington 1579 W
     Louckforde William, Fremington 1605 W
Lockier, Lockyear, Lockyer
     Frances, Georgeham 1623 [W]
     Lockyear George, Northam 1756 W
     Lockier Simon, Georgeham 1613 [W]; forename blank in Ms;
          supplied from parish register
     Lockyer Thomas, Fremington 1595 [W]
     Lockier Thomas, Winkleigh 1629 [W]
Lodey Jonathan, South Molton 1772 A
Lolwear Robert, Barnstaple 1675 W
Loman, Looman, Luman
     Andrew, Northam 1669 A
     Anthony, Monkleigh 1762 W
     Elizabeth, Monkleigh 1774 W
     James, Clovelly 1707 W
     Looman John, Weare Giffard 1692 A
     John, Clovelly 1704 W
     Looman Thomas, Bulkworthy 1753 W
     Thomasine, Northam 1685 W
     William, Northam 1684 W
     Luman William, Bideford 1715 W
     William, Frithelstock 1740 W
London Thomasine, Frithelstock 1712 A
     William, Bideford 1660 W
Lone, Lonne
     Lonne ..., North Tawton 1607 [W]
     Lonne Alexander, North Tawton 1574 W
     Joan, North Tawton 1578 W
     Lone or Lonne John, North Tawton 1590 [W] and 1595 [W]
     Lonne Lawrence, Bondleigh 1589 W
     Lonne Robert, South Molton 1593 [W]
     Lonne Roger, North Tawton 1613 [W] "of Lake Way" in
          register; forename blank in Ms; supplied from parish register
Loney Henry, Great Torrington 1592 [W]
Long, Longe
     Longe Catherine, Hartland 1575 W
     Longe Elias, Fremington 1576 W
     Longe Faith, North Molton 1639 W
     James, Great Torrington 1662 A
     Longe Joan, Barnstaple 1626 [W]
     Long alias Barns Joan, Brendon 1680 A
     Longe John, Barnstaple 1581 W
     John, Countisbury 1671 W
     John, Great Torrington 1853 W
     Joseph, Buckland Brewer 1842 W
     Sarah, Great Torrington 1853 W
     Longe William, South Molton 1621 [W]
     Longe Willmot, Barnstaple 1627 [W]
Longden see Langdon
Longe see Long
Longman, Langman
     Langman Henry, South Molton 1631 [W]
     John, Merton 1753 A
     John, Sheepwash 1850 W
     Langman Margery, South Molton 1635 W

Rebecca, Great Torrington 1773 A
Langman Robert, Peters Marland 1570 W
Thomas, Northam 1707 A
William, Merton 1803 W*
Lonne see Lone
Looman see Loman
Loosemore, Loosmore, Losemore
Losemore ..., Thelbridge 1608 [W]
Ann, Barnstaple 1819 W
Francis, Meshaw 1793 W
Hugh, Barnstaple 1752 A
James, Rose Ash 1624 [W]
James, Rose Ash 1673 W and O
James, Rose Ash 1701 A
Loosmore James, Rose Ash 1762 W
James, Burrington 1777 A
James, Meshaw 1818 W
James, Molland 1845 W
James, Atherington 1858 W
Joan, Rose Ash 1743 W
Losemore John, Creacombe 1565 W
Losemore John, Creacombe 1597 [W]
John, Cruwys Morchard 1626 [W]
John, Atherington 1713 A
John, Chulmleigh 1733 W
John, Meshaw 1738 W
John, Tawstock 1752 A
John, Meshaw 1764 W
John, Cruwys Morchard 1775 W
John, Barnstaple, carrier 1810 W
John, Rose Ash 1819 W
John, Meshaw 1843 W
Losemore Lodovic, Twitchen 1713 W
Margaret, South Molton 1801 W
Mary, Challacombe 1633 W
Mary, Rose Ash 1714 W
Nicholas, Rose Ash 1738 W
Nicholas, Landkey, yeoman 1799 W
Penelope, Barnstaple 1752 A
Richard, Burrington 1750 W
Richard, South Molton 1839 W
Robert, Cruwys Morchard 1623 [W]
Robert, Meshaw 1680 W
Robert, Knowstone 1814 W
Robert, Knowstone 1839 W
Losemore Roger, Cruwys Morchard 1594 [W]
Leusmore Roger, Burrington 1757 W
Sarah, Meshaw 1822 A to John, brother
Thomas, South Molton 1794 A
Thomas, Bideford 1797 W
William, Atherington 1751 W
William, Atherington 1823 W
William, Meshaw 1843 W
William, Meshaw 1856 W
Lord, Lorde
Elizabeth, Parracombe 1815 W
Joan, Martinhoe 1836 A
John, Challacombe 1747 W
Mathew, Instow 1724 A
Samuel, Challacombe 1754 A
Samuel, Martinhoe 1823 W
Samuel, Barnstaple 1836 W
Lorde Thomas, Atherington 1710 A
Thomas, Martinhoe 1771 A
Thomas, Martinhoe, yeoman 1811 A
William, Tawstock 1717 A
William, Martinhoe 1827 W
William, Martinhoe 1853 W
Lorimer, Lorimere, Lorymer
..., Huntshaw 1609 [W]
Lorymer ..., Heanton Punchardon 1616 [W]
Anthony, Georgeham 1613 [W]; forename blank in Ms;
supplied from parish register
Lorymer Christian, Parracombe 1592 [W], 1593 [W] and 1595
[W]

Edward, Parracombe 1622 [W]
Lorymer Elizabeth, Huntshaw 1592 [W]
Lorymer George, Bideford 1618 [W]
Lorymer Hugh, Yarnscombe 1615 [W] and 1616 [W]
Lorymer John, Huntshaw 1591 [W] and 1592 [W]
John, Alverdiscott 1619 [W]
Lorimere Richard, Weare Giffard 1578 W
Lorymer Richard, Yarnscombe 1632 [W]
Lorimere Roger, Weare Giffard 1577 A
Thomas, Alverdiscott 1643 W
Lorymer Walter, Alwington 1587 A
Walter, Alverdiscott 1600 W
Lorymer William, Alverdiscott 1595 [W]
Loromie, Loromy see Laramy
Lorymer see Lorimer
Lorynne Richard, Chittlehampton 1581 W
Lose ..., Martinhoe 1614 [W]
Losemore see Loosemore
Lother James, Clovelly 1826 W
Lott Betsy, Hartland 1823 W
Louckforde see Lockford
Louse Margaret, Shebbear 1689 W
Loveband, Lovebande, Lovebone
..., Combe Martin 1603 [W]
Lovebande ..., St Giles in the Wood 1604 [W]
Ann, Atherington 1794 W
Anthony, Yarnscombe 1788 W
Lovebone Christian, Westleigh 1675 A
Crispin, St Giles in the Wood 1591 [W]
Dorothy, Yarnscombe 1620 [W]
Edward, Merton 1675 W
Gilbert, Petrockstowe 1611 [W]; forename blank in Ms;
supplied from parish register
Henry, Peters Marland 1662 A
Henry, Merton 1664 W
Jane, Yarnscombe 1710 W
Joan, Yarnscombe 1643 W
Joan, Abbotsham 1693 A
Joan, Westleigh 1729 W
John, St Giles in the Wood 1602 W
Mary, St Giles in the Wood 1603 W
Mary, Yarnscombe 1821 W
Mathew, Yarnscombe 1626 [W]
Mathew, Yarnscombe 1688 A
Richard, Yarnscombe 1593 [W]
Richard, Westleigh 1663 A
Richard, Westleigh 1717 W
Richard, Yarnscombe 1738 W
Richard, Yarnscombe, yeoman 1806 W
Thomas, Yarnscombe 1598 [W]
Thomas, Yarnscombe 1712 W
Thomas, Yarnscombe, yeoman 1808 W
Thomasine, Yarnscombe 1590 [W]
Loveday Henry, West Worlington 1663 W
Lovell John, Cruwys Morchard 1634 W
Lovereigne see Lovering
Loveridge Robert, Barnstaple 1588 W
Lovering, Lovereigne, Loverin, Loveringe, Loveryn, Loverynge,
Loverne, Loveryn
Loveringe ..., Combe Martin 1603 [W] and 1612 [W]
Loveringe ..., Tawstock 1607 [W]
Loveringe ..., Mortehoe 1609 [W]
Loveringe Beaton, Combe Martin 1605 W
Loverne Catherine, Brendon 1636 W
Daniel, Monkleigh 1770 W
Daniel, Northam 1847 W
Davis, Yarnscombe 1687 W
Elizabeth, Tawstock 1808 W
Elizabeth, Barnstaple 1812 W
Elizabeth, Parracombe 1850 W
Loveringe Ellen, Instow 1587 W
Ezekiel, Ilfracombe 1830 W
George, Parracombe 1805 A
George, Combe Martin 1843 W
Loveryn Giles, Combe Martin 1681 A

Hannah, Tawstock 1853 W
Heyman, Tawstock 1848 W
Loverne Jane, Winkleigh 1687 W
Joan, South Molton 1710 A
Loveringe John, Mortehoe 1585 W
Loveringe John, Combe Martin 1597 [W]
Loveringe John, Bittadon 1628 [W] and 1630 O
John, Weare Giffard 1670 W
John, Yarnscombe 1670 A and 1672 [W] codicil only or
　compotatus account
Loverin John, Tawstock 1682 W
John, Weare Giffard 1707 W
John, Bideford 1719 W
John, Weare Giffard 1726 W
Lovereigne John, ship *Pembroke* 1750 W
John, Weare Giffard 1762 W
John, Ilfracombe 1812 W
Johnson, Tawstock 1698 A
Joseph, Bideford 1699 A
Loveringe Margaret, Tawstock, widow 1602 [W]; forename
　blank in Ms; supplied from parish register
Loveringe Margaret, Tawstock 1603 W
Loveringe Mary, Tawstock 1602 W
Mary, Great Torrington 1771 A
Mary, Barnstaple 1822 W
Mary, Pilton 1857 W
Mary Ann, Northam 1854 W
Nicholas, ship *Captain* 1757 A
Philip, Landcross 1771 A
Rebecca, Combe Martin 1837 W
Richard, East Worlington 1565 W
Loverynge Richard, Instow 1573 W
Loveringe Richard, Marwood 1607 [W]; forename blank in
　Ms; supplied from parish register
Loverin Richard, Woolfardisworthy 1692 A
Richard, Combe Martin 1836 A to Jane, widow
Richard, Parracombe 1849 W
Loverynge Robert, Instow 1569 W
Robert, Winkleigh 1670 W
Samuel, Tawstock 1832 A to Mary, widow
Sarah, Tawstock 1767 W
Sarah, Weare Giffard 1827 A to John of Black Torrington, son
Susan, Barnstaple 1852 W
Thomas, Tawstock 1676 A
Thomas, Combe Martin 1694 W
Thomas, Berrynarbor 1752 W
Thomas, Tawstock 1840 W
Loveringe William, King's Nympton 1584 W
Loveringe William, Mortehoe 1598 [W]
Loveringe William, Barnstaple 1626 [W]
Loveryn William, Combe Martin 1681 W
William, Tawstock 1700 W
William, Weare Giffard 1735 W
William, Kentisbury 1778 W
William, Weare Giffard 1794 W
William, Georgeham 1796 W
William, Tawstock, yeoman 1798 W
William, Ilfracombe, chandler 1807 W
William, Barnstaple 1837 W
Lovett Edward, Tawstock, esquire 1703 W
Joan, Tawstock 1709 A
Lovice Humphrey, Sheepwash 1635 A and 1638 O
Lowdey see Lawday
Lowman George, Rose Ash 1711 W
Robert, Clovelly 1568 W
Lubbone, Lubban
Lubban Anthony, High Bickington 1676 A
Baldwin, Yarnscombe 1589 A
Edward, St Giles in the Wood 1589 W
John, Yarnscombe 1589 A
Lucas, Luckes, Luckis, Lukes, Lukis
Alice, East Down nd W
Lukes Dorothy, Combe Martin 1818 W
Eleanor, Barnstaple 1676 W
Elizabeth, Ilfracombe 1620 [W]

George, East Down 1573 W
Luckis John, Stoke Rivers 1672 W
Lukis John, Barnstaple 1764 A
Lukis John, Barnstaple 1796 A
Lukis John, Marwood 1798 W
Margaret, Challacombe 1675 W
Luckes Mary, Shirwell, widow 1796 W
Morgan, Marwood 1672 W
Roger, Challacombe 1675 A
Lukis William, Marwood 1794 W
Luckford, Luckfor
Elizabeth, Fremington, widow 1607 [W]; forename blank in
　Ms; supplied from parish register
Luckfor John, Fremington 1574 W
Luckham, Luckomb, Luckome
Luckomb ..., Winkleigh 1612 [W]
John, Tawstock 1632 [W]
Luckome Walter, Fremington 1623 [W]
Luckie Prudence, Georgeham 1626 [W]
Luckis see Lucas
Luckomb, Luckome see Luckham
Luckman Thomas, Charles 1581 W
Lucy, Lucye
..., South Molton 1727 A
Lucye John, Charles 1585 W
Lucye Thomas, Charles 1585 W
Luff Edmund, High Bickington 1767 W
Nicholas, Winkleigh 1673 [W]
Lugg, Lugge
Adam, Barnstaple 1673 W
Lugge Christopher, Dolton 1624 [W]
Christopher, Atherington 1677 W
Lugge Joan, Dolton 1564 W
Lugge Joan, Barnstaple 1624 [W]
Lugge Joan and Thomas, Barnstaple 1631 [W]
John, Barnstaple 1667 A
John, Atherington 1678 W
John, Pilton 1734 W
Lugge Philip, Dolton 1625 [W]
Richard, Chulmleigh 1670 A
Thomas, Barnstaple 1684 A
Lugge Thomas and Joan, Barnstaple 1631 [W]
Lugge William, Dolton 1636 W
Lugger Elizabeth, Pilton 1681 W
Ralph, Roborough 1632 [W] and 1634 O
Thomas, High Bickington 1670 A
William, Roborough 1621 [W]
William, Chittlehampton 1672 A
Luke Ann, Fremington 1623 [W]
Anthony, Fremington 1630 [W]
Humphrey, Sheepwash 1640 W
Mary, Fremington 1625 [W]
Mary, Parkham 1814 W
Robert, South Molton 1633 W
William, Fremington 1631 [W]
Luker Philip, Fremington 1800 A
Lukes, Lukis see Lucas
Lulyer James, Great Torrington 1744 A
Luman see Loman
Lune see Lunne
Lunean Ann, Barnstaple 1707 W
Lunnacomb see Lanercombe
Lunne, Lune
..., North Tawton 1609 [W]
Lune Edward, Winkleigh 1573 W
Lune Elizabeth, Winkleigh 1582 W
Joan, North Tawton 1620 [W] and 1631 [W]
John, North Tawton 1634 W
William, North Tawton 1632 [W]
Luorthie see Leworthy
Luppincott, Luppencotte, Luppingcot, Luppingcott, Lyppincote,
　Lyppingcott
Luppingcott alias Leigh ... 1594 [W]
Lyppingcott Agnes, Fremington 1604 W
Luppencotte Ann, Alverdiscott, widow 1582 W

Luppingcott Anthony, Bideford 1620 [W]
Luppingcott Arthur, Westleigh 1592 [W]
Harry 1789 W
Lyppincote John, Alverdiscott 1569 W
Luppingcot Philip, Alverdiscott 1568 W
William, Alverdiscott 1671 A and 1679 A
Lurthie Emott, High Bray 1571 W
Luscombe Elizabeth, Ilfracombe 1805 W
Mary, Ilfracombe 1831 W
Nathaniel, Ilfracombe 1790 W
Thomas, Ilfracombe 1737 A
Luttrell, Lutterell
Alice, Kentisbury 1671 W
Andrew, Hartland 1625 [W], 1626 O and 1642 O
Lutterell Andrew, Kentisbury 1709 W
Lutterell Anthony, Hartland 1663 W
Lutterell Edward, Hartland 1666 A
Jane, Hartland 1680 W
John, Hartland 1672 W
Mary, Berrynarbor, widow 1632 [W]
Nicholas, Hartland 1637 W
Nicholas, Hartland, esquire 1695 A
Prudence, Hartland 1639 A
Thomas, Hartland 1695 W
Luworthie see Leworthy
Lux alias Lock Thomas, Coldridge 1690 A
Luxton, Luxon, Luxston
..., Brushford 1608 [W] and 1614 [W]
..., Winkleigh 1612 [W]
..., Coldridge 1613 [W]
Abraham, North Tawton 1665 A
Luxston Alice, Winkleigh 1586 W and 1588 W
Ann, Burrington 1677 W
Bartholomew, Abbotsham 1694 A
Bernard, Winkleigh 1582 W
Bernard, Brushford 1621 [W]
Bernard, Winkleigh 1640 W
Bernard, Ashreigney 1734 W and 1741 W
Catherine, Winkleigh 1578 W
Charles, Chittlehampton 1808 W
Christopher, North Tawton 1758 W
Dorothy, Brushford 1783 A
Dorothy, North Tawton, widow 1800 W
Edward, Dolton 1636 W
Edward, Buckland Brewer 1671 W and 1680 A
Elizabeth, Brushford 1672 W
Luxon Elizabeth, Bideford 1681 W
Elizabeth, Winkleigh 1699 A
Luxon Elizabeth, Bideford 1723 A
Elizabeth, St Giles in the Wood 1729 A
Luxon Elizabeth, Bideford 1776 W
Francis, Ashreigney 1644 W
George, Winkleigh 1660 W
Luxon George, Brushford 1693 A
Luxon George, Northam 1762 W
George, Witheridge 1784 W and 1791 W
George, Coldridge 1793 W
George, Winkleigh 1794 W
George, King's Nympton 1836 A to Mary, widow
Henry, Winkleigh, yeoman 1821 A to John, yeoman, son
Henry, Knowstone, yeoman 1856 A to Henry, yeoman and
  Mary, sp., children
Hugh, Winkleigh 1568 W
Hugh, Winkleigh 1692 W and 1697 W
Hugh, Winkleigh 1724 W
Humphrey, Iddesleigh 1615 [W]
Jacob, Dolton 1741 W
Luxon Jane, Washford Pyne 1699 W
Joan, Winkleigh 1593 [W] and 1598 [W]
John, Winkleigh 1576 W, 1587 W and 1588 W
John, Bideford 1664 W
John, Winkleigh 1666 A
John, Winkleigh 1676 W and 1694 A
John, Winkleigh 1712 W
John, Burrington 1725 W

John, Wembworthy 1769 A
John, Ashreigney 1782 W
John, Coldridge 1828 W
John, Wembworthy 1829 W
John, Coldridge 1833 W
Margaret, Burrington 1675 A
Luxston Mark, Winkleigh 1589 W
Mary, Winkleigh 1628 [W]
Mary, Bideford 1643 W
Mary, Winkleigh 1690 W and 1707 W
Mary, South Molton 1831 A
Peter, Winkleigh 1612 [W]; forename blank in Ms; supplied
  from parish register
Peter, Winkleigh 1627 [W]
Luxon Peter, Bideford 1714 W
Peter, Bondleigh 1803 A
Philip, Bideford 1664 W
Philip, Alverdiscott 1667 W
Luxon Philip, Bideford 1698 A
Rachel, Winkleigh 1665 W
Richard, Burrington 1635 W
Richard, Winkleigh 1662 W
Robert, North Tawton 1645 W
Robert, Coldridge 1682 W
Luxon Robert, North Tawton 1723 W
Robert, Brushford 1730 W
Robert, Rackenford 1732 W
Robert, Brushford 1753 W
Robert, Eggesford 1769 W
Robert, Winkleigh 1811 W
Robert, Brushford 1813 W
Robert, Northam 1824 W
Robert, Romansleigh 1825 A to Elizabeth, widow
Luxon Samuel, Bideford 1690 W
Samuel, Washford Pyne 1707 W
Samuel, Tawstock 1728 A
Samuel, Ashreigney 1777 W
Scipio, St Giles in the Wood 1691 W
Luxon Scipio, King's Nympton 1707 W
Susan, Brushford 1830 W
Thomas, Buckland Brewer 1599 [W]
Thomas, Winkleigh 1602 W
Thomas, Winkleigh, snr. 1640 W
Thomas, Winkleigh 1675 W
Thomas, Fremington 1781 W
William, Winkleigh 1579 W
William, Rackenford 1763 W
William, Rackenford 1791 W
Lyckey see Lickey
Lyddon
John, South Molton 1743 A
John, South Molton 1827 W
Mary, East Anstey 1726 A
Philip, Ashreigney 1803 W
Philip, Ashreigney 1819 A
Samuel, ship *Sunderland* 1761 A
Thomas, Molland 1738 A
William, East Anstey 1698 W
William, East Anstey 1721 A
William, Rackenford 1770 W
William, Oakford, thatcher 1808 W
William, Twitchen 1853 A to Mary, widow
Lyde Alexander, Chittlehampton 1639 A and O
Anthony, High Bickington 1639 W
John, High Bickington 1571 W
Richard, Chittlehampton 1578 W
Richard, Atherington 1589 W
Lye John, Lapford 1589 A
Walter, Goodleigh 1567 W
Lyell see Lyle
Lykey see Lickey
Lyle, Liell, Lile, Lisle, Lyell, Lyll
Liell Anthony, Buckland Brewer 1597 [W]
Lyll Digory, Welcombe 1633 W
Lile James, Clovelly 1666 [W]

Lisle James, Northam 1715 W
John, Hartland 1634 [W]
Lile John, Hartland 1664 A
Lyell John, Northam 1693 W
John, Hartland 1703 O
John, Clovelly 1708 W
Lile John, Northam 1711 A
Lile John, Bideford 1833 W
Lyell Margery, Frithelstock 1579 W
Philip, Clovelly 1712 W
Lyell Richard, Buckland Brewer 1620 [W]
Liell Stephen, North Molton 1592 [W]
Thomas, Alwington 1678 A
Thomas, Northam 1703 W
Lile Thomas, Bideford 1853 W
Lyll William, Alwington 1627 [W]
Lyell William, Buckland Brewer 1668 A
Lill William, Northam 1692 A
Lyell William, Northam 1757 A
Lyllecrop, Lylleycrop, Lylleycropp, Lyllicrop, Lyllycropp,
   Lyllycrap, Lyllycropp see Lillicrop
Lymbeare, Lymbeere, Lymber, Lymbere, Lymberie, Lymberry,
   Lymbery, Lymbeer, Lymebere, Lymebury see Limbery
Lynch, Lynche
Lynche John, Great Torrington 1589 W
John, Alwington 1686 A
John, Berrynarbor 1720 W
John, Combe Martin 1781 W
John, Marwood 1852 W
Judith, Alwington 1680 [W]
Peter, Peters Marland 1685 W
Lynche Richard, Parkham 1578 W
Thomas, Parkham 1688 A
Lynche William, Bideford 1635 A
William, Alwington 1702 W
Lyncomb, Lincombe, Lynncomb
John, Charles 1577 W
Lynncomb Peter, Wembworthy 1580 W
Richard, Charles 1577 A
Lincomb Roger, Charles 1578 W
Roger, Charles 1579 W
Thomas, Charles 1577 W
Lyne, Lynes, Lyons
Ann, Dolton 1811 W
George, Winkleigh 1712 W
John, Winkleigh 1693 W
Lyons Nicholas, Mortehoe 1587 A
Thomas, Dolton 1855 W
Lynes Thomasine, Ilfracombe 1623 [W]
Lynes William, Bideford 1637 O
Lynncomb see Lyncomb
Lynton Henry, South Molton 1721 A
Lyons see Lyne
Lyssett see Lisset
Lytell see Little
Lyttecotte Agnes, Shebbear 1571 W

Maber William, Barnstaple 1857 W
Mabin, Mabyn
Apphia, Hartland 1732 A
Mabyn Christian, Bideford 1627 [W]
Mabyn Digory, Alwington 1627 [W]
John, Hartland 1715 W
Mably Thomas, Chittlehampton 1669 W
Mabyn see Mabin
Macey William, Instow 1853 W
McGie Arthur, Lynton 1764 W
Mackenny William, Heanton Punchardon 1694 W
Mackerell, Mackinel, Mackrell
Mackinel Daniel, Bideford 1743 A
Hugh, East Worlington 1595 [W]
Mackrell Richard, East Worlington 1563 W
Richard, South Molton 1627 [W]
Mackland alias Baker ..., East Worlington 1601 W

Macqueen Margaret Cowper, Barnstaple, widow 1842 A to
   Mary Ann Cooper of Barnstaple, sp., sister
Mackrell see Mackerell
Madden Ann, South Molton 1831 W
Maddocks, Maddicks, Maddock, Maddocke, Maddox,
   Madduke, Madock
Madock Elizabeth, Winkleigh 1792 W
Madduke George, Northam 1723 W
Honor, High Bickington 1641 W
Maddox John, Northam 1720 W
Maddicks John, Northam 1742 W
Maddicks Lydia, Northam 1756 W
Margaret, High Bickington 1631 W
Maddox Mary, Northam 1726 W
Maddocke Robert, North Tawton 1571 W
Maddicks Roger, Abbotsham 1775 W and 1777 W
Thomas, Northam 1701 W
Maddock William, Winkleigh 1776 W
Madford, Madforde, Medford
Madforde Bernard, North Molton 1563 W
Madforde Elizabeth, North Molton 1567 W
Medford George, Barnstaple 1674 A
John, Great Torrington 1631 [W]
Medford Peter, Barnstaple 1637 A
Medford Roger, West Anstey 1643 W
Vincent, South Molton 1592 [W]
William, North Molton 1593 [W]
Medford William, Barnstaple 1689 W
Madge, Maidge, Maydge
Maidge ..., Clovelly 1602 A
Maidge ..., Peters Marland 1611 [W]
Edward, Meeth 1592 [W]
Elizabeth, Instow 1625 [W]
Emma, Dolton 1571 A
Gabriel, Instow 1631 [W]
Gilbert, Woolfardisworthy 1696 A
Humphrey, Great Torrington 1721 W
James, Instow 1677 A
Maydge Joan, Northam 1645 W
Joan, Northam 1704 W
John, Knowstone 1579 W
Maydge John, Peters Marland 1587 A
Maidge John, Peters Marland 1593 [W]
Maidge John, Buckland Filleigh 1600 W
Maidge John, Meeth 1616 [W]
Maidge John, Clovelly 1618 [W]
John, Clovelly 1737 W
John, Dolton 1742 A
John, Meeth 1813 W
John, Meeth 1835 W
Lawrence, Buckland Filleigh 1672 W
Maidge Lewis, Peters Marland 1605 W
Philip, Dolton 1721 W
Philip, Meeth 1790 W
Philip, Meeth 1831 W
Robert, Northam 1633 A
Maydge Robert, Peters Marland 1670 A
Maidge Thomas, Hartland 1595 [W]
Maydge Ulysses, Peters Marland 1629 [W]
William, Peters Marland 1564 W
William, Northam 1626 [W]
William, Great Torrington 1767 W; A dbn
William, Clovelly 1774 A
Madock see Maddocks
Madren ..., Ilfracombe 1600 A
Magent, Maggent
Peter, Dolton 1634 W
Maggent Philip, Dolton 1586 W
Mager see Major
Magford see Mogford
Maggent see Magent
Maggs George alias Moses, Great Torrington 1834 A
Magrath John, Northam 1777 A
Maidge see Madge

Maier see Mare
Mainard see Maynard
Maine, Main, Mayn, Mayne
..., Shirwell 1606 [W]
..., Chittlehampton 1608 [W]
..., Bideford 1611 [W]
Mayne Abraham, Shirwell 1599 [W]
Mayne Agnes, Atherington 1846 W
Mayne Arthur, Woolfardisworthy 1662 W
Mayne Christopher, South Molton 1577 W
Christopher, Abbotsham 1699 W
Mayne Edmund, Barnstaple 1633 A
Mayne Edward, Marwood 1743 A
Main Edward, Fremington 1766 W
Mayne Elizabeth, Frithelstock 1721 W
Mayne Elizabeth see also Thomas Wilmot
Mayne Griffith, West Down 1633 W
Hannah see Susan Langdon
Henry, Shirwell 1703 W
Mayne James, Lynton 1629 [W]
Mayne James, Atherington 1838 W
Jane, Barnstaple 1842 A
Mayne John, Chittlehampton 1567 W and 1577 W
Mayne John, Bratton Fleming 1573 [W]
Mayne John, Eggesford 1580 W
Mayne John, Shirwell 1580 [W]
Mayne John, Georgeham 1602 W
Mayne John, Clovelly 1603 W
Mayne John, Marwood 1623 [W]
Mayne John, Chittlehampton 1633 [W]
Mayne John, Bratton Fleming 1635 W
Mayne John, North Molton 1637 W
John, Tawstock 1699 A
Mayne John, Fremington 1726 W
Mayne John, Stoke Rivers 1792 A
Mayne John, Atherington 1800 W
Main John, Clovelly 1824 W
Mayne Margaret, Barnstaple 1773 A
Mary, Woolfardisworthy 1677 A
Mary, Tawstock 1697 W
Mary, Abbotsham 1701 W
Peter, Frithelstock 1689 A
Mayne Philip, Woolfardisworthy 1726 W
Mayne Richard, Tawstock 1584 A
Mayne Richard, Winkleigh 1594 [W]
Mayne Richard, Georgeham 1630 [W]
Mayne Richard, Bratton Fleming 1637 W
Robert, Frithelstock 1673 A
Mayne Robert, Atherington 1727 A
Robert, Bideford 1818 W
Mayne Robert, Atherington 1833 W
Mayne Roger, Frithelstock 1712 W
Sarah, Bideford 1809 A (limited)
Mayne Thomas, Bideford 1573 W
Mayn Thomas, Ashreigney 1575 W
Mayne Thomas, Bideford 1589 A
Mayne Thomas, Bideford 1663 A
Mayne Thomas, Abbotsham 1733 W
Mayne William, Georgeham 1602 W
William, Barnstaple 1612 [W]; forename blank in Ms;
    supplied from parish register
Mayn William, Georgeham 1676 W
Mayne William, Woolfardisworthy 1700 W
William, Bideford, mariner 1810 W
Mayne William, Ilfracombe 1853 W
Mair, Maire see Mare
Major, Mager, Mayger, Meager
Abraham, Northam 1713 W
Harry, Shebbear 1839 W
Meager Joan, Bideford 1582 W
Meager John, Barnstaple 1615 [W]; forename blank in Ms;
    supplied from parish register
John, Tawstock 1761 A
Meager Nicholas, Abbotsham 1750 W
Mager Roger, Abbotsham 1718 W

Mayger Thomas, Bideford 1575 W
Meager Willmot, Abbotsham 1723 W
Malcomb Thomas, Bideford 1735 W
Mallett, Mallet
Gilbert, Bow 1846 W
Hugh, Iddesleigh 1823 A to Hugh, esquire, son
Humphrey, Langtree 1838 W
Mallet John, Woolleigh [Ullegh in Ms], Beaford 1570 W
John, Iddesleigh 1661 [W]
John, Merton, gentleman 1801 W
John, Great Torrington 1802 W
Mary, Great Torrington 1838 A to George, son
Oliver, Iddesleigh 1621 [W]
Oliver, Iddesleigh 1661 W
Richard, Iddesleigh 1616 [W]
Mallet Richard, Alverdiscott 1643 A
Robert, Dowland 1765 W
William, Iddesleigh 1586 W
William, Iddesleigh 1781 W
Mallony Nicholas, North Molton 1663 W
Malton Richard, Instow 1664 W
Man Adam, Northam 1680 A
Catherine, Northam 1743 W
George, Molland 1745 W
Gilbert, Clovelly 1615 [W]
John, Northam 1702 W
John, Zeal Monachorum 1728 W
John, ship *Boyne* 1743 A
Joseph, Molland 1763 W
Thomas, Northam 1704 A
Thomas, Zeal Monachorum 1735 W
William, Bow 1664 W
Manaton see Mannaton
Mandley, Mandly see Manley
Manfeild John, Bideford 1664 A
Manley, Mandley, Mandly, Manly, Maundley
Amesia, Northam 1680 W
Ann, Cruwys Morchard 1633 A
George, Cruwys Morchard 1626 [W]
Grace, North Molton 1843 A
Hugh, South Molton 1843 W
Joan, Cruwys Morchard 1675 A
John, Cruwys Morchard 1635 W
John, Chulmleigh 1676 A
Manly John, Cruwys Morchard 1692 A
Manly John, Combe Martin 1765 W
John, Marwood, cordwainer 1803 W
Leonard, Northam 1679 W
Manly Nicholas, Chulmleigh 1668 W
Nicholas, Chulmleigh 1679 A
Manly Richard, Cruwys Morchard 1741 W
Manly Richard, Cruwys Morchard 1814 W
Robert, Fremington 1616 [W]
Manly Robert, Cruwys Morchard 1670 W
Roger, Barnstaple 1791 A
Thomas, Cruwys Morchard 1624 [W] and 1627 O
Mandly Thomas, Cruwys Morchard 1702 W
Maundley Thomas, Cruwys Morchard 1710 W
Mandley Thomas, Cruwys Morchard 1730 A
Manin, Maninge see Manning
Mannaton, Manaton
Ann, Chittlehampton 1829 W
Francis, Chittlehampton 1799 W
John, Northam 1696 W
Manaton John, Chittlehampton 1824 W
Manaton Robert, Chittlehampton 1758 W
Manning, Manin, Maninge, Mannen, Manninge, Manynge,
    Monynge
Manninge ..., Bratton Fleming 1603 [W]
Mannen ..., Yarnscombe 1606 [W]
Andrew, Ashreigney, yeoman 1802 W
Andrew, Ashreigney 1818 W
Ann, Buckland Brewer 1641 W
Ann, Chittlehampton, widow 1809 W
Charles, South Molton 1833 W

Charles, South Molton 1851 W
Connaught, Tawstock 1661 [W]
Monynge Daniel, Great Torrington 1586 A
Manninge Elizabeth, Buckland Brewer 1626 [W]
Elizabeth, Bishop's Nympton, widow 1857 A to Betsy, sp.,
  daughter
Francis, Chulmleigh 1706 A
Francis, Chulmleigh 1759 A
Gertrude, Great Torrington 1727 W
Henry, Wembworthy 1669 A
Honor, Tawstock 1685 W
Hugh, West Down 1850 W
James 1741 A
Manninge Joan, Rose Ash 1591 [W]
Maninge Joan, Rose Ash 1620 [W]
Manninge John, Stoodleigh 1577 W
Manynge John, Rose Ash 1578 W
John, Chulmleigh 1738 W
John, Chulmleigh 1777 W
John, Cheldon 1789 A
John, Cheldon 1803 W*
John, Burrington 1846 W
John, Chittlehampton 1848 W
Martha, Bideford, sp. 1808 W
Manninge Oliver, Great Torrington 1591 [W]
Manninge Paschal, Tawstock 1615 [W]
Manninge Peter, Molland 1634 A
Peter, Chulmleigh 1729 W and 1736 A
Manin Richard, North Tawton 1695 W
Richard, Bideford 1726 W
Richard, North Tawton 1734 W
Robert, Chulmleigh 1791 W
Robert, Iddesleigh 1843 W
Manninge Thomas, St Giles in the Wood 1619 [W]
Thomas, Buckland Brewer 1684 A
Thomas, Arlington 1795 W
William, Tawstock 1697 W
William, Parkham 1746 A
William, Chittlehampton, yeoman 1800 W
William, Puddington 1829 W
William, Chittlehampton 1832 W
William, Witheridge 1851 W
William, Dowland 1857 W
Mansell John, Arlington 1692 A
Michael, Arlington 1641 W
Mantle George, mariner 1741 W
Many, Manie
Edward, Barnstaple 1701 W
Manie Robert, Chittlehampton 1597 [W]
Manie see Many
Manynge see Manning
Mappowder Thomas, Little Torrington 1689 W
Marcar see Marker
March Mary, Barnstaple 1823 W
Richard, Barnstaple 1816 W
Marchant, Marchante, Merchant, Merchante
Ann, Tawstock 1670 W
Merchant Anthony, Tawstock 1698 A and 1711 A
Anthony, Parracombe 1771 W
Merchante Elizabeth, Georgeham 1578 W
Elizabeth, Tawstock 1632 [W]
Humphrey, Tawstock 1666 W
Merchant Humphrey, Tawstock 1711 A
Merchant Humphrey, Parracombe 1787 W
Marchante John, Alwington 1587 W
John, Tawstock 1596 [W] and 1602 W
John, Georgeham 1624 [W]
John, Fremington 1675 A
Merchant John, Tawstock 1715 W
Merchant John, Tawstock 1761 A
Merchant Nicholas, Tawstock 1698 W
Richard, Fremington 1593 [W]
Richard, Parracombe 1779 W
Merchant Thomas, Tawstock 1699 A
Marcom see Martin Thomas (1855)

Mardon, Merdon
Merdon John, Bow 1695 W
John, South Molton 1847 W
Mare, Maier, Mair, Maire, Mayre
Alexander, Loxhore 1592 W
Mayre alias Richord Ann, Tawstock 1692 A
Dorothy, Burrington 1622 [W]
Edward, Burrington 1775 A
Mayre George, Shirwell 1566 W
Maire Henry, South Molton 1752 A
Hugh, Ilfracombe 1564 W
Maier Hugh, Loxhore 1615 [W]
Hugh, South Molton 1757 W
Mayre Joan, Ashreigney 1623 [W]
Maire Joan, South Molton 1774 W
Mare alias More John, Barnstaple 1581 W
Maire John, Zeal Monachorum 1687 A
John, Tawstock 1745 W
Mair John, Charles 1763 A
John, Coldridge 1778 A
Maire Mabel, Zeal Monachorum 1578 W
Mare alias Somer Nicholas, Ilfracombe, widower 1568 W
Peter, South Molton 1759 A
Philip, Berrynarbor 1708 W
Richard, Zeal Monachorum 1663 W
Maire Robert, Chittlehampton 1725 W
Robert, Chittlehampton 1763 W
Thomas, North Tawton 1732 A
Maire Thomas, South Molton, husbandman 1813 A to John and
  Thomas, sons
Mair Walter, Satterleigh 1753 W
Mair Walter, Warkleigh, Ackland 1788 W
Maier William, Shirwell 1611 [W] "Moore of West Plaistow" in
  register; forename blank in Ms; supplied from parish register
William, Ashreigney 1679 W
  see also Mayer
Markendale Barbara, Northam 1698 A
Marell see Morrell
Marker, Marcar
Marcar Emanuel, Chulmleigh 1626 [W]
Emanuel, Chulmleigh 1667 W
Joan, Chulmleigh 1666 W
John, Burrington 1644 W
Roger, Chulmleigh 1674 W
Sarah, Chulmleigh 1728 W
William, Chulmleigh 1667 W
William, Chulmleigh 1725 W
William, Tawstock 1772 A
William, Tawstock 1856 W
Markey William, High Bray 1851 and 1854 W
Marks, Marke
Marke Alice, Goodleigh 1640 A
Hannah, Bideford 1821 W
John, Pilton 1714 W
John, Bideford 1795 W
Marke Michael, Barnstaple 1582 A
Marke Philip, West Down 1642 W
Marke Richard, Ilfracombe 1744 A
Robert, St Giles in the Wood 1688 W
Thomas, Bideford 1740 W
William, Bideford 1812 W
Marles see Mearles
Marley, Marly
Christian, Rose Ash 1597 [W]
Marley alias Parramore George, Chulmleigh 1641 W
Marly George, Fremington 1735 W
Marly George, Oakford 1738 A
Jenny, Barnstaple 1851 W
John, Rose Ash 1588 W
John, Rose Ash 1637 A
Marly John, Stoodleigh 1774 W
Joseph, Knowstone 1696 W
Margery, Rose Ash 1564 W
Oliver, Rose Ash 1628 [W]
Richard, Stoodleigh 1719 W

Marly alias Hunt Sarah, Molland 1710 A
Thomas, Oakford, yeoman 1810 A
William, Ashreigney 1695 A
William, Atherington 1751 W
Marquiss John, Woolfardisworthy (East or West), snr. 1845 W
Marrell see Morrell
Marriott Daniel, Barnstaple 1783 W
Marris see Morris
Marsford David, Buckland Filleigh 1563 W
Marsh, Marshe
..., Ashford 1608 [W]
..., Chittlehampton 1610 [W]
..., Tawstock 1612 [W]
Alexander, Barnstaple 1614 [W]; forename blank in Ms;
    supplied from parish register
Alexander, West Down 1739 A
Marshe Alice, Barnstaple 1628 [W]
Bartholomew, South Molton 1595 [W]
Catherine, Northam 1748 A
Christiana, Marwood 1728 W
Elizabeth, South Molton 1750 W
George, Lynton 1744 A
George, South Molton 1826 W
John, Pilton 1603 W
Marshe John, Northam 1621 [W]
Marshe John, Ashford 1628 [W], 1630 [W] and 1634 W
Marshe John, Loxhore 1638 W
John, Chittlehampton 1673 W
John, West Anstey 1707 W
John, South Molton 1822 A
Mersh Lodovic, Chittlehampton 1694 W
Marshe Margery, Ashford 1573 W
Mary, Peters Marland 1748 A
Matthias, Bideford 1740 W and 1743 A
Nicholas, Fremington 1617 [W]
Marshe Patience, Instow 1630 [W]
Rachel, Yarnscombe 1714 A
Richard, Yarnscombe 1714 A
Richard, Brendon 1744 A
Richard, North Molton 1779 A
Marshe Robert, Instow 1629 [W]
Robert, Bideford 1691 W
Marshe Scipio, Ashford 1637 A
Thomas, Northam 1615 [W]
Thomas, Chittlehampton 1679 A
Thomas, Northam 1733 A
Thomas, Northam 1747 W A dbn 1767
Marshe William, Ashford 1621 [W]
William, Northam 1689 W
William, West Anstey 1698 W
William, South Molton 1772 A
William, South Molton, innkeeper 1811 W
Marshe Willmot, Chittlehampton 1621 [W]
Marshall, Marshel, Marshell, Mershell
..., King's Nympton 1604 [W]
Ann, Barnstaple 1790 A
Ann, Tawstock, widow 1810 A
Bridget, Frithelstock 1766 W
David, Dolton 1611 [W]; forename blank in Ms; supplied
    from parish register
Dorcas, Barnstaple 1746 W
Marshell Edmund, High Bickington 1720 W
Edward, Winkleigh 1713 A
Eleanor, Chittlehampton 1601 W
Elizabeth, Northam 1720 W
Elizabeth, Pilton 1828 A (Eliza) to John Marshall, guardian of
    children
Elizabeth, South Molton 1850 W A with will annexed dbn
    passed at the Principal Registry, Jun 1884
Francis, Sheepwash 1791 W
George, Hartland, snr. 1705 W
George, Beaford 1796 W
Grace Boyle, Barnstaple, sp. 1856 A to John Boyle Marshall,
    brother

Hammond, Barnstaple 1790 A
Henry, Rose Ash 1675 W
Henry, Rose Ash 1730 W
Henry, Tawstock, blacksmith 1809 A; A dbn 1810
Hugh, Barnstaple 1718 W
Joan, Great Torrington 1579 W
Mershall John, Warkleigh 1566 W
John, Beaford 1708 W
John, Chulmleigh 1709 A
Marshel John, Welcombe 1712 W
John, Barnstaple, snr. 1716 W
John, Petrockstowe 1718 W
John, Rackenford 1725 A
John, Barnstaple 1734 W
John, Loxhore 1739 W
John, Merton 1748 W
John, Hartland 1782 W
John, Winkleigh 1782 W
John, Rose Ash, yeoman 1809 W; 1810 A dbn
John, Chulmleigh 1817 W
John, South Molton 1836 A
John, Beaford 1840 W
John, Hartland 1843 W
John, Chulmleigh 1852 W; 1853 second act dbn
John see also Elizabeth
Joseph 1741 A
Joseph, South Molton 1778 W
Margaret, Beaford 1819 A
Mary, Welcombe 1677 W
Mary, Bideford 1722 A
Mary, Chulmleigh 1825 W
Maurice, Dolton 1629 [W]
Michael, Winkleigh 1636 W
Nicholas, Hartland 1743 W
Peter, Chulmleigh 1718 A
Philip, ship *Colchester* 1600 W
Philip, Great Torrington 1639 A
Richard, Hartland 1765 W
Richard, Hartland 1839 A to Margaret, widow
Richard, Northam, Appledore 1841 A to Ann, widow
Robert, Chulmleigh 1845 W
Thomas, Great Torrington 1575 A
Thomas, King's Nympton 1603 W
Thomas, Bideford 1681 W
Thomas, Bideford 1710 A
Thomas, Beaford 1741 W
Thomas, Northam 1745 A
Thomas, Winkleigh 1786 A
Thomas, South Molton 1822 W
Thomas, Barnstaple 1851 W
Thomas, East Putford, draper 1854 A to Thomas Fry of
    Parkham near Bideford, stranger in blood
William, Bideford 1728 W
William, Bideford 1751 W
William, Frithelstock 1760 A
William, Tawstock 1814 W
Marshe see Marsh
Marshel, Marshell see Marshall
Martin, Martaine, Marten, Martine, Martyn, Martyne
Marten ..., North Tawton 1601 A
Martyne ..., Bondleigh 1608 [W]
Marten ..., Bideford 1609 [W]
Marten ..., Northam 1613 [W]
Marten alias Johns ..., Bideford 1697 A
Adam, Barnstaple 1680 A
Martyn Adam, Barnstaple 1732 W
Adam, Barnstaple 1830 A to John, Philip and James, brothers
Marten Alice, Frithelstock 1641 W
Marten Andrew, Great Torrington, snr. 1627 [W]
Andrew, Great Torrington 1660 W
Marten Andrew, Frithelstock 1673 W
Martyn Andrew, Merton, snr. 1713 W
Andrew, Merton 1715 W
Martyn Andrew, Great Torrington 1737 A
Arthur, Frithelstock 1688 W and 1694 W

Arthur, Bideford 1746 A
Bartholomew, Bow 1677 W
Marten Catherine, Chittlehampton 1597 [W]
Charity, Barnstaple 1833 A to Alexander of Swimbridge,
  brother
Marten Christopher, Filleigh 1623 [W]
Martyn Christopher, Frithelstock 1641 W
Digory, Meeth 1706 A
Marten Edward, Sheepwash 1597 [W]
Edward, Shebbear 1703 W
Edward, Combe Martin 1746 W
Edward, Abbotsham, yeoman 1801 A
Edward, Bideford 1803 W
Elias, Merton 1696 W
Marten Elizabeth, Barnstaple 1597 [W]
Marten Elizabeth, Barnstaple 1665 W
Elizabeth, Filleigh 1693 W
Martyn Elizabeth, Hartland 1734 A
Elizabeth, Filleigh 1742 W
Elizabeth, Barnstaple 1829 W
Francis, Tawstock 1663 W
Martine Francis, Chawleigh, jnr. 1726 A
Francis, Winkleigh 1820 W
Geoffrey, Chittlehampton 1563 A
George, West Buckland 1716 W
Martyn George, Bideford 1732 A
Grace, Bideford, widow 1808 W
Marten Henry, South Molton 1639 A
Marten Henry, Shebbear 1708 W
Martyn Henry, Yarnscombe 1721 W
Henry, Barnstaple 1857 W
Hugh, Filleigh 1664 A
Marten alias Honychurch Humphrey, North Tawton 1585 W
Humphrey, Pilton 1714 W
Morten Joan, West Buckland 1581 W
Marten Joan, Bideford 1626 [W]
Marten John, Northam 1578 W
Martyn John, Barnstaple 1580 A
Marten John, Frithelstock 1585 W
Martyne John, Marwood 1585 W and 1586 W
Marten alias Honichurch John, North Tawton 1587 W
Martyn John, George Nympton 1587 A
Marten John, Chittlehampton 1589 W
Marten John, Barnstaple 1591 [W]
Marten John 1596 [W]
Marten John, Bideford 1608 [W]; forename blank in Ms;
  supplied from parish register
John, Chittlehampton 1626 [W]
Marten John, Hartland 1635 W
John, Frithelstock 1661 W
John, Frithelstock 1696 W
Martin or Martyn John, Merton 1699 W
John, Filleigh 1704 W
John, Frithelstock 1717 A
John, Bideford 1747 A
John, Shebbear 1749 W
John, Iddesleigh 1781 W
John, Frithelstock 1816 W
John, Barnstaple 1832 W
John, Bideford 1855 W
Joyce, Ilfracombe 1751 A
Martyn Leonard, Bideford 1734 W
Marten Mary, Barnstaple 1619 [W] and 1625 [W]
Martaine Mary, Northam 1704 A
Martyn Mary, Barnstaple 1735 W
Mary Ann wife of Henry see Grace Keys
Marten Nicholas, Frithelstock 1633 [W]
Nicholas, Northam 1663 W
Oliver, Sheepwash 1789 W
Marten Peter, Barnstaple 1608 [W]; forename blank in Ms;
  supplied from parish register
Philip, Barnstaple 1834 W
Marten Ralph, Chittlehampton 1563 W
Marten alias Arnolde Richard, Barnstaple 1564 W
Marten Richard, Langtree 1592 [W]
Richard, Petrockstowe 1703 W

Richard, Bideford 1705 W and 1707 W
Richard, South Molton 1714 W
Martine Richard, Petrockstowe 1725 W
Martyn Richard, Filleigh 1736 W
Richard, Little Torrington 1739 W
Richard, Petrockstowe 1768 W
Marten Robert, George Nympton 1630 [W]
Marten Robert, Great Torrington 1641 A
Samuel, South Molton, saddler 1798 W
Sarah, Bideford, sp. 1853 A to William, labourer, brother
Marten Thomas, Barnstaple 1590 [W]
Marten Thomas, Great Torrington 1590 [W]
Marten Thomas, North Tawton 1599 [W]
Marten Thomas, Filleigh 1637 A and 1638 O
Thomas, Filleigh 1684 W
Thomas, Northam 1686 A
Thomas, Hartland 1722 A
Thomas, Ilfracombe 1817 W
Thomas, Barnstaple, butcher 1820 A to Catherine wife of G.
  Kelly, daughter
Thomas, Ilfracombe 1855 A (Marcom) to Mary Ann Dovell of
  Combe Martin, daughter
Thomasine, South Molton 1776 W
Marten William, Bideford 1578 W
Martyne William, Meshaw 1588 W
Marten William, Barnstaple 1622 [W]
Marten William, Winkleigh 1623 [W] and 1624 [W]
Marten William, Frithelstock 1641 W
Martyn William, Shebbear 1727 A
Martyn William, Peters Marland 1738 W
William, Shebbear 1742 W
William, Frithelstock 1778 A
Martindale William, Zeal Monachorum 1621 [W]
Martyn, Martyne see Martin
Mary or May Edward, Merton 1671 W
Robert, Pilton 1671 W
Masford Catherine, Buckland Filleigh 1575 A
Mason, Masson
  ..., Winkleigh 1608 [W]
Henry, Barnstaple 1664 A
John, Bideford 1772 W
Judith, Barnstaple 1621 [W]
Mathew, Barnstaple 1703 A
Mason alias Masson Mathew, Barnstaple 1707 [W]
Masters Richard, Barnstaple 1619 [W]
Masticke Agnes, Alwington 1586 W
Mathers, Mather
George, Chulmleigh 1686 W
Mather George, Chulmleigh 1791 W
Thomas, Wembworthy 1622 [W]
Mathews, Mathew, Mathewe, Matthew, Matthews
Mathew ..., Great Torrington 1609 [W]
Mathew ..., Barnstaple 1610 [W]
..., Ilfracombe 1660 W
Adrian, Rackenford 1721 A
Agnes, Chulmleigh 1733 W
Mathewe Ann, Barnstaple 1619 [W] and 1628 [A]
Mathew Arthur, Alverdiscott 1684 W
Matthews Benjamin, Bideford 1758 A
Mathew Catherine, Alverdiscott 1688 W
Matthews George, Chulmleigh 1726 A
George, Clovelly 1746 A
Matthews James, South Molton 1841 W
Mathew John, Barnstaple 1583 A
Mathewe John, Bideford 1584 A
Mathewe John, Wembworthy 1587 W
Mathew John, West Worlington 1599 [W]
Mathewe John, Chawleigh 1624 [W]
Matthews John, Georgeham 1693 A
John, Bideford 1739 W
John, Rackenford 1780 W
John, Bideford 1800 W
Mathew, Georgeham 1723 W
Mathew Miles, Great Torrington 1598 [W]
Mathewe Nicholas, Alverdiscott 1577 W

Mathewe Nicholas, North Molton 1585 W
Mathew Nicholas, Atherington 1603 [W]; forename blank in
  Ms; supplied from parish register
Mathew Nicholas, Atherington 1637 A
Mathewe Philip, Coldridge 1604 W
Mathew Richard, Yarnscombe 1590 [W]
Mathew Richard, Great Torrington 1601 W
Richard, Weare Giffard 1740 W
Richard, Heanton Punchardon 1852 W
Roger, Buckland Brewer 1781 W
Mathew Thomas, Barnstaple 1612 O forename blank in Ms;
  supplied from parish register
Mathew Thomas, Alverdiscott 1641 W
Matthew Thomas, Barnstaple 1680 A
Thomas, St Giles in the Wood, husbandman 1806 A
Matthews Thomas, Yarnscombe 1846 A
Mathewe Thomasine, Barnstaple, widow 1611 [W]; forename
  blank in Ms; supplied from parish register
Mathewe William, Alverdiscott 1563 W
Mathew William, Great Torrington 1617 [W]
William, Pilton 1749 A
William, Bideford, shipowner 1802 W
Matthews William, Great Torrington 1856 A
Mattacott, Matcott, Mattacot, Mattacote, Mattcott
Mattcott Agnes, Fremington 1633 W
Matcott Agnes, Merton 1709 A
Mattacote Alice, St Giles in the Wood, widow 1570 W
Arthur, Fremington 1618 [W]
Mattcott Baldwin, Fremington 1633 W
Mattcott Bartholomew 1620 [W]
Henry, Fremington 1582 W
Mattcot John, Fremington 1573 A
John, St Giles in the Wood 1615 [W]
John, Fremington 1617 [W]
John, St Giles in the Wood 1618 [W]
Mattcott John, St Giles in the Wood 1619 [W]
Mattcott John, Pilton 1623 [W]
Matcott John, St Giles in the Wood 1704 W
Julian, Fremington 1596 [W]
Lucy, St Giles in the Wood 1564 W
Mattacot Nicholas, Fremington 1574 W
Robert, Fremington 1571 W
Mattcott Robert, St Giles in the Wood 1640 A
Thomas, Chittlehampton 1630 [W]
Mattcott Thomasine, St Giles in the Wood 1629 [W] and 1631
  [W]
Matcott William, St Giles in the Wood 1689 W
Matthew, Matthews see Mathews
Maule John, Cruwys Morchard 1587 W
Maunder, Mawnder
..., Rackenford 1611 [W]
Agnes, Stoodleigh 1767 A
Alexander, Cruwys Morchard 1644 W
Alexander, Cruwys Morchard 1663 W and 1669 [W]
Alice, Cruwys Morchard 1586 W
Baldwin, Cruwys Morchard 1698 A
Bartholomew, Rackenford 1597 [W]
Christopher, Warkleigh 1636 W
Elizabeth, Washford Pyne 1691 W
Elizabeth, Rackenford 1848 W
George, Stoodleigh 1566 W
George, Puddington 1662 W
George, Heanton Punchardon 1665 W
George, Rackenford 1844 W
Henry, Molland 1848 W
James, South Molton 1853 W
Joan, Rackenford 1622 [W]
John, Cruwys Morchard 1593 [W] and 1598 [W]
John, Stoodleigh 1607 W and 1617 [W]
John, Eggesford 1661 W
John, Washford Pyne 1674 W
John, Stoodleigh 1731 A
John, Cruwys Morchard 1845 W

Mawnder Julian, Stoodleigh 1565 W
Mary, Thelbridge 1637 A
Mary, Thelbridge 1644 W
Mary, Washford Pyne 1790 W
Mary, Cruwys Morchard 1818 W
Robert, Cruwys Morchard 1579 W
Roger, Eggesford 1704 A
Roger, Romansleigh 1741 W and 1765 W
Roger, South Molton 1777 W
Sarah see Joan Moore
Thomas, Cruwys Morchard 1586 W and 1588 A
Thomas, Goodleigh 1623 [W]
Thomas, Stoodleigh 1625 [W]
Thomas, Witheridge 1637 W
Thomas, Eggesford 1639 A
Thomas, Stoodleigh 1820 W
Walter, East or West Worlington 1709 A
Walter, West Worlington 1734 W
Mawnder William, Cruwys Morchard 1565 W
William, Rackenford 1610 [W]; forename blank in Ms;
  supplied from parish register
William, Warkleigh 1631 [W]
William, Meshaw 1686 W
Wilmot, Stoodleigh 1611 [W]; forename blank in Ms;
  supplied from parish register
Maundley see Manley
Maunsey John, Fremington 1579 A
Maurice Nicholas, Combe Martin 1683 W
Mavericke David, Ilfracombe 1620 [W]
Mawnder see Maunder
May, Maye, Meaye
..., Northam 1602 [W]
Agnes, Twitchen 1639 W
Alnette, Hartland 1602 W
Alnette, Hartland 1632 [W]
Maye Amiel, Marwood 1586 W
Andrew, Fremington 1712 A
Ann, Great Torrington 1804 W
Ann, Barnstaple 1837 W
Ann, Barnstaple 1857 W
Anthony, Huntshaw 1632 [W]
Barbara, Peters Marland 1644 W
Maye Catherine, Marwood 1588 W
Catherine, South Molton 1620 [W]
Catherine, North Molton 1687 A
Charles, Littleham (near Bideford) 1728 W
Daniel, Weare Giffard 1741 A
David, Hartland 1636 W
Dionysius, Witheridge 1628 [W]
Dorothy, Barnstaple 1762 W
Dorothy, North Tawton 1772 W
Edmund, St Giles in the Wood 1620 [W]
Maye Edward, Marwood 1571 W
Edward, Martinhoe 1592 W
May or Mary Edward, Merton 1671 W
Edward, Lapford 1822 W
Eleanor, Petrockstowe 1696 W
Elizabeth, Monkleigh 1682 W
Elizabeth, Chawleigh 1820 W
Elizabeth, Barnstaple 1829 W
Elizabeth, Fremington 1831 W
Emanuel, Fremington 1762 W
Emanuel, South Molton, surgeon, bachelor 1805 W
Emotta, Hartland 1684 A
Francis, Goodleigh 1640 A
Francis, Hartland 1695 A
Gabriel, Hartland 1673 W
George, Instow 1592 [W]
George, South Molton 1682 A
George, Hartland 1693 W
George, High Bickington 1753 A
George, Barnstaple 1846 W
Henry, North Molton 1791 W
Henry, North Molton, shopkeeper 1808 W
Honor, Hartland 1696 W

Hugh, Thelbridge 1668 W
Hugh, Thelbridge 1790 W
Isaac, Tawstock 1817 W
Isott, North Tawton 1590 [W]
Isott, Martinhoe 1636 W
James, Hartland 1668 W
James, Barnstaple 1678 W
James, Northam 1684 A
James, Barnstaple 1750 A
James, Chawleigh 1771 W and 1772 W
James, Chittlehampton 1822 W
Jane, Petrockstowe 1693 W
Jane, Lapford 1824 W
Joan, South Molton 1597 [W]
Joan, Goodleigh, widow 1605 [W]; forename blank in Ms;
   supplied from parish register
Joan, Goodleigh 1627 [W]
Joan, Barnstaple 1628 [W]
Maye John, Marwood 1566 W and 1570 W
Maye John, Knowstone 1573 W
John, Hartland 1592 [W]
John, Instow 1600 W
Maye John, Martinhoe 1602 W
John, Hartland 1606 W
John, Pilton 1616 [W]
John, Barnstaple 1619 [W]
John, Witheridge 1623 [W]
John, Bratton Fleming 1631 [W] and O
John, Peters Marland 1638 A and 1641 O
John, Barnstaple 1640 A
John, South Molton 1640 A
John, Goodleigh 1644 A
John, Little Torrington 1671 W
John, Witheridge 1685 W
John, Peters Marland 1690 A
John, Hartland 1694 A
John, North Molton 1698 W
John, Langtree 1729 W
John, Ilfracombe 1749 A
John, Great Torrington 1763 W
John, Bratton Fleming 1777 W
John, Cheldon 1796 A
John, Barnstaple, cordwainer 1805 W
John, Shirwell, blacksmith 1823 A to Ann, widow
John, Barnstaple 1829 A to Richard Jere, creditor
John, Lapford 1854 W
John, Woolfardisworthy 1855 W
Margaret, North Molton 1740 W
Martha, East Buckland 1745 W
Mary, Great Torrington 1773 W
Mary, Barnstaple 1787 A
Mary, Rose Ash 1703 W
Mary and William, Knowstone 1623 [W] and 1625 O
Nicholas, Peters Marland 1706 A
Paschal, South Molton 1703 W
Philip, Hartland 1641 W
Philip, Molland 1670 A
Prudence, Barnstaple 1837 A
Rebecca, Great Torrington 1769 A
Richard, Barnstaple 1596 [W]
Richard, Hartland 1623 [W]
Richard, Great Torrington 1629 [W]
Richard, Yarnscombe 1629 [W]
Richard, Thelbridge 1677 W
Richard, Bideford, snr. 1691 W
Richard, North Molton 1806 W
May or Mary Robert, Pilton 1671 W
Robert, Buckland Filleigh 1687 W
Robert, Tawstock 1698 A
Robert, Bratton Fleming 1709 W
Robert, Thelbridge 1765 W
Samuel, Peters Marland 1691 A
Samuel, Fremington 1741 W
Sarah, Tawstock 1855 W
Sarah, Lapford 1856 W

Thomas, Goodleigh 1619 [W] and 1622 O
Thomas, Great Torrington 1619 [W]
Thomas, Peters Marland 1626 [W]
Thomas, South Molton 1627 [W]
Thomas, Fremington 1628 [W]
Thomas, Oakford 1685 W
Thomas, Great Torrington 1703 A
Thomas, Great Torrington 1756 W
Thomas, West Putford 1838 W
Maye William, Chestowe 1570 W
Meaye William, Pilton 1584 W
William, Petrockstowe 1602 [W]; forename blank in Ms;
   supplied from parish register
William, Goodleigh 1605 [W]; forename blank in Ms; supplied
   from parish register
William, Pilton 1619 [W]
William, Barnstaple 1668 W
William, Bideford 1673 [W]
William, Hartland 1695 W
William, Rose Ash 1700 W
William, Langtree 1728 W
William, South Molton 1765 A
William, Barnstaple 1766 W
William, Buckland Filleigh 1781 W
William, Buckland Filleigh 1808 W
William, St Giles in the Wood 1818 W
William, Parkham 1842 W
William and Mary, Knowstone 1623 [W] and 1625 O
William Morris, Great Torrington 1838 W
Maydge see Madge
Maye see May
Mayer, Mayor, Meyre
   George, North Tawton 1616 [W]
   Henry, Tawstock 1672 W "Moore" in register; forename blank
      in Ms; supplied from parish register
   Mayor Hugh, Charles 1680 W
   John, Winkleigh 1584 W
   John, Ashreigney 1624 [W]
   John, Tawstock 1630 [W] and 1636 W
   John, Marwood 1638 W
   Marian, Tawstock 1597 [W]
   Peter, South Molton 1663 W
   Robert, Witheridge 1597 [W]
   Meyre Robert, Brushford 1638 W
   Robert, North Tawton 1645 A
   Samuel, Zeal Monachorum 1672 A
   Stephen, North Tawton 1635 [W]
   Thomas, Burrington 1597 [W]
   Thomas, North Tawton 1597 [W]
   Walter, Tawstock 1642 A
   Mayer alias Upcott William, Witheridge 1589 A
      see also Mare
Mayger see Major
Mayn see Maine
Maynard, Mainard
   Mainard George, South Molton 1663 W
   Mainard Thomas, Sheepwash 1664 W
   William, Burrington 1828 A to Catherine, widow
   William, Burrington 1841 W
Mayne see Maine
Mayor, Mayre see Mare, Mayer
Maysey see Moysey
Meacombe Richard, Petrockstowe 1586 W
Meadway Humphrey 1640 W
   William 1630 [W]
Meager see Major
Meare, Mear, Mere
   ..., Tawstock 1607 [W]
   Cicely, Dowland 1577 W
   James, Tawstock 1586 A
   Jane, Woolfardisworthy 1620 [W]
   Joan, Tawstock 1643 A
   Mear Joan, Tawstock 1644 A
   John, Witheridge 1571 W
   Mere alias Upcoate John, Witheridge 1574 W

John, Lapford 1620 [W]
Mear Margaret, Zeal Monachorum 1675 W
Mear Mary, Fremington 1774 W
Peter, Fremington 1733 W
Mear Robert, Lynton 1600 W
Meare alias Upcott Thomas, Witheridge 1644 A
Mear Thomas, Bideford 1780 W
William, Witheridge 1615 [W]
Mearles, Marles, Mirles
Marles Elizabeth, Burrington 1772 A
Susan, Ashreigney 1743 A
Mirles William, Roborough 1586 I
Meash Richard, North Molton 1763 W
Meaye see May
Meddon, Medon
Anthony, Buckland Brewer 1673 [W]
Baldwin, Buckland Brewer 1667 A
Catherine, Buckland Brewer 1586 W
Catherine, Bideford, sp. 12 May 1803 W; A dbn 1813
Elizabeth, Alwington 1673 A
John, Buckland Brewer 1606 W
John, Buckland Brewer, jnr. 1639 W
John, Buckland Brewer 1644 W
John, East Putford 1664 W
John, Newton St Petrock 1673 [W]
John, Newton St Petrock 1690 A
John, Alwington 1711 W
John, Alwington 1733 W
John, Alwington 1776 A
John, Alwington 1812 W
John, Alwington 1829 A, 1831 A and 1837 A
Medon alias Smyth Nicholas, Combe Martin 1661 W
Philip, Iddesleigh 1625 [W]
Thomas, Buckland Brewer 1622 [W]
Thomas, Alwington 1696 W
Thomas, Alwington 1721 A
Thomasine, Bideford 1712 A
Valentine, Buckland Brewer 1667 A
William, Buckland Brewer 1622 [W]
William, Alwington 1641 [W]
William, Buckland Brewer 1670 A
William, Bideford 1691 A
William, Bideford 1712 A
William, Alwington 1715 W
Medford see Madford
Medland, Medlande
Henry, Iddesleigh 1597 [W]
Hugh, Great Torrington 1736 W
Jane, Chulmleigh 1668 W
Medlande Robert, Parkham 1617 [W]
William, Great Torrington 1667 W
Medon see Meddon
Medway, Medwaye
Anthony, Martinhoe 1602 W
Richard, Martinhoe 1574 A
Medwaye William, Martinhoe 1580 W
Medylton see Middleton
Meek John, Clovelly 1729 W
Meicer John, Northam 1691 A
Meldon, Melton
Melton Hugh, North Molton 1688 W
Joseph, Molland 1716 A
Thomas, South Molton 1669 W
William, Oakford 1683 A
Melhuish, Melhuich, Melhuishe, Melhush, Melhushe,
   Melhuysh, Melhuyshe, Mellhuyshe, Melluish, Meshnish
..., High Bickington 1603 [W]
..., High Bickington 1665 W
Alice, Cruwys Morchard 1611 [W]; forename blank in Ms;
   supplied from parish register
Melhuyshe Anthony, Martinhoe 1619 [W]
Melhuyshe David, Knowstone 1563 W
Dorcas, Heanton Punchardon 1738 A
Melhuyshe Edward, Oakford 1637 W
Melhuyshe Ferdinand, Cruwys Morchard 1637 W

Francis, Cruwys Morchard 1676 W
George, Cruwys Morchard 1602 W and 1604 W
Melhuyshe George, Puddington 1623 [W]
Grace, Cruwys Morchard 1616 [W]
Grace, Little Torrington 1711 W
Grace see also George Berry
Melhuyshe Hugh, Witheridge 1578 W
Melhuishe Humphrey, Cruwys Morchard 1645 W
Humphrey, Chittlehampton 1679 W
Humphrey, Chittlehampton 1708 W
Humphrey, Thelbridge 1714 W
Melluish Humphrey, Puddington 1748 W
Jane, Witheridge 1845 W
Mellhuyshe Joan, Witheridge 1574 W
Joan, Cruwys Morchard 1609 [W]; forename blank in Ms;
   supplied from parish register
Melhushe John, Martinhoe 1573 W
Melhuyshe John, Cruwys Morchard 1621 [W]
Melhuysh John, Martinhoe 1644 W
John, Chittlehampton 1738 W
John, Puddington 1738 W
John, Cruwys Morchard 1832 W
Lodovic, Cruwys Morchard 1644 A
Lodovic, Witheridge 1687 W
Mary, Chawleigh 1731 W
Mary, Washford Pyne 1753 W
Mary, Tawstock 1755 W
Nicholas, Witheridge 1694 W
Paul, Merton 1668 W
Philip, Huish 1685 W
Melhuishe Richard, Warkleigh 1595 [W]
Richard, Woolfardisworthy 1682 W
Melluish Richard, Woolfardisworthy 1723 W
Richard, Cruwys Morchard 1753 W
Melhuishe Robert, Cruwys Morchard 1591 [W]
Meshnish Robert, Woolfardisworthy 1769 A
Robert, Oakford 1842 W
Roger, Northam 1745 W
Meshnish Rose, Woolfardisworthy 1771 W
Melhushe Thomas, Cruwys Morchard 1575 W
Thomas, Merton 1662 W
Thomas, Ashreigney 1668 W
Thomas, Cruwys Morchard 1698 W and 1699 W
Thomas, Northam, esquire 1704 W
Thomas, Little Torrington 1707 W
Melhuich Thomas, Puddington 1773 W
Thomas, Woolfardisworthy, yeoman 1817 A to Robert, son
William, Martinhoe 1565 W
Meller ..., Combe Martin 1602 [W] and 1605 [W]
John, Combe Martin 1592 [W]
Thomas, St Giles in the Wood 1595 [W]
Mellett, Mellet
..., Twitchen 1612 [W]
Mellet Elizabeth, North Molton 1584 W
Mellhuyshe, Melluish see Melhuish
Melton see Meldon
Menhinnit, Menhinit
Joseph, West Down, yeoman 1809 W
Menhinit Joseph, West Down 1851 W
Mennard, Mennerd, Meunard
Ambrose, Shebbear 1592 [W]
John, Little Torrington 1597 [W]
Mary, Shebbear 1591 [W]
Mennerd Philip, Shebbear 1606 [W]; forename blank in Ms;
   supplied from parish register
Mennard or Meunard Robert, Shebbear 1590 [W]
Merchant, Merchante see Marchant
Merdon see Mardon
Mere see Meare
Meredith John, Bideford 1735 A
   William, Northam 1723 A
Merefeild, Merifilde see Merryfield
Merrice see Morris
Merrick see Myrick
Merridee Thomas, Bideford 1732 W

Merrifelde, Merrifield see Merryfield
Merrill Richard, Great Torrington 1728 W
Merryfield, Merefeild, Merifilde, Merrifelde, Merrifield,
    Merryfeild, Meryfild, Myrifild
    Elizabeth, Bideford 1737 W
    Merryfeild George, North Tawton 1622 [W]
    Meryfild John, Langtree 1570 W
    Merryfeild John, Iddesleigh 1642 A
    Merrifield Mary, Westleigh 1805 W
    Merefeild Philip, Bideford 1605 [W]; forename blank in Ms;
      supplied from parish register
    Merifilde Roger, Iddesleigh 1571 W
    Merrifelde Thomas, Iddesleigh 1569 W
    Merryfeild Thomas, Langtree 1622 [W]
    Myrifild Thomas, King's Nympton 1685 W
    Thomas, Bideford 1732 W and 1736 W
Merryman Lawrence, Fremington 1721 W
Mersey George, Great Torrington 1709 A
Mersh see Marsh
Mershall see Marshall
Merson Elizabeth, North Molton 1815 [W]
    Elizabeth Tanner, North Molton 1845 W
    Francis, North Molton 1822 A to Elizabeth Tanner Merson,
      widow
    John, North Molton 1845 W
    Richard, North Molton 1857 W
Mervin John, Heanton Punchardon 1730 W
    John, Parkham 1771 W
    Margaret, Barnstaple 1723 W
    Richard, Heanton Punchardon 1689 A
Meryfild see Merryfield
Meshnish see Melhuish
Metherell, Metherel
    Edmund, Barnstaple 1721 W
    Grace, Frithelstock 1725 A
    Metherel John, Winkleigh 1713 W
    Margaret, Barnstaple 1755 A
    Metherel Thomas, Hartland 1762 W
    Metherel William, Hartland 1752 W
Meunard or Mennard Robert, Shebbear 1590 [W]
Meyre see Mayer
Michael, Michall, Michaell
    Daniel, Barnstaple 1682 W
    Michall alias Back Mary, South Molton 1831 W
    Michaell Thomas, Dolton 1586 A
Michell, Mictchell see Mitchell
Middleton, Medylton, Middelton, Midleton, Midlton,
    Myddleton
    ..., Northam 1613 [W]
    Midlton Anthony, Bideford 1667 W
    Myddleton Clase, Abbotsham 1634 A
    Myddleton Clase, Abbotsham 1635 W
    Elizabeth wife of Robert see John Clark
    Midleton George, Bideford, snr. 1684 W
    Midleton George, Bideford 1702 W
    Midleton Henry, Abbotsham 1584 W
    Joan, Abbotsham, widow 1607 [W]; forename blank in Ms;
      supplied from parish register
    Medylton John, Instow 1564 W
    Middelton John, Abbotsham 1603 W
    Midleton Richard, Bideford 1682 W
    Richard, Meeth 1765 A
Myddleton see Middleton
Midland Thomas, Dolton 1831 W
Midleton, Midlton see Middleton
Mildon, Mylden, Myldon
    ..., Knowstone 1613 [W]
    Amy, Chittlehampton 1832 W
    Ann, Chittlehampton 1795 A
    Bartholomew, Chittlehampton 1802 A
    Bartholomew, Chittlehampton 1827 W
    Myldon Elizabeth, Molland 1573 A
    Elizabeth, South Molton 1782 W
    George, Chittlehampton 1764 W
    Henry, Knowstone 1641 W
    Henry, Knowstone 1733 W

Henry, Chittlehampton 1804 W
Henry, King's Nympton 1852 W
Mylden Joan, Bow 1633 W
Joan, Chittlehampton 1763 W
Myldon John, Molland 1569 W
John, South Molton 1622 [W]
John, Chawleigh 1627 [W]
John, Oakford 1641 W
John, South Molton 1674 W
John, Chittlehampton 1731 W
John, West Worlington 1738 A
John, Chittlehampton 1753 W and 1769 W
John, Chittlehampton 1829 W
John, Chittlehampton 1833 A to William of South Molton,
    brother
Lawrence, Knowstone 1597 [W]
Mary, Chittlehampton 1841 W
Myldon Nicholas, Roborough 1578 W
Peter, Chittlehampton 1790 W
Peter, Chittlehampton 1810 W
Peter, Chittlehampton 1825 A to Elizabeth, widow
Rebecca, Chittlehampton 1774 W
Myldon Robert, Winkleigh 1589 W
Robert, Berrynarbor 1704 A
Thomas, South Molton 1716 W
Thomas, South Molton 1750 W
William, Oakford 1643 A
William, King's Nympton, yeoman 1797 W
Milford, Milforde, Millford, Mylford
    ..., Lapford 1614 [W]
    Mylford Agnes, Lapford 1603 W
    Alice, Bow 1617 [W], 1625 [W] and 1634 W
    Arthur, Shirwell 1683 A
    Millford Chamond, Bondleigh 1668 W
    Christopher, Bondleigh 1743 A
    Mylford Edward, Lapford 1602 W
    Millford Hannah, Zeal Monachorum 1703 A
    Henry, Dolton 1663 W
    Henry, Tawstock 1731 W
    Mylford James, Lapford 1583 W
    Mylford Joan, Lapford 1576 W
    Millford Joan, Bondleigh 1698 W
    Mylford John, Zeal Monachorum 1577 W
    John, Lapford 1629 [W]
    Millford John, Bondleigh 1698 W
    Margaret, Wembworthy 1713 W
    Michael, Zeal Monachorum 1699 A
    Peter, Coldridge 1621 [W]
    Reginald, Bow 1616 [W]
    Richard, Lapford 1595 [W]
    Milforde Roger, Zeal Monachorum 1567 W
    Roger, Lapford 1668 A
    Samuel, Iddesleigh 1670 [W]
    Mylford Thomas, Lapford 1583 W
    Thomas, Chittlehampton 1622 [W]
    William, Buckland Brewer 1642 A
Mill, Myll
    Christopher, Pilton, butcher 1822 A to Grace, widow
    Myll Henry, Warkleigh 1583 W
    Hugh, Newton Tracey, yeoman 1814 A to John White, son
    Myll James, Chittlehampton 1581 A
    Myll John, Parkham, snr. 1572 W
    John, Clovelly 1692 W
    John, Beaford 1805 A
    John, Merton, yeoman 1807 W
    John, Merton 1810 W
    Mary, Bideford 1692 A
    Mary, Bideford, widow 1810 W
    Richard, Welcombe 1721 W
    Richard, Hartland 1767 W
    Robert, Chulmleigh 1595 [W]
    Robert, North Molton 1600 W
    Robert, Beaford 1833 W
    Sarah, Hartland 1752 A
    Stephen, Shebbear 1832 W

Thomas, East Putford 1673 [W]
Thomas, Barnstaple 1830 A
William, Welcombe 1666 W
William, Bideford 1695 W and 1714 A
William, Buckland Brewer 1735 A
William, Bideford 1761 A
William, Fremington 1795 A
William, Northam 1826 A to Elizabeth, widow
Millar see Miller
Millard, Millerd
    Ann, Winkleigh 1739 W
    Millerd Oliver, Instow 1701 W
Millegan Joseph, Filleigh 1820 A
Miller, Millar
    Catherine, Fremington 1710 W
    Millar Edward, Combe Martin 1674 W
    Elizabeth, Fremington 1621 [W]
    George, Northam 1624 [W] and 1626 O
    George, Instow 1693 W
    James, Instow 1619 [W]
    John, Northam 1621 [W]
    John, East Down 1622 [W]
    John, Lynton 1661 W
    John, Goodleigh 1665 A
    John, Instow 1700 A
    John, Chulmleigh 1828 W
    Millar Robina Craig, Ilfracombe 1844 W
    Thomas, Chulmleigh 1848 W
Millerd see Millard
Milles see Mills
Millford see Milford
Milling Thomas, Challacombe 1636 A
Millman, Milman
    Francis, Shebbear 1721 W
    James, Buckland Filleigh 1735 A
    James, Buckland Filleigh 1820 W
    Mary, Buckland Filleigh 1782 W
    Milman Miles, Shebbear 1621 [W]
    Richard, Langtree 1665 W
    Shadrach, Shebbear 1689 W
    Susan, Shebbear 1803 W
    William, Buckland Filleigh 1717 W
    William, Shebbear 1798 W
    William, Barnstaple, mariner 1855 A to Mary, widow
Mills, Milles, Mylls
    Milles Alice, Barnstaple 1622 [W]
    Alice, Warkleigh 1677 W
    Catherine, Bideford 1847 W
    Christopher, Pilton 1846 A; A dbn
    Edward, South Molton 1683 W
    Elias, Burrington 1843 A to Jane, widow
    Mills alias Rudge Elizabeth, South Molton 1679 A
    Milles Francis, Clovelly 1615 [W]
    Hugh, Beaford 1729 A
    Humphrey, Satterleigh 1786 W
    Humphrey, Burrington 1820 A
    Humphrey, Tawstock 1820 A
    Humphrey, Barnstaple 1856 W
    Mylls James, Barnstaple 1633 A
    James, Langtree 1846 W
    James Nancekivell see John Essery
    Jenny, Barnstaple 1852 W
    Joan, Filleigh 1678 W
    Mylls John, Barnstaple 1633 [W]
    John, Barnstaple 1671 W
    John, Northam 1711 W
    John, Hartland 1763 W
    John, Warkleigh, yeoman 1799 W
    John, South Molton 1822 W
    Mills alias Coplestone Mary, Bideford 1695 A
    Nicholas, East Putford 1678 A
    Richard, North Tawton 1645 A
    Richard, Barnstaple 1706 W
    Samuel, Northam 1669 A
    Mylls Simon, Barnstaple 1580 A

Thomas, Filleigh 1678 [W]
William, South Molton 1678 W
William, Loxhore 1766 W
William, Barnstaple 1819 W
William, Warkleigh 1829 W
William, Chittlehampton 1856 W
Millward, Millwood see Milward
Milman see Millman
Milton, Mylten, Mylton
    Anstis, South Molton 1780 W
    Mylton Edward, Chawleigh 1639 W
    Elizabeth, High Bray 1767 A
    James, Bideford 1735 W
    Joan, Burrington 1733 A
    Mylten John, Witheridge 1571 W
    John, Langtree 1597 [W]
    John, Twitchen 1688 W
    John, Atherington 1704 A
    John, Great Torrington 1739 W
    John, Atherington 1766 A
    John, Fremington 1776 W
    John, Atherington 1847 W
    John see also Thomas Cheek
    Margaret, Bideford 1742 A
    Richard, Chittlehampton 1669 [W]
    Robert, Chittlehampton 1769 A
    Robert, Chittlehampton 1793 A
    Susan, Chittlehampton 1745 W
    Thomas, Atherington 1738 A
    Thomas, North Molton, miller 1807 W
    William, Atherington 1699 A and 1725 A
    William, South Molton 1730 W
    William, Molland 1856 W
Milward, Millward, Millwood
    Agnes, Barnstaple 1740 W
    Francis, St Giles in the Wood 1841 W
    Millwood John, Goodleigh 1692 W
    John, Barnstaple 1724 W
    Millward Thomas, St Giles in the Wood, yeoman 1800 W
    William, Roborough 1844 W
Mineard William, Dolton 1773 A
Mirfield, Murfeild, Murfeilde, Myrfild
    Murfeild Ann, Dolton 1668 A
    Myrfild Ebbot, Iddesleigh 1573 A
    Murfeilde Joan, Petrockstowe 1603 W
    Murfeild John, Bideford 1643 A
    Murfeild Thomas, Petrockstowe 1597 [W]
Mirles see Mearles
Mitchell, Michell, Mictchell, Mitchel, Mutchell, Mychell
    ..., Dolton 1615 [W]
    Michell ..., Bow 1624 [W]
    Amiel, Ashreigney 1687 A
    Amiel, Ashreigney 1719 A
    Amiel, Ashreigney 1793 W
    Amiel, Witheridge 1834 W
    Michell Catherine, Great Torrington 1624 [W]
    Dorothy, Great Torrington 1705 W
    Elizabeth, Beaford 1728 W
    George, Ashreigney 1751 W
    George, Ashreigney 1840 A to Eleanor, widow
    Grace, Barnstaple 1715 A
    Grace see also Elizabeth Lock
    Hannah, Ashreigney 1762 W
    Honor, Great Torrington 1848 W
    James, Barnstaple 1720 W
    Mitchel Jane or Mary, Merton 1715 W
    Michell alias Uppington John, South Molton 1577 W
    Mychell John, Beaford 1578 W
    Mychell John, Barnstaple 1634 A
    John, Beaford 1688 W and 1700 W
    John, Ashreigney 1712 W
    John, Great Torrington 1735 A
    John, Merton 1795 W
    John, Chulmleigh 1826 W
    Mary, Witheridge 1825 W

Ogilby, Bideford 1707 A
Philip, Ashreigney 1725 A
Philip, Ashreigney 1835 W
Michell Phineas, Great Torrington 1645 W
Phineas, Great Torrington 1660 W
Phineas, Great Torrington 1692 A
Mitchell alias Whitlock Richard, Ashreigney 1663 [W]
Richard, Burrington 1722 W
Richard, North Tawton 1781 W
Michell Robert, Barnstaple 1622 [W] and 1628 [W]
Samuel, Northam 1721 W
Samuel, Chulmleigh 1814 W
Michell Thomas, Little Torrington 1624 [W]
Mutchell Walter, Ashreigney 1674 [W]
Michell William, Beaford 1599 [W]
William, Ashreigney 1777 W
Moase, Moise
Moise ..., Chawleigh 1600 A
Amy, Buckland Filleigh 1836 W
Moise Ann, Buckland Brewer 1854 W
James, Woolfardisworthy 1850 W
James, Parkham 1856 W
Miriam, Bideford 1826 W
Richard, Frithelstock 1846 W
Rowland, Bideford, mason 1811 A
Rowland, Bideford 1836 A
Rowland, Frithelstock 1839 W
Moccom, Moccomb see Morcombe
Mock, Mocke
..., Buckland Brewer 1612 [W]
..., Heanton Punchardon 1612 [W]
Mocke Agnes, Fremington 1567 W
Mocke Ann, Buckland Brewer 1585 A
Edward, West Buckland 1617 W
Mocke James, Loxhore 1624 [W]
Mocke John, Highampton 1577 A
John, Shebbear 1664 W
John, Winkleigh 1672 A
John, Loxhore 1680 A
Joseph, Braunton 1846 A
Mary, Chittlehampton 1692 A
Mocke Nicholas, Yarnscombe 1571 W
Samuel, Shirwell 1775 W
Thomas, Chittlehampton 1687 W
Thomas, Buckland Brewer 1688 A
Thomas, Warkleigh 1749 W
William, Bideford 1827 W
Mockford Thomas, ship *Edinburgh* 1749 W
Mocknell Sarah, Bideford 1756 A
Modgford see Mogford
Modland Ann, Great Torrington 1745 W
Moell see Mole
Moer see Moore
Moffatt, Muffatt
Muffatt William, Northam 1749 A
Mogan, Mogen
Alban, Barnstaple 1731 A
Mogen alias Morrice Joan, George Nympton 1607 [W];
   forename blank in Ms; supplied from parish register
Mogeridg, Mogeridge see Muggeridge
Moges, Moggis
Joseph, Barnstaple 1743 A
Moggis alias Moggeridge William, Challacombe 1606 W
Mogford, Magford, Modgford, Mogforde
..., Rose Ash 1601 A
..., Bondleigh 1606 [W]
..., Rackenford 1609 [W]
..., East Worlington 1612 [W] and O
..., Rose Ash 1617 [W]
Agnes, Chittlehampton 1581 W
Alfred, Witheridge 1694 W
Ann, Stoodleigh 1588 W
Modgford Beatrice, Mortehoe 1576 W
David, Rose Ash 1629 [W]
Elizabeth, Cheldon 1615 O

Elizabeth, Bideford 1759 A
George, Oakford 1575 A
Modgford George, Rackenford 1577 A
George, Filleigh 1626 [W]
George, Filleigh 1636 [W] and O
Henry, Knowstone 1635 A
Humphrey, Great Torrington 1619 [W]
Mogforde John, Petrockstowe 1571 W
John, West Worlington 1592 [W]
Mogforde John, Chulmleigh 1592 [W]
John, Knowstone 1595 [W]
Magford alias Mugford John, Hartland 1601 W
John, Cruwys Morchard 1613 [W]; forename blank in Ms;
   supplied from parish register
John, Meshaw 1615 [W]
John, Knowstone 1623 [W]
John, Rose Ash 1641 W
John, Oakford 1692 W
John, Oakford 1727 W
John, Witheridge 1727 A
John, Knowstone 1731 W
Jude, Rose Ash 1629 [W]
Lodovic, Oakford 1710 W
Lucretia, Knowstone 1805 A
Margaret, West Worlington 1626 [W]
Peter, South Molton 1740 W
Richard, West Worlington 1593 [W]
Richard, Hartland 1626 [W]
Richard, Chittlehampton 1645 A
Robert, Alwington, yeoman 1810 W
Mogford alias Creusey Vincent, Chittlehampton 1565 W
Mogforde William, Mortehoe 1566 W
William, Rose Ash 1671 W
William, Hartland 1694 A
William, Knowstone, tailor 1796 A
William, Oakford, yeoman 1808 W
Mogforde Willmot, Knowstone 1564 W
Willmot, Burrington 1639 W
   see also Mugford
Moggeride, Moggeridg, Moggeridge, Moggridg, Moggridge see
   Muggeridge
Moggis see Moges
Mogridge, Mogrudge see Muggeridge
Mogworthy see Muxworthy
Moire see Moore
Moise see Moase
Molande see Molland
Mole, Moell, Moll, Molle
Molle ..., North Molton 1612 [W]
Molle Anthony, North Molton 1589 W
Molle Charles, North Molton 1617 [W] and 1619 [W]
Molle Clement, Fremington 1621 [W]
Edward, Ilfracombe 1624 [W]
Edward, Clovelly 1640 O
Molle Elizabeth, North Molton, widow 1612 [W]; forename
   blank in Ms; supplied from parish register
Elizabeth, High Bray 1620 [W]
Molle Helen, Fremington 1628 [W]
Henry, North Molton 1599 [W]
Molle Henry, North Molton 1684 W
Moll John, Stoke Rivers 1563 W
Moell John, North Molton 1583 A
Molle John, North Molton 1596 [W]
Molle John, Rose Ash 1597 [W]
Molle John, Pilton 1622 [W]
John, North Molton, jnr. 1717 W
John, North Molton 1774 W
Mathew, West Anstey 1725 W
Miriam, North Molton, widow 1808 A
Moll Rachel, Barnstaple 1740 W
Molle Richard, Rose Ash 1566 W
Molle Richard, East Down 1593 [W]
Thomas, Frithelstock 1605 W
Thomas, Ilfracombe 1671 W
Molle William, Littleham (near Bideford) 1622 [W]

William, North Molton 1640 O
Moll William, North Molton 1660 W
   see also Moule
Molford ...., King's Nympton 1610 [W]
   Grace, North Tawton 1644 W
   Roger, Cadbury 1597 [W]
   Roger, Burrington 1641 W
   Roger, Burrington 1672 W
   Susan, Great Torrington 1617 [W]
   Zenobia, Burrington 1676 W
Moll see Mole
Molland, Molande
   ..., Yarnscombe 1603 [W]
   ..., Lapford 1607 [W]
   ..., Burrington 1611 [W]
   Agnes, Burrington 1624 [W]
   Agnes see also John Blackmore
   Arthur, Ashreigney 1743 A
   Charity, Ashreigney 1733 W
   Edmund, King's Nympton 1639 W
   George, Alverdiscott 1604 W
   Henry, South Molton 1741 A
   Hugh, Ashreigney 1719 W and 1727 W
   James, Huntshaw 1681 A
   James, Huntshaw 1736 A
   James, Beaford 1784 W
   James, Ashreigney 1830 W and A to Margaret, widow
   Joan, Lapford 1623 [W]
   Joan, King's Nympton 1625 [W]
   Joan or John, Lapford 1573 W
   Joan or John, Burrington 1585 W
   John, King's Nympton 1575 A
   John, King's Nympton 1593 [W]
   John, South Molton 1643 A
   John, Lapford 1707 W
   John, Burrington 1733 W
   John, Lapford 1734 A
   John, Huntshaw 1753 W
   John, Ashreigney 1755 W
   John, High Bickington 1762 W
   John, East Worlington 1767 A
   John, Winkleigh 1796 W
   John, Ashreigney 1797 W*
   Margaret, Burrington 1620 [W]
   Margery, Ashreigney 1733 W
   Mathew, High Bickington 1766 A
   Nicholas, King's Nympton 1639 W
   Philip, Ashreigney 1720 W and 1725 W
   Philip, High Bickington 1757 A
   Philip, Beaford 1787 A
   Philip, Roborough 1840 W
   Richard, Ashreigney 1752 W
   Richard, Roborough 1761 W
   Robert, Lapford 1699 W
   Robert, Lapford 1762 W
   Roger, Burrington 1639 W
   Roger, Great Torrington 1691 W
   Roger, Parkham 1694 W
   Samuel, Chulmleigh 1726 W
   Samuel, Winkleigh 1741 A
   Molande Thomas, Burrington 1618 [W]
   Thomas, Burrington 1639 A
   Thomas, Ashreigney 1729 W
   Thomas, Lapford 1732 A
   Thomas, Ashreigney 1777 A
   Thomas, Winkleigh 1848 W
   Thomasine, Huntshaw 1698 A
   William, Ashreigney 1718 W
   William, Ashreigney 1750 A
   William, North Tawton 1827 A to Mary, widow
Molle see Mole
Mollens see Mullins
Molton, Moulton
   ..., Romansleigh 1611 [W]
   Elizabeth, High Bickington 1574 A

James, Bideford 1662 A
John, High Bickington 1582 W
Molton alias Tolly John, Instow 1601 W
John, South Molton 1630 [W]
John, Westleigh 1721 W
Marian, South Molton 1631 [W]
Moulton Mary, Westleigh 1725 W
Philip, Romansleigh 1575 W
Philip, Hartland 1684 A
Richard, Dolton 1570 W
Richard, Instow 1615 [W]
Robert, Romansleigh 1597 [W]
Thomasine, Instow 1595 [W]
William, Romansleigh 1679 A
Moncke see Monk
Monckleigh, Monckley see Monkleigh
Moneland Richard, Burrington 1564 W
Monjoy see Mountjoy
Monk, Moncke, Muncke
   Muncke Anthony, Martinhoe 1580 W
   Moncke Anthony, Martinhoe 1620 [W]
   Moncke Catherine, Parkham 1595 [W]
   Moncke Jane, Martinhoe 1623 [W]
   Moncke John, Martinhoe 1599 [W]
   John, Great Torrington 1795 W
Monkleigh, Monckleigh, Monckley, Monkley
   Monckleigh Ann, Buckland Brewer 1600 W
   Monckleigh Bridget, Great Torrington 1618 [W]
   Monkley Elizabeth, Great Torrington 1833 W
   Monckley John, Great Torrington 1730 W
   Monkley John, Hartland, mason 1797 W
   Monkley Samuel, Great Torrington 1767 W
Monne see Moone
Monnier James, Barnstaple 1746 A
   James, Barnstaple 1806 A
Monsey see Mounsey
Monynge see Manning
Moone, Moon
   ..., Little Torrington 1603 [W]
   Ann, Bideford 1732 W
   Elizabeth, Chulmleigh 1626 [W]
   Moon Elizabeth, Bideford 1780 W
   George, Fremington 1758 W
   Hugh, Fremington 1675 W
   Joan, Bideford, widow 1571 W
   Monne John, Bideford 1527 W
   John, Chulmleigh 1619 [W]
   John, Dolton 1663 W
   John, Marwood 1663 A
   Moon John, Tawstock 1738 W
   Joseph, Mortehoe 1711 W and 1715 W
   Joseph, West Down 1728 W
   Lambert, Atherington 1633 A
   Margaret, Mortehoe 1689 W
   Moon Margaret, High Bickington 1746 W
   Mary, Fremington 1670 W
   Philip, Great Torrington 1629 [W]
   Richard, Littleham (near Bideford) 1684 A
   Richard, West Down 1695 A
   Richard, West Down 1722 W
   Moon Richard, West Down 1765 W
   Moon Richard, Bideford 1775 W
   Moon Robert, Parracombe 1809 W
   Rowland, Frithelstock 1768 W
   Moon Sarah, Bideford 1776 W
   Moon Thomas, ship *Hampton Court* 1763 W
   Moon Thomas, Barnstaple 1793 W
   Moon Thomas, Barnstaple, broker 1805 W
   Moon Thomas, Bideford 1815 W
   Moon Thomas, Barnstaple 1833 W
   William, Great Torrington 1633 W
   William, Bideford 1698 A
   Moon William, Bideford 1726 W
   Moon William, High Bickington 1741 A
   Moon William, Bideford 1756 W

Moore, Moer, Moire, More, Mowre
Moore alias Smaldon ..., South Molton 1603 W
..., Chulmleigh 1608 [W]
..., Loxhore 1608 [W]
..., Huntshaw 1609 [W]
..., North Tawton 1609 [W]
..., Nymet Rowland 1611 [W]
..., Stoke Rivers 1611 [W]
..., West Anstey 1611 [W]
..., Mariansleigh 1613 [W]
Abraham, Shebbear 1705 A
Agnes, Great Torrington 1625 [W]
Agrippa, Winkleigh 1772 W
Alexander, Bideford 1621 [W]
Alexander, Combe Martin 1641 W
Alice, Chawleigh 1620 [W]
Alice, Arlington 1637 W
Alice, Chulmleigh 1673 [W]
Alice, Tawstock 1727 W
Amesius, Molland 1682 W
More Ananias, Witheridge 1738 W
Ananias, Witheridge 1793 W
Ann, Bideford 1638 W
Ann, Chittlehampton 1682 W
Ann, Bow 1721 W
Ann, Great Torrington 1783 W
More Anthony, Molland 1566 W
Arthur, Buckland Brewer 1641 A
Bartholomew, High Bray 1702 W
Courtenay, Alverdiscott, gentleman 1707 [W]
More David, Arlington 1587 W
David, Loxhore 1723 W
Moire Edward, Zeal Monachorum 1573 W
Edward, Eggesford 1643 A
Elizabeth, Tawstock 1603 W
Emanuel, Molland 1613 [W]; forename blank in Ms; supplied
   from parish register
Emanuel, Molland 1670 A
Emma, Tawstock, sp. 1851 [W] to John and William
Frances, North Molton 1688 W
Francis, Loxhore 1725 A
Francis, Bideford 1735 A
George, Thelbridge 1617 [W]
George, Great Torrington 1621 [W]
George, Woolfardisworthy 1642 A
George, Molland 1683 W
George, Ashreigney 1700 W
George, Barnstaple 1728 W
George, Great Torrington 1746 A
George, Great Torrington 1757 W
George, Twitchen 1844 W
Grace, High Bray 1644 W
Grace, Winkleigh 1672 W
Gregory, East Anstey 1706 A
Griffith, Frithelstock 1691 A
Hannah, Bideford 1755 W
Henry, Abbotsham 1664 W
Henry, Tawstock 1671 W
Henry, Tawstock 1702 W
Henry, Tawstock 1733 W
Henry, Molland 1775 A
Henry, Molland 1843 W
Hugh, Challacombe 1598 [W]
Hugh, West Worlington 1621 [W]
Hugh, Tawstock 1754 W
Hugh, Tawstock 1802 A
James, Langtree 1693 W
James, Barnstaple 1696 A
Jane, Bideford 1643 A
Jane, Bideford 1764 W
Joan, Bideford 1595 [W]
Joan, Roborough 1595 [W]
Joan, Molland 1599 [W]
Joan, Huntshaw 1620 [W]
Joan, Kentisbury 1623 [W]

Joan, Molland 1775 W
Joan, Molland, widow 1847 A to Sarah wife of David
   Maunder, yeoman, daughter
John, Westleigh 1570 W
John, Lapford 1573 W
More John, Arlington 1576 W
More John, Zeal Monachorum 1580 W
More alias Mare John, Barnstaple 1581 W
More John, St Giles in the Wood 1588 W
Moer John, Twitchen 1589 A
More John, Weare Giffard 1589 W
John, Twitchen 1590 [W]
John, Bideford 1593 [W]
John, Mariansleigh 1596 [W]
John, North Tawton 1601 W
John, Iddesleigh, snr. 1619 [W]
John 1622 [W]
John, Great Torrington 1629 [W]
John, High Bickington 1633 [W]
John, St Giles in the Wood 1635 W
John, Dolton 1639 A
John, Thelbridge 1639 A
John, Great Torrington 1669 A
John, Bow 1674 W
John, Fremington 1674 W
John, Parkham 1676 A
John, Great Torrington 1687 W
John, Loxhore 1690 W
John, Molland 1690 W
John, Sheepwash 1705 A
John, Beaford 1707 A
John, Oakford 1731 W
John, North Tawton 1733 W
John, Molland 1744 A
John, Bideford 1745 W
John, Tawstock 1766 W
John, Hartland 1774 W
John, Newton St Petrock 1780 W
John, Twitchen, yeoman 1810 A
John, Molland 1815 W
John, Tawstock 1830 W
John, Molland 1848 W
John, Hartland 1851 W
John, Great Torrington 1856 W
Jonathan, High Bickington 1823 W
Joseph, Sheepwash 1679 W
Mowre Margaret, Westleigh 1582 W
More Margaret, Thelbridge 1587 W
Margaret, Tawstock 1705 W
Margaret, South Molton 1832 W
More Margery, Westleigh 1571 W
Margery, Iddesleigh 1635 W
Mary, Tawstock 1617 [W]
Mary, Sheepwash 1680 A
Mary, Twitchen 1853 W
Mathew, Tawstock 1668 W
Michael, Tawstock 1682 A
Nicholas, Tawstock 1704 W
Nicholas, St Giles in the Wood 1716 W
Nicholas, Tawstock 1727 A
Peter, Great Torrington 1639 W
Philip, Molland 1670 A and 1672 C
Philip, Sheepwash 1710 W
Philip, Ilfracombe 1792 W
Moor Philip, South Molton 1812 W
More Richard, Molland 1585 W
More Richard, Rackenford 1587 W
Moer Richard, Bideford 1589 A
Richard, Instow 1591 [W]
Richard, Weare Giffard 1595 [W] and 1596 [W]
Richard, Bratton Fleming 1619 [W]
Richard, Molland 1670 A
Richard, Tawstock 1706 W
Richard, Molland 1750 W and 1761 W
Richard, High Bickington, butcher 1809 A

Robert, Molland 1599 [W]
Robert, Shebbear 1604 W
Robert, Tawstock 1613 [W]; forename blank in Ms; supplied
  from parish register
Robert, Sheepwash 1623 [W]
Robert, Winkleigh 1637 W
Robert, Chittlehampton 1732 W
Roger, Great Torrington 1673 [W]
Roger, Great Torrington 1717 A
Roger, Great Torrington 1743 W
Roger, Pilton, cordwainer 1802 A
Samuel, Twitchen 1821 W
Sarah, Tawstock 1841 W
Simon, Tawstock 1587 W
Simon, Winkleigh 1643 A
Simon, Lapford 1691 W
Susan, Bideford 1831 W
Theobald, Great Torrington 1599 [W]
More Thomas, Beaford 1568 W
More Thomas, Bow 1587 W
Thomas, South Molton 1591 [W]
Thomas, Tawstock 1615 [W]; forename blank in Ms; supplied
  from parish register
Thomas, Molland 1622 [W]
Thomas, Dolton 1643 W
Thomas, Winkleigh 1669 W
Thomas, Molland 1683 W
Thomasine, Newton St Petrock 1604 W
Thomasine, Great Torrington 1668 W
Walter, Witheridge 1667 W
Walter, Tawstock 1699 W
William, Arlington 1563 W
William, Molland 1600 W
William, Bideford 1605 W
William, Shirwell 1609 [W]; forename blank in Ms; supplied
  from parish register
More William, North Tawton 1636 W
William, Bratton Fleming 1668 W
Winifred, High Bray 1716 [W]
Mooreman, Moorman, Moreman
Moorman Agnes, North Molton 1774 W
Moreman Charity, North Molton 1777 W
Edward, North Molton 1674 A
Elizabeth, North Molton 1688 W
Moorman Elizabeth, North Molton 1718 W
Frances, North Molton 1684 A
George, North Molton 1684 A
Moreman George, Great Torrington 1826 A to Agnes, widow
Henry, High Bray 1733 W and 1746 W
John, North Molton, snr. 1670 W
John, High Bray 1754 W
Mary, North Molton 1718 W
Richard, North Molton 1691 A; forename blank in Ms;
  supplied from parish register
Richard, South Molton 1691 W
Richard, North Molton, snr. 1716 W
Moorman Richard, North Molton 1716 W
Moorman Richard, North Molton 1796 W*
Robert, North Molton 1749 A and 1759 A
Moorman Roger, North Molton 1640 W
Moreman Thomas, North Molton 1583 A
Moorman Thomas, North Molton 1672 [W]
Thomas, Barnstaple 1694 W
Moorman Thomas, North Molton 1718 W
Moreman alias Noreman William, North Molton 1575 W
Morcombe, Moccom, Moccomb, Morcom, Morcomb
Agnes, Meeth 1588 W
Augustine, Hartland 1580 W
Morcomb Christopher, Sheepwash 1680 W
Dorothy, Littleham (near Bideford) 1632 [W]
Elizabeth, Woolfardisworthy 1629 [W]
Ferdinand, Sheepwash 1690 W
Morcomb Ferdinand, Langtree 1703 W
Jane, Frithelstock 1681 W

Moccomb Jason, Littleham (near Bideford) 1606 [W];
  forename blank in Ms; supplied from parish register
Morcomb John, Hartland 1577 W
John, Meeth 1584 W
John, Littleham (near Bideford) 1592 [W] and 1593 [W]
John, Parkham 1625 [W] and 1626 O
John, Shebbear 1630 [W]
John, Littleham (near Bideford) 1632 W
Morcomb John, Littleham (near Bideford) 1645 A
Morcomb John, Littleham (near Bideford) 1676 A
Morcom John, Ashford, jnr. 1817 A to John, yeoman, father
Morcom John, Ashford 1818 W
Morcomb Johnson, Bideford 1679 A
Morcomb Margery, Parkham 1565 W
Margery, Parkham 1598 [W]
Margery, Shebbear 1635 W
Morcomb Mary, Northam 1736 W
Nicholas, Newton St Petrock 1685 W
Morcomb Philip, Woolfardisworthy 1602 W
Philip, Barnstaple 1672 W
Morcomb Philip, Littleham (near Bideford) 1735 A
Philip, Parkham 1854 W
Morcomb Richard, Meeth 1684 A
Morcomb Robert, Hartland 1612 [W]; forename blank in Ms;
  supplied from parish register
Robert, Sheepwash 1626 [W] and 1627 O
Samuel, Sheepwash 1691 A
Morcomb Sarah, Huntshaw 1735 A
Morcomb Sybil, Sheepwash 1702 W
Thomas, Parkham 1564 W
Morcomb Thomas, Shebbear 1706 W
Morcomb Thomas, Bideford 1725 A
Morcom Thomas, Combe Martin 1855 A
Thomasine, Barnstaple 1614 [W]; forename blank in Ms;
  supplied from parish register
William, Sheepwash 1582 A and 1585 O account
William, Northam 1618 [W]
Morcomb William, Meeth 1641 A
Morcom William, Ashford 1830 W
Morcombe alias Claril Willmot, High Bickington 1580 W
Morcomb Wilmot, Hartland 1607 [W]; forename blank in Ms;
  supplied from parish register
More see Moore
Moreman see Mooreman
Mores see Morris
Morewene, Morewyne see Morwen
Morgan
Morgan alias Wood ..., Barnstaple 1644 W
Agnes, Ilfracombe 1678 W
Alexander, Barnstaple 1580 W
Ann, Barnstaple 1767 W
Ann, Barnstaple 1824 W
Catherine, Rackenford 1758 W
Edward, Northam 1769 W
Elizabeth, Barnstaple 1735 W
Evan, Bideford 1676 A
George, Chulmleigh 1694 A
Grace, Barnstaple 1768 W
James, Northam 1625 [W]
James, Barnstaple 1744 A
Jane, Bideford 1736 W
John, Tawstock 1586 A
John, Barnstaple 1760 W
John, South Molton 1794 W
Margaret, Bideford 1680 A
Meredith, East Anstey 1664 A
Philip, Bideford 1665 W
Thomas, Barnstaple 1732 W
William, Little Torrington 1661 [W]
William, Barnstaple, maltster 1797 W
Morice see Morris
Morish see Morrish
Morley George, Stoodleigh 1665 W
Morrell, Marell, Marrell, Morrill
  ..., Iddesleigh 1602 [W]

..., Stoodleigh 1609 [W]
..., Atherington 1611 [W] and 1612 [W]
Alexander, Stoodleigh 1664 A
Bernard, Knowstone 1630 [W]
Catherine, Cruwys Morchard 1636 A
Edward, Woolfardisworthy 1626 [W]
Gertrude, Combe Martin 1669 W
Morrill Grace, Great Torrington 1726 W
Henry, Knowstone 1593 [W]
Marrell John, East Worlington 1587 A
John, Cruwys Morchard 1590 [W]
John, Stoke Rivers 1602 W
John, Barnstaple 1627 [W] and 1629 [W]
John, Yarnscombe 1630 [W]
John, Molland 1638 W
John, Berrynarbor 1643 W
John, Westleigh 1764 W
Leonard, Knowstone 1600 W
Margaret, South Molton 1666 W
Mary, Berrynarbor 1599 [W]
Mary, Knowstone 1623 [W]
Nicholas, Combe Martin 1599 [W]
Nicholas, Combe Martin 1665 [W]
Philip, Knowstone 1634 W
Marell Richard, Chulmleigh 1639 W
Richard, Woolfardisworthy 1673 W
Thomas, Stoke Rivers 1605 W
Thomas, St Giles in the Wood 1639 A
Walter, South Molton 1603 W
William, Kentisbury 1623 [W]
Morris, Marris, Merrice, Mores, Morice, Morrice, Morrise,
     Murris
Anthony, Rose Ash 1700 W
David, Ilfracombe 1830 A to Mary, widow
Eleanor, Combe Martin 1675 W and 1690 W
Eleanor, Hartland 1749 W
Elizabeth, Meshaw 1580 W
Morrice alias Mogen Joan, George Nympton 1607 [W];
     forename blank in Ms; supplied from parish register
Joan, Bideford 1706 A
Mores John, Meshaw 1565 W
John, Berrynarbor 1582 W
Morice John, Cruwys Morchard 1591 [W]
John, Northam 1693 A
John, Berrynarbor 1697 W
John, Mortehoe 1728 A
Merrice John, Parkham 1738 W
John, West Down 1742 W
John, Chittlehampton 1753 A
John, East Buckland 1816 W
John, Lapford 1826 W
John, South Molton 1828 W
John, Chittlehampton 1837 W
Morrise Morgan, Bideford 1731 W
Mores Nicholas, Ilfracombe 1570 W
Nicholas, Barnstaple 1575 W
Marris Nicholas, Barnstaple 1576 A
Murris Richard, Barnstaple 1580 A
Richard, Knowstone 1588 W
Richard, Bideford 1744 A
Richard, Huntshaw 1758 A
Robert, Stoke Rivers 1702 A
Simon, North Tawton 1700 W
Susan, Combe Martin 1688 A
Thomas, Molland 1675 W
Thomas, North Tawton 1678 A
Thomas, Bideford 1708 A
Thomas, Barnstaple 1741 W
Thomasine, Stoke Rivers 1703 W
William, Meshaw 1573 W
William, Berrynarbor 1588 A
William, Cruwys Morchard 1633 W
William, Combe Martin 1689 W
William, Chittlehampton 1828 A to Agnes, widow
Morrish, Morish, Morrysh, Moryshe
Alice, South Molton 1679 W

Anthony, Monkleigh 1750 W
Bartholomew, North Tawton 1685 W
Morrish alias Osmont Christian, Marwood 1579 W
Edmund, North Tawton 1675 W
Elizabeth, Bideford 1817 W
George, North Tawton 1678 A
George, Lapford 1778 W
German, South Molton 1661 A
Henry, Mariansleigh 1724 A
Humphrey, Rackenford 1683 W
James, Bondleigh 1733 W
Jane, Buckland Brewer 1856 W
Morrysh Joan, Berrynarbor 1588 W
Moryshe John, Stoodleigh 1573 W
John, Barnstaple 1683 [W]
John, Stoodleigh 1686 A
Morish John, Bideford 1704 W
John, Rackenford 1712 A
John, Berrynarbor 1725 W
John, East Anstey 1759 W
John, East Putford 1784 W
John, East Buckland 1786 W
John, Bideford 1820 W
Mary Ann see Morrison
Peter, Landcross 1716 A
Morish Philip, Shebbear 1704 A
Philip, Bideford 1812 W
Richard, Northam 1829 A to Mary, widow
Robert, Parkham 1750 W
Thomas, Bideford 1732 W
Thomas, High Bray 1759 W
Thomas, High Bray 1789 W
William, Berrynarbor 1661 A
William, Parkham 1689 A
William, Ilfracombe 1717 W
William, Ilfracombe 1783 W, 1788 W, 1792 W
Morrison Elizabeth, Great Torrington 1743 W
Mary Ann, Bideford 1833 A (Morrish) to Edward Lethbridge,
     guardian to children
Morrysh see Morrish
Morse, Morshe
..., Coldridge 1607 [W] and 1616 [W]
Hercules, Frithelstock 1625 [W]
Morshe John, South Molton 1578 W
John, Coldridge 1591 [W]
John, Chawleigh 1594 [W]
Nicholas, Molland 1619 [W]
Philip, North Molton 1635 W
Robert, Knowstone 1619 [W] and 1637 A
William, Chawleigh 1596 [W]
Mortimer, Mortemar, Mortimore, Mortymer
Mortemar Agnes, Great Torrington 1686 W
Andrew, High Bickington 1619 [W]
Eleanor, Fremington 1637 W
George, Witheridge 1629 [W]
George, Kentisbury 1703 W
Gilbert, Witheridge 1597 [W]
John, Witheridge 1592 [W]
Mortimore John, Great Torrington 1794 W
Mortimore Mark, Bow 1621 [W]
Nicholas, Winkleigh 1613 [W]; forename blank in Ms;
     supplied from parish register
Mortimer alias Tanner Richard, Lapford 1563 W
Mortymer alias Tanner Thomas, Witheridge 1589 W
Thomas, Bow 1621 [W]
Thomas, Berrynarbor 1705 W
Mortimore William, Weare Giffard 1578 W
Mortymer William, Fremington 1615 [W]
William, Great Torrington 1674 W
William, Kentisbury 1675 W
Morwene, Morewyne, Morwen
Morewyne Lodovic, Little Torrington 1574 W
Lodovic, Little Torrington 1575 W
Morwen Thomas, Little Torrington 1575 A
Moryng Lewis, Little Torrington 1574 W

Moryshe see Morrish
Moses William, Woolfardisworthy 1599 [W]
Mosey Anthony, East or West Worlington 1710 W
  Edward, Great Torrington 1692 W
Moss Michael, Witheridge 1824 A
  William, Monkleigh 1691 W
Motley Mottley Dorothy, Barnstaple 1750 A
Mougen, Mougon
  Maurice, George Nympton 1595 [W]
  Mougon Rose, Barnstaple 1627 [W]
Moule, Moul, Moull, Moulle, Mowle
  Ann, North Molton 1758 W
  Moull Charity, Newton St Petrock 1636 W
  Clement, Fremington 1623 [W]
  Moull Edward, Clovelly 1636 A
  Mowle Elizabeth, Ilfracombe 1754 W
  Elizabeth, North Molton 1783 W
  Henry, Barnstaple 1806 W*
  Henry, Fremington 1818 W
  Henry, Georgeham 1845 W
  Henry, Fremington 1853 W
  Hugh, Tawstock, snr. 1645 W
  Hugh, Fremington 1691 W
  Hugh, Tawstock 1699 A
  Moul James, Littleham (near Bideford) 1631 [W]
  John, North Molton 1669 W
  Mowle John, Tawstock 1681 W
  John, Tawstock 1684 W
  John, North Molton 1689 W and 1690 W
  Luke, West Anstey 1757 A
  Michael, North Molton 1671 A
  Michael, North Molton 1673 [W]
  Mowle Susan, North Molton 1709 W
  Susan, Charles 1840 A to Harry of High Bray, brother
  Mowle Thomas, Ilfracombe 1701 W
  Mowle Thomas, Ilfracombe 1754 W
  Walter, Tawstock 1627 [W]
  Walter, Clovelly 1705 A
  William, Littleham (near Bideford), jnr. 1624 O
  Moull William, North Molton 1636 [W]
  Moul William, North Molton 1751 W
  Moulle William, Barnstaple, maltster 1802 W
    see also Mole
Moulton see Molton
Mounce, Mouncey see Mounsey
Moungey, Mounjoy see Mountjoy
Mounsey, Monsey, Mounce, Mouncey
  Monsey ..., Great Torrington 1608 [W]
  Monsey ..., Mortehoe 1614 [W]
  Alexander, Mortehoe 1642 A
  Edward, Mortehoe 1705 A
  Mouncey Elizabeth, Weare Giffard 1762 W
  Mouncey Honor, Merton 1775 W
  Mouncey John, Weare Giffard 1762 W
  Mouncey John, Pilton 1782 W
  Mounce Sarah, Great Torrington 1826 A to Elizabeth wife of
    John Skinner of Newton St Petrock, sister
Mountjoy, Monjoy, Moungey, Mounjoy, Mountjoye, Mungey,
  Munjoy
  ..., Newton St Petrock 1608 [W]
  ..., Bideford 1609 [W]
  Ann, South Molton 1789 W
  Charles, Bideford, yeoman 1808 W
  Charles, Great Torrington 1851 W
  Clase, Bideford 1753 W
  Monjoy Elizabeth, Hartland 1715 W
  Elizabeth, Hartland 1782 W
  Monjoy George, Chittlehampton 1696 W
  Mountjoye Hugh, Hartland 1589 W
  Hugh, Hartland 1666 W
  Munjoy Hugh, Hartland 1733 W
  Hugh, Hartland 1823 W
  Isott, Hartland 1667 W
  Isott, Hartland 1706 W
  James, Barnstaple 1639 W

Mungey James, Barnstaple 1672 W
  James, South Molton 1764 W and 1776 W
  James, South Molton 1839 A
  James, South Molton 1844 W
  Moungey Jane, Hartland 1571 W
  Moungey John, Great Torrington 1606 W
  Munjoy John, Hartland 1686 W
  John, Newton St Petrock 1721 W
  John, Bideford 1751 A
  John, Hartland 1796 W
  Mounjoy Lawrence, Hartland 1692 A
  Mary, Hartland 1715 W
  Munjoy Nicholas, Hartland 1677 W
  Prudence, South Molton 1794 W
  Monjoy Richard, Chittlehampton 1677 W
  Richard, Barnstaple 1850 W re-sworn 6 Mar 1851
  Mounjoy Simon, Chittlehampton 1689 W
  Monjoy William, Chittlehampton 1707 A
  Monjoy William, Hartland 1707 W
  William, Hartland 1769 A
  William, Hartland 1827 W
Mountstephen, Mountstephens
  Mountstephens Edward, Knowstone 1668 [W]
  Edward 1696 W
  Edward, Knowstone 1708 W
Mourte Olimpe, Bideford 1700 W
Mowle see Moule
Mowre see Moore
Moxey John, Bow 1733 A
Moxworthy see Muxworthy
Moyse, Moyes
  Agnes, Clovelly 1625 [W]
  Baldwin, Burrington 1725 W
  Catherine, Iddesleigh 1605 W
  Moyes Elizabeth, Frithelstock 1733 W
  Frances, Iddesleigh 1642 W
  George, Iddesleigh 1592 [W]
  Giffard, Iddesleigh 1660 W
  Grace, Hartland 1748 W
  Grace, Frithelstock 1783 W
  Humphrey, Monkleigh 1691 W
  Joan, Iddesleigh 1596 [W]
  Joan, Burrington 1643 W
  John, Burrington 1588 W
  John, Clovelly 1620 [W]
  John, Iddesleigh 1637 W
  John, Burrington, snr. 1638 W
  John, Buckland Brewer 1691 A
  John, Bideford 1725 A
  John, Burrington 1726 W
  Judith, Great Torrington 1762 W
  Mary, Bideford 1732 W
  Michael, Iddesleigh 1603 W
  Michael, Iddesleigh 1633 A
  Moyes Philip, Great Torrington 1758 W
  Richard, Iddesleigh 1597 [W]
  Moyes Richard, Great Torrington 1807 W
  Robert, Burrington 1667 A
  Robert, Hartland 1748 A
  Sebastian, Burrington 1690 A
  Thomas, Roborough 1720 A
  William, Dolton 1586 A
  William, Bondleigh 1680 W
  Moyes William, Frithelstock 1776 W
  William, Buckland Brewer 1842 W
Moysey, Maysey, Mozey
  Maysey Edward, Great Torrington 1616 [W]
  Mozey Grace, Witheridge 1675 A
  Grace, Yarnscombe 1724 W
  John, Northam 1606 W
  Robert, Bideford 1684 A
  William, Burrington 1589 W
Mucgrave see Musgrave
Mudd Catherine, Atherington 1644 W
  Daniel, Atherington 1641 A

Hugh, Chittlehampton 1587 A
Hugh, Barnstaple 1727 A
John, Chittlehampton 1574 W
John, Chittlehampton 1593 [W]
Mudde Thomas, Barnstaple 1621 [W]
Muden Susan, Instow 1767 W
William, Instow 1763 W
Mudge Joan, Barnstaple 1615 [W]; forename blank in Ms;
  supplied from parish register
Richard, Chittlehampton 1595 [W]
William, Barnstaple 1600 A; forename blank in Ms; supplied
  from parish register
Muffatt see Moffatt
Mugford, Muggford
Benjamin, Hartland 1731 A
Grace, Bideford 1830 W
Muggford Honoria, Hartland 1696 A
Humphrey, Great Torrington 1633 W
John, Hartland 1601 W
John, West Buckland 1674 A
John, Hartland 1731 W and 1734 A
John, Knowstone 1747 A
John Francis, Northam, mariner 1856 A to John, cordwainer,
  father
Mary, Hartland 1840 W
Muggford Mathew, Hartland 1698 A
Robert, Hartland 1673 [W]
Robert, Bideford 1844 A
Muggford William, Hartland 1695 A
William, Tawstock 1765 A
William, Hartland 1772 W
William, Hartland 1817 W
  see also Mogford
Muggeridge, Mogeridge, Moggeridg, Moggeridge, Moggridg,
  Moggridge, Mogridge, Mogrudge, Muggeride, Mugridge
Mogeridge ..., Challacombe 1610 [W]
Mogridge Abraham, Bratton Fleming 1726 W and 1740 A
Mogridge Abraham, Bratton Fleming, yeoman 1801 W
Mogridge Abraham, Charles, yeoman 1809 A
Mogridge Abraham, Charles, schoolmaster and butcher 1852
  A to Elizabeth Pickard
Mogeridge Agnes, Stoke Rivers 1776 W
Moggridge Andrew, Chulmleigh 1714 A
Mogridge Catherine, Molland 1597 [W]
Mogeridge David, Bratton Fleming 1601 W
Mogeridge David, Kentisbury 1618 [W]
Moggeridge Elizabeth, Molland 1661 A
Mogridge Elizabeth, Challacombe 1672 W
Mogridge Elizabeth, Bratton Fleming 1742 A
Mogridge Elizabeth, Bratton Fleming 1763 A
Mogridge Elizabeth, Simonsbath, Somerset 1847 W
Moggerid Henry, Stoke Rivers 1694 W
Mogridge Hugh, Bratton Fleming 1597 [W]
Mogridge Humphrey, Challacombe 1630 [W]
Moggridg Ilett, Brendon 1699 W
Mogridge Jane, Molland 1670 A probably an account made
  after the 1670 A 1672
Mogridge John, Bratton Fleming 1528 [W]
Mogrudge John, Molland 1569 W
Moggeridge John, Bratton Fleming 1598 [W]
Mogridge John, Challacombe 1645 W
Moggerid John, Molland 1664 W
Moggerid John, Molland 1665 W
Mogridge John, East Buckland 1670 W probably an account
  made after the 1670 A 1672
Moggeridge John, Yarnscombe 1685 W
Moggerid John, Stoke Rivers 1692 W
Moggridge John, Bratton Fleming, jnr. 1705 A
Moggridge John, Bratton Fleming 1714 W
Mogridge John, Stoke Rivers 1738 A
Mogridge Margaret, Bratton Fleming 1743 W
Moggerid Mary, Shirwell 1666 A
Mugridge Mary, Molland 1762 W
Moggerid Philip, Molland 1661 W

Mogridge Philip, Molland 1674 W
Moggeridge Philip, Molland 1686 W
Mogridge Philip, Molland 1733 W
Mogridge Philip, Molland 1758 W
Mugridge Philip, Chittlehampton 1762 W
Mogridge Philip, Oakford 1786 A
Mogridge Philip, Knowstone 1817 W
Mogeridge Rebecca, Bratton Fleming 1693 W
Mogridge Richard, Bratton Fleming 1623 [W]
Mogridge Richard, Brendon 1677 W
Mogridge Sarah, Witheridge 1822 A to John Partridge, brother
Muggeride Thomas, ship *Antelope* 1748 W
Mogridge Thomas, Bratton Fleming 1830 W
Mogridge Walter, Parracombe 1836 A
Moggeride alias Moggis William, Challacombe 1606 W
Moggeridg William, Shirwell 1664 A
Moggeridg William, Shirwell 1666 A
Mogridge William, Countisbury 1812 W
Mugridge William, Alverdiscott 1833 W
Mogridge William, Bratton Fleming 1846 W
Muggford see Mugford
Mugridge see Muggeridge
Mugworthy see Muxworthy
Mules, Mullis
Abraham, Tawstock 1692 A
Agnes, Barnstaple 1628 [W]
Alice, Tawstock 1592 [W]
Alice, Tawstock 1660 W
Ann, Chittlehampton 1626 [W]
Ann, Chawleigh 1809 W
Brian, Dolton 1593 [W]
Catherine, Tawstock 1632 [W]
Christopher, Huntshaw 1672 W
Christopher 1759 A
Christopher, Beaford 1763 W
Dorothy, Beaford 1767 A
Dorothy, Bideford 1820 W
Elizabeth, Barnstaple 1603 W
Elizabeth, Mortehoe 1632 [W]
Mullis Elizabeth, Alverdiscott 1833 W
Elizabeth, Marwood 1850 W
Mullis Emanuel, Alverdiscott 1851 W
Geoffrey, Barnstaple 1566 W
George, Northam 1616 [W]
George, Northam 1698 W
George, Filleigh 1702 W
George, West Down, snr. 1705 W
George, Mortehoe 1758 W and 1774 W
Grace, Beaford 1685 W
Grace, Beaford 1717 W
Hannah, Ilfracombe 1821 W
Henry, Mortehoe 1622 [W]
Henry, Ilfracombe, snr. 1714 W
Jane, Barnstaple 1719 A
Joan, Barnstaple, widow 1570 W
Joan, Northam 1623 [W]
Joan, Mortehoe 1628 [W]
Joan, St Giles in the Wood 1718 W
John, Tawstock 1580 W
John, Warkleigh 1600 W
John, Roborough 1602 A; forename blank in Ms; supplied
  from parish register
John, Barnstaple 1613 [W]; forename blank in Ms; supplied
  from parish register
John, Warkleigh 1623 [W]
John, Roborough 1636 A
John, Tawstock 1670 A
John, Northam 1673 W
John, Mortehoe 1685 A
John, Beaford 1711 W
John, Mortehoe 1719 W
John, Clovelly 1726 [W]
John, Tawstock 1737 W and 1742 W
John, Chittlehampton 1744 A
John, Mortehoe 1754 W and 1757 W

Mullis John, Northam 1771 W
John, Ilfracombe 1795 W
John, Fremington, yeoman 1800 W
John, Bideford 1802 W
Mullis Loveday, Alverdiscott 1733 W
Mullis Mary, Frithelstock 1783 W
Mary, Marwood, widow 1821 A to Jonathan Hawkes Mules of
   Ilminster, Somerset, clerk, son
Philip, Barnstaple 1581 W
Philip, Mortehoe 1587 W
Philip, Mortehoe 1755 W and 1757 W
Rebecca, Combe Martin 1768 A
Richard, Ilfracombe 1704 A
Mullis Richard, Alverdiscott 1762 W
Mullis Richard, Frithelstock 1783 W
Robert, Beaford 1731 W
Rose, High Bickington 1719 A
Susan, Tawstock 1696 W
Thomas, Fremington 1585 O account
Thomas, Tawstock 1585 W and 1596 [W]
Thomas, Newton Tracey 1596 [W]
Thomas, Warkleigh 1620 [W]
Thomas, Ilfracombe 1745 W
William, Mortehoe 1566 [W]
William, Warkleigh 1596 [W]
William, High Bickington 1622 [W]
William, Bideford 1683 W
Mullis William, Alverdiscott 1716 W
Mullis William, Bideford 1756 A
Mullis William, Bideford 1777 W
Mullis William, Alverdiscott, carpenter 1811 A
Mullis William, Horwood 1825 W
Mullis William, Alverdiscott 1846 A
Mullins, Mollens, Mulland, Mullen, Mullens
   Grace see Ann Berry
Mollens John, Barnstaple 1695 W
Mullen Margaret, Burrington 1749 A
Mary, Barnstaple 1643 W
Mullens Robert, Barnstaple 1637 A
Mulland Thomas, Burrington 1835 W
Mullis see Mules
Mumford Henry, Clovelly 1712 A and 1725 A
Muncke see Monk
Mungey, Munjoy see Mountjoy
Murch Abraham, Lapford 1708 W
Elizabeth, High Bickington 1738 W
Elizabeth, Yarnscombe 1763 W
James, High Bickington 1706 A
James, Bideford 1765 W
James, Yarnscombe 1768 W
Richard, Rackenford 1743 A
Thomas, Chittlehampton 1842 W
William, Winkleigh 1697 A
Murfeild, Murfeilde see Mirfield
Murle see Murrell
Murray John, Bideford 1709 A
Murrell, Murle
John, Iddesleigh 1593 [W]
Richard, Lapford 1599 [W]
Murle Richard, Lapford 1626 [W]
Murring Richard, Buckland Brewer 1590 [W]
Murris see Morris
Musgrave, Mucgrave
Mucgrave Mary, Barnstaple 1723 A
Richard, South Molton 1697 W
Mussaven, Mustavin
Mary, Northam 1679 W
Mustavin Robert, Northam 1661 A
Thomas, Goodleigh 1672 W
Mussell, Mussel
Elizabeth, Fremington 1695 A
Gabriel, Instow 1670 W
Joan, Abbotsham, widow 1607 [W]; forename blank in Ms;
   supplied from parish register
John, Abbotsham 1575 W

John, Alwington 1579 W
John, Abbotsham 1605 W
Joseph, Weare Giffard 1672 A
Julian, Weare Giffard 1666 W
Peter, Northam 1592 [W]
Mussel Thomas, Bideford 1635 W
Valentine, Abbotsham 1600 W
William, Alwington 1589 A
Musselwhite Elizabeth, Pilton 1768 W
Mustavin see Mussaven
Mutchell see Mitchell
Muxworthy, Moxworthy, Muxery, Muxeworthy, Muxworthie
..., North Molton 1603 [W] and 1612 [W]
Mogworthy ..., Cheldon 1610 [W] and 1611 [W]
Muxworthie Agnes, High Bray 1577 W
Agnes, High Bray 1639 W
Muxworthy alias Aukland Archelaus 1798 A
Catherine, High Bray 1663 A
Daniel, Great Torrington 1684 W
Daniel, High Bray 1697 A
Daniel, Fremington 1819 W
Elias, St Giles in the Wood 1616 [W]
Elias, St Giles in the Wood 1693 W
Muxworthie Elizabeth, High Bray 1586 A
Erasmus, Stoodleigh 1635 A
George, Yarnscombe 1808 W
Grace, Fremington 1821 W
Henry, North Molton 1634 W
Hugh, Tawstock 1667 A
Joan, High Bray 1617 [W]
Muxworthie John, Kentisbury 1574 W and A
Moxworthy John, Westleigh 1577 W
Muxworthie John, Alverdiscott 1578 W
Muxworthie John, Chittlehampton 1593 [W]
John, High Bray 1604 W
John, snr. High Bray 1608 [W]; forename blank in Ms; supplied
   from parish register
John, Westleigh 1615 [W] and 1616 O
John, High Bray 1619 [W] and 1627 [W]
John, North Molton 1673 W
Muxery John, Witheridge 1689 A
John, High Bray 1710 W
Mugworthy John, West Buckland 1760 A
Mary, Challacombe 1689 A
Mary, Tawstock 1822 W
Muxworthie Richard, Fremington 1595 [W]
Richard, North Molton 1604 W
Richard, Stoodleigh 1633 W
Muxworthie Roger, High Bray 1569 W
Roger, Georgeham 1609 [W]; forename blank in Ms; supplied
   from parish register
Muxery alias Rawle Sybil, Brendon 1683 A
Muxworthie Thomasine, High Bray 1598 [W]
Walter, Challacombe 1665 W
Muxworthie William, High Bray, snr. 1569 W
Muxworthie William, High Bray 1572 W
William, North Molton 1624 [W]
William, Tawstock 1812 W
Moxworthy William, North Tawton 1827 A to Thomasine,
   widow
William, Tawstock 1844 A to Ann wife of John Williams,
   widow
Mychell see Mitchell
Myddleton see Middleton
Myicord John, Dolton 1673 W
Mylden, Myldon see Mildon
Mylford see Milford
Myll see Mill
Mylls see Mills
Mylten, Mylton see Milton
Myneod William, Tawstock 1612 [W] "Mynnywoode" in register;
   forename blank in Ms; supplied from parish register
Myrfild see Mirfield
Myrick Philip, Ilfracombe 1755 A
Myrifild see Merryfield

Naish see Nash

Nankivell, Nancekievell, Nancekievill, Nancekivel, Nancekevell,
    Nancekivil, Nancekivill, Nanskevill, Nincekivell
  Nancekievell Elizabeth, Parkham 1812 A to Ann Lee, daughter
  Nancekievill John, Parkham 1771 A
  Nancekievill John, Langtree 1832 W
  Nancekivill John, Woolfardisworthy 1833 W
  Nancekievell Mary, Parkham 1813 W
  Nancekivell Mathew, Clovelly 1800 W
  Nanskevill Robert, Petrockstowe 1735 A
  Nancekievell Thomas, Parkham, farmer 1798 W
  Nincekivell Thomas, Langtree 1830 A to Thomas and Mary
    Risdon, children
  Nancekivell Thomas, Parkham 1846 W
  Nancekivil William, Parkham 1798 W
  William, Langtree, yeoman 1808 W
  Nancekivell William, Woolfardisworthy 1831 W
  Nancekivell William, Parkham 1842 W
  Nancekivell William, Ashreigney 1848 W

Naraway, Naroway see Narraway

Narracott John, Burrington 1711 W
  Samuel, Roborough 1737 A

Narraway, Naraway, Naroway, Narroway, Norraway
  Ann, Alverdiscott 1757 W
  Elizabeth, Barnstaple 1761 A and 1772 A
  Naraway James, Westleigh 1815 W
  Narroway John, Chittlehampton 1708 W
  John, Barnstaple 1824 W
  Mary, Bideford 1838 A
  Norraway Samuel, Alverdiscott 1749 A
  Naroway Thomas, Westleigh 1710 A
  William, Alverdiscott 1757 A
  William, Little Torrington, yeoman 1803 A

Nash, Knashe, Naish
  Avis, Great Torrington 1721 W
  Knashe Joan, Ilfracombe 1573 A
  Naish John, Heanton Punchardon 1686 W
  John, Bideford 1730 A
  Mary, Littleham (near Bideford) 1672 W
  Thomas, Bideford 1727 A
  William, Barnstaple 1643 A

Nasica John, Barnstaple 1694 A

Nations, Nation
  Nation Charles, Parkham 1703 A
  Francis, Great Torrington 1728 W
  Nation Joan, Great Torrington 1703 W
  John, St Giles in the Wood 1752 W and 1757 A
  John, Merton 1785 W
  Willmot, Merton 1783 W

Natt George, Bratton Fleming 1708 W
  John, Combe Martin 1720 W
  John, Fremington, yeoman 1797 W

Ne ... (name unfinished) Edward, North Tawton 1663 A

Neale, Neal, Neall, Neeld, Neele, Neil, Neild, Nele, Neyle,
  Neyll, Nylde
  ..., Great Torrington 1605 [W]
  Neil Anthony, Fremington 1705 W
  Arthur, Barnstaple 1735 A
  Neyll Baldwin, Fremington 1573 W
  Neyle Catherine, Littleham (near Bideford) 1604 W
  Neall Dennis, Parkham 1586 W
  Eleanor, Alwington 1627 [W]
  Neeld George, Barnstaple 1628 [W]
  Neall Gregory, Martinhoe 1588 W
  Neele Henry, Fremington 1632 [W]
  Neild Henry, Chulmleigh 1735 W
  Hugh, Parkham 1680 A
  Jane, Berrynarbor 1591 [W]
  Neall Joan, Parkham 1583 W
  John, Landcross 1584 A
  Nele John, Parkham 1584 W
  John, Fremington 1591 [W]
  Neal John, Hartland 1834 W
  Margaret, Fremington 1591 [W]
  Neeld Mary, Barnstaple 1624 [W]

Neeld Michael, Iddesleigh 1621 [W]
Nylde Richard, Fremington 1586 W
Richard, Parkham 1633 A
Richard, Berrynarbor 1670 A
Richard, Bideford 1679 A
Robert, Alwington 1608 [W]; forename blank in Ms; supplied
  from parish register
Thomas, Littleham (near Bideford) 1583 W
William, Parkham 1569 W
Nele William, Parkham 1630 [W]

Neathaway see Nethaway
Neathercott see Nethercott
Necke see Nicks
Neeld, Neele see Neale
Neick see Nicks
Neil, Neild, Nele see Neale

Nelson Francis, Merton 1777 A

Nenoe, Neno, Nenow, Nenowe, Nino, Ninoe, Ninone
  Nenow ..., Dolton 1607 [W]
  Nenowe ..., Huish 1607 [W]
  Nenow ..., Iddesleigh 1612 [W]
  Nenowe Agnes, Iddesleigh 1621 [W]
  Nenow Anthony, Heanton Punchardon 1638 W
  Nenowe Armanell, Winkleigh 1636 W
  Daniel, Iddesleigh 1762 A
  Neno Daniel, Dolton, yeoman 1809 W
  Nenowe Egline, Iddesleigh 1579 W
  Nenow Elizabeth, Iddesleigh 1643 W
  Ninone John, North Tawton 1681 A
  Nenow Margery, Winkleigh 1597 [W]
  Nenowe Michael, North Tawton 1629 [W]
  Rebecca, Winkleigh 1733 W
  Neno Richard, Huish 1565 W
  Nenowe Richard, Huish 1634 W
  Nino Richard, Chulmleigh 1695 W
  Nenowe Robert, Martinhoe 1635 W
  Ninoe Robert, Iddesleigh 1762 W
  Nenowe Simon, Iddesleigh 1566 W
  Tobias, Iddesleigh 1750 W and 1764 A
  Nenow William, Winkleigh 1586 W
  Nenowe William, Bideford 1604 [W]; forename blank in Ms;
    supplied from parish register
  Nenowe William, Iddesleigh 1641 A
  William, Meeth 1726 W

Nethaway, Neathaway, Netheway
  ..., Huish 1600 W
  ..., Frithelstock 1602 [W] and 1609 [W]
  Andrew, Meeth 1703 A
  Anthony, Littleham (near Bideford) 1695 W
  Arthur, Frithelstock 1644 W
  Catherine, Monkleigh 1787 W
  Catherine, Monkleigh 1814 W
  Christopher, Frithelstock 1639 W
  Ezekiel, Langtree 1760 W
  Henry, Langtree 1690 A and 1695 A
  Hugh, Ashreigney 1626 [W]
  Joan, Langtree 1705 W
  John, Langtree 1628 [W]
  John, Littleham (near Bideford) 1629 [W]
  John, Langtree 1697 W
  John, Bideford 1723 A
  Margaret, Langtree 1702 W
  Neathaway Mary, Langtree 1709 W
  Mathew, Langtree 1672 A
  Peter, Langtree 1671 W
  Peter, Langtree 1749 A
  Netheway Peter, Langtree, yeoman 1796 W
  Peter, Langtree 1832 W
  Roger, Frithelstock 1760 A
  Samuel, Langtree 1690 W
  Netheway Samuel, Langtree 1796 W
  Stephen, Huish 1693 W
  Thomas, Dowland 1677 W
  Thomas, Littleham (near Bideford) 1717 W and 1735 A

Nethercott, Neathercott, Nethercot, Nethercote
    Nethercot alias Cote Henry, Ilfracombe 1578 W
    Hugh, East Down 1577 W
    Nethercote alias Shuchefielde John, Oakford 1566 W
    Mary, Burrington 1781 W
    Neathercott Richard, Burrington 1771 A
    Robert, Ashreigney 1835 W
    Nethercot alias Cote Willmot, Ilfracombe 1578 W
Netherwinde Richard, Tawstock 1594 [W]
Newbery Richard, West Anstey 1719 W
Newcombe, Newcomb
    ..., Little Torrington 1606 [W]
    Newcomb ..., Bondleigh 1613 [W]
    Newcomb ..., Broadnymet 1613 [W]
    Agnes, Bideford 1639 W
    Newcomb Catherine, Chawleigh 1642 A
    Newcomb Christopher, Winkleigh 1741 W
    Christopher, Winkleigh, yeoman 1809 W
    Elizabeth, Monkleigh 1745 W
    Newcomb John, Martinhoe 1586 W
    John, Bondleigh 1623 [W]
    Newcomb John, Bondleigh, snr. 1681 W
    John, Roborough 1765 A
    John, Chawleigh 1823 W
    John, Bulkworthy 1825 W
    Mary, Frithelstock 1827 W
    Richard, South Molton 1636 A
    Richard, Bideford 1638 W
    Robert, Broadnymet 1572 W
    Robert, Bondleigh 1590 [W]
    Newcomb Robert, Roborough 1725 W
    Newcomb Robert, Roborough 1730 W
    Sarah, Winkleigh 1743 W
    Simon, Great Torrington 1583 W
    Simon, Chawleigh 1818 A to Christopher of Winkleigh,
      brother
    Newcomb Thomas, Chawleigh 1740 A
    Thomas, Winkleigh 1829 W
    William, Bow 1577 A
    William, Winkleigh 1641 W
    William, Knowstone 1697 W
    Newcomb William, Shebbear 1714 W
    William, High Bickington 1775 W
    William, Shebbear 1802 W
    William, Bulkworthy 1824 W
    William, Frithelstock 1825 W
    William, Monkleigh 1841 W
    Newcomb Zachariah, Winkleigh 1674 [W]
Newcourt John, Pickwell, Georgeham 1603 W
    John, Pickwell, Georgeham, esquire 1612 [W]; forename
      blank in Ms; supplied from parish register
    John, Georgeham 1632 [W]
    Tobias, Georgeham 1662 A
Newell Rachel, Ilfracombe 1784 W
    Richard, Ilfracombe 1766 W
    Thomas, Ilfracombe 1722 W
    William, Clovelly 1727 A
Newman John, Bideford 1697 W
    Samuel see Robert Brook
    Thomas, Alverdiscott 1679 A
Newton Alice, West Anstey 1725 W
    John, Witheridge 1579 W
    John, Molland 1731 W
    John, Westleigh 1735 A
    Peter, Filleigh 1837 W
    Richard, Molland 1762 A
    Roger, Alverdiscott 1703 W
    Thomas, Chulmleigh 1624 [W]
    William, West Anstey 1712 W
    William, West Anstey 1750 A
    William, Molland 1756 A
Neyle, Neyll see Neale
Nicholas Thomas, Ilfracombe 1792 A
Nichols, Nichol, Nicholl, Nicholles, Nicholls, Nickells, Nickle,
    Nickoll, Nickolls, Nicoll, Nycoll, Nycolle, Nycolls
    Nicholl ..., Chawleigh 1600 O account

Nicholl ..., Woolfardisworthy 1603 [W], 1609 [W] and 1614
  [W]
Nicholls ..., Northam 1603 [W]
Nicholl ..., Great Torrington 1609 [W]
Nicholl ..., Mortehoe 1610 [W]
Nicholl ..., Bideford 1611 [W]
Nicholl ..., Goodleigh 1614 [W]
Nicholl ..., Martinhoe 1614 [W]
Nicholls alias Greene ..., Tawstock 1666 W
Nickle Abraham, High Bray 1664 A
Nicholl Agnes, Hartland 1596 [W]
Nicholl Agnes, Langtree 1597 [W]
Nicholl Agnes, Hartland, widow 1607 [W]; forename blank in
  Ms; supplied from parish register
Nicholl Agnes, Northam 1703 W
Nicoll alias Gene Alexander, Kentisbury 1582 W
Nicholl Alexander, Kentisbury 1592 [W]
Nicholl Alexander, Challacombe 1597 [W]
Nicholl Alexander, Northam 1667 W
Nicholl Alice, Combe Martin 1619 [W]
Nicholl Alice, Marwood 1624 [W]
Nicholl Andrew, Clovelly 1697 W
Nicholl Ann, Hartland 1637 W
Nicholls Ann, Great Torrington 1692 W
Nicholls Ann, Yarnscombe 1730 W and 1732 W
Nicholl Anthony, Newton Tracey 1584 W
Nicholl Anthony, Fremington 1622 [W]
Nicholls Anthony, Fremington 1714 W and 1721 A
Nicholls Arthur, Barnstaple 1717 A
Nicholls Arthur, Chittlehampton 1732 W
Nickolls Catherine, Northam 1735 W
Nicholl Catherine 1763 W
Nicholl Christopher, Marwood 1622 [W]
Nicholl Christopher, Hartland 1635 W
Nicholl Christopher, Barnstaple 1666 A
Nicholls Christopher, Marwood 1672 W
Nicholls Daniel, Northam 1776 W
Nicholl Dennis, Northam 1745 A
Nicholles Edward, Kentisbury 1572 W
Nicholls alias Agger Edward, Woolfardisworthy 1579 W
Nicholl Edward, Combe Martin 1619 [W]
Nicholls Edward, Mariansleigh 1682 W
Nickle Edward, Berrynarbor 1690 W
Edward, Lynton, gentleman 1806 W
Nicholl Eleanor, Mortehoe 1693 W
Nicholl Elias, Tawstock 1604 W
Nicholl Elizabeth, Woolfardisworthy 1592 [W]
Nicholls Elizabeth, Chittlehampton 1690 W
Nicholls Elizabeth, Knowstone 1704 A
Nicholls Elizabeth, Barnstaple 1736 W
Elizabeth, Alwington 1848 W
Nicholl Ellen, Satterleigh 1641 W
Nicholl Emma, Berrynarbor 1643 W
Nicholl Emma, Hartland 1643 A
Nicholl Emma, Woolfardisworthy 1643 A
Nicholl Ezekiel, Welcombe 1703 W
Nycolls Francis, Hartland 1583 A
Nicholl George, Buckland Brewer 1564 W
Nicholl George, Instow 1666 W
Nicholls George, West Down 1694 W
George, Yarnscombe 1711 W
Nicholls George, Alverdiscott 1715 W
Nicholl Gilbert, Marwood 1633 W
Nicholls Grace, Barnstaple 1779 W
Nicholls Gregory, Chittlehampton 1689 W
Nicholl Henry, Mortehoe 1595 [W]
Nicholls Henry, Bideford 1748 A
Nicholls Henry, Coldridge 1754 W
Nicholls Honor, Chittlehampton 1736 W
Nicholl Hugh, Langtree 1597 [W]
Nicholl Hugh, Hartland 1625 [W] and 1640 W
Nicholls Hugh, Clovelly 1664 W
Nicholl Hugh, Hartland 1699 W
Nickols Hugh, Molland 1805 W
Nicholl James, Barnstaple 1645 W

Nicholls James, Barnstaple 1672 W
Nicholls James, Hartland 1717 W
Nicholls James, Yarnscombe 1731 W
Nicholls Jane, Filleigh 1684 W and 1686 A
Nicholls Jane, Northam 1769 W
Nicholl Jennifer, Parracombe 1619 [W]
Nycoll Joan, Pilton 1573 W
Nycolle Joan, Hartland 1573 A
Nicolls Joan, Hartland 1583 W
Nicholl Joan, Northam 1626 [W]
Nicholls Joan, Marwood 1636 W
Nicholls Joan, Welcombe 1742 W
Nicholl John, Pilton, jnr. 1566 W
Nicolle John, Pilton, snr. 1566 W
Nycholls John, Puddington 1567 W
Nycoll John, Hartland 1568 W
Nicoll alias Agger John, Woolfardisworthy (West) 1569 W
Nicholl John, Brownsham, Hartland 1571 W
Nicolls John, High Bray 1572 W
Nycolle John, Burrington 1573 W
Nichol John, Fremington 1579 A
Nicholl John, Barnstaple 1581 W
Nicoll John, Burrington 1583 W
Nicholle John, Barnstaple 1584 W
Nicholl John, Chawleigh 1593 [W]
Nicholl John, Hartland 1603 [W] "of Loveland" in register;
  forename blank in Ms; supplied from parish register
Nicholl John, Woolfardisworthy 1603 W
Nicholl alias Geyne John, Shirwell 1606 W
Nicholl John, Berrynarbor 1612 [W] "John Nichols alias
  Geene" in register; forename blank in Ms; supplied from
  parish register
Nicholl John, Newton Tracey 1624 [W]
Nicholl John, Woolfardisworthy 1637 W
Nicholl alias Adger John, Woolfardisworthy 1643 W
Nicholl John, Woolfardisworthy 1661 W
Nicholl John, Pilton 1663 W
Nicholls John, Parracombe 1671 W
Nicholls John, Chittlehampton 1675 A
Nicholls John, Woolfardisworthy 1675 A
Nicholls John, Great Torrington 1678 A
Nicholl John, Marwood 1684 W
Nicholls John, Fremington 1691 A
Nicholls John, Chittlehampton 1695 A
Nickels John, George Nympton 1702 W
Nicholls John, Wembworthy 1714 A
Nicholls John, West Down 1718 W
Nicholls John, Hartland 1721 W
Nicholls John, Bideford 1732 W
Nickolls John, Woolfardisworthy 1735 A
Nicholls John, Northam 1768 W
Nicholls John, Chittlehampton 1776 A
Nickels John, Wembworthy 1821 W
Nicholls John, Heanton Punchardon 1842 W
Nickols Jonathan, Stoodleigh 1823 W
Nicholls Joseph, Hartland 1702 A
Nicholl Julia 1661 W
Nicholls Julian, Pilton 1794 A and 1798 A
Nicholls Justinian, Hartland 1709 W
Nicholls Margaret, Mariansleigh 1691 A
Nicholl Marian, Merton 1679 A
Nicholl Martin, Hartland 1635 A
Nicholl Mary, Shebbear 1603 W
Nicholl Mary, Marwood 1621 [W]
Nicholls Mary, Buckland Brewer 1671 A
Nicholl Mary, Marwood 1684 W
Nicholls Mary, Bideford 1765 W
Nickolls Mary, Chittlehampton 1826 A to William, son
Nicholls Maurice, Tawstock 1743 A
Nicholls Melchior, Northam 1728 W
Nicholls Nicholas, Tawstock 1708 W
Nicholl Oliver, Newton Tracey 1594 [W]
Nicholl Osmond, Instow 1666 A
Nicholls Patience, Chulmleigh 1731 W
Nicholl Peter, Littleham (near Bideford) 1616 [W]

Nicholl Peter, Hartland 1622 [W]
Nicholl Peter, Northam 1663 A
Nicholls Peter, Northam 1670 W
Nicholls Peter, Georgeham 1677 A
Nicholls Peter, Hartland 1683 W
Nicholls Peter, Parracombe 1702 A
Nicholls Peter, Hartland 1710 W
Peter, Northam 1716 A
Nicholls Peter, Hartland, jnr. 1751 A
Nicholls Peter, Hartland 1755 W
Nicholls Peter, Hartland 1795 A
Nycoll Philip, Mortehoe, snr. 1568 W
Nycoll Philip, Ashford 1573 W
Nicholl Philip, Northam 1622 [W]
Nicholl Philip, Woolfardisworthy 1637 W
Nicholl Philip, Clovelly 1677 A
Nicholls Philip, Great Torrington 1714 W
Nicholls Philip, Fremington 1732 W
Nicholls Philip, Great Torrington 1739 A
Nicholls Phillippa, Hartland 1715 A
Nicholl Rebecca, Wembworthy 1715 A
Nicholls Rebecca, Barnstaple 1743 W
Nicoll alias Edger Richard, Woolfardisworthy 1583 W
Nicholl Richard, Hartland 1584 W
Nicholl Richard, Barnstaple 1635 A
Nicholls Richard, Marwood 1638 W
Nicholls Richard, Berrynarbor 1670 W
Nicholl Richard, Fremington 1674 A
Nicholls Richard, Trentishoe 1676 W
Nicholls Richard, Instow 1687 W
Nicholls Richard, Barnstaple 1690 W, 1708 W
Nicholls Richard, Barnstaple 1717 A, 1728 A
Nicholls Richard, Northam 1736 A
Nicholls Richard, Bideford 1744 W
Nicholls Richard, Stoke Rivers 1777 A
Nicholls Richard, Woolfardisworthy 1778 A
Nicholls Richard, Parracombe 1792 W
Nicholls Richard, Parracombe 1837 A
Nicoll Robert, Hartland 1576 W
Nicholl Robert, Woolfardisworthy 1599 [W]
Nicholl Robert, Newton Tracey 1627 [W]
Nicholl Robert, Northam 1627 [W]
Nicholls Robert, Barnstaple 1680 A
Nicholls Robert, Barnstaple 1709 W
Nicholls alias Green Robert, Ilfracombe 1714 W
Nicholls Robert, Barnstaple 1725 W
Nickolls Robert, Great Torrington 1735 A
Nicholls Robert, Welcombe 1742 W
Nicolls Roger, Marwood 1577 W
Roger, Chittlehampton 1719 A
Nicholls Sarah, Northam 1818 W
Sarah wife of John see also Elizabeth Cooper
Nycholl Thomas, Witheridge 1565 W
Nycolls alias Ager Thomas, Woolfardisworthy (East or West),
  jnr. 1566 W
Nicoll Thomas, Mortehoe 1576 W
Nicoll Thomas, East Putford 1577 W
Nicholl Thomas, High Bray 1590 [W]
Nicholl Thomas, Parracombe 1596 [W]
Nicholl Thomas, Woolfardisworthy 1596 [W]
Nicholl Thomas, Hartland 1606 W
Nicholl Thomas, Alverdiscott 1635 W
Nickle Thomas, Chittlehampton 1637 W
Nicholl Thomas, Arlington 1639 W
Nicholls Thomas, Buckland Filleigh 1677 W
Nicholls Thomas, Barnstaple 1684 A
Nicholls Thomas, Pilton 1725 W
Nicholls Thomas, Northam 1736 W
Nicholls Thomas, South Molton 1752 W
Nicholls Thomas, Northam, mariner 1807 W
Nicholls Thomas, Meshaw 1814 W
Nicolls Thomasine, Burrington 1583 W
Nicholl Thomasine, Hartland 1613 [W]; forename blank in
  Ms; supplied from parish register
Nicholl Thomasine, Chawleigh 1615 [W]

Nichol Thomasine, High Bray 1637 W
Nicholl Thomasine, Hartland 1641 W
Nicholl Thomasine, Fremington 1667 W
Nicholls Tobias, Northam 1691 A
Nycholl Walter, Bratton Fleming 1576 W
Nicholl Walter 1640 W
Nicoll William, Ilfracombe 1588 W
Nicholl William, Hartland 1590 [W]
Nicholls William, Northam 1591 [W]
Nicoll William, Hartland 1606 W; forename blank in Ms;
    supplied from parish register
Nicholl William, Northam 1619 [W]
Nicholl William, Pilton 1624 [W]
Nicholl William, Hartland 1638 W
Nicholls William, Barnstaple 1643 W
Nicholl William, Georgeham 1662 A
Nicholls William, Langtree 1674 W
Nicholls William, West Down 1694 W
Nicholl William, Bideford 1708 A
Nicholls William, Horwood 1711 W
Nicholls William, Welcombe 1713 W
Nicholls William, Pilton 1716 W
Nicholls William, Barnstaple 1728 W
Nicholls William, Pilton 1728 A
Nickells William, Woolfardisworthy 1742 W
Nicholls William, Northam 1745 W
Nicholls William, Northam 1748 A
Nicholls William, Northam 1748 W
Nicholls William, Marwood 1756 A
Nickells William, Pilton 1758 A
Nicholls William, Wilton, Hartland 1760 A
Nicholls William, Chittlehampton 1791 W
Nicholls William, Chittlehampton 1792 A
Nicholls William, Chittlehampton, yeoman 1804 A
Nicholls William, Great Torrington, miller 1816 A to William
    of Frithelstock and John of Bideford, sons
William, Little Torrington 1848 W
Nick see Nicks
Nickells, Nickels, Nickle, Nickolls, Nickols see Nichols
Nicks, Necke, Neick, Nick, Niec, Nycke
    Neick Agnes, Mariansleigh, widow 1608 [W]; forename blank
        in Ms; supplied from parish register
    Francis, Arlington 1721 A
    Niec Francis, Arlington 1833 A to Mary, daughter
    Nick James, Barnstaple 1643 W
    Nycke William, Coldridge 1575 W
    Necke William, Mariansleigh 1588 W
Nicoll, Nicolle, Nicolls see Nichols
Niles John, Northam 1734 W
    Thomas, Northam 1734 W
Nincekivell see Nankivell
Nino, Ninoe, Ninone see Nenoe
Noett see Nott
Nogle Ann, Tawstock 1796 W
    Daniel, Challacombe, yeoman 1798 W
    John, North Molton 1702 W and 1710 W
    John, North Molton 1738 W
    John, Tawstock 1790 A
Noone Bartholomew, Filleigh 1583 A
    Richard, South Molton 1635 W
Norcott see Northcott
Nordon, Northdon, Norton
    Blaise, Washford Pyne 1593 [W]
    Northdon Margaret, Winkleigh 1568 W
    Mary, Monkleigh 1608 [W] "Bowman alias Norton" in
        register; forename blank in Ms; supplied from parish register
Noreman see Norman
Nores see Norris
Norley Mary, Bideford 1680 A
Norman, Noreman
    ..., Mortehoe 1613 [W]
    ..., Parracombe 1615 [W]
    Agnes, Parracombe 1604 W
    Agnes, Ilfracombe 1767 A
    Alice, Challacombe 1625 [W]

Ann, Buckland Brewer 1820 A to Samuel, son
Catherine, Shebbear 1580 A
Cecilia, Tawstock 1577 W
Crispin, Buckland Brewer 1755 W
Dorothy, Iddesleigh 1718 W
Dorothy, Northam 1741 W
Eleanor, Ilfracombe 1715 W
Elizabeth, Berrynarbor 1623 [W] and 1639 A
Elizabeth, Buckland Brewer 1853 A (Eliza) to John, yeoman,
    father
Elizabeth see also John Thorne
Ellen, Parracombe 1588 W
George, Berrynarbor 1639 W
George, Berrynarbor 1830 W
George, Meeth 1847 W
Grace, Barnstaple 1806 W
Henry, Tawstock 1626 [W] and 1628 O
Joan, Frithelstock 1644 W
John, Parracombe 1570 W
John, Loxhore 1590 [W]
John, Tawstock 1597 [W]
John, Parracombe 1617 O
John, Berrynarbor 1622 [W]
John, Challacombe 1622 [W]
John, Parracombe 1622 [W]
John, Barnstaple 1636 W
John, Langtree 1637 W
John, Frithelstock 1643 A
John, Ilfracombe 1708 A
John, Ilfracombe 1720 W
John, Berrynarbor 1789 W
John, Frithelstock 1829 W
John, High Bickington 1836 W
Margery, Fremington, widow 1613 [W]; forename blank in
    Ms; supplied from parish register
Mary, Northam 1668 W
Mary, Berrynarbor 1778 A
Mary, Berrynarbor, sp. 1799 A
Mary, Northam 1839 W
Mathew, St Giles in the Wood 1732 W
Nathaniel, West Down 1705 A
Nicholas, Ilfracombe 1761 A
Nicholas, Goodleigh 1785 W
Nicholas, Tawstock 1857 W
Oliver, Parracombe 1571 W
Philip, Great Torrington 1594 [W]
Richard, Martinhoe 1585 W
Richard, Roborough 1629 [W]
Richard, Yarnscombe 1629 [W]
Richard, Parracombe 1641 A
Richard, Ilfracombe 1665 A
Richard, Roborough 1693 W
Richard, Ilfracombe 1698 W
Richard, Combe Martin 1721 W
Richard, St Giles in the Wood 1735 A
Richard, Northam 1738 W
Richard, Berrynarbor, yeoman 1799 A
Robert, Ilfracombe 1705 W
Robert, High Bickington, yeoman 1802 W
Robert, High Bickington 1831 W
Samuel, Parkham 1787 W
Samuel, Buckland Brewer, yeoman 1801 W
Sarah, Ilfracombe 1856 W
Susan, High Bickington 1805 W*
Thomas, Parracombe 1588 W
Thomas, Berrynarbor 1627 [W]
Thomas, Stoodleigh 1732 W
Thomas, Northam 1735 W
Thomas, Frithelstock 1848 W
Thomasine, Combe Martin 1667 W
Timothy, Ilfracombe 1696 A
Walter, Combe Martin 1678 A and 1681 A
Noreman William, North Molton 1575 W
William, Challacombe 1579 W

William, Fremington 1608 [W]; forename blank in Ms;
   supplied from parish register
William, Challacombe 1621 [W]
William, Barnstaple 1636 W
William, Northam 1695 A
William, Ilfracombe 1709 A
William, Berrynarbor 1826 A
William, Ilfracombe 1843 W
Norris, Nores, Norrice, Norrish, Norrishe
Norrice Abraham, Chulmleigh 1667 A
  Agnes, Ashreigney 1578 A
Norrishe Ambrose, Ashreigney 1636 W
  Ambrose, Ashreigney 1728 W
Norrish Ann, Huntshaw 1851 A
  Anthony, Coldridge 1620 [W]
Norrish Christian, South Molton 1766 W
  Elizabeth, Molland 1636 A
Norrish Elizabeth, Rackenford 1797 W
  Engys, Pilton 1636 W
Nores Joan, Winkleigh 1570 W
Norrish Joan, South Molton 1762 W
Norrishe John, Molland 1578 W
Norrice John, Barnstaple 1610 [W]; forename blank in Ms;
   supplied from parish register
Norrishe John, Fremington 1624 [W]
Norrishe John, Chulmleigh 1625 [W]
Norrishe John, King's Nympton 1632 [W]
Norrish John, Fremington 1733 A
  John, South Molton 1744 W
Norrish John, North Molton 1822 W
  Martin, Hartland 1597 [W]
  Mary, Barnstaple 1621 [W]
Norrish Mary Ann, Loosemore, Oakford 1854 A
Norrish Philip, Ashreigney 1666 W
Norrishe Richard, Ashreigney 1627 [W]
Norrish Richard, East Anstey 1698 A
Norrishe Robert, Molland 1635 W
Norrish Samuel, Rackenford 1778 W
Norrish Samuel, Rackenford 1825 W
  Susan, Barnstaple 1636 W
  Thomas, South Molton 1563 W
Nores William, Ashreigney 1565 W
  William, North Molton 1587 W
Norrish William, Ashreigney 1707 W
Norrishe Willmot, Ashreigney 1625 [W]
Norraway see Narraway
Norrice, Norrish, Norrishe see Norris
Northam Alice, Meeth 1631 [W]
  David, Yarnscombe 1597 [W]
  Henry, Dolton 1612 [W]; forename blank in Ms; supplied
   from parish register
Nortyam Henry, Meeth 1712 A
  John, Barnstaple 1619 [W]
  Nicholas, Huish 1636 A
  Peter, Meeth 1665 W
  Samson, Dolton 1664 W
  Thomas, Ilfracombe 1732 W
Northcott, Norcott, Northcote
  ..., Frithelstock 1611 [W]
  ..., Nymet Rowland 1612 [W]
  Alfred, Buckland Brewer 1772 A
  Alice, Great Torrington 1582 W
  Bridget, Monkleigh 1690 [W] and 1708 A
Northcote Christopher, Coldridge 1709 W
  Christopher, Chawleigh 1771 W and 1780 W
  Edward, Combe Martin 1749 W
  Elizabeth, Chawleigh 1664 [W]
  Elizabeth, Buckland Brewer 1734 W
  George, Burrington 1702 W
Northcote George, Iddesleigh 1712 W
  George, Lapford 1763 W
Northcote George, Lapford 1817 W
Northcote George, Thelbridge 1850 W
  Giles, Fremington 1639 W
  Giles 1704 A

Norcott Joan, East Putford 1788 W
Northcott alias Taylder John, Landcross 1581 W
  John, Woolfardisworthy 1619 [W]
  John, Brushford 1624 [W]
  John, Nymet Rowland, snr. 1634 [W]
  John, Lapford 1671 W
  John, Monkleigh 1681 W
  John, Chawleigh, jnr. 1702 W
  John, snr. 1702 W
  John, Bideford 1715 A
  John, Iddesleigh 1715 W
Norcott John, Combe Martin 1856 W
  Mary, Bow 1739 W
  Peter, Coldridge 1622 [W]
  Philip, Chulmleigh 1624 [W]
  Philip, Burrington 1668 W
  Radigon, Frithelstock 1616 [W]
  Richard, Combe Martin 1668 A
  Richard, Bideford 1690 W
  Richard, Combe Martin 1700 A
  Richard, Thelbridge 1848 W
Northcote Robert, Chawleigh 1727 A
  Robert, Bow 1735 A
  Roger, Bondleigh 1623 [W]
  Roger, Lapford 1696 W
  Roger, Lapford 1772 W
  Roger, Barnstaple 1852 W
  Samuel, Parkham 1623 [W]
  Sybil, Parkham 1631 [W]
  Stephen, Parkham 1624 [W]
  Stephen, East Putford 1640 W
  Stephen, Buckland Brewer 1715 A
Norcott Stephen, East Putford 1725 W
  Stephen, Lapford 1774 W
  Stephen, Cruwys Morchard 1823 A
  Thomas, Parkham 1619 [W]
  Valentine, Dolton 1593 [W]
  William, West Anstey 1601 W
  William, Fremington 1690 A
  William, Chawleigh 1728 W
  William, Lapford 1737 W
Norcott William, Berrynarbor 1822 W
Northdon see Nordon
Northley, Northleigh
  Northleigh Elizabeth, Bow 1835 W
  Thomas, Bow 1809 W
Northway Thomas, Westleigh 1745 A
Norton, Nortune
  ..., Buckland Filleigh 1609 [W]
  Ann, Witheridge 1666 W
  Nortune John, Petrockstowe 1578 W
  Robert, Witheridge 1645 A
Norwood Roger, Great Torrington 1589 W
Nosworthy William, Bow 1634 W
Nott, Not, Notte, Nout
  ..., Witheridge 1604 [W]
  Nott or Nutt ..., Barnstaple 1637 O
  Agnes, Rose Ash 1718 A
  Agnes, Chittlehampton 1743 W
  Alexander, Pilton 1723 A
  Alphonse, Chawleigh 1564 W
  Amesius, Chulmleigh 1707 A
  Ann, Bratton Fleming 1628 [W] and 1630 O
  Ann, Chittlehampton 1704 W
  Ann, Chulmleigh 1732 W
  Ann wife of John see Ann Carter
  Arthur, Beaford 1750 W
  Barbara, Chawleigh 1622 [W]
  Charity, Chittlehampton 1668 A
  Charity, Rose Ash 1724 W
  Christopher, Witheridge 1604 W
  Christopher, High Bickington 1703 W
  Christopher, South Molton 1722 A
  Edward, Filleigh 1739 A
  Edward, Filleigh 1787 W

Edward, West Buckland 1833 W
Elias, Rose Ash 1715 W
Elias, Chittlehampton 1736 W
Elias, Chittlehampton 1760 W
Elizabeth, St Giles in the Wood 1592 [W]
Elizabeth, King's Nympton 1722 W
Elizabeth, Merton 1785 W
Ellen, South Molton 1814 W
Frances, Chittlehampton 1804 W*
Not alias Dun George, South Molton 1720 A
George, Combe Martin 1742 A
George, Chulmleigh 1769 W
George, Barnstaple 1770 A
Grace, South Molton 1663 W
Grace, Bideford 1672 W
Grace, Shirwell 1732 A
Grace, South Molton 1850 W
Gregory, Bratton Fleming 1720 A
Henry, Rose Ash 1565 W
Hugh, Cheldon 1597 [W]
Humphrey, Great Torrington 1603 W
Joan, Rose Ash, widow 1573 W
Noett Joan 1573 W
Joan, Burrington 1620 [W]
Joan, Lapford 1628 [W]
Joan, Trentishoe 1686 A
Nout John, Combe Martin 1571 W
Notte John, Molland 1574 W
John, St Giles in the Wood 1586 A
John, Mariansleigh 1591 [W]
John, Witheridge 1591 [W]
John, Cheldon 1592 [W]
John, Cheldon 1619 [W]
John, Chittlehampton 1636 A and O
John, Stoodleigh 1665 W
John, Chittlehampton 1667 A
John, Beaford 1670 W and 1672 W
John, Rose Ash 1675 W
John, Chittlehampton 1686 A
John, Lapford, snr. 1688 W
John, Chittlehampton 1723 W
John, South Molton 1737 W
Noett John, Rose Ash 1739 W
John, Filleigh 1743 W
John, Chulmleigh 1745 W
John, Cheldon 1756 A
John, North Molton 1773 W
John, Witheridge 1774 A
John, Merton 1794 W
John, East Down, gentleman 1800 W
John, Shirwell, yeoman 1805 W
Judith, Beaford 1701 W
Lodovic, Mariansleigh 1628 [W]
Margery, Chittlehampton 1669 W
Mary, Ilfracombe 1592 [W]
Mary, Stoodleigh 1666 W
Not alias Dun Mary, South Molton 1720 W
Mary, South Molton 1722 A
Mary, South Molton 1758 A
Mary, Chawleigh 1777 W
Mary, Merton 1831 W
Mary and William, South Molton 1743 A
Michael, South Molton 1824 W
Moses, Witheridge 1695 W
Philip, Chawleigh 1710 W
Richard, Rose Ash 1572 W
Robert, Heanton Punchardon 1699 W
Robert, Roborough 1728 A
Robert, Chittlehampton 1775 W
Samuel, Northam 1743 W
Sarah, South Molton 1737 W
Susan, Chittlehampton 1684 W
Susan, Berrynarbor 1798 A
Thomas, St Giles in the Wood 1565 W
Thomas, Great Torrington 1568 W

Notte Thomas, Chittlehampton 1572 W
Thomas, South Molton 1624 [W]
Thomas, Stoodleigh 1665 W
Thomas, Peters Marland 1678 W
Thomas, Merton 1776 W
Not William, Chulmleigh 1565 W
William, North Molton 1589 W
William, Rackenford 1589 A
Notte William, Monkleigh 1617 [W]
William, Ashreigney 1621 [W]
William, North Molton 1631 [W]
William, Chulmleigh 1663 W
William, Chittlehampton 1665 W
William, George Nympton 1706 W
William, South Molton 1710 W
William, East Down 1723 W
William, High Bickington 1741 W
William, South Molton 1746 A; A dbn 1758
William, Rose Ash 1753 W
William, Challacombe, yeoman 1816 A to John of
    Chittlehampton, son
William, Meshaw 1850 W
William, Shirwell 1852 W
William and Mary, South Molton 1743 A
Noy John, Hartland 1639 W
Nutcombe, Nuttcombe
    Elizabeth, West Worlington 1762 W
    Nuttcombe John, Ilfracombe 1631 [W]
Nutt, Nutte
    Nutt or Nott ..., Barnstaple 1637 O
    Agnes, Mariansleigh 1663 W
    Alice, Combe Martin 1725 W
    Ann, Chittlehampton 1676 W
    Anthony, Burrington 1662 W
    Anthony, Georgeham 1776 A
    Christian, Berrynarbor 1782 W
    Clement, Combe Martin 1597 [W]
    David, Combe Martin 1622 [W]
    David, Combe Martin 1698 A
    Edward, Combe Martin 1642 A
    Edward, Combe Martin 1660 W
    Nutte Elizabeth, Charles 1578 W
    Humphrey, South Molton 1758 W
    Joan, Combe Martin 1597 [W]
    Joan, Combe Martin 1769 W
    John, Combe Martin, snr. 1637 W
    John, Chittlehampton 1672 W
    John, Bideford 1691 A
    John, Tawstock 1756 A
    John, Berrynarbor 1762 W
    Nicholas, Combe Martin 1621 [W]
    Nicholas, Combe Martin 1663 W
    Nicholas, Combe Martin 1737 W and 1752 W
    Nicholas, Ilfracombe 1760 W
    Richard, Parracombe 1626 [W]
    Richard, Combe Martin 1661 A
    Richard, Combe Martin 1723 W
    Richard, Combe Martin 1781 W
    Sarah, Ilfracombe 1763 [W]
    Susan, Bideford 1768 W
    Thomas, Monkleigh 1620 [W]
    William, Combe Martin 1573 W
    William, Bratton Fleming 1670 W
    William, Alverdiscott 1684 W
    William, South Molton 1838 W and 1852 W
Nuttcombe see Nutcombe
Nycholl, Nycholls see Nichols
Nycke see Nicks
Nycoll, Nycolle, Nycolls see Nichols
Nylde see Neale

Oadam see Odam
Oake, Oke
    Oke ..., Coldridge 1616 [W]
    John, Fremington 1589 A

Oke Richard, Hartland 1832 W
Oke Walter, Northam 1856 W
Oataway see Oatway
Oates, Oatts, Oatty
   Oatts ...., Buckland Brewer 1601 A
   Oatty Anthony, Georgeham 1630 O
   Gertrude, Georgeham 1707 A
   Oates alias Watts Tristram, Georgeham 1642 W
Oatway, Oataway, Oateway, Oattaway, Otaway
   Oatway Amos, Ilfracombe 1717 W
   Oataway Dorothy, Ilfracombe, widow 1806 W
   Oataway James, Yarnscombe 1831 W
   John, Yarnscombe 1836 W
   Mary, Great Torrington 1817 W
   Nathaniel, Great Torrington, millwright 1798 A
   Otaway Richard, Ilfracombe 1733 W
   Richard, Bideford 1780 W
   Oateway Stephen, High Bickington 1688 W
   Oattaway William, Ilfracombe 1765 W
Odam, Oadam
   Charity, South Molton 1619 [W]
   Clement, South Molton 1722 W
   Clement, ship *Sandwich* 1749 A
   Clement, Chawleigh 1762 W
   David, Barnstaple 1679 W and 1689 W
   George, Georgeham 1783 W
   George, South Molton 1851 W
   Hugh, South Molton 1664 W
   James, South Molton 1847 W
   John, Romansleigh, jnr. 1566 W
   John, Chulmleigh 1626 [W]
   John, South Molton 1721 W
   John, South Molton 1746 A
   Oadam Mary, Chulmleigh 1628 [W]
   Peter, Chittlehampton 1586 W
   Richard, South Molton 1638 W
   Robert, South Molton 1632 [W]
   Thomas, South Molton 1605 W
   William, South Molton 1719 W
Odford Thomas, Bideford 1678 A
O'Donaghue Cosgaipre, Hallifield, Shebbear 1842 W
Oissell alias Weiche Joan, High Bickington, widow 1581 W
Oke see Oake
Old, Olde
   Olde Agnes, Parkham 1636 A
   Olde Grace, Woolfardisworthy 1803 A
   Humphrey, Northam 1722 A
   Jasper, Clovelly 1672 W
   Olde John, Buckland Brewer 1588 A
   John, East Putford 1681 W
   Olde Mathew, Parkham 1627 [W]
   Patience, Woolfardisworthy 1691 W
   Olde Richard, Clovelly 1616 [W]
   Richard, Hartland 1696 W
   Susan, Abbotsham, widow 1815 A to John, labourer, son
   William, East Putford 1691 W
   William, Woolfardisworthy 1732 A
Oldam Edward, Buckland Brewer 1714 W
Olding, Olden, Oldinge, Oulden, Ouldon
   Oulden George, Lapford 1702 A
   Ouldon John, Lapford 1676 W
   Olden Peter, Great Torrington 1623 [W] and 1624 O
   Oldinge Robert, South Molton 1592 [W]
   Thomas, Coldridge 1716 A
   Oldinge William, Lapford 1615 [W]
Oleborough ..., Barnstaple 1605 [W]
Oliver, Olyver
   ..., Brendon 1611 [W]
   ..., Heanton Punchardon 1616 [W]
   Alexander, Hartland 1599 [W]
   Anthony, Pilton 1622 [W]
   Catherine, Barnstaple 1733 W
   Digory, Shebbear 1643 W
   Elizabeth, Barnstaple 1700 W
   Emanuel, Bideford 1637 W

Ezekiel, Ashreigney 1628 [W]
George, South Molton 1703 W
George, Woolfardisworthy 1753 W and 1759 A
Henry, Stoke Rivers 1595 [W]
Henry, South Molton 1748 A
Honor, Barnstaple 1621 [W]
James, Barnstaple 1616 [W]
James, Barnstaple 1679 W
Joan, Great Torrington 1630 [W]
Joan, North Molton 1754 W
John, Hartland 1583 A
John, Barnstaple 1592 [W]
John, Bideford 1714 A
John, South Molton 1729 W
John, Bideford 1731 A
John, South Molton 1753 A
John, North Molton 1812 W
Maria wife of Peter Hurdon see Peter Harding
Mary, Barnstaple 1698 W
Mary, Bideford 1833 W
Mary, South Molton, widow 1849 A to Eleanor Hunsworthy
   Pollock, widow and Mary Eliza Oliver, sp., both of Pilton,
   daughters
Mary Eliza, Ilfracombe 1853 W
Nicholas, South Molton 1632 [W]
Nicholas, Bideford 1706 A
Olyver Philip, Hartland 1573 W
Philip, Hartland 1579 A
Richard, Barnstaple 1609 [W]; forename blank in Ms;
   supplied from parish register
Olyver Robert, Barnstaple 1589 W
Robert, Barnstaple 1660 A
Robert, Bideford 1703 A
Samuel, Bideford 1769 W
Thomas, Bideford, snr. 1749 W
Thomas, ship *Edinburgh* 1750 A
Thomas, South Molton 1752 W
Thomasine, Northam 1622 [W]
William, South Molton 1687 A
William, Barnstaple 1697 A
William, Chittlehampton 1716 A
William, Lynton 1737 W
William, South Molton 1764 W
William, Bideford 1825 W
Onyon Thomas, Northam 1618 [W]
Orchard, Orchar
   ..., Petrockstowe 1607 [W] and 1610 [W]
   Elizabeth, Bideford 1769 A
   George, Abbotsham 1735 W
   Orchar Joan, Pilton 1731 A
   Orchard alias Tooker John, Frithelstock 1568 W
   Orchard alias Tooker John, Langtree 1575 A
   Orchard alias Tooker John 1582 W
   John, Northam 1675 A
   John, Northam 1706 A
   Mary, Pilton 1664 W
   Sarah, Bideford 1754 W
   Thomas, Northam 1752 W
   William, Hartland 1708 W
Ormond Mary Ann, Barnstaple, sp. 1852 A to Fanny Loverey
   Ormond
Orrell Mary, Hartland 1707 W
   Richard, Hartland 1688 W
Orton Nathaniel, Shirwell 1741 W
Osborne, Osbarne, Osborn, Osbourne, Osburne
   Osbarne ..., Abbotsham 1613 [W]
   Osburne Charity, Abbotsham 1626 [W]
   Osborn Edward, Langtree 1812 W
   Elizabeth, Abbotsham 1578 A
   Elizabeth, Northam 1719 W
   Osbourne George, Barnstaple 1660 W
   Osbarne Hugh, Iddesleigh 1603 W
   James, Northam 1709 A
   James, Bideford 1721 W
   Osburne John, Abbotsham 1643 W

Osbourne John, Abbotsham 1661 W
John, Bideford 1681 A
Osbourne John, Huish 1695 W
John, Welcombe 1697 W
Osbourne Lodovic, Petrockstowe 1682 W
Richard, Tawstock 1713 A
Osbourne Robert, Tawstock 1687 A
Osborn Samuel, Huish 1716 W
Thomas, Petrockstowe 1639 W
Osbourn Thomas, South Molton 1675 A
Thomas, Newton St Petrock 1698 A
William, Berrynarbor 1575 W and 1576 W
Osell see Oswell
Osler John, Great Torrington 1791 W
Osmond, Osmonde Osmont
Osmont alias Morrish Christian, Marwood 1579 W
Christopher 1725 A
George, Winkleigh 1663 A
Henry, South Molton 1620 [W]
Isota, Winkleigh 1624 [W]
Joan, South Molton 1692 W
Osmonde John, Zeal Monachorum 1566 W
John, High Bray 1593 [W]
John, Winkleigh 1640 A
Osmand John, South Molton 1703 W
Lodovic, Winkleigh 1623 [W]
Oswell, Osell, Ossell
Elizabeth and George, Instow 1629 [W]
George and Elizabeth, Instow 1629 [W]
Osell alias Weche Joan, High Bickington 1580 W
Ossell alias Wyche John, Westleigh 1569 W
Osell alias Wiche Peter, Fremington 1580 W
Simon, Littleham (near Bideford) 1625 [W]
Ossell Stephen, Westleigh 1612 [W] "Welch alias Ossell" in
register; forename blank in Ms; supplied from parish register
Otaway see Oatway
Ottery Joan, South Molton 1739 W
Ouldon see Olding
Owen, Owens, Ownes
Ann, South Molton 1817 [W]
Owens Charles, Ilfracombe 1698 A
Owens Eleanor, Bideford 1719 W
Owens Francis, Northam 1733 W
Henry, Dolton, gentleman 1808 W
Jane, Dolton 1832 A to Frances, widow
Joan, Barnstaple 1766 A
John, Barnstaple 1644 W
John, Parkham 1695 W
Ownes John, Westleigh 1707 A
Margaret, Northam 1631 [W]
Robert, Marwood 1593 [W]
Owens Robert, Northam 1702 A
Oyens Samuel, Bideford 1798 A
Owens Sarah, Ilfracombe 1717 W
Thomas, South Molton 1814 W
Thomas, Dolton 1839 W
Oxenham, Oxeham
... 1637 W
Abraham, Barnstaple 1838 W
Ann, Northam 1776 W
Betty, Charles 1844 W
Clement, Cruwys Morchard 1598 [W]
Oxeham Edward, Molland 1817 W
Gideon, Great Torrington 1637 A
Grace, Winkleigh 1729 W
Jane, Winkleigh 1710 A
Joan, Stoodleigh 1760 W
John, Weare Giffard 1731 W
John, Northam 1769 W
John, Westleigh 1783 A
Julian, Meshaw 1579 A
Mary, Oakford 1716 W
Richard, Winkleigh 1699 W
Richard, Winkleigh 1735 W
Robert, Oakford 1740 W

Robert, Oakford, gentleman 1800 W
Thomas, Oakford 1704 W
Thomas, Northam 1848 W

Packer ..., Chulmleigh 1607 [W]
..., Chulmleigh 1614 [W]
Ann, Lapford 1766 W
Elizabeth, Coldridge 1711 W
Elizabeth, Lapford, widow 1806 W
Elizabeth wife of Arthur see Elizabeth Cornish Leigh
George, Lapford 1697 W
George, Lapford 1793 W
George, Lapford, yeoman 1806 W
George, Lapford 1832 W
Grace, Bondleigh 1730 W
James, Coldridge 1754 W
John, Coldridge 1643 W
John, Bondleigh 1730 W
John, Coldridge 1742 A
John, Witheridge 1787 W
John, East Worlington 1801 A
John, Barnstaple 1827 W
Mary, Great Torrington 1807 W
Mary, Chulmleigh 1830 W
Richard, South Molton 1838 A to Elizabeth, widow
Richard, Tawstock 1849 W
Thomas, Zeal Monachorum 1673 A and O
Thomas, Lapford 1743 W
William, Lapford 1738 W
William, Lapford 1768 A
Paddon, Padon
..., Burrington 1614 [W]
Agnes, Burrington 1616 [W]
Catherine, High Bickington 1757 W
Catherine, Ilfracombe 1804 W
Daniel, Atherington 1631 [W]
Elizabeth, Great Torrington 1641 W
George, Bondleigh 1592 [W]
George, Burrington 1615 [W]
George, Dowland 1661 W
George, Winkleigh 1684 W
George, Winkleigh 1748 A
George, Winkleigh, jnr. 1844 W
Hugh, Dolton 1710 A
Hugh, Pilton 1713 W
Isott, Shebbear 1605 W
James, Alwington 1843 A to Samuel of Parkham, brother
Joan, Winkleigh 1582 W
Joan, Ashreigney 1631 [W]
Joan, Alwington 1638 A
Joan, Wembworthy 1643 A
Joan, Winkleigh 1665 W
John, Ashreigney 1567 W
John, Burrington 1594 [W]
John, Winkleigh 1607 [W]; forename blank in Ms; supplied
from parish register
John, Burrington 1632 [W]
John, Bow 1711 A
John, Iddesleigh 1725 W
John, High Bickington 1745 W
John, Iddesleigh 1747 W
John, Atherington 1793 A
John, High Bickington 1814 W
John, Iddesleigh 1815 W
John, Atherington 1817 W
Judith, Atherington 1670 W
Margaret, Wembworthy 1633 W
Margery, Dowland 1690 W
Mary, Westleigh 1709 W
Mary, Dolton 1727 W
Nicholas, Winkleigh 1571 W
Peter, Barnstaple 1643 A
Philip, Dolton 1679 A
Philip, Dolton 1734 W
Richard, Burrington 1598 [W] and 1602 W

Richard, Filleigh 1641 A
Robert, Ashreigney 1617 [W]
Padon Robert, Westleigh 1705 [W]
Samuel, Parkham 1856 W
Susan, Iddesleigh 1807 W
Thomas, Wembworthy 1586 A
Thomas, Wembworthy 1631 [W]
Thomas, Burrington 1641 W
Thomas, Winkleigh 1675 W
Thomas, Dolton 1727 W
William, Chittlehampton 1629 [W]
William, Iddesleigh 1675 W
William, Great Torrington 1680 A
William, Winkleigh 1729 W
William, Cruwys Morchard 1780 W
Willmot, Iddesleigh 1674 W
Pafford, Pafforde, Pawford
John, North Tawton 1573 W
John, North Tawton 1719 W and 1733 W
Pafforde Mark, North Tawton 1573 W
Pagam Lewis, Yarnscombe 1592 [W]
Page, Paidge, Paige, Payge
Payge Ann, Bideford 1637 W
Bartholomew, Sheepwash 1758 W
Beaton, Chulmleigh 1754 W
Paige Grace, South Molton 1829 W
Paige Grace, South Molton 1838 A to John Allen Paige and
    William B. Paige, brothers
Paidge James, Westleigh 1593 [W]
Paige James, Shebbear 1813 W
Paige Jane, South Molton 1838 A to John Allen Paige, Ann
    and Mary Eliza, brother and sisters
Paige John, Barnstaple 1670 A
John, Roborough 1837 W
Mary, High Bickington 1845 W
Paige Robert, Sheepwash 1817 W
Paige William, Badcock 1844 W
Paine, Pain, Payn, Payne, Peine
Payne ..., St Giles in the Wood 1602 [W]
Peine ..., Rose Ash 1603 [W]
..., Bideford 1607 [W] and 1609 [W]
..., St Giles in the Wood 1609 [W]
..., Nymet Rowland 1611 [W]
Payne Agnes, St Giles in the Wood 1619 [W]
Alice, Tawstock 1565 W
Payne Elizabeth, Great Torrington 1729 W
Payne George, St Giles in the Wood 1593 [W]
Payne Helen Webber, Winkleigh 1837 W removed by
    monition into the Consistory Court in Exeter
Payn Henry, Bideford 1669 A
Henry, St Giles in the Wood 1692 W
Payne Henry, St Giles in the Wood 1748 A
Payne James, Barnstaple 1837 A
Payne John, Nymet Rowland 1574 W
Payne John, Barnstaple 1602 [W]; forename blank in Ms;
    supplied from parish register
Payne John, Alwington 1627 [W]
Payne John, Rose Ash 1638 A
Payne John, Tawstock 1643 W
Pain John, Bideford 1679 A
Payne John, St Giles in the Wood 1703 W
Payne John, Barnstaple 1813 W
Payne Lawrence, St Giles in the Wood 1735 W
Peyne Margery, Barnstaple 1623 [W]
Payne Mary, Barnstaple 1836 W
Payn Nicholas, Barnstaple 1586 W
Payne Robert, St Giles in the Wood 1675 W
Payne Rose, Barnstaple 1622 [W]
Payne Stephen, Bideford 1598 [W]
Payne Walter, Bideford, jnr. 1712 A
Payne William, Cheldon 1573 W
Payne William, Rose Ash 1593 [W]
Peyne William, Alwington 1604 [W]; forename blank in Ms;
    supplied from parish register
Payne William, Barnstaple 1628 [W]

Payne William, Great Torrington 1717 W
Payne William, Barnstaple 1741 W
Painter, Paynter
Hannah, Pilton 1836 W
Henry, North Molton 1715 A
Paynter John, Langtree 1586 W
Paynter Philip, Parkham 1587 W
Paynter Richard, South Molton 1583 W
Robert, North Molton 1781 W
Paynter William, South Molton 1590 [W]
Palbridge Mary see Robert Pike
Palford Joan, North Tawton 1589 W
Palfreman, Palfreeman, Palfremen, Palfriman, Palfryman
Edmund, Tawstock 1776 W
Palfryman Edward, Molland 1691 A
James, South Molton 1854 W
Palfreeman Jane, Tawstock 1794 A
Joan, Twitchen 1712 A
John, Molland 1739 W
John, Molland 1774 W
John, Molland 1845 A
John, Countisbury, surgeon 1848 A to James, brother
John, Countisbury 1855 A
Margaret see William Kingdon
Richard, Filleigh 1762 W
Robert, Molland 1596 [W]
Palfriman Robert, Twitchen 1706 W
Palfriman Thomas, Molland 1704 W
Thomas, West Buckland 1814 W
Palk, Palke
Palke William, South Molton 1760 W
William, South Molton 1789 A
Palmer ..., Chittlehampton 1602 [W]
..., Frithelstock 1605 [W]
..., Parkham 1607 [W]
..., Northam 1610 [W]
..., Barnstaple 1611 [W]
..., Northam 1614 [W]
Agnes, Northam 1587 W
Agnes, Monkleigh 1771 W
Alice, Westleigh, widow 1564 W
Ann, Frithelstock 1693 W
Anthony, Barnstaple 1596 [W]
Anthony, Barnstaple 1693 W
Cad-Edwards, Instow 1857 W
Charity, Buckland Brewer 1743 A and 1744 A
Christopher, Great Torrington 1682 W and 1684 A
Christopher, Buckland Brewer 1749 A
Christopher, Little Torrington 1784 W
Daniel, Shebbear 1636 W
Elizabeth, Barnstaple 1745 W
Elizabeth, Langtree 1836 W
Emanuel, Great Torrington 1644 A
Emanuel, Little Torrington 1670 W
Esther, Barnstaple 1704 W
Fortune, Langtree 1770 A
Gabriel, Northam 1632 [W]
George, Frithelstock 1602 W
George, Frithelstock 1663 W
George, Monkleigh 1711 W
George, Bideford 1781 W
Grace, Great Torrington 1633 W
Henry, Northam 1618 [W]
Henry, Heanton Punchardon 1635 A and 1637 O
Hugh, Parkham 1609 [W]; forename blank in Ms; supplied
    from parish register
Humphrey, Atherington 1704 A
Humphrey, Monkleigh 1721 W
Jacob, Barnstaple 1737 W
Jane, Great Torrington 1602 [W]
Jane, Great Torrington 1750 W
John, Burrington 1565 W
John, Parkham 1579 W
John, Langtree 1585 A
John, Yarnscombe 1592 [W]

John, Frithelstock 1620 [W]
John, Little Torrington 1676 A
John, Frithelstock 1680 A
John, Barnstaple 1698 A
John, Beaford 1700 W
John, Northam 1701 W
John, Barnstaple 1706 A
John, Beaford 1706 A
John, Frithelstock 1709 A
John, Monkleigh 1715 W
John, Barnstaple 1718 W
John, Monkleigh 1726 W
John, Frithelstock 1748 A
John, Barnstaple 1758 W
John, Great Torrington 1767 A
John, Bideford 1836 W
John, Great Torrington 1838 W
John, Peters Marland 1838 W
Joseph, ship *Port Malon* 1746 A
Joseph, South Molton 1795 W
Margaret, High Bickington 1625 [W]
Mary, Atherington 1704 A
Mary, Buckland Filleigh 1739 W
Mathew, Buckland Brewer 1721 W
Nicholas, Barnstaple 1636 W
Philip, Northam 1587 W
Philip, Molland 1782 W
Richard, Yarnscombe 1565 W
Richard, Parkham 1573 A
Richard, South Molton 1587 W
Richard, Marwood 1607 [W]; forename blank in Ms; supplied
   from parish register
Richard, South Molton 1738 W
Robert, Huntshaw 1599 [W]
Robert, Parkham 1697 W
Samuel, Northam 1695 A and 1703 A
Samuel, Great Torrington 1725 W
Sarah, North Molton 1772 W
Simon, St Giles in the Wood 1635 W
Stephen, Frithelstock 1613 [W]; forename blank in Ms;
   supplied from parish register
Susan, Barnstaple 1666 A
Susan, Barnstaple 1738 W
Thomas, Parkham 1672 W
Thomas, Fremington 1679 W
Thomas, Northam 1703 A
Thomas, Barnstaple 1726 W
Thomas, North Tawton 1760 A
Thomasine, Yarnscombe 1588 W
Thomasine, Parkham 1624 [W]
Walter, Parkham 1593 [W]
Walter, Parkham 1623 [W]
Walter, Bideford 1744 W
William, Great Torrington 1592 [W]
William, Parkham 1598 [W]
William, Barnstaple 1612 [W]; forename blank in Ms;
   supplied from parish register
William, Great Torrington 1626 [W] and 1628 O
William, Frithelstock 1685 W
William, North Tawton 1737 A
William, Buckland Brewer 1773 W
William, Barnstaple 1780 W
Palmes William, Molland, miller 1804 W
William, Petrockstowe, yeoman 1806 W
William, Frithelstock, yeoman 1808 W
William, Peters Marland 1850 W
Willmot, Northam 1623 [W]
Paltridge Richard, Chulmleigh 1823 W and 1824 W
Richard, Chulmleigh 1844 W
Panter, Paunter
Paunter ..., Clovelly 1609 [W]
Paunter John, Parkham 1594 [W]
James, North Molton 1769 A
Richard, Abbotsham, snr. 1633 A
Roger, Abbotsham 1632 [W]

Thomas, Abbotsham 1629 [W]
Paunter Willmot, Parkham 1620 [W]
Parcell James, Ilfracombe 1707 A
Parcken, Parckens see Parkins
Parcker see Parker
Parcking, Parckinge see Parkins
Parckman see Parkman
Pardon, Peardon
Aaron see Sarah Pincombe
Henry, Merton 1766 A
Peardon John, Bideford 1675 W
Peardon John, Bideford 1678 W
John, Bideford 1733 W
Mary, Merton 1803 W
Peardon Robert, St Giles in the Wood 1681 W
Parett see Parrott
Parinter see Parminter
Parish, Paris, Parres, Parris
Paris John, Ilfracombe 1678 A
John, Bideford 1839 W
Parris Margaret, Bow 1573 W
Parrishe Mary, South Molton 1630 [W] and 1639 O
Parris Michael, Sheepwash 1575 W
Parrishe Richard, South Molton 1630 [W] and 1639 O
Parres Walter, Buckland Filleigh 1565 W
Parke John, Bow 1626 [W]
Robert, Barnstaple 1707 W
Parke alias Smithe William, Mariansleigh 1567 W
Parkehouse see Parkhouse
Parker, Parcker
Parcker ..., Chittlehampton 1602 [W] and 1607 [W]
..., Georgeham 1602 [W]
..., Meeth 1602 [W]
Parcker ..., Clovelly 1609 [W]
Parcker ..., Beaford 1611 [W]
Parcker Agnes, Georgeham, widow 1611 [W]; forename blank
   in Ms; supplied from parish register
Alice, Fremington 1578 W
Parcker Alice, Chittlehampton 1615 [W]
Amos, Georgeham 1741 A
Anthony, Tawstock 1578 W
Anthony, Chittlehampton 1599 [W]
Charles, Chittlehampton 1737 A
Charlotte, Barnstaple 1850 W
Christopher, Marwood, labourer 1820 A to Mary
Edward, Barnstaple 1665 A
Egline, Frithelstock 1671 W
Elizabeth, Chittlehampton 1829 W
Elizabeth, Ashreigney 1841 W
Francis, Clovelly 1644 A
Grace, Barnstaple 1690 A
Henry, Ashreigney 1593 [W]
Hugh, Fremington 1665 W
Hugh, Oakford 1730 A
James, Instow 1623 [W]
James, Berrynarbor 1636 W
James, Berrynarbor 1753 W
James, West Down, yeoman 1799 W
John, Witheridge 1564 W
John, Meshaw 1578 A
John, Chulmleigh 1588 W
John, Rackenford 1588 W
Parcker John, Georgeham 1609 [W]; forename blank in Ms;
   supplied from parish register
Parcker John, Georgeham 1617 [W]
Parcker John, Georgeham, jnr. 1618 [W]
John, Little Torrington 1629 [W]
John, Chittlehampton 1637 W
John, Fremington 1638 W and 1639 W
John, Countisbury 1663 W
John, Cruwys Morchard 1690 A
John, Instow 1698 W
John, Shebbear 1739 A
John, Georgeham 1762 A
John, Lapford 1765 W

John, Fremington 1775 W
John, Ilfracombe 1838 W
Mathew, Chittlehampton 1630 [W]
Mayhow, Meeth 1674 W
Nicholas, Georgeham 1597 [W]
Phineas, Barnstaple 1628 [W]
Phineas, Barnstaple 1695 W
Richard, Rackenford 1574 W
Richard, Fremington 1603 W
Parker alias Keeper Richard, Berrynarbor 1663 W another will
　　dated 1665
Parcker Robert, Clovelly 1617 [W]
Robert, Rackenford 1669 W
Roger, Witheridge 1753 W
Rose, Fremington 1594 [W]
Samuel, Buckland Brewer 1857 W
Squire, High Bickington, yeoman 1801 A
Susan, Fremington 1667 W
Thomas, Berrynarbor 1584 A
Thomas, Berrynarbor 1592 [W]
Thomas, Barnstaple 1610 [W]; forename blank in Ms;
　　supplied from parish register
Thomas, Berrynarbor 1632 [W]
Thomas, Chittlehampton 1839 A to Amy, widow
Thomas, Ilfracombe 1844 W
Thomasine, Instow 1628 [W]
Thomasine, Witheridge 1714 W
William, Instow 1665 W
William, Ilfracombe 1675 A
William, Ilfracombe 1704 W
William, Oakford 1739 W
William, Lapford 1741 W
William, Chittlehampton 1758 W
William, Chittlehampton 1822 W
William, Ashreigney 1833 W
Parkhouse, Parkehouse, Parkhowse
Parkhowse Elizabeth, Witheridge 1627 [W]
Humphrey, Witheridge 1685 W
Humphrey, Rackenford 1709 A and 1725 A
John, South Molton 1641 W
John, Witheridge 1663 [W]
John, Rackenford 1684 W
John, Witheridge 1685 A
John, Witheridge 1687 W
John, Witheridge, snr. 1698 W
John, Monkleigh 1718 W
John, Langtree, snr. 1800 W
John, Ashreigney, yeoman 1806 A
John, Ashreigney, thatcher 1808 A
Margaret, Knowstone 1598 [W]
Mary, Frithelstock 1822 W
William, Witheridge 1677 W
William, Weare Giffard 1791 A
William, Monkleigh, limeburner 1844 A to Elizabeth, widow
Parkins, Parcken, Parckens, Parcking, Parckinge, Parkin,
　　Parking, Parkinge, Parkyn, Parkyne, Parkyns, Parrkinge,
　　Perken, Perkin, Perking, Perkins, Perkyn, Perkyns
Parcken ..., Shebbear 1607 [W]
Parcken ..., Sheepwash 1610 [W]
Parcken ..., Huntshaw 1611 [W]
Parcken ..., Pilton 1614 [W]
Perkins ..., Buckland Filleigh 1699 [W]
Perkyn Agnes, Petrockstowe 1637 A
Parckinge Alexander, Countisbury 1618 [W]
Parkin Alexander, Fremington, yeoman 1855 A to Prudence,
　　widow
Parkin Alice, Beaford 1723 W
Perkyn Ambrose, Arlington 1637 W
Perkyn Amesius, Kentisbury 1636 W
Parcken Amos, Trentishoe 1606 W
Andrew, Bratton Fleming 1667 A
Perkin Ann, South Molton 1670 W
Parkin Ann, Ilfracombe 1742 W
Perkin Ann, Petrockstowe 1750 W
Parkin Ann, Bideford, sp. 1799 W

Parkin Ann, Loxhore 1850 W
Perkyn Charity, Arlington 1635 W
Parkin Charity, Merton 1682 W
Parckens Christopher, Chittlehampton 1589 W
Perken David, Brendon 1584 W
Parkyn David, Fremington 1624 [W]
Perken Edmund, Petrockstowe 1581 W
Perkyn Edmund, Huish 1627 [W]
Parcken Edward, North Tawton 1601 W
Parckinge Edward, Arlington 1616 [W]
Parkyn Edward, Arlington 1630 [W] and 1632 [W]
Perkin Edward, North Tawton 1668 A
Perkin Edward, King's Nympton 1716 A
Parkin Eleanor, Petrockstowe 1730 A
Perken Elizabeth, Petrockstowe 1575 W
Perkyn Elizabeth, Pilton 1636 W
Parkin Elizabeth, Barnstaple 1676 W
Perkin Elizabeth, St Giles in the Wood, widow 1799 W
Parkin Elizabeth, Barnstaple 1846 W
Parkin Emma, South Molton 1748 W
Parkin George, South Molton 1728 W
Parkin George, South Molton 1766 W
Parkin George, Arlington 1841 W
Perkin George, Frithelstock 1854 W
Perkin Grace, Parkham 1691 A
Parcking Henry, Woolfardisworthy 1618 [W]
Perking Henry, Petrockstowe 1671 A
Perkin Henry, Buckland Filleigh 1761 W
Perkin Henry, Langtree 1821 W
Parkin Hugh, High Bray 1778 W
Perkin Humphrey, Great Torrington 1753 A
Perkyn James, Fremington 1636 W
Parkin James, Ilfracombe 1735 W
Perkin Jane, Brendon 1681 W
Perkin Joachim, Chittlehampton 1680 A
Parken Joan, Martinhoe, widow 1572 W
Parckinge Joan, Fremington 1605 W
Perkyn Joan, Fremington 1640 W
Perkin Joan, Petrockstowe 1683 A
Parkin Joan, Barnstaple 1731 W
Parkin Joan, South Molton 1745 A
Parken John, Challacombe 1565 W
Parkinge John, Martinhoe 1569 W
Parkyns John, Westleigh 1573 A
Parken John, Chittlehampton 1587 W
Parkin John, Brendon 1592 [W]
Parkinge John, Ashreigney 1597 [W]
Parckinge John, Arlington 1604 [W] "of Cleve Town";
　　forename blank in Ms; supplied from parish register
Parckinge John, Meeth 1618 [W]
Perkyn John, Petrockstowe 1622 [W]
Perkyn John, Pilton 1629 [W]
Perking John, Arlington 1631 [W]
Perkyn John, Brendon, snr. 1637 A
Perkyn John, Ilfracombe 1638 W
Perkin John, Brendon 1670 W
Parkin John, Barnstaple 1673 [W]
Perkin John, Heanton Punchardon 1678 A
Perkin John, Parkham 1687 W
Parkin John, Brendon 1698 A
Parkin John, Great Torrington 1726 A and 1734 A
Parkin John, High Bickington 1749 A
Perkin John, ship *Ripton* 1751 W
Parking John, Tawstock 1778 W
Perkin John, St Giles in the Wood 1783 W
Parkin John, Brightley, Chittlehampton, yeoman 1807 W
Parkin Joseph, Buckland Filleigh 1729 W
Parrkinge Lambert, Marwood 1573 A
Parckinge Leonard, Huish 1606 W
Parcken Lewis, Brendon 1600 W
Parcken Lewis, Buckland Filleigh 1601 W
Parkin Margaret, Heanton Punchardon 1689 A
Perkin Mary, Wembworthy 1695 A
Perkin Nicholas, Barnstaple 1716 W
Perkins Paul, Lynton 1667 W

Parkin Philip, Charles 1679 W
Parkin Philip, Bideford 1776 W
Parkin Philip, Bratton Fleming, yeoman 1807 W
Parckinge Richard, Barnstaple 1616 [W]
Perkins Richard, Bideford 1716 W
Parkin Richard, South Molton 1739 A
Parkin Richard, Pilton, miller 1807 W
Parkyn Robert, Sheepwash 1630 [W]
Perkin Robert, Sheepwash 1670 O
Perkin Robert, West Buckland 1709 W
Parkin Robert, Brendon 1718 W and 1727 W
Parkin Robert, Brendon 1742 W
Parken Roger, Brendon 1585 W
Perkin Roger, Petrockstowe 1680 W
Parkin Roger, Chittlehampton 1845 W
Perkin Samuel, Barnstaple 1716 W
Parkin Samuel, Tawstock, yeoman 1799 W
Parkin Silvester, Burrington 1706 W
Parken Thomas, Petrockstowe 1571 W
Parckinge Thomas, Sheepwash 1616 [W]
Perkin Thomas, Roborough 1642 W
Parkin Thomas, Tawstock 1817 W
Perkyn Walter, Huish 1637 W
Perkin Walter, Huntshaw 1643 W
Parkin Walter, North Tawton 1716 W
Parkyne William, Filleigh 1583 W
Parken William, Meeth 1587 [W] and 1599 [W]
Parcken William, Barnstaple 1606 W
Parckinge William, Petrockstowe 1608 [W]; forename blank
   in Ms; supplied from parish register
Perkyn William, Roborough 1635 W
Perkin William, South Molton 1667 A
Perkin William, Arlington 1673 A and 1674 O
Perkin William, Parracombe 1689 A
Perkin William, South Molton 1694 W
Parkin William, Northam 1744 W
Parkin William, Bratton Fleming 1764 W
Parkin William, Arlington 1782 A
Parkin William, 40th Regiment of Foot 1805 A
Parkin William, Arlington, yeoman 1811 A
Parkin William, Barnstaple 1828 W
Parkin William, Warkleigh 1837 W
Parkin William, Chittlehampton, yeoman 1845 A to Mary,
   widow
Perkin William, Northam 1856 W
Parkeman see Parkman
Parken, Parkin, Parking, Parkinge see Parkins
Parkman, Parckman, Parkeman
   Parckman ..., Bratton Fleming 1612 [W]
   Parkeman Hugh, Brendon 1721 W
   Joan, Fremington 1622 [W]
   Parckman John, Fremington 1607 [W] "of Collacott" in
      register; forename blank in Ms; supplied from parish register
   John, Countisbury 1634 A
   John, Fremington 1643 W
   John, Fremington 1792 W
   John, South Molton 1797 W*
   Thomas, North Molton 1621 [W]
   Thomas, Fremington 1627 [W]
   William, Northam 1777 A
   William, Ilfracombe 1795 W
Parkyn, Parkyne, Parkyns see Parkins
Parlabyn John, North Tawton 1577 W
   Mark, North Tawton 1623 [W]
Parminter, Parinter, Parmenter, Parmiter, Parmynter, Parmyter
   Agnes, Ilfracombe 1828 W
   Cornelius, Bideford 1723 A
   Damaris, Bideford 1709 [W]
   Deborah, Georgeham 1706 W
   Dorothy, Pilton 1687 W
   Dorothy, Barnstaple 1694 W
   Edward, Pilton 1676 W
   Parmyter Edward, Berrynarbor 1677 W
   Edward, Barnstaple, mason 1811 A
   Elizabeth, Barnstaple 1783 W

   Ephraim, West Down 1708 A
   George, Barnstaple 1731 A
   George, Ilfracombe 1738 W
   George, Ilfracombe 1785 W
   Parmiter Henry, Ilfracombe 1607 [W]; forename blank in Ms;
      supplied from parish register
   Parmiter Henry, Brendon 1643 W
   Henry, West Down 1674 W
   Henry, Marwood 1733 W
   Henry, Tawstock 1734 A
   Henry, West Down 1741 A
   Parinter James, Georgeham 1694 W
   James, Berrynarbor 1794 W
   James, Barnstaple 1852 W
   Jane, Georgeham 1736 W
   Joan, Fremington 1716 A
   Joan, Stoke Rivers 1734 W
   Joan, Ilfracombe 1777 W
   Joan, Ilfracombe 1838 W
   Parmiter John, West Down 1577 W
   Parmenter John, West Down 1632 [W]
   John, West Down 1672 W
   John, West Down 1702 W
   John, Ilfracombe 1722 W
   John, Barnstaple 1733 A
   John, West Down 1736 W
   John, Barnstaple 1742 A
   John, Barnstaple 1743 W
   John, Northam 1749 W
   John, Ilfracombe 1751 A
   John, Ilfracombe 1752 W
   John, Northam 1796 W
   John, Ilfracombe, mariner 1801 W
   John, Ilfracombe 1830 W and 1832 W
   John, West Down 1853 W
   Margaret, Barnstaple 1826 A to James, brother
   Mary, Ilfracombe 1678 W
   Parmynter Mary, Georgeham 1692 W
   Mary, Barnstaple 1694 W
   Mary, West Down 1747 W
   Mary, Barnstaple 1774 W and 1782 W
   Moses, Georgeham 1701 A
   Nicholas, Ilfracombe 1682 W
   Parmiter Peter, Ilfracombe 1673 [W]
   Peter, Georgeham 1679 W
   Peter, Ilfracombe 1679 W and 1693 W
   Peter, West Down 1713 W
   Peter, Georgeham 1784 W
   Parmenter Philip, West Down 1625 [W]
   Parmenter Philip, Barnstaple 1644 A
   Parmiter Philip, Ilfracombe 1693 W
   Philip, Georgeham 1698 W
   Richard, Barnstaple 1721 W
   Richard, Northam 1742 W
   Richard, Bideford 1761 W
   Richard, West Down 1764 W
   Richard, Pilton 1806 A
   Richard, Ilfracombe 1818 W
   Robert, Barnstaple 1674 [W]
   Salmon Mary, Ilfracombe 1810 W
   Sarah, Barnstaple 1746 W
   Sarah, Ilfracombe 1764 W and 1776 W
   Susan, Ilfracombe 1840 W
   Parmiter Thomas, Ilfracombe 1598 [W]
   Thomas, Ilfracombe 1671 A
   Thomas, Stoke Rivers 1690 W
   Thomas, Georgeham 1729 W
   Thomas, Pilton 1755 W
   Thomas, Shirwell 1855 W
   Thomasine, Stoke Rivers, sp. 1800 W
   Parmiter William, Ilfracombe 1677 W
   Parmiter William, Ilfracombe, jnr. 1704 A
   Parinter William, Pilton 1714 W
   William, Stoke Rivers 1719 W and 1734 A
   William, Pilton 1759 A

William Richards, Pilton, yeoman 1820 A to Thomas and
James, brothers
William Richards, Pilton 1834 A
Parnacott, Parnacot
..., Petrockstowe 1607 [W] and 1612 [W]
Parnacott alias Holman ..., Peters Marland 1674 A
Parnacot Agnes, Shebbear, widow 1567 W
Ann, Petrockstowe 1635 W
Ann 1674 A
Parnacott alias Holman Ann, Peters Marland 1674 [W]
Anthony, Martinhoe 1632 [W]
Avis, Shebbear 1597 [W]
Catherine, Petrockstowe 1717 A and 1726 A
Elizabeth, Sheepwash 1756 A
Joan, Clovelly 1631 [W]
John, Martinhoe 1581 W
John, Shebbear 1588 W and 1592 [W]
John, Langtree 1629 [W] and 1630 O
John, Stoke Rivers 1631 [W]
Joseph, Petrockstowe 1667 W
Joseph, Petrockstowe 1712 W and 1714 W
Joseph, Petrockstowe 1725 W and 1726 A
Joseph, Petrockstowe 1792 A
Joseph, Petrockstowe 1844 W
Mary, Peters Marland 1780 W
Richard, Shebbear 1612 [W]; forename blank in Ms; supplied
from parish register
Samuel, Petrockstowe 1751 A
Thomas, Ashreigney 1579 A
Thomas, Little Torrington 1595 [W]
Walter, Martinhoe 1588 A
William, Parkham 1617 [W]
William, Martinhoe 1641 W
Parr, Parre
Henry, Parkham 1847 W
Parre John, Sheepwash 1583 W and 1585 W
John, Pilton 1827 W
Susan, Petrockstowe 1777 W
Parramore, Parrimore
Parramore alias Marley ..., Georgeham or Chulmleigh 1641 W
Andrew, South Molton 1623 [W]
Andrew, South Molton 1730 W
Joan, South Molton 1743 W
Parrimore John, Ilfracombe 1677 W
Joshua, South Molton 1753 W
Stephen, Frithelstock 1625 [W]
Parratt see Parrott
Parre see Parr
Parres see Parish
Parrett see Parrott
Parrimore see Parramore
Parrishe see Parish
Parrott, Parett, Parratt, Parrett
Parrett ..., Combe Martin 1609 [W]
Evan, Martinhoe 1599 [W]
Parrett Every, Bideford 1766 W
Parett Humphrey Price, Northam 1836 W
Parrett John, Lynton 1711 A
Parrett Mary, Bideford 1780 W
Mary, Northam 1857 W
Parrett Rebecca, Barnstaple 1713 W
Parratt Walter, Witheridge 1579 W
Parrett William, Weare Giffard 1606 W
Parrkinge see Parkins
Parry John, Barnstaple 1666 W
Parryn Thomas, Martinhoe 1592 [W]
Parsell Joan, Ilfracombe 1788 W
Parslen see Parslow
Parsley Bartholomew, Fremington 1683 W and 1706 A
Henry, Fremington 1742 A
John, Fremington 1703 W and 1713 A
Nathaniel, Chulmleigh 1693 W
Roger, Chittlehampton 1737 A
William, Fremington 1776 W

Parslow, Parslen
George, Barnstaple 1825 A to Susanna, daughter
Humphrey, Oakford 1680 W
Parslen Humphrey, Oakford 1721 A
Lodovic, Burrington 1713 W
Parsons, Parson, Person, Persons
Parson Alfred, Little Torrington 1573 W
Amos, Shebbear 1850 W
Parson Andrew, Burrington 1578 W
Persons Anthony, Bow 1742 A
Arthur, Shebbear 1732 A
Arthur, Shebbear 1763 W
Digory, Pilton 1630 [W]
Elizabeth, Buckland Brewer 1619 [W]
Henry, Welcombe 1645 W
James, Great Torrington 1664 W
James, Shebbear 1722 A
James, West Putford 1851 W
James and Martha, Shebbear 1726 W
Parson Joan, Langtree 1574 W
Joan, Langtree 1592 [W]
Parson John, Bideford 1592 [W]
John, Shebbear 1596 [W]
Person John, Shebbear 1597 [W]
Parson John, Bideford 1622 [W] and 1633 A
Parson John, Langtree 1634 W
John, Bideford 1661 W
Parson John, Hartland 1693 W
John, Barnstaple 1761 A
Martha and James, Shebbear 1726 W
Person Richard, Bideford 1571 W
Parson Richard, Langtree 1591 [W]
Parson Richard, Barnstaple 1644 W
Richard, King's Nympton 1830 W
Parson Samuel, Hartland 1693 W
Parson Thomas, Bideford 1616 [W]
Parson Thomas, Petrockstowe 1666 A
Thomas, Pilton 1702 W
Parson Walter, Bideford 1626 [W]
William, Bideford 1604 W
William, Chulmleigh 1843 W
Partridge, Partridg, Partrudge
Amos, Challacombe 1768 W
Beaton, Dolton 1692 W
Catherine P, West Buckland 1852 A
Charlons, Roborough 1756 W
Partridg Christopher, Rackenford 1714 W
Elizabeth, Witheridge 1734 W
Elizabeth, Rose Ash, sp. 1809 W
Elizabeth, Coldridge 1844 W
George, Puddington 1731 W
Partridg James, Rose Ash 1664 W
James, Rose Ash 1679 W
James, Witheridge 1728 W
James, Thelbridge 1756 W
James, East Worlington 1791 A
James, Rackenford 1805 W
James, Thelbridge 1812 W
James, Thelbridge 1813 A to Mary Ann, mother
James, Witheridge, yeoman 1814 A to Mary, widow
James, Rose Ash 1855 W
Jane, Knowstone 1777 W
Jane, Rose Ash 1778 W
Partridg John, Witheridge 1665 W
John, Cruwys Morchard 1680 A
Partrudge John, Cruwys Morchard 1684 A
Partridg John, Puddington 1697 W
Partridg John, Burrington 1710 A
John, Cheldon 1715 W
John, Chawleigh 1725 A
John, Lapford 1761 W and 1763 W
John, Rose Ash 1763 W
John, Chawleigh 1772 W
John, Rackenford 1772 W
John, Beaford 1774 W

John, Bideford 1774 W
John, Washford Pyne 1792 W
John, King's Nympton 1825 W
John, Witheridge 1846 W
John see Sarah Muggeridge
Mary, Witheridge 1669 W
Partridg Mary, Challacombe 1713 W
Mary, Roborough 1791 W
Mary Ann, Thelbridge 1841 A to Sarah, sp., daughter
Peter, Washford Pyne 1687 W
Partridg Richard, Lapford 1691 W
Partridg Richard, Nymet Rowland 1709 A
Partridg Richard, Witheridge 1709 [W]
Richard, Thelbridge 1785 A
Richard, Coldridge, yeoman 1798 W
Richard, Coldridge 1829 A to Betsy Reed of Chulmleigh,
   daughter
Roger, Lapford 1758 W
Samuel, Chawleigh 1748 W
Samuel, Witheridge, yeoman 1808 W
Sarah, Thelbridge 1784 W
Stephen, Dolton 1669 A
Stephen and Thomas, Dolton 1674 A
Susan, Witheridge 1679 W
Susan, West Anstey 1856 W
Thomas, Dolton 1669 A
Thomas, Lapford 1775 W
Thomas and Stephen, Dolton 1674 A
Walter, Rackenford 1679 W
Partridg William, Witheridge 1687 A
William, Challacombe 1728 W
William, Bratton Fleming 1759 W
William, Bratton Fleming 1794 W
William, Washford Pyne 1821 W
William, Northam 1842 W
Pasch William, Bideford 1741 A
Paschow, Paschowe
   John, Newton St Petrock 1605 W
   Paschowe John, Welcombe 1644 A
   Richard, Chawleigh 1597 [W]
Pasemore see Pasmore
Pasford, Pasforde, Pawford
   Andrew, North Tawton 1628 [W]
   Pasforde Edmund, North Tawton 1624 [W]
   Pawford John, North Tawton 1573 W
   John, North Tawton 1633 W
   John, North Tawton 1675 W
   Mary, North Tawton 1636 W
   Michael, North Tawton 1623 [W]
   Richard, North Tawton, snr. 1624 [W] and 1627 O
Pasforde see Pasford
Paslew, Paslewe, Paslow
   Paslow Ann, Horwood 1591 [W]
   Paslewe David, Bideford 1592 [W]
   Edward, Bideford 1629 [W]
   Hugh, Burrington 1635 W
   Paslewe James, Horwood 1566 W
   William, Arlington 1622 [W]
Pasley, Pasly, Payshleigh
   Payshleigh Alice, South Molton 1631 [W]
   Henry, Fremington 1707 A
   Pasly John, Fremington 1706 A
Paslow see Paslew
Pasly see Pasley
Pasmore, Pasemore, Passmore
   ..., Goodleigh 1601 A
   ... 1602 [W]
   ..., Goodleigh 1608 [W]
   ..., Challacombe 1610 [W]
   ..., Chulmleigh 1613 [W]
   Agnes, Chulmleigh 1599 [W]
   Alexander, Challacombe 1598 [W]
   Alexander, Challacombe 1628 [W]
   Passemore Alice, Chulmleigh 1566 W
   Alice, Countisbury 1589 W

Alice, Tawstock 1630 [W]
Alphonse, Challacombe 1572 W
Ambrose, Barnstaple 1688 W
Amesius, Challacombe 1635 A
Passmore Andrew, South Molton, wheelwright 1815 A to
   John, son
Ann, Chittlehampton 1674 W
Anstis, North Molton 1634 W
Bartholomew, Monkleigh 1703 W
Passmore Betty, Filleigh 1847 W
Charles, Ashford 1743 W
Passmore Daniel, Great Torrington 1724 W
Davy, Brendon 1563 W
Dennis, High Bray 1617 [W]
Dorothy, Chulmleigh 1709 A
Passmore Edmund, North Molton 1823 W
Elizabeth, Chittlehampton 1580 W
Elizabeth, North Molton 1710 A
Elizabeth, Tawstock 1715 W
Ellen, Goodleigh 1632 [W]
Passmore Emanuel, Chulmleigh 1748 W
Francis, Goodleigh 1672 W
Francis, Chulmleigh 1706 A and 1708 A
Passmore Francis, St Giles in the Wood 1815 W
Gabriel, Bideford 1633 A
Pasemore George, Tawstock 1587 W
George, Goodleigh 1697 W
George, Georgeham 1713 W
Gertrude, West Worlington 1711 [W]
Giles, Goodleigh 1633 W
Grace, Burrington 1625 [W]
Passmore Grace, North Molton 1826 A to Thomas, son
Passmore Henry, Chulmleigh 1772 A
Passmore Hugh, North Molton 1841 W
Passmore Hugh, Filleigh 1856 W
Jane, Tawstock 1760 W
Passmore Jane, Tawstock 1816 W
Joan, Goodleigh 1618 [W]
Joan, North Molton 1628 [W]
Joan, North Molton 1668 A
Passmore Joan, Beaford 1729 W
Joan, North Molton 1758 W
John, Pilton 1573 W
Passmore John, Brendon 1575 A
John, Tawstock 1583 A
John, Challacombe 1587 W
Pasemore John, Brendon 1589 W
John, Brendon 1602 W
John, Tawstock 1606 W
John, High Bray 1619 [W] and 1623 O
John, North Molton 1636 [W]
John, Goodleigh 1645 W
John, Goodleigh 1663 A and 1668 A
John, Brendon 1680 W
John, Goodleigh 1684 A
John, Bratton Fleming 1687 W
John, North Molton 1690 W
John, Chulmleigh 1710 W and 1717 W
Passmore John, Bratton Fleming 1721 W
John, Dowland 1743 W
Passmore John, Chulmleigh 1748 W
John, Chittlehampton 1755 W
John, Tawstock 1759 W
John, Chittlehampton 1762 W
Passmore John, Chawleigh 1772 W
John, Tawstock 1759 W
Passmore John, North Molton 1781 A
John, Bideford 1783 W
John, North Molton 1784 A
Passmore John, Filleigh 1786 W
Passmore John, North Molton 1787 A
Passmore John, Charles 1796 W*
Passmore John, North Tawton, yeoman 1799 W
Passmore John, Wembworthy 1800 A
Passmore John, Peters Marland, yeoman 1802 W
Passmore John, North Molton 1818 W

Passmore John, South Molton, jnr. 1826 W
Passmore John, Charles 1838 A to John of East Buckland, son;
    A dbn granted at Exeter Oct 1879
Passmore John, Lynton 1843 W
Passmore John, Ashreigney 1852 W
John the eldest, Monkleigh 1608 [W]; forename blank in Ms;
    supplied from parish register
Passmore Jonathan, North Molton 1772 W
Lawrence, Goodleigh 1639 W
Martha, Northam 1768 W
Mary, Buckland Filleigh 1696 W
Mary, Chulmleigh 1745 W
Passmore Mary Caroline, Ilfracombe 1833 A to Elizabeth of
    Gay Street, sister
Mathew, High Bray 1611 [W]; forename blank in Ms;
    supplied from parish register
Michael, Goodleigh 1616 [W]
Michael, Twitchen 1776 W
Passmore Michael, North Molton, yeoman 1807 W
Nathaniel, Monkleigh 1716 A
Nicholas, North Molton 1717 A
Passmore Nicholas, North Molton 1807 W
Passmore Nicholas, Combe Martin 1815 W
Passmore Patience, Chulmleigh 1721 W
Passmore Pauline, Chulmleigh 1732 W
Peter, Chulmleigh 1661 W
Peter, Beaford 1717 W
Philip, North Molton 1616 [W]
Philip, North Molton 1743 W, 1759 W, 1762 W
Passmore Philip, North Molton, woolcomber 1804 W
Passmore Philip, North Molton 1822 W
Richard, Chulmleigh 1570 W
Richard, Goodleigh 1623 [W]
Richard, Northam 1753 W
Richard, Bratton Fleming 1755 W
Passmore Richard, North Molton 1777 W
Richard, Chawleigh 1784 W
Passmore Richard, Buckland Brewer 1787 W
Passmore Richard, Stoke Rivers, yeoman 1800 W
Passmore Richard, Filleigh 1826 A to John E. Cutcliffe of
    South Molton, guardian to the children
Passmore Richard, King's Nympton 1837 W
Passmore Richard, Alwington 1842 W
Passmore Richard, Barnstaple 1845 W
Passmore Robert, Chulmleigh 1565 W
Robert, Goodleigh 1619 [W]
Robert, Bratton Fleming 1690 A
Passmore Robert, North Molton 1827 W
Roger, Cheldon 1693 A
Passmore Roger, St Giles in the Wood, yeoman 1809 W
Passmore Sarah, Lynton, sp. 1848 A to Philip, yeoman,
    brother
Stukeley, Beaford 1636 W
Stukeley, Bideford 1691 A
Susanna wife of Richard see Michael Lock
Thomas, Goodleigh 1626 [W] and 1633 W
Thomas, Marwood 1704 W
Thomas, Barnstaple 1710 A
Passmore Thomas, Ilfracombe 1844 W
Passmore William, Goodleigh 1581 W
William, South Molton 1605 W
William, Challacombe 1643 W
William, Bratton Fleming 1690 W
William, Chittlehampton 1698 W
William, North Molton 1702 W
Passmore William, South Molton 1740 W
William, Great Torrington 1755 A
William, Dowland 1757 A
William, North Molton 1759 W
William, West Worlington 1764 W
William, West Worlington 1790 W
Passmore William, snr. 1803 W
Passmore William, North Molton 1833 W
Passmore William, Burrington 1839 W
Passmore William, North Molton 1842 W
Passenger Christopher, Brendon 1637 A

Passey Adam, Northam 1632 [W]
Passmore see Pasmore
Paterudge see Patridge
Patrydge see Patridge
Patridge, Pateridge, Paterudge, Patrydge, Patteridge, Pattridge,
    Pattrudge
    Pateridge ..., Bondleigh 1603 [W]
    Pateridge ..., Witheridge 1614 [W]
    Patrydge Hugh, Washford Pyne 1639 W
    Paterudge Joan, Bondleigh 1583 W
    Patrighe John, Dolton 1564 [W]
    John, Witheridge 1594 [W]
    Pateridge John, Romansleigh 1615 [W]
    Patrydge John, South Molton 1637 W
    Leonard, Witheridge 1593 [W]
    Mary, North Molton 1628 [W]
    Pattridge Philip, Dolton 1573 W
    Pateridge Richard, Witheridge 1604 W
    Robert, Mariansleigh 1597 [W]
    Patteridge Stephen, Puddington 1600 W
    Thomas, Dolton 1629 [W]
    Walter, Burrington 1579 A
    Pattrudge William, Bondleigh 1572 W
    William, Dolton 1594 [W]
    William, High Bickington 1599 [W]
Patt John, Petrockstowe 1719 W
Patteridge see Patridge
Pattison Patterson Honor, Great Torrington 1812 W
    James, Ilfracombe 1764 W
    Joan, Ilfracombe 1789 W
Pattridge, Pattrudge see Patridge
Patty George, Bideford 1639 A
Paul, Paule, Paull see Pawle
Paunter see Panter
Paverleigh Thomas, Westleigh 1617 [W]
Pavy Philip, Tawstock 1674 W
Pawe Nicholas, High Bickington 1666 W
    William, Dolton 1603 W
Pawford see Pasford
Pawle, Paul, Paule, Paull, Pawl, Pawles
    ..., South Molton 1613 [W]
    Ann, South Molton 1614 [W]; forename blank in Ms; supplied
        from parish register
    Paul Anthony, South Molton 1631 [W]
    Catherine 1747 W
    Christopher, Burrington 1729 A
    Paul George, South Molton 1619 [W]
    George, Great Torrington 1620 [W]
    Henry, South Molton 1688 W
    Hugh, South Molton 1710 W
    Jane, Barnstaple 1747 W
    Pawle alias Lange John, Barnstaple 1570 W
    John, Kentisbury 1593 [W]
    John, Barnstaple 1595 [W]
    John, Oakford 1722 W
    John, South Molton 1727 W
    Paul John, ship *Monmouth* 1746 W
    Judith, South Molton 1694 A
    Mary, Barnstaple 1740 W
    Paul Peter, South Molton 1630 [W]
    Robert, South Molton 1592 [W]
    Paul Robert, Chittlehampton 1712 W
    Pawl Roger, South Molton 1710 W
    Paul Thomas, Beaford 1711 A
    William, South Molton 1598 [W]
    Pawles William, Pilton 1624 [W]
    Paule William Chappel, Barnstaple, gentleman 1842 A to
        William Chappel Pawle, son
Pawlin, Pawlen, Pawlyn, Powlyn
    Pawlen ... 1568 [W]
    Pawlyn ..., Hartland 1604 [W]
    Pawlyn ..., Charles 1607 [W] and 1615 [W]
    Pawlyn Agnes, Charles 1602 W
    Catherine, Barnstaple 1694 A
    Pawlyn Edmund, Charles 1593 [W]

Pawlyn Henry, South Molton 1642 W and A
   Joan, Hartland 1565 W
Pawlen Margaret, St Giles in the Wood 1569 W
Pawlyn Peter, Winkleigh 1580 A
Pawlen Richard, Hartland 1600 A (buried 1598); forename
   blank in Ms; supplied from parish register
Pawlyn Richard, Charles 1615 [W]
   Powlyn Robert, St Giles in the Wood 1567 W
Pawles see Pawle
Pawlyn see Pawlin
Payge see Page
Payn, Payne see Paine
Paynter see Painter
Paynton Edward, Great Torrington 1619 [W]
Payor William, Barnstaple, victualler 1807 W
Payshleigh see Pasley
Payton George, Ilfracombe 1731 A
Peace, Pease
   Anthony, Great Torrington 1708 W
   Pease Elizabeth, Atherington 1727 W
   George, North Molton 1734 W
   Jane, Bideford 1764 W
   Peace alias Pearce Margaret, Tawstock 1819 W
   Richard, Bideford 1759 A
   William, ship *Lark* 1749 W
   William, Frithelstock 1757 W
Peacomb John, King's Nympton 1694 W
Peagan Richard, Wembworthy 1662 W
Peake, Peeke, Peik, Peike, Peke, Peyke
   Peeke Ann, Dowland 1622 [W]
   Anthony, Combe Martin 1699 W
   Anthony, Combe Martin 1738 W
   Anthony, Combe Martin 1762 A
   Peak Anthony, Combe Martin, yeoman 1807 W
   Anthony, Combe Martin 1825 A to Elizabeth, widow
   Peik Blaise, Iddesleigh 1606 W
   Peeke Catherine, Zeal Monachorum 1635 W
   David, Combe Martin 1675 A
   David, West Down 1730 W
   David, Mortehoe 1735 A
   David, Barnstaple 1739 W
   David, Combe Martin 1805 W
   Peike Edmund, Buckland Brewer 1605 W
   Peeke Elizabeth, Bondleigh 1565 W
   Peike Giles, Parkham 1605 [W] "Pycke" in register; forename
   blank in Ms; supplied from parish register
   Peike Humphrey, Chawleigh 1594 [W]
   Peeke James, Chawleigh 1670 W
   Jane, Barnstaple 1765 W
   Peeke Joan, Abbotsham 1641 W
   Peke John, Combe Martin 1566 W
   John, South Molton 1574 W
   Peeke John, Combe Martin, snr. 1585 W
   John, South Molton 1596 [W]
   Peyke John, Mariansleigh 1597 [W]
   Peike John, Chawleigh 1601 W
   John, Combe Martin 1665 W
   John, Combe Martin 1671 W
   John, Combe Martin 1713 W
   John, West Down 1748 W
   John, West Down 1771 A
   John, West Down 1795 W
   Peak John, Combe Martin 1827 W
   John, Trentishoe 1831 W
   John, West Down 1838 A to Susan, widow
   John, Shirwell 1847 W
   Lodovic, Combe Martin 1704 W
   Peike Margaret, Parkham 1590 [W]
   Nicholas, Shirwell 1599 [W]
   Nicholas, West Down 1767 W
   Nicholas, Ilfracombe 1780 W
   Peak Nicholas, West Down 1808 W
   Nicholas, Combe Martin 1855 W
   Peeke Rawlina, Bow 1636 W
   Peik Richard, Zeal Monachorum 1602 W

   Richard, Combe Martin 1619 [W]
   Peeke Richard, Parkham 1622 [W]
   Peeke Richard, Winkleigh 1622 [W]
   Peeke Richard, Abbotsham 1635 W
   Richard, Northam 1714 W
   Richard, Combe Martin 1720 A
   Peeke Robert, Winkleigh 1636 W
   Peeke Robert, West Anstey, snr. 1670 W
   Peeke Walter, Bow 1624 [W] and 1626 [W]
   Peike William, Chawleigh 1617 [W]
Pealer William, Zeal Monachorum 1841 W
Pearce see Pearse
Pearde, Peard
   ..., Welcombe 1607 [W]
   ..., Abbotsham 1612 [W]
   ..., Hartland 1612 [W]
   ..., Tawstock 1613 [W]
   Agnes, Barnstaple 1621 [W]
   Alexander, Marwood 1603 W
   Peard Alice, Barnstaple 1666 A
   Peard Ann, Fremington 1733 W
   Peard Armanell, Welcombe 1635 W
   Peard Baldwin, Tawstock 1621 [W]
   Peard Charles, Barnstaple 1670 A; A dbn
   Peard Christiana, Bideford 1722 W
   David, Welcombe 1590 [W]
   Peard Devereux, Barnstaple 1674 A
   Peard Dorothy, Barnstaple 1723 A
   Peard Elizabeth, Barnstaple 1695 W
   Peard Hannah, Barnstaple 1777 W
   Peard Henry, West Down 1645 W
   Peard Humphrey, Brendon 1591 [W]
   Peard Humphrey, Berrynarbor 1633 W
   Peard Humphrey, West Down 1711 W
   Peard James, Frithelstock 1843 W
   Peard Jane, Great Torrington, widow 1799 W
   Peard Joan, Lynton Welcombe 1568 W
   Joan, Tawstock, widow 1571 W
   John, Downe, Welcombe 1564 W
   Peard John, Welcombe 1582 W
   John, Marwood 1591 [W]
   John, Goodleigh 1602 W
   John, Hartland 1612 O forename blank in Ms; supplied from
   parish register
   John, Barnstaple 1615 [W]; forename blank in Ms; supplied
   from parish register
   John, Barnstaple 1629 [W]
   Peard John, Pilton 1638 A
   Peard John, Barnstaple 1680 W and 1692 W
   Peard John, Ilfracombe 1696 W
   Peard John, Bideford 1713 A
   Peard John, Bideford 1720 A
   Peard John, Combe Martin 1769 A
   Peard John, Combe Martin 1811 A
   Peard John, Frithelstock 1836 W
   Peard John, Monkleigh 1843 W
   Peard Julian, Barnstaple 1642 W
   Peard Margaret, Marwood 1712 W
   Peard Mary, Ilfracombe 1715 W
   Mathew, Welcombe 1627 [W]
   Peard Mendon 1703 W
   Peard Nicholas, Yarnscombe 1678 A
   Peard Nicholas, Abbotsham 1693 A
   Peter, West Down 1611 [W]; forename blank in Ms; supplied
   from parish register
   Peard Philip, Frithelstock 1732 W
   Peard Philip, Great Torrington 1793 W
   Peard Richard, Lynton 1565 W
   Richard, West Down 1616 [W]
   Peard Richard, Georgeham 1620 [W]
   Richard, Barnstaple, snr. 1622 [W] and 1624 O
   Peard Richard, West Down 1696 W
   Peard Richard, Barnstaple 1729 W
   Peard Richard, West Down 1745 A
   Peard Robert, West Down 1570 W

Peard Samuel, Barnstaple 1695 W
Peard Sarah, Frithelstock 1841 W
Simon, Hartland 1626 [W] and 1629 [W]
Peard Thomas, Alverdiscott 1597 [W]
Thomas, West Down 1602 W
Peard Thomas, Welcombe 1636 W
Peard Thomas, Northam 1678 A
Peard Thomas, Northam 1681 W
Peard Thomas, Bideford 1692 A
Peard Thomas, Barnstaple 1731 W
Peard Thomas, West Down 1772 W
Peard Thomas, West Down 1797 W
Peard Thomas, Frithelstock 1830 W
Peard Walter, Ilfracombe 1706 A
William, Hartland 1621 [W]
Peard William, Welcombe 1691 W
Peard William, Barnstaple 1718 A
Peard William, Barnstaple 1756 A
Peard William, Barnstaple 1759 W
Peardon see Pardon
Peare John, Ilfracombe 1699 W
Margaret, Ilfracombe 1719 A
Pearne, Pearn
Elizabeth, Little Torrington 1662 A
Pearn Frances, Merton 1678 A
Philip, Merton 1710 W
Pearse, Pearce, Peerce, Peers, Peerse, Peirce, Peirs, Peirse,
Peres, Pers, Perse
..., Shebbear 1605 [W]
..., Satterleigh 1608 [W]
..., West Anstey 1609 [W]
..., Arlington 1611 [W]
..., Northam 1614 [W]
..., Rose Ash 1615 [W]
..., South Molton 1615 O
Peirse ..., Hartland 1690 [W]
Agnes, Hartland 1686 W
Perse Alexander, Molland 1578 W
Alice, Hartland 1644 W
Ambrose, Chulmleigh 1728 A
Ambrose, Hartland 1750 A
Ann, Cheldon 1616 [W]
Pearce Ann, Mariansleigh 1829 W
Pearce Anstis, Tawstock 1785 A
Anthony, Instow 1728 W
Balthazar, Shebbear 1691 A
Charity, Romansleigh 1770 W
Pearce Charity, High Bickington 1791 W
Pearce Charles, Atherington 1698 W
Pearce Christopher, South Molton 1830 W
Peirce Daniel, Petrockstowe 1687 W
David, Barnstaple 1616 [W]
Dennis, East Worlington 1721 W
Edmund, Shebbear 1699 W
Edward, Combe Martin 1735 A
Elizabeth, Bideford 1731 W
Elizabeth, Marwood, sp. 1822 A to James, cordwainer, brother
Emblem, Knowstone 1793 W
Pers Emott, Knowstone 1592 [W]
Frances, Hartland 1704 W
Pearce Francis, Mariansleigh 1819 W
Peirce Gabriel, Hartland 1683 W
George, Chulmleigh 1591 [W]
Peirse alias Holmes Giles, Creacombe 1695 W
Hannah, Bideford 1748 W
Henry, Roborough 1616 [W]
Henry, North Molton 1637 W
Henry, Barnstaple 1733 W
Pearce Henry 1741 W
Henry, Great Torrington 1825 W
Hugh, King's Nympton 1620 [W]
Peirs Hugh, South Molton 1680 A
James, Pilton 1804 W
James, Marwood 1840 W
Joan, Atherington 1580 W

Peers Joan, Shebbear 1589 W
Joan, Great Torrington 1591 [W]
Joan, Wembworthy 1669 W
Joan, Shebbear 1682 W
Peerce John, Oakford 1563 W
Peers John, Warkleigh 1565 W
Peerse John, King's Nympton 1572 W
Peers John, Marwood 1586 A
Peers John, Shebbear 1589 W
John, Kentisbury 1591 [W]
John, Shebbear 1599 [W]
John, Cheldon 1615 [W]
John, Buckland Brewer 1616 [W]
John, Shebbear 1626 [W]
John, Hartland 1627 [W]
Pearce John, Great Torrington 1631 [W]
Pearce John, Chittlehampton 1633 W
John, Rose Ash 1633 W
John, Tawstock 1639 W
John, South Molton 1641 W
John, Hartland 1644 W
Peirse John, North Molton 1666 W
John, Marwood 1669 W
Pearce John, Pilton 1676 A
John, Combe Martin 1678 W
Peirse alias Holmes John, Rose Ash 1681 W
Peirse John, Bideford 1695 W
John, Georgeham 1706 A
Peirse John, Parracombe 1715 A
John, Northam 1725 W
John, Chittlehampton 1740 W
John, Ilfracombe 1748 A
Pearce John, Bondleigh 1783 W
Pearce John, Tawstock 1785 W
Pearce John, Chittlehampton 1788 A
Lawrence, Atherington 1692 A
Margaret, Hartland 1734 W
Pearce alias Peace Margaret, Tawstock 1819 W
Margery, Dolton 1571 W
Margery, Great Torrington 1635 A
Peirse Margery, Buckland Filleigh 1696 W
Martin, West Anstey 1629 [W]
Mary, Northam 1624 [W]
Peirse Mary, Petrockstowe 1688 A
Pearce Mary, Great Torrington 1832 W
Melior, Satterleigh 1710 W
Michael, Chulmleigh 1733 A
Nicholas, King's Nympton 1660 A
Oliver, South Molton 1600 W
Oliver, Pilton 1723 A
Patience, Monkleigh 1722 A
Peres alias Holmes Peter, Rose Ash 1582 W
Pearce Philip, South Molton 1639 W
Philip, South Molton, snr. 1704 A
Philip, South Molton 1705 [W] and 1719 A
Pearce Phillippa, Littleham (near Bideford) 1645 A
Pearce Richard, Trentishoe 1630 [W]
Pearce Richard, Merton 1664 A
Peirse Richard, Hartland 1667 W
Richard, Shebbear 1679 W
Peers Richard, Yarnscombe 1682 W
Peirce Richard, South Molton 1682 A
Richard, Warkleigh 1717 W
Richard, Monkleigh 1723 A dbn
Richard, Hartland 1723 A
Richard, Bideford 1728 W and 1732 W
Richard, Instow 1742 W
Pearce Richard, Abbotsham 1773 W
Pearce Richard, Bideford 1782 W
Richard, West Anstey 1813 W
Pearce Richard, Marwood 1844 A to Mary wife of Thomas
Jones, widow
Pers Robert, Dolton 1565 W
Peers Robert, George Nympton 1584 A
Robert, South Molton 1615 [W]

Robert, Yarnscombe 1616 [W]
Robert, Shebbear 1623 [W]
Robert, Hartland, snr. 1637 W
Robert, South Molton 1640 W
Peirse Robert, Shebbear 1664 [W]
Robert, Hartland 1670 W
Peirse Roger, South Molton 1695 W
Samuel, High Bickington 1708 W
Sarah, Barnstaple 1711 W
Pearce Simon, Kentisbury 1623 [W]
Pearce Stephen, Petrockstowe 1637 W
Susanna see Edward Cockram
Theophilus, Barnstaple 1618 [W]
Thomas, Great Torrington 1591 [W] and 1595 [W]
Thomas, Atherington 1595 [W]
Pearce Thomas, Coldridge 1663 W
Thomas, East Worlington 1671 A and 1673 O
Thomas, Shebbear 1674 W
Thomas, Monkleigh 1690 A
Thomas, Instow 1792 W
Thomasine, West Anstey 1630 O
Walter, Barnstaple 1591 [W]
Walter, Yarnscombe 1615 [W]
Walter, Northam 1616 [W]
Peers Walter, Petrockstowe 1624 [W]
William, Molland 1596 [W]
William, Abbotsham 1616 [W]
William, Barnstaple 1669 A
Peirce William 1745 A
Pearce William, High Bickington 1787 A
Pearce William, Chulmleigh, yeoman 1797 W
Pearson William Wallace, Bideford 1849 W
Pease see Peace
Peat, Peate
John, Northam 1718 W
Richard, Buckland Filleigh 1585 A
Peate William, Alwington 1695 W
Peckard, Peccard, Peccarde, Pechard, Peckarde, Peckart,
Peckerd, Pecket, Pekett
..., Woolfardisworthy 1605 [W] and 1614 [W]
Peccard Arthur, Buckland Brewer 1625 [W]
Bartholomew, Parkham 1733 W
Beaton, Buckland Brewer 1643 A
Christiana, St Giles in the Wood 1622 [W] and 1624 O
Emma, Buckland Brewer 1638 A
Gabriel, Hartland 1611 [W]; forename blank in Ms; supplied
from parish register
Peccard George, Knowstone 1626 [W]
George, Westleigh 1724 A
Pechard Henry, mariner 1747 A
James, High Bickington 1806 W*
Peccarde John, Woolfardisworthy 1572 W
Pekett John, Burrington 1572 W
Peccard John, Welcombe 1624 [W]
John, Bideford 1643 W
John, Great Torrington 1725 W
Peccard Peter, Woolfardisworthy 1666 W
Ralph, St Giles in the Wood 1621 [W]
Pecket Ralph, St Giles in the Wood 1677 W
Richard, Woolfardisworthy 1596 [W]
Richard, Buckland Brewer 1735 A
Robert, Great Torrington 1759 W
Sebastian, Woolfardisworthy 1626 [W]
Peckerd Thomas, Clovelly 1573 W
Thomas, Woolfardisworthy 1599 [W]
Peckarde Thomas, Knowstone 1618 [W]
Thomas, Ilfracombe 1619 [W]
Peckett Thomas, Coldridge 1633 W
Thomas, Woolfardisworthy 1636 W
Thomas, Woolfardisworthy 1725 W
Thomas, Westleigh 1746 W
Peckart Tristram, Fremington 1689 W
William, Buckland Brewer 1598 [W]
William, Buckland Brewer 1622 [W]
William, Frithelstock 1672 W

William, Great Torrington 1688 A
William, Great Torrington 1711 W
William, Littleham (near Bideford) 1743 A
Pects Christopher, Buckland Brewer 1729 W
Pedler, Pedlar
Alexander, Frithelstock 1773 W
Pedlar Edmund, Lynton 1710 A
Henry, Monkleigh 1669 A
Humphrey, Monkleigh 1688 W
Pedler alias Dove Mary, Monkleigh 1666 A
Mary, Monkleigh 1679 W
Mary, Zeal Monachorum 1851 W
Richard, Abbotsham 1711 W
Thomas, Monkleigh 1796 W
Thomas, Barnstaple 1841 W
Pedlar William, Chittlehampton 1734 W
Pedrick John, Barnstaple 1810 W
Pee Emma, Northam 1669 W
Peeke see Peake
Peerce, Peers, Peerse see Pearse
Peery see Perry
Peggins John, North Tawton, clerk 1614 [W] "Peckinsus" in
register; forename blank in Ms; supplied from parish register
Peik, Peike, Peke see Peake
Peine see Paine
Peirce, Peirs, Peirse see Pearse
Pekett see Peckard
Pelavyne see Pellaven
Pelland Henry, North Tawton 1617 [W]
William, Buckland Brewer 1596 [W]
Pellaven, Pelavyne, Pellivant, Pelvine
..., Chittlehampton 1608 [W] and 1614 [W]
..., High Bickington 1612 [W]
Alice, High Bickington 1603 W
Pellivant Andrew, Hartland 1633 A
Joan, Chittlehampton 1587 W
Pelavyne John, High Bickington 1566 W
John, High Bickington 1585 W
John, Bondleigh 1599 [W]
John, High Bickington 1637 W
John, Petrockstowe, jnr. 1642 W
Pelvine or Pyllaver Mathew, Chittlehampton 1573 A
Roger, High Bickington 1604 W
William, High Bickington 1585 W
Pellett John, Winkleigh 1737 A
Pellew Joan, Newton St Petrock 1673 [W]
Pellivant, Pelvine see Pellaven
Penbethey, Penbitha
Penbitha Jacob, Chittlehampton 1725 A
Jacob, Barnstaple, joiner 1796 W
Pencomb, Penckomb, Pencombe, Pencome
Christopher, South Molton 1585 W
Emma, North Molton 1588 W
Pencome John, South Molton 1571 W
Pencombe John, North Molton 1576 W
Penckomb Margery, Tawstock, widow 1611 [W]; forename
blank in Ms; supplied from parish register
Pencombe Philip, Tawstock 1564 W
Pencombe Richard, Chittlehampton 1588 W
Thomas, South Molton 1601 W
Pencombe William, North Molton 1564 W
Pender George, High Bickington 1643 A
John, Burrington 1598 [W]
Margery, Bideford 1679 W
Marian, Atherington 1634 [W]
Richard, Atherington 1684 W
Penecote see Pennacott
Penford John, Chulmleigh 1597 [W]
John, Burrington 1598 [W]
Penford alias Bullyn John, Chulmleigh 1602 W
Richard, Cheldon 1592 [W]
Pengelly, Pengelley, Pengilly
Pengilly Henry, Woolfardisworthy 1783 W
Pengelley James, Woolfardisworthy 1801 W
Pengilly James, Frithelstock 1837 W

Pengilly Philip, Woolfardisworthy 1790 W
  Roger, Barnstaple 1844 W
Pengilly Sarah, Northam 1856 A
  William, Frithelstock 1707 A
Pengilly William, Clovelly 1819 W
Penhale George, Shebbear 1840 W
Penhorwood ..., Westleigh 1608 [W]
  Alexander, Little Torrington 1663 W
  Alexander, Fremington 1680 W
  Alexander, Little Torrington 1707 [W]
  Alexander, Northam 1801 W
  Alexander, Northam 1834 W
  Eleanor, Tawstock 1696 W
  Elizabeth, Bideford 1720 W
  George, Frithelstock 1772 A
  James, Tawstock 1690 W
  Joan, Tawstock 1626 [W]
  John, Tawstock 1595 [W]
  John, Little Torrington 1623 [W]
  John, Hartland 1643 W
  John, Hartland 1678 A
  John, Little Torrington 1681 A
  John, Great Torrington 1737 A
  John, Northam 1846 W double probate passed at Exeter Apr
    1869
  Joseph, Barnstaple 1694 A
  Mary, Great Torrington 1695 A
  Peter, Westleigh 1585 W
  Robert, Westleigh 1586 W
  Roger, Hartland 1635 W
  Roger, Buckland Brewer 1697 W
  Sarah see Thomas Hutchings
  Thomas, Hartland 1671 A
  Thomas, Westleigh 1695 A
  Thomas, Westleigh 1701 W
  Thomas, Tawstock 1710 W
  Thomas, Northam 1840 W
  Thomasine, Westleigh 1595 [W]
  William, Westleigh 1591 [W]
  William, Northam 1644 W
  William, Bideford 1701 W
  William, Tawstock 1703 W
Penington see Pennington
Pennacott, Penecote, Penincott, Pennicott, Pennycott,
    Pennycotte, Pernacot
  Pennycotte Elizabeth, Lapford 1577 A
  Pernacot Robert, Shebbear 1565 W
  Sebastian, Chulmleigh 1602 W
  Penincott Sebastian, Chulmleigh 1719 A
  Sybil, Chulmleigh 1662 W
  Penecote William, Chulmleigh 1572 W
  Pennycott William, Chulmleigh 1631 [W]
  Pennicott William, Burrington 1675 [W]
  William, Burrington 1697 W
Penne Christopher, Frithelstock 1588 W
Penney see Penny
Pennicott see Pennacott
Pennington, Penington
  Penington Eleanor, Barnstaple 1633 A
  Mary, Hartland 1857 W
  William, Hartland 1839 W
Pennsford see Pensford
Penny, Penney
  ..., Combe Martin 1613 [W]
  Alan, Abbotsham 1748 W
  Elizabeth, Bideford 1722 A
  Elizabeth, Barnstaple, widow 1805 W
  Penney Jane, Northam 1855 W
  John, Barnstaple 1753 W
  John, Barnstaple 1799 A
  Penney John, Abbotsham, yeoman 1811 A
  Penney John, Northam 1849 W
  Penney Mary, Bideford 1848 W
  Sarah, Abbotsham 1759 A
  William, Merton 1730 A

Penney William, Northam 1852 W
Pennycott, Pennycotte see Pennacott
Penray see Penry
Penrose Agnes, Fremington 1693 A
  Agnes, Barnstaple 1727 A
  Amos, Petrockstowe 1707 W
  Ann, Tawstock 1731 W
  Caleb, Tawstock 1706 W and 1721 W
  Catherine, Fremington 1666 W
  Christopher, Fremington 1615 [W]; forename blank in Ms;
    supplied from parish register
  Elizabeth, Barnstaple 1740 W
  George, Barnstaple 1644 A
  Helen, Bideford 1606 W
  Henry, Langtree 1629 [W]
  Henry, Petrockstowe 1670 W
  John, Fremington 1678 W
  John, Barnstaple 1714 A
  John, Bideford 1714 A
  Julian, Woolfardisworthy 1667 W
  Margaret, Petrockstowe 1707 [A]
  Philip, Great Torrington 1661 W
  Rachel, Tawstock 1728 W
  Richard, Parkham 1697 A
  Robert, Fremington 1645 W
  Robert, Barnstaple 1687 A
  Thomas, Burrington 1594 [W]
  William, North Molton 1662 A
Penry, Penray
  Penry alias Gread Catherine, Barnstaple 1699 A; forename
    blank in Ms; supplied from parish register
  David, Instow 1680 A
  Mary, Bideford 1698 A
  Thomas, Ashford 1676 W
  Thomas, Ashford 1676
Pensford, Pennsford
  Pennsford Jane, Wembworthy 1756 A
  Pennsford John, Wembworthy 1754 A and 1756 A
Pepell, Peple
  Peple George, Heanton Punchardon 1758 W
  Pepell alias Caulie John, Buckland Brewer 1572 W
Peper see Pepper
Peple see Pepell
Pepper, Peper
  ..., South Molton 1611 [W]
  ..., Abbotsham 1612 [W], 1613 [W] (3), 1614 [W]
  Peper Agnes, South Molton 1585 A
  George, South Molton, mason 1811 W
  George, West Worlington 1829 W
  George see also George Webber
  John, Frithelstock 1589 A
  Richard, Buckland Filleigh 1622 [W]
  Thomas, Abbotsham 1597 [W]
Percye Richard, Burrington 1617 [W]
Perdon Philip, Merton 1673 W
Peres see Pearse
Periam Cecilia, West Down 1588 W
  Geoffrey, Ilfracombe 1603 W
  Thomas, Westleigh 1582 W
Perimean see Perryman
Perin, Perinne see Perrin
Perken, Perkin, Perking, Perkins, Perkyn see Parkins
Pernacot see Pennacott
Perrian see Perrin
Perriman see Perryman
Perrin, Perin, Perinne, Perrian, Perryn, Peryan, Peryn, Pyrine
  Perin ..., Mortehoe 1609 [W] and 1611 [W] (2)
  ..., Ilfracombe 1612 [W]
  Perryn Agnes, Georgeham 1598 [W]
  Perryn Cecilia, Shirwell 1637 A
  Perryn Cecilia, Georgeham 1640 O
  Perryn Charles, Georgeham 1734 W
  Perryn Elizabeth, Great Torrington 1643 W
  Perryn Elizabeth, Bideford 1757 A
  Perryn George, West Down 1683 W

Peryan George, Barnstaple 1689 A
Perryn Grace, West Down 1687 W
Grace, Bideford 1694 W
Perryn Gregory, Georgeham 1623 [W]
Henry, Bideford 1716 W
Honor, Buckland Brewer 1682 W
Perryn Hugh, Great Torrington 1619 [W]
Humphrey, Heanton Punchardon 1684 W
James, Fremington 1823 W
James, Berrynarbor 1840 W
Joan, West Down 1700 W
Peryn John, West Down 1576 W
Peryn John, Mortehoe 1604 [W]
Perryn John, West Down 1623 [W]
Perryn John, Ilfracombe 1636 W
John, Georgeham 1675 A
Perrian John, Mortehoe 1677 W
Perin John, Ilfracombe 1678 A
John, Merton 1689 A
John, Marwood 1693 A
Pyrine John, Bideford 1711 W
John, Berrynarbor 1820 W
Perryn Margaret, Pilton 1637 W
Mary, Georgeham 1710 W
Perryn Mathew, Merton 1727 A
Perryn Oliver, Ilfracombe 1624 [W]
Peryn Petronell, Georgeham 1601 W
Perryn Philip, Shirwell 1636 W
Peryn Ralph, West Down 1680 W
Robert, West Down 1741 W
Perin Samuel, Bideford 1717 W
Susan, Sheepwash 1683 W
Perryn Thomas, West Down 1623 [W]
Perin Thomas, Merton 1670 W
Perryn Thomas, Heanton Punchardon 1707 A
Thomas, Bideford 1710 W
Tryphena, Barnstaple 1669 A
Perin Walter, Mortehoe 1570 W
Peryn Walter, Heanton Punchardon 1585 W
Perryn William, Mortehoe 1597 [W]
Perryn William, Georgeham 1600 W
Perryn William, Great Torrington 1623 [W]
Perryn William, West Down 1675 A
Peryn William, West Down 1675 A
Perrome William, Lynton 1623 [W] and 1624 O
Perry, Peery
Abraham, Fremington 1663 [W]
Dorothy, Pilton 1662 A
Edward, Barnstaple 1774 W and 1775 W
Henry, Barnstaple 1597 [W]
Peery Joan, Roborough 1629 [W]
John, Barnstaple 1691 W
John, Pilton 1724 A
John, Barnstaple 1748 A
Richard, West Anstey 1617 [W]
Richard, Northam 1852 W
Robert, Ilfracombe 1689 W
Perry alias Knight Tristram, Pilton 1697 A
William, Barnstaple 1643 A
Perryman, Perimean, Perriman, Peryan, Peryman
Alice, Georgeham 1621 [W]
Benjamin, Ilfracombe 1818 W
Deborah, Instow 1759 W
Peryman Edward, West Down 1601 W
Perriman Edward, Bideford 1706 [A]
Elizabeth, Instow 1684 W
Elizabeth, Fremington 1824 W
Perriman Faithful, Instow 1684 A
Peryman George, Georgeham 1617 [W]
George, Georgeham 1742 W
George, Instow 1743 W
Peryman Humphrey, Georgeham 1613 [W]; forename blank in
  Ms; supplied from parish register
Perriman Joan, Georgeham 1687 W
John, Georgeham 1645 W

Perriman John, Barnstaple 1690 A
Perriman John, Instow 1719 W
John, Witheridge 1743 A
John, Georgeham 1749 W
Perriman Mary, South Molton 1721 W
Mary, South Molton, widow 1855 A to Thomas, yeoman, son
Perriman Nathaniel, Instow 1680 A
Perriman Nathaniel, Instow 1708 A
Peryman Nicholas, West Down 1586 W
Perriman Richard, West Down 1696 W
Perriman Richard, Georgeham 1697 W
Perriman Richard, South Molton 1720 W
Richard, South Molton 1726 W
Richard, Little Torrington 1799 W
Perimean Solomon, Barnstaple 1709 A
Perryn see Perrin
Peryman see Perryman
Peryn see Perrin
Pers, Perse see Pearse
Person, Persons see Parsons
Peryan see Periam
Pester Agnes, North Molton 1573 W
Joan, Monkleigh, widow 1570 W
Petell see Pettle
Peter, Peters
..., West Down 1600 W
..., Langtree 1602 [W]
Agnes, Bow 1637 O
George, Rackenford 1618 A
Peters John, Wembworthy 1777 A
Peters John, Wembworthy 1839 W
Peters Lewis, Wembworthy 1736 A
Philip, Rackenford 1618 [W]
Peters Philip, Pilton 1626 [W]
Peter alias Burren Richard, West Down 1600 W
Peters Simon, Wembworthy 1822 W
Peters Thomasine, West Down 1627 [W]
William, Mariansleigh 1580 W
William, Cruwys Morchard 1635 A
Peters William, Langtree 1738 W
Peters William, Huish 1845 W
Peterfield Robert, Bideford 1721 A
Peters see Peter
Petharick see Petherick
Petherbridge, Pethebridg, Pethebridge, Pithebridge
Anthony, Alverdiscott 1775 W
Pethebridge Anthony, Fremington 1815 W
Pethebridge Anthony, Alverdiscott 1826 A to Mary, widow
Elizabeth, Yarnscombe 1832 W
George, Yarnscombe 1818 A to Elizabeth, widow
Pithebridge Henry, Atherington 1676 W
Pethebridg Henry, Yarnscombe 1711 A
Henry, Yarnscombe 1824 W
Pethebridg Jane, Atherington 1707 A
Pethebridge Joan, Burrington 1730 W
Pethebridge Joan, Alverdiscott 1827 W
John, Alverdiscott 1822 W
Pethebridge John, Alverdiscott, yeoman 1853 A to Elizabeth,
  widow
Pethebridge Mary, Alverdiscott 1844 W
Richard, Atherington 1762 W
Richard, Newton Tracey 1779 W
Pethebridge Richard, Alverdiscott 1825 W
Pethebridge Richard, Yarnscombe 1840 W
Thomas, Fremington 1856 W
Pethebridge William, Petrockstowe 1583 A
Petherick, Petharick, Pethericke, Pethick
Petharick ..., Woolfardisworthy 1614 [W]
..., Clannaborough 1615 [W]
Pethick Alexander, Weare Giffard, yeoman 1806 A to William
Pethick Alexander, Weare Giffard, yeoman 1816 A to John,
  yeoman, grandson dbn left by William
Daniel, Monkleigh 1754 W
Elias alias Elijah, Tawstock 1680 W
Elizabeth, Tawstock 1683 W

Elizabeth, Hartland 1691 W
Jane, Merton 1697 A
Pethericke John 1595 [W]
John, Woolfardisworthy 1679 W
John, Hartland 1771 W
John, Bideford 1781 A
John, Parkham, labourer 1809 A
Joseph, Monkleigh 1663 A
Robert, Swimbridge 1853 W
Pethick William, Woolfardisworthy 1671 W
Pethick William, Frithelstock 1675 W
Willmot, Eggesford 1731 A

Pett
Pett alias Aplye Agnes, South Molton 1588 W
George Coates, Alverdiscott, yeoman 1814 A to Mary, widow
John, Petrockstowe 1821 W
Mary, Shebbear 1837 A to William, son
Richard, Shebbear 1822 A to Mary, widow
William, Buckland Filleigh 1828 W
William, Shebbear 1837 A

Pettell see Pettle
Petten see Petton

Pettle, Petell, Pettell
Edmund, Monkleigh 1625 [W]
Elizabeth, Monkleigh 1784 W
Elizabeth, Monkleigh, wife 1811 W
Emma, Abbotsham 1663 A
Gabriel, Monkleigh 1634 W
Henry, Monkleigh 1623 [W]
John, Monkleigh 1765 W
John, Northam, jnr. 1811 W
Mary, Monkleigh 1825 A
Richard, Monkleigh 1760 W
Richard, Great Torrington 1852 W
Pettell Thomas, Langtree 1598 [W]
Pettell William, Monkleigh 1573 W
William, Abbotsham 1664 W
William, Abbotsham, yeoman 1842 A to John, yeoman, son

Petton, Petten
..., Bideford 1611 [W]
Petten John, Rackenford 1635 W
Peter, Hartland 1596 [W]
Petten Richard, Northam 1700 W
Thomas, Hartland 1606 W
Petton alias Juell Thomas, Hartland 1606 W

Pettwood Thomas, Ashreigney 1814 W

Pevis, Pevice, Pevise
George, St Giles in the Wood 1581 A
Pevise Hannah, South Molton 1704 W
John, Satterleigh 1703 W
John, Warkleigh 1703 W
Pevice Lodovic, West Anstey 1712 W
Pevise Thomas, Alverdiscott 1701 A

Pewtner Christopher 1708 W
Mary, Barnstaple 1730 W
Nathaniel, Barnstaple 1750 W

Peyke see Peake
Peyne see Paine

Phare, Phrare
..., West Down 1612 [W]
Alexander, Georgeham 1751 W
Grace, Marwood 1689 A
Joan, Pilton 1593 [W]
John, Mortehoe 1677 A
Phare alias Fair John, Mortehoe 1677 A
Nathaniel, Georgeham 1707 A
Samuel, Frithelstock 1662 A
Thomas, Pilton 1593 [W]
Phrare Thomas 1661 W
Walter, West Down 1603 [W] "Fare" in register; forename
    blank in Ms; supplied from parish register
    see also Fare

Phelp see Philp
Pherries see Ferris
Philip, Philipe, Philippe, Philips see Phillips

Philkins see Filkins
Phillips, Filipps, Philip, Philipe, Philippe, Philips, Phillip,
    Phillipp, Phillipps, Phyllipes
..., Bideford 1607 [W]
..., Combe Martin 1613 [W]
Phillipp Agnes, Littleham (near Bideford) 1574 W
Phillip Ann, Warkleigh 1670 W
Ann, Great Torrington 1733 W
Ann, Westleigh 1740 W
Ann, Bideford 1745 A
Anthony, Frithelstock 1732 W
Philips Avis, Lapford 1593 [W]
Catherine, Northam 1672 W
Catherine, Tawstock 1679 A
Philip Charles, Zeal Monachorum 1749 W
David, Northam 1744 A
Phillipps Dorothy, West Down 1694 W
Phillip Elizabeth, Georgeham 1671 [W]
Elizabeth, Bideford 1702 W
Philips Elizabeth, Pilton 1756 A
Emanuel, Arlington 1817 W
Phillipps Ephraim, Bideford 1694 W
Philippe George, Great Torrington 1567 W
George, Georgeham 1665 W
George, Fremington 1727 A
George, Huntshaw 1850 W
Henry, West Down 1840 W
Hugh, West Buckland 1844 W
James Page, Ilfracombe 1848 W
Philips Jane, Mortehoe 1715 A
Jane, Bideford 1829 W
Joan, Combe Martin 1682 W
Fillipps John, Pilton 1594 [W]
Philipps John, Pilton 1594 [W]
John, Berrynarbor 1614 [W]; forename blank in Ms; supplied
    from parish register
Philipp John, Georgeham 1621 [W]
John, Pilton 1667 A
John, Warkleigh 1669 A
John, Georgeham 1682 A
Phillip John, Parracombe 1687 W
John, Frithelstock 1704 A
John, Westleigh 1726 W
John, Ilfracombe 1744 W
John 1745 A
John, mariner 1748 A
Philip John, Witheridge 1749 A
Philips John, West Down 1751 W
John, Ilfracombe 1766 W
John, Coldridge 1769 A
John, Fremington 1769 A
John, Barnstaple 1770 W
John, West Down 1791 W
John, Alverdiscott 1798 W*
John, Huntshaw 1812 W
John, West Worlington, yeoman 1815 A to Ann, widow
John, Barnstaple 1823 W
John, East Worlington 1826 W
John, West Down, blacksmith 1828 W
John, West Down, carpenter 1828 A to Mary, widow
John, Buckland Brewer 1832 W
Joseph, Georgeham 1714 W
Joshua, Bideford 1837 A
Mary, Frithelstock 1716 W
Mary, Pilton 1773 W
Mary, Merton 1777 A
Philips Mathew, Ilfracombe 1751 W
Philipps Owen, Pilton 1637 A
Owen, Berrynarbor 1697 W
Philip, Ilfracombe 1710 A
Phyllis, Barnstaple 1675 W
Rebecca, Ilfracombe 1857 A
Richard, Northam 1573 W
Phillipps Richard, South Molton 1584 W
Philipe Richard, Hartland 1589 W

Richard, Bow 1668 W
Richard, Combe Martin 1680 A
Richard, Bideford 1732 W
Philip Richard, Chawleigh 1763 A
Richard, Westleigh 1765 A
Richard, Chawleigh 1769 W
Richard, Buckland Brewer 1781 W
Philips Richard, Chulmleigh, yeoman 1810 W
Robert, Bideford 1702 A
Robert, Barnstaple 1763 W
Philip Robert, West Worlington 1788 W
Robert, Burrington 1800 A
Salome, High Bickington 1615 [W]
Samuel, East Worlington 1858 [W]
Thomas, Barnstaple 1690 A
Thomas, Loxhore 1697 A
Thomas, Bideford 1707 W
Thomas, Rose Ash 1743 W
Philips Thomas, Northam 1753 W
Philips Thomas, Alverdiscott 1754 A
Thomas, Rose Ash, yeoman 1802 W
Thomas, Satterleigh, farmer 1855 A to William, innkeeper,
    son
Thomasine, Barnstaple 1665 W
Phyllipes Thomasine, Fremington 1572 W
Walter, Ilfracombe 1729 A
Phillipe alias Brocke William, North Tawton 1573 W
Phellippe William, Northam 1581 A
Philipps William, Alverdiscott 1627 [W]
William, Alverdiscott 1661 A
William, Alverdiscott 1681 A and 1687 A
William, Yarnscombe 1693 W
William, Bideford 1697 W
Phillipps William, Bideford 1719 A
William, Alwington 1726 A
William, Loxhore 1737 W
William, Bideford 1745 A
William, Fremington 1749 A
William, Fremington 1769 A
William, Pilton 1771 W
William, West Down 1792 W
William, Frithelstock, yeoman 1801 W
William, Bideford 1833 A to Mary, widow
William, Pilton 1836 W
William, Chawleigh 1838 A to Frances, widow
William, Barnstaple 1846 W
Phillyis
John, Heanton Punchardon 1725 A
Richard, Alverdiscott 1723 A
Phyllipes see Phillips
Philman ..., Barnstaple 1602 A
Philp, Filp, Filpe, Phelp, Philpe
Philpe ..., Ashreigney 1607 [W]
Philpe ..., Winkleigh 1610 [W]
Filpe Anthony, Georgeham 1615 [W]
Anthony, Georgeham 1615 [W]
Anthony, Georgeham 1705 [W]
Philpe Edward, Witheridge 1688 W
Elizabeth, Marwood 1669 A
Philpe George, Great Torrington 1575 W
Philpe John, Georgeham 1633 W
Phelp John, Zeal Monachorum 1698 A
John, Zeal Monachorum 1706 A
Filp Nicholas, Hartland 1596 [W]
Philpe Nicholas, Hartland 1596 [W]
Philpe Richard, Georgeham 1628 [W]
Robert, Northam 1676 W
Robert, East Worlington 1685 W
Robert, Northam 1735 W
Philpe Thomas, Northam 1588 W
Filpe Thomas, Langtree 1591 [W]
Thomas, Langtree 1591 [W]
Filpe Thomas, South Molton 1595 [W]
Philpe Thomas, South Molton 1595 [W]
Philpe Thomas, Mortehoe 1617 [W]
Philpe William, Bideford 1576 A

Philpe William, Yarnscombe 1620 [W]
Phisick ..., Filleigh 1612 [W]
Joan, Filleigh 1617 [W]
Phrare see Phare
Phrase, Phraze
Phraze Edward, Barnstaple 1681 A
Henry, Ilfracombe 1640 W
Phraze John, Newton St Petrock 1669 [W] and 1672 O
Phraze John, Barnstaple 1766 A
Phyllipes see Phillips
Picke, Pyck, Pycke
John, Winkleigh 1581 W
Pyck Ambrose, Bondleigh 1588 W
Pycke John, Parkham 1586 W
Pick Sophia Melhuish, Braunton, widow 1857 A to Joshua
    Peyton Pick, surgeon, son
Pickard, Pickardy, Pickerd, Pickerde, Pickhard, Pycard, Pyckerd
Pickerd Agnes, Parkham 1567 W
Ann, Parkham 1838 A (1836) to James, son
Bartholomew, Parkham 1780 W
Bartholomew, Northam 1823 W
Edward, Buckland Brewer 1682 A
Elizabeth, Loxhore 1786 W
Elizabeth, Northam 1831 W
Elizabeth see Abraham Muggeridge
Giles, Langtree 1594 [W]
Henry, Ilfracombe 1631 [W]
James, Northam 1676 A
James, Parkham, yeoman 1817 A to Ann, widow
James, Ashreigney, yeoman 1854 A to Grace, widow
Jasper, Northam 1828 W
Joan, Barnstaple 1752 W
Pickerde John, Northam 1582 W
Pyckerd John, Buckland Brewer 1586 W
John, Buckland Brewer 1596 [W]
John, Buckland Brewer 1629 [W]
John, Welcombe 1682 W
John, Bideford 1692 A
John, Littleham (near Bideford) 1778 W
John, Northam 1854 W and 1856 A
Jonathan, Chulmleigh 1835 W
Margaret, Northam 1678 A
Maria, Chulmleigh 1826 A to Jonathan, father
Pickardy Mary, Bideford 1691 A
Mary, Parkham 1788 W
Mary, Northam 1850 W
Nicholas, ship *Portland* 1749 A
Priscilla, St Giles in the Wood 1678 W
Pyckerd Richard, Northam 1587 A
Richard, Northam 1669 W
Robert, Bratton Fleming 1820 W
Robert, Ashreigney 1847 W
Roger, Bideford 1716 W
Samuel, Northam 1737 W
Pyckerd Thomas, Ilfracombe 1568 W
Pickerd Thomas, Molland 1575 W
Pickhard Thomas, Instow 1741 W
Pycard Thomasine, Woolfardisworthy 1574 W
Valentine, Frithelstock 1643 A
Pickering, Pickring
Pickering alias Bale Ann, Martinhoe 1645 A
Jonas, Bideford 1705 [W]
Pickring Richard, Kentisbury 1670 W
Pickett Anthony, Roborough 1617 [W]
John, Iddesleigh 1564 W
John, St Giles in the Wood 1591 [W]
William, North Tawton 1752 A
William, North Tawton 1757 W
Pickring see Pickering
Pidcock Joan, Combe Martin 1731 A
Samuel, Combe Martin 1721 W
Pidgeon Henry, Great Torrington 1854 W Estate Duty records
    supplied christian name which blank in Ms
Pidler Alexander, Little Torrington, yeoman 1810 W
John, Frithelstock, yeoman 1802 W

Margery, Frithelstock 1821 W
Richard, Monkleigh 1720 A
Pidsley, Pydaley
Pydaley John, Wembworthy 1640 W
Margery, Knowstone 1595 [W]
Thomas, South Molton 1641 A
Piell see Pile
Pike, Pikes, Pyke, Pykes
Alice, Wembworthy 1680 W
Andrew, Wembworthy 1680 W
Benedict, Meshaw 1633 W
Benjamin, Shirwell 1775 A
Pyke Benjamin, Barnstaple 1802 A
Pyke Elizabeth, Ashreigney 1736 W
Pyke Elizabeth, Northam 1793 W
Emblem, Peters Marland 1673 [W]
Pikes George, Pilton 1667 A and 1671 O
George, Winkleigh 1676 W
Pyke or Pyle George, Ilfracombe 1686 W
Pyke George, Winkleigh 1722 A
George, South Molton 1768 A
George, Chawleigh 1817 W and 1818 W
Pyke Grace, Barnstaple 1802 A
Pyke Hugh, Winkleigh 1564 W
Pyke Isaac, Instow 1766 W
James, Clovelly 1691 A
John, Bondleigh 1617 [W]
John, Pilton 1660 W
John, Bideford 1688 W
John, Abbotsham 1692 A
John, Chawleigh 1694 A
Pyke John, Northam 1720 W
Pyke John, Fremington 1721 A
Pyke John, Bow 1728 A
Pyke John, Chawleigh 1735 W
Joseph, Northam 1712 W
Pyke Mary, Bow 1741 W
Pyke Mary, Bideford 1847 W
Pyke Mary see also John Jewell
Pyke Nicholas, Coldridge 1564 W
Pyke Nicholas, Oakford 1769 A
Pyke Richard, Coldridge 1574 A
Richard, Winkleigh 1676 A
Richard, Chawleigh 1766 A
Richard, Chawleigh 1770 W
Richard, Lapford 1846 W
Robert, Chawleigh 1694 W
Robert, West Anstey 1719 A
Robert, West Anstey 1784 A
Robert, Chulmleigh, maltster 1815 A to Mary Palbridge,
daughter
Pyke Roger, Coldridge 1566 W
Samuel, Abbotsham 1709 W
Samuel, Northam 1753 W
Pyke Samuel, Northam, esquire 1804 W transmitted to
Doctors' Commons, 5 Nov 1814
Thomas, Chawleigh 1848 W
William, Northam 1671 A and 1672 O
William, Bondleigh 1687 A
William, Chawleigh 1707 W
William, Winkleigh 1711 W
Pyke William, Bondleigh 1733 W and 1747 W
Pyke William, Chawleigh 1748 W
William, Wembworthy 1766 A
William, Chawleigh 1792 W
Pyke William, Georgeham 1833 W
Pyke William, Chawleigh 1845 A
Pile, Piell, Pille, Pills, Pyell, Pyle, Pyll, Pylle
Ann, Great Torrington 1778 W
Pyell Anthony, Martinhoe 1587 A
Piell Anthony, Martinhoe 1615 [W]
Pyle Anthony, Martinhoe 1635 [W]
Pyle Anthony, Combe Martin 1664 W
Anthony, Combe Martin 1739 A
Benjamin, Combe Martin 1704 A

Pyle Benjamin, Lynton 1745 W
Bridget, Chittlehampton 1679 W
Piell Cecilia, Martinhoe 1618 [W]
Pyle Clement, Combe Martin 1664 W
David, Challacombe 1720 W
David, Challacombe 1763 W
David, Challacombe 1854 W
Edmund, Trentishoe, yeoman 1800 A
Piell Edward, Trentishoe 1599 [W]
Pyle Edward, Martinhoe 1698 A
Pills Elizabeth, Bideford 1738 W
Elizabeth, Trentishoe 1831 A to Elizabeth Burgess of
Kentisbury and Grace Burgess of Trentishoe, daughters
Pyell Frances, Martinhoe 1630 [W]
Pyle or Pyke George, Ilfracombe 1686 W
Pyle Henry, Parracombe 1629 [W]
James, Lynton 1753 W
Jane, Martinhoe 1627 [W]
Piell Joan, Martinhoe 1592 [W]
Joan, Arlington 1779 W
Pyle John, Martinhoe 1625 [W]
Pyle John, Martinhoe 1667 A
Pille John, Instow 1704 W
John, Lynton 1727 W
Pills John. Bideford 1738 W
John, Challacombe 1748 W
John, Challacombe 1831 W and 1848 A
Joseph, Arlington 1770 W
Mary, Monkleigh 1715 W
Mary, Winkleigh 1751 W
Pyle Mary, Arlington 1768 A
Mary, Arlington 1784 W
Philip, Arlington 1778 W
Philip, Bratton Fleming 1821 W
Philip, Arlington 1848 A
Pyll Richard, Martinhoe 1579 W
Richard, Stoke Rivers 1582 W
Pyle Richard, Coldridge 1666 W
Richard, Ilfracombe 1680 W
Thomas, Ilfracombe 1734 A
Pyell William, Martinhoe 1624 [W]
Pills William, Bideford 1740 A
Pill William, Northam 1742 W
Pill William, Bideford 1842 A
William, Arlington 1846 W
Pylle Thomas, Martinhoe 1579 W
Pyle Thomas, Arlington 1819 W
Pyle Thomasine, Parracombe 1703 W
Pillavin, Pillafant, Pillaven, Pillifant, Pyllaver
Elizabeth, Heanton Punchardon 1696 W
George, Ashford 1713 W
Grace, Heanton Punchardon 1760 W
Pillaven John, Heanton Punchardon 1726 W
Pillafant John, Westleigh 1851 W
Pillifant Margaret, Sampford Courtenay 1800 W
Pyllaver or Pelvine Mathew, Chittlehampton 1573 A
Pillaven Robert, Barnstaple 1645 W
Pylven William, Chittlehampton 1570 W
Pille see Pile
Pillgrim Priscilla, Bideford 1829 W
Pillifant see Pillavin
Pilman, Pillman, Pylman, Pylmon
Pylmon ..., Little Torrington 1578 W
..., Huntshaw 1607 [W] and O
Anthony, Langtree 1606 W
Henry, Huntshaw 1644 W
Pillman John, Hartland 1840 W
Jonah, Little Torrington 1675 W
Pylman Joseph, Bratton Fleming 1643 W
Richard, Little Torrington 1578 W
Pylman Richard, Little Torrington 1602 W
Richard, Goodleigh 1616 [W]
Thomas, Little Torrington 1717 W
Thomas, Little Torrington 1738 A
Pillman Thomas, Clovelly 1826 A to Betty, widow

Pillman Ursula, Hartland 1852 W
Pillman Ursula see also Thomas King
Pylman Walter, Northam 1587 W
Pylman William, Huntshaw 1643 W
Pim, Pym
Elizabeth, Huish 1853 W
John, Bideford 1843 W
Pym Philip, East Down 1668 A
Pym Thomas, Bideford 1692 W
Pinard Henry, Warkleigh 1762 W
Pince, Pynse
Pynse Catherine, Rose Ash 1618 [W]
Mary, Buckland Brewer 1839 A to Elizabeth Prowse, daughter
William, Great Torrington, carrier 1797 A
Pinchoe Catherine, Ilfracombe 1605 W
Pincombe, Pinckombe, Pincomb, Pynckomb, Pyncomb,
Pyncombe
Pynckomb ..., South Molton 1614 [W]
Pynckomb ..., North Molton 1615 O
Pyncombe Amy, Molland 1636 W
Pincomb Amy, South Molton 1710 W
Pyncombe Ann, South Molton 1630 [W]
Pyncombe Anthony, Warkleigh 1596 [W]
Pincomb Anthony, Ashreigney 1662 W
Pincomb Anthony, Buckland Filleigh 1701 W
Pincomb Anthony, Beaford 1715 A
Arthur, Beaford 1728 W
Arthur, Roborough, tailor 1800 W effects under £100
Bridget, South Molton 1681 A
Pinckombe Dorothy, North Molton, widow 1610 [W];
forename blank in Ms; supplied from parish register
Edith, Tawstock, widow 1572 W
Pyncombe Edward, Tawstock 1594 [W]
Pincomb Edward, Roborough 1696 A
Pincomb Elizabeth, Roborough 1704 W
Elizabeth, Merton 1722 W
Pincomb Elizabeth, Heanton Punchardon 1745 A
Pyncombe Emott, East Buckland 1620 [W]
Pinckomb George, North Molton 1610 [W]; forename blank in
Ms; supplied from parish register
Pyncombe George, North Molton 1624 O
George, Barnstaple 1673 A
Pyncomb Henry, South Molton 1644 A
Pincomb James, Molland 1678 W
Pincomb James, Filleigh 1708 W
Pyncombe Joan, Yarnscombe 1628 [W]
Pynckomb John, Barnstaple 1616 [W]
Pyncombe John, Molland 1625 [W]
Pincomb John, Rose Ash 1676 W
John, North Molton 1689 W
Pincomb John, Roborough 1695 W
Pincomb John, Rose Ash 1703 W
Pyncombe John, South Molton 1711 A
Pincomb John, Merton 1713 A
John, Langtree 1737 W
Pyncombe Lodovic, West Buckland 1625 [W]
Pyncombe Mary, Molland 1637 W
Pincomb Mary, Buckland Filleigh 1662 W
Mary, Beaford 1729 W
Pincomb Mathew, Huish 1672 A
Pincomb alias Tinnacomb Methusaleh, Welcombe 1665 [W]
Pyncombe Peter, Bideford 1622 [W]
Pyncombe Peter, Barnstaple 1729 W
Pyncombe Petronell, North Molton 1591 [W]
Pincomb Petronell, Warkleigh 1705 W
Pyncombe Philip, Bideford 1632 [W]
Philip, Roborough 1727 W
Phillippa see Mary Ann Tarr
Richard, Bideford 1592 [W]
Richard, Chittlehampton 1673 A
Pincomb Robert, Barnstaple 1710 A
Pincomb Robert, Great Torrington 1742 A
Robert, Heanton Punchardon 1744 W and 1748 W
Samuel, Bideford 1705 [W]
Sarah, Roborough, widow 1824 A to Aaron Pardon, carpenter,
grandson and guardian of deceased

Pincomb Stephen, Tawstock 1682 W
Pincomb Thomas, Bideford 1663 W
Pincomb Thomas, Alwington 1685 W
Pincomb Thomas, St Giles in the Wood 1711 A
Thomas, ship *Shrewsbury* 1746 A
Thomas, High Bickington 1753 A
Thomas, Twitchen, yeoman, jnr. 1851 A to Harriet
Pyncombe William, North Molton 1567 W
Pynckham William, Bideford 1570 W
Pyncombe William, Alwington 1637 A and 1637 O
Pyncombe William, South Molton 1637 W
William, Bideford 1641 W
Pyncomb William, South Molton 1692 W
Pincomb William, Abbotsham 1693 W
William, Chittlehampton 1693 W
Pincomb William, Northam 1734 W
William, Bideford 1748 W
William, Beaford 1812 W
William, Roborough, labourer 1820 A to Abraham, brother
Pine, Pyne
Pyne Alice, Nymet Rowland 1579 W
Pyne Bridget, Bratton Fleming 1669 W
Pyne Dorothy, East Down 1639 W
Pyne Dorothy, Barnstaple 1690 W
Pyne Edward, East Down, esquire 1663 W
Pyne Edward, Bratton Fleming, snr. 1675 A
Pine Edward, East Down, snr. 1707 W
Pyne Elizabeth, East Down 1717 W
Elizabeth, East Down 1720 W
Emblem, Shirwell 1673 [W]
Pyne Eusebius, Yarnscombe 1721 A
Eusebius, Tawstock 1742 A
Francis, Shirwell 1714 A
Pyne Francis, St Giles in the Wood 1732 A
Pyne George, Coldridge 1621 [W]
Pyne George, Shirwell 1632 [W]
Grace, East Down 1768 A
Pyne Honor, East Down 1574 W
Pyne Jane, Tawstock 1720 A
Pyne John, Chulmleigh 1601 W
Pyne John, Bideford 1661 W
Pyne John, Chulmleigh 1668 W
Pyne John, West Down 1681 W
Pyne John, Tawstock, jnr. 1705 [W]
Pyne John, Horwood 1705 [W]
John, Oakford 1823 W
Mary, Oakford 1705 [W]
Pyne Mary, West Down 1708 W
Mary, Shirwell 1747 W
Pyne Nicholas, Burrington 1620 [W]
Pyne Nicholas, Bideford 1663 A
Pyne Patience, Bideford 1692 A
Pyne Philip, East Down, esquire 1600 W
Pyne Philip, Tawstock 1752 A
Pyne Richard, Bideford 1624 [W] and 1625 O
Pyne Richard, Oakford 1704 W
Pyne Richard, Rackenford 1802 A
Richard, Oakford 1830 W
Pyne Samuel, Ilfracombe 1697 A
Pyne Theobald, Chulmleigh 1597 [W]
Thomas, Oakford 1826 W
Pyne Tobias, Countisbury 1696 A
Pyne William, Chulmleigh 1635 W and 1639 O
Pyne William, Warkleigh 1714 W
William, Oakford 1734 W
William, Oakford 1814 W and 1820 W
Pyne Willmot, Coldridge 1640 A
Pintoe Richard, Ilfracombe 1706 W
Piper, Pyper
Andrew, Alverdiscott 1605 [W]; forename blank in Ms;
supplied from parish register
Arthur, Peters Marland 1691 W
Dionysius, Loxhore 1632 [W]
Edmund, Peters Marland 1662 W
Edmund, Newton St Petrock 1742 A

Edward, Buckland Filleigh 1685 W
Elizabeth, Monkleigh 1836 W and 1838 W
Grace, Peters Marland 1718 W
James, Iddesleigh 1679 W
James, Newton St Petrock 1691 A
James, Newton St Petrock 1697 W
James, Iddesleigh 1737 W
Pyper Joan, Martinhoe 1575 W
John, Filleigh 1594 [W]
John, Huish, jnr. , yeoman 1799 A
John, Roborough, yeoman 1806 A
John, Iddesleigh 1812 A to Elizabeth, grandmother
Joseph, Peters Marland 1682 A
Joseph, Peters Marland 1683 W
Ruth, Newton St Petrock 1742 A
Samuel, Iddesleigh 1820 W
Thomas, Buckland Filleigh 1619 [W]
Thomas, Peters Marland 1623 [W] and 1627 [W]
William, Iddesleigh 1825 W
Pippin Robert, Northam 1799 W
Pitaman see Pitman
Pitford, Pittford, Pytford
   Pytford Christopher, High Bickington 1636 A and O
   Christopher, South Molton 1677 W
   Faithful, South Molton 1661 W
   George, Ashreigney 1593 [W]
   Pytford Margery, Barnstaple 1636 W
   Pittford Mary, South Molton 1663 W
   Pytford Thomas, Chulmleigh 1596 [W]
Pithebridge see Pethebridge
Pitman, Pitaman, Pytman
   Pytman Alice, Romansleigh 1588 A
   Alice, Little Torrington 1622 [W]
   Humphrey, Knowstone 1716 W
   Pitaman or Pyeman Richard, Romansleigh 1581 W
   Thomas, Northam 1684 W
   Walter, Romansleigh 1602 W
Pitt see Pitts
Pitter Eleanor, Tawstock 1606 W
Pittes see Pitts
Pittford see Pitford
Pitton, Pytton
   Charity, Huntshaw 1642 W
   Hugh, Hartland 1682 W
   Pytton John, Hartland 1573 A
   Pytton John, Hartland 1573 W
   Pytton alias Jule John, Bideford 1580 W
   Nicholas, Hartland 1595 [W]
   Philip, Hartland 1616 [W]
   Richard, Hartland 1717 W
   Thomas, Hartland 1684 A
   Thomas, Hartland 1700 W
   Thomas, Northam 1709 W
   Thomas, Ilfracombe 1715 A
   William, Hartland 1601 W
   Pytton Willmot, Huntshaw 1642 A
Pitts, Pitt, Pittes, Pytts
   Pytts Agnes, Atherington 1574 W
   Anthony, Bideford 1715 W
   Pitt Elizabeth, Bideford 1756 A
   Garrett, Tawstock 1631 [W]
   Henry, Chittlehampton 1628 [W] and 1629 [W]
   Henry, Iddesleigh 1689 W
   Honor, Monkleigh 1669 W
   Humphrey, Shirwell 1745 W
   James, Winkleigh 1667 W
   James, Clannaborough 1777 A
   Joan, Chittlehampton 1598 [W]
   Joan, Great Torrington 1666 A
   Pytts John, Atherington 1573 W
   Pittes John, Atherington 1617 [W]
   John, Newton Tracey 1621 [W]
   John, Great Torrington 1627 [W]
   John, Atherington 1634 W
   John and Sarah, Bideford 1678 A

Lawrence, Atherington 1602 [W]; forename blank in Ms;
   supplied from parish register
Lawrence, Tawstock 1631 [W]
Marian, Atherington 1620 [W]
Richard, Tawstock 1591 [W]
Richard, Tawstock 1625 [W]
Richard, Great Torrington 1706 W
Robert, Tawstock 1599 [W]
Roger, Tawstock 1591 [W]
Samuel, Bideford 1752 W
Pitt Samuel, Bideford 1756 W
Sarah and John, Bideford 1678 A
Thomas, Tawstock 1599 [W]
Thomas, Shirwell 1639 [W]
Thomas, Tawstock 1640 W
Thomas, Barnstaple 1678 A
Thomas, Pilton 1719 W
Thomasine, Atherington, widow 1610 [W]; forename blank in
   Ms; supplied from parish register
William, Langtree 1625 [W]
William, Bow 1708 W
William, Bideford 1732 A
Pittwood, Pitwod, Pitwood, Pytwode, Pytwood
   Pitwood ..., Wembworthy 1601 A
   Pitwood ..., Wembworthy 1614 [W]
   Gilbert, Lapford 1681 W
   Humphrey, Chawleigh 1660 W
   Pytwode John, Wembworthy 1575 W and 1588 A
   Pitwod John 1589 A account
   John, Wembworthy 1660 W
   John, Chulmleigh 1664 A
   Pitwood John, Burrington 1775 A
   John, Huntshaw 1833 W
   John, Ashreigney 1845 W
   Pitwood Mary, Ashreigney, widow 1809 W
   William, Ashreigney, yeoman 1798 W
Please, Plaice, Plaise, Pleace, Pleyse
   ..., South Molton 1609 [W]
   ..., Puddington 1613 [W]
   Andrew, West Anstey 1668 W
   Andrew, West Anstey 1704 A
   Pleace Cornelius, Bideford 1743 W
   Pleace Elizabeth, Peters Marland, sp. 1797 W
   Pleace Elizabeth, Puddington 1799 W
   Frederick, Combe Martin 1845 [W]
   John, West Anstey 1570 W, 1583 [W], 1587 W &1603 W
   John, West Anstey 1665 W
   Pleace John, West Anstey 1695 W
   Plaice John, Woolfardisworthy 1705 [W]
   Pleace John, Pilton 1773 A
   John, Cruwys Morchard, husbandman 1799 W
   Pleace Martin, ship *Torbay* 1756 A
   Mary, West Anstey 1672 W
   Mary, Eggesford, widow 1802 W
   Pleyse Philip, Molland 1685 A
   Pleace Rebecca, Barnstaple 1741 W
   Plaise Richard, West Anstey, snr. 1566 W
   Richard, West Anstey 1576 W
   Pleace Robert, Winkleigh 1620 [W]
   Roger, Puddington 1602 W
   Simon, Warkleigh 1728 W
   Pleace Walter, Combe Martin 1828 A
   William, Puddington 1637 A
   William, Puddington 1640 [W]
   William, South Molton 1697 W
   Pleace William, Puddington 1753 W
   William, Warkleigh 1772 W
   Pleace William, Cruwys Morchard 1800 W
Plastead Daniel, Bideford 1676 W
Plattyn William, Wembworthy 1570 W
Plealand Margaret, Shebbear 1626 [W]
Plem see Plym
Pleyse see Please
Plimshole, Plymshole
   Plymshole Catherine, Newton Tracey 1695 A

Francis 1799 W
William, Bideford 1789 W
Plowman ...., Lynton 1606 [W]
...., Brendon 1608 [W]
David, Lynton 1598 [W]
John, Lynton 1580 W, 1591 [W] and 1594 [W]
John, Brendon 1596 [W]
Roger, Lynton 1580 W
Thomas, South Molton 1587 W
Thomas, Berrynarbor 1593 [W]
William, Lynton 1593 [W]
Plucknett, Plucknet
Andrew, Great Torrington 1689 A
John, Northam 1857 W
Plucknet Thomas, Great Torrington 1679 A
Plumpton, Plympton
Plympton Cyprian, Knowstone 1663 A
Thomas, Combe Martin 1585 A
Plym, Plem
Ann, Barnstaple 1638 W
Plem George, Barnstaple 1620 [W]
George, Barnstaple 1725 A
Humphrey, Tawstock 1633 W
Richard, Barnstaple 1664 W
Samuel, Barnstaple 1735 W and 1749 A
Plympton see Plumpton
Plymshole see Plimshole
Poat John, Bideford 1773 A
Pocock, Pococke, Powcoke, Powkoke
Powcoke Henry, Sheepwash 1577 W
Pococke Joan, Sheepwash 1565 W
Pococke Robert, Sheepwash 1567 W
Thomas, Sheepwash 1573 A
Powkoke Thomas, Sheepwash 1577 W
Podger Abraham, Warkleigh 1727 W
Elizabeth, Warkleigh 1746 W
James, Warkleigh 1697 W
Margaret, Loxhore 1783 W
Pointz, Points, Poyntz
Points ...., Buckland Brewer 1609 [W]
Poyntz Edward, Arlington 1678 W
Edward, Bittadon 1692 W
Poyntz Eleanor, Barnstaple 1670 W
Poyntz Eleanor, Barnstaple 1694 A
Poynts Hugh, Newton St Petrock 1593 [W]
Poyntz Jane, Combe Martin 1750 W
Points John, Marwood 1615 [W]
Poyntz John, Barnstaple 1666 W
Poyntz John, Barnstaple 1685 W
Poynts Margaret 1623 [W]
Poyntz Philip, Bideford 1697 [W]
Poynts alias Poynes Richard, Metcombe, Marwood 1572 W
Poyntz Temperance, Arlington 1724 W
Polglase John, Buckland Filleigh 1565 W
Polkinghorne, Polkinghore, Polkinghorn, Pulkinghorne
Polkinghore John, St Giles in the Wood 1802 W
Polkinghorn William, Weare Giffard 1712 A
Pulkinghorne William, Great Torrington 1833 A
Pollard, Pollarde, Pollord
...., Chulmleigh 1609 [W]
...., Clovelly 1612 [W]
...., Meshaw 1612 [W]
...., South Molton 1612 [W]
Alice, Chulmleigh 1583 A
Andrew, Northam 1682 W
Andrew, Clovelly 1705 [W]
Ann, South Molton 1695 W
Pollarde Anthony, Chulmleigh 1580 W
Arthur, South Molton 1667 W
Arthur, Instow 1681 W
Baptist, Clovelly 1727 W
Catherine, Pilton 1707 or 1797 W
Cecilia, Horwood 1663 W
Dorothy, Chulmleigh 1665 W
Elizabeth, Frithelstock 1585 W

Elizabeth, Tawstock 1673 [W]
Eusebius 1684 W
Francis, Clovelly 1742 W
George, Atherington 1596 [W]
George, Northam 1760 W
Honor, Cheldon 1638 W
Pollard alias Day Honor, High Bickington 1664 A
Joan, South Molton 1597 [W]
Joan, Tawstock 1674 A
John, Buckland Filleigh 1623 [W]
John, South Molton, gentleman 1624 [W]
John, Northam 1629 [W]
John, South Molton 1691 W
John, Bideford 1693 A
John, Mariansleigh 1770 A
John, Witheridge 1835 W
Lodovic, Langtree 1699 W
Margaret, South Molton 1638 A
Mary, Atherington 1628 [W]
Mary, Filleigh 1637 W
Mary, South Molton 1690 W
Richard, Cheldon 1627 [W]
Richard, High Bickington 1685 A
Robert, Knowstone 1573 W
Robert, South Molton 1597 [W]
Robert, Clovelly 1629 [W]
Robert, South Molton 1670 A
Robert, Fremington 1680 W
Robert, Clovelly 1695 A
Robert, Clovelly 1728 A
Samuel, South Molton 1694 W
Samuel, Barnstaple 1704 A
Susan, Northam 1759 A and 1763 A
Thomas, Fremington 1623 [W]
Thomas, Abbotsham 1640 [W]
Thomas, Barnstaple 1701 W
Pollord Thomas, Northam 1743 W
Thomas, B ... 1759 W
Thomas, Bishop's Nympton 1807 A
Thomasine, Northam 1684 A
William, Hartland 1626 [W]
William, Northam 1639 A
William, Northam 1736 W
William, Barnstaple 1739 A
William, Clovelly 1743 W
William, Northam 1749 A
William, Barnstaple 1782 W
Pollock Eleanor, Ilfracombe, Almsworthy 1854 A
Eleanor Hunsworthy see Mary Oliver
Pollord see Pollard
Pomeroy, Pomery, Pomrey, Pomrie, Pomroy, Pomry
Pomrie ...., 1568 [W]
Pomery Grace, Northam 1606 W
Grace, Abbotsham 1723 A
Grace, Littleham (near Bideford) 1723 A
Pomry John, Buckland Filleigh 1638 W
Pomery John, Alwington 1696 W
Pomroy John, Abbotsham 1700 A
Pomroy Mary, Alwington 1705 [W]
Philip, Abbotsham 1661 A
Pomroy Richard, Barnstaple 1831 W
Pomrie Stephen, Sheepwash 1569 W
Pomery Thomas, Northam 1606 W
Pomroy Thomas, Barnstaple 1838 A to James
William, Heanton Punchardon 1748 A
Pomrey William, Northam 1836 W
Ponsford, Ponsforde, Pounsford
Pounsford Anthony, Chawleigh 1642 W
Digory, Rackenford 1685 W
Pounsford George, Hugh, Winkleigh 1592 [W]
Pounsford George, Little Torrington 1720 A
Pounsford Jane, Chulmleigh 1663 W
Judith see James Burgess
Pounsford Michael, High Bickington 1637 W
Pounsford Sarah, Bideford 1793 A

Tebbet, Chawleigh 1589 W
Pounsford Thomas, Bow 1643 W
Pounsford Thomas, King's Nympton 1643 W
Pounsford Thomas, Bideford 1695 W
Pounsford Thomas, Chulmleigh 1716 A
Ponsforde Walter, Chawleigh 1567 W
William, Chittlehampton 1826 W
Pood Samuel, Bideford 1704 A
Pooe Mary, Burrington 1715 W
Pooke Henry, Knowstone 1722 W
Thomas, Knowstone 1666 W and 1678 W
Thomas, Knowstone 1713 A
Thomas, Knowstone 1756 A
Poole, Pool, Poule
Pool Abraham, Bideford 1706 A
Christian, Great Torrington 1591 [W]
Edward, Hartland 1666 W
Pool Eleanor, Great Torrington 1709 A
Elizabeth, Ilfracombe 1717 A
Frances S. see Robert Ackland
George, Burrington 1586 W
George, Great Torrington 1709 A
Giles, Great Torrington 1703 A
Jane, Great Torrington 1714 A
John, Great Torrington 1582 A
John, Burrington 1591 [W]
John, Burrington 1636 W
John, Chulmleigh 1639 W
John, Great Torrington 1742 W
Samuel, Great Torrington 1668 W
Samuel, Great Torrington 1704 A
Samuel, Great Torrington 1719 W
Samuel, mariner 1747 W
Sarah, Ilfracombe 1717 A
Thomas, Satterleigh 1625 [W]
Thomas, Great Torrington, clothier 1805 A
Poule alias Harnaman or Hornman William, Rose Ash 1564 W
William, Chulmleigh 1630 [W]
Pooley, Powley
Elizabeth, Hartland 1827 W
John, ship St George 1757 W
Powley William, Bideford 1579 A
William, Hartland 1788 W
Pope ...., Lapford 1607 [W]
..., Meshaw 1609 [W]
..., Bratton Fleming 1612 [W] and 1614 [W]
Agnes, Kentisbury 1728 W
Alice, High Bray 1621 [W]
Ambrose, Cruwys Morchard 1669 W
Ann, St Giles in the Wood, sp. 1840 A to Mary Goss and Jane Dennis, sisters
Christopher, Washford Pyne 1690 W
Edmund, Northam 1676 A
Edward, Great Torrington 1675 W
George, Lapford 1597 [W] and 1598 [W]
George, Fremington 1619 [W]
George, Warkleigh 1739 A
George, Fremington 1815 A
Henry, High Bray 1603 W
Henry, Bratton Fleming 1643 A
James, Barnstaple 1677 W
Jane, Sandford 1857 W
Joan, Zeal Monachorum 1703 A
Joan, Chittlehampton 1719 W
John, South Molton 1606 W
John, West Buckland 1622 [W]
John, Barnstaple 1623 [W]
John, West Buckland 1666 W
John, Chittlehampton 1705 [W]
John, Clovelly 1740 A
John, Chittlehampton 1741 W
John, St Giles in the Wood, yeoman 1811 W
John, St Giles in the Wood 1839 W
Leonard, Shebbear 1621 [W]
Margery, Shebbear 1636 W

Martha, Barnstaple 1730 A
Mary, Bratton Fleming 1730 W
Methusaleh, Bratton Fleming 1642 W
Michael, Barnstaple 1645 A
Nicholas, Lapford 1594 [W]
Penelope, St Giles in the Wood 1840 A to Mary Goss and Jane Dennis, sisters
Philip, Northam 1674 W
Philip, Zeal Monachorum 1702 W
Richard, High Bray 1571 W
Richard, High Bray 1602 W
Richard, Shebbear 1681 W
Richard, Northam 1691 A
Richard, Frithelstock 1698 W
Richard, Kentisbury 1728 W
Richard, Bratton Fleming 1752 A
Richard, Chittlehampton 1769 A
Scipio, Winkleigh 1785 A
Thomas, Fremington 1596 [W]
Thomas, Puddington 1632 [W] and 1635 O
Thomas, Winkleigh 1766 W
Walter, Ilfracombe 1680 A
William, Ilfracombe 1702 A
William, Barnstaple 1707 A
Popham, Popeham
..., Great Torrington 1608 [W] and 1614 [W]
..., Little Torrington 1614 [W]
Popham alias Willmote ..., North Molton 1685 A
Agnes, Parracombe 1767 W
Alice, Kentisbury 1684 A
Anthony, Combe Martin 1663 W
Hugh, Lynton 1679 W
Hugh, Lynton 1717 W
Humphrey, Parracombe 1747 W
Jerome, Berrynarbor 1638 A and 1640 O
John, Great Torrington 1579 W
John, Lynton 1685 A
John, ship Terrible 1759 W
John, Filleigh 1782 W
John, Northam 1787 W
Margery, Great Torrington, widow 1608 [W]; forename blank in Ms; supplied from parish register
Mary, Lynton 1685 A
Nicholas, Kentisbury 1707 A
Nicholas, Great Torrington 1827 W
Richard, Little Torrington 1604 W
Richard, Lynton 1628 [W]
Richard, Great Torrington 1640 W
Robert, Great Torrington 1590 [W]
Robert, Berrynarbor 1848 W
Popeham Thomas, Hartland 1565 W
Thomas, Great Torrington 1593 [W]
Thomas, Northam 1854 W
William, Great Torrington 1602 W
William, Westleigh 1672 A
Portayne see Portin
Porter James, East Down 1749 W
Portin, Portayne, Portine, Portnie, Portyn
Christian, Ilfracombe 1610 [W]; forename blank in Ms; supplied from parish register
Portayne Henry, Ilfracombe 1587 W
Portnie Thomas, Ilfracombe 1583 A
Portyn Thomasine, Tawstock, widow 1615 [W]; forename blank in Ms; supplied from parish register
Portine William, Tawstock 1588 W
Poslett Elias, Great Torrington 1725 A
Elizabeth, Great Torrington 1712 W
Paul, Great Torrington 1639 A
Potham William, Winkleigh 1783 W
Potter ..., Iddesleigh 1614 [W]
Elizabeth, Great Torrington 1755 A
George, Barnstaple 1717 W
John, Newton St Petrock or Petrockstowe 1698 A
Mary, Great Torrington 1702 W
Mary, Great Torrington 1734 W

Mary, Eggesford 1796 A
Philip, Great Torrington 1688 A
Philip, Great Torrington 1718 A
Philip, Great Torrington 1721 [W] and 1730 A
Philip, Great Torrington 1760 A
Robert, Georgeham 1826 W
Samuel, Bondleigh 1849 W
William, Bideford 1834 W
Pougsley see Pugsley
Poule see Poole
Pounce George, Bideford 1741 W
Pounchard see Punchard
Pounsford see Ponsford
Pountaine Ann, Barnstaple 1738 W
    Thomas 1726 W
Pow, Powe
    Powe ..., Clovelly 1607 [W]
    Powe ..., Dolton 1609 [W]
    Powe Agnes, Coldridge 1688 W
    Ann, Tawstock 1693 W
    Arthur, High Bickington 1708 W and 1715 W
    Christopher, Alwington 1835 W
    Elizabeth, Dolton 1638 W
    Elizabeth, Northam 1678 W
    Francis, Petrockstowe 1737 W
    George, Frithelstock 1639 W
    Gregory, Martinhoe 1621 [W]
    James, Bideford 1702 A
    Powe John, Dowland 1572 W
    Powe John, Parkham 1579 W
    Powe John, Dolton 1589 W
    John, Coldridge 1625 [W]
    John, Parkham 1629 [W]
    John, Dowland 1630 [W]
    John, Parkham 1665 A
    Powe John, Tawstock 1689 W
    John, Buckland Brewer 1695 A
    John, High Bickington 1702 W
    Powe John, Bideford 1711 A
    Powe John, High Bickington 1715 W
    Powe John, Atherington 1724 W
    Powe John, Westleigh 1735 W
    John, Alwington 1824 A to William, son
    Powe Judith, Pilton 1765 A
    Margaret, Yarnscombe 1808 W
    Mary, Bideford 1721 W
    Powe Nicholas, Parkham 1584 W
    Powe Nicholas, High Bickington 1724 A
    Philip, Parkham 1669 W
    Powe Robert, High Bickington 1597 [W]
    Robert, Dolton 1636 W
    Robert, Fremington 1717 A
    Powe Robert, Bideford 1826 A to Frances, widow
    Powe Robert, Dolton 1612 [W]; forename blank in Ms;
        supplied from parish register
    Samuel, Fremington 1734 W
    Powe Simon, Georgeham 1693 A
    Powe Simon, Pilton 1741 A
    Powe Stephen, Dolton 1567 W
    Stephen, Dolton 1625 [W]
    Thomas, Dowland 1627 [W]
    Thomas, Northam 1664 A
    Thomas, Iddesleigh 1695 W
    Thomas, Pilton, husbandman 1804 W
    William, Frithelstock 1620 [W]
    Powe William, Dolton 1626 [W]
    William, Frithelstock 1635 [W]
    William, Fremington 1716 W and 1717 W
    Powe William, Georgeham 1735 W
    Powe William, Westleigh 1735 W
    William, Alwington 1781 W
    Powe William, Westleigh 1831 A to Elizabeth, widow
Powcoke see Pocock
Powe see Pow

Powell, Powle
    Powle Christopher, Barnstaple 1788 W
    Elizabeth, Great Torrington 1690 W
    Francis, Mortehoe 1717 W
    George, Bideford, snr. 1685 W
    Powle John, Great Torrington 1583 A account
    John, Hartland 1623 [W]
    John, West Down 1755 A
    Powle Judith, Barnstaple 1788 W
    Mary, Bideford 1696 W
    Mathew, Barnstaple 1630 [W]
    Nicholas, Barnstaple 1644 W
    Richard, Great Torrington 1581 A
    Richard, Bideford 1697 W
    Sarah, Heanton Punchardon 1697 A
    Thomas, Great Torrington 1681 A
    Thomas, Great Torrington 1686 W
    William, Bideford 1687 A
    William, Bideford 1756 A
Power Alfred, Bideford 1714 W
    Ann, Bideford 1749 W
    John, Bideford 1702 W
    John, Barnstaple 1726 A
    Powyer John, Ilfracombe 1807 A
    Margery, Abbotsham 1582 [W]
    Michael, ship *Saltash* 1757 W
    Patrick, Bideford 1739 A
    Sarah, Bideford 1714 A
    Poyer Thomas, Heanton Punchardon 1714 W
    Walter, Abbotsham 1583 W
    William, Bideford 1743 W
Powkoke see Pocock
Powle see Powell
Powlesland George, Meeth 1843 A to Ann, widow
Powley see Pooley
Powlyn see Pawlyn
Powse Richard, Bideford 1591 [W]
Powste John, Sheepwash 1585 A
Poyle Jane, Great Torrington 1573 W
Poyner John, Barnstaple 1564 W
Poynter Hugh, Newton St Petrock 1586 A
Poyntington William, Cruwys Morchard 1589 W
Poynts, Poyntz see Pointz
Prance, Praunce
    Praunce ..., Woolfardisworthy 1607 [W]
    Praunce Abel, Bideford 1711 W
    Praunce Anthony, Woolfardisworthy 1623 [W]
    Praunce Elizabeth, Woolfardisworthy 1641 W
    Elizabeth, Bideford 1727 W
    Praunce Giles, Parkham 1774 W
    Praunce Grace, Woolfardisworthy 1625 [W]
    Isott, Woolfardisworthy 1673 W
    Praunce James, Bideford 1701 W
    Jane, Northam 1724 W
    Praunce Joan, Chulmleigh 1615 [W]
    Joan, Northam 1763 W
    Praunce John, Buckland Brewer 1590 [W]
    Praunce John, Northam 1599 [W]
    Praunce John, Parkham 1661 W
    Praunce John, Woolfardisworthy 1728 W
    John, Woolfardisworthy 1733 W
    John, Parkham 1782 A
    John, Parkham 1819 W
    Praunce Margaret, Woolfardisworthy 1641 W
    Praunce Mary, Woolfardisworthy 1668 A
    Mary wife of John see Betty Jeffery
    Phyllis, Northam 1801 W
    Praunce Nicholas, Buckland Brewer 1597 [W]
    Praunce Robert, Buckland Brewer 1565 W
    Praunce Robert, Buckland Brewer 1619 [W]
    Praunce Robert, Woolfardisworthy 1635 W
    Praunce Robert, Woolfardisworthy 1641 W
    Praunce Robert, Buckland Brewer 1694 A
    Praunce Roger, Northam 1618 [W]
    Samuel, Bideford 1721 W

Stephen, Bideford 1725 W
Praunce Stephen, Alwington 1729 W
Praunce Thomas, Bideford 1711 A
Praunce Thomas, Parkham 1716 W
Praunce Thomasine, Buckland Brewer 1594 [W]
Praunce Thomasine, Woolfardisworthy 1671 W
Praunce William, Abbotsham 1573 W
Praunce William, Woolfardisworthy 1581 W
William, Woolfardisworthy 1582 W
Praunce William, Buckland Brewer 1589 A
Praunce William, Buckland Brewer 1606 W
Praunce William, Parkham 1690 A
Praunce William, Woolfardisworthy 1702 A
William, Alwington 1720 A
William, Northam 1727 A
Praunce William, Parkham 1774 A
Praned Robert, Northam 1757 W
Praster John, Parkham 1566 W
Pratt Robert, Great Torrington 1638 A
Praughter, Proughter
    Proughter Joan, North Molton 1620 [W]
    John, North Molton 1616 [W] "Prother" in register; forename
    blank in Ms; supplied from parish register
Praunce see Prance
Preddis, Preddys, Predys, Priddis, Pridis
    Pridis ..., Great Torrington 1610 [W] and 1614 O
    Andrew, Great Torrington 1591 [W]
    Predys Ellen, North Molton 1564 W
    Preddys John, Great Torrington 1622 [W]
    Preddys Peter, Barnstaple 1631 [W]
    Preddys Richard, Barnstaple, jnr. 1641 A
Predham see Pridham
Preges Robert, North Molton 1619 [W]
Preist see Priest
Prescott, Priscott
    ..., Stoodleigh 1608 [W]
    Ann, Stoodleigh 1724 W
    Priscott Betsy, Combe Martin 1845 A
    Elizabeth, King's Nympton 1667 [W]
    Priscott Elizabeth, Shirwell 1780 A
    Frances, Oakford 1663 W
    Priscott John, Shirwell 1780 A
    Priscott John, Shirwell 1816 A to Grace, widow
    Priscott John, Shirwell 1854 W
    John, South Molton 1855 W
    Priscott Richard, Tawstock 1854 W
    Thomas, Stoodleigh 1713 W
    Thomas, Stoodleigh 1766 A
    Thomas, Chawleigh, yeoman 1810 W
    Priscott Thomas, Loxhore 1836 W
    Priscott Thomas, Heanton Punchardon 1853 W
    William, Stoodleigh 1590 [W]
    William, King's Nympton 1660 A
    Priscott William, Ilfracombe, mariner 1809 A
Presse Margaret, Knowstone 1600 W
Presson Andrew, Bow 1602 W
    Marian, Tawstock 1593 [W]
Prest, Preste see Priest
Prestly, Prestleigh
    Dorothy, Northam 1620 [W]
    Prestleigh Robert, North Tawton 1604 W
Preston John, Clannaborough 1574 W
    John, Georgeham 1857 W
    Richard, Bow 1678 A
    William, Clannaborough 1587 W
Price Edward, Northam 1775 W
    James, Romansleigh 1791 W
    James, Ilfracombe 1820 W
    John, Bideford 1660 W
    John, West Worlington 1733 A
    John, Bideford 1755 A
    Margaret, Barnstaple 1684 A
    Michael, West Worlington 1758 A
    Mildred, West Worlington 1818 W
    Richard, East Worlington 1676 W

Robert, Georgeham 1704 A
Samuel, East Worlington 1791 W
Samuel, East Worlington, jnr. 1791 W
Samuel, East Worlington, yeoman 1805 A
Thomas, Barnstaple 1680 W
Thomas, Barnstaple 1707 A
William, Bideford 1698 W
Priddis see Preddis
Prideaux Ann, Bideford 1726 W
    Francis, Bideford 1671 W
    Humphrey, Bideford 1664 W
    Joan, Barnstaple 1673 W
Pridham, Predham, Pridman, Prodham, Prudham, Prydham
    Predham ..., Langtree 1606 [W]
    Predham ..., North Tawton 1611 [W]
    Prydham Abraham, Sheepwash 1640 A
    Predham Agnes, Great Torrington, widow 1613 [W];
        forename blank in Ms; supplied from parish register
    Agnes, Parkham 1672 A
    Ann, Thelbridge 1682 W
    Predham alias Jewle Dorothy, Great Torrington 1606 W
    Elizabeth, Witheridge 1763 W
    Elizabeth, Burrington 1780 W
    Gilbert, Burrington 1763 W
    Prodham Henry, Langtree 1572 W
    Humphrey, St Giles in the Wood 1681 A
    Prydham Joan, Langtree 1619 [W]
    Predham John, Langtree 1605 W
    John, Langtree 1663 W
    John, Lapford 1682 A
    John, Lapford 1704 W
    John, Great Torrington 1776 A
    Prydham Mary, Fremington 1625 [W]
    Mary, Coldridge 1764 A
    Mildred, Thelbridge 1716 A
    Nicholas, Peters Marland 1596 [W]
    Prydham Nicholas, Fremington 1630 [W]
    Peter, Thelbridge 1671 W
    Peter, Thelbridge 1739 W
    Peter, Cruwys Morchard 1781 A
    Prudham Richard, Langtree 1570 W
    Predham Richard, Fremington 1621 [W]
    Richard, Thelbridge 1714 W
    Simon, Thelbridge 1730 W
    Simon, Witheridge 1750 A
    Thomas, Coldridge 1675 W
    Thomas, Thelbridge 1682 A
    Thomas, Coldridge 1723 W
    Thomas, Clovelly 1733 A
    Thomas, Chulmleigh 1753 W
    Thomas, Bideford 1838 W
    Thomas Charles, Bideford 1834 W
    Thomasine, Langtree 1616 [W]
    Predham William, Langtree 1600 W
    Prydham William, Langtree 1632 [W]
    William, Bideford 1703 A
    William, Chulmleigh 1802 W
    William, Parkham 1848 W
Pridis see Preddis
Pridman see Pridham
Priest, Preist, Prest, Preste, Prieste, Prist, Pryst
    Preist ..., Abbotsham 1604 [W] and 1608 [W]
    Preste Agnes, Hartland 1582 W
    Pryst Agnes, Hartland 1603 W
    Prieste Alice, Nymet Rowland 1563 W
    Preste Alice, Hartland 1569 W
    Prieste Catherine, Hartland 1571 W
    Prest Christopher, Hartland 1582 W
    Preist Edward, Ilfracombe 1719 W
    Prist Elizabeth, Bideford 1718 W
    Elizabeth, Ilfracombe 1728 W
    Preist Henry, Pilton 1636 A
    Prest Hugh, Woolfardisworthy 1575 A
    Preste Hugh, Hartland 1582 W
    Prest Hugh, Clovelly 1744 W

James, Chittlehampton, yeoman 1803 W
Prest Lawrence, Great Torrington 1574 A
Prest Mark, Nymet Rowland 1602 W
Mary, North Molton 1825 W
Prieste Thomas, Hartland 1563 W
William, Barnstaple 1827 A
Prim Thomas, Mortehoe 1733 W
Prince Bernard, Clovelly 1849 A
Mary, Instow 1739 W
Richard, Little Torrington 1632 [W]
Richard, Clovelly, yeoman 1847 A to Susan wife of Samuel
   Vine, mariner, daughter
Prior Benjamin, Chulmleigh 1750 A
Betty, South Molton 1818 W
Henry, North Molton 1598 [W]
John, Bideford 1796 W
Mary, South Molton 1814 W
William, South Molton, innholder 1808 W
Priscott see Prescott
Prist see Priest
Pritchard, Pritchet
Pritchet Benjamin, Westleigh, mariner 1705 [W]
John, West Anstey 1777 W
Prithybridge Henry, Yarnscombe 1772 W
Prodham see Pridham
Prolle, Prole, Proule, Prowle
Prowle ..., Martinhoe 1776 W
Alexander, Martinhoe 1758 W
Joan, Martinhoe 1758 A
Proule John, Martinhoe 1740 W
Prole John, Georgeham 1813 W
Proughter see Praughter
Proule see Prolle
Prouse see Prowse
Proust see Prust
Prout, Proute, Prowt, Prowte
Elizabeth, Hartland 1708 W
Prowte Francis, Barnstaple 1716 W
Prowte Hugh, Bideford 1619 [W]
Prowte Joan, Bideford 1623 [W]
Prowte John, Hartland 1576 W and 1578 W
John, Northam 1734 W
John, Northam, Appledore 1853 A to Hannah, widow
Proute Mathew, Barnstaple 1694 A
Proute Nicholas, Hartland 1681 W
Peter. Bideford, cordwainer 1808 W
Richard, Huntshaw 1676 A
Prowt William, Abbotsham 1586 A
William, Barnstaple 1823 W
Prower ...., Great Torrington 1611 [W]
Daniel, Abbotsham 1635 A
John, Abbotsham 1687 W
Margery, Abbotsham 1581 [W]
Prowle see Prolle
Prowse, Prouse
Prouse ..., Clovelly 1608 [W] and 1614 [W]
Prouse ..., Combe Martin 1610 [W] and 1612 [W]
Agnes, Alwington 1580 W
Ann, Clovelly 1630 [W]
Elizabeth, Heanton Punchardon 1720 W
Elizabeth see also Mary Pince
Prouse Hugh, Clovelly 1826 W
James, Clovelly 1750 A
James, Hartland 1820 W
Prouse James, Hartland 1834 A to Ann, widow
Joan, Langtree 1619 [W] and 1624 O
Joan, Abbotsham 1625 [W]
Prose John, Clovelly 1566 W
Prouse John, Langtree 1618 [W]
Prouse John, Buckland Brewer 1851 W
Paschal, Berrynarbor 1694 A
Peter, Clovelly 1622 [W]
Richard, Bow 1571 W
Thomas, West Anstey 1717 A
Thomas, Barnstaple 1785 W

Thomas, Woolfardisworthy 1841 W
Thomasine, Clovelly 1640 W
William, Hartland 11 Mar 1834 W; 2nd grant 7 Aug 1849
Prouse William, Buckland Brewer 1841 W
Prowt, Prowte see Prout
Prudham see Pridham
Prust, Proust, Pruishe, Pruist, Pruiste, Pruste, Pryshe
Pruist ..., Woolfardisworthy 1604 [W]
Pruishe ..., Abbotsham 1606 [W]
Pruiste ..., Woolfardisworthy 1611 [W]
..., Alverdiscott 1690 A
Ann, Welcombe 1628 [W]
Azariah, Hartland 1661 W and 1669 O
Pruist Charles, Hartland 1592 [W]
Charles, Hartland 1668 A
Christopher, Bideford, snr. 1713 A
Edmund, Clovelly 1721 W
Pruste Elias, Welcombe 1619 [W]
Elizabeth, Bideford 1662 W
Elizabeth, Hartland 1781 W
George, Great Torrington 1686 W
George, Alverdiscott 1689 A
Grace, Hartland 1727 A
Henry, Clovelly 1662 W
Honor, Hartland 1679 W
Pruste Hugh, Hartland 1595 [W] and 1598 [W]
Hugh, Barnstaple 1720 A
Hugh, Hartland 1812 A to John and Thomas, Elizabeth
   Saunders and Grace Cholwell, children
James, Hartland 1630 [W]
Jane, Hartland 1643 A
Jeremiah, Great Torrington 1728 A
Joan, Hartland 1620 [W]
Joan, Bideford 1722 W
John, Elmscott, Hartland 1568 W
John, Hartland 1573 W
Pruist John, Hartland 1607 [W] "of Etson" in register;
   forename blank in Ms; supplied from parish register
Pruste John, Welcombe, snr. 1619 [W]
John, Pilton 1623 [W]
John, Hartland 1627 [W]
John, Hartland 1664 W and 1673 A
John, Hartland 1699 A
John, Clovelly 1724 W
Joseph, Hartland 1713 A
Joseph, Hartland 1714 W
Joseph, Bideford 1714 A and 1719 A
Joseph, Hartland 1736 A
Judith, Hartland 1676 W
Juliana, Monkleigh 1689 A
Lawrence, Welcombe 1630 [W]
Margaret, Hartland 1605 W
Margaret, Bideford 1622 [W]
Mary, Bideford 1642 A
Melchior, Northam 1687 A
Melchior, Northam 1707 A
Nicholas, Welcombe 1565 W
Nicholas, Welcombe 1636 W
Nicholas, Hartland 1684 W
Nicholas, Hartland 1714 W
Nicholas, ship *Bedford* 1749 W
Nicholas, Clovelly 1752 W
Paul, Clovelly 1749 A
Pruist Peter, Hartland 1604 W
Peter, Northam 1661 A
Peter, Hartland 1686 A
Peter, Bideford 1694 W
Philip, Welcombe 1631 [W], 1632 [W] and 1635 W
Philip, Hartland 1644 W
Philip, Hartland 1723 A
Phillippa, Clovelly 1663 W
Rebecca, Hartland 1681 A
Proust Richard, Elmscott, Hartland 1581 W
Richard, Welcombe 1631 [W]
Richard, Clovelly 1764 A

Robert, Instow 1638 W
Robert, Hartland 1679 A
Samson, Hartland 1595 [W]
Samson, Hartland 1669 W
Samuel, Welcombe 1670 A
Samuel, Bideford 1708 A
Sarah, Northam 1720 W
Pryshe Thomas, Hartland 1606 W
Thomas, Hartland 1669 W and 1674 W
Thomas, Woolfardisworthy 1682 W
Thomas, Parkham 1705 [W]
Thomas, Northam 1707 W
Thomas, Hartland 1778 W
Pruiste Tristram, Welcombe 1618 [W]
William, Hartland 1717 W
William, Hartland 1790 W
William, Hartland 1817 W
William, Hartland 1833 W
Pruist Willmot, Hartland 1616 [W]
Willmot, Hartland 1675 W
Prutherck David, Welcombe 1702 A
Prydham see Pridham
Pryshe see Prust
Puddicombe, Pudecombe
John, Burrington 1722 W
John, High Bickington 1766 W
John, Beaford 1821 W
John, Westleigh 1850 W
Pudecombe Robert, Burrington 1814 W
Robert, Merton 1836 W
William, Burrington 1729 W
William, Merton, yeoman 1810 W
William, Fremington 1834 W
Pudner Elias, Barnstaple 1703 A
George, East Putford 1715 W
John, Great Torrington 1592 [W] and 1602 W
John, Great Torrington 1678 A
Nicholas, Little Torrington 1637 [W]
Simon, Little Torrington 1677 A
Thomas, Bideford 1581 A
Thomas, Bideford 1590 [W]
William, Barnstaple 1716 W
Pugsley, Pougsley, Pugesley, Puggeslegh, Puggesleghe,
Puggesleighe, Puggsley, Puggsly, Pugsleigh, Pugsly
Pugsleigh ..., Loxhore 1597 [W], 1610 [W] and 1611 [W]
..., Countisbury 1690 W
Pugsleigh Alice, Georgeham 1606 W
Pugsleigh Ambrose, Loxhore 1624 [W]
Ambrose, Loxhore 1643 W
Ambrose, Kentisbury 1669 A
Ambrose, Tawstock 1677 A
Puggsley Ann, Yarnscombe 1662 W
Anthony, Loxhore 1688 W
Anthony, Loxhore 1730 W
Pugsly Anthony, Loxhore 1781 A
Anthony, Loxhore 1830 W
Charity, Loxhore 1704 W
Charity, Loxhore 1727 W
Pugsleigh Christian, Georgeham 1626 [W]
David, Arlington 1592 [W]
Dorothy, Ilfracombe 1801 W*
Edward, Fremington 1643 A
Edward, Loxhore 1743 W
Elizabeth, Loxhore 1592 [W]
Elizabeth, Stoke Rivers 1592 [W]
Pugsleigh Elizabeth, Loxhore 1618 [W]
Elizabeth, Tawstock 1801 W
Pugsleigh Emma, Langtree 1621 [W]
George, Fremington 1780 W
George, Marwood 1806 W*
George, Bideford 1831 W
Puggsley Helen, Loxhore 1682 W
Henry, Berrynarbor 1673 W
Pugsleigh Humphrey, Barnstaple 1626 [W]
Humphrey, West Buckland 1768 W

Humphrey, West Buckland 1800 W
Puggesleghe James, Georgeham 1573 A
James, Georgeham 1596 [W]
James, Loxhore 1831 W
Jane, Charles 1787 A
Joan, Stoke Rivers 1592 [W]
Joan, Fremington 1596 [W]
Pugsleigh Joan, Georgeham 1617 [W]
Puggsley Joan, Georgeham 1667 A
Joan, Berrynarbor 1676 W
Joan, High Bray 1716 W
Joan, High Bray 1724 A
Joan, Marwood 1739 A
Joan, Loxhore 1752 W
Joan, South Molton 1758 W
Joan, Bratton Fleming 1760 W
Joan, High Bray 1776 W
Puggeslegh John, Loxhore 1571 W
Pugsleigh John, Fremington 1581 A
Pugsleigh John, Barnstaple 1608 [W]; forename blank in Ms;
supplied from parish register
Pugsleigh John, Loxhore 1618 [W]
Pugsleigh John, High Bray 1625 [W]
Pugsleigh John, Instow 1631 [W]
Puggsley John, Filleigh 1668 W
Pougsley John, Barnstaple 1690 W
Puggsly John, Bratton Fleming 1701 W
Pugesley John, ship *Anston* 1756 W
Jonah, Loxhore 1671 A
Leonard, Loxhore 1644 W
Pugsley alias Knill Mary, Barnstaple 1697 A
Puggesleighe Mathew, Loxhore 1571 W
Pugsleigh Nicholas, Barnstaple 1632 [W] and 1635 O
Nicholas, West Buckland 1733 W
Pugsleigh Peter, Kentisbury 1622 [W]
Puggsley Peter, Loxhore 1685 W
Richard, Barnstaple 1578 A
Pugsleigh Richard, Challacombe 1605 W
Pugsleigh Richard, Shirwell 1608 [W]; forename blank in Ms;
supplied from parish register
Pugsleigh Richard, Georgeham 1616 [W]
Pugsleigh Richard, Pilton 1626 [W]
Richard, Weare Giffard 1662 W
Richard, West Buckland 1686 A
Richard, Alverdiscott 1740 [W]
Pugsleigh Robert, Shirwell 1629 [W]
Robert, George Nympton 1705 [W]
Robert, Satterleigh 1763 W
Robert, Combe Martin 1770 A
Thomas, Barnstaple 1664 W
Thomas, Bideford 1670 W
Thomas, heretofore of Barnstaple, but late of Newton Tracey
1834 W
Thomas, Newton Tracey 1846 A
Pugsley William, Great Torrington 1592 [W]
Pugsleigh William, Loxhore 1606 W
Pugsleigh William, Barnstaple 1636 A and 1640 O
Pugsleigh William, Shirwell 1636 A
William, Bulkworthy 1688 A
Puggsley William, Barnstaple 1698 W
William, East Down 1708 W
William, East Down 1784 A
William, Fremington, yeoman 1805 W
William, Barnstaple 1827 W
William, Martinhoe 1852 W
William, Ilfracombe 1853 W
Pulham
Pulham alias Vicary ..., North Molton 1676 W
Alice, North Molton 1635 A
Christian, North Molton 1633 W
Henry, Knowstone 1594 [W]
Lawrence, Knowstone 1592 [W]
Mary, North Molton 1727 W
Nicholas, Knowstone 1593 [W]

Nicholas, North Molton 1615 [W] "Vicarye alias Pulham" in
    register; forename blank in Ms; supplied from parish register
Pulham alias Vicary William, North Molton 1676 W
Pulkinghorne see Polkinghorne
Pullan alias Vicary Agnes, North Molton 1679 A
Pulley, Pully
    ..., Arlington 1608 [W]
    Pully Christopher, High Bickington 1630 [W]
    Henry, Bideford 1839 W
    Lodovic, High Bickington 1672 [W]
    Sarah, Northam, widow 1846 A to John Colwill of Hartland,
      yeoman, brother
    Pully Thomas, High Bickington 1689 A
Pulsford, Pulsor
    Agnes, Fremington 1663 W
    Christopher, Great Torrington 1767 A
    David, East Anstey 1625 [W]
    George, ship *Amazon* 1747 A
    Humphrey, East Anstey 1663 W
    John, Barnstaple 1661 W
    John, East Anstey 1663 W
    John, East Anstey, yeoman 1805 W
    Pulsor Margaret, East Anstey 1608 [W] "Pulsford" in register;
      forename blank in Ms; supplied from parish register
    Robert, East Anstey 1623 [W]
    Thomas, Great Torrington 1768 W
    Thomas, North Molton 1813 W
    Thomasine, Barnstaple 1673 A
    William, North Molton 1712 W
Pulsworthy, Pulsworthie
    Pulsworthie John, East Anstey, jnr. 1566 W
    John, Twitchen 1637 A
Punchard, Pounchard, Puncharde
    Pounchard ... 1605 [W]
    ..., Martinhoe 1611 [W]
    Punchard alias Tucker ..., Mortehoe 1661 A
    Adrian, Berrynarbor 1644 W
    Agnes, Tawstock 1631 [W]
    Alice, Pilton 1780 W
    Anthony, Tawstock 1620 [W]
    Collett, Fremington 1565 W
    Fanny, Northam 1852 A
    Francis, Pilton, carpenter 1797 W
    George, Barnstaple 1603 [W]; forename blank in Ms; supplied
      from parish register
    George, Instow 1686 W
    George, Fremington 1607 [W]; forename blank in Ms;
      supplied from parish register
    Humphrey, Tawstock 1591 [W]
    Humphrey, Atherington 1834 W
    Puncharde John, Fremington 1567 W
    Puncharde John, Martinhoe 1572 W
    John, Pilton 1585 A
    Pounchard John, Tawstock 1586 W
    Pounchard Margaret, Tawstock 1584 W
    Margaret, Bideford 1590 [W]
    Pounchard Mary, Tawstock 1584 W
    Oliver, Wembworthy 1602 W
    Peter, Ilfracombe 1601 A; forename blank in Ms; supplied
      from parish register
    Pounchard Philip, Bideford 1589 W
    Richard, High Bray 1675 W
    Richard, Bratton Fleming 1762 A
    Richard, Pilton 1768 W
    Richard, Atherington, yeoman 1806 W
    Punchard alias Collander Sarah, Pilton 1670 A
    Stephen, Tawstock 1570 W
    Walter, Huntshaw 1635 W
    William, Tawstock 1627 [W]
Punchardon Richard, Barnstaple 1726 W
Puncke James, Little Torrington 1717 A
Punyar David, Berrynarbor 1599 [W]
Purchase Catherine, North Molton 1837 W
    Charles Davey, North Molton, gentleman 1851 A to Mary
      wife of George Shapland

Daniel, North Molton 1833 W
John, North Molton 1749 W
Nicholas, South Molton 1691 A
Nicholas, North Molton 1735 W
Nicholas, North Molton 1768 W
Nicholas, North Molton 1840 W
Thomas, Barnstaple 1804 A
Pycard see Pickard
Pyck, Pycke see Pick
Pyckerd see Pickard
Pydaley see Pidsley
Pyell see Pile
Pyeman or Pitman Richard, Romansleigh 1581 W
Pyke, Pykes see Pike
Pyle, Pyll, Pylle see Pile
Pylman, Pylmon see Pilman
Pylven see Pillavin
Pym see Pim
Pynchs Thomas, Ilfracombe 1597 [W]
Pynckham, Pynckomb, Pyncomb, Pyncombe see Pincombe
Pyne see Pine
Pynse see Pince
Pyper see Piper
Pyrine see Perrin
Pytford see Pitford
Pytman see Pitman
Pytton see Pitton
Pytts see Pitts
Pytwode, Pytwood see Pittwood

Quance Bartholomew, Abbotsham 1641 W
    Gabriel, Northam 1633 A and 1635 O
    Grace, Northam 1681 W
    Joan, Westleigh 1678 W
    Joan see also William Ashplant
    John, Northam 1636 [W]
    John, Northam 1680 W
    John, Hartland 1707 W
    John, Merton 1781 W
    John, Shebbear, gentleman 1809 W
    John, Merton 1829 W
    John, Merton, yeoman 1853 A to Ann wife of William
      Rowtcliffe, yeoman, mother
    Margaret, Northam 1680 A
    Mary, Northam 1732 W
    Patience, Northam 1688 A
    Peter, Clovelly 1626 [W]
    Richard, Northam 1695 A
    Richard, Merton, yeoman 1805 W
    Richard, Little Torrington 1847 W
    Samuel, Northam 1682 W
    Susan, Northam 1680 A
    Thomas, Northam 1664 A
    Thomas, Parkham 1664 A
    Walter, Northam 1618 [W]
    William, Clovelly 1617 [W]
    William, Merton 1799 W*
    William, Bideford 1836 A to Elizabeth, widow
    William, Shirwell 1840 W
Quantick, Quanticke, Quantock, Quantocke
    ..., Chittlehampton 1608 [W]
    Quantick alias Tibs Clase, Chittlehampton 1693 W
    Quantick Elizabeth, Chulmleigh 1743 A
    Quantock Henry, Warkleigh 1738 A
    Quanticke John, Chittlehampton 1600 W
    Quanticke John, Chittlehampton 1600 W
    Quantocke John, West Buckland 1633 W
    Quanticke John, Winkleigh 1634 W
    Quanticke John, Chittlehampton 1637 [W]
    Quantocke Nicholas, Winkleigh 1586 W
    Quanticke Robert, West Buckland 1601 W
    Robert, South Molton 1615 [W]
    Quantock Roger, King's Nympton 1589 W
    Roger, King's Nympton 1603 W
    Samuel, South Molton 1769 W

Sarah, South Molton 1838 W
Thomas, Chittlehampton 1601 W
Thomas, Chulmleigh 1749 A
Quanticke Walter, Chittlehampton 1622 [W]
Quartly, Quartley
Quartley Henry, Molland 1725 A
James, Molland, yeoman 1802 W
John, Molland 1832 W
Mary, Molland 1764 W
William, Molland 1763 W
Quellem Charles, Tawstock 1725 W
Quent see Quint
Quesnyme William, St Giles in the Wood, curate of High
    Bickington 1577 W
Quick, Quicke, Quycke
    ..., Stoodleigh or Oakford 1609 O
    ..., High Bickington 1613 [W]
    Quicke Agnes, Mariansleigh, widow 1563 W
    Quycke Agnes, Barnstaple 1632 [W]
    Alexander, Berrynarbor, husbandman 1804 W
    Quycke Alice, Oakford 1583 W
    Quycke Alice, Barnstaple 1631 [W]
    Quycke Anthony, Barnstaple 1620 [W]
    Quycke Catherine, Barnstaple 1624 [W]
    Quicke Cicely, Stoodleigh 1572 W
    Quycke Ebbot, High Bickington 1581 W
    Eleanor, Chawleigh 1695 W
    Quycke Elizabeth, High Bickington 1624 [W]
    Elizabeth, Huntshaw 1777 A
    Quycke Emblem, High Bickington 1636 A
    Quicke Emott, Knowstone 1592 [W]
    George, Barnstaple 1836 W
    Henry, Witheridge 1688 W
    Quicke Hugh, Chawleigh 1564 W
    Quycke Hugh, Cruwys Morchard 1586 W
    Humphrey, East Buckland 1814 W
    James, Huntshaw 1786 W
    Jane, Northam 1673 [W]
    Joan, Merton 1839 W
    Quicke John, Oakford 1567 W
    Quycke John, High Bickington 1575 W
    Quicke John, Tawstock 1591 [W]
    Quycke John, High Bray 1594 [W]
    Quycke John, Knowstone 1627 [W]
    Quicke John, Wembworthy 1642 W
    John, Barnstaple 1645 W
    John, Chulmleigh 1664 W
    John, Peters Marland 1678 A
    John, Dolton 1768 A
    John, Merton 1827 W
    Joseph, St Giles in the Wood, yeoman 1802 W
    Joseph, High Bickington 1841 A
    Margaret, High Bickington 1645 W
    Quycke Margery, High Bickington 1619 [W]
    Mary, Barnstaple 1840 W and 1841 W
    Michael, Oakford 1597 [W]
    Michael, Fremington 1601 W
    Quicke Peter, Barnstaple 1610 [W]; forename blank in Ms;
        supplied from parish register
    Peter, Barnstaple 1616 [W]
    Philip, Barnstaple 1830 W
    Quicke Richard, Cruwys Morchard 1568 W
    Quicke Richard, North Tawton 1585 W
    Richard, Oakford 1608 [W]; forename blank in Ms; supplied
        from parish register
    Robert, Peters Marland 1827 W
    Samuel, Cheldon 1670 A and 1673 O
    Samuel, Lapford 1701 W
    Quick alias Cobner Susan, Northam 1673 [W]
    Quicke alias Cobner Susan, Northam 1673 A
    Quicke Thomas, Ashreigney 1592 [W]
    Thomas, Northam 1674 [W]
    Thomas, West Down 1684 W
    William, High Bickington 1644 [W]
    William, Cruwys Morchard 1772 A

William, Pilton 1850 [W]
Quint, Quent, Quinte
    Edward, East Putford 1592 [W]
    Quinte Thomas, East Putford 1603 W
    Quent William, East Putford 1625 [W]
Quodford Thomasine, Roborough 1591 [W]
Quycke see Quick
Quyson Giles, Ashford 1577 W

Rabgent, Rabient
    ..., Chawleigh 1613 [W]
    Rabient Theobald, Chawleigh 1638 W
Rachards see Richards
Rackely, Bouchier or Buchard George, North Molton 1674 W
Rackett Grace, Rose Ash 1663 A
Radd, Radde
    Radde ..., Fremington 1606 [W]
    Radde ..., Roborough 1613 [W]
    John, Langtree, jnr. 1569 W
    Radde William, Abbotsham 1590 [W]
        see also Rodd
Raddon John, Winkleigh 1603 W
    Leonard, North Tawton 1762 W
    William, Bow 1597 [W]
    William, Bow 1597 [W]
Radelegh see Radley
Radford, Radforde
    ..., Burrington 1614 [W]
    ..., Chulmleigh 1614 [W]
    ..., South Molton 1614 [W]
    Ambrose, Ashreigney 1595 [W]
    Ann, Burrington 1633 W
    Ann, Thelbridge 1661 W
    Ann, North Molton 1838 W
    Christiana, Oakford 1722 W
    Christopher, Oakford 1575 W
    Dorothy, Oakford 1635 W
    Edward, Romansleigh 1751 W
    Elias, Burrington 1690 A
    Elizabeth, Molland 1630 [W]
    Elizabeth, Chawleigh 1636 W
    Elizabeth, Witheridge 1757 W
    Frances, Witheridge 1685 W
    Radforde George, Chawleigh 1627 [W]
    George, Chulmleigh 1684 W
    George, West Worlington 1698 W
    George, Chawleigh 1786 A
    George, Oakford, labourer 1819 A to William, brother
    Grace, Ashreigney 1667 W
    Harriet Prestwood, South Molton 1835 W
    Hugh, Burrington 1677 A
    Humphrey, Witheridge 1586 W
    Humphrey, Stoodleigh 1615 [W] and 1620 W
    Jane, Witheridge 1621 [W]
    Jane, Oakford 1672 W
    Jane, Eggesford 1682 W
    Jane, East Anstey 1698 W
    Joan, Oakford 1597 [W] and 1697 A
    John, Witheridge 1576 [W]
    John, Oakford 1598 [W]
    John, Ashreigney 1606 W
    John, Oakford 1665 A
    John, Witheridge 1681 W
    John, Oakford 1684 W
    John, Burrington 1685 A
    John, Burrington 1720 W and 1723 W
    John, South Molton 1727 W
    John, East Worlington 1739 W
    John, Oakford 1739 [W]
    John, East Worlington 1756 W
    John, Oakford 1767 A
    John, Oakford 1790 W
    John, Thelbridge 1809 W
    Lewis, Witheridge 1587 W

Lodovic, Thelbridge 1661 W
Radforde alias Reede Margaret, Chawleigh 1615 [W]
Margery, Burrington 1708 W
Mary, Oakford 1779 W
Mary wife of Benjamin see Mary Hatche
Polinora, Chulmleigh 1695 [W]
Prestwood Love, Lapford 1835 A to Charles, brother, gone to
    America
Richard, Coldridge 1617 [W]
Richard, Eggesford 1666 W
Richard, Oakford 1677 W
Richard, Oakford 1720 W
Richard, Chawleigh 1780 W
Richard, Oakford, yeoman 1808 W and 1811 W
Scipio, South Molton 1643 W
Stephen, Oakford 1730 A
Susan, Chawleigh 1812 W
Thomas, Chawleigh, gentleman 1613 [W]; forename blank in
    Ms; supplied from parish register
Thomas, East Anstey 1667 W
Thomas, East Worlington 1668 W
Thomas, East Worlington 1671 W
Thomas, Chawleigh 1703 A
Thomas, Ashreigney 1706 W
Thomas, Stoodleigh 1732 W
Thomas, East Worlington 1740 W
William, Burrington 1580 W
William, Oakford 1639 [A]
William, Oakford 1685 W
William, Stoodleigh 1714 W
William, Oakford 1725 W
William, Cruwys Morchard 1744 W
William, North Molton, surgeon 1807 W
William, Chittlehampton 1822 W
William, Ilfracombe, mariner 1823 A to Mary, widow
William, Lapford 1835 A to Charles of Paignton, brother,
    gone to America
William, Lapford 1835 A to Charles of Paignton, father
Radley, Radelegh, Radlie
    ..., North Molton 1603 [W]
    Agnes, North Molton 1663 W
    Radelegh Elizabeth, North Molton 1587 W
    Elizabeth, High Bray 1820 W
    Radlie George, North Molton 1677 A
    George, High Bray 1774 W
    George, Goodleigh, yeoman 1799 W
    George, High Bray 1831 W
    George White, South Molton, yeoman 1846 A to Mary,
        mother
    James, South Molton 1854 W
    John, North Molton 1715 W
    Margaret, High Bray 1781 A
    Mary, High Bray 1856 W
    Richard, North Molton, snr. 1628 [W]
    Richard, South Molton 1663 W
    Richard, North Molton 1820 W
    Samuel, Tawstock 1833 W
    Sarah, Fremington 1793 A
Radmore , Radmoore
    Calvin, Chittlehampton 1719 W
    Calvin, Atherington 1721 A
    Calvin, Roborough 1797 A
    Calvin, Chittlehampton 1807 W*
    Charity, Brushford 1683 W
    Jane, Brushford 1689 W
    John, Brushford 1623 [W]
    John, Brushford 1627 [W]
    Nathaniel, Winkleigh 1749 A
    Richard, Clovelly 1565 W
    Richard, Brushford 1697 A
    Radmoore Richard, Brushford 1706 A
    Robert, Atherington, yeoman 1799 W
    William, Brushford 1571 W
Raimont see Raymont
Rainer John, Barnstaple 1621 [W]

Rainold, Rainolde, Rainolds see Reynolds
Rainsie see Ramsey
Raishley, Raishly see Rashley
Ramsey, Rainsie
    Rainsie John, Little Torrington 1621 [W]
    John, Barnstaple, carrier 1810 A
    Mary, Ilfracombe 1798 W
Ramster John, Barnstaple 1744 A
Ramstred Henry, Stoodleigh 1575 W
Randall, Randel, Randell, Randle
    Randle ..., Ilfracombe 1603 [W]
    Randle ..., North Tawton 1611 [W]
    Randle ..., Warkleigh 1611 [W]
    Randle Abraham, Peters Marland 1624 [W]
    Randle Agnes, Barnstaple 1704 W
    Randle Ann, Chittlehampton 1706 A
    Randle Anthony, Kentisbury, esquire 1616 [W] and 1618 O
    Randle Anthony, Bideford 1663 A
    Randle Bartholomew, Kentisbury 1667 W
    Randle Benjamin, Clovelly 1753 A
    Randell Catherine, Hartland 1563 W
    Charles, Clovelly 1697 A
    Randle Christiana, Warkleigh 1662 W
    Randle David, Mortehoe 1633 A
    David, Northam 1745 W
    Randell Elizabeth, Warkleigh, widow 1567 W
    Randell Elizabeth, Hartland 1596 [W]
    Elizabeth, Great Torrington 1712 A
    Elizabeth, Great Torrington 1715 W
    Randle Francis, Clovelly 1705 W
    George, Chittlehampton 1699 A
    George, Barnstaple 1702 W
    Giles, Barnstaple 1703 W
    Giles, Barnstaple 1728 W
    Grace, Combe Martin 1692 A
    Hugh, Barnstaple 1733 W
    Randle Humphrey, Kentisbury 1668 W
    James, Hartland 1703 W
    James, Monkleigh 1733 W
    Randle Joan, Tawstock, widow 1605 [W]; forename blank in
        Ms; supplied from parish register
    Randel Joan, Hartland 1802 W
    Randell John, Warkleigh 1565 W
    Randell John, Clovelly 1593 [W]
    Randle John, Frithelstock 1621 [W]
    John, Chulmleigh 1664 A
    John, Hartland 1692 A
    Randle John, Clovelly 1745 W
    Randle John, Brendon 1754 W
    John, Barnstaple 1831 A to Ann of Highgate, widow
    Judith, Clovelly 1709 W
    Randle Lucy, Warkleigh 1625 [W]
    Randle Margaret, Kentisbury 1637 A
    Randle Margaret, St Giles in the Wood 1643 [W]
    Mary, St Giles in the Wood 1693 W
    Mary, Warkleigh 1693 A
    Robert, Buckland Brewer 1571 W
    Randle Robert, Warkleigh 1638 W
    Randle Robert, Clovelly 1754 W
    Theophilus, St Giles in the Wood 1685 W
    Randle Thomas, Frithelstock 1626 [W]
    Thomas, Bideford 1702 W
    Thomas, Barnstaple 1709 W
    Thomas, ship *Captain* 1756 A
    Randle William, North Tawton 1603 W
    William, Great Torrington 1690 A
    William, Great Torrington 1717 W
    William, Great Torrington 1723 W
    William, Hartland 1798 A
    William, Hartland 1801 W
Rapson Joseph, Oakford 1816 W
Rashley, Raishley, Raishly, Rashly, Rayshley
    Raishley ..., King's Nympton 1611 [W]
    Alice, Georgeham 1667 A
    Christopher, Georgeham 1662 A
    Francis, Georgeham 1688 A

Rayshley James, Georgeham 1620 [W]
Rashly Jane, Georgeham 1695 W
Raishley Joan, King's Nympton 1615 O
Joan, Georgeham 1674 W
John, Georgeham 1716 W
Peter, Ilfracombe 1688 W
Peter, Georgeham 1729 W
Raishley Richard, Georgeham 1607 [W]; forename blank in
Ms; supplied from parish register
Samuel, Georgeham 1733 A
Rashly Thomas, North Molton 1592 [W]
Raishly Thomas, King's Nympton 1597 [W]
Walter, Ilfracombe 1704 W
Ratcliffe, Ratche, Ratclie, Ratclif, Roclife, Roclyff
James, Tawstock 1761 A
Roclife alias Bucher Joan, King's Nympton 1582 W
Ratcliffe alias Butcher Joan, King's Nympton 1674 A
Ratclie or Roclyff alias Boocher John, King's Nympton 1572
W
Roclyff or Ratclie or Ratche alias Boocher John, King's
Nympton 1572 W
Roclyff John, Barnstaple 1585 W
Ratclif John, King's Nympton 1615 [W]
John, Bow 1670 A
Richard, Tawstock, yeoman 1806 W
Walter, Chittlehampton 1619 [W]
William, Barnstaple 1622 [W] and 1624 O
Rattenbury, Rattenberry, Rattenburie, Rottenberye, Rottenbury,
Rottenburye, Rottonburie
..., Shirwell 1613 O
Rottenbury Agnes, Winkleigh 1748 A
Ann, Winkleigh 1830 A
Anthony, Winkleigh 1852 W
Rattenberry Elizabeth, Sheepwash 1685 A
Francis, Shirwell 1623 [W]
Rattenberry Francis, Tawstock 1690 A
Rattenberry George, Huish 1667 W
George, Goodleigh 1719 W
Rottenberry George, Fremington 1856 W
Rattenberry George Hern, Fremington 1851 W
Grace, High Bickington 1733 W
Grace, Winkleigh 1812 W
Hannibal, Ashreigney 1641 A
Rottenbury Henry, Fremington 1789 W
Hugh, Iddesleigh 1597 [W]
Rattenberry Hugh, Winkleigh 1681 A
Rattenberry Hugh, Winkleigh 1714 W
Hugh, Ashreigney 1722 W
Hugh, Winkleigh 1722 W
Hugh, Winkleigh 1757 W
Hugh, Winkleigh, yeoman 1808 A
Hugh, Atherington 1841 W
Humphrey, Ashreigney 1669 A and 1671 A
Humphrey, High Bickington 1729 W
James, Ashreigney 1706 A
James, Wembworthy 1815 W
James, Pilton 1854 W
Jenophia, Shirwell 1621 [W] and 1628 O
Joan, Monkleigh 1636 W
Joan, Shirwell 1678 W
Rottonburie John, Iddesleigh, jnr. 1576 W
Rattenburie John, Woolfardisworthy 1587 W
John, Iddesleigh 1594 [W]
John, Dowland 1632 [W]
John, Iddesleigh 1636 W
Rattenberry John, Winkleigh 1684 A
John, East Down 1739 W
John, Winkleigh 1740 W
Rottenbury John, Martinhoe 1777 A
Rottenbury John, Parracombe 1783 A
John, Winkleigh 1814 W
John, Merton 1822 W
John, Winkleigh 1826 A to Eleanor, widow
John, Ashreigney 1827 A to Sarah, widow
John, Washford Pyne 1842 W
Margaret, Shirwell 1622 [W], 1623 [W] and 1628 O

Marian, Huish 1637 W
Martha, Ashreigney 1726 W
Mary, Washford Pyne 1854 W
Michael, Monkleigh 1635 W
Rottenberye Richard, Iddesleigh 1569 W
Richard, Winkleigh 1599 [W]
Richard, Winkleigh 1821 A to Mary wife of John Stoneman of
North Tawton, sister and Anthony, brother
Samuel, Instow 1694 W
Simon, Sheepwash 1581 W
Simon, Shirwell 1618 [W]
Walter, Dowland 1598 [W]
Rottenburye William, Dolton 1570 W
William, Huish 1601 W
Rottenbury William, North Tawton 1747 A
Willmot, Ashreigney 1702 W
Ravening Henry, Barnstaple 1662 A
Henry, Barnstaple 1689 W
Rawe, Raw
Catherine, Lapford 1602 W
Raw Hugh, Great Torrington 1660 A
John, Northam 1584 W
Rawle, Rawll
Agnes, Brendon 1771 A
Alexander, Pilton 1623 [W]
Arthur, Arlington 1636 W
Catherine, High Bickington, widow 1644 W
David, Lynton 1580 W
David, Fremington 1595 [W]
David, Lynton 1749 W
Edward, Tawstock 1730 W
Edward, Tawstock 1765 W
Elizabeth, Pilton 1666 W
Elizabeth, Marwood 1727 A
Grace, Tawstock 1772 W
Rawles Gregory, Pilton 1642 W
Helen, Mortehoe 1634 W
Helen, Kentisbury 1668 W
Henry, Brendon 1687 A
Henry, Brendon 1758 W
Humphrey, Countisbury 1671 A
Joan, King's Nympton, widow 1635 W
John, Fremington 1605 W
John, Brendon 1626 [W]
Rawles John, Pilton 1666 W
John, Brendon 1670 W
John, Countisbury 1672 W
John, Countisbury 1673 A
John, Brendon 1715 W
John, Bratton Fleming 1721 W
John, Brendon 1769 A
John, Bideford 1829 W
Lawrence, Kentisbury 1661 W
Margaret, Bideford 1839 W
Nicholas, Parracombe 1627 [W]
Rawles Richard, Barnstaple 1670 W
Roger, Brendon 1595 [W]
Roger, Brendon 1671 W
Susan, Bratton Fleming 1754 W
Rawle alias Muxery Sybil, Brendon 1683 A
Rawll Thomas, Lynton 1586 W
Thomas, King's Nympton 1630 [W]
Thomas, ship *Alade* 1759 A
Urithe, South Molton 1642 A
William, Brendon 1617 [W]
William, Coldridge 1677 A
William, Chittlehampton 1697 A
William, Bideford 1763 W
William, Bideford, weigher 1807 W
William, Arlington 1821 A to Eleanor Carden of East Down,
sister
William, Bideford 1828 W
Rawleigh, Rawley, Rawly
..., Buckland Filleigh 1613 [W]
..., Buckland Filleigh 1708 A

Rawly Christopher, Great Torrington 1710 A
  Christopher, Buckland Filleigh 1716 A
Rawley John, Iddesleigh 1634 W
  John, Buckland Filleigh 1663 W
  Margery, Buckland Filleigh 1663 W
  Mary, Great Torrington 1715 W
  Robert, Buckland Filleigh 1685 W
  Samuel, Great Torrington 1684 W
  William, Peters Marland 1721 W
Rawling John, Welcombe 1720 W
Rawll see Rawle
Ray John, North Tawton 1852 W
Raymont, Raimont, Rayment, Raymett, Raymon, Reamon,
    Reamond, Reamont, Reymant, Reymond, Reymont
  Reamont ..., Dolton 1611 [W]
  Reymond Alice, East Worlington 1580 W
  Raimont Andrew, Dolton 1606 W
  Augustine, Coldridge 1677 W
  Raymett Augustine, Coldridge 1758 A
  Raimont Henry, Lapford 1608 [W]; forename blank in Ms;
    supplied from parish register
  James, Winkleigh 1840 W
  Reamon Joan, Welcombe, widow 1571 W
  Raimont Joan, Lapford 1605 W
  Raimont Joan, Dolton 1611 O forename blank in Ms; supplied
    from parish register
  Reamond John, Welcombe 1565 W
  Reamont John, Lapford 1589 W
  John, Lapford 1595 [W] and 1597 [W]
  John, Coldridge 1786 W and 1787 W
  Mary, Chawleigh 1822 W
  Reymant Nicholas, Buckland Brewer 1625 [W]
  Reymont Nicholas, Lapford 1637 W
  Raymon Petherick, Abbotsham 1566 W
  Richard, Bondleigh 1824 W
  Richard, Eggesford 1839 W
  Reymont Robert, Lapford 1634 A and 1637 O
  Reamont William, Challacombe 1590 [W]
  Reyment William, Great Torrington 1831 A
  William Lacey, Coldridge 1821 W
Raymor see Reamore
Raynolds, Raynolls see Reynolds
Rayshley see Rashley
Read, Reade see Reed
Reamer see Reamore
Reamon, Reamond, Reamont see Raymont
Reamor, Raymor, Reamer, Reamore, Remer, Remor, Remore,
    Reymor
  Elizabeth, Barnstaple 1696 W
  Reymor Frances, Monkleigh 1667 W
  Francis Richard, Alwington 1618 [W]
  Reamer George, Tawstock 1638 O
  Hugh, Arlington 1669 W
  Joan, Arlington 1681 W
  John 1595 [W]
  Raymor John, Pilton 1671 A
  John, Barnstaple 1694 W
  Remore Richard, Tawstock 1572 W
  Reymor Robert, Great Torrington 1674 W
  Reymor Sarah, Barnstaple 1712 W
  Reamore Thomas, Challacombe 1617 [W]
  Reamer Thomas, Tawstock 1637 A
  Remor Thomas, Littleham (near Bideford) 1685 W
  William, Parracombe 1632 [W]
  Remer William, Bideford 1677 W
  Reymor Willmot, Arlington 1667 W
Reche see Rich
Reckard, Reckerd, Record see Rickard
Redd see Reed
Reddy Cornelius, Northam 1712 W
Rede see Reed
Redford Rodfourde ..., Oakford 1572 W
Redlar, Redler see Ridler
Redmore, Ridmur
  Amelia, Ilfracombe 1846 A

  Ann, East Down 1828 W
  George, Ilfracombe 1829 W
  Ridmur Joan, Bideford 1687 W
  John, Ilfracombe 1774 W
  Nicholas, Berrynarbor 1783 W
  William, Kentisbury 1837 W
Redwood Robert, East Worlington, yeoman 1811 A
Ree Ann, Great Torrington, widow 1811 W
Reed, Read, Reade, Redd, Rede, Reede, Reid
  Reede ..., Ashford 1602 [W]
  Reede ..., Fremington 1604 [W]
  Reede ..., Rose Ash 1604 [W]
  Reede ..., Bideford 1609 [W] and 1613 [W]
  Reede ..., Zeal Monachorum 1613 [W]
  ..., Pilton 1614 [W]
  Reede ..., Mariansleigh 1615 [W]
  Reade alias Blackmore ... 1695 A
  Reede Adam, Ilfracombe 1620 [W]
  Adam, Ilfracombe 1671 W
  Adrian, Combe Martin 1598 [W]
  Reede Agnes, Atherington 1574 A
  Rede Agnes, Atherington 1575 W
  Reede Agnes, Ilfracombe 1612 [W]; forename blank in Ms;
    supplied from parish register
  Reede Agnes, East Down 1691 W
  Agnes, Ilfracombe 1726 W
  Agnes, Lapford 1741 W
  Agnes, Winkleigh 1778 W
  Alice, Ilfracombe 1586 W
  Reed alias Southmore Alice, Coldridge 1586 W
  Alice, Combe Martin, widow 1640 W
  Andrew, Twitchen 1598 [W]
  Read Ann, Challacombe 1642 A
  Ann, Great Torrington 1711 W
  Ann, Bishop's Nympton 1819 A
  Reede Anstis, Marwood 1638 A
  Reede Anthony, Marwood 1628 [W] and 1629 [W]
  Anthony, Lapford 1663 W
  Betsy see Richard Partridge
  Brian, Buckland Brewer 1773 W
  Catherine, Great Torrington 1733 W
  Catherine, Cruwys Morchard 1570 W
  Christian, Lapford 1784 W
  Reede David, Challacombe 1567 W
  Rede David, Warkleigh 1570 W
  David, Loxhore 1587 A
  David, Hartland 1639 A
  Reede David, Hartland 1639 A
  David, Ilfracombe 1713 W
  Reede Dorcas, Ilfracombe 1684 W
  Dorothy, Barnstaple 1780 W
  Dorothy, Great Torrington 1814 W
  Reede Edith, Beaford 1625 [W] and 1630 [W]
  Edward, Mortehoe 1583 W
  Reede Edward, Ilfracombe 1604 [W]; forename blank in Ms;
    supplied from parish register
  Reede Edward, Ilfracombe 1627 [W]
  Edward, Combe Martin 1711 A
  Edward, Barnstaple 1780 W
  Edward, Chawleigh, yeoman 1820 A to Richard, brother
  Edward, Ashreigney 1854 W
  Edward see also Martha Brown
  Eleanor, Barnstaple 1778 A
  Elizabeth, Hartland 1582 W
  Reede Elizabeth, Coldridge 1620 [W]
  Elizabeth, Warkleigh 1645 W
  Reede Elizabeth 1686 W
  Elizabeth, Barnstaple 1731 A
  Elizabeth, Ilfracombe 1819 W
  Elizabeth, Ilfracombe 173.. W year shown incompletely
  Emma, Ilfracombe 1597 [W]
  Reede Emma, Ilfracombe 1686 W
  George, Northam 1591 [W]
  Reade George, Tawstock 1643 W
  George, Chulmleigh 1664 A

George, Charles 1668 W
George, Burrington 1676 A
George, Chawleigh 1716 W
George, Chawleigh 1755 W
George, Ilfracombe 1766 W
George, Chawleigh, yeoman 1796 W
George, Chawleigh 1815 W
Reede Helen, Mariansleigh 1619 [W]
Henry, Hartland 1585 A
Reede Henry, Hartland 1692 A
Henry, Chawleigh 1731 W
Henry, Brushford 1771 W
Henry, Chawleigh 1812 W
Henry, Chawleigh 1823 A (Chudleigh) to Henry, son
Hugh, King's Nympton 1592 [W]
Reede Hugh, Combe Martin 1633 W
Hugh, Hartland 1639 W
Hugh, Barnstaple 1670 A
Reede James, Tawstock 1582 W
Reede James, Ilfracombe 1621 [W]
Reed alias Blackmore James, Barnstaple 1674 A
Reede James, Northam 1690 W
Redd James, Martinhoe 1744 W
James, Marwood 1744 W
James, Ilfracombe 1766 W and 1769 W
Reede Jane, Chawleigh 1688 W
Jane, Meshaw 1723 W
Reede Joan, Roborough, widow 1563 W
Joan, Ilfracombe 1592 [W]
Joan, Combe Martin 1597 [W]
Reade Joan, Tawstock 1601 W
Joan, Ilfracombe 1605 [W]; forename blank in Ms; supplied
    from parish register
Joan, Coldridge 1641 A
Reede John, Eddistone, Hartland 1563 W
Reede John, Alwington 1564 W
Rede John, Hartland 1567 W
Reede John, Brendon 1572 W
Rede John, Zeal Monachorum 1573 W
Rede John, Combe Martin 1575 A
John, Woolfardisworthy 1575 W
Reede John, Ilfracombe 1578 W
Redd John, Kentisbury 1580 W
Reade John, Berrynarbor 1586 W
John, Great Torrington 1592 [W]
John, Barnstaple 1593 [W]
John, South Molton 1593 [W]
John, Combe Martin 1597 [W]
John, Huntshaw 1598 [W]
Reede John, Heanton Punchardon 1620 [W]
Reede John, Marwood 1624 [W]
Reede John, Woolfardisworthy (East or West), snr. 1627 [W]
Reede John, Barnstaple 1627 [W]
Reede John, Hartland 1627 [W]
Redd or Rodd John, Challacombe 1637 W
John, Woolfardisworthy 1667 W
John, Coldridge 1681 W
John, East Down 1683 W
John, North Molton 1693 W
Read John, Ilfracombe 1694 W
John, Ilfracombe 1698 W
John, Rose Ash 1699 W
Reade John, Berrynarbor 1703 A
Reade John, Barnstaple 1707 A
John, Parracombe 1709 A
Redd John, Pilton 1727 A
John, Barnstaple, mariner 1751 A
John, St Giles in the Wood 1770 A
John, Marwood 1786 W
John, Lapford 1802 W
John, Coldridge 1805 W
John, Ilfracombe 1808 A
John, Lapford 1817 W
John, Chawleigh 1839 A to Mary, widow
John, Meeth 1843 A to John of 195 Regent Street, London,
    son

John, Rackenford 1850 W
John, Ilfracombe, yeoman 1852 A to John
John Richards, Trentishoe 1841 A to Thomas, brother
Jonathan, Shirwell 1709 A
Judith, Combe Martin 1708 W
Julian, Ilfracombe 1668 W
Reede Mabel, King's Nympton 1690 W
Rede Margaret, Mariansleigh 1567 W
Reede alias Radforde Margaret, Chawleigh 1615 [W]
Reede Marian, Ashford 1620 [W]
Mark, Barnstaple 1644 W
Reade, Blackmore alias Mark, Barnstaple 1695 A; forename
    blank in Ms; supplied from parish register
Martha, Chawleigh 1797 A*
Reede Mary, South Molton 1636 W
Reede Mary, Instow 1759 W
Mary, Lapford 1768 A
Mary, Barnstaple 1785 A
Mary, Barnstaple 1813 W
Mary, King's Nympton 1854 W
Reede Nathaniel, Goodleigh 1675 A
Nathaniel, Goodleigh 1709 W
Rede Nicholas, Georgeham 1581 W
Nicholas, Zeal Monachorum 1597 [W]
Reede Nicholas, King's Nympton 1604 W
Reede Nicholas, Coldridge 1620 [W]
Reede Paschal, South Molton 1619 [W]
Reede Peter, Twitchen 1624 [W]
Philip, East Buckland 1675 W
Philip, Barnstaple 1757 W
Read Ralph, Alverdiscott 1679 W
Richard, Coldridge 1594 [W]
Richard, Georgeham 1597 [W]
Reede Richard, Great Torrington 1618 [W] and 1619 O
    account made by the executors
Reede Richard, Woolfardisworthy 1621 [W]
Reede Richard, Combe Martin 1624 [W]
Reede Richard, Beaford 1628 [W]
Reede Richard, Hartland 1639 W
Richard, Combe Martin 1673 [W]
Reede Richard, Kentisbury 1687 W
Richard, Wembworthy 1726 W
Richard, Combe Martin 1729 W
Richard, Chawleigh 1751 A
Richard, North Tawton 1761 A
Richard, Coldridge 1781 W
Richard, Chawleigh 1816 W
Richard, Coldridge 1821 W
Richard, Cheldon 1824 A to Sarah, widow
Richard, Chawleigh 1840 W
Richard, Knowstone 1845 W
Rede Robert, King's Nympton 1570 W
Robert, Ilfracombe 1591 [W]
Reede Robert, Warkleigh 1618 [W]
Rede Roger, Pilton 1569 W
Roger, Coldridge 1599 [W]
Roger, Lapford 1731 W
Roger, Lapford 1772 W
Roger, Rose Ash 1777 A
Roger, Rackenford, yeoman 1801 W
Samuel, Ilfracombe 1713 W
Samuel, King's Nympton 1841 W
Sarah, Cheldon, widow 1826 A to Martha Sheet, mother and
    guardian to children
Simon, Hartland 1591 [W]
Simon, Barnstaple 1721 W and 1731 W
Reid Sophia, Pilton 1822 A to Sophia Deborah Reid, daughter
Rede Thomas, Berrynarbor 1580 W
Thomas, Challacombe 1590 [W]
Thomas, King's Nympton 1593 [W]
Reede Thomas, Great Torrington 1615 [W]
Thomas, Bratton Fleming 1663 A
Reade Thomas, Ilfracombe 1669 W
Thomas, Atherington 1676 W
Read Thomas, Ilfracombe 1679 W

Thomas, Welcombe, snr. 1700 W
Thomas, Marwood 1712 W
Read Thomas, Beaford 1716 W
Redd Thomas, Hartland 1725 A
Thomas, Combe Martin 1749 A
Redd Thomas, St Giles in the Wood 1750 W
Thomas, Wembworthy 1772 W
Thomas, Combe Martin 1813 W
Thomas, Ilfracombe 1815 W
Thomas, Wembworthy 1835 W
Thomas, Monkleigh, labourer 1852 A to Mary Copp
William, Chawleigh 1591 [W]
William, Combe Martin 1591 [W]
William, Atherington 1599 [W]
Reede William, Ilfracombe 1606 W
William, Combe Martin 1671 W
William, Northam 1680 W
William, Combe Martin 1681 A
Reede William, Clovelly 1690 W
William, North Molton 1726 W
William, North Molton 1735 W
William, lately belonging to HMS *Weymouth* 1741 A
William, Ilfracombe 1750 W
William, Barnstaple 1780 A
William, Barnstaple 1785 W
William, Ilfracombe 1822 A to Mary, widow
William, Heanton Punchardon 1842 W
William, Buckland Brewer 1843 W
Reeder Elizabeth, Barnstaple 1789 W
Reepe William, Barnstaple 1615 [W]
Reeson John, Littleham (near Bideford) 1829 A to Mary, widow
Reeve, Reeves, Reive, Reve, Reves, Reyve
Reive ..., North Tawton 1603 [W]
Abraham, Coldridge 1672 W
Ann, Bideford 1753 W and A
Reve Edward, Combe Martin 1590 [W]
Reyve Emma, Kentisbury 1622 [W]
Reive George, Alverdiscott 1616 [W]
Honor, North Tawton 1671 W
Reive John, Great Torrington 1590 [W]
Reves John, Northam 1636 A.
John, Bideford 1706 W
John, Bideford 1745 W
Reeves John, Bideford 1808 W
Reeve Lawrence, Bideford 1716 A
Peter, Bondleigh 1670 W
Reyve Thomas, Alverdiscott 1619 O
Reyve Thomas, Kentisbury 1619 [W]
Thomas, North Tawton 1670 A
Reeve William, Bideford 1714 W
William, Bideford 1741 W
Reid see Reed
Reive see Reeve
Relley Humphrey, Northam 1752 W
Remer see Reamore
Remon John, Alwington 1750 W
Remor, Remore see Reamore
Remphry, Remphrey
George, Chittlehampton 1708 A
James, Georgeham 1732 W
Remphrey James, Georgeham 1820 W
Thomas, Pilton 1668 W
Rendell, Rendall, Rendel, Rendle
Elizabeth, Warkleigh 1575 W
Rendle Elizabeth, Chittlehampton 1813 A to James, son
Rendle George, Northam 1682 A
Rendle George, Goodleigh, mason 1815 A to William, father
Rendle James, Chittlehampton 1779 W
Rendle James, Chittlehampton 1825 W
James, Barnstaple 1835 W and 1839 A
Rendle James, East Buckland 1847 W
Rendle James, Hartland 1856 W
Jane, Barnstaple 1852 W
John, Hartland 1577 W
Rendle John, Chittlehampton, yeoman 1806 A
Rendel John, West Buckland, heretofore of Landkey 1825 W

Rendle John, North Tawton 1837 W
Rendle John, Chittlehampton 1852 W
Rendall Lodovic, Chittlehampton 1719 A
Richard, Tawstock 1579 A
Richard, Tawstock 1591 [W]
Rendle Robert, Northam 1627 [W]
Rendle Robert, North Molton 1810 W
Simon, Chittlehampton 1578 W
Rendle Simon, Tawstock 1636 W
Rendle Stephen, Great Torrington 1621 [W]
Rondell Thomas, Frithelstock 1577 A
Rendie see Rendy
Rendle see Rendell
Rendy, Rendie, Rendye
Rendye John, North Molton 1575 W
Rendie John, Shebbear 1614 [W]; forename blank in Ms;
    supplied from parish register
John, Rose Ash 1667 A
Rendye Peter, Shebbear 1579 W
Rendye Roger, Rose Ash 1618 [W]
Roger, Rose Ash 1676 W
Rene see Reene
Renie Joan, St Giles in the Wood 1591 [W]
Joan, Little Torrington 1598 [W]
Joan, Lynton 1599 [W]
John, Bideford 1599 [W]
John, Lynton 1599 [W]
Rennells, Rennels see Reynolds
Rennor Alice, Tawstock 1661 W
Renolds see Reynolds
Rensbere Nicholas, Great Torrington 1587 A and 1588 A
    account
Renton Thomas, Ilfracombe 1776 A
Resdon Grace, Pilton 1806 W
Retallicke Christiana, Buckland Brewer 1726 A
Reve, Reves see Reeve
Revrie Lawrence, Chittlehampton 1687 W
Rew, Rewe
Rewe ..., Combe Martin 1603 [W]
..., Little Torrington 1614 [W]
Rewe Abraham, St Giles in the Wood 1579 W
Rewe Avis, Alverdiscott 1582 W
Rewe Catherine, Langtree 1630 [W]
Christian, Langtree 1639 W
Henry, South Molton 1694 A
Isaac, Langtree 1709 W
Joan, North Molton 1692 A
Joan, Northam 1708 W
Rewe John, Combe Martin 1578 W
John, Northam 1703 W
Rewe Margaret, South Molton 1618 [W]
Rewe Robert, South Molton 1581 W
Rewe Robert, Alverdiscott 1587 W
Robert, South Molton 1674 A
Robert, South Molton 1704 A
Rewe Thomas, Alverdiscott 1617 [W]
Thomas, Abbotsham 1706 W
Rewe Thomasine, Alverdiscott 1623 [W]
Rewe William, Alverdiscott 1575 W
William, High Bickington 1666 W
William, Langtree 1670 A
Reymant, Reymond, Reymont see Raymont
Reynolds, Rainold, Rainolde, Rainolds, Raynolds, Raynolls,
    Rennells, Rennels, Renolds, Reynell, Reynold, Reynoll,
    Reynolls
Rainolds ..., Ilfracombe 1614 [W]
Rainold Agnes, Ilfracombe 1612 [W] "Rendle" in register;
    forename blank in Ms; supplied from parish register
Renolds Ann, Rackenford 1684 W
Barbara, North Tawton 1593 [W]
Raynolds Catherine, Ilfracombe 1621 [W]
Reynoll Honor, Ilfracombe 1675 A
John, Ilfracombe 1666 W
Reynell John, Fremington 1680 A
Reynell John, Instow 1741 W

John, Yarnscombe 1767 A
Reynell Mary, Fremington 1668 W
Reynold Michael, Clovelly 1631 [W]
Rainolde Richard, Ilfracombe 1607 [W] "Reandle" in register;
    forename blank in Ms; supplied from parish register
Reynell Roger, North Tawton 1710 A
Raynolls Thomas, Marwood 1693 A
Thomas, Marwood 1703 A
Thomas, Marwood 1747 A
Reynolls Thomas, Marwood 1817 W
Rennels Thomas, Barnstaple 1824 W
Renolds William, Bideford 1728 A
Rennells William, Ilfracombe 1845 A
Reyve see Reeve
Riccard Russell Marlyn see John Saunders
Rice, Rise, Ryce, Ryse
Ann, Heanton Punchardon 1716 A
Ann, Ilfracombe 1780 A
David, Westleigh near Bideford 1690 A
Dorothy, Fremington 1685 W
Dorothy, Chulmleigh 1741 W
Edward, Barnstaple 1665 W
Eleanor, Instow 1697 W
Elizabeth, Instow 1765 A
Evan, Bideford 1713 A
Francis, West Down 1784 W
George, Barnstaple 1703 W
George, ship *Northumberland* 1761 W
George, ship *Sunderland* 1761 A
George, Barnstaple 1833 W
Henry, Barnstaple 1696 W
James, Instow 1781 A
Ryce Joan, Pilton 1632 [W]
Joan, Buckland Brewer 1720 W
Joan, Bittadon 1755 W
John, Pilton 1621 [W]
John, Coldridge 1624 [W]
John, Fremington 1677 W
John, Fremington 1697 W
John, Ilfracombe 1762 A
John, Weare Giffard 1767 W
Lodovic, West Worlington 1628 [W]
Mabel, Woolfardisworthy 1601 W
Nicholas, Westleigh near Bideford 1718 W
Paul, Pilton 1617 [W]
Philip, Chulmleigh 1804 A
Philip, Hartland 1840 W
Ryse Richard, Pilton 1576 W
Richard, Barnstaple 1627 [W]
Robert, Woolfardisworthy 1590 [W]
Robert, Zeal Monachorum 1690 A
Sarah, Ilfracombe 1782 W
Sarah, Chulmleigh 1825 W
Simon, Barnstaple 1596 [W]
Stephen, Bittadon 1754 W
Susan, Chittlehampton 1807 A
Thomas, Winkleigh 1675 A
Rise Thomas, Coldridge 1688 W
Thomas, Ilfracombe 1772 W
Thomas, Trentishoe 1781 A
William, Ilfracombe 1673 [W]
William, Bideford 1705 A
Rich, Reche, Riche
Elizabeth, Shebbear 1597 [W]
Hugh, Cruwys Morchard 1712 A
Humphrey, Buckland Filleigh 1623 [W] and 1624 O
Reche Joan, Buckland Brewer, widow 1563 W
Riche John, North Molton 1567 W
John, Cruwys Morchard 1681 W
John, Cruwys Morchard 1707 A
Riche Thomas 1630 [W]
Thomas, Barnstaple 1773 A
Richards, Rachards, Richard, Richardes, Richord, Rychards
..., Combe Martin 1607 [W]
Richardes ..., Ilfracombe 1610 [W]

..., Kentisbury 1612 [W]
Agnes, Mariansleigh 1636 W
Richards alias Rook Agnes, Combe Martin 1701 W
Agnes, Beaford 1704 W
Agnes, Ilfracombe 1761 W
Andrew, Lynton, yeoman 1809 W
Ann, Countisbury 1639 W
Richard Ann, Bratton Fleming 1666 W
Richord alias Mayre Ann, Tawstock 1692 A
Ann, Fremington 1722 A
Richard Ann, Buckland Brewer 1782 W
Ann, Brendon 1812 W
Ann, High Bickington 1856 W
Bezaleel, High Bickington 1828 W
Christopher, South Molton 1670 W
David, Ilfracombe 1712 A
David, Countisbury 1734 W
Richard Deborah, Kentisbury 1763 W
Dorothy, Bow 1676 W
Edmund Barrow, Shirwell 1847 W second christian name
    from FreeBMD; only initial in Ms
Edward, Marwood 1711 A
Edward, Pilton 1730 W and 1747 W
Edward, Georgeham 1751 W
Edward, Pilton 1795 A
Edward, Lynton, labourer 1857 A to Elizabeth, widow
Elizabeth, Kentisbury 1754 W
Elizabeth, Brendon 1771 W
Elizabeth, Marwood 1802 W
Elizabeth, Trentishoe 1822 W
Elizabeth, Marwood 1843 W
Francis, Kentisbury 1698 A and 1713 A
George, Tawstock 1628 [W]
George, Tawstock 1712 W
George, High Bickington 1743 W
George, Bideford, yeoman 1803 W
George, Burrington 1848 W
Grace wife of Andrew see Jane Stanbury
Grace Cobley, Kentisbury 1845 A
Helen, South Molton 1620 [W]
Henry, East Down 1679 A
Henry, Bratton Fleming 1681 A
Henry, Yarnscombe 1831 A to Mary, widow
Henry, High Bickington 1855 W
Henry and Mary, Kentisbury 1668 A
Honour, Tawstock, widow 1609 [W]; forename blank in Ms;
    supplied from parish register
James, Rackenford 1597 [W]
James, Barnstaple 1747 W
Richard James, Bideford 1763 W
James, Kentisbury 1767 A
James, Kentisbury 1832 W
James, Brendon 1846 W
James, Barnstaple 1853 W
Jedidiah, High Bickington 1829 W
Joan, Tawstock 1639 W
Joan, South Molton 1680 W
Richardes John, Mariansleigh 1568 W
John, Roborough 1592 [W]
John, Meeth 1595 [W]
John, Northam 1631 [W]
John, Kentisbury 1639 W
John, Barnstaple 1641 [W]
John, Kentisbury 1664 W
John, Barnstaple 1673 [W]
John, Kentisbury 1680 W
John, Tawstock 1702 A
John, South Molton 1706 W
Rachards John, Challacombe 1713 W
John, Kentisbury 1741 W
John, Ilfracombe 1746 A
John, East Down 1747 W
John, Ilfracombe 1749 W
John, Brendon 1763 W
John, Kentisbury 1763 A

John, High Bickington 1764 A and 1780 A
John, Chulmleigh 1788 W
John, Trentishoe 1788 W
John, Georgeham 1793 A
John, Brendon 1798 W
John, Shirwell, mason 1810 A
John, Marwood 1812 A to Thomas Clement, creditor
John, Lapford 1813 W
John, South Molton 1821 W
John, Barnstaple 1827 W
John, Shirwell 1835 A to Alice, widow
John 1839 A
John, Barnstaple 1846 W
John, Countisbury 1849 W
John, Loxhore 1852 W
Joseph, Lapford 1784 W
Joshua, South Molton 1774 W
Margaret, South Molton 1675 A
Mary, Kentisbury 1713 A
Mary, Northam 1728 W
Mary, Burrington 1739 A
Mary, South Molton 1778 W
Mary, Ilfracombe 1783 A
Mary, Countisbury, widow 1809 W
Mary, Lynton 1845 W
Mary and Henry, Kentisbury 1668 A
Nathaniel, Combe Martin 1826 W
Richard Nicholas, Berrynarbor 1621 [W]
Nicholas, Parracombe 1667 A and 1671 O
Nicholas, Northam 1720 W
Ogilby, East Down 1746 W
Peter, Burrington 1681 A
Peter, Countisbury 1771 A
Peter, Lapford 1781 W
Petronell, Tawstock 1622 [W]
Philip, Ilfracombe 1683 A
Philip, Fremington 1727 W and 1733 W
Philip, Northam 1818 W
Philip, Georgeham 1825 W
Rychards Richard, Martinhoe 1580 W
Richard, Countisbury 1636 A and 1642 A
Richard, Parracombe 1682 W
Richard, East Down 1745 W
Richard, Lynton 1777 W
Richard, East Down 1826 W
Richard, Langtree 1836 W
Robert, Barnstaple 1628 W
Robert, Lapford 1693 W
Robert, Tawstock 1747 W
Roger, Tawstock 1603 W
Sage, Barnstaple 1709 W
Richard Samuel, Burrington 1722 A
Samuel, Fremington 1722 A
Samuel, High Bickington 1795 W
Samuel, Ashreigney 1839 A
Sarah, Brendon 1812 W
Simon, Tawstock 1603 W
Simon, South Molton 1668 A
Thomas, Rackenford 1591 [W]
Thomas, North Tawton 1637 W
Thomas, Bideford 1670 A
Thomas, Mariansleigh 1718 W
Thomas, North Molton 1740 W
Thomas, Abbotsham 1778 W
Thomas, Littleham (near Bideford) 1779 W
Thomas, Pilton 1812 A to Mary, widow
Thomas, Ilfracombe 1828 A
Thomas, Yarnscombe 1829 W proved 30 Jul 1829; A dbn
   1835 to Mary Arthur of Atherington
Thomas, High Bickington, yeoman 1848 A to Thomas,
   yeoman, son
Thomas, Kentisbury 1853 A
Richardes William, Mariansleigh, snr. 1571 W
William, Chulmleigh 1597 [W]
William, Frithelstock 1626 [W]
Richard William, Tawstock 1632 [W]

William, Kentisbury 1690 W
William, Tawstock 1709 A
William, High Bickington 1729 A
William, Parracombe 1733 W
William, Georgeham 1739 A
William, Shirwell 1747 W
William, Kentisbury 1749 W
William, Abbotsham 1762 W
William, Northam 1763 A
William, Loxhore 1783 W
William, Kentisbury 1784 A
William, Lynton 1792 W
William, Barnstaple 1794 W
William, Kentisbury, gentleman 1798 W
William, Lynton 1803 W
William, Brendon, yeoman 1805 A
William, Cruwys Morchard 1815 W
William, Marwood 1819 W
William, Eggesford 1830 A to Elizabeth, widow
William, Lynton 1842 W
Riche see Rich
Richman Eleanor, Heanton Punchardon, widow 1805 W
   William, Heanton Punchardon 1776 A
Richord see Richards
Rickard, Reckard, Reckerd, Record, Rickeard, Rykerd
   Rykerd John, West Buckland 1580 W
   Rickeard John, North Hele, Buckland Brewer 1588 W
   Reckard John, Frithelstock 1630 [W] and O
   Record or Rickard Mary, Northam, Appledore 1840 A.
   Reckerd William, Buckland Brewer 1632 [W]
   Record William, Northam 1697 A
   Reckard Willmot, Buckland Brewer 1643 W
Rickett Andrew, Tawstock 1703 A
   Henry, Ilfracombe 1702 A
   Philip, East Down 1625 [W]
   Philip, Ilfracombe 1745 W
   Robert, Rose Ash 1722 A
   William, Northam 1675 W
Ricks, Rycke
   John, Dowland 1774 W and 1783 W
   Rycke William, Rose Ash 1574 W
Ridd, Ridde
   Agnes, Stoke Rivers 1699 W
   Alexander, Challacombe 1718 W
   Ambrose, East Buckland 1714 A
   Amos, formerly of Instow, but late of Pixyheam in Westleigh
     1830 W
   Elizabeth, Bratton Fleming 1754 W
   Francis, Challacombe 1776 A
   Grace, Combe Martin 1827 A to Susanna, daughter
   Humphrey, Challacombe 1731 W
   Humphrey, Challacombe 1824 A to Rebecca, widow
   Ridd alias Rudd James, Atherington 1833 W
   Jane, Tawstock 1839 W
   Joan, Bratton Fleming 1740 W
   John, Combe Martin 1677 A
   John, Bratton Fleming 1710 W
   John, Challacombe, snr. 1729 W
   John, Challacombe 1739 W
   John, Bratton Fleming 1749 W and 1758 W
   John, Challacombe 1777 W
   John, Combe Martin, surgeon 1821 A to Grace, widow,
     mother
   John, Bratton Fleming 1825 W
   John, Bratton Fleming 1850 W
   Ridde Lawrence, Heanton Punchardon 1672 W
   Mary Ann see Thomas Dennis
   Philip, Challacombe 1693 W
   Philip, Bratton Fleming 1733 A
   Philip, Bratton Fleming, soldier 1760 W
   Philip, Challacombe 1791 A
   Philip, Chittlehampton 1812 W
   Rebecca, Bratton Fleming 1685 W
   Rebecca, Bratton Fleming 1768 W
   Richard, Challacombe 1816 W

Richard, Challacombe 1835 W
Susan, Challacombe 1711 W
Ride or Rydde Thomas, High Bray 1584 W
Thomas, Bratton Fleming 1745 W
Thomas, Arlington 1775 W
Thomas, Barnstaple, shipwright 1801 A
Thomas, Tawstock 1824 W
William, Challacombe 1644 A
William, Combe Martin 1672 W
William, Challacombe 1677 W
William, Challacombe 1723 W and 1729 W
William, Bratton Fleming 1735 W
William, Challacombe 1769 A and 1782 A
William, Combe Martin, yeoman, jnr. 1824 A to William of
    Challacombe, father
William, Bratton Fleming, labourer 1848 A to Jane, widow
William, Bratton Fleming 1852 W
Willmot, Challacombe 1687 W
Riddle, Rydol
    Rydol Joan, Chawleigh 1754 W
Rider ..., Northam 1605 [W]
    Edward, King's Nympton 1667 W
    Margaret, Clovelly 1662 A
    Thomas, Tawstock 1616 [W]
Ridge, Ridg, Rydge
    Beaton, Meeth 1696 W
    James, Bratton Fleming 1839 W
    John, Dolton 1710 A
    Ridg John, Winkleigh, jnr. 1715 W
    John, Arlington 1836 W and 1851 W
    Mary, Dolton 1729 W
    Thomas, Buckland Filleigh 1767 W
    Thomas, East Down 1836 W
    Rydge William, Bideford 1627 [W]
    William, Dolton 1739 W
    William, Tawstock 1774 W
    William, Arlington 1852 W
    William, Ilfracombe 1854 W
Ridgman, Rydgeman
    John, Northam 1602 W
    Rydgeman William, Northam 1640 W
Ridler, Redlar, Redler, Rydlar
    Redler ..., Horwood 1611 [W]
    Redlar Ann, Westleigh near Bideford 1672 W
    Jane, Bideford 1678 W
    Rydlar John, Landcross 1624 [W]
    Redler Mary, South Molton 1841 W
    Redler Nicholas, Bideford 1664 W
    Redler Thomas, South Molton 1837 W
Ridley Elizabeth, Beaford 1694 W
    William, Barnstaple, snr. 1709 W
Ridmur see Redmore
Riglin William, Mortehoe 1692 A
Rigsby, Rigsbie
    Alice, Buckland Brewer 1668 [W]
    Ann, Buckland Brewer 1674 W
    Rigsbie John, Buckland Brewer 1615 [W] and 1616 O
    John, Shebbear 1727 W
    John, Shebbear 1780 A and 1792 A
    John, Hartland 1814 W
    John, Monkleigh 1857 W
    Rebecca, Buckland Brewer 1674 W
    Rigeby Roger, Shebbear 1743 A
    William, Buckland Brewer 1660 W
    William, Buckland Brewer 1693 W
Riley William, Marwood 1853 W
Ringstead, Ringsteade
    Ringsteade ..., Burrington 1608 [W]
    Roger, Chulmleigh 1590 [W]
    Thomasine, Chulmleigh 1593 [W]
Rippin, Rippen
    Alice, Witheridge 1791 W
    Henry, Ashreigney 1849 W
    John, Cruwys Morchard 1775 A
    Rippen John, Burrington 1827 W

Mary, Burrington 1847 W
Richard, Ashreigney, yeoman 1807 W
William, Burrington 1831 A to Elizabeth, widow
Risdon, Rysdon, Rysedon
    ..., Great Torrington 1602 [W]
    ..., Sheepwash 1612 [W]
    Abraham, Buckland Brewer 1693 W
    Daniel, Pilton 1772 W
    Edward, Sheepwash 1601 [W]
    Rysdon Elizabeth, Parkham 1633 W
    Elizabeth, Buckland Brewer 1685 W
    Elizabeth, Sheepwash 1721 W
    Elizabeth, Bulkworthy 1839 W
    Rysdon George, Sheepwash 1628 [W]
    George, Parkham 1666 A and 1670 O
    Giles, St Giles in the Wood 1645 A
    Giles, Parkham 1732 A
    Grace, Pilton, widow 1806 W
    Hannah, Woolfardisworthy 1775 W
    James, Bideford 1642 A
    Joan, Sheepwash 1599 [W]
    Joan, Great Torrington 1603 W
    John, Bideford 1720 A
    John, Petrockstowe 1772 W
    Joseph, Buckland Filleigh 1707 W
    Joseph, Buckland Filleigh 1753 A
    Rysdon Margery, Sheepwash 1630 [W]
    Mary see Thomas Nankivell
    Rysdon Philip, Buckland Brewer, gentleman 1640 W
    Philip, Bideford 1711 W
    Philip, Woolfardisworthy 1750 A
    Rysedon Richard, Sheepwash 1578 W
    Richard, Woolfardisworthy 1775 A
    Rysdon Robert, Sheepwash 1583 W
    Rysdon Thomas, Petrockstowe 1628 [W]
    Thomas see Thomas Nankivell
    Rysdon Tristram, St Giles in the Wood 1640 A
    William, Chulmleigh 1662 A
    William, St Giles in the Wood, gentleman 1703 W
Rise see Rice
Rivers John, South Molton 1776 W
Roach, Roch, Roche
    Abraham, Bideford 1703 A
    Roche Alice, Zeal Monachorum 1640 A
    Roch Henry, Fremington 1593 [W]
    Isott, Parracombe 1755 W
    Joan, Bideford 1714 W
    John, Barnstaple 1711 A
    Lodovic, Northam 1729 W
    Roch Margaret, Barnstaple 1774 W
    Roche Paul, Molland 1572 W
    Richard, Parracombe 1785 A
    Richard, Parracombe, yeoman 1817 A to Joan, widow
    Roch Robert, Zeal Monachorum 1632 [W]
    Roche Thomas, Winkleigh 1627 [W]
    Thomas, Parracombe 1720 W and 1734 W
    William, Parracombe 1824 W
Roame, Roam
    Catherine, Winkleigh 1669 W
    Grace, Winkleigh 1669 W
    Roam Richard, Winkleigh 1672 A
Roash Abraham, Bideford 1742 W
Robbens, Robbins, Roben see Robins
Robenson see Robinson
Roberts ..., Chawleigh 1609 [W]
    Agnes, Ilfracombe 1799 A
    Anthony, Combe Martin 1682 A
    Archelaus and Bartholomew, West Down 1667 [A]
    Charles, West Down 1713 W
    Christian, West Down 1631 [W]
    David, Arlington 1697 W
    David, St Giles in the Wood 1751 A
    Edward, South Molton 1744 W
    George, Combe Martin 1688 W
    George, Chulmleigh 1746 A

Grace, Rose Ash 1717 W
Humphrey, Chawleigh 1587 A account
Humphrey, Chawleigh 1587 A
Joan, Combe Martin 1592 [W]
John, Combe Martin 1626 [W]
John, West Down 1667 A
John, Rose Ash 1694 W
John, West Down 1700 A
John, North Molton, woolcomber 1811 W
John, North Molton 1823 W
Joseph, Clovelly 1828 W
Mary, West Down 1666 W
Mary wife of John see Charles Smith
Nicholas, West Down 1631 [W]
Phyllis, Combe Martin 1630 [W]
Priscilla, West Down 1712 A and 1713 A
Robert, Chulmleigh 1626 [W]
Roger, Chulmleigh 1625 [W]
Samuel, Barnstaple 1827 A
Thomas, Barnstaple 1690 A
William, Ashreigney 1639 W
William, Combe Martin 1704 W and 1709 W
William, Barnstaple 1722 W
Robins, Robbins, Robens, Robyns
..., Mortehoe 1610 [W]
..., Northam 1613 [W]
Robbins ..., Bow 1624 [W]
Robbins Ann, Ilfracombe 1747 A
Anthony, Buckland Brewer 1726 A
Robbins Arthur, Barnstaple 1762 A
Catherine, Northam 1608 [W]; forename blank in Ms;
    supplied from parish register
Elizabeth, Shirwell 1839 W
Robyns George, Weare Giffard, servant to Mr Fortescue 1601
    A; forename blank in Ms; supplied from parish register
Robbins Hugh, Hartland 1687 W
Robens James, Stoodleigh 1567 W
Robbins James, Horwood 1626 [W]
Jeremiah, Great Torrington 1717 W and A
Robbins Jerome, Great Torrington 1686 A
Robens Joan, Ilfracombe 1579 W
Robens Joan, Great Torrington 1586 A account
Joan, Huish 1736 W
Robens John, Bideford 1588 A
John, Woolfardisworthy 1596 [W]
Robyns John, Ilfracombe 1604 W
Robbens John, Rackenford 1619 [W]
Robbens John, Shebbear 1621 [W]
Robbins John, Chulmleigh 1660 [W]
Robbins John, Parkham 1664 A
Robbins John, Bow 1668 W and A
John, Parkham 1672 O
John, Parkham 1677 W
John, Yarnscombe 1710 A
John, Buckland Brewer 1736 W
John, mariner 1742 W
Robbins John, Dolton 1758 A
Robbins John, Shebbear 1761 A
Robbins John, Woolfardisworthy 1784 A
Robbins John, Marwood 1791 A
John, Yarnscombe 1826 W
John, Marwood 1836 W
Robens Margaret, Fremington 1584 W
Margery, Woolfardisworthy 1595 [W]
Robbins Margery, Hartland 1691 W
Robbins Mark, Zeal Monachorum 1687 W
Robbins Mary, Zeal Monachorum 1683 A
Mary, Bideford 1829 W
Robbins Nicholas, Yarnscombe, farmer 1806 W
Robens Owen, Barnstaple 1574 A
Robens Paschal, Woolfardisworthy 1586 W
Patience, Northam 1686 A
Roben Peter, Hartland 1606 [W]; forename blank in Ms;
    supplied from parish register
Robens Petherick, Mortehoe 1601 W

Philip, Great Torrington 1590 [W]
Richard, Parkham 1641 A
Robbins Richard, Shebbear 1701 W
Robbins Richard, Huish 1712 W
Richard, Bideford, saddler 1796 A
Robbins Robert, Woolfardisworthy 1771 A
Robbins Robert, Woolfardisworthy, gentleman 1804 A
Robens Roger, Great Torrington 1591 [W]
Samuel, Parkham 1669 A
Susan, Beaford 1733 W
Robens Thomas, Ilfracombe 1579 W
Thomas, Ilfracombe 1640 A
Thomas, Ilfracombe 1667 A
Thomas, Northam 1679 W
Robbins Thomas, Buckland Brewer 1691 W
Robbins Thomas, Marwood 1747 W
Robbins Thomas, East Putford 1773 W
Robbins Thomas, Barnstaple 1793 W
Thomas, Bittadon, yeoman 1801 W
Robbens William, Huntshaw 1622 [W]
William, West Down 1672 W
Robinson, Robenson
Mary, Iddesleigh 1816 W
Robenson Richard, Fremington 1574 W
Robyns see Robins
Roch, Roche see Roach
Rock, Rocke
Agnes, Mariansleigh 1716 W
Rocke Alice, Martinhoe, widow 1572 W
Eli, King's Nympton 1740 W
Elizabeth, King's Nympton 1685 W
Henry, Mariansleigh 1675 W
Rocke Joan, High Bickington 1589 W
Rocke Joan, Mariansleigh 1589 W
Rocke Joan, Bideford 1736 A
John, Combe Martin 1588 A
John, Bideford 1747 W
John, Barnstaple, papermaker 1811 W
John, Combe Martin 1846 A
Mary, Mariansleigh 1664 A
Mary, Northam 1745 W
Mary, East or West Anstey 1765 A
Mary, Mariansleigh 1829 W
Mathew, Barnstaple 1759 W
Peter, Mariansleigh 1662 W
Peter, Mariansleigh 1685 A
Peter, King's Nympton 1709 W
Peter, Mariansleigh 1733 W
Philip, Arlington 1814 W
Rocke Richard, Frithelstock 1591 [W]
Richard, Arlington 1820 A to Elizabeth, widow
Thomas, Mariansleigh 1680 A
Thomas, Mariansleigh 1694 W
William, Bideford 1736 W
William, Mariansleigh 1737 W
Rocke William, Bideford 1737 W
William, Barnstaple 1822 W
William, Mariansleigh 1848 W
Rockleigh
Rowklegh William, Burrington 1577 A
Roclife, Roclyff see Ratcliffe
Rodd, Rod, Rodde
Ann, George Nympton 1847 W
Catherine, Chulmleigh 1693 A
Edmund, Great Torrington 1691 W
Edmund, Frithelstock 1738 W
Rode James, Ilfracombe 1833 W
John, Littleham (near Bideford) 1590 [W]
Rod John, Ashreigney 1604 W
John, Roborough 1674 [W]
John, High Bickington 1784 A
John, St Giles in the Wood 1826 W
Rodde Michael, Abbotsham 1579 W
Robert, East Worlington 1682 A
Susan, St Giles in the Wood 1750 W

Thomas, Lapford 1820 W
Thomas, Langtree 1821 W
Thomasine, Roborough 1688 W
William, Roborough 1573 W
William, Charles 1678 W
William, Roborough 1679 W
William, Parkham 1752 W
William, St Giles in the Wood 1789 W
William, St Giles in the Wood 1800 W
William, Ilfracombe, mariner 1803 A
  see also Radd
Roffe Thomas, Meeth 1718 [W]
Rogerman, Rogeman
  ..., Chittlehampton 1612 [W]
  Alice, Abbotsham 1661 W
  Francis, Charles 1667 W
  Henry, Woolfardisworthy 1619 [W]
  Henry, Hartland 1703 W
  Hugh, Clovelly 1620 [W]
  Hugh, Sheepwash 1661 W
  Hugh, Clovelly 1700 W
  John, Woolfardisworthy 1591 [W]
  John, Woolfardisworthy 1604 W
  John, South Molton 1660 W
  John, Bideford 1704 A
  Mabel, High Bickington 1592 [W]
  Rogeman Ralph, Clovelly 1763 W
  Richard, Clovelly 1683 W
  Simon, Frithelstock 1591 [W]
  Thomas, Woolfardisworthy 1625 [W]
  Thomas, Woolfardisworthy 1674 W
  Thomas, Chulmleigh 1722 A
  Thomas, Abbotsham 1740 W
  Thomas, Hartland 1755 A
Rogers, Roger
  ..., Northam 1605 [W]
  Roger Alice, Georgeham 1601 W
  Ann, Kentisbury 1816 W
  Ann, Instow, widow 1849 A to Francis Hammett, gentleman,
    brother
  Christian, Heanton Punchardon 1775 A
  Christopher, Lapford 1637 W
  Christopher, Bondleigh 1737 W
  David, Instow 1734 W
  Elizabeth, Pilton 1760 A
  Emma, Buckland Brewer, widow 1608 [W]; forename blank
    in Ms; supplied from parish register
  George, Shirwell 1685 W
  George, East Down 1719 W
  Gregory, Shirwell 1752 W
  Hannah, Ilfracombe 1802 W
  Roger James, Bideford 1729 W
  Jane, Winkleigh 1690 W
  Joan, Bondleigh 1632 [W]
  John, Atherington 1602 W; forename blank in Ms; supplied
    from parish register
  John, Pilton 1619 [W]
  John, Little Torrington 1624 [W]
  John, Atherington 1633 W
  John, Lapford, jnr. 1640 W
  John, Georgeham, snr. 1644 W
  John, Alverdiscott 1674 A
  John, Hartland 1688 W
  John, Pilton 1693 W
  John, Instow 1708 A
  John, Shirwell 1767 A
  John, King's Nympton, yeoman 1807 W
  Lawrence, East Worlington 1621 [W]
  Margaret, Instow 1739 W
  Margaret, Bondleigh 1767 A
  Margery, Tawstock 1664 W
  Margery, Bondleigh 1696 W
  Mary, Northam 1758 W
  Mary, King's Nympton 1786 W
  Nicholas, Barnstaple 1724 W

Owen, Buckland Brewer 1605 W
Petronell, Bondleigh 1640 A
Philip, Pilton 1737 W
Philip, Bondleigh 1743 A
Philip, Loxhore 1762 W
Priscilla, Pilton 1696 W
Richard, Bondleigh 1627 [W], 1632 [W], 1633 A and 1635 O
Richard, Bondleigh 1707 W
Roger Robert, Georgeham 1568 W
Robert, Winkleigh 1645 W
Roger, Pilton 1684 W
Rowland, Northam 1739 W and 1742 W
Samuel, Ilfracombe 1788 A
Stephen, Georgeham 1592 [W]
Thomas, South Molton 1632 [W]
Thomas, Northam 1637 A
Thomas, Northam 1750 W
Walter, Atherington 1602 [W]; forename blank in Ms;
  supplied from parish register
William, Ilfracombe 1576 A
William, Little Torrington 1586 A
William, Northam 1679 W
William, Woolfardisworthy 1681 A
William, King's Nympton 1707 W
William, Northam 1746 W
Roland see Rowland
Roler Phyllis, Goodleigh 1626 [W]
Rolle, Roll, Rowle
  ..., Great Torrington 1606 [W]
  Alexander, Northam 1701 W
  Charles, Tawstock, gentleman 1709 W
  Rowle Edward, Tawstock 1756 A
  Rowle Elizabeth, Barnstaple 1743 W
  Henry, Petrockstowe 1595 [W]
  Henry, Tawstock 1699 A
  Roll Joachim, Chittlehampton 1638 A
  Roll Joan, Petrockstowe 1634 W
  Lucilla, St Giles in the Wood 1742 W
  Margaret, Great Torrington 1592 [W]
  Margaret, Great Torrington 1592 [W]
  Roll Margaret, Great Torrington 1660 W
  Margaret, Bideford 1725 [W]
  Maurice, Meeth 1696 W
  Maurice, Meeth c1604 [W]
  Thomas, Petrockstowe 1604 W
  William, Barnstaple 1680 W
Rolson William, Nymet Rowland 1596 [W]
Rolston alias Durant Mary, North Tawton 1710 A
Rombelew, Rombelewe, Rombelow, Rombelowe see Rumbelow
Romsham, Romson, Rumsam, Runson, Rumsom, Rumson,
  Rumsum
  ..., Combe Martin 1614 [W]
  Anthony, Kentisbury 1634 A
  Rumsam George, Combe Martin 1826 A to Elizabeth of East
    Down, widow
  Romsom James, Combe Martin 1595 [W]
  John, Kentisbury 1587 A
  John, Ashreigney 1644 W
  Rumsum John, Ilfracombe 1841 W
  William, Combe Martin 1590 W
  Rumson William, Barnstaple 1670 A and 1672 O
  Rumsom William, Barnstaple 1724 W
  Rumson William, Ilfracombe 1851 W
Rood Thomasine, Littleham (near Bideford) 1591 [W]
Rooke, Rook, Rookes
  ..., Parracombe 1611 [W]
  Rookes ..., Coldridge 1611 [W]
  ..., Combe Martin 1613 [W]
  Rook alias Richards Agnes, Combe Martin 1701 W
  Agnes, Knowle-Water, Heanton Punchardon, sp. 1798 W
  Alexander, Bratton Fleming 1602 W
  Anthony, Martinhoe 1604 W
  Anthony, Combe Martin 1666 A
  Bartholomew, Northam 1706 A
  Bartholomew, Northam 1742 W and 1754 W

Catherine, Northam 1737 W
David, Lynton 1584 W
Eleanor, Challacombe 1684 W
Elizabeth, Bideford 1789 W
George, Barnstaple 1673 A
George, Challacombe 1680 A
George, Northam 1693 A
Gertrude, Shirwell 1743 W
Grace, Oakford 1663 A
Henry, Langtree 1637 W
Henry, Fremington 1756 W; 1763 A dbn
Hilary, Combe Martin 1589 W
Humphrey, Combe Martin 1663 A and 1669 O
Humphrey, Loxhore 1724 W
Hursey, Trentishoe 1630 [W]
Rook alias Aysh Jane, Combe Martin 1668 A
Joan, Mariansleigh 1615 [W]
Joan, Countisbury 1669 A
Joan, Northam 1752 A
John, Lynton 1592 [W]
John, Combe Martin 1595 [W]
John, Ilfracombe 1599 [W]
John, Martinhoe 1616 [W]
John, Barnstaple 1622 [W]
John, Parracombe 1628 [W]
John, Trentishoe 1628 [W]
John, Bratton Fleming 1637 [W]
John, High Bickington 1645 A
John, Combe Martin 1661 W
John, Lynton 1663 W
John, Great Torrington 1668 A
John, Knowstone 1671 W
John, Bratton Fleming 1675 A
John, mariner, jnr. 1705 A
John, Barnstaple 1720 W
Rookes John, Atherington 1720 W
John, Northam 1755 A
Mary, Bratton Fleming 1619 [W]
Mary, Knowstone 1671 W
Nicholas, Combe Martin 1615 [W]
Rookes Ralph, Coldridge 1571 W
Richard, Frithelstock 1591 [W]
Richard, Trentishoe 1641 A
Rook Richard, Combe Martin 1664 W
Richard, Tawstock 1691 A
Richard, Winkleigh 1711 W
Robert, Great Torrington 1692 A
Samuel, Iddesleigh 1753 A
Simon, Trentishoe 1625 [W]
Thomas, Lynton 1586 W
Thomas, Challacombe 1624 [W]
Thomas, Challacombe 1685 A
Thomas, Bratton Fleming 1690 W
Thomas, Parracombe 1693 W
Rook Thomas, Marwood 1803 A
William, Bratton Fleming 1590 [W]
William, Pilton 1591 [W]
William, Arlington 1643 W
William, Combe Martin 1668 W
Rook William, Georgeham, yeoman 1813 A to Eleanor,
    widow
Rook William, Bideford 1818 W
Rook William, Dolton 1836 A
Roper, Rooper
Rooper alias Setter Bartholomew, Chittlehampton 1588 A
John, South Molton 1583 W
Rooper alias Sitter Richard, South Molton 1585 W
Richard, South Molton 1620 [W]
Richard, Barnstaple 1726 A
Robert, South Molton 1618 [W]
Rosier, Rosyer
Ann, Berrynarbor 1705 W
Ann, Chulmleigh 1715 W
Rosser Dorothy, Barnstaple 1737 W
Edward, Great Torrington 1715 W
Rosyer Elizabeth, Yarnscombe 1578 W

Elizabeth, Northam 1733 W
Elizabeth, Northam 1761 W
Grace, Chulmleigh 1730 W
Grace, Barnstaple 1737 A; A dbn 1758
John, Barnstaple 1670 W
Richard, Barnstaple 1677 W
William, Northam 1732 A
William, Northam 1736 W
Ross Margaret see Henry Ellis Heard
Rossiter John, Heanton Punchardon 1695 A
Mary, Atherington 1668 W
Rosyer see Rosier
Rother Elizabeth, Combe Martin 1638 A
Rottenberry, Rottenberye, Rottenbury, Rottenburye, Rottonburie
    see Rattenbury
Rouse see Rowse
Routley, Routly, Routtley, Rowtley
Rowtley Alexander Francis Snow, West Anstey 1756 W
Anthony, George Nympton 1731 W
Grace, Bondleigh 1828 A to James, son
Routtley Hugh, South Molton 1739 W
John, Huntshaw 1746 A
Routly Joyce, Atherington 1724 W
Richard, Bondleigh 1816 A to James, son
Row see Rowe
Rowcliff, Rowckcleffe, Rowckclyf, Rowclif, Rowclife,
    Rowclifes, Rowcliffe, Rowclyffe, Rowkclyffe, Rowtcliff,
    Rowtleffe
Rowcliffe ..., Meeth 1600 A
Rowcliffe ..., Burrington 1602 [W]
..., Brendon 1604 [W]
..., King's Nympton 1614 [W]
Agnes, South Molton 1675 W
Rowcliffe Aldred, Yarnscombe 1618 [W]
Rowcliffe Alice, Tawstock 1730 A
Rowcliffe Alice, Buckland Brewer 1821 W
Andrew, Merton 1687 W
Rowtleffe Andrew, Merton 1762 W
Rowtcliff Andrew, Merton, yeoman 1807 W
Rowtcliff Andrew, Merton 1844 W and 1851 W
Rowtcliffe Ann wife of William see John Quance
Rowcliffe Anthony, Martinhoe 1644 W
Arthur, South Molton 1682 W
Rowcliffe Beatrice, Burrington 1626 [W]
Rowcliffe Charles, Dolton 1743 W
Daniel, Chittlehampton 1664 W
Daniel, King's Nympton 1709 W
Rowclifes Daniel, Burrington 1724 A
Edward, Chittlehampton 1707 W
Rowclif Edward, Chittlehampton 1774 W
Rowcliffe Elizabeth, King's Nympton 1592 [W]
Elizabeth, Yarnscombe 1711 A
Rowcliffe Elizabeth, George Nympton 1768 W
Faithful, Cheldon 1642 W
Rowcliffe George, Yarnscombe 1622 O
Rowcliffe George, Meeth 1631 [W]
Henry, Sheepwash 1714 W
Hugh, Chulmleigh 1701 W
Rowcliffe Hugh, South Molton 1821 W
Rowcliffe Joan, South Molton 1734 W
Routcliffe Joan, Buckland Brewer 1757 W
Rowcliffe John, Ilfracombe 1591 [W]
Rowcliffe John, Ashreigney 1596 [W]
Rowcliffe John, Burrington 1620 [W] and 1632 [W]
Rowcliffe John, Chittlehampton 1636 A
Rowcliffe John, King's Nympton 1640 O
John, King's Nympton 1661 [W]
John, Burrington 1664 W and 1670 A
John, King's Nympton 1716 W
Rowcliffe John, South Molton 1735 A
Rowcliffe John, Buckland Brewer 1753 W
Rowcliffe John, Chittlehampton 1759 A
Rowcliffe John, Burrington 1789 W
Rowcliffe John, Atherington 1804 A
Rowcliffe John, Buckland Brewer 1812 W
John, Buckland Brewer 1842 W

Rowcliffe John, South Molton 1844 W
Joseph, Burrington 1670 W
Rowcliffe Philip, Martinhoe 1633 W and 1635 W
Rowcliffe Philip, High Bickington 1638 W
Priscilla, Merton 1680 A
Rowcliffe Roger, King's Nympton 1602 W
Roger, Chittlehampton 1615 [W]
Roger, Chittlehampton 1682 W
Roger, Chittlehampton 1709 A
Samuel, Merton 1692 A
Sarah, Chittlehampton 1693 W
Rowcliffe Thomas, Burrington 1573 W
Rowclyffe Thomas, King's Nympton 1585 W
Thomas, Burrington 1606 [W]; forename blank in Ms;
    supplied from parish register
Rowcliffe Thomas, Yarnscombe 1621 [W]
Thomas, Chittlehampton 1675 A
Thomas, King's Nympton 1684 W
Rowcliffe Thomas, George Nympton 1768 W
Rowckcleffe William, Huish 1569 W
Rowckclyf William, Yarnscombe 1587 A
Rowkclyffe William, Burrington 1589 W
Rowclife William, King's Nympton 1601 W
William, South Molton 1663 W
William, King's Nympton 1664 W
William, Buckland Brewer 1718 A
Rowtcliffe William, Merton, yeoman 1811 W
Rowcliffe William, South Molton 1854 W
Rowtcliffe Willmot, Merton 1822 W
Rowden, Rowdon
Rowdon ..., Chulmleigh 1608 [W]
Rowdon ..., Thelbridge 1610 [W]
Rowdon ..., South Molton 1611 [W]
Rowdon ..., Lapford 1615 [W]
Ambrose, South Molton 1734 W
Rowdon Bartholomew, Chulmleigh 1596 [W]
Rowdon Christopher, King's Nympton 1592 [W]
Dennis, South Molton 1706 W
Rowdon Eleanor, Lapford 1831 W
Rowdon Elizabeth, Bow 1809 A
Francis, Barnstaple 1766 A
Hannah, South Molton 1823 A
Rowdon Henry, South Molton 1625 [W]
Rowdon Isaac, Romansleigh 1623 [W]
Rowdon Jane, South Molton 1618 [W]
Rowdon Joan, Thelbridge, widow 1569 W
Rowdon Joan, South Molton 1583 W
Joan, South Molton 1589 W
Rowdon Joan, South Molton 1597 [W]
Rowdon Joan, Chulmleigh 1605 W
Rowdon Joan, Brushford 1617 [W]
John, Zeal Monachorum 1741 A
John, Bow, blacksmith 1809 W
Margaret, Zeal Monachorum 1742 A
Mark, Bow 1735 A
Nathaniel, Zeal Monachorum 1716 A
Rowdon Nicholas, King's Nympton 1591 [W]
Rowdon Richard, King's Nympton 1591 [W]
Rowdon Robert, Lapford 1580 W
Rowdon Robert, Ashreigney 1643 A
Robert, South Molton 1684 W
Rowdon Robert, Chittlehampton 1738 A
Robert, Chittlehampton, tailor 1806 W
Rowdon Roger, Chawleigh 1608 [W]; forename blank in Ms;
    supplied from parish register
Rowdon Sybil, Lapford 1567 W
Thomas, South Molton 1821 A to John of Thorverton, father
Rowdon William, South Molton 1587 W
William, Woolfardisworthy 1677 W
William, Barnstaple 1777 A
Rowe, Row, Rowes
..., Abbotsham 1600 A
..., Instow 1600 A
..., Bow 1601 A (2)
..., Buckland Brewer 1601 A
..., North Tawton 1607 [W]

..., Abbotsham 1612 [W]
..., Langtree 1613 [W]
..., West Anstey 1613 [W]
Abraham, Bideford 1717 W
Abraham, Chulmleigh 1748 W
Alexander Francis Snow, Bideford 1832 A to George M.,
    brother
Row Ann, Hartland 1709 A
Ann, Hartland 1831 W
Anthony, Bideford 1668 W
Armanell, North Tawton 1713 W
Azariah, Coldridge 1688 W
Baldwin, South Molton 1687 A
Catherine, Tawstock 1669 W
Charles, Bideford 1667 W
Charles, Alwington 1714 W
Christopher, Chulmleigh 1565 W
Row Christopher and Martha, North Tawton 1644 W
David, Buckland Brewer 1597 [W]
David, Ilfracombe 1711 A
Edmund, North Tawton 1591 [W]
Edmund, Beaford 1665 W
Row Edward, Beaford 1664 W
Edward, Beaford 1675 W
Elizabeth, Lapford 1589 A
Elizabeth, Chulmleigh 1626 [W]
Elizabeth, Littleham (near Bideford) 1725 A
Row Elizabeth, Barnstaple 1726 W
Row Elizabeth, Bradworthy 1843 W
George, Chulmleigh 1564 W
George, Beaford 1662 A
George, Barnstaple 1698 A
George, Monkleigh 1704 A
George, Burrington 1721 W
Grace, Hartland 1830 A to Thomas Velley Row, James
    Somers Rowe and George Henry Sellick and others; A dbn
    passed at the Principal Registry 27 Jun 1871, and again 28
    Mar 1873
Henry, Chawleigh 1590 [W]
Henry, North Tawton 1595 [W]
Henry, Abbotsham 1625 [W]
Henry, Bondleigh 1633 W
Row Henry, Hartland 1720 W
Row Henry, North Tawton 1737 W
Henry, Burrington 1759 W
Henry, Hartland 1760 A
Henry, Weare Giffard 1841 A
Henry, Buckland Brewer 1850 W
Honor, Abbotsham 1733 W
Humphrey, Buckland Brewer 1573 W
Row Isaac, Burrington 1781 W
James, Marwood 1826 A to Elizabeth, widow
Joan, Hartland, widow 1604 [W]; forename blank in Ms;
    supplied from parish register
Joan, Meeth 1672 W
Joan, North Tawton 1681 W
Joan, Bideford 1685 A
John, Tawstock 1578 W
Row John, Hartland 1583 W
John, Abbotsham 1591 [W]
John, Nymet Rowland 1593 [W]
John, St Giles in the Wood 1597 [W]
Row John, Barnstaple 1619 [W]
John, Chulmleigh 1619 [W]
Row John, Abbotsham 1622 [W]
John, Lapford 1628 [W]
Rowes John, Clovelly 1629 [W]
John, Alwington 1634 W and 1640 O
Row John, North Tawton, jnr. 1636 W
John, Abbotsham 1640 W
Row John, Langtree 1661 W
John, Beaford 1662 A
John, Abbotsham 1667 W and 1669 A
John, Tawstock 1685 W
John, Abbotsham 1692 A

Row John, Tawstock 1695 W
Row John, Barnstaple 1703 A
John, Barnstaple 1708 A
John, North Tawton 1720 A
John, Bideford 1721 W
John, South Molton 1735 W
John, Bow 1738 A
John, Chittlehampton 1751 W
John, Bratton Fleming 1763 W
John, South Molton 1772 W
Row John, Buckland Brewer 1777 W
John, Burrington 1778 A
John, Alverdiscott 1837 W
John, Burrington 1839 W
John, Northam 1847 W
Row Jonah, Bow 1637 W
Row Joseph, Barnstaple 1635 W
Joseph, Bulkworthy 1778 A
Row Joseph, St Giles in the Wood 1852 W
Row Lodovic, Ilfracombe 1663 W
Lucas, Hartland 1623 [W]
Row Margaret, North Tawton 1638 W
Margaret, Barnstaple 1682 W
Margery, Bow 1565 W
Margery, North Tawton 1593 [W]
Row Martha and Christopher, North Tawton 1644 W
Mary, Monkleigh 1682 W
Mary, Northam 1715 W
Mary, Tawstock 1721 W
Mary, South Molton 1738 W
Mary, Buckland Brewer 1755 W
Mary, Littleham (near Bideford) 1767 W
Mary, Barnstaple 1790 W
Mary, Northam 1854 W
Mary Ann, Hartland 1849 A
Row Mathew, Abbotsham 1603 W
Matilda, Hartland 1584 W
Michael, Ashreigney 1688 W
Michael, Stoke Rivers 1711 W
Michael, Ashreigney 1734 A
Nicholas, Lapford 1586 W
Nicholas, Langtree 1615 [W]
Peter, Chulmleigh 1568 W
Peter, Tawstock 1643 W
Peter, Hartland 1709 W
Philip, Tawstock 1751 A
Pinilla, Great Torrington 1751 W
Prudence, Bratton Fleming, widow 1796 W
Richard, Chulmleigh 1578 W
Richard, Great Torrington 1591 [W] and 1592 A account
Richard, Abbotsham 1633 A and 1635 O
Row Richard, Abbotsham 1681 W
Richard, Alwington 1683 W
Richard, Barnstaple 1736 A
Robert, North Tawton 1590 [W]
Robert, Burrington 1592 [W]
Robert, South Molton 1618 [W]
Robert, North Tawton 1619 [W]
Row Robert, South Molton 1669 A
Robert, King's Nympton 1812 A to Agnes, widow
Roger, Barnstaple 1622 [W]
Scipio, Bideford 1699 A
Thomas, Buckland Brewer 1586 W
Thomas, Hartland 1590 [W] and 1597 [W]
Thomas, Bideford 1640 W
Row Thomas, Hartland 1678 W
Thomas, Bideford 1697 W
Thomas, Abbotsham 1700 W
Thomas, Clovelly 1741 A
Row Thomas, Bideford 1745 A
Thomas, Bideford 1750 A
Thomas, Hartland 1760 A
Thomas, Hartland 1770 W
Thomasine, Tawstock 1568 W and 1579 W
Row Thomasine, Meeth 1679 W

Row Thomasine, Abbotsham 1696 W
Walter, North Tawton 1569 W
William, Hartland 1592 [W]
William, North Tawton 1614 [W]; forename blank in Ms;
    supplied from parish register
William, Alwington 1625 [W]
Row William, Monkleigh 1637 A and 1640 O
William, Hartland 1670 W
William, Hartland 1690 W
William, Abbotsham 1692 W
William, Hartland, jnr. 1700 W
William, Ashreigney 1703 A
William, Barnstaple 1703 A
William, Littleham (near Bideford) 1752 W
William, Hartland 1753 W
Row Willmot, North Tawton 1638 W
Row Willmot, Hartland 1677 W
Row Willmot, Abbotsham 1719 W
Rowkclyffe see Rowcliff
Rowin Edward, Alverdiscott 1636 W
Rowklegh see Rockleigh
Rowland, Roland, Rowlande
    ..., Zeal Monachorum 1610 [W]
    Alison, Lapford, widow 1565 W
    Bridget, Hartland 1767 A
    Elizabeth, Beaford 1755 W
    Elizabeth, Beaford 1772 W
    Jane, Hartland 1698 [W]
    John, Beaford 1725 A
    Rowlande Margaret, Hartland 1566 W
    Mary, Great Torrington 1715 W
    Nicholas, Hartland 1690 A
    Richard, Hartland 1740 A
    Roland Robert, Zeal Monachorum 1588 W
    Roger, Barnstaple 1577 W
    Roger, North Tawton 1633 W
    Thomas, Witheridge 1628 [W]
    William, Bow 1597 [W]
    William, Bideford 1814 W
Rowle see Rolle
Rowley Alice, Barnstaple 1703 W
    Henry, Barnstaple 1694 A
Rowse, Rouse
    Ezekiel, Buckland Brewer 1677 W
    Ezekiel, Buckland Brewer 1700 A
    Joan, Langtree 1706 W
    Martha, Langtree 1720 W
    Mary, Buckland Brewer 1720 W
    Stephen, Petrockstowe 1603 W
    William, Great Torrington 1839 A to Richard Baker Rouse,
        brother
Rowstone Christian, South Molton 1579 W
Rowtcliff, Rowtleffe see Rowcliff
Rowtley see Routley
Roynon ..., Pilton 1682 W
Rud see Rudd
Rudall, Rudal, Ruddell, Rudell, Rudle
    Alexander, Nymet Rowland 1790 W
    Arthur, Chulmleigh 1779 W
    George, Chawleigh 1627 [W] and 1629 O
    Rudell George, Lapford 1784 W
    George, Eggesford 1853 W
    Rudle John, Instow 1684 W
    Ruddell John, Ashreigney 1784 W
    Philip, Chulmleigh 1770 W and 1775 W
    Rudal Roger, West Worlington 1763 W
    Rudal Roger, Lapford, yeoman 1802 W
    Samuel, Coldridge 1693 W
    Samuel, Chawleigh 1766 W
Rudd, Rud, Rudde, Rydd, Rydde
    Abraham, Heanton Punchardon 1693 W
    Agnes, Challacombe 1723 W
    Alexander, Westleigh near Bideford 1674 A
    Alexander, Lynton 1705 W
    Ambrose, Goodleigh 1680 W

Ambrose, Burrington 1821 A to James of Yarnscombe, uncle
Francis, Atherington 1675 W
Rudde George, Tawstock 1671 W
Henry, Ilfracombe 1779 W
Rud Henry, Tawstock 1805 W*
Rydd Hilary, Combe Martin 1639 [W]
Rudd alias Ridd James, Atherington 1833 W
Rudde Joan, Marwood 1580 A
Rydde Joan, Challacombe 1580 W
John, Combe Martin 1664 W
John, Ashford 1667 W
John, Stoke Rivers 1681 W
John, Westleigh near Bideford 1700 A
John, Tawstock 1787 W
John, Marwood 1792 W
John, Tawstock, yeoman 1804 W
John, Tawstock 1841 W
Lucas, Combe Martin 1667 A
Peter, Hartland 1664 A
Philip, Challacombe 1710 W
Prudence, Combe Martin 1739 W
Rydd Richard, Combe Martin 1636 A
Rydd Robert, Combe Martin 1631 [W]
Rydde or Ride Thomas, High Bray 1584 W
Rudde Thomas, Challacombe 1629 [W]
Rudde William, Ashford 1589 W
William, Barnstaple 1637 W
William, Tawstock 1761 W
William, Atherington 1793 W
Ruddell see Rudall
Rude ..., Combe Martin 1604 [W]
..., Charles 1607 [W] (2)
..., King's Nympton 1610 [W]
..., Charles 1614 [W]
Agnes, Charles 1603 W
Agnes, Instow 1783 A (2)
Alice, Fremington 1588 A
Christopher, Charles 1626 [W]
Eleanor, King's Nympton 1722 W
Elizabeth, Fremington 1588 A
Elizabeth, Instow 1783 A
James, Ashford 1603 W
James, Instow 1740 W
James, Fremington, yeoman 1804 A
James, Great Torrington 1856 W
Joan, Charles 1674 A
John, King's Nympton 1615 O
John, Fremington 1623 [W]
John, Instow 1718 W
John, Bideford 1743 A
John, Instow 1761 W
John, Instow 1824 W
Macklin, Bratton Fleming 1591 [W]
Mary, King's Nympton 1730 W
Mary, Barnstaple 1834 W
Michael, High Bray 1617 [W]
Prudence, Fremington 1741 A
Richard, Fremington 1579 W
Richard, Arlington 1608 [W]; forename blank in Ms; supplied
from parish register
Richard, Knill, Instow 1801 A
Thomas, King's Nympton 1702 W
William, Ilfracombe 1606 W
Rudell see Rudall
Rudge, Rudg
Agnes, Dolton 1706 W
E., High Bickington 1683 A
Elizabeth, Dowland 1671 W
Rudge alias Mills Elizabeth, South Molton 1679 A
George, Lapford 1598 [W]
John, Washford Pyne 1579 W
John, Bideford 1635 A
John, South Molton 1636 A
John, Warkleigh 1696 W
John, Winkleigh 1726 W

Peter, Trentishoe, snr. 1630 [W]
Simon, Dolton 1697 W and 1698 A
Stephen, Alwington 1594 [W]
Thomas, Lapford 1645 A
Rudg Thomas, Dolton 1661 W
Thomas, Dowland 1689 A
Thomas, Meeth 1702 W
William, Dowland 1668 W
William, Tawstock 1688 A
Rudgman Joy, Frithelstock 1615 [W]
Rudle see Rudall
Rudmore Calvin, Brushford 1688 W
George, Clovelly 1623 [W]
Giles, Clovelly 1615 [W]
John, Clovelly 1635 W
John, Goodleigh 1681 W
John, Clovelly 1693 A
Robert, Clovelly 1629 [W]
William, Clovelly 1690 W
Rugge Anthony, Chulmleigh 1598 [W]
Elizabeth, Chulmleigh 1626 [W]
Elizabeth, Northam 1758 W
Jacob, Northam 1755 W
Robert, South Molton 1575 W
Simon, Chulmleigh 1585 W
Rule, Rull
Elizabeth, West Anstey 1662 W
Hugh, Witheridge 1624 [W]
Rull John, Chittlehampton 1633 W
Lodovic, South Molton 1668 A and 1671 O
Peter, King's Nympton 1642 A
Thomas, Witheridge 1617 [W]
Rumbelow, Rombelew, Rombelewe, Rombelow, Rombelowe,
Rumbelewe
Rombelew ..., Pilton 1610 [W]
Rombelew Alice, Goodleigh 1589 W
George, North Molton 1684 A
Rombelow John, Chittlehampton 1606 W
John, North Molton 1741 W
John, King's Nympton 1764 A
John, North Molton 1848 W
Paul, Chulmleigh 1784 W
Rombelowe Peter, Chulmleigh 1567 W
Richard, South Molton 1696 W
Rombelewe Robert, Oakford 1593 W
Sarah, King's Nympton 1803 W
William, South Molton 1833 W
Rumsam, Rumsom, Rumson, Rumsum see Romsham
Rundle Joan, Newton St Petrock 1679 W
Russell, Russel
Elizabeth, Alwington 1622 [W]
Henry, Alwington 1590 [W]
Hugh, Parkham 1586 [W]
Jane, Bideford 1707 W
Jane, Bideford 1725 A
John, Yarnscombe 1592 [W]
John, Yarnscombe 1599 [W]
Morgan, Bideford 1706 W
Owen, Ilfracombe 1583 W
Paschal, Clovelly 1583 A
Patrick, Northam 1579 W
Russel Richard, Loxhore 1832 W
Susan, Woolfardisworthy 1741 W
Thomas, Northam 1784 W
Thomas, George Nympton 1830 W
William, Northam 1589 W
William, Bideford 1601 W
William, High Bray 1834 A
Ruston, Russon
Dorothy, Atherington 1625 [W]
Henry, Bideford 1584 W
Joan, Atherington 1624 [W]
John, Great Torrington 1588 A
Peter, Atherington 1625 [W] and 1627 O
Russon Roger, Chittlehampton 1669 A

Simon, Atherington 1598 [W]
William, South Molton 1569 W
William, Chittlehampton 1703 A
Ruthery Arthur, Northam 1707 A
Ryan Mary, North Tawton 1828 A
Ryce see Rice
Rychards see Richards
Rycke see Ricks
Rydd, Rydde see Rudd
Rydge see Ridge
Rydgeman see Ridgman
Rydlar see Ridler
Rydol see Riddle
Rykerd see Rickard
Rysdon see Risdon
Ryse see Rice
Rysedon see Risdon
Ryson Anthony, Parkham 1576 W

S .....y William, Trentishoe 1719 W
Sachwell John, West Anstey 1567 W
Sackery John, Barnstaple 1676 W
Sagarde see Saggarde
Sage, Saidge, Saige, Sayge, Seage
    Saige ..., High Bickington 1610 [W]
    Agnes, Fremington 1576 W
    Seage Agnes, Chulmleigh 1747 W
    Ambrose, Chulmleigh 1746 W
    Sayge Ann, Barnstaple 1636 W
    Sayge Augustine, North Molton 1628 [W]
    Seage Caleb, Great Torrington 1707 W
    Catherine, South Molton 1686 W
    Sayge Catherine, Chulmleigh 1627 [W]
    Clara, High Bickington 1661 W
    Deborah, High Bickington 1696 W
    Edmund, Chulmleigh 1700 W
    Edward, Little Torrington 1707 A
    Eleanor, King's Nympton 1678 W
    Sayge Elizabeth, High Bickington 1625 [W]
    Sayge Elizabeth, Barnstaple 1631 [W]
    Saidge Henry, Ashreigney 1607 [W]; forename blank in Ms;
        supplied from parish register
    Humphrey, Landcross 1721 A
    Joan, Burrington 1693 W
    Seage Joan, Littleham (near Bideford) 1693 W
    Joan, High Bickington 1746 W
    Saige John, George Nympton 1599 [W]
    Saige John, Chulmleigh 1644 W
    John, Ashreigney 1660 W
    John, King's Nympton 1679 W
    John, Chawleigh 1711 W
    John, Chittlehampton 1766 A
    Seage John, Barnstaple 1822 W
    John, High Bickington 1825 A to Rachel, widow
    Seage John, Langtree 1829 W
    Seage John, Bideford 1841 W
    John, Stoodleigh 1848 W
    Seage John, Atherington 1855 A
    Saige Margery, George Nympton 1597 [W]
    Seage Mary, Barnstaple 1822 A to William Locke of
        Goodleigh, brother
    Saidge Nicholas, Ashreigney 1615 [W]
    Saidge Philip, Ashreigney 1616 [W]
    Sayge Philip, Woolfardisworthy 1625 [W]
    Sayge Philip, High Bickington 1635 W
    Philip, High Bickington 1777 W
    Richard, Chittlehampton 1665 A
    Sayge Robert, Rose Ash 1640 A
    Sayge Roger, Barnstaple 1625 [W]
    Silvester, Northam 1703 A
    Sayge Thomas, Ashreigney 1591 [W]
    Sayge Thomas, North Molton 1624 [W]
    Sayge Thomas, Tawstock 1628 [W]
    Thomas, Ashreigney 1676 A
    William, Fremington 1563 W

William, Stoke Rivers 1582 W
William, Northam 1675 W
William, High Bickington 1769 A
William, High Bickington 1816 W
William, High Bickington 1832 W
Seage William, West Buckland 1836 W
Seage William, Bratton Fleming 1857 W
Saggarde, Sagarde
    John, Bideford 1611 [W]; forename blank in Ms; supplied
        from parish register
    Sagarde Robert, Abbotsham 1566 W
Saidge, Saige see Sage
Sailes Robert, Northam 1766 W
St. Hill Peter, Tawstock 1761 W
Salisbury, Salisbery, Sallsbury, Salsbury, Salusberie
    Sallsbury Griffith, Pilton 1620 [W]
    Joan, Barnstaple 1643 A
    Salsbury John, Barnstaple 1630 [W]
    Salisbery Jonas, Barnstaple 1610 [W]; forename blank in Ms;
        supplied from parish register
    Salisburie Maurice, Pilton 1615 [W]; forename blank in Ms;
        supplied from parish register
    Sallsbury Richard, Barnstaple 1620 [W]
    Salusburie Robert, Barnstaple 1585 W
    Salsbury Robert, Barnstaple 1639 A
    Sallsbury William, Buckland Brewer 1623 W
Salmon, Saloman
    Ann, Northam 1747 A
    Saloman Edmund, Great Torrington 1630 [W]
    Elizabeth, Ilfracombe, widow 1801 W
    James, Ilfracombe 1732 A
    Joseph, Ilfracombe, mariner 1804 W
    Robert, Ilfracombe 1778 W
    Thomas, Northam 1790 W and 1799 A
    Thomas, Barnstaple 1818 A to Elizabeth, widow
    Thomasine, Great Torrington 1595 [W]
Salsbury see Salisbury
Salter James, Weare Giffard 1569 W
    John, Instow 1746 W
Salterne, Saltern, Saltren
    Arthur, Bideford 1595 [W]
    George, Huntshaw 1624 [W]
    George, Woolfardisworthy 1698 A
    Grace, Bideford 1628 [W] and 1630 O
    Saltern Humphrey, Huntshaw 1836 W
    Joan, Huntshaw 1564 W
    Joan, Huntshaw 1594 [W]
    Joan, Abbotsham 1665 W
    Saltren Joan, Monkleigh 1783 W
    John, Bideford 1592 [W]
    John, Parkham 1606 W
    John, Huntshaw, snr. 1621 [W] and 1624 O
    John, Parkham 1666 A
    John, Woolfardisworthy 1687 A
    Saltern John, Monkleigh 1740 W
    Margaret, Woolfardisworthy 1685 A
    Oliver, Weare Giffard 1593 [W]
    Saltern Patience, Parkham 1670 [W]
    Richard, Bideford 1585 A
    Saltern Robert, ship *Augusta* 1746 A
    Saltren Roger, Bideford 1573 A, 1579 A and 1581 A account
    Saltren Stephen, Huntshaw 1581 A
    Thomas, Weare Giffard 1630 [W] and 1632 O
    Thomas, Weare Giffard, widower 1640 W
    Thomas, Parkham 1665 W
    Saltren Thomas, Woolfardisworthy 1677 W and 1684 W
    Thomas, Monkleigh 1690 A
    Thomas, Monkleigh 1700 W
    Saltern Thomas, Woolfardisworthy 1728 W
    Saltren Thomas, Parkham 1756 W
    Walter, Weare Giffard 1592 [W] and 1595 [W]
    Walter, Weare Giffard 1616 [W]
    Walter, Parkham 1633 W
Salusburie see Salisbury
Sames see Sams

Sampson, Samson, Sempson
..., Northam 1603 [W]
..., North Tawton 1607 [W]
 Abraham, North Tawton 1630 [W] (2)
 Alexander, George Nympton 1645 A
 David, Instow 1767 A
 Elizabeth, Witheridge 1682 W
 Elizabeth, Instow 1791 W
 George, George Nympton 1640 A
 Humphrey, North Tawton 1604 W
 Humphrey, Horwood 1624 [W]
 Jeremiah, Bideford 1709 A
 John, Witheridge 1630 [W]
 Samson John, Witheridge 1693 A
 John, North Tawton 1694 W
 John, North Tawton 1706 W
 John, Winkleigh 1736 A
 Samson John, Instow 1748 A
 Marcker, North Tawton 1600 W
 Sempson Margaret, Northam, widow 1612 [W]; forename
  blank in Ms; supplied from parish register
 Samson Mary, Northam 1705 W
 Mary, heretofore of Bondleigh, since of Broadwood Kelly, but
  late of Bideford 1834 A to William, widower
 Richard, Northam 1596 [W]
 Sempson Richard, Northam 1611 [W]; forename blank in Ms;
  supplied from parish register
 Samson Richard, Bideford 1745 A
 Richard, Fremington, yeoman 1797 W
 Richard, Chulmleigh 1815 W
 Sarah, Bideford 1713 W
 Thomas, North Tawton 1629 [W]
 Thomas, Instow 1770 W
 Samson Thomas, Fremington, mariner 1821 A to Mary,
  widow
 William, Fremington 1797 W
Sams, Sames
 Sames ..., Ilfracombe 1607 [W]
 Mary, Barnstaple 1710 A
Samson see Sampson
Sanders see Saunders
Sanderson Sarah, Northam 1823 W
Sandford Robert, Great Torrington 1848 W
Sandicke or Downeman William, West Down 1584 W
Sanger, Zanger
 ..., King's Nympton 1613 [W]
 Agnes, Meshaw 1685 W
 Alexander, Mariansleigh 1591 [W]
 Edward, Swimbridge 1847 W
 Elizabeth, Mariansleigh 1703 W
 Joan, Mariansleigh 1593 [W]
 John, Mariansleigh, snr. 1640 W
 John, Mariansleigh 1781 A
 John, Romansleigh 1826 W
 Jonathan, Mariansleigh 1686 W
 Zanger Jonathan, Romansleigh 1742 W
 Nicholas, Mariansleigh 1753 W
 Richard, Woolfardisworthy 1591 [W]
 Roger, Mariansleigh 1665 W
 Roger, Meshaw 1684 W
 Roger, Mariansleigh 1734 W
 Sarah, Mariansleigh 1669 W
 Zanger Susan, North Molton 1665 W
Sapledon or Stapledon Petronell, Hartland 1630 [W]
Sardles John, Mariansleigh, cordwainer 1799 W
 William, South Molton 1849 W
Sarell, Sarel, Sarele, Sarells, Sarrill
 Edward, Bideford, maltster 1810 W
 Sarells John, Bideford 1740 A
 Richard, Abbotsham 1629 [W]
 Sarel Robert, Georgeham, yeoman 1798 W
 Thomas, Barnstaple 1645 A
 Sarrill Thomas, Bideford 1685 W
 Sarele William, Bideford 1773 W
Satchfield Richard, Stoodleigh 1626 [W]
Saterleigh John, Molland 1591 [W]

Saul, Saule, Saull, Sawle
 Saule ..., Nymet Rowland 1600 A.
 Saule ..., Burrington 1614 [W]
 Saull Elizabeth, Eggesford 1812 W
 John, Ashreigney 1621 [W]
 Saule John, Burrington 1671 [W]
 Philip, Chawleigh 1636 A
 Richard, Molland 1622 [W]
 Thomas, North Tawton 1760 W
 Sawle William, Chittlehampton 1596 [W]
 Sawle William, Wembworthy 1606 W
 Saule William, Ashreigney 1608 [W]; forename blank in Ms;
  supplied from parish register
 William, Yarnscombe 1632 [W]
 Saull William, Eggesford 1794 W
Saunders, Sanders, Saunder
 ..., Meshaw 1601 A
 ..., Meshaw 1602 [W]
 Saunder ..., Northam 1603 [W]
 ..., Instow 1606 [W]
 ... 1703 [W]
 Sanders Abraham, Langtree 1847 W
 Saunder Agnes, Tawstock 1618 [W]
 Saunders alias Hill Agnes, Buckland Brewer 1707 A
 Ambrose, Bideford 1711 W
 Andrew, Pilton 1706 W
 Andrew, Wembworthy 1785 A
 Andrew, Chulmleigh 1833 W
 Ann, Chawleigh 1854 W
 Saunder Anthony, Fremington 1606 W
 Anthony, Buckland Brewer 1633 A
 Anthony, Chittlehampton 1725 A
 Anthony, Chulmleigh 1754 W
 Sanders Anthony, Chittlehampton 1768 A
 Anthony, Wembworthy, yeoman 1808 W
 Arthur, Chittlehampton 1723 W and 1725 A
 Arthur, Ashreigney 1817 A
 Saunder Arthur, Chittlehampton 1834 A to James, father
 Baldwin, Cruwys Morchard 1628 [W]
 Bartholomew, Meshaw 1682 A
 Charles, Great Torrington 1690 A
 Christopher, Hartland 1661 [W]
 Christopher, Tawstock 1667 W
 Christopher, Great Torrington 1706 O
 Sanders Daniel, Clovelly 1640 W
 Deborah, Hartland 1721 W
 Edmund, Knowstone 1769 A
 Edmund or Edward, Little Torrington 1840 W
 Saunder Edward, Bulkworthy 1593 [W]
 Edward, Northam 1728 W
 Edward, Tawstock 1732 A
 Edward, Chittlehampton, miller 1815 A (Ned) to Mary, widow
 Edward, Chittlehampton 1834 W
 Edward or Edmund, Little Torrington 1840 W
 Elizabeth, Barnstaple 1628 [W]
 Elizabeth, Chittlehampton 1679 W
 Elizabeth, Tawstock 1733 W
 Elizabeth, Chittlehampton 1751 A
 Elizabeth, Brendon 1778 W
 Elizabeth, Chittlehampton 1794 W, 1801 W (2), 1803 W and
  1805 A
 Sanders Elizabeth, Great Torrington, widow 1811 W
 Elizabeth, Beaford 1833 W
 Elizabeth, Chulmleigh 1839 W
 Elizabeth, Alverdiscott 1847 W
 Elizabeth, Great Torrington 1848 W
 Elizabeth, Woolfardisworthy 1848 W
 Elizabeth see also Hugh Prust
 Erasmus, Chulmleigh 1690 A
 Esther, Bideford 1700 W
 Frances, Tawstock 1677 W
 Frances, Little Torrington 1851 W
 Francis, Tawstock 1727 W
 Francis, Chittlehampton 1793 W
 Francis, Shebbear, yeoman 1797 A

Francis, Bideford 1801 W
Sanders Geoffrey, Chawleigh 1857 W
George, Bideford 1620 [W]
George, Lynton 1641 A
George, East Worlington 1685 W
George, Brendon 1753 W
George, Chittlehampton 1768 W
Saunder George, Chittlehampton 1784 W; 1811 2nd probate
George, Chittlehampton 1789 W
Saunder George, Chittlehampton 1850 W
Saunder Henry, Chittlehampton 1645 W
Saunder Hugh, Welcombe 1624 [W]
Hugh, Molland 1679 W
Hugh, Great Torrington 1696 A
Hugh, Meshaw 1710 W
Hugh, Yarnscombe 1710 W
Humphrey, Clovelly 1743 W
James, Clovelly 1630 [W]
James, East Down 1703 W
James, Weare Giffard 1727 A
Saunder James, Chittlehampton 1839 W
Sanders James, South Molton, glover 1845 A to James H.,
    fellmonger
Saunder James, Chittlehampton 1850 W
Jane, Great Torrington 1721 A
Saunder Joan, Woolfardisworthy 1590 [W]
Joan, Wembworthy 1790 W
Joan, Great Torrington 1815 W
Saunder John, Heanton Punchardon 1583 W
Saunder John, Chittlehampton 1587 A
Sander John, Fremington 1589 W
Saunder John, Hartland 1593 [W]
Saunder John, Petrockstowe 1593 [W]
Saunder John, Meshaw 1594 [W]
Saunder John, East Worlington 1596 [W]
John, Yarnscombe 1604 W
John, Tawstock 1608 [W]; forename blank in Ms; supplied
    from parish register
John, Bideford 1630 [W]
Saunder John, Woolfardisworthy (East or West), snr. 1632
    [W]
Saunder John, High Bickington 1635 W
John, Petrockstowe 1640 A
Saunder John, Clovelly 1644 A
John, Meshaw 1663 W
John, Shebbear 1671 A
John, Chittlehampton 1676 W
John, Burrington 1678 W
John, Warkleigh 1707 W
Saunder John, Chittlehampton 1708 W
John, Clovelly 1720 W
John, Wembworthy 1730 W
John, Chittlehampton 1731 W
John, Bideford 1761 A
John, Brendon 1761 W
John, Ilfracombe 1762 A
John, Chittlehampton 1772 W
John, Wembworthy 1781 W
John, South Molton 1784 W
John, Tawstock 1791 W
John, Filleigh, cooper 1806 A
John, Knowstone, yeoman 1807 A
John, Shebbear 1807 W
John, Bideford 1817 W
John, Chulmleigh 1824 W
John, Tawstock 1829 W
John, Fremington 1840 W
John, Parkham 1848 W
John, Woolfardisworthy, labourer 1848 A to William of
    Welcombe, brother
John, Beaford 1849 W
John, Loxhore, gentleman 1849 A to George, brother, dead his
    execs. Russell Marlyn Riccard and John Facey of
    Chittlehampton, gentlemen
John, Chawleigh 1850 W
Sanders John, Newton St Petrock 1854 W

Jonah, Yarnscombe 1662 A
Juliana, Langtree 1666 W
Luke, Bideford 1683 W
Saunder Margaret, Northam 1620 [W]
Margaret, Barnstaple 1694 A
Margaret, Bideford, widow 1799 A
Saunder Margery, Clovelly 1571 W
Martha, Weare Giffard 1698 W
Mary, Yarnscombe, snr. 1624 [W]
Mary, Bideford 1684 W
Mary, Molland 1691 A
Mary, Chittlehampton 1694 W
Mary, Northam 1747 W
Mary, North Molton 1786 W
Mary, Wembworthy 1790 A
Mary, Great Torrington 1815 W
Saunder Michael, North Molton 1637 A
Nicholas, Tawstock 1625 [W]
Nicholas, Bideford 1637 [W]
Sanders Nicholas, Buckland Brewer, innkeeper 1856 A to
    Mary, widow
Obedience, Instow 1670 A
Peter, Clovelly 1697 A
Peter, Clovelly 1766 W
Philip, Buckland Brewer 1816 W
Richard, Heanton Punchardon 1585 W
Richard, East Worlington 1631 [W]
Saunder Richard, Northam 1676 W
Richard, Weare Giffard 1677 A
Richard, Northam 1707 A
Richard, Weare Giffard 1709 A
Richard, Weare Giffard 1718 W
Richard, Wembworthy 1763 W
Richard, Roborough 1774 W
Sanders Richard, Langtree 1848 W
Saunder Robert, Great Torrington 1579 W
Robert, Coldridge 1623 [W]
Robert, Great Torrington 1628 [W]
Robert, Heanton Punchardon 1643 A
Robert, Great Torrington 1736 A
Robert, Beaford 1739 W
Robert, Chulmleigh 1761 A
Robert, Beaford 1793 W
Robert, Beaford, yeoman 1817 A to Elizabeth, widow
Robert, Winkleigh 1833 W
Robert, Great Torrington 1844 W
Sanders Robert, Langtree 1854 W
Roger, Monkleigh 1820 A to Mary, widow
Sanders Ruth, Kentisbury 1672 O
Saunder or Kinge Samson, Parkham 1571 W
Samuel, Abbotsham 1703 W
Samuel, Great Torrington 1717 A
Samuel, Parkham 1777 W
Samuel, Alverdiscott, yeoman 1820 A to William, brother
Sanders Samuel, Northam 1840 W
Sarah, Bideford, widow 1804 W
Sanders Sarah, Alverdiscott, sp. 1814 A to John, brother
Simon, Pilton 1693 W
Saunder Stephen, Fremington 1635 W
Susan, Great Torrington 1801 A
Susan, Alverdiscott 1847 W
Saunder Thomas, Clovelly 1568 W
Saunder Thomas, Monkleigh 1588 W
Saunder Thomas, Clovelly 1595 W
Saunder Thomas, Abbotsham 1597 [W]
Saunder Thomas, Bulkworthy 1615 [W]
Thomas, Dolton 1619 [W]
Thomas, Roborough 1619 [W]
Thomas, Barnstaple 1636 A
Thomas, Fremington 1682 W
Thomas, Buckland Brewer 1692 A
Sanders Thomas, East Worlington 1813 W
Sanders Thomas, Burrington 1825 W
Thomasine, Buckland Brewer, widow 1568 W
Unity, Marwood 1724 W

Urithe, Chulmleigh 1626 [W]
Walter, Great Torrington 1664 W
Walter, Tawstock 1684 A
Walter, Bideford 1740 A
Saunder William, Petrockstowe 1565 W
William, Woolfardisworthy 1577 W
William, Petrockstowe 1623 [W]
Saunder William, Hartland 1631 [W]
William, Instow 1637 A
William, Yarnscombe 1637 A
William, Wembworthy 1663 W
William, Meshaw 1679 A
William, Burrington 1690 W
William, Kentisbury 1694 W and 1698 A
William, West Worlington 1699 W
William, Beaford 1709 A
William, Burrington 1715 A
Sanders William, St Giles in the Wood 1775 W
William, Wembworthy 1788 W
William, Bideford, mariner 1800 W
William, Alverdiscott, yeoman 1805 W
William, Buckland Brewer, miller 1805 A
William, Wembworthy, labourer 1805 A
William, seaman of HMS *Bellona* 1809 A
William, Great Torrington 1836 W
Sanders William, Woolfardisworthy 1837 A to Elizabeth,
     widow
William, Newton Tracey 1852 W
Sanders William, Combe Martin, cordwainer 1856 A to
     Elizabeth Jones Sanders, widow
Savage John, Barnstaple 1625 [W] and 1626 O
Sawdon see Sowden
Sawle see Saul
Saws alias Sayer Rebecca, Northam 1724 A
Sawtell Robert, South Molton 1857 W
Sawyer Robert, Tawstock 1598 [W]
Sayer Joan, Tawstock 1591 [W]
John, Tawstock 1623 [W]
Mary, Tawstock 1627 [W]
Sayer alias Saws Rebecca, Northam 1724 A
Robert, Huntshaw 1643 A
Thomas, Tawstock 1636 W
Thomas, Northam 1705 W
Sayge see Sage
Sayward see Seaward
Scamp, Scam, Scampe, Skambe, Skame, Skampe
..., Hartland 1604 [W]
Scampe ..., Bideford 1607 [W]
Scampe ..., Mortehoe 1614 [W]
Abel, Burrington 1669 A
Agnes, Burrington 1668 W
Scampe Alice, Georgeham, widow 1614 [W]; forename blank
     in Ms; supplied from parish register
Skambe Andrew, Sheepwash 1630 [W]
Scampe Augustine, West Down 1627 [W]
Skampe Augustine, West Down 1638 W
Augustine, Heanton Punchardon 1698 W
Catherine, West Down 1714 W
Scambe Dionysia, Peters Marland 1622 [W]
Edward, Georgeham 1731 W
Elizabeth, Barnstaple 1670 W (2)
Scampe Florence, Mortehoe 1633 [W]
Scampe George, West Down 1622 [W]
George, East Down 1759 W
Henry, Petrockstowe 1663 W
Hugh, Northam 1737 A
Joan, Northam 1682 A
Joan Coats, Ilfracombe 1851 W
Scam John, Sheepwash 1597 [W]
Scampe John, Georgeham 1614 [W]; forename blank in Ms;
     supplied from parish register
Scampe John, Huish 1631 [W]
Scampe John, West Down, snr. 1634 A
John, Burrington 1661 A
John, Northam 1682 A
John, Great Torrington 1720 A

Scam John, Barnstaple 1721 W
John, Instow 1773 W
John, Instow 1826 W
Jonathan, Georgeham 1712 W
Lodovic, Northam 1662 A
Margaret, Instow, widow 1800 W
Scampe Marian, Barnstaple 1638 A
Skampe Mary, Georgeham 1625 [W]
Mary, Georgeham 1733 W
Scampe Peter, West Down 1610 [W]; forename blank in Ms;
     supplied from parish register
Scampe Peter, West Down 1632 [W]
Scampe Peter, West Down 1644 W
Peter, Pilton 1730 W
Peter, West Down 1738 A
Peter, Northam 1745 W
Peter, Pilton 1825 W
Peter, Barnstaple 1836 W
Philip, Ilfracombe 1784 W
Philip, West Down 1819 W
Scampe Richard, Bideford 1603 W
Scampe Richard, Georgeham 1619 [W]
Scampe Richard, Georgeham 1634 A
Richard, Georgeham 1685 A
Richard, Georgeham 1700 W
Robert, Georgeham, mason 1811 W
Robert, West Down 1856 A
Scampe Robert, Georgeham 1602 [W]; forename blank in Ms;
     supplied from parish register
Rose, Pilton 1668 W
Scampe Thomas, Georgeham 1571 W
Skame Thomas, Bideford 1580 W
Skampe Thomas, West Down 1585 W and 1586 A
Skampe Thomas, Georgeham 1598 [W]
Thomas, Ilfracombe 1824 W
Thomasine, Georgeham 1765 W
Scambe William, Hartland 1601 W
William, Marwood 1676 A
William, Merton 1677 W
Scampe William, Instow 1780 W
Scawen John, Bideford 1682 A
Sciance, Scyence
James, Barnstaple 1799 W
James, Barnstaple 1815 W
Scyence Nicholas, Barnstaple 1610 [W]; forename blank in
     Ms; supplied from parish register
Scibbowe see Skibbowe
Score, Scoare, Scure, Skear, Skeare, Skoare, Skore
Skear ..., Martinhoe 1604 O
Scoare Agnes, Lynton, widow 1611 [W]; forename blank in
     Ms; supplied from parish register
Scure Alice, Burrington 1586 W
Ann, Lynton 1645 A
Ann, Lynton 1685 W
Skore Bartholomew, Georgeham 1639 W
Catherine, Shirwell 1728 W
Edward, Pilton 1689 W
Edward, Shirwell 1710 W
Edward, Pilton 1734 W
Edward, Barnstaple 1744 W
Skore Elizabeth and Thomas, East Down 1597 [W]
George, Barnstaple 1741 W
Jane, Hartland 1723 W
Scoare Joan, Lynton, widow 1611 [W] "at Caffens" in register;
     forename blank in Ms; supplied from parish register
John, Brendon 1570 W
John, Lynton 1575 W
Skore John, Lynton 1582 W
Scoare John, Lynton 1590 [W]
Skeare John, Langtree 1592 [W]
Skore John, Martinhoe 1623 [W]
John, Martinhoe 1635 A and 1638 O
John, Hartland 1700 W
John, Parkham 1831 W
Peter, Parracombe 1716 W

Skear Richard, Martinhoe 1595 [W]
Scoare Richard, Lynton 1613 [W] "at Caffens" in register;
   forename blank in Ms; supplied from parish register
Richard, Barnstaple 1674 A
Score or Scow Richard, Fremington 1712 W
Skore Robert, Brendon 1585 W
Robert, Lynton 1640 W
Robert, Kentisbury 1729 W
Skoare Roger, Brendon 1584 W
Skoare Simon, Lynton 1584 W
Skore Thomas, Lynton 1580 W
Thomas, Martinhoe 1644 W
Thomas, Hartland 1731 W
Skore Thomas and Elizabeth, East Down 1597 [W]
Timothy, Parracombe 1678 W
William, Hartland 1723 A
William, Hartland 1841 A
Willmot, Pilton 1671 W
Scott, Scot, Scote, Scotte, Skot, Skott, Skotte
Abraham, High Bray 1644 [W]
Agnes, High Bray 1672 W
Alexander, High Bray 1696 W
Ann, West Buckland 1737 W
Ann, High Bickington 1763 W
Skotte Anthony, Frithelstock 1623 [W]
Baldwin, South Molton 1758 W
Skott Charity, High Bray 1624 [W]
Christian, Pilton 1790 W
Scott alias Chaple Christiana, Chittlehampton 1703 A
Daniel, High Bray 1755 W
Edward, Sheepwash 1640 A
Elizabeth, Goodleigh 1708 W
Elizabeth, South Molton 1767 W
Elizabeth, Barnstaple 1818 W
Frances, High Bray 1677 W
Scotte George, High Bray 1589 W
Gilbert, South Molton 1848 W
Hannah, Fremington 1754 W
Henry, Frithelstock 1616 [W]
James, High Bray 1670 A
James, High Bray 1687 W
James, Chittlehampton 1726 W
James, East Buckland 1733 W
James, South Molton 1758 W
James, Black Torrington 1858 W
Jane, High Bray 1693 W
Scotte Joan, Frithelstock 1597 [W]
Joan, High Bray 1637 W
Joan, High Bray 1735 A
Skott John, High Bray 1625 [W], 1626 [W] and 1627 O
Skott John, High Bray 1628 [W]
John, Frithelstock, snr. 1639 W
John, Bideford 1668 A
John, Chittlehampton 1670 W
John, Tawstock 1670 W
John, South Molton 1681 W
John, Georgeham 1684 W
John, Langtree 1684 W
John, West Down 1704 W
John, High Bray 1716 W
John, High Bray 1731 A and 1732 A
John, Georgeham 1745 W
John, Fremington 1747 W
John, Barnstaple 1766 W
Joseph, Sheepwash 1722 A
Leonard, Petrockstowe 1611 [W]; forename blank in Ms;
   supplied from parish register
Mary, South Molton, widow 1803 W
Mary, South Molton 1817 W
Mary, Barnstaple 1835 A
Skott Mathew, Frithelstock 1628 [W]
Nathaniel, Frithelstock 1596 [W]
Philip, South Molton 1600 W
Philip, Braunton 1813 W
Richard, Fremington 1598 [W]

Scotte Richard, Tawstock 1611 [W]; forename blank in Ms;
   supplied from parish register
Richard, Newton Tracey 1640 W
Richard, High Bray 1672 A
Richard, George Nympton 1724 A
Skot Robert, Buckland Filleigh 1567 W
Roger, High Bray 1690 W
Samuel, Alverdiscott 1693 W
Septimus, Bideford, gentleman 1850 A to Henry of Oldham,
   gentleman, nephew
Simon, Chittlehampton 1681 A
Scote Thomas, Brendon 1565 W
Thomas, High Bray 1630 [W]
Thomas, Tawstock 1633 W
Thomas, Bideford 1695 W
Thomas, South Molton 1708 W
Thomas, South Molton 1750 A
Thomas, High Bickington 1763 W
Thomas, Chittlehampton 1776 W
Thomas, South Molton 1792 W
Skotte William, High Bray 1567 W
Scot William, Ashreigney 1588 W
William, High Bray 1600 W and 1601 W
William, Birchill, Langtree 1638 W
William, West Buckland 1737 W
William, South Molton 1750 W
William, High Bickington 1781 W
William, South Molton, innholder 1803 W
William, Mariansleigh 1824 W
William, Roborough 1833 W
Scow or Score Richard, Fremington 1712 W
Screech, Scriche, Skreech
Agnes, Barnstaple 1747 W
John, Bideford 1688 W
Skreech Mary, Bideford 1688 A
Scriche Maud, Chawleigh, widow 1569 W
Screene John, Shirwell 1686 A
Scriche see Screech
Scriggins, Scriggin, Scriggon, Scriggons, Scroggen, Scroggon,
   Skriggin, Skriggon, Skrygon
Skrygon Elizabeth, Great Torrington 1638 W
Scriggin Elizabeth, Dolton 1699 W
Skrygon George, Great Torrington 1625 [W]
George, Great Torrington 1721 W
Skriggin Henry Cottey, Merton 1693 W
Jeremiah, Great Torrington 1741 A
Skrygon John, Dolton, snr. 1634 W
John, Merton 1713 W
Skrygon Lawrence, Great Torrington 1625 [W]
Scriggon Philip, Merton 1690 A
Skriggon Philip, Beaford 1679 W
Scriggon Richard, Merton 1690 W
Scriggon Robert, Dolton 1686 W
Scriggons Robert, Great Torrington 1700 W
Skrygon Simon, Dolton 1637 W
Scroggen Thomas, Beaford 1682 W
Scroggon Thomas, Beaford 1702 W
Skriggon William, Clovelly 1669 W
William, Merton 1708 W
William, Merton, yeoman 1801 W
Scudamore Mary, Monkleigh 1609 [W] "Mrs" in register;
   forename blank in Ms; supplied from parish register
Scure see Score
Scyence see Sciance
Scynner see Skinner
Seacombe see Secombe
Seage see Sage
Seager, Seagar, Segar, Zeagar, Zegar
Zeagar Christian, Barnstaple 1676 W
Seagar Christiana, Barnstaple 1676 W
Segar Robert, Clannaborough 1625 [W]
Zegar Walter, St Giles in the Wood 1576 W
William, Woolfardisworthy 1598 [W]
Seale, Seall see Zeale

Sealy, Ceely, Seely
  Ceely Ann, Wembworthy 1679 W
  Ceely Ann, Wembworthy 1742 [W]
  Armiger, Barnstaple 1827 A to Mary, widow
  Seely Arthur, Molland 1682 W
  William, Molland 1713 A
Seaman, Seyman
  Anthony, Knowstone 1602 W
  Henry, Knowstone 1617 [W]
  Seyman or Zeman John, Knowstone 1573 W
  John, South Molton 1644 A
  Richard, Knowstone 1637 A
  Robert, Knowstone 1583 W
  Robert, Knowstone 1698 A
Searle, Searell, Searells, Searl, Searles, Serles
  ..., Rackenford 1604 [W]
  ..., Chawleigh 1610 [W]
  ..., North Tawton 1612 [W]
  Searles Ann, Winkleigh 1823 W
  Anthony, Chawleigh 1590 [W] and 1591 A account
  Searells Bartholomew, Barnstaple 1639 A
  Catherine, Burrington 1743 W
  Christiana, Wembworthy 1681 W
  Edward, Lapford 1781 W
  George, Chawleigh 1675 A
  Henry, Berrynarbor 1667 A
  Searles Henry, South Molton 1801 W
  Humphrey, Chawleigh 1634 W
  Searell Joan, Coldridge 1620 [W]
  Searell Joan, Chawleigh 1627 [W]
  Searell Joan, Chulmleigh 1628 [W]
  Searles Joan, Witheridge 1749 W
  Searles John, Zeal Monachorum 1664 W
  John, Chawleigh 1692 A
  John, Burrington 1728 W
  Serle John, South Molton 1732 A
  Searl John, Coldridge 1771 W
  John, Chittlehampton 1803 W*
  Margaret, Coldridge 1640 W
  Margaret, Chulmleigh 1667 W
  Margaret, Lapford 1681 A
  Searls Margaret, South Molton 1807 W
  Mary, Chulmleigh 1705 A
  Searle alias Delbridg Mary, Knowstone 1716 [W]
  Searell Nicholas, Lapford 1635 W
  Philip, Chulmleigh 1662 A
  Philip, Chulmleigh 1695 A
  Philip, Chawleigh 1700 A
  Philip, Chawleigh 1759 A
  Richard, Combe Martin 1633 A
  Searle alias Laurence Richard, Bideford 1661 A
  Richard, Lapford 1664 A
  Richard, Chittlehampton 1765 W
  Richard, Chittlehampton, yeoman 1798 A
  Serles Samuel, South Molton 1816 W
  Searles Sarah, Northam 1753 W
  Searell Theobald, King's Nympton 1625 [W]
  Thomas, Lapford 1598 [W]
  Thomas, Great Torrington 1615 [W]
  Searell Thomas, Lapford 1630 [W]
  Thomas, Wembworthy 1679 W
  Walter, Chawleigh 1606 W
  William, Rackenford 1597 [W]
  William, Combe Martin 1696 W
  William, Wembworthy 1719 W
Searson Jane, Great Torrington 1819 W
Seaward, Sayward, Seward, Seyward
  Sayward ..., Alwington 1609 [W]
  Benjamin, Barnstaple 1799 W
  Elizabeth, Barnstaple, widow 1817 A to John Berry of
    Shoreditch, Middlesex, gentleman, nephew
  Seyward John, King's Nympton 1626 [W]
  Seward Richard, Bideford 1615 [W]
  Thomas, Bow 1645 W
  Thomas, North Tawton 1774 W

  Thomas, North Tawton, yeoman 1811 A
Seccombe, Seacombe, Seckomb, Sercombe
  Abraham, Northam 1625 [W]
  Seacombe Agnes, Northam 1635 W
  Seckomb John, Shebbear 1608 [W]; forename blank in Ms;
    supplied from parish register
  John, Littleham (near Bideford) 1643 W
  Samuel, Chawleigh 1765 A
  Sercombe William, Hartland 1588 W
Seely see Sealy
Segar see Seager
Seldon, Zeldon
  Zeldon Alexander, Witheridge 1715 W
  Cecilia, Barnstaple 1692 A
  Charles, Bondleigh, yeoman 1802 W
  Dorothy, Monkleigh 1585 A
  Edward, Barnstaple 1681 A
  Joan, Bondleigh 1818 W
  John, Bondleigh 1761 A
  John, Bondleigh, yeoman 1810 A
  John, Bondleigh 1840 W
  Joseph, Barnstaple 1690 A
  Raymond, Frithelstock 1782 W
  Raymond, Frithelstock, jnr. 1827 A to Elizabeth, widow
  Raymond, Frithelstock 1840 W
  Richard, Pilton 1643 W
  Richard, Pilton 1664 A
  Richard, Bondleigh, yeoman 1810 W
  Robert, Buckland Brewer 1837 W
  Samuel, Buckland Brewer, yeoman 1852 A to William
  Sarah, Barnstaple 1707 A
  Thomas, Puddington 1812 W
  William, Meeth 1771 W
  William, Goodleigh 1829 W
Sellake see Sellick
Seller, Sellar
  Sellar ..., Horwood 1610 [W]
  Sellar Alice, Horwood 1615 [W]
  Baldwin, Monkleigh 1566 W
  Elizabeth, Parkham 1573 W
  Joan, Alwington, widow 1589 W
  Joan, Monkleigh 1599 [W]
  Joan, Frithelstock 1603 W
  John, Great Torrington 1622 [W] and 1623 O
  John, Frithelstock 1628 [W]
  John, Frithelstock 1639 W
  John, Alwington 1641 W
  John, Instow 1733 W
  Margaret, Tawstock 1672 A
  Richard, Bideford 1589 W
  Sellar Robert, Barnstaple 1617 [W]
  Sellar Thomas, Bideford 1608 [W]; forename blank in Ms;
    supplied from parish register
  William, Frithelstock 1580 W
Sellick, Sellake
  Agnes, Combe Martin 1715 W
  George Henry see Grace Rowe
  Sellake John, Chulmleigh 1574 A
  Sellake John, Cruwys Morchard 1587 W
  Thomas, Barnstaple 1837 W
  Sellake William, East Worlington 1593 [W]
  William, Combe Martin 1706 W
  see also Zellake
Sellivant see Sullivan
Selly, Selley, Sellie, Selye
  ..., Molland 1616 [W]
  Selley Agnes, Molland 1694 W
  Selley Agnes, Tawstock 1753 W
  Alice, Mariansleigh 1738 W
  Amos, King's Nympton 1778 A
  Selley Christopher, Warkleigh 1758 W
  Selley Edward, Tawstock 1751 W
  Selley George, Washford Pyne 1837 W
  Hugh, Molland 1639 W
  Hugh, Molland 1724 A

Selley Hugh, Chittlehampton 1833 A to Hugh, son
Selye Jenny, Abbotsham, widow 1564 W
   Joan, East Anstey 1619 [W]
Sellie John, Abbotsham 1588 W
   John, Chulmleigh 1603 W
   John, Abbotsham 1622 [W]
   John, Abbotsham 1661 A
   John, Knowstone 1690 W
   Martha, Romansleigh 1763 A
   Martin, Molland 1664 W
   Meliora, Warkleigh 1638 A
   Raymond, Rackenford 1625 [W]
   Richard, Abbotsham 1627 [W]
   Robert, Knowstone 1683 A
   Robert, North Molton 1724 A
   Sellie Thomas, Countisbury 1580 W
   Thomas, Knowstone 1695 W
   William, Roborough 1707 W
   William, Mariansleigh 1769 A
   Willmot, Abbotsham 1596 [W] (2)
Selman Lawrence, Witheridge 1594 [W]
   Richard, Witheridge 1616 [W]
Selye see Selly
Sempson see Sampson
Sennett, Semett
   Semett George, Atherington 1726 A
   Jane, Bideford 1748 W
Sequence Alice, Georgeham, widow 1568 W
   Alice, Barnstaple 1572 W
Sergeant, Serjeant
   Honor see Joseph Veale Dark
   Serjeant John, Buckland Filleigh 1723 W
   John, Little Torrington 1783 W
Sercombe see Secombe
Serjeant see Sergeant
Serle, Serles see Searle
Semett see Sennett
Setter Ann, South Molton 1740 W
   Setter alias Rooper Bartholomew, Chittlehampton 1588 A
   Elizabeth, Ilfracombe 1800 W
   William, ship *Crown* 1749 A
Seward see Seaward
Sexon see Shaxtona
Seyman see Seaman
Seyward see Seaward
Shabbrooke, Shabrooke see Shambrooke
Shadwick, Shaddock
   Henry, Hartland 1845 A
   Shaddock Thomas, Newton Tracey 1779 A
Shambrooke, Shabbrooke, Shabrooke
   Shabbrooke ..., Coldridge 1611 [W]
   Shabbrooke Humphrey, Puddington 1661 W
   Shabrooke James, Chittlehampton 1734 W
   Michael, Ilfracombe 1768 W
   Shabbrooke Nicholas, Coldridge 1635 W
   Thomas, Ilfracombe 1743 A
Shancke, Shanke
   Edward, Yarnscombe 1623 [W]
   Joan, Barnstaple 1591 [W]
   Joan, Parkham 1597 [W]
   John, Westleigh 1594 [W]
   Rebecca, Yarnscombe 1730 W
   Stephen, Yarnscombe 1687 A
   Walter, Fremington 1565 W
   Shanke Stephen, Yarnscombe 1687 A
Shapcott, Shapcote, Shepcott
   Shepcott ..., Knowstone 1611 [W] (2)
   Alexander, Oakford 1639 W
   Alice, South Molton 1796 W
   Andrew, West Anstey 1676 W
   Edward, Molland 1748 W
   Edward, Molland 1776 W
   Elizabeth, King's Nympton 1848 W
   George, Cruwys Morchard 1672 W
   Grace, Barnstaple 1830 W

   Henry, Knowstone 1624 [W]
   Henry, South Molton 1790 W
   Shepcott Joan, Cruwys Morchard, widow 1607 [W]; forename
     blank in Ms; supplied from parish register
   Joan, Molland 1739 A
   John, Molland, woolcomber 1797 A
   Magdalen, Cruwys Morchard 1691 A
   Margaret, West Anstey 1668 W
   Philip, Knowstone 1624 [W]
   Shepcott Robert, Cruwys Morchard 1602 W
   Shepcott Robert, West Anstey 1602 W
   Samuel, Witheridge 1662 W
   Sarah, Molland, widow 1806 W
   Shepcott William, Molland 1620 [W]
   William, Knowstone 1624 [W]
   Shapcote William, Molland 1714 A
   William, Barnstaple, shopkeeper 1815 A to Grace, widow
   William, King's Nympton, mason 1844 A to Betsy, daughter
   William, Bishop's Nympton 1855 W
Shapland, Shaplon, Shaplond, Shopland
   ..., Stoke Rivers 1600 A
   ..., Stoke Rivers 1607 [W] (2)
   ..., West Buckland 1607 [W]
   Shapland alias Smyth ... 1609 [W]
   ..., North Molton 1612 [W]
   Abel, Chulmleigh 1740 W
   Benedict, Chulmleigh 1775 W
   Charity, King's Nympton 1840 W
   Christopher, North Molton 1615 [W]; forename blank in Ms;
     supplied from parish register
   Christopher, North Molton 1626 [W] and 1628 [W]
   Christopher, North Molton 1679 A (2)
   Christopher, North Molton 1719 W
   Christopher, Goodleigh 1759 W
   Christopher, North Molton 1760 W
   Christopher, North Molton 1776 W
   Christopher, George Nympton, yeoman 1802 W
   Christopher, North Molton 1804 A
   Christopher, Goodleigh 1812 W
   Christopher, George Nympton 1825 W second probate
   Christopher, North Molton 1841 A
   Christopher, North Molton 1845 A to Margaret Buckingham
     of West Buckland, Wilmott of North Molton and Charity of
     Bishop's Nympton, sisters
   Elizabeth, North Molton 1682 W
   Elizabeth, Georgeham 1851 W
   George, North Molton 1612 [W]; forename blank in Ms;
     supplied from parish register
   George, Burrington 1624 [W]
   George, North Molton 1667 W
   George, North Molton, snr. 1703 W
   George, North Molton 1732 A
   George, North Molton 1778 W, 1780 W and 1781 W
   George, Tawstock 1784 W
   George, North Molton, yeoman 1817 A to Richard, son
   George, King's Nympton 1824 W
   George, North Molton 1833 W
   Shopland George 1836 A
   George, North Molton 1843 A
   Grace, North Molton 1636 W
   Grace, Barnstaple 1796 W
   Grace, Fremington 1828 W
   Grace, South Molton 1837 W
   Shopland Henry, Tawstock, yeoman 1799 W
   Hugh, Twitchen 1753 W
   Hugh, Charles 1778 W
   Hugh, Twitchen 1814 W
   Shopland Jane, Tawstock 1774 A
   Jane, Tawstock 1827 W
   Joan, Barnstaple, widow 1644 W
   Joan, North Molton 1682 A
   Joan, Northam 1753 W
   Joan, Charles 1781 W
   John, Burrington 1590 [W]
   Shopland John, North Molton 1596 [W]

John, St Giles in the Wood 1620 [W]
John, South Molton 1637 W
Shopland John, Bratton Fleming 1641 W
John, North Molton 1665 W
John, West Buckland 1698 W
John, Burrington, jnr. 1704 A
John, North Molton 1736 W and 1740 W
John, Bideford 1746 W
John, Bratton Fleming 1770 W
John, South Molton 1775 W
Shaplon John, Buckland Brewer 1786 W
John, Tawstock, yeoman 1801 A
John, Rose Ash 1804 A
John, Charles, yeoman 1809 W
John, Chittlehampton 1812 A to Mary, widow
John, North Molton 1817 W
John, South Molton 1824 W
John, Tawstock 1831 A to Joanna, widow
Shopland John, Wembworthy 1832 W
Shopland John, Barnstaple 1834 W
Shopland John, Bideford 1836 W
John, Goodleigh 1845 W
Shopland John, Bideford 1849 W
Joseph, North Molton 1754 W
Joseph, King's Nympton 1829 W
Joseph, King's Nympton 1852 W
Julian, Bratton Fleming 1643 W
Mary, North Molton 1641 W
Mary, South Molton 1757 A
Mary, George Nympton 1816 W
Shopland Mary, Wembworthy 1836 W
Mary, Fremington 1837 A
Mary wife of George see Charles Davey Purchase
Michael, Twitchen, yeoman 1807 A
Nicholas, North Molton 1722 W
Nicholas, North Molton 1737 A
Nicholas, Twitchen 1773 A
Philip, North Molton 1663 W
Richard, North Molton 1577 W and 1585 W
Richard, Burrington 1644 W
Richard, North Molton 1762 W
Richard, North Molton 1852 W
Robert, North Molton 1572 W
Shaplond Robert, West Buckland 1575 W and A
Roger, Burrington 1671 A
Simon, North Molton 1638 W
Sybil, North Molton 1641 W
Thomas, Frithelstock 1591 [W]
Thomas, Burrington 1626 [W]
Thomas, South Molton 1631 [W]
Thomas, North Molton 1635 A
William, Bratton Fleming 1616 [W]
William, North Molton 1623 [W] and 1631 [W]
Shopland William, East Buckland 1709 A
William, North Molton 1744 W
William, North Molton 1759 W
William, East Buckland 1764 A
William, High Bray, yeoman 1805 W
William, Barnstaple 1820 W
William, South Molton, maltster 1822 A to Elizabeth, widow
William, Twitchen, yeoman 1826 A to Winifred, widow
William, Tawstock, labourer 1842 A to Sarah, widow
William, Georgeham 1848 W
William, North Molton 1848 W
William, Barnstaple, baker 1856 A to Frances, widow
Shapley, Shaplegh, Shapleigh, Shaply
Agnes, Clovelly 1590 [W]
Grace, Barnstaple 1705 W
James, Clovelly 1636 W
Shaply James, Parkham 1700 W
James, Bideford 1729 W
Joan and John, Hartland 1598 [W]
John, Clovelly 1596 [W]
John, Parkham 1684 W
John, Clovelly 1707 W

John, Parkham 1732 W
John, Bideford 1768 W
John, Bideford 1786 W and 1789 W
John and Joan, Hartland 1598 [W]
Joseph, Pilton 1643 A
Mary, Bideford 1740 W
Nicholas, Clovelly 1667 W
Shapleigh Robert, Clovelly 1690 W
Thomas, Welcombe 1601 W
Thomas, Bideford 1708 W
Shaplegh William, Bideford 1588 W
William, Clovelly 1625 [W]
William, Northam 1706 W
William, Bideford 1742 W
Shaplon, Shaplond see Shapland
Shaply see Sharpley
Shappen see Shapton
Shapster, Shapter
Agnes, Northam 1628 [W]
Christopher, Northam 1640 A
Shapter alias Cutler John, Barnstaple 1568 W
Shapter John, Highampton 1589 A
Shapton, Shappen
Shappen ..., South Molton 1613 [W]
..., Great Torrington 1614 [W]
Bartholomew, Bideford 1690 W
Edward, Satterleigh 1622 [W]
Elizabeth, Chittlehampton 1631 [W]
Elizabeth, Buckland Brewer 1852 W
Joan, South Molton 1644 A
John, South Molton 1580 W
John, South Molton 1643 A
John, Frithelstock 1749 W
Shapton or Shaxton Philip, Chawleigh 1622 [W]
Richard, Satterleigh 1629 [W]
Robert, South Molton 1606 W
Samuel, Buckland Brewer 1825 W
Sarah, Bideford 1769 W
Shapton or Shaxton Simon, North Tawton 1635 W
Susan, Buckland Brewer 1790 W
Thomas, Chittlehampton 1603 W
Walter, South Molton 1586 W
William, Chittlehampton 1630 [W]
William, North Molton 1633 W
William, South Molton 1745 W
    see also Shaxton
Sharland, Sharlande
Sharlande Edward, Instow 1617 [W]
Edward, Witheridge 1770 W
Elizabeth, Huntshaw 1685 A
George, South Molton 1676 W
George, Fremington 1729 W
George, Cruwys Morchard 1832 W
Henry, Shirwell 1685 W
Joan, Chawleigh 1731 A
John, Shirwell 1613 [W]; forename blank in Ms; supplied
    from parish register
John, Fremington 1680 A
John, Marwood 1729 W
John, Chulmleigh 1798 A
John, Marwood 1805 W
John, Barnstaple, carpenter 1809 W; re-proved 4 May 1812
John, Pilton 1837 W
Mary, South Molton 1692 W
Richard, Lapford 1741 W
Sarah, Barnstaple 1840 W
Thomas, Shirwell 1665 W
William, Ashford 1789 W
William, Ashford, yeoman 1798 W
    see also Shorland
Sharles William, Barnstaple 1623 [W]
Sharman see Sherman
Sharpsheir ..., South Molton 1613 [W]
Sharsell Mary, Great Torrington 1737 W
Richard, Barnstaple 1586 W

Stephen, Merton 1729 W
Stephen, Bideford 1733 W
Shastridge, Shestruge
    Shestruge Geoffrey, High Bickington 1563 W
    Richard, High Bickington 1586 W
Shatoke see Shattick
Shatt, Shett
    Shett Elizabeth, Chawleigh 1712 A
    Francis, Ashreigney 1755 W
Shattick, Shatoke, Shatticke
    Shatoke Henry, North Molton 1566 W
    Shatticke Joan, Pilton, widow 1640 A
    Shatticke Thomas, North Molton 1598 [W]
    Thomas, North Molton 1612 [W]; forename blank in Ms;
      supplied from parish register
Shaxton, Sexon, Shaxon, Shaxsen, Shaxson, Shaxston
    ..., Filleigh 1605 [W]
    ..., Coldridge 1614 [W]
    Shaxston Francis, Dolton 1682 W
    Francis, Northam 1754 A.
    Shaxon Francis, Northam, yeoman 1809 A
    Henry, Nymet Rowland 1705 W
    Joan, Coldridge 1605 W
    Shaxsen John, North Tawton 1571 W
    John, Lapford 1641 W
    John, Northam 1762 W
    Shaxson John, Northam 1771 W
    Margaret, Northam 1756 W
    Martha, Bideford 1785 W
    Shaxton or Shapton Philip, Chawleigh 1622 [W]
    Richard, Coldridge 1596 [W]
    Richard, Lapford 1643 W
    Richard, Burrington 1712 A
    Richard, Bideford 1725 W
    Richard, Bideford 1745 A
    Shaxton or Shapton Simon, North Tawton 1635 W
    Shaxson Susan, Northam 1789 A
    Shaxsen Thomas, North Tawton 1587 W
    Shaxon Thomas, Northam 1784 W
    Shaxson Thomas, Northam 1834 W
    Sexon Thomas, Landkey 1854 W
    William, Nymet Rowland 1672 A
    William, Merton 1744 W
    see also Shapton
Sheane, Shenne
    John, Clovelly 1598 [W]
    Shenne or Sherme Simon, Abbotsham 1686 W
Shearme see Sherme
Shear see Sheere
Shearland Gabriel, Bideford 1588 W
    Simon, Goodleigh 1587 W
Shears see Sheere
Shebbear, Shebbeare, Shebber, Shebbere, Shebeare
    ..., Abbotsham 1606 [W], 1607 [W], 1608 [W] &1611 [W]
    Agnes, Abbotsham 1640 W
    Shebbeare Agnes, Abbotsham 1695 W
    Ann, Abbotsham 1738 A
    Shebbeare Elizabeth, Abbotsham 1661 W
    Elizabeth, Witheridge 1721 W
    Henry, Northam 1606 W
    John, Buckland Brewer 1599 [W]
    John, Northam, jnr. 1622 [W]
    John, Northam 1637 O
    John, Northam 1638 W
    Shebbeare John, Abbotsham 1687 A
    Shebber John, Abbotsham 1724 W
    Mary, Littleham (near Bideford) 1643 W
    Shebbeare Mathew, Abbotsham 1701 W
    Phillippa, Abbotsham 1641 W
    Richard, Abbotsham 1625 [W]
    Shebber Robert, Abbotsham 1589 W
    Robert, Abbotsham 1630 [W]
    Shebeare Samuel, Abbotsham 1746 A
    Shebbere Thomas, Abbotsham 1575 W
    Shebbeare Thomas, Abbotsham 1624 [W]

Shebbeare Thomas, Abbotsham 1690 W
Thomasine, Abbotsham 1597 [W]
Shebbeare William, Abbotsham 1666 W and 1669 W
William, Abbotsham 1677 W
Shebbeare William, Abbotsham 1687 A
Shebbeare William, Abbotsham 1703 W
Shebbrocke see Shobrooke
Shebear see Shebbear
Shebrooke see Shobrooke
Sheere, Shear, Shears, Sheer
    Christopher, Ashreigney 1786 W
    Christopher, Huish 1820 W
    George, ship *Straford* 1749 W
    Grace, East Putford 1694 A
    Sheer James, Buckland Brewer 1756 A
    Shears John, Petrockstowe 1705 A
    John, Beaford 1839 W; A dbn 1843
    Richard, Bideford 1643 A
    Samuel, Ilfracombe 1727 A
    Shear William, Hartland 1670 W
    William, Ashreigney 1713 W
    Shears William, Ashreigney, snr. 1785 W
    William, Beaford 1788 W
    William, Beaford, yeoman 1802 A
    Willmot, Ashreigney 1770 A
Sheet Martha see Sarah Reed
Shelly Richard, Abbotsham 1661 W
Shelston Richard, Coldridge 1660 W
    Robert, Winkleigh 1690 W
Shenne see Sheane
Shepande see Shepherd
Shepcott see Shapcott
Shepherd, Shepande, Sheperd, Shepheard, Sheppard, Sheppeard,
    Shepyeard
    Shepyeard ..., Martinhoe 1613 [W]
    Shepheard alias Hooper ..., West Down 1690 A
    Shepyeard Alexander, Ilfracombe 1605 [W]; forename blank
      in Ms; supplied from parish register
    Shepheard Ann, Pilton 1619 [W]
    Shepheard Anthony, Merton 1670 A
    Sheppeard Bartholomew, Mortehoe 1632 [W]
    Sheppeard Caleb, Barnstaple 1638 A
    Sheppeard Christopher, Martinhoe 1576 W
    Sheppeard Daniel, Mortehoe 1635 W
    Shepheard Digory, Hartland 1666 W
    Shepheard Edward, Barnstaple 1666 [W]
    Shepande Elizabeth, Iddesleigh 1581 W
    Shepheard Elizabeth, Hartland 1662 W
    Sheppard Elizabeth, Great Torrington 1854 W
    Shepyeard Henry, Pilton 1610 [W]; forename blank in Ms;
      supplied from parish register
    Shepheard Humphrey, Merton 1665 W
    Shepheard Isott, Petrockstowe 1672 W
    Shepheard James, Chulmleigh, jnr. 1703 A
    Shepheard James, Westleigh 1705 A
    James, Westleigh 1712 A
    James, Chulmleigh 1713 W
    James, Barnstaple 1733 W
    Shepheard John, West Down 1598 [W]
    Shepheard John, West Down 1644 W
    Shepheard alias Hooper John, Instow 1663 W
    Shepheard John, Barnstaple 1693 A
    Sheperd John, mariner 1741 W
    Sheppard John, Great Torrington 1822 W
    John, Great Torrington 1830 W
    Shephard Martha, Great Torrington 1802 A
    Mary, Bideford 1776 W
    Shephard Mary, Barnstaple 1782 W
    Shepyeard Nicholas, Tawstock 1615 [W]
    Nicholas, Barnstaple 1775 W
    Shephard Nicholas, Barnstaple, gentleman 1806 W
    Sheppard Ralph, Welcombe 1591 [W]
    Sheppeard Richard, Mortehoe 1637 A
    Sheppeard Richard, Mortehoe 1640 W and O
    Shepherd alias Hooper Richard, West Down 1811 W

Sheppeard Robert, Martinhoe 1640 W
Shepheard alias Hooper Roger, Instow 1703 A
Shephard Sarah, Barnstaple 1816 W
Shepperd Thomas, Pilton 1571 W
Shepperd Thomas, Yarnscombe 1577 W
Shepyeard Thomas, Burrington 1617 [W]
Shepheard Thomas, Hartland 1646 A
Shepperd Thomas, Abbotsham 1855 W
Shepheard William, Pilton 1596 [W]
William, Parkham 1825 W
William, Bideford 1856 W
Sherbrooke, Sherbruck
Ann, Great Torrington 1771 W
John, Cruwys Morchard 1766 A
Sherbruck Thomas, Heanton Punchardon 1772 W
Sherland, Sherlande, Sherlond
..., South Molton 1609 [W] and O
Sherlande ..., Instow 1610 [W]
Alice, South Molton 1631 [W]
Bartholomew, Goodleigh 1633 [W] and O
Elizabeth, South Molton 1670 A
Gine, Ashford 1627 [W]
Sherlond John, Shirwell 1572 W
Philpott, Ashford 1663 W
Richard, Shirwell 1627 [W]
Robert, Ashford 1625 [W]
Thomas, South Molton 1606 W
Thomas, Huntshaw, snr. 1671 W
Sherlande William, Fremington 1614 [W]; forename blank in
    Ms; supplied from parish register
Sherlond Willmot, Tawstock, widow 1568 W
Sherman, Sharman
Catherine, Westleigh 1732 W
Elizabeth, Barnstaple 1623 [W]
George, Westleigh 1718 W
John, Fremington 1629 [W]
Sharman John, Northam 1676 A dbn
Leonard, Bideford 1605 W
Robert, Fremington 1623 [W]
Ruth, Littleham (near Bideford) 1693 W
Simon, Fremington 1627 [W] and 1628 [W]
Thomas, Littleham (near Bideford) 1686 A
Thomasine, Bideford 1619 [W]
Sherman alias Braunton Willmot, Northam 1645 W
Willmot, Fremington 1687 W
Sherme, Shearme, Sherm, Sherne
Sherm Charles, Woolfardisworthy 1671 W
Edmund, Northam 1639 W
Sherm Hugh, Hartland 1715 W
Sherne John, Hartland 1605 W
John, Northam 1667 A
Phillippa, Abbotsham 1690 A
Shearme Phillippa, Abbotsham 1695 A
Salome, Hartland 1606 W
Sherne Simon, Hartland 1620 [W]
Sherme or Shenne Simon, Abbotsham 1686 W
William, Hartland 1633 W
Sherwill Hugh, Knowstone 1599 [W]
Sherwood John, Bideford 1631 [W]
Shestruge see Shastridge
Shett see Shatt
Shewbroke, Shibbrocke see Shobrooke
Shilston, Shillson
Bernard, Winkleigh 1616 [W]
Shillson John, Winkleigh 1837 W
Nicholas, Coldridge 1583 W
Thomas, North Tawton 1628 [W]
Shoare see Shore
Shobrooke, Shebbrocke, Shebrooke, Shewbroke, Shibbrocke,
    Shobbrook, Shobrook
Elizabeth, Zeal Monachorum 1740 W
Shebrooke Henry, Barnstaple 1732 W
Shobbrook Humphrey, Woolfardisworthy 1679 A
Humphrey, South Molton 1715 W
Shobrook James, Barnstaple 1842 W

Shobrook Jane, Barnstaple 1854 W
Shebbrocke John, Coldridge 1570 W
John, Barnstaple 1795 A
Salome, Barnstaple 1790 W
Shewbroke Thomas, Woolfardisworthy 1584 W
Thomas, South Molton 1596 [W]
Thomas, South Molton 1643 W
Shobrook Thomas, Chittlehampton 1694 W
Thomas, Chittlehampton 1722 A
Shobbrook Thomas, Burrington 1840 W
Thomasine, Lapford 1705 W
Shibbrocke William, Washford Pyne 1583 W
Shebrooke William, Nymet Rowland 1727 W
Shobrook William, Brushford, yeoman 1809 W
Shobbrook William, Chawleigh 1839 W
Sholford
Roger, Lynton 1573 W
Roger, Lynton 1610 [W] "Shelford" in register; forename
    blank in Ms; supplied from parish register
Shoote see Shute
Shopland see Shapland
Shore, Shoare, Shure
Elizabeth, North Tawton 1755 A
John, North Tawton 1597 [W]
Shure Ralph, Roborough 1585 W
Rebecca, Instow 1803 A
Shoare Richard, North Tawton 1669 W
Richard, North Tawton 1733 W
Richard, North Tawton 1764 W
Thomas, North Tawton 1783 A
Shorland Elizabeth, Barnstaple 1687 W
Henry, Tawstock 1691 W
Henry, Rackenford 1704 W
John, South Molton 1661 A
John, Oakford 1716 W
John, Pilton 1739 W
Mary, Ilfracombe 1662 W
Mary, Fremington 1683 W
Mary, Fremington 1762 A
Mary and Simon, Goodleigh 1665 A
Simon, Goodleigh 1664 A
Simon and Mary, Goodleigh 1665 A
William, Instow 1681 A
    see also Sharland
Short, Shorte
Shorte ..., Chulmleigh 1603 [W]
..., Bideford 1604 [W]
Shorte ..., Clovelly 1607 [W]
Shorte ..., Rose Ash 1612 [W] and 1614 [W]
Shorte ..., Woolfardisworthy 1613 [W]
Ann, Langtree 1689 A
Ann, Sheepwash 1716 W
Shorte Baldwin, Littleham (near Bideford) 1580 W
Bernard, Ashreigney 1820 W
Bernard, Ashreigney 1837 W
Shorte Catherine, Rose Ash 1620 [W]
Edith, Sheepwash 1668 W
Shorte Edmund, Buckland Brewer 1642 A
Shorte Elizabeth, Great Torrington 1629 [W] and 1632 A
Elizabeth, Dolton 1707 A
Elizabeth see also Jenny Broom
Shorte Ellen, Littleham (near Bideford) 1615 [W]
Emma, Bideford 1669 A
Shorte Gabriel, Littleham (near Bideford) 1616 [W]
Gabriel, Littleham (near Bideford) 1670 W
George, Bideford 1706 A
George, Dolton 1709 W
George, Yarnscombe 1717 W
George, Northam 1740 W
George, Bideford 1741 W
George, Atherington 1763 A
Grace, Bideford 1759 A
Gregory, Dolton 1815 W
Humphrey, Meeth 1644 A
Humphrey, North Tawton 1678 A

Humphrey, Meeth 1714 A
James, Abbotsham 1726 W
Shorte Joan, Clovelly 1566 W
Shorte Joan, Horwood 1596 [W]
Shorte Joan, Ilfracombe 1615 [W]
Shorte Joan, Rose Ash 1619 [W]
Joan, Hartland 1743 W
John, Landcross 1565 W
John, Monkleigh 1568 W
John, Clovelly 1570 W
Shorte John, Rose Ash 1572 W
Shorte John, Martinhoe 1579 W
Shorte John, Great Torrington 1616 [W]
Shorte John, Littleham (near Bideford) 1617 [W]
Shorte John, Buckland Brewer 1622 [W]
Shorto John, Northam 1636 A and 1640 O
John, Great Torrington 1643 [W]
John, Barnstaple 1671 W
John, Littleham (near Bideford) 1681 W
John, Dolton 1689 W
John, Northam 1711 A
John, Woolfardisworthy 1711 A
John, Littleham (near Bideford) 1715 A
John, Barnstaple 1721 W
John, Woolfardisworthy 1730 W
John, Woolfardisworthy 1751 W
John, Bow 1787 W
John, Woolfardisworthy 1795 W
John, Instow, yeoman 1802 W
John, Hartland 1846 W
John, South Molton 1848 W
Joseph, Weare Giffard 1829 W
Shorte Leonard, Dolton 1691 W
Margaret, Woolfardisworthy 1759 W
Shorte Margery, Landcross, widow 1568 W
Shorte Martin, Clovelly 1622 [W]
Shorte Mary, Buckland Brewer 1640 A
Mary, Buckland Brewer 1670 W
Mary, Bideford 1681 A
Mary, Barnstaple 1759 W
Nathaniel, Landcross 1705 A
Shorte Nicholas, Littleham (near Bideford) 1613 [W];
    forename blank in Ms; supplied from parish register
Obadiah, Hartland 1700 W
Shorte Peter, Ashreigney 1617 [W]
Shorte Philip, Alverdiscott 1643 A
Philip, Great Torrington 1764 A
Rebecca, widow 1803 A
Richard, Woolfardisworthy 1704 A
Richard, Ashreigney 1705 W
Richard, Instow 1740 A
Richard, Ashreigney 1820 W
Richard, Woolfardisworthy 1830 W
Richard, Woolfardisworthy 1851 W
Shorte Robert, Stoke Rivers 1580 W and 1581 A
Shorte Robert, Hartland 1623 [W]
Shorte Robert, Littleham (near Bideford) 1626 [W]
Shorte Robert, Buckland Brewer 1629 [W]
Shorte Roger, Clovelly 1616 [W]
Roger, Hartland 1739 W
Shorte Rose, Bratton Fleming 1620 [W]
Samuel, Bideford 1727 W
Samuel, Tawstock 1730 W
Samuel, Tawstock 1762 W
Sarah, Meeth 1666 A
Susan, Ashreigney 1851 W
Shorte Thomas, Cruwys Morchard 1604 [W]; forename blank
    in Ms; supplied from parish register
Shorte Thomas, Bratton Fleming 1610 [W]; forename blank in
    Ms; supplied from parish register
Shorte Thomas, Littleham (near Bideford) 1645 W
Thomas, Sheepwash 1667 W
Shorte Thomas, Lapford 1671 W
Thomas, Shebbear 1762 W
Thomas, Parkham 1793 A

Thomas, Woolfardisworthy 1808 W
Shorte Thomasine, Abbotsham 1588 W
Thomasine, Brendon 1685 A
Shorte William, Clovelly 1571 W
Shorte William, Horwood 1596 [W]
Shorte William, Ilfracombe 1603 W
Shorto William, Tawstock 1635 W
William, Dolton 1689 W
William, Bideford 1720 W
William, Abbotsham 1724 W
William, Bideford 1786 W
William, Weare Giffard 1858 W
Shortar James, Bideford 1744 W
Shorte see Short
Shortridge, Shortrudg, Shortrudge
    Shortrudg Ann, Witheridge 1713 W
    Elizabeth, Witheridge 1684 A
    Isott, Parkham, widow 1811 A
    James see Stephen Balch
    Shortrudge Joan, Witheridge 1686 W
    John, Woolfardisworthy 1802 W
    Richard, Witheridge 1645 A
    Richard, Witheridge 1672 A and O
    Richard, Witheridge 1679 W; A dbn 1679
    Richard, Witheridge 1763 A
    Richard, Parkham, yeoman 1808 W
    Susan, Witheridge 1788 A
    Thomas, High Bickington 1589 A
Shout see Shute
Shropshere John, Chittlehampton 1598 [W]
Shuchefielde alias Nethercote John, Oakford 1566 W
Shure see Shore
Shute, Shoote, Shout, Shurt, Shurte, Shutt, Shutte
    Shutt ..., Burrington 1600 A
    Shutt ..., Dolton 1604 [W]
    Shutte ..., Parkham 1608 [W]
    Shutte ..., Ashreigney 1611 [W]
    Shurte Ann, Northam 1629 [W]
    Anthony, Buckland Brewer 1593 [W] (2)
    Anthony, Ashreigney 1688 W
    Bernard, Ashreigney 1620 [W]
    Shutte Elizabeth, Burrington 1603 W
    Elizabeth, Dolton 1817 W
    Shutt Henry, Dolton 1720 W
    Honor, High Bickington 1669 O
    Shutt Honor, High Bickington 1688 W
    Shutt Hugh, Chittlehampton 1673 O
    Shutt Hugh, Ashreigney 1695 W
    Shoote Jane, Dolton 1628 [W] and 1633 W
    Shutt Jasper, Hartland 1692 W
    Shutt Jasper, Hartland 1731 W
    Shutt Jeremiah, South Molton 1693 W
    Shutt Joan, Molland 1670 A and O
    Shutt Joan, Dolton 1742 A
    John, Stoodleigh 1588 W
    Shutte John, Yarnscombe 1600 W
    John, Dolton 1622 [W]
    Shutt John, Ashreigney 1625 [W]
    Shurte John, Bideford 1628 [W]
    John, Barnstaple 1628 [W]
    John, Bideford 1629 [W] (2) and O, 1631 [W]
    Shutt John, Ashreigney 1633 W
    Shutt John, Dolton, snr. 1637 [W]
    Shutt John, Dolton 1643 W
    John, Ashreigney 1701 W
    Shutt John, High Bickington 1725 W
    Shutt John, Parkham 1729 W
    Shutt John, Hartland 1741 A
    John, Dolton 1743 W
    Shutt John, Chittlehampton 1762 A
    John, Ashreigney 1769 W
    John, Ashreigney 1786 A
    John, Dolton 1813 W
    John, Atherington 1841 W
    John, Hartland 1841 W

Jonathan, Ashreigney 1712 W
Shout Martin 1573 W
Shurt Mary, Bideford 1680 W
Mary, Ashreigney 1705 W
Shutt Mary, Northam 1746 W
Shutt Nicholas, Parkham 1598 [W]
Shutt Nicholas, High Bickington 1666 A
Shutt Nicholas, High Bickington 1689 A
Shutt Paschal, Dolton 1709 A
Richard, Dolton 1741 W
Shutt Richard, Parkham 1759 W
Richard, Zeal Monachorum 1766 A
Richard, Dolton 1777 W
Shutt Richard, Abbotsham 1834 W
Richard, Dolton 1839 A to John Friend, nephew
Shutt Sarah, Hartland 1802 A
Sebastian, Parkham 1593 [W]
Thomas, Great Torrington 1593 [W]
Shutt Thomas, Hartland 1714 W
Thomas, Chittlehampton 1797 A
Thomas, Buckland Filleigh 1855 A
William, Roborough 1573 W
William, Ashreigney 1622 [W]
Shutt William, Parkham 1640 W
Shutt William, Molland 1670 W
Shutt William, High Bickington 1742 A
William, Dolton, yeoman 1799 W
Willmot, Martinhoe 1585 W
Silke James, Buckland Filleigh 1843 W
Jane, Weare Giffard 1727 W
Jane, Buckland Filleigh 1793 A
John, Buckland Filleigh 1814 W
Susan, Buckland Filleigh 1814 W
Silley, Sylley, Sylly, Zelly
Zelly Elizabeth, Romansleigh 1790 A
Philip, Oakford 1587 W
Sylly Raymond, Rackenford 1633 W
Sylley Richard, Rackenford 1617 [W]
Robert, Rackenford 1642 A
Sillifant see Sullivan
Simens see Simons
Simkin Lucy, Northam 1830 W
Simmons see Simons
Simms, Syme, Syms
Syms Ann, St Giles in the Wood 1690 A
Syme John, St Giles in the Wood 1733 W
Syms Thomas, St Giles in the Wood 1716 A
Syms William, St Giles in the Wood 1670 A
William, Barnstaple 1753 A
Simons, Simens, Simmons, Simon, Symonde, Symone, Symons
..., Chulmleigh 1608 [W]
Symons Abel, Yarnscombe 1850 W
Symons Adam, Marwood 1729 W
Simon Agnes, Hartland 1565 W
Symons Agnes, Marwood 1600 W
Symons Agnes, Pilton 1675 W
Symons Agnes, Barnstaple 1723 W
Symons Alexander, Great Torrington 1734 A
Ambrose, Atherington 1624 [W]
Symons Ambrose, Yarnscombe, yeoman 1806 W
Symons Ann, Pilton 1674 A
Symons Anthony, Barnstaple 1605 W
Anthony, Woolfardisworthy 1638 W
Simmons Benjamin, Great Torrington 1768 A
Symons Catherine, Instow 1697 W
Symons Charles, Weare Giffard 1708 A
Symons Charles, Marwood 1710 W
Symons Charles, Heanton Punchardon 1738 W
Symonde Charles, Ilfracombe 1851 W
Symons Christopher, Rose Ash 1595 [W]
Symons Christopher, Barnstaple 1622 [W]
Christopher, South Molton 1680 W
Symons Christopher, Goodleigh 1700 A
Symons Christopher, Chittlehampton 1710 A
Symons David, Northam 1666 A

Edward, Weare Giffard 1627 [W]
Symons Edward, Instow 1663 W
Symons Edward, Barnstaple 1749 A
Symons Edward, East Buckland 1751 W
Edward, Pilton 14 Mar 1766 W; 2nd grant 1813 W
Symons Edward, Langtree, yeoman 1846 A to Thomas, son
Symons Eleanor, Combe Martin 1758 W
Symons Elizabeth, Tawstock, widow 1610 [W]; forename
  blank in Ms; supplied from parish register
Symons Elizabeth, Barnstaple 1799 W
Simmons Francis, Marwood 1751 W
Symons George, Bideford 1665 W
Symons George, Combe Martin 1752 W
Simens George, Combe Martin 1759 W
Symons George, Heanton Punchardon 1779 W
Symons Grace, Barnstaple 1690 A
Symons Hannah, Barnstaple 1749 W
Symons Henry, Heanton Punchardon 1728 W
Symons Henry, Great Torrington 1758 W
Symons Hugh, Chittlehampton 1743 W
Symons Hugh, ship *Colchester* 1763 W
Symons Humphrey, Ilfracombe 1661 W
Symons Humphrey, Great Torrington 1665 W
Symons Humphrey, Combe Martin 1747 A
Symons James, ship *Boyne* 1748 W
Symons Jane, Pilton 1813 W
Symons Joan, Alwington 1590 [W]
Joan, Marwood 1592 [W]
Joan, Shirwell 1592 [W] and 1596 [W]
Joan, Westleigh 1597 [W]
Symons Joan, Pilton 1604 W
Symons Joan, Instow 1618 [W]
Symons Joan, Marwood 1661 W
Symons Joan, Barnstaple 1689 A
Symons Joan, Pilton 1763 W
Symon John, Woolfardisworthy 1568 W
Simon John, Marwood 1572 W and 1573 W
Symons John, Shirwell, snr. 1573 W
Symons John, Alwington 1579 W
John, Martinhoe 1585 W
John, Shirwell 1590 [W]
Symon John, Chulmleigh 1593 [W]
Symons John, Marwood 1598 [W]
Symons John, Parkham 1601 W
John, Barnstaple 1615 [W]
John, Instow 1615 [W]
John, Barnstaple 1637 W
John, Shirwell 1640 W
Symons John, Marwood 1642 W
Symons John, Barnstaple 1643 A
Symons John, Marwood 1643 W
Symons John, Barnstaple 1645 A
Symons John, Trentishoe 1667 W
John, Northam 1676 A
John, Marwood 1677 A (2)
Symons John, Atherington 1684 A
John, Shirwell 1685 W
Symons John, Marwood 1698 W
Symons John, Shirwell, snr. 1701 W
Symons John, Westleigh 1709 W
Symons John, Fremington 1726 W
Symons John, Buckland Brewer 1729 W
Symons John, Bideford 1743 A
Symons John, Pilton 1753 W
John, Burrington 1776 A
Symons John, Yarnscombe 1805 W*
Symons John, Tawstock 1822 W
Symons John, Ashreigney 1824 W
Symons Joseph, Witheridge 1617 [W]
Symons Joseph, Heanton Punchardon 1665 W
Symons Joseph, Pilton 1684 W
Symons Joseph, Pilton 1812 W
Symons Joseph, Yarnscombe 1834 W
Julian, Atherington 1637 W

Symons Lawrence, Barnstaple 1615 [W]; forename blank in
  Ms; supplied from parish register
Mary, Shirwell 1679 W
Symons Mary, Marwood 1701 W
Symons Mary, Shirwell 1713 A
Symons Mary, Great Torrington 1720 W
Symons Mary, Heanton Punchardon 1789 W
Symons Mary, Barnstaple, widow 1810 A
Symons Mary, Yarnscombe 1846 W
Symonds Mary see Mary Lavercomb
Symons Mathew, Northam 1682 W
Symons Nathaniel, Barnstaple 1675 A
Symons Nicholas, Barnstaple 1645 W
Symons Nicholas, East Down 1675 A
Simens Oliver, Hartland 1819 W
Symons Peter 1580 W
Symons Philip, Berrynarbor 1714 A
Symons Philip, Alverdiscott 1727 A
Philip, Sheepwash 1581 A
Phyllis, Instow 1670 W
Symons Rebecca, Northam 1710 A
Symons Richard, Marwood 1587 W
Symons Richard, Northam 1610 [W]; forename blank in Ms;
  supplied from parish register
Symons Richard, Heanton Punchardon 1618 [W]
Symons Richard, Heanton Punchardon 1673 [W]
Symons Richard, Great Torrington 1707 A
Symons Richard, Marwood 1754 A
Symons Richard, Barnstaple, yeoman 1810 W
Symons Richard, Yarnscombe 1835 W
Symonde Richard Pyke, West Down 1831 W
Symon Robert, Pilton 1617 [W]
Symons Robert, Barnstaple 1630 [W]
Roger, Great Torrington 1615 [W]
Roger, Great Torrington 1670 A
Rose, Instow 1584 A
Symons Stephen, Marwood 1640 A
Symons Susan, Great Torrington 1814 W
Simon Thomas, Martinhoe 1574 W
Symons Thomas, Westleigh 1587 W
Thomas, Clovelly 1591 [W]
Thomas, Shirwell 1611 [W]; forename blank in Ms; supplied
  from parish register
Thomas, Shirwell 1627 [W]
Thomas, Charles 1628 [W]
Symons Thomas, Weare Giffard 1637 A
Symons Thomas, Goodleigh 1709 W
Symons Thomas 1741 A
Symons Timothy, Great Torrington 1668 A
Simones Walter, Witheridge 1574 W
William, Great Torrington 1636 [W]
Symons William, Marwood 1666 W
Symons William, Barnstaple 1669 A
Symons William, Northam 1697 A
William, Marwood 1706 W
Symons William, Pilton 1826 W
Symons William, Tawstock 1854 W
Symons Winifred, Pilton 1631 [W]
Simpson, Sympson
Sympson Thomas, Bideford 1707 A
William, Northam 1701 W
Sinckock see Sincocke
Sinclair John, Northam 1855 W
Sincocke, Sinckock, Sincock, Syncock, Syncocke, Syncoke
Syncock Alfred, Little Torrington 1699 A
Christopher, Hartland 1621 [W]
Syncock Dorothy, Westleigh 1725 W
Edith, Westleigh 1633 W
Elizabeth, Great Torrington 1597 [W]
Syncocke Elizabeth, Great Torrington 1598 [W]
Syncock James, Little Torrington 1696 A
Joan, Warkleigh 1635 W
Syncock John, Little Torrington 1696 W
Syncock Nicholas, Westleigh 1700 A
Sincock Philip, Northam 1667 A

Syncock Richard, Great Torrington 1617 [W] and 1619 O
Richard, Westleigh 1623 [W] and 1626 [W]
Syncock Samuel, Bideford 1695 A
Syncoke Simon, Hartland 1580 W
Thomas, Great Torrington 1592 [W]
Thomas, Westleigh 1626 [W]
Sincock Thomas, Great Torrington 1643 A
Sinckock Thomas, Buckland Brewer 1612 [W]; forename
  blank in Ms; supplied from parish register
Sing, Singe
Singe ..., Lapford 1610 [W]
Singe ..., Winkleigh 1611 [W]
Andrew, Great Torrington 1710 A and 1715 A
Daniel, Great Torrington 1695 A
Singe John, Lynton 1645 W
John, Beaford 1667 W
John, Great Torrington 1843 W
John, King's Nympton 1847 W
Lodovic, Fremington 1680 W
Thomasine, Fremington 1690 A
Singe William, Great Torrington 1592 [W]
Sink Richard, Bideford 1758 W
Sitter David, Barnstaple 1773 A
Edward, Barnstaple 1813 W
Sitter alias Rooper Richard, South Molton 1585 W
Sitton Andrew, Bratton Fleming 1724 W
Skambe, Skame, Skampe see Scamp
Skear, Skeare see Score
Skibbow, Scibbowe, Skibboll, Skibbowe, Skybbow
Skibbowe ..., Chulmleigh 1611 O
Skibbow alias Isaack Agnes, Burrington 1660 A
Skybbow Ann, Chulmleigh 1638 W
Scibbowe Anstis, King's Nympton 1601 W
Honor, King's Nympton 1702 W
Skibbowe alias Isacke John, King's Nympton 1569 W
Skybbow Julian, Wembworthy 1633 W
Skibboll Roger, King's Nympton 1632 [W]
Skihle see Skitch
Skinner, Scynner, Skayner, Skimer, Skiner, Skyner, Skynner
..., Knowstone 1608 [W]
Abraham, Ilfracombe 1617 [W]
Alexander, Tawstock 1783 W
Alexander, Chittlehampton 1784 W
Alexander, South Molton 1833 W
Ann, Georgeham 1667 W
Ann, South Molton 1853 W
Augustine, Fremington 1691 W and 1695 W
Avis, Barnstaple 1623 [W]
Bartholomew, Bideford 1643 W
Catherine, North Molton 1806 W
Catherine, Knowstone 1593 [W]
Catherine, Ilfracombe 1605 W
Cecilia, Ilfracombe 1684 A
Skynner Christian, Beaford 1588 W
Christopher 1736 A
Daniel, Great Torrington 1643 A
Edmund, Barnstaple 1760 A and 1762 A
Edward, Chulmleigh 1631 [W]
Edward, Barnstaple 1645 A
Eli, High Bickington 1772 A
Elizabeth, Hartland 1643 A
Elizabeth, Chittlehampton 1766 W
Elizabeth, Chittlehampton 1782 A
Elizabeth, Barnstaple 1786 W
Elizabeth, Fremington 1834 W
Elizabeth and Susan, Ilfracombe 1638 A
Elizabeth wife of John see also Sarah Mounsey
Ephraim, Barnstaple 1625 [W]
George, Chulmleigh 1641 W
George, Chittlehampton 1665 W
George, George Nympton 1684 A
George, Chulmleigh 1739 A
George, Chulmleigh 1767 A
George, King's Nympton 1840 A to William, brother
Giles, King's Nympton 1835 W

Skynner Henry, Ilfracombe 1586 W
Henry Cottey 1836 A
Humphrey, South Molton 1642 W
Humphrey, Burrington 1668 A
Humphrey, Ilfracombe 1712 A
Isott, Chittlehampton 1632 [W]
James, Chittlehampton 1596 [W]
James, West Anstey 1728 W
Jane, Clovelly 1723 W
Jane, Rose Ash 1829 A (Jenny) to William, father
Jeremy, St Giles in the Wood 1705 W
Joan, East Buckland 1764 W
Skynner John, Chulmleigh 1564 W
Skayner John, Cruwys Morchard 1579 W
Skyner John, Great Torrington 1579 W
Skynner John, Horwood 1588 W
Skynner John, Martinhoe 1588 W
John, Chittlehampton 1598 [W] and 1599 [W]
Skimer John, East Anstey 1604 W
Skiner John, Woolfardisworthy 1606 W
John, Ilfracombe 1607 [W]; forename blank in Ms; supplied
   from parish register
Scynner John, Barnstaple 1616 [W]
Scynner John, Goodleigh 1617 [W]
John, Beaford 1620 [W]
John, Ilfracombe 1625 [W]
John, Chulmleigh 1632 [W]
John, Clovelly 1663 W
John, Mortehoe 1665 W
John, Chulmleigh 1666 W
John, South Molton 1667 A
John, Goodleigh 1671 A and 1674 O
John, Cruwys Morchard 1672 W
John, Sheepwash 1694 A
John, Goodleigh 1701 W
John, Great Torrington, jnr. 1704 A
John, Great Torrington, snr. 1704 W
John, Chulmleigh 1709 W
John, Pilton 1711 A
John, Chittlehampton 1713 W
John, King's Nympton 1715 A
John, South Molton 1727 A
John, Bideford 1738 W
John, Chittlehampton 1749 A
John, Barnstaple 1754 W
John, Chawleigh 1768 A
John, North Tawton 1774 W
John, West Buckland 1778 W
John, Bideford 1779 A
John, King's Nympton 1785 W
John, Chittlehampton 1787 W
John, Chittlehampton, yeoman 1809 A
John, Ashreigney 1817 A
John, Witheridge 1840 A to Mary, widow
John, Loxhore 1855 W
Lodovic, Atherington 1623 [W]
Malachi, Thelbridge 1593 [W]
Margaret, Charles 1563 W
Margaret, Martinhoe 1590 [W]
Margaret, Chulmleigh 1639 W
Margaret, South Molton 1677 W
Margaret, Bondleigh 1722 W
Margaret, South Molton 1829 W
Martha, North Tawton 1755 W
Skynner Mary, Barnstaple 1575 A
Mary, Creacombe 1665 A
Mary, Burrington 1669 W
Mary, Goodleigh 1696 W
Mary, Mortehoe 1741 A
Mary, Northam 1741 A
Mary, Barnstaple 1746 A
Mary, Chittlehampton 1766 A
Mary, Barnstaple 1793 W
Mary, South Molton 1836 A
Mary, Witheridge 1849 W

Mathew, Cruwys Morchard 1708 A
Michael, Rose Ash 1638 W
Michael, Clovelly 1716 W
Michael, Barnstaple 1850 W
Nancy, Barnstaple 1850 W
Skynner Nicholas, Beaford 1576 W
Skener Nicholas, Martinhoe 1580 W
Nicholas, Beaford 1628 [W]
Nicholas, Chulmleigh 1668 A and 1671 O
Nicholas, Chawleigh 1746 A
Peter, Clovelly 1706 W
Philip, Thelbridge 1622 W
Philip, Yarnscombe 1641 A
Philip, Burrington 1728 W
Richard, Georgeham 1665 W
Richard, Ilfracombe 1684 W
Richard, Bideford 1703 A
Richard, Bondleigh 1716 A
Richard, King's Nympton 1716 W
Richard, Chawleigh 1767 W
Robert, Huntshaw 1637 A
Robert, Berrynarbor 1766 W
Samuel, Chittlehampton 1770 A
Sebart, Burrington 1642 W
Sebastian, Chulmleigh 1693 W
Susan, Chittlehampton 1834 W
Susan and Elizabeth, Ilfracombe 1638 A
Skynner Thomas, Burrington 1566 W
Skynner Thomas, Goodleigh 1570 W
Thomas, Goodleigh 1593 [W]
Thomas, Barnstaple 1609 [W]; forename blank in Ms;
   supplied from parish register
Thomas, Goodleigh 1619 [W]
Thomas, Molland 1673 A
Thomas, Chittlehampton 1759 W
Thomas, Chittlehampton 1786 W
Thomas, King's Nympton 1824 W
Thomas, Chittlehampton 1832 W
Thomas, South Molton, yeoman 1845 A to Alexander,
   yeoman, brother
Thomas, Charles 1848 W
Walter, Beaford 1590 [W]
Walter, Zeal Monachorum 1595 [W]
Walter, Goodleigh 1620 [W]
Walter, Mortehoe 1625 [W]
Walter, Burrington 1673 W
Skyner William, Combe Martin 1578 A
Skynner William, Combe Martin 1579 A account
William, South Molton 1690 W
William, Burrington 1733 W
William, Barnstaple 1770 A
William, Chulmleigh 1772 W
William, Chittlehampton 1825 W
Skirry Richard, Pilton 1592 [W]
Skitch, Skihle, Skyche, Skytch, Skytche
   Skyche Elizabeth, Tawstock 1578 A
Elizabeth, Newton Tracey 1708 W
George, Tawstock 1597 [W]
Humphrey, Tawstock 1618 [W]
Humphrey, Newton Tracey 1708 W
Skytche John, Tawstock 1573 W
Skytch John, Tawstock 1602 W
John, Newton Tracey 1678 W
John, Buckland Brewer 1755 W
Nicholas, Instow 1708 W
Thomas, Tawstock 1695 W
Thomas, Bideford 1747 A
Thomas, Frithelstock 1763 A
Skihle William, Frithelstock 1746 W
Skoare, Skore see Score
Skot, Skott, Skotte see Scott
Skreech see Screech
Skriggin, Skriggon, Skrygon see Scriggins
Skybbow see Skibbow
Skyche see Skitch

Skyner, Skynner see Skinner
Skytch, Skytche see Skitch
Slade, Slad
   Daniel, Bideford 1685 W
   Slad Elizabeth, Twitchen 1575 W
   Elizabeth, Rose Ash 1665 W
   Elizabeth, Newport, Bishop's Tawton 1852 W
   Joan, Abbotsham 1598 [W]
   Joan, Marwood 1759 A
   Slade alias Glade John, Twitchen 1571 W
   John, Twitchen 1593 [W]
   John, Little Torrington 1757 W
   John, Barnstaple 1767 W
   John, Creacombe 1849 W
   John, Langtree 1856 W
   Jolomia, Little Torrington 1722 W
   Prudence, Little Torrington 1760 A
   Richard, Langtree 1821 W
   Robert, Abbotsham 1583 W
   William, St Giles in the Wood 1668 A
   William, Little Torrington 1719 A
Slader, Sladen, Sladder
   ..., North Molton 1604 [W]
   Catherine, King's Nympton 1602 W
   Christiana, Chittlehampton 1622 [W]
   Dorothy, Mariansleigh 1643 W
   Eleanor, North Molton 1771 W
   Elizabeth, North Molton 1789 W
   Elizabeth, North Molton 1819 W
   George, High Bray 1624 [W]
   George, Mariansleigh 1624 [W]
   George, North Molton 1728 W
   George, Trentishoe 1820 W
   Honor, Chittlehampton 1803 W
   James, Buckland Brewer 1629 [W]
   Joan, North Molton 1721 A
   Joan widow of Michael 1825 W
   Joan, North Molton 1852 A
   Sladder John, North Molton 1572 W
   John, East Worlington 1583 W
   John, South Molton 1637 W and 1639 O
   John, North Molton 1763 W and 1767 W
   John, Barnstaple 1794 A
   John, North Molton, yeoman 1798 W
   John, Parracombe 1798 W
   Margaret, North Molton 1799 W
   Mark, North Tawton 1589 W
   Sladen Mary, North Molton 1767 W
   Mary, Rose Ash 1824 W
   Mary wife of William see Michael Lock
   Michael, Winkleigh 1613 [W]; forename blank in Ms;
     supplied from parish register
   Michael, North Molton 1678 W, 1684 W, 1686 A, 1691 A and
     1699 A
   Michael, North Molton 1727 W
   Michael, North Molton 1788 W
   Peter, North Molton 1701 W
   Peter, North Molton 1814 W
   Theophilus, St Giles in the Wood 1758 W
   Thomas, North Molton 1572 W and 1597 [W]
   Thomas, North Molton 1638 W
   Thomas, North Molton 1665 W
   Thomas, North Molton 1768 W
   Thomas, North Molton 1787 W
   Thomas, North Molton 1853 A
   William, South Molton 1622 [W]
   William, North Molton 1683 W
   William, Little Torrington 1717 W
   William, North Molton 1719 A
   William, Little Torrington 1725 A
   William, North Molton 1778 W
   William, North Molton, yeoman 1800 W
   William, North Molton 1808 W
   William, North Molton 1823 W
Slaterne Willmot, Bideford 1696 W

Sleaper see Sleeper
Slee, Sley
   ..., Chulmleigh 1602 [W] (2) and A
   ..., East Down 1604 [W]
   ..., Shirwell 1608 [W] and 1611 [W]
   ..., Berrynarbor 1609 [W]
   ..., Coldridge 1618 O
   Alice, Coldridge 1620 [W]
   Ambrose, Great Torrington 1828 W
   Augustine, Coldridge 1621 [W]
   Catherine, Barnstaple 1794 A
   Daniel, Heanton Punchardon 1724 W
   Eleanor, Barnstaple 1760 W
   Elizabeth, Pilton 1681 W
   Faith, Coldridge 1680 A
   Francis, Pilton 1744 A
   George, Marwood 1662 W
   George, Coldridge 1669 W
   George, East Down 1700 W
   George, Winkleigh 1713 A
   George, Barnstaple 1737 W
   George, Barnstaple 1789 W
   Grace, Winkleigh 1716 W
   Henry, Pilton 1662 W
   Henry, Pilton 1704 W
   Hugh, East Down 1565 W
   Humphrey, Coldridge 1591 [W]
   Joan, Ilfracombe 1589 A
   Joan, Coldridge 1621 [W]
   Joan, Barnstaple 1636 W
   Joan, Goodleigh 1637 W
   Sley John, East Down 1575 A
   Sley John, Shirwell 1578 A
   John, North Molton 1594 [W]
   John, East Down 1596 [W]
   John, Fremington 1603 W
   John, Lynton 1622 [W]
   John, Pilton 1640 W
   John, Romansleigh 1644 A
   John, Pilton 1661 A
   John, Shirwell 1661 W
   John, Eggesford 1667 W
   John, Shirwell 1682 A
   John, Great Torrington 1828 W; A dbn 1835
   John, Marwood 1836 W
   Margaret, Coldridge, widow 1569 W
   Margaret, Coldridge 1696 W
   Mark, Barnstaple 1754 A
   Mary, Barnstaple 1663 A
   Mary, Pilton 1681 W
   Nathaniel, Eggesford 1645 A
   Nathaniel, Hartland 1664 W
   Nathaniel, Winkleigh 1707 A
   Nathaniel, Lapford 1738 W
   Nicholas, East Down 1695 W
   Oliver, Fremington 1568 W
   Rebecca, East Down 1712 W
   Richard, Pilton 1660 W
   Richard, Pilton 1673 [W] and 1680 W
   Richard, Eggesford 1684 W
   Richard, Coldridge 1695 W
   Richard, Winkleigh 1738 A
   Richard, Barnstaple 1742 W
   Richard, Roborough, yeoman 1797 W
   Richard, Zeal Monachorum 1830 A to Charity, widow
   Robert, Shirwell 1630 [W]
   Robert, Pilton 1642 A
   Roger, East Down 1590 [W]
   Roger, Lynton 1634 W
   Roger, Coldridge 1699 W
   Simon, Shirwell 1568 W
   Susan, Winkleigh 1793 W
   Thomas 1587 A
   Thomas, Coldridge, snr. 1617 [W]
   Thomas, Lynton 1625 [W]

Thomas, Coldridge 1629 [W]
Thomas, Pilton 1669 W
Thomas, Winkleigh 1684 W
Thomas, Coldridge 1690 A
Valentine Thorn, Great Torrington 1857 W second christian
   name from FreeBMD; initial only in Ms
Walter, Pilton 1630 [W]
William, Coldridge 1584 W
William, Bideford 1692 W
William, Shirwell 1743 A
William, Coldridge 1762 W
William, Winkleigh 1780 A
Sleeper, Sleaper
..., Goodleigh 1612 [W]
Agnes, Goodleigh 1623 [W]
Hugh, Berrynarbor 1693 W
Mark, Fremington 1596 [W]
Robert, Goodleigh 1596 [W]
Sleaper Sabine, Goodleigh 1570 W
Simon, Instow 1636 W
Slensbury ..., Marwood 1611 [W]
Sley see Slee
Sleyman John, Bideford 1644 W
Slocombe, Slocomb, Slowcomb, Slowcombe
Slocomb Agnes, Countisbury 1703 A
Agnes, Countisbury 1764 W
Amesius, East Down 1622 [W]
Ann, Shirwell 1639 W
Slocomb Anthony, Kentisbury 1643 A
Slocomb Anthony, Combe Martin 1709 A
Slocomb Anthony, Combe Martin 1710 W
Christopher, Countisbury 1738 W and 1744 W
Christopher, Countisbury 1781 A
Slocomb David, Challacombe 1604 W
Slowcombe Elizabeth, East Down 1580 W
Slocomb George, Barnstaple 1645 A
Slowcomb George, Kentisbury 1663 A
George, Heanton Punchardon 1708 A
George, Instow 1786 W
Slowcombe Henry, Arlington 1575 W
Hugh, Countisbury 1692 W and 1693 A
Hugh, Marwood 1743 W
James, Tawstock 1781 W
Slocomb Joan, Barnstaple 1617 [W]
Joan, Kentisbury 1627 [W]
Slocomb Joan, Heanton Punchardon 1713 A
Slowcomb John, Challacombe 1577 W
John, Kentisbury 1589 W
John, Challacombe 1595 [W] and 1604 W
John, Tawstock 1734 A
John, Brendon 1773 W
John, Berrynarbor, yeoman 1810 W
Nicholas, Heanton Punchardon 1692 A
Slowcomb Philip, East Down 1577 W
Slocomb Richard, Tawstock 1716 A
Richard, Countisbury 1733 W
Richard, Berrynarbor 1750 A
Thomas, Kentisbury 1630 [W]
Thomas, West Down 1836 A to Sarah, widow
Walter, East Down 1622 [W]
Walter, Fremington 1753 A
William, Shirwell 1743 A
Sloe see Slow
Sloely see Sloley
Sloggett John, Sheepwash 1772 W
Sloley, Sloely, Sloly, Slowley, Slowly, Slowlye
Agnes, Shirwell 1635 W
Alexander, Northam 1734 W
Amos, Martinhoe 1786 W
Amos, Martinhoe 1854 W and 1857 W
Amos see also Esther Challacombe
Slowly Catherine, Barnstaple 1686 W
Sloly Catherine, Fremington 1627 [W]
Christian, Marwood 1760 W
Slowley Clase, Countisbury 1579 W

Slowley David, Fremington 1596 [W]
David, Brendon 1619 [W]
Slowly David, Alverdiscott 1639 A
Sloly David, Lynton 1678 A
Dorothy, Barnstaple 1632 W and 1638 W
Slowly Dorothy, Fremington 1688 W
Elizabeth, Shirwell 1714 W
Slowly George, Barnstaple 1621 [W]
Sloly George, West Buckland 1696 W
Slowly Grace, Chittlehampton 1621 [W]
Hugh, Kentisbury 1777 W
Hugh, Fremington 1820 W
James, Fremington 1667 W
Sloly James, High Bray 1703 W
James, Barnstaple 1756 A
Slowley Joan, Shirwell 1596 [W]
Sloly Joan, Shirwell 1626 [W]
Sloly Joan, Alverdiscott 1640 W
Sloly Joan, Fremington 1695 W
Sloly Joan, High Bray 1705 W
Slowlye John, Alverdiscott 1615 [W]
Slowly John, Fremington 1621 [W]
John, Shirwell, snr. 1636 W
Slowly John, Frithelstock 1668 W
Slowly John, Tawstock 1690 W
Sloly John, Barnstaple 1714 W
Slowly John, Tawstock 1728 W
John, Tawstock 1734 A
John, Martinhoe 1805 W
Slowlie John, snr., Shirwell 1611 [W]; forename blank in Ms;
   supplied from parish register
Sloly Judith, West Buckland 1697 A
Slowly Margaret, East Buckland 1621 [W] and 1623 O
Martha, Kentisbury 1753 A
Sloely Mathew, Parracombe 1685 W
Richard, Barnstaple 1626 [W]
Slowley Richard, Fremington 1669 A
Slowly Robert, Combe Martin 1689 [W]
Robert, Kentisbury 1745 W
Robert, Kentisbury 1821 W
Robert, Kentisbury 1839 A to Thomas, brother
Slowly Roger, Tawstock 1596 [W]
Slowly Simon, Barnstaple 1623 [W]
Sloly Simon, Barnstaple 1718 W
Sophia, Barnstaple 1768 W
Slowly Stephen, Shirwell 1624 [W]
Slowly Thomas, Fremington 1639 A
Walter, Barnstaple 1773 W
Sloly Walter, Bideford 1818 W
Slowly William, Barnstaple 1620 [W]
William, Bow 1636 W
William, Brendon 1661 A
Slowly William, Great Torrington 1670 W
William, Barnstaple 1717 W
William, Brendon 1783 W
William, Brendon 1814 W
Sloman, Slooman see Slowman
Slow, Sloe
Sloe ..., Chawleigh 1604 [W]
Alden, Chawleigh 1597 [W]
John, Chawleigh 1590 [W]
Slowcomb, Slowcombe see Slocombe
Slowley, Slowlie, Slowly, Slowlye see Sloley
Slowman, Sloman, Slooman, Sluman
Slooman Bartholomew, Pilton 1636 W
Bartholomew, Bideford 1674 W
Sloman Elizabeth, Bideford 1678 W
Slooman Elizabeth, Ilfracombe 1855 W
Slooman George, Fremington 1686 A
George, Westleigh 1773 W
Slooman George, Tawstock 1816 W
Joan, North Tawton 1584 W
John, Northam 1586 W
John, Pilton 1615 [W]
Sloman John, Northam 1618 [W]

Slooman John, Tawstock 1688 W
Slooman John, Westleigh 1731 W
John, Tawstock 1775 A
John, Westleigh 1798 A
Sloman Lawrence, Hartland 1738 W
Mark, North Tawton 1597 [W]
Robert, Bow 1577 W
Slooman Robert, Tawstock 1829 W
Slooman Samuel, Tawstock 1832 A to Catherine, widow
Sarah, Atherington 1829 [W]
Thomas, Bideford 1588 W
Slooman Thomas, Great Torrington 1639 W
Thomasine, Westleigh 1744 W
Slooman William, Hartland 1633 W
Slooman William, Pilton 1636 W
Sluman William, Barnstaple 1852 W
Zachariah, Tawstock 1742 W
Slye alias Arche Alice, Chulmleigh, widow 1572 W
Smaldon, Smalldon, Smoldon
　Smalldon Elizabeth, Tawstock 1801 W*
　George, Yarnscombe 1641 W
　George, Yarnscombe 1684 W and 1685 W
　Smoldon George, Chittlehampton 1844 W
　Smalldon James, Tawstock 1835 W
　Smaldon alias Moore John, South Molton 1603 W
　John, Tawstock 1841 W
　Smaldon alias Trout Margery, Charles 1683 W
Smaldridge see Smallridge
Smale ..., High Bickington 1612 [W]
　..., Peters Marland 1612 [W]
　Ambrose, South Molton 1699 W
　Amos, Winkleigh 1643 A
　Andrew, Chittlehampton 1616 [W] and 1617 [W]
　Andrew, Goodleigh 1639 W
　Andrew Edmund, East Putford 1837 W
　Ann, Bow 1714 A
　Archelaus, Northam 1689 W
　Arthur, Barnstaple 1661 W
　Avis, Shebbear 1676 W
　Catherine, Chawleigh 1676 W
　Catherine, Westleigh 1790 [W]
　Christian, Chawleigh 1676 W
　Dionysia, Frithelstock 1663 W
　Edith, Meeth 1710 W
　Edmund, Shebbear 1597 [W]
　Edmund 1604 [W]
　Edmund, Frithelstock 1673 [W]
　Edmund, Shebbear 1685 W
　Edmund, Bideford 1704 [W]
　Edmund, Shebbear 1714 W
　Edward, Pilton 1606 W
　Edward, Dolton 1746 A
　Eleanor, Langtree 1792 A
　Elizabeth, Twitchen 1640 [W]
　Elizabeth, Peters Marland 1679 W
　Elizabeth, Bideford 1687 A
　Elizabeth, Northam 1730 W
　Ezekiel, Barnstaple 1704 W
　Ezekiel, Barnstaple 1739 W
　Gabriel, Sheepwash 1625 [W]
　George, South Molton 1643 W
　George, Bideford 1731 W
　Henry, Barnstaple 1677 W
　Henry, Barnstaple 1716 W
　Henry, Dolton 1731 A
　Hugh, Cruwys Morchard 1631 [W]
　Israel, Bideford 1629 [W] and 1631 [W]
　James, Tawstock 1663 W
　James, Shebbear 1812 W
　Jane, Shebbear 1775 W
　John, Welcombe, snr. 1566 W
　John, Chittlehampton 1573 W
　John, Mariansleigh 1592 [W]
　John, Shebbear 1605 W

John, Buckland Brewer 1613 [W]; forename blank in Ms;
　supplied from parish register
John, Meeth 1616 [W]
John, Tawstock 1618 [W]
John, Instow 1632 [W]
John, Frithelstock 1637 W
John, Chawleigh, snr. 1639 W
John, Frithelstock 1645 W
John, Chittlehampton 1663 W
John, Shebbear 1668 A
John, Chawleigh 1669 A
John, Hartland 1676 A
John, Meeth 1690 W
John, Bideford 1710 W
John, Northam 1722 W
John, Bideford 1726 A
John, Bideford 1743 W
John, Westleigh 1763 W
John, Langtree 1778 W
John, Woolfardisworthy 1779 W
John, Frithelstock, gentleman 1803 W
John, Bideford, shipwright 1806 W; A dbn
John, Frithelstock 1837 W
Leonard, Northam 1697 W
Lodovic, Chittlehampton 1636 W
Lodovic, Yarnscombe 1643 A
Margery, Chittlehampton 1617 [W]
Martha, Shebbear 1728 A
Mary, Tawstock 1625 [W]
Mary, Barnstaple 1666 W
Mary, Yarnscombe, snr. 1675 W
Mary, Great Torrington 1732 W
Mary, Northam 1803 W
Mary, Bideford, widow 1806 A
Mary, Shebbear 1813 W
Mary, Chawleigh 1847 W
Mathew, Welcombe 1602 W
Mathew, Barnstaple 1687 A
Maurice, Meeth 1689 W
Nicholas, Monkleigh 1613 [W]; forename blank in Ms;
　supplied from parish register
Petronell, Shebbear 1597 [W]
Ralph, Northam 1717 W
Richard, Pilton 1622 [W]
Richard, Great Torrington 1641 A
Richard, Westleigh 1665 A
Richard, Westleigh 1694 W
Robert, Warkleigh 1637 W
Robert, Puddington 1669 W
Robert, Tawstock 1672 W
Robert, Yarnscombe 1674 W
Robert, Shebbear 1685 W
Roger, Chawleigh 1598 [W]
Roger, Littleham (near Bideford) 1604 W
Roger, Coldridge 1669 W
Sabine, Chittlehampton 1705 A
Samuel, Dowland 1754 W
Susan, Barnstaple 1671 W
Susan, Yarnscombe 1706 W
Thomas, Sheepwash 1573 A
Thomas, Barnstaple 1602 W
Thomas, Hartland 1640 W
Thomas, Great Torrington 1664 A
Thomas, Dowland 1740 W
Thomas, Ashreigney 1777 W
William, Shebbear 1565 W
William, South Molton 1643 W
William, Tawstock 1669 W
William, Chittlehampton 1674 W
William, Great Torrington, jnr. 1713 W
William, Frithelstock 1719 W
William, Tawstock 1724 W
William, Shebbear 1727 W
William, Chittlehampton 1736 W

William, Shebbear 1755 W
William, Merton, yeoman 1806 W
William, Witheridge 1822 W
William, Frithelstock 1839 A (Small) to John, father
Smalecorne, Smaleorne
   Smaleorne Robert, Fremington 1726 A
   Samuel, Barnstaple 1631 [W]
Smaleridg, Smalerudge see Smallridge
Smalewood see Smallwood
Small John, Bideford 1853 W
   William, Chittlehampton 1584 A
   William, Frithelstock 1839 A to John, father
Smallacombe Elizabeth, Shebbear 1592 [W]
   John, Shebbear 1592 [W]
Smalldon see Smaldon
Smallridge, Smaldridge, Smaleridge, Smalerudge, Smallridg
   Smaldridge Anthony, Chittlehampton, yeoman 1806 A
   Edward, Chittlehampton 1715 A
   Smallridg Honor, Chittlehampton 1701 W
   Smalerudge John, Chittlehampton 1596 [W]
   John, Chittlehampton 1616 [W]
   John, Northam 1741 W
   John, Chittlehampton, labourer 1808 W
   Smaldridge John, Tawstock 1814 W
   John, Tawstock 1851 W
   Mary, Chittlehampton 1670 W
   Smaleridg William, Northam 1711 A
Smallwood, Smalewood, Smallwood
   Smalwood Elizabeth, Molland 1599 [W]
   Smalewood Robert, Molland 1596 [W]
Smart, Smarte
   Dionysia, Cruwys Morchard 1661 A
   Smarte Elizabeth, Knowstone 1577 W
   James, Bideford 1693 T
   Smarte William, Knowstone 1623 [W] and 1624 O
   William, Cruwys Morchard 1661 A
Smith, Smithe, Smyth, Smythe
   Smyth ..., Bow 1609 [W]
   Smyth alias Shapland ... 1609 [W]
   Smyth ..., Great Torrington 1610 [W]
   Smyth ..., Stoke Rivers 1610 [W]
   Smyth ..., South Molton 1611 [W]
   Smyth ..., Parracombe 1612 [W]
   Smyth ..., Coldridge 1613 [W]
   Smyth ..., West Anstey 1613 [W]
   Smyth ..., Zeal Monachorum 1613 [W]
   Smyth ..., Chulmleigh 1614 [W]
   ..., Combe Martin 1615 [W]
   Smyth alias Whiddon ... 1707 A
   Smyth Aaron, Charles, farmer 1852 A to Richard
   Abraham, Abbotsham 1791 W
   Smyth Adam, Barnstaple 1728 W
   Smyth Agnes, Parracombe 1634 W
   Smyth Agnes, Hartland 1635 W
   Smyth Alice, Zeal Monachorum 1623 [W]
   Smyth Alice, Combe Martin 1684 A
   Smyth Amesius, Meshaw 1628 [W]
   Smyth Ann, North Molton 1636 A
   Smyth Ann, Combe Martin 1665 W
   Smyth Ann, Barnstaple 1689 W
   Ann, Barnstaple 1780 A
   Ann, North Molton 1787 W
   Ann see also Francis or Frances Bale or Ball
   Smyth Anthony, Marwood 1625 [W]
   Anthony, Berrynarbor 1704 W
   Smyth Bartholomew, Filleigh 1597 [W]
   Smithe Bernard, Clovelly 1570 W
   Catherine, Great Torrington, widow 1641 W
   Smyth Catherine, South Molton 1663 [W]
   Smyth Catherine, Barnstaple, widow 1707 [W]
   Catherine, Combe Martin 1780 [W]
   Smyth Cecilia, Fremington 1627 [W]
   Smyth Charity, Ilfracombe 1626 [W]
   Charles, St Giles in the Wood 1705 A
   Smyth Charles, St Giles in the Wood 1734 A

Charles, Bideford 1845 W to Mary wife of John Roberts of
   Bristol, surveyor of customs, daughter
Smyth Christian, Stoke Rivers 1587 W
Christian, Combe Martin 1672 W
Christmas, Bideford 1845 A
Smyth Daniel, North Molton 1667 W
Smyth Daniel, North Molton 1726 W
Smyth Dennis, Zeal Monachorum 1589 W
   Dudley, Chulmleigh 1746 A
   Dudley, Chulmleigh 1759 A
Smyth Edward, Marwood 1641 W
   Edward, Marwood 1663 W
   Edward, Barnstaple 1671 W
Smyth Edward, Shirwell 1738 W
   Edward, Shirwell 1776 W
Smyth Elizabeth, North Molton 1742 A
   Elizabeth, Ilfracombe 1747 W
   Elizabeth, North Molton 1760 W
   Elizabeth, Combe Martin 1791 A
   Elizabeth, Ilfracombe 1856 W
   Elizabeth, George Nympton 1857 W
Smyth George, East Down 1589 W
Smyth George, North Molton 1740 W
   George, Marwood 1775 A
Smith alias Bale George, Combe Martin 1776 W
Smyth George, Marwood 1793 W
   George, Marwood, yeoman 1803 A
Smyth George, Marwood, yeoman 1845 A to Mary, widow
Smyth George, Marwood 1850 W
Smyth George, Charles, farmer 1852 A to Richard
   Grace, Great Torrington 1650 [W]
   Grace 1669 W
   Grace, South Molton 1759 W
   Grace, East Worlington 1820 W
Smythe Henry, High Bray 1570 W
Smyth Henry, West Anstey 1587 W
Smyth Henry, Filleigh 1618 [W]
   Henry, Hartland 1678 A
Smyth Henry, Barnstaple 1691 A
Smyth Henry, North Molton 1703 W
Smyth Henry, North Molton 1739 W
   Henry, North Molton 1762 W
   Henry, North Molton 1787 A
Smyth Henry, Filleigh, yeoman 1797 W
Smyth Henry, Filleigh 1818 W
   Henry, North Molton, yeoman 1845 A (South Molton) to John
   and George, sons
Smyth Henry, Charles 1852 W
Smythe Isott, Hartland 1577 W
   James, Great Torrington 1763 W
   James, North Molton 1769 W
Smyth James, North Molton, yeoman 1807 W
Smyth James, Chulmleigh 1839 W
   Jane, Berrynarbor 1614 [W]; forename blank in Ms; supplied
   from parish register
Smythe Joan, East Anstey 1574 W
Smyth Joan, Martinhoe 1587 W
Smyth Joan, Barnstaple 1596 [W]
Smyth Joan, West Anstey 1598 [W]
Smyth Joan, Great Torrington 1636 W
   Joan, North Molton 1672 W
Smyth Joan, Marwood 1685 A
Smyth Joan, Northam 1697 A
Smyth Joan, South Molton 1710 W
Smyth Joan, Charles 1853 W
Smythe John, North Molton 1568 W
Smythe John, Clovelly 1571 W
Smyth John, Hartland 1576 W
Smythe John 1580 W
Smythe John, Dolton 1583 W
Smyth John, West Anstey 1588 W
Smyth John, Meshaw 1593 [W] and 1598 [W]
Smyth John, Barnstaple 1603 W
Smyth John, Coldridge 1605 W

Smyth John, Marwood 1607 [W]; forename blank in Ms;
    supplied from parish register
Smyth John, Stoke Rivers 1619 [W]
Smyth John, Ilfracombe 1623 [W] and 1625 [W]
Smyth John, Berrynarbor 1624 [W]
Smyth John, Weare Giffard 1627 [W]
Smeath John, Knowstone 1637 A
Smyth John, Challacombe 1638 W
Smyth John, Great Torrington 1664 W
John, Atherington 1676 A
John, Atherington 1679 W
John, Ashreigney 1680 W
Smyth John, Frithelstock 1681 W
Smyth John, King's Nympton 1691 A
Smyth John, Northam 1692 A
John, Fremington 1694 A
John, Bow 1695 W
Smyth John, Barnstaple 1704 A
Smyth John, North Molton 1707 W
Smyth John, Great Torrington 1722 W
John, ship *Midway* 1746 A
John, North Molton 1762 W
John, Bideford 1770 W
Smyth John, Charles 1783 W
John, Chittlehampton 1802 W
John, Chittlehampton, yeoman 1807 W
John, Ilfracombe, maltster 1808 A
John, Witheridge, yeoman 1809 W
Smyth John, Charles, yeoman 1810 W
John, Merton 1814 W
John, Georgeham 1831 A
John, Martinhoe 1832 A to John of Lynton, son
John, South Molton 1842 W
Smyth John, Marwood 1847 W
John, George Nympton 1851 W
Smyth John, Charles 1852 W
John, Alverdiscott 1857 W
Smyth John, Charles 1857 W
John Trout, South Molton 1837 W
Smyth Joseph, Mortehoe 1599 [W]
Joseph, Bideford 1669 A
Smyth Macklin, Marwood 1640 W
Smyth Margaret, Frithelstock 1633 W
Smyth Margery, Clovelly, widow 1564 W
Smyth Marian, Tawstock 1586 W
Smyth Martha, North Molton 1741 W
Mary, Barnstaple 1615 [W]
Smyth Mary, Marwood 1629 [W]
Smyth alias Stanbury Mary, Barnstaple 1664 A
Mary, Great Torrington 1672 A
Smyth Mary, Marwood 1707 W
Smyth Mary, Marwood 1724 W
Mary, Combe Martin 1828 T
Mary, Mortehoe 1853 T
Smyth Mary Ann, Charles, sp. 1852 A to Richard
Smyth Mecholina, Marwood 1695 W
Smythe Nicholas, Stoke Rivers 1573 A
Smyth Nicholas, Frithelstock 1605 W
Nicholas, Alwington 1615 [W]
Smyth Nicholas, Great Torrington 1616 [W]
Smyth alias Medon Nicholas, Combe Martin 1661 W
Smyth Nicholas, Combe Martin 1737 A
Oliver, Marwood 1745 W
Smythe Pentecost, Chulmleigh 1579 W
Smyth Peter, Parracombe 1628 [W]
Peter, Georgeham 1854 W
Smyth Philip, Barnstaple 1622 [W] and 1629 [W]
Smyth Philip, St Giles in the Wood, clerk 1630 [W]
Philip, Ilfracombe 1815 W
Smyth Richard, Barnstaple 1620 [W]
Richard, Georgeham 1644 W
Smyth Richard, South Molton 1644 A
Smyth Richard, Combe Martin 1665 W
Smyth alias Wheadon Richard, Ilfracombe 1724 W
Smyth Richard, Ilfracombe 1726 W

Smyth Richard, North Molton 1740 A
Richard, Combe Martin 1771 W
Richard, Chittlehampton, yeoman 1798 W
Richard, Chittlehampton 1804 W
Richard, South Molton 1830 W
Smythe Robert, Clovelly 1571 W
Smyth Robert, South Molton 1581 W
Smyth Robert, Bideford 1723 A
Smith alias Southwood Robert, King's Nympton 1774 W
Robert, Mortehoe 1854 W
Smyth Roger, Frithelstock 1631 [W]
Sarah, Bideford 1770 W
Smyth Silvester, Lynton 1591 [W]
Smyth Simon, Marwood 1695 W
Smyth Simon, Marwood 1729 W
Smyth Susan, Barnstaple 1683 W
Smyth Susan, Bow 1694 A
Susan, Marwood 1793 W
Susan, Bideford, widow 1802 W
Tamar, Georgeham 1834 W
Tammy, Georgeham 1851 W
Smyth Thomas, High Bray 1577 W
Smyth Thomas, Ilfracombe 1617 [W]
Smyth Thomas, South Molton 1626 [W]
Smyth Thomas, North Molton 1638 W
Thomas, North Molton 1644 W
Thomas, Alwington 1671 W
Thomas, North Molton 1680 W
Smyth alias Weddon Thomas, Lynton 1688 W
Smyth Thomas, Marwood 1693 A
Thomas, Ilfracombe 1694 A
Thomas, Marwood 1694 W
Smyth Thomas, Bideford 1694 W
Thomas, North Molton 1706 A
Smyth Thomas, Lapford 1707 W
Smyth Thomas, North Molton 1733 W
Thomas, Bideford 1742 T
Thomas, Clovelly 1745 T
Thomas, Hartland 1747 A
Thomas, North Molton 1763 W
Thomas, Marwood 1773 W
Thomas, Bideford 1777 W
Thomas, Countisbury 1783 W
Thomas, Combe Martin, mariner 1799 W
Thomas, Combe Martin 1808 W
Thomas, Northam 1818 W
Smyth Thomasine, Barnstaple 1615 [W]
Smyth Thomasine, Marwood 1702 A
Smyth Thomasine, North Molton 1733 A
Smyth Walter, Berrynarbor 1614 [W]; forename blank in Ms;
    supplied from parish register
Smyth William, North Molton 1623 [W]
Smyth William, Winkleigh 1630 [W] and 1633 O
Smyth William, Ilfracombe 1638 W
Smyth William, Pilton 1639 W
Smyth William, Ilfracombe 1697 W
Smyth William, North Molton 1724 A
William, Ilfracombe 1748 A
Smyth William, North Molton 1779 W and 1780 A
Smyth William, South Molton, tanner 1796 W
William, Bideford, innholder 1818 A to Ann, widow
William, Northam 1829 W
William, Mortehoe 1831 W
Smyth William, East Buckland 1837 W
Smyth William, King's Nympton 1837 W
William, North Molton 1843 W and 1844 O
William, Northam 1851 W
Smithe alias Parke William, Mariansleigh, snr. [no year given]
    W
Smithe see Smith
Smithson, Smythston, Smythton
    George, Shirwell 1588 W
    James, Fremington 1622 [W]
    Smythson John, Ilfracombe 1620 W
    Smythstone Nicholas, Ilfracombe 1565 W

Smythson Philip, Barnstaple 1640 W
Smythson Thomas, Ilfracombe 1641 A
Smyth see Smith
Smytham alias Gybbons William, Little Torrington, Langtree
    1574 A
Smytham alias Gebbens William, Langtree 1603 W
Smythe see Smith
Smythson, Smythston see Smithson
Smoldon see Smaldon
Snapp, Snap
    John, Bideford 1696 W
    Snap Margaret, Great Torrington 1687 W
Snearman William, East Putford 1759 W
Snelcock, Snelcocke
    ..., Mortehoe 1622 [W]
    Snelcocke Henry, Coldridge 1575 W
Snell .... Challacombe 1600 W
    ..., Zeal Monachorum 1611 [W]
    ..., Nymet Rowland 1612 [W]
    ... 1664 [W]
    Andrew, Zeal Monachorum 1639 W
    Andrew, Zeal Monachorum 1761 W
    Andrew, North Tawton, yeoman 1796 W
    Andrew, Zeal Monachorum 1830 W
    Ann, Dowland 1625 [W]
    Anthony, Chawleigh 1618 [W]
    Anthony, Chawleigh 1689 W
    Anthony, Atherington 1707 W
    Anthony, Chawleigh 1712 A
    Anthony, Chawleigh 1716 W
    Anthony, Atherington 1741 A
    Anthony, Chawleigh 1748 W
    Anthony, High Bickington 1753 W and 1755 W
    Anthony, Chawleigh 1763 W
    Anthony, Beaford 1793 W
    Anthony, Chawleigh 1796 A
    Anthony, Beaford, yeoman 1799 W
    Anthony, St Giles in the Wood 1845 W
    Anthony, Little Torrington 1851 W
    Bernard, Winkleigh 1645 A
    Betty, Zeal Monachorum 1843 W
    Catherine, High Bickington 1846 W
    Charles, Merton 1762 A
    Charles, Dolton 1819 A
    Christopher, North Tawton 1736 W
    Edmund, Chulmleigh 1627 [W] and 1630 O
    Edward, Ashreigney 1701 W
    Edward, Barnstaple 1827 W
    Eleanor, Ashreigney 1726 W
    Snell alias Furson Elizabeth, Eggesford 1693 A
    Elizabeth, South Molton 1728 A
    Elizabeth, Chawleigh 1733 W
    Elizabeth, Zeal Monachorum 1844 W
    Francis, St Giles in the Wood 1755 A
    Francis, St Giles in the Wood 1838 A to Susanna, widow
    George, Chawleigh 1629 [W] and 1631 [W]
    George, George Nympton 1636 A
    George, Chawleigh 1667 A
    George, Dolton 1700 W
    George, Dolton 1734 W
    George, Merton 1794 W
    George, High Bickington, husbandman 1808 W
    George, Dolton 1829 W
    George, Zeal Monachorum 1852 W
    Henry, Chawleigh 1590 [W] and 1596 [W]
    Henry, Chawleigh 1639 W
    Henry, King's Nympton 1724 W
    Henry, St Giles in the Wood 1727 W
    Henry, St Giles in the Wood 1755 A
    James, Winkleigh 1735 A and 1741 A
    James, Beaford 1831 A to Thomas, father
    James, Beaford 1843 A to Anthony of Little Torrington,
      brother
    James, Heanton Punchardon 1855 W
    Jane, Dolton 1713 W
    Jane, Fremington 1857 W

    Joan, Chawleigh 1730 W
    John, Chawleigh 1585 W
    John, Zeal Monachorum 1586 W
    John, Chawleigh 1640 [W]
    John, Chawleigh 1664 W
    John, Chulmleigh 1682 W
    John, Ashreigney 1707 A
    John, Chawleigh 1716 W and 1722 A
    John, St Giles in the Wood 1717 W
    John, Ashreigney 1728 W
    John, Chawleigh 1755 W and A dbn 1755
    John, Chittlehampton 1781 W
    John, Burrington 1782 W
    John, North Tawton 1793 W
    John, Tawstock 1799 W
    John, Merton, yeoman 1808 W
    John, High Bickington 1813 W
    John, Bideford, yeoman 1814 A to Elizabeth, widow
    John, Beaford 1820 W
    John, High Bickington 1838 W
    John, North Tawton 1841 W
    John, Burrington 1844 W
    John, Burrington 1855 W
    John see Thomas Isaac
    Margery, Atherington 1721 W
    Mary, High Bickington 1758 A
    Mary, North Tawton 1800 A
    Mary, Beaford, widow 1808 W
    Mary, Winkleigh 1818 W
    Mary, Eggesford 1822 A
    Mary, Petrockstowe 1832 A
    Mary, Zeal Monachorum 1832 A to Elizabeth of Great
      Torrington, daughter
    Mary, Chawleigh 1850 W
    Mathew, George Nympton 1614 [W]; forename blank in Ms;
      supplied from parish register
    Michael, Yarnscombe, yeoman 1810 W
    Nicholas, Dolton 1643 W
    Richard, Zeal Monachorum, landlord 1802 W
    Robert, Fremington 1584 A
    Robert, North Tawton 1597 [W]
    Robert, Chawleigh 1644 W
    Robert, Chawleigh 1682 A
    Robert, Chawleigh 1706 W
    Robert, Atherington 1717 A
    Robert, Chulmleigh 1723 W
    Robert, Chawleigh 1747 W
    Robert, Burrington, yeoman 1806 W
    Robert, Winkleigh, yeoman 1811 W
    Rose, Chawleigh 1682 A
    Samuel, Zeal Monachorum 1825 W
    Simon, Burrington 1785 W
    Simon, Northam 1801 A
    Thomas, Zeal Monachorum 1676 W
    Thomas, Meshaw 1714 T
    Thomas, Winkleigh 1715 A
    Thomas, Winkleigh 1777 A
    Thomas, Beaford 1847 W
    Thomas, Great Torrington 1852 W
    Thomasine, Chawleigh 1716 W
    William, Zeal Monachorum 1593 [W] and 1597 [W]
    William, Chawleigh 1604 [W]; forename blank in Ms;
      supplied from parish register
    William, Eggesford 1622 [W]
    William, Chawleigh 1684 W
    William, Chulmleigh, snr. 1700 W
    William, Chawleigh 1700 A
    William, Chawleigh 1703 W
    William, Chawleigh 1725 W
    William, Fremington 1760 W
    William, Chawleigh 1772 W
    William, Burrington 1792 W
    William, Chawleigh, yeoman 1798 W
    William, Beaford, yeoman 1800 W
    William, St Giles in the Wood, yeoman 1800 A

William, Chawleigh 1815 W
William, Beaford 1819 W
William, Chawleigh 1828 W
William, Fremington 1848 W
Snitall Simon, Huish 1631 [W]
Sniveney or Suiveney Richard, Barnstaple 1703 A
Snow, Snowe
  Snowe ..., Northam 1602 [W]
  Snowe ..., Twitchen 1604 [W]
  Snowe ..., West Anstey 1607 [W]
  Snowe ..., South Molton 1608 [W]
  ..., Welcombe 1609 [W]
  Snowe ..., Coldridge 1609 [W]
  ..., West Anstey 1611 [W]
  Snowe ..., Burrington 1612 [W]
  Snowe ..., Woolfardisworthy 1612 [W]
  Agnes, Hartland 1595 [W]
  Agnes, Combe Martin 1776 A
  Agnes, Berrynarbor 1777 A
  Alexander, Cruwys Morchard 1707 A
  Snowe Alice, Hartland 1583 W
  Snowe Alice, West Anstey 1622 [W]
  Snowe Alice, Berrynarbor 1623 [W]
  Amesius, Littleham (near Bideford) 1682 A
  Snowe Ann, Winkleigh 1637 W
  Ann, Rackenford 1846 W
  Ann and George, Yarnscombe 1697 A
  Snowe Bernard, Hartland 1605 W
  Charlotte, Mortehoe 1838 W
  Snowe Christian, Hartland 1605 W
  Christian, Monkleigh 1827 W
  Snowe Dorothy, West Anstey 1615 [W]
  Edward, Witheridge, snr. 1734 W
  Edward, Witheridge 1735 A and 1737 A
  Edward, Ashford 1755 W
  Edward, Creacombe, yeoman 1796 W
  Elizabeth, Twitchen 1638 A
  Elizabeth, Bratton Fleming 1694 W
  Elizabeth, Ilfracombe 1745 W
  Elizabeth, Chittlehampton, widow 1806 W
  Elizabeth, Great Torrington 1856 W
  Ezekiel, Twitchen 1624 [W]
  Frances, Berrynarbor 1691 A
  Francis, Twitchen 1620 [W]
  Francis, Berrynarbor 1727 W
  Francis, Ilfracombe 1736 W
  Francis, Berrynarbor 1746 W
  George, Pilton 1585 A
  Snowe George, King's Nympton 1588 W
  Snowe George, Romansleigh 1613 [W]; forename blank in
    Ms; supplied from parish register
  Snowe George, Bideford 1631 [W] and 1632 [W]
  George, Chulmleigh 1772 A
  George, Chulmleigh 1826 W
  George and Ann, Yarnscombe 1697 A
  Gertrude, Chulmleigh 1849 W
  Grace, Bratton Fleming 1687 W and 1693 A
  Henry, South Molton 1672 W
  Henry, South Molton 1718 A
  Henry, Warkleigh 1740 W
  Henry, Warkleigh 1771 A
  Henry, Ilfracombe 1786 A
  Honor, Barnstaple 1754 A
  Snowe Hugh, Clovelly 1605 W
  Hugh, Hartland 1770 W
  Snowe Humphrey, Ilfracombe 1611 [W]; forename blank in
    Ms; supplied from parish register
  Snowe Humphrey, Berrynarbor 1635 W
  Humphrey, Ilfracombe, snr. 1643 A
  Humphrey, Ilfracombe 1683 W
  Humphrey, Ilfracombe 1703 A
  Humphrey, Ilfracombe 1734 A
  Isott, Littleham (near Bideford) 1596 [W]

Snowe Jerome, Hartland 1612 [W]; forename blank in Ms;
  supplied from parish register
Jerome, Berrynarbor 1705 A
Snowe Joan, Oakford, widow 1563 W
Snowe Joan, Yarnscombe 1570 W
Snowe Joan, Pilton 1602 W
Joan, Clovelly 1627 [W]
Joan, South Molton 1676 W
Joan, Berrynarbor 1736 W
Snowe John, South Molton 1566 W
Snowe John, Yarnscombe 1568 W
Snowe John, Oakford 1577 A
John, Oakford 1585 W
Snowe John, King's Nympton 1590 [W]
Snowe John, Hartland 1593 [W]
Snowe John, Northam 1604 W
Snowe John, Molland 1609 [W]; forename blank in Ms;
  supplied from parish register
Snowe John, Atherington 1613 [W] and 1615 O
Snowe John, Berrynarbor 1615 [W]; forename blank in Ms;
  supplied from parish register
Snowe John, Oakford 1625 [W]
Snowe John, East Down 1631 [W]
John, Mortehoe 1672 W
John, Oakford 1679 A
John, Great Torrington 1681 A
John, Marwood 1683 W and 1691 A
John, Ilfracombe 1691 A
John, Bratton Fleming 1693 W
John, Berrynarbor 1725 [W]
John, Ilfracombe 1735 A
John, Marwood 1751 A
John, Stoke Rivers 1768 W
John, Berrynarbor 1777 A
John, Barnstaple 1792 W
John, Monkleigh 1792 W
John, Tawstock 1804 W
John, Molland 1829 A to Ann, widow
John, Oakford, shoemaker 1854 A to James of South Molton,
  son
John, Barnstaple 1856 W
Joseph, Berrynarbor 1706 W, 1716 A, 1719 A & 1725 A
Julian, Mortehoe 1837 W
Margaret, Stoke Rivers 1757 A
Snowe Martin, Hartland 1579 W
Snowe Martin, South Molton 1591 [W]
Mary, Littleham (near Bideford) 1700 W
Mary, Clovelly, sp. 1806 W
Mary, Countisbury 1824 W
Nicholas, Ilfracombe 1640 W
Nicholas, Hartland 1641 W
Nicholas, Ilfracombe 1680 W
Nicholas, Warkleigh 1759 W
Nicholas, Chittlehampton 1763 A
Oliver, Fremington 1604 W
Snowe Oliver, Hartland 1620 [W]
Snowe Pather, Hartland 1631 [W]
Pather, Barnstaple 1639 A
Snowe Peter, Hartland 1568 W
Peter, Hartland 1603 W
Philip, Pilton 1599 [W]
Philip, Bideford 1706 A
Philip, Ilfracombe 1718 W
Snowe Radigon, Littleham (near Bideford) 1586 W
Snowe Richard, Hartland 1565 W
Snowe Richard, Coldridge 1600 W
Snowe Richard, Ilfracombe 1620 [W]
Snowe Richard, Winkleigh 1627 [W]
Snowe Richard, Barnstaple 1635 A
Richard, Hartland 1700 W
Richard, Barnstaple 1714 A
Richard, Molland 1754 A
Richard, Pilton 1792 W
Snowe Robert, West Anstey 1583 W

Robert, George Nympton 1595 [W]
Snowe Robert, Rose Ash 1617 [W]
Robert, West Anstey 1644 W
Robert, Hartland 1701 W
Robert, Witheridge 1716 W
Snowe Thomas, Ash Rose [Rose Ash] 1563 W
Snowe Thomas, Shirwell 1572 W
Thomas, West Anstey 1585 A
Thomas, Littleham (near Bideford) 1591 [W]
Thomas, Romansleigh 1597 [W]
Snowe Thomas, Hartland 1629 W
Thomas, Hartland, snr. 1639 A, 1640 O and 1643 A
Thomas, Chulmleigh 1644 W
Thomas, Clovelly 1666 W
Thomas, West Anstey 1681 W
Thomas, Chulmleigh 1716 A
Thomas, Monkleigh 1746 W
Thomas, Sheepwash 1750 A
Thomas, Newton Tracey 1781 W
Thomas, Chulmleigh 1782 A
Thomas, Molland 1804 W
Thomas, Monkleigh, yeoman 1807 W
Thomas, Knowstone 1854 W
Snowe Walter, Chulmleigh 1629 O
Snowe Walter, Pilton 1629 [W] (2)
Walter, Berrynarbor 1687 W
Walter, Combe Martin 1769 A
Snowe William, Ilfracombe 1599 [W]
Snowe William, Chawleigh 1602 T
Snowe William, Oakford 1626 [W]
Snowe William, Chulmleigh 1627 [W]
Snowe William, Hartland 1629 [W] and 1635 A
Snowe William, Littleham (near Bideford) 1638 [W]
William, Alwington 1673 A
William, Ilfracombe 1675 W, 1680 A and 1688 A
William, Frithelstock 1696 W
William, Ilfracombe 1710 W
William, Littleham (near Bideford) 1715 A
William, Tawstock 1719 A
William, Marwood 1739 W
William, Ilfracombe 1763 A
William, Littleham (near Bideford) 1763 W
William, Clovelly 1775 W
William, Littleham (near Bideford) 1786 W
William, Fremington, yeoman 1802 W
William, Mortehoe 1821 W
William, Hartland 1846 W
William, West Down 1846 W
Soaper see Soper
Socoden Humphrey, Lapford 1711 A
Sole Roger, George Nympton 1595 [W]
Soley, Sowllie
  Benjamin, Ilfracombe 1702 W
  Sowllie John, Countisbury 1580 W
Some Nicholas, Berrynarbor 1597 [W]
Somer, Somers see Summers
Somerton or Summerton Susanna, South Molton 1824 A to
  Henry Edworthy of Pilton, brother
Somerwill, Somervil, Somervile, Somerwell, Sommerwill,
  Summerwill
  Somervile Alexander, North Molton 1684 A
  Summerwill Elizabeth, Marwood, widow 1803 W
  Henry, Molland 1621 [W] and 1623 O
  Joan, Charles 1591 [W]
  John, East Buckland 1618 [W]
  Somervil John, High Bray 1716 W
  John, Ilfracombe 1746 W
  John, Newton Tracey 1751 W
  John, Tawstock 1783 W
  Sommerwill John, Marwood, yeoman 1802 W
  Sommerwill John, Tawstock 1815 W
  Somerwell Mary, Newton Tracey 1764 A
  Philip, Witheridge 1593 [W]
  Richard, Tawstock 1603 W
  Sommerwill Robert, North Molton 1724 W

Roger, Witheridge 1608 [W]; forename blank in Ms; supplied
  from parish register
Thomas, South Molton 1605 W
Thomas, High Bray 1631 [W]
Sommerwill Thomas, Marwood, yeoman 1804 W
William, Charles 1582 A
Sommer, Sommers see Summers
Sonacott George, North Molton 1618 [W]
Soners see Summers
Sonier Peter, Tawstock 1739 W
Soper, Soaper
  Soaper George, Bideford 1741 W
  William, Ilfracombe 1805 W
Sorrell Robert, Abbotsham 1594 W
Souden, Soudon see Sowden
Soutch George, Barnstaple 1591 [W]
  Walter, Newton St Petrock 1604 W
Southamore see Southmore
Southcoate see Southcott
Southcombe, Southcomb, Suthcomb, Suthcombe
  Southcomb alias Woodley Alice, Coldridge, widow 1568 W
  Southcomb Anthony, East Buckland 1715 [W]
  Anthony, East Buckland 1751 W
  Anthony, North Molton 1836 A to John, son
  Southcomb Elizabeth, Mariansleigh 1694 W
  Suthcomb Elizabeth and Humphrey, Atherington 1643 A
  Southcomb George, Rose Ash 1696 W
  George, Rose Ash 1763 W
  Grace, Rose Ash 1819 W
  Southcomb Henry, Chawleigh 1611 [W]; forename blank in
    Ms; supplied from parish register
  Henry, Rose Ash 1749 W and 1751 W
  Hugh, South Molton 1692 W
  Suthcombe Humphrey, Mariansleigh 1639 A
  James, Rose Ash, farmer 1809 W
  Suthcombe Joan, Cheldon 1623 [W]
  Joan, Burrington 1742 W
  Joan, East Buckland 1763 W
  Sowthcome John, Iddesleigh 1571 W
  Southcomb John, Cheldon 1618 [W]
  Suthcomb John, St Giles in the Wood 1643 W
  John, Rose Ash 1685 A
  Southcomb John, Mariansleigh 1700 A
  John, Rose Ash 1723 W
  John, Rose Ash 1750 W
  John, Rose Ash 1842 W
  Juliana, Rose Ash 1707 W
  Southcomb Leonard, Parkham 1666 W
  Southcomb Lodovic, Rose Ash 1663 W
  Southcomb Lodovic, Rose Ash 1674 A
  Margaret, Mariansleigh 1580 W
  Southcomb Robert, Mariansleigh 1672 W
  William, East Buckland 1781 W
Southcott, Southcoate, Southcote, Southcotte, Sowthcotte
  ..., Bideford 1610 [W]
  ..., Parkham 1612 [W]
  Alice, Petrockstowe 1594 [W]
  Ann, Westleigh 1713 W
  Edward, Weare Giffard 1698 A
  Southcote Emott, Parkham 1573 W
  George, Alwington 1579 W
  George, Fremington 1617 [W]
  Hannibal, Northam 1671 W
  Hugh, Northam 1600 W
  Sowthcotte Joan, Westleigh 1572 W
  Joan, Weare Giffard 1702 A
  Joan, Weare Giffard 1727 W
  Southcote John, Parkham 1568 W
  Southcotte John, Bideford 1579 A
  John, Parkham 1585 A
  John, Westleigh 1618 [W]
  John, Parkham 1676 [W] and A dbn
  Southcoate John, Bideford 1697 A
  John, Westleigh 1698 W
  Suthcott Leonard, Westleigh 1636 [W]

Leonard, Northam 1697 A
Suthcott Margery, Newton St Petrock 1633 W
Neville, Weare Giffard 1633 A and 1634 O
Neville, Weare Giffard 1686 A
Nicholas, Alwington 1579 W
Philip, Weare Giffard 1693 A
Philip, Weare Giffard 1706 W
Richard, Tawstock 1664 A
Simon, Petrockstowe 1581 A
Stephen, Weare Giffard 1613 [W]; forename blank in Ms;
    supplied from parish register
Thomas, Westleigh 1661 W
Suthcott Thomasine, Westleigh 1633 W
William, Bideford 1605 W
William, Northam 1621 A and 1625 O
William, Parkham 1695 A
Southell Richard, Buckland Brewer 1629 [W]
Southmore, Southamore
Southamore ..., Coldridge 1599 [W]
Southmore alias Reed Alice, Coldridge 1586 W
Richard, Coldridge 1594 [W]
Southwell Edward, ship *Lark* 1751 A
Southwood, Southwoode, Sowthwoode
..., Lapford 1602 [W]
Southwoode ..., Thelbridge 1602 [W]
..., Chulmleigh 1609 [W] and 1614 [W]
Alexander, St Giles in the Wood 1631 [W]
Sowthwoode Ambrose, Chulmleigh 1572 W
Arthur, Langtree 1600 W
Augustine, Coldridge 1597 [W]
Christian, Witheridge 1593 [W]
Edward, ship *Lark* 1748 A
Elizabeth, Chulmleigh 1639 A
Elizabeth, Chulmleigh 1666 A
Enoch, Chulmleigh 1708 W
George, Chulmleigh 1605 W
Hugh, Chulmleigh 1635 W
Joan, Thelbridge 1592 [W]
Southwoode Joan, St Giles in the Wood 1618 [W]
John, Chulmleigh, snr. 1567 W
John, Thelbridge 1583 W
John, Barnstaple 1622 [W]
John, Chawleigh 1623 [W]
John, King's Nympton 1638 A
John, St Giles in the Wood 1668 W
John, Chittlehampton 1682 [W]
Southward John, Barnstaple 1825 W
Lawrence, Thelbridge 1689 W
Lawrence, Thelbridge 1748 W
Peter, St Giles in the Wood 1638 W
Philip, Witheridge 1585 W
Philip, St Giles in the Wood 1602 W
Philip, South Molton 1634 W
Richard, Witheridge 1615 [W]
Richard, Chulmleigh 1627 [W]
Richard, Barnstaple 1638 [W]
Robert, Chulmleigh 1594 W
Southwood alias Smith Robert, King's Nympton 1774 W
Roger, Chittlehampton 1691 A
Roger, Fremington 1750 W
Samuel, Chulmleigh 1669 W
Sarah, Chulmleigh 1779 W
Thomas, Chawleigh 1597 [W]
Thomas, Bondleigh 1774 W
Thomas, Chulmleigh 1778 A
Tristram, Mariansleigh 1645 A
Southwoode William, St Giles in the Wood 1602 W
William, Thelbridge 1640 A
William, Thelbridge 1693 W
William, Bideford 1848 W
Southyeo
Southyeo alias Venner Ann, Great Torrington 1642 A
William, Great Torrington 1635 [W]
Soward John, Bow 1690 A
Sowden, Sawdon, Souden, Soudon, Sowdon
Soudon Alexander, Northam 1760 W

Sowdon Christopher, West Worlington 1663 A
Daniel, Northam 1743 W
Soudon Daniel, Northam 1744 A
Sowdon Dorothy, Burrington 1723 W
Elizabeth, Rose Ash 1845 W
Sowdon Henry, Lapford 1603 W
James, Molland 1849 W
Joan, Washford Pyne 1709 W
Sowdon John, Lapford 1623 [W]
Sowdon John, Chulmleigh 1624 [W]
Sowdon John, Burrington 1631 [W]
Sowdon John, Lapford 1672 A
Sowdon John, Burrington 1674 W
John, Chittlehampton 1702 W
John, Thelbridge 1741 A
John, Lapford 1764 A
Sowdon John, Rose Ash 1825 W
Joseph, Lapford 1691 A
Sawdon Lawrence, Lapford 1587 W
Sowdon Lawrence, Lapford 1595 [W]
Sowdon Lodovic, Burrington 1633 W
Mildred, Witheridge 1828 W
Sowdon Philip, Witheridge 1664 W and 1669 A
Souden Philip, Chawleigh 1739 W
Sowdon Richard, Lapford 1758 W
Sowdon Richard, East Worlington 1822 W
Sowdon Roger, Burrington 1640 A
Roger, Burrington 1705 A
Sowdon Thomas, Lapford 1731 A
Thomas, Lapford 1732 W
Sowdrake Robert, Pilton 1601 W
Sowford Elizabeth, Dolton 1565 W
Sowllie see Soley
Sowthcome see Southcombe
Sowthcotte see Southcott
Sowthwoode see Southwood
Sparcke see Sparks
Sparckwill Richard, Hartland 1611 [W]; forename blank in Ms;
    supplied from parish register
Spare James, Parkham 1720 W
Mary, Parkham 1729 W
William, Meeth 1769 W
Sparks, Sparcke, Spark, Sparke
Sparke Anthony, Barnstaple 1625 [W]
Sparke Catherine, Yarnscombe 1622 [W]
Spark Elizabeth, Northam 1758 W
Sparcke James, Clovelly 1617 [W]
Spark Joanna, Fremington 1587 W
Sparke John, Yarnscombe 1620 [W]
Sparke Margaret, Yarnscombe 1683 W
Sparke Mary, Heanton Punchardon 1671 A
Spark Richard, Great Torrington 1644 A
Sparke Robert, Northam 1748 A
Spark Robert, Northam 1751 A
Sparke William, Northam 1746 W
Sparke William, Sheepwash 1835 A to Joanna, widow
Sparman, Spearman
..., Chittlehampton 1615 [W]
Spearman Abraham, Shebbear 1774 W
Spearman Abraham, Shebbear 1790 W
Spearman Abraham, Shebbear, yeoman 1808 W
Spearman Abraham, Shebbear 1837 W
Ann, Barnstaple 1773 W
Bartholomew, Georgeham 1672 [W]
Christopher, Bratton Fleming 1590 [W]
Elizabeth, Barnstaple 1768 W
Spearman George, Shebbear 1777 W
Margaret, Bideford 1631 [W]
Spearman Margery, Parkham 1710 A
Robert, Barnstaple 1608 [W]; forename blank in Ms; supplied
    from parish register
Robert, Stoke Rivers 1640 [W]
Spearman Thomas, Shebbear 1736 A (2)
Thomas, Barnstaple 1760 W

Spearman Timothy, Hartland 1715 A
Spearman Uriah, Weare Giffard 1845 W
William, Bratton Fleming 1589 W
Spearman William, Hartland 1715 A
Sparrow, Sparrowe
  Elizabeth, Barnstaple 1633 W
  Sparrowe James, Barnstaple 1600 A; forename blank in Ms;
    supplied from parish register
  Sparrowe James, Barnstaple 1609 [W]; forename blank in Ms;
    supplied from parish register
  Sparrowe John, Barnstaple 1594 [W]
  Julian, Barnstaple 1690 [W]
  Sparrowe Philip, Barnstaple 1613 [W]; forename blank in Ms;
    supplied from parish register
Speake John, Tawstock 1625 [W]
Speare, Spear
  Spear Christopher, Petrockstowe 1792 A
  John, Winkleigh 1572 W
  John, Ashreigney 1681 W
  Margery, Winkleigh 1571 W
  Michael, Roborough 1667 W
  Michael, Meeth 1713 W
  Thomas, Winkleigh 1580 W
Spearman see Sparman
Speed William, Barnstaple 1741 W
Spencer, Spensar, Spenser
  ...., Hartland 1607 [W]
  Alexander, Mariansleigh 1625 [W]
  Spenser Alexander, Rose Ash 1697 W
  Alexander, Rose Ash 1770 W
  Beata, Bideford 1832 O
  Elizabeth, Mariansleigh 1720 W
  Elizabeth, South Molton, jnr. 1851 W
  Francis, East Worlington 1821 W
  Spenser George, Mariansleigh 1697 A
  George, Mariansleigh 1733 W
  George, East Worlington, butcher 1809 W
  Henry, Chawleigh 1631 [W]
  Henry, Mariansleigh 1667 W
  Jane, Satterleigh 1628 [W]
  Joan, Mariansleigh 1587 W
  Joan, Rose Ash 1793 W
  John, Witheridge 1573 W
  John, Satterleigh 1604 W
  John, Chulmleigh 1662 W
  John, Mariansleigh, snr. 1672 W
  Sarah, Bideford 1827 W
  Spensar Thomas, Witheridge 1573 W
  William, Bideford 1768 A
Spicer Bartholomew, Pilton 1748 W
  Hugh, Rose Ash 1663 W
  Mary, Pilton 1731 W
  Richard, Pilton 1692 W
  Samuel, Pilton 1720 W
Spinner John, Knowstone 1791 W
Spinster Simon, Pilton 1625 [W]
  Thomas 1597 [W]
Spinway Hugh, Combe Martin 1723 A
Spiring Mary, Bideford 1762 A
Spooner Elizabeth, Rose Ash 1714 W
Spopton ...., South Molton 1747 W
Spour see Spurr
Sprague, Sprage
  Sprage George, South Molton 1625 [W]
  George, South Molton 1682 A
  Henry, South Molton 1687 A
  Mary, South Molton 1687 A
Spray, Spraye see Spry
Sprigg, Spriggs
  Anthony, South Molton 1740 W
  Spriggs Phillippa, Hartland 1636 A
  Sarah, Georgeham 1755 W
  Simon, Chittlehampton 1739 W
Spry, Spray, Spraye
  Spray George, Bideford 1812 W

Joan, Bideford 1690 W
Joan, Huish 1782 W
Joan, Witheridge 1813 W
Thomas, Bideford 1747 W
Spray Thomasine, Chawleigh 1638 W
Walter, Bideford 1682 A
Walter, Bideford 1701 W
Spraye William, Instow 1573 W
William, Witheridge 1781 W
William, Buckland Filleigh 1827 W
Spurr, Spour, Spur
  Spour Elizabeth, Rose Ash 1714 W
  Spour Peter, Northam 1710 W
  Valentine, Buckland Brewer 1668 W
  Spur Valentine, Buckland Brewer 1709 W
Spurrier Spuyer Ann, Lynton, widow 1808 A
  James, Barnstaple, widower 1610 [W] "Sparrow" in register;
    forename blank in Ms; supplied from parish register
Spurway, Spurwaie
  Avis, Barnstaple, widow 1856 A to Caroline, sp., daughter
  Edward, Oakford 1741 W
  Elizabeth, Oakford 1683 A
  John, Barnstaple 1831 A
  Richard, Witheridge 1631 [W] and 1632 O
  Spurwaie Robert, Oakford 1607 [W] "of Carleton" in register;
    forename blank in Ms; supplied from parish register
  William, Oakford 1724 W
Squance ...., Northam 1601 [W]
  Daniel, Great Torrington 1750 W
  Daniel, Beaford 1778 W
  Daniel, Great Torrington 1799 W
  David, Hartland 1615 [W]
  Elizabeth, Northam 1853 W
  Gertrude, Great Torrington 1772 W
  Hannah, Great Torrington 1828 W
  John, Hartland 1599 [W]
  John, Parkham 1709 W
  John, Bow 1763 W
  John, Huntshaw, gentleman 1805 W
  John, Parkham 1813 W
  Mary, Great Torrington 1762 W
  Thomas, Tawstock 1825 W second probate
  William, Parkham 1846 W
Square Simon, North Tawton 1686 A
  Simon, High Bickington 1725 W
Squarlock John, Instow 1692 A
Squire, Squier, Squyer, Squyr, Squyre, Sqyre
  ...., East Anstey 1604 [W]
  ...., Parracombe 1604 [W]
  ...., Chittlehampton 1607 [W] and 1608 [W]
  ...., Wembworthy 1607 [W]
  ...., Huntshaw 1608 [W]
  ...., Winkleigh 1610 [W]
  ...., Bondleigh 1612 [W]
  ...., High Bickington 1811 A
  Squyre Agnes, North Molton 1598 [W]
  Andrew, Wembworthy 1606 W
  Andrew, Bideford 1665 W
  Andrew, Wembworthy 1675 [W]
  Ann, Shebbear, widow 1613 [W]; forename blank in Ms;
    supplied from parish register
  Squyer Ann, Burrington 1635 W
  Ann, High Bray 1776 W
  Ann, Bideford 1850 W
  Arthur, Bideford 1801 A
  Squyre Bartholomew, Tawstock 1624 [W]
  Squyre Christopher, North Molton 1591 [W]
  Christopher, Iddesleigh 1616 [W]
  Squyer Christopher, Parracombe 1628 [W]
  Christopher, North Molton 1666 W
  Christopher, South Molton 1700 W
  Daniel, Beaford 1717 A
  Squyer Dorothy, Filleigh 1644 A
  Dorothy, Bulkworthy 1849 W
  Squyer Eleanor, Burrington 1632 [W]

Elizabeth, South Molton 1712 A
Emanuel, Chulmleigh 1728 W
Squyre Emma, Goodleigh 1624 [W] and 1626 [W]
Ferdinand, Bideford 1666 W
Squyer Francis, Chulmleigh 1626 [W]
Francis, St Giles in the Wood 1731 W
Francis, St Giles in the Wood, carpenter 1810 W
Francis, St Giles in the Wood 1836 W
Squyre George, Burrington, widow 1624 [W]
George, South Molton 1660 W
George, Chittlehampton 1700 W
Squyr Henry, North Molton 1588 W
Henry, St Giles in the Wood 1772 A
Henry, St Giles in the Wood 1789 A
Hugh, Burrington 1735 A
Hugh, Bulkworthy 1738 A
Humphrey, Bideford 1856 W
James, Sheepwash, yeoman 1801 W
Jane, St Giles in the Wood 1680 A
Jane, Brendon 1748 W
Squyre Joan, Burrington 1565 [W]
Squyre Joan, Witheridge 1565 W
Squyre Joan, Wembworthy 1596 [W]
Squyre Joan, North Molton 1597 [W]
Joan, North Molton 1608 [W]; forename blank in Ms; supplied
   from parish register
Joan, Chittlehampton 1669 A
Squier alias Hooper Joan, Bideford 1679 A
Joan, Mariansleigh 1686 W
Squyre John, Wembworthy 1588 W
Squyer John, Burrington 1596 [W]
John, Bondleigh 1603 W
John, Coldridge 1604 W
John, North Molton 1614 [W] "of Enthye" in register;
   forename blank in Ms; supplied from parish register
Squyer John, Warkleigh 1628 [W]
Sqyre John, Bondleigh 1633 O
Squier John, Warkleigh, snr. 1643 W
John, Goodleigh 1664 W
John, Cruwys Morchard 1665 W
John, Mariansleigh 1668 W
John, Winkleigh 1668 W
John, South Molton 1674 W
John, Frithelstock 1676 W
John, Bideford 1701 W
John, North Molton 1704 A
John, North Molton 1710 W and A
John, Bulkworthy 1711 W
John, Bulkworthy 1728 A
John, Brendon 1745 W
John, Buckland Brewer 1791 A
John, Frithelstock 1791 W
John, Bulkworthy, shopkeeper 1806 W
John, Lynton, yeoman 1824 A to Agnes, widow
John, Roborough 1850 W
Jonah, Winkleigh 1679 A
Jonah, Petrockstowe 1841 A
Lewis, Shebbear 1606 W
Margaret, Charles 1694 A
Squyer Mark, Winkleigh 1623 [W]
Squyre Martha, King's Nympton 1635 W
Squyer Mary, Chulmleigh 1634 A
Mary, King's Nympton 1669 W
Mary, Frithelstock 1683 W
Mary, Barnstaple 1842 A
Michael, North Molton 1704 W
Squier Michael, North Molton 1725 W
Michael, North Molton 1787 W
Michael, North Molton 1823 W
Michael, North Molton 1842 W
Squyre Nicholas, Chulmleigh 1565 W
Squyre Paschal, Shebbear 1624 [W]
Paschal, Charles 1674 W
Squyer Peter, Lynton 1635 W
Philip, Brendon 1742 A

Philip, Fremington 1744 A
Philip, North Molton 1762 W
Philip, Lynton, yeoman 1802 W
Philip, Bulkworthy 1833 W
Squyre Philpott, Chulmleigh, widow 1567 W
Squyer Richard, North Molton 1566 W and 1568 W
Squier Richard, Bondleigh 1569 W
Squyre Richard, Chulmleigh 1577 W
Squyre Richard, St Giles in the Wood 1621 [W]
Squyre Richard, Great Torrington 1639 W
Richard, Chittlehampton 1669 A
Richard, Goodleigh 1683 A
Richard, North Tawton 1758 W
Richard, Chittlehampton 1767 W
Squyre Robert, North Molton 1586 A
Robert, St Giles in the Wood 1702 W
Robert, Great Torrington 1760 A
Roger, North Molton 1611 [W]; forename blank in Ms;
   supplied from parish register
Samuel, Burrington, jnr. 1717 W
Samuel, High Bickington, yeoman 1811 A
Squyre Susan, North Molton 1597 [W]
Squyre Susan, North Molton 1599 [W]
Susan, Sheepwash 1815 W
Sybil, North Molton 1615 [W]
Thomas, North Molton 1567 W
Squyre Thomas, Shebbear 1599 [W]
Thomas, Huntshaw 1618 [W]
Squyer Thomas, Chulmleigh 1626 [W]
Thomas, Parkham 1703 W
Squyer Thomasine, Burrington 1636 W
Valentine, Frithelstock 1665 W
Walter, Warkleigh 1567 W
Squyer William, North Molton 1570 W
Squyer William, Winkleigh 1577 W
William, Bondleigh 1617 [W]
Squyer William, Bideford 1638 A
Squyre William, North Molton 1640 W
William, Lynton 1669 A
William, Lynton 1684 W
William, Berrynarbor 1688 A
William, South Molton 1700 W
William, Hartland 1701 W
William, Hartland 1701 W
William, Peters Marland 1709 A
William, North Molton 1740 W
William, Bondleigh 1758 W
William, Martinhoe 1765 W
William, North Molton 1802 W*
William, St Giles in the Wood 1838 W
William, Bratton Fleming 1847 W
William, Lynton 1856 A
Willmot, Parracombe 1755 W
Squirrell, Squyrell
   Squyrell James, Pilton 1622 [W]
   Squyrell John, Pilton 1631 W
   Squyrell Mary, Pilton 1631 A
Squyer, Squyr, Squyre see Squires
Squyrell see Squirrell
Sqyre see Squires
Stabb Nicholas Wilking, Ilfracombe, gentleman 1857 A to
   Thomas, surgeon, father; limited A of goods not covered by
   former grant passed at Exeter, Jun 1866
Stabbick Elizabeth, Rose Ash 1836 A
Stabledon see Stapledon
Stacy, Stacey
   Edward, Merton 1674 A
   Stacey James, Peters Marland 1845 W
   Stacey John, Merton 1828 A
   Malachi, Bideford 1727 A
   Thomas, Bideford 1681 A
Staddon, Staddin, Stadon
   Catherine, Fremington 1721 W
   Edward, Combe Martin 1768 W
   George, Tawstock 1719 W

George, Northam 1764 A
John, Barnstaple 1640 A
Mary, Combe Martin 1783 A
Staddin Michael, Northam 1668 A
Robert, Barnstaple 1635 W
Thomas, Monkleigh 1573 W
Stadon Thomasine, Bratton Fleming 1574 W
William, Combe Martin 1661 A
Stadham John, Bratton Fleming 1602 W
Stadler William, Combe Martin 1688 W
Stadon see Staddon
Stafford, de Stafford, Stafforde, Stawford
de Stafford ..., esquire 1613 [W]
Stawford Ann, Witheridge 1636 W
George, Bideford 1605 [W]; forename blank in Ms; supplied
from parish register
James, Witheridge 1619 O
Nicholas, Chulmleigh 1627 [W]
Philip, Chulmleigh 1633 W
Robert, Stafford, Dolton 1604 W
Robert, Bideford 1806 A
Thomas, Dolton, esquire 1674 A
Thomasine, Great Torrington 1605 W
William, Roborough 1622 [W]
Staley Augustine, South Molton 1704 A
Stambery, Stambury see Stanbury
Stamp Philip, West Down 1711 W
Stanbury, Stambery, Stambury, Stanberie, Stanberry,
Stanberrye, Standbury
..., Great Torrington 1610 [W]
Stanbury alias Smyth ..., Barnstaple 1664 A
Abraham, Barnstaple. cooper 1803 W
Agadius, Ilfracombe 1728 W
Agnes, East Down, widow 1566 W
Agnes, Hartland 1635 W
Agnes, Barnstaple 1749 A
Alexander, Bideford 1625 [W]
Standbury Ann, Kentisbury 1676 W
Ann, Littleham (near Bideford) 1856 A
Bridget, Great Torrington 1619 [W]
Charles, Barnstaple 1694 A
Stambery Charles, Bideford 1708 W
Charles, Northam 1747 W
Elisha, Dolton 1777 W
Stambury Elizabeth, Barnstaple 1817 W
Elizabeth, Barnstaple 1834 A A dbn 1835
Gabriel, Bideford 1697 A
George, Barnstaple 1604 [W]; forename blank in Ms; supplied
from parish register
George, East Down 1689 A
Stambury George, Barnstaple 1726 W
George, Tawstock 1788 W
Stambury George, Tawstock 1827 W
Grace, Pilton 1740 W
Hannah, Berrynarbor 1705 W
Hannah, Berrynarbor 1729 A
Jane, Instow 1697 A
Jane, Ilfracombe, sp. 1851 A to Grace wife of Andrew
Richards
Stanberie John, East Down, snr. 1564 W
Stanberry John, East Down 1662 W
John, Barnstaple 1667 A
John, Ilfracombe 1678 A
Stanberrye John, Great Torrington [no year given] W
John, Barnstaple 1701 A
John, Shirwell 1702 W
Stambury John, Alwington 1716 W
John, Goodleigh 1730 W
John, Dolton, yeoman 1801 W
Joseph, Northam, mariner 1705 A
Margaret, Ilfracombe 1733 W
Nicholas, East Down 1598 [W]
Nicholas, Ilfracombe, snr. 1640 W
Nicholas, Berrynarbor 1729 A
Nicholas, Kentisbury 1729 W
Nicholas, Berrynarbor 1730 A

Philip, Berrynarbor 1685 A
Stambury Philip, Ilfracombe 1722 W
Richard, Pilton 1635 W
Richard, Barnstaple 1665 A
Richard, Ilfracombe 1668 W
Stambury Richard, Ilfracombe 1721 W
Richard, Ilfracombe 1743 A
Richard, King's Nympton 1840 W
Robert, East Down 1636 W
Robert, East Down 1670 A
Robert, East Down 1736 W
Robert, Shirwell 1739 A
Roger, Barnstaple 1662 A
Ruth, Kentisbury 1671 A
Sarah, Northam 1790 W
Thomas, Hartland 1704 W
Thomas, Pilton 1737 W
Thomas, Northam 1765 W
Thomasine, Barnstaple 1611 [W]; forename blank in Ms;
supplied from parish register
Thomasine, Dolton 1691 W
Thomasine 1719 A
William, Barnstaple 1597 [W]
William, Barnstaple 1623 [W] and 1629 [W]
William, Berrynarbor 1637 W
William, Berrynarbor 1664 W and 1666 W
William, Hartland 1693 A
William, Alwington 1694 W
William, Shirwell 1732 A
William, Northam 1744 W
William, Dolton 1766 W
William, Bratton Fleming 1775 A
William, Barnstaple 1839 W
Standish Charles, Barnstaple 1705 W
Dorothy, Barnstaple 1742 W
Edward, Barnstaple 1707 W
Joan, Tawstock 1736 W
Standon Nicholas, Bideford 1584 A
Stanely see Stanley
Stanlake, Stenlake
Stenlake ..., Newton St Petrock 1603 [W]
Stenlake Gertrude, Shebbear 1725 W
Stenlake John, Clovelly 1637 A and 1640 O
John, Winkleigh 1767 W
Stenlake Luke, Newton St Petrock 1605 W
Stanley, Stanely
Stanely Charles, East Buckland 1617 [W]
Edward, Barnstaple 1682 A and 1686 A
Stanely Edward, Abbotsham 1689 A
Stanely John, Abbotsham 1719 W
Mary, Barnstaple 1686 A
Stanely Richard, East Buckland 1597 [W]
Stanning John, Shebbear 1682 W
Margaret, Shebbear 1687 W
Stanton, Staunton
Staunton Francis, Weare Giffard 1679 A
James, Yarnscombe 1637 A
Jasper, Weare Giffard 1740 W
John, Brendon 1620 [W]
Lawrence, Brendon 1620 [W]
William Fry, heretofore of Stoke Damerel, but late of Little
Torrington 1833 W
Willmot, Weare Giffard 1692 A
Stapledon, Stabledon, Stapleton
..., Langtree 1608 [W]
..., Georgeham 1609 [W] and 1611 [W]
..., Shebbear 1613 [W]
Agnes, Georgeham, widow 1612 [W]; forename blank in Ms;
supplied from parish register
Amos, Alverdiscott 1605 W
Anthony, Buckland Brewer 1675 W
Baldwin, Hartland 1672 A
Bartholomew, Westleigh 1594
Bartholomew, Westleigh 1628 [W]
Bartholomew, Westleigh 1708 [W]

Stabledon Bartholomew, Instow 1716 A
Bartholomew, Landcross 1836 W
Edmund, Burrington 1674 W
Edmund, Burrington 1686 W
Edmund, Burrington 1711 W
Elizabeth, Langtree 1674 W
Elizabeth, Frithelstock 1743 W
James, Horwood 1639 W
James, Westleigh 1693 A
James, Bideford 1736 W
Stapleton James, Westleigh 1759 W
Stapleton James, Fremington 1840 W
Joan, Georgeham 1570 W
Joan, Buckland Brewer 1624 [W]
Stabledon Joan, High Bray 1695 W
John, Buckland Brewer 1624 [W]
John, Westleigh 1638 A
John, Hartland 1639 W
John, Parkham 1667 W
John, Alverdiscott 1669 A and 1672 O
John, Bideford 1679 W
Stabledon John, Beaford 1690 W
John, Burrington 1696 W
John, Buckland Brewer 1728 W
John, Buckland Brewer 1749 A
Stapleton John, Buckland Brewer 1761 W
John, Buckland Brewer 1793 W
Stapleton John, East Putford 1836 W
Stapleton John, late of the City of London 1852 A
Stapleton John, Bideford, shipowner 1854 A to Robert
    Mugford Stapleton of Bude, Cornwall, master mariner,
    father
Joseph, Buckland Brewer 1773 A
Joseph, Buckland Brewer 1792 A
Joseph, Buckland Brewer 1853 W
Lucy, Northam 1673 W
Mary, Buckland Brewer 1762 W
Nicholas, Langtree 1577 W
Nicholas, Bideford 1628 [W]
Nicholas, Tawstock 1748 W
Stapledon or Sapledon Petronell, Hartland 1630 [W]
Philip, Alverdiscott 1666 A
Philip, Buckland Brewer 1678 W
Stabledon Philip, Parkham 1701 W
Philip, Buckland Brewer 1748 A
Philip, Buckland Brewer, yeoman 1804 W
Rebecca wife of Arthur see Thomas Heard
Richard, Woolfardisworthy 1571 W
Richard, Woolfardisworthy 1635 W
Richard, Winkleigh 1638 A and 1640 O
Richard, Parkham 1745 A
Richard, Roborough, yeoman 1852 A to Mary
Sarah, Littleham (near Bideford) 1772 W
Thomas, Alverdiscott 1573 W
Thomas, Westleigh 1573 W
Thomas, Woolfardisworthy 1586 W
Thomas, Winkleigh 1620 [W] and O
Thomas, Westleigh 1637 A
Thomas, Newton Tracey 1640 O
Thomas, Winkleigh 1676 W
Stabledon Thomas, Frithelstock, snr. 1712 W
Thomas, Winkleigh 1715 W
Thomas, Frithelstock 1726 A
Thomas, Frithelstock 1739 A
Thomas, Bideford 1796 W
Thomas, Bideford, yeoman 1810 W
Thomas, Buckland Brewer 1812 W
Thomas, Buckland Brewer, yeoman 1855 A to Thomas, son
Thomasine, High Bray 1691 W
Walter, Hartland 1581 W
William, Langtree 1594 [W]
William, Alverdiscott 1604 W
William, Bideford 1666 A
William, Bideford 1669 [W]
William, Frithelstock 1673 A
Stabledon William, Buckland Brewer 1701 A

William, Buckland Brewer 1800 W and 1802 W
Stapleton William, Buckland Brewer 1824 W
Starland Thomas, Tawstock 1599 [W]
Staunton see Stanton
Stavely, Staveley
  Abraham, Abbotsham 1698 W
  Staveley Ann Chappell, Bideford 1851 W
  Elizabeth, Chittlehampton 1669 W
  George, Pilton 1727 W
  Staveley George, Bideford 1837 W
  John, Abbotsham 1671 A
  John, Pilton 1726 W
  Richard, Bideford 1632 A and 1633 O
  Richard, Chittlehampton 1667 [W]
  Thomas, Pilton 1727 W
Stawell Edmund, Bondleigh 1770 W and A
  Richard, Bondleigh 1783 W
  Thomas, Bondleigh 1770 W
  William Palmer, High Bickington 1850 W
Stawford see Stafford
Stawte see Stoat
Stedeford George, Atherington 1856 A
Steed John Oliver, Barnstaple 1847 W
Steer, Steere, Stere, Steure, Sture
  Abraham, Northam 1827 W
  Sture Alice, Great Torrington 1620 [W]
  Augustine, Chulmleigh 1703 W
  Bernard, Chulmleigh 1717 W
  Steere Charles, Witheridge 1741 A
  Steure Frideswide, Roborough 1567 W
  Steere Joan, Chulmleigh 1729 W
  Sture John, South Molton 1581 W
  John, Parracombe 1597 [W]
  John, Arlington 1670 A and O
  Steere John, Wembworthy, labourer 1819 A to Mary wife of
    Richard Cowler, widow
  Sture Lodovic, Lynton 1633 W
  Sture Philip, Brushford 1570 W
  Sture Richard, Bow 1594 [W]
  Richard, Huntshaw, jnr. 1823 W
  Richard, Abbotsham 1833 W
  Steere Robert, Witheridge, jnr. 1728 A
  Steere Robert, Witheridge 1735 W
  Steere Robert, Brushford 1740 A
  Susan, Abbotsham 1839 W
  Stere William, Mortehoe 1567 W
Steeven, Steevens, Steevins see Stephens
Steggins see Stiggins
Stemson, Stempson
  Alexander, South Molton 1740 A
  George, Cruwys Morchard 1690 A
  Stempson Samuel, Witheridge 1736 A
Stenlake see Stanlake
Stentiford Richard, Zeal Monachorum 1804 W
  William, Wembworthy 1736 W
Stepard Sarah, Frithelstock 1745 W
Stepers Joan, Coldridge 1728 W
Stephens, Steeven, Steevens, Steevins, Stephain, Stephan,
  Stephen, Stephings, Stevens, Stevings, Stevins
  ..., Dolton 1602 [W]
  ..., St Giles in the Wood 1609 [W]
  ..., South Molton 1610 [W]
  ..., Landcross 1612 [W]
  ..., Ilfracombe 1613 [W]
  ..., Thelbridge 1614 [W]
  Agnes, Marwood 1619 [W]
  Steeven Agnes, Woolfardisworthy 1623 [W]
  Agnes and William, Creacombe 1617 [W]
  Stephen Alice, Woolfardisworthy 1626 [W]
  Amos, West Anstey 1617 [W]
  Stevins Ann, Coldridge 1689 W
  Stephen Anthony, Woolfardisworthy 1591 [W]
  Austin, Oakford 1610 [W]; forename blank in Ms; supplied
    from parish register
  Steevens Baldwin, St Giles in the Wood 1630 [W]

Beaton, Northam 1595 [W]
Stevins Catherine, Buckland Brewer 1700 A
Charles, Dolton 1608 [W]; forename blank in Ms; supplied
    from parish register
Christian, East Buckland 1574 W
Christopher, Northam 1741 W
Christopher, Barnstaple 1779 A
Stephen Constance, Tawstock 1592 [W]
David, Tawstock 1593 [W]
David, Ilfracombe 1626 [W]
Edward, Burrington 1827 W
Stevens Eleanor, East Anstey 1704 W
Elizabeth, Eggesford 1625 [W]
Stevens Elizabeth, Chulmleigh 1663 W
Stevins Elizabeth, Barnstaple 1675 A
Stevens Elizabeth, Buckland Brewer 1702 W
Elizabeth, Frithelstock 1754 W
Stevens Francis, Chulmleigh 1842 W
Stephen George, Roborough 1631 [W]
Steephens George, Mortehoe 1634 W
Steevens George, Beaford 1642 A
Stevins George, Tawstock 1681 A
Stevins George, Coldridge 1687 W
Stevins George, Dolton 1697 A
Stevins George, West Anstey 1698 W
George, Pilton 1753 A
Gilbert, Bondleigh 1640 A
Steevins Giles, Ilfracombe 1720 W
Stephan Gregory, Mortehoe 1625 [W]
Henry, Dolton 1624 [W]
Stevens Henry, Chulmleigh 1669 W
Stevins Henry, Buckland Brewer 1687 W
Stevins Henry, Chulmleigh 1691 A and 1700 A
Stevings Henry, Bideford 1705 W
Henry, Frithelstock 1749 W
Stevens Henry, Ilfracombe 1765 W
Steevins Henry, Ilfracombe 1835 W
Stevens Henry, Winkleigh 1846 W
Honor, Mortehoe 1630 [W]
Stephen Hugh, Barnstaple 1615 [W]; forename blank in Ms;
    supplied from parish register
Stevins Hugh, Buckland Brewer 1733 W
Hugh, Barnstaple 1755 A
Hugh, Barnstaple 1783 W
James, Barnstaple 1613 [W]; forename blank in Ms; supplied
    from parish register
Stevins James, Northam 1689 W
Stevins James, Clannaborough 1697 W
Stevens Jane, Buckland Brewer 1702 W
Stephings Jane, Ilfracombe 1829 W
Stephen Jenkin, Bideford 1662 W
Joan, Ilfracombe 1580 W
Stephen Joan, West Anstey 1606 W
Joan, Lynton, widow 1607 [W]; forename blank in Ms;
    supplied from parish register
Joan, Oakford 1614 [W]; forename blank in Ms; supplied from
    parish register
Steevens alias Jacob Joan, Bow 1641 W
Stevins Joan, West Anstey 1705 W
Joan, Tawstock 1734 W
Stephen John, High Bray 1572 W
Stephain John, Ilfracombe 1577 W
Stevens John, Tawstock 1578 A
Steven John, Langtree 1579 W
Steven John, Tawstock 1579 W
John, West Anstey 1580 W
Stephen John, Northam 1583 W
John, Northam 1584 A
John, St Giles in the Wood 1585 W
Stephen John, Barnstaple 1587 W
Stephen John, Heanton Punchardon 1587 W
Stephen John, Northam 1589 W
John, Brendon 1598 [W]
Stephens alias Holmes John, Barnstaple 1601 W
John, Lynton 1604 W

John, Monkleigh 1609 [W]; forename blank in Ms; supplied
    from parish register
John, Cheldon 1619 [W]
John, Lynton 1629 [W]
Steevins John, Bow 1641 A
Steevins John, Woolfardisworthy 1643 A
John, Barnstaple, gentleman 1675 W
Stevens John, Winkleigh 1676 W
Stevins John, Ilfracombe 1682 A
Stevens John, Northam 1689 W
Stevins John, Molland 1698 W
John, Northam 1701 W
Stevins John, Ilfracombe 1703 A and 1709 A
Stevins John, Northam 1710 W
Stevins John, Witheridge 1710 W
Stevins John, North Molton 1712 A
John, Northam 1722 W
John, St Giles in the Wood 1722 W
John, Barnstaple 1724 A
Steevins John, Ilfracombe 1747 A
John, Winkleigh 1826 W
Stevens John, Winkleigh 1851 W
Joseph, Fremington, maltster 1804 W
Lawrence, Brendon 1604 W
Stephan Margaret, Brendon 1570 W
Stephen Margaret, Northam 1588 W
Stevens Margaret, Ilfracombe 1719 W
Stevens Margery, Wembworthy 1739 A
Stevens Mary, Barnstaple 1674 W
Stevins Mary, Ilfracombe 1682 W
Stevins Mary, Heanton Punchardon 1745 W
Mary, Winkleigh 1750 A and 1752 A
Michael, High Bray 1630 [W]
Stevins Nicholas, Bideford 1716 A
Peter, King's Nympton 1619 [W]
Philip, Roborough 1617 [W]
Steevens Philip, Molland 1670 W
Steevins Philip, Ilfracombe 1732 W
Stevens Philip, Bideford 1839 W
Richard, Lynton 1587 W
Richard, West Anstey 1600 W
Richard, South Molton, esquire 1635 A and 1636 O
Steevens Richard, Molland 1640 W
Richard, Huntshaw 1675 W
Stevins Richard, Bideford 1704 W
Stevens Richard, Monkleigh 1742 A
Richard, Meshaw 1750 A
Richard, Winkleigh 1780 W
Richard, Roborough 1790 W
Richard, Heanton Punchardon 1810 W
Richard, Northam, mariner 1810 A
Stevens Richard, Winkleigh 1830 W
Stephan Robert, Ilfracombe 1568 W
Robert, Woodland, West Anstey 1572 W
Stephen Robert, Barnstaple 1629 [W]
Robert, Tawstock 1724 A
Stevens Robert, Instow 1857 W
Robert, Witheridge 1615 [W]; forename blank in Ms; supplied
    from parish register
Roger, West Anstey 1598 [W]
Stevens Samuel, Winkleigh, yeoman 1805 W
Stevens Samuel, Winkleigh 1837 W
Stevens Samuel, Winkleigh 1850 W
Stevens Samuel, Winkleigh 1857 W
Stevins Simon, Ilfracombe 1693 W
Stevins Simon, Ilfracombe 1705 W
Stevings Simon, Ilfracombe 1741 W
Simon, Ilfracombe 1760 W
Stevens Simon, Winkleigh 1835 W
Stephen Thomas, Chulmleigh 1571 W
Thomas, Witheridge 1580 W
Thomas, Woolfardisworthy 1590 [W]
Stephen Thomas, Witheridge 1614 [W]; forename blank in
    Ms; supplied from parish register
Steevens Thomas, Ashreigney 1637 A

Thomas, Northam 1640 A
Stevins Thomas, West Anstey 1687 W
Stevens Thomas, Bideford 1776 W
Stevens Thomas, Great Torrington 1800 A
Thomas, Great Torrington 1815 W
Stevens Thomas, Bideford, blacksmith 1853 A to Thomas,
    blacksmith and Robert, labourer, sons
Stevens Thomasine, Barnstaple 1742 W
Steevens Tristram, Barnstaple 1669 A
Walter, Barnstaple 1596 [W]
Styvine William, Woolfardisworthy 1582 W
Stephen William, Dolton 1589 W
William, West Down 1597 [W]
William, St Giles in the Wood 1598 [W]
William, Chawleigh 1604 W
Stephen William, Woolfardisworthy 1605 W
William, Marwood 1611 [W]; forename blank in Ms; supplied
    from parish register
William, Mortehoe 1615 [W] and 1623 A
William and Agnes, Creacombe 1617 [W]
William, West Anstey 1629 [W]
Steevens William, Beaford 1640 [W]
Stevens William, Roborough, snr. 1642 W
Steevins William, Ilfracombe 1645 W
Steevins William, Winkleigh 1676 W
Stevins William, Buckland Brewer 1685 W
Stevins William, Witheridge 1690 A
William, Rose Ash 1703 [W]
Stevens William, Ashreigney 1707 A
Stevens William, Northam 1707 A
William, Northam 1731 [W]
William, Chulmleigh 1741 [W]
William, Dolton 1743 [W]
Steevens William, South Molton 1774 W
William, Roborough 1803 [W]
Stevens William, Instow 1812 W
Stevens William, Winkleigh 1819 W
Stevens William, South Molton 1823 W
Stevens William, Merton 1850 W
Stere see Steer
Sterlake Richard, Great Torrington 1582 W
Sterling Avis, Tawstock 1668 A
Sterry, Sterrie, Sterye, Stirrey
    Sterrie ..., Instow 1611 [W]
    Sterye Genson, Instow 1564 W
    Henry, Ilfracombe 1597 [W]
    Thomas, Clovelly 1617 [W]
    Stirrey Welthian, Ilfracombe 1625 [W]
Steven, Stevens, Stevings, Stevins see Stephens
Steward, Stewart
    Elizabeth, South Molton 1699 A
    Stewart John, Wembworthy 1763 A
Stick, Sticke, Stycke
    Stick alias Cartwith or Cartway ..., Rose Ash 1671 A and 1673
      O
    Stycke Anthony, Newton Tracey 1639 [W]
    Elizabeth, Rose Ash 1699 W
    Sticke John, Frithelstock 1570 W
    Stycke John, Pilton 1624 [W]
    Stycke John, Warkleigh 1645 W
    Sticke Richard, Coldridge 1591 [W]
    Stycke Richard, Newton Tracey 1632 [W]
    Richard, Coldridge 1676 A
    Sticke Robert, Frithelstock 1643 W
    William, Great Torrington 1709 W
Stiddiford William, Chittlehampton 1793 A
Stiggins, Steggins
    Steggins Alexander, Great Torrington 1606 W
    Ann, Great Torrington 1631 [W]
    Jeremiah, Merton 1698 W
Stile Thomas, North Molton 1577 A
Stirrey see Sterry
Stirtson see Stutson
Stoat, Stawte, Stoate, Stote, Stott, Stowte
    Stote ..., Stoke Rivers 1614 [W]

Stote Agnes, East Anstey 1573 W
Stote Agnes, North Molton 1630 [W]
Stoate Alexander, North Tawton 1711 W
Stote Christopher, Northam 1607 [W]; forename blank in Ms;
    supplied from parish register
Stote David, Countisbury 1580 W
Stote David, Barnstaple 1586 W
Stot Edward, Ilfracombe 1639 W
Edward, Pilton 1720 W
Edward, Trentishoe 1745 W
Stoal Edward, Barnstaple 1753 W
Stote George, Brendon 1586 W
Stote George, Ashford 1635 W and 1638 O
George, Heanton Punchardon 1780 W
Hannah, Barnstaple 1826 A
Stote Henry, Stoke Rivers 1590 [W]
Stote Henry, Chittlehampton 1640 A
Hezekiah, Barnstaple 1720 W
Jenny, Barnstaple 1837 W
Stote Joan, Brendon 1566 W
Joan, Stoke Rivers 1675 W
Stote John, Stoke Rivers 1576 A
Stote John, Ashford 1587 W
Stote John, Trentishoe 1592 [W]
Stote John, Barnstaple 1623 [W]
Stoate John, East Buckland 1627 [W]
Stoate John, North Molton 1627 [W]
Stoate John, Brendon 1678 A
Stoate John, Brendon 1685 W
Stoate John, Goodleigh 1750 W
Stott John, Northam 1765 W
John Smale, Barnstaple 1830 W
Stoate Joseph, Pilton 1750 W
Stote Margaret, Northam 1620 [W]
Stote Mary, Barnstaple 1761 W
Mary, Heanton Punchardon 1788 W
Stote Peter, Goodleigh 1627 [W]
Stowte Richard, Mortehoe 1622 [W]
Stawte Richard, Barnstaple 1623 [W]
Stote Robert, Brendon 1564 W
Robert, Heanton Punchardon 1761 W
Stote Thomas, Barnstaple 1617 [W]
Thomas, Barnstaple 1723 W
Stote William, Brendon 1586 W
Stote William, Parracombe 1635 W
Stote William, South Molton 1705 W
Stoate William, North Molton 1727 A
William, Barnstaple 1836 W
William Richards, Alwington 1820 W
Stock, Stocke
    Grace, South Molton 1717 W
    John, South Molton 1710 W
    Stocke Richard, North Molton 1627 [W]
Stockaie ..., Rose Ash 1607 [W]
Stockam see Stockham
Stocke see Stock
Stockham, Stockam, Stockhame
    ..., Bideford 1608 [W] and 1614 [W]
    Stockhame alias Comen John, Knowstone 1574 W
    Stockam Richard, George Nympton 1637 A
Stodden Edward, Combe Martin 1632 [W]
    Stodden alias Baglehole Henry, Hartland 1601 W
    Richard, Stoodleigh 1589 W
    Stodden alias Blackeford Robert, Barnstaple 1601 W
Stofford, Stoufford, Stowford, Stowforde
    James, Witheridge 1618 [W]
    Stowforde John, Bulkworthy or Buckland Brewer 1563 W
    John, Stowford, esquire 1592 [W]
    John, Buckland Brewer 1612 [W] "of Bulkworthy"; forename
      blank in Ms; supplied from parish register
    Stowford Samuel, Meshaw 1700 W
    Stowford Thomas, Great Torrington 1579 A
    Stowford Thomasine, Sheepwash 1570 W
    Walter, Parkham 1599 [W]
    Walter, Parkham 1634 A

Stoufford William, Romansleigh 1697 A
Stoie see Stoye
Stoke Joan, Brendon 1632 [W]
  John, Stoke Rivers 1573 W
Stoker Joseph, Great Torrington 1857 W
Stoley John, Fremington 1851 W
  John, Kentisbury 1857 W
Stone Christopher, West Worlington 1733 W
  Christopher, Stoodleigh 1754 A
  Henry, Lapford 1786 A
  Joan, South Molton 1740 A
  Joan, East Worlington 1761 W
  Joan, Chulmleigh, widow 1807 W
  John, Witheridge 1734 W
  John, Heanton Punchardon 1774 W
  John, Mariansleigh 1774 A
  John, Knowstone, yeoman 1801 W
  Joseph, Barnstaple 1757 W
  Joseph, Abbotsham 1809 W*
  Margaret, West Worlington 1733 W
  Philip, Northam 1727 W
  Richard, Stoodleigh 1597 [W]
  Richard, Romansleigh 1757 A
  Richard, Chawleigh 1771 W
  Richard, Great Torrington 1840 W
  Richard, Hartland 1841 A to Betty, widow
  Stephen, Eggesford 1778 W
  Thomas, Cruwys Morchard 1730 A
  Thomas, Abbotsham 1790 W
  Thomas, Kentisbeare, snr. 1816 W
  Thomas, Northam 1830 W
  Thomas, Knowstone 1842 W
  Stone alias Chrispene William, Berrynarbor 1582 W
  William, Oakford 1632 [W]
  William, Witheridge 1715 A
  William, Meshaw 1732 A
  William, Chulmleigh 1813 W
  William, Abbotsham 1830 W
Stonehouse, Stonhouse
  Stonhouse Jane, North Tawton 1776 A
  Jonathan, North Tawton 1765 A
Stoneman ..., Coldridge 1609 [W]
  Agnes, Great Torrington 1844 A to Gertrude and Agnes,
    daughters
  Alexander, North Tawton 1787 W
  Benjamin, Langtree 1785 W
  Catherine, North Tawton 1785 W
  Christopher, Nymet Rowland 1693 W
  Christopher, Bow 1710 A
  Christopher, Bondleigh 1795 W
  George, Great Torrington 1846 W
  Hannah, Great Torrington 1735 A
  Henry, Great Torrington 1710 A
  Henry, Great Torrington, snr. 1711 W
  Henry, Brushford 1729 W
  Henry, Great Torrington 1735 W
  Henry, Brushford 1740 W
  Henry, Barnstaple 1745 W
  Henry, Great Torrington 1747 W
  Henry, Great Torrington 1789 W
  Henry, Great Torrington 1839 W and 1845 A
  John, Nymet Rowland 1633 W
  John, Nymet Rowland 1682 W
  John, Frithelstock 1738 W
  John, Buckland Brewer, yeoman 1796 A
  John, North Tawton 1825 W and 1830 W
  Magdalen, Brushford 1735 W
  Mary, Zeal Monachorum, widow 1808 W
  Mary, North Tawton 1837 W
  Mary wife of John see Richard Rattenbury
  Peter, Chulmleigh 1676 W
  Peter, Chulmleigh 1759 A
  Peter, North Molton, woolcomber 1808 W
  Peter, North Molton 1846 W
  Philip, Langtree 1829 W

  Richard, Great Torrington 1693 W
  Richard, Bideford 1720 A
  Richard, Brushford 1760 W
  Robert, North Molton 1721 A
  Thomas, South Molton 1709 W
  Thomas, North Molton 1721 A
  Thomas, South Molton 1726 W
  Thomas, Great Torrington 1767 W
  Thomas, Bondleigh, yeoman 1809 W
  William, Coldridge 1788 A
Stoner Elizabeth, South Molton 1582 A
Stonhouse see Stonehouse
Stot, Stote, Stott see Stoat
Stoufford see Stofford
Stowe David, Martinhoe 1622 [W]
Stower, Stowers
  Andrew, South Molton 1691 W
  Richard, Chawleigh 1677 W
  Stowers Sarah, Ilfracombe 1678 A
Stowford, Stowforde see Stofford
Stowte see Stoat
Stowy Christopher, Bideford 1677 W
Stoye, Stoie, Stoy
  Anthony, Molland 1626 [W]
  Joan, Martinhoe 1629 [W]
  Stoie Matilda, Martinhoe 1585 W
  Stoy or Stay Philip, Georgeham 1704 A
  Stoy William, Bow 1777 A
Stoyle ..., Marwood 1834 W
  Henry, West Down 1688 A
  Henry, Combe Martin 1724 A
  Hilary, Winkleigh 1634 W
  James, Zeal Monachorum 1846 W
  John, Combe Martin 1724 A
  John, Westleigh 1787 W
  John, South Molton 1799 W
  John, Coldridge 1831 W
  John, Barnstaple 1855 W
  Robert, Wembworthy 1639 W
  Thomas, Instow 1713 W
  Thomas, ship *York* 1750 W
Stradling Jane, Barnstaple 1751 W
Strain Martha, Shirwell 1765 A
Strange, Strang, Straunge
  Dorothy, Northam 1856 W
  Edmund, Northam 1704 A
  Elizabeth, Littleham (near Bideford) 1591 [W]
  Elizabeth, Littleham (near Bideford) 1629 [W]
  George, Bideford 1667 W
  George, Bideford 1736 W
  John, Bideford 1593 [W]
  John, Northam 1632 [W]
  Strang John, Bideford 1710 A
  John, Northam 1726 W
  John, Bideford 1785 W
  Jonathan, Bideford 1753 W
  Strang Mary, Bideford 1661 A
  Robert, Littleham (near Bideford) 1566 W
  Straunge Robert, Burrington 1572 W
  Sarah, Bideford 1789 [W]
  Thomas, Northam 1766 W
  Urithe, Northam 1633 W
  William, Northam 1766 A
  William, Bideford 1787 W
Stranger Thomas, North Molton 1837 W
Straunge see Strange
Strawbridg James, Rose Ash 1716 W
Streblehill, Strebelhill, Stribilhill, Styblehill
  ..., Warkleigh 1608 [W]
  Strebelhill ..., Chittlehampton 1612 [W]
  Styblehill Ellen, Chittlehampton 1643 W
  Richard, Tawstock 1572 W
  Stribilhill William, Winkleigh 1575 W
Streblinge, Streblyne, Streplyn see Striblin

Street, Streete, Streets, Streke
   Ann, Lynton 1740 A
   Streke Editha, Pilton 1683 W
   Ephraim, Countisbury 1719 A
   Streets James, Pilton 1832 W
   Streete Joan, Tawstock 1629 [W]
   John, Countisbury 1718 A
   Joseph, Pilton 1667 W
   Martha, Chulmleigh 1846 W
   Mary, Pilton 1671 W
   Streete Mary, Pilton 1683 W
   Thomas, Pilton 1714 W
Stribilhill see Streblehill
Striblin, Streblinge, Streblyne, Streplyn, Strible, Striblen,
     Stribling, Striblinge, Striblyn, Striplin, Stripline, Stryblin,
     Strybling, Stryblinge, Stryblyn
   Striblinge ..., Instow 1608 [W]
   Striblinge ..., Goodleigh 1610 [W]
   Stryblyn Agnes, Chittlehampton 1586 W
   Stryblyn Alice, Bideford 1637 A
   Striblin Ambrose, Northam 1631 [W]
   Stryblin Andrew, South Molton 1629 [W]
   Strybling Anthony, Instow 1633 W
   Arthur, Goodleigh 1686 W
   Stribling Christopher, Bideford 1692 A
   Striblyn Damaris, Tawstock 1669 W
   Striblyn David, Challacombe 1711 W
   Streblinge Edward, Goodleigh 1588 W
   Striblinge Edward, Northam 1597 [W]
   Striblyn Edward, Goodleigh 1616 [W]
   Striblyn Edward, Tawstock 1669 A
   Striblyn Edward, Tawstock 1710 W
   Elizabeth, Bideford 1673 [W]
   Elizabeth, Tawstock 1678 W
   Striblyn Elizabeth, Tawstock 1694 W
   Striblyn Emott, North Molton 1644 W
   Stryblinge Francis, Goodleigh 1625 [W]
   Stryblinge George, Instow 1593 [W]
   Striblinge George, North Molton 1612 [W]; forename blank in
     Ms; supplied from parish register
   Striblyn George, Tawstock 1692 W
   Striblyn Giles, Barnstaple 1662 W
   Stribling Jane, Tawstock 1712 A
   Jane, High Bickington 1749 W
   Striblyn Jasper, North Molton 1660 W
   Striblyn Jeremiah, Tawstock 1698 W
   Stribling Jeremiah, Barnstaple 1806 W
   Streplyn Joan, Bideford, widow 1563 W
   Striplin Joan, Great Torrington 1579 W
   Striblinge Joan, Bideford 1618 [W]
   Striblyn Joan, Westleigh 1641 W
   Striblyn Joan, South Molton 1699 A
   Strible John, Chittlehampton 1585 W
   Stryblyn John, Fremington 1594 [W]
   Stryblyn John, Tawstock 1602 W; forename blank in Ms;
     supplied from parish register
   Striblinge John, Tawstock 1610 [W]; forename blank in Ms;
     supplied from parish register
   Striblyn John, Filleigh 1615 [W]
   Striblin John, Challacombe 1622 [W]
   Striblyn John, Northam, snr. 1643 W
   Striblyn John, Bideford 1645 W
   John, Bideford 1675 W
   Striblyn John, Tawstock 1676 W
   John, Tawstock 1684 W
   Striblyn John, Tawstock 1693 A
   Striblyn John, High Bickington 1696 A
   Striblyn John, Tawstock 1700 A
   Striblyn John, Tawstock 1701 W
   Stribling John, High Bickington 1742 A
   Strybling Lawrence, Fremington 1640 W
   Streblyne Mabel, Tawstock 1566 W
   Stribling Margaret, Pilton 1683 A
   Striblinge Margery, Warkleigh 1640 W
   Striblyn Margery, Fremington 1660 A

   Striblyn Mary, Tawstock 1714 W
   Stribling Mary, Barnstaple 1829 W
   Striblinge Mathew, Yarnscombe 1597 [W]
   Stribling Michael, Bratton Fleming 1734 W
   Stribling Nicholas, Tawstock 1693 W
   Striblen Peter, High Bickington 1578 W
   Stribling Philip, Bideford 1701 W
   Stribling Richard, Tawstock 1591 [W]
   Strybling Richard, High Bickington 1635 W
   Stribling Richard, Fremington 1643 A
   Stribling Richard, Bideford 1644 A
   Richard, Fremington 1679 W
   Stripline Richard, Barnstaple 1705 W
   Stryblyn Robert, Instow 1577 W
   Striblinge Robert, Chittlehampton 1618 [W]
   Stribling Robert, Abbotsham 1689 W
   Stribling Robert, Goodleigh 1738 A
   Striblinge Samuel, Tawstock 1615 [W]; forename blank in
     Ms; supplied from parish register
   Striblyn Samuel, Horwood 1675 A
   Striblen Thomas, Barnstaple 1586 W
   Stryblinge Thomas, Pilton 1622 [W]
   Stryblinge Thomas, Pilton 1624 [W]
   Strybling Thomas, Goodleigh 1632 [W]
   Stribling Thomas, Barnstaple 1822 W
   Strybling Walter, Goodleigh 1637 W
   Streblinge William, Chittlehampton 1588 W
   Stryblinge William, Tawstock 1593 [W]
   Stryblinge William, Tawstock 1622 [W]
   Strybling William, Warkleigh 1635 W
   Strybling William, Pilton 1639 A
   Striblyn William, High Bickington 1664 W
   William, Tawstock 1678 W
   Striblyn William, Warkleigh 1700 A
   Stribling William, High Bickington 1746 W
   Stryblinge Willmot, Filleigh 1640 W
   Stribling Willmot, Bratton Fleming 1739 W
Stroade, Strode see Stroud
Strong, Stronge
   Stronge ..., Great Torrington 1609 O
   Stronge Cyprian, Great Torrington 1630 [W]
   John, Tawstock 1737 W
Stroud, Stroade, Strode
   John, Woolfardisworthy 1736 A
   Strode John, Barnstaple 1748 A
   Mary, Woolfardisworthy 1770 W
   Philip, Woolfardisworthy 1704 W
   Strode Richard, Tawstock, gentleman 1632 [W]
   Stroad Sarah, Barnstaple 1755 A
   Thomas, Weare Giffard 1707 W
   Thomas, Woolfardisworthy 1734 W and 1738 W
   William, Alwington 1684 A and 1685 A
Stuckey, Stucey
   Abraham, Ashreigney 1753 A
   Stucey John, Merton 1740 A
   John, Wembworthy 1805 A
Stukely, Stucklegh, Stuckleigh, Stuckley, Stucley
   ..., West Worlington 1667 W
   Stucley Ann, Chulmleigh 1794 W
   Stucley Chivenor, Chulmleigh 1777 W
   Edmund, West Worlington 1661 W
   Frances, Meshaw 1629 [W]
   Stucley Hugh, West Worlington 1578 A
   Stuckleigh Hugh, Hartland 1579 W
   Stuckley Joan, Hartland 1595 [W]
   John, West Worlington, esquire 1636 A
   Stucley John, West Worlington 1641 W
   Stuckley John, Northam 1721 A
   Stucley Lewis, West Worlington 1580 W
   Scipio, Burrington 1629 [W]
   Thomas, Bideford 1709 A
   Timothy, Wembworthy, snr. 1697 W
   Stucley William, Chulmleigh 1789 W
Stumper David, Shirwell 1682 W
Sture see Steere

Stutson, Stirtson
  Stirtson John, Northam 1701 W
  John, Northam 1721 A
Styblehill see Streblehill
Stycke see Stick
Sucker or Tocker Thomasine, Washford Pyne 1570 W
Suivaney or Sniveney Richard, Barnstaple 1703 A
Sullivan, Sellivant, Sillifant, Sulifant
  Alice, Great Torrington 1580 W
  Sellivant Elizabeth 1632 [W]
  Sulifant John, Little Torrington 1705 A
  Sillifant Thomas, Great Torrington 1694 A
Sully Ann, Molland 1843 W
  John, East Anstey 1696 W
Summers, Somer, Somers, Sommer, Sommers, Soners, Sumer, Summer
  Sommer ..., Winkleigh 1602 [W] and 1603 [W]
  Somer ...., Fremington 1609 [W]
  Somer ...., Tawstock 1612 [W]
  Somer ...., Combe Martin 1614 [W]
  Somer Agnes, Tawstock 1602 W
  Agnes, Fremington 1702 W and 1710 W
  Somer Ambrose, Ilfracombe 1582 W
  Sommer Avery, Tawstock 1586 A
  Somer Avis, Tawstock 1599 O account
  Sumer Bernard, Brushford 1670 W
  Summer David, Berrynarbor 1643 A
  Dorcas, Bideford 1727 W
  Sommers Dorcas, Chittlehampton 1739 A
  Dorothy, North Tawton 1719 A
  Sommer Ebbot, Iddesleigh 1633 W
  Summer Eleanor, Tawstock 1708 W
  Somer Elias, Tawstock 1578 W
  Elizabeth, North Tawton 1708 W
  Sommers Elizabeth, Tawstock 1742 W
  Somer Emma, Bideford 1804 W
  Sommer George, Chittlehampton 1602 W
  George, Fremington 1719 A
  Sommers George, Fremington 1742 W
  Sommers George, Ilfracombe 1749 A
  Hannah, Ilfracombe 1760 A
  Henry, Chittlehampton 1667 A
  Somers Henry, Ilfracombe 1669 A
  Soners Henry, Ilfracombe 1745 W
  Somer Henry, Tawstock 1763 W
  Somer Humphrey, Winkleigh 1580 A
  Sommer Humphrey, Berrynarbor 1618 [W]
  Summer Humphrey, Winkleigh 1661 W
  Sommers Isaac, Ilfracombe 1758 W
  Sommers Jesse, Chittlehampton 1747 A
  Somer Joan, Fremington 1617 [W]
  Summer Joan, Yarnscombe 1626 [W]
  Summer Joan, Winkleigh 1631 [W]
  Summer Joan, Bideford 1634 W
  Summer Joan, Martinhoe 1645 W
  Sommers Joan, Tawstock 1682 W
  Summer Joan, Winkleigh 1708 W
  Somer John, Winkleigh 1570 W
  Somer John, Meeth 1582 A and 1583 O account
  Somer John, Berrynarbor 1594 [W]
  Somer John, Tawstock 1603 [W] "of Templand" in register; forename blank in Ms; supplied from parish register
  Sommer John, Tawstock 1636 W
  Summer John, Chittlehampton 1662 W
  Sumers John, Barnstaple 1670 A
  Sommers John, Berrynarbor 1672 O
  Somers John, Berrynarbor 1674 A and 1680 A
  Somers John, Fremington 1681 W
  John, Winkleigh 1688 W
  Somers John, Tawstock 1696 W
  John, South Molton 1710 A
  Sommers John, Pilton, esquire 1714 W
  Sommers John, Ilfracombe 1716 A
  Sommers John, Barnstaple 1723 A
  Sommers John, Ilfracombe 1741 A

Sommers John, Winkleigh 1748 A
Somers John, Berrynarbor 1766 W
John, Berrynarbor 1799 W*
Sommers John, Loxhore 1834 A to Mary, daughter
Somer Lawrence, Tawstock 1596 [W]
Sommers Lawrence, Barnstaple 1742 W
Sommers Margaret, Barnstaple 1737 W
Somer Margery, Great Torrington 1603 [W]
Sommers Margery, North Tawton 1736 A
Somer Mary, Barnstaple 1592 [W]
Somers Mary, Chittlehampton 1678 W
Sumers Mary, Berrynarbor 1680 W
Mary, Winkleigh 1752 W
Somer Mathew, Chittlehampton 1578 W
Summer Milner, Hartland 1664 W
Somer alias Mare Nicholas, Ilfracombe, widow 1568 W
Summer Nicholas, Berrynarbor 1633 W
Summer Nicholas, Ilfracombe 1664 W
Sommers Nicholas, Tawstock 1684 W
Nicholas, Ilfracombe 1708 W
Sommers Nicholas, Ilfracombe 1738 A
Summer Peter, Tawstock 1663 W
Somers Philip, Barnstaple 1698 A
Somer Richard, Tawstock 1597 [W]
Sommers Richard, North Tawton 1769 W
Somer Robert, Martinhoe 1582 A
Sommer Robert, High Bickington 1619 [W]
Somers Robert, Barnstaple 1670 W
Robert, Tawstock 1685 A
Sommer Robert, Chittlehampton 1746 A
Somers Robert, Tawstock 1779 W
Somer Robert, Tawstock, yeoman 1800 W
Roger, Fremington 1680 W
Summer Sarah, Ilfracombe 1664 A
Sarah, Barnstaple 1720 W
Somer Simon, Berrynarbor 1597 [W]
Simon, Ilfracombe 1710 W
Sommers Simon, Ilfracombe 1747 W
Summer Stephen, Hartland 1662 W
Somer Thomas, North Tawton 1588 W
Somer Thomas, Barnstaple 1592 [W]
Somer Thomas, Tawstock 1594 [W]
Somer Thomas, Bondleigh 1597 [W]
Sommer Thomas, Tawstock 1615 [W]
Summer Thomas, Ilfracombe 1668 A
Sommers Thomas, Ilfracombe 1669 A
Somer Thomas, Fremington 1670 [W]
Thomas, Bideford 1724 W
Sommers Thomas, Barnstaple 1729 W
Sommers Thomas, Tawstock 1734 W
Sommers Thomas, Barnstaple 1741 W
Sommers Thomas, Ilfracombe 1744 A
Somer Walter, Tawstock 1590 [W]
Somer William, Bondleigh 1599 [W]
Somer William, Iddesleigh 1599 [W]
Sumers William, Chittlehampton 1673 A
Summer William, North Tawton 1697 W
Somer William, Chittlehampton 1717 [W]
Sommers William, Ilfracombe 1734 W
Sommer William, Chittlehampton 1739 W
Sommers William, Ilfracombe 1747 W
William, Ilfracombe 1751 A
William, Chittlehampton 1781 A
William, Chittlehampton 1819 W
Sommer Willmot, Ilfracombe 1633 A
Summerton see Somerton
Summerwill see Somerwill
Sumpter Edward, Berrynarbor 1626 [W]
  Nicholas, St Giles in the Wood 1570 W
Surridge, Surrage, Surridg
  John, Pilton 1741 W
  Surrage Robert, Oakford 1676 W
  Surridg William, Knowstone 1704 W
Suryar Elizabeth, High Bray 1749 W
Susan see Suzan

Sussex Francis, Barnstaple 1760 A
    John, Weare Giffard 1827 W to William of Alverdiscott, son
    Mulford, Weare Giffard 1814 W
    Susanna, Weare Giffard 1827 A to Mary wife of William
        Kidwell, daughter
    William, Newton Tracey 1794 W
Suthcomb, Suthcombe see Southcombe
Suthcott see Southcott
Sutten see Sutton
Sutter ..., South Molton 1614 [W]
    Agnes, Ilfracombe 1583 A
    Davy, Ilfracombe 1582 W
    James, Ilfracombe 1687 W
    John, Coldridge 1571 W
    John, Mortehoe 1703 W
    Nicholas, Ilfracombe 1691 W
    Philip, Ilfracombe 1689 W
    Robert, South Molton 1618 [W]
    William, Ilfracombe 1663 A
Sutton, Sutten
    Anthony, Bratton Fleming 1714 A
    Augustine, South Molton 1597 [W]
    Christopher Burnoll, Bideford 1829 W
    Isaac, Barnstaple 1621 [W]
    Isaac, Barnstaple 1621 [W]
    Joan, Burrington 1590 [W]
    John, Northam 1605 W
    Sutten Petronell, South Molton 1599 [W]
    Robert, South Molton 1565 W
    Robert, Burrington 1592 [W]
Suzan, Susan, Suzance, Suzanne
    ..., Bideford 1623 [W]
    Christopher, Bideford 1631 [W]
    Suzanne Christopher, Bideford 1614 [W]; forename blank in
        Ms; supplied from parish register
    Petronell, Bideford 1635 [W]
    Susan William, Bideford 1571 W
    Suzance William, Heanton Punchardon 1600 W
Swaine, Swayne
    Agnes, Barnstaple 1667 A
    Edward John, Barnstaple 1683 A
    Swayne John, Barnstaple 1663 W
    John, Barnstaple 1682 A
    John, Ilfracombe 1698 W
    John, Ilfracombe 1715 [W]
    Swayne John, Barnstaple 1720 W
    Swayne John, Barnstaple 1808 A
    Nicholas, Barnstaple 1682 A
    Swayne Nicholas, Barnstaple 1694 W
Swanley Richard, Ilfracombe 1578 W
Sweete, Sweet, Sweett, Swete, Swett, Swyte
    ..., Dolton 1637 W
    ..., Great Torrington 1727 A
    Sweet Catherine, Georgeham 1639 W
    Sweet Charles, Great Torrington 1716 A
    Sweet Charles, Great Torrington 1744 W
    Christopher, Georgeham 1620 [W]
    Eleanor, Georgeham 1683 A
    Eleanor, Georgeham 1693 W
    Elizabeth, Georgeham 1606 W
    Sweet Elizabeth, Georgeham 1680 W
    Sweet Emma, Georgeham 1678 W
    Emotta and Robert, Tawstock 1627 [W]
    George, Georgeham 1630 [W] and 1632 [W]
    Sweet George, Tawstock 1643 A
    Sweet George, Tawstock 1667 W
    Hugh 1801 W
    James, Georgeham 1636 W
    Joan, Shebbear, widow 1608 [W]; forename blank in Ms;
        supplied from parish register
    Joan, Tawstock 1625 [W]
    Sweet Joan, Barnstaple 1673 [W]
    Sweet John, Georgeham 1596 [W]
    Sweett John, Tawstock 1616 [W]
    John, Georgeham 1633 [W]

Sweet John, Georgeham 1675 W
Sweet John, Georgeham 1742 W
Sweet John, Great Torrington 1743 W
Sweet John, Bideford 1847 W
John, snr., Georgeham 1712 W "of South Hole" in register;
    forename blank in Ms; supplied from parish register
Sweett Julian, Tawstock 1581 W
Kiveren, Buckland Brewer 1682 A
Sweet Margaret, Great Torrington 1718 W
Sweet Margaret, Great Torrington 1754 A
Sweet Margery, Tawstock 1673 W
Swett Mary, Barnstaple 1583 W
Mary, Georgeham 1695 W
Mathew, Georgeham 1661 W
Peter, Great Torrington 1663 W
Phillippa, Barnstaple 1623 [W]
Richard, Tawstock 1579 W
Richard, Barnstaple 1581 W
Richard, Barnstaple 1667 T
Swete Robert, Georgeham 1567 W
Robert and Emota, Tawstock 1627 [W]
Sweet Samuel, Great Torrington 1703 W
Stephen, Barnstaple 1605 [W]; forename blank in Ms;
    supplied from parish register
Swyte Thomas, Tawstock 1568 W
Sweett Thomas, Shebbear 1600 T
Thomas, Georgeham 1616 [W]
Thomas, Barnstaple 1622 [W]
Urithe, Northam 1668 W
Swift Roger, Chulmleigh 1641 W
Swire Philip, Lynton 1721 W
Swyne Thomas, Chulmleigh 1626 [W]
Swyte see Sweete
Sydenham Jane, Barnstaple 1689 A
    Sydenham alias Harford Jane 1690 A
    Simon, Bideford 1645 A
Sylley, Sylly see Silley
Syme, Syms see Simms
Symon, Symonde, Symons see Simons
Sympson see Simpson
Syms see Simms
Synabus Michael, Fremington 1695 W
Syncock, Syncocke, Syncoke see Sincocke
Synsooner John, Barnstaple 1750 W

Tackle see Takell
Taige Margaret 1760 W
Tailbushe, Taylebushe
    Taylebushe Arthur, Pilton 1622 [W] and 1624 O
    Tailbushe Christopher, Pilton 1564 W
Tailder, Taildor, Taylder
    ..., Great Torrington 1605 [W]
    Taylder Alexander, Great Torrington 1725 W
    Ann, Georgeham 1617 [W]
    Taylder Ann, North Molton 1725 W
    Taylder Blanche, Westleigh 1626 [W]
    Edith, Shirwell 1614 [W]; forename blank in Ms; supplied
        from parish register
    Taylder Elizabeth, High Bickington 1632 [W] and 1641 A
    Taylder Frances, Bideford 1628 [W]
    Taylder Henry, Northam 1626 [W]
    Taylder alias Northcott John, Landcross 1581 W
    Taylder John, Barnstaple 1583 A
    Taylder John, Dolton 1586 [W]
    Taylder John, Northam 1588 A
    Taylder John, Chittlehampton 1590 [W]
    John, Great Torrington 1601 W
    John, Georgeham 1617 W
    Taylder John, Bideford 1619 [W]
    Taylder John, High Bickington 1623 [W]
    Taylder John, Northam 1640 W (2)
    Taylder John, Huish 1714 W
    Taylder Mathew, Huish 1727 W
    Taylder Philip, Bideford 1598 [W]
    Taylder Richard, Tawstock 1593 [W]

Taylder Richard, Kentisbury 1619 [W]
Taylder Robert, Hartland 1595 [W]
Taylder Robert, East Putford 1622 [W]
Taylder Robert, Westleigh 1684 W
Stephen, Barnstaple 1605 W
Taylder Thomas, Tawstock 1588 W
Thomas, Bideford 1606 W
Taylder Thomas, High Bickington 1632 [W]
Taylder William, Chittlehampton 1588 W
Taildor William, Westleigh 1612 [W]; forename blank in Ms;
    supplied from parish register
Taylder William, Yarnscombe 1626 [W]
Taylder Willmot, Bideford 1601 W
Tailor, Tailour see Taylor
Takell, Tackle
..., South Molton 1602 [W]
Alexander, Chawleigh 1634 A and 1643 A
Arthur, South Molton 1645 A
Geoffrey, Rose Ash 1618 [W]
Henry, South Molton 1623 [W]
John, Knowstone 1565 W and 1571 W
John, South Molton 1597 [W]
John, South Molton 1663 A
Nicholas, Barnstaple 1617 [W]
Richard, Goodleigh 1632 [W]
Rose, Lapford 1597 [W]
Thomas, Rose Ash 1587 A
Thomas, Cruwys Morchard 1594 [W]
Tackle Thomas, Fremington 1738 A
Talamey, Talamy see Tallamy
Talbett James, Georgeham 1573 W
Tallamy, Talamey, Talamy, Tallamey, Tallamye, Tallemey
Ann, Buckland Brewer 1693 W
Anthony, Bideford 1690 A
Anthony, Buckland Brewer 1720 W
Elizabeth, Frithelstock 1730 W
Talamy Gregory, Buckland Brewer 1718 W
Tallamey John, Buckland Brewer 1594 [W]
Tallemey John, Buckland Brewer 1618 [W]
John, Frithelstock 1689 W
Talamy John, Frithelstock 1704 A
John, Bideford 1736 A
John, Bideford 1755 W
Talamey John, Buckland Brewer 1785 A
Jonathan, Bideford 1726 W
Patience, Bideford 1728 A
Philip, Northam 1695 W
Richard, Bideford 1752 A
Tallamye Robert, Landcross 1620 [W]
William, Bideford 1741 W
William, Bideford 1819 W
Talley see Tolley
Tallin, Talling, Tallyn, Tallyng, Tawlon, Tolland, Tollen
Tallyn Anthony, Georgeham 1686 W
Anthony, Goodleigh 1769 W
Tawlon Anthony, Northam 1787 W
Tallyng Catherine, Northam 1687 A
Tallyn Catherine, Weare Giffard 1800 A
Elizabeth, Ilfracombe 1783 W
Tallyn George, Georgeham 1747 W
Talling George, Georgeham 1751 A
Tallyn James, Northam 1685 A
Tallyn James, Northam 1709 A
Tollen John, West Down 1590 [W]
Tollen John, West Down 1609 [W]; forename blank in Ms;
    supplied from parish register
John, Barnstaple 1756 W
John, Georgeham 1767 A
John, Bratton Fleming, gentleman 1807 A
Joseph, Northam 1760 A
Tallyn Mary, Georgeham 1716 W
Tallyn Nicholas, Bratton Fleming 1719 T
Tallyn Peter, Mortehoe 1704 A
Philip, Tawstock 1760 A
Tallyn Philip, Tawstock, yeoman 1808 A

Tallyn Prudence, Northam 1680 W
Tolland Sarah wife of John see Robert Kent
Tally Thomas, Bratton Fleming 1680 W
Tallyn Thomas, Bratton Fleming 1725 W
Tallyn Thomasine, Bratton Fleming, widow 1809 W
Tallyn William, Bratton Fleming 1642 W
Tallyn William, Georgeham 1721 W
William, Mortehoe 1748 W
Talman see Tawman
Tamlyn, Tamblin, Tamlin
Amos, Arlington 1743 W
Amos, Tawstock 1765 W
Amos, Tawstock, yeoman 1800 W (2)
Anthony, Marwood 1637 W
Anthony, Tawstock, yeoman 1807 W
Charles, Marwood 1636 W
Charles, Atherington 1716 W
Charles, Atherington 1798 W
Elizabeth, Marwood 1636 W
Elizabeth, Marwood 1669 W
Elizabeth, Tawstock, widow 1849 W to Elizabeth, sp.,
    daughter
Elizabeth, East Down 1851 W
Elizabeth, East Down, sp. 1852 A to William and Mary wife
    of William
Esther, Tawstock 1641 W
Grace, East Down 1675 W
Grace, East Down 1823 W
James, Arlington 1728 W
Tamlin James, Twitchen 1757 W
James, Arlington 1771 W
James, Arlington 1794 W
James, Arlington, yeoman 1802 W
James, Arlington 1829 W
James, Parracombe 1841 W
John, Marwood 1622 W
John, Arlington 1709 W
John, Barnstaple, yeoman 1799 W
John, North Molton, yeoman 1806 W
John, North Molton 1810 W
John, Stoke Rivers, yeoman 1810 W
John, Bratton Fleming, gentleman 1816 A to Elizabeth, widow
Tamlin John, Chittlehampton 1834 W
John, Bratton Fleming 1845 A
Mary, Pilton 1670 W
Mary, Arlington 1731 A
Mary, North Molton, widow 1808 W
Mary, Sheepwash 1828 W
Mary, Stoke Rivers 1842 W
Mathew, Marwood 1664 W
Oliver, Marwood 1672 W
Peter, Marwood 1645 W
Philip, East Down 1670 A
Prudence, Arlington, sp. 1802 A
Richard, Marwood 1683 A
Robert, Marwood 1668 W
Tamlin Robert, Chittlehampton 1842 W
Roger, Marwood 1622 [W]
Rowland, Atherington 1725 W
Samuel, Bratton Fleming 1842 W
Thomas, Marwood 1599 [W]
William, Marwood 1595 [W]
William, Arlington 1684 A
William, Arlington 1713 W
Tamlin William, Stoke Rivers 1758 W
William, East Down, yeoman 1796 W
William, Stoke Rivers, yeoman 1807 A
William, North Molton 1813 W
William, East Buckland 1831 W
William, East Down 1831 W
Tamlin William, Chulmleigh 1836 W
Tamblin William, King's Nympton 1841 W
Tamlin William, Chittlehampton 1841 W
William, East Down 1849 W
    see also Tomlyn

Tancock, Tancocke
George, North Tawton 1723 W
James, Winkleigh 1837 A
James, Winkleigh 1838 A to Mary, widow
Mary, North Tawton 1686 W
Thomas, Chawleigh 1839 W
Tancocke William, Witheridge 1737 W
Tanner ..., Oakford 1608 [W]
..., Witheridge 1613 [W]
Andrew, Coldridge 1690 A
Anthony, High Bickington 1667 W
Eleanor, Fremington 1637 W
Elizabeth, Chittlehampton 1605 W
Elizabeth, Rose Ash 1763 A
Elizabeth, Creacombe 1793 W
Elizabeth, King's Nympton 1856 W
George, Witheridge 1629 [W]
George, Witheridge 1663 W
George, Rose Ash 1685 W
Grace, Chittlehampton 1826 W
Hugh, Knowstone 1565 W
Humphrey, Rose Ash 1695 W
Joan, Chittlehampton 1641 [W]
Joan, Rose Ash 1711 W
John, Witheridge 1592 W
John, Rose Ash 1675 W
John, Rose Ash 1730 W
John, Rose Ash 1749 W
John, Cruwys Morchard 1777 W
John, Chulmleigh 1785 W
John, Witheridge 1839 A to Sarah of Creacombe, widow
Jonathan, Rose Ash 1771 A
Jonathan, Rose Ash 1823 A
Jonathan, Rose Ash 1848 W
Mary, Great Torrington 1629 [W]
Mathew, Creacombe 1685 W
Oliver, Georgeham 1699 A
Tanner alias Mortimer Richard, Lapford 1563 W
Richard, Elworthy, Somerset 1851 W
Robert, Creacombe 1698 W
Robert, West Anstey 1747 W
Robert, Witheridge 1753 W
Robert, Rose Ash 1814 W
Robert, South Molton 1836 A to Jonathan, father
Roger, Chittlehampton 1707 W
Tanner alias Tocker Thomas, King's Nympton 1572 W
Thomas, Witheridge 1574 W
Tanner alias Mortimer Thomas, Witheridge 1589 W
Thomas, Chulmleigh 1726 A
Thomas, Chulmleigh 1733 W
Thomas, Creacombe 1738 W
Thomas, Barnstaple 1839 W
William, Fremington 1615 [W]
William, Witheridge 1629 [W]
William, Creacombe 1747 W
William, Rose Ash 1853 W
Tanney George, Northam 1702 A
Tannway or Tarraway Joan, Hartland 1737 A
Tansell Christian, Charles 1591 [W]
Hugh, George Nympton 1578 A
John, King's Nympton 1585 W
Lawrence, Tawstock 1565 W
Margaret, Rose Ash, widow 1567 W
Thomas, King's Nympton 1594 [W]
William, Rose Ash 1565 W
Tanton, Tantton
Elizabeth, Meeth 1816 W
John, Meeth, yeoman 1811 W
John, St Giles in the Wood 1824 W
John, Peters Marland 1849 W
Tantton Mary, Barnstaple 1744 W
Richard, Meeth 1850 W
Samuel, Meeth 1690 A
Thomas, St Giles in the Wood 1835 W
Thomas, Peters Marland 1853 W

Thomas, Petrockstowe 1853 W
William, St Giles in the Wood, yeoman 1801 W
William, Shebbear 1837 A to Susanna, widow
Taplor Edward, Merton 1753 A
Tapp, Tappe
Tappe ... 1600 W
Tappe ..., Twitchen 1615 [W]
Ann, Barnstaple 1802 W
Ann, Rose Ash 1823 W
Tappe Christian, North Tawton 1575 W
Elizabeth, North Molton 1684 W
Elizabeth, Mariansleigh 1759 A
Gilbert, North Tawton 1673 W
Grace, Twitchen 1673 W
Hugh, Rose Ash 1704 A
Hugh, Twitchen 1783 W
James, North Molton 1824 W
Jane, Twitchen 1764 W
Tappe John, North Tawton 1565 W
Tappe John, North Molton, snr. 1588 W
Tappe John, North Molton 1620 [W]
Tappe John, Coldridge 1629 [W]
John, Twitchen 1662 A
John, Twitchen 1665 W
John, Twitchen 1748 W
John, Ashford 1759 A
John, Twitchen 1784 A
John, South Molton, woolcomber 1797 W
John, Cruwys Morchard 1812 W
John, Twitchen 1812 W
Jonathan, Chulmleigh 1831 A
Margaret, West Anstey 1698 W
Mary, Northam 1685 W
Mary, Rackenford 1800 A
Mary, Twitchen or Parkham, sp. 1808 W
Mary, Rose Ash 1835 W
Michael, North Molton 1701 W
Michael, North Molton 1733 W
Michael, South Molton 1759 A
Oliver, Great Torrington 1591 [W]
Philip, Molland 1690 W
Philip, South Molton 1759 W
Philip, Rose Ash 1831 A
Philip see also William Hewett
Richard, Chittlehampton 1795 W
Richard, North Molton 1820 W
Tappe Roger, Twitchen 1616 [W]
Roger, Twitchen 1675 W
Roger, Twitchen 1764 W
Roger, Knowstone 1814 W
Thomas, Fremington 1583 W
Thomas, North ... 1665 W
Thomas, Twitchen, yeoman 1800 W
Thomas, North Molton 1806 W
Urithe, North Molton 1662 W
William, Twitchen 1710 [W]
William, North Molton 1727 W
William, Twitchen 1752 W
William, Knowstone 1780 W
William, Mariansleigh 1780 A
William, South Molton 1781 W
William, Twitchen, yeoman 1798 W
William, Twitchen 1816 W
William, South Molton 1839 W
see also Topp
Tapscott, Tappscott
Hugh, South Molton 1690 W
James, Chittlehampton 1690 A
Tappscott Susan, South Molton 1696 A
Thomas, South Molton 1753 A
Tardrew, Tardrewe, Terdrew, Terdrewe, Terthrew, Terthrewe
Anthony, Alwington 1735 W
Catherine, Parkham 1695 A
Terthrewe Elizabeth, Buckland Brewer 1629 [W]

Tardrewe John, Buckland Brewer 1615 [W] "of Hemberye";
    forename blank in Ms; supplied from parish register
Terthrew John, Buckland Brewer 1641 W
Mary, Instow 1697 A
Nathaniel, Hartland 1712 W
Nathaniel, Parkham 1715 W
Philip, Bideford 1851 W
Terdrew Richard, Parkham 1714 W
Robert, Monkleigh 1701 W
Susan, Parkham 1719 W
Terdue Thomas, East Putford 1685 A
Thomas, Parkham 1691 W
Terdrewe William, Monkleigh 1635 W
William, Bideford 1703 W
Tarr, Tare, Tarre
    Tare or Fare Alexander, Ilfracombe 1718 A
    Betty, Rackenford 1752 W
    Tarre Edith, Molland 1592 [W]
    James, Knowstone 1852 W
    Tarre John, Molland 1583 A
    John, West Anstey 1819 W
    Lodovic, King's Nympton 1696 W
    Mary Ann, Fremington, sp. 1856 A to Phillippa Pincombe, of
        Twitchen, aunt
    William, Rackenford 1749 A
    William, West Anstey 1765 W
    William, Knowstone 1786 W
        see also Torr
Tarraway or Tannway Joan, Hartland 1737 A
Tarre see Tarr
Tarrens, Torrens
    Christopher, Northam 1628 [W]
    Peter, Northam 1622 [W]
    Torrens William, Northam 1644 A
Tasker John, Chittlehampton 1716 A; forename blank in Ms;
    supplied from parish register
    Lodovic, Charles 1662 A
Tate Charles, High Bickington 1703 A
Tatem Frances, Northam 1855 A
    Robert, Northam 1850 A
    William Henry, Northam, Appledore, mariner 1855 A to Mary
        Ann, widow
Tatton see Tawton
Tawley see Tolley
Tawlon see Tallin
Tawman, Talman
    Talman ..., Petrockstowe 1612 [W]
    Ann, Ilfracombe 1820 W
    Fulk, Petrockstowe 1625 [W]
    John, Petrockstowe 1628 [W]
Tawnsend see Townsend
Tawton, Tatton
    ..., Winkleigh 1602 [W]
    ..., Dowland 1612 [W]
    Agnes, Meeth 1588 W
    Alice 1589 W
    Bernard, Winkleigh 1615 [W]
    Bridget, Meeth 1639 A
    Catherine, Meeth 1792 W
    Edward, Meeth 1640 A (2)
    Elizabeth, Coldridge 1618 [W]
    Elizabeth, Barnstaple 1630 [W]
    Gertrude, Pilton 1732 A
    Isott, Iddesleigh, widow 1568 W
    James, Great Torrington 1661 W
    Joan, Iddesleigh 1601 W
    Joan, Barnstaple 1620 [W]
    John, Meeth 1573 W
    John, Winkleigh 1582 W
    John, Iddesleigh 1589 A
    John, Iddesleigh 1590 [W]
    John, Meeth 1602 W
    John, Fremington 1615 [W]
    John, Meeth 1717 W
    Lewis, Peters Marland 1605 W

Mark, Barnstaple 1622 [W]
Mary, Little Torrington 1779 W
Mary, Meeth 1827 W
Matilda, Petrockstowe 1579 W
Nathaniel, Great Torrington 1643 [W]
Philip, Meeth 1763 W
Phyllis, Fremington 1637 W
Ralph, Fremington 1718 W
Rebecca, Little Torrington 1730 W
Robert, Meeth 1725 W
Rowland, Iddesleigh 1569 W
Samuel, Meeth 1785 W
Thomas, Winkleigh 1597 [W]
Thomas, Meeth 1630 [W]
Thomas, Barnstaple 1636 W
Thomas, Barnstaple 1663 W
Thomas, Northam, shipwright 1811 W
Urithe, Iddesleigh 1569 W
Walter, Meeth 1687 W
Walter, Meeth 1700 W
Tatton Walter, Sheepwash 1748 A
William, Iddesleigh 1573 W
William, Barnstaple 1591 [W]
William, Winkleigh 1618 W and O
William, Monkleigh 1636 W
William, Bideford 1730 W
William, Northam 1797 W
William, Northam 1818 A; A dbn 1842
Taylebushe see Tailbush
Taylor, Tailor, Tailour, Tayler, Tayloure
    Tailor ..., Pilton 1611 [W]
    Agnes, Sheepwash 1622 [W]
    Alexander, Great Torrington 1776 W
    Tailor Ann, Yarnscombe 1616 [W]
    Anthony, Tawstock 1639 W
    Cecilia, Dolton 1566 W
    Christiana, Coldridge 1690 A
    Elizabeth, Merton 1771 W
    Elizabeth, Westleigh 1817 W
    Elizabeth, Chawleigh 1818 W
    Esther, Huish 1729 W
    Frances, Bideford 1629 O
    George, Chulmleigh 1704 W
    George, Chulmleigh, jnr. 1705 W
    Gilbert, Charles 1694 W
    Gregory, Warkleigh 1569 W
    Tailour Harry, Northam 1564 W
    Henry, East Anstey 1740 W
    James, Barnstaple 1723 W
    James, East Worlington, yeoman 1809 W
    Jeremiah, Fremington 1733 W
    Jeremiah, Fremington 1769 W
    Joan, Tawstock 1688 W
    Joan, Great Torrington 1710 W
    Tayloure John, Ashreigney 1573 W
    John, Great Torrington 1597 [W]
    John, Great Torrington 1632 [W]
    John, Bideford 1643 W
    John, Tawstock 1685 W
    John, Oakford 1686 A
    John, Huish 1690 W
    John, Lynton 1695 W
    John, Northam 1705 W
    Tayler John, High Bickington 1719 W
    John, East Down 1723 W
    Tayler John, Tawstock 1727 W
    John, West Buckland 1728 W
    John, Buckland Brewer 1734 A
    Joseph, East Anstey 1769 A
    Leonard, Pilton 1622 [W]
    Lewis, St Giles in the Wood 1599 [W]
    Mary, East Anstey 1758 A
    Mary, Great Torrington 1795 W
    Mary, Fremington, widow 1810 W
    Mary, Fremington 1831 W

Mathew, Dolton 1665 A
Michael, High Bickington 1667 W
Nectan, Dowland 1624 [W]
Nicholas, Tawstock 1673 [W]
Nicholas and Ursula, Roborough 1697 A
Nicholas, Heanton Punchardon 1708 A and 1714 A
Nicholas, Tawstock 1756 W
Nicholas, Fremington 1827 A to Mary, widow
Philip, Huish 1714 W
Philip, Great Torrington 1752 W
Prudence, Tawstock 1724 W
Rebecca, Barnstaple 1774 A
Richard, Instow 1596 [W]
Richard, Great Torrington 1707 W
Tayler Richard, Abbotsham 1720 W
Richard, St Giles in the Wood 1770 A
Richard, Barnstaple, maltster 1808 W
Richard, Bideford 1842 W
Richard, Bideford 1854 W
Robert, Great Torrington 1709 W
Robert, Westleigh 1801 A; A dbn 1817 to Richard of
   Bideford, carpenter, son
Samuel, Ilfracombe 1741 W
Stephen, Abbotsham 1692 W
Susan, Great Torrington 1694 W
Thomas, Brushford 1580 W
Thomas, Huish 1662 W
Thomas, Dolton 1675 A
Thomas, Bideford 1734 W
Thomas, Westleigh 1742 W
Thomas, Great Torrington 1823 W
Tailor Thomasine, Barnstaple 1608 [W]; forename blank in
   Ms; supplied from parish register
Ursula and Nicholas, Roborough 1697 A
William, Challacombe 1738 A
William, Great Torrington 1787 W
William, Cruwys Morchard 1825 W
William, Filleigh 1851 W
William, Tawstock 1853 W
Teague Richard, Fremington 1744 W
Tearell see Terrell
Tebbe see Tibbs
Teddy Thomas, Peters Marland 1593 [W]
Temlet Elizabeth, Oakford 1574 W
Temple Elizabeth, North Molton 1731 A
Tenckombe see Tincomb
Tepper, Tipper
   ..., South Molton 1601 A
   ..., South Molton 1613 [W] and 1614 [W]
Alice and Anthony, South Molton 1642 [W]
Anthony, South Molton 1708 W
Arthur, South Molton 1660 W
Christopher, South Molton 1618 [W] and O
Christopher, South Molton 1689 W
Edward, South Molton 1739 W
Edward, South Molton 1752 W
Tipper Francis, South Molton 1758 A
George, South Molton, mason 1806 W
George, South Molton 1811 W
George, South Molton 1824 W
Grace, South Molton 1749 A
James, South Molton 1827 W
John, King's Nympton 1675 W
John, South Molton 1675 A
John, South Molton 1723 W
Tipper John, South Molton 1726 W
Tipper John, South Molton 1757 A; A dbn 1758
Oliver, South Molton 1684 W
Thomas, Lynton 1856 W
Thomasine, King's Nympton 1686 A
William, South Molton 1576 W
William, South Molton 1631 [W]
Tipper William, South Molton 1758 W
Terdrew, Terdrewe see Tardrew
Terrell, Tearell, Terel, Tirrell, Tyrrill
   Emotta, Westleigh 1621 [W]

Tirrell Joan, Northam 1705 W
Terell John, Westleigh 1615 [W]
Tyrrill John, Barnstaple 1710 W
Tirrell John, Barnstaple 1712 W
Terell Philip, Alwington 1601 W
Terell Thomas, Iddesleigh 1572 W
Tearell Thomas, Westleigh 1626 [W]
Terry, Terrey, Tyrry
   Tyrry ..., Georgeham 1660 A
Anthony, Alwington 1718 W
Arthur, Tawstock 1731 W
Hugh, Tawstock 1731 A
Hugh, Tawstock, yeoman 1807 W
John, Tawstock 1675 W
John, Burrington 1709 W
John, Alwington 1710 A
John, Burrington 1755 A
Terrey John, Georgeham 1758 W
Mary, Tawstock 1758 A
Peter, Barnstaple 1668 W
Peter, Barnstaple 1669 W
Priscilla, Alwington 1693 W
Prudence, Tawstock 1829 W
William, Tawstock 1732 A
Terthrew, Terthrewe see Tardrew
Terwicks Richard, Gorwood, Buckland Brewer 1589 W
Tethcott see Tothacott
Tetherley, Tetherlegh, Tetherly, Titheleigh, Titherleigh,
   Titherley, Titherly, Tytherlegh, Tytherleigh
   Titheleigh ..., Hartland 1607 [W]
Titherleigh ..., Northam 1613 [W]
Tytherleigh ..., Northam 1614 [W]
Titherleigh Alice, Northam 1632 W
Titherleigh Arthur, Frithelstock 1629 [W]
Titherly Arthur, Langtree 1700 A
Titheleigh Christopher, Frithelstock 1625 [W]
Titherly Edward, Northam 1686 A
Titherleigh Giles, Great Torrington 1711 W
Tetherly Honor, Langtree 1735 W
Titherleigh James, Northam 1622 [W]
Tytherleigh James, Fremington 1624 [W]
Tetherly Jane, Northam 1752 W
Tytherleigh Joan, Northam 1607 [W]; forename blank in Ms;
   supplied from parish register
Tytherlegh John, Northam 1576 [W]
Tetherlegh John, Great Torrington 1587 A & O account
Titherleigh John, Northam 1592 [W] and 1593 [W]
Titherly John, Northam 1736 W and 1742 W
Titherley John, Langtree 1770 A
Titherly John, Langtree 1783 W
Titherley Martha, Frithelstock 1684 A
Titherley Mary, Northam 1688 W
Titherley Nicholas, Frithelstock 1699 W
Tytherly Phillippa, Peters Marland 1672 A
Tetherleigh Richard, Northam 1566 W
Tytherleigh Richard, Great Torrington 1602 W
Tetherly Richard, Langtree 1738 W
Tetherly Samuel, Northam, jnr. 1742 W
Tetherly Samuel, Northam 1752 W; A dbn 1755
Tetherly Samuel, Northam 1802 A
Samuel, Northam 1837 W
Titherley Susan, Northam 1757 W
Tytherly Valentine, Northam 1596 [W]
Tetherleigh William, Frithelstock 1592 [W]
Titherly William, Little Torrington 1715 A
Tetherly William, Northam 1729 W
Tetherly William, Bideford 1741 A
Tew, Tue
   Tue Alice, Huntshaw 1593 [W]
Elizabeth, Fremington 1662 A
James, Fremington 1591 [W]
John, Fremington 1573 W
Tue John, Tawstock 1601 W
Tue John, Fremington 1638 W

Tue Richard, Fremington 1611 [W]
Robert, Fremington 1637 W
Thassell Robert, Bulkworthy or Buckland Brewer 1563 W
Thelbridge Elizabeth, Barnstaple 1590 [W]
Richard, Wembworthy 1771 W
Thelder Charles 1582 W
Thomas Abraham, Witheridge 1752 W
Agnes, Northam 1705 W
Agnes, Thelbridge 1726 W
Alexander, Molland 1616 [W]
Alice, Westleigh 1663 W
Andrew, South Molton 1642 W
Andrew, Witheridge 1696 A
Andrew, North Tawton 1770 A
Anthony, Newton Tracey 1596 [W]
Anthony, Cruwys Morchard 1630 [W]
Baldwin, Tawstock 1576 W
Charles, Northam 1740 W
Charles, Marwood 1745 W
Charles, West Down 1768 A
Charles, West Down 1832 W
Christiana, South Molton 1702 A
Christopher, Northam 1662 A
David, Witheridge 1574 W
David, Challacombe 1636 A
David, Pilton 1643 A
David, High Bickington 1673 A
David, Instow 1677 W
Edmund, Barnstaple 1665 W
Edward, Instow 1745 W
Elias, Tawstock 1617 W
Elizabeth, Thelbridge 1689 W
Elizabeth, Kentisbury 1793 W
Elizabeth, Parkham 1855 W
Elizabeth see also Ann Edwards
Esther, Berrynarbor 1787 W
Frances, Westleigh 1643 W
Geoffrey, Challacombe 1596 [W]
George, Barnstaple 1729 W
George, Chittlehampton 1734 W
Grace, Bideford 1686 W
Gregory, Bideford 1679 A
Hannah, South Molton 1800 A
Henry, King's Nympton 1686 A
Henry, King's Nympton 1704 A
Henry, Shirwell 1734 W
Henry, Heanton Punchardon 1751 W
Henry, ship *Captain* 1756 W
Honor, Westleigh 1667 W
Honor, Northam 1715 A
Hugh, Witheridge 1645 W
Hugh, Fremington, yeoman 1810 W
Isabel, Barnstaple 1777 W
James, Witheridge 1645 A
James, Barnstaple 1688 A
James, Northam 1696 W
James, North Molton 1759 W
James, Tawstock 1795 W
James, Great Torrington, surveyor 1854 A to William of
  Trowbridge, Wiltshire, railway contractor's clerk, brother
Jane, North Molton 1636 W
Jane, Northam 1825 W
Jane, Molland 1838 A to James, brother
Jenkin, Great Torrington 1690 A
Joan, Newton Tracey, widow 1613 [W]; forename blank in
  Ms; supplied from parish register
Joan, Fremington 1644 W
Thomas alias Davy Joan, Witheridge 1673 W
Joan, Shirwell 1734 W
John, Fremington 1568 W
Thomas alias Tomes John, South Molton 1598 [W]
John, Newton Tracey 1604 W
John, Northam 1627 [W]
Thomas alias Davy John, Thelbridge 1663 A
John, Bideford 1673 W

John, Ilfracombe 1688 A
John, Bittadon 1704 A
John, Thelbridge 1706 A
John, Thelbridge 1709 W
John, Great Torrington 1720 A
John, Abbotsham 1722 W
John, Barnstaple 1737 A and 1740 A
John, Witheridge, snr. 1739 W
John, Barnstaple 1740 A
John, Witheridge 1745 W
John, Barnstaple 1747 W
John, Beaford 1757 W
John, Countisbury 1757 W
John, Ilfracombe 1757 W
John, Brendon 1758 A
John, Tawstock 1760 W
John, Thelbridge 1765 A
John, Pilton 1781 W
John, Barnstaple 1782 W
John, Northam 1784 W
John, Northam 1804 W
John, South Molton 1814 W
John, Goodleigh 1827 W
John, Barnstaple 1835 W
John, Pilton 1835 W
Margaret, Romansleigh 1593 [W]
Margaret, Barnstaple 1700 W
Margaret, Pilton 1837 W
Mary, Barnstaple 1680 W
Mary, Molland 1685 W
Mary, Barnstaple 1829 W
Mildred, Witheridge 1764 W
Morgan, Bideford 1690 A
Nicholas, Barnstaple 1732 W
Nicholas, Barnstaple, potter 1815 A to Abel Hartner Thomas,
  captain, R.N., son
Thomas alias Thome Pauline, Barnstaple 1570 W
Philip, Witheridge 1661 W
Philip, Barnstaple 1668 W
Philip, Shirwell 1668 W
Philip, Northam 1854 A
Priscilla, Barnstaple 1751 W
Richard, Witheridge 1609 [W]; forename blank in Ms;
  supplied from parish register
Richard, Chulmleigh 1615 [W]
Richard, Witheridge 1638 A
Richard, Washford Pyne 1645 W
Richard, Thelbridge 1678 A
Richard, Witheridge 1688 W
Richard, Rose Ash 1731 W
Richard, Northam 1748 W
Richard, Barnstaple 1749 W
Richard Palmer, Barnstaple 1822 W
Robert, Cruwys Morchard 1625 [W]
Robert, Tawstock 1636 W
Robert, George Nympton 1637 W
Robert, Northam 1682 A
Robert, Witheridge 1743 A
Robert, ship *Expedition* 1748 A
Robert, Kentisbury 1766 W
Robert, Tawstock 1769 A
Robert, Kentisbury 1790 W
Robert, High Bickington 1829 A to Jane, widow
Robert, Lynton 1833 W
Samuel, Thelbridge 1792 W
Thomas, Northam 1705 A
Tristram, Horwood 1643 W
Walter, Cruwys Morchard 1611 [W]; forename blank in Ms;
  supplied from parish register
Walter, Newton Tracey 1616 [W]
Walter, Morchard Bishop or Cruwys Morchard 1676 A
Walter, Witheridge 1752 W
William, Newton Tracey 1591 [W]
William, Cruwys Morchard 1603 W
William, Witheridge 1627 [W]

William, Rose Ash 1636 A
William, Westleigh 1667 W
William, Northam 1706 A
William, Northam 1713 W
William, Kentisbury 1758 W
William, Pilton 1759 A
William, Berrynarbor 1766 W
William, St Giles in the Wood 1769 W
William, Parracombe 1786 W
William, Barnstaple 1809 W
William, St Giles in the Wood 1834 W
William, Great Torrington 1857 A
Thome Bernard, Chittlehampton 1666 W
  John, King's Nympton 1563 W
  Marian, King's Nympton 1571 W
  Oliver, Barnstaple 1569 W
  Thome or Thomas Pauline, Barnstaple 1570 W
  William, King's Nympton 1588 A
Thompson, Thomson, Tomson
  Dorothy, Barnstaple 1693 W
  Tomson George, Beaford 1672 A
  George, Fremington 1717 W
  Thomson John, Brendon 1576 W
  Martha, Barnstaple 1775 W
  Prudence, Chulmleigh 1666 W
Thore Joan, Twitchen 1626 [W]
Thorne, Thorn
  ..., Tawstock 1602 [W]
  ..., Marwood 1607 [W]
  ..., Buckland Filleigh 1609 [W]
  ..., North Tawton 1611 [W]
  ..., Twitchen 1611 [W]
  ..., South Molton 1614 [W]
  Abraham, North Molton 1761 W
  Adam, Marwood 1615 [W]
  Adam, Marwood 1629 [W] and 1631 [W]
  Adam, Marwood 1691 W
  Adam, Marwood 1739 W
  Adrian, North Molton 1625 [W]
  Agnes, Witheridge, widow 1563 W
  Agnes, North Molton 1569 W
  Agnes, High Bray 1583 A
  Agnes, High Bray 1593 [W]
  Agnes, Tawstock 1594 [W]
  Agnes, Roborough 1664 W
  Agnes, North Molton 1703 W
  Alexander, North Molton 1791 [W]
  Alfred, Romansleigh 1633 W
  Thorn Alfred, Romansleigh 1643 A
  Alice, Chawleigh 1591 [W]
  Alice, North Molton 1606 W
  Alice, North Molton 1835 W
  Ann, Burrington 1684 W
  Ann, South Molton 1725 W
  Ann, Tawstock 1783 W
  Thorn Ann, Molland 1803 A
  Ann, South Molton 1837 W
  Ann, Yarnscombe 1855 W
  Arthur, Ashreigney 1665 W
  Catherine, Shirwell 1589 W
  Charity, Chittlehampton 1747 W
  Charles, North Molton, snr. 1671 W
  Charles, North Molton 1690 A
  Charles, North Molton 1704 W
  Charles Hooper, Kentisbury 1834 A to Fanny, mother
  Christian, Shirwell 1706 W
  Christopher, Tawstock 1569 W
  Christopher, Charles 1635 W
  Christopher, Shirwell 1693 W
  Thorn Christopher, Goodleigh 1782 A
  Clemice, Parracombe, widow 1571 W
  David, Combe Martin 1576 W
  David, Molland 1637 W
  David, Marwood 1638 W
  David, Combe Martin 1645 W

David, Ilfracombe 1703 A
Dionysia, King's Nympton 1628 [W]
Ebbot, Warkleigh 1726 A
Edmund, Chulmleigh 1572 W
Edmund, Chulmleigh 1662 W
Edward, Fremington 1730 W
Edward, Fremington 1758 W
Eleanor, Barnstaple 1623 [W]
Eleanor, Sheepwash 1661 W
Eleanor, Fremington 1744 W
Eleanor, North Molton 1816 W
Elizabeth, Twitchen 1590 [W]
Elizabeth, North Molton 1615 [W]
Elizabeth, King's Nympton 1632 [W]
Elizabeth, Twitchen 1635 W
Elizabeth, North Molton 1636 W
Elizabeth, High Bickington 1644 W
Elizabeth, Newton St Petrock 1671 W
Elizabeth, Bideford 1683 W
Elizabeth, Great Torrington 1689 W
Elizabeth, Marwood 1695 W
Elizabeth, Fremington 1785 W
Elizabeth, Tawstock 1813 W
Emotta, South Molton 1667 W
Thorn Francis, Abbotsham 1787 W
Geoffrey, Romansleigh 1593 [W]
George, Ashford 1625 [W]
George, Barnstaple 1681 W
George, Chulmleigh 1681 A
George, Northam 1703 A
George, Barnstaple 1749 W
George, North Molton 1770 A
George, Warkleigh, yeoman 1796 W
George, Witheridge, yeoman 1806 W
Grace, Stoodleigh 1623 [W]
Grace, Marwood 1683 W
Grace, Barnstaple 1725 A
Henry, Molland 1614 [W]; forename blank in Ms; supplied
  from parish register
Henry, South Molton 1624 [W]
Henry, King's Nympton 1688 W
Henry, Fremington 1698 A
Henry, Georgeham 1720 A
Henry, King's Nympton 1766 W
Thorn Henry, North Molton 1779 A
Thorn Henry, Fremington 1794 A
Honor, Twitchen 1591 [W]
Honor, South Molton 1847 W
Hugh, Great Torrington 1563 W
Hugh, Twitchen 1577 W
Hugh, East Down 1636 W
Hugh, Oakford 1639 W
Humphrey, Warkleigh 1668 W
Humphrey, Warkleigh 1694 A
James, Barnstaple 1631 [W]
James, Great Torrington 1842 W
James, North Molton 1857 W
Jane, North Molton 1670 W
Thorn Jane, Satterleigh 1680 A
Thorn Jane, Alverdiscott 1772 A
Jane, Fremington 1799 W
Jeremiah, Newton St Petrock 1705 W and 1708 W
Jeremiah, Langtree 1761 A
Joan, Newton St Petrock 1573 W
Joan, North Molton 1575 W
Joan, Twitchen 1575 W
Joan, South Molton 1587 W
Joan, North Molton 1588 W and 1591 [W]
Joan, Fremington 1601 W
Joan, North Molton 1601 W
Joan, Shirwell 1617 [W]
Joan, Twitchen 1618 [W]
Joan, Trentishoe 1639 A
Joan, South Molton 1665 A
Joan, Barnstaple 1686 W

Joan, South Molton 1700 W
Joan, Pilton 1736 A
Joan, North Molton 1754 A
Joan and John, North Molton 1670 W
John, Newton St Petrock 1570 W
John, Shirwell 1572 W
John, Chittlehampton 1581 W
John, Westleigh 1586 [W]
John, Shirwell 1589 W
John, North Molton 1591 [W] and 1595 [W]
John, Warkleigh 1595 [W]
John, Beaford 1596 [W]
John, Parracombe 1596 [W]
John, Chittlehampton 1597 [W]
John, Martinhoe 1597 [W]
John, Roborough 1597 [W]
John, Twitchen 1597 [W]
John, High Bray 1598 [W]
John, North Molton 1598 [W]
John, Clovelly 1601 W
John, North Molton 1604 W
John, Barnstaple 1605 W
John, Shirwell 1613 [W]; forename blank in Ms; supplied
    from parish register
John, North Molton 1615 [W] and 1618 O
John, Northam 1616 [W]
John, High Bray 1617 [W]
John, Barnstaple 1622 [W]
John, North Molton 1622 [W]
John, Molland 1626 [W]
John, Twitchen 1627 [W]
John, North Molton 1629 [W]
John, North Molton, snr. 1634 W
John, Countisbury 1637 W
John, Buckland Filleigh 1639 A
John, Parracombe 1639 W
John, Newton St Petrock 1660 W
John, North Molton 1661 W
John, Marwood 1663 A
John, Pilton 1664 W
John, Rackenford 1666 W
John, Heanton Punchardon 1667 A
John, North Molton 1667 W
John, King's Nympton 1670 W
Thorn John, King's Nympton 1677 W
John, North Molton 1686 W
John, King's Nympton 1688 W
John, Barnstaple 1689 W
John, North Molton, snr. 1690 A
John, Barnstaple 1691 A
John, Bideford 1693 A
John, Twitchen 1694 W
John, King's Nympton 1695 W
John, North Molton 1698 W
John, Rackenford 1700 A
John, South Molton 1700 W
John, North Molton 1705 W
John, Parracombe 1710 W
Thorn John, North Molton 1711 W and 1718 W
Thorn John, South Molton 1719 W
John, Barnstaple 1720 A
John, Warkleigh 1723 A
John, North Molton 1733 W
John, Chulmleigh 1734 W
John, Ashford 1736 W
John, ship *Mermaid* 1749 W
John, North Molton 1751 W
John, Langtree 1754 W
John, Stoke Rivers 1756 A
John, Alverdiscott 1765 A
Thorn John, North Molton 1767 A
John, South Molton 1771 W
John, Charles 1785 W
John, Molland 1787 W
John, High Bray 1791 A
John, Marwood 1797 A

John, North Molton 1798 A
John, Alverdiscott 1801 W
John, South Molton, gentleman 1805 W
John, South Molton, yeoman 1810 A
John, Barnstaple, mason 1814 A to Elizabeth Norman,
    daughter
John, North Molton, shopkeeper 1816 A to Alice, widow
John, North Molton 1822 W
John, Chittlehampton 1827 A to John, son
John, North Molton 1829 W
John, South Molton 1830 W
John, Winkleigh 1831 W
Thorn John, Loxhore 1836 W
John, South Molton 1839 W
Thorn John, Ashreigney 1841 W
John, Shebbear 1843 W
John, Newton St Petrock 1845 W
John, High Bray 1846 W
John, South Molton, saddler 1856 A to William, innkeeper,
    brother
John and Joan, North Molton 1670 W
Jonah, Alverdiscott 1602 W
Joseph, Buckland Filleigh 1641 [W]
Julian, Barnstaple 1618 [W] and 1627 [W]
Thorn Julian, North Molton 1641 [W]
Lawrence, Barnstaple 1639 W
Leonard, Tawstock 1640 W
Lodovic, King's Nympton 1673 W
Lucy, North Molton 1702 A
Macklin, Marwood 1599 [W]
Margaret, Northam 1611 [W]; forename blank in Ms; supplied
    from parish register
Margaret, Romansleigh, widow 1614 [W]; forename blank in
    Ms; supplied from parish register
Margaret, South Molton 1669 A
Mary, Barnstaple 1640 W
Mary, Marwood 1663 A
Mary, Barnstaple 1666 A
Mary, Barnstaple 1676 W
Mary, Chittlehampton 1732 A
Mary, Great Torrington 1741 W
Mary, Ilfracombe 1741 A
Mary, Stoke Rivers 1757 A
Thorn Mary, George Nympton 1768 W
Mary, Pilton 1775 W
Mary, Chawleigh 1780 W
Mary, Barnstaple 1790 W
Mary, Alverdiscott 1821 W
Mary, Ilfracombe 1854 W
Mathew, Marwood 1607 [W]; forename blank in Ms; supplied
    from parish register
Mathew, Winkleigh 1626 [W]
Mathew, Marwood 1683 W
Michael, North Molton 1672 W
Thorn Michael, North Molton 1716 A
Michael, North Molton 1725 W
Michael, West Buckland 1763 W
Michael, North Molton 1777 W
Michael, South Molton 1849 W
Neriah, Winkleigh 1599 [W]
Neriah, West Down 1691 W
Neriah, ship *Augusta* 1756 A
Neriah, Barnstaple 1764 W
Nicholas, King's Nympton 1623 O
Nicholas, Countisbury 1643 A
Nicholas, Barnstaple 1672 W
Thorn Nicholas, Countisbury 1709 W
Nicholas, North Tawton 1750 W
Paul, Mariansleigh 1587 W
Peter, North Molton 1583 W
Peter, North Molton 1598 [W]
Peter, Romansleigh 1711 A
Philip, North Molton 1613 [W]; forename blank in Ms;
    supplied from parish register
Philip, Northam 1664 A

Philip, Shirwell 1690 A
Rachel, South Molton 1794 W and 1800 W
Richard, Buckland Filleigh 1570 W
Richard, High Bickington 1579 W
Richard, Chittlehampton 1603 W
Richard, Stoke Rivers 1616 [W]
Richard, King's Nympton 1619 [W]
Richard, Chulmleigh 1643 W
Richard, Yarnscombe 1644 W
Richard, Martinhoe 1672 W
Richard, South Molton 1672 W
Richard, Shirwell 1713 A
Richard, Newton St Petrock 1731 W
Richard, Ilfracombe 1732 W
Richard, Rose Ash 1740 W
Richard, High Bray 1745 W
Richard, Rose Ash 1762 W
Richard, Goodleigh 1792 W
Richard, North Molton, yeoman 1810 A
Richard, Little Torrington 1825 W
Richard, Kentisbury 1829 W
Richard, North Molton 1843 A
Robert, Chulmleigh 1564 W
Robert, Ashford 1573 W
Robert, High Bickington 1591 [W]
Robert, Chawleigh 1618 [W]
Robert, Barnstaple 1619 [W]
Robert, Satterleigh 1687 W
Robert, Rackenford 1695 [W]
Thorn Robert, Cruwys Morchard 1767 W
Thorn Robert, Witheridge 1779 A
Robert, South Molton 1837 W
Sarah, Chulmleigh 1681 W
Sarah, Barnstaple 1685 A
Thorn Sarah, South Molton 1760 W
Sarah, Barnstaple 1829 W
Sarah, North Molton 1848 W
Simon, Parracombe 1593 [W]
Simon, Barnstaple 1692 W
Stephen, Barnstaple 1623 [W]
Thomas, North Molton 1564 W
Thomas, North Molton 1579 W
Thomas, Parracombe 1579 W
Thomas, Tawstock 1586 [W]
Thomas, North Molton 1589 W
Thomas, Chulmleigh 1592 [W]
Thomas, Barnstaple 1599 [W]
Thomas, Shirwell 1600 W
Thomas, Twitchen 1603 W
Thomas, Romansleigh 1623 [W]
Thomas, Countisbury 1665 W
Thomas, North Molton 1667 W
Thomas, Martinhoe 1674 W
Thomas, Bideford 1676 A
Thomas, North Molton 1687 W and 1689 A
Thomas, Tawstock 1721 W
Thomas, Fremington 1785 A
Walter, North Molton 1570 W
Walter, Countisbury 1592 [W]
Walter, King's Nympton 1627 [W]
Walter, Northam 1636 O; A dbn
Walter, Charles 1685 W
Walter, Countisbury 1714 W
Walter, Ilfracombe, gentleman 1855 A to George of
   Swimbridge and Elizabeth Buckingham wife of Thomas
   Jose of Landkey, brother and sister; later to Mary of
   Swimbridge, widow
William, Alverdiscott 1573 A
William, South Molton 1573 W
William, Petrockstowe 1575 W
William, Weare Giffard 1575 A
William, Langtree 1576 A
William, Mariansleigh 1584 W
William, South Molton 1586 [W]
William, Chulmleigh 1591 [W]
William, Parracombe 1596 [W]

William, King's Nympton 1602 W
William, South Molton 1604 W
William, North Molton 1630 [W]
William, Chittlehampton 1631 [W] and 1633 O
William, East Down 1638 W
Thorn William, Petrockstowe 1642 W
William, North Molton 1661 W and A
William, Marwood 1682 W
William, North Molton, jnr. 1690 W
William, Warkleigh 1696 [W]
Thorn William, South Molton 1705 W
William, North Molton 1710 A
William, Ilfracombe 1715 [W]
William, North Molton 1724 W
William, Fremington 1725 W
William, Great Torrington 1737 W
William, King's Nympton 1739 W
William, Brendon 1741 W
William, Great Torrington 1741 W
William, South Molton 1741 W
William, ship *Namur* 1752 A
William, North Molton 1754 W
William, Dolton 1757 W
William, ship *Louisa* 1757 A
William, Fremington 1770 W
William, South Molton 1782 W
William, Ilfracombe 1790 W
William, King's Nympton 1795 W
William, North Tawton, yeoman 1806 W
Thorn William, St Giles in the Wood, yeoman 1811 A
William, Barnstaple 1811 W
William, Filleigh 1815 W
William, Rackenford 1815 W
William, Brendon 1820 W
William, North Molton 1823 W
William, Barnstaple 1825 W
William, Cruwys Morchard 1827 W
William, Warkleigh 1827 W
William, King's Nympton 1829 W
William, Martinhoe 1829 W
William, South Molton 1831 W
William, Barnstaple 1837 W
William, Molland 1837 W
William, North Molton 1837 W
William, Tawstock 1837 W
William, Langtree 1839 W
William, North Molton 1841 W and 1847 W
William, Knowstone 1850 W
William, North Molton 1853 A
William, Stoke Rivers 1857 W
Willmot, Twitchen 1585 A
Willmot, George Nympton 1610 [W]; forename blank in Ms;
   supplied from parish register
Willmot, North Molton 1635 [W]
Thresher Peter, Witheridge 1730 A
Threwe Thomas, Parkham 1567 W
   Threwe alias Drewe William, Buckland Brewer 1577 W
Thuell John, King's Nympton 1775 W
Tibbs, Tebbe, Tibb, Tibbe, Tibs, Tybbe, Tybbs
   Tibb Ann, Hartland 1675 W
   Tibb Ann, Northam 1686 W
   Tibb Ann, Hartland 1700 W
   Arthur, Warkleigh 1670 A
   Tibs alias Quantick Clase, Chittlehampton 1693 W
   Elizabeth, Chulmleigh 1781 W
   Tibbe John, Hartland 1576 W
   Tybbe John, Hartland 1622 A
   Tybbs John, Pilton 1637 W
   John, Chittlehampton 1736 A
   Tebbe Richard, Hartland 1591 [W]
   Tybbe Robert, Georgeham 1579 W
   Thomas, Chittlehampton 1723 A
   Tebbe Walter, Hartland 1604 W
   William, Burrington 1742 A
   William, Burrington 1760 A

William, Chulmleigh 1777 W
Tybbe Willmot, Hartland 1586 [W]
Tibo Elias, Barnstaple 1720 A
Tibond Elizabeth, Barnstaple 1741 A
Tibs see Tibbs
Tickle, Tickell, Tycle
George, King's Nympton 1629 [W]
Tycle John, Winkleigh 1577 W
Tickell John, King's Nympton 1679 A
John, Chawleigh 1712 W
Robert, King's Nympton 1711 A
Tickell see Tickle
Tidball, Tidboald
John, Chittlehampton 1722 W
Tidball alias Tout John, Chittlehampton 1773 W; forename
    blank in Ms; supplied from parish register
Tidboald Mary, Stoodleigh 1724 A
Richard, Chittlehampton 1739 A
Tidboald Thomas, Stoodleigh 1722 W
Tidboald Walter, Stoodleigh 1733 A
Tidboald Walter, Rackenford, yeoman 1808 W
William, North Molton 1847 W
Tidlake, Tydlake
Tydlake ..., Rackenford 1597 [W]
Tillard William, South Molton 1665 W
Tiller Alfred, South Molton 1680 A
Elizabeth, South Molton 1670 O
Thomas, South Molton 1730 W
William, South Molton 1670 O
Timewell, Tymewell, Tymewill
Tymewill ..., Chulmleigh 1608 [W]
Tymewill Elizabeth, Rackenford 1605 W
Tymewell Elizabeth, Chulmleigh 1621 [W]
Tymewill John, Rackenford 1621 [W]
Tymewell Thomas, Winkleigh 1626 [W]
Tincomb, Tenckombe, Tinnacomb, Tynkcombe
Tenckombe ..., North Tawton 1610 [W]
Joan, Witheridge 1693 W
Tinnacomb alias Pincomb Methusaleh, Welcombe 1665 [W]
Tynkcombe Robert, Barnstaple 1605 [W]; forename blank in
    Ms; supplied from parish register
Tinson Grace, South Molton, widow 1807 W
James, Barnstaple 1810 W
James, Barnstaple 1845 W
Mary, Barnstaple 1844 W
Mary, Northam, sp. 1848 A to Elizabeth wife of William
    Collacott of South Molton, mason, snr., sister
Tipper see Tepper
Tippet, Tippetts
James, Hartland 1675 A
Tippetts Richard, Barnstaple 1768 W
Tirrell see Terrell
Titheleigh, Titherleigh, Titherley, Titherly see Tetherley
Tocker, Tocke, Toker
Christopher, South Molton 1586 [W]
Edward, Kentisbury 1575 W
Elizabeth, Kentisbury 1575 W
Ellen, Trentishoe 1588 A
Toker Emma, Marwood 1583 A
Toker Harry, Combe Raleigh 1569 W
Henry, Dolton 1586 [W]
Henry, Eggesford 1588 W
John, North Molton 1565 W
Toker John, Marwood 1568 W
Toker alias Toner John, Chulmleigh 1572 W
John, Trentishoe 1573 W
John, West Buckland 1573 W
John, West Down 1575 W
Tocker alias Orchard John, Langtree 1575 A
John, Georgeham 1576 W
Tocker alias Orchard John 1582 W
John, Southam 1583 W
John, Mortehoe 1586 [W]
Toker Lye, Berrynarbor 1572 W
Toker Lye, Rackenford 1579 W

Toker Nicholas, Chulmleigh 1584 W
Peter, Great Torrington 1588 W
Richard, Yarnscombe 1573 W
Richard, St Giles in the Wood 1580 W
Richard, Zeal Monachorum 1589 A
Robert, Ilfracombe 1583 A
Robert, Dolton 1586 [W]
Simon, Woolfardisworthy 1578 W
Toker Thomas, Trentishoe 1566 W
Tocker alias Tanner Thomas, King's Nympton 1572 W
Thomas, Marwood 1582 W
Tocke Thomas, South Molton 1592 [W]
Tocker alias Sucker Thomasine, Washford Pyne 1570 W
Thomasine, Roborough 1578 A
Valentine, Marwood 1582 W
Walter, Trentishoe 1587 A
Toker Walter Rowly, Parracombe 1567 W
William, Dowland 1587 W
Todd Mathew, Great Torrington 1744 A
William, Barnstaple 1854 W
Togood see Toogood
Toke see Tooke
Toker see Toocker
Told Joshua, West Buckland 1723 W
William, Tawstock 1775 W
Toll Richard, Great Torrington 1742 W
Tolland, Tollen see Tallin
Tolley, Talley, Tawley, Tolly
... 1607 O
Alice, Thelbridge 1598 [W]
Tawley Ann, Thelbridge 1636 W
Ann, Witheridge 1664 W
Tawley Ann, Lapford 1684 W
Talley Ann, Stoodleigh 1817 W
Ann, Washford Pyne 1852 W
Edward, Thelbridge 1621 [W] and 1623 [W]
Edward, Meshaw 1788 W
Elizabeth, East Worlington 1694 W
Tolly Hugh, Molland 1738 A
Hugh, Mariansleigh, yeoman 1816 A to Mary, widow
James, Washford Pyne 1629 [W]
Tolly James, Lapford 1680 A
James, Thelbridge 1825 A to Elizabeth, widow
Tolly alias Molton John, Instow 1601 W
Tawley John, Chulmleigh 1691 A
Tolly John, Thelbridge 1696 W
John, Lapford 1711 W
Talley John, Stoodleigh, gentleman 1798 W
John, Meshaw 1828 W
John, Rose Ash 1842 W
Talley Jude, Stoodleigh 1801 W
Mary, Romansleigh 1832 A to John of Meshaw and Edward of
    West Worlington, sons
Talley Mathew, Stoodleigh 1713 A
Roger, Great Torrington 1591 [W]
William, Lapford 1670 A
William, Witheridge 1705 W
William, Washford Pyne 1851 W
Tollomye Agnes, Buckland Brewer 1616 [W]
Tolly see Tolley
Tolver Ann, Barnstaple, widow 1807 W
Tome, Tom, Tombe, Tomes, Tomme, Toms
..., Marwood 1600 A
..., Chulmleigh 1610 [W]
..., Chittlehampton 1611 [W]
..., King's Nympton 1611 [W]
Toms alias Yeamacott ..., Chulmleigh 1698 T
Tomes ..., Berrynarbor 1786 W
Toms Abraham, Barnstaple 1697 A
Toms David, Barnstaple 1712 A
Tom Edward, West Buckland 1642 W
Tom George, West Buckland 1630 [W]
Toms George, Dolton 1682 A
Tomme Henry, Chittlehampton 1598 [W]
Tom Henry, Pilton 1664 W

Joan, King's Nympton 1617 [W]
Tomes alias Thomas John, South Molton 1598 [W]
Tomme John, West Buckland 1599 [W]
Tom John, South Molton 1639 W
Toms John, Newton St Petrock 1690 A
Tombe John, Peters Marland 1738 W
Toms Lewis, South Molton, gentleman 1817 A to Humphrey
   of Bishop's Nympton, gentleman, brother
Tomme Lodovic, King's Nympton 1636 W
Tom Lodovic, King's Nympton 1696 A
Tom Martha, King's Nympton 1639 A
Tom Mary, Warkleigh 1671 O
Tomm Mary, King's Nympton 1699 W
Toms Mary, Heanton Punchardon 1735 A
Tomme Richard, Romansleigh 1592 [W]
Richard, Langtree 1617 [W]
Toms Richard, Peters Marland 1690 A
Toms alias Yearnacott Robert 1693 A
Tomme Rose, West Buckland 1621 [W]
Toms Samson, Petrockstowe 1677 W
Tomme Thomas, King's Nympton 1596 [W]
Tom Thomas, King's Nympton 1688 A
Toms Thomasine, Huntshaw 1708 W
Toms William, Parracombe 1768 A
Toms William, East Buckland 1774 W
Toms William, Berrynarbor, yeoman 1808 W
Toms William, Combe Martin 1835 A to John of Ilfracombe,
   son
Tomells Ann, Bideford 1638 W
John, Bideford 1588 W
Tomlyn Elizabeth, Marwood, widow 1570 W
Grace, Marwood 1661 W
Tomlyn alias Webber Joan, Marwood 1603 [W]; forename
   blank in Ms; supplied from parish register
John, Marwood 1607 [W]; forename blank in Ms; supplied
   from parish register
John, Pilton 1666 A
Oliver, Barnstaple 1624 [W]
Roger, Peters Marland 1624 O
Thomas, Marwood 1583 W
Thomas, Shirwell 1626 [W]
William, Loxhore 1660 W
   see also Tamlyn
Tomson see Thompson
Toner alias Toker John, Chulmleigh 1572 W
Tonkin, Tonken
Renatus, Frithelstock 1743 W
Tonken William, Frithelstock 1764 W
Tonysende see Townsend
Toogood, Togood
Agnes, Ilfracombe 1599 [W]
Edward, Ilfracombe 1621 [W]
John, Ilfracombe 1593 [W]
John, Ilfracombe 1680 W
Togood Mary, Ilfracombe 1707 W
Toocker, Tooker, Toucker, Towker
..., Puddington 1600 O account
..., Great Torrington 1601 A
..., Welcombe 1601 A
..., Combe Martin 1602 [W]
..., Sheepwash 1602 [W]
Tooker ..., High Bickington 1602 [W]
..., Combe Martin 1606 [W]
..., Shirwell 1607 [W]
..., Kentisbury 1610 [W]
..., Clovelly 1611 [W] (2)
..., Parracombe 1611 [W]
..., Mortehoe 1612 [W] (2) and 1614 [W]
..., Parracombe 1612 [W]
..., Winkleigh 1612 [W]
Tooker alias Punchard ..., Mortehoe 1661 A
Tooker alias Bowden ..., Ashford 1666 A
Adrian, Bratton Fleming 1628 [W]
Agnes, Combe Martin 1616 [W]
Agnes, Molland 1616 [W] and 1617 [W]

Agnes, East Anstey 1619 [W]
Alfred, Mortehoe 1633 W
Alice, St Giles in the Wood 1621 [W]
Tooker Anastasia, George Nympton 1641 A
Tooker Ann, Lynton 1668 A
Anstis, South Molton 1597 [W]
Anthony, Marwood 1603 W
Bartholomew, Stoke Rivers 1640 W (2)
Catherine, Mortehoe 1600 W
Tooker Charles, Marwood 1641 A
Towker Christian, Washford Pyne 1567 W
Tooker Christopher, Great Torrington 1643 W
Tooker David, Parracombe 1661 A
Edmund, East Anstey 1610 [W]; forename blank in Ms;
   supplied from parish register
Tooker Elizabeth, East Buckland 1583 A
Elizabeth, Bideford, widow 1605 [W]; forename blank in Ms;
   supplied from parish register
Emanuel, Peters Marland 1618 [W]
Emma, Heanton Punchardon 1593 [W]
Francis, Alwington 1601 W
Tooker Geoffrey, Mortehoe 1569 W
Tooker George, Parracombe 1586 [W]
Henry, St Giles in the Wood 1620 [W]
Hugh, Great Torrington 1622 [W]
Tooker Hugh, Bratton Fleming 1644 A
Jacquet, Berrynarbor 1631 [W]
James, Barnstaple 1596 [W]
James, Georgeham 1597 [W]
James, Kentisbury 1597 [W]
Towker Joan, Bratton Fleming 1567 W
Joan, Ilfracombe 1597 [W]
Joan, Georgeham, widow 1611 [W]; forename blank in Ms;
   supplied from parish register
Joan, Hartland, widow 1612 [W]; forename blank in Ms;
   supplied from parish register
Joan, Dowland 1618 [W]
Joan, Peters Marland 1624 [W]
Joan, Bratton Fleming 1631 [W]
Joan, Yarnscombe 1634 [W]
Joan, Chawleigh 1640 W
Tooker Joan, Great Torrington, widow 1643 A
Tooker alias Orchard John, Frithelstock 1568 W
John, Kentisbury 1572 W
Tooker John, Georgeham 1589 [W]
John, Bratton Fleming 1590 [W]
John, Brendon 1590 [W]
John, Mortehoe 1592 [W]
John, Kentisbury 1593 [W]
John, Mortehoe 1593 [W]
John, Zeal Monachorum 1593 [W]
John, Ilfracombe 1594 [W]
John, Puddington 1596 [W]
John, North Molton 1599 [W]
John, Zeal Monachorum 1599 [W]
John, Heanton Punchardon 1600 A; forename blank in Ms;
   supplied from parish register
John, Georgeham 1600 W
John, Mortehoe 1601 W
John, Winkleigh 1605 [W]
John, Hartland 1606 W
John, Lynton 1610 [W]; forename blank in Ms; supplied from
   parish register
John, Petrockstowe 1610 [W]; forename blank in Ms; supplied
   from parish register
John, St Giles in the Wood 1615 [W]
John, Northam 1617 [W]
John, Parracombe 1617 [W] and 1619 [W]
John, Zeal Monachorum 1619 [W]
John, Berrynarbor 1624 [W] and 1627 O
John, Challacombe 1631 [W]
John, Northam 1634 A
John, Berrynarbor 1636 W and 1642 W
John, Clovelly 1636 A
John, Monkleigh 1636 W

John, Yarnscombe 1638 A
Tooker alias Bowden John, Barnstaple 1643 W
John, Barnstaple 1645 A
Tooker John, North Molton 1664 A
Tooker John, Martinhoe 1676 A
Tooker John, Marwood 1680 W
John son of Emma, widow, Georgeham 1607 [W]; forename
    blank in Ms; supplied from parish register
Julia, Kentisbury 1623 [W]
Lawrence, Hartland, snr. 1639 [W]
Margaret, Loxhore 1639 W
Tooker Margaret, Ilfracombe 1662 W
Tooker Mary, Bideford 1671 W
Tooker Mary, Martinhoe 1680 W
Mathew, Barnstaple, jnr. 1630 [W]
Mathew, Barnstaple 1634 A
Tooker Matilda, South Molton 1585 W
Tooker Michael, Roborough 1643 A
Nicholas, Monkleigh 1629 [W]
Tooker Nicholas, Zeal Monachorum 1642 W
Tooker Nicholas, Bideford 1661 W
Oliver, Chawleigh 1596 [W]
Tooker Paschal, Ilfracombe 1584 W
Paul, Georgeham 1632 [W]
Peter, Yarnscombe 1604 W
Peter, Witheridge 1625 [W]
Philip, Berrynarbor 1611 [W]; forename blank in Ms; supplied
    from parish register
Tooker Philip, Parracombe 1666 A
Tooker Philip, Langtree 1765 A
Tooker Richard, Yarnscombe 1581 W
Richard, Heanton Punchardon 1590 [W]
Richard, Marwood 1609 [W] "of Middle Marwood" in
    register; forename blank in Ms; supplied from parish register
Richard, Burrington 1616 [W]
Richard, South Molton 1616 [W]
Richard, Chittlehampton 1622 [W]
Richard, Parracombe 1627 [W]
Toucker Richard, Buckland Brewer 1639 W
Richard, Little Torrington 1640 A
Tooker Richard, Great Torrington 1641 W
Tooker Robert, Mortehoe 1586 A
Robert, Martinhoe 1597 [W]
Robert, Northam 1612 [W]; forename blank in Ms; supplied
    from parish register
Robert, Coldridge 1632 [W]
Tooker Robert, Mortehoe 1642 A
Tooker Robert, Mortehoe 1664 A
Roger, Yarnscombe 1606 W
Samuel, South Molton 1638 W
Tooker Thomas, Combe Martin 1593 [W]
Thomas, East Anstey 1619 [W]
Thomas, South Molton 1622 [W]
Thomas, St Giles in the Wood 1634 W
Thomas, East Buckland 1639 W
Tooker Thomas, Bow 1698 W
Tooker Thomasine, Kentisbury 1581 W
Tooker Thomasine, Martinhoe 1675 [W]
Tooker Tobias, Georgeham 1671 W
Tooker Toocker Walter, Dolton 1621 [W]
Tooker Toocker Walter, Chawleigh 1638 W
Tooker William, Zeal Monachorum 1589 W
William, Fremington 1593 [W]
William, North Molton 1595 [W]
William, Combe Martin 1604 W
William, South Molton 1606 W
William, Hartland 1622 [W]
William, Combe Martin 1626 [W] and 1627 [W]
William, Zeal Monachorum 1628 [W]
William, North Molton 1628 [W] and 1630 O
William, South Molton 1639 W
William, Great Torrington 1643 W
Tooker William, St Giles in the Wood 1644 W
Tooker William, West Down 1714 W
Willmot, Georgeham 1594 [W]

Willmot, North Molton 1627 [W]
Willmot, Zeal Monachorum 1628 [W]
Tooke, Toke
    John, Witheridge 1694 A
    Toke William, Chawleigh 1596 [W]
Tooker see Toocker
Tooslowe John, St Giles in the Wood 1637 W
Toore see Torr
Toozer see Tozer
Topp, Topps
    Arthur, Bideford 1628 [W]
    Topps Catherine, North Molton 1636 A
    Francis, Northam 1631 [W]
    Topps Joan, Bideford 1565 W
    Joan, Twitchen 1638 W
    Roger, South Molton 1677 A
    Thomas, Northam, snr. 1643 W
    Topps Thomasine, Winkleigh 1597 [W]
    Willmot, Twitchen 1591 [W]
        see also Tapp
Topper John, Alwington 1588 W
Topps see Topp
Tore see Torr
Torer Richard, Bow 1688 A
Torkey Thomas, Fremington 1578 A
Tornshend see Townsend
Torr, Toore, Tore
    Toore Alice, Clovelly 1589 W
    Jane, Westleigh 1855 W removed by monition, 3 Nov 1856
    Toore John, Abbotsham 1569 W
    John, Westleigh, Revd 1836 A
    Tore Peter, Abbotsham 1569 W
    Tore Philip, Clovelly 1581 W
        see also Tarr
Torrens see Tarrens
Torrington Alice, Meshaw 1618 [W]
    Bartholomew, Romansleigh 1700 W and 1707 W
    Henry, Meshaw 1700 W and A
    Henry, Chittlehampton 1726 A
    Henry, Meshaw, yeoman 1808 W
    John, Romansleigh 1707 W
    John, Meshaw 1729 A
    John, High Bray 1800 A
    John, North Molton 1806 A
    Lodovic, South Molton 1674 T
    Mary, Meshaw 1731 A
    Torrington alias Warren Mary, King's Nympton 1763 A
    Robert, King's Nympton 1668 [W]
    Robert, King's Nympton 1731 A
    William, Meshaw 1615 [W]
    William, Meshaw 1749 A
    William, Meshaw 1836 W
Torsell John, Lapford 1775 W
Tory John, Northam 1680 W
Toser see Tozer
Toss Richard, Buckland Filleigh 1582 W
Tossell, Tossel
    Agnes, Bow 1633 W
    Christian, King's Nympton 1640 W
    Edward, King's Nympton 1748 A
    Elizabeth, Marwood 1787 W
    George, King's Nympton 1741 W
    George, Chulmleigh 1754 A
    Gregory, King's Nympton 1694 W
    Humphrey, Chulmleigh, yeoman 1803 W
    Joan, Tawstock 1591 [W]
    Joan, Brendon 1627 [W]
    John, King's Nympton 1639 A
    John, Barnstaple 1685 A
    John, King's Nympton 1690 W
    John, King's Nympton 1742 W
    John, King's Nympton 1758 W
    Tossel John, Ashreigney 1767 W
    John, King's Nympton 1780 W
    John, Marwood 1784 W

Tossel John, King's Nympton, yeoman 1810 W
John, Pilton 1846 W
Mary, Tawstock 1625 [W]
Tossel Nicholas, Pilton 1813 W
Susan, Ashreigney 1779 W
Thomas, George Nympton 1599 [W]
Walter, King's Nympton 1598 [W]
William, King's Nympton 1832 W
Tosser see Tozer
Tothacott, Tethcott, Tythecott
Joan, Buckland Brewer, widow 1608 [W]; forename blank in
  Ms; supplied from parish register
John, Northam 1599 [W] (2)
John, Northam 1599 [W]
Nicholas, Buckland Brewer 1598 [W]
Tythecott Philip, Littleham (near Bideford) 1744 W
Richard, Buckland Brewer 1643 W
Tethcott Thomas, Buckland Brewer 1588 A
Toucker see Toocker
Tounsend see Townsend
Tourner see Turner
Tout, Toute, Toutt, Towte
Toute Ann, Barnstaple 1679 W
Towte Bernard, Barnstaple 1672 A
Towte Catherine, Great Torrington 1618 [W]
Edmund, Ashreigney 1816 W
Toute Elizabeth, North Molton 1724 W
Elizabeth, Ashreigney 1754 W
Elizabeth, Ashreigney 1817 W
Towte George, Ashreigney 1751 W
George, Ashreigney 1763 W
Towte Hugh, Burrington 1702 W
Towte Hugh, Burrington 1732 A
Hugh, Wembworthy 1763 A
James, Stoke Damerel 1799 A
John, Fremington 1642 W
John, Barnstaple 1678 W
Toutt John, Burrington 1727 W
Towte John, Witheridge 1753 W
Tout alias Tidball John, Chittlehampton 1773 W
John, North Molton, saddler 1809 A
Mary, Chittlehampton, widow 1848 A to John Jenkins, mason,
  brother
Michael, Burrington 1704 A
Philip, Chittlehampton 1848 W
Towte Simon, Ashreigney 1769 A
Thomas, South Molton 1836 [W]
Toute William, Burrington 1775 W
William, Chawleigh 1826 A to Joanna, widow
Towte Willmot, Burrington 1714 W
Touzin Mary, Bideford 1795 W
Towers John, Ulverston, Lancashire 1794 A
Towill see Towle
Towker see Toocker
Towle, Towill
Towill Richard, Chawleigh 1564 A
Richard, Great Torrington, cooper 1811 W
Towyll Thomas, Countisbury 1583 W
William, Petrockstowe 1802 W original transmitted to
  Doctor's Commons, 20 Feb 1815
Towte see Tout
Towyll see Towle
Townsend, Tawnsend, Tonysende, Tornshend, Tounsend
..., Frithelstock 1607 [W]
Agnes, Shebbear 1660 W
Edmund, Petrockstowe 1781 W
Tonysende Elizabeth, Peters Marland 1564 W
Elizabeth, Frithelstock 1633 W
Jasper, Huntshaw 1743 A
Joan, Frithelstock 1677 [W]
John, Shebbear 1645 W
Tawnsend John, Northam 1729 W
Marcus, Huntshaw 1705 W
Philip, Chulmleigh 1778 W
Richard, Frithelstock 1606 W

Tounsend William, Buckland Brewer 1584 W
Tornshend William, High Bickington 1746 W
Towton John, Petrockstowe 1583 W
Tozer, Toozer, Toser, Tosser
..., Zeal Monachorum 1614 [W]
Charles, Bow 1787 W
Tosser Edmund, Bow 1583 A
Giles, Zeal Monachorum 1703 W
Giles, Zeal Monachorum 1765 A and 1766 A
James, Bow 1644 A
Toser John, Bow 1571 W
John, North Tawton 1671 A
Lawrence, Bow 1601 W
Mark, Bow 1632 [W]
Mark, Bow 1716 W
Toozer Nicholas, Winkleigh 1601 W
Richard, Bow 1633 W
Richard, Bow 1676 W
Tosser Robert, Broadnymet 1586 [W]
Robert, Chawleigh 1608 [W]; forename blank in Ms; supplied
  from parish register
Robert son of Mark, Bow 1611 [W]; forename blank in Ms;
  supplied from parish register
Robert, Zeal Monachorum 1702 W
Samuel, Bow 1668 W
Samuel, Bow 1743 W
Thomas, North Tawton 1694 A
Thomas, Bow 1726 W
William, Bow 1631 [W]
William, Bow 1731 W
William, North Tawton 1732 W
William, Zeal Monachorum 1766 W
Trace Ann, Weare Giffard 1805 W*
Christopher, Roborough 1632 W
John, Langtree 1722 A
Peter, King's Nympton 1625 [W]
Thomas, Martinhoe 1642 W (2)
Thomas, Little Torrington 1784 W
William, High Bickington 1571 W
William, Roborough 1632 [W]
William, Beaford 1640 A (2)
Tracy, Tracey, Traci, Tracie
Tracie ..., Dowland 1608 [W]
..., Bideford 1613 [W]
Tracey Ann, Ashreigney 1673 [W]
Anthony, Bideford 1597 [W]
Argent, Bow 1624 [W]
Christopher, Northam 1597 [W]
Christopher, Bideford 1687 W
Henry, Roborough 1625 [W]
Tracey Henry, Bow 1764 W
James, Bideford 1723 W
Jane, Bideford 1673 [W]
Joan, Northam 1593 [W]
Joan, Roborough 1617 [W]
Trassie John, Roborough 1582 W
John, Northam 1588 W
John, East Worlington 1645 W
John, Bideford 1686 W
John, Bideford 1704 A
John, Bideford 1707 W
John, Bow 1724 W
Joseph, Roborough 1694 W
Margery, Roborough 1700 W
Peter, King's Nympton 1679 W
Priscilla, Northam 1751 A
Ralph, Zeal Monachorum 1603 W
Ralph, Roborough 1693 [W]
Tracey Richard, High Bickington 1627 [W]
Tracey Roger, Bideford 1631 [W]
Samuel, Bideford 1667 W
Samuel, Bideford 1695 W
Tracey Sarah, King's Nympton 1741 A
William, Northam 1666 W
William, Northam 1684 A

William, Shebbear 1734 W
Tracey William, Shebbear 1792 A
Traci William, Weare Giffard 1805 W
Traisnell Susan, Bideford, widow 1811 W
Trameer Richard, Little Torrington 1643 A
Tranter Susan, Great Torrington 1828 W
Trapnell Edward, Pilton 1623 [W]
Trathen, Trathing
    John, Woolfardisworthy 1830 W
    Trathing William, Merton 1786 A
Tratt see Trott
Travers, Travis
    Travis Christopher, Northam 1639 W
    Eleanor, North Tawton 1627 [W]
Treable see Treble
Trebarft William, Alwington 1712 A
Treble, Treable, Trebble, Trebel, Trebell
    Ann, North Molton 1742 W
    Christian, Mariansleigh 1736 W
    English, North Molton 1662 W
    George, North Molton 1608 W; forename blank in Ms;
        supplied from parish register
    Grace, South Molton 1844 W
    Trebble John, High Bray 1631 [W]
    John, Romansleigh 1643 A
    John, Mariansleigh 1713 A
    John, South Molton 1719 W
    John, Romansleigh 1744 W
    John, North Molton 1758 W
    John, North Molton 1829 W
    John, Barnstaple 1852 W
    Trebble Richard, North Molton 1620 [W]
    Richard, Parkham 1790 W
    Stephen, Romansleigh 1697 A
    Thomas, North Molton 1703 A
    Thomas, North Molton 1715 A
    Thomas, Mariansleigh 1733 W
    Trebell Thomas, Abbotsham 1836 W
    Trebble Walter, Yarnscombe 1634 W
    William, Romansleigh 1578 W
    William, North Molton 1705 A
    William, South Molton 1712 A
    William, Barnstaple 1736 W
    Trebel William, South Molton 1745 A
    Treable William, North Molton 1851 W
Tredue William, Barnstaple 1685 W
Tredull John, Cheldon 1726 A
Treeby Christian, Great Torrington 1837 W
Tregeare, Tregear
    Edward, Martinhoe 1718 W
    Edward 1717 [W]
    Tregear John, Frithelstock 1595 [W]
Tregearthen John, Clovelly 1764 A
Tregeney ..., Clovelly 1612 [W]
Tregilas Edmund, Barnstaple 1634 A
    William, Barnstaple 1637 W
Treleviain see Trevilian
Trembles ..., Alwington 1615 [W]
    Roger, Alwington 1604 W
Tremblett, Tremlett, Trimlett
    Tremlett John, Rackenford 1589 W
    Tremlett John, Winkleigh 1677 W
    John, Bow 1695 A
    John, Romansleigh 1695 W
    Trimlett John, Winkleigh 1700 W
    Robert, North Tawton 1841 W
Tremeire ..., Woolfardisworthy 1614 [W]
Tremlett see Tremblett
Trench Peter, Littleham (near Bideford) 1710 W
Trencher Beatrice, Frithelstock, widow 1611 [W]; forename
    blank in Ms; supplied from parish register
    John, Witheridge 1612 [W]; forename blank in Ms; supplied
        from parish register
    John, Great Torrington 1696 [W]
    Richard, Frithelstock 1628 [W]

Trenerry John, Barnstaple 1823 A
Trescott Rebecca, Bideford 1718 W
Tresher Samuel, Puddington 1770 A
Tresteyae Mary, Bideford 1754 W
Tretencott ..., Mariansleigh 1612 [W]
Trevett George, Cruwys Morchard 1579 W
Trevilian, Treleviain, Trevillian
    ..., Ashreigney 1609 [W]
    Trevillian Agnes, Atherington 1596 [W]
    Trevillian Joan, Buckland Brewer 1626 [W]
    Lewis, Ashreigney, gentleman 1608 [W]; forename blank in
        Ms; supplied from parish register
    Treleviain Nicholas, Buckland Brewer 1748 W
    Thomas, Yarnscombe 1565 W
    Thomas, Yarnscombe 1668 A
Trevithnam Thomas, Bideford 1690 W
Trevor Ann, Barnstaple 1630 [W]
    James, Atherington 1711 W and 1715 A
Treweakes Elizabeth, Buckland Brewer, widow 1611 [W]
    "Terwicks" in register; forename blank in Ms; supplied from
        parish register
Treweeler Tobias, North Molton 1728 A
Trewin Elizabeth, Fremington 1749 A
    Elizabeth, St Giles in the Wood 1843 W
    James, South Molton 1734 A
    John, St Giles in the Wood 1836 W
    John Perry, Shebbear, yeoman 1852 A Frewin of Holsworthy
        to Isaac
Trewman Grace, Chulmleigh 1626 [W]
    Robert, Chulmleigh 1623 [W]
Trick, Tricke, Trickes, Tricks, Trix, Trixe, Trycke, Tryke
    ..., Newton St Petrock 1607 [W]
    ..., Buckland Brewer 1611 [W]
    Tricke ..., Langtree 1614 [W]
    Trix Abraham, Pilton 1698 A
    Trixe Anthony, Chulmleigh 1602 W
    Tricke Arthur, Meddon, Hartland 1567 W
    Tricke Arthur, Alwington 1624 [W]
    Tricke Arthur, Parkham 1640 W
    Charles, Hartland 1827 A to William of Woolfardisworthy,
        brother
    Tricks Edward, Bideford 1628 [W]
    Eli, Welcombe 1641 A
    Trix Elisha, Witheridge 1723 A
    Trixe Elizabeth, Tawstock, widow 1613 [W] "Triggs" in
        register; forename blank in Ms; supplied from parish register
    Emanuel, Hartland 1685 W
    Emanuel, Hartland 1751 W
    Emanuel, Hartland 1766 W
    Frances, Great Torrington 1840 W
    Trix Francis, Chittlehampton 1699 A
    Trix Francis, Chittlehampton 1780 W
    Hugh, Langtree, husbandman 1808 W
    Trix Joan, Chulmleigh 1563 W
    Tricks Joan, Bideford 1630 [W]
    Trix Joan, Chulmleigh 1690 W
    Trix Joan, King's Nympton 1824 W
    Tricke John, Bulkworthy 1579 W
    Trycke John, Parkham 1579 W
    Tryke John, Buckland Brewer 1584 W
    Trixe John, Wembworthy 1618 [W]
    Tricke John, Abbotsham 1619 [W]
    Trickey John, Hartland 1619 [W]
    Tricke John, Welcombe, snr. 1625 [W]
    John, Welcombe 1669 W
    John, Hartland 1688 W
    John, Hartland 1693 A
    John, Woolfardisworthy 1721 A
    John, Hartland 1727 A
    John, Woolfardisworthy 1755 A
    John, Hartland 1766 W
    John, Bideford 1800 W
    John, Hartland, mason 1809 A
    John, Weare Giffard 1832 A to John, son
    John, Welcombe 1836 W

John, Hartland 1849 W
John, Dolton 1854 W
John Way, Bideford, mariner 1850 A to Ann, widow
Joseph, Beaford 1850 W
Leonard, Welcombe 1708 W
Trix Lodovic, Chulmleigh 1635 A
Tricke Margaret, Abbotsham 1637 A
Margaret, Frithelstock 1723 A
Tricke Mary, Alwington 1638 A and 1640 O
Mary, Woolfardisworthy 1739 A
Tricke Nicholas, Newton Tracey 1590 [W]
Tricks Nicholas, Chulmleigh 1678 W
Peter, Woolfardisworthy 1690 W
Tricke Richard, Welcombe 1576 W
Richard, Welcombe 1590 [W]
Trickes Richard, Bideford 1610 [W]; forename blank in Ms;
    supplied from parish register
Trix Richard, Chulmleigh 1686 W
Trix Richard, Chulmleigh 1724 W
Robert, Hartland 1667 W
Sarah, Hartland 1826 W
Susan, Hartland 1759 W
Susan, West Putford 1762 W
Susan, Woolfardisworthy 1793 W
Tricke Thomas, Hartland 1565 W
Trycke Thomas, Welcombe 1578 W
Tricke Thomas, Buckland Brewer 1587 W
Thomas, Welcombe 1712 A
Thomas, Hartland 1778 W
Thomas, Welcombe 1830 W
Thomas, Hartland 1850 W
Tricke William, Hartland 1639 W
William, Hartland, yeoman 1797 W
Trix William, South Molton, yeoman 1803 W
Trix William, King's Nympton 1829 W
William, Hartland 1840 W
Trix William, South Molton 1854 W
William, Woolfardisworthy 1857 W
Tricker Daniel, Langtree 1728 W
Dorothy, Tawstock 1662 W
Giles, Tawstock 1639 W
John, Tawstock 1703 W
Trickes see Trick
Tricks see Trick
Trigg Agnes, Pilton 1854 W
Alexander, Bratton Fleming 1620 [W]
Edmund, Bratton Fleming 1624 [W]
Frances, Tawstock 1623 W
Joan, Bratton Fleming 1624 [W]
John, Bratton Fleming 1599 [W]
John, Chulmleigh 1731 W
John, Barnstaple 1740 W
Mary, Chulmleigh 1737 W
Richard, Bratton Fleming 1667 A
Robert, Bratton Fleming 1681 A
Robert, Bratton Fleming 1737 A
Thomasine, Bratton Fleming 1709 W
Thomasine, Bratton Fleming 1710 W
Trim William, Barnstaple 1830 W
Trimlett see Tremblett
Tripcony Alice, Westleigh 1619 [W]
Tripe, Tripp, Trype
George, Lapford 1690 W
George, North Tawton 1757 W
John, Wembworthy 1597 [W]
Trype Lewis, Instow 1581 W
Tripp Richard, Newton St Petrock 1620 [W]
Tristeen Nicholas, Bideford 1733 W
Trix, Trixe see Trick
Trobridge Humphrey, Wembworthy 1643 W
Tromp John, Marwood 1830 W
Troot, Troote see Trott
Trothen John, Buckland Brewer, yeoman 1797 W
Trott, Tratt, Troot, Troote, Trotte
..., Great Torrington 1610 [W]

Trotte ..., Great Torrington 1670 [W]
Troote Alice, Twitchen 1564 W
Christian, Great Torrington 1752 A
James, Great Torrington 1597 [W]
Joan, Bideford 1758 W
Tratt John, Ilfracombe 1592 [W]
John, Parkham 1793 W
Mary, Parkham 1795 W
Troote Nicholas, South Molton 1615 [W]; forename blank in
    Ms; supplied from parish register
Troot Richard, North Molton 1599 [W]
Samuel, Bideford 1708 A
Trotte Simon, Great Torrington 1607 [W]; forename blank in
    Ms; supplied from parish register
Stephen, Bideford 1731 W
Troote Thomas, Buckland Brewer 1643 A
Tratt William, Winkleigh 1564 W
William, Great Torrington 1849 W
Troughton William, Shebbear 1672 W
Trout, Troute, Troutt, Trowte
Troute ..., Yarnscombe 1611 [W]
Edith, Dolton 1641 W
Troutt James, North Tawton 1593 [W]
Trowte John, North Tawton 1578 W
Trowte John, North Tawton 1601 W
Troute John, Rose Ash 1620 [W]
Trout alias Smaldon Margery, Charles 1683 W
Richard, Marwood 1716 A
Troute Robert, Rose Ash 1588 W
Robert, Great Torrington 1592 [W]
Troute Thomas, East Worlington 1583 A
Trowte Thomas, Twitchen 1624 [W]
Trowte Walter, Twitchen 1585 W
Trudgeon, Trudgian
Trudgian Bennett, Great Torrington 1673 [W]
Garnett, Great Torrington 1701 W
Truker see Tucker
Trycke see Trick
Trype see Tripe
Tucke John, Hartland 1669 A
Tucker, Truker
Tucker alias Punchard ..., Mortehoe 1661 A
Tucker alias Churley ..., South Molton 1676 A
Tucker alias Bowden ..., Ashford 1677 W
....Adam, Parkham 1816 A dbn to Mary, sp. goods
    unadministered by Adam
Agnes, Parracombe 1571 A
Agnes, Georgeham 1766 W
Alexander, East Buckland 1672 A
Alexander, Chittlehampton 1764 W
Alexander, Loxhore, yeoman 1800 W
Alice, Georgeham 1714 W
Andrew, Barnstaple 1643 W
Ann, Ilfracombe 1636 A
Ann, West Buckland 1695 A
Ann, Thelbridge 1745 W and 1747 W
Ann, Marwood 1746 W
Ann, South Molton 1787 A
Ann, Georgeham 1833 W
Ann, Molland, wife 1852 A to John
Anthony, Shebbear 1611 W
Anthony, Tawstock 1762 A
Anthony, Yarnscombe 1835 W
Armanell, Witheridge 1693 W
Arthur, Barnstaple 1729 A
Baldwin, South Molton 1643 A
Bartholomew, Ilfracombe 1677 W
Catherine, Marwood 1683 W
Catherine, Great Torrington 1824 A to Mary Blackwell,
    daughter
Christopher, Great Torrington 1677 W
Christopher, South Molton 1692 A
Christopher, Molland 1732 A
Daniel, Mortehoe 1673 [W]
David, Bratton Fleming, yeoman 1802 W

Dorothy, Berrynarbor 1718 W
Edward, Bideford 1662 W
Edward, Northam 1688 W
Edward, Kentisbury 1691 W
Edward, High Bray 1697 W
Edward, Hartland 1737 A
Edward, Hartland 1744 W
Edward, Tawstock 1767 W
Edward, Instow 1776 W
Edward, Georgeham 1849 W
Eleanor, Shirwell 1695 W
Eleanor, Berrynarbor 1701 W
Eleanor, Barnstaple 1777 W
Eli, Langtree 1710 A
Eli, Langtree 1844 W
Elizabeth, Parkham 1663 A
Elizabeth, Barnstaple 1725 W
Elizabeth, Berrynarbor 1726 W
Elizabeth, Mortehoe 1741 W
Elizabeth, Kentisbury 1743 W
Elizabeth, Barnstaple 1748 A
Elizabeth, Fremington 1828 W
Elizabeth, Great Torrington 1840 W
Elizabeth Frances, Barnstaple 1727 A
Emanuel, South Molton 1699 W
Emanuel, Instow 1728 W
Emma, Ilfracombe 1691 W
Emott, Marwood 1741 W
Francis, Mortehoe 1723 W
Francis, South Molton 1782 W
Francis, Frithelstock 1785 W
George, Barnstaple 1700 A
George, Ilfracombe 1704 A
George, Goodleigh 1763 A
George, Georgeham 1829 W
George, Kentisbury 1844 W
George, formerly of Pilton, late of Kentisbury 1852 W
Giles, West Worlington, yeoman 1804 W
Giles, Lapford, farmer 1854 A to Joseph of Chulmleigh,
   brother
Grace, Zeal Monachorum 1679 A
Grace, Marwood 1712 A
Grace, North Molton 1733 W
Grace, North Molton 1744 W
Grace, Goodleigh 1782 A
Henry, North Molton 1666 [W]
Henry, Barnstaple 1757 W
Henry, Goodleigh 1766 W
Humphrey, Creacombe 1692 A
James, Georgeham 1694 A
James, Goodleigh 1761 A
James, Goodleigh 1762 W
James, Chittlehampton 1814 W
James, Nymet Rowland 1844 A
Jane, Northam 1674 A
Jane, High Bickington 1683 W
Jane, Wembworthy 1692 W
Jane, West Buckland 1695 W
Jane, Barnstaple 1780 A
Jane, Barnstaple 1803 A
Jasper, Chittlehampton 1724 W
Joan, Shirwell 1664 W
Joan, Yarnscombe 1686 W
Joan, Barnstaple 1688 A
Joan, Instow 1773 W
Truker John, Winkleigh 1577 A
John, Twitchen 1579 W
John, Mortehoe 1616 W
Tucker alias Bowden John, Barnstaple 1661 O
John, Northam 1666 W
John, Hartland 1672 O
John, Great Torrington 1673 W
John, Yarnscombe 1679 W
John, Bideford 1685 A
John, High Bray 1687 A
John, Georgeham 1688 A

John, Parracombe 1694 A
John, Georgeham 1695 A
John, Georgeham 1699 W
John, North Molton 1699 W
John, South Molton 1700 A
John, Goodleigh 1707 W
John, Instow 1712 W
John, Marwood 1712 W
John, Challacombe 1716 W
John, Berrynarbor 1729 A
John, Berrynarbor 1744 A
John, South Molton 1745 W
John, Chittlehampton 1752 A
John, Zeal Monachorum 1755 A
John, Instow 1757 W
John, Great Torrington 1758 W
John, South Molton 1758 W
John, Eggesford 1760 A
John, Frithelstock 1762 A
John, Tawstock 1764 W
John, Georgeham 1765 W
John, Brendon, yeoman 1799 A
John, Chittlehampton, yeoman 1805 W
John, Mortehoe 1812 W
John, Tawstock, carpenter 1815 A to Elizabeth, widow
John, Langtree 1836 W
John, Mortehoe 1849 W
John, Bulkworthy 1853 W
John, Langtree 1855 W
Jones, Berrynarbor 1726 A
Joseph, Marwood 1746 W
Joseph, High Bray 1762 A
Joseph, Northam 1802 A
Joshua, Tawstock 1722 W
Margaret, Shirwell 1695 A
Margaret, Goodleigh 1715 A
Margaret, Great Torrington 1734 A
Margaret, Arlington 1766 A
Margaret and Richard, Shirwell 1695 A
Mary, Burrington 1663 A
Mary, Georgeham 1693 W
Mary, Shirwell 1695 W
Mary, Bratton Fleming 1799 W* (1798)
Mary, Barnstaple 1820 W
Mary, Atherington 1822 W
Mary, Yarnscombe 1843 W
Mary, Ilfracombe 1855 W
Mary, Georgeham 1856 W
Mathew, Mortehoe 1755 W
Mathew, Langtree, jnr. 1774 W
Mathew, Langtree 1774 W
Michael, Chittlehampton 1810 W
Nicholas, Marwood 1688 A
Paul, Barnstaple 1707 A
Peter, Burrington 1660 W
Peter, North Molton 1669 W
Peter, Molland 1686 A
Peter, Wembworthy 1686 W
Peter, Parracombe 1704 A
Peter, Mortehoe 1725 A
Peter, Mortehoe 1738 A and 1742 A
Peter, Parracombe 1831 W
Peter, West Worlington 1851 W
Tucker alias Bowden Philip, Barnstaple 1669 A
Tucker alias Bowdon Philip, Ashford 1669 A
Philip, Great Torrington 1724 W
Philip, Great Torrington 1740 A
Philip, Parracombe 1771 W
Rebecca, South Molton 1688 W
Richard, Burrington 1679 A
Richard, Witheridge 1679 A
Richard, Marwood 1681 W
Richard, Great Torrington, snr. 1684 W
Richard, Northam 1692 W
Richard, Shirwell, snr. 1695 W

Richard, Goodleigh 1706 A
Richard, Combe Martin 1714 W
Richard, Kentisbury 1728 W
Richard, Atherington 1761 [W]
Richard, Trentishoe 1813 W
Richard, Georgeham 1838 W
Richard, Lynton 1839 A to Mary of East Down, widow
Richard and Margaret, Shirwell 1695 A
Robert, North Tawton 1688 W
Robert, East Buckland 1708 W
Robert, Great Torrington 1757 W and 1758 W
Robert, Bulkworthy 1837 W
Robert, Rose Ash 1853 W
Robert, Woolfardisworthy 1853 W
Samuel, South Molton 1689 W
Samuel, Mortehoe 1732 W
Sarah, Combe Martin 1749 A
Stephen, Great Torrington 1717 A
Stephen, Weare Giffard 1730 A
Stephen, Great Torrington 1816 W
Susan, Barnstaple 1755 W
Susan, Mortehoe 1772 W
Thomas, Berrynarbor 1670 W
Thomas, Berrynarbor 1682 W
Thomas, Great Torrington 1711 A
Thomas, Ilfracombe 1718 A
Thomas, North Tawton 1734 W
Thomas, Berrynarbor 1742 W
Thomas, ship *York* 1756 W
Thomas, Barnstaple 1773 A
Thomas, West Down, yeoman 1803 W
Thomas, Ilfracombe 1823 A to Justina, widow
Thomasine, Georgeham 1711 A
Tristram, Georgeham 1699 A
Ursula, Georgeham 1683 W
Valentine, Instow 1707 W
Walter, Langtree 1681 W
William, South Molton 1574 W
William, Parracombe 1586 [W]
William, Great Torrington 1663 W
William, Twitchen 1666 W
William, Witheridge 1667 A
William, Great Torrington 1679 A
William, South Molton 1682 W and 1686 A
William, Clannaborough 1699 W
William, Parracombe 1700 W
William, Buckland Brewer 1704 W
William, Northam 1705 W
William, Buckland Brewer 1706 [W]
William, Ilfracombe 1718 A
William, Langtree 1727 W
William, Great Torrington 1732 A
William, North Molton 1734 W
William, High Bray 1739 W
William, Kentisbury 1766 A
William, Barnstaple 1804 W
William, Trentishoe, yeoman 1804 W
William, Welcombe, yeoman 1811 W
William, Pilton 1812 W
William, Atherington, yeoman 1814 A to Mary, widow
William, Buckland Brewer 1828 W
William, Barnstaple 1832 W
William, Kentisbury 1848 W
Tuckerfield Thomas, Bow 1593 [W]
Tuckett John, Bideford, potter 1796 W
Susan, Bideford, widow 1811 W
William, South Molton 1853 W
Tuckfield, Tuckfylde
Tuckfylde Alnot, Bow 1585 W
John, Pilton 1748 A
John, Ilfracombe 1785 W
Thomas, Ilfracombe 1763 W
Tue see Tew
Tull William, Bideford 1740 A
Tuplin, Tupling
Ann, Northam 1847 [W]

Grace, Tawstock 1845 W
Tupling Gregory, Northam 1822 W
William, Tawstock 1834 W
Turbett, Turbet
John, Barnstaple 1712 W
Turbet Thomas, Barnstaple 1575 W
Turell Amy, Northam 1758 W
Turner, Tourner
..., Great Torrington 1602 [W]
..., King's Nympton 1607 [W]
..., Martinhoe 1608 [W]
Abraham, South Molton 1703 W
Agnes, King's Nympton 1596 [W]
Agnes, Burrington 1636 A and 1640 O
Alice, Langtree 1634 A
Alice, Langtree 1635 W
Andrew, Burrington 1757 W
Baldwin, Chulmleigh 1566 W
Catherine, Buckland Brewer 1667 A
Christopher, East Worlington 1745 W
Cresset, Chulmleigh 1672 W
Edward, Bondleigh 1636 A
Elizabeth, Chulmleigh 1575 W
Francis, High Bickington 1694 W
George, Filleigh 1590 [W]
George, Bow 1594 [W]
George, King's Nympton 1595 [W]
George, Chittlehampton 1726 A
Grace, Rackenford 1742 W
Hannah, Meeth 1858 W
Henry, Burrington 1622 [W]
Henry, Burrington 1662 A
Hugh, Martinhoe 1600 W
Humphrey, South Molton 1722 A
James, Barnstaple 1598 [W]
James, Barnstaple 1629 [W]
James, Burrington 1713 W
James, East Worlington 1728 W
Jane, Warkleigh 1785 W
Joan, Buckland Brewer 1638 [W]
John, Ashreigney 1565 W
John, Buckland Brewer 1565 W
Tourner John, Northam 1571 W
John, Burrington 1580 W
John, King's Nympton 1586 [W]
John, Burrington 1590 [W] (2)
John, Buckland Brewer 1591 [W]
John, Winkleigh 1603 W
Turner alias Webber John, Winkleigh 1603 W
John, Winkleigh 1620 [W]
John, Burrington 1638 W
John, Filleigh 1676 W
John, Chulmleigh 1688 A
John, Langtree 1700 W
John, Witheridge 1708 W
John, South Molton 1726 W
John, Chulmleigh 1740 A
John, East Worlington 1761 W
John, South Molton 1763 W and 1765 W
John, St Giles in the Wood 1794 W
John, South Molton 1818 W
John, St Giles in the Wood 1818 W
John, Combe Martin 1848 W and 1856 W
Joseph, Ashreigney 1856 W
Joshua, Barnstaple 1842 W
Tourner Walter, Horwood 1567 W
William, Barnstaple 1627 [W]
William, Buckland Brewer 1686 W
William, Buckland Brewer 1712 W
William, Beaford 1759 W
William, Hartland 1848 W
William, Lynton 1855 W
William Thorne, Ilfracombe 1853 W
Turney Henry, Barnstaple 1591 [W]

Turpitt James, West Down, snr. 1729 W
  Margaret, Great Torrington 1736 A
Tuychen Henry, St Giles in the Wood 1621 [W]
  Ralph, Buckland Brewer 1643 A
  William, Roborough 1668 W
Tybbe, Tybbs see Tibbs
Tycle see Tickle
Tydlake see Tidlake
Tyer Philip, Bideford 1686 W
Tyeth Grace, Bideford 1790 W
  William Short, Bideford 1850 W
Tymblett Robert 1696 A
Tymewell, Tymewill see Timewell
Tynkcombe see Tincomb
Tyrrill see Terrell
Tyrry see Terry
Tyte George, Barnstaple 1839 W
  John, Barnstaple 1855 W
Tythecott see Tothacott
Tytherlegh, Tytherleigh, Tytherly see Tetherley

Udenham William, South Molton 1640 W
Udy, Udie
  Udie Eleanor, Great Torrington 1575 W
  Eleanor, Great Torrington 1723 A
  Elizabeth, Barnstaple 1698 A
  Lodovic, Great Torrington 1722 A
  Udie Richard, Great Torrington 1575 A
  Richard, Great Torrington 1620 [W]
  Richard, Great Torrington 1668 A
  Udie Samuel, Great Torrington 1615 [W]
  Thomas, Barnstaple 1695 W
Unbles Elizabeth, Bideford 1731 W
  John, Bideford 1726 W
Underhill Barbara, North Tawton 1781 W
  Barnabas, Great Torrington 1621 [W]
  Elizabeth, Coldridge 1563 W
  Elizabeth, Dolton 1673 [W]
  Elizabeth, North Tawton 1707 W
  George, North Tawton 1698 W
  Hugh, Bondleigh 1698 A
  Hugh, Shebbear, yeoman 1821 A to Mary, widow
  Jane, Coldridge 1686 W
  John, Coldridge 1590 [W]
  John, Coldridge 1660 W
  John, Iddesleigh 1661 W
  John, Bideford, snr. 1713 W
  John, North Tawton 1775 W
  Joseph, Wembworthy 1776 A
  Joseph, Wembworthy 1835 W and 1844 W
  Mary, Bideford 1833 W
  Moses, Brushford 1777 A
  Phyllis, Iddesleigh 1664 A
  Robert, Winkleigh 1741 A
  Simon, Iddesleigh 1623 [W]
  Simon, Winkleigh 1686 W
  William, North Tawton 1685 W and 1686 W
  William, North Tawton 1725 W
Upcott, Upcoate, Upcot
  ..., Chulmleigh 1611 [W]
  ..., Martinhoe 1611 [W]
  Agnes, Thelbridge 1636 A
  Ann, North Molton 1599 [W]
  Bennett, Tawstock 1616 [W]
  Dorothy, Burrington 1622 [W]
  Upcot Eleanor, Northam 1570 W
  George, North Molton 1615 [W] and 1621 [W]
  George, North Molton 1636 A
  Grace, North Tawton 1638 W
  Upcote Harry, Roborough 1569 W
  Henry, Roborough 1593 [W]
  Hugh, Roborough 1640 A
  Hugh, Shirwell 1695 W
  Joan, Witheridge 1575 W
  Joan, North Molton 1597 [W]

Joan, Huish 1693 A
Joan, South Molton 1739 A
Upcoate alias Mere John, Witheridge 1574 W
John, Northam 1591 [W]
John, East Worlington 1616 [W]
John, Roborough 1622 [W]
John, Goodleigh 1722 A
Lawrence, Martinhoe 1597 [W]
Mary, Beaford 1734 W (2)
Mary, Pilton, sp. 1847 A to Elizabeth Flexman of Pilton,
  widow, sister
Philip, Martinhoe 1575 W and 1586 O account
Richard, Northam 1591 [W]
Richard, Marwood 1697 A
Robert, Witheridge 1597 [W]
Susan, Pilton, sp. 1847 A to Elizabeth Flexman of Pilton,
  widow, sister
Thomas, Frithelstock 1580 A
Thomas, Northam 1592 [W]
Thomas, North Tawton 1597 [W]
Thomas, Martinhoe 1600 W
Upcott alias Meare Thomas, Witheridge 1644 A
Upcott alias Mayer William, Witheridge 1589 A
William, Eggesford 1599 [W]
William, Witheridge 1615 [W]
William, High Bickington 1632 [W]
William, Oakford 1632 [W]
Upcotte William, Northam, snr. 1670 [W]
William, Ashford 1730 W
Upham ..., Chittlehampton 1614 [W]
  Alexander, Cruwys Morchard 1746 W
  Askal, South Molton 1731 A
  Francis, ship *Toy* 1750 A
  Hugh, South Molton 1678 W
  Israel, Warkleigh 1637 A
  John, East Anstey 1578 W
  John, Chittlehampton 1632 [W]
  John, Chittlehampton 1687 W
  Margery, Great Torrington 1627 [W]
  Simon, Fremington 1740 A
  Theophilus, Barnstaple 1717 A
  William, East Anstey 1591 [W]
Uphill Alice, Instow [no year given] W
  Archelaus, Instow 1682 W
  Mary, Instow 1695 W
  William, Northam 1587 A
Upjohn Peter, Bideford 1795 W
Uppacott John, Chawleigh 1606 W
  William, North Molton 1588 W
Uppington ..., Witheridge 1611 [W]
  Beatrix, High Bray 1600 W
  Uppington alias Michell John, South Molton 1577 W
  Robert, Witheridge 1590 [W]
  Robert, Rackenford 1678 W
  Thomas, Witheridge 1627 [W] and 1630 [W]
Upricharde ..., North Molton 1603 [W]
Upright Faith, Roborough 1738 W
  Henry, Bondleigh 1592 [W]
  Joan, Newton St Petrock 1637 A
  John, Roborough 1734 W
  William, Bondleigh 1638 W
  William, North Tawton 1780 W
Upton ..., Great Torrington 1610 [W]
  Theophilus, Barnstaple 1711 A
Uryne Elizabeth, Woolfardisworthy (East or West), widow 1566
  [W]
Ustock Judith, Combe Martin 1706 [W]

Vagg Elizabeth, Ilfracombe 1850 A
Vagures alias Fugurs William, Cruwys Morchard 1663 W
Valdon, Valden
  Valden Margaret, Monkleigh 1638 W
  Walter, Monkleigh 1636 W
Vale, Veyell, Veylle
  Veylle Anthony, Monkleigh 1581 W

Veyell Thomas, Shebbear 1571 W
Valentine, Fallentyne
  Fallentyne John, Hartland 1583 W
Vallacott see Vellacott
Vallance Ann, Bideford 1664 W
Vallecott see Vellacott
Vallett Charles, Great Torrington 1794 W
  James, Great Torrington 1725 A
  Priscilla, Great Torrington 1742 A
  Robert, Northam 1662 A
  Roger, Great Torrington 1709 W
  Sarah, Great Torrington 1764 W
  Wilmot, Northam, widow 1614 [W]; forename blank in Ms;
    supplied from parish register
Valline Bowden, Bideford 1586 W
Valter Charles, Bratton Fleming 3 May 1771 W; 1783 A dbn
Van see Vanne
Vandon see Vawden
Vanne, Van, Vane
  ..., Great Torrington 1605 [W]
  ..., Little Torrington 1613 [W]
  Elizabeth, Great Torrington 1591 [W]
  George, Great Torrington 1626 [W]
  George, Great Torrington 1632 [W]
  John, Little Torrington 1601 W
  Lewis, Great Torrington 1601 W
  Mabel, Great Torrington 1630 [W]
  Vane Rees, East Down [no year given] A
  Vane Richard, Great Torrington 1587 W
  Van William, Great Torrington, snr. 1634 W
Vanstone, Vanston, Venstone
  Vanston ..., Winkleigh 1613 [W]
  Vanston ..., High Bickington 1614 [W]
  Benjamin, Iddesleigh 1785 A
  Christopher, Dolton 1835 W
  Eleanor, High Bickington 1629 [W]
  Emetta, Merton 1699 W
  Vanston Isott, Wembworthy 1605 W
  James, Sheepwash 1775 W
  James, Sheepwash 1829 W
  John, Martinhoe 1628 [W]
  John, Shirwell 1665 W
  John, High Bickington 1713 W
  Vanston Peter, Winkleigh 1617 [W]
  Vanston Richard, Dowland 1601 W
  Samuel, Winkleigh 1678 A
  Sybil, Langtree 1635 W
  Simon, Buckland Filleigh 1782 A
  Stephen, Buckland Filleigh 1691 A
  Venstone Stephen, Woolfardisworthy 1741 A
  Stephen, Woolfardisworthy, yeoman 1808 W
  Stephen, Langtree 1831 W
  Thomas, Great Torrington 1636 W
  Vanston William, Winkleigh 1602 W
  William, High Bickington 1708 W
Varneham see Vernham
Varrant Arthur, Chawleigh 1641 A
Vater see Vawter
Vaudon see Vawden
Vaughan Elizabeth, Barnstaple 1714 W
  John, Northam 1697 A
  John, Northam 1711 A
  Thomas, Northam 1703 A
Vauter see Vawter
Vawden, Vandon, Vaudon, Vawdon
  Grace, King's Nympton 1769 W
  Vaudon Hannibal, King's Nympton 1679 W
  Hannibal, King's Nympton 1751 W
  Vandon Joan, King's Nympton 1704 W
  Vawdon Thomas, Petrockstowe 1602 W
  Vandon or Vaudon William, Burrington 1643 W
Vawter, Vater, Vauter, Voater
  Vater Abraham, Chittlehampton 1783 W
  Vauter Agnes, Molland 1614 [W]; forename blank in Ms;
    supplied from parish register

Vawter Thomas, South Molton 1563 W
Voater Thomas, South Molton 1626 [W]
Veale, Veal, Viell, Ville
  Ville Agnes, Barnstaple 1825 W
  Alice, Monkleigh 1621 [W]
  Anthony, Monkleigh 1603 W
  Eleanor, Northam 1749 W
  Elizabeth, Great Torrington 1681 A
  Elizabeth, Great Torrington 1719 W
  Veal Elizabeth, Alwington 1837 W
  Veal George, Alwington 1787 W
  Veal George, Buckland Brewer 1820 W
  George, Parkham 1832 A to Grace, widow
  James, Great Torrington 1739 W
  Jane, Alwington 1770 W
  John, Littleham (near Bideford) 1691 A
  Joseph, Alwington 1821 W
  Oliver, Barnstaple 1829 W
  Oliver see also George Kingston
  Richard, Shebbear 1624 O
  Veal Richard, Alwington 1823 W
  Robert, Shebbear 1624 [W]
  Robert, Winkleigh 1628 [W]
  Viell Roger, Great Torrington 1582 W
  Thomas, Bideford 1705 W
  Ville Thomas, Barnstaple 1819 W
  William, Northam 1746 A
  William, ship *Fox* 1750 A
Veare, Veire
  ..., Atherington 1601 [W]
  Veire Elizabeth, Northam 1611 [W]; forename blank in Ms;
    supplied from parish register
  John, Atherington 1591 [W]
  Roger, Northam 1603 W
Veasey, Veasy, Veisie
  Veisie David, Stoodleigh 1568 W
  Veasy Margery, Winkleigh 1624 [W]
  William, Twitchen 1675 W
Vedden Thomas, St Giles in the Wood 1810 W
Veire see Veare
Veisie see Veasey
Vellacott, Vallacott, Vallecott, Vellacote
  Agnes, Fremington 1856 W
  Alexander, Lynton 1783 W
  Ann, Lynton 1708 W
  Ann, Heanton Punchardon 1726 W
  Anthony, Berrynarbor 1677 W
  Anthony, Heanton Punchardon 1733 A
  Dorothy, Berrynarbor 1764 W
  Edward, Kentisbury 1675 W
  Eleanor, Pilton 1621 [W] (2)
  Eleanor, Barnstaple 1847 W
  Elizabeth, Fremington 1782 W
  Geoffrey, Berrynarbor 1746 W
  Humphrey, North Molton 1820 A to Elizabeth, widow
  Jeremiah, Heanton Punchardon 1840 W
  Joan, North Molton 1591 [W]
  Joan, North Molton 1695 W
  John, Pilton 1596 [W]
  John, Heanton Punchardon 1683 W
  John, Lynton 1685 A
  John, Kentisbury 1691 W
  John, Lynton 1726 W
  Vallacott John, Kentisbury 1728 W
  John, Brendon 1755 A
  John, Brendon 1768 A
  John, Heanton Punchardon 1777 W
  John, Kentisbury 1785 W
  John, Lynton, yeoman 1810 A
  John, Heanton Punchardon, gentleman 1820 A to Jeremiah,
    gentleman, son
  Mathew, North Molton 1578 W
  Michael, North Molton 1733 A
  Nicholas, Berrynarbor 1644 A
  Nicholas, Combe Martin 1667 W

Nicholas, Stoke Rivers 1731 W and 1733 W
Peter, Combe Martin 1711 W
Prudence, Stoke Rivers 1735 W
Richard, Lynton 1664 A
Richard, Lynton 1697 W
Richard, Lynton 1793 W
Richard, Lynton, yeoman 1801 A
Robert, Georgeham 1756 A
Sarah, Lynton 1803 W
Vellacote Thomas, North Molton 1568 W
Thomas, North Molton 1784 W
Thomas, Great Torrington 1790 A
Walter, Barnstaple 1637 W
William, Kentisbury 1593 [W]
Vallecott William, Kentisbury 1597 [W]
William, Lynton 1681 W
William, North Molton 1685 A
William, Northam 1716 W
William, Lynton 1753 W
William, Georgeham 1790 W
William, Lynton 1829 W
Velley, Velleigh, Vellie, Velly
  Velly Charles, Hartland 1724 W
  Charles, Barnstaple 1764 A A dbn 1764
  Velly Elizabeth, Barnstaple 1760 W
  John, Hartland 1694 W
  John, Hartland 1785 A
  Velly Lodovic, Fremington 1630 [W]
  Velly Nicholas, Hartland 1636 [W] and 1637 O
  Velly Nicholas, Welcombe 1698 W
  Vellie Peter, Fremington 1608 [W] "Wolley" in register;
    forename blank in Ms; supplied from parish register
  Velleigh Thomas, Fremington 1576 W
  Wakeman, Barnstaple 1763 A A dbn 1781
  Velly William, Hartland 1699 W
Vellyon Simon, Bideford 1724 W
Venn, Ven
  Ann, Little Torrington 1824 W
  Christian, West Worlington 1793 A
  Venn alias Venner Elizabeth, Chittlehampton 1573 W
  Henry, Chulmleigh 1789 W
  Henry, Chulmleigh, yeoman 1808 W
  James, Little Torrington 1820 W
  John, East Anstey 1673 W
  Nicholas, Stoodleigh 1720 A
  Richard, Wembworthy 1740 A
  Robert, Coldridge 1643 W
  Ven Robert, East Worlington 1714 W
  Robert, Witheridge 1738 A and 1746 A
  Sarah, South Molton 1737 W
  Sarah, South Molton 1758 A
  Thomas, Stoodleigh 1733 W
  William, South Molton 1845 W
Venner, Vennar, Vennor, Veynor
  ..., Chittlehampton 1601 A
  ..., West Anstey 1602 [W]
  ..., Warkleigh 1608 [W]
  ..., Knowstone 1610 [W]
  ..., Stoodleigh 1611 [W]
  ..., Martinhoe 1615 [W]
  Agnes, Molland 1582 W
  Alice, King's Nympton 1581 W
  Andrew, Martinhoe 1629 [W]
  Ann, West Anstey 1625 [W]
  Venner alias Southyeo Ann, Great Torrington 1642 A
  Ann, Goodleigh 1820 W
  Christopher 1569 W
  Christopher, Iddesleigh 1603 W
  Christopher, Cruwys Morchard 1621 [W]
  Christopher, Stoodleigh 1855 W; A with W dbn passed at
    Exeter, Dec 1865
  Elizabeth, Warkleigh 1566 W
  Venner alias Venn Elizabeth, Chittlehampton 1573 W
  Elizabeth, Barnstaple 1632 [W]
  Elizabeth, Warkleigh 1681 W
  George, Great Torrington 1624 [W]

George, Witheridge 1799 W
Gertrude, Great Torrington 1637 W
Henry, Chittlehampton 1586 W
Honor, Goodleigh, widow 1802 W
Hugh, West Anstey 1591 [W]
Humphrey, Oakford 1563 W
Humphrey, Chawleigh 1749 A
Jacquet, Chittlehampton 1644 T
John, Ashreigney 1564 W
John, Chittlehampton 1579 W
John, Roborough 1587 A
John, Martinhoe 1591 [W] and 1601 W
John, King's Nympton 1606 W
John, Warkleigh 1620 [W]
John, Stoodleigh 1639 A
John, Chittlehampton 1641 W
John, Warkleigh 1679 W
John, Oakford 1778 W
John, West Anstey 1857 W
Mary, Tawstock 1627 [W]
Nathan, Chittlehampton 1636 W
Nicholas, Littleham (near Bideford) 1579 W
Peter, Great Torrington 1634 A
Philip, King's Nympton 1578 A
Philip, Merton 1700 W
Vennor Philip, Frithelstock 1766 W
Veynor Richard, Molland 1564 W
Robert, Chittlehampton 1572 W and 1577 W
Robert, Bondleigh 1580 [W] relating to a bequest to John,
  Richard, Jane and Ralph, children of John Labet of
  Torrington
Robert, Barnstaple 1619 [W]
Robert, Merton 1691 W
Robert, West Worlington 1693 W
Vennor Robert, Goodleigh, jnr. 1766 W
Roger, Oakford 1676 [W]
Roger, Oakford 1693 [W]
Stephen, Littleham (near Bideford) 1590 [W]
Thomas, Martinhoe 1598 [W] and 1599 [W]
Thomas, Burrington 1601 W
Thomas, Littleham (near Bideford) 1625 [W]
Thomas, Littleham (near Bideford) 1663 W
Thomas, Pilton 1822 W
Walter, Pilton 1642 W
William, King's Nympton 1566 W
William, Satterleigh 1574 W and 1581 O account
Vennar William, Winkleigh 1583 A
William, Littleham (near Bideford) 1588 A
William, Warkleigh 1598 [W]
William, Chittlehampton 1620 [W] and O
William, Roborough 1621 [W]
William, Chittlehampton 1637 W
William, Chittlehampton 1703 W
Vennicombe see Vinnacomb
Venning, Venninge, Vennings
  Vennings Henry, Great Torrington, snr. 1634 [W]
  Venninge John, Barnstaple 1613 [W]; forename blank in Ms;
    supplied from parish register
  John, Bideford 1709 A
  Martha, East Putford 1688 W
  Stephen, Bideford 1697 W
Vennycombe see Vinnacomb
Venstone see Vanstone
Venton Bartholomew, Sheepwash 1698 W
  Elizabeth, Sheepwash 1700 A
  John, Petrockstowe 1625 [W], 1627 [W] and 1629 O
  Robert, Buckland Filleigh 1626 [W]
  Stephen, Petrockstowe 1784 W
  Thomas, Petrockstowe 1635 A
  Thomas, Petrockstowe 1669 W
  Willmot, Chulmleigh 1781 W
Venys Walter, Instow 1564 W
Vercheld, Verchell, Verchild, Verchilde, Verchylide, Verechild
  see Fairchild
Verman Ethelred, Northam 1698 A

Grace, Northam 1741 W
John, Northam 1676 W
John, Northam 1846 W
Margery, South Molton 1661 A
Mary, Northam 1742 W
Philip, Northam 1692 W
Richard, Northam 1717 W
Richard, Bideford 1746 A
Verman alias Vernon Richard, Northam 1809 A
Robert, Northam 1704 A
Thomas, Northam 1679 W
Thomas, South Molton 1694 W
Thomas, Northam 1755 A
Verneham see Vernham
Verney ..., West Down 1855 W
John, Pilton 1851 A
Vernham, Varneham, Verneham
..., South Molton 1604 [W]
Agnes, Northam 1628 [W] and O
Alexander, Ashford 1590 [W]
Verneham Christopher, Pilton 1607 [W]; forename blank in
Ms; supplied from parish register
Varneham David, South Molton 1598 [W]
Verneham John, Northam 1606 W
John, South Molton 1644 A
Verneham Leonard, Pilton 1605 [W]; forename blank in Ms;
supplied from parish register
Richard, Pilton 1593 [W]
Richard, Northam 1664 W
Verneham Robert, Abbotsham 1591 [W]
Thomas, Northam 1738 W
Vernon Frances, Northam 1697 W
Henry, South Molton 1763 W
James, South Molton 1832 W
Richard, Northam 1783 A
Vernon alias Vernam Richard, Northam 1809 A
Richard, Northam 1836 W; 1837 W transmitted to Doctor's
Commons
Samuel Pyke, Northam 1848 W
Sarah, South Molton 1841 A to Elizabeth, sp., daughter
William, South Molton 1690 W
William, South Molton 1717 A
William, South Molton 1854 W
Vershied John, Tawstock 1602 W
Vesey, Veysey
Charity, Rackenford 1713 W
Charles, Great Torrington 1857 W
Veysey George, Rose Ash, yeoman 1797 W
Veysey Humphrey, Creacombe, yeoman 1800 W
Veysey James, formerly of Creacombe but of Oakford 1814 W
9 Oct 1847
Veysey James, Bishop's Nympton 1852 A to Joan
Veysey Joan, Stoodleigh 1823 W
Veysey John, Woolfardisworthy 1761 W
Veysey John, Fremington, yeoman 1810 W
Veysey John, Creacombe 1823 W
Veysey John, Molland 1835 W
Joseph, Rackenford 1686 W
Mary, East Buckland 1709 W
Veysey Richard, Stoodleigh 1813 W
Veysey Richard, Rackenford 1852 W
Robert, East Anstey 1770 W
Thomas, Hartland 1661 W
Veysey Thomas, Rose Ash 1779 W
Veysey Thomas Tanner, Creacombe 1817 W
Walter, Rackenford 1691 W
William, East Buckland 1704 W
Veysey William, Mariansleigh 1776 W
Veysey William, Creacombe 1802 W
Veyell, Veylle see Vale
Veysey see Vesey
Vicary, Vicarie, Vicarye, Viccary, Vickery, Vicry, Vycary
..., Mariansleigh 1603 [W]
..., North Molton 1610 [W], 1612 [W] and 1613 [W]
..., North Tawton 1624 [W]

Vicary alias Pulham ..., North Molton 1676 W
Viccary ..., Winkleigh 1693 W
Vicary alias Pullan Agnes, North Molton 1679 A
Alexander, Rose Ash 1643 W
Viccary Alexander, Molland 1662 A
Viccary Alexander, Witheridge 1709 W
Viccary Alexander, Rose Ash 1717 W
Vicarie Alice, North Molton 1568 W
Alice, North Molton 1635 A
Ann, King's Nympton 1643 W
Viccary Ann, Rose Ash 1753 W
Ann, Molland, widow 1857 A to John Cockram of Bishop's
Nympton, yeoman, brother
Viccary Arthur, King's Nympton 1704 W
Viccary Augustine, Barnstaple 1703 A
Vickery Charity, Marwood 1854 W
Christian, North Molton 1633 W
Christopher, Stoodleigh 1633 A and 1635 O
Viccary Christopher, Rose Ash 1743 W
Christopher, Rose Ash 1756 W
Christopher, Rose Ash 1787 A
Christopher, Fremington 1835 W
David, King's Nympton 1641 W
Viccary David, Combe Martin 1708 A
Dorothy, Molland 1600 W (2)
Elizabeth, North Molton 1741 A
Elizabeth, Barnstaple 1761 A
Vicry Elizabeth, Bideford 1773 W
Vickery Elizabeth, Cruwys Morchard 1840 W
Frances, Rose Ash, jnr. 1636 A
Frances, Rose Ash 1640 O
Viccary Francis, Bow, mariner 1745 W
Vicarie George, Winkleigh 1611 [W]; forename blank in Ms;
supplied from parish register
Vicarie George, Winkleigh 1615 [W]
George, North Molton 1618 [W] and O "of Sonacott" in
register; forename blank in Ms; supplied from parish register
Viccary George, Mariansleigh 1685 W
Viccary George, Bideford 1696 A
Viccary George, Mariansleigh 1728 A
Vickery George, Romansleigh 1855 W; A and W dbn passed
at Exeter, Feb 1867
German, Romansleigh 1638 A
Gertrude, Chulmleigh, widow 1806 W
Vycary Grace, Rose Ash 1619 [W]
Henry, Creacombe 1592 [W]
Henry, Knowstone 1593 [W] and 1594 [W]
Henry, Rose Ash 1600 W
Vicarye Henry, Rose Ash 1600 W
Henry, Knowstone 1636 [W]
Viccary Henry, King's Nympton 1677 A
Henry, Barnstaple 1786 A and 1792 A
Hugh, Warkleigh 1635 A
James, Great Torrington 1717 W
Viccary James, Burrington 1738 A
James, Lapford 1830 W
Jane, Meshaw 1820 A to John, son
Jasper, Molland 1600 W
Vicarie Joan, Huntshaw 1570 W
Joan, Molland 1672 W
Joan, Bideford 1710 W
Vicarie John, Twitchen 1569 W
Vicarye John, North Molton 1572 W
Vicarye John, Witheridge 1572 W
Vicarie John, Rackenford 1579 A
Vicarie John, South Radworthy, North Molton 1581 W
John, Knowstone 1593 [W]
John, North Molton 1595 [W] and 1604 [W]
John, Molland 1606 W
John, Atherington 1618 [W]
John, Molland 1626 [W]
John, Witheridge, snr. 1627 [W]
John, Witheridge 1628 [W] and 1631 [W]
John, Winkleigh 1636 A and 1640 O
John, Chittlehampton 1637 A

John, Tawstock 1643 W
Viccary John, South Molton 1661 A
Viccary John, Winkleigh 1664 A
Viccary John, King's Nympton 1690 A
Viccary John, Barnstaple 1691 A
Viccary John, Combe Martin 1691 A
Viccary John, North Molton 1701 A
Viccary John, South Molton 1708 W
John, Burrington 1716 W
John, Great Torrington 1717 A
Viccary John, Great Torrington 1717 W
John, North Molton 1734 A
John, North Molton 1757 W
John, Chulmleigh, schoolmaster 1802 W
Vickery John, Lapford, yeoman 1806 W
John Merril, Great Torrington 1807 W*
Vickary Joseph, Bideford 1720 A
Joseph, Rose Ash 1769 A
Joseph, Woolfardisworthy 1823 W
Joseph, Oakford 1827 W
Vickery Judith, Chawleigh 1760 A
Lawrence, Knowstone 1592 [W]
Vicarie Margaret, Molland 1583 W
Margaret, Barnstaple 1742 W
Margaret, Rose Ash 1820 W
Mary, Chittlehampton 1633 O
Viccary Mary, North Molton 1754 A
Viccary Mathew, Barnstaple 1690 A
Vicarie Michael, Rose Ash 1587 W
Nicholas, Knowstone 1593 [W]
Vicarie Nicholas, North Molton 1615 [W] "Vicarye alias
    Pulham" in register; forename blank in Ms; supplied from
    parish register
Nicholas, Oakford 1638 W
Viccary Nicholas, West Anstey 1686 W
Oliver, North Molton 1604 W
Vicarie Paul, Twitchen 1578 W
Philip, South Molton 1616 [W]
Philip, King's Nympton, snr. 1634 W
Philip, King's Nympton 1677 A
Viccary Philip, King's Nympton 1677 W
Philip, Cruwys Morchard 1834 W
Vicarie Richard, Huntshaw 1568 W
Vicarye Richard, Knowstone 1572 W
Richard, Molland 1591 [W]
Richard, South Molton 1615 [W]
Richard, Witheridge 1640 [W]
Richard, North Molton 1643 W
Viccary Richard, Combe Martin 1690 A
Viccary Richard, Bideford 1704 W
Viccary Richard, Chawleigh 1746 W
Vickery Richard, Chawleigh 1773 A
Richard, Rose Ash 1812 W
Richard, Barnstaple 1837 W
Vicarie Robert, Stoodleigh 1567 W
Vicarie Robert, Knowstone 1577 W
Vicarie Robert, Molland 1578 W
Robert, Chittlehampton 1625 [W]
Viccary Robert, Rose Ash 1668 A
Roger, Chulmleigh 1834 W
Viccary Susan, King's Nympton 1686 A
Susan see also Sarah Grater
Vicarie alias Webberie Thomas, South Molton 1563 W
Viccary Thomas, Molland 1582 W
Thomas, Mariansleigh 1585 W
Thomas, North Molton 1615 [W]
Thomas, Twitchen 1624 [W]
Thomas, Brendon 1626 [W]
Thomas, Molland 1627 [W]
Thomas, East Worlington 1720 W
Vickers Thomas, Shebbear 1742 W
Vicry Thomas, Burrington 1772 W
Thomas, West Worlington 1830 A to John of Witheridge,
    brother
Thomas, Ashreigney 1837 W

Thomasine, King's Nympton 1678 W
Thomasine, Oakford, widow 1810 W
Walter, North Molton 1622 [W]
Vicarie William, Rose Ash 1583 W
William, Mariansleigh 1592 [W]
William, North Molton 1604 W
William, Chittlehampton 1637 A
Vicary alias Pulham William, North Molton 1676 W
Viccary William, North Molton 1682 W and 1690 A
Viccary William, Molland 1691 A
Viccary William, King's Nympton 1694 A
Viccary William, West Buckland 1707 A
William, East Anstey 1712 W
William, Great Torrington 1728 W
William, North Molton 1741 W
William, Great Torrington 1746 A
Viccary William, Barnstaple 1747 W
Viccary William, North Tawton 1748 A
Viccary William, Meeth 1750 A
William, North Tawton 1830 W
Vice Joan, Barnstaple 1628 [W]
John, Great Torrington 1756 A
John, Great Torrington 1780 A
Mary, St Giles in the Wood 1755 A
Mary, St Giles in the Wood 1756 A
Rebecca Merrill, Great Torrington, sp. 1816 A to Rebecca,
    mother
Vickery, Vicry see Vicary
Victor Richard, Berrynarbor 1727 W
Viell see Veale
Vigures, Viggers, Vygures
..., Parkham 1605 [W]
Abraham, Cruwys Morchard 1670 W
Vygures Alexander, Shebbear 1628 [W]
Ambrose, Great Torrington 1717 W
Vygures Catherine, Buckland Brewer 1623 [W] (2)
Vygures George, Great Torrington 1632 [W]
George, Ilfracombe 1742 W
Humphrey, Monkleigh 1690 W
Humphrey, Monkleigh 1736 A
Jane, Marwood 1741 W
Joan, Buckland Brewer 1588 W
Vygures Joan, Great Torrington 1625 [W]
John, Buckland Brewer 1603 W
John, Alwington 1669 A
John, Parkham 1681 A
John, Great Torrington 1687 W
John, Fremington 1705 A
John, Woolfardisworthy 1713 W
Viggers John, Berrynarbor 1852 W
Lodovic, Bideford, clerk 1642 A
Mary, Northam 1645 W
Vygures Mary, Great Torrington 1726 W
Richard, Little Torrington 1663 A
Robert, Parkham 1683 W
Samuel, Little Torrington 1669 A and 1672 O
Samuel, Great Torrington 1704 W
Samuel, Ilfracombe 1764 A
Vygures Thomas, Parkham 1635 W
Thomas, Buckland Brewer 1606 [W] "Fugars" in register;
    forename blank in Ms; supplied from parish register
Vygures William, Hartland 1619 [W]
Vygures William, Petrockstowe 1628 [W]
William, Buckland Brewer 1695 A
Ville see Veale
Vinary Ann, Great Torrington 1727 W
John, Barnstaple 1721 W
John, Great Torrington 1727 W
Vincent George, Fremington 1639 A
John, Barnstaple 1638 W
Vine, Vion, Vyne
Vion Alexander, Barnstaple 1690 W
Vion Alexander, Barnstaple 1707 W
Vyne Ann, Hartland 1674 W
Bernice, Bideford 1854 W

Elizabeth, Hartland 1690 A
Vyne Emanuel, Hartland 1703 W
Emanuel, Hartland 1742 A
Emanuel, Hartland 1765 W
Vyne Grace, Hartland 1662 W
Vyne Henry, Hartland 1633 [W]
Vyne Hugh, Hartland 1599 [W]
Hugh, Pilton 1745 A
James, Hartland 1754 A
Vyne John, Hartland 1595 [W]
Vyne John, Hartland 1644 A
Vyne John, Hartland 1661 W
John, Hartland 1690 W
John, Hartland 1749 W
Margaret, Hartland, sp. 1848 A (1849) to John Trick Vine,
    gentleman, brother
Mary, Hartland 1849 W
Michael, Hartland 1743 W
Michael, Hartland, mariner 1820 A to John, brother
Nicholas, Hartland 1669 A
Vyne Peter, Hartland 1687 W
Peter, Hartland 1746 W
Vyne Richard, Hartland 1663 W
Richard, Hartland 1679 W
Vyne Richard, Hartland 1689 A
Vyne Richard, Horwood 1703 W
Richard, Hartland 1743 W and 1744 A
Sarah, Hartland 1748 W
Sarah, Hartland 1856 W
Susan wife of Samuel see Richard Prince
Vyne Thomasine, Hartland 1596 [W]
Vyne William, Northam 1619 [W]
William, Hartland 1834 W
Vineing James, Great Torrington 1693 A
Joseph, Woolfardisworthy 1691 A
Viney see Vinney
Vinnacomb, Vennicombe, Vennycombe
Gilbert, Atherington 1709 A
Vennicombe Richard, North Tawton 1598 [W]
Vennycombe William, North Tawton 1622 [W]
Vinney, Viney, Vyney
Vyney Alice, Abbotsham [no year given] [W]
Vyney John, Alwington 1606 W
Vyney Richard, Bideford 1627 [W]
Vinney John, Great Torrington 1590 [W]
Viney Thomasine, Great Torrington 1594 [W]
Vissick, Visicke, Vizick
Vizick George, Filleigh 1661 A
Visicke John, Hartland 1628 [W]
Robert, Northam 1695 W
Susan, Great Torrington 1699 W
Vittary, Vittry
Arthur, Meeth 1729 W
Vittry Mary, Fremington 1703 A
Mary, Burrington 1729 W
Vizick see Vissick
Voater see Vawter
Vodden, Voden
Lawrence, St Giles in the Wood 1733 W
Lawrence, St Giles in the Wood 1831 W
Voden Margery, Petrockstowe, widow 1569 W
Martha, St Giles in the Wood 1784 A
Thomas, St Giles in the Wood 1775 W
Thomas, St Giles in the Wood, yeoman 1810 W
Thomas, Dolton, yeoman 1811 A
Thomas, St Giles in the Wood 1855 W
Vogwill, Vogwell
Henry, Petrockstowe 1739 A
John, Petrockstowe 1721 W
Vogwell Thomas, Petrockstowe 1717 W
Voysey, Voisey, Voysie
..., West Worlington 1705 A
Agnes, Barnstaple 1644 W
Alexander, Oakford 1670 W
Alexander, Knowstone 1716 A

Alexander, Clovelly 1719 A
Alice, Great Torrington 1619 [W]
Charles, George Nympton 1709 W
Voisey Charles, George Nympton 1747 W
George, Great Torrington 1591 [W] and 1592 [W]
Voisey George, Stoodleigh 1610 [W]; forename blank in Ms;
    supplied from parish register
Voisey Giles, Winkleigh 1612 [W]; forename blank in Ms;
    supplied from parish register
Hugh, Chulmleigh 1689 W
Hugh, Molland 1697 W
Humphrey, Creacombe 1737 W
Voisey James, Rackenford 1618 [W]
Voysie John, Rose Ash 1578 A
John, Rackenford 1635 W
John, Barnstaple 1636 W
John, George Nympton 1711 A
John, Fremington 1762 W
Voisey John, Knowstone 1769 A (2)
John, Knowstone 1780 A
John, Woolfardisworthyv 1811 W
John, Washford Pyne 1834 W
Marian, Stoodleigh 1594 [W]
Mary, Stoodleigh 1630 [W]
Voisey Mary, George Nympton 1771 W
Nicholas, Stoodleigh 1583 W
Nicholas, Barnstaple 1632 [W]
Peter, Woolfardisworthy, yeoman 1808 W
Richard, Great Torrington 1598 [W]
Voisey Richard, Ilfracombe 1826 W
Robert, Washford Pyne 1684 W
Voisey Robert, Oakford 1748 W
Robert, Witheridge 1774 W
Robert, Witheridge 1785 W
Voysie William, Great Torrington 1583 W
William, Barnstaple 1630 [W]
William, Rackenford 1679 A
Voisin Pierre, Barnstaple 1729 W
Vonston William, Winkleigh 1573 W
Voscombe Elizabeth, Buckland Brewer 1639 W
John, Buckland Brewer 1580 W
Voss, Vosse
Voss alias Foss John, High Bickington 1679 A
Vosse John, High Bickington 1679 A
Vouler alias Ley Oliver, Tawstock 1565 W
Vycary see Vicary
Vye Catherine, Ilfracombe 1788 A
Eleanor, Ilfracombe 1801 A
Elizabeth, Ilfracombe 1727 T
George, Ilfracombe 1681 A
George, Ilfracombe 1772 T
George, Ilfracombe 1792 W
George, Ilfracombe 1845 T
John, Ilfracombe 1720 W
John, Ilfracombe 1783 W
John, Ilfracombe, yeoman 1810 W
Mary, Ilfracombe, widow 1847 W to Mary wife of George
    Bolton, major in 30th Foot
Nathaniel, Ilfracombe 1709 W
Nathaniel, Ilfracombe 1739 W and 1742 A
Richard, Ilfracombe 1765 W
Sarah, Ilfracombe 1768 W
Thomas, Ilfracombe 1760 A
Thomas, Ilfracombe 1798 A
Thomas, Ilfracombe 1823 W
Thomasine, Ilfracombe 1781 A
William, Ilfracombe 1735 W
William, Ilfracombe 1813 W
William, Ilfracombe 1841 W
Vygures see Vigures
Vyle George, Barnstaple 1638 W
Robert, Barnstaple 1640 W and A
Vyney see Vinney

Wade John, Ilfracombe 1814 W
  Lodovic, Satterleigh 1717 W
  Richard, Clovelly 1766 A
  Sarah, Ilfracombe 1779 W
  Sarah, Clovelly 1788 A
  Thomas, Wembworthy 1635 [W]
  Thomas, master mariner 1827 W
  William, North Tawton 1595 [W]
  William, Rackenford 1630 [W]
Wadland, Wadlan, Wadlande, Wadlin
  Wadlande ..., Fremington 1610 [W]
  Elizabeth, Bideford 1732 W
  Hannah, Dolton 1852 W
  Henry, Dolton 1857 W
  Joan, Bideford 1692 W
  John, Bideford 1686 W
  John, Bideford 1697 W
  John, Bideford 1725 W and 1732 W
  John, Huish 1772 W
  Neville, Weare Giffard 1677 A
  Philip, Ilfracombe 1764 W
  Wadlande Richard, Bideford 1602 W
  Richard, Bideford 1679 A
  Richard, Bideford 1723 W
  Samuel, Roborough 1832 W
  Sarah, Bideford 1704 W
  Thomas, Bideford 1761 A
  William, Weare Giffard 1676 A
  Wadlan William, Langtree 1855 W
Wadman Stephen, Landcross 1582 W
Waeland see Walland
Waimouth see Waymouth
Wainsborough Thomas, Oakford 1733 A
Waishington see Washington
Wakeham James, Shebbear 1676 A
Wakeley, Wakely
  John, Bideford 1687 A
  Nicholas, Hartland 1744 A
  Wakely Silvester, Hartland 1766 W
  Wakely William, Bideford 1697 A
Wakeman Phillippa, Barnstaple 1757 W
  William, Barnstaple 1810 W
Wakerell Thomas, Chawleigh 1620 [W] and 1623 O
Walch see Welsh
Waldon, Wallden, Weldon, Weldowe
  ..., Bideford 1607 [W]
  ..., Clovelly 1609 [W]
  Barnabas, Fremington 1615 [W]
  Elizabeth, Welcombe 1630 [W]
  Henry, Alverdiscott 1789 W
  Isota, Hartland 1620 [W]
  John, Hartland 1569 W and 1573 W
  John, Northam 1616 [W]
  John, Hartland 1631 [W]
  Lawrence, Hartland 1580 W
  Lawrence, Hartland 1704 W
  Lawrence, Hartland 1759 W
  Weldon Margaret, Fremington 1573 W
  Margaret, Great Torrington 1640 W
  Mary, Great Torrington, widow 1808 A
  Mary, Great Torrington 1838 A to Lewis G., nephew
  Peter, Hartland 1602 W
  Peter, Hartland 1633 W
  Wallden Philip, Woolfardisworthy 1586 W
  Rebecca, Hartland 1759 A
  Richard, Hartland 1631 [W]
  Richard, Hartland 1700 W
  Robert, Great Torrington, snr. 1632 [W]
  Weldowe Thomas, Fremington 1563 W
  Thomas, Great Torrington 1661 A
  Thomas, Bideford 1689 A
  William, Great Torrington 1831 A to Mary, sister
Waldron Abraham, Chittlehampton, carpenter 1809 W
  Anstis, South Molton 1640 W
 Wale William, North Molton 1626 [W]

Walker ..., North Molton 1610 [W]
  Christian, Alwington 1588 W
  Edward, Pilton 1747 W
  Francis, Coldridge 1616 [W]
  John, Witheridge 1737 W
  Mary, Witheridge 1777 W
  Phillippa, Barnstaple 1757 W
  Phineas, Pilton 1748 W
  Sarah, Pilton 1754 W
  Thomas, Witheridge, yeoman 1801 W
Walkey Jane, Bideford 1832 W
  John, Georgeham 1596 [W]
  John, Great Torrington 1784 W and 1793 W
  John, Bideford 1820 W
  John, Great Torrington 1827 W
Wall, Walle, Walls
  Walle George, Witheridge 1597 [W]
  John, Barnstaple, jnr. 1636 A, 1637 O and 1638 O
  Richard, Witheridge 1570 W
  Richard, Instow 1639 A
  Sarah, Barnstaple 1790 W
  Walls Thomas Ilfracombe, yeoman 1804 W
  Walls Thomas, Great Torrington 1834 W
Walland, Waeland, Wallam, Wallan, Wallen, Wallond, Wallyn,
  Welland, Welling, Woland, Wolland, Woolland
  Wallen ..., Zeal Monachorum 1611 [W]
  Agnes, Brendon 1664 W
  Alice, Bratton Fleming 1575 W
  Christopher, Fremington 1599 [W]
  Wolland Elizabeth, Trentishoe, widow 1796 W
  Welland George, East Anstey 1577 W
  Woolland Grace, Burrington 1764 W
  Gregory, Countisbury 1620 [W]
  Gregory, Barnstaple 1637 W
  Hannah, Tawstock 1815 W
  Welling alias Llewellin Henry, Barnstaple 1688 A; forename
    blank in Ms; supplied from parish register
  Wallen Humphrey, Zeal Monachorum 1687 A
  Ilett, Brendon 1643 A
  Joan, Brendon 1642 W
  Wallam John, Bow 1571 W
  Wolland John, Brendon 1579 W
  Wallan John, Brendon 1584 W
  John, Bratton Fleming 1591 [W]
  Wallen John, Zeal Monachorum 1595 [W]
  Wallen John, Zeal Monachorum 1662 W
  Wallen John, Eggesford 1689 A
  Woland John, Romansleigh 1703 A
  John, Trentishoe 1773 A
  John, Parracombe, husbandman 1811 W
  Woolland Lawrence, Ashreigney 1763 W
  Wallyn Love, Bow 1573 W
  Mar ..., Bratton Fleming 1626 [W]
  Philip, Brendon 1619 [W]
  Wallan Richard, Countisbury 1583 W
  Richard, Brendon 1663 W
  Wallen Richard, Warkleigh 1709 A
  Wallen Roger, Zeal Monachorum 1595 [W]
  Waeland Sarah, Dolton 1831 W
  Wallond Thomas, Bratton Fleming 1574 W
  Welland William, South Molton 1644 A
Wallden see Waldon
Walle see Wall
Wallen see Walland
Waller Daniel, Great Torrington 1695 A
  Richard, Countisbury 1585 A
Wallis Elizabeth, Buckland Brewer 1697 A
  George, Peters Marland 1679 A
Wallond see Walland
Walls see Wall
Wallshe see Walshe
Wallwyn Richard, Zeal Monachorum 1569 W
Wallyn see Walland
Walrond Edward, Great Torrington 1712 A
  John, Cruwys Morchard 1591 [W]

Walscott, Walskotte
   ..., South Molton 1611 [W]
   Walskotte alias Goulde Alice, Warkleigh 1582 W
   John, South Molton 1598 [W]
Walshe, Wallshe
   Wallshe David, Peters Marland 1583 W
   Harry, High Bray 1571 W
   John, Eddistone, Hartland 1570 W
Walskotte see Walscott
Walter, Walters
   ..., Littleham (near Bideford) 1605 [W]
   ..., Bideford 1608 [W]
   Andrew, Great Torrington 1666 A
   Andrew, Witheridge 1764 W
   Ann, Horwood 1703 W
   Anthony, Martinhoe 1578 W
   Anthony, Great Torrington 1623 [W]
   Bartholomew, Shebbear 1618 [W]
   Bartholomew, Shebbear 1668 W
   Charles, Marwood 1697 W
   Christopher, Great Torrington 1636 W
   David, Fremington 1662 A
   Edward, Great Torrington 1619 [W]
   Edward, Shebbear 1677 W
   Edward, Shebbear 1742 W
   Edward, Shebbear 1800 W
   Edward, Shebbear 1856 W
   Walters Elizabeth, Ilfracombe 1857 W
   George, Shebbear 1730 W
   George, Great Torrington 1736 A
   George, Shebbear 1783 W
   Grace, Marwood 1673 [W]
   Gregory, Barnstaple 1622 [W]
   Henry, Shebbear 1631 [W]
   Walters Ilett, Ilfracombe 1837 W
   Isott, Great Torrington 1665 W
   James, Barnstaple 1588 A and 1589 A
   James, Shebbear 1736 W
   James, Hartland 1856 [W]
   James, Newton St Petrock 1856 [W]
   Jane, Marwood 1675 O
   Jane, Georgeham 1712 W
   Jane, Witheridge 1765 [W]
   Joan, Georgeham 1629 [W]
   Joan, High Bray 1669 A
   John, Alwington 1571 W
   Walter alias Hosier John, Barnstaple 1579 W
   John, Littleham (near Bideford) 1583 W and 1593 [W]
   John, Georgeham 1601 W
   John, Northam 1618 [W]
   John, Georgeham 1628 [W]
   Walters John, Bideford 1628 [W]
   John, Marwood 1630 [W]
   John, Shebbear 1632 [W]
   John, Hartland 1634 A
   John, Abbotsham 1639 W
   John, Bideford 1678 W
   John, Great Torrington 1696 W
   John, Witheridge 1705 W
   John, Hartland 1716 A
   John, Alverdiscott 1755 W
   John, Northam 1758 W
   John, Great Torrington 1779 W
   John, Woolfardisworthy 1781 W
   John, Alverdiscott, yeoman 1809 W
   Joseph, Shebbear 1769 A
   Joseph, Fremington 1849 W
   Walters Joseph Henry, Ilfracombe 1847 W
   Margaret, Shebbear 1643 W
   Walter alias Ayre Mary, Buckland Brewer 1677 [W]
   Mary, Shebbear 1700 W
   Mary, Shebbear 1783 W
   Mary, Peters Marland, sp. 1808 W
   Walters Mary, Ilfracombe 1851 W
   Nicholas, Tawstock 1662 W

   Nicholas, Great Torrington 1753 A
   Paschal, Frithelstock 1570 W
   Peter, Frithelstock 1679 A
   Philip, Shebbear 1841 W
   Prudence, Marwood 1675 W
   Rebecca, Bideford 1778 W
   Richard, Hartland 1598 [W]
   Richard, Great Torrington 1640 [W]
   Richard, Hartland 1699 A
   Richard, Great Torrington 1729 W
   Richard, Bideford 1745 W
   Richard, Hartland, yeoman 1848 A to Eliza, widow
   Robert, Marwood 1673 A
   Walters Samuel, Ilfracombe, boat builder 1805 W
   Stephen, Marwood 1661 A
   Thomas, Shebbear, jnr. 1640 W
   Thomas, Shebbear 1664 A
   Thomas, Shebbear 1712 W
   Thomas, Witheridge 1726 W and 1728 W
   Thomas, Shebbear 1768 A
   Walters Thomas, Ilfracombe 1782 A
   Walters Thomas, Ilfracombe 1822 W
   Thomasine, Barnstaple 1625 [W]
   Timothy, Great Torrington 1643 W
   Tristram, Buckland Filleigh 1689 W
   William, Countisbury 1579 W
   William, Frithelstock 1599 [W]
   William, Littleham (near Bideford) 1633 W
   William, Marwood 1644 W
   William, Hartland 1662 W
   William, Alverdiscott 1698 W
   William, Witheridge 1707 W
   William, Hartland 1726 W
   William, Bideford 1750 W
   Walters William, Ilfracombe 1821 W
   William Henry, Bideford, farmer 1853 W
Walterman Alice, Hartland, widow 1572 W
Walton William, Barnstaple 1851 W
Wannacott see Wonnacott
Warcop, Warcrop, Warkop
   Warcrop Edward, Barnstaple 1623 [W]
   Edward, Barnstaple 1624 [W]
   Warkop Henry, Barnstaple 1610 [W]; forename blank in Ms;
     supplied from parish register
Ward, Warde
   Warde ..., Rackenford 1608 [W]
   Warde Agnes, Countisbury 1617 [W]
   Warde Agnes, Brendon 1618 [W]
   Warde Agnes, Martinhoe 1631 [W]
   Agnes, Fremington 1674 W
   Warde Alexander, Barnstaple 1597 [W]
   Warde Alice, Countisbury 1620 [W]
   Alice, Shirwell 1724 W
   Warde Ann, Bideford 1614 [W]; forename blank in Ms;
     supplied from parish register
   Ann, Burrington 1665 W
   Ann, Atherington 1799 W*
   Warde Anthony, Kentisbury 1616 [W]
   Warde Anthony, Berrynarbor 1617 [W]
   Warde Anthony, Countisbury 1618 [W]
   Bartholomew, Dowland 1679 W
   Bartholomew, Dolton 1757 W
   Bartholomew, Merton 1837 W
   Christopher, Pilton 1640 W
   Warde David, Twitchen 1597 [W]
   Diana, Chittlehampton 1688 W
   Edward, Combe Martin 1739 A
   Warde Elizabeth, Barnstaple 1578 W
   Elizabeth, Petrockstowe 1771 A
   Elizabeth, Langtree 1808 W
   Emblem, Huntshaw 1752 A
   Francis, Combe Martin 1666 W
   Francis, Shirwell 1687 W
   Francis, Shirwell 1711 W

Francis, Shirwell 1736 W and 1744 A
Francis, Shirwell 1763 A
George, Ilfracombe 1732 A
Warde Henry, Pilton 1598 [W]
Hugh, Abbotsham 1733 A
Humphrey, Challacombe 1670 W
Humphrey, East Down, jnr. 1690 W
Humphrey, Challacombe 1720 W
Warde James, Parracombe 1596 [W]
Warde James, Georgeham 1617 [W]
James, Shirwell 1702 W
James, Barnstaple 1711 W
James, Shirwell 1734 W
Warde Joan, Combe Martin 1572 W
Joan, North Molton 1573 W
Warde Joan, Countisbury 1577 W
Warde Joan, Pilton, widow 1608 [W]; forename blank in Ms;
    supplied from parish register
Joan, Brendon 1689 W
Warde John, Countisbury 1567 W
Warde John, Challacombe 1571 W
Warde John, Berrynarbor 1581 W
Warde John, Countisbury 1581 W
John, Fremington 1583 W
John, Kentisbury 1586 W
John, Barnstaple 1587 A
Warde John, Oakford 1591 [W]
Warde John, Barnstaple 1592 [W]
Warde John, Trentishoe 1592 [W]
Warde John, Kentisbury 1593 [W]
Warde John, Barnstaple 1614 [W]; forename blank in Ms;
    supplied from parish register
Warde John, Bideford 1614 [W]; forename blank in Ms;
    supplied from parish register
Warde John, Great Torrington 1615 [W]
Warde John, Brendon 1619 [W]
John, Challacombe 1622 [W]
Warde John, Martinhoe 1625 [W]
Warde John, Brendon 1626 [W]
Warde John, Tawstock 1637 A
John, Great Torrington, snr. 1671 [W]
John, High Bickington, mariner 1678 W
John, Great Torrington 1688 W
John, Beaford 1741 A
John, Brendon 1754 W
John, King's Nympton 1765 W
John, East Down 1766 W
John, Merton 1794 W
John, Brendon 1820 W
John, Parkham 1834 A to Grace, widow
John, Merton 1852 W
Lewis, Great Torrington 1756 A
Lewis, Great Torrington 1856 A
Lodovic, Dolton 1689 W
Marian, Shirwell 1722 W
Mary, Challacombe 1703 W
Mary, High Bickington 1707 W
Mary, West Buckland 1845 W
Warde Matilda, Kentisbury 1625 [W]
Nicholas, Shirwell 1724 W
Nicholas, Combe Martin 1743 W
Peter, Tawstock 1645 A
Philip, Great Torrington 1679 A
Warde Richard, Combe Martin 1580 A
Warde Richard, Oakford 1597 A
Warde Richard, Countisbury 1636 W
Richard, Brendon 1675 W
Richard, Beaford 1724 W and 1732 W
Richard, Bideford 1741 W
Richard, Buckland Brewer 1783 W
Richard, Lynton 1857 W
Richard see also Richard Dyer
Robert, Dolton 1734 W
Robert, East Down 1737 W
Robert, Merton 1770 W

Robert, Chawleigh 1772 W
Robert, Merton 1842 W
Warde Thomas, West Down 1581 W
Warde Thomas, Pilton 1608 [W]; forename blank in Ms;
    supplied from parish register
Warde Thomas, North Molton 1624 [W]
Thomas, Chittlehampton 1669 W
Thomas, Chittlehampton 1701 W
Thomas, Combe Martin 1705 W
Thomas, Great Torrington 1734 W
Thomas, Chittlehampton 1753 A
Thomas, Buckland Brewer or Filleigh 1787 A
Thomasine, Brendon 1692 A
Warde William, Trentishoe 1575 W
William, Pilton 1591 [W]
Warde William, Martinhoe 1591 [W]
Warde William, North Molton 1600 W
Warde William, Challacombe 1617 [W]
Warde William, East Buckland 1627 [W]
William, Barnstaple 1634 A
Warde William, Martinhoe 1636 A
William, Combe Martin 1641 A
William, Challacombe 1688 W
William, Shirwell 1707 A
William, Dolton 1726 W
William, Combe Martin 1738 W
William, Barnstaple 1746 W
William, Winkleigh 1756 W
William, Merton 1793 W
William, Chawleigh 1812 W
William, Iddesleigh 1827 W
William, West Buckland 1837 W
Willmot, Georgeham 1698 A
Warden, Worden
Edward, Yarnscombe 1696 W
Worden John, Buckland Brewer 1622 [W]
Worden Walter, Northam 1596 [W]
Ware ..., Martinhoe 1612 [W]
Alice, Martinhoe 1602 W
Ananias, Petrockstowe, yeoman 1808 W
Ananias, Peters Marland 1840 A to Eliza of Little Torrington,
    widow
Ananias, Great Torrington 1844 W
Ann, Tawstock 1832 W
Ann, Tawstock 1847 W
Armanell, Iddesleigh 1637 W
Daniel, Iddesleigh 1635 W
Daniel, Tawstock 1818 W
Daniel, Great Torrington 1850 W
Dunstan, Martinhoe 1625 [W] and 1626 O
Elizabeth, Merton 1666 W
Elizabeth, Bideford 1843 W
George, Northam 1628 [W]
Henry, Merton 1690 W
Hugh, Cheldon 1619 [W] and O
John, Hartland 1629 [W]
John, Martinhoe 1639 W
John, Northam 1667 W
John, Parkham 1697 [A]
John, High Bickington 1732 W
John, Bideford 1843 A to John, grandfather
John, Peters Marland 1846 W
Margery, Bow 1687 W
Mary, Chittlehampton 1626 [W]
Mary, Dolton 1734 A
Mathew, Martinhoe 1595 [W]
Mitchell, High Bickington 1588 W
Philip, Tawstock 1636 W
Richard, Parracombe 1663 W
Richard, Winkleigh 1679 A
Robert, Chittlehampton 1579 A
Robert, Merton 1730 A
Robert, Petrockstowe 1851 W
Thomas, Chittlehampton 1597 [W]
Thomas, Northam 1622 [W]

Thomas, Meshaw, labourer 1853 A to Elizabeth, widow
Tryphena, Martinhoe 1622 [W]
William, Chittlehampton 1598 [W]
Waring William, Marwood 1824 W
Warley John, Atherington 1662 A
Susan, Atherington 1689 W
Warman John, Barnstaple 1669 A
John, Barnstaple 1723 A and 1725 A
John, Bideford 1829 W
Margaret, Barnstaple 1667 A
Mary, Pilton 1698 A
Warman alias Warmington Richard, Tawstock 1780 W
Sarah, Barnstaple 1689 W
Simon, Pilton 1680 A
Simon, Barnstaple 1756 W
Stephen, Barnstaple 1724 W
Warmington, Warminton
David, Weare Giffard 1709 A
Elizabeth, Merton 1744 A
Francis, Clovelly 1731 A
Hezekiah, Weare Giffard 1720 W
John, Bideford 1837 A
John, Buckland Filleigh 1853 W
Warmington alias Warman Richard, Tawstock 1780 W
Warminton Richard, Pilton 1815 W
Thomas, Woolfardisworthy 1587 W
William, Bideford 1738 W
William, Clovelly 1780 W
William, Welcombe 1835 W
Warminton William, Pilton 1844 W
Warram, Warrame
Agnes, Wembworthy 1591 [W]
Warrame John, Wembworthy 1588 W
William, Wembworthy 1588 W
Warre Augustine, West Worlington 1594 [W]
Robert, West Worlington 1580 W
Warren Aaron, Barnstaple 1822 W
Agnes, Bratton Fleming 1626 [W]
Alice, Chulmleigh 1615 [W] and 1616 [W]
Warring Alice, Chittlehampton 1673 W
Warring Anstis, Chittlehampton 1673 W
Baldwin, Twitchen 1619 [W]
Ebbot, Coldridge 1676 A
Elizabeth, North Molton 1720 W
Emma, Coldridge 1598 [W] and 1599 [W]
George, Westleigh 1606 W
George, South Molton 1625 [W]
Henry, South Molton 1729 W
Joan, Coldridge 1577 W
Joan, Woolfardisworthy 1677 W
Warring Joan, Yarnscombe 1707 W
Joan, Bratton Fleming 1714 W
John, Clovelly 1587 W
John, Coldridge 1595 [W]
John, South Molton 1636 W
John, Chittlehampton 1668 W
John, Brushford 1680 A
John, Witheridge 1706 W
John, Bratton Fleming 1707 [W]
John, South Molton 1748 W
John, Witheridge 1749 A
John, Bishop's Nympton 1806 A
John, Twitchen 1806 A
John, Bow 1812 W
Mary, Weare Giffard 1714 A
Warren alias Torrington Mary, King's Nympton 1763 A
Mathew, Swimbridge 1853 W
Michael, Woolfardisworthy 1675 W
Nathaniel, Barnstaple 1626 [W]
Peter, Lapford 1622 [W]
Richard, Filleigh 1617 [W]
Richard, Witheridge 1706 A
Robert, Ilfracombe 1695 A
Roger, Chulmleigh 1602 W
Thomas, North Molton 1730 W

William, Coldridge 1569 W
William, Langtree 1569 W
William, Dolton 1615 [W]
William, Coldridge 1617 [W]
William, Langtree 1617 [W]
William, Coldridge 1676 W
William, Zeal Monachorum 1678 A
William, Barnstaple 1681 A
William, North Molton 1713 W
William, South Molton 1737 W
William 1789 W
Warwick Catherine, Bideford 1641 W
Washer Edward, East Anstey 1679 W
Edward, East Anstey 1684 A
Richard, Tawstock 1685 A
Washington, Waishington
Waishington ..., Barnstaple 1606 [W]
Rahab, Barnstaple 1588 W
Thomas, Bideford 1688 W
Watcher Mary, Clovelly 1734 W
Richard, Buckland Brewer 1713 A
Waterman ..., Great Torrington 1613 [W]
..., Langtree 1614 [W]
Edward, Newton St Petrock 1578 A
Edward, Westleigh 1614 [W]; forename blank in Ms; supplied
from parish register
James, St Giles in the Wood 1582 W
James, St Giles in the Wood 1661 W
John, Hartland 1570 W
John, Shirwell 1582 W
John, Langtree 1591 [W] (2) and 1603 W
John, Woolfardisworthy 1603 W
Walter, Langtree 1583 W
William, Woolfardisworthy 1574 A
Waters Elizabeth, Little Torrington 1823 W
Watersale John, Kentisbury 1591 [W]
Wather John, Clovelly 1717 W
Wathern John, Bideford 1717 W
Watkins Christopher, Bideford 1835 [W]
George, Ilfracombe 1813 W
James, Tawstock 1703 A
Mary, Northam 1736 A
Mary, Bideford 1853 W
Richard, Bideford, mariner 1809 W
Sarah, South Molton 1731 W
Watling Thomas, Barnstaple 1664 W
Wats see Watts
Watson Clement, Roborough 1773 A
Elizabeth, Barnstaple 1715 W
Jane, Barnstaple 1674 W
Jane, Bideford 1729 A
John, Barnstaple 1674 W
Mary, Northam 1708 W
Peter, Pilton 1702 W
Watts, Wats, Wattes
Wattes ..., Abbotsham 1609 [W]
Agnes, Georgeham 1697 W (2)
Anthony, South Molton 1705 A and 1707 A
Anthony, Horwood [no year given] [W]
Baldwin, Fremington 1606 W
Bartholomew, Georgeham 1672 A
Bartholomew, Mortehoe 1717 W
Edward, Abbotsham 1615 [W]
Elizabeth, Abbotsham 1625 [W]
Elizabeth, Barnstaple 1718 W
Emanuel, Pilton 1744 A
Emanuel, Pilton, mariner 1747 A
George, Pilton 1812 W
Henry, Georgeham 1682 W
Henry, Georgeham 1713 W
Henry, Berrynarbor 1829 W
Humphrey, Tawstock 1722 A
James Perrin, Combe Martin 1856 A to Esther, sister
Joan, Berrynarbor 1633 A
John, Ilfracombe 1824 W

John, West Down 1827 W
John, Combe Martin 1845 W
John, Goodleigh 1857 W
Joseph, Ilfracombe 1834 W
Joseph, Berrynarbor 1847 W
Margaret, Fremington 1597 [W]
Margaret, Tawstock 1708 A
Mary, Northam 1643 A
Mary, Pilton 1829 W
Mary, West Down 1832 W
Wats Pentecost, Fremington 1592 A
Pollard, Barnstaple 1704 W
Richard, Rose Ash 1632 [W]
Roger, Fremington 1637 W
Watts alias Hamount Thomas, High Bray 1577 W
Thomas, Abbotsham 1593 [W]
Thomas, Ilfracombe 1804 W
Thomas, Marwood 1834 A
Thomas, Berrynarbor 1840 W
Thomas, Weare Giffard 1855 W
Watts alias Oates Tristram, Georgeham 1642 W
Tristram, Georgeham 1704 W
Tristram, Ilfracombe 1821 W
William, North Molton 1621 [W]
William, Tawstock 1713 W
William, Barnstaple 1839 W
William, Ilfracombe 1839 W
William, South Molton, ostler 1848 A to Thomasine, widow
William, Chittlehampton 1853 W
Way, Waye, Wey
..., Cheldon 1606 [W]
Agnes, Clovelly 1789 W
Waye Anthony, Beaford 1604 W
Wey Catherine, Chawleigh 1772 W
Waye Charity, Lynton 1725 W
Wey Christopher, Chittlehampton 1713 W
Wey Digory, Hartland 1681 W
Waye Edward, Eggesford 1577 A
Waye Edward, Lynton 1721 W
Wey Edward, North Molton 1756 A
Elizabeth, Hartland 1750 W
Elizabeth, South Molton, widow 1806 W
Joan, Coldridge 1691 A
John, Clovelly 1626 [W]
John, Hartland 1735 W
John, North Molton 1740 W
John, Chulmleigh 1745 W
John, Hartland 1747 W
John, Clovelly 1769 W
John, Hartland 1793 W
John, Hartland 1817 W
Waye Lewis, Little Torrington 1587 W
Wey Margaret, Clovelly 1686 W
Mary, Coldridge 1661 W
Mary, Chulmleigh 1754 A
Wey Patrick, Hartland 1589 W
Peter, Hartland 1675 A
Wey Peter, Hartland 1715 A
Richard, Cruwys Morchard 1627 [W]
Richard, Great Torrington 1727 W
Robert, Coldridge 1643 W
Robert, Eggesford 1673 W
Robert, Chawleigh 1683 W
Robert, Chawleigh 1706 A
Thomas, Clovelly 1682 W
Thomas, Hartland 1708 A
Waye William, Little Torrington 1585 W
Waye William, Petrockstowe 1602 W
William, Cruwys Morchard 1635 A
William, Cruwys Morchard 1637 [W]
William, Eggesford 1665 W
William, Clovelly 1704 A
William, Rackenford 1706 W
William, Hartland 1707 W
William, Chawleigh 1733 A

William, Hartland 1773 W
William, Hartland 1796 A
Wayborn James or William, Oakford, yeoman 1808 W
Waye see Way
Waymouth, Waimouth
Waimouth ..., Bideford 1613 [W]
Philip, Northam 1636 A
Weak, Weake see Weekes
Weamont John, Clovelly 1592 [W]
Weare, Wear, Where
Alfred, Hartland 1626 [W]
Ananias, Iddesleigh 1702 W
Catherine, Iddesleigh 1718 W
Christiana, Chawleigh 1726 W
Wear Hannah, North Tawton 1761 A
Where Humphrey, East Putford 1665 W
Where John, Northam 1639 A
John, High Bickington 1716 W
Martin, Oakford 1641 W
Mathew, Merton 1663 A
Obadiah, Iddesleigh 1701 W
Wear Obadiah, High Bickington 1758 W
Wear Obadiah, Bideford 1767 W
Robert, Merton 1701 W
Weatt see Wheat
Weaver John, South Molton 1596 [W]
Webb, Webbe
Webbe ..., Woolfardisworthy 1604 [W]
Edward, Clovelly 1684 W
Elizabeth, Woolfardisworthy 1734 W
Elizabeth, Pancrasweek 1857 W
Webbe John, St Giles in the Wood 1568 W
Webbe John, Woolfardisworthy 1570 W
John, Woolfardisworthy (East or West), snr. 1589 W
John, Great Torrington 1706 [W]
Mary, Atherington 1709 W
Philip, Littleham (near Bideford) 1668 W
Philip, Alwington 1693 W
Philip, Buckland Brewer 1725 A
Webbe Richard, Woolfardisworthy 1626 [W]
Thomas, Woolfardisworthy 1587 W
Welthian, Barnstaple 1638 W
William, Georgeham 1854 W
Webbare see Webber
Webbe see Webb
Webber, Webbare
..., King's Nympton 1579 W
..., Chawleigh 1589 W
..., King's Nympton 1594 [W]
..., Chawleigh 1605 [W]
..., Iddesleigh 1607 [W]
..., Chulmleigh 1608 [W]
..., North Tawton 1610 [W]
..., East Putford 1612 [W]
..., Barnstaple 1614 [W]
..., East Putford 1614 [W]
..., Knowstone 1614 [W]
Agnes, Barnstaple 1700 W
Alexander, Barnstaple 1739 W
Alice, South Molton 1603 W
Alice, Chittlehampton 1606 W
Ambrose, Challacombe 1776 W
Andrew, Chulmleigh 1675 W
Ann, Chawleigh 1599 [W]
Ann, King's Nympton 1791 W
Ann, Beaford, widow 1802 W
Ann, Chulmleigh 1831 W
Ann, Beaford 1846 W
Anthony, St Giles in the Wood 1587 W
Anthony, Chulmleigh 1716 W
Armanell, Wembworthy 1628 [W]
Armanell, Chawleigh 1707 W
Webbare Barden, Tawstock 1589 A
Betty, Burrington 1843 A to Elizabeth wife of John Foss and
    John, children

Webber alias Bullen Cecilia, Bideford 1706 A
Charity, Iddesleigh 1633 W
Charles, Chawleigh 1620 [W]
Charles, Hartland 1690 A
Charlotte Helland, South Molton 1841 W
Christopher, West Down 1581 W
Damaris, Barnstaple 1739 A
Daniel, Stoodleigh 1755 W
Dorothy, South Molton 1776 A
Dorothy, North Molton 1788 A
Edmund, Great Torrington 1573 W
Edmund, Northam 1704 W
Edward, Chulmleigh 1616 [W]
Edward, Chulmleigh 1681 A
Edward, Combe Martin 1764 W
Edward, Challacombe 1847 W
Eleanor, Chawleigh 1638 W
Elizabeth, West Down 1589 W
Elizabeth, Chulmleigh 1617 [W]
Elizabeth, Knowstone 1663 W
Elizabeth, Chulmleigh 1708 W
Elizabeth, Chawleigh, widow 1709 A
Elizabeth, Chulmleigh 1764 W
Elizabeth, Dolton 1767 W
Elizabeth, Romansleigh 1773 W
Elizabeth, Coldridge, widow 1807 A
Emma, Parracombe 1590 [W]
Enoch, Chulmleigh 1644 W
Esther, Challacombe 1671 W
Webber alias Austin Esther 1701 A
Faith, Georgeham 1699 W
Frances, Morchard Bishop 1854 W
George, King's Nympton 1595 [W]
George, Yarnscombe 1615 [W]
George, Chawleigh 1618 [W]
George, Chulmleigh 1660 W
George, Chawleigh 1685 W
George, Chawleigh 1725 W and 1728 W
George, Chulmleigh 1750 W
George, Chulmleigh, yeoman 1807 W
George, West Worlington, yeoman 1814 A to George Pepper,
    William Webber, John Lethaby and Grace Hunt, nephews
    and niece
George, King's Nympton 1817 W
George, High Bickington 1820 A
George, Chulmleigh 1821 W
George, Chulmleigh 1828 A to Susanna, widow
George, Georgeham 1825 W
George, Chulmleigh 1838 W
George, North Molton, farmer 1850 A to Mary wife of John
    Buckingham of Twitchen, daughter
Giles, Chawleigh 1781 W
Grace, North Tawton 1746 W
Grace, Satterleigh 1802 W
Grace, Chulmleigh, widow 1804 W
Hannah, Challacombe 1803 A
Henry, Chawleigh 1588 A
Henry, Wembworthy 1617 [W]
Henry, Chawleigh 1623 [W]
Henry, Pilton 1732 A
Henry, Combe Martin 1749 A
Henry, ship *Folkestone*, cutter 1768 W
Honor, Northam 1728 W
Hugh, Dolton 1565 W
Humphrey, West Down 1589 W
Humphrey, Combe Martin 1780 A
James, South Molton 1618 [W] and O
James, Chittlehampton 1821 W
James, Challacombe 1851 W
James, Knowstone 1854 W
Jane, Chulmleigh 1724 A
Jeremiah, Dolton 1708 W
Jeremiah, Ilfracombe 1747 W
Jerome, West Down 1636 A
Joan, Littleham (near Bideford), widow 1571 W

Joan, Great Torrington 1582 W
Joan, Little Torrington 1583 W
Joan, Combe Martin 1586 A
Joan, Littleham (near Bideford) 1600 W
Webber alias Tomlyn Joan, Marwood 1603 [W]; forename
    blank in Ms; supplied from parish register
Joan, Chulmleigh 1627 [W]
Joan, South Molton 1628 [W]
Joan, Molland 1635 W
Joan, Chulmleigh 1679 A
Joan, Chulmleigh 1712 A
Joan, Knowstone 1822 W
John, Clovelly 1572 W
John, West Anstey 1582 W
Webber alias Hawkens John, Burrington 1585 W
John, Little Torrington 1587 W
John, Woolfardisworthy 1589 A
John, Chulmleigh 1590 [W] and 1592 [W]
John, Eggesford 1591 [W]
John, West Worlington 1599 [W]
John, Littleham (near Bideford) 1600 W
Webber alias Turner John, Winkleigh 1603 W; forename
    blank in Ms; supplied from parish register
John, Winkleigh 1620 [W]
John, Chulmleigh 1622 [W]
John, Satterleigh 1625 [W]
John, Woolfardisworthy 1634 A
John, West Anstey 1635 W
John, Burrington 1638 A
John, Chulmleigh 1666 A
John, Chawleigh 1669 O
John, Chulmleigh 1670 W
John, Twitchen 1671 A
John, Romansleigh 1675 A
John, Barnstaple 1676 A
John, Ilfracombe 1678 A
John, North Molton 1691 A
John, Chulmleigh 1695 A
John, Chawleigh 1696 A
John, Romansleigh 1697 W
John, Chulmleigh 1704 A
John, Bideford 1706 W
John, Chawleigh 1706 W
John, South Molton 1706 A
John, Bideford 1707 A
John, Chawleigh 1707 A and 1712 A
John, Chulmleigh 1728 W
John, Chulmleigh 1729 A
John, Barnstaple 1735 W
John, Beaford 1735 W
John, Wembworthy 1739 W
John, Dolton 1741 W
John, Mariansleigh 1743 W
John, Beaford 1746 W
John, Pilton 1747 W
John, Northam 1753 W
John, Chulmleigh 1770 W
John, Ilfracombe 1774 W
John, East Anstey 1779 W
John, Stoodleigh 1789 W
John, Chulmleigh, yeoman 1807 W
John, Meeth 1814 W
John, Woolfardisworthy 1815 W
John, High Bickington 1816 W
John, South Molton 1824 W
John, Chawleigh 1830 W
John, Chulmleigh 1841 W and 1845 [A]
Julia, Georgeham 1661 W
Margaret, Georgeham 1629 [W]
Margaret, Burrington 1638 A
Martha, High Bickington 1619 [W]
Martha, Winkleigh 1686 W
Martin, Molland 1633 W
Martin, North Molton 1778 W
Martin, North Molton, yeoman 1855 A to Martin, son

Mary, West Worlington 1697 W
Mary, Chulmleigh 1735 W
Mary, Pilton 1747 W
Mary, Stoodleigh 1786 W
Mary, Beaford 1812 W
Mary, King's Nympton 1849 W
Mary see also Grace Dennis
Mathew, Chawleigh 1624 [W]
Nicholas, Chawleigh 1589 W
Nicholas, Beaford, snr. 1703 W
Nicholas, Dolton 1711 A
Nicholas, Beaford 1762 W
Nicholas, Beaford 1780 A
Nicholas, Beaford, yeoman, jnr. 1851 A to Nicholas
Oliver, Knowstone 1596 [W]
Peter, Georgeham 1606 W
Peter, Chulmleigh 1678 W
Peter, Georgeham 1695 W
Philip, Chulmleigh 1695 A and 1697 A
Philip, Beaford 1724 [W]
Philip, Romansleigh 1740 W
Philip, Chulmleigh 1771 W
Philip, Winkleigh 1804 W
Rebecca, Northam 1734 W
Richard, Chawleigh 1572 W
Richard, Pilton 1574 A
Richard, Lapford 1587 W
Richard, North Tawton 1615 [W]
Richard, Chulmleigh 1618 [W]
Richard, High Bickington 1641 [W]
Richard, Ilfracombe 1666 W
Richard, Chulmleigh 1689 W
Richard, Northam 1690 W
Richard, Combe Martin 1698 A
Richard, Barnstaple or Northam 1703 W
Richard, Romansleigh 1704 W
Richard, Chulmleigh 1729 W and 1739 W
Richard, Mariansleigh 1748 W and 1751 W
Richard, Chawleigh 1824 W
Richard, Cruwys Morchard 1827 W
Richard, Romansleigh 1831 W
Richard, Meshaw 1846 W
Robert, Chulmleigh 1573 W and 1575 A
Robert, Chittlehampton 1626 [W]
Robert, Pilton 1668 W
Robert, East Anstey 1719 W
Robert, South Molton, minor 1720 W
Robert, Northam 1740 W
Robert, West Anstey 1773 A
Robert, Yarnscombe, yeoman 1797 W
Robert, North Molton 1821 W
Roger, South Molton 1598 [W]
Roger, West Worlington 1641 W
Samuel, North Molton, yeoman 1797 A
Sarah, North Molton 1821 W
Simon, Bideford 1719 A
Susan, Chulmleigh 1616 [W]
Susan, Romansleigh 1734 W
Thomas, West Down 1589 W
Thomas, Chulmleigh 1599 [W]
Thomas, Chulmleigh 1616 [W] and 1625 [W]
Thomas, Buckland Brewer 1631 [W]
Thomas, Chulmleigh 1632 [W]
Thomas, Chawleigh 1643 W
Thomas, Winkleigh 1676 W
Thomas, Chulmleigh 1682 W
Thomas, Northam 1688 W
Thomas, Fremington 1692 A
Thomas 1707 A
Thomas, Romansleigh 1728 W
Thomas, King's Nympton 1763 W and 1769 A
Thomas, Coldridge 1774 A
Thomas, Dolton 1815 W
Thomas, West Anstey 1822 W
Thomas, Dolton 1823 W

Thomas, Meeth 1841 W removed under monition
Thomas, Alwington 1851 W
Thomas Selley, Barnstaple, accountant 1855 A (Thomas
    Selby) to Frances, widow
Thomasine, West Anstey 1602 W
William, Littleham (near Bideford) 1588 A
William, Burrington 1628 [W]
William, Chawleigh 1660 W
William, Chulmleigh 1663 W
William, North Molton 1679 A
William, Chulmleigh 1689 W
William, Cheldon 1701 W
William, Chulmleigh 1722 W
William, Beaford 1724 W
William, Northam 1724 W
William, Chulmleigh 1728 W and 1729 W
William, Coldridge 1747 W
William, Combe Martin 1752 A
William, Coldridge 1763 A
William, King's Nympton 1780 A
William, Beaford 1787 A
William, Romansleigh 1791 W
William, King's Nympton, gentleman 1802 W
William, Beaford 1804 A
William, Rackenford 1822 W
William, Wembworthy 1826 W
William, Beaford 1834 W
William, Witheridge 1847 W
William, West Anstey 1851 W
William Partridge, Meshaw, gentleman 1847 W
Willmot, Molland 1621 [W]
Willmot, Romansleigh 1706 A
Webbery, Webberie
    Dorothy, Huish 1599 [W]
    Webberie alias Vicarie Thomas, South Molton 1563 W
Weche see Weech
Wedden see Whiddon
Wedgery see Widgery
Wedlake ... 1610 [W]
    Agnes, Chulmleigh 1590 [W]
    Wedlake alias Braylegh Ann, West Buckland 1587 A
    Eleanor, Creacombe 1745 W
    Wedlake alias Beare George, Barnstaple 1601 W
    Grace, Charles, widow 1808 W
    Henry, Chittlehampton 1620 [W]
    Henry, Filleigh 1623 [W]
    Wedlake alias Braylegh John, Martinhoe 1588 W
    Wedlake alias Brailey John, South Molton 1776 W
    John, Charles, yeoman 1801 W
    Lodovic, Chittlehampton 1620 [W]
    Michael, Tawstock 1616 [W]
    Thomas, Charles, yeoman 1806 A
    Thomas, Charles, yeoman 1809 A
    Wedlake alias Braylie William, East Buckland 1601 W
    William, Chittlehampton 1625 [W]
    William, Goodleigh 1810 W and 1814 W
        see also Widlake
Weech, Weche, Weiche
    Elizabeth and George, Instow 1629 [W]
    Weche alias Osell Joan, High Bickington 1580 W
    Weiche alias Oissell Joan, High Bickington, widow 1581 W
    Simon, Littleham (near Bideford) 1625 [W]
Weedon Ann, St Giles in the Wood 1713 W
Weekes, Weak, Weake, Weeks, Weke, Wheak, Wheake
    ..., Little Torrington 1693 A
    Wheake alias Bennet ..., Ilfracombe 1705 W
    ..., Merton 1734 W
    Alice, Bondleigh 1598 [W]
    Ann, Winkleigh 1629 [W]
    Wheake Ann, Arlington 1731 W
    Christopher, North Tawton 1614 [W]; forename blank in Ms;
        supplied from parish register
    Weeks Christopher, Winkleigh 1704 W
    Weeks Christopher, Iddesleigh 1752 W
    Elizabeth, Martinhoe 1630 [W]

Weke alias Bennett Emma, West Down 1577 W
Grace, St Giles in the Wood 1742 A
Weeks Henry, Iddesleigh 1776 W
Weeks Henry, East Worlington 1826 W
Wheake Joan, Marwood 1616 [W]
Weekes alias White Joan, North Tawton 1664 A
John, Winkleigh 1620 [W]
Wheake John, Berrynarbor 1621 [W]
Wheake alias Bennett John, Arlington 1732 W
Weak John, Arlington 1785 W
Weeks John, Iddesleigh 1828 A to Sarah, widow
Joseph, Burrington 1628 [W]
Weeks Josiah, Barnstaple 1851 W
Mary, North Tawton 1630 [W]
Wheak Peter, Pilton 1601 W
Wheake Philip, Shirwell 1685 W
Weake Philip, Arlington 1732 W
Richard, Winkleigh 1600 W
Richard, Parkham 1601 W
Richard, Clannaborough 1630 [W] and 1631 [W]
Weeks Richard, Barnstaple 1812 W
Robert Henry, Bideford 1852 W
Weeks Roger, Zeal Monachorum 1636 W
Weeks Sarah, Iddesleigh 1796 W
Simon, North Tawton 1611 [W]; forename blank in Ms;
    supplied from parish register
Simon, Bideford 1625 [W]
Weeks Thomas, Winkleigh 1728 W
Thomas, Oakford 1732 W
William, Coldridge 1742 W
Weeks William, South Molton, innkeeper 1813 A to Mary,
    widow; transmitted to Doctor's Commons, 1813
Weeks William, Iddesleigh 1821 W
Weetron Letitia, Little Torrington 1726 W
Weiche see Weech
Weight Charles, Barnstaple 1753 W
James, Burrington, yeoman 1811 A
Welch see Welsh
Weldon, Weldowe see Waldon
Welland, Welling see Walland
Wellington Alice, St Giles in the Wood 1684 A
    Elizabeth, Sheepwash 1691 W
    Elizabeth, Great Torrington 1698 W
    Elizabeth, Way 1748 W
    Grace, Great Torrington 1687 A
    Grace, Bideford 1711 A
    Joan, St Giles in the Wood 1693 W
    Lewis, St Giles in the Wood 1684 W
    Lewis, St Giles in the Wood 1789 A
    Nicholas, Great Torrington 1634 W
    Peter, Bideford 1726 W
    Peter, St Giles in the Wood 1728 A
    Richard, Great Torrington 1643 W
    Thomas, Great Torrington 1686 W
Wellisford see Welsford
Wellocott see Woollacott
Wells Thomas, Bideford 1723 A
Welsford, Wellisford, Wellsford
    Elizabeth, Bideford 1751 A
    Wellsford Hercules, Bideford 1747 W
    Wellisford Humphrey, Buckland Filleigh 1640 [W]
Welsh, Walch, Welch, Welshe, Wylsh
    Walch ..., Hartland 1602 [W]
    ..., Great Torrington 1607 [W]
    ..., Little Torrington 1612 [W]
    Wylsh ..., Barnstaple 1660 A
    Agnes, Great Torrington 1734 W
    Anthony, Little Torrington, gentleman 1712 A
    Welch David, Sheepwash 1704 A
    Eleanor, Langtree 1663 W
    Welshe Elizabeth, Little Torrington 1635 W
    Welshe Henry, High Bray 1624 [W]
    Welshe Henry, Filleigh 1629 [W]
    Welshe Joan, Hartland, widow 1572 W
    Welshe John, Witheridge 1573 W

Welshe John, High Bray 1620 [W]
Welshe John, High Bray 1645 W
Welch John, Great Torrington 1720 A
John, Great Torrington 1725 W
John, Bideford 1746 W
Joseph, Langtree 1669 W
Philip, Great Torrington 1696 W
Ralph, Buckland Brewer 1601 W
Roger, Little Torrington 1663 W
Welshe Thomas, Great Torrington 1582 W
Thomas, High Bray 1640 W
Welch Thomas, Great Torrington 1702 A
Thomas, Bideford 1805 W
Welshe William, Peters Marland 1570 W
Welshe William, Barnstaple 1594 [W]
Welshe William, Ilfracombe 1599 [W]
Welshman Susan, Chulmleigh 1816 W
Welshow John, Stoodleigh 1686 W
Welston see Wilston
Wenpen Audrey, Martinhoe 1602 W
Wenpenny see Winpenny
Wenslade see Winslade
Wensley Anthony Reed, North Tawton 1851 W
    James, Puddington 1841 W
    John, North Tawton 1819 W
    Roger, Chulmleigh 1842 W
Wenter see Winter
Weott see Wheat
Werry Charles, Great Torrington, snr. 1713 A
    Charles, Great Torrington 1767 A
Wescomb, Wescombe see Westcombe
Weslade see Westlade
Weslake see Westlake
Wesland, Weslande, Weslond see Westland
West Elizabeth, Weare Giffard 1846 W
    James, Chulmleigh, yeoman 1798 W
    John, Witheridge 1673 A
    John, Meeth 1847 W
    Mary, Ilfracombe 1671 W
    Mary, Weare Giffard, sp. 1842 A to Sarah, sp., sister
    Thomas 1588 W
    William, North Molton 1721 A
Westacot, Westacott see Westcott
Westaway Andrew Snell, Petrockstowe 1839 W
    Jane, King's Nympton 1636 W
    Richard, Winkleigh 1808 A
    William, Barnstaple 1743 A
Westcombe, Wescomb, Wescombe
    Wescombe ..., Barnstaple 1610 [W] and O
    Wescombe ..., Chulmleigh 1610 [W] and 1611 [W] (2)
    Wescombe George, Barnstaple 1636 W
    Wescombe Henry, Chulmleigh 1635 A
    Wescomb Jennifer, Barnstaple 1644 A
    Wescombe John, Chulmleigh, snr. 1566 W
    Wescombe John, Chulmleigh 1591 [W]
    Wescomb Lettice, Barnstaple, widow 1606 [W]; forename
        blank in Ms; supplied from parish register
    Richard, Chulmleigh 1569 W
    Wescombe Richard, Northam 1572 W
    Wescomb William, Barnstaple 1698 A
Westcott, Wescott, Westacott
    Wescott ..., South Molton 1605 [W]
    Westacott ..., Bideford 1609 [W]
    Alexander, Romansleigh 1625 [W]
    Anthony, Chulmleigh 1592 [W]
    Anthony, Great Torrington 1701 W
    Catherine, North Molton, sp. 1857 A to John, farmer, brother
    Westacott Christopher, Winkleigh 1728 A
    Christopher, North Molton 1780 W
    Christopher, North Molton, yeoman 1811 A
    Westacott Elizabeth, South Molton 1821 W
    Elizabeth, North Molton 1848 A to Henry, yeoman, brother
    Wescott Frances, Berrynarbor 1666 A
    George, Great Torrington 1673 W
    Westacott George, ship *Burford* 1746 W

Westacott George, North Molton 1763 A
Westacott George, Bideford 1836 A
George, North Molton 1836 W and 1842 W
Grace, Barnstaple 1689 W
Henry, North Molton 1796 A
Westacott Henry, Pilton 1815 W
Wescott Hugh, Winkleigh 1599 [W]
Hugh, North Molton 1643 W
Westacott Jane, Barnstaple 1741 W
Westacott Jasper, Great Torrington 1737 A
Wescote Joan, Tawstock 1573 A
Joan, North Molton 1828 W
Westacott John, Northam 1608 [W]; forename blank in Ms;
    supplied from parish register
John, Chulmleigh 1620 [W] and 1623 [W]
Westacott John, Clovelly 1625 [W]
John, North Molton 1728 W
John, Oakford 1785 W
John, North Molton 1786 A
Westacott John, George Nympton 1837 A to Ann, widow
Westacott John, Langtree 1843 W
John, North Molton 1847 W
Westacott John, Barnstaple 1851 W
Westacott John, Chulmleigh 1853 W
Westacott Margaret, North Molton 1734 W
Margaret, North Molton, widow 1803 W
Margaret, North Molton 1850 W to John, yeoman, nephew
Margaret, North Molton 1857 W
Westacott Martin, Barnstaple 1717 W
Mary, Barnstaple 1696 W
Mary, North Molton, sp. 1810 A
Westacott Mary, Barnstaple 1825 A
Wescott Nicholas, Roborough 1597 [W]
Nicholas, Littleham (near Bideford) 1791 W
Westacott Philip, Goodleigh 1770 W
Richard, Tawstock 1564 W
Westacott Richard, Little Torrington 1744 W
Robert, Chulmleigh 1587 W
Robert, Tawstock 1618 [W]
Westacott Robert, Yarnscombe 1621 [W]
Robert, Northam 1688 A
Westacott Robert, Chulmleigh 1714 W
Westacott Robert, Chulmleigh 1745 W
Westacott Robert, Barnstaple 1813 W and 1822 W
Westacott Rose, Northam 1675 W
Wescott Sybil, North Molton 1593 [W]
Wescott Thomas, Winkleigh 1573 W
Thomas, Wembworthy 1682 W
Westacot Thomas, Barnstaple 1739 W
Westacott Thomas, Fremington 1754 W
Thomas, Littleham (near Bideford) 1766 W
William, North Molton 1738 W
Westacott William, Chittlehampton 1760 W
Westacott William, South Molton 1771 W
William, North Molton 1805 A
William, High Bray 1840 W
William, North Molton 1847 W and 1851 W
Westacott Willmot, Romansleigh 1638 W
Western, Wesherne, Westerne, Westherne, Westhorne,
    Westhurne, Westren
Westerne ..., Knowstone 1603 [W] and 1611 [W]
Westerne ..., Martinhoe 1609 [W]
Westerne ..., Washford Pyne 1610 [W]
Westerne ..., Cruwys Morchard 1612 [W]
Alice, Hartland, sp., jnr. 1822 A to Alice, widow, mother
Westherne Anthony, Great Torrington 1619 O
Wesherne Anthony, Great Torrington 1629 [W]
Westerne Catherine, West Anstey 1660 W
David, North Tawton 1674 W
Dorothy, Oakford 1679 W
Westhorne Elizabeth, Twitchen 1567 W
Westherne Emott, Knowstone 1637 W
Westerne George, North Tawton 1664 W
Hannah, Winkleigh 1790 W
Westherne Henry, Marwood 1635 W

Henry, Bondleigh, yeoman 1801 A
Henry, Bondleigh 1817 W
Wesherne Humphrey, Cruwys Morchard 1628 [W]
Westerne Humphrey, Oakford 1664 W
Isaac, Bow 1759 A
Westorne James, North Tawton 1703 W
James, North Tawton 1790 W
Westhorne Joan, Knowstone 1580 W
Westerne Joan, King's Nympton 1699 W
Westerne Joan, Woolfardisworthy 1710 A
Westhurne John, East Anstey 1577 W
Westerne John, South Molton 1584 W
Westerne John, Beaford 1615 [W]; forename blank in Ms;
    supplied from parish register
Westherne John, East Anstey 1631 [W]
Western John, East Down 1644 W
John, Oakford 1672 A
John, Brushford 1739 W
John, North Tawton 1749 W
John, North Tawton 1777 W
Westren John, Brushford 1783 W
John, Bow, carpenter 1811 W
John, Witheridge 1822 A to Jane, widow
Westren John, Brushford 1830 W
Jonathan, Great Torrington 1803 A
Jonathan, Great Torrington 1838 W
Westerne Margaret, South Molton 1601 W
Westherne Margery, Washford Pyne 1632 [W]
Mary, Hartland 1818 W
Westerne Peter, Nymet Rowland 1665 W
Peter, Great Torrington 1791 A
Peter, Chulmleigh, woolcomber 1796 A
Peter, Chulmleigh 1815 W
Westherne Richard, Chulmleigh 1599 [W]
Richard, Great Torrington 1728 A
Richard, Hartland 1820 W
Westhorne Robert, Coldridge 1621 [W]
Westherne Robert, Oakford 1632 [W]
Westerne Roger, Cruwys Morchard 1603 [W]; forename blank
    in Ms; supplied from parish register
Samuel, Bideford 1824 W
Westhorne Thomas, Twitchen 1567 W
Westerne Thomas, Twitchen 1597 [W]
Westerne Thomas, Cruwys Morchard 1602 W
Westherne Thomas, *Newton to ..* 1630 [W]
Thomas, Nymet Rowland 1705 W
Thomas, Brushford 1777 A
Thomas, Witheridge 1825 W
Thomas, Ashreigney 1829 W
Thomas, Bondleigh 1839 W
Thomas, Witheridge 1840 A to Susanna, widow
Westren Thomas, Braunton 1844 W
Thomasine, King's Nympton 1710 A
William, North Tawton 1716 W
William, Bow 1786 W
William, Newton St Petrock 1817 W
Westlade Agnes, Fremington 1618 [W]
Agnes, Fremington 1626 [W]
Agnes, Fremington 1742 W
James, Fremington 1664 A and 1674 A
John, Fremington 1690 W
John, Fremington 1710 W
John, Bideford 1742 W
Joseph, Fremington 1679 W
Mary, Fremington 1676 W and 1684 W
Richard, Instow 1642 W
Weslade Thomas, Northam 1584 A
William, Fremington 1664 A
William, Fremington 1690 W
William, Fremington 1738 W
Westlake, Weslake
Agnes, Heanton Punchardon 1662 [W]
Ann, Chittlehampton 1667 W
Anthony, Heanton Punchardon 1620 [W]
Charles, Great Torrington 1680 A and 1692 A

Daniel, Great Torrington 1780 A
George, Northam 1754 W
Grace, Barnstaple 1802 W
Hugh, Chittlehampton 1691 W
John, Sheepwash 1620 [W]
John, Bondleigh, yeoman 1806 W
Mary see John Hutchings
Weslake Phenes wife of William, Alverdiscott 1613 [W];
    forename blank in Ms; supplied from parish register
Richard, Bondleigh, yeoman 1802 W
Roger, Great Torrington 1643 A
Simon, Sheepwash 1628 [W]
Westlake alias Beaple Thomas, Fremington 1643 W
Westland, Weslond, Westlande, Westlane
    Westlande Catherine, Chawleigh 1589 W
    Weslond Edmund, North Tawton 1579 A
    Westlane George, Puddington 1606 W
    Westlane George, Puddington 1714 A
    John, Rose Ash 1591 [W]
    Wesland Maud, North Tawton 1579 W
Westlick Joseph, Clovelly 1851 W
    Richard, Hartland 1830 W
    Richard, Hartland 1856 W
    Thomas, Hartland, labourer 1855 A to Thomas, tailor, son
Westorne see Western
Weston William, Instow 1785 W
Westren see Western
Wether see Wither
Wethercomb John, St Giles in the Wood 1580 W
Wetheridge see Witheridge
Wetherly, Witherly
    William, Northam 1708 A
    Witherly William, Northam 1715 [W]
Wetherowe John, Stoodleigh 1580 W
Wethers see Wither
Wetherudge see Witheridge
Wevells, Wevills
    Alexander, Burrington 1668 W
    Wevills John, Great Torrington 1580 W
    Thomasine, Great Torrington 1591 [W]
Wey see Way
Whayler John, Clovelly 1602 W
Wheadon see Whiddon
Whealer see Wheeler
Wheat, Weatt, Weott
    Weatt ..., Northam 1611 [W]
    Weatt Agnes, Barnstaple 1624 [W]
    Weott Ann, Atherington 1619 [W]
Wheak, Wheake see Weekes
Wheatley John, Barnstaple 1774 W
Wheaton, Wheatton
    Andrew, Eggesford 1588 W
    Ann, Eggesford 1591 [W]
    John, Eggesford 1624 [W]
    Peter, Eggesford 1587 A
    Wheatton Thomas, Eggesford 1607 [W]; forename blank in
        Ms; supplied from parish register
Wheeler, Whealer, Wheler, Whiller
    Wheler ..., Barnstaple 1604 [W]
    Wheler ..., Shebbear 1611 [W]
    Wheler ..., Charles 1614 [W]
    Whiller Alexander, Barnstaple 1717 W
    Wheler Christopher, Charles 1592 [W]
    Wheler Elias, Barnstaple 1596 [W]
    Elizabeth, Huntshaw 1727 A
    Emma, East Buckland 1628 [W]
    Hugh, Clovelly 1736 A
    Humphrey, Barnstaple 1622 [W]
    John, Clovelly 1623 [W]
    John, Stoke Rivers 1631 [W]
    John, Stoke Rivers 1693 A
    Whealer John, Fremington, yeoman 1800 W
    Judith, Barnstaple 1724 W
    Wheler Lawrence, Tawstock 1599 [W]
    Whiller Margaret, Heanton Punchardon 1688 W

Rebecca, Fremington 1803 W
Richard, Bideford, cabinet maker 1803 W
Wheler Robert, Tawstock 1600 W
Thomas, Clovelly 1622 [W]
William, Buckland Brewer 1666 A
Wheitfield see Whitfield
Where see Weare
Whetefeld, Whetfeld see Whitfield
Whetsford ..., East Worlington, Ilfracombe 1610 [W]
Whetstone, Whetson
    Whetson Joan, Northam 1616 [W]
    Joan 1621 [W]
    Robert, Northam 1589 A
    Simon, Chawleigh 1625 [W]
Whetyn see Whiddon
Whidby Thomas, Barnstaple 1729 A
Whiddon, Wedden, Wheadon, Whetyn, Whyddon
    Whetyn ..., Woolfardisworthy 1563 W
    Whiddon alias Smyth ..., Ilfracombe 1707 A
    Dorothy, King's Nympton 1680 W
    Elizabeth, Georgeham 1688 A
    George, Ashford 1699 W
    James, Georgeham 1689 A
    Whyddon Joan, Georgeham 1633 W
    Whyddon John, Arlington 1624 [W]
    John, Georgeham 1689 W
    Whyddon Mary, Georgeham 1631 [W]
    Wheadon alias Smyth Richard, Ilfracombe 1724 W
    Richard, Trentishoe 1797 A
    Robert, King's Nympton 1664 W
    Silvester, Lynton 1591 [W]
    Thomas, King's Nympton 1688 W
    Wedden alias Smyth Thomas, Lynton 1688 W
    Vincent, King's Nympton 1643 W
    Vincent, King's Nympton 1694 W
Whiffe ..., Bow 1609 [W]
Whiller see Wheeler
Whimple see Wimple
Whinet Ann, Barnstaple 1717 W
Whinslade see Winslade
Whippaine Joan, North Tawton 1595 [W]
Whiston, Whyston
    Whyston John, Great Torrington 1578 W
    Pentecost and Robert, Northam 1590 [W]
    Thomas, Northam 1595 [W]
Whitaker George, Bideford 1843 A to Elizabeth, widow
    Whiteacre Susan, Pilton 1857 W
Whitchurch, Whitechurch
    Richard, Barnstaple 1707 W
    Whitechurch Richard, Barnstaple 1708 [W]
    Whitechurch Richard, Barnstaple 1709 A; forename blank in
        Ms; supplied from parish register
    Richard, Barnstaple 1780 W
White, Whitt, Whyt, Whyte
    ..., North Molton 1594 [W]
    ..., Great Torrington 1611 [W]
    ..., Combe Martin 1613 [W]
    ..., Bow 1620 [W]
    Alexander, Peters Marland 1625 [W]
    Alexander, Sheepwash 1756 A
    Alice, Bow 1571 W
    Anastasia, Peters Marland 1636 W
    Ann, Bratton Fleming 1769 W
    Ann, Pilton 1849 W
    Anthony, Martinhoe 1598 [W]
    Arthur, Sheepwash 1722 W
    Arthur, Sheepwash 1766 W
    Augustine, Ilfracombe 1746 W
    White alias Corne Beaton, South Molton 1579 A
    Charles, Shebbear, snr. 1837 W
    Daniel, Northam 1746 W
    Edward, Bideford 1572 W
    Elizabeth, Great Torrington 1630 [W] and 1633 A
    Frances, Washford Pyne 1707 W
    Francis, Washford Pyne 1710 W and 1711 W

Frederick, Clovelly 1783 A
George, Alwington 1572 W
George, Lapford 1642 A
George, Instow, jnr. 1667 W
Grace, Great Torrington 1627 [W]
Henry, Countisbury 1639 W
Henry, Great Torrington 1827 W
White alias Calle James, Barnstaple 1581 A account
James, Ilfracombe 1705 W
James, Mortehoe 1758 W and 1764 A
White alias Weakes Joan, North Tawton 1664 A
Joan, Instow 1729 W
Joan, Goodleigh, widow 1819 A to Mary wife of John Yeo,
    daughter
John, Buckland Brewer 1565 W
John, Winkleigh 1565 W
John, Chawleigh 1572 W
Whyte John, Bideford 1573 W
Whyt John, North Molton 1580 W
Whyte John, Alwington 1583 A
Whyte John, Stoke Rivers 1583 W
Whyte John, Bow 1586 W
John, North Molton 1594 [W]
John 1597 [W]
John, Winkleigh 1603 W
John, Lynton 1607 [W]; forename blank in Ms; supplied from
    parish register
John, Winkleigh 1627 [W]
John, Knowstone 1633 W
John, Ilfracombe 1641 [W]
John, Lapford 1645 A
John, Dolton 1672 A
John, Twitchen 1694 W
John, Northam 1705 W
John, Pilton 1705 A
John, Dolton 1773 O
John, Mariansleigh 1822 W
John 1826 W
John see also Hugh Mill
Joseph, Bideford 1841 W
Judith, Barnstaple 1727 W
Lodovic, Peters Marland 1661 A
Margaret, Peters Marland 1646 A
Margery, Barnstaple, widow 1563 W
Martha, Peters Marland 1713 W
Mary, Bideford 1742 W
Mary, Pilton 1771 W
Mary, Bideford 1790 W
Nathaniel, Fremington 1643 A
Nicholas, Barnstaple 1624 [W]
Nicholas, Barnstaple 1662 A
Obadiah, Ilfracombe 1674 A
Oliver, Instow 1663 W
Peter, Rose Ash 1765 W
Peter, Bideford 1815 W
Petronell, Northam 1745 A
Philip, Fremington 1725 W
Whitt Richard, Barnstaple 1578 W
Whyte Richard, Ilfracombe 1583 A
Richard, Great Torrington 1630 [W]
Richard, North Tawton 1776 W
Richard, Woolfardisworthy 1830 W
Robert, Bow 1568 W
Robert, Stoodleigh 1614 [W] and 1615 O
Robert, Beaford 1691 W
Robert, Instow 1714 W
Robert, Zeal Monachorum 1719 W
Robert, Oakford 1728 W
Robert, Zeal Monachorum 1739 [W]
Robert, Witheridge 1803 A
Robert, Witheridge 1828 W
Roger, Monkleigh 1567 [W]
Rowland, Dolton 1691 A
Samuel, Barnstaple 1836 W and 1838 W
Samuel, Bideford 1837 W and 1844 W

Sarah, Mariansleigh 1845 W
Thomas, Great Torrington 1585 W
Thomas, Lapford 1639 A and O
Thomas, Great Torrington 1677 W
William, Beaford 1586 W
Whyte William, Chawleigh 1588 W
William, Dolton 1599 [W]
William, Winkleigh 1614 [W]; forename blank in Ms;
    supplied from parish register
William, Great Torrington 1615 O
William, Shebbear, yeoman 1804 W
William, Tawstock 1846 W
Whiteacre see Whitaker
Whitear, Whiteare see Whitehair
Whitechurch see Whitchurch
Whitefeild, Whitefeilds, Whitefield, Whitefilde see Whitfield
Whitehair, Whitear, Whiteare, Whitehaire, Whitehayer,
    Whitehear, Whiteheard, Whiteheare, Whiteheir, Whithair,
    Whithayor, Whithear, Whitheare, Whither, Whittear
    Whitear ..., Petrockstowe 1607 [W]
    Whitear ..., Peters Marland 1614 [W]
Whitehayer Ann, Little Torrington 1628 [W]
Ann, Northam 1777 A
Whithear Catherine, Northam 1785 W
Whithear Elizabeth, Northam 1734 A
Whithayor Gabriel, South Molton 1639 W
Whither George, Buckland Filleigh 1679 W
Whiteheare George, Brendon 1685 W
Whitehear Gertrude, Ilfracombe 1721 W
Whitehayer Grace, Peters Marland 1625 [W]
Whitehayer Hu. . ., Chittlehampton 1643 W
Whithayer Joan and John 1597 [W]
Whitear alias Wither Joan, Ilfracombe 1605 W
Whiteheare Joan, South Molton 1682 W
Whitheare John, Peters Marland 1564 W
Whithayer Joan and John 1597 [W]
Whitear John, Peters Marland 1604 W
Whittear John, Martinhoe 1617 [W]
Whitehayer John, Chittlehampton 1624 [W]
Whither John, Langtree 1680 A
Whitehaire Lucy, Buckland Brewer 1718 W
Whithear Mary, South Molton 1719 W
Whitehear Peter, Ilfracombe 1677 W
Whitehayer Philip, Pilton 1626 [W]
Whiteheir Richard, South Molton 1678 A
Whitear Robert, Ilfracombe 1600 W
Whiteare Robert, Northam 1724 W
Whiteheard Temperance, Langtree 1683 W
Whitehear Thomas, Northam 1751 W
Whitheare Walter, Petrockstowe 1667 W
Whitehayer William, Great Torrington 1623 [W]
Whitehayer William, Ilfracombe 1631 [W]
Whiteheare William, Ilfracombe 1664 W
Whithair William, Northam, shopkeeper 1 Dec 1780 W; A
    dbn 1811
Whithear William, Northam 1781 W
Whitehorne Thomas, Woolfardisworthy 1701 W
Thomas, Woolfardisworthy 1747 A
Whitelock, Whitelocke
Christian, Langtree 1753 A
Whitelocke Joan, Alwington 1626 [W]
Whitelocke John, Parkham 1622 [W] and 1630 [W]
Whitelocke John, Frithelstock 1632 [W]
Whitelocke John, Burrington 1637 W
John, Langtree 1752 W
Whitelocke Philip, Langtree 1757 W
Whitelocke Richard, Langtree 1598 [W] and 1599 [W]
Whitelocke Robert, Alwington 1628 [W]
Whitelocke William, High Bickington 1590 [W]
Whitelocke William, Woolfardisworthy 1624 [W]
William, Woolfardisworthy 1664 W
Whitepaine William, Zeal Monachorum 1628 W
William, Zeal Monachorum 1684 W
Whiteson Jane, Northam 1624 [W]
Whiteway John, Barnstaple 1628 [W]

Thomas, Barnstaple 1622 [W]
Whiteyeare Leonard, Bondleigh 1703 W
Whitfield, Wheitfield, Whetefeild, Whetfeld, Whitefeild,
    Whitefeilds, Whitefeild, Whitefilde, Whitefild, Whitfeilde,
    Whitfild, Whitfild, Whitfilde, Whytfylde, Witefield
Whitfeild ..., South Molton 1613 [W]
Whitfeild ..., Heanton Punchardon 1614 [W]
Whitefield alias Glover ..., Frithelstock 1693 A
Whitefeild Abraham, Berrynarbor 1743 [W]
Whitefeild Adam, Barnstaple 1675 A
Whitefeild Alexander, Challacombe 1712 W
Alexander, Berrynarbor 1741 A
Whitfilde Alice, North Molton, widow 1572 W
Whetfeld Alice, Heanton Punchardon 1588 W
Whitfeild Ambrose, Challacombe 1617 [W]
Whitefeild Ann, Barnstaple 1853 W
Whitfeilde Arthur, Parkham 1602 W
Whitefeild Catherine, Tawstock 1631 [W]
Whitefeild Christian, Bideford 1674 W
Whitfilde Christopher, Goodleigh 1567 W
Whitefeild Edward, High Bray 1620 [W]
Whitfeld Eleanor, Tawstock 1582 A
Whitefeild Eleanor, Tawstock 1624 [W]
Whitefeild Elizabeth, Chittlehampton, widow 1811 W
Whitefeild Elizabeth, Barnstaple 1830 A to James, tailor, son
Whitfeild Emma, Countisbury 1640 A
Whetfeld George, Abbotsham 1588 A
Whitefeild Grace, Parkham 1697 A
Whitefeild Humphrey, Bideford 1627 [W]
Whitefield James, Barnstaple 1829 W
Whitefeild Jane, Bideford 1640 W
Whitefeild Joan, Challacombe 1594 [W]
Whitfild John, Ilfracombe 1582 W
Whytfylde John, Heanton Punchardon 1582 W
Whitefeild John, High Bickington 1592 [W]
Whitefeild John, Tawstock 1593 [W]
Whitefeild John, Martinhoe 1599 [W]
Whitfeilde John, Tawstock 1615 [W]
Whitfeild John, North Molton 1617 [W]
Whitefeild John, Challacombe 1619 [W]
Whitefeild John, Martinhoe 1624 [W]
Whitefeild John, Parkham 1630 [W]
Whitefeild John, Bideford 1637 A
Whitefeild John, Barnstaple 1641 A
Whitefeild John, Littleham (near Bideford) 1641 A
Whitefeild John, Tawstock 1641 W
Whitefields John, Bideford 1644 W
Whitefeild John, Chittlehampton 1691 A
Witefield John, Martinhoe 1693 A
Whitefield John, Bideford 1695 A
Whetefeild John, Bideford 1703 W
Whitefeild John, Bideford 1703 A
Whitefeild John, Northam 1743 W
Whitefield John, ship *Plymouth* 1748 A
Whitefeild John, Barnstaple 1761 A
John, Bideford 1773 W
Wheitfeild John, Bideford 1785 A
Whitefeild John, Parracombe 1805 W
....John, Martinhoe 1825 A to Elizabeth, widow
Whitefeild Joseph, Bideford 1720 A
Whitefeild Julia, Barnstaple 1691 W
Whitefeild Lodovic, Tawstock 1630 [W]
Whitefield Margaret, High Bray 1637 W
Whitefeild Mathew, Tawstock 1595 [W]
Whitefeild Mathew, Heanton Punchardon 1671 W
Whitefield Patience, Bideford 1763 W
Whitefeild Peter, Tawstock 1633 A
Whitefeild Philip, Heanton Punchardon 1643 W
Whitefilde Richard, Chawleigh 1569 W
Whitfilde Richard, Brendon 1589 W
Whitefeild Richard, Abbotsham 1599 [W]
Whitefeild Richard, High Bray 1632 [W]
Whitfeild Robert, Parkham 1613 [W]; forename blank in Ms;
    supplied from parish register
Whitefeild Robert, Parkham 1684 W

Robert, Chittlehampton 1731 W
Robert, Clovelly 1764 A
Whitefeild Roger, Tawstock 1592 [W]
Whitefield Sarah, Barnstaple 1830 A
Whitefield Simon, Chittlehampton [no year given] A
Whitfilde Thomas, High Bray 1567 W
Whitfeilde Thomas, Tawstock 1610 [W] and 1619 O
Whitefeild Thomas, Bideford 1640 W
Whitefeild Thomas, Bideford 1668 A
Whitefeild Thomas, Bideford 1703 A
Whitefeild Thomas, Bideford 1728 A
Thomas, Clovelly 1764 W
Whitfeild Thomasine, Tawstock 1603 W
Whitefeild Thomasine, Bideford 1643 W
Whitefeild Willmot, Bratton Fleming 1624 [W]
Whitford John, Bow 1619 [W]
Joyce, South Molton 1831 A
Whithair, Whithayer see Whitehair
Whithead Alison, Arlington or Atherington 1605 W
Whithear, Whitheare, Whither see Whitehair
Whitley Giles, Berrynarbor 1588 W
Whitlock, Whitlocke, Whyteloke, Whytlocke, Whytloke
    ..., North Tawton 1607 [W]
    ..., Woolfardisworthy 1608 [W] and 1610 [W]
    ..., Langtree 1609 [W]
Whitlocke ..., East Buckland 1610 [W]
    ..., Great Torrington 1613 [W] and 1614 [W]
Whitlocke Catherine, Frithelstock 1638 W and 1640 O
Christopher, Langtree 1837 W and 1838 W
Whitlocke Digory, Alwington 1638 W
Ebbot, Warkleigh 1696 W
Elizabeth, Shebbear 1725 A
Whitlocke Elizabeth, Woolfardisworthy 1739 A
Honor, Langtree 1775 W
Whytloke Joan, Langtree 1575 W
Whitlocke John, Langtree 1565 W
Whyteloke John, Parkham 1575 W
John, Abbotsham 1796 A
John, Langtree 1825 W
John, Langtree 1848 W
John, Bideford 1850 W
Whytlocke Mary, Martinhoe 1573 W
Mary, Woolfardisworthy 1759 W
Mary, Chittlehampton 1774 W
Mathew, Buckland Brewer 1606 W
Peter, Alwington 1605 W
Philip, Hartland 1664 A
Philip, Langtree 1708 A (2)
Philip, Langtree 1759 W
Whitlocke Richard, Langtree 1570 W
Whitlock alias Mitchell Richard, Ashreigney 1663 [W]
Richard, Langtree 1687 W
Richard, Langtree 1726 A
Witlock Richard, Hartland 1762 W
Richard, Langtree 1798 A
Richard, Langtree 1803 W
Thomas, Alwington 1601 W
Thomas, Langtree 1643 A
Thomas, Langtree 1715 W
Thomas, Monkleigh 1722 A
Whitlocke William, Monkleigh 1567 W
William, Warkleigh 1684 W
Willmot, Chittlehampton 1715 W
Whitpin, Whytpayne
Whytpayne Richard, North Tawton 1578 A
Whitrow, Whitrawe, Whitrowe
Whitrowe ..., Huntshaw 1603 [W]
Whitrowe ... 1604 [W]
Bernard, Barnstaple 1777 W
Elizabeth, Barnstaple 1783 A
Whitrowe John, West Anstey 1615 [W]
John, Witheridge 1789 W
Margery, Great Torrington 1710 W
Whitrawe Robert, Lapford 1574 A

Whitrowe William, Bideford 1608 [W]; forename blank in
  Ms; supplied from parish register
Whitson, Whitstone
  Aaron, Bideford 1700 W
  Agnes, Northam 1618 [W]
  Benjamin, Northam 1663 W
  Charles, Littleham (near Bideford) 1788 W
  Christopher, Northam 1622 [W]
  Elizabeth, Northam 1604 [W]; forename blank in Ms; supplied
    from parish register
  Elizabeth, Littleham (near Bideford) 1841 W
  Emett, Northam 1644 W
  Hannah, Northam 1736 W
  James, Barnstaple 1741 W
  Joan, Northam 1607 [W]; forename blank in Ms; supplied
    from parish register
  Whitstone John, Northam 1578 W
  John, Northam 1620 [W]
  John, Northam, snr. 1622 [W]
  John, Northam 1637 A and 1645 A
  Julia, Northam 1635 A
  Mark, Bideford 1700 W
  Mark, Northam 1707 W
  Mary, Northam 1665 A
  Mathew, Huntshaw 1640 W
  Peter, Abbotsham 1671 W
  Phillippa, Northam 1736 W
  Richard, Northam 1614 [W]; forename blank in Ms; supplied
    from parish register
  Richard, Northam 1637 W
  Richard, Bideford 1663 W
  Robert, Northam 1636 W
  Robert, Northam 1668 W
  Thomas, Northam 1608 [W]; forename blank in Ms; supplied
    from parish register
  William, Northam 1622 [W]
  William, Northam, jnr. 1660 A
  William, Northam, snr. 1660 A
  William, Northam 1680 W
  William, Littleham (near Bideford) 1836 W
Whitt see White
Whittear see Whitehair
Whitton Mary, Bideford 1847 W
Who, Whoo, Whooe
  Whoo Augustine, Bideford 1585 W
  Whooe Christopher, Buckland Brewer 1664 W
  Whoo Elizabeth, Buckland Brewer 1579 W
  Whoo Elizabeth, Bideford 1586 W; forename blank in Ms;
    supplied from parish register
  Whooe John, Barnstaple 1596 [W]
  Mary, Marwood 1624 [W]
  Thomasine, Abbotsham 1634 W
Whyddon see Whiddon
Whynslade see Winslade
Whyston see Whiston
Whyt, Whyte see White
Whyteloke see Whitlock
Whytfylde see Whitfield
Whytherudge see Witheridge
Whytlocke, Whytloke see Whitlock
Whytpayne see Whitpin
Wiatt see Wyatt
Wichalls, Wichalse, Wichehalse
  ..., Barnstaple 1604 [W] and 1611 O
  Wichehalse John, Barnstaple 1619 [W]
  Nicholas, Barnstaple 1607 [W]; forename blank in Ms;
    supplied from parish register
  Wichalse Robert, Tawstock, gentleman 1643 W
Wiche, Wyche
  Wyche alias Ossell John, Westleigh 1569 W
  Wiche alias Osell Peter, Fremington 1580 W
Wichehalse see Wichalls
Wickett John, Pilton 1699 A
  Mary, Bondleigh 1623 [W]
Wickey Ann, Barnstaple 1719 A

  Edward, Bratton Fleming 1744 W
  Elizabeth, Barnstaple 1736 A
  George, Barnstaple 1750 A
  Henry, Georgeham 1678 W
  Henry, Barnstaple 1728 W
  Jacquet, Georgeham 1615 [W]
  Margaret, Barnstaple 1730 A
  Richard, Georgeham 1669 [W]
  Stephen, Georgeham 1708 A
  Tabitha, Barnstaple, sp. 1803 A
Wickham Mary, Northam 1830 W
  Richard, Northam 1796 A
Wicott John, Bideford 1688 W
  Robert, Bideford 1688 A
Widden see Widdon
Widdeslade John, Buckland Brewer 1616 [W]
Widdon, Widden, Wydden, Wyddon
  Wyddon Agnes, Parracombe 1634 W
  Wydden Anthony, Marwood 1625 [W]
  Wydden Cecilia, Fremington 1727 [W]
  Wyddon John, King's Nympton 1635 W
  Widden Philip, Ashford 1740 W
  Richard, Trentishoe 1793 A
Widgery, Wedgery
  Wedgery Elkanah, South Molton 1837 W
  James, South Molton 1720 W
  Joan, South Molton 1756 W
  John, South Molton 1773 W
  John, South Molton, butcher 1811 W
  John, South Molton 1856 W
  Marmaduke, South Molton 1700 A and 1702 A
  Marmaduke, South Molton 1739 W
  Wedgery Mary, South Molton 1615 W
  Peggy, South Molton 1829 A
  Philip, South Molton 1779 W
  Samuel, South Molton 1749 W
  Samuel, South Molton, yeoman 1805 W
  Samuel, South Molton 1835 W
  Sarah, South Molton 1775 A
  William, South Molton 1836 A
  William, South Molton 1857 W
Widlake, Wydlake, Wydlakes
  Wydlake alias Braylie ..., Filleigh 1601 W
  ... 1608 [W]
  Widlake alias Brayly Agnes, Fremington 1680 W
  Wydlake Andrew, Filleigh 1630 [W]
  Wydlake Andrew, Chittlehampton 1633 A
  Christian, East Buckland 1617 [W]
  Christopher, High Bray 1775 W
  Edward, Charles 1820 W
  Wydlake Elizabeth, West Buckland 1623 [W]
  Wydlake Elizabeth, Filleigh 1637 W
  Widlake alias Brayly Francis, Fremington 1680 A; forename
    blank in Ms; supplied from parish register
  Wydlake Henry, Chittlehampton 1623 O
  Widlake alias Braylie Hugh, Filleigh 1602 W
  Widlake alias Brailegh James, West Buckland 1570 W
  Wydlake alias Bralie John, North Molton 1572 A
  Wydlake alias Bralie John, Warkleigh 1584 W
  Wydlake alias Brelye John, Filleigh 1584 W
  Wydlakes John, Fremington 1623 [W]
  Wydlake John, Huntshaw 1626 O
  Wydlake John, North Molton 1630 [W]
  Wydlake John, Fremington, snr. 1636 A
  Wydlake John, Chittlehampton 1639 A
  Widlake alias Brauly John, South Molton 1667 A
  Widlake alias Brauly Mary, Chittlehampton 1641 W
  Widlake alias Brauly Nicholas, South Molton 1665 A
  Wydlake Petronell, Great Torrington 1628 [W]
  Philip, Tawstock 1820 A to Mary, widow
  Wydlake Richard, West Buckland 1626 [W]
  Wydlake Thomas, Kentisbury 1629 [W]
  Wydlake Thomas, Ashreigney 1630 [W]
  Widlake alias Brauly Thomas, George Nympton 1704 W
  Thomas, Charles 1809 A

William, East Buckland 1564 W
Widlake alias Brayly William, Filleigh 1669 O
William, Goodleigh, yeoman 1810 W
   see also Wedlake
Wiett see Wyatt
Wigleigh Jonathan, Molland 1745 W
Wilce Mary, South Molton 1712 W
Wilcox, Wilcock, Wilcocke, Wilcocks, Willcock, Willcocks,
   Willcoke, Willcox
   Wilcocke Agnes, Buckland Brewer [no year given] [W]
   Wilcocks Alexander, Buckland Brewer 1640 A
   Willcock Alice, Hartland 1666 W
   Wilcocke Bernard, Great Torrington 1597 [W]
   Willcox Elizabeth, North Tawton 1780 A
   Giles, Chawleigh 1725 A
   Willcox Grace, Chawleigh 1762 W
   Wilcocks Henry, Bideford 1745 W
   Willcock Henry, Northam 1781 A
   Willcock Honor, Hartland 1733 A
   Wilcocke James, Hartland 1629 [W]
   Wilcocks Jane, Rose Ash 1848 W
   Wilcock Joan, Buckland Brewer 1612 [W]; forename blank in
     Ms; supplied from parish register
   Wilcocks Joan, Buckland Brewer 1623 [W]
   Wilcocks John, Buckland Brewer 1638 W
   Wilcocke John, Ashreigney 1640 W
   Willcock John, North Molton 1718 W
   Willcox John, Chulmleigh 1731 A
   Wilcocks John, Chulmleigh 1745 W
   Willcock John, Bideford, jnr. 1813 W
   Wilcock Lawrence, Cruwys Morchard 1604 [W]; forename
     blank in Ms; supplied from parish register
   Willcock Mary see John Hoar
   Wilcocke Peter, Buckland Brewer 1639 W
   Wilcocks Philip, Ashreigney 1671 W
   Willcox Philip, Burrington 1788 W
   Willcoke Richard, Great Torrington 1583 A
   Wilcocks Richard, Buckland Brewer 1637 A
   Wilcocke Robert, Hartland 1571 W
   Roger, North Tawton 1728 W
   Roger, North Tawton 1780 A
   Wilcocks Samuel, Dolton 1644 A
   Wilcocks Samuel, Witheridge 1813 W
   Wilcocks Samuel, Witheridge 1854 A
   Wilcox Simon, North Tawton 1734 W
   Wilcoke Thomas, Buckland Brewer 1576 W
   Wilcocke Thomas, Langtree 1582 W
   Thomas, North Tawton 1741 A
   Willcocks Thomas, Witheridge 1798 W
   Willcox Thomas, Burrington 1818 W
   Willcocks William, Countisbury 1855 W
Wild Joseph, Northam 1718 A
Wiley Emma, Barnstaple 1748 W
Wilkay, Wilkaye see Wilkey
Wilke, Wylke
   Wylke John, Tawstock 1573 W
   Margaret, Goodleigh 1574 W
   William, Fremington 1573 W
Wilken see Wilkins
Wilkeridge Thomas, Berrynarbor 1755 W
Wilkey, Wilkay, Wilkaye, Wilkye
   ..., Atherington 1606 [W]
   ..., Pilton 1613 [W]
   Wilkay Alice, Fremington 1634 A
   Ambrose, Pilton 1605 W
   Ann, Instow 1676 W
   Wilkay Anthony, Woolfardisworthy 1626 [W]
   Anthony, Woolfardisworthy 1680 W
   Anthony, Bratton Fleming 1690 W
   Anthony, Bratton Fleming 1755 W
   Wilkay Arthur, Heanton Punchardon 1630 [W]
   Catherine, Barnstaple 1841 W
   Wilkay Catherine, East Buckland 1620 [W]
   Wilkay Eleanor, Pilton 1635 W
   Wilkye Elizabeth, Bratton Fleming 1577 W

   Elizabeth, Pilton 1663 W
   George, Bratton Fleming 1665 A
   George, Barnstaple 1712 W
   George, Barnstaple 1788 W
   George, Barnstaple 1829 W
   Harry, Barnstaple 1567 W
   Wilkay Helen, Pilton 1628 [W]
   Wilkay Henry, Georgeham 1635 W
   Henry, Barnstaple 1644 A
   James, Fremington 1684 W
   Wilkye alias Holway Joan, Chittlehampton 1575 A
   Wilkaye John, Tawstock 1587 W
   John, Bideford 1603 W
   John, Pilton 1605 W
   John, Northam 1682 W
   John, Barnstaple 1695 W and 1704 W
   Margaret, Heanton Punchardon 1581 W
   Margaret, Barnstaple 1707 W
   Wilkay Nicholas, Barnstaple 1622 [W]
   Nicholas, South Molton 1664 W
   Wilkaye alias Holwaye Richard, High Bickington 1582 W
   Richard, Barnstaple 1605 W
   Richard, Bratton Fleming 1617 [W]
   Richard, Northam 1711 W
   Wilkay Robert, Bratton Fleming 1623 [W]
   Simon, Clovelly 1602 W
   Wilkaye Stephen, Tawstock 1583 A
   Thomas, Kentisbury 1603 W
   Wilkey alias Holway Thomas, Wembworthy 1606 W
   Thomas, ship *Pembroke* 1750 A
   Wilkay Walter, Barnstaple 1623 [W]
   William, Pilton 1605 W
   William, Charles 1688 W
   William, Barnstaple 1842 W
Wilkins, Wilken
   Betty, Molland 1811 A
   Wilken George, Pilton 1735 A
   Joseph, High Bickington 1752 A
   Robert, Great Torrington 1756 A
Wilkinson John, Barnstaple 1837 A to John Gibble, creditor
Wilkye see Wilkey
Will James, Witheridge 1565 W
   Robert, Pilton 1577 W
   Robert, Lynton 1621 [W]
Willcock, Willcocks, Willcoke, Willcox see Wilcox
Willes see Willis
Willett, Willott
   George, Bideford 1621 [W] and 1623 O
   Isott, Alwington 1679 W
   John, Northam 1587 W
   John, Abbotsham 1688 W
   Mary, Alwington 1710 W
   Mary, Abbotsham 1721 W
   John, Alwington 1673 A
   Willott John, Buckland Brewer 1714 W
   Richard, Alwington 1693 W
   Thomasine, Bideford 1718 W
   William, Abbotsham 1635 [W]
   William, Abbotsham 1689 A
Willey, Wylly
   Wylly Joan, Mortehoe 1574 W
   Joseph, Rose Ash 1601 W
Williams, Willyams, Wyllyams
   ..., Barnstaple 1602 [W]
   ..., Great Torrington 1608 [W]
   ..., Ilfracombe 1610 [W]
   ..., Barnstaple 1611 [W]
   Abraham, Hartland 1729 A
   Agnes, South Molton 1678 W
   Alexander, Instow 1582 W
   Alice, Northam 1682 A
   Ann, Northam 1623 [W]
   Ann, North Molton 1660 W
   Ann, High Bickington 1723 W
   Ann, Bideford 1767 W

Ann, Pilton 1857 W
Ann wife of John see William Muxworthy
Anthony, North Molton 1619 [W]
Anthony, Barnstaple 1742 A
Anthony, Bideford 1755 W
Arthur and John, Great Torrington 1636 A
Catherine and Robert, Bideford 1635 A
Charity, Bideford 1744 W
Charles, Buckland Filleigh 1740 W
Charles, Winkleigh 1817 W
Charles, Barnstaple 1849 W
Christiana, North Molton 1687 A
Christopher, Molland 1612 [W]; forename blank in Ms;
    supplied from parish register
Christopher, Little Torrington 1726 A
Daniel, Great Torrington 1841 W
David, Barnstaple 1661 A
David, Heanton Punchardon 1689 A
David, Northam 1729 W
David, Bideford 1762 W
Deborah, Hartland 1715 A
Digory, Bideford 1794 W
Edward, Instow 1672 W
Edward, Littleham (near Bideford) 1714 A
Edward, Northam 1727 W
Edward, Barnstaple 1761 W
Edward, Barnstaple 1784 W
Edward, Weare Giffard 1791 A
Edward, Bideford 1818 W
Edward, Great Torrington 1843 W
Eleanor, Great Torrington 1716 W
Elizabeth, Pilton 1598 [W]
Elizabeth, Winkleigh 1637 A
Elizabeth, Northam 1684 W
Elizabeth, Ilfracombe 1695 A
Elizabeth, Pilton 1750 A
Elizabeth, Little Torrington 1763 W
Elizabeth, North Molton 1763 W
Elizabeth, Barnstaple, widow 1807 W
Elizabeth, Bideford 1814 W
Elizabeth, Northam 1847 W
Emma, Trentishoe 1590 [W]
Francis, High Bickington 1749 W
Francis, Bideford 1752 A
Willyams Geoffrey, Ilfracombe 1586 W
George, Bideford 1675 A
George, Great Torrington 1685 W
George, Ilfracombe 1742 W
George, Northam 1746 W
George, Georgeham 1832 W
George, Chulmleigh 1843 W
George, Northam 1851 W and 1853 W
George, Shebbear 1855 W
Grace, Northam 1733 W
Griffith, Chulmleigh 1740 W
Hannibal, Ilfracombe 1728 A
Henry, Georgeham 1637 A
Henry, Cruwys Morchard 1693 W
Henry, West Down 1703 W
Henry, North Molton 1746 W
Henry, Shirwell 1774 W
Honor, Great Torrington, widow 1853 A to Joseph F., son
Hugh, Witheridge 1610 [W]; forename blank in Ms; supplied
    from parish register
Wyllyams James, North Molton 1573 W
James, North Molton 1598 [W]
James, Great Torrington 1626 [W] and 1634 A
James, Great Torrington 1661 A
James, Northam 1727 A
James, Combe Martin 1832 W; A dbn granted 13 Feb 1833
Jane, Ilfracombe 1764 W
Jane, Northam 1823 W
Janora, Ashreigney 1623 [W] and 1624 O
Jasper, Hartland 1697 A
Jenkin, Northam 1636 A

Jenkin, Barnstaple 1705 A
Jerome, Parracombe 1700 A
Joan, Great Torrington 1590 [W]
Joan, Buckland Brewer or Buckland Filleigh 1621 [W]
Joan, Roborough 1632 [W]
Joan, Marwood 1737 A
John, Witheridge 1579 W
John, Bideford 1581 A
John, Great Torrington 1586 W
John, Parkham 1602 [W]; forename blank in Ms; supplied
    from parish register
John, Frithelstock 1603 W
John, Winkleigh 1611 [W]; forename blank in Ms; supplied
    from parish register
John, Frithelstock 1636 A
John, Bideford 1643 A
John, Barnstaple 1664 W
John, Barnstaple 1690 A
John, Northam 1698 W
John, West Down 1704 A
John, Barnstaple 1706 A
John, East Down 1706 W
John, Northam 1708 W
John, Bideford 1721 W
John, Hartland 1723 W
John, Bideford 1730 W and 1740 A
John, Northam 1741 T
John, Clovelly 1744 T
John, ship *Torbay* 1746 A
John, Bideford 1747 W
John, Great Torrington 1758 A
John, Littleham (near Bideford) 1786 A
John, Chulmleigh 1814 W
John, Bideford 1816 W
John, Georgeham 1817 W
John, Northam 1826 A to Mary Evans, daughter
John, Pilton 1842 W
John, Northam 1845 W and 1848 W
John, Chulmleigh 1847 W
John, Frithelstock 1636 A
Jonathan, Buckland Brewer 1615 [W]
Joseph, Barnstaple 1698 A (2)
Joshua, Northam, joiner 1851 A to Elizabeth
Joshua, Northam, Appledore, maltster, jnr. 1852 A to Maria
Josiah, Bideford 1706 A
Lawrence, Hartland 1699 W
Lewis, Barnstaple 1797 A
Lodovic, South Molton 1675 W
Margaret, Northam 1631 [W]
Margaret, Bideford 1752 A
Margaret, Northam 1795 W
Margaret, Great Torrington, widow 1806 W
Margaret, Bideford 1849 W
Margery, Petrockstowe 1692 W
Margery, Shirwell 1736 [W]
Martha, Bideford 1735 W
Mary, Barnstaple 1684 W
Mary, Winkleigh 1725 A
Mary, Buckland Filleigh 1740 W
Mary, Combe Martin 1845 W
Mary, Winkleigh, widow 1846 A to Walter, victualler, son
Mary, Winkleigh 1853 W
Mary, Chulmleigh 1854 W
Mary see also Esther Chibbett
Mathew, West Down 1745 W
Mathew, Abbotsham 1762 W
Michael, Northam 1724 A
Nathaniel, Northam 1706 A
Nicholas, Instow 1632 [W]
Nicholas, Witheridge 1698 W
Peter, Martinhoe 1626 [W]
Philip, Barnstaple 1597 [W]
Philip, Buckland Brewer 1714 W
Philip, Barnstaple 1796 A
Priscilla, Pilton 1668 W

Priscilla, Great Torrington 1770 W
Rees, Newton Tracey 1679 A
Richard, Bideford 1579 A
Richard, Woolfardisworthy 1593 [W]
Richard, Martinhoe 1617 [W]
Richard, Georgeham 1625 [W]
Richard, Molland 1665 W
Richard, Bideford 1670 A
Richard, Nymet Rowland 1685 W
Richard, High Bickington 1746 W
Richard Thomas, ship *Bristol*, jnr., infant 1856 A to Richard
   Thomas William Besley of Bowden, Cheshire, esquire,
   nephew
Robert, Roborough 1597 [W]
Robert, Ashreigney 1623 [W]
Robert, Northam 1673 W
Robert, Landcross 1694 W
Robert, Hartland 1699 A
Robert, Bratton Fleming 1717 W
Robert, ship *Preston* 1749 A
Robert, Winkleigh 1854 W
Robert and Catherine, Bideford 1635 A
Rowland, Westleigh 1712 W
Samuel, Ilfracombe 1781 W
Silvester, Marwood 1791 [W]
Thomas, Molland 1597 [W]
Thomas, Mortehoe 1636 W
Thomas, Northam 1682 W
Thomas, Pilton 1708 A
Thomas, Bideford 1712 A
Thomas, Ilfracombe 1713 W
Thomas, North Molton 1745 W
Thomas, Bideford 1749 W
Thomas, ship *Lively* 1749 A
Thomas, Ilfracombe 1770 A
Thomas, Langtree, yeoman 1797 W
Thomas, North Molton, yeoman 1810 W
Thomas, Northam 1813 W
Walter, Bideford 1704 A
Walter, Ilfracombe 1707 A
Walter, Fremington 1762 W
Walter, Winkleigh 1813 W
William, Parkham 1578 W and 1579 A
William, Frithelstock 1590 [W]
William, Chittlehampton 1682 A
William, Northam 1730 A
William, Chulmleigh 1741 A
William, ship *Rye* 1748 W
William, Petrockstowe 1777 A
William, Fremington 1784 W
William, Ilfracombe 1835 A to Mary, widow
William, Fremington 1841 W
William, Northam 1842 W, 1843 W and 1852 W
William, South Molton 1855 W
Willmot, Woolfardisworthy 1633 A
Willis, Willes, Willice
   Willes ..., Hartland 1609 [W]
   Willice ..., Trentishoe 1614 [W] (2)
   Ann, Trentishoe 1750 W
   Willes Anthony, Bideford 1626 [W]
   Arthur, Great Torrington 1713 W
   Catherine, Combe Martin 1824 A to Timothy H. of
      Barnstaple, shopkeeper, son
   Willes Charity, Pilton 1617 [W]
   Charles, Barnstaple 1705 A
   Willice Christian, Bideford 1602 [W]; forename blank in Ms;
      supplied from parish register
   Elizabeth, Ilfracombe 1747 A
   Grace, Bideford 1695 W
   Hannah, Great Torrington 1780 W
   Henry, Combe Martin 1855 W
   Hursey, Trentishoe 1630 [W]
   Joan, Fremington 1733 W
   Willice John, Littleham (near Bideford) 1616 [W]
   John, Northam 1686 A

John, Fremington 1727 A
Margery, Littleham (near Bideford) 1625 [W]
Margery, Trentishoe 1711 W
Mary, Ilfracombe 1841 W
Willes Nicholas, Cruwys Morchard 1566 W
Willice Philip, Trentishoe 1580 W
Philip, Martinhoe 1685 W
Willes Richard, Bideford 1581 A
Richard, Trentishoe 1675 W
Willett Richard, Alwington 1683 W
Richard, Great Torrington 1684 A
Willice Richard, Trentishoe 1738 W
Richard, Combe Martin 1839 A
Robert, Bideford, snr. 1706 [W]
Robert, Bideford 1722 A
Robert, Combe Martin 1759 W
Robert, Combe Martin 1802 W
Robert, Combe Martin 1853 W
Willes Thomas, Bideford 1596 [W]
Thomas, Trentishoe 1694 W
Thomas, Fremington 1779 W
Thomas, Combe Martin 1854 W
Willice Thomas, Barnstaple 1603 [W]; forename blank in Ms;
   supplied from parish register
Timothy Harding, Combe Martin, yeoman 1807 W
Timothy Harding, Barnstaple 1838 W
William, Combe Martin 1622 [W] and 1624 O
William, Parracombe 1639 W
William, Combe Martin 1690 W and 1692 A
William, Trentishoe 1715 W
William, Combe Martin, shoemaker 1815 A to Henry,
   labourer, son
William, Great Torrington 1835 W
William, Combe Martin 1851 W
Willmets, Willmetts, Willmot, Willmote, Willmotes, Willmots,
   Willmott, Willmotte, Willmotts see Wilmot
Willott see Willett
Willowbye Ann, Great Torrington 1636 A
Wills Anthony, Pilton 1615 [W]
   Baldwin, South Molton 1684 W
   Bethuel, Bideford 1796 W
   Christian, North Molton 1632 [W]
   Daniel, South Molton 1761 W
   Daniel, South Molton 1833 A
   Digory, Northam 1703 A
   Elizabeth, Littleham (near Bideford) 1669 W
   George, Pilton 1637 W
   Grace, Thelbridge 1733 W
   James, Georgeham 1732 W
   James, Great Torrington 1840 A to Thomas, brother
   Jane, Bideford 1796 A
   John, Barnstaple 1619 [W]
   John, Great Torrington 1703 A
   John, Bideford 1709 A
   John, Great Torrington 1749 A and 1753 A
   John, Bideford, maltster 1796 W
   Joseph, South Molton 1743 W
   Joseph, Barnstaple 1841 W
   Mary, Trentishoe 1639 W
   Mary, Bideford 1662 W
   Nicholas, Barnstaple 1616 [W]
   Nicholas, South Molton 1639 A
   Nicholas, North Molton 1759 A
   Noah, South Molton, husbandman 1810 A
   Peter, Bideford 1699 W
   Richard, Little Torrington 1596 [W]
   Richard, Great Torrington 1842 W
   Robert, Bideford 1599 [W]
   Robert, North Molton 1619 [W]
   Robert, Cruwys Morchard 1623 O
   Samuel, Bideford 1737 A
   Susan, South Molton 1854 A
   Thomas, South Molton 1758 A
   Thomas, Great Torrington 1782 W
   Thomas, Great Torrington 1848 W

Thomas, Northam 1852 W
Thomas, South Molton 1854 A
William, Tawstock 1622 [W]
Willmot, Welcombe 1636 A
Willson see Wilson
Willyams see Williams
Willyngs John, Frithelstock 1583 W
Wilment alias Wilmot Joseph, Bideford, shopkeeper 1820 A to
     Nathaniel
Wilmington Richard, Bideford 1674 [W]
Wilmot, Willmets, Willmetts, Willmot, Willmote, Willmotes,
     Willmots, Willmott, Willmotte, Willmotts, Wilmott(e)
Willmote alias Popham ..., North Molton 1685 A
Willmets Benjamin, Barnstaple, maltster 1822 A to John, son
Willmotts Fulk, Bideford 1636 A
Willmott James, Great Torrington 1588 A
Willmots James, Filleigh 1716 W
Willmotts James, Filleigh 1745 W
Willmetts James, Goodleigh 1788 A
Willmets James, Barnstaple 1829 A to Mary, widow
Wilmotte John, Shebbear 1607 [W]; forename blank in Ms;
     supplied from parish register
Wilmot John, Yarnscombe 1671 W
Willmets John Balment, Barnstaple 1819 W
Wilmot alias Wilment Joseph, Bideford 1820 A
Willmotts Margaret, Stoke Rivers 1678 W
Willmotes Margaret, Yarnscombe 1701 W
Willmetts Mary, Goodleigh 1788 A
Willmott Nicholas, Dolton 1626 [W]
Wilmott Richard, Burrington 1564 W
Willmott Richard, Peters Marland 1634 W
Richard, Barnstaple 1841 A
Willmotts Thomas, Filleigh 1697 A
Willmetts Thomas, North Molton 1813 A to Elizabeth Mayne
     of Stoke Rivers and Catherine Lewis, two next of kin
Thomasine, High Bickington 1567 W
Wilshire Ann, Northam 1791 W
Wilson, Willson, Wylson
Agnes, Chawleigh 1731 W
Anthony, Chulmleigh 1645 W
Elizabeth, Barnstaple 1628 [W]
George, Little Torrington 1797 A*
Willson John, Lapford 1586 W
Wylson Lawrence, Barnstaple 1589 O bond
Peter, Zeal Monachorum 1588 W
Peter, Chawleigh 1716 A
Phillippa, Ashreigney 1683 A
Robert, Bideford 1834 W
Roger, Lapford 1706 W
William, Chawleigh 1746 A
William, Little Torrington 1855 W
Wilston, Welston
Welston John, Barnstaple 1591 [W]
Mathew, Nymet Rowland 1575 A
Richard, Zeal Monachorum 1593 [W]
Wimple, Whimple
Whimple Henry, Barnstaple, mariner 1802 W; A dbn 1805
James, Barnstaple 1741 A
John, Pilton 1767 W
Mary, Barnstaple 1805 W
Whimple Simon, Pilton 1781 A
Whimple Simon, Pilton 1781 W
Wind Alice, South Molton 1666 A
Windegood John, Fremington 1627 [W]
Winford John, South Molton, glazier 1805 W
Mary, Great Torrington 1772 A
Winpenny, Wenpenny, Wynpenny
Andrew, Barnstaple 1678 A
Wynpenny Catherine, Barnstaple 1640 A
Wynpenny Hugh, Barnstaple 1629 [W]
Wenpenny John, Martinhoe 1578 W
Wynpenny John, Barnstaple 1637 W
Mary, Barnstaple 1663 W
Winslade, Wenslade, Whinslade, Whynslade, Winslad,
     Wynslade
Grace, Northam 1714 W

Whynslade Joan, Beaford 1579 W
Whinslade Joan, Satterleigh 1580 W
John, Buckland Brewer 1597 [W]
Winslade alias Eascott John, Northam 1606 W
John, Northam 1706 W
Wynslade Luke, Frithelstock 1566 W
Philip, Beaford 1565 W
Richard, Satterleigh 1578 W and 1588 O account
Wenslade Richard, Fremington 1589 W
Wenslade Rose, Satterleigh 1582 W
Uzziah, Bideford 1705 A
Walter, Beaford 1591 [W]
Winslad William, Northam 1775 W
Winsley Samuel, Chulmleigh 1857 W
Winson John, Ashreigney 1837 W
Thomas, Great Torrington 1847 W
Winstanley Joseph, Barnstaple 1727 W
Winter, Wenter
Wenter ..., Tawstock 1603 [W]
Winter alias Downe Thomas, East Worlington 1582 W
Wiott see Wyatt
Wisdon ..., Zeal Monachorum 1613 [W]
Edward, Bow 1590 [W]
John, South Molton 1619 [W]
John, Barnstaple 1624 [W]
Philip, Chawleigh 1588 W
William, Coldridge 1578 [W]
Wise, Wyes, Wyse
..., Chittlehampton 1603 [W]
..., Hartland 1610 [W]
..., Northam 1614 [W]
Ann, Barnstaple 1767 W
Wyes Arthur, Buckland Brewer 1618 [W]
Elizabeth, Bideford 1741 A
Emblem, Barnstaple 1623 [W]
George, Bideford 1741 A
Grace, Bideford 1827 W
Hugh, Peters Marland, clerk 1569 W
Joan, Clovelly 1630 [W]
John, Northam 1706 [W]
Nathaniel, Littleham (near Bideford) 1711 W
Nathaniel, Bideford 1748 W
Nathaniel, Bideford 1819 W
Wyse Roger, Clovelly 1571 [W]
Sarah, Northam 1730 W
Simon, Chittlehampton 1603 W
Thomas, Clovelly 1620 [W]
Thomas, Northam 1691 A
William, Northam 1613 [W]; forename blank in Ms; supplied
     from parish register
Wish Mary, Bideford 1775 W
Wisland, Wysland
..., Chawleigh 1604 [W]
Philip, Chawleigh 1614 [W]; forename blank in Ms; supplied
     from parish register
Wysland Richard, Chawleigh 1580 W
Witchalse, Withalse
Bridget, Lynton 1661 A and 1668 A
Dorothy, Lynton 1663 A
Elizabeth, Tawstock 1664 W
Hugh, Lynton 1695 A
Withalse Mary, Chittlehampton 1693 W
Thomas, Chittlehampton 1686 W
Witefield see Whitfield
Witham George, Buckland Brewer or Filleigh 1838 W
Withalse see Witchalse
Withcomb, Withecomb
Withcomb Abraham, St Giles in the Wood 1618 [W]
Withcomb John, Bratton Fleming 1702 W
Withcomb Phillippa, St Giles in the Wood, widow 1572 W
Withcomb Thomas, St Giles in the Wood 1572 W
Withecomb Thomas, High Bickington 1790 W
Withcomb Thomas, Instow 1820 W
Wither, Wether, Wethers, Withers, Wyther
Agnes, Berrynarbor 1624 [W]

Wyther Andrew, Great Torrington 1665 A
Withers Anthony, Great Torrington 1592 [W]
Elizabeth, Rackenford 1598 [W]
Wyther Hugh, Huish 1676 W
Jane, Rackenford 1598 [W]
Withers Joan, Berrynarbor 1591 [W]
Wither alias Whitear Joan, Ilfracombe 1605 W
John, Stoodleigh 1574 W
Wethers John, Great Torrington 1566 W
Withers John, Great Torrington 1591 [W]
Withers John, Berrynarbor 1594 [W]
John, Berrynarbor 1603 T
Wyther Richard, Moortown, Great Torrington 1571 W
Wether alias Hichcocke Richard, Knowstone 1574 A
Wither alias Hychcocke Richard, Creacombe 1574 A
Wyther Roger, West Anstey 1563 W
Wethers William, Parkham 1583 A
Witheridge, Wetheridge, Wetherudge, Whytherudge, Witheridg,
    Witherydge, Wytherydge
..., Northam 1609 [W]
..., Clovelly 1611 [W]
Edward, Martinhoe 1615 [W]
Wytherydge Edward, Georgeham 1636 W
Witherydge Elizabeth, Parkham 1621 [W]
Elizabeth, East Down 1763 W; A dbn 1770
Francis, Combe Martin 1737 W
Giles, Littleham (near Bideford) 1610 [W]; forename blank in
    Ms; supplied from parish register
Hannah, Ilfracombe 1737 A
James, Fremington 1603 [W]; forename blank in Ms; supplied
    from parish register
Joan, Fremington, widow 1612 [W]; forename blank in Ms;
    supplied from parish register
Witherydge Joan, Bulkworthy 1620 [W]
Witheridg Joan, Fremington 1689 W
Wetherudge John, Stoke Rivers 1577 W
Wetheridge John, Barnstaple 1581 O account
Wetheridge John, Berrynarbor 1585 A
Wetherudge John, Stoke Rivers 1588 A
John, Northam 1602 [W]; forename blank in Ms; supplied
    from parish register
Witherydge John, Berrynarbor 1627 [W]
Witherydge John, Combe Martin 1629 [W]
Witheridg John, Buckland Brewer 1660 A
Witheridg John, Berrynarbor 1663 W
Witheridg John, Instow 1666 A
John, Berrynarbor 1729 W and 1739 A
John, Combe Martin 1792 W
Witherydge Mary, Berrynarbor 1623 [W], 1624 [W] and 1636
    O
Mary, Littleham (near Bideford) 1664 W
Mary, Combe Martin, widow 1808 A
Mary, Combe Martin, widow 1821 A to John, labourer,
    grandson
Wetherudge Nicholas, Berrynarbor 1586 W
Witherydge Nicholas, Berrynarbor 1619 [W], 1624 [W, 1627
    [W] and 1636 O
Witheridg Nicholas, Berrynarbor 1708 W
Nicholas, Ilfracombe 1732 W
Oliver, Barnstaple [no year given] [W]
Philip, Parkham 1617 [W]
Witherydge Richard, Barnstaple 1627 [W]
Whytherudge Robert, Goodleigh 1578 W
Robert, Barnstaple 1644 W
Roger, Fremington 1608 [W]; forename blank in Ms; supplied
    from parish register
Roger 1680 W
Thomas, Buckland Brewer 1615 [W]
Wytherydge Thomas, Berrynarbor 1638 W
Witheridg Thomas, Peters Marland 1661 W
Witheridg Thomas, Berrynarbor 1697 W
Thomas, Berrynarbor 1745 W
Wetherudge William, Littleham (near Bideford) 1576 W
William, Littleham (near Bideford) 1600 W
Wytherydge William, Barnstaple 1640 A
William, South Molton 1737 A

William, Combe Martin 1792 A
Witherly see Wetherly
Withers see Wither
Withey Agnes, Combe Martin 1666 W
John, Combe Martin 1665 W
Witheycombe, Wythycombe
    Wythycombe Nicholas, King's Nympton 1630 [W]
    Richard, Bratton Fleming 1817 W
Withingham Charles, Ilfracombe, shipwright 1801 W
    Dorothy, Ilfracombe 1758 W "Witheringham" in register;
        forename blank in Ms; supplied from parish register
    Dorothy, Ilfracombe 1796 A
Witts Thomas, Great Torrington 1623 [W]
Woadam see Wodam
Woats Anthony, Georgeham 1628 [W] and 1630 O
Wodam, Woadam
    John, Chulmleigh 1626 [W]
    Woadam Mary, Chulmleigh 1628 [W]
Wodley see Woodley
Woland see Walland
Wolcott Alice, North Tawton 1580 W
    John, North Tawton 1580 W
Wolfe, Wolf, Wolff, Woulfe
    Wolff Derwent, Lapford 1573 W
    Elizabeth, Lapford 1589 W
    Evan, Chulmleigh 1567 W
    Isaac, Barnstaple, pedlar 1808 A
    Woulfe Joan, Yarnscombe 1589 W
    Wolf Richard, Lapford 1582 A
    Richard, Lapford 1585 [A] account
    Robert, Bideford 1614 [W]; forename blank in Ms; supplied
        from parish register
Wollacombe, Wollacomb, Woolacombe, Woolcomb
    Wollacomb Alexander 1617 [W]
    Christiana, Bideford 1625 [W]
    Henry, Mortehoe 1620 [W]
    John, Roborough 1591 [W]
    John, Roborough, esquire 1609 [W]; forename blank in Ms;
        supplied from parish register
    Wollacomb John, esquire 1663 W
    Mary, Roborough 1598 [W]
    Mary, Roborough 1626 [W]
    Woolacombe Peter, Great Torrington 1714 A
    Woolcomb alias Bowden Phyllis, Witheridge 1665 W
Wollacott see Woollacott
Wolland see Walland
Wollifford John, Clovelly 1761 A
Wollscott see Woollacott
Wolridge, Wolrydge see Woolridge
Wolson ..., Heanton Punchardon 1611 [W]
    John, Fremington 1604 W
Wolsworthie Margaret, Knowstone 1578 W
Wolway see Woolway
Wonnacott, Wannacott, Wonacot, Wonacott, Wonncote
    Edward, Dolton 1585 W
    Wonnacott alias Wollacott Elizabeth, South Molton 1600 W
    Wonacott Francis, East Down 1822 W
    Wonacot John, Bondleigh 1564 W
    John, Dolton 1598 [W]
    John, Shebbear 1825 W and A to Joseph Chidley, guardian to
        Mary
    Michael, Sheepwash 1768 A
    Wonncote Philip, Dolton 1580 W
    Thomas, Dolton 1663 [W]
    Wannacott William, Shebbear 1752 A
    William, Shebbear 1844 W
    Wonacott William, Combe Martin 1846 W
Wood, Woode
    ..., Newton St Petrock 1593 [W]
    Woode ..., Knowstone 1605 [W]
    ..., Chulmleigh 1606 [W]
    Woode ..., North Tawton 1607 [W]
    Woode ..., Georgeham 1610 [W]
    Woode ..., Eggesford 1612 [W]
    Wood alias Coomb ..., High Bickington 1663 W

Agnes, Hartland 1568 W
Agnes, Georgeham 1623 [W]
Agnes, Knowstone 1623 [W]
Alexander, Cruwys Morchard 1641 W
Woode Alice, Georgeham 1623 [W] and 1624 O
Woode Ann, Eggesford, Worshipful Mrs 1608 [W]; forename
    blank in Ms; supplied from parish register
Ann, Cruwys Morchard 1638 W
Catherine, Abbotsham 1661 W
Woode Christopher, Cruwys Morchard 1578 W
Christopher, North Tawton, esquire 1662 W
Christopher, North Tawton 1670 W
Edward, Lynton 1628 [W]
Eleanor, Barnstaple 1733 W
Elizabeth, Shirwell 1645 A
Woode English, Chulmleigh 1603 [W]
Francis, Barnstaple 1703 A
Woode Isott, Ashreigney 1622 [W]
James, Bideford 1699 W
John, Hartland 1568 W
John, Iddesleigh 1580 W
John, Shebbear 1592 [W]
John, Knowstone 1598 [W]
John, Chulmleigh 1599 [W]
Wood alias Hayne John, Chulmleigh 1627 [W]
John, Winkleigh 1643 W
Wood alias Morgan John, Barnstaple 1644 W
John, Knowstone 1678 W
John, Barnstaple 1680 W
John, Barnstaple 1715 W
John, Iddesleigh 1720 W
John, Northam 1752 W
John, Witheridge 1771 W
John, Littleham (near Bideford) 1794 W
Joseph, Knowstone 1780 W
Joseph, George Nympton 1833 W
Julia, Northam 1724 W
Leonard, Westleigh 1826 W
Woode Margaret, Tawstock 1631 [W] and 1633 O
Woode Marmaduke, Tawstock 1617 [W]
Mary, Barnstaple 1682 W
Nicholas, Puddington 1640 W
Nicholas, Iddesleigh 1674 W
Philip, Shirwell 1637 W
Richard, Eggesford 1597 [W]
Richard, Abbotsham 1642 A
Richard, Bideford 1709 A
Richard, Northam 1718 W
Richard, Ilfracombe 1719 W
Robert, Knowstone 1632 [W]
Woode Sybil, Rose Ash 1630 [W]
Simon, Winkleigh 1641 A
Thomas, Alwington 1606 [W]; forename blank in Ms;
    supplied from parish register
Thomas, Alwington 1624 [W]
Thomas, North Tawton 1629 [W]
Thomas, Cruwys Morchard 1706 W
Thomas, Rackenford 1784 W
Walter, Chulmleigh 1583 A
Woode William, Georgeham 1615 [W]
William, Barnstaple 1787 W
Woodbear, Wodbere Joan, Stoodleigh 1580 W
Joan, Stoodleigh 1621 [W]
Wodbere see Woodbear
Woodcock Charity, High Bickington 1801 W
Joan, Romansleigh 1679 A
Woocock John, High Bickington 1793 W
Thomasine, Romansleigh 1709 W
William, Romansleigh 1605 A
Woode see Wood
Woodley, Wodley, Woodleigh
..., Puddington 1613 [W]
Woodley alias Southcomb Alice, Coldridge, widow 1568 W
Joan, Puddington 1593 [W]
Wodley John, Puddington 1588 W

Woodleigh John, North Tawton 1761 W
Robert, Great Torrington 1763 A
Woodman Ann, Littleham (near Bideford) 1594 W
Ann, Littleham (near Bideford) 1599 [W]
Elizabeth, Littleham (near Bideford) 1594 [W]
John, Littleham (near Bideford) 1577 W
William, Littleham (near Bideford) 1573 W
Woodrofe Elizabeth, Barnstaple 1621 [W]
Grace, Barnstaple 1624 [W]
Woodrufe William, Barnstaple 1635 O; A dbn
Woodward, Woodwarde
..., Lapford 1606 [W]
..., Witheridge 1607 [W]
Emott, Lapford 1565 W
John, Witheridge 1617 [W] and 1619 O
Lodovic, Witheridge 1624 [W]
Lodovic, Witheridge 1636 A
Mary, Witheridge 1625 [W], 1636 A and O
Woodwarde Richard, Lapford 1564 W
Stukeley, Eggesford 1637 W
Thomas, Washford Pyne 1592 [W]
Woodyeats William, Cruwys Morchard 1706 W
Woolacombe see Wollacombe
Woolaway see Woolway
Woolcock Jenkin, Georgeham 1667 W
Woolcomb see Wollacombe
Woollacott, Wellocott, Wollacott, Wollscott, Woolacot,
    Woolacott, Woolcott
Wollacott ..., High Bickington 1610 [W]
Abigail, High Bickington 1758 W
Agnes, Burrington 1669 W
Ann, Chittlehampton 1766 W
Anthony, Burrington 1716 W
Avis, High Bickington 1644 W
Wollacott alias Wonnacott Elizabeth, South Molton 1600 W
Elizabeth, Bow 1797 W
Wollacott George, High Bickington 1586 W
Wollacott Henry, High Bickington 1666 A
Henry, Tawstock, yeoman 1808 W
Wollacott Henry, High Bickington, blacksmith 1840 W
Woolacott Henry, Tawstock 1844 W
Woolcott Hugh, Rose Ash 1716 W
Wollacott Joan, High Bickington 1579 W
Joan, High Bickington 1698 A
Joan, Alverdiscott 1717 W
Joan, Clovelly 1721 W
Wollacott John, North Tawton, snr. 1588 W
Wollacott John, High Bickington 1601 W
Wollacott John, North Tawton 1623 [W]
Wollacott John, High Bickington 1632 [W]
Woolacott John, High Bickington 1741 A
Wollacott John, High Bickington 1744 W
Joan, High Bickington 1761 W
John, Chittlehampton 1763 W
John, Atherington 1787 W
Woolcott John, South Molton, woolcomber 1799 W
Woolacott John, High Bickington 1799 W
Wollacott Josiah, Atherington 1716 A
Wollacott Margery, Dowland 1779 W
Wollacott Mary, High Bickington 1666 A
Mary, High Bickington 1780 W
Wollacott Philip, High Bickington 1632 [W]
Philip, High Bickington 1679 [W]
Wollacott Robert, High Bickington 1604 W
Wollacott Robert, Clovelly 1674 A
Robert, High Bickington 1703 W
Woolacott Robert, Barnstaple 1820 W
Woolacott Robert, High Bickington 1855 W
Wollscott Roger, South Molton 1594 [W]
Roger, Chittlehampton 1724 W
Roger, High Bickington 1729 W
Wollacott Thomas, High Bickington 1591 [W]
Wollacott Thomas, Meeth 1626 [W]
Wollacott Thomas, High Bickington 1630 [W]
Wollacott Thomasine 1592 [W]

Wollacott William, Westleigh 1619 [W]
William, High Bickington 1661 W
William, Clovelly 1712 A
William, High Bickington 1735 A
Wellocott William, High Bickington 1756 W
Woolacott William, Burrington, husbandman 1842 A to Sarah,
    widow
Wollacott Willmot, High Bickington 1604 W
Woolland see Walland
Woollway see Woolway
Woolridge, Wolridge, Wolrydge
    Wolridge ..., Northam 1611 [W]
    Wolrydge Hugh, Ashreigney 1625 [W]
    Wolrydge Joan, Ashreigney 1634 W
    John, Ashreigney 1601 W
Woolway, Wolway, Woolaway, Woollway
    Wolway ..., Burrington 1594 [W]
    Woollway Christiana, Chawleigh 1762 A
    Francis, South Molton 1839 W
    Giles, Chawleigh 1769 W
    Giles, Chawleigh 1831 W
    Woolaway John, Chittlehampton 1783 W
    John, Burrington, yeoman 1799 W
    John, Chawleigh, miller 1809 W
    John, Chawleigh, yeoman 1810 W
    John, Chawleigh, yeoman 1811 W
    John, Chawleigh 1820 W
    John, Chawleigh 1852 W
    Wolway Lodovic, Tawstock 1620 [W]
    Thomas, Burrington 1789 W
    Woollway William, South Molton 1830 W
Worden see Warden
Worgan John, Northam 1641 W
Worstcott Elizabeth, Wembworthy 1820 W
Worth, Worthe
    Eleanor, Ashreigney 1670 A and 1672 O
    Grace, Barnstaple 1632 [W]
    Joan, Barnstaple 1624 [W]
    John, Shebbear 1717 W
    Paul, Barnstaple 1615 [W]; forename blank in Ms; supplied
        from parish register
    Paul, Barnstaple 1622 [W] and 1624 [W]
    Worthe Roger, Barnstaple 1565 A
Worthen Thomas, Bideford 1644 A
Wotten Richard, Northam 1578 W
Woulfe see Wolfe
Wrath alias Harden Richard, Knowstone 1587 W
Wraye, Wrey
    Wrey Ann, Barnstaple 1813 W
    Anthony 1576 [W]
Wreford, Wreaford, Wrefforde, Wreyford
    Wreyford ..., Burrington 1614 [W]
    Agnes, Lapford 1775 W
    Wreaford Elizabeth, Bow 1680 W
    John, Chulmleigh 1840 W
    Mathew, Witheridge, yeoman 1818 A to Grace, widow
    Wrefforde Michael, North Tawton 1602 W
    Wreyford Richard, North Tawton 1620 [W]
    Wreford alias Dart Silvanus, Bow 1842 W
    Silvanus Dart, Bow 1842 W
    William, Zeal Monachorum 1812 W
Wren Dorothy, Bideford 1759 W
    Edward, Bideford 1715 W
    Elizabeth, Bideford 1762 W
    Grace, Bideford 1813 A
    Josiah, Bideford 1791 W
    Josiah, Bideford 1817 W
    Robert, Bideford 1712 A
    Robert, Bideford 1751 W
    Sarah, Bideford, widow 1801 W
    Thomas, Bideford 1686 W
    William, Bideford 1699 A
    William, Bideford 1744 W
Wrey see Wraye
Wreyford see Wreford

Wright ..., Ashford 1609 [W] and 1611 [W]
    ..., Cruwys Morchard 1611 [W]
    Elizabeth, Cruwys Morchard 1747 [W]
    George, Georgeham 1731 W
    George, Georgeham 1777 W
    Henry, Cruwys Morchard 1583 W
    Humphrey, Cruwys Morchard 1692 A
    James, Burrington 1811 A
    Joan, Cruwys Morchard 1743 W
    Joan, Chulmleigh 1771 W
    John, Puddington 1690 A
    John, Cruwys Morchard 1720 A
    Margaret, Cruwys Morchard 1722 W
    Oliver, Bideford 1639 W
    Richard, Great Torrington 1705 A
    Richard, Combe Martin 1831 A to Mary, widow
    Robert, Puddington 1664 A
    Thomas, Cruwys Morchard 1685 W
    Thomas, Cruwys Morchard 1743 W
    Thomasine, Ashford 1639 A
    Ursula, Georgeham 1800 W
    William, Ashford 1600 W
    William, Ashford 1623 [W]
    William, Ashford 1685 A
    William, Georgeham 1753 W
Wyatt, Wiatt, Wiett, Wiott, Wyat, Wyett, Wyott
    Wiatt ..., Barnstaple 1611 [W]
    ..., Stoke Rivers 1611 [W]
    Wiatt ..., Chittlehampton 1614 [W]
    Adam, Barnstaple 1611 [W]; forename blank in Ms; supplied
        from parish register
    Wyat Alice, Barnstaple 1579 W
    Wiatt Alice, Ilfracombe 1604 W
    Catherine, Barnstaple 1587 A
    Wiott Catherine, Ilfracombe 1705 W
    Elizabeth, Northam 1815 W
    Wyott Grace, Ilfracombe 1642 A
    Wyott Grace, Ilfracombe 1759 W
    Wyat Hannah, Northam 1723 A
    Wyott Henry, Shirwell 1623 [W]
    Wyott James, Northam 1763 A
    Wyott Joan, Stoke Rivers 1619 [W]
    Wyott Joan, Shirwell 1679 W
    John, Ashford 1585 W
    Wyott John, Ilfracombe 1634 W
    Wyott John, Barnstaple 1636 W
    Jonathan, Tawstock 1697 A
    Jonathan, Tawstock 1730 W
    Julia, Northam 1630 [W]
    Wyott Margaret, Barnstaple 1593 [W]
    Wyott Margaret, Alwington 1627 [W]
    Wyott Nicholas, Ilfracombe 1731 W
    Wyott Nicholas, Ilfracombe 1748 W
    Pauline, Shirwell 1585 A
    Wiatt Philip, Roborough 1614 [W]; forename blank in Ms;
        supplied from parish register
    Wyott Philip, Alwington 1634 A
    Wiett Philip, Abbotsham 1708 W
    Wyat Richard, Ashford 1577 W
    Robert, Marwood 1603 W
    Wiatt Robert, Goodleigh 1606 [W] "Wayt" in register;
        forename blank in Ms; supplied from parish register
    Wyott Robert, Ilfracombe 1687 W
    Wyott Robert, Ilfracombe 1785 W
    Wyott Sarah, Ilfracombe 1768 W
    Susan, Ilfracombe 1736 W
    Wyett Thomas, Alwington 1575 A
    Wyat Thomas, Barnstaple 1577 W
    Wyott Thomas, Ashford 1599 [W]
    Wyett Thomas, Great Torrington 1721 W
    William, Barnstaple 1587 A
    William, Heanton Punchardon 1603 W
    Wyott William, Ilfracombe 1704 A
    Wyat William, Ilfracombe 1735 W
    Wyott William, Ilfracombe, mariner 1747 A

Wybard Agnes, Heanton Punchardon 1723 W
Wybron, Wybern
  Wybern James, Oakford 1803 W
  James, Marwood 1823 W
  James, Marwood 1843 W
Wyche see Wiche
Wycod Abraham, Bideford 1663 A
Wydden, Wyddon see Widdon
Wydlake, Wydlakes see Widlake
Wyes see Wise
Wyett see Wyatt
Wylke see Wilke
Wylly see Willey
Wyllyams see Williams
Wylsh see Welsh
Wylson see Wilson
Wyne Walter, South Molton 1626 [W]
Wynge Charity, Tawstock 1636 W
  Lawrence, Tawstock 1627 [W]
Wynpenny see Winpenny
Wynslade see Winslade
Wyott see Wyatt
Wyse see Wise
Wysland see Wisland
Wyther see Wither
Wytherydge see Witheridge
Wythycombe see Witheycombe
Wyvell Mary, Burrington 1664 A

Yae see Yeo
Yalland see Yolland
Yandle, Yandall, Yendell
  George, Rose Ash 1833 A to Sarah, widow
  John, Rose Ash 1803 W
  Yendell Sarah, Bishop's Nympton 1852 A
  Yandall Thomas, Lynton 1705 A
  Yandell Thomas, North Molton 1841 W
  William, East Anstey 1644 W
Yard, Yarde, Yeard, Yearde
  Alexander, Chulmleigh 1663 W
  Ann, South Molton 1744 W
  Yarde Catherine, King's Nympton 1592 [W]
  Edward, Bideford 1749 W
  Yarde Joan, Ilfracombe 1573 W
  Yarde John, Rose Ash 1570 W
  Yeard John, Rose Ash 1588 A
  Yeard John, Rose Ash 1616 [W] and 1618 [W]
  Mary, Bideford 1753 A
  Richard, King's Nympton 1573 W
  Yeard Richard, Satterleigh 1637 W
  Yarde Roger, Barnstaple 1581 A
  Yeard Thomas, Satterleigh 1845 [W]
  Yearde William, Rose Ash 1617 [W]
  Yearde William, Rose Ash 1617 [W]
Yardley, Yardly
  William, East Buckland 1670 W
  Yardly William, East Buckland 1692 W
Yea see Yeo
Yeainacott see Yealmacott
Yealand, Yealland see Yolland
Yealmacott, Yeainacott, Yeamacott
  ..., King's Nympton 1611 [W]
  Yeamacott alias Toms ..., Chulmleigh 1698 W
  Joan, King's Nympton 1617 [W]
  Yeainacott Lodovic, King's Nympton 1636 [W]
  Yeamacott alias Toms Robert 1693 A
  Thomas, King's Nympton 1596 [W]
Yeard, Yearde see Yard
Yeark William, Abbotsham 1702 W
Yearly John, ship *Ripon* 1748 [W]
  William, East Buckland 1734 A
Yearnacott see Yealmacott
Yelland see Yolland
Yellaton, Yeollaton
  Yeollaton ..., Mortehoe 1607 [W]

  John, Kentisbury 1627 [W] and 1630 O
  Thomas, Ilfracombe 1663 A
Yeo, Yae, Yea, Yoe, Yoo, Yowe
  ..., Shebbear 1602 [W]
  Yea ..., Woolfardisworthy 1604 [W]
  ..., North Tawton 1610 [W]
  ..., Shebbear 1611 [W]
  ..., Bideford 1614 [W]
  Agnes, Shebbear 1664 W
  Alexander, Chulmleigh 1640 W
  Alexander, Stoke Rivers 1713 A
  Andrew, Hartland 1624 [W]
  Yoe Ann, Huish 1573 W
  Ann, Northam 1759 W
  Arthur, Great Torrington 1707 W
  Avis, Northam, widow 1566 W
  Betty, Barnstaple 1856 W
  Catherine, Northam 1630 [W]
  Charity, Barnstaple 1615 [W]
  Charles, Northam 1731 A
  Christopher, Filleigh 1664 W
  Christopher, South Molton 1669 W
  Christopher, Northam 1680 A
  David, Chittlehampton 1576 W
  Yoo Edmund, Northam 1764 W
  Elizabeth, King's Nympton 1594 [W]
  Elizabeth, Meeth 1692 A
  Elizabeth, Peters Marland 1715 W
  Elizabeth, Arlington 1825 W
  Elizabeth, Great Torrington 1826 A to Christopher C. Bennett
    of Great Torrington and Samuel Bennett of Peters Marland,
    creditors
  Elizabeth, Northam 1832 W
  Elizabeth, Barnstaple 1837 W
  Yowe Francis, Northam 1581 W
  Francis, Weare Giffard 1681 W
  Francis, Welcombe 1714 A
  George, Huish, esquire 1672 W
  George, Northam 1695 A
  Grace, Hartland 1715 A
  Grace, Hartland 1745 A
  Helen, Woolfardisworthy 1623 [W]
  Henry, Alverdiscott, yeoman 1808 A
  Yea Hugh, King's Nympton 1630 [W]
  Humphrey, Littleham (near Bideford) 1758 W
  Isott, Woolfardisworthy 1674 W
  James, Hartland 1666 A
  Jane, Hartland 1669 O
  Jane, Chittlehampton 1687 W
  Yoe Joan, Bideford 1577 W
  Joan, Dolton 1610 [W]; forename blank in Ms; supplied from
    parish register
  Joan, Huish 1702 W
  John 1573 A
  John, Dolton 1591 [W]
  John, Northam 1598 [W]
  John, Abbotsham 1632 [W]
  John, North Tawton 1633 W
  John, Meeth, gentleman 1644 W
  John, Barnstaple 1668 W
  John, Bideford 1682 W
  John, Monkleigh 1690 W
  John, Great Torrington 1710 W
  John, Northam, snr. 1736 W
  John, Northam 1740 [W]
  John, Stoke Rivers 1745 A
  John, King's Nympton 1818 W
  John, Goodleigh 1833 W
  Jonathan 1679 W
  Leonard, Huish 1641 W
  Margaret, Zeal Monachorum 1630 [W]
  Margery, North Tawton 1599 [W]
  Mark, North Tawton 1631 [W] and 1633 O
  Mary, West Down 1600 A; forename blank in Ms; supplied
    from parish register

Mary, Woolfardisworthy 1663 W
Mary, Burrington 1776 W
Mary, Barnstaple 16 Feb 1793 W; A dbn 1812
Mary, Goodleigh 1856 W
Mary see also Joan White
Melchior, Northam 1702 W
Melchior, Northam 1734 W
Yea Michael, High Bickington 1624 [W]
Morgan, ship *Looe* 1762 A
Nicholas, Huish 1640 W
Parnell, North Tawton 1599 [W]
Peter, Great Torrington 1744 A
Petronell, Barnstaple 1817 W
Philip, Sheepwash 1704 A
Philip, Hartland 1745 W
Phillippa, Hartland 1711 A
Rebecca, Monkleigh 1690 W
Richard, King's Nympton 1587 A
Richard, Hartland 1696 W
Yoe Richard, Monkleigh 1764 W
Robert, Shebbear 1572 W
Yowe Robert, Shebbear 1582 O account
Robert, Weare Giffard 1637 A
Robert, Shebbear 1666 [W]
Robert, North Tawton 1674 W
Yae Roger, Rose Ash 1573 A
Roger, Charles 1673 W
Roger, Chittlehampton 1745 A
Samuel, Peters Marland 1687 A
Samuel, Barnstaple 1706 A
Sarah, Barnstaple 1855 W
Thomas, Bideford 1568 W
Thomas, Abbotsham 1602 W
Thomas, Bow 1621 [W]
Thomas, Woolfardisworthy 1672 W
Thomas, Northam 1711 A
Thomas, Littleham (near Bideford) 1778 W
William, North Tawton 1586 W and A
William, Northam 1610 [W]; forename blank in Ms; supplied
    from parish register
William, Barnstaple 1615 [W]
William, Beaford 1622 O
William, Northam 1629 [W]
William, West Buckland 1632 [W]
William, Bideford 1667 W
William, Northam 1671 A
William, Northam 1675 W
William, Shebbear 1685 W
William, North Tawton 1698 W
William, Alwington 1736 W
William, Northam 1750 W
William, Swimbridge 1854 A
William, Shirwell, yeoman 1856 A to Mary, widow
Willmot, Shirwell 1722 W
Yeoland, Yeolland see Yolland
Yeollaton see Yellaton
Yeoman Cornelius, Bideford 1716 W
Yeovans alias Davy alias Evans Joan, Heanton Punchardon,
    widow 1672 W
Yoe see Yeo
Yoldon see Youlden
Yolland, Yalland, Yelland, Yeoland, Yeolland, Yollande
    Yealand Mary, Pilton 1676 W
    Yollande ..., Langtree 1607 [W]
    ..., Winkleigh 1611 [W]
    Yeoland Alexander, South Molton 1665 A
    Yeoland alias Comb Alexander, Pilton 1685 A
    Alice, Bow 1594 [W]
    Christian, St Giles in the Wood 1635 W
    Yelland Daniel, Dolton 1800 W
    Elizabeth, Pilton 1643 A
    George, Pilton 1622 [W]
    James, Pilton 1641 A
    Joan, Pilton 1630 [W]
    Yeolland alias Combe Joan, Pilton, snr., widow 1675 W
    Yealland Joan, Chawleigh 1737 W

Yelland Joan, Rose Ash 1758 W
John, Langtree 1631 [W]
John, St Giles in the Wood 1633 W
Yeoland alias Coomb John, Pilton 1667 W, 1670 W and 1673
    W
Yeoland John, Molland 1698 W
Yeoland John, Bulkworthy 1733 W
Yeoland alias Cooniber Mary, Pilton 1663 W
Yeoland Mary, Newton St Petrock 1723 W
Yeoland Mathew, Peters Marland 1727 W
Yeolland Philip, Goodleigh 1602 W
Philip, Chulmleigh 1643 W
Philip, Chawleigh 1645 A
Yeoland Philip, Chawleigh 1727 W
Yelland Philip, Oakford 1769 W; 1770 A.T.
Richard, Langtree 1623 [W]
Yeoland alias Coomb Richard, Pilton 1663 W
Yollande Robert, Kentisbury 1594 [W]
Robert, Tawstock 1632 [W]
Yeoland Robert, Chulmleigh 1731 W
Yeolland Robert, Winkleigh 1737 W
Sybil, Langtree 1638 W
Thomas, Goodleigh 1594 [W]
Thomas, Chawleigh 1603 [W]; forename blank in Ms;
    supplied from parish register
Thomas, South Molton 1680 W
Yeoland Thomas, Chawleigh 1700 W
William, Pilton 1591 [W]
William 1592 [W]
William, Pilton 1624 [W]
William, Winkleigh 1637 W
Yeoland alias Comb William, Barnstaple 1663 W
William, Bondleigh 1663 W
Yeoland William, Pilton 1681 W
Yelland William, Rose Ash 1748 W
Yoo see Yeo
Yorke, Yorck, Yorcke
    Yorcke Elizabeth, Abbotsham 1588 A
    Jasper, Bideford 1670 W
    Yorck John, Abbotsham 1588 W
Youatt Caleb, Newton Tracey, yeoman 1803 W
    James, Newton Tracey, yeoman 1811 W
    John, Great Torrington, butcher 1852 A to Elizabeth
Youlden, Yoldon
    Henry, Monkleigh 1715 W
    John, High Bickington 1680 W
    Yoldon Lodovic, High Bickington 1625 [W]
    Yoldon Thomas, Peters Marland 1691 A
Young, Younge
    Charles, Bideford 1775 A
    Francis, Wembworthy 1642 A
    Francis, Wembworthy 1688 W
    Francis, Brushford 1760 A
    Francis, Bideford 1855 W
    Younge Henry, Ashreigney 1619 [W]
    John, Alverdiscott 1672 A
    John, Huntshaw 1752 W
    Younge John, Brushford 1758 A
    John, Huntshaw 1797 W
    Younge Margery, Chulmleigh 1620 [W]
    Younge Philip, Northam 1717 W
    Richard, Northam 1748 A
    William, Brushford 1748 W
    Willmot, Bideford 1629 W
Yowe see Yeo

Zachary, Zachery
    Zachery John, Barnstaple 1676 W
    Mary, Barnstaple 1702 W
    Zachery Thomas, Barnstaple 1710 W
    Willmot, Barnstaple 1736 A
Zanger see Sanger
Zeagar see Seager
Zeale, Seale, Seall, Zeal
    Seale ..., North Molton 1611 [W]

Seale ..., Rose Ash 1615 [W]
Zeale alias Eames ... 1690 W
Alexander, Knowstone 1770 W
Christian, North Molton 1723 W
Elizabeth, North Molton 1663 A
George, North Molton 1644 [W]
George, Knowstone 1704 A
Zeal George, Chittlehampton 1793 A
Zeal George, South Molton, yeoman 1809 A
Zeal Gregory, Knowstone, husbandman 1799 W
Henry, Rose Ash 1624 [W]
Henry, Rose Ash 1692 W
Henry, Rose Ash 1705 A
Zeal Joan, Mariansleigh 1776 W
John, Rose Ash 1615 [W]
Zeal John, North Molton 1638 W and 1642 W
Seall alias Eame John, Rose Ash 1585 W
John, North Molton 1702 W
Zeal John, Georgeham 1814 W

John, Barnstaple 1822 W
Mary, Rose Ash 1712 W
Zeal Mary, Barnstaple 1826 W
Zeal Michael, North Molton 1636 W
Zeal Michael, North Molton 1688 W
Michael, North Molton 1749 A and 1751 A
Robert, North Molton 1732 W
Zeal Robert, North Molton 1776 W
Thomas, High Bray 1727 A
William, North Molton 1733 W
Zegar see Seager
Zealloke see Zellake
Zeldon see Seldon
Zellake, Zealloke
... Alice, Sheepwash 1616 [W]
Zealloke Richard, Witheridge 1582 W
Thomas, Yarnscombe 1679 W
  see also Sellick
Zelly see Silley

Places in Devon

Places not in Devon